LaunchPad

LaunchPad for *How Children Develop*, Canadian Sixth Edition

Available April 2020 at launchpadworks.com

Each chapter in LaunchPad for *How Children Develop*, Canadian Sixth Edition, features a collection of activities carefully chosen to help master the major concepts. The site serves students as a comprehensive online study guide, available any time, with opportunities for self-quizzing with instant feedback, exam preparation, and further exploration of topics from the textbook. For instructors, all units and activities can be instantly assigned, and students' results and analytics are collected in the Gradebook.

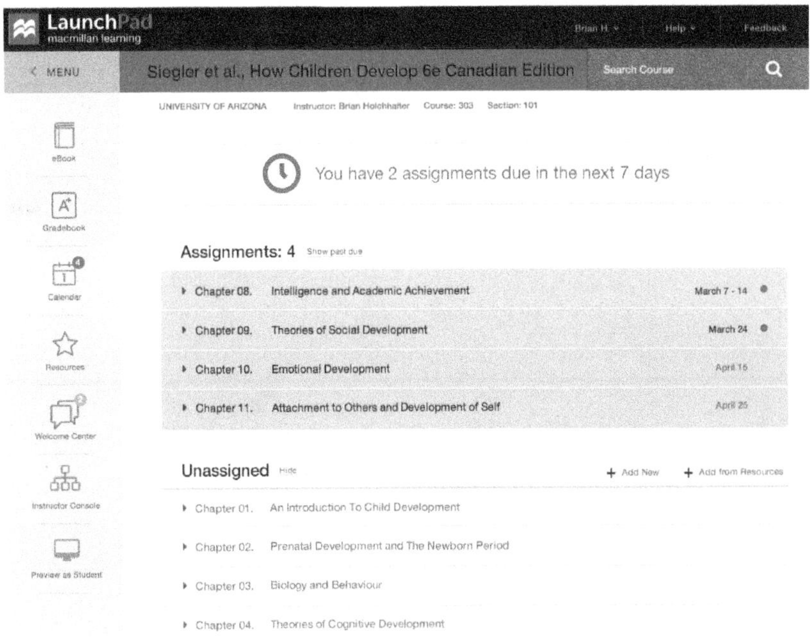

FOR STUDENTS

- Full e-book of *How Children Develop*, Canadian Sixth Edition
- Chapter Summaries
- LearningCurve Quizzing
- Student Video Activities
- Interactive Flashcards
- Research Exercises

FOR INSTRUCTORS

- Gradebook
- Presentation Slides
- Clicker Questions
- Electronic Figures, Photos, and Tables
- Instructor Resources

How Children DEVELOP

CANADIAN SIXTH EDITION

How Children DEVELOP

CANADIAN SIXTH EDITION

Robert Siegler
Teachers College, Columbia University

Elizabeth T. Gershoff
The University of Texas at Austin

Jenny R. Saffran
University of Wisconsin–Madison

Nancy Eisenberg
Arizona State University

Susan Graham
University of Calgary

and

Campbell Leaper
University of California, Santa Cruz
Author of Chapter 15: Gender Development

worth publishers
Macmillan Learning
New York

This is dedicated to the ones we love

Senior Vice President, Content Strategy: Charles Linsmeier
Program Director, Social Sciences: Shani Fisher
Executive Program Manager for Psychology: Daniel DeBonis
Development Editor: Andrew Sylvester
Assistant Editor: Anna Munroe
Executive Marketing Manager: Katherine Nurre
Marketing Assistant: Chelsea Simens
Associate Media Editor: Stephanie Matamoros
Director, Content Management Enhancement: Tracey Kuehn
Senior Managing Editor: Lisa Kinne
Senior Content Project Manager: Vivien Weiss
Senior Workflow Project Manager: Paul Rohloff
Photo and Video Researcher/Permissions Editor: Jennifer Atkins
Executive Permissions Editor: Cecilia Varas
Senior Media Project Manager: Eve Conte
Director of Design, Content Management: Diana Blume
Design Services Manager: Natasha Wolfe
Interior Text Designer: Victoria Tomaselli
Art Manager: Matthew McAdams
Cover Design: John Callahan
Production Supervisor: Robert Cherry
Composition: Lumina Datamatics, Inc.
Printing and Binding: King Printing Co., Inc.
Cover Art: Jeannine Fallert/Illustration Source

Library of Congress Control Number: 2019954721

ISBN-10: 1-319-17302-0
ISBN-13: 978-1-319-17302-9

Printed in the United States of America

3 4 5 6 24 23 22

Worth Publishers
One New York Plaza
Suite 4600
New York, New York 10004-1562
www.macmillanlearning.com

About the Authors

ROBERT SIEGLER is the Schiff Foundations Professor of Psychology and Education at Teachers College, Columbia University. His research focuses on how children learn mathematics. He is author of the cognitive development textbook *Children's Thinking* and has written or edited several additional books on child development. His books have been translated into Japanese, Chinese, Korean, German, Spanish, French, Greek, Hebrew, and Portuguese. He has presented keynote addresses at the conventions of the Cognitive Development Society, the Japanese Psychological Association, the German Psychological Association, the American Psychological Society, and the Conference on Human Development. He also has served as Associate Editor of the journal *Developmental Psychology*, co-edited the cognitive development volume of the 1998 and 2006 editions of the *Handbook of Child Psychology*, and served on the National Mathematics Advisory Panel from 2006 to 2008. Dr. Siegler received the American Psychological Association's Distinguished Scientific Contribution Award in 2005, was elected to the National Academy of Education in 2010, was named Director of the Siegler Center for Innovative Learning at Beijing Normal University in 2012, and was elected to the Society of Experimental Psychologists in 2016.

JENNY R. SAFFRAN is the Vilas Distinguished Achievement Professor and College of Letters & Science Distinguished Professor of Psychology at the University of Wisconsin–Madison, and is an investigator at the Waisman Center. Her research is focused on learning in infancy and early childhood, with a particular emphasis on language. Dr. Saffran's research has been continually funded by the Eunice Kennedy Shriver National Institute of Child Health and Human Development for over 20 years. She has received numerous awards for her research and teaching, including the Boyd McCandless Award from the American Psychological Association for early career contributions to developmental psychology and the Presidential Early Career Award for Scientists and Engineers from the National Science Foundation. In 2015, she was elected to the American Academy of Arts and Sciences.

SUSAN GRAHAM is a Professor in the Department of Psychology at the University of Calgary and the Director of the Owerko Centre at the Alberta Children's Hospital Research Institute. She is a fellow of the Association for Psychological Science and Canadian Society for Brain, Behaviour, and Cognitive Science. She has received a number of awards for her research and mentorship, including a Canada Research Chair, the Killam Annual Professor Award, and the Izzak Walton Killam Award for Graduate Supervision and Mentoring. She is currently the Editor-in-Chief for the *Journal of Cognition and Development*. After completing her undergraduate degree at the University of Manitoba, she moved to Concordia University to complete her graduate studies. She received her PhD in Clinical Psychology in 1996. Her research program focuses on language and cognitive development during the infancy and preschool years and has been continuously funded by the Natural Sciences and Engineering Research Council of Canada and the Social Sciences and Humanities Research Council of Canada.

STEVEN NOREYKO PHOTOGRAPHY

ELIZABETH T. GERSHOFF is the Amy Johnson McLaughlin Centennial Professor of Human Development and Family Sciences and Associate Director of the Population Research Center, both at the University of Texas at Austin. Her research focuses on how parental and school discipline affect child and youth development and on how parent education and early childhood education programs, such as the federal Head Start program, can improve the lives of at-risk children. Dr. Gershoff has been awarded numerous federal grants from the Centers for Disease Control and Prevention, the National Institute for Child Health and Human Development, the National Institute for Mental Health, and the National Science Foundation to support her research. She was lead author of the volume *Societal Contexts of Child Development,* which won the 2014 Society for Research on Adolescence Social Policy Award for Best Edited Book, and of a new book, *Ending the Physical Punishment of Children: A Guide for Clinicians and Practitioners.* She was an Associate Editor at the journal *Developmental Psychology* and is President-Elect of the Society for Child and Family Policy and Practice, which is Division 37 of the American Psychological Association. She is an internationally recognized expert on the effects of physical punishment on children, and her research on the topic has been recognized with a Lifetime Legacy Achievement Award from the Center for the Human Rights of Children at Loyola University Chicago and the Nicholas Hobbs Award from Division 37 of the American Psychological Association.

NANCY EISENBERG is Regents' Professor of Psychology at Arizona State University. Her research interests include social, emotional, and moral development, as well as socialization influences, especially in the areas of self-regulation and adjustment. She has published numerous empirical studies, as well as books and chapters on these topics. She has also been editor of *Psychological Bulletin* and the *Handbook of Child Psychology* and was the founding editor of the Society for Research in Child Development journal *Child Development Perspectives.* Dr. Eisenberg has been a recipient of Research Scientist Development Awards and a Research Scientist Award from the National Institutes of Health (NICHD and NIMH). She has served as President of the Western Psychological Association and of Division 7 of the American Psychological Association and is president-elect of the Association for Psychological Science. She is the 2007 recipient of the Ernest R. Hilgard Award for a Career Contribution to General Psychology, Division 1, American Psychological Association; the 2008 recipient of the International Society for the Study of Behavioral Development Distinguished Scientific Contribution Award; the 2009 recipient of the G. Stanley Hall Award for Distinguished Contribution to Developmental Psychology, Division 7, American Psychological Association; and the 2011 recipient of the William James Fellow Award for Career Contributions in the Basic Science of Psychology from the Association for Psychological Science.

Brief Contents

Contents

NOSTALGIA/ILLUSTRATION SOURCE

JOSE ORTEGA/ILLUSTRATION SOURCE

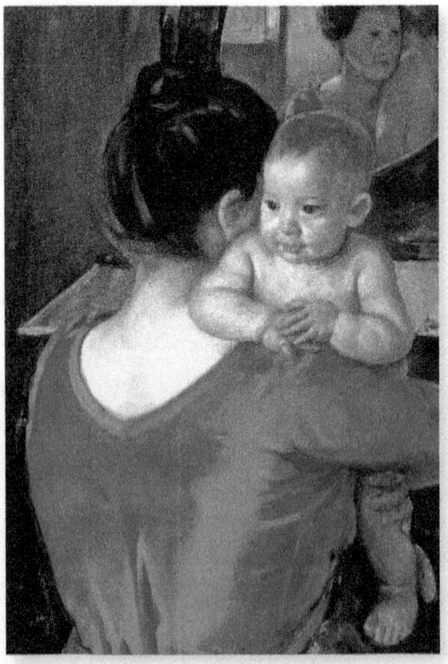

MOTHER AND CHILD, 1900 (OIL ON CANVAS)/CASSATT, MARY STEVENSON (1844-1926)/BROOKLYN MUSEUM OF ART/BROOKLYN MUSEUMOF ART, NEW YORK, USA/BRIDGEMAN IMAGES

CHAPTER

6 Development of Language and Symbol Use 194

LUCAS TALKING TO A DOG, 2006 (OIL ON BOARD)/BEALING, NICOLA (CONTEMPORARY ARTIST)/NICOLA BEALING (CONTEMPORARY ARTIST)/ PRIVATE COLLECTION/BRIDGEMAN IMAGES

CHAPTER

7 Conceptual Development 232

THE LITTLE JOKER (OIL ON CANVAS)/BROWN, JOHN GEORGE (1831-1913)/ CHRISTIES IMAGES/PRIVATE COLLECTION/BRIDGEMAN IMAGES

HERITAGE IMAGES/GETTY IMAGES

CRICKET, SRI LANKA, 1998 (OIL ON CANVAS)/ MACARA, ANDREW/ANDREW MACARA/ PRIVATE COLLECTION/BRIDGEMAN IMAGES

NEVER MIND!, 1884 (OIL ON CANVAS)/ MORGAN, FREDERICK (1856-1927)/ CHRISTIES IMAGES/PRIVATE COLLECTION/ BRIDGEMAN IMAGES

REFUGEE MOTHER AND BABY, GOMA, 1997 (OIL ON CANVAS)/MCDONNELL, HECTOR (B.1947)/HECTOR MCDONNELL (BACS)/PRIVATE COLLECTION/ BRIDGEMAN IMAGES

FAMILY IN THE PARK, 1999 (OIL ON CANVAS)/BOOTMAN, COLIN /COLIN BOOTMAN /PRIVATE COLLECTION/BRIDGEMAN IMAGES

GEOFFREY CLEMENTS/ GETTY IMAGES

FINE ART PHOTOGRAPHIC LIBRARY, LONDON/ ART RESOURCE, NY

LAURIE WIGHAM/GETTY IMAGES

KITE FLYING, 2000 (W/C ON PAPER)/SELIGMAN, LINCOLN/LINCOLN SELIGMAN/PRIVATE COLLECTION/BRIDGEMAN IMAGES

Preface

This is an exciting time in the field of child development. Recent years have brought new theories, new ways of thinking, new areas of research, and innumerable new findings. We originally wrote *How Children Develop* to describe this ever-improving body of knowledge of children and their development and to convey our excitement about the progress that is being made in understanding the developmental process. We are pleased to continue this endeavour with the publication of the Canadian sixth edition of *How Children Develop.*

As teachers of child development courses, we appreciate the challenge that instructors face in trying to present these advances and discoveries—as well as the major older ideas and findings—in a one-semester course. Therefore, rather than aim at encyclopedic coverage, we focus on identifying the most important developmental phenomena and describing them in sufficient depth to make them meaningful and memorable to students. In short, our goal has been to write a textbook that makes the child development course coherent and enjoyable for students and teachers alike.

Classic Themes

The basic premise of the book is that all areas of child development are unified by a small set of enduring themes. These themes can be stated in the form of questions that child-development research tries to answer:

1. How do nature and nurture together shape development?
2. How do children shape their own development?
3. In what ways is development continuous, and in what ways is it discontinuous?
4. How does change occur?
5. How does the sociocultural context influence development?
6. How do children become so different from one another?
7. How can research promote children's well-being?

These seven themes provide the core structure of the book. They are introduced and illustrated in Chapter 1; highlighted repeatedly, where relevant, in the subsequent 14 content chapters; and utilized in the final chapter as a framework for integrating findings relevant to each theme from all areas of development. The continuing coverage of these themes allows us to tell a story that has a beginning (the introduction of the themes), a middle (discussion of specific findings relevant to them), and an ending (the overview of what students have learned about the themes). We believe that this thematic emphasis and structure will not only help students understand enduring questions about child development but will also leave them with a greater sense of satisfaction and completion at the end of the course.

Contemporary Perspective

The goal of providing a thoroughly contemporary perspective on how children develop has influenced the organization of our book as well as its contents. Whole new areas and perspectives have emerged that barely existed when most of today's child-development textbooks were originally written. The organization of *How Children Develop* is designed to present these new topics and approaches in the context of the field as it currently stands, rather than trying to shoehorn them into organizations that once fit the field but no longer do.

Consider the case of Piaget's theory and current research relevant to it. Piaget's theory often is presented in its own chapter, most of which describes the theory in full detail and the rest of which offers contemporary research that demonstrates problems with the theory. This approach often leaves students wondering why so much time was spent on Piaget's theory if modern research shows it to be wrong in so many ways.

The fact is that the line of research that began more than 50 years ago as an effort to challenge Piaget's theory has emerged since then as a vital area in its own right—the area of conceptual development. Research in conceptual development provides extensive information on children's understanding of such fascinating topics as human beings, plants and animals, and the physical universe. As with other research areas, most studies in this field are aimed primarily at uncovering evidence relevant to current claims, not those of Piaget.

We adapted to this changing intellectual landscape in two ways. First, our chapter "Theories of Cognitive Development" (Chapter 4) describes the fundamental aspects of Piaget's theory in depth and honours his legacy by focusing on the aspects of his work that have proven to be the most enduring. Second, a first-of-its-kind chapter called "Conceptual Development" (Chapter 7) addresses the types of issues that inspired Piaget's theory but concentrates on modern perspectives and findings regarding those issues. This approach allows us to tell students about the numerous intriguing proposals and observations that are being made in this field, without the artificiality of classifying the findings as "pro-Piagetian" or "anti-Piagetian."

The opportunity to create a textbook based on current understanding also led us to assign prominent positions to such rapidly emerging areas as epigenetics, behavioural genetics, brain development, prenatal learning, infant cognition, acquisition of academic skills, emotional development, prosocial behaviour, and friendship patterns. All these areas have seen major breakthroughs in recent years, and their growing prominence has led to even greater emphasis on them in this edition.

Getting Right to the Point

Our desire to offer a contemporary, streamlined approach led to other departures from the traditional organization. It is our experience that today's students take child-development courses for a variety of practical reasons and are eager to learn about *children*. Traditionally, however, they have had to wait two or three or even four chapters—on the history of the field, on major theories, on research methods, on genetics—before actually getting to the study of children. We wanted to build on their initial motivation from the start.

Rather than beginning the book, then, with an extensive examination of the history of the field, we include in Chapter 1 a brief overview of the social and intellectual context in which the scientific study of children arose and provide historical background wherever it is pertinent in subsequent chapters. Rather than have an early chapter of "blockbuster" theories that covers all the major cognitive and social theories at once (at a point far removed from the content chapters to which the theories apply), we present a chapter on cognitive developmental theories just before the chapters that focus on specific aspects of cognitive development, and we similarly present a chapter on social developmental theories just before the chapters that focus on specific aspects of social development.

Likewise, rather than have a separate chapter on genetics, we include basic aspects of genetics as part of Chapter 3, "Biology and Behaviour," and then discuss the contributions of genetics to some of the differences amongst individuals throughout the book. When we originally chose this organization, we hoped that it would allow us, from the first weeks of the course, to kindle students' enthusiasm for finding out how children develop. Judging by the overwhelmingly positive response we have received from students and instructors alike, it has.

Features

The most important feature of this book is the exposition, which we have tried to make as clear and compelling as possible. As in previous editions, we have given extra attention to making it accessible to a broad range of students.

To further enhance the appeal and accessibility of the text, we have retained three types of discussion boxes that explore topics of special interest:

- "Applications" boxes focus on how child development research can be used to promote children's well-being. Amongst the applications that are summed up in these boxes are genetic testing, which probes the depths of an individual's genetic makeup; board-game procedures for improving preschoolers' understanding of numbers; the Better Beginnings, Better Futures program; interventions to reduce child abuse; programs, such as PATHS, for helping rejected children gain acceptance from their peers; and Positive Youth Development and Service Learning Programs, which seek to reduce problem behaviours and increase positive behaviours.
- "Individual Differences" boxes focus on populations that differ from the norm with regard to the specific topic under consideration, or on variations amongst children in the general population. Some of these boxes highlight developmental problems such as autism, ADHD, dyslexia, specific language impairment, visual impairments, and conduct disorder, whereas others focus on differences in the development of children that centre on attachment status, gender, socioeconomic status, and cultural differences.
- "A Closer Look" boxes examine important and interesting research in greater depth than would otherwise be possible: the areas examined range from brain-mapping techniques to explorations of gender nonbinary identity to the developmental impact of homelessness and disparities between poverty and health.

In place of the brief section summaries used in previous editions, we cap each major section with a thought-provoking Review Question. These prompts serve the dual purpose of encouraging deeper thinking about the material and of forcing the student to pause before diving ahead in the chapter.

We have also retained a number of other features intended to improve students' learning. These features include boldfacing key terms and supplying definitions both within the immediate text and in marginal glossaries; extensive, bulleted Summaries at the end of each chapter; Test Yourself quizzes for students to quickly test their comprehension and understanding of the material in preparation for exams or simply as a way to review; and Critical Thinking Questions intended to promote deeper consideration of essential topics.

The Canadian Edition

Our goal in writing this Canadian edition was to create a textbook that retains the essential and updated coverage of the American edition, but would also engage Canadian students by situating the content in Canadian and international contexts, highlighting the remarkable scientific accomplishments of Canadian developmental scientists, drawing on Canadian issues, and including current Canadian data and statistics whenever possible. We integrate discussion of research conducted with Canadian children and families throughout the chapters, highlighting the research conducted at universities across Canada. Finally, we have included photographs and figures that reflect the Canadian context and Canadian research.

To illustrate how we have incorporated a Canadian perspective, we highlight below some of the specific information included across different chapters. Please note that this is by no means an exhaustive list of the Canadian content incorporated in each chapter!

Chapter 1

- We have included recent statistics about the prevalence of spanking in Canada, recent developments in practices regarding legal interviews of and testimony from children in Canada, and recent rates of child poverty in Canada.
- We also incorporate findings from the study of children who were adopted from Romanian orphanages to families in Canada.
- We include a description of the Tri-Council Policy Statement: Ethical Conduct for Research Involving Humans, which governs research involving human subjects in Canada.

Chapter 2

- We incorporate Canadian statistics about maternal smoking, the use of alcohol and drugs during pregnancy, fetal alcohol syndrome (FAS), sudden infant death syndrome (SIDS), the rate of teenage pregnancies, infant mortality rates (including comparison of rates across some provinces and territories, with a focus on the north), newborns with low birth weight, and multiple births.
- We also discuss recent developments related to environmental pollutants affecting Inuit communities and the Grassy Narrows and White Dog First Nations people.
- We present research from studies conducted in Alberta investigating the effects of maternal prenatal depression on children's brain structure.
- We present data on hospitalization rates for First Nation and Inuit infants compared to non-Indigenous infants in a discussion of structural racism.

Chapter 3

- We discuss recent research from the University of Toronto on genetic mutations that may lead to autism, findings from the Quebec Newborn Twin Study, information about mandated daily physical activity in schools, and McMaster University's Early Development Inventory and other interventions to address issues related to the effects of poverty on children's health and well-being.

Chapter 5

- We highlight research by Canadian researchers including Kang Lee, who looked at other-race effect (ORE) in children; Sarah Laurence, Daphne Maurer, and Catherine Mondloch, who study face perception of infants; Laurel Trainor, Sandra Trehub, and Glen Schellenberg, who study infants' responses to music; and Diane Poulin-Dubois, who researches infants' observational learning and imitation.

Chapter 6

- We cite research from McGill University that provides insight into language and the brain, comparing brain activation in the left hemisphere for hearing speakers of English and deaf signers of American Sign Language (ASL) and Langue des Signes Québécoise (LSQ).
- We also describe research from Canadian researchers such as Laurel Trainor (McMaster University), Janet Werker (University of British Columbia), Diane Poulin-Dubois (Concordia University), and Geoff Hall (University of British Columbia), whose research has shaped our understanding of language development.
- The discussion of bilingualism includes details specific to the Canadian context.

Chapter 7

- We present a multi-country study from J. Bradley Wigger about the prevalence of imaginary companions, as well as research from the Angus Reid Institute on beliefs in fantasy and the supernatural.

Chapter 8

- We describe results of the Better Beginnings, Better Futures program in Ontario and of the Aboriginal Head Start Program in Urban and Northern Communities, as well as Canadian studies on gifted children and the development of reading abilities.
- We also discuss Canadian research on how reading at home affects the development of reading skills, as well as a recent Canadian study on children's use of invented spelling.

Chapter 9

- We present data on the prevalence of ADHD diagnoses among Canadian children.
- We discuss screen time rates among children in Alberta, and present recommendations from the Canadian Pediatric Society. We also discuss social media trends among Canadian adolescents.

Chapter 10

- We discuss the Roots of Empathy program, originally developed in Toronto, which aims to encourage prosocial behaviour and decrease aggressive behaviour, and the Alberta Family Wellness Initiative, which works to develop practices and policy related to mental health.

- We present a new study conducted in Alberta exploring the inter-generational effects of Adverse Childhood Experiences (ACEs).
- We present findings on acccss to mental health care across Canada, and we offer data on the prevalence of mood disorders among Canadian children.

Chapter 11

- We highlight Canadian research on paternal and maternal attachment, bicultural integration and ethnic identity, and sexual-minority adolescents, including a discussion of the impact of Gay Straight Alliances in Canadian schools.

Chapter 12

- This chapter has been heavily revised to present recent changes to the Canadian family structure, including statistics related to lone parents, first-time parents, adolescent parents, grandparents raising children, same-sex parents, teen parents, and divorced and stepparent families, with supporting graphs detailing various family structures by child's age and province.
- We discuss child maltreatment in the context of the Public Health Agency of Canada's description of various forms of abuse, and present recent data from Ontario on rates of abuse.
- Within the discussion of the economic context, we present data and research on child poverty and homelessness in Canada.
- We reference research on Canadian family-leave policies and the effects and availability of childcare, including a detailed presentation of the Alberta Child Care Accreditation Standards.

Chapter 13

- This chapter includes discussion of Canadian research on peer relations, including studies by researchers such as Hildy Ross, Bill Bukowski, François Poulin, Sara Pedersen, Frank Vitaro, Shelley Hymel, Robert Coplan, and Wendy Craig.
- We include statistics from Canadian studies on time spent with friends, adolescents' use of technology, bullying, and cyberbullying.

Chapter 14

- This chapter includes Canadian studies on the relationship between cultural and socioeconomic differences and morality, temperament and prosocial behaviour, aggression, the connection between socioeconomic status and antisocial behaviour, and the prevalence of Oppositional Defiance Disorder.
- We discuss community service projects in Ontario and other provinces.
- This chapter opens with a discussion of the tragic murder of Canadian soldier Captain Nathan Cirillo.

Chapter 15

- This chapter highlights Canadian research on academic achievement, including degree attainment by women in STEM-related fields, gender bias in observed aggressive behaviour, and sexual harassment and physical aggression in dating relationships.

New and Expanded Coverage

In every edition, we endeavour to address new developments in the field and bring in fresh examples drawn from current events. In addition to the Canadian focus just described, we have expanded our coverage of a number of research areas that have become increasingly important in recent years for both the students of child development and the instructors who teach it. We have sought in this Canadian sixth edition to balance the inclusion of this new material with judicious cuts and consolidation of coverage. We have worked to remove outdated and less relevant material, eliminate overlapping coverage across chapters, and present core concepts in a more concise manner. The result is a leaner, more visually appealing text that delivers the same wealth of coverage found in prior editions, but in a manner that we hope you, and more importantly your students, will find more manageable and digestible.

In the following paragraphs, we outline some of the most significant highlights of the Canadian sixth edition. We hope you find it to be useful and appealing.

Chapter 1

- Updated presentation of long-term consequences and later findings in Box 1.1: The Romanian Adoption Study.
- Updates and revisions made throughout the presentation section on Enduring Themes in Child Development, notably in Theme 2: The Active Child (expanded discussion of play), Theme 4: Mechanisms of Change (additional examples and recent research added), and Theme 5: The Sociocultural Context (updated discussion of SES).

Chapter 2

- Exposition updated and tightened throughout, most notably in the discussions of conception, early and prenatal development, teratogens, infant sleep, and crying.
- Updated the subsection on Fetal Experience, including a new discussion of prenatal visual preferences and of phylogenetic continuity.
- Updates to the discussion of Drugs and Maternal Factors in the section on Teratogens, including a significant revision of the section on Maternal Emotional State.
- Updated and revised subsection on Intervention Programs included in the section on Negative Outcomes at Birth.

Chapter 3

- Significant reorganization and update to the discussion of heredity in the section on Parents' Genotype–Child's Genotype.
- Updated (and reduced length of) Box 3.1: Genetic Testing, with new content covering non-invasive prenatal testing.
- Expanded and updated discussion of methylation, including a new figure, and epigenetic effects.
- In the section on Behavioural Genetics, revised and updated the discussion of Heritability, particularly the discussion of misconceptions, and expanded and updated the discussion of molecular genetics research design with new coverage of candidate gene studies.

- In the section on Brain Development, added new figures and expanded discussions of arborization, neurogenesis, and synapse production and elimination.
- New subsection on Vaccines added to section on Physical Growth and Development.

Chapter 4

- Opening section discussing Piaget's Theory of Cognitive Development has been shortened for a more concise presentation.
- Presentation of Sociocultural Theories has been restructured and shortened.
- New research added to the discussion of executive functioning in the section on Information-Processing Theories.

Chapter 5

- Section on Cognition has been eliminated, with topics distributed to other sections in the chapter (as well as to Chapter 7).
- Section on Learning has been retitled Learning and Memory, and a corresponding subsection on Memory has been added.
- Expanded and updated discussion of Taste and Smell.
- New Table 5.1 charting Infant Reflexes has been added to this section.

Chapter 6

- All Boxes shortened and updated with current research.
- Section on Components of Language has been revised to be more concise.

Chapter 7

- Expanded discussion of causal understanding now includes a discussion of object knowledge (adapted from material previously found in Chapter 5).
- Expanded discussion of Naïve Psychology in Infancy, with additional material previously found in Chapter 5, now adapted and updated for this section.

Chapter 8

- Updated discussion of the impact of technology, such as video games, on fluid intelligence.
- Updated discussion of the effects of poverty on measures of intelligence and academic achievement, including a new figure showing current poverty rates across several countries.
- Discussion of intervention programs updated to reflect recent findings.
- Revamped and shortened presentation of Gardner's theory of multiple intelligences and Sternberg's theory of successful intelligence.
- Updates throughout the section on Acquisition of Academic Skills, including new coverage of the simple view of reading and new research on math achievement and math anxiety.

Chapter 9

- Each section covering a major theoretical approach has been streamlined for a more concise presentation.
- Updated discussion of Parental Leave, including a new figure plotting the length of maternity leave in a sampling of countries.
- Subsection SES and development has been cut from the chapter, and the subsection on child maltreatment has been moved from this chapter to Chapter 12, to allow for an expanded and updated subsection on Children and the Media.

Chapter 10

- Coverage has been streamlined and updated throughout, most notably to the sections on Understanding Emotions and Emotion Regulation.
- New research added throughout the sections on the Emergence of Emotions.
- Relocation and restructuring of the sections on the Role of Family and on Temperament, for better flow through the chapter.

Chapter 11

- Coverage has been streamlined and updated throughout, particularly in the coverage of Attachment Theory in the opening section and in the section on The Self.
- New research included in the discussions of parenting and attachment styles and on genetic influences on attachment styles.
- Significant revisions and updates throughout the discussion of Identity, including new research added on acculturation in the context of children of immigrants, and new survey data related to sexual-minority youth.

Chapter 12

- Substantial updates to the section on Family Structure.
- Section on Child Maltreatment added to this chapter, expanding and updating material previously found in Chapter 9.
- Box 12.3: Preventing Child Abuse, previously included in Chapter 9, has been updated and reworked to focus on strategies recommended by the Centers for Disease Control and Prevention.
- Substantial revisions and updates to Box 12.5: Family Leave Policies.

Chapter 13

- Significant streamlining of material throughout chapter to make for a more concise presentation.
- New major section on Play opens the chapter, with a new Box 13.1: The Development of Children's Social Play.
- Box 13.2: Culture and Children's Peer Experience has been substantially revised.
- Subsection on Cyberbullying has been thoroughly updated.

Chapter 14

- Discussion of Piaget's Theory of Moral Judgment and Kohlberg's Theory of Moral Reasoning have been reworked for a more concise treatment.
- Heavily revised coverage of Social Domain Theory of moral development, including the introduction of several new key terms.
- New research added to the discussion of Cultural and Socioeconomic Differences in moral reasoning, including a series of new figures based on a study done on charitable giving.
- Updated and streamlined section on Prosocial Behaviours for a more concise presentation; discussion of Hamlin's helper/hinderer study added from Chapter 5.
- Updated and streamlined section on Antisocial and Aggressive Behaviours, including the addition of a new subsection on Interventions for Aggressive and Antisocial Children.

Chapter 15

- Extensive updating and restructuring throughout the chapter, including a focus on issues and research related to transgender and gender-nonbinary populations, where applicable.
- New opening section on Sex and Gender, including the introduction of several new key terms; discussion of major gender differences across several dimensions, including new Box 15.1: Challenges to the Gender Binary; Table 15.1: Summary of Average Gender Differences has also been moved from later in the chapter to this opening section.
- Section on Theoretical Approaches to Gender Development has been updated and restructured, with a new discussion of Integrative Theoretical Approaches, including a new figure diagramming the gender self-socialization model.
- Revised and updated section on Milestones in Gender Development, including a new discussion of ambivalent sexism in the discussion of development during adolescence.
- Final section Patterns of Gender Development has been updated and reorganized with a new subsection on STEM-Related Skills.

Supplements

How Children Develop, Canadian Sixth Edition, features a wide array of multimedia tools that are designed for the individual needs of students and teachers. For more information about any of the items listed below, please visit the online catalog at www.macmillanlearning.com.

LaunchPad with LearningCurve Quizzing

A comprehensive web resource for teaching and learning psychology

LaunchPad combines Macmillan Learning's award-winning media with an innovative platform for easy navigation. For students, it is the ultimate online study guide with rich interactive tutorials, videos, e-book, and the LearningCurve adaptive quizzing system. For instructors, LaunchPad is a full course space where class documents can be posted, quizzes are easily assigned and graded, and students' progress can be assessed and recorded. Whether you are looking for the most effective study tools or a robust platform for an online course, LaunchPad is a powerful way to enhance your class.

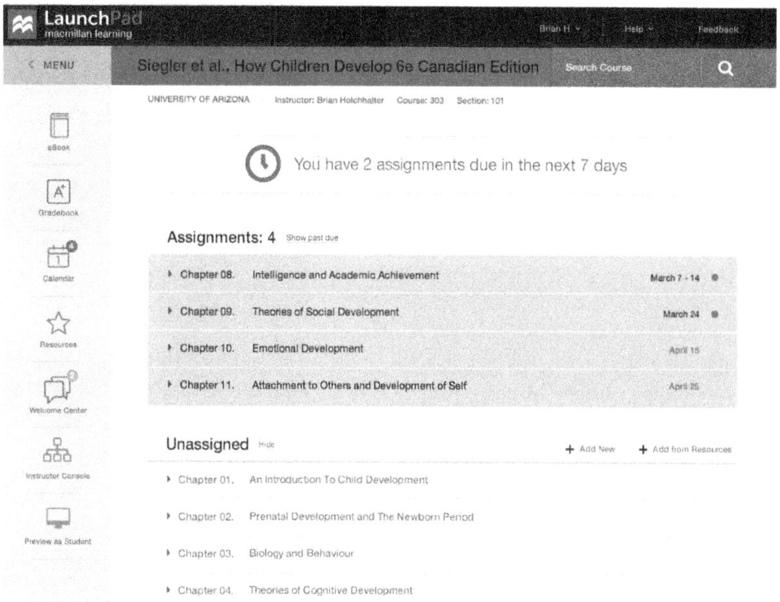

LaunchPad for *How Children Develop*, Canadian Sixth Edition, can be previewed and purchased at launchpadworks.com.

How Children Develop, Canadian Sixth Edition, and LaunchPad can be ordered together with ISBN-10: 1-319-34650-2 / ISBN-13: 978-1-319-34650-8.

LaunchPad for *How Children Develop*, Canadian Sixth Edition, includes the following resources:

- The **LearningCurve** quizzing system was designed based on the latest findings from learning and memory research. It combines adaptive question selection, immediate and valuable feedback, and a game-like interface to engage students in a learning experience that is unique to them. Each LearningCurve quiz is fully integrated with other resources in LaunchPad through the Personalized Study Plan, so students will be able to review with Worth's extensive library of videos and activities. And state-of-the-art question analysis reports allow instructors to track the progress of individual students, as well as their class as a whole.

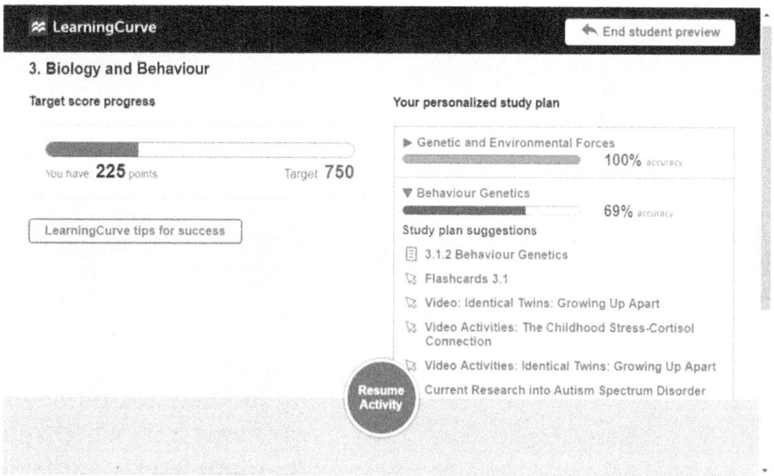

- **An interactive e-book** allows students to highlight, bookmark, and make their own notes, just as they would with a printed textbook. Digital enhancements include full-text search and in-text glossary definitions.
- **Student Video Activities** include more than 100 engaging video modules that instructors can easily assign for student assessment. Videos cover classic experiments, current news footage, and cutting-edge research, all of which are sure to spark discussion and encourage critical thinking.
- **Deep integration** is available between LaunchPad products and most learning management systems, including Blackboard, Brightspace by D2L, Canvas, and Moodle. These deep integrations offer educators single sign-on and gradebook sync, now with auto refresh. These best-in-class integrations offer deep linking to all Macmillan digital content at the chapter and asset levels, giving professors maximum flexibility within their LMS.

Presentation and Faculty Support

Presentation Slides

Presentation slides are available in two formats that can be used as they are or can be customized. One set includes all the textbook's illustrations and tables. The second set consists of lecture slides that focus on key themes and terms in the book and include text illustrations and tables. Both of these prebuilt PowerPoint presentations are available through LaunchPad at launchpadworks.com.

Presentation Videos

Worth's video clips for developmental psychology span the full range of topics for the child development course. With hundreds of clips to choose from, this premium collection includes research and news footage on topics ranging from prenatal development to the experience of child soldiers to empathy in adolescence. These clips are made available to instructors for lecturing in the classroom and also through LaunchPad.

Instructor's Resource Manual

Written by Lynne Baker-Ward of North Carolina State University, and revised by Barinder Bhavra, this innovative *Instructor's Resource Manual* includes handouts for student projects, reading lists of journal articles, course-planning suggestions, and supplementary readings, in addition to lecture guides, chapter overviews, and learning objectives. The *Instructor's Resource Manual* can be downloaded in LaunchPad at launchpadworks.com.

Macmillan Community

Macmillan Community is an online forum where teachers can find and share favourite teaching ideas and materials, including videos, animations, images, PowerPoint slides, news stories, articles, web links, and lecture activities. It is also the home of Worth's abundant social media content, including tweets, blog posts, webinars, and more! Browse the site and share your favourite materials for teaching psychology at https://community.macmillan.com.

Assessment

Test Bank

The Test Bank for *How Children Develop* by Kyle Danielson of the University of Toronto, Scarborough, features more than 100 multiple-choice and essay questions for each chapter. Each question is keyed to the textbook by topic, type, and level of difficulty. The Test Bank is available through LaunchPad at launchpadworks.com.

Acknowledgments

So many people have contributed (directly and indirectly) to this textbook that it is impossible to know where to start or where to stop in thanking them. All of us have been given exceptional support by our spouses and significant others—Jerry Harris, Xiaodong Lin, Seth Pollak, John Gerlach, and Andrew Gershoff—and by our children—Benjamin Clore; Michael Harris; Todd, Beth, and Aaron Siegler; Avianna McGhee; Eli and Nell Pollak; Sam and Madeline Gerlach; and Noah and Ella Gershoff—as well as by our parents, relatives, friends, and other loved ones. Our advisors in college and graduate school, Richard Aslin, Ann Brown, Les Cohen, Ted Dix, Harry Hake, George Holden, Robert Liebert, Jim Morgan, Paul Mussen, Elissa Newport, Jim Pate, and Diane Poulin-Dubois, helped to launch our careers and taught us how to recognize and appreciate good research.

We also have all benefited from collaborators who shared our quest for understanding child development and from a great many exceptionally helpful and generous colleagues, including Larry Aber, Karen Adolph, Martha Alibali, Renee Baillargeon, Sharon Carver, Craig Chambers, Zhe Chen, Robert Crosnoe, Suzanne Curtin, Richard Fabes, Cindy Fisher, Susan Gelman, Geoff Hall, Aletha Huston, Andrew Grogan-Kaylor, Melanie Jones, David Klahr, Patrick Lemaire, Casey Lew-Williams, Angeline Lillard, Liz Nilsen, John Opfer, Penny Pexman, Elizabeth Planalp, Karl Rosengren, Kristin Shutts, Tracy Spinrad, David Uttal, Carlos Valiente, and Erica Wojcik. We owe special thanks to our assistants, Sheri Towe and Theresa Treasure, who helped in innumerable ways in preparing the book, and to Shanting Chen and Kathleen Holloway for their thorough work reviewing the video library that accompanies this edition.

We would also like to thank the many reviewers who contributed to this and previous editions. For the Canadian edition, we thank **Alba Agostino,** Ryerson University; **Daniel Ansari,** University of Western Ontario; **Christina Besner,** Champlain College Lennoxville; **Ann Bigelow,** St. Francis Xavier University; **Tanya Broesch,** Simon Fraser University; **Tina Bonnett,** Fanshawe College; **Carie M. Buchanan,** St. Thomas More College–University of Sakatchewan; **Arloene Burak,** University of Victoria; **Jeremy Carpendale,** Simon Fraser University; **Kyle Danielson,** University of British Columbia; **Kelly Dean Schwartz,** University of Calgary; **Cass Foursha-Stevenson,** Mount Royal University; **Kathleen Hughes,** University of Calgary; **Jacqueline Kampman,** Thompson Rivers University; **Padmapriya Kandhadai,** University of British Columbia; **Elizabeth Kelley,** Queen's University; **Cheryl Kier,** Athabasca University; **Tru Kwong,** Mount Royal University; **Danielle Labossière,** Grenfell Campus, Memorial University of Newfoundland; **Linda Langevin,** Medicine Hat College; **Vivian Li,** University of British Columbia; **Tina Malti,** University of Toronto; **Anna Matejka,** University of Toronto Mississauga; **Lillian May,** University of British Columbia; **Nancy Ogden,** Mount Royal University; **Gene Ouellette,** Mount Allison University; **Angelina Paolozza,** University of Toronto; **Alissa Pencer,** Dalhousie University; **Jocelyn Proulx,** University of Manitoba; **Danielle Quigley,** Douglas College; **Valerie San Juan,** University of Calgary; **Daniel Séguin,** Mount Saint Vincent University; **Veronica Smith,** University of Alberta; **Christina Starmans,** University of Toronto; **Alexandra Twyman,** University of Western Ontario; **Tara Vongpaisal,** MacEwan University; **Kelly Warren,** Grenfell Campus, Memorial University of Newfoundland; **Janet F. Werker,** University of British Columbia; **Sandra Wiebe,** University of Alberta; **Lynne Zarbatany,** University of Western Ontario.

For the American edition: **Daisuke Akiba,** Queens College, City University of New York; **Kimberly Alkins,** Queens College, City University of New York; **Hiram Allen,** College of New Rochelle; **Dina Anselmi,** Trinity College; **Lynne Baker-Ward,** North Carolina State University; **Hilary Barth,** Wesleyan University; **Christie Bartholomew,** Kent State University; **Christopher Beevers,** University of Texas at Austin; **Martha Bell,** Virginia Tech; **Cynthia Berg,** University of Utah; **Rebecca Bigler,** University of Texas at Austin; **Margaret Borkowski,** Saginaw Valley State University; **Lyn Boulter,** Catawba College; **Renia Brown-Cobb,** Virginia State University; **Eric Buhs,** University of Nebraska–Lincoln; **G. Leonard Burns,** Washington State University; **Allison**

Butler, Bryant University; **Wendy Carlson,** Shenandoah University; **Erik W. Cheries,** University of Massachusetts Amherst; **Mel Joseph Ciena,** University of San Francisco; **Kristi Cordell-McNulty,** Angelo State University; **Myra Cox,** Harold Washington College; **Maria Crisafi,** Columbia University; **Kimberly Cuevas,** University of Connecticut; **Emily Davidson,** Texas A&M University–Main Campus; **Peggy DeCooke,** The State University of New York at Purchase; **Ed de St. Aubin,** Marquette University; **Marissa Diener,** University of Utah; **Julie Earles,** Wilkes Honors College, Florida Atlantic University; **Sharon Eaves,** Shawnee State University; **Jessica Espinosa,** Miami Dade College; **Guadalupe Espinoza,** California State University, Fullerton; **Elisa Esposito,** Widener University; **Urminda Firlan,** Grand Rapids Community College; **Dorothy Fragaszy,** University of Georgia; **Jeffery Gagne,** University of Texas–Arlington; **Jennifer Ganger,** University of Pittsburgh; **Alice Ganzel,** Cornell College; **Catherine Gaze,** Elmhurst College; **Janet Gebelt,** Westfield State University; **Peter Gerhardstein,** Binghamton University; **Melissa Ghera,** St. John Fisher College; **Helana Girgis,** Hartwick College; **Susan Graham,** University of Calgary; **Andrea Greenhoot,** University of Kansas; **Jessica Greenlee,** Virginia Commonwealth University; **Shelia Greenlee,** Christopher Newport University; **Frederick Grote,** Western Washington University; **John Gruszkos,** Reynolds University; **Hanna Gustafsson,** University of North Carolina; **Alma Guyse,** Midland College; **Louise Hainline,** Brooklyn College; **Lauren Harris,** Michigan State University; **Sybil Hart,** Texas Tech University; **Karen Hartlep,** California State University–Bakersfield; **Patricia Hawley,** University of Kansas–Main; **Joan Henley,** Arkansas State University; **Susan Hespos,** Northwestern University; **Doris Hiatt,** Monmouth University; **Aline Hitti,** University of San Francisco; **Susan Holt,** Central Connecticut State University; **Wendy Jung,** Tulane University; **Lana Karasik,** The College of Staten Island; **Lisa Huffman,** Ball State University; **Kathryn Kipp,** University of Georgia; **Rosemary Krawczyk,** Minnesota State University; **Amber Kreischer,** University of Texas at Austin; **Raymond Krukovsky,** Union County College; **Tara Kuther,** Western Connecticut State University; **Martin Lampert,** Holy Names University; **Richard Lanthier,** George Washington University; **Elida Laski,** Boston College; **Kathryn Lemery,** Arizona State University; **Barbara Licht,** Florida State University; **Jeffrey Liew,** Texas A&M University; **Angeline Lillard,** University of Virginia; **Lori Markson,** Washington University in St. Louis; **Marsha J. McCartney,** University of Kansas; **Wayne McMillin,** Northwestern State University; **Martha Mendez-Baldwin,** Manhattan College; **Scott Miller,** University of Florida; **Keith Nelson,** Pennsylvania State University–Main Campus; **Paul Nicodemus,** Austin Peay State University; **Tracy Nishida,** Arizona State University; **Katherine O'Doherty,** Vanderbilt University; **Christin Ogle,** American University; **John Opfer,** The Ohio State University; **Beverly Pead,** Springfield Technical Community College; **Ann Repp,** University of Texas at Austin; **Nicole Rivera,** North Central College; **Shannon Ross-Sheehy,** University of Tennessee; **Sarah Sanborn,** Clemson University; **Leigh A. Shaw,** Weber State University; **Jennifer Simonds,** Westminster College; **Rebekah Smith,** University of Texas–San Antonio; **Tara Stoppa,** Eastern University; **Mark Strauss,** University of Pittsburgh–Main; **Spencer Thompson,** University of Texas–Permian Basin; **Marisel Torres-Crespo,** Hood College; **Lisa Travis,** University of Illinois Urbana–Champaign; **Roger Webb,** University of Arkansas–Little Rock; **Keri Weed,** University of South Carolina–Aiken; **Sherri Widen,** Boston College; **Fei Xu,** The University of California, Berkeley.

We would especially like to thank Campbell Leaper, University of California, Santa Cruz, for his major contributions to the revision of our chapter on gender development (Chapter 15). We are indebted to Campbell for bringing to the Canadian sixth edition his expertise and keen insight in this important area.

Thanks are particularly due to our friends and collaborators at Worth Publishers. As Executive Program Manager for Psychology, Daniel DeBonis provided exceptional support and any number of excellent suggestions. We would also like to thank Marge Byers, who nurtured our first edition from its inception and helped us to realize our vision. Peter Deane, our development editor for the first four editions, is in a class by himself in both skill and dedication. Peter's creative thinking and firm understanding of the field enhanced the content of the book in innumerable ways. We are deeply grateful to him. Special thanks go to the development editor for the latest two editions, Andrew Sylvester, who provided consistently outstanding help throughout the process, as well as to assistant editor Anna Munroe, senior content project manager Vivien Weiss, director of content management enhancement Tracey Kuehn, art manager Matthew McAdams, cover designer John Callahan, interior designer Victoria Tomaselli, design manager Natasha Wolfe, executive permissions editor Cecilia Varas, photo researcher Jennifer Atkins, senior workflow project manager Paul Rohloff, and compositor Lumina Datamatics, and Subramaniam Vengatakrishnan and Prasanna Kalyanaram in particular, for their excellent work. They have helped create a book that we hope you will find a pleasure to look at as well as to read. Executive marketing manager Katherine Nurre provided outstanding promotional materials to inform professors about the book. Associate media editor Stephanie Matamoros managed the superb package of ancillary material. We also want to thank the Canadian marketing and sales teams led by Jen Cawsey. The enthusiasm and support provided by Jen, as well as Kasia Bulgarski, Jennifer Mills, Kiyo Monteith, Kate Nicoll, Robbie Patterson, Jordan Scholefield, and Katy Turenne, are greatly appreciated!

CHAPTER

1

An Introduction to Child Development

NOSTALGIA/ILLUSTRATION SOURCE

Water Baby and the Moon

Reasons to Learn About Child Development

Historical Foundations of the Study of Child Development

Enduring Themes in Child Development | Methods for Studying Child Development

THEMES

NATURE AND NURTURE ■ THE ACTIVE CHILD ■ CONTINUITY/DISCONTINUITY

MECHANISMS OF CHANGE ■ THE SOCIOCULTURAL CONTEXT

INDIVIDUAL DIFFERENCES ■ RESEARCH AND CHILDREN'S WELFARE

In 1955, a group of child-development researchers began a unique study. Their goal, like that of many developmental researchers, was to find out how biological and environmental factors influence children's intellectual, social, and emotional growth. What made their study unique was that they examined these diverse aspects of development for all 698 children born that year on the Hawaiian island of Kauai and continued studying the children's development for 40 years.

With the parents' consent, the research team, headed by Emmy Werner, collected many types of data about the children. To learn about possible complications during the prenatal period and birth, they examined physicians' records. To learn about family interactions and the children's behaviour at home, they arranged for nurses and social workers to observe the families and to interview the children's mothers when the children were 1 year old and again when they were 10 years old. The researchers also interviewed teachers about the children's academic performance and classroom behaviour during the elementary school years and examined police, family court, and social service records that involved the children, either as victims or perpetrators. Finally, the researchers administered standardized intelligence and personality tests to the participants when they were 10 and 18 years old and interviewed them at ages 18, 32, and 40 to find out how they saw their own development (Werner, 2005).

Results from this study illustrated some of the many ways in which biological and environmental factors combine to produce child development. For example, children who experienced prenatal or birth complications were more likely than others to develop physical handicaps, mental illness, and learning difficulties. But whether they developed such problems—and if so, to what degree—depended a great deal on their home environment. Parents' income, education, and mental health, together with the quality of the relationship between the parents, especially influenced children's development. By age 2, toddlers who had experienced severe prenatal or birth problems but who lived in harmonious middle-income families were nearly as advanced in language and motor skills as were children who had not experienced early problems. By the time the children were 10-year-olds, prenatal and birth problems were consistently related to psychological difficulties *only* if the children also grew up in poor rearing conditions.

What of children who faced both biological and environmental challenges—prenatal or birth complications *and* adverse family circumstances? The majority of these children developed serious learning or behaviour problems by age 10. By age 18, most had acquired a police record, had experienced mental health problems, or had become an unmarried parent. However, one-third of such at-risk children showed impressive resilience, growing up into young adults who, in the words of Werner, "loved well, worked well, and played well" (1989, p. 108D).

Michael was one such resilient child. Born prematurely, with low birth weight, to teenage parents, he spent the first 3 weeks of his life in a hospital, separated from his mother. By his 8th birthday, Michael's parents were divorced, his mother had deserted the family, and he and his three brothers and sisters were being raised by their father, with the help of their elderly grandparents. Yet by age 18,

Michael was successful in school, had high self-esteem, was popular with his peers, and was a caring young man with a positive attitude toward life. The fact that there are many children like Michael—children who show great resilience in the face of adversity—is among the most heartening findings of research on child development.

Reading this chapter will increase your understanding of these and other basic questions about child development. It will also introduce you to some historical perspectives on these fundamental questions, as well as to the perspectives and methods that modern researchers use to address them. But first, we would like you to consider a basic question for those taking this course: Why study child development?

ADRIAN WYLD/AP IMAGES

This family has lived in a one-room tent for approximately 2 years. Will these children be resilient enough to overcome their disadvantaged environment? The answer will depend in large part on how many risk factors they face, their personal characteristics, and the nature of the parenting they receive.

Reasons to Learn About Child Development

For us, as both parents and researchers, the sheer enjoyment of watching children and trying to understand them is reason enough for studying child development. What could be more fascinating than the development of a child? But there are also practical and intellectual reasons for studying child development. Understanding how children develop can improve child rearing, promote the adoption of wiser social policies regarding children's welfare, and answer basic questions about human nature. We examine each of these reasons in the following sections.

Raising Children

Trying to be a good parent raises endless questions. If I drink wine occasionally while I'm pregnant, will it harm my baby even before she's born? Once she's born, is it okay to take her outside in the cold weather? Should I raise my son at home for his first few years, or would going to day care be better for his development? My daughter is 3 years old and not speaking yet—should I worry, and is there some way to help her? Should I try to teach my 5-year-old to read early, or will she learn when she's ready? How can I help my kindergartner deal with her anger? My teenager seems lonely and says that no one likes him; how can I help?

Child-development research can help answer such questions. For example, one problem that confronts almost all parents is how to help their children control their anger. One tempting reaction is to spank children who express anger in inappropriate ways, such as fighting, name-calling, and talking back. In Canada, about 25% of parents report spanking their children (Fréchette & Romano, 2015; Perron et al., 2014). Research shows, however, that spanking makes problem behaviours worse, and the effects are long-lasting. One large-scale study showed that the more often parents spanked their kindergartners, the more often the same children argued, fought, and acted inappropriately at school when they were 3rd-graders. This relation has held true for children from various backgrounds, and it has held true above and beyond the effects of other relevant factors, such as parents' income and education (Gershoff et al., 2012).

Fortunately, research suggests several effective alternatives to spanking (Denham, 1998, 2006). One is expressing sympathy: when parents respond to their children's anger with sympathy, the children are better able to cope with the situation causing the distress. Another effective approach is helping angry children find positive alternatives to expressing their feelings. For example, encouraging them to do something they enjoy helps them cope with their hostility.

Posters like this are used in the turtle technique to remind children of ways to control anger.

These strategies and similar ones, such as time-outs, can also be used effectively by others who contribute to raising children, such as day-care personnel and teachers. One demonstration of this was provided by a special curriculum devised for helping preschoolers (3- and 4-year-olds) who were angry and out of control (Denham & Burton, 1996). This curriculum encourages preschool teachers to help children recognize their own and other children's emotions, as well as to teach children techniques for controlling their anger and peaceably resolving conflicts with other children. One approach that children were taught for coping with anger was the "turtle technique." When children felt themselves becoming angry, they were to move away from other children and retreat into their "turtle shell," where they could think through the situation until they were ready to emerge from the shell.

The curriculum was quite successful. Children who participated in it became more skillful in recognizing and regulating anger when they experienced it. For example, one boy, who had regularly gotten into fights when angry, told the teacher after a dispute with another child, "See, I used my words, not my hands" (Denham, 1998, p. 219). The benefits of this program can be long term. In one test, positive effects were still evident as long as 4 or 5 years after children completed the curriculum (Jennings & Greenberg, 2009). As this example suggests, knowledge of child-development research can be helpful to everyone involved in the care of children.

Choosing Social Policies

Another reason to learn about child development is to be able to make informed decisions about the wide variety of social-policy questions that affect children in general. For example, does playing violent video games increase aggressive behaviour? How much trust should judges and juries place in preschoolers' testimony in child-abuse cases? Should children who struggle in school be held back, or should they be promoted to the next grade so that they can be with children of the same age?

Consider the issue of whether playing violent video games makes children and adolescents more aggressive. This issue has been hotly contested by politicians, advocacy groups, and researchers, with some arguing that such games are sufficiently harmful that their sale to minors should be forbidden. The Entertainment Software Association of Canada is responsible for rating video games in terms of age-appropriateness, content, and interactive features, and most retailers in Canada, using this rating system, require age verification for the purchase of games rated M (mature) (Entertainment Software Rating Board, n.d.).

To provide a thorough evaluation of the evidence, Ferguson (2015; also see Furuya-Kanamori & Doi, 2016) reviewed findings from 101 studies conducted on the topic. He used a statistical technique known as **meta-analysis**, a method for combining the results from independent studies to reach conclusions based on all of them. This meta-analysis indicated that the effect of playing violent video games on children's and adolescents' aggression was minimal. Minimal is not the same as nonexistent—playing violent video games did appear to increase aggressive behaviour by a small amount—but the meta-analysis contradicted claims that violent video games are a major cause of children's and adolescents' aggression. Such quantitative analyses of the impact of various activities on children's behaviour are

meta-analysis a method for combining the results from independent studies to reach conclusions based on all of them useful evidence in deciding whether the benefits of preventing potentially harmful activities outweigh the costs of impinging on people's freedom to do what they want.

Another issue of social policy in which child-development research has played an important role concerns how much trust to put in preschoolers' courtroom testimony. Research suggests that tens of thousands of children testify in legal cases in Canada about crimes they either experienced or witnessed (Cunningham & Stevens, 2011). Many of these children are very young: in 2012, about 40% of children who were victims of sexual offences in Canada were 11 years of age or younger (Statistics Canada, 2014). Many of these children face the prospect of testifying in court. The stakes are extremely high in such cases. If juries believe children who falsely testify that they were abused, innocent people may spend years in jail. If juries do not believe children who accurately report abuse, the perpetrators will go free and probably abuse other children. What can be done to promote reliable testimony from young children and to avoid leading them to report experiences that never occurred?

Psychological research has helped answer such questions. In one experiment, researchers tested whether biased questioning affects the accuracy of young children's memory for events involving touching one's own and other people's bodies. The researchers began by having 3- to 6-year-olds play a game, similar to "Simon Says," in which the children were told to touch various parts of their body and those of other children. A month later, a social worker was sent to interview the children about their experiences during the game (Ceci & Bruck, 1998). Before the social worker conducted the interviews, she was given a description of each child's experiences. However, unknown to her, the description she heard included inaccuracies. The social worker was given instructions much like those in a court case: "Find out what the child remembers."

As it turned out, the version of events that the social worker had heard often influenced her questions to children. If, for example, children's accounts of an event contradicted what the social worker believed to be the case, she tended to question the children repeatedly about the event ("Are you sure you touched his foot? Is it possible you touched some other part of his body?"). In response to the social worker's questions, children often changed their responses, with 34% of 3- and 4-year-olds eventually corroborating at least one of the social workers' incorrect beliefs. Children were led to "remember" not only plausible events that never happened but also implausible ones that the social worker had been told about. For instance, some children "recalled" their knee being licked and a marble being inserted in their ear.

Studies of this type have yielded a number of conclusions regarding children's testimony in legal proceedings. One important finding is that when 3- to 5-year-olds are not asked leading questions, their testimony is usually accurate as far as it goes, though they leave out a great deal of information (Bruck, Ceci, & Principe, 2006; Howe & Courage, 1997). However, when prompted by leading questions, young children's testimony is often inaccurate, especially when the leading questions are asked repeatedly. The younger the children are, the more their recall tends to reflect the biases of the interviewer's questions (Otgaar et al., 2018). In addition, realistic props, such as anatomically correct dolls and drawings, which are often used in judicial cases

In courtrooms such as this one, asking questions that will help children to testify accurately is of the utmost importance.

ST. PETERSBURG TIMES/SCOTT MCINTYRE/THE IMAGE WORKS

BOX 1.1 A CLOSER LOOK The Romanian Adoption Study

A particularly poignant illustration of the way in which scientific research can increase understanding of human nature comes from studies of how children's ability to overcome the effects of early maltreatment is affected by its timing, that is, by when in the child's life the maltreatment begins and ends. This research examines children whose early life was spent in horribly inadequate orphanages in Romania in the late 1980s and early 1990s (McCall et al., 2011; Nelson et al., 2007; Rutter, O'Connor, & The English and Romanian Adoptees Study Team, 2004). Children in these orphanages had almost no contact with any caregiver. For reasons that remain unknown, the brutal Communist dictatorship of that era demanded that staff workers not interact with the children, even when giving them their bottles. Staff members provided the infants with so little physical contact that the crown of many infants' heads became flattened from the babies' lying on their backs for 18 to 20 hours per day.

Shortly after the collapse of Communist rule in Romania, a number of these children were adopted by families around the world, including Canada and Great Britain. When these children arrived in their adoptive homes, most were severely malnourished, with more than half being in the lowest 3% of children their age in terms of height, weight, and head circumference. Most also showed varying degrees of intellectual disability and were socially immature. The parents who adopted them knew of their deprived backgrounds and were highly motivated to provide loving homes that would help the children recover from the damaging effects of their early mistreatment.

To evaluate the long-term effects of their early deprivation, the physical, intellectual, and social development of about 150 of the Romanian-born children adopted into homes in Great Britain were examined at age 6 years. To provide a basis of comparison, the researchers also followed the development of a group of British-born children who had been adopted into loving British families before they were 6 months of age. Simply put, the question was whether human nature is sufficiently flexible that the Romanian-born children could overcome the extreme deprivation of their early experience.

By age 6 years, the physical development of the Romanian-born children had improved considerably, both in absolute terms and in relation to the British-born comparison group. However, the Romanian children's early experience of deprivation continued to influence their physical development, with the extent of negative effects depending on how long the children had been institutionalized. Romanian-born children who were adopted by British families before age 6 months, and who had therefore spent the smallest portion of their early lives in the orphanages, weighed about the same as British-born children when both were 6-year-olds. However, Romanian-born children adopted between the ages of 6 and 24 months, and who therefore had spent more of their early lives in the orphanages, weighed less; and those adopted between the ages of 24 and 42 months weighed even less (Rutter et al., 2004).

Intellectual development at age 6 years showed a similar pattern. The Romanian-born children who had been adopted before age 6 months demonstrated levels of intellectual competence comparable with those of the British-born group. Those who had been adopted between ages 6 and 24 months did somewhat less well, and those adopted between ages 24 and 42 months did even more poorly (Rutter et al., 2004). The intellectual deficits of the Romanian children adopted after age 6 months were just as great when the children were retested at age 11, indicating that the

in the hopes of improving recall of sexual abuse, turn out not to improve recall of events that occurred but to actually increase the number of inaccurate claims, perhaps by blurring the line between fantasy and reality (Poole, Bruck, & Pipe, 2011).

Research on child eyewitness testimony has had a large practical effect: In various jurisdictions in Canada, multidisciplinary guidelines have been developed to assist police, child welfare workers, physicians, and other professionals in interviewing children and preparing them for court (see the Canadian Child Abuse Association for examples of these guidelines). Training programs have been developed by researchers at Wilfrid Laurier University and the University of Regina to improve how police and social workers conduct investigative interviews with children (Price & Roberts, 2011). In addition to helping courts obtain more accurate testimony from young children, such research-based conclusions illustrate how knowledge of child development can inform social policies more generally.

Understanding Human Nature

A third reason to study child development is to better understand human nature. Many of the most intriguing questions regarding human nature focus on infancy and childhood. For example, does learning start only after children are born, or can it occur in the womb? Can later upbringing in a loving home overcome the detrimental effects of early rearing in a loveless institutional setting? Do children vary in personality and intellect from the day they are born, or are they similar at birth, with differences arising only because they have different experiences?

negative effects of the early deprivation persisted for many years after they were adopted into the loving homes (Beckett et al., 2006; Kreppner et al., 2007). However, by the time the children had become young adults (22- to 25-year-olds), their intellect was in the normal range (Sonuga-Barke et al., 2017).

The early experience in the orphanages had even more prolonged damaging effects on the children's social development (Kreppner et al., 2007). Almost 20% of the Romanian-born children who were adopted after age 6 months showed extremely abnormal social behaviour at age 6 years, such as not looking at their parents in anxiety-provoking situations and willingly going off with strangers (versus 3% of the British-born comparison group who did so). Even in early adulthood, many had difficulty controlling their emotions and forming friendships (Rutter et al., 2009). Unlike with intellectual development, these negative effects on social and emotional development persisted into adulthood (Sonuga-Barke et al., 2017), with children from the Romanian orphanages having far greater rates of using mental health services than those in the control group (43% versus 10%). In contrast to the differences in intellectual development, which diminished over time, the differences in mental health problems increased between ages 15 and 23 years.

This atypical social development was accompanied by abnormal brain activity. Brain scans obtained when the children were 8 years old showed that those adopted after living for a substantial period in the orphanages had unusually low levels of neural activity in the **amygdala**, a brain area involved in emotional reactions (Chugani et al., 2001). Subsequent studies have identified similar brain abnormalities among children who spent their early lives in poor-quality orphanages in Russia and East Asia (Nelson et al., 2011; Tottenham et al., 2010).

These findings reflect a basic principle of child development that is relevant to many aspects of human nature: *The timing of experiences influences their effects.* In the present case, children were sufficiently flexible to overcome the effects of living in the Romanian institutions if the deprivation ended by age 6 months; living in the institutions until older ages, however, had effects that were rarely overcome completely, even when children spent many subsequent years in loving and stimulating environments. The adoptive families clearly made a huge positive difference in their children's lives, but the later the age of adoption, the greater the long-term harmful effects of early deprivation.

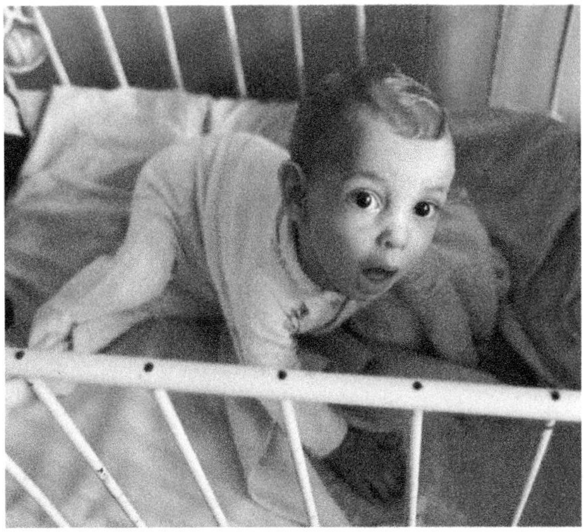

PETER TURNLEY/GETTY IMAGES

This infant is one of the children adopted from a Romanian orphanage in the 1990s. How successfully he was likely to develop depended not only on the quality of caregiving he received in his adoptive home but also on the amount of time he spent in the orphanage and the age at which he was adopted.

Studying infants and young children offers an opportunity to learn what people are like before they are affected by the innumerable influences of family and society. One major group of contemporary philosophers and psychologists, known as *nativists,* argues that evolution has created many remarkable capabilities that are present even in early infancy, particularly in areas of special importance, such as understanding basic properties of physical objects, plants and animals, and other people. Another major group of philosophers and psychologists, known as *empiricists,* has argued that infants possess general learning mechanisms that allow them to learn a great deal quite quickly, but that infants and young children lack the specialized capabilities that nativists attribute to them.

amygdala an area of the brain that is involved in emotional reactions

Until recently, people could only speculate about questions regarding human nature. Now, however, developmental scientists have methods that enable us to observe, describe, and explain the process of development, and thus to deepen our understanding of how we become who we are. Box 1.1 provides one fascinating example of the questions that these methods can address.

REVIEW QUESTIONS

In addition to the examples discussed in this section, can you think of other situations where a better understanding of child development may benefit society? What reasons do you have for studying child development? ■

Historical Foundations of the Study of Child Development

From ancient Greece to the early years of the twentieth century, a number of profound thinkers observed and wrote about children. Their goals were like those of contemporary researchers: to help people become better parents, to improve children's well-being, and to understand human nature. Unlike contemporary researchers, however, these early philosophers usually based their conclusions on general beliefs and informal observations of only a few children.

Beginning in the early twentieth century, when the benefits of using the scientific method had become evident in medicine and many other areas, psychologists began to apply the scientific method to analyzing human behaviour. Still, the issues the early thinkers raised are sufficiently important, and their insights sufficiently deep, that their views continue to influence contemporary thinking about child development.

Early Philosophers' Views of Children's Development

The classic Greek philosophers Plato and Aristotle, who lived in the fourth century B.C., proposed some of the earliest recorded and most influential ideas about children's development. They were particularly interested in how children are influenced by their nature and by the nurture they receive. Both philosophers believed that the long-term welfare of society depended on the proper raising of children. Careful upbringing was essential because children's basic nature would otherwise lead to their becoming rebellious and unruly. Plato viewed the rearing of boys as a particular challenge:

> Now of all wild things, a boy is the most difficult to handle. Just because he more than any other has a fount of intelligence in him which has not yet "run clear," he is the craftiest, most mischievous, and unruliest of brutes.
>
> (*The Laws,* bk. 7, 1961, p. 1379)

Consistent with this view, Plato emphasized self-control and discipline as the most important goals of education (Borstelmann, 1983).

Aristotle agreed with Plato that discipline was necessary, but he was more concerned with fitting child rearing to the needs of the individual child. In his words:

> It would seem . . . that a study of individual character is the best way of making education perfect, for then each [child] has a better chance of receiving the treatment that suits him.
>
> (*Nicomachean Ethics,* bk. 10, chap. 9, p. 1180)

Plato and Aristotle differed considerably in their views of how children acquire knowledge. Plato believed that children have innate knowledge. For example, he believed that children are born with a concept of "animal" that, from birth onward, automatically allows them to recognize that dogs, cats, and other creatures they encounter are animals. In contrast, Aristotle believed that all knowledge comes from experience and that the mind of an infant is like a blackboard on which nothing has yet been written.

Roughly 2000 years later, the English philosopher John Locke (1632–1704) and the French philosopher Jean-Jacques Rousseau (1712–1778) refocused attention on the question of how parents and society in general can best promote children's development. Locke, like Aristotle, viewed the child as a *tabula rasa,* or blank slate, whose development largely reflects the nurture provided by the child's parents and the broader society. He believed that the most important goal of child rearing is the growth of character. To build children's character, parents need to set good examples of honesty, stability, and gentleness. They also need to avoid indulging the child, especially early in life. However, once discipline and reason have been instilled, Locke believed that

> authority should be relaxed as fast as their age, discretion, and good behavior could allow it. . . . The sooner you treat him as a man, the sooner he will begin to be one.
>
> (Cited in Borstelmann, 1983, p. 20)

In contrast to Locke's advocating discipline before freedom, Rousseau believed that parents and society should give children maximum freedom from the beginning. Rousseau claimed that children learn primarily from their own spontaneous interactions with objects and other people, rather than through instruction by parents or teachers. He even argued that children should not receive any formal education until about age 12, when they reach "the age of reason" and can judge for themselves the worth of what they are told. Before then, they should be allowed the freedom to explore whatever interests them.

Although formulated long ago, these and other philosophical questions continue to underlie many contemporary debates about human nature. However, the contemporary debates are based to a much greater extent on the results of carefully conducted research. For example, after reviewing many research studies, Kagan (2000) concluded that children have an innate moral sense, encompassing five abilities that even our closest primate relatives lack. These include the ability to infer the thoughts and feelings of others, to apply the concepts of good and bad to one's own behaviour, to reflect on past actions, to understand that negative consequences could have been avoided, and to understand one's own and others' motives and emotions. A great deal of evidence relevant to these and other issues about human nature will be presented in the chapters that follow.

Social Reform Movements

The contemporary field of child psychology also has roots in early social reform movements that were devoted to improving children's lives by changing the conditions in which they lived. During the Industrial Revolution of the 1700s, 1800s, and early 1900s, a great many children in Europe and the United States worked as poorly paid labourers with few if any legal protections. Some were as young as 5 and 6 years; many worked up to 12 hours a day in factories or mines, often in extremely hazardous circumstances. These harsh conditions worried a number of social reformers, who began to study how such circumstances affected the children's development. For example, in a speech before the British House of Commons in 1843, the Earl of Shaftesbury noted that the narrow tunnels where children dug out coal had

> very insufficient drainage [and] are so low that only little boys can work in them, which they do naked, and often in mud and water, dragging sledge-tubs by the girdle and chain. . . . Children of amiable temper and conduct, at 7 years of age, often return next season from the collieries greatly corrupted . . . with most hellish dispositions.
>
> (Quoted in Kessen, 1965, pp. 46–50)

The Earl of Shaftesbury's effort at social reform brought partial success—a law forbidding employment of girls and of boys younger than 10. In addition to bringing about the first child labour laws, this and other early social reform

BETTMANN/GETTY IMAGES

During the eighteenth, nineteenth, and early twentieth centuries, many young children worked in coal mines and factories. Their hours were long, and the work was often unhealthy and dangerous. Concern over the well-being of such children led to some of the earliest research on child development.

movements established a legacy of research conducted for the benefit of children and provided some of the earliest recorded descriptions of the adverse effects that harsh environments can have on children.

Darwin's Theory of Evolution

Later in the nineteenth century, Charles Darwin's work on evolution inspired a number of scientists to propose that intensive study of children's development might lead to important insights into human nature. Darwin himself was interested in child development, and in 1877 he published an article in which he presented his careful observations of the growth of his infant son, William. Darwin's "baby biography"—a systematic description of William's day-to-day development—represented one of the first methods for studying children.

Such intensive studies of individual children's growth continue to be a distinctive feature of the modern field of child development. Darwin's evolutionary theory, which employs variation, natural selection, and inheritance as its fundamental concepts, also continues to influence the thinking of modern developmentalists on a wide range of topics: infants' attachment to their mothers (Bowlby, 1969), innate fear of natural dangers such as spiders and snakes (Hoehl et al., 2017), sex differences (Geary, 2010a), aggression and altruism (Tooby & Cosmides, 2005), and learning mechanisms (Siegler, 1996).

REVIEW QUESTION

Throughout history, philosophers and researchers such as Plato, Darwin, and Kagan have sought to understand what makes people different from even our closest primate relatives. In what ways other than their moral sense do you think human children differ most from the animals most similar to us? ■

Enduring Themes in Child Development

The modern study of child development begins with a set of fundamental questions. Everything else—theories, concepts, research methods, data, and so on—is part of the effort to answer these questions. Although experts in the field might choose different particular questions as the most important, there is widespread agreement that the seven questions in Table 1.1 are among the most important. These questions form a set of themes that we will highlight throughout the book as we examine specific aspects of child development. In this section, we introduce and briefly discuss each question and the theme that corresponds to it.

1 *Nature and Nurture:* How Do Nature and Nurture Together Shape Development?

nature our biological endowment; the genes we receive from our parents

The most basic question about child development is how nature and nurture interact to shape the developmental process. **Nature** refers to our biological endowment, in particular, the genes we receive from our parents. This genetic inheritance influences every aspect of our makeup, from broad characteristics such as physical appearance, personality, intellect, and mental health to specific preferences, such as political attitudes and propensity for thrill-seeking (Plomin et al., 2012). **Nurture** refers to the wide range of environments, both physical and social, that influence our development, including the womb in which we spend the prenatal period, the homes in which we grow up, the schools that we attend, the broader communities in which we live, and the many people with whom we interact.

Popular depictions often present the nature–nurture question as an either/or proposition: "What determines how a person develops, heredity *or* environment?" However, this either/or phrasing is misleading. All human characteristics—our intellect, our personality, our physical appearance, our emotions—develop through the *joint* workings of nature and nurture, that is, through the constant interaction of our biology and our environment. Accordingly, rather than asking whether nature *or* nurture is more important, developmentalists ask how nature *and* nurture work together to shape development.

That this is the right question to ask is vividly illustrated by findings on the development of schizophrenia. Schizophrenia is a label for a family of serious mental illnesses, often characterized by hallucinations, delusions, confusion, and irrational behaviour. There is an obvious genetic component to this disease. Children who have a schizophrenic parent have a much higher probability than other children of developing the illness later in life, even when they are adopted as infants and therefore are not exposed to their parents' schizophrenic behaviour (Kety et al., 1994). Among identical twins—that is, twins whose genes are identical—if one twin has schizophrenia, the other has a roughly 40% to 50% chance of also having schizophrenia, as opposed to the roughly 1% probability for the general population (see Figure 1.1; Cardno & Gottesman, 2000; Gejman, Sanders, & Duan, 2010; Gottesman, 1991).

At the same time, the environment is also clearly influential, since roughly 50% to 60% of children who have an identical twin with schizophrenia do not become schizophrenic themselves; and children who grow up in troubled homes are more likely to become schizophrenic than are children raised in a stable household. Most important, however, is the interaction of genes and environment. A study of adopted children, some of whose biological parents were schizophrenic, indicated that the only children who had any substantial likelihood of becoming schizophrenic were those who had a schizophrenic parent *and* who also were adopted into a troubled family (Tienari, Wahlberg, & Wynne, 2006).

A remarkable recent series of studies has revealed some of the biological mechanisms through which nature and nurture interact. These studies show that just as the **genome**—each person's complete set of hereditary information—influences behaviours and experiences, behaviours and experiences influence the genome (Meaney, 2010; Slavich & Cole, 2013). This might seem impossible, given that each person's DNA is constant throughout life. However, the genome includes not only DNA but also proteins that regulate gene expression by turning gene activity on and off. These proteins change in response to experience and, without structurally altering DNA, can produce enduring changes in cognition, emotion, and behaviour. This discovery has given rise to a new field called **epigenetics**, the study of stable changes

TABLE 1.1 Basic Questions About Child Development

1. How do nature and nurture together shape development? *(Nature and nurture)*
2. How do children shape their own development? *(The active child)*
3. In what ways is development continuous, and in what ways is it discontinuous? *(Continuity/discontinuity)*
4. How does change occur? *(Mechanisms of change)*
5. How does the sociocultural context influence development? *(The sociocultural context)*
6. How do children become so different from one another? *(Individual differences)*
7. How can research promote children's well-being? *(Research and children's welfare)*

nurture the environments, both physical and social, that influence our development

genome each person's complete set of hereditary information

epigenetics the study of stable changes in gene expression that are mediated by the environment

FIGURE 1.1 Genetic relatedness and schizophrenia The closer the biological relation, the stronger the probability that relatives of a person with schizophrenia will have the same mental illness. (Data from Gottesman, 1991)

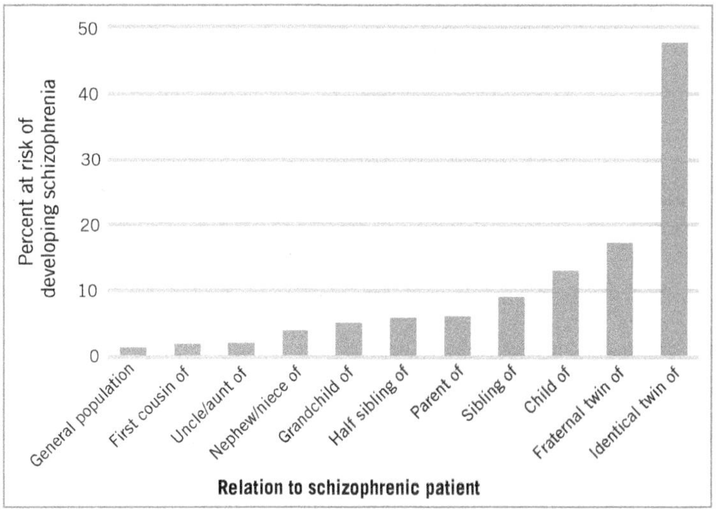

NICHOLAS KAMM/GETTY IMAGES

How do you think nature and nurture together led Justin Trudeau, son of former Canadian prime minister Pierre Trudeau, to become prime minister himself in 2015?

in gene expression that are mediated by the environment. Stated simply, epigenetics examines how experience gets under the skin.

Evidence for the enduring epigenetic impact of early experiences and behaviours comes from research on **methylation**, a biochemical process that reduces expression of a variety of genes and is involved in regulating reactions to stress (Lam, Hastie et al., 2012). One study showed that the amount of stress that mothers reported experiencing during their children's infancy was related to the amount of methylation in the children's genomes 15 years later (Essex et al., 2013). Other studies showed increased methylation in the cord-blood DNA of newborns of depressed mothers (Oberlander et al., 2008) and in adults who were abused as children (McGowan et al., 2009), leading researchers to speculate that such children are at heightened risk for depression as adults (Rutten & Mill, 2009).

methylation a biochemical process that influences behaviour by suppressing gene activity and expression

As these examples illustrate, developmental outcomes emerge from the constant bidirectional interaction of nature *and* nurture. To say that one is more important than the other, or even that the two are equally important, drastically oversimplifies the developmental process.

2 *The Active Child:* How Do Children Shape Their Own Development?

Children's own actions also contribute to their development. Even in infancy and early childhood, this contribution can be seen in a multitude of areas, including attention, language use, and play.

Infants shape their own development through selective attention. Even newborns attend more to objects that move and make sounds than to other objects. This preference helps them learn about important parts of the world, such as people, other animals, and inanimate moving objects, including cars and trucks. When looking at people, infants' attention is particularly drawn to faces, especially their mother's face; given a choice of looking at a stranger's face or their mother's, even 1-month-olds choose to look at Mom (Bartrip, Morton, & de Schonen, 2001). At first, infants' attention to their mother's face is not accompanied by any visible emotion, but by the end of the second month, infants smile and coo more when focusing intently on their mother's face than at other times. This smiling and cooing by the infant elicits smiling and talking by the mother, which elicits further cooing and smiling by the infant, and so on (Lavelli & Fogel, 2005). In this way, infants' preference for attending to their mother's face leads to social interactions that can strengthen the mother–infant bond.

One of the earliest ways children shape their own development is through their choice of where to look. From the first month of life, seeing Mom is a high priority.

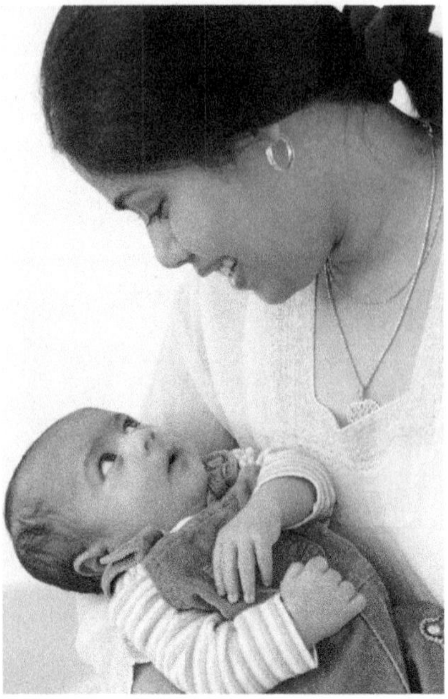

RUTH JENKINSON/GETTY IMAGES

Once children begin to speak, usually between 9 and 15 months of age, their contribution to their own development becomes more evident. For example, toddlers (1- and 2-year-olds) often talk when they are alone in a room. Only if children were internally motivated to learn language would they practice talking when no one was present to react to what they are saying. This "crib speech" is entirely normal, and the practice probably helps toddlers learn language.

Young children's play provides many other examples of how their internally motivated activity contributes to their development. Children play by themselves for the sheer joy of doing so, but they also learn a great deal in the process. Anyone who has seen a baby bang a spoon against the tray of a high chair or intentionally drop food on the floor would agree that, for the baby, the activity is its own reward.

At the same time, the baby is learning about the noises made by colliding objects, about the speed at which objects fall, and about the limits of his or her parents' patience.

Young children's fantasy play seems to make an especially large contribution to their knowledge of themselves and other people. Starting at around age 2 years, children sometimes pretend to be different people in make-believe dramas. For example, they may pretend to be superheroes doing battle with monsters or play the role of parents taking care of babies. The particular play activities vary across cultures, but the existence of play and its developmental pattern are similar, even in cultures that actively discourage playing (Carlson, Taylor, & Levin, 1998).

In addition to being inherently enjoyable, play teaches children valuable lessons, including how to cope with fears, resolve disputes, and interact with others (Lillard, 2017). Older children's play, which typically is more organized and rule-bound, promotes additional useful capabilities, such as the self-control needed for turn-taking, adhering to rules, and controlling one's emotions in the face of setbacks (Hirsh-Pasek, Zosh et al., 2015). As we discuss later in the chapter, children's contributions to their own development strengthen and broaden as they grow older and become increasingly able to choose and shape their environments.

AMI PARIKH/SHUTTERSTOCK

Play contributes to children's development in many ways, including the spatial understanding and attention to detail required to complete puzzles.

3 *Continuity/Discontinuity:* In What Ways Is Development Continuous, and in What Ways Is It Discontinuous?

Some scientists envision children's development as a **continuous** process of small changes, like that of a pine tree growing taller and taller. Others see the process as a series of occasional, sudden, **discontinuous** changes, like the transition from caterpillar to cocoon to butterfly (Figure 1.2). The debate over which of these views best describes child development has continued for decades.

Researchers who view development as *discontinuous* start from a common observation: children of different ages seem *qualitatively different*. A 4-year-old and a 6-year-old, for example, seem to differ not only in how much they know but in the way they think about the world. To appreciate these differences, consider two conversations between Beth, the daughter of one of the authors, and Beth's mother. The first conversation took place when Beth was 4 years old; the second, when she was 6. Both conversations occurred after Beth had watched her mother

continuous development the idea that changes with age occur gradually, in small increments, like that of a pine tree growing taller and taller

discontinuous development the idea that changes with age include occasional large shifts, like the transition from caterpillar to cocoon to butterfly

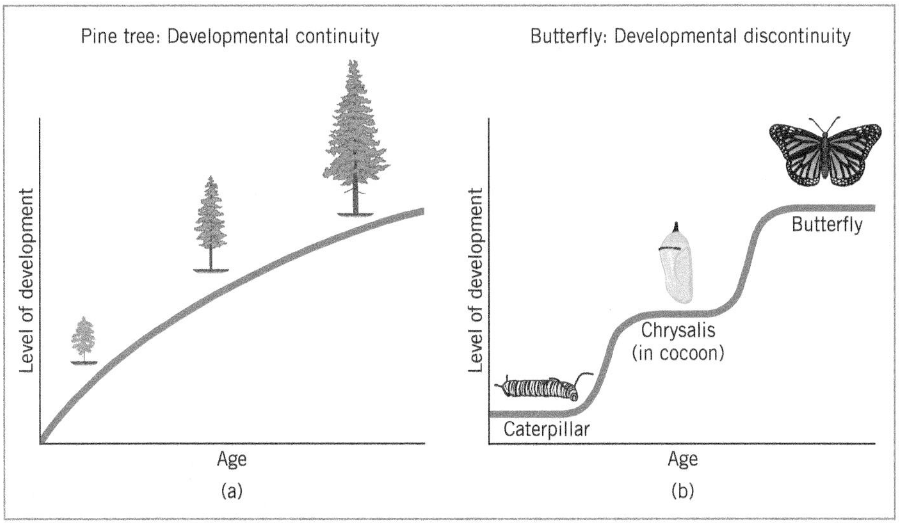

FIGURE 1.2 Continuous and discontinuous development Some researchers see development as a continuous, gradual process, akin to a tree's growing taller with each passing year. Others see it as a discontinuous process, involving sudden dramatic changes, such as the transition from caterpillar to cocoon to butterfly. Each view fits some aspects of child development.

pour all the water from a typical drinking glass into a taller, narrower glass. Here is the conversation that occurred when Beth was 4:

Mother: Is there still the same amount of water?
Beth: No.
Mother: Was there more water before, or is there more now?
Beth: There's more now.
Mother: What makes you think so?
Beth: The water is higher; you can see it's more.
Mother: Now I'll pour the water back into the regular glass. Is there the same amount of water as when the water was in the same glass before?
Beth: Yes.
Mother: Now I'll pour all the water again into the tall thin glass. Does the amount of water stay the same?
Beth: No, I already told you, there's more water when it's in the tall glass.

Two years later, Beth responded to the same problem quite differently:

Mother: Is there still the same amount of water?
Beth: Of course!

What accounts for this change in Beth's thinking? Her everyday observations of liquids being poured cannot have been the reason for it; Beth had seen liquids poured on a great number of occasions before she was 4, yet she failed to develop the understanding that the volume of liquid remains constant. Experience with the specific task could not explain the change either, because Beth had no further exposure to the task between the first and second conversation. Then why as a 4-year-old would Beth be so confident that pouring the water into the taller, narrower glass increased the amount, and then as a 6-year-old be so confident that it did not?

This conservation-of-liquid-quantity problem is actually a classic technique designed to test children's level of thinking. It has been used with thousands of children around the world, and virtually all the children studied, no matter what their culture, have shown the same type of change in reasoning as Beth did (though usually at somewhat older ages). Furthermore, such age-related differences in understanding pervade children's thinking. Consider two letters sent to the host of the children's television show *Mr. Rogers' Neighborhood*, one by a 4-year-old and one by a 5-year-old (Rogers, 1996, pp. 10–11):

Dear Mr. Rogers,
I would like to know how you get in the TV.

(Robby, age 4)

Dear Mr. Rogers,
I wish you accidentally stepped out of the TV into my house so I could play with you.

(Josiah, age 5)

Clearly, these are not ideas that an older child would entertain. As with Beth's case, we have to ask, "What is it about 4- and 5-year-olds that leads them to form such improbable beliefs, and what changes occur that make such notions laughable to 6- and 7-year-olds?"

One common approach to answering these questions comes from **stage theories**, which propose that development occurs in a progression of distinct age-related stages, much like the butterfly example in Figure 1.2b. According to these theories, a child's entry into a new stage involves relatively sudden, qualitative

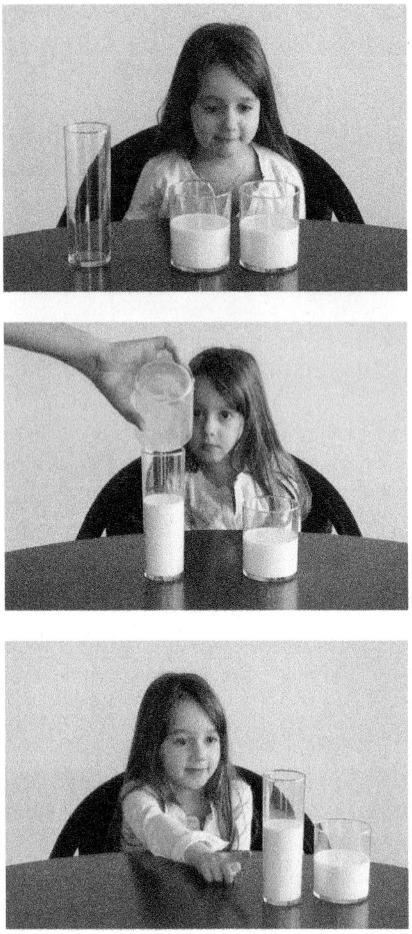

ALL: BIANCA MOSCATELLI/WORTH PUBLISHERS

Children's behaviour on Piaget's conservation-of-liquid-quantity problem is often used to exemplify the idea that development is discontinuous. The child first sees equal amounts of liquid in similarly shaped glasses and an empty, differently shaped glass. Then, the child sees the liquid from one glass poured into the differently shaped glass. Finally, the child is asked whether the amount of liquid remains the same or whether one glass has more. Young children, like this girl, are unshakable in their belief that the glass with the taller liquid column has more liquid. A year or two later, they are equally unshakable in their belief that the amount of liquid in each glass is the same.

stage theories approaches proposing that development involves a series of large, discontinuous, age-related phases changes that affect the child's thinking or behaviour in broadly unified ways and move the child from one coherent way of experiencing the world to a different coherent way of experiencing it.

Among the best-known stage theories is Jean Piaget's theory of **cognitive development**, the development of thinking and reasoning. This theory holds that between birth and adolescence, children go through four stages of cognitive growth, each characterized by distinct intellectual abilities and ways of understanding the world. For example, according to Piaget's theory, 2- to 5-year-olds are in a stage of development in which they can focus on only one aspect of an event, or one type of information, at a time. By age 7, children enter a different stage, in which they can simultaneously focus on and coordinate two or more aspects of an event and can do so on many different tasks.

cognitive development the development of thinking and reasoning

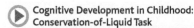

Cognitive Development in Childhood: Conservation-of-Liquid Task

WORTH PUBLISHERS

According to this view, when confronted with a problem like the one that Beth's mother presented to her, most 4- and 5-year-olds focus on the single dimension of height and therefore perceive the taller, narrower glass as having more water. In contrast, most 7- and 8-year-olds consider both relevant dimensions of the problem simultaneously. This allows them to realize that although the column of water in the taller glass is higher, the column also is narrower, and the two differences offset each other.

In the course of reading this book, you will encounter a number of other stage theories, including Sigmund Freud's theory of psychosexual development, Erik Erikson's theory of psychosocial development, and Lawrence Kohlberg's theory of moral development. Each of these stage theories proposes that children of a given age show broad similarities across many situations and that children of different ages tend to behave very differently.

Although such stage theories have been highly influential, in the past 20 years, many researchers have concluded that most developmental changes are gradual rather than sudden, and that development occurs skill by skill rather than in a broadly unified way (Munakata, Snyder, & Chatham, 2012; Thelen & Smith, 2006). This view of development is less dramatic than that of stage theories, but a great deal of evidence supports it. One such piece of evidence is the fact that a child often will behave in accord with one proposed stage on some tasks but in accord with a different proposed stage on other tasks (Fischer & Bidell, 2006). This variable level of reasoning makes it difficult to view the child as being "in" either stage.

Much of the difficulty in deciding whether development is continuous or discontinuous is that the same facts can look very different, depending on one's perspective. A classic study by Tanner (1961) addressed the seemingly simple question of whether children's height increases continuously or discontinuously. Figure 1.3a shows a boy's height, measured yearly from birth to age 18. When one looks at the boy's height at each age, development seems smooth and continuous, with growth occurring rapidly early in life and then slowing down.

Cognitive Development: The Balance-Scale Problem

WORTH PUBLISHERS

However, when you look at Figure 1.3b, a different picture emerges. This graph illustrates the same boy's growth, but it depicts the amount of growth from one year to the next. The boy grew every year, but he grew most during two periods: from birth to age 2½ and from ages 13 to 15. These are the kinds of data that lead people to talk about discontinuous growth and about a separate stage of adolescence that includes a physical growth spurt.

So, is development fundamentally continuous or fundamentally discontinuous? The most reasonable answer seems to be, "It depends on how

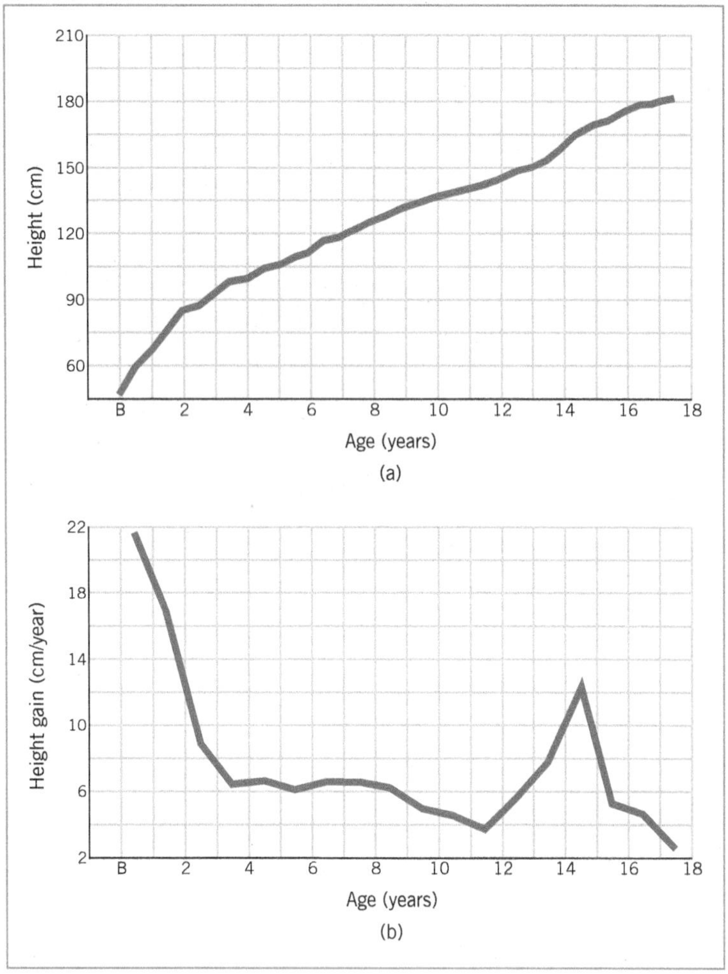

FIGURE 1.3 Continuous and discontinuous growth Depending on how it is viewed, changes in height can be regarded as either continuous or discontinuous. (a) Examining a boy's height in absolute terms from birth to 18 years makes the growth look gradual and continuous. (Data from Tanner, 1961) (b) Examining the increases in the same boy's height from one year to the next over the same period shows rapid growth during the first 2½ years, then slower growth, then a growth spurt in adolescence, then a rapid decrease in growth; viewed this way, growth seems discontinuous.

you look at it and how often you look." Imagine the difference between the perspective of an uncle who sees his niece every 2 or 3 years and that of the niece's parents, who see her every day. The uncle will almost always be struck with the huge changes in his niece since he last saw her. The niece will be so different that it will seem that she progressed to a higher stage of development. In contrast, the parents will most often be struck by the continuity of her development; to them, she just seems to grow up steadily. Throughout this book, we will consider the changes, large and small, sudden and gradual, that have led some researchers to emphasize the continuities in development while others emphasize the discontinuities.

4 *Mechanisms of Change:* How Does Change Occur?

Perhaps the deepest mystery about children's development is expressed by the question "How does change occur?" In other words, what are the mechanisms that produce the remarkable changes that children undergo with age and experience? Different developmentalists use the term "mechanisms" in somewhat different ways, but all attempts to specify mechanisms share the goal of producing increasingly precise accounts of the processes that produce an outcome of interest. Developmental mechanisms can be behavioural, neural, or genetic. Thus, mathematical development has been explained through the behavioural mechanism of improved strategies (Siegler, 2016), the neural mechanism of increased interconnection between the frontal cortex and the intraparietal sulcus (Rosenberg-Lee, Barth, & Menon, 2011), and the genetic mechanism of the presence or absence of specific alleles (Davis et al., 2014).

One particularly interesting analysis of mechanisms of developmental change involves the roles of brain activity, genes, and learning experiences in the development of *effortful attention* (e.g., Rothbart, Sheese, & Posner, 2007). Effortful attention involves voluntary control of one's emotions and thoughts. It includes processes such as inhibiting impulses (e.g., obeying requests to put all of one's toys away, as opposed to putting some away but then getting distracted and playing with the remaining ones); controlling emotions (e.g., not crying when failing to get one's way); and focusing attention (e.g., concentrating on one's homework despite the inviting sounds of other children playing outside). Difficulty in exerting effortful attention is associated with behavioural problems, weak math and reading skills, and mental illness (Blair, 2016; Diamond & Lee, 2011).

To specify the physiological mechanisms underlying effortful control, researchers have examined brain activity of people as they performed tasks that require such control. These studies have shown that when people are controlling thoughts and emotions, brain activity is especially intense in connections between the limbic

neurotransmitters chemicals involved in communication among brain cells

area—a part of the brain that plays a large role in emotional reactions—and the anterior cingulate and prefrontal cortex—brain structures involved in setting and attending to goals (Gazzaniga, Ivry, & Mangun, 2013). Connections among these brain areas develop considerably during childhood, and their development appears to be one mechanism that underlies improving effortful attention during childhood. As we might predict, based on our understanding of nature and nurture, development of these areas reflects environmental circumstances as well as genetics. For example, spending one's childhood in poverty has a negative effect on the brain activity needed to suppress negative emotions and improve effortful attention many years later in adulthood (Kim, Evans et al., 2013).

Other studies have examined the genetic mechanisms that influence brain activity during effortful attention and the way in which those genetic mechanisms influence the effects of parenting. Specific genes have been found to influence the production of key **neurotransmitters**—chemicals involved in communication among brain cells. Variations in these genes among children are associated with variations in the quality of performance on tasks that require effortful attention (Canli et al., 2005; Diamond et al., 2004). These genetic influences do not occur in a vacuum. Infants with a particular form of one of the genes in question show differences in effortful attention related to the quality of parenting they receive; lower-quality parenting is associated with lower ability to regulate attention (Sheese et al., 2007). Among children who do not have that form of the gene, quality of parenting has less effect on effortful attention.

Learning can change the wiring of the brain system that produces effortful attention. Rueda and colleagues (2005) presented 6-year-olds with a 5-day training program that used computerized exercises to improve capacity for effortful attention. Examination of electrical activity in the anterior cingulate indicated that those 6-year-olds who had completed the computerized exercises showed improved effortful attention. These children also showed improved performance on intelligence tests, which makes sense given the sustained effortful attention required by such tests. Thus, the experiences that children encounter influence their brain processes and gene expression, just as brain processes and genes influence children's reactions to their experiences. More generally, a full understanding of the mechanisms that produce developmental change requires specifying how genes, brain structures and processes, and experiences interact.

Another illustration of developmental mechanisms involves the changing role of sleep in promoting learning and generalization (Gómez & Edgin, 2015). Infants spend a great deal of their lives sleeping; for example, 6-month-olds average 14–15 hours of sleep per day (Ohayon et al., 2004). This prolonged sleep serves an important function in promoting learning (Diekelmann & Born, 2010). However, the type of learning that it promotes changes with the maturation of the *hippocampus,* a brain structure that is particularly important for learning and remembering.

During the first 18 months following birth, sleep appears to promote learning of general, frequently encountered patterns but not learning of the specifics of material presented only once or twice (Gómez, Bootzin, & Nadel, 2006). In contrast, after age 24 months, children tend to show the opposite pattern: when tested shortly after napping, they often remember the specifics of what they learned better than peers who did not nap during that period, but their memory for general patterns is no better than those of peers who did not nap (Kurdziel, Duclos, & Spencer, 2013).

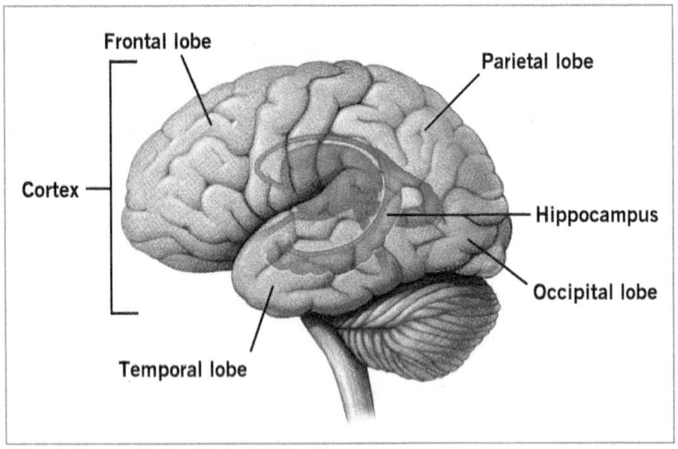

FIGURE 1.4 The human cortex The four main lobes of the cortex: frontal, parietal, occipital, and temporal. The hippocampus, which is also shown, is deeper inside the brain than it appears in this figure, whereas the cortex covers outer portions of the brain.

Werchan and Gómez (2014) described mechanisms that could underlie this change from infancy to the preschool period. Their explanation was based on a major theory of memory, called *Active Systems Consolidation Theory* (McClelland, McNaughton, & O'Reilly, 1995), which posits that two interconnected brain areas, the hippocampus and the cortex, simultaneously encode new information during learning (see Figure 1.4). The hippocampus can learn details of new information after one or two experiences; the cortex produces abstraction of general patterns over many experiences. The theory posits that in older children and adults, hippocampal memories are replayed during sleep, which allows opportunities for the cortex to extract general patterns from the specific memories stored in the hippocampus. The mechanism works in the opposite direction as well; learning general patterns improves the retention of details of new experiences of the same type (Mullally & Maguire, 2014).

These findings and theories led Werchan and Gómez (2014) to hypothesize that the benefits of sleep on infants' memory for general patterns reflect functioning of the cortex, whereas the benefits of sleep on preschoolers' memory for specific experiences reflect functioning of the hippocampus. They proposed that prior to 18 to 24 months of age, the hippocampus is too immature to enable the rapid learning of the details of specific experiences; therefore, sleeping does not benefit memory for these specifics. However, the cortex is mature enough at this age to extract general patterns. Considerable evidence supports this claim (Edgin et al., 2015; Friedrich et al., 2015). Thus, sleep is not a waste of time; it is essential for learning and for healthy development in general.

5 *The Sociocultural Context:* How Does the Sociocultural Context Influence Development?

Children grow up in a particular set of physical and social environments, in a particular culture, under particular economic circumstances, at a particular time in history. Together, these physical, social, cultural, economic, and historical circumstances constitute the **sociocultural context** of a child's life—which influences every aspect of children's development.

A classic depiction of the components of the sociocultural context is Urie Bronfenbrenner's (1979) bioecological model (discussed in depth in Chapter 9). The most obviously important components of children's sociocultural contexts are the people with whom they interact—parents, grandparents, brothers, sisters, day-care providers, teachers, friends, and classmates—and the physical environment in which they live—their house, childcare centre, school, neighbourhood, and so on. Another important but less tangible component of the sociocultural context is the institutions that influence children's lives, including educational systems, religious institutions, sports leagues, social organizations, and others.

Yet another important set of influences are the general characteristics of the child's society: its economic and technological advancement; its values, attitudes, beliefs, and traditions; its laws and political structure; and so on. For example, the simple fact that most toddlers and preschoolers growing up in Canada today go to childcare outside their homes reflects a number of these less tangible sociocultural factors, including the historical era (50 years ago, far fewer children in Canada attended childcare centres); the economic structure (there are far more opportunities today for women to work

sociocultural context the physical, social, cultural, economic, and historical circumstances that make up any child's environment outside the home); cultural beliefs (e.g., that receiving childcare outside the home does not harm children); and cultural values (e.g., the value that mothers of young children should be able to work outside the home if they wish). Attendance at childcare centres, in turn, partly determines the people children meet and the activities in which they engage.

One method that developmentalists use to understand the influence of the sociocultural context is to compare the lives of children who grow up in different cultures. Such *cross-cultural comparisons* often reveal that practices that are rare or nonexistent in one culture are common in others. The following comparison of young children's sleeping arrangements in different societies illustrates the value of such cross-cultural research.

OWEN FRANKEN

In many countries, including Denmark, the country in which this mother and child live, mothers and children sleep together for the first several years of the child's life. This sociocultural pattern is in sharp contrast to the Canadian practice of having infants sleep separately from their parents soon after birth.

In most families in Canada and the United States, newborn infants sleep in their parents' bedroom, either in a crib or in the same bed. However, when infants are 2 to 6 months old, parents usually move them to another bedroom where they sleep alone (Greenfield, Suzuki, & Rothstein-Fisch, 2006). This seems natural to most people raised in North America because it is how they and others whom they know were raised. From a worldwide perspective, however, such sleeping arrangements are unusual. In most other societies, including nations such as Italy, Japan, and South Korea, young children almost always sleep in the same bed as their mother for the first few years, and somewhat older children also sleep in the same room as their mother, sometimes in the same bed (e.g., Nelson, Schiefenhoevel, & Haimerl, 2000; Whiting & Edwards, 1988).

How do these differences in sleeping arrangements affect children? To find out, Morelli and colleagues (1992) interviewed mothers in middle-class U.S. families in Salt Lake City, Utah, and in rural Mayan families in Guatemala. These interviews revealed that by age 6 months, the large majority of the U.S. children had begun sleeping in their own bedroom. As the children grew out of infancy, the nightly separation of child and parents became a complex ritual, surrounded by activities intended to comfort the child, such as telling stories, reading children's books, singing songs, and so on. About half the children were reported as taking a comfort object, such as a blanket or teddy bear, to bed with them.

In contrast, interviews with the Mayan mothers indicated that their children typically slept in the same bed with them until the age of 2 or 3 years and continued to sleep in the same room with them for years thereafter. The children usually went to sleep at the same time as their parents. None of the Mayan parents reported bedtime rituals, and almost none reported their children taking comfort objects, such as dolls or stuffed animals, to bed with them.

Why do sleeping arrangements differ across cultures? Interviews with the Mayan and U.S. parents indicated that cultural values were foremost. Mayan culture prizes interdependence among people. The Mayan parents expressed the belief that having a young child sleep with the mother is important for developing a good parent–child relationship, for avoiding the child's becoming distressed at being alone, and for helping parents spot any problems the child is having. They often expressed shock and pity when told that infants in the United States typically sleep separately from their parents (Greenfield et al., 2006). In contrast, U.S. culture prizes independence and self-reliance, and the U.S. mothers expressed the belief that having babies and young children sleep alone promotes these values, as well as allowing intimacy between husbands and wives (Morelli et al., 1992).

TABLE 1.2 Child Poverty in Canada (Persons under 18 years), 2013 to 2017

	Child Poverty Rate	Total Number of Children Living in Poverty (in thousands)
2013	14.5%	974
2014	12.4	836
2015	13.3	900
2016	11.0	755
2017	9.0	622

Data from Statistics Canada, 2019.

These differences illustrate both how practices that strike us as natural may differ greatly across cultures and how the simple conventions of everyday life often reflect deeper values.

Contexts of development differ not just between cultures but also within them. In modern multicultural societies, many contextual differences are related to ethnicity, race, and **socioeconomic status (SES)**—a measure of social class that is based on income and education. Virtually all aspects of children's lives—from the food they eat to the parental discipline they receive to the games they play—vary with ethnicity, race, and SES.

The socioeconomic context exerts a particularly large influence on children's lives. In economically advanced societies, including Canada, most children grow up in reasonably comfortable circumstances, but millions of other children do not. In 2017 in Canada, 9% of children lived below the poverty level; in absolute numbers, that figure represents approximately 622,000 children, down from 11% in 2016 (see Table 1.2; Statistics Canada, 2019). Although declining in Canada, poverty rates are especially high for Indigenous children in Canada (MacDonald & Wilson, 2016).

As documented in a report to the Royal Society of Canada, children from economically disadvantaged families tend to do less well than other children in many ways, and these effects can be long-lasting (Boivin & Hertzman, 2012). In infancy, they are more likely to have serious health problems. Beginning at age 3 years and continuing through at least age 20, their brains, on average, have less surface area, especially in areas that support spoken language, reading, and spatial skills (Noble et al., 2015). Throughout childhood and adolescence, they tend to have more emotional problems, smaller vocabularies, lower IQs, and lower math and reading scores on standardized achievement tests (Evans, Li, & Whipple, 2013). In adolescence, they are more likely to have a baby or drop out of school (Penman-Aguilar et al., 2013).

These negative outcomes are not surprising when we consider the huge array of challenges that poor children face. Compared with children who grow up in more affluent circumstances, they are more likely to live in dangerous neighbourhoods, to attend lower-quality childcare centres and schools, and to be exposed to high levels of air and water pollution (Bell & Ebisu, 2012). In addition, their parents read to them less, provide fewer books in the home, and are less involved in their schooling (Hart & Risley, 2003). Children in low-income families also are more likely than children from more affluent families to grow up in single-parent homes or to be raised by neither biological parent. The accumulation of these disadvantages over years of development, often termed **cumulative risk**, seems to be the greatest obstacle to poor children's successful development (Evans & Cassells, 2014; Morales & Guerra, 2006).

Yet, as we saw in Werner's study of the children of Kauai, described at the beginning of the chapter, many children do overcome the obstacles that poverty presents. Such resilient children are more likely than others to have three characteristics: (1) positive personal qualities, such as high intelligence, an easygoing personality, and an optimistic outlook on the future; (2) a close relationship with at least one parent; and (3) a close relationship with at least one adult other than their parents, such as a grandparent, teacher, coach, or family friend (Chen & Miller, 2012; Masten, 2007). As these characteristics suggest, children's resilience reflects not just their personal qualities but also the interactions they have with other people (Masten, 2014).

socioeconomic status (SES) a measure of social class based on income and education

cumulative risk the accumulation of disadvantages over years of development

6 *Individual Differences:* How Do Children Become So Different from One Another?

Everyone who has experience with children is struck by their uniqueness—their differences not only in physical appearance but in everything from activity level and temperament to intelligence, persistence, and emotionality. These differences among children emerge quickly. Some infants in their first year are shy, others outgoing. Some infants play with or look at objects for prolonged periods; others rapidly shift from activity to activity. Even children in the same family often differ substantially, as you probably already know if you have siblings.

Scarr (1992) identified four factors that can lead children from a single family (as well as children from different families) to turn out very different from one another:

1. Genetic differences
2. Differences in treatment by parents and others
3. Differences in reactions to similar experiences
4. Different choices of environments

The most obvious reason for differences among children is that every individual is genetically unique. This is true even of so-called "identical twins." At conception, the genomes of these children are identical, but mutations or copying errors result in several hundred gene differences being present, on average, even before birth (Li et al., 2014). The genomes of all other children are much more different from each other; for example, other siblings, including fraternal twins, differ in 50% of the genes on which people differ (the vast majority of genes are identical for all humans; they're what make us human).

A second major source of variation among children is differences in the treatment they receive from parents and other people. This differential treatment is often associated with preexisting differences in the children's characteristics. For instance, parents tend to provide more sensitive care to easygoing infants than to difficult ones; by the second year, parents of difficult children are often angry with them, even when the children have done nothing wrong in the immediate situation (van den Boom & Hoeksma, 1994). Teachers likewise tend to provide positive attention and encouragement to pupils who are learning well and are well behaved, but with pupils who are doing poorly and are disruptive, they tend to be openly critical and to deny the pupils' requests for special help (Good & Brophy, 1996).

In addition to being shaped by objective differences in the treatment they receive, children also are influenced by their subjective interpretations of their treatment. A classic example occurs when each of a pair of siblings feels that their parents favour the other. Siblings also often react differently to events that affect the whole family. In one study, 69% of negative events, such as parents' being laid off or fired, elicited fundamentally different reactions from siblings (Beardsall & Dunn, 1992). Some children were very concerned at a parent's loss of a job; others were sure that everything would be okay.

A fourth major source of differences among children relates to the previously discussed theme of the *active child:* as children grow older, they increasingly choose activities and friends for themselves and thus influence their own subsequent development. They may also accept or choose niches for

Different children, even ones within the same family, often react to the same experience, such as this roller coaster ride, in completely different ways.

LOOK DIE BILDAGENTUR DER FOTOGRAFEN GMBH/ALAMY

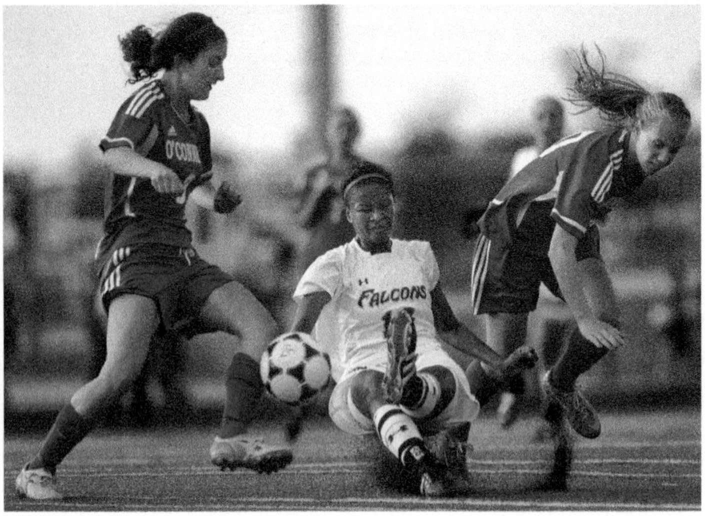

THE WASHINGTON POST/GETTY IMAGES

Adolescents who participate in sports and other extracurricular activities are more likely to complete high school, and less likely to get into trouble, than peers who are not engaged in these activities. This is another example of how individuals make choices that influence their development.

themselves: within a family, one child may become "the smart one," another "the popular one," another "the naughty one," and so on. A child labelled by family members as "the nice one" may strive to live up to the label; so, unfortunately, may a child labelled "the troublemaker."

As discussed in the sections on nature and nurture and on mechanisms of development, differences in biology and experience interact in complex ways to create the infinite diversity of human beings. A study of 11- to 17-year-olds found that the grades of children who were highly engaged with school changed in more positive directions than would have been predicted by their genetic background or family environments alone (Johnson, McGue, & Iacono, 2006). The same study revealed that children of high intelligence were less negatively affected by adverse family environments than were other children. Thus, children's genes, their treatment by other people, their subjective reactions to their experiences, and their choice of environments interact in ways that make each child unique.

7 *Research and Children's Welfare:* How Can Research Promote Children's Well-Being?

Improved research-based understanding of child development often leads to practical benefits. Several examples have already been described, including the program for helping children deal with their anger and the recommendations for fostering valid eyewitness testimony from young children.

Another type of practical benefit arising from child-development research involves educational innovations. Children's reasoning, remembering, conceptualizing, and problem solving is inherently related to education; throughout the book, especially in Chapters 4 and 8, we review many examples of educational innovations stemming from child-development research. One fascinating example comes from studies of children's differing beliefs about intelligence and how those differing beliefs influence their learning (see Box 1.2).

REVIEW QUESTION

Which of the seven fundamental questions about child development most interests you? Why? ■

Methods for Studying Child Development

As illustrated in the preceding section, modern scientific research has advanced understanding of fundamental questions about child development well beyond that of the ancient Greek philosophers who first raised the questions. This progress reflects the successful application of the scientific method to the study of child development. In this section, we describe the scientific method and examine how its use has advanced our understanding of child development.

The Scientific Method

scientific method an approach to testing beliefs that involves choosing a question, formulating a hypothesis, testing the hypothesis, and drawing a conclusion

The basic assumption of the **scientific method** is that all beliefs, no matter how probable they seem and no matter how many people share them, may be wrong. Therefore, until beliefs have been repeatedly tested, they must be viewed

BOX 1.2 INDIVIDUAL DIFFERENCES Can Children Learn to Be More Intelligent?

Carol Dweck and her colleagues (Dweck, 2012; Yeager & Dweck, 2012) have found that some children (and adults) believe that intelligence is a fixed entity. They see each person as having a certain amount of intelligence that is set at birth and cannot be changed by experience. Other children (and adults) believe intelligence is a changeable characteristic that increases with learning and that the time and effort people put into learning is the key determinant of their intelligence.

People who believe that intelligence increases with learning tend to react to failure in more effective ways (Dweck, 2006). When they fail to solve a problem, they more often persist on the task and try harder. Such persistence in the face of failure is an important quality. As the great British Prime Minister Winston Churchill once said, "Success is the ability to go from one failure to another with no loss of enthusiasm." In contrast, people who believe that intelligence is a fixed entity tend to give up when they fail.

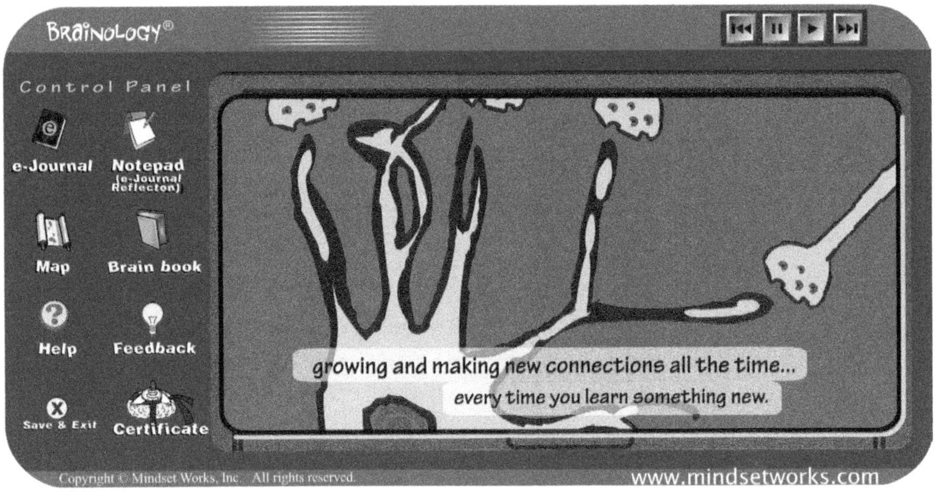

MINDSET WORKS, INC.

Screenshot from Brainology, a commercially available educational program based on the findings of Blackwell, Trzesniewski, and Dweck (2007). The software, like the research study, emphasizes that learning makes children smarter by building new connections within the brain.

Building on this research regarding the relation between beliefs about intelligence and persistence in the face of difficulty, Blackwell, Trzesniewski, and Dweck (2007) devised an effective educational program for middle school students from low-income backgrounds. They presented randomly selected students with research findings about how learning alters the brain in ways that improve subsequent learning and thus "makes you smarter." Other randomly selected students from the same classrooms were presented with research findings about how memory works. The investigators predicted that the students who were told about how learning affects the brain would change their beliefs about intelligence in ways that would help them persevere in the face of failure. In particular, the changed beliefs were expected to improve students' learning of mathematics, an area in which children often experience initial failure.

The researchers' prediction was borne out. Children who were presented information about how learning changes the brain and enhances intelligence subsequently improved their math grades, whereas the other children did not. Children who initially believed that intelligence was an inborn, unchanging quality, but who came to believe that intelligence reflected learning, showed especially large improvements. Perhaps most striking was that when the children's teachers (who did not know which type of information each child had received) were asked if any of their students had shown unusual improvement in motivation or performance, the teachers cited more than three times as many students who had been given information about how learning builds intelligence. Subsequent reviews of research on mindset instruction indicate that such effects are real, though they often are small (Burnette et al., 2012; Sisk et al., 2018).

Providing children with information about how learning changes the brain and thus builds intelligence is, of course, not the only way to increase their motivation to learn. Another effective method involves presentation of *struggle stories,* which relate how famous or notable people—for example, great scientists such as Albert Einstein and Marie Curie—needed to overcome failures and difficult life circumstances on the way to success. Studies conducted in the United States and in China have shown that hearing such struggle stories improves children's science learning (Hong & Lin-Siegler, 2012; Lin-Siegler et al., 2016).

Interview with Carol Dweck

as **hypotheses**, that is, as testable predictions of the presence or absence of phenomena or relations rather than as truth. If a hypothesis is tested, and the evidence repeatedly does not support it, the hypothesis must be abandoned no matter how reasonable it seems.

Use of the scientific method involves four basic steps:

1. Choosing a question to be answered
2. Formulating a hypothesis regarding the question
3. Developing a method for testing the hypothesis
4. Using the resulting data to draw a conclusion regarding the hypothesis

hypotheses testable predictions of the presence or absence of phenomena or relations

To illustrate these steps, let's make the *question* to be answered "What abilities predict which children will become good readers?" A reasonable *hypothesis* might be "Kindergartners who can identify the separate sounds within words will become better readers than those who cannot." A straightforward *method* for testing this hypothesis would be to select a group of kindergartners, test their ability to identify the separate sounds within words, and then, several years later, test the reading skills of the same children. Research has, in fact, shown that kindergartners who are aware of the component sounds within words later tend to read more skillfully than their peers who lacked this ability as kindergartners. This pattern holds true regardless of whether the children are learning English, Norwegian, or Swedish (Furnes & Samuelsson, 2011). The pattern also holds whether children are learning Canadian-English as a first or second language (Chiappe & Siegel, 1999). These results support the *conclusion* that kindergartners' ability to identify sounds within words predicts their later reading skill.

The first, second, and fourth of these steps are not unique to the scientific method. Great thinkers of the past also asked questions, formulated hypotheses, and drew conclusions that were reasonable, given the evidence available to them. What distinguishes scientific research from nonscientific approaches is the third step: the methods used to test the hypotheses. When rigorously employed, these research methods yield high-quality evidence that allows investigators to progress beyond their initial hypotheses to draw firmly grounded conclusions.

The Importance of Appropriate Measurement

For the scientific method to work, researchers must use measures that are directly relevant to the hypotheses being tested. Even measures that initially seem reasonable sometimes turn out to be less informative than originally thought. For example, a researcher who hypothesized that a supplemental food program would help children suffering from malnutrition might evaluate the program on the basis of weight gain from just before the program to just after it. However, weight is an inadequate measure of nutrition: providing unlimited doughnuts would probably produce weight gain but would not improve nutrition; many people who consume large amounts of junk food are obese yet malnourished (Via, 2012).

Regardless of the particular measure used, many of the same criteria determine whether a measure is a good one. One key criterion has already been noted—the measure must be directly relevant to the hypothesis. Two other qualities that good measures must possess are *reliability* and *validity*.

Reliability The degree to which independent measurements of a behaviour under study are consistent is referred to as **reliability**. One important type of consistency, **interrater reliability**, indicates how much agreement there is in the observations of different raters who witness the same behaviour. Sometimes the observations are qualitative, as when raters classify a baby's attachment to her mother as "secure" or "insecure." Other times, the observations are quantitative, as when raters score on a scale of 1 to 10 how upset babies become when they are presented with an unfamiliar noisy toy or a boisterous stranger. In both cases, interrater reliability is attained when the raters' evaluations are in close agreement—as when, for example, Baby A in a group being observed for a particular behaviour gets a 6 or 7 from all the raters, Baby B gets a 3 or 4 from all of them, Baby C consistently gets an 8 or 9, and so on. Without such agreement, one cannot have confidence in the research findings because there is no way to tell which (if any) of the ratings were accurate.

reliability the degree to which independent measurements of a given behaviour are consistent

interrater reliability the amount of agreement in the observations of different raters who witness the same behaviour

A second important type of consistency is **test–retest reliability**. This type of reliability is attained when measures of a child's performance on the same test, administered under the same conditions, are similar on two or more occasions. Suppose, for example, that researchers presented a vocabulary test to a group of children on two separate occasions, one week apart. If the test is reliable, the children who scored highest on the first testing should also score highest on the second because none of the children's vocabularies would have changed much over such a short period. As in the example of interrater reliability, a lack of test–retest reliability would make it impossible to know which result (if either) accurately reflected each child's status.

test–retest reliability the degree of similarity of a participant's performance on two or more occasions

validity the degree to which a test measures what it is intended to measure

internal validity the degree to which effects observed within experiments can be attributed to the factor that the researcher is testing

external validity the degree to which results can be generalized beyond the particulars of the research

Validity The **validity** of a test or experiment refers to the degree to which it measures what it is intended to measure. Researchers strive for two types of validity: internal and external. **Internal validity** refers to whether effects observed within experiments can be attributed with confidence to the factor that the researcher is testing. For instance, suppose that a researcher tests the effectiveness of a type of psychotherapy for depression by administering it to a number of depressed adolescents. If, three months later, many of the adolescents are no longer depressed, can it be concluded that this type of psychotherapy caused the improvement? No, because the students' recovery may have been due to the mere passage of time. Moods fluctuate, and many people who are depressed at any given time will be happier at a later date even without psychotherapy. In this example, the passage of time is a source of internal *invalidity* because the factor believed to cause the improvement (the psychotherapy) may have had no effect.

External validity, in contrast, refers to the ability to generalize research findings beyond the particulars of the research in question. Studies of child development are almost never intended to apply only to the particular children and research methods involved in a given study. Rather, the goal is to draw conclusions that apply to children more generally. Thus, the findings of a single experiment are only the first step in determining the external validity of the results. Additional studies with participants from different backgrounds and with research methods that vary in their particulars are invariably needed to establish the external validity of the findings. (Table 1.3 summarizes the key properties of behavioural measures.)

External validity, internal validity, and reliability are related in important ways. An unreliable measure, one in which the ratings of different people are not strongly related, cannot be valid because there is no way to tell which rater, if any, is accurately assessing the behaviour being rated. Similarly, measures that are invalid with the original sample and experimental situation provide no reason

TABLE 1.3 Key Properties of Behavioural Measures

Property	Question of Interest
Relevance to hypotheses	Do the hypotheses predict in a straightforward way what should happen on these measures?
Interrater reliability	Do different raters who observe the same behaviour classify or score it the same way?
Test–retest reliability	Do children who score higher on a measure at one time also score higher on the measure at other times?
Internal validity	Can effects within the experiment be attributed to the variables that the researcher intentionally manipulated?
External validity	How widely can the findings be generalized to different children in different places at different times?

structured interview a research procedure in which all participants are asked to answer the same questions

questionnaire a method that allows researchers to gather information from a large number of participants simultaneously by presenting them a uniform set of printed questions

clinical interview a procedure in which questions are adjusted in accord with the answers the interviewee provides

to believe that the measures would be valid for different samples or situations. Thus, reliability is necessary for internal validity, and both are necessary for external validity.

Contexts for Gathering Data About Children

Researchers obtain data about children in three main contexts: *interviews, naturalistic observation,* and *structured observation.* In the following sections, we consider how gathering data in each context can help answer different questions about children.

Interviews and Questionnaires

The most obvious way to collect data about children is to go straight to the source and ask the children themselves about their lives. **Structured interviews**, sets of predetermined questions administered to participants, are especially useful when the goal is to collect self-reports on the same topics from everyone being studied.

With young children, the questions are usually presented orally; however, with children of reading age, printed **questionnaires** are usually used. Such questionnaires make it easier for researchers to obtain data from many children simultaneously. Both oral interviews and printed questionnaires provide a quick and straightforward way for researchers to learn about children's feelings, beliefs, and behaviours.

A second type of interview, the **clinical interview**, is especially useful for obtaining in-depth information about an individual child. In this approach, the interviewer begins with a set of prepared questions, but if the child says something intriguing, the interviewer can depart from the script to follow up on the child's lead.

The usefulness of clinical interviews can be seen in the case of Bobby, a 10-year-old child who was assessed for symptoms of depression (Schwartz & Johnson, 1985). When the interviewer asked him about school, Bobby said that he did not like it because the other children disliked him and he was bad at sports. As he put it, "I'm not really very good at anything" (p. 214). To explore the source of this sad self-description, the interviewer asked Bobby what he would wish for if three wishes could be granted. Bobby replied, "I would wish that I was the type of boy my mother and father want, I would wish that I could have friends, and I would wish that I wouldn't feel sad so much" (p. 214). Such heartrending comments provide a sense of the painful subjective experience of this depressed child, one that would be impossible to obtain from methods that were not tailored to the individual.

One-on-one clinical interviews like this one can elicit unique in-depth information about a child.

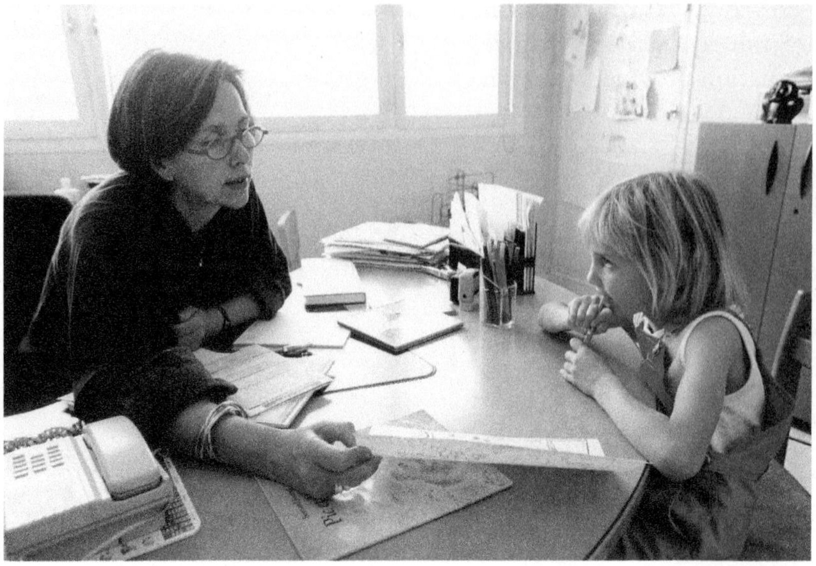

VOISIN/PHANIE/SCIENCE SOURCE

As with all contexts for collecting data, interviews have both strengths and weaknesses. On the positive side, they can yield a great deal of data quickly and provide in-depth information about individual children. On the negative side, answers to interview questions often are biased. Children (like adults) often avoid disclosing facts that show them in a bad light, misremember the way that events happened, and fail to understand their own motivations (Wilson & Dunn, 2004).

These limitations have led many researchers to use observational methods that allow them to witness the behaviour of interest for themselves.

naturalistic observation examination of ongoing behaviour in an environment not controlled by the researcher

structured observation a method that involves presenting an identical situation to each participant and recording the participant's behaviour

Naturalistic Observation

When the primary research goal is to describe how children behave in their usual environments—homes, schools, playgrounds, and so on—**naturalistic observation** is the method of choice for gathering data. In this approach, observers station themselves unobtrusively in the background of the chosen setting, allowing them to see the relevant behaviours while minimizing the chances that their presence will influence those behaviours.

A classic example of naturalistic observation is Gerald Patterson's (1982) comparative study of family dynamics in "troubled" and "typical" families. The troubled families were defined by the presence of at least one child who had been labelled "out of control" and referred for treatment by a school, court, or mental health professional. The typical families were defined by the fact that none of the children in them showed signs of serious behavioural difficulties. Income levels and children's ages were similar for the troubled and typical families.

To observe the frequency with which children and parents engaged in negative behaviours—teasing, yelling, whining, criticizing, and so on—research assistants repeatedly observed dinnertime interactions in both troubled and typical homes, always staying silent in the background.

The researchers found that the behaviours and attitudes of both parents and children in the troubled families differed strikingly from those of their counterparts in the typical families. Parents in the troubled families were more self-absorbed and less responsive to their children than were parents in the typical households. Children in the troubled families responded to parental punishment by becoming more aggressive, whereas children in the typical households responded to punishment by becoming less aggressive. In the troubled families, interactions often fell into a vicious cycle in which the child acted in a hostile or aggressive manner, the parent reacted angrily, the child escalated the level of hostility, the parent ratcheted up the aggression even further, and so on. As Patterson's study suggests, naturalistic observations are particularly useful for illuminating everyday social interactions, such as those between children and parents.

Although naturalistic observation can yield detailed information about certain aspects of children's everyday lives, it also has important limitations. One is that naturally occurring contexts vary on many dimensions, so it is often hard to know which ones influenced the behaviour of interest. For example, it was clear in the Patterson study that the interactions of troubled families differed from those of the more harmonious families, but the interactions and family histories differed in so many ways that it was impossible to specify how the current situation arose. A second limitation of naturalistic studies is that many behaviours of interest occur only occasionally in the everyday environment, which reduces researchers' opportunities to observe them. A means for overcoming both limitations is the method known as *structured observation*.

Psychologists sometimes observe family interactions around the dinner table, because mealtime comments can evoke strong emotions.

MONKEY BUSINESS IMAGES/DREAMSTIME.COM

Structured Observation

When using **structured observation**, researchers design a situation that will elicit behaviour that is relevant to a hypothesis and then observe how different children

COURTESY OF SUWANNA AND DAVID SIEGLER

Temptation is everywhere, but children who are generally compliant with their mother's requests when she is present are also more likely to resist temptation when she is absent (like this boy, the nephew of one of the authors, whose reach, despite appearances, stopped just short of the cake).

behave in that situation. The researchers then relate the behaviours to characteristics of the child, such as age, sex, or personality, and to the child's behaviour in other situations that are also observed.

In one such study, Kochanska, Coy, and Murray (2001) investigated the links between 2- and 3-year-olds' compliance with their mother's requests to forego appealing activities and their compliance with her requests that they participate in unappealing ones. Mothers brought their toddlers to a laboratory room that had a number of especially attractive toys sitting on a shelf and a great many less attractive toys scattered around the room. The experimenter asked each mother to tell her child that he or she could play with any of the toys *except* the ones on the shelf. Raters observed the children through a one-way mirror over the next few minutes and classified them as complying with their mother's request wholeheartedly, grudgingly, or not at all. Then the experimenter asked the mother to leave the room and observed whether the child played with the "forbidden" toys in the mother's absence.

The researchers found that children who had complied wholeheartedly in the first instance tended to avoid playing with the forbidden toys for a longer time in the second. Moreover, these children were also more likely to comply with their mother's request that they put away the many toys on the floor after she left the room. When retested near their 4th birthday, most children showed the same type of compliance as they had as toddlers. Overall, the results indicated that the quality of young children's compliance with their mother's requests is a somewhat stable, general property of the mother–child relationship.

This type of structured observation offers an important advantage over naturalistic observation: it ensures that all the children being studied encounter identical situations. This allows direct comparisons of different children's behaviour in a given situation and, as in the research just discussed, also makes it possible to establish the generality of each child's behaviour across different situations. On the other hand, structured observation does not provide as extensive information about individual children's subjective experience as do interviews, nor can it provide the open-ended, everyday kind of data that naturalistic observation can yield.

As these examples suggest, which data-gathering approach is best depends on the goals of the research. (Table 1.4 summarizes the advantages and disadvantages of interviews, naturalistic observation, and structured observation as contexts for gathering data.)

Correlation and Causation

People differ along an infinite number of **variables**, that is, attributes that vary across individuals and situations, such as age, sex, activity level, socioeconomic status, particular experiences, and so on. A major goal of child-development research is to determine how these and other major characteristics of children and influences on them are related to one another, both in terms of associations and in terms of cause–effect relations. In the following sections, we consider the research designs that are used to examine each type of relation.

Correlational Designs

The primary goal of studies that use **correlational designs** is to determine whether children who differ in one variable also differ in predictable ways in other variables. For example, a researcher might examine whether toddlers' aggressiveness is related to the number of hours they spend in day care or whether adolescents' popularity is related to their self-control.

variables attributes that vary across individuals and situations, such as age, sex, and popularity

correlational designs studies intended to indicate how two variables are related to each other

TABLE 1.4 Advantages and Disadvantages of Three Contexts for Gathering Data

Data-Gathering Situation	Features	Advantages	Disadvantages
Interview/questionnaire	Children answer questions asked either in person or on a questionnaire.	Can reveal children's subjective experience. Structured interviews are inexpensive means for collecting in-depth data about individuals. Clinical interviews allow flexibility for following up on unexpected comments.	Reports are often biased to reflect favourably on interviewee. Memories of interviewees are often inaccurate and incomplete. Prediction of future behaviours often is inaccurate.
Naturalistic observation	Children's activities in one or more everyday settings are observed.	Useful for describing behaviour in everyday settings. Helps illuminate social interaction processes.	Difficult to know which aspects of situation are most influential. Limited value for studying infrequent behaviours.
Structured observation	Children are brought to laboratory and presented prearranged tasks.	Ensures that all children's behaviours are observed in same context. Allows controlled comparison of children's behaviour in different situations.	Context is less natural than in naturalistic observation. Reveals less about subjective experience than interviews.

The association between two variables is known as their **correlation**. When variables are strongly correlated, knowing a child's score on either variable allows accurate prediction of the child's score on the other. For instance, the number of hours per week that children spend reading correlates highly with their reading-test scores (Guthrie et al., 1999); this means a child's reading-test score can be accurately predicted if one knows how much time the child spends reading. It also means that the number of hours the child spends reading can be predicted if one knows the child's reading-test score.

Correlations range from 1.00, the strongest positive correlation, to −1.00, the strongest negative correlation. The direction is positive when high values of one variable are associated with high values of the other, and when low values of one are associated with low values of the other; the direction is negative when high values of one variable are associated with low values of the other. Thus, the correlation between time spent reading and reading-test scores is positive because children who spend high amounts of time reading also tend to have high reading-test scores; the correlation between obesity and amount of exercise that a child gets is negative because more obese children tend to exercise less.

Correlation Does Not Equal Causation

When two variables are strongly correlated and there is a plausible cause–effect relation between them, it often is tempting to infer that one causes the other. However, correlations do not justify inferences about causal relations between the variables. This is true for two reasons. The first is the **direction-of-causation problem**: a correlation does not indicate which variable is the cause and which variable is the effect. In the preceding example, greater time spent reading *might* cause increased reading achievement, but the cause–effect relation could run in the opposite direction: greater reading skill might cause children to spend more time reading, because reading faster and with greater comprehension makes reading more fun.

The second reason why correlation does not imply causation is the **third-variable problem**: the correlation between two variables may actually be the result of some third, unspecified variable. In the reading example, for instance, rather

correlation the association between two variables

direction-of-causation problem the concept that a correlation between two variables does not indicate which, if either, variable is the cause of the other

third-variable problem the concept that a correlation between two variables may stem from both being influenced by some third variable than greater reading achievement being caused by greater reading time, or vice versa, both of these aspects of reading could be caused by growing up in a family that values and rewards knowledge and intelligence.

Recognizing that correlation does not imply causation is crucial for interpreting research results. Even findings published in prestigious research journals can easily be misinterpreted. For example, based on a correlation between children younger than 2 years sleeping with a nightlight and their later becoming nearsighted, an article in the prestigious journal *Nature* concluded that the light was harmful to visual development (Quinn et al., 1999). Not surprisingly, the claim received considerable publicity in the popular media (e.g., Torassa, 2000). Subsequent research, however, showed that the inference about causation was wrong. The nearsighted children generally had nearsighted parents, and the nearsighted parents, for unknown reasons, more often placed nightlights in their infants' rooms (Gwiazda et al., 2000; Zadnik et al., 2000). Thus, inheritance of genes that predispose children to become nearsighted, rather than the use of nightlights, might have been the cause that led to the correlation. As the example illustrates, even seemingly straightforward inferences of causation, based on correlational evidence, frequently prove to be wrong.

If correlation does not imply causation, why do researchers often use correlational designs? One major reason is that the influence of many variables of interest—age, sex, race, and social class among them—cannot be studied experimentally (see the next section) because researchers cannot manipulate them; that is, they cannot assign participants to one sex or another, to one SES or another, and so on. Consequently, these variables can be studied only through correlational methods. Correlational designs are also valuable when the goal is to describe relations among variables rather than to identify cause–effect relations among them. If, for example, the research goal is to discover how moral reasoning, empathy, anxiety, and popularity are related to one another, correlational designs would almost certainly be employed.

Experimental Designs

If correlational designs are insufficient to indicate cause–effect relations, what type of approach is sufficient? The answer is **experimental designs.** The logic of experimental designs can be summarized quite simply: if children in one group are exposed to a particular experience and subsequently behave differently from a comparable group of children who were not exposed to the experience or were exposed to a different experience, then the subsequent differences in behaviour must have resulted from the differing experiences.

Two techniques are crucial to experimental designs: *random assignment* of participants to groups, and *experimental control.* **Random assignment** involves assigning participants to one experimental group or another according to chance, so that the groups are comparable at the outset. In the same way that flipping a coin many times results in a roughly 50-50 distribution of heads and tails, assigning many children to experimental groups by a random process results in groups whose members are equivalent on all or almost all variables. This comparability is crucial for being able to infer that it was the varying experiences to which the groups were exposed in the experiment that caused the later differences between them. Otherwise, those differences might have arisen from some preexisting difference between the people in the groups.

Say, for instance, that researchers wanted to compare the effectiveness of two interventions for helping depressed mothers improve their relationship with their

experimental designs a group of approaches that allow inferences about causes and effects to be drawn

random assignment a procedure in which each participant has an equal chance of being assigned to each group within an experiment infant—namely, providing the mothers with home visits from trained therapists versus providing them with supportive phone calls from such therapists. If the researchers provided the home visits to families in one neighbourhood and the supportive phone calls to families in another neighbourhood, it would be unclear whether any differences in mother–infant relationships following the experiment were caused by differences between the effectiveness of the two types of support or by differences between the families in the two areas. Depressed mothers in one neighbourhood might suffer from less severe forms of depression than mothers in the other, or they might have greater access to other support, such as close families, mental health centres, or parenting programs.

In contrast, when groups are created through random assignment and include a reasonably large number of participants (typically 30 or more per group), initial differences between the groups tend to be minimal. For example, if 100 families with mothers who suffer from depression are divided randomly into two experimental groups, each group is likely to include a few mothers who are extremely depressed, a few with mild forms of depression, and many in between, as well as a few infants who have been severely affected by their mother's depression, a few who have been minimally affected, and many in between. The logic implies that groups created through random assignment should be comparable on all variables except the different treatment that people in the experimental groups encounter during the experiment.

The second essential characteristic of an experimental design, **experimental control**, refers to the ability of the researcher to determine the specific experiences that children in each group encounter during the study. In the simplest experimental design, one with two conditions, the groups are often referred to as the "experimental group" and the "control group." Children in the **experimental group** are presented the experience of interest; children in the **control group** are treated identically except that they are not presented the experience of interest or are presented with a different experience that is expected to have less effect on the variables being tested.

The experience that children in the experimental group receive, and that children in the control group do not receive, is referred to as the **independent variable**. The behaviour that is hypothesized to be affected by exposure to the independent variable is referred to as the **dependent variable**. Thus, if a researcher hypothesized that showing schoolchildren an anti-bullying video would reduce school bullying, the researcher might randomly assign some children in a school to view the video and other children in the same school to view an equally interesting video about a different topic. In this case, the anti-bullying video would be the independent variable, and the amount of bullying after the children watched it would be the dependent variable. If the independent variable had the predicted effect, children who saw the anti-bullying video would show less bullying after watching it than would children who saw the other video.

One illustration of how experimental designs allow researchers to draw conclusions about causes and effects is a study that tested the hypothesis that having television shows running in the background while infants and toddlers play lowers the quality of that play (Schmidt et al., 2008). The independent variable was whether or not a television program was on in the room where the participants were playing; the dependent variables were a variety of measures of children's attention to the television program and of the quality of their play. The television program being played was *Jeopardy!*, which presumably would have been of little interest to the 1- and 2-year-olds in the study. Indeed, the

experimental control the ability of researchers to determine the specific experiences of participants during the course of an experiment

experimental group the group of participants in an experimental design who are presented the experience of interest

control group the group of participants in an experimental design who are not presented the experience of interest but in other ways are treated similarly

independent variable the experience that participants in the experimental group receive and that those in the control group do not receive

dependent variable a behaviour that is measured to determine whether it is affected by exposure to the independent variable

PICTURE PARTNERS/ALAMY

The quality of infants' and toddlers' play is adversely affected by a television being on in the same room.

toddlers looked at it an average of only once per minute and only for a few seconds at a time. Nonetheless, the television show disrupted the children's play, reducing the length of play episodes and the children's focus on them. These findings indicate that there is a causal, and negative, relation between background exposure to television shows and the quality of young children's play.

Experimental designs are the method of choice for establishing causal relations, a central goal of scientific research. However, as noted earlier, experimental designs cannot be applied to all issues of interest. For example, hypotheses about why boys tend to be more physically aggressive than girls cannot be tested experimentally because gender cannot be randomly assigned to children. In addition, many experimental studies are conducted in laboratory settings; this improves experimental control but can raise doubts about the external validity of the findings—that is, whether the findings from the lab apply to the outside world. (The advantages and disadvantages of correlational and experimental designs are summarized in Table 1.5.)

Research Designs for Examining Children's Development

A great deal of research on child development focuses on how children change or remain the same as they grow older and gain experience. To study development over time, investigators use three types of research designs: cross-sectional, longitudinal, and microgenetic.

Cross-Sectional Designs

The most common and easiest way to study changes and continuities with age is to use the **cross-sectional** approach. This method compares children of different ages on a given behaviour, ability, or characteristic by studying them at roughly the same time—for example, within the same week or month. In one cross-sectional study, Evans, Xu, and Lee (2011) examined the development of dishonesty in Chinese 3-, 4-, and 5-year-olds. The children played a game in which winning a prize required guessing the type of object hidden under an upside-down paper cup. Before the child could guess, the experimenter said she needed to leave the room and asked the child not to peek while she was gone. The cup was so packed with candies that if the child peeked, some would spill out; putting them all back under the cup was almost impossible.

cross-sectional design a research method in which participants of different ages are compared on a given behaviour or characteristic over a short period

TABLE 1.5 Advantages and Disadvantages of Correlational and Experimental Designs

Types of Design	Features	Advantages	Disadvantages
Correlational	Comparison of existing groups of children or examination of relations among each child's scores on different variables.	Only way to compare many groups of interest (boys–girls, rich–poor, etc.). Only way to establish relations among many variables of interest (IQ and achievement, popularity and happiness, etc.).	Direction-of-causation problem. Third-variable problem.
Experimental	Random assignment of children to groups and experimental control of procedures presented to each group.	Allows causal inferences because design rules out direction-of-causation and third-variable problems. Allows experimental control over the exact experiences that children encounter.	Need for experimental control often leads to artificial experimental situations. Cannot be used to study many differences and variables of interest, such as age, sex, and temperament.

At all ages, many children peeked and then denied doing so. However, 5-year-olds lied more often, and their lies were more ingenious, than those of the younger children. For example, many 5-year-olds explained the presence of candies on the table by saying that they accidentally knocked over the cup with their elbow; others destroyed the evidence by eating it. Three-year-olds were the least-skilled fibbers, generating implausible excuses such as that the candies came out by themselves or that some other child entered the room and knocked over the cup.

Cross-sectional designs are useful for revealing similarities and differences between older and younger children. However, they do not yield information about the stability of behaviour over time or about the patterns of change shown by individual children. This is where longitudinal approaches are especially valuable.

longitudinal design a method of study in which the same participants are studied twice or more over a substantial length of time

Longitudinal Designs

The **longitudinal** approach involves following the same children over a substantial period (usually at least a year) and observing changes and continuities in these children's development at regular intervals during that time. The study at the beginning of this chapter on the development of children in Kauai from before birth to age 40 is one example of a longitudinal study. Another good example of what the longitudinal approach can tell us is Brendgen and colleagues' (2001) examination of Québec children's popularity with classmates. Each child's popularity was examined each year from the time they were 7-year-olds to the time they were 12-year-olds. The popularity of most children proved to be quite stable over this period; many were popular in the large majority of years, and many others were unpopular throughout.

At the same time, some individuals showed idiosyncratic patterns of change from year to year; the same child might be popular at age 8, unpopular at age 10, and of average popularity at age 12. Such information about the stability of individual differences over time and about individual children's patterns of change could only have been obtained in a longitudinal design, that is, in a design where the same children were examined repeatedly over time.

Although longitudinal designs are very useful for revealing stability and change over time, cross-sectional designs are far more common. The reasons for the greater prevalence of cross-sectional designs are mainly practical. Studying the same children over long periods involves the difficult task of locating the children for each re-examination. Inevitably, some children move away or stop participating for other reasons. Such loss of participants may call into question the validity of the findings because the children who do not continue may differ from those who participate throughout. Another threat to the validity of longitudinal designs is the possible effects of repeated testing. For example, repeatedly taking IQ tests could familiarize children with the type of items on the tests, thus improving the children's scores for reasons other than changes to their intelligence. Therefore, longitudinal designs are used primarily when the main issues are stability and change in individual children over time—issues that can only be studied longitudinally. When the central developmental issue involves age-related changes in typical performance, cross-sectional studies are more commonly used.

Being excluded is no fun for anyone. Longitudinal research has been used to determine whether the same children are unpopular year after year or whether popularity changes over time.

MASTERFILE/MASTERFILE

IMAGE COURTESY OF XIN LI AND LUJIE CHEN

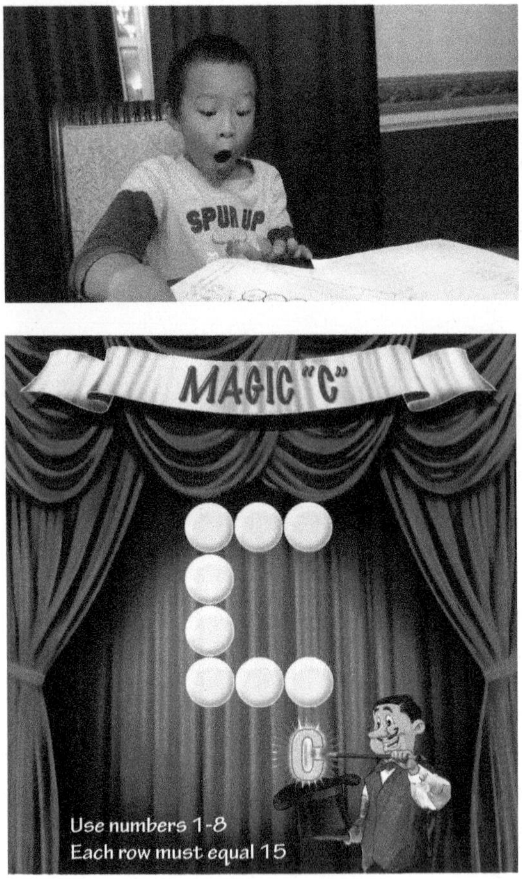

The excitement of discovery is evoked by an insight while this child was trying to solve a problem in the game "Magic C."

Microgenetic Designs

An important limitation of both cross-sectional and longitudinal designs is that they provide only a broad outline of the process of change. **Microgenetic designs**, in contrast, are specifically designed to provide an in-depth depiction of the processes that produce change (Lavelli & Fogel, 2013; Miller & Coyle, 1999). The basic idea of this approach is to recruit children who are thought to be on the verge of an important developmental change, heighten their exposure to the type of experience that is believed to produce the change, and then intensively study the change *as it is occurring*. Microgenetic designs are like longitudinal ones in repeatedly testing the same children over time. They differ in that microgenetic studies typically include a greater number of sessions presented over a shorter time than in a longitudinal study.

Siegler and Jenkins (1989) used a microgenetic design to study how young children discover the *counting-on strategy* for adding two small numbers. This strategy involves counting up from the larger addend the number of times indicated by the smaller addend. For example, when asked the answer to 3 + 5, a child who was counting-on would start from the addend 5 and say or think "6, 7, 8" before answering "8." Prior to discovering this strategy, children usually solve addition problems by counting from 1. Counting from the larger addend, rather than from 1, reduces the amount of counting, producing faster and more accurate solutions.

To observe the discovery process, the researchers selected 4- and 5-year-olds who did not yet use counting-on but who knew how to add by counting from 1. Over an 11-week period, these children received many addition problems several times per week—far more experience than U.S. children would normally have with addition before entering school—and each child's behaviour on every problem was video-recorded. This approach allowed the researchers to identify exactly when each child discovered the counting-on strategy.

Examination of the problems immediately preceding the discovery revealed a surprising fact: necessity is not always the mother of invention. Children often discovered the counting-on strategy while solving easy problems that they previously solved correctly by counting from 1.

The microgenetic method also revealed that children's very first use of the new strategy often was accompanied by insight and excitement, like that shown by Lauren:

> *Experimenter:* How much is 6 + 3?
> *Lauren: (long pause)* 9.
> *E:* OK, how did you know that?
> *L:* I think I said . . . I think I said . . . oops, um . . . 7 was 1, 8 was 2, 9 was 3.
> *E:* How did you know to do that? Why didn't you count 1, 2, 3, 4, 5, 6, 7, 8, 9?
> *L: (with excitement)* 'Cause then you have to count all those numbers.
> (Siegler & Jenkins, 1989, p. 66)

Despite Lauren's insightful explanation of counting-on and her excitement over discovering it, she and most other children only gradually increased their use of the new strategy on subsequent problems, though they eventually used it quite often. Many other microgenetic studies have also shown that generalization of new strategies tends to be slow (Kuhn & Franklin, 2006).

As this example illustrates, microgenetic methods provide insight into the process of change over brief periods. However, unlike standard longitudinal

microgenetic design a method of study in which the same participants are studied repeatedly over a short period

TABLE 1.6 Advantages and Disadvantages of Designs for Studying Development

Design	Features	Advantages	Disadvantages
Cross-sectional	Children of different ages are studied at a single time.	Yields useful data about differences among age groups. Quick and easy to administer.	Uninformative about stability of individual differences over time. Uninformative about similarities and differences in individual children's patterns of change.
Longitudinal	Children are examined repeatedly over a prolonged period.	Indicates the degree of stability of individual differences over long periods. Reveals individual children's patterns of change over long periods.	Difficult to keep all participants in study. Repeatedly testing children can threaten external validity of study.
Microgenetic	Children are observed intensively over a relatively short period while a change is occurring.	Intensive observation of changes while they are occurring can clarify process of change. Reveals individual change patterns over short periods in considerable detail.	Does not provide information about typical patterns of change over long periods. Does not yield data regarding change patterns over long periods.

methods, microgenetic designs do not yield information about stability and change over long periods. They therefore are typically used when the basic pattern of age-related change has already been established and the goal becomes to understand how the changes occur. (Table 1.6 outlines the strengths and weaknesses of the three approaches to studying changes with age and experiencc: cross-sectional, longitudinal, and microgenetic designs.)

Ethical Issues in Child-Development Research

All research with human beings raises ethical issues, and this is especially the case when the research involves children. Researchers have a vital responsibility to anticipate potential risks that children in their studies may encounter, to minimize such risks, and to ensure that the benefits of the research outweigh any potential harm.

In Canada, hospital- and university-based research with humans is governed by the Tri-Council Policy Statement: Ethical Conduct for Research Involving Humans. This policy statement lays out a code of ethical conduct for investigators to follow. Some of the most important ethical principles in the policy statement are as follows:

- Be sure that the research does not harm children physically or psychologically.
- Obtain informed consent for participating in the research, preferably in writing, from parents or other responsible adults and also from children if they are old enough that the research can be explained to them. The experimenter should inform children and relevant adults of all aspects of the research that might influence their willingness to participate and should explain that refusing to participate will not result in any adverse consequences to them.
- Preserve individual participants' anonymity, and do not use information for purposes other than that for which permission was given.
- Discuss with parents or guardians any information yielded by the investigation that is important for the child's welfare.
- Try to counteract any unforeseen negative consequences that arise during the research.
- Correct any inaccurate impressions that the child may develop in the course of the study. When the research has been completed, explain the main findings to participants at a level they can understand.

Recognizing the importance of such ethical issues, universities and governmental agencies have established institutional review boards made up of independent scientists and sometimes others from the community. These boards evaluate the proposed research to ensure that it does not violate ethics guidelines. However, the individual investigator is in the best position to anticipate potential problems and bears the ultimate responsibility for seeing that his or her study meets high ethical standards.

REVIEW QUESTION

The concept of the active child suggests that, through their actions, children contribute to their own development. What challenges might the concept of the active child present for the various data-gathering strategies discussed in this section? ■

CHAPTER SUMMARY

Reasons to Learn About Child Development

- Learning about child development is valuable for many reasons: it can help us become better parents, inform our views about social issues that affect children, and improve our understanding of human nature.

Historical Foundations of the Study of Child Development

- Great thinkers such as Plato, Aristotle, Locke, and Rousseau raised basic questions about child development and proposed interesting hypotheses about them, but they lacked the scientific methods to answer the questions.

Enduring Themes in Child Development

- The field of child development is an attempt to answer a set of fundamental questions:
  1. How do nature and nurture together shape development?
  2. How do children shape their own development?
  3. In what ways is development continuous, and in what ways is it discontinuous?
  4. How does change occur?
  5. How does the sociocultural context influence development?
  6. How do children become so different from one another?
  7. How can research promote children's well-being?
- Every aspect of development, from the most specific behaviour to the most general trait, reflects people's biological endowment (their nature) as well as the experiences that they have had (their nurture).
- Even infants and young children actively contribute to their own development through their patterns of attention, use of language, and choices of activities.
- Many developments can appear either continuous or discontinuous, depending on how often and how closely we look at them.
- The mechanisms that produce developmental changes involve a complex interplay among experiences, genes, and brain structures and activities.
- The contexts that shape development include the people with whom children interact directly, such as family and friends; the institutions in which they participate, such as schools and religious organizations; and societal beliefs and values, such as those related to race, ethnicity, and social class.
- Individual differences, even among siblings, reflect differences in children's genes, in their treatment by other people, in their interpretations of their own experiences, and in their choices of environments.
- Principles, findings, and methods from child-development research are being applied to improve the quality of children's lives.

Methods for Studying Child Development

- The scientific method has made possible great advances in understanding children. It involves choosing a question, formulating a hypothesis relevant to the question, developing a method to test the hypothesis, and using data to decide whether the hypothesis is correct.
- For a measure to be useful, it must be directly relevant to the hypotheses being tested, reliable, and valid. Reliability means that independent observations of a given behaviour are

consistent. Validity means that a measure assesses what it is intended to measure.

- Among the main situations used to gather data about children are interviews, naturalistic observation, and structured observation. Interviews are especially useful for revealing children's subjective experience. Naturalistic observation is particularly useful when the primary goal is to describe how children behave in their everyday environments. Structured observation is most useful when the main goal is to describe how different children react to the identical situation.
- Correlation does not imply causation. The two differ in that correlations indicate the degree to which two variables are associated, whereas causation indicates that changing the value of one variable will change the value of the other.
- Correlational designs are especially useful when the goal is to describe relations among variables or when the variables of interest cannot be manipulated because of technical or practical considerations.
- Experimental designs are especially valuable for revealing the causes of children's behaviour.
- Data about development can be obtained through cross-sectional designs (examining different children of different ages), through longitudinal designs (examining the same children at different ages), or through microgenetic designs (presenting the same children repeated relevant experiences over a relatively short period and analyzing the change process in detail).
- It is vital for researchers to adhere to high ethical standards. Among the most important ethical principles are striving to ensure that the research does not harm children physically or psychologically; obtaining informed consent from parents and, where possible, from children; preserving participants' anonymity; and correcting any inaccurate impressions that children form during the study.

Test Yourself

1. The "turtle shell" technique is an example of a successful intervention that helps preschoolers cope with what?
   a. The sense of isolation
   b. Feelings of embarrassment
   c. Bullying from peers
   d. Their own anger
2. What is meta-analysis?
   a. The reproduction of a past study in order to confirm or debunk the results
   b. A philosophical exploration of an experiment or case study
   c. A method for combining and analyzing the results from several independent studies
   d. A list of all published articles related to a specific area of research
3. Studies have shown that children's testimony is usually accurate when which of the following conditions are met?
   a. The interviewer does not ask leading questions.
   b. One of the child's parents is present.
   c. The child and the interviewer are alone when the testimony is given.
   d. The child is repeatedly prompted during the interview.
4. According to developmentalists, which of the following is true?
   a. Development is most heavily influenced by nature.
   b. Development is most heavily influenced by nurture.
   c. Development is influenced by the joint workings of nature and nurture.
   d. Nature and nurture are essentially the same.
5. The concept of the "active child" refers to ____________.
   a. observations of children at play
   b. whether an infant sleeps through the night
   c. the importance of physical activity to child development
   d. how children contribute to their own development
6. In recent decades, researchers have come to the conclusion that, after infancy, most developmental changes occur ____________.
   a. gradually
   b. suddenly
   c. discontinuously
   d. externally
7. In the context of mechanisms of developmental change, the study of the development of "effortful attention" provides insights into
   a. continuous versus discontinuous development.
   b. the role of brain activity, genes, and learning experiences.
   c. the complexity of the child's sociocultural environment.
   d. the role of the researcher in judging the validity of a study.
8. The physical, social, cultural, economic, and historical circumstances that make up a child's environment are known as the ____________.
   a. developmental foundation
   b. sociocultural context
   c. developmental stage
   d. socioeconomic status

9. The first basic step in using the scientific method involves
   a. developing a research plan.
   b. choosing a question.
   c. formulating a hypothesis.
   d. drawing a conclusion.
10. In order to generalize her findings beyond the individuals who participated in her study, Dr. Liu needs to conduct additional research using participants from a variety of backgrounds. What quality of behavioural research is Dr. Liu addressing?
    a. Interrater reliability
    b. Internal validity
    c. Test–retest reliability
    d. External validity
11. The experience that children in an experimental group receive—and which children in a control group do *not* receive—is referred to as the ____________.
    a. dependent variable
    b. independent variable
    c. random assignment
    d. correlational design
12. A team of researchers is studying whether stable individual differences exist in sleeping behaviour at various ages. They decide to test 3-month-olds, 6-month-olds, and 9-month-olds. What type of design are they using to examine this question?
    a. Longitudinal
    b. Cross-sectional
    c. Naturalistic observation
    d. Microgenetic
13. Which type of design is used to study developmental change as it is occurring by observing participants numerous times over a relatively short span of time?
    a. Longitudinal
    b. Cross-sectional
    c. Structured observation
    d. Microgenetic
14. By administering the same test to the same group of participants under similar conditions two or more times, a researcher can measure ____________ reliability.
    a. internal
    b. external
    c. test–retest
    d. interrater
15. According to the Tri-Council guidelines, which of the following is *not* a stated ethical principle for conducting research with children?
    a. Information about the child uncovered through the course of the study must not be revealed to the parent or guardian, regardless of its importance for that child's welfare.
    b. Unforeseen consequences must be dealt with when they arise during research.
    c. Researchers must correct any inaccurate impressions that the child may develop as a result of the study.
    d. The research must not harm the child, physically and psychologically.

LaunchPad
macmillan learning

DON'T STOP NOW! Research shows that testing yourself is a powerful learning tool. Visit LaunchPad to access the LearningCurve adaptive quizzing system, which gives you a personalized study plan to help build your mastery of the chapter material through videos, activities, and more. **Go to launchpadworks.com.**

Critical Thinking Questions

1. What areas of child development interest you most? Can you generate a study that would ask and perhaps answer an important question about one of those areas? What research method would your proposed experiment use?
2. What do you hope to learn from this course? Are you most interested in how to raise children, social policies to help children, or what child development tells us about human nature?
3. Have you needed to be resilient in overcoming problems that arose in your life? If so, what types of difficulties did you overcome, how did you do so, and what do you think allowed you to do so?
4. Do children have different natures, or are differences among children purely due to differences in their experiences? What personal observations, research findings, and reasoning led to your conclusion?
5. Why do you think that the children who spent less than 6 months in orphanages in Romania were able to catch up physically, intellectually, and socially, whereas those who spent more time in the orphanages and left at older ages have not been able to catch up? Do you think they will catch up in the future?

6. In what ways is it fortunate, and in what ways unfortunate, that children shape their own development to a substantial extent?
7. Did reading about sleeping arrangements in the United States and in other cultures influence what you would like to do if you have children? Explain why or why not.
8. Given what you learned in this chapter about child-development research, can you think of practical applications of the research (other than the ones described) that seem both feasible and important to you?

Key Terms

amygdala, p. 7
clinical interview, p. 26
cognitive development, p. 15
continuous development, p. 13
control group, p. 31
correlation, p. 29
correlational designs, p. 28
cross-sectional design, p. 32
cumulative risk, p. 20
dependent variable, p. 31
direction-of-causation problem, p. 29
discontinuous development, p. 13
epigenetics, p. 11
experimental control, p. 31
experimental designs, p. 30
experimental group, p. 31
external validity, p. 25
genome, p. 11
hypotheses, p. 23
independent variable, p. 31
internal validity, p. 25
interrater reliability, p. 24
longitudinal design, p. 33
meta-analysis, p. 4
methylation, p. 12
microgenetic design, p. 34
naturalistic observation, p. 27
nature, p. 10
neurotransmitters, p. 17
nurture, p. 11
questionnaire, p. 26
random assignment, p. 30
reliability, p. 24
scientific method, p. 22
sociocultural context, p. 18
socioeconomic status (SES), p. 20
stage theories, p. 14
structured interview, p. 26
structured observation, p. 27
test–retest reliability, p. 25
third-variable problem, p. 29
validity, p. 25
variables, p. 28

Answers to Test Yourself

1. d, **2.** c, **3.** a, **4.** c, **5.** d, **6.** a, **7.** b, **8.** b, **9.** b, **10.** d, **11.** b, **12.** b, **13.** d, **14.** c, **15.** a

CHAPTER

2 Prenatal Development and the Newborn Period

JOSE ORTEGA / ILLUSTRATION SOURCE

JOSE ORTEGA, *Mother and Child*

Prenatal Development | Hazards to Prenatal Development | The Birth Experience | The Newborn Infant

THEMES

NATURE AND NURTURE ■ THE ACTIVE CHILD ■ THE SOCIOCULTURAL CONTEXT

INDIVIDUAL DIFFERENCES ■ CONTINUITY/DISCONTINUITY

RESEARCH AND CHILDREN'S WELFARE

Picture the following scenario: a developmental psychologist is investigating a very young research participant's ability to learn. First, she plays a recording of a nonsense word for the young participant (*tatata*). The participant hears this word multiple times a day, for several months. The psychologist wants to use brain responses to find out whether the participant has learned the novel word. But before the psychologist can measure the participant's brain waves, something very important has to happen: the participant has to be born!

This scenario is not at all fanciful. Indeed, as you will discover later in this chapter, it describes one of many studies that has revolutionized our understanding of prenatal development (Partanen, Kujala, Tervaniemi et al., 2013). Fetuses can detect and learn from a range of stimuli coming from both the outside world and inside the mother's body, and they are affected by these stimuli after birth.

This chapter will examine prenatal development—a time of astonishingly rapid and dramatic change. We will also consider some of the ways in which these processes can be disrupted by environmental hazards. Then, we will explore the birth process and some of the most salient aspects of neonatal behaviour. Finally, we will outline issues associated with low birth weight and premature birth.

Most of the themes described in Chapter 1 play prominent roles in our discussion of the earliest periods of development. The most notable will be *nature and nurture,* because prenatal development relies on the continual interplay of biological and environmental factors. The *active child* theme will also be featured: the activity of the fetus contributes in numerous vital ways to its development. Another theme we will highlight is the *sociocultural context* of prenatal development and birth. There is substantial cultural variation in how the birth process unfolds. The theme of *individual differences* comes into play throughout prenatal development and early postnatal life. *Continuity/discontinuity* is also prominent: despite the dramatic contrast between prenatal and postnatal life, the behaviour of newborns shows clear connections to their experience inside the womb. Finally, the theme of *research and children's welfare* is central to our discussion of how poverty can affect prenatal development and birth outcomes, as well as to our description of intervention programs designed to foster healthy development for preterm infants.

Prenatal Development

Hidden from view, the process of prenatal development has always been mysterious and fascinating, and beliefs about the origins of human life and development before birth are an important part of the lore and traditions of all societies. (Box 2.1 describes one set of cultural beliefs about the beginning of life that is quite unlike those of Western societies.)

In the fourth century B.C.E., Aristotle posed a fundamental question that influenced Western thought for the next 15 centuries: Does prenatal life start with a fully formed individual, composed of a full set of tiny parts, or do the many

BOX 2.1 A CLOSER LOOK Beng Beginnings

Few topics have generated more intense debate and dispute in Canada in recent decades than the issue of when life begins—at the moment of conception, the moment of birth, or sometime in between. The irony is that few who engage in this debate recognize how complex the issue is or the degree to which societies throughout the world have different views on it.

Consider, for example, the perspective of the Beng, a people in the Ivory Coast of West Africa. According to the Beng, every newborn is a reincarnation of an ancestor (Gottlieb, 2004). In the first weeks after birth, the ancestor's spirit, its *wru,* is not fully committed to an earthly life and therefore maintains a double existence, travelling back and forth between the everyday world and *wrugbe,* or "spirit village." (The term can be roughly translated as "afterlife," but "before-life" might be just as appropriate.) It is only after the umbilical stump has dropped off that the newborn is considered to have emerged from *wrugbe* and become a person. If the newborn dies before this point, there is no funeral, for the infant's passing is perceived as a return to the *wrugbe.*

These beliefs underlie many aspects of Beng parenting practices. One is the frequent application of an herbal mixture to the newborn's umbilical stump to hasten its drying out and dropping off. In addition, there is the constant danger that the infant will become homesick for its life in *wrugbe* and decide to leave its earthly existence. To prevent this, parents try to make their babies comfortable and happy so they will want to stay in this life. Among the many recommended procedures is elaborately decorating the infant's face and body to elicit positive attention from others. Sometimes diviners are consulted, especially if the baby seems to be unhappy; a common diagnosis for prolonged crying is that the baby wants a different name—the one from its previous life in *wrugbe.*

So when does life begin for the Beng? Because each infant is a reincarnation of an ancestor, in one sense, an individual's life begins well before birth. In another sense, however, life begins sometime after birth, when the *wru* commits to life and the individual is considered to have become a person.

Beng Infant Caretaking Practices

The mother of this Beng baby has spent considerable time painting the baby's face in an elaborate pattern. She does this every day in an effort to make the baby attractive so other people will help keep the baby happy in this world.

parts of the human body develop in succession? Aristotle argued in favour of the latter, which he termed **epigenesis**—the emergence of new structures and functions during development (we will revisit this idea in Chapter 3 in its more modern form, *epigenetics*). Seeking support for his idea, he took what was then a very unorthodox step: he opened chicken eggs to observe organs in various stages of development.

Conception

Each of us originated as a single cell that resulted from the union of two highly specialized cells—a sperm from our father and an egg from our mother. These **gametes**, or germ cells, are unique not only in their function but also in the fact that each one contains only half the genetic material found in other cells. Gametes are produced through **meiosis**, a form of cell division in which the eggs and sperm receive only one member from each of the 23 chromosome pairs contained in all other cells of the body. This reduction to 23 chromosomes in each gamete is necessary for reproduction, because the union of egg and sperm must contain the normal amount of genetic material (23 *pairs* of chromosomes).

The process of reproduction starts with the launching of an egg (the largest cell in the human female body) from one of the woman's ovaries into the adjoining fallopian tube (see Figure 2.1). As the egg moves through the tube toward the uterus, it emits a chemical substance that acts as a sort of beacon, a "come-hither" signal that attracts sperm toward it. If an act of sexual intercourse takes place near

epigenesis the emergence of new structures and functions in the course of development

gametes (germ cells) reproductive cells—egg and sperm—that contain only half the genetic material of all the other cells in the body

meiosis cell division that produces gametes

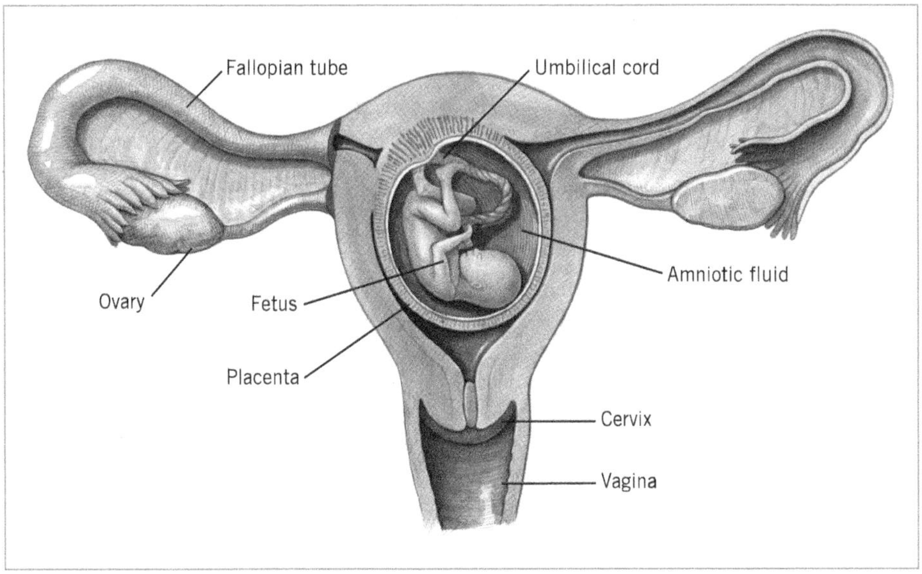

FIGURE 2.1 Female reproductive system A simplified illustration of the female reproductive system, with a fetus developing in the uterus (womb). The umbilical cord runs from the fetus to the placenta, which is burrowed deeply into the wall of the uterus. The fetus is floating in amniotic fluid inside the amniotic sac.

the time the egg is released, **conception**, the union of sperm and egg, is possible. In every ejaculation, as many as 500 million sperm are pumped into the woman's vagina. Each sperm, a streamlined vehicle for delivering the man's genes to the woman's egg, consists of little more than a pointed head packed full of genetic material (the 23 chromosomes) and a long tail that whips around to propel the sperm through the woman's reproductive system.

conception the union of an egg from the mother and a sperm from the father

To be a candidate for initiating conception, a sperm must travel for about 6 hours, journeying 15 to 18 centimetres from the vagina up through the uterus to the egg-bearing fallopian tube. The rate of attrition on this journey is enormous: of the millions of sperm that enter the vagina, only about 200 ever get near the egg (see Figure 2.2). Many of the sperm get tangled up with other sperm milling about in the vagina; others wind up in the fallopian tube that does not currently

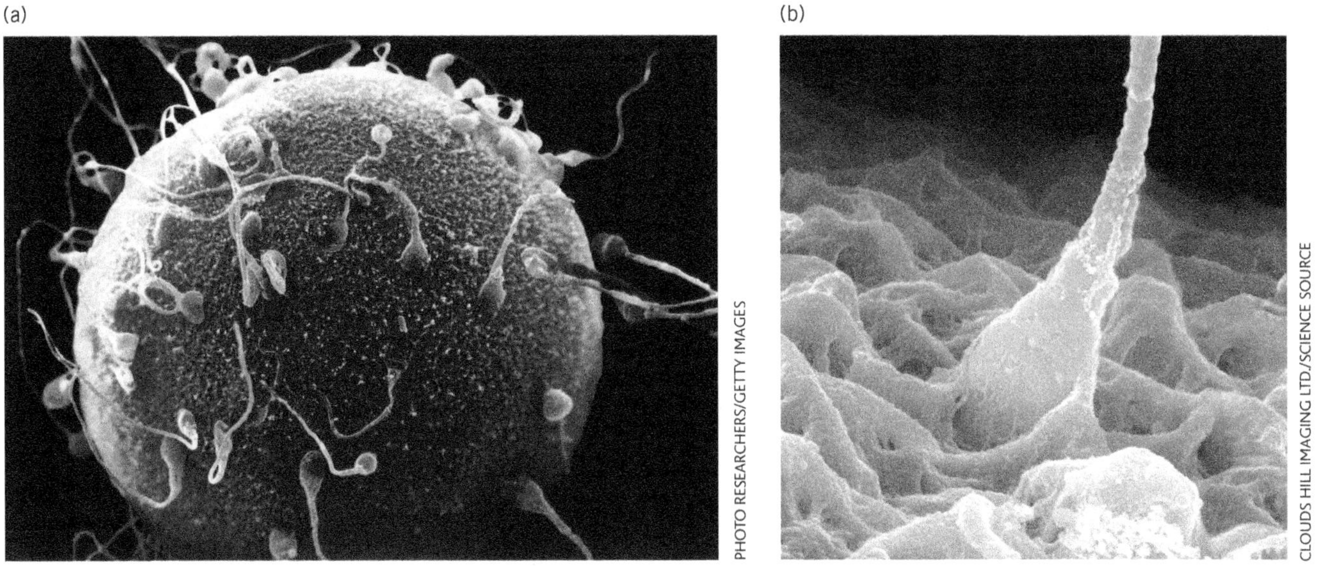

FIGURE 2.2 (a) Sperm nearing the egg Of the millions of sperm that enter the vagina, only a few ever get near the egg. The egg is the largest human cell (the only one visible to the naked eye), but sperm are among the smallest. **(b) Sperm penetrating the egg** This sperm is whipping its tail around furiously to drill itself through the outer covering of the egg.

BOX 2.2 INDIVIDUAL DIFFERENCES Do Girls Outnumber Boys?

Do girls outnumber boys? Because the answer to that question depends on the various forces that influence development and survival, it ultimately depends on when in the lifecycle you ask. There are slightly more male newborns (51.3%) across generations and around the world. This is the case, despite the fact that male fetuses are more susceptible to spontaneous abortion than females in both the 1st week and last several weeks of pregnancy (though it is worth noting that female fetuses are more susceptible in weeks 10–15) (Orzack et al., 2015).

The apparent frailty of male fetuses, paired with the fact that males outnumber females at birth, would seem to imply that male embryos must significantly outnumber female embryos (Austad, 2015). In fact, conception is equally likely to result in male and female embryos (Orzack et al., 2015). Researchers took advantage of the increased use of reproductive technologies and prenatal genetic tests to determine the sex of nearly 140,000 3- to 6-day-old fetuses, and they found an almost exact 50-50 split between males and females. It appears that female fetuses are actually less likely than male fetuses to survive early gestation, resulting in the slight male bias at birth.

Females win the next big competition—birth. During labour and delivery, males are more likely to experience fetal distress than females, even controlling for the males' larger size and head circumference (DiPietro, Costigan, & Voegtline, 2015). Indeed, for decades, and across many cultural contexts, infant mortality rates have been higher for boys than for girls (Drevenstedt et al., 2008). Male fetuses are more sensitive than females are to teratogens (harmful external agents), including opioids and alcohol, which affects their viability and ability to thrive after birth (e.g., DiPietro & Voegtline, 2017). Male infants' heightened vulnerability is not limited to the immediate postnatal period. Males are also more likely than females to die from sudden infant death syndrome (SIDS, discussed in more detail in Box 2.3; Mage & Donner, 2014) and have higher rates of incidence of a wide range of developmental disabilities, including attentional disorders and autism spectrum disorders.

Societal and cultural forces also play a role, sometimes to devastating effect. In many societies, both historically and currently, male offspring are more highly valued than female offspring, and parents resort to infanticide to avoid having daughters. For example, Inuit families in Canada's North traditionally depended on male children to help in the hunt for food, and in former times, Inuit girls were often killed at birth. Until 2015, the Chinese government strictly enforced a "one-child" policy, a measure designed to reduce population growth by forbidding couples to have more than one child. This policy resulted in many parents killing or abandoning their female babies (or giving them up for adoption to Western families) in order to make room for a male child.

A more technological approach is currently practiced in some countries that place a premium on male offspring: prenatal tests are used to determine the gender of the fetus, and female fetuses are selectively aborted. These cases dramatically illustrate the sociocultural model of development described in Chapter 1: cultural values, government policy, and available technology all affect developmental outcomes. Though not addressed in the studies cited here, it is important to note that not every individual can be categorized as male or female, and that an infant's designated sex at birth may differ from their eventual gender identity. These issues are addressed more fully in Chapter 15.

It is important to remember that our understanding of the effects of environmental forces on developmental outcomes is far from complete. New research is exploring the impact of climate change on sex ratios—both in terms of higher temperatures, which may increase the ratio of boys conceived compared to girls, and stress-related teratogens as a result of extreme weather events and subsequent environmental effects, which may negatively affect the number of male fetuses that survive through birth (Fukuda et al., 2014). Evidence at this point does not support definitive statements about the impact of climate change on birth sex ratios, but emerging research in this area reminds us of the complex network of forces at play.

harbour an egg. And a substantial portion of the sperm have serious genetic or other defects that prevent them from propelling themselves vigorously enough to reach and fertilize the egg. Thus, any sperm that do get to the egg are likely to be healthy and structurally sound, revealing a Darwinian-type "survival of the fittest" process operating during conception. (Box 2.2 describes the consequences of this selection process for the conception of males and females.)

As soon as one sperm's head penetrates the outer membrane of the egg, a chemical reaction seals the membrane, preventing other sperm from entering. The tail of the sperm falls off, the contents of its head gush into the egg, and the nuclei of the two cells merge within hours. The fertilized egg, known as a **zygote**, now has a full complement of human genetic material, 23 chromosomes from the egg and 23 chromosomes from the sperm.

zygote a fertilized egg cell

embryo the developing organism from the 3rd to 8th week of prenatal development

fetus the developing organism from the 9th week to birth

mitosis cell division that results in two identical cells

Developmental Processes

Four major developmental processes underlie the transformation of a zygote into an **embryo** and then a **fetus**. The first is *cell division,* known as **mitosis**. Within about 12 hours after conception, the zygote divides into two equal parts, each containing a full complement of genetic material. These two cells then divide into four, those four into eight, those eight into sixteen, and so on. Through continued cell division over the course of 38 weeks, the barely visible zygote becomes a newborn consisting of trillions of cells.

A second major process is *cell migration,* the movement of newly formed cells away from their point of origin. Among the many cells that migrate are the neurons that originate deep inside the embryonic brain and then, like pioneers settling new territory, travel to the outer reaches of the developing brain.

The third process in prenatal development is *cell differentiation.* Initially, all of the embryo's cells, referred to as **embryonic stem cells**, can give rise to any of the more than 200 possible cell types in the human body. (It is this unique flexibility that makes embryonic stem cells the focus of a great deal of research in regenerative medicine.) After several cell divisions, however, these cells start to specialize. Since all cells in the body share an identical set of genes, what factors determine which type of cell a given stem cell will become? While much about this process remains unknown, it is clear that the cell's location influences its future development via chemical and cell-to-cell contact with neighbouring cells, and that gene expression—which genes in the cell are switched on—distinguishes one type of cell from another.

The fourth developmental process is something you would not normally think of as developmental at all—*death.* The role of this genetically programmed "cell suicide," known as **apoptosis**, is readily apparent in hand development: the formation of fingers depends on the death of the cells in between the ridges in the hand plate, as seen in Figure 2.3. In other words, death is preprogrammed for the cells that disappear from the hand plates. Apoptosis has been referred to as a "ticking death timer" because it follows a specific timeline, programmed into the cells themselves.

Finally, hormones have a major influence throughout prenatal development. For example, hormones play a crucial role in sexual differentiation. All human fetuses, regardless of the genes they carry, can develop either male or female genitalia. The presence of *androgens,* a class of hormones that includes testosterone, leads to the development of male genitalia. If androgens are absent, female genitalia develop. The source of androgens is the male fetus itself, at around the 8th week after conception. This is just one of the many ways in which the fetus influences its own development. Other important hormones include steroids such as glucocorticoids, which limit fetal growth and help fetal tissues mature. Toward the end of gestation, the fetus increases production of these hormones in order to facilitate maturation of key organs, such as the lungs, that are needed for life outside the womb. Later in this chapter, we will discuss the role played by glucocorticoids in the influence of maternal stress on the fetus.

We now turn our attention to the general course of prenatal development.

Early Development

On its journey through the fallopian tube to the womb, the zygote doubles its number of cells roughly twice a day. By the 4th day after conception, the cells arrange themselves into a hollow sphere with a bulge of cells, called the *inner cell mass,* on one side.

embryonic stem cells embryonic cells, which can develop into any type of body cell

apoptosis genetically programmed cell death

The Prenatal Period: Conception to Birth

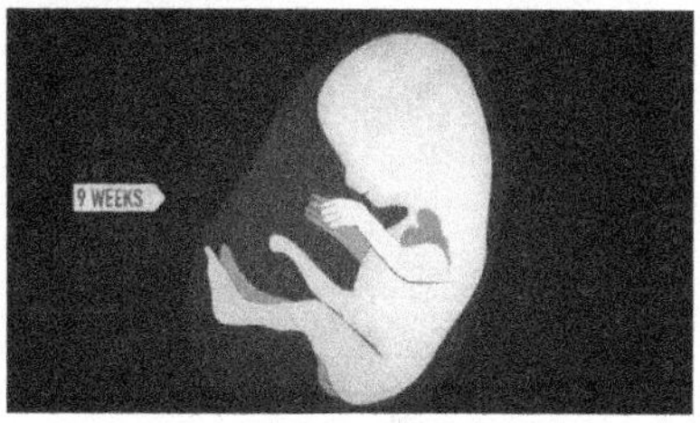

WORTH PUBLISHERS

FIGURE 2.3 Fetal hand plate The role of apoptosis, or cell death, is clearly seen in the development of the hand, which requires the death of the cells in between the ridges of the hand plate in order for the fingers to separate.

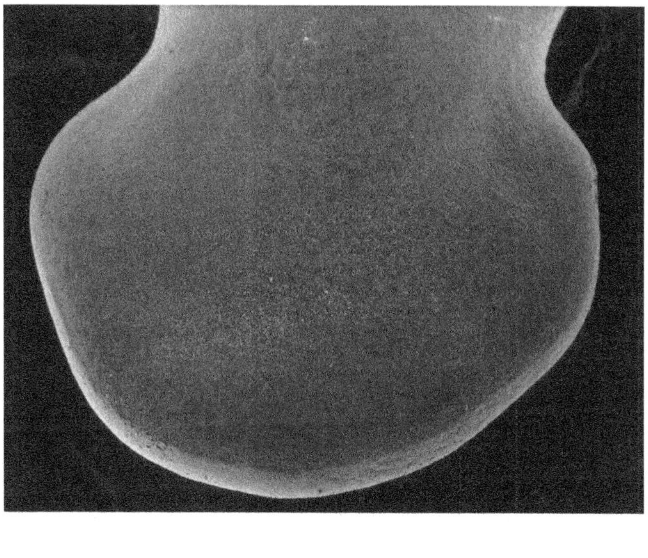

SPL/SCIENCE SOURCE

identical (monozygotic) twins twins that result from the splitting in half of the zygote, resulting in each of the two resulting zygotes having exactly the same set of genes

fraternal (dizygotic) twins twins that result when two eggs happen to be released into the fallopian tube at the same time and are fertilized by two different sperm; fraternal twins have only half their genes in common

neural tube a groove formed in the top layer of differentiated cells in the embryo that eventually becomes the brain and spinal cord

amniotic sac a transparent, fluid-filled membrane that surrounds and protects the fetus

placenta a support organ for the fetus; it keeps the circulatory systems of the fetus and mother separate, but a semipermeable membrane permits the exchange of some materials between them (oxygen and nutrients from mother to fetus, and carbon dioxide and waste products from fetus to mother)

umbilical cord a tube containing the blood vessels connecting the fetus and placenta

This is the stage at which **identical (monozygotic) twins** most often originate. They result from a splitting in half of the inner cell mass, thus they have exactly the same genetic makeup. In contrast, **fraternal (dizygotic) twins** result when two eggs happen to be released from the ovary into the fallopian tube and both are fertilized. Because they originate from two different eggs and two different sperm, fraternal twins are no more alike genetically than non-twin siblings with the same parents.

By the end of the 1st week following conception, if all goes well (which it does for less than half the zygotes that are conceived), the zygote embeds itself in the uterine lining and becomes dependent on the mother for sustenance. The embedded ball of cells then starts to differentiate. The inner cell mass becomes the embryo, and the rest of the cells become an elaborate support system—including the *amniotic sac* and *placenta*—that enables the embryo to develop. The inner cell mass is initially a single layer thick, but during the 2nd week, it folds itself into three layers, each with a different developmental destiny. The top layer becomes the nervous system, the nails, teeth, inner ear, lens of the eyes, and the outer surface of the skin. The middle layer becomes muscles, bones, the circulatory system, the inner layers of the skin, and other internal organs. The bottom layer develops into the digestive system, lungs, urinary tract, and glands. A few days after the embryo has differentiated into these three layers, a U-shaped groove forms down the centre of the top layer. The folds at the top of the groove move together and fuse, creating the **neural tube** (Figure 2.4). One end of the neural tube will swell and develop into the brain, and the rest will become the spinal cord.

The elaborate support system that develops along with the embryo is essential to the embryo's survival. The **amniotic sac** is a membrane filled with a clear, watery fluid in which the fetus floats. The amniotic fluid operates as a protective buffer for the developing fetus, providing it with a relatively even temperature and cushioning it against jolting. The **placenta** is a rich network of blood vessels, weighing roughly one pound, that extends into the tissues of the mother's uterus. While we might assume that the placenta comes from the mother, 90% of the cells in the placenta come from the fetus itself. Far from just being afterbirth, the placenta is a complex organ that plays a critical role in the healthy development of the fetus.

FIGURE 2.4 Neural tube In the 4th week, the neural tube begins to develop into the brain and spinal cord. In this photo, the neural groove, which fuses together first at the centre and then outward in both directions as if two zippers were being closed, has been "zipped shut" except for one part still open at the top. Spina bifida, a congenital disorder in which the skin over the spinal cord is not fully closed, can originate at this point. After closing, the top of the neural tube will develop into the brain.

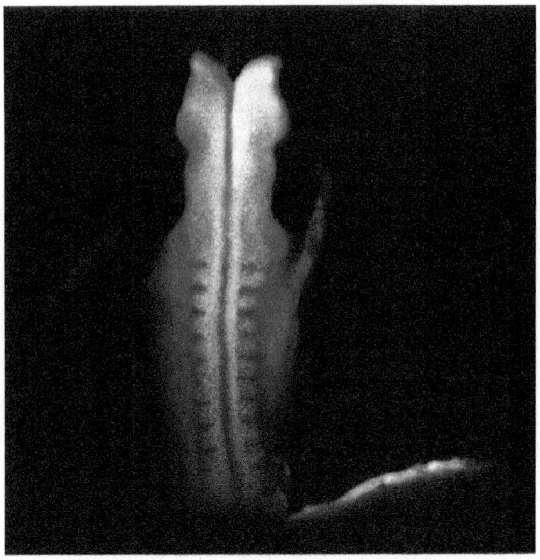

ANATOMICAL TRAVELOGUE/SCIENCE SOURCE

Crucially, the placenta is semipermeable: it permits the exchange of materials carried in the bloodstreams of the fetus and its mother, but it prevents the blood of the mother and fetus from mixing. Oxygen, nutrients, minerals, and some antibodies—all of which are just as vital to the fetus as they are to you—are transported to the placenta by the mother's circulating blood. They then cross the placenta and enter the fetal blood system. Waste products (e.g., carbon dioxide and urea) from the fetus cross the placenta in the opposite direction and are removed from the mother's bloodstream by her normal excretory processes. The placental membrane also serves as a defensive barrier against a host of dangerous toxins and infectious agents that can inhabit the mother's body but would be harmful or even fatal to the fetus. Unfortunately, being semipermeable, the placenta is not a perfect barrier, and, as you will see shortly, a variety of harmful elements can cross it and attack the fetus. These support system structures are illustrated in Figure 2.1.

The amniotic sac is connected to the placenta via the **umbilical cord**, which is a tube containing the blood vessels that run to the fetus.

An Illustrated Summary of Prenatal Development

The course of prenatal development from the 4th week post-conception on is illustrated in Figures 2.5 through 2.11, and significant milestones are highlighted in the accompanying text. Notice that earlier development takes place at a more rapid pace than later development and that the areas nearer the head develop earlier than those farther away (e.g., head before body, hands before feet)—a general tendency known as **cephalocaudal development**.

Figure 2.5: At 4 weeks after conception, the embryo is curved so tightly that the head and the tail-like structure at the other end are almost touching. The round area near the top of the head is where the eyes will form, and the round gray area near the back of the "neck" is the primordial inner ear. A primitive heart is visible; it is already beating and circulating blood. An arm bud can be seen in the side of the embryo; a leg bud is also present but less distinct.

Figure 2.6: (a) In this 5½-week-old fetus, the nose, mouth, and palate are beginning to differentiate into separate structures. (b) Just 3 weeks later, the nose and mouth are almost fully formed. Cleft palate, one of the most common birth defects worldwide, involves malformations of this area and originates sometime between 5½ and 8 weeks prenatally, as these structures are developing.

Figure 2.7: The bulging forehead of this 9-week-old fetus reflects extremely rapid brain growth. Rudimentary eyes and ears are forming. All the internal organs are present. Sexual differentiation has started. Ribs are visible, fingers and toes have emerged, and nails are growing.

Figure 2.8: This image of an 11-week-old fetus clearly shows the heart, which has achieved its basic adult structure. You can also see the developing spine and ribs, as well as the major divisions of the brain.

Figure 2.9: During the last 5 months of prenatal development, the growth of the lower part of the body accelerates. At this age, the external genitalia are substantially developed, and a different camera angle would have revealed the sex of this fetus.

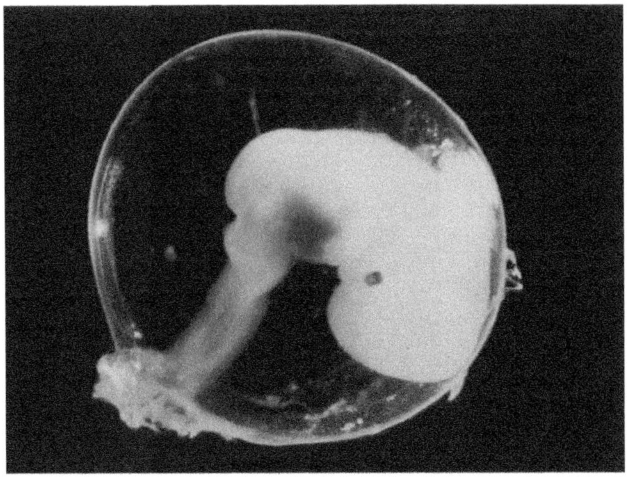

BIOPHOTO ASSOCIATES/SCIENCE SOURCE

| FIGURE 2.5 **Embryo at 4 weeks.**

cephalocaudal development the pattern of growth in which areas near the head develop earlier than areas farther from the head

(a) (b)

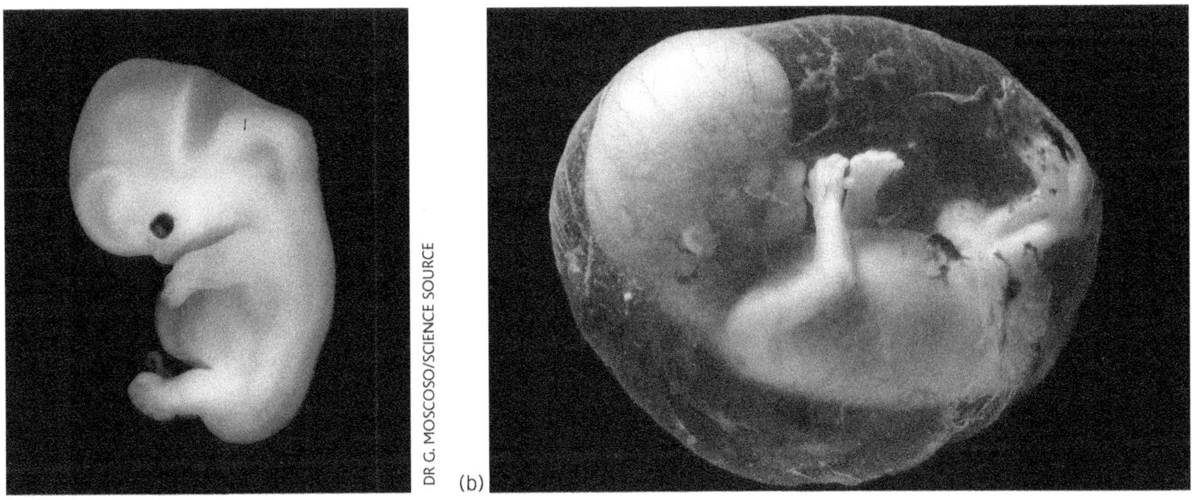

DR G. MOSCOSO/SCIENCE SOURCE

STEVE ALLEN/THE IMAGE BANK/GETTY IMAGES

| FIGURE 2.6 **Face development from (a) 5½ to (b) 8½ weeks.**

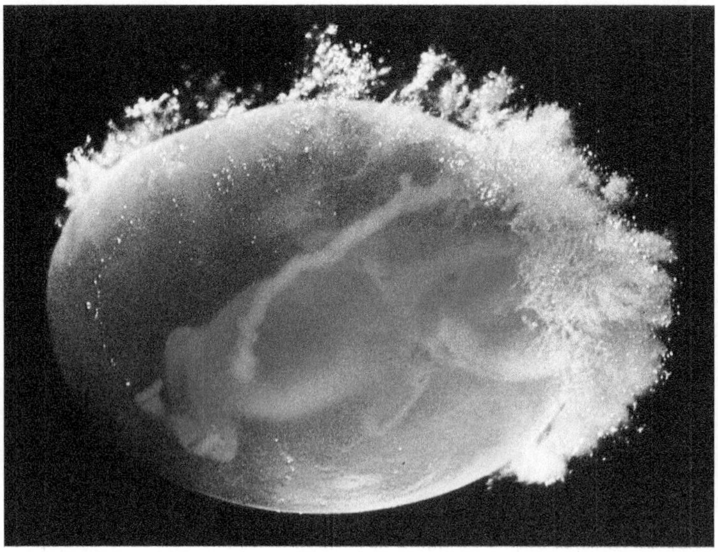

ALAIN POL, CNRI/SCIENCE PHOTO LIBRARY/GETTY IMAGES

FIGURE 2.7 Fetus at 9 weeks.

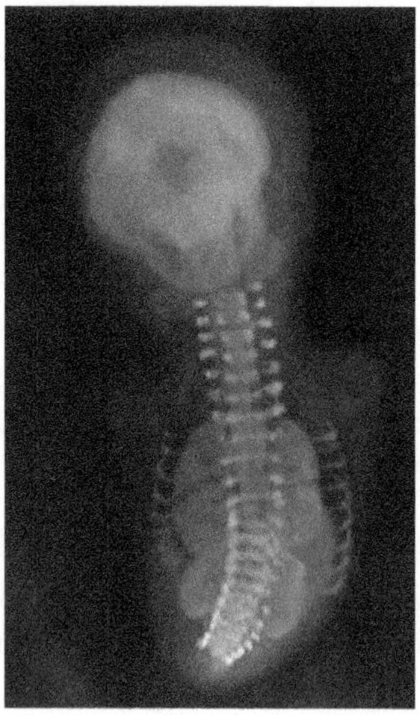

ANATOMICAL TRAVELOGUE/SCIENCE SOURCE

FIGURE 2.8 Fetus at 11 weeks.

Figure 2.10: This 18-week-old fetus is covered with very fine hair, and a greasy coating protects its skin from its long immersion in liquid. The components of facial expressions are present—the fetus can raise its eyebrows, wrinkle its forehead, and move its mouth.

Figure 2.11: The brain and lungs of a 28-week-old fetus are sufficiently developed that it would have a chance of surviving on its own, without medical intervention. The eyes can open, and they move, especially during periods of rapid eye movement (REM) sleep. The auditory system is functioning, and the fetus reacts to a variety of sounds.

During the last 3 months of prenatal development, the fetus grows dramatically in size, essentially tripling its weight. It also develops a wide repertoire of behaviours and learns from its experiences, as described in the next section. Table 2.1 summarizes the major milestones in prenatal development.

ANATOMICAL TRAVELOGUE/SCIENCE SOURCE

FIGURE 2.9 Fetus at 16 weeks.

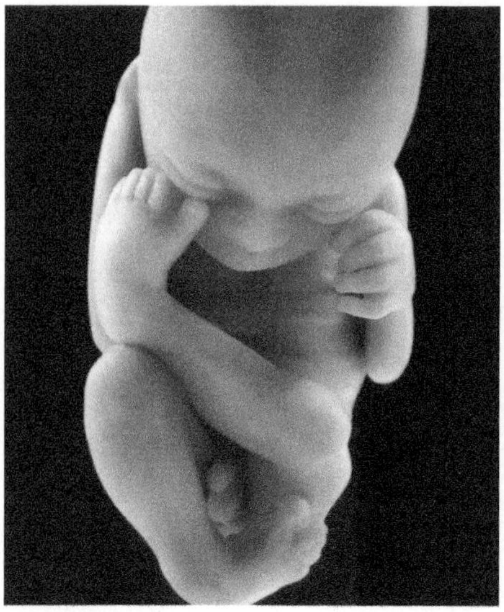

ARNO MASSEE/SCIENCE SOURCE

FIGURE 2.10 Fetus at 18 weeks.

TABLE 2.1 Milestones in Prenatal Development

Trimester	Weeks	Major Milestones
1	1	Zygote travels from fallopian tube to womb and embeds in uterine lining; cells arrange into a ball and begin to form embryo and support system.
	2–3	Embryo forms three layers, which will become the nervous system and skin; muscles, bones, and circulatory system; and digestive system, lungs, and glands; neural tube also develops.
	4	Neural tube continues to develop into the brain and spinal cord; primitive heart is visible, as are leg and arm buds.
	5–9	Facial features differentiate; rapid brain growth occurs; internal organs form; fingers and toes emerge; sexual differentiation has started.
	10–12	Heart develops its basic adult structures; spine and ribs develop more fully; brain forms major divisions.
2	13–24	Lower body growth accelerates; external genitalia are fully developed; body develops hairy outer covering; fetus can make basic facial expressions; fetal movements can be felt by mother.
3	25–38	Fetus triples in size; brain and lungs are sufficiently developed at 28 weeks to allow survival outside of womb; visual and auditory systems are functional; fetus is capable of learning and behaviours begin to emerge.

Fetal Experience and Behaviour

Is the womb a haven of peace and quiet? Although the uterus and the amniotic fluid buffer the fetus from much of the stimulation impinging on the mother, the fetus still experiences an abundance of sensory stimulation and is capable of learning and developing behaviours.

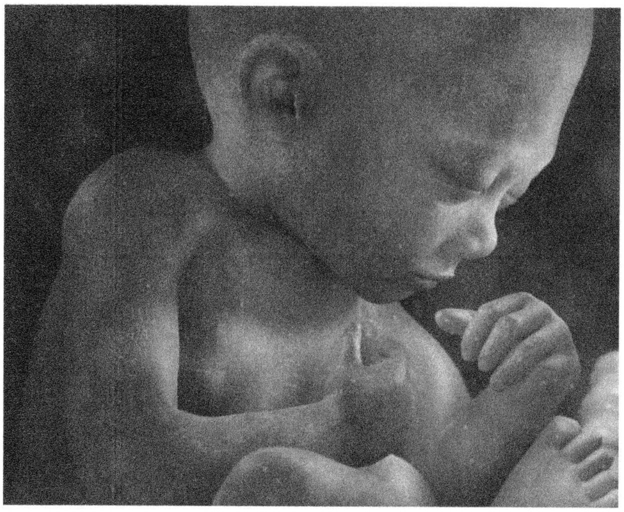

MEDI-MATION/SCIENCE PHOTO LIBRARY

FIGURE 2.11 Fetus at 28 weeks.

Studies of fetal behaviour reveal many results consistent with the themes laid out in Chapter 1. Prenatal experiences shape the developing fetus (*nature and nurture*). The fetus participates in, and contributes to, its own development: the formation of organs and muscles depends on fetal activity, and the fetus rehearses the behavioural repertoire it will need at birth (*the active child*). There is also evidence for both *continuity and discontinuity.* To give just one striking example, 32-week-old fetuses whose heart rates were generally slower and who moved less were more behaviourally inhibited at 10 years of age (DiPietro et al., 2018). Despite their very different environments (discontinuity), fetuses and children show surprising similarities (continuity).

Movement

From 5 or 6 weeks after conception, the fetus moves spontaneously. One of the earliest distinct patterns of movement to emerge (at around 7 weeks) is, remarkably enough, hiccups. Although the reasons for prenatal hiccups are unknown, one theory posits that they are a *burping* reflex, preparing the fetus for eventual nursing by removing air from the stomach to make more room for milk (Howes, 2012).

Swallowing is another important reflex that helps to prepare the fetus for survival outside the womb. Fetuses swallow amniotic fluid, most of which is excreted back out into the amniotic sac. The tongue movements associated with swallowing promote the normal development of the palate. In addition, the

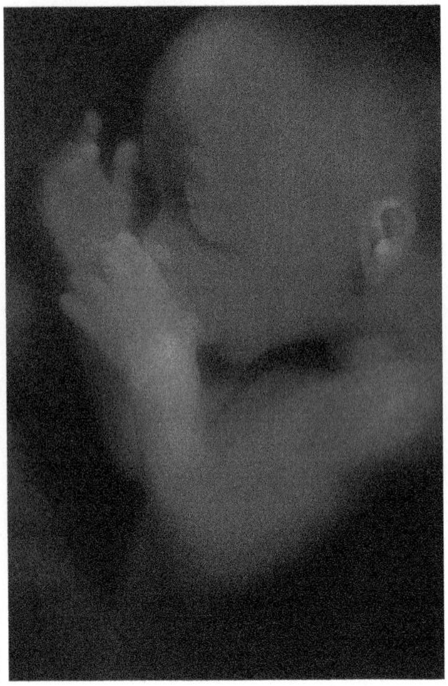
NEIL BROMHALL/SCIENCE PHOTO LIBRARY/GETTY IMAGES

FIGURE 2.12 Fetal arm and hand movements.

passage of amniotic fluid through the body helps the digestive system mature properly.

Another form of fetal movement anticipates breathing after birth. For breathing to occur, the respiratory system must be mature and functional. Beginning as early as 10 weeks after conception, the fetus promotes its respiratory readiness by exercising its lungs through "fetal breathing," moving its chest wall in and out. No air is taken in, of course; rather, small amounts of amniotic fluid are pulled into the lungs and then expelled. Fetal breathing is initially infrequent and irregular but then increases in rate and stability. By the third trimester, fetuses "breathe" roughly once per second (Ulusar, Sandhal, & Mendilcioglu, 2017).

Touch

The fetus experiences tactile stimulation as a result of its own activity. Fetuses have been observed not only grasping their umbilical cords but also rubbing their face and sucking their thumbs. Indeed, the majority of fetal arm movements during the second half of pregnancy result in contact between their hand and mouth (Myowa-Yamakoshi & Takeshita, 2006), as the fetus in Figure 2.12 demonstrates. Remarkably, fetuses' choice of thumb to suck predicts later handedness; fetuses who suck their right thumb are more likely to be righthanded adolescents, whereas fetuses who suck their left thumb are more likely to be lefthanded adolescents (Hepper, Wells, & Lynch, 2005).

As the fetus grows larger, it bumps against the walls of the uterus increasingly often. By full term, fetal heart rate responds to maternal movements, suggesting that their vestibular systems—the sensory apparatus in the inner ear that provides information about movement and balance—is also functioning before birth (Cito et al., 2005; Lecanuet & Jacquet, 2002).

Sight

Although it is not totally dark inside the womb, the visual experience of the fetus is minimal. Despite minimal stimulation, fetuses can process visual information by the third trimester of pregnancy, and, much like newborn infants, fetuses have visual preferences. In a recent study, researchers used 4-D ultrasound to measure what third-trimester fetuses preferred to look at by projecting light patterns onto pregnant women's abdomens (see Figure 2.13; Reid et al., 2017). Fetuses preferred light displays that are top-heavy (resembling correctly oriented faces) over those that are bottom heavy (resembling inverted faces). These data suggest that infants' predispositions to look toward face-like stimuli may not require postnatal experience (though see Scheel et al., 2018, for an alternative view). We continue the discussion of face perception and preference in infants in Chapter 5, Box 5.1.

Taste

The amniotic fluid contains a variety of flavours, and fetuses like some better than others. Indeed, the fetus has a sweet tooth. The first evidence of fetal taste preferences came from a study performed more than 60 years ago (described by Gandelman, 1992). A physician named DeSnoo (1937) devised an ingenious treatment for women with excessive amounts of amniotic fluid. He injected saccharin into their amniotic fluid, hoping that the fetus would help the mother out by ingesting increased amounts of the sweetened fluid, thereby diminishing the excess. And, in fact, tests of the mothers' urine showed that the fetuses ingested more amniotic fluid when it had been sweetened, demonstrating that flavour preferences exist before birth.

Smell

Amniotic fluid takes on odours from what the mother has eaten. Obstetricians have long reported that during birth they can smell scents like curry and coffee in the amniotic fluid of women who had recently consumed them. Smells can be transmitted through liquid, and amniotic fluid comes into contact with the fetus's odour receptors through fetal breathing, providing fetuses with the opportunity for olfactory experience. Prenatal scent learning plays an important role in many species' early developmental processes, demonstrating the principle of **phylogenetic continuity**: humans share many characteristics and developmental processes with nonhuman animals due to our shared evolutionary history. For example, during the birth process in rats, the nipples on the underside of the mother rat's belly are smeared with amniotic fluid. The scent of the amniotic fluid is familiar to the rat pups from their time in the womb, and it lures the pups to the mother's nipples for nursing. When the mother rat's nipples are washed immediately after birth, newborn rats fail to attach to her nipples (Teicher & Blass, 1977). This classic finding clearly demonstrates that nurture begins prenatally: experiences before birth play an important role in post-natal developmental processes.

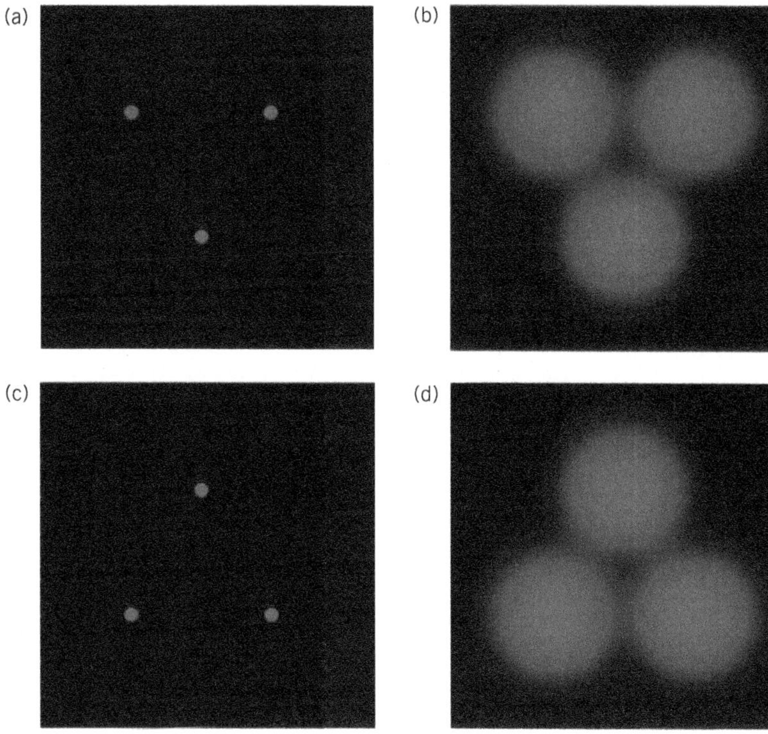

FIGURE 2.13 Light-pattern projection Fetuses prefer light displays that are top-heavy, resembling correctly oriented faces (a, b) over bottom-heavy displays (c, d). The images on the left show the unobstructed light display, and the images on the right illustrate how this display would look to the fetus.

Hearing

The prenatal environment is surprisingly noisy. Fetuses float in a soundscape dominated by their mother's heartbeat, blood flow, and breathing. From the fetuses' vantage point, digestive sounds occur roughly 5 times per second (Parga et al., 2018)! The noise level in the uterus ranges from about 70–95 decibels (roughly the noise level of a vacuum to a lawnmower). The mother's voice is particularly prominent. We know that the fetus hears its mother because its heart rate changes when the mother starts speaking (Voegtline et al., 2013).

During the last trimester, external noises elicit changes in fetal movements and heart rate as well, suggesting that the fetus also perceives sounds outside the mother's body. For instance, Canadian researchers found that fetal heart rate increases when recordings of the mother's or father's voices are played near the pregnant mother's abdomen (Lee & Kisilevsky, 2014). Similarly, changes in heart-rate patterns suggest that fetuses can distinguish between music and speech played near the mother's abdomen (Granier-Deferre et al., 2011).

The uterine auditory experience appears to be particularly well-suited to early brain development. In a study by Webb and colleagues (2015), a group of hospitalized preterm infants spent several hours each day listening to recordings of their mothers' uterine sounds (including voices and heartbeats). At 1 month of age, their brain development was compared to another group of preterm infants who were only exposed to regular hospital sounds. The preterm

phylogenetic continuity the idea that because of our common evolutionary history, humans share many characteristics, behaviours, and developmental processes with non-human animals, especially mammals

habituation a simple form of learning that involves a decrease in response to repeated or continued stimulation

dishabituation the introduction of a new stimulus rekindles interest following habituation to a repeated stimulus

infants exposed to womb sounds had larger auditory cortexes than the control group, suggesting that maternal sounds may facilitate brain development before full gestation.

Because sound is such a prevalent feature of the fetal environment, it plays a major role in prenatal learning, as we discuss next.

Fetal Learning

To this point, we have emphasized the impressive behavioural and sensory capabilities of the fetus. Even more impressive is the extent to which the fetus learns from its experiences in the last 3 months of pregnancy, after the central nervous system is adequately developed to support learning.

In the example of fetal learning that opened this chapter, infants remembered specific prenatal auditory experiences that were presented via audio speakers adjacent to the mother's abdomen, such as repetitions of a single nonsense word (Partanen, Kujala, Tervaniemi et al., 2013) or a melody like *Twinkle Twinkle Little Star* (Partanen, Kujala, Näätänen et al., 2013). More direct evidence for fetal learning comes from studies of habituation, one of the simplest forms of learning. Much like adults and children, fetuses grow bored if a stimulus is repeated over and over again. This process is called **habituation**: a decrease in response to repeated or continued stimulation (see Figure 2.14). Habituation provides evidence of learning and memory: the stimulus loses its novelty (and becomes boring) only if the stimulus is remembered from one presentation to the next. When a perceptible change in the stimulus occurs, it becomes interesting again—a process known as **dishabituation**. Fetuses as young as 30 weeks gestation show habituation to both visual and auditory stimuli, indicating that their central nervous systems are sufficiently developed for learning and short-term memory to occur (Matuz et al., 2012; Muenssinger et al., 2013).

Fetuses also learn from their extensive experience with their mother's voice. To test this idea, Queens University's Barbara Kisilevsky and her colleagues (2003) tested term fetuses in one of two conditions. Half of the fetuses listened to a recording of their mother reading a poem, played through speakers placed on their mother's abdomen. The other half listened to recordings of the same poem read by another woman. Fetal heart rate increased in response to the mother's voice but decreased in response to the other woman's voice. These findings suggest that the fetuses recognized (and were aroused by) the sound of their own mother's voice relative to a stranger's voice. For this to be the case, fetuses must be learning and remembering the sound of their mother's voice.

After birth, do newborns remember anything about their fetal experience? The answer is a resounding yes! They still prefer to listen to their own mother's voice rather than to the voice of another woman (DeCasper & Fifer, 1980). Furthermore, newborns prefer to listen to a version of their mother's voice that has been filtered to sound the way it did in the womb, rather than to another woman's filtered voice (Moon & Fifer, 1990; Spence & Freeman, 1996). Newborns prefer to listen to the language they heard in the womb over another language (Mehler et al., 1988; Moon, Cooper, & Fifer, 1993). Finally, newborns remember the sounds of specific stories heard in the

FIGURE 2.14 Habituation Habituation occurs in response to the repeated presentation of a stimulus. As the first stimulus is repeated and becomes familiar, the response to it gradually decreases. When a novel stimulus occurs, the response recovers. The decreased response to the repeated stimulus indicates the formation of memory for it; the increased response to the novel stimulus indicates discrimination of it from the familiar one, as well as a general preference for novelty.

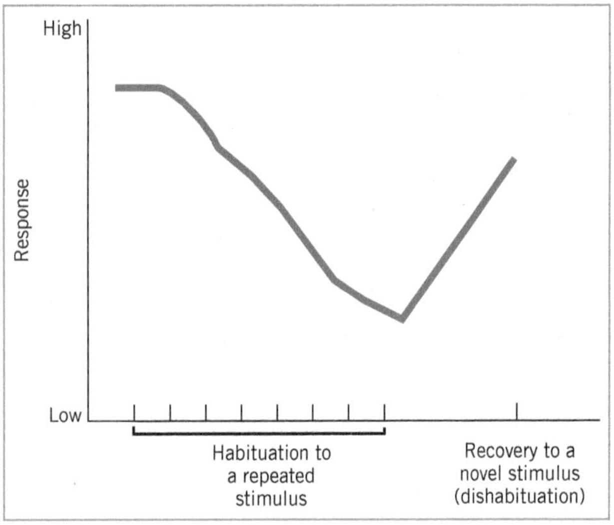

womb (DeCasper & Spence, 1986). Figure 2.15 describes the technique these researchers used to study prenatal learning.

Fetuses also learn from the tastes and smells they encounter in the womb. Like the rat pups discussed earlier, newborn humans remember the scent of amniotic fluid. They orient to their own amniotic scent and prefer scents reflecting flavours that their mother ate while she was pregnant, like anise (licorice) or garlic (for a review, see Anzman-Frasca et al., 2018). Long-lasting taste preferences have also been observed. In one study, pregnant women drank carrot juice for three weeks near the end of their pregnancy (Mennella, Jagnow, & Beauchamp, 2001). When tested at around 5½ months of age, their babies reacted more positively to cereal prepared with carrot juice than to the same cereal prepared with water. These flavour preferences suggest a *persistent* effect of prenatal learning that may shed light on the origins and strength of cultural food preferences. A child whose mother ate a lot of chili peppers, ginger, and cumin during pregnancy, for example, might be more favourably disposed to Indian food than would a child whose mother's diet lacked those flavours.

Does this evidence of fetal learning suggest that there is a benefit to "prenatal education" programs, where specific music, languages, voices, or other experiences can be used to enhance cognitive abilities after birth? Probably not. In the first place, the fetal brain is unlikely to be sufficiently developed to process much about language meaning. In addition, the liquid environment in the womb filters out detailed speech and music sounds, leaving only pitch contours and rhythmic patterns. In short, the fetus learns about general sounds but not any specific content.

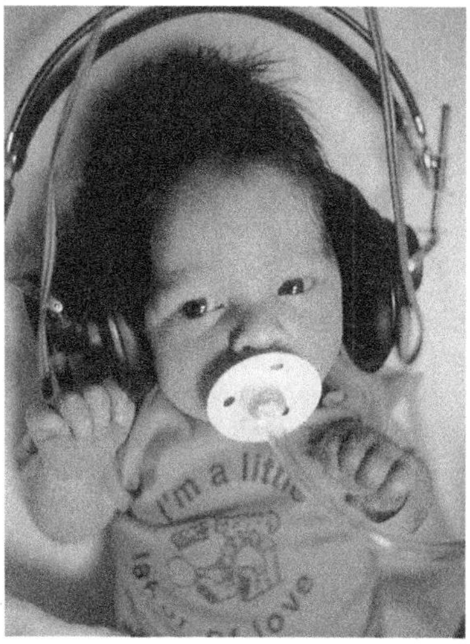

MELANIE J. SPENCE, THE UNIVERSITY OF TEXAS AT DALLAS

FIGURE 2.15 **Prenatal learning** This newborn can control what he gets to listen to. His pacifier is hooked up to a computer, which is in turn connected to an audio player. If the baby sucks in one pattern (predetermined by the researchers), he will hear one recording. If he sucks in a different pattern, he will hear a different recording. Researchers have used this technique to investigate many questions about infant abilities, including the influence of fetal experience on newborn preferences.

REVIEW QUESTION

Fetal development includes periods of rapid change, as well as periods of slower growth. Throughout the gestation process, the fetus goes through phases during which different organs and systems develop. How do the different periods of fetal development illustrate aspects of continuity and discontinuity? ■

Hazards to Prenatal Development

Regrettably, prenatal development is not always free of error or misfortune. The most dire, and by far the most common, misfortune is *spontaneous abortion*—commonly referred to as *miscarriage.* Most miscarriages occur before the woman even knows that she is pregnant. The majority of embryos that are miscarried very early have severe defects, such as a missing chromosome or an extra one, that make further development impossible. In Canada and the United States, between 6% and 15% of clinically recognized pregnancies end in miscarriage (Arck et al., 2008; Rai & Regan, 2006). This number is similar to the rate in a very different culture, rural Kenya (18.9%), suggesting that the factors that influence miscarriage are present across a wide range of life circumstances (Dellicour et al., 2016).

Across their childbearing years, at least 25% of women—and possibly as many as 50%—experience at least one miscarriage. Few women realize how common this experience is, making it all the more painful if it happens to them. Yet more

teratogen an external agent that can cause damage or death during prenatal development

sensitive period the period of time during which a developing organism is most sensitive to the effects of external factors

dose–response relation a relation in which the effect of exposure to an element increases with the extent of exposure (prenatally, the more exposure a fetus has to a potential teratogen, the more severe its effect is likely to be)

Challenges During Pregnancy

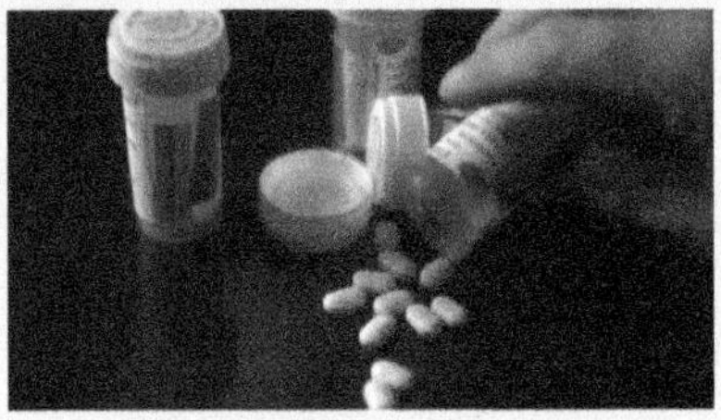

ONESTONEMEDIA/GETTY IMAGES

This young artist exhibits the harmful prenatal effects of exposure to thalidomide. It seems likely that his mother took the drug in the 2nd month of her pregnancy, when the arm buds are developing—an unfortunate example providing clear evidence of the importance of timing in how environmental agents can affect the developing fetus.

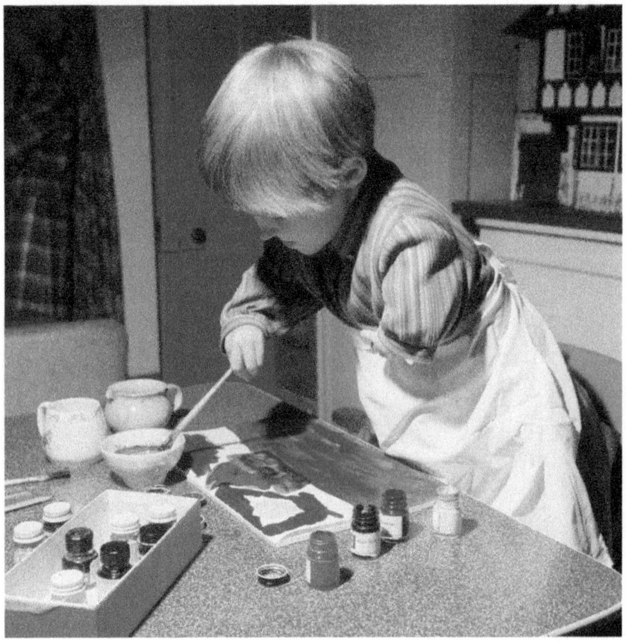

PAUL FIEVEZ/GETTY IMAGES

agonizing is the experience of the approximately 1% of women who experience *recurrent miscarriages,* or the loss of three or more consecutive pregnancies. Encouragingly, though, many women who have had recurrent miscarriages successfully carry subsequent pregnancies to term (Cohain, Buxbaum, & Mankuta, 2017).

For fetuses that survive the danger of miscarriage, there is still a range of factors that can lead to unforeseen negative consequences. Here, we consider some of the many environmental risk factors. Genetic factors will be discussed in Chapter 3.

Teratogens

A vast number of environmental agents, called **teratogens,** have the potential to harm the fetus. The effects of potential teratogens are heavily influenced by timing (one of the basic developmental principles discussed in Chapter 1). Many teratogens cause damage only if they are present during a **sensitive period** in prenatal development. The major organ systems are most vulnerable to damage at the time when their basic structures are being formed. Because the timing is different for each system, the sensitive periods are different for each system, as shown in Figure 2.16.

The most dramatic illustration of the importance of timing comes from the use of the drug thalidomide in the early 1960s. Thalidomide was prescribed to treat morning sickness (among other things) and was considered to be so safe that it was sold over the counter in numerous countries, including Canada (the last country to withdraw thalidomide from the market). At the time, it was believed that such medications would not cross the placental barrier. However, many pregnant women who took this new, presumably safe drug gave birth to babies with major limb deformities; some babies were born with no arms and with flipperlike hands growing out of their shoulders. In a striking illustration of sensitive period effects, serious defects occurred only if the pregnant woman took the drug between the 4th and 6th week after conception—the time when her fetus's limbs were emerging and developing (look again at Figures 2.5 to 2.11). Taking thalidomide either before the limbs started to develop or after they were basically formed had no harmful effect.

As you can see in Figure 2.16, the sensitive periods for many organ systems occur before the woman might realize she is pregnant. Because a substantial number of pregnancies are unplanned, sexually active people of childbearing age should be aware of factors that could compromise the health of a child they might conceive.

Another crucial factor influencing the severity of teratogenic effects is the amount and duration of exposure. Most teratogens show a **dose–response relation:** the greater the fetus's exposure to a potential teratogen, the more likely it is that the fetus will suffer damage and the more severe any damage is likely to be.

Teratogens frequently occur in combination, making it difficult to separate out their effects. For families living in poverty, for example, it is hard to tease apart the effects of poor maternal nutrition, exposure to pollution, inadequate prenatal care, and psychological stress. The presence of multiple risk factors can have a *cumulative* impact on development, as we discuss further at the end of this chapter in the section on multiple-risk models.

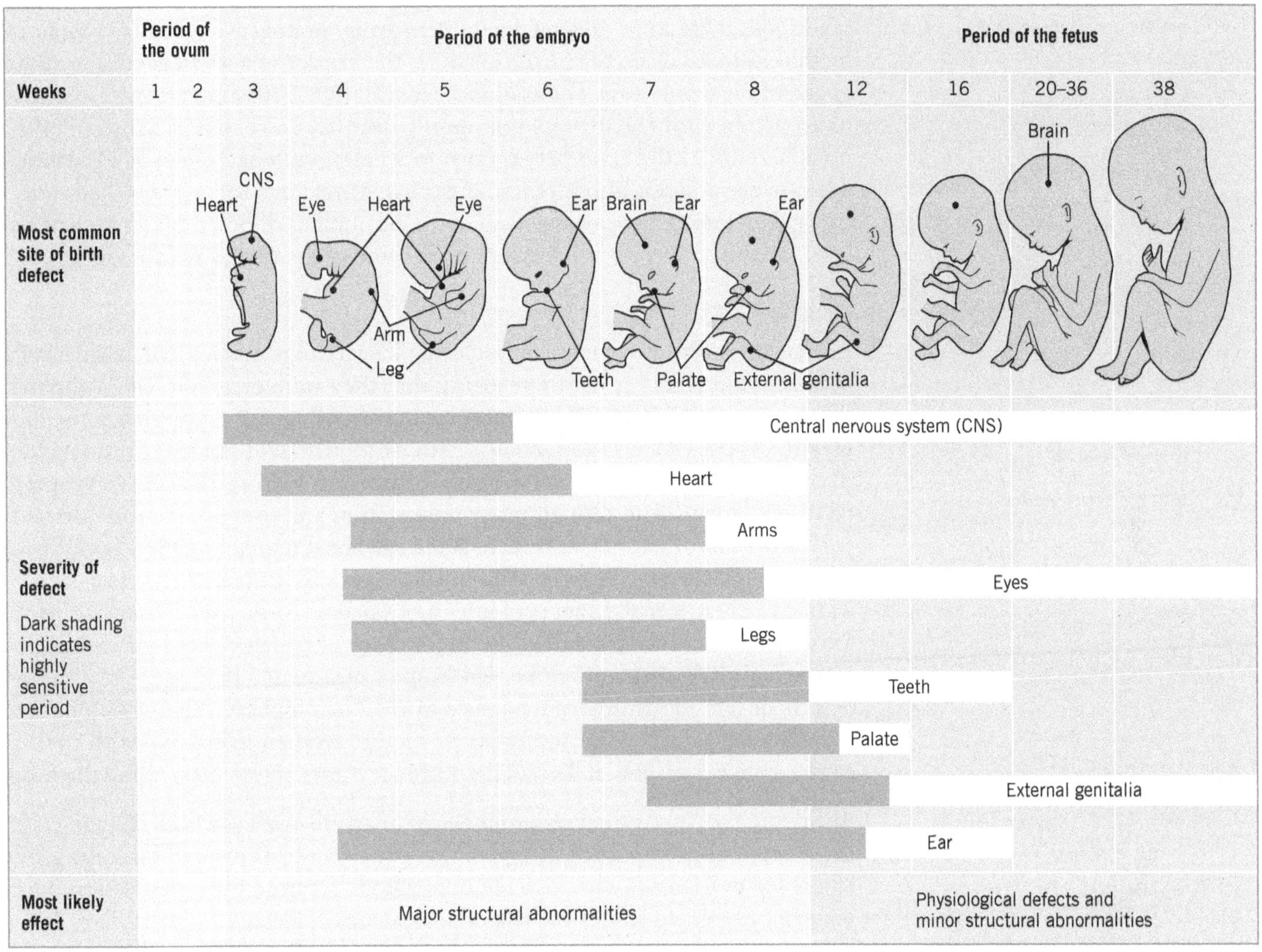

FIGURE 2.16 Sensitive periods of prenatal development The most sensitive or critical period of prenatal development is the embryonic period. During the first 2 weeks, before implantation in the uterus, the zygote is generally not susceptible to environmental factors. Every major organ system of the body undergoes all or a major part of its development between the 3rd and the 9th week. The dark green portions of the bars in the figure denote the times of most rapid development when major defects originate. The light green portions indicate periods of continued but less rapid development when minor defects may occur. (Information from Moore & Persaud, 1993)

Negative effects of prenatal experience may not be immediately evident. *Fetal programming* refers to the belated emergence of effects of prenatal experience that "program the physiological set points that will govern physiology in adulthood" (Coe & Lubach, 2008). For instance, in the case of inadequate prenatal nutrition, the fetus's metabolism adjusts to the level of nutritional deficiency experienced in the womb and does not reset itself after birth. In a postnatal environment with abundant food, this programming sets the stage for the development of overweight and obesity issues.

Evidence comes from studies of individuals who were conceived in the Netherlands in 1944, during what was known as the Dutch Hunger Winter (Schulz, 2010). At this point in World War II, the German occupying force in the Netherlands limited rations to as little as 400 to 800 calories per day. Women in the earlier stages of pregnancy during the famine had babies of normal birth weights. However, these infants grew up to have high rates of obesity. The fetuses' metabolisms were apparently set prenatally, while they were experiencing undernutrition, and were not reset when nutrition reached normal levels. Thus, the physiology of these individuals was a poor match for the food-rich environment available later in their lives, leading to an increased risk of obesity.

The effects of teratogens can also vary according to *individual differences* in genetic susceptibility (probably in both the mother and the fetus). Thus, a substance that is harmless to most people may trigger problems in individuals whose genes predispose them to be affected by it. Identifying teratogens is further complicated by the existence of *sleeper effects,* in which the impact of a given agent may not be apparent for many years. For example, between the 1940s and 1960s, the hormone diethylstilbestrol (DES) was commonly used to prevent miscarriage and had no apparent ill effects on babies born to women who had taken it. However, in adolescence and adulthood, these offspring turned out to have elevated rates of cervical and testicular cancers. An enormous number of potential teratogens have been identified, but we will focus only on some of the most common ones.

Drugs

In Canada, 6.7% of women reported using illegal drugs in the three months before becoming pregnant or before realizing that they were pregnant, while about 1% of women reported using drugs after recognizing that they were pregnant (Public Health Agency of Canada, 2009). Almost all drugs of abuse—both legal and illegal—have been shown to be, or are suspected of being, dangerous for prenatal development. And though many prescription and over-the-counter drugs are perfectly safe for pregnant women, some are not. Pregnant women (and women who have reason to think they might soon become pregnant) should take medications only under the supervision of a physician. Some prescription drugs that are in common use by women of childbearing age, such as the acne medication isotretinoin (Accutane), are known human teratogens that cause severe birth defects or fetal death. Indeed, because of the unambiguous relationship between Accutane and birth defects, physicians require women to comply with multiple contraceptive measures and ongoing pregnancy tests before prescribing the drug.

Antidepressants Antidepressant medications raise particularly challenging issues for women contemplating pregnancy. These medications can be hugely beneficial for individuals experiencing depression. Treatment for depression during pregnancy can help reduce the risk of postpartum depression, which affects 10% to 30% of new mothers, and which is especially likely for women with previous histories of depression (Brummelte & Galea, 2016). In Canada, roughly 3% to 5% of pregnant women take antidepressant medication (Bérard & Sheehy, 2014; Smolina et al., 2015). Evidence regarding whether or not these medications are harmful to the fetus is inconclusive (Lusskin et al., 2018), raising difficult questions for pregnant women who are depressed. Should they choose a pharmaceutical intervention for their depression and risk negative outcomes from the medication? Or should they choose not to treat their mood disorder and risk negative outcomes from the depression itself?

One potential solution to this issue is the use of non-pharmaceutical treatments for depression, which many pregnant women say they would prefer (Dimidjian & Goodman, 2014). Behavioural interventions, including cognitive behaviour therapy and mindfulness-based cognitive therapy, hold promise as ways to treat perinatal depression without the use of medication (e.g., Dimidjian et al., 2017).

Opioids Another issue of increasing concern is the use of prescription opioid medications (e.g., Vicodin, Percocet, Oxycodone, Fentanyl) and the related use of illicit opioids, such as heroin. Because they are designed to mimic the effects of neurotransmitters, they have the potential to wreak havoc on the developing brain. Prescribed for pain management or used illegally, opioids can be highly damaging to fetuses, who can become addicted themselves. Neonatal abstinence syndrome (NAS) is a form of drug withdrawal seen when fetuses exposed to opioids in the womb are born. In Canada, prevalence of NAS has continued to rise (Brogly et al., 2017); for example, between 1992 and 2011, the rate of NAS increased 0.28 per 1000 live births to 4.29 per 1000 live births (Turner et al., 2015).

Common effects of NAS include low birth weight, problems with breathing and feeding, and seizures. Treatment for these newborns often requires medications such as methadone or morphine to manage withdrawal symptoms. As we mentioned earlier, teratogens often occur in clusters. In the case of opioids, the co-presence of other maternal drug use (e.g., antidepressants or marijuana) increases the likelihood that the newborn will have NAS (Sanlorenzo, Stark, & Patrick, 2018).

Marijuana Marijuana is of particular interest to researchers because it is so frequently used by women of reproductive age, and its usage may increase in Canada now that cannabis has been legalized. Even prior to legalization, which occurred in October 2018, marijuana use among pregnant women was on the rise; in Ontario, marijuana use during pregnancy grew from 1.2% in 2012 to 1.8% in 2017, with the highest rate (6.5%) among 15- to 24-year-olds (Corsi et al., 2019). Data on the effects of marijuana on fetal development are inconclusive because many users of marijuana also smoke cigarettes and/or use alcohol, and the effects of each drug are difficult to tease apart; some studies suggest that the combination of marijuana and tobacco is particularly problematic (Ryan et al., 2018). Prenatal exposure to marijuana is also associated with a range of problems involving attention, impulsivity, learning, and memory in older children (Behnke et al., 2013).

The effects of opioids and marijuana on fetal development can be devastating, but the two drugs that wreak the most widespread havoc on fetal development are cigarettes (nicotine) and alcohol, which we turn to next.

Cigarette smoking When a pregnant woman smokes a cigarette, both she and her fetus get less oxygen. Indeed, the fetus makes fewer breathing movements while its mother is smoking, and the fetuses of smokers metabolize some of the cancer-causing agents contained in tobacco. Secondhand smoke has an indirect effect on fetal oxygen as well, through the mother's intake of cigarette gases when someone is smoking nearby.

The main developmental consequences of maternal smoking are slowed fetal growth and low birth weight, both of which compromise the health of the newborn. In addition, smoking is linked to increased risk of sudden infant death syndrome (SIDS) (discussed in Box 2.3) and a variety of other problems, including lower IQ, hearing deficits, ADHD (see Box 9.3), and cancer. As with other teratogens, there is a dose–response relationship: greater smoking intensity (as measured in the number of cigarettes per day) predicts worse outcomes, including stillbirths (e.g., Marufu et al., 2015). And, as with other teratogens, timing matters: the effects of smoking are greatest early in gestation (e.g., Behnke et al., 2013). However, in spite of the well-documented and widely advertised negative effects of maternal smoking on fetal development, approximately 12% of pregnant women in Canada continue to smoke during pregnancy (Lange et al., 2015).

E-cigarettes (e-cigs) are becoming increasingly prevalent as an alternative to conventional cigarettes. Many pregnant women believe that vaping is healthier for their fetuses than cigarette smoking (Wagner, Camerota, & Propper, 2017). While e-cigs

Smoking endangers the health of the fetus.

GABBY JONES/BLOOMBERG VIA GETTY IMAGES

BOX 2.3 APPLICATIONS Sudden Infant Death Syndrome

For parents, nothing is more terrifying to contemplate than the death of their child. New parents are especially frightened by the specter of **sudden infant death syndrome (SIDS)**. SIDS refers to the sudden, unexpected, and unexplained death of an infant younger than 1 year. The most common SIDS scenario is that an apparently healthy baby, usually between 2 and 5 months of age, is put to bed for the night and found dead in the morning. In Canada, SIDS accounts for 21.3% of post-neonatal deaths, making it the leading cause of infant mortality between 28 days and 1 year of age (Public Health Agency of Canada, 2013). Furthermore, infants from socioeconomically disadvantaged and Indigenous populations have higher incidences of SIDS than do other populations in Canada (Collins et al., 2012; Gilbert et al., 2013).

The causes of SIDS are not well understood, but they likely involve an interaction between an underlying biological issue that places the infant at risk and an environmental stressor—for example, limited access to oxygen due to an obstruction of the nose and mouth. Recent research suggests that at least some infants who succumbed to SIDS had altered levels of serotonin, a neurotransmitter (Haynes et al., 2017). Decreased serotonin may make it more difficult for young infants to detect and respond to a lack of oxygen by turning their head away from bedding or other soft materials, especially during sleep.

A subset of cases result from a rare genetic mutation in the breathing muscles that puts infants at greater risk of respiratory challenge in situations that impair breathing (Männikkö et al., 2018). Researchers studying SIDS hope to identify biomarkers, like neurotransmitters or genetic mutations, that will help physicians flag infants at heightened risk for SIDS (Bright, Vink, & Byard, 2018).

To decrease the risk of SIDS, the most important steps that parents can take entail removing any barriers to their baby's breathing. First, putting infants to sleep on their backs reduces the possibility of breathing obstructions. Sleeping on the stomach increases the risk of SIDS more than any other single factor. A campaign encouraging parents to put their infants to sleep on their back—the "back to sleep" movement—contributed to a dramatic reduction in the number of SIDS victims. Second, parents should not smoke because it decreases the oxygen available in the infant's environment. If they do smoke, they should not smoke around the baby. Third, bedding should be firm; soft bedding can trap air around the infant's face, causing the baby to inhale carbon dioxide instead of oxygen. For more recommendations, the Public Health Agency of Canada posts resources for parents and caregivers.

One unanticipated consequence of the "back to sleep" movement has been that North American infants are now beginning to crawl slightly later than those in previous generations, presumably because of reduced opportunity to strengthen their muscles by pushing up off their mattress. Parents are encouraged to give their babies supervised "tummy time" to exercise their muscles during the day.

In Canada, death from SIDS declined by more than 71% between 1981 and 2009, likely due to Safe Sleep campaigns supported by the Public Health Agency of Canada and the Canadian Pediatric Society.

avoid some of the issues related to smoke exposure, the use of nicotine in any form is a risk factor for fetal development and can affect fetal cardiac, respiratory, and nervous systems. In addition, because e-cigs are largely unregulated, they range greatly in the amount of nicotine they contain, with some brands containing far more nicotine than cigarettes do (Jiang et al., 2018). Thus, the perception of the benefits of e-cigs relative to traditional cigarettes may lead pregnant women to overlook the risks.

Alcohol Maternal alcohol use is the leading cause of fetal brain injury and is generally considered to be the most preventable cause. In Canada, 1 in 10 pregnant women report using alcohol during their pregnancies (Popova et al., 2017b). This rate is similar to the worldwide estimate of the prevalence of alcohol use during pregnancy, but there are substantial cultural differences (Popova et al., 2017a). Rates are highest in European countries (25% overall, with the highest rate in Ireland at 60%), and lowest in countries in the Middle East, where Saudi Arabia, Qatar, and Oman report rates of 0% (though it is worth noting that stigma may lead women in some countries to underreport alcohol use). These data suggest

sudden infant death syndrome (SIDS) the sudden, unexpected death of an infant less than 1 year of age that has no identifiable cause that alcohol use during pregnancy reflects broader cultural views about the use of alcohol, especially by women.

When a pregnant woman drinks, the alcohol in her blood crosses the placenta into both the fetus's bloodstream and the amniotic fluid. Thus, the fetus gets alcohol both directly—in its bloodstream—and indirectly, by drinking an amniotic-fluid cocktail. Concentrations of alcohol in the blood of mother and fetus quickly equalize, but the fetus has less ability to metabolize and remove alcohol from its blood, so it remains in the fetus's system longer.

Maternal drinking can result in **fetal alcohol spectrum disorder (FASD)**, which comprises a continuum of alcohol-related birth defects. Babies born to alcoholic women often exhibit extreme negative outcomes, known as *fetal alcohol syndrome* (FAS). The most obvious symptoms of FAS are characteristic facial structures, like the eyes, nose, and lips shown in Figure 2.17. Other forms of FAS can include varying degrees of intellectual disability, attention problems, and hyperactivity. Recent analyses suggest that the rates of FAS in Canada are much greater than previously suspected, with a prevalence estimated to be between 2% and 3% based on a study of 7- to 9-year-olds tested in the Greater Toronto area (Popova et al., 2018).

Even moderate drinking during pregnancy (i.e., less than one drink per day) can have both short- and long-term negative effects on development. So can occasional drinking if it involves binge drinking (four drinks or more on a single occasion). In Canada, it is estimated that 1% to 2% of pregnant women engaged in at least one incident of binge drinking during the previous month (Lange et al., 2017). The negative effects can include low birth weight, increased risk for ADHD, and delays in cognitive development and school achievement (e.g., Behnke et al., 2013). Given the research to date, the Society of Obstetricians and Gynaecologists of Canada recommends that pregnant women avoid alcohol altogether (Carson et al., 2017).

RICK'S PHOTOGRAPHY/SHUTTERSTOCK

FIGURE 2.17 Facial features of FAS This child displays the three primary diagnostic facial features of fetal alcohol syndrome: small eyes (as measured across); the absence of, or flattening of, the vertical groove between the nose and the upper lip (smooth philtrum); and a thin upper lip. This facial phenotype is one of the diagnostic criteria for FAS.

Environmental Pollutants

The bodies and bloodstreams of most Americans (including women of childbearing age) contain a noxious mix of toxic metals, synthetic hormones, and various ingredients of plastics, pesticides, and herbicides that can be teratogenic (Moore, 2003). These substances often have significant negative effects on the fetus. For instance, the infants of Inuit mothers, whose diets are high in Arctic fish, are exposed to lead, mercury, and polychlorinated biphenyls (PCBs) both prenatally and postnatally. This type of exposure has been associated with later difficulties in attention, cognition, and neuromotor development (Boucher et al., 2014; Boucher et al., 2012; Deprés et al., 2005). Air pollution from the burning of fossil fuels is associated with low birth weight and neurotoxicity and disproportionately affects low-income populations, both in North America and around the world (Perera, 2016). Often, different forms of pollution act in combination. For example, China's rapid industrialization has led to a dramatic increase in pollution-related birth defects due to the unregulated burning of coal, water pollution, and pesticide use (e.g., Ren et al., 2011).

While progress has been made nationwide in eradicating some pollutants, the situation in Grassy Narrows and White Dog First Nations provides clear evidence that environmental hazards continue to pose risks. In the 1970s, peoples from the Grassy Narrows and White Dog First Nations, who lived near Dryden, Ontario, began experiencing symptoms consistent with methylmercury poisoning

fetal alcohol spectrum disorder (FASD) the harmful effects of maternal alcohol consumption on a developing fetus. Fetal alcohol syndrome (FAS) involves a range of effects, including facial deformities, intellectual disabilities, attention problems, hyperactivity, and other defects. Fetal alcohol effects (FAE) is a term used for individuals who show some, but not all, of the standard effects of FAS.

LUCAS OLENIUK/TORONTO STAR VIA GETTY IMAGES

Decades after the English–Wabigoon River System was originally contaminated by mercury dumping, the First Nations peoples who live and fish there are still suffering the effects.

(Takaoka et al., 2014). A chemical and pulp mill was dumping mercury into the English–Wabigoon River System and poisoning the fish that were the First Nations' main source of food and income. Four decades after the mill stopped dumping mercury into the river system, mercury levels in fish remain above safe levels, and people are still developing the symptoms of Minamata disease (named after a coastal town in Japan that suffered a similar case of factory-related methylmercury poisoning); these symptoms include numbness in the limbs, difficulty walking a straight line, vision and hearing impairments, headaches, and exhaustion. Such incidents highlight the impact that decisions by individuals, groups, and local governments can have on environmental factors, which can in turn have significant and sometimes disastrous consequences on fetal and child development. And these issues are not easily remedied; only in 2017 did the Ontario government pledge funds to remediate the river system.

Maternal Factors

Because the mother-to-be provides the most immediate environment for her fetus, some of her characteristics can affect prenatal development. These characteristics include age, nutritional status, health, and stress level.

Age

A pregnant woman's age is related to the outcome of her pregnancy. Infants born to girls 15 years or younger are 3 to 4 times more likely to die before their 1st birthday than are those born to mothers who are between 23 and 29 (Phipps, Blume, & DeMonner, 2002). However, the rate of teenage pregnancy in Canada is declining, and in 2014, the teen birth rate for teenagers under 17 years old fell to the lowest recorded level (5.4 births per 1000 females younger than 17; Public Health Agency of Canada, 2017).

The increasing age at which many women become pregnant is also cause for concern. In recent decades, many women in industrialized countries wait until their 30s or 40s to have children. Techniques to treat infertility have continued to improve, increasing the likelihood of conception for older parents. Like many other risk factors, there is a dose–response relationship, with risk of negative outcomes for both mother and fetus increasing with maternal age. For example, children born to older mothers and/or older fathers are at heightened risk for developmental disorders such as autism spectrum disorder (ASD; Sandin et al., 2016).

The causal pathways linking older mothers and fathers to their infants' developmental outcomes are likely different, since only mothers contribute to prenatal environments and birth circumstances (Lee & McGrath, 2015). Fathers' contributions may lie more in mutations and other chromosomal abnormalities, as we will discuss in Chapter 3.

Nutrition

The fetus depends on its mother for all its nutritional requirements. If a pregnant woman has an inadequate diet, her unborn child may also be nutritionally deprived. An inadequate supply of specific nutrients can have dramatic consequences. For instance, women who get too little folic acid (a form of B vitamin) are at high risk for having an infant with a neural-tube defect such as spina bifida (see Figure 2.4). While prenatal vitamins are frequently used to address these concerns, many women do not know they are pregnant during the crucial early periods of gestation. Many processed foods, such as breakfast cereals, are fortified with folic acid to help ensure that women receive adequate nutrition during the early weeks of pregnancy.

Because malnutrition is more common in impoverished families, it often coincides with the host of other risk factors associated with poverty, making it difficult to isolate its effects on prenatal development. However, one unique study of development in extreme circumstances made it possible to assess certain effects of malnutrition *independent of socioeconomic status.* As we discussed earlier, people of all income and education levels suffered severe famine in parts of the Netherlands during World War II. Children conceived during the Dutch Hunger Winter have been followed into adulthood. In late middle age, individuals who had experienced malnutrition as fetuses showed impaired performance on attentional tasks and had prematurely aged brains, compared with those who had not (de Rooij et al., 2010; Franke et al., 2018).

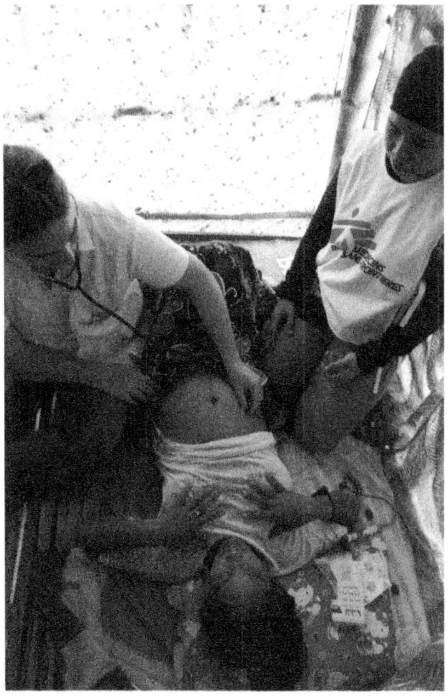

JEOFFREY MAITEM/GETTY IMAGES

This expectant mother, living in an evacuation camp in the Philippines, is being examined by a Doctors Without Borders medical worker. She worries about how she is going to feed her child. Whether caused by displacement due to war or natural disaster, pervasive poverty, or some other factor, concern for maternal nutrition is a situation all too common throughout the world.

Disease

Although most maternal illnesses that occur during a pregnancy have no impact on the fetus, some do. For example, if contracted early in pregnancy, rubella (also called the 3-day measles) can have devastating developmental effects, including major malformations, deafness, blindness, and intellectual disabilities. The Society of Obstetricians and Gynaecologists of Canada recommends that women who do not have immunities against rubella be vaccinated before becoming pregnant (Dontigny et al., 2018).

Sexually transmitted infections (STIs) are also quite hazardous to the fetus. Cytomegalovirus (CMV), a type of herpes virus that is present in 50% to 70% of women of reproductive age in North America, is the most common cause of congenital infection (affecting 1% to 5% of births; Manicklal, 2013). CMV can damage the fetus's central nervous system and cause a variety of other serious defects, including hearing loss. Genital herpes can also be very dangerous: if the infant comes into contact with active herpes lesions in the birth canal, blindness or even death can result. HIV infection is sometimes passed to the fetus in the womb or during birth, but the majority of infants born to women who are HIV-positive or who have AIDS do not become infected themselves. HIV can also be transmitted through breast milk after birth, but research suggests that breast milk contains a carbohydrate that may actually protect infants from HIV infection (Bode et al., 2012).

Zika, a mosquito-borne viral infection, burst onto the world scene in 2016. While the illness itself is mild and often goes undetected, it can cause a serious birth defect called microcephaly, a condition in which the baby's head is much smaller than expected. Depending on the severity of the problem, issues can range from hearing and vision loss to seizures and intellectual disability. Microcephaly occurs in roughly 6% of fetuses whose mothers were infected by Zika (Honein et al., 2017). Consistent with our earlier discussion of sensitive periods, higher rates of microcephaly are observed for women whose Zika infections occurred during the first trimester of pregnancy. The virus appears to infect fetuses' cortical-neural progenitor cells, resulting in stunted brain growth (Tang et al., 2016). The only preventative option is to avoid mosquito bites in areas where the virus has spread. Women of reproductive age should also take heed of the fact that Zika can be transmitted sexually and through body fluids (Kim et al., 2018).

This Brazilian infant suffers from microcephaly, likely due to her mother's Zika infection during pregnancy.

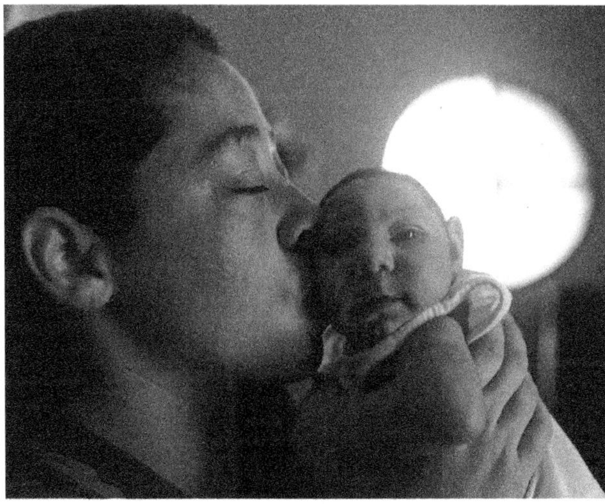

[E]AE/NEWSCOM/XINHUA NEWS AGENCY/RIO DE JANEIRO

Maternal Emotional State

Effects of maternal stress during pregnancy have been observed on myriad aspects of infant and child development, ranging from infant cognitive development to later psychiatric diagnoses (for review, see Van den Bergh et al., 2017). Brain-imaging studies with infants and young children reveal both structural and functional effects of prenatal maternal state on the developing brain (Van den Bergh, Dahnke, & Mennes, 2018). For example, Alberta researchers showed that maternal prenatal depression was associated with changes in brain structure in children aged 2 to 5 years (Lebel et al., 2016). A primary mechanism for these effects is alternations in the hypothalamic–pituitary–adrenal (HPA) axis and the hormone cortisol, a glucocorticoid which helps regulate stress in both the mother and the fetus. As discussed earlier in this chapter, glucocorticoids slow the growth of the fetus. The concept of *fetal programming*, also discussed previously, shapes research in this area and suggests that the altered hormonal environment for the fetus may lead to long-term changes in how children and adults cope with stress via disrupted HPA axis functioning.

In some wealthy countries, including the United States, pregnant women from minority ethnic groups report greater rates of prenatal stress than do women in majority ethnic groups (Liu et al., 2016). Pregnant women in less wealthy countries report even greater levels of stress (Glover et al., 2018). Their anxiety may relate to scarcity of resources, as in cases of high food insecurity, or to war or domestic violence. Women in developing countries may also have increased fears about the outcomes of their pregnancies due to high rates of infant and maternal mortality where they live. For instance, researchers in rural Nigeria found that in a group of 262 women giving birth, 5 women died and 52 experienced severe complications (Mbachu et al., 2017). These sorts of statistics, combined with their firsthand knowledge about the dangers of childbirth, likely add yet another layer of stress for many women in developing countries.

Like other types of teratogens, it is difficult to tease apart the specific effects of maternal stress from other factors that often co-occur with stress. For example, expectant mothers who are stressed during pregnancy are likely to still be stressed after giving birth. Genetic factors may also link both maternal stress and postnatal outcomes. One clever study took advantage of the increased use of assistive reproductive technology—*in vitro* fertilization (IVF)—to attempt to tease apart these factors (Rice et al., 2010). In this study, mothers were either genetically related or unrelated to their fetuses. The results revealed effects of maternal stress on birth weight and later antisocial behaviour, in both related and unrelated mother–fetus pairs, suggesting that the prenatal environment, not shared genetics, was the strongest predictor of later outcomes. However, for measures of child anxiety, the results suggest that postnatal maternal stress, not prenatal maternal stress, was the strongest predictor of later outcomes.

This area of research reveals a complex interplay between prenatal and postnatal factors in developmental outcomes. It also points to the importance of finding ways to help minimize maternal stress both pre- and postnatally. The increased popularity of prenatal yoga and meditation classes suggests that there may be straightforward ways to reduce at least some aspects of pregnancy-related stress, with potential benefits for both mother and fetus.

Prenatal exercise classes, as well as yoga or meditation classes, may help reduce pregnancy-related stress.

MANGO PRODUCTIONS/GETTY IMAGES

REVIEW QUESTION

A wide variety of environmental agents can have a negative impact on prenatal development, from drugs to pollution to maternal factors like stress, illness, or nutrition. How can research into these hazards be used to influence public policy aimed at reducing their prevalence and impact? ■

The Birth Experience

Approximately 38 weeks after conception, contractions of the muscles of the uterus begin, initiating birth. Typically, the fetus has already contributed to the process by rotating into the normal head-down position. In addition, the maturing lungs of the fetus may release a protein that triggers the onset of labour. Uterine contractions, as well as the baby's progress through the birth canal, are extremely painful for the mother.

Is birth as painful for the newborn as for the mother? Actually, there is good reason to believe that birth is not particularly painful for the baby. Compare how much pain you feel when you pinch and pull on a piece of skin on your forearm versus when you wrap your hand around your forearm and squeeze as tightly as you can. The stretching is painful, but the squeezing is not. The mother's pain comes from her tissues being greatly stretched, but the baby experiences squeezing.

The Birth Experience

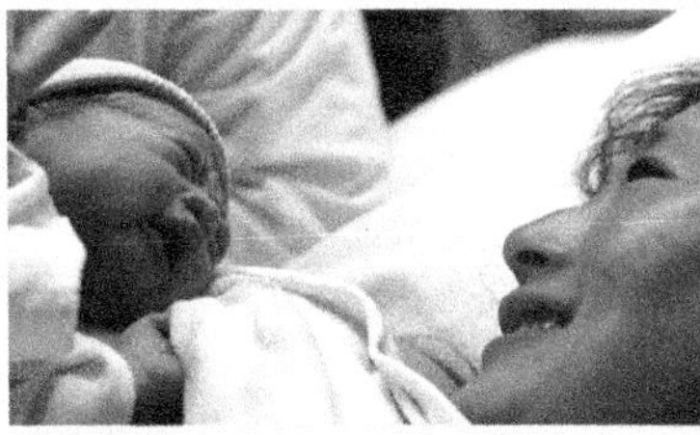

REGINE MAHAUX AND ERIC DAEM/GETTY IMAGES

The squeezing that the fetus experiences during birth serves several important functions. First, it temporarily reduces the overall size of the fetus's disproportionately large head, allowing it to pass safely through the mother's pelvic bones. This is possible because the skull is composed of separate plates that can overlap one another slightly during birth (see Figure 2.18). The squeezing of the fetus's head during birth also stimulates the production of hormones that help the fetus withstand mild oxygen deprivation during birth and help regulate breathing after birth. The squeezing of the fetus's body forces amniotic fluid out of the lungs, in preparation for the newborn's first, crucial gasp of air.

Diversity of Childbirth Practices

Although the biological aspects of birth are pretty much the same everywhere, childbirth practices vary enormously. All cultures pursue the dual goals of (1) safeguarding the *survival and health* of both mother and baby and (2) ensuring the

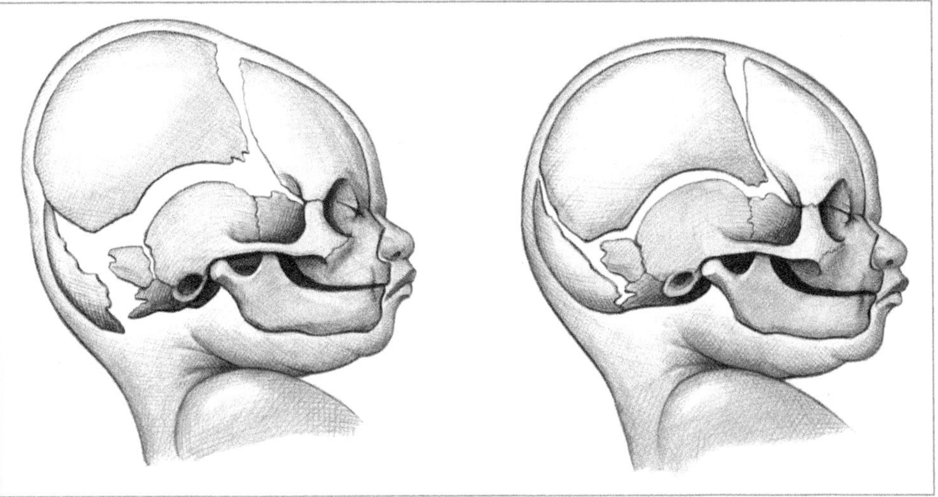

FIGURE 2.18 Head plates Pressure on the head during birth can cause the separate plates of the skull to overlap, resulting in a temporarily misshapen head. Fortunately, the condition rapidly corrects itself after birth. The "soft spot," or fontanel, is simply the temporary space between separate skull plates in the top of the baby's head.

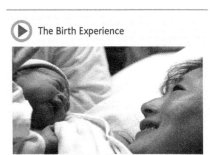

social integration of the new person. Groups differ, however, regarding the relative importance they give to these goals. An expectant mother on the South Pacific island of Bali assumes that her husband and other kin, along with any children she may already have, will all want to be present at the joyous occasion of the birth of a new child. Her female relatives, as well as a midwife, actively help her throughout the birth, which occurs in her home. Having already been present at many births, the Balinese woman knows what to expect from childbirth, even when it is her first child (Diener, 2000).

A very different scenario unfolds in twenty-first century North America, where the woman in labour usually withdraws almost totally from her everyday life. In most cases, she enters a hospital to give birth, typically attended by a small group of family or close friends. The birth is supervised by a variety of medical personnel, most of whom are strangers. Unlike her Balinese counterpart, the first-time Canadian mother has probably never witnessed a birth, so she may not have very realistic expectations about the birth process. Also, unlike her counterparts in most societies, a Canadian woman in labour has a 28% chance of having a surgical delivery by cesarean (also called C-section)—a rate that is high relative to other countries but has been in decline for the past few years (Canadian Institutes for Health Information, n.d.; Martin, Hamilton, & Osterman, 2018).

C-sections are intended to assist infants and mothers facing birth complications, and indeed they have saved untold numbers of lives. However, there are other reasons for the high number of surgical deliveries in Canada, including a vastly increased rate of multiple births (discussed in the next section), scheduling convenience for the physician and/or the parents, maternal obesity, prior C-sections (which may necessitate future C-sections), and physicians' attempts to decrease risk of lawsuits concerning medical malpractice should problems arise from a vaginal birth (e.g., Yang et al., 2009). Indeed, one study found that among a sample of American women who had a C-section, nearly half did not appear to have any pregnancy complications (Witt et al., 2015).

The Balinese approach to childbirth emphasizes the social goal of immediately integrating the newborn into the family and community—hence the presence of many kin and friends to support mother and baby. In contrast, the belief that childbirth is safer in a hospital setting outweighs the resulting social isolation of mother and baby. And indeed, while the rates of home births are increasing in North America, it is unclear whether home births are riskier than hospital births. One recent study found that in the United States, infant mortality in hospital births attended by certified midwives was significantly lower than infant mortality in home births attended by certified midwives (Grünebaum et al., 2016). It is worth noting, however, that in Ontario where home births are more common (20% of all births) and well-integrated into the healthcare system, the mortality rates for home and hospital births are equivalent, possibly because it is standard practice to transfer home-birthing mothers to the hospital when complications arise (as was the case for 25% of home births in this Canadian sample; Hutton et al., 2015).

The medical model of childbirth prevails in Canada.

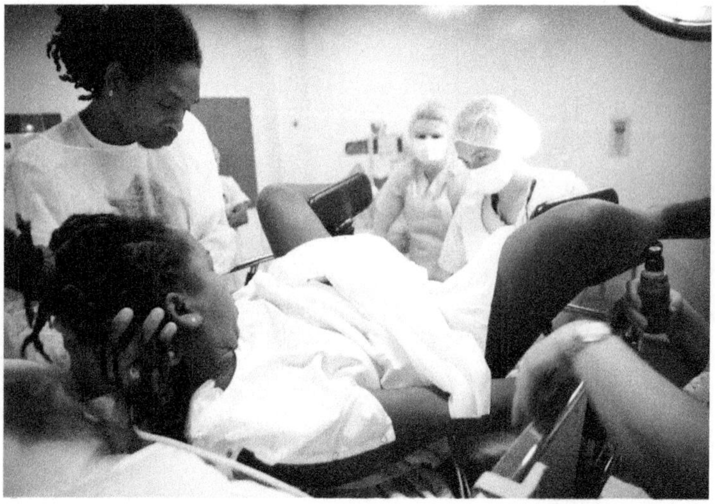

ABK / BSIP / THE IMAGE WORKS

The practices in both Canada and Bali have been changing to some degree. In Canada, the social dimensions of birth are increasingly recognized by doctors and hospitals, which often now employ certified midwives for expectant parents who prefer a less medicalized birth plan. As in Bali, various family members—sometimes even including the parents' other children—are encouraged to be present to support the labouring mother and to share a family experience. Another increasingly common practice in Canada is the use of *doulas,* individuals trained to assist women in terms of both emotional and physical comfort during labour and delivery. This shift has been accompanied by decreased use of delivery drugs, enhancing the woman's participation in childbirth and her ability to interact with her newborn, including engaging in activities such as skin-to-skin contact, which promotes stabilization of physiological processes in the transition from the womb to the outside world (e.g., Rutgers & Meyers, 2015).

In addition, many expectant parents attend childbirth education classes through their birth centre or educational organizations like Lamaze, where they learn some of what their Balinese counterparts pick up through routine attendance at births. Social support is a key component of these programs; the pregnant woman's partner, or some other supportive person, is trained to assist her during the birth. Such childbirth programs are generally beneficial, and obstetricians routinely advise expectant couples to enroll in them. At the same time that these changes are occurring in Canada, Western medical practices are being increasingly adopted in societies like Bali, in an effort to improve newborn survival rates.

As a final example of alternate birthing practices, let's consider the Ju/'hoansi women of rural Botswana and Namibia, who often give birth outdoors and alone despite the dangers posed by animal predators, including lions. This practice is deeply intertwined with spiritual and cultural beliefs that have endured for centuries and reflects a specific view of individual development that sees the birth experience as a key event in a person's maturation (Biesele, 1997). Though extreme when viewed from other cultural perspectives, and dangerous from a modern medical standpoint, the birthing traditions of the Ju/'hoansi illustrate the complex ways that childbirth, among other aspects of child development, are linked to the greater social and cultural context.

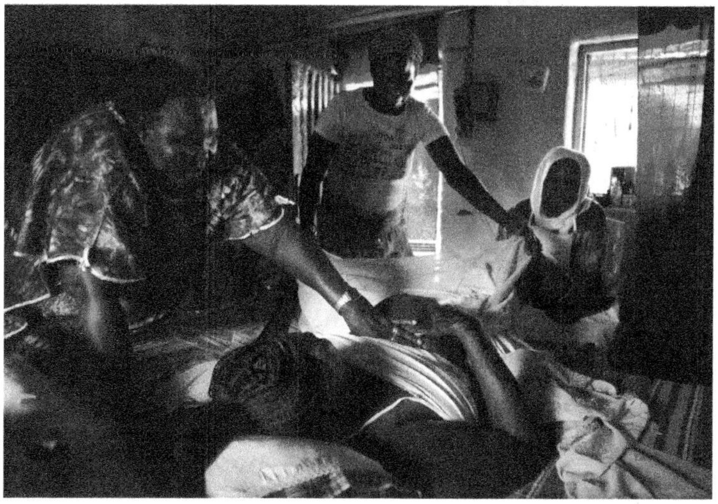

Similar to Balinese practices, this childbirth in South Sudan is quite different from the norm in Canada. The baby was born at home, with the help of a grandmother, great aunt, and a qualified birth attendant.

REVIEW QUESTIONS

The diverse range of birthing practices highlights the influence of sociocultural context, and these practices can have a direct impact on the newborn. Consider the birth experiences that you have encountered: In what ways did these experiences reflect cultural practices that are beneficial to the newborn and mother? What alternate practices should have been implemented for the benefit to the newborn and mother? ■

The Newborn Infant

Healthy newborns begin interacting with their new environment right away, exploring and learning about newfound physical and social entities. Newborns' exploration of this uncharted territory is very much influenced by their state of arousal.

state level of arousal and engagement in the environment, ranging from deep sleep to intense activity

rapid eye movement (REM) sleep an active sleep state characterized by quick, jerky eye movements under closed lids and associated with dreaming in adults

non-REM sleep a quiet or deep sleep state characterized by the absence of motor activity or eye movements and more regular, slow brain waves, breathing, and heart rate

State of Arousal

State refers to a continuum of arousal, ranging from deep sleep to intense activity. As you well know, your state dramatically affects your interaction with the environment—with what you notice, do, learn, and think about. It also affects the ability of others to interact with you.

Figure 2.19 depicts the average amount of time in a 24-hour period that newborns typically spend in each of six states, ranging from quiet sleep to crying. Within this general pattern, however, there is a great deal of individual variation. To appreciate how these differences might affect parent–infant interactions, imagine yourself as the parent of a newborn who cries more than the average baby, sleeps little, and spends less time in the awake–alert state. Now imagine yourself with a baby who cries relatively little, sleeps well, and spends an above-average amount of time quietly attending to you and the rest of his or her environment (see Figure 2.20). Clearly, you would have many more opportunities for pleasurable interactions with the second newborn.

The two newborn states that are of particular concern to parents—sleeping and crying—have both been studied extensively.

FIGURE 2.19 Newborn states This figure shows the average proportion of time, in a 24-hour day, that Western newborns spend in each of the six states of arousal. There are substantial individual and cultural differences in how much time babies spend in the different states.

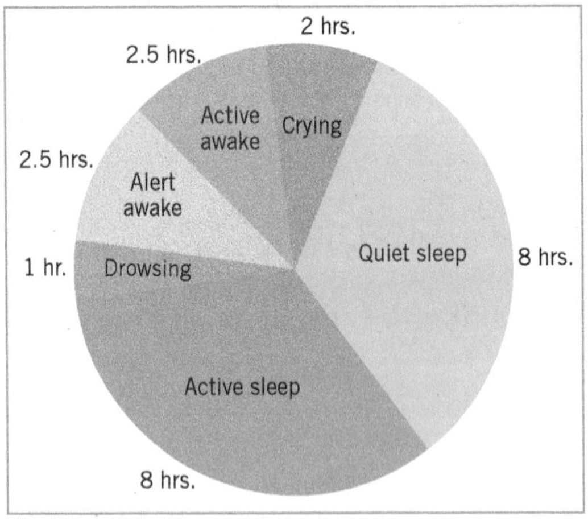

Sleep

Two facts about sleep and its development are of particular importance. First, the average newborn sleeps twice as much as young adults do. Second, the pattern of two different sleep states—*REM sleep* and *non-REM sleep*—changes dramatically with age. **Rapid eye movement (REM) sleep** is an active sleep state associated with dreaming in adults; it is characterized by quick, jerky eye movements under closed lids, a distinctive pattern of brain activity, body movements, and irregular heart rate and breathing. **Non-REM sleep**, in contrast, is a quiet sleep state characterized by the absence of motor activity or eye movements and more regular, slow brain waves, breathing, and heart rate. REM sleep constitutes fully 50% of a newborn's total sleep time. The proportion of REM sleep declines quite rapidly to only 20% by 3 or 4 years of age and remains low for the rest of life.

Why do infants spend so much time in REM sleep? Some researchers believe that it helps develop the infant's visual system. Because newborns spend so much time asleep, they do not have much opportunity to amass waking visual experience. The high level of internally generated brain activity that occurs during REM sleep may help to make up for the natural deprivation of visual stimulation, facilitating the early development of the visual system in both fetus and newborn. Another way in which REM sleep may be adaptive for neonates is that the natural jerking movements (called *myoclonic twitching*) that occur exclusively during REM sleep may give infants opportunities to build sensorimotor maps (Blumberg, 2015). These twitching movements are most frequent during early development and may help the infant with the difficult problem of linking motor patterns with the specific sensations that they evoke.

Another distinctive feature of sleep in the newborn period is that neonates' slumbering brains do not become disconnected from external stimulation to the same extent that the brains of older individuals do. This stimulation allows newborns to learn during sleep. In one study, infants were exposed to recordings of foreign vowel sounds while they slumbered in the newborn nursery. When tested in the morning, their brain activity revealed that they recognized the sounds they had heard while asleep (Cheour et al., 2002).

FIGURE 2.20 Quiet-alert state The parents of this quiet-alert newborn have a good chance of having a pleasurable interaction with the baby.

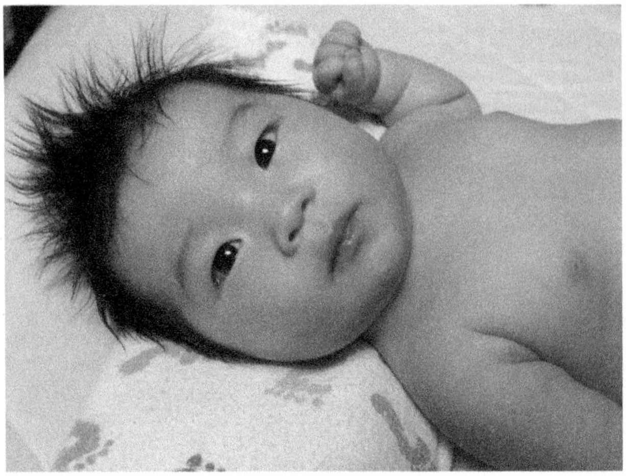

ROY HSU/GETTY IMAGES

Although newborns are likely to be awake during part of their parents' normal sleep time, they gradually develop the more mature pattern of sleeping through the night. Nighttime awakenings typically diminish over the course of the first postnatal year. However, there is a subset of infants who continue to wake regularly. Roughly one-third of parents of 6-month-olds in the United States report that their infants continued to wake up at least once every night (Weinraub et al., 2012). Even by 12 months of age, only about half of the infants in a Canadian study slept for at least 8 hours at a stretch (Pennestri et al., 2018).

A number of sleep techniques have been proposed to help parents and infants who are struggling with sleep. A recent randomized-control study was designed to determine whether behavioural sleep interventions work and whether they cause undue stress for parents and infants (Gradisar et al., 2016). The results suggest that, compared with a sleep-education control group, infants in a graduated-extinction group—in which parents slowly increased their delays in responding to their crying infant—showed greater improvement in sleep behaviours, with no negative effects on infant stress (cortisol levels) or infant–mother attachment. The study also demonstrated successful effects of another behavioural method, bedtime fading, in which the infant's bedtime is shifted later to ensure sleepiness, and then gradually moved earlier. Both groups showed large decreases in nocturnal wakefulness, with concomitant positive effects on maternal stress.

In contrast with Canadian parents, Kipsigis parents in rural Kenya are relatively unconcerned about their infants' sleep patterns. Kipsigis babies are almost always with their mothers. During the day, infants are often carried on their mother's back as she goes about her daily activities; at night they sleep with her and are allowed to nurse whenever they awaken. As a consequence, these babies distribute their sleeping throughout the night and day for several months (Harkness & Super, 1995; Super & Harkness, 1986). Thus, cultures vary not only in terms of where babies sleep, as you learned in Chapter 1, but also in terms of how strongly parents attempt to influence when their babies sleep.

Sleep in Infancy and Toddlerhood

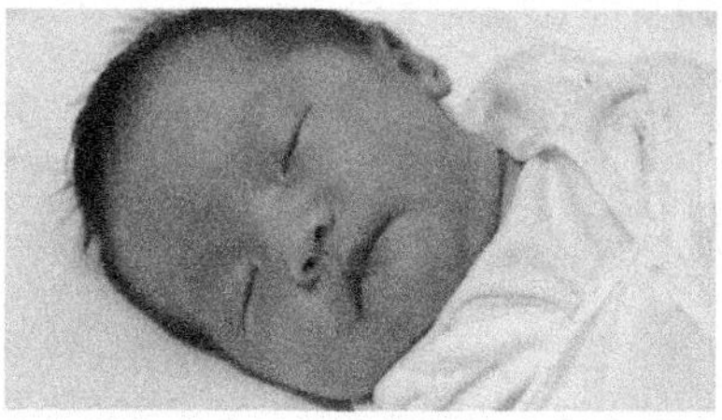

LIM CHEWHOW/SHUTTERSTOCK

GARY S CHAPMAN/GETTY IMAGES

Most Canadian parents want to avoid the 2 A.M. fate of this young father. They regard their baby's sleeping through the night as a developmental triumph—the sooner, the better.

Crying

Infants cry for many reasons—including illness, pain, and hunger—that require the attention of caregivers. As unpleasant as it is, crying is a normal behaviour. Rather than diminishing over the first few months, as many new parents expect, it actually increases, peaking around 6 to 8 weeks of age. Crying behaviour tends to decrease in frequency around 3 to 4 months of age, potentially because infants now have somewhat more control over their environment. During this period, crying bouts tend to increase in the late afternoon and evening, a phenomenon familiar to most caregivers of young infants.

Parents, especially first-timers, are often puzzled and anxious about why their baby is crying, and especially why their infants' crying bouts increase in frequency—and sometimes intensity—over the first 2 months. In extreme cases, caregivers may react with a form of child abuse known as *shaken baby syndrome,* which can result in severe head trauma or death (e.g., Barr et al., 2015). Relatively minimal parental education can play an important role in demystifying infant crying. For example, the Period of PURPLE program, developed by Ron Barr at the University of British Columbia in conjunction with the National Centre on Shaken Baby Syndrome, is provided in hospitals after birth and via public-educational outreach programs.

This baby is sleeping in a baby box provided to new parents as part of a recent study funded by the Alberta government.

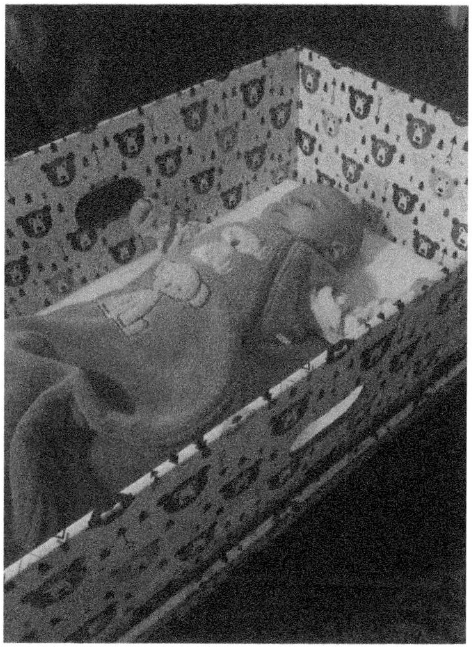

KAREN BENZIES

swaddling a soothing technique, used in many cultures, that involves wrapping a baby tightly in cloths or a blanket

colic excessive, inconsolable crying by a young infant for no apparent reason

This informational intervention can be highly effective in decreasing emergency room visits based on parental concerns about crying (Barr et al., 2015). More significantly, the intervention decreased the number of infants admitted to the hospital in British Columbia for abusive head trauma (Barr et al., 2018). Understanding that crying is a normal developmental process can significantly decrease parental stress and—in extreme cases—parent-caused injury to infants.

Soothing What are the best ways to console a crying baby? Most of the traditional standbys—rocking, singing lullabies, stroking the baby, holding the baby up to the shoulder, giving the baby a pacifier, distracting the baby—work reasonably well. Many effective soothing techniques involve moderately intense and continuous or repetitive stimulation. One very common soothing technique is **swaddling**, which involves wrapping a young baby tightly in cloths or a blanket, thereby restricting limb movement. The tight wrapping provides a constant high level of tactile stimulation and warmth. This technique is practiced in cultures as diverse and widespread as those of the Navajo and Hopi in the American Southwest (Chisholm, 1983), the Quechua in Peru (Tronick, Thomas, & Daltabuit, 1994), and rural villagers in Turkey (Delaney, 2000). It is also increasing in popularity in North America; numerous popular baby-carrying devices compress the infant close to the caregiver's body, leaving the caregiver's hands free for daily activities.

Never Shake: Preventing Shaken Baby Syndrome

COURTESY CHILDREN'S TRUST FUND OF MISSOURI

One question that often concerns parents is whether or not to respond to their infant's signals of distress. Will quick and consistent supportive responses reward the infant for fussing and crying and hence increase these behaviours? Or will a rapid response give the infant a sense of security that leads to less fussing and crying? The literature suggests that both perspectives are valid. In one classic study, Bell and Ainsworth (1972) found that prompt responding to infant cries predicted less crying several months later. Yet in another classic study, Hubbard & van IJzendoorn (1991) found that infants whose cries were ignored during the first 9 weeks cried less during the next 9 weeks.

While most research in this area has focused on Western families, there are substantial cultural differences in parental responding that may influence these patterns. For example, mothers in the rural island communities of Fiji are more likely to rapidly respond to their infant's negative facial displays of affect than are urban mothers in the United States (Broesch et al., 2016). As with many aspects of parenting, there is likely not one "right" answer to the question of how and when to respond to infant distress. Cultural norms and individual differences among infants jointly influence families' preferred responses to parenting challenges.

Colic No matter how or how much their parents try to soothe them, some infants are prone to excessive, inconsolable crying for no apparent reason during the first few months of life, a condition referred to as **colic**. Indeed, one of your authors was a colicky baby who resisted being held. The causes of colic are unknown and may include allergic responses to the mother's diet (ingested via breast milk), formula intolerance, immature gut development, and/or excessive gassiness. Unfortunately, colic is not a rare condition: around 18% of young Canadian infants—and their parents—suffer

ANDREY BURKOV / DREAMSTIME

Carrying infants close to the parent's body results in less crying. Many North American parents are now emulating the traditional carrying methods of societies like the Quechua in Peru. Swaddling should be avoided when babies are lying on their stomachs or sides, due to increased risk for SIDS (Pease et al., 2016).

from it (Wolke et al., 2017). Fortunately, it typically ends by about 3 months of age and has no long-term effects. One of the best things parents with a colicky infant can do is seek social support, which can provide relief from the stress, frustration, and sense of inadequacy they may feel because they are unable to relieve their baby's distress.

Coping with Colic

COURTESY KIDSINTHEHOUSE.COM

Parenting in Infancy and Toddlerhood

WORTH PUBLISHERS

Negative Outcomes at Birth

Neonatal caregivers worldwide use an evaluation tool called the **Apgar score** to quickly assess the health of newborn infants immediately following birth. A cumulative score is derived from ratings on skin tone, pulse rate, facial responses (typically grimacing), arm and leg activity, and breathing strength. Perfect scores are rare, reflecting the traumatic effect that even a normal birth can have on the newborn, but a consistently low score can indicate serious health problems.

Although most clinically recognized pregnancies in an industrialized society result in the full-term birth of a healthy baby, sometimes the outcome is less positive. The worst result, obviously, is the death of an infant. A much more common negative outcome is low birth weight, which can have long-term consequences.

Infant Mortality

Infant mortality—death during the first year after birth—is now relatively rare in the industrialized world, thanks to decades of improvements in public health and general economic levels. In Canada, the 2018 infant mortality rate was estimated to be 4.5 deaths per 1000 live births (Central Intelligence Agency [CIA], 2018).

Although the Canadian infant mortality rate is declining over time in absolute terms, it is high compared with that of other industrialized nations. The *relative* ranking of Canada has generally gotten worse over the past several decades, partially because the infant mortality rates in many other countries have had a higher rate of improvement and partially because of a wide variation in birth registration practices across countries. In Canada, the United States, Wales, and England, a live birth is registered if the infant shows any signs of life at birth, regardless of birth weight or gestational age. In contrast, other countries use other criteria to register a live birth, such as gestational age (e.g., >22 weeks), birth weight (e.g., >500 g), or length of survival (e.g., at least 24 hours after birth; Deb-Rinker et al., 2015).

The rates of infant mortality in Canada are starkly different for different provinces and territories. For instance, infants born in Nunavut and the Northwest Territories (NWT) are two to three times more likely to die before their first birthday as infants born in British Columbia and Nova Scotia. Indeed, the infant mortality rate for Nunavut and NWT is similar to the rates observed in many developing countries. Why do so many babies die in the Canadian North, given that we are a highly developed country? There are many reasons having to do with limited access to health care, a greater prevalence of *macrosomic births* (births of very large babies), and higher rates of poverty (Luo et al., 2012).

In less developed countries, especially those suffering from a breakdown in social organization due to war, famine, or persistent extreme poverty, the infant mortality rates can be staggering. In Afghanistan and Somalia, for example, roughly 1 of every 10 infants dies before age 1 (CIA, 2018).

Low Birth Weight

Most Canadian newborns weigh between 2500 grams and 4500 grams. Infants who weigh less than 2500 grams at birth are considered to be of **low birth weight (LBW)**. Many LBW infants are **premature**, or preterm; that is, they are born

Apgar score method for evaluating the health of the newborn immediately following birth based on skin tone, pulse rate, facial response, arm and leg activity, and breathing

infant mortality death during the first year after birth

low birth weight (LBW) a birth weight of less than 2500 grams

premature any child born at 37 weeks after conception or earlier (as opposed to the normal term of 38 weeks)

EMILIO MORENATTI/AP IMAGES

Afghanistan has the highest infant mortality rate in the world (CIA, 2018). Among the causes are extreme poverty, poor nutrition, and poor sanitation. The great majority of the population lacks access to clean water, leading to a great many infant deaths related to dysentery, severe diarrhea, and other illnesses.

at 37 weeks or earlier after conception. About 7.8% of babies born in Canada between 2015 and 2017 were premature (Statistics Canada, 2019a). Other LBW infants are referred to as **small for gestational age:** they may be either preterm or full-term, but they weigh substantially less than is normal for their gestational age, which is based on weeks since conception.

In 2017, 6.5% of babies born in Canada were LBW (Statistics Canada, 2019a). As a group, LBW newborns have a heightened level of medical complications, as well as higher rates of neurosensory deficits, more frequent illness, lower IQ scores, and lower educational achievement. *Very LBW* babies (VLBW; those weighing less than 1500 grams) are particularly vulnerable; these infants accounted for around 1% of live births in Canada (Statistics Canada, 2019b).

Low Birth Weight in India

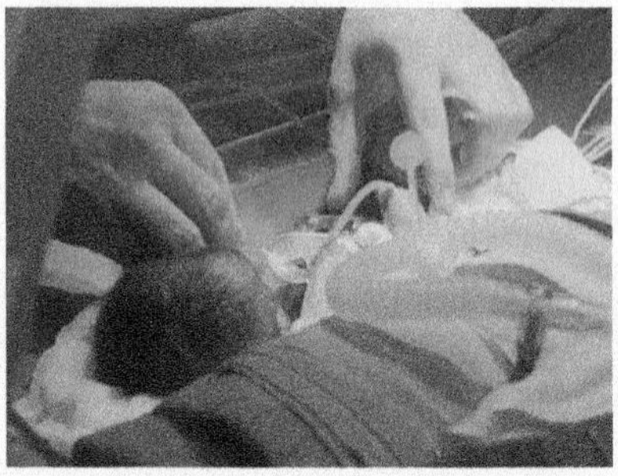

UNICEF

There are numerous causes of LBW and prematurity, including several discussed in the section on teratogens: smoking, alcohol, and environmental pollutants such as lead and mercury. In some rapidly developing countries, such as China, high levels of airborne pollution have been linked to both LBW and preterm birth, likely due to impaired oxygen transport across the placenta (Fleischer et al., 2015). Another cause is the skyrocketing rate of twin, triplet, and other multiple births as a result of the development of increasingly successful treatments for infertility. (The use of fertility drugs typically results in multiple eggs being released during ovulation; the use of in vitro fertilization [IVF] usually involves the placement of multiple laboratory-fertilized embryos in the uterus.) Between 1991 and 2017, the rate of multiple births in Canada increased from 2% to 3.1% (Statistics Canada, 2019c). This is a concern because the rates of LBW among multiples are quite high: 53.8% of multiples weigh less than 2500 grams (Statistics Canada, 2019b). The numbers for higher-order births (triplets and up) have also increased dramatically in recent years. This is a concern because the rates of LBW among multiples are quite high: 55% for twins and higher than 95% for triplets and above (Martin, Hamilton, Osterman et al., 2018).

small for gestational age babies who weigh substantially less than is normal for whatever their gestational age

BETTMANN/CONTRIBUTOR/GETTY

The Dionne quintuplets, born in 1934 in a farmhouse in Ontario, are the first known quintuplets to have survived infancy. The identical sisters were born two months prematurely. During infancy, the government removed them from their family and placed them in a specially built hospital with an observation area for tourists. In the 1930s, they were the biggest tourist attraction in Canada. In 1998, the Ontario government formally apologized to the surviving sisters.

Long-term outcomes As a group, children who were LBW infants have a higher incidence of developmental problems: the lower their birth weight, the more likely they are to have persistent difficulties. For example, 8-year-old Australian children who were born LBW showed a greater incidence of sensory impairments, poorer academic achievement, and more behaviour problems than their term-birth peers (Hutchinson et al., 2013). Other studies suggest links between VLBW and childhood psychiatric issues, especially those involving inattention, anxiety, and social difficulties (e.g., ADHD, autism; Johnson & Marlow, 2011). The hypothesized pathways between LBW and these negative outcomes include white-matter reduction, ventricular enlargement, and other abnormal brain development outcomes.

However, it is important to note that these comparisons often confound SES with birth-weight status. For example, in the aforementioned study by Hutchinson and colleagues (2013), the sample of term-birth families had higher educational attainment and employment status than the preterm sample. Indeed, a German study demonstrated that the strongest predictor of outcomes for VLBW infants is maternal education (Voss et al., 2012). The authors concluded that special services and additional support may be especially important for families of at-risk infants with less educational background.

The good news is that for the *majority* of LBW children, the negative effects of their birth status gradually diminish, generally ending up within the normal range on most developmental measures. Figure 2.21 depicts a particularly striking example (Teoh et al., 2006). Indeed, one follow-up study of extremely LBW infants (<1000 grams) found that by 18 to 22 months of age, 16% were unimpaired and 22% were only mildly impaired (Gargus et al., 2009).

FIGURE 2.21 Small miracles Rumaisa and Hiba Rahman, shown here shortly after their birth in Chicago in 2004, were born 15 weeks premature. Rumaisa weighed just 260 grams at birth, making her the world's smallest surviving infant. Her sister was slightly heavier, at 567 grams. Despite the significant challenges these sisters faced in their early lives, they both reached appropriate developmental milestones in motor and language abilities, perhaps because they were able to reach 25 weeks in the womb (Rochman, 2011).

PHOTO BY OSCAR IZQUIERDO/LOYOLA UNIV. MEDICAL CENTER VIA GETTY IMAGES

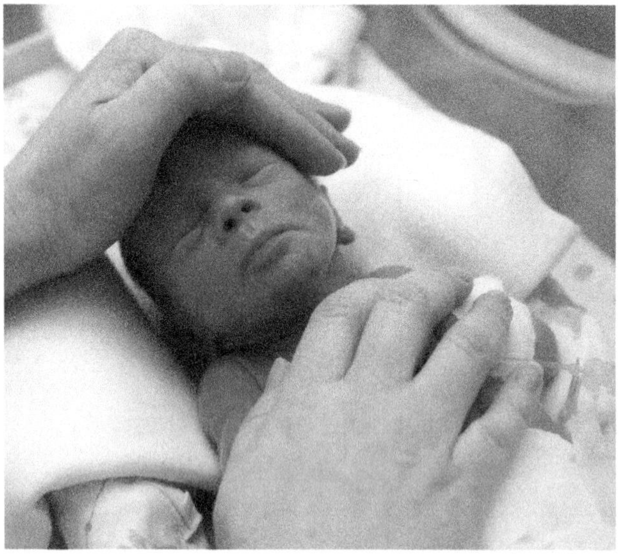
PROFIMEDIA.CZ A.S. / ALAMY

FIGURE 2.22 Infant massage Everybody enjoys a good massage, including infants (Badr et al., 2015). Hospitalized newborns may particularly benefit from massage (e.g., Field, 2017). As an added bonus, parents also benefit from massaging their infants (Vicente, Veríssimo, & Diniz, 2017).

Intervention programs Supporting LBW newborns and their families is a prime example of our theme about the role of research in improving the welfare of children. Until relatively recently, hospitals minimized parents' contact with their LBW infants, mainly because of fear of infection. Parents are now encouraged to have as much physical contact and social interaction with their hospitalized infant as the baby's condition allows. Indeed, *kangaroo care*—a variant of the skin-to-skin care discussed earlier, in which caregivers act as incubators to help maintain infants' skin temperature and to promote breast-feeding—decreases mortality and increases growth, breast-feeding, and attachment (Conde-Agudelo & Díaz-Rossello, 2014). Recent data suggest that breast milk, in and of itself, promotes healthy brain development in preterm infants (Blesa et al., 2019); we will return to the topic of breast-feeding in Chapter 3.

Being touched—cuddled, caressed, and carried—is a vital part of a newborn's life. Many LBW infants experience little stimulation of this kind because of the precautions that must be taken with them, including keeping them in special *isolettes* where they are hooked up to life-support machines. Because LBW infants are often premature, they may spend weeks or months in the neonatal intensive care unit (NICU). For these infants, their exposure to touch in the hospital affects how they respond to touch later on. As one study showed, babies who experienced more gentle touching by caregivers in the NICU later showed stronger neural responses to touch than did babies who had less experience with gentle touching in the NICU. In contrast, babies who experienced more painful experiences in the NICU later showed decreased brain responses to touch than did babies who experienced less pain in the NICU (Maitre et al., 2017). Thus, early atypical experiences in the NICU can shape infants' later responses to something as ubiquitous as touch, as shown in Figure 2.22.

Hospitals have designed education programs to help parents of preterm infants learn about the revised timetable of their baby's early development: developmental milestones will be delayed, often linked more tightly to gestational age at birth than to chronological age after birth. For example, their preterm infant will not begin to smile at them at around 6 weeks of age, the time when full-term infants usually reach this milestone. Instead, they may have to wait several more weeks for their baby to look them in the eye and break into a heart-melting smile. Thus, preterm infants are potentially more challenging to care for while being less rewarding to interact with.

One consequence of these challenges is that children who were born preterm are more likely to be victims of parental child abuse than are full-term infants. Indeed, a recent study of infant hospitalizations due to child abuse found that the two strongest predictors were preterm birth and extended stay in the NICU (Mason et al., 2018). Interventions that provide parents with training in child development, and/or focus on helping parents to become more responsive to their LBW infants, have yielded numerous positive effects, including improved behavioural outcomes, greater weight gain, higher IQs, and myriad other improved outcomes relative to their LBW peers (Nordhov et al., 2012; Wassenaer-Leemhuis et al., 2016). Successful intervention programs also include support sessions, in the hospital and during home visits, designed to encourage parents to talk about their experiences and express their feelings.

Though these interventions can improve outcomes for specific conditions, it is important to note the impact of cumulative risk: the more risks the infant endures, the lower the chances of a good outcome. Because this principle is so important for all aspects of development, we examine it in greater detail in the following section.

Multiple-Risk Models

Risk factors tend to occur together. For example, a pregnant woman who engages in substance abuse is also likely to be under a great deal of stress and unlikely to eat well, take vitamins, seek prenatal care, have a strong social support network, or take good care of herself in other ways. Furthermore, whatever the cumulative effects of these prenatal risk factors, they will likely be compounded after birth if the mother continues her unhealthy lifestyle.

As you will see repeatedly throughout this book, a negative developmental outcome—whether in terms of prenatal or later development—is more likely when multiple risk factors are involved. In a classic demonstration of this fact, Michael Rutter (1979) reported a heightened incidence of psychiatric problems among English children growing up in families with four or more risk factors (including marital distress, low SES, paternal criminality, and maternal psychiatric disorder; Figure 2.23). Thus, the likelihood of developing a disorder is slightly elevated for the child of parents who fight a lot; but if the child's family is also poor, the father engages in criminal behaviour, and the mother suffers from emotional problems, the child's risk is multiplied nearly tenfold. Across numerous developmental domains, there are cumulative effects of risk factors: the more risk factors, the worse the potential outcomes. These cumulative risk effects impact aspects of child functioning, ranging from attachment to language development to well-being (Evans, Li, & Whipple, 2013).

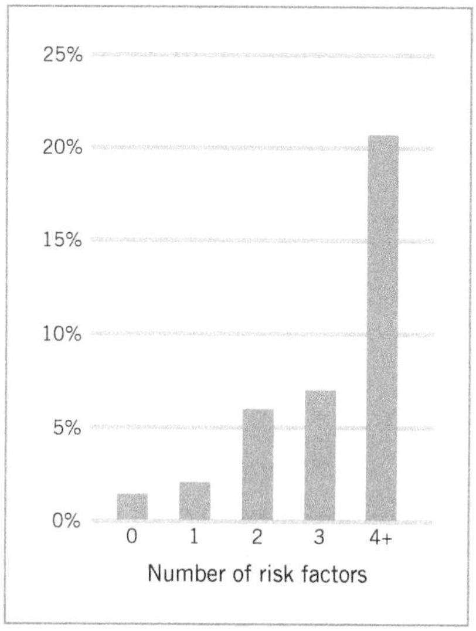

FIGURE 2.23 Multiple risk factors Children who grow up in families with multiple risk factors are more likely to develop psychiatric disorders than are children from families with only one or two problematic characteristics. (Data from Rutter, 1979)

Consider some of the risk factors for fetal development that we have discussed: inadequate prenatal care, poor nutrition, illness, emotional stress, cigarette smoking, drug abuse, and exposure to environmental and occupational hazards. All these factors are more likely to be experienced by a woman living below the poverty line than by a middle-class woman. It is no wonder, then, that on the whole, the outcome of pregnancy is less positive for infants of lower-SES parents than for babies born to middle-class parents. This is not just the case in Canada. In Japan, which has less income disparity than Canada, there is a link between income and birth outcomes (Fujiwara, Ito, & Kawachi, 2013).

Structural racism—which describes behaviours and beliefs that harm specific racial and ethnic groups and can result in residential segregation, uneven access to healthcare, and high rates of incarceration—also impacts fetal and newborn health (Bailey et al., 2017). For example, hospitalization rates in Quebec are significantly higher in both First Nations and Inuit infants as compared to non-Indigenous infants (He et al., 2017). In the United States, consistent with research on the role of maternal stress in fetal development, pregnant women in minority communities who report higher levels of concern about racial discrimination are more likely to have preterm infants than those who report lower levels of concern (Braveman et al., 2017). Improving the quality of hospitals and other medical facilities that serve minority communities is one promising approach currently being taken to address pregnancy-related health disparities (Howell, 2018). We will return to these issues in Box 3.4: Poverty and Health Disparities.

Much of the discussion in this chapter has focused on the many ways in which early developmental processes can go wrong. There are, of course, individuals who, faced with multiple and seemingly overwhelming developmental hazards, even beginning before birth, nevertheless do well. In studying such children, researchers

developmental resilience successful development in spite of multiple and seemingly overwhelming developmental hazards

employ the concept of **developmental resilience** (Masten, Best, & Garmezy, 1990; Sameroff, 1998). Resilient children—like those in the Kauai study discussed in Chapter 1—often have two factors in their favour: (1) certain personal characteristics, especially intelligence, responsiveness to others, and a sense of being capable of achieving their goals; and (2) responsive care from someone. Returning to our theme of *individual differences,* personal traits combined with a supportive environment can help us understand remarkable successes in the face of developmental challenges.

REVIEW QUESTION

A central theme in child development is the ways in which nature and nurture work together to shape developmental processes. How do nature and nurture interact in experiences such as newborn sleep patterns, crying, and the effects of multiple risks that an infant might face? ■

CHAPTER SUMMARY

Prenatal Development

- Nature and nurture combine forces in prenatal development. Much of this development is generated by the fetus itself, making the fetus an active player in its own progress. Substantial continuity exists between what goes on before and after birth in that infants demonstrate the effects of what has happened to them in the womb.
- Prenatal development begins at the cellular level with conception, the union of an egg from the mother and a sperm from the father to form a single-celled zygote. The zygote multiplies and divides on its way through a fallopian tube.
- The zygote undergoes the processes of cell division, cell migration, cell differentiation, and cell death. These processes continue throughout prenatal development.
- When the zygote becomes implanted on the uterine wall, it becomes an embryo. From that point, it is dependent on the mother to obtain nourishment and oxygen and to get rid of waste products through the placenta.
- Fetal behaviour begins 5 or 6 weeks after conception with simple movements, undetected by the mother, that become increasingly complex and organized into patterns. Later, the fetus practices behaviours vital to independent living, including swallowing and a form of intrauterine "breathing."
- The fetus experiences a wealth of stimulation both from within the womb and from the external environment. The fetus learns from this experience, as demonstrated by studies showing that both fetuses and newborns can discriminate between familiar and novel sounds, especially in speech, and exhibit persistent taste preferences developed in the womb.

Hazards to Prenatal Development

- There are many hazards to prenatal development. The most common fate of a fertilized egg is spontaneous abortion (miscarriage).
- A wide range of environmental factors can be hazardous to prenatal development. These include teratogens from the external world and certain maternal characteristics, such as age, nutritional status, physical health, behaviour (especially the use of legal or illegal drugs), and emotional state.

The Birth Experience

- Approximately 38 weeks after conception, the baby is ready to be born. Usually, the behaviour of the fetus helps to initiate the birth process.
- Being squeezed through the birth canal has several beneficial effects on the newborn, including preparing the infant to take his or her first breath.
- Cultural practices surrounding childbirth vary greatly and are in part related to the goals and values emphasized by the culture.

The Newborn Infant

- Newborns' states of arousal range from deep sleep to active crying.
- The amount of time infants spend in the different arousal states varies greatly, both across individuals and across cultures.

- REM sleep seems to compensate for the lack of visual stimulation that results from the darkness of the womb, and for the fact that newborns spend much of their time with their eyes shut, asleep.
- The sound of a baby crying can be very aversive, and adults employ many strategies to soothe distressed infants.
- The infant mortality rate in Canada is high relative to that of other developed countries. It is much higher for babies born to low-SES parents.
- Infants born weighing less than 5½ pounds (2500 grams) are referred to as being of low birth weight. LBW infants are at risk for a variety of developmental problems, and the lower the birth weight, the greater the risk of lasting difficulties.
- A variety of intervention programs have been designed to improve the course of development of LBW babies, encompassing time in the hospital as well as after the infant returns home.
- The multiple-risk model refers to the fact that infants with a number of risk factors have a heightened likelihood of continued developmental problems. Poverty is a particularly insidious risk to development, in part because it is associated with numerous negative factors.
- Some children display resilience even in the face of substantial challenges. Resilience seems to result from certain personal characteristics and from responsive care from someone.

Test Yourself

1. The single cell that forms when two gametes merge during conception is called the
a. zygote.
b. ova.
c. sperm.
d. embryo.

2. Which process of prenatal development is critical to the specialization of cells?
a. Cell division
b. Synaptogenesis
c. Cell differentiation
d. Apoptosis

3. Harry and Ron are genetically identical twins and are referred to as ____________. Althea (a genetic female) and Stephen (a genetic male) are also twins but are clearly ____________ twins.
a. monozygotic; identical
b. dizygotic; fraternal
c. dizygotic; monozygotic
d. monozygotic; dizygotic

4. Which of the following systems protects the developing embryo from dangerous toxins?
a. Amniotic sac
b. Placenta
c. Umbilical cord
d. Neural tube

5. The disproportionately large head of a 5-month-old fetus is a typical result of the normal process of
a. cephalocaudal development.
b. proximal–distal development.
c. lateral development.
d. bottom-up development.

6. Which of the following senses is the least active while the fetus is in the womb?
a. Hearing
b. Smell
c. Taste
d. Sight

7. Logan's dad is thrilled as Logan laughs each time he shows him a new toy: a monkey that squeaks when he pushes on its belly. After repeated exposure to the squeaking monkey, Logan becomes bored and no longer laughs. This process is known as
a. habituation.
b. dishabituation.
c. classical conditioning.
d. operant conditioning.

8. The DeCasper and Spence study, in which pregnant women read aloud twice a day from the same book during their last 6 weeks of pregnancy, was designed to assess
a. fetal attention.
b. fetal learning.
c. infant attention.
d. infant learning.

9. Which of the following does *not* influence the severity of the effect of a teratogen on a developing fetus?
a. Timing of exposure
b. Quantity of exposure
c. Duration of exposure
d. Number of previous pregnancies of the mother

10. Which is *not* a symptom of fetal alcohol syndrome?
a. Facial deformities
b. Intellectual disability
c. Underactivity
d. Attention problems

11. Studies suggest that the squeezing that a fetus experiences during delivery serves several important functions. Which of the following is *not* one of them?
   a. It temporarily reduces the size of the infant's head, allowing it to pass safely through the pelvic bones.
   b. It squeezes fluid from the ear canals, allowing the baby to hear.
   c. It stimulates the production of hormones that help the fetus withstand mild oxygen deprivation.
   d. It forces amniotic fluid out of the lungs, in preparation for the baby's first breaths.
12. Which of the following is a characteristic of non-rapid eye movement (non-REM) sleep?
   a. Irregular heart rate
   b. Irregular breathing
   c. Quick, jerky eye movements
   d. Slow brain waves
13. Which of the following describes an infant who is most likely suffering from colic?
   a. Vivian cries for several hours a day for unexplained reasons.
   b. Jeremy cries loudly when he is hungry.
   c. LaTosha cries when she is placed in her crib.
   d. Emelie rarely cries.
14. Which of the following interventions are parents of low-birth-weight infants encouraged to use to support development and promote survival?
   a. Parental training in child development
   b. Gentle massage
   c. Kangaroo care
   d. All of the above
15. What does the multiple-risk model suggest about negative developmental outcomes?
   a. Each risk factor will produce a unique negative outcome.
   b. The presence of one risk factor increases the likelihood that another risk factor will emerge in the future.
   c. The more risk factors that are present, the more likely and worse the potential outcomes will be.
   d. The presence of more risk factors increases the likelihood that a child will develop resilience.

Critical Thinking Questions

1. A recent cartoon showed a pregnant woman walking down a street carrying an MP3 player with a set of very large headphones clamped around her protruding abdomen. What point was it making? What research might have provided the basis for the woman's behaviour, and what assumptions is she making about what the result might be? If you or your partner were pregnant, do you think you would do something like this?
2. We hear a great deal about the terrible and tragic effects that illegal drugs like cocaine can have on fetal development. In this chapter, tobacco and alcohol use are identified as two of the most common harmful behaviours. How do the effects of these various substances differ from each other, and should that influence how we as a society perceive their use by pregnant women?
3. Suppose you were in charge of a public-health campaign to improve prenatal development in Canada and you could focus on only one factor. What would you target and why?
4. Pick a country or culture that you are not very familiar with and research the common beliefs and practices with respect to conception, pregnancy, and childbirth. Do their practices appeal to you more than the practices with which you are familiar? Are there beliefs or practices that could be used beneficially with the ones that you are familiar with?
5. Speculate on why the infant mortality rate in Canada has steadily gotten worse compared with that of other countries. Suggest some potential policy changes or healthcare initiatives that might help to address these causes.
6. Explain the basic idea of the multiple-risk model and how it relates to poverty in terms of prenatal development and birth outcomes.

Key Terms

amniotic sac, p. 46
Apgar score, p. 69
apoptosis, p. 45
cephalocaudal development, p. 47
colic, p. 68
conception, p. 43
developmental resilience, p. 74
dishabituation, p. 52
dose–response relation, p. 54
embryo, p. 44
embryonic stem cells, p. 45
epigenesis, p. 42
fetal alcohol spectrum disorder (FASD), p. 59
fetus, p. 44
fraternal (dizygotic) twins, p. 46
gametes (germ cells), p. 42
habituation, p. 52
identical (monozygotic) twins, p. 46
infant mortality, p. 69
low birth weight (LBW), p. 69
meiosis, p. 42
mitosis, p. 44
neural tube, p. 46
non-REM sleep, p. 66
phylogenetic continuity, p. 51
placenta, p. 46
premature, p. 69
rapid eye movement (REM) sleep, p. 66
sensitive period, p. 54
small for gestational age, p. 70
state, p. 66
sudden infant death syndrome (SIDS), p. 58
swaddling, p. 68
teratogen, p. 54
umbilical cord, p. 46
zygote, p. 44

Answers to Test Yourself

1. a, **2.** c, **3.** d, **4.** b, **5.** a, **6.** d, **7.** a, **8.** b, **9.** d, **10.** c, **11.** b, **12.** d, **13.** a, **14.** d, **15.** c

CHAPTER

3 Biology and Behaviour

TILLY WILLIS/PRIVATE COLLECTION/BRIDGEMAN IMAGES

TILLY WILLIS, *Waiting* (oil on canvas, 2005)

THEMES

NATURE AND NURTURE ■ THE ACTIVE CHILD

CONTINUITY/DISCONTINUITY ■ MECHANISMS OF CHANGE

INDIVIDUAL DIFFERENCES ■ RESEARCH AND CHILDREN'S WELFARE

Dramatizations of twins separated at birth have fascinated us for centuries, starting with Shakespeare's masterpiece *The Comedy of Errors* and continuing with modern films, such as *Twins* (1988), the *Parent Trap* (in 1961 and again in 1998), and *Three Identical Strangers* (2018). While in reality such situations are rare, they provide a potentially invaluable opportunity to tease apart nature and nurture by illustrating how the same genomes function in different environments.

THOMAS WANSTALL / THE IMAGE WORKS

When reunited at the age of 31, identical twins Gerald Levey and Mark Newman discovered, among many other similarities, that they were both volunteer firemen with droopy moustaches; long sideburns; and a penchant for hunting, fishing, and John Wayne movies. They even drank the same brand of beer, from a can, which they held with their pinkie tucked under the bottom and crushed when they had emptied it.

The Minnesota Study of Twins Reared Apart was designed to do exactly that (Bouchard et al., 1990). More than 100 pairs of twins reared apart were brought to Minneapolis to undergo a battery of tests. Among the identical twin pairs in this study, Gerald Levey and Mark Newman (shown in the photo at right) were separated at birth and reared separately in middle-class Jewish homes in the New York area. The twins showed many striking similarities, both physical and behavioural, including a similar work history and their roles as volunteer firemen. The Minnesota study's team of investigators was struck by the extent of the similarities they found in the separated twins; they identified genetic contributions to "almost every behavioral trait so far investigated from reaction time to religiosity" (Bouchard et al., 1990).

As striking as these similarities may be, it would be a great oversimplification to suggest that all of the traits shared by separated twins are genetic. For example, it would be a stretch to argue that the men in the photograph share a set of genes that predetermined they both would become firemen. Genes code for proteins, not for anything as complex as an occupation. As we saw in Chapter 1, it is also the case that experience alters gene expression, a process known as *epigenetics.* Thus, even twins who share the same DNA will not share the same pattern of gene expression. Epigenetic effects are being explored in a unique ongoing study involving identical twins Scott and Mark Kelly, who are both astronauts. Scott spent a year on the International Space Station while Mark stayed on Earth. Even several years after returning to Earth, researchers found that Scott's pattern of gene expression remained measurably different from Mark's (Garrett-Bakelman et al., 2019).

NASA PHOTO / ALAMY

Identical twins Mark and Scott Kelly have added a unique chapter to the twin studies annals. Both are astronauts and Scott's recent stay of nearly a year aboard the International Space Station while his brother stayed on Earth has provided NASA with the opportunity for a groundbreaking study of the effects of extended space travel, including exposure to radiation, carbon monoxide, and the micro-gravity environment.

Understanding how genes and environment interact is essential to understanding development at every point in the life span. This chapter focuses on the key biological factors that are in play from the moment of conception through adolescence, including the inheritance and influence of genes, the development and early functioning of the brain, and physical development and maturation. It highlights several of the themes set out in Chapter 1. Issues of *nature and nurture,* as well as *individual differences* among children, are central topics. *Mechanisms of change* are prominent in our discussions of the developmental role played by genetic factors and of the processes involved in brain development. *Continuity/discontinuity* in development is also highlighted throughout the chapter. We again emphasize the role of the *active child* in charting the course of development. Finally, the theme of *research and children's welfare* is also prominent, especially as we focus on gene-based disorders and on factors that influence healthy physical development.

genome the complete set of DNA of any organism, including all of its genes

genotype the genetic material an individual inherits

Nature and Nurture

Long before there was any understanding of the principles of heredity, people were aware that some characteristics "run in families" and that this tendency was somehow related to procreation. For as long as there have been domesticated animals, for example, farmers have practiced selective breeding to improve characteristics of their livestock, such as the size of their horses and the milk yield of their goats, cows, or yaks. Our modern understanding of how characteristics are transmitted from parent to offspring originated with Gregor Mendel, a nineteenth-century Austrian monk who observed distinct patterns of inheritance in cross-bred pea plants. A much deeper understanding of how genetic influences operate came in the 1950s with James Watson, Francis Crick, and Rosalind Franklin's identification of the structure of DNA, the basic component of hereditary transmission.

In recent decades, we have seen enormous progress in deciphering the genetic code. Researchers have mapped the entire **genome**—the complete set of an organism's genes—of myriad species of plants and animals, including humans, chickens, mice, and chimpanzees. Plans are afoot to sequence the genomes of all known species (Lewin et al., 2018). Along with these innovations in gene sequencing have come innovations in *gene synthesis,* a method for producing DNA. In 2016, scientists announced a plan to synthesize an entire human genome (Boeke et al., 2016). While this project has been scaled back to focus on creating cells that are immune to viral infection (Dolgin, 2018), human gene synthesis remains a topic with a great deal of potential for scientific and medical advances. Yet it is also fraught with ethical concerns. Indeed, the November 2018 announcement by a Chinese scientist about the first genome-edited newborns—twins, one of whose genes was edited to resist HIV—was met with widespread outrage in the scientific community. Many critics raised concerns about the unintended consequences such manipulation might hold for brain function and behaviour not just of these individuals, but also of any progeny that also inherits the new genes (Cohen, 2018). Researchers have also raised concerns that the specific gene variant manipulated in this procedure could be related to reduced life expectancy, perhaps due to increased vulnerability to other viruses (Wei & Nielsen, 2019).

Twins Reared Apart

© BBC WORLDWIDE

Comparisons of the genomes of various species have revealed numerous surprises. One was the number of genes that humans have: the current estimate of roughly 20,000 to 21,000 protein-coding genes (Willyard, 2018) is far fewer than previous estimates, which ranged from 35,000 to more than 100,000 genes (Ezkurdia et al., 2014). A second surprise was that most of those genes are possessed by all living things. Most human genes are devoted, in decreasing order, to making us animals, vertebrates, mammals, primates, and—finally—humans. A third surprise is that genes themselves make up only about 1% of the human genome. Much of the rest of our genome is made up of non-coding DNA—once thought to be "junk" DNA—that plays a crucial role in regulating the activity of protein-coding genes.

CP PHOTO / LETHBRIDGE HERALD-IAN MARTENS

In the 1970s and 1980s, six brothers from the Sutter family reached the National Hockey League. Altogether, they played nearly 5,000 games and won the Stanley Cup six times. The phenomenal athletic ability of these brothers is almost certainly due to a combination of nature—the genes they inherited from their parents—and nurture—the encouragement and support they received from their parents.

Genetic and Environmental Forces

To simplify our discussion of the complex interactions among genetic and environmental factors, we will organize it around the model of hereditary and environmental influences shown in Figure 3.1. Three key elements of the model are the **genotype**, which is inherited genetic material;

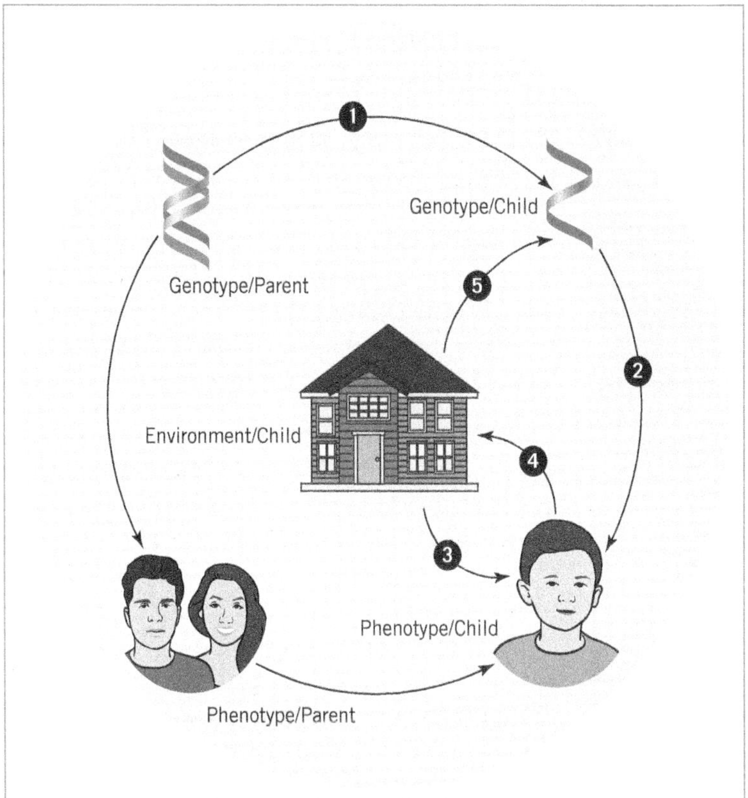

FIGURE 3.1 **Development** Development is a combined function of genetic and environmental factors. The five numbered relations are discussed in detail in the text.

the **phenotype**, the observable expression of the genotype, including *both* body characteristics and behaviour; and the **environment**, which incorporates every aspect of individuals and their surroundings (including prenatal experience) other than the genes themselves.

These three elements are involved in five relations that are fundamental in the development of every child: (1) parents' genetic contribution to children's genotypes; (2) the contribution of children's genotypes to their own phenotypes; (3) the contribution of children's environments to their phenotypes; (4) the influence of children's phenotypes on their environments; and (5) the influence of children's environments on their genotypes. We will consider each of these relations in turn.

Genes and Development

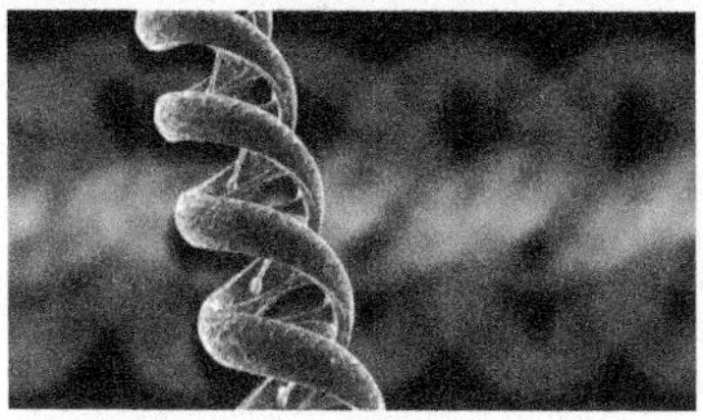

A LUNA BLUE/SHUTTERSTOCK

phenotype the observable expression of the genotype, including both body characteristics and behaviour

environment every aspect of individuals and their surroundings other than genes

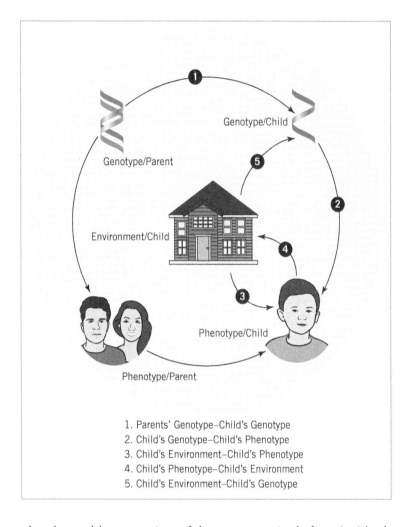

1 Parents' Genotype–Child's Genotype

Relation 1 involves the transmission of genetic material from parent to offspring. You caught a glimpse of this process in Chapter 2, when we discussed the gametes (one from the mother and one from the father) that conjoin to create a zygote. The nucleus of every cell in the body contains **chromosomes**, long threadlike molecules made up of two twisted strands of **DNA (deoxyribonucleic acid)**. DNA carries all the biochemical instructions involved in the formation and functioning of an organism. These instructions are "packaged" in **genes**, the basic unit of heredity in all living things. Each gene is a segment of DNA that is the code for the production of particular proteins.

chromosomes molecules of DNA that transmit genetic information; chromosomes are made up of DNA

DNA (deoxyribonucleic acid) molecules that carry all the biochemical instructions involved in the formation and functioning of an organism

genes sections of chromosomes that are the basic unit of heredity in all living things

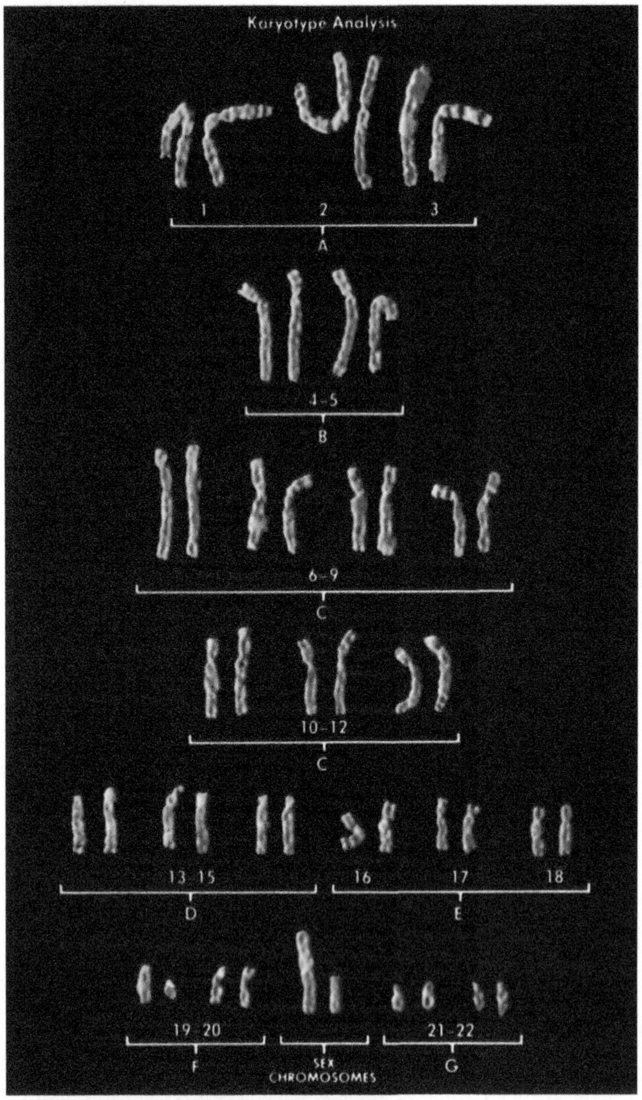

BIOPHOTO ASSOCIATES/SCIENCE SOURCE

FIGURE 3.2 Karyotype This colour-enhanced micrograph, called a karyotype, shows the 23 pairs of chromosomes in a genetically male human. As you can see, the chromosomes of each homologous pair are roughly the same size except for the sex chromosomes (middle of bottom row): the Y chromosome is much smaller than the X chromosome. A genetically female human's karyotype would contain two X chromosomes.

Some proteins are the building blocks of the body's cells; others regulate the cells' functioning. Genes affect development and behaviour only through the manufacture of proteins.

Human heredity Humans have a total of 46 chromosomes, divided into 23 pairs, in the nucleus of each cell (see Figure 3.2). Each chromosome pair carries, usually at corresponding locations, genes of the same type—that is, sequences of DNA that are relevant to the same traits. Because each parent passes along one chromosome to their offspring, every individual has two copies of each gene, one on the chromosome inherited from the father and one on the chromosome from the mother.

Genetic diversity and individual differences Genes guarantee that humans will be similar to one another in certain ways, both at the species level (e.g., humans are bipedal and have opposable thumbs) and at the individual level (i.e., family resemblances). Genes also guarantee differences at both levels. Several mechanisms contribute to genetic diversity among people.

One mechanism that promotes variability among individuals is the *random assortment* of chromosomes in the formation of egg and sperm. During gamete division, the 23 pairs of chromosomes are shuffled randomly, with chance determining which member of each pair goes into each new egg or sperm. When a sperm and an egg unite, the odds are essentially zero that any two individuals—even members of the same family—will have the same genotype (except, of course, identical twins). Further variation is introduced by a process called **crossing over**: when gametes divide, the two members of a pair of chromosomes sometimes swap sections of DNA. As a result, some of the chromosomes that parents pass on to their offspring are constituted differently from their own.

A second mechanism that enhances variability is **mutation**, a change in a section of DNA. Some mutations are random, spontaneous errors; others are caused by environmental factors. Those that occur in gametes (germ cells) can be passed on to offspring. Many inherited disorders originate from a mutated gene, as discussed in Box 3.2 in the next section.

Most mutations are harmful. Occasionally, however, a mutation enhances the individual's genetic fitness by increasing disease resistance or allowing the individual to adapt to some crucial aspect of the environment. Such mutations provide the basis for evolution: individuals with the favourable mutated gene are more likely to survive long enough to produce offspring, who, in turn, are likely to possess the mutated gene, thus heightening their own chance of surviving and reproducing. Across generations, these favourable genes proliferate in the gene pool of the species.

crossing over the process by which sections of DNA switch from one chromosome to the other; crossing over promotes variability among individuals

mutation a change in a section of DNA

sex chromosomes the chromosomes (X and Y) that determine an individual's designated sex at birth

Sex determination The **sex chromosomes**, which determine an individual's designated sex at birth, are an exception to the general pattern of chromosome pairs just described. Genetic females have two identical, largish sex chromosomes called X chromosomes, but genetic males have one X chromosome and one much smaller Y-shaped chromosome. Because a female has only X chromosomes, the division of her germ cells results in all her eggs having an X. However,

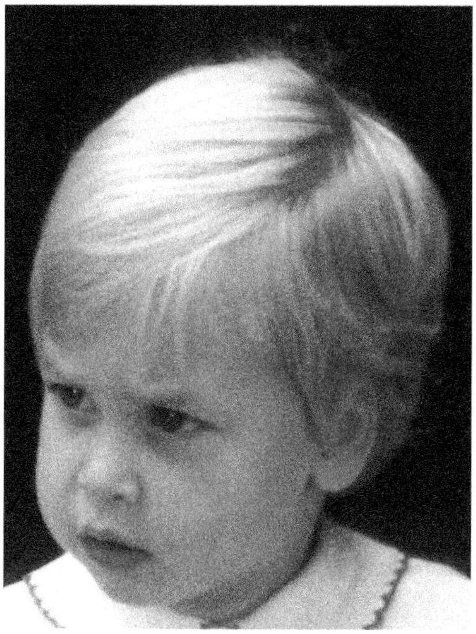

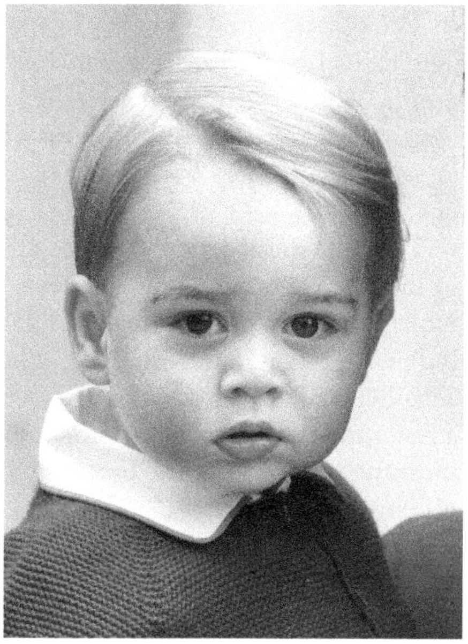

Children inherit half of their genes from their biological mother and half from their biological father. But mechanisms like random assortment and crossing over, as well as forces influencing the child's phenotype, shape the degree to which a child will resemble one parent and the degree to which they will vary. In the case of the British royals pictured here, Prince George (right) bears a strong resemblance to his father, Prince William (left) at age 2.

because a male is XY, half his sperm contain an X chromosome and half contain a Y. For this reason, the genetically male parent always determines the genetic sex of offspring. If an X-bearing sperm fertilizes an egg, a female (XX) zygote results; if a Y-bearing sperm fertilizes an egg, a male (XY) zygote results. A gene on the Y chromosome encodes the protein that triggers the prenatal formation of testes by activating genes on other chromosomes, triggering the production of the hormone testosterone (as discussed in Chapter 2). Sexual development is discussed in detail in Chapter 15.

2 Child's Genotype–Child's Phenotype

We now turn to Relation 2 in Figure 3.1, the relation between one's genotype and one's phenotype. Keep in mind that phenotypes include both physical characteristics, such as height and eye colour, and behavioural characteristics, such as temperament and intelligence. Genes also influence unobservable, intermediate aspects of the phenotype that impact behaviour, most notably, our brain and nervous systems. These intermediate phenotypes, known as **endophenotypes**, mediate the pathways between genes and behaviour.

Although every cell in your body contains copies of all the genes you received from your parents, only some of those genes are expressed. At any given time in any cell in the body, some genes are active (turned on), while others are not. Some genes that are hard at work in neurons, for example, are totally at rest in toenail cells.

Gene expression: Developmental changes From conception to death, genes influence an individual's development and behaviour only if they are switched on and off in the right place, at the right time, and for the right length of time. Some genes are turned on in only a few cells and for only a few hours and then are switched off permanently. This pattern is typical during embryological development when, for instance, the genes that are turned on in certain cells lead them to specialize for arm, hand, and fingerprint formation. Other genes are involved in the basic functioning of almost all cells almost all the time.

endophenotypes intermediate phenotypes, including the brain and nervous systems, that do not involve overt behaviour

regulator genes genes that control the activity of other genes

alleles two or more different forms of a gene

dominant allele the allele that, if present, gets expressed

recessive allele the allele that is not expressed if a dominant allele is present

homozygous having two of the same allele for a trait

heterozygous having two different alleles for a trait

The switching on and off of genes is controlled primarily by **regulator genes**. The activation or inactivation of one gene is always part of a chain of genetic events. When one gene is switched on, it causes another gene to turn on or off, which has an impact on the status of yet other genes. Thus, genes never function in isolation. Rather, they belong to extensive networks in which the expression of one gene is a precondition for the expression of another, and so on.

The fact that regulator genes can repeatedly switch other genes on and off in different patterns means that a given gene can function multiple times in multiple places during development. This on-again, off-again functioning of individual genes results in enormous diversity in genetic expression. By analogy, consider the fact that this book is written with only 26 letters, and probably only a few thousand different words made up of combinations of those letters. The meaning comes from the order in which the letters have been "switched on and off" by the authors.

External factors also affect the switching on and off of genes. A dramatic example is the effect of thalidomide on limb development (described in Chapter 2), in which the sedative interferes with the functioning of genes underpinning normal growth factors. Another example relates to vision: early visual experience is necessary for the normal development of the visual system because it causes the switching on of certain genes, which, in turn, switch on other genes in the visual cortex (Maya-Vetencourt & Origlia, 2012). The ramifications of decreased visual experience are observed in cases of children with cataracts that are not removed early in life, as discussed later in this chapter.

Gene expression: Dominance patterns Many of an individual's genes are never expressed; some others are only partially expressed. What factor determines whether a gene is expressed? One-third of human genes have two or more different forms, known as **alleles**. The alleles of a given gene influence the same trait or characteristic (e.g., eye colour), but they contribute to different developmental outcomes (e.g., brown, blue, hazel, gray eyes).

Perhaps the simplest pattern of gene expression—discovered by Mendel—is referred to as the *dominant–recessive pattern*. Some genes have only two alleles, one of which is **dominant** and the other **recessive**. In this pattern, there are two possibilities: (1) a person can inherit two of the same allele—two dominant or two recessive—and thus be **homozygous** for the trait in question; or (2) the person can inherit two different alleles—one dominant and the other recessive—and thus be **heterozygous** for the trait. When an individual is homozygous, the corresponding trait will be expressed. When an individual is heterozygous for a trait, the instructions of the dominant allele will be expressed (see Figure 3.3).

FIGURE 3.3 Mendelian inheritance patterns Pictured here are the Mendelian inheritance patterns for the offspring of two brown-haired parents who are both heterozygous for hair colour. The allele for brown hair (B) is dominant and that for blond hair (b) is recessive. Note that these parents have three chances out of four of producing children with brown hair. They have two chances in four of producing brown-haired children who carry the gene for blond hair.

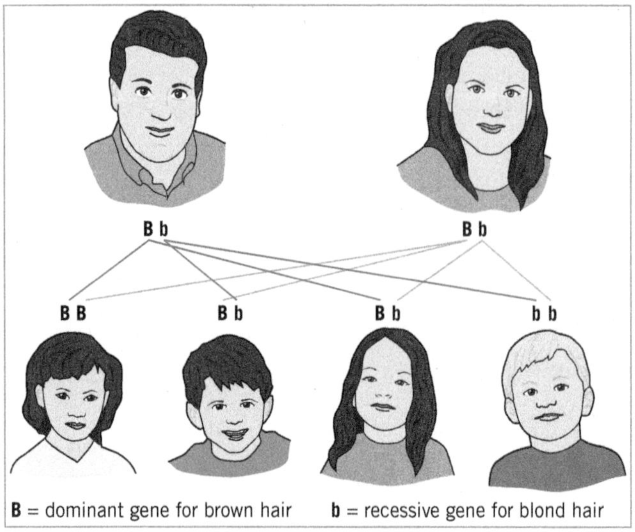

The sex chromosomes present an interesting wrinkle in the story of dominance patterns. The X chromosome carries roughly 1,500 genes, whereas the much smaller Y chromosome carries only about 200. Thus, when a genetic female inherits a recessive allele on the X chromosome from her mother, she is likely to have a dominant allele on the chromosome from her father to suppress it, so she will not express the trait in question. In contrast, when a genetic male inherits the same recessive allele on the X chromosome from his mother, he likely will not have a dominant allele from his father to override it, so he will express the trait. Genetic males are thus more likely than females to suffer a variety of sex-linked inherited disorders caused by recessive alleles on their X chromosome (see Box 3.2).

Despite the traditional emphasis given to the dominant–recessive pattern of inheritance, it actually pertains to relatively few human traits—such as hair colour, blood type, abundance of body hair, and the like—as well as to a large number of genetic disorders (see Box 3.2). Inheritance patterns are vastly more complicated for most of the traits and behaviours that are of primary interest to developmental scientists, ranging from physical characteristics such as height and obesity to psychological constructs such as aggression and temperament. For example, the variability in human intelligence is currently believed to be linked to more than 500 different genes (Coleman et al., 2019). These traits, and most others we will discuss in this textbook, follow a **polygenic inheritance** pattern: many different genes contribute to any given phenotypic outcome. For this reason, you should be skeptical whenever you encounter news headlines announcing the discovery of "a gene for" a complex human trait or predisposition. As noted, more than 500 genes contribute to individual differences in human intelligence, a polygenic trait that is not determined by any single gene.

polygenic inheritance inheritance pattern in which traits are governed by more than one gene

phenylketonuria (PKU) a disorder related to a defective recessive gene on chromosome 12 that prevents metabolism of the amino acid phenylalanine

3 Child's Environment–Child's Phenotype

We now come to Relation 3 in our model—the impact of the environment on the child's phenotype. (Remember, the environment includes everything not in the genetic material itself, including the array of prenatal experiences discussed in Chapter 2.) Because of the continuous interaction of genotype and environment, a given genotype may develop differently in different environments.

One example of a phenotype produced by a genotype–environment interaction is **phenylketonuria (PKU)**, a disorder related to a defective recessive gene on chromosome 12. Individuals who inherit this gene from both parents cannot metabolize phenylalanine, an amino acid present in many foods (especially red meats) and in aspartame, an artificial sweetener. If they eat a normal diet, phenylalanine accumulates in the bloodstream, causing impaired brain development and intellectual disabilities. However, if infants with the PKU gene are identified shortly after birth and kept on a stringent diet free of phenylalanine, intellectual impairment can be avoided. Thus, a given genotype results in very different phenotypes—intellectual disability or relatively normal intelligence—depending on environmental circumstances. Because early detection of PKU is so effective, all newborns in Canada and the United States are screened for PKU, as well as for a number of other genetic disorders. In Box 3.1, we describe the role of genetic testing, including screening prior to pregnancy, fetal genetic testing, and newborn screening.

A second example comes from an important study showing that the effects of abusive parenting interact with the child's genotype to produce different adult outcomes (Caspi et al., 2002). The researchers wanted to determine why some severely maltreated children become violent and antisocial as adults, whereas others who are exposed to the same abuse do not. To do so, they focused on the MAOA gene, an X-linked gene that inhibits brain chemicals associated with aggression. The results, shown in Figure 3.4, revealed the importance of a *combination* of environmental *and* genetic factors leading to antisocial outcomes. Young men who had a relatively inactive version of the MAOA gene, and who had experienced severe maltreatment, grew up to be more antisocial than other men who had also

BOX 3.1 APPLICATIONS Genetic Testing

As knowledge about genetics continues to increase, opportunities to use that knowledge to improve human health have become far more widespread. One such application, *genetic testing,* can be performed at any point in an individual's life in order to diagnose or predict the likelihood of developing a disease or disorder.

Genetic testing is frequently used prior to pregnancy to determine whether prospective parents are carriers of a specific disorder. **Carrier genetic testing** is typically offered to people of Eastern European Jewish descent because they have an increased likelihood of carrying the recessive gene for Tay Sachs, a severe birth defect that culminates in death by age 5. Testing is also typically offered to people of African descent because they have an increased likelihood of carrying the recessive gene for sickle-cell disease, in which red blood cells have an atypical sickle shape causing chronic anemia and pain (discussed further in Box 3.2). Some prospective parents opt for *in vitro fertilization* (IVF) with *preimplantation genetic diagnosis,* in which the fertilized eggs are tested for a specific genetic disorder. Eggs that do not carry the gene are chosen for implantation into the mother's uterus.

Prenatal testing involves genetic testing during pregnancy to assess risk for a range of genetic disorders, and it is especially encouraged for pregnancies with an elevated risk of a genetic disorder (e.g., fetuses with older parents, as discussed in Chapter 2). Prenatal *screening tests* analyze maternal blood for information about degree of risk. A recent innovation called *non-invasive prenatal testing* (NIPT) uses fragments of fetal DNA that enter the mother's bloodstream. NIPT can be used as early as the 9th week of a pregnancy to test for *aneuploidy* (missing or extra chromosomes), which is associated with conditions such as trisomy 13 (Patau syndrome), trisomy 18 (Edwards syndrome), and trisomy 21 (Down syndrome), depending on the location of the aneuploidy. More invasive prenatal *diagnostic tests* detect genetic anomalies using fetal cells, either from the placenta (*chorionic villus sampling,* or CVS, usually done between 10 and 13 weeks of pregnancy) or from amniotic fluid (*amniocentesis,* usually done between 15 and 20 weeks of pregnancy). Genetic counselors, who receive extensive training in both genetics and counselling, help families interpret the findings of genetic tests and offer resources to facilitate the difficult decisions that often accompany the diagnosis of a genetic disorder.

Newborn screening occurs in every province in Canada (Therrell et al., 2015). Newborns receive a tiny pinprick to their heel to get a blood sample, which is then tested for 30 to 50 different genetic and non-genetic disease biomarkers, including PKU (as discussed earlier). As the cost of gene sequencing technology continues to decrease, it may be possible to provide parents with more extensive information about their newborn infant's predisposition for particular diseases. Indeed, a recent study suggests that genomic sequencing of newborns illuminates a range of potential health issues not detected by current newborn screening protocols (Ceyhan-Birsoy et al., 2019). This type of information could be useful in guiding a lifetime of medical care. However, whole-genome screening also raises important ethical concerns. Would insurance companies be justified for raising rates if newborn screening reveals an untreatable disease or detects a disorder that won't exhibit symptoms for decades? And could extensive genetic information lead to discrimination?

In 2017, the Canadian government passed the Genetic Non-Discrimination Act, intended to prohibit the use of genetic information in decisions about insurance or employment. However, as genetic information becomes ever more easily accessible to individuals through companies such as 23andme, the intersection between genetic testing and discrimination protections remains murky. It is also unclear how people without any training in human genetics will interpret the results of mail-order genetic tests. Whenever possible, parents should seek out trained professionals such as genetic counselors before making important decisions about their child's care.

▶ Newborn Genetic Testing

experienced severe maltreatment but who possessed a more active version of the MAOA gene. More concretely, 85% of the maltreated group with the relatively inactive gene developed some form of antisocial behaviour, and they were almost 10 times more likely to be convicted of a violent crime.

As this study makes clear, neither factor by itself (possessing the inactive MAOA gene or being abused) predisposed boys to become highly aggressive. The higher incidence of antisocial behaviour was observed only for the group of boys who possessed *both* the genetic and environmental risk factors. As the authors of that study note, knowledge about specific genetic risk factors that make people more susceptible to particular environmental effects could strengthen multiple-risk models, such as those discussed in the preceding two chapters.

Parental contributions to the child's environment Parents are central to children's environments through their interactions with their offspring and with each other, the experiences and encouragement they offer, and so on. Less obvious is the idea that parents' own genetic makeup influences the environment parents provide for their children. These types of *gene–environment correlations* are observed frequently in the study of child development. Parents' behaviour toward

carrier genetic testing genetic testing used to determine whether prospective parents are carriers of specific disorders

prenatal testing genetic testing used to assess the fetus's risk for genetic disorders

newborn screening tests used to screen newborn infants for a range of genetic and non-genetic disorders their children (e.g., how warm or reserved they are, how patient or short-fused) is genetically influenced, as are the kinds of preferences, activities, and resources to which they expose their children. For example, parents for whom reading is challenging—perhaps related to genetic factors, such as reading disabilities like dyslexia, which are known to be highly heritable (and highly polygenic)—are less likely to provide a reading-oriented environment for their children than parents who are skilled readers (e.g., Snowling & Melby-Lervåg, 2016).

The idea that parents' genes influence their own abilities and preferences, which in turn influence the environment they provide for their children, was elegantly tested in a recent study that investigated the effects of parental genes on children's educational outcomes (Kong et al., 2018). The researchers characterized the genotypes of trios—a child and their two biological parents—and found that the child's educational outcomes were predicted, in part, by parental alleles that the child did *not* inherit. These non-transmitted parental alleles play an important role in the creation of the child's environment, a phenomenon that the researchers describe as *genetic nurture.* By affecting the parents' phenotypes (and thereby influencing the family environments), the parents' genes affected their children's educational success.

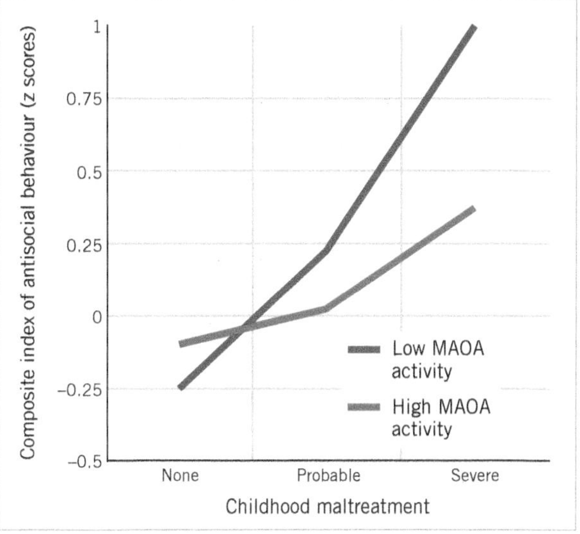

FIGURE 3.4 Genotype and environment This graph shows the level of antisocial behaviour observed in young men as a function of the degree to which they had been maltreated in childhood. Young men who had experienced severe maltreatment were in general more likely to engage in antisocial behaviour than were those who had experienced none. However, the effect was much stronger for those individuals who had a relatively inactive MAOA gene (red). (Data from Caspi et al., 2002, p. 852)

4 Child's Phenotype–Child's Environment

Relation 4 in our model restates the *active child* theme—children as a source of their own development. Each child evokes certain kinds of responses from others. The older child of one of your authors was a very outgoing baby. Because of his engaging personality, he created an environment filled with people—family and strangers alike—smiling and talking to him. The younger child, by contrast, was a very shy infant who actively avoided contact with strangers; her temperament limited the types of interactions she had with unfamiliar adults. Thus, these two children, despite living in the same home with the same parents, experienced very different early environments by virtue of their own behaviour.

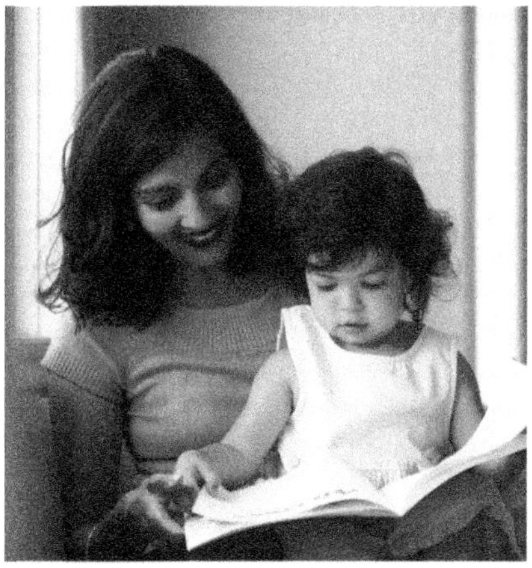

PHOTODISC / THINKSTOCK

This parent enjoys reading novels for pleasure and reads extensively for her work. She is providing a rich literary environment for her young child. The child may become an avid reader both because his mother's genetic makeup contributed to his enjoyment of reading and because of the physical environment (lots of books) and the social environment (encouragement of an interest in books) available in the home.

Children also create their own environments by actively selecting surroundings and experiences that match their interests and personalities. As soon as infants start reaching, crawling, and walking, they begin to *select* objects for exploration rather than relying on their parents' choices of play objects. Beginning in the preschool years, children choose playmates whom they enjoy and activities that interest them. Returning to the reading example, children who enjoy books will read more than children who find reading tedious. The more they read, the more skilled they become, leading them to choose increasingly more challenging books; this, in turn, leads them to acquire advanced vocabulary, improve their language comprehension, and enhance their general knowledge base, resulting in greater success in school. Children's ability to shape their own environments has profound effects on intellectual development, as we will see in Chapter 8.

5 Child's Environment–Child's Genotype

The fifth relationship in our model is perhaps the most surprising. Geneticists previously believed that the genotype was "fixed" at conception. But as discussed in Chapter 1 (page 11), the field of **epigenetics** has turned this conventional wisdom

epigenetics the study of stable changes in gene expression that are mediated by the environment

Children play an increasingly larger role in creating their own environments as they seek out activities and objects that interest them, often to the chagrin of their parents.

on its head. Although the structure of the genetic code remains "fixed" during one's lifetime, the expression of the genetic code is altered. Recall that a specific gene does not lead to a specific phenotype but that, instead, the genetic encoding of proteins alters the ways in which genes are *expressed* as phenotypes. Epigenetic mechanisms, mediated by the environment, can alter the functioning of genes and create stable changes in their expression—and some of these changes can be passed on to the next generation.

The epigenetic mechanism most commonly studied in humans is *methylation,* which silences gene expression. Methyl molecules block transcription in the promotor region of the gene, turning off gene activity, as illustrated in Figure 3.5. DNA methylation typically operates like a dimmer switch, regulating the amount of protein produced by a given gene (Lester, Conradt, & Marsit, 2016). Epigenetic processes involving methylation are of particular interest to developmental scientists because they provide evidence for long-term epigenetic effects of early adverse experiences on gene expression, impacting later health and well-being (e.g., Provenzi et al., 2016).

Key evidence for how methylation exerts epigenetic effects on behaviour comes from studies of rodents. Like humans, rodent mothers vary in the quality of their maternal behaviour. Typical rat mothering involves licking and grooming behaviour, which activates glucocorticoid receptor genes (recall from Chapter 2 that glucocorticoids are involved in stress reactivity). But some rat mothers do not perform these maternal behaviours at the same rate—a non-human analog to human child neglect. And indeed, rat pups whose mothers were unresponsive show less activity in the glucocorticoid receptor gene (Weaver et al., 2004).

As adults, these rat offspring were more fearful and showed aberrant stress responses. Because they were working with rats, the research team was able to use a research design that is not possible with human infants: they cross-fostered the rat pups, assigning some of the pups to be raised by mothers to whom they were genetically unrelated. This manipulation allowed the researchers to show that the effects they observed—stable alternations of DNA methylation as a function of maternal behaviour—were truly due to the rat pups' postnatal environments, rather than to prenatal or genomic differences.

FIGURE 3.5 Gene methylation Early experiences, such as stresses, nutrition, toxins, and other environmental factors, influence methyl molecules, which bind to DNA base pairs and block transcription in the gene's promoter region, altering gene expression.

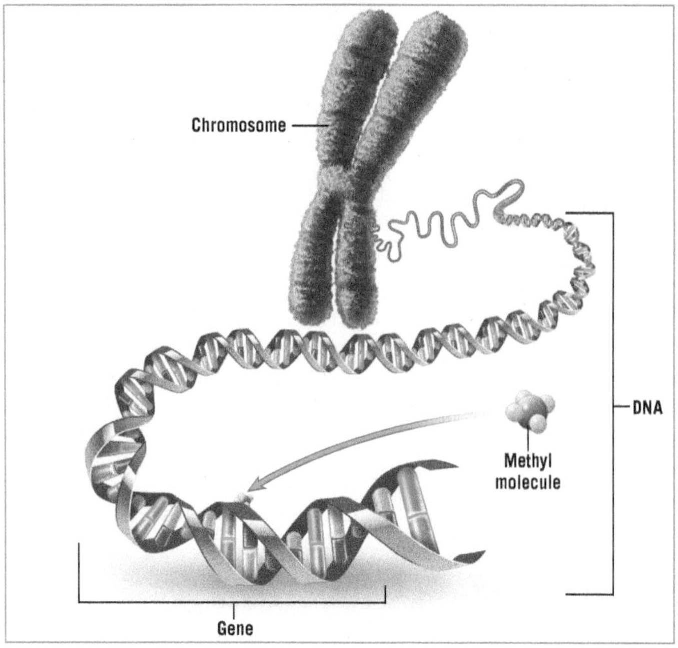

As you saw in Chapter 1, early stress also affects methylation in humans (e.g., Conradt, 2017). For example, children who experienced severe early-life stress in the form of child maltreatment show similar patterns of methylation in the glucocorticoid receptor gene as the rodents who received poor parental care (Romens et al., 2015). More recently, researchers used a whole-genome screen to examine both methylation and gene expression in a group of 9- to 12-year-old girls who had experienced levels of childhood adversity ranging from mild to severe (Papale et al., 2018). The results revealed a large number of genes (more than 100!) whose methylation levels varied in association with the amount of stress the girls had experienced.

Another recent study revealed epigenetic changes related to childhood abuse in the sperm cells of adult males—cells that are of particular interest as a possible mechanism for passing epigenetic changes from parent to child (Roberts et al., 2018). Given all of the genetic reshuffling that occurs at conception, as discussed earlier in this chapter, much of the methylation in germ cells is erased. Nevertheless, this research suggests a possible epigenetic route for the cross-generational transmission of stress.

Our discussion of the relationships between genotypes, phenotypes, and environments emphasized the challenges in understanding how genes impact the development of individuals. Nevertheless, the conceptualization we have presented is greatly simplified. This is particularly true for the fifth relationship—epigenetics—which, when considered in full, suggests that the line between genes and environment is blurry at best. In the next section, we will explore the research designs and tools that researchers in the field of behaviour genetics have used to make headway in teasing apart nature and nurture in the study of human development.

ERIC ISSELEE/SHUTTERSTOCK

Grooming behaviour by rat mothers activates glucocorticoid receptor genes in offspring. The offspring of rat mothers who did not perform these maternal behaviours at the typical rate were more fearful and showed aberrant stress responses.

REVIEW QUESTION

The model of development depicted in Figure 3.1 illustrates several of the themes of this book: the interplay of nature and nurture, the influence of the active child on their own development, and the various mechanisms that can influence development, among others. Select one theme and explain how it is represented in each of the five relationships discussed in this section. ■

Behaviour Genetics

Why do the individuals in any group of human beings vary in terms of how smart, sociable, depressed, aggressive, and religious they are? Researchers in the field of **behaviour genetics** assume that all behavioural traits are, to some extent, **heritable**. Individual differences in a trait, therefore, are influenced to some degree by genetically transmissible factors (e.g., Plomin, 2018). Behaviour geneticists try to tease apart genetic and environmental contributions by taking advantage of the differences observed among a population. Two premises underlie this endeavour: (1) To the extent that genetic factors are important for a given trait or behaviour, individuals who are genotypically similar should be phenotypically similar, and (2) to the extent that shared environmental factors are important, individuals who were reared together should be more similar than people who were reared apart.

Quantitative Genetics Research Designs

Quantitative behaviour geneticists use statistical methods to study "naturally occurring genetic and environmental variation" in a population by comparing the phenotypes of individuals who vary in the amount of genomic DNA they share (Plomin, DeFries, & McClearn, 2008, p. 70). The mainstay of quantitative behaviour genetics is the *family study,* which attempts to determine whether phenotypic traits are correlated with the degree to which people are genetically related—parents and children, identical and fraternal twins, non-twin siblings, or adoptive family members. (As you may recall from Chapter 1, the strength and direction of a correlation indicate the extent to which two variables are related;

behaviour genetics the science concerned with how variation in behaviour and development results from the combination of genetic and environmental factors

heritable refers to characteristics or traits that are genetically transmitted

KRIS TIMKEN/GETTY IMAGES

RON LEVINE/GETTY IMAGES

Twin studies compare correlations for identical twins (top) and same-sex fraternal twins (bottom) to estimate the heritability of a given trait.

the higher the correlation, the more precisely scores on one variable can be predicted from scores on the other.) The resulting correlations are compared to see if they are (1) higher for more closely related individuals than for less closely related people, and (2) higher for individuals who share the same environment than for individuals who do not.

The *twin-study* design is a specialized form of the family study used to compare the correlations for identical (monozygotic, or MZ) twins with those for same-sex fraternal (dizygotic, or DZ) twins. As you will recall, identical twins have 100% of their genes in common (though gene expression is affected by epigenetic factors, as discussed in the preceding section), whereas fraternal twins share, on average, 50% of their genomic DNA (just like non-twin siblings). For twins who grow up together, the degree of similarity of the environment is generally assumed to be equal. Known as the *equal environments assumption*, the claim is that both types of twins shared the same prenatal environment, were born at the same time (so experienced societal changes similarly), grew up in the same family and community, and are always the same age when tested. If the correlation between identical twins on a given trait or behaviour is substantially higher than that between fraternal twins, it is assumed that genetic factors are substantially responsible for the difference.

It is important to note, however, that the equal environments assumption has been questioned for a range of reasons (e.g., Felson, 2014; Richardson & Norgate, 2005). For example, parents of MZ twins may treat them more similarly than parents of DZ twins. And even among MZ twin pairs, there are notable differences in the degree of placental sharing (known as *chorionicity*), complicating measures of prenatal environmental similarity (Van Beijsterveldt et al., 2016). While many MZ twin pairs fully share a placenta, others do not, making their prenatal environments more akin to those of DZ twins. Thus, it is overly simplistic to assume that environments of MZ twin pairs and DZ twin pairs are always equally similar to one another.

Another family-study design is the *adoption* study. In this approach, researchers examine whether adopted children's scores on a given measure are correlated more highly with those of their biological parents and siblings or with those of their adoptive parents and siblings. Genetic influences are inferred to the extent that children resemble their biological relatives more than they do their adoptive ones.

We began this chapter with the ideal behaviour genetics design—the *adoptive twin* study—in which identical twins who grew up together are compared to identical twins who were separated shortly after birth and raised apart. If the correlations for twins reared apart are similar to those for twins reared together, it suggests that environmental factors have little effect. Conversely, to the extent that the correlations between identical twins who grew up in different environments are lower than those for identical twins who grew up together, environmental influence is inferred. As we mentioned earlier, however, children's phenotypes also shape their environments (Relations 2 and 4). Furthermore, adoption agencies generally place separated twins with families of backgrounds similar to one another. Therefore, even adoptive twin study designs are vulnerable to confounding of environmental and genetic factors.

heritability a statistical estimate of the proportion of the measured variance on a trait among individuals in a given population that is attributable to genetic differences among those individuals

Heritability

To estimate how much of the variability in measures of a given trait is attributable to genetic and environmental factors, behaviour geneticists derive heritability estimates from correlations of the type shown in Table 3.1. **Heritability** is a statistical estimate of how much of the measured variance on a phenotypic trait among individuals in a given population is attributable to genetic differences among those individuals.

Heritability analyses have been applied to many diverse aspects of human behaviour, several of which you will encounter in other chapters of this book. One large meta-analysis of more than 17,000 traits—with more than 14 million twin pairs—found that heritability was greater than zero for every trait investigated in the analysis (Polderman et al., 2015). These traits include psychological traits like temperament, which we will discuss further in Chapter 10, as well as many other aspects of personality, cognition, and psychopathology (Plomin et al., 2016; Vukasović & Bratko, 2015).

One well-studied trait is intelligence. Table 3.1 summarizes the results of more than 100 family studies of IQ through adolescence. The pattern of results reveals both genetic and environmental influences. Genetic influence is revealed by the presence of generally higher correlations for individuals with higher degrees of genetic similarity. Most notable is the finding that identical (MZ) twins resemble each other in IQ more than do same-sex fraternal (DZ) twins. At the same time, environmental influences are reflected in the fact that identical twins are not identical in terms of IQ. Further evidence for the influence of environmental factors is that MZ twins reared together are more similar than those reared apart.

As compelling as they seem, heritability measures have also been widely criticized. Part of the criticism stems from ways that the term "heritability" is often misinterpreted or misused by the public. The concept of heritability is

TABLE 3.1 Summary of Family Studies of Intelligence

	Average Familial IQ Correlations (R)	
Relationship	**Average R Reared-together Biological Relatives**	**Number of Pairs**
MZ twins	0.86	4672
DZ twins	0.60	5533
Siblings	0.47	26,473
Parent–offspring	0.42	8433
Half siblings	0.35	200
Cousins	0.15	1176
	Reared-apart Biological Relatives	
MZ twins	0.72	65
Siblings	0.24	203
Parent–offspring	0.24	720
	Reared-together Nonbiological Relatives	
Siblings	0.32	714
Parent–offspring	0.24	720

Note: MZ = monozygotic; DZ = dizygotic
Source: McGue et al. (1993).

commonly (and mistakenly) applied to individuals, despite the fact that, as we have emphasized, *heritability applies only to populations.* The heritability of intelligence, for example, is generally considered to be approximately 50%. This means that, *for the population studied,* roughly 50% of the variation in IQ scores is due to genetic differences among the members of the population. It does *not* mean that 50% of your IQ score is due to your genetic makeup and 50% is due to your experience.

Furthermore, *a heritability estimate applies only to a particular population living in a particular environment.* Consider the case of height. Research conducted almost exclusively with North Americans and Europeans—most of them adequately nourished—puts the heritability of height at around 90%. But what if some segment of this population had experienced a severe famine during childhood, while the rest remained well fed? Would the heritability estimate for height still be 90%? No—because the variability due to environmental factors (poor nutrition) would *increase* dramatically; therefore, the variability that could be attributed to genetic factors would *decrease* to the same degree.

Another common misperception is that heritability estimates are inherent to the trait in question and are not affected by the context in which the trait is measured. But *heritability estimates necessarily reflect the environments of the populations of individuals from which they are derived.* Consider hypothetical heritability estimates of reading ability for children in two different countries: Brazil, where there is considerable variability in educational opportunities, and Finland, where nearly all children have excellent educational opportunities (Bishop, 2015). The heritability estimate of reading ability for children in Brazil would likely be much lower than in Finland. For children in Brazil, individual differences in reading outcomes will be more heavily influenced by the environment because educational experiences are far more variable than in Finland. Thus, heritability estimates may appear larger within populations with more homogeneous environments.

A related observation is that even for the same trait in the same population, *heritability estimates can change as a function of developmental factors.* Sometimes these patterns are counterintuitive. For instance, as twins get older, the degree of variance in intelligence accounted for by their genetic similarity actually increases (Haworth et al., 2010). These results are consistent with the idea that people actively construct their own environment: the phenotype–environment correlation (Relation 4) discussed earlier. Younger children have little or no choice about their educational setting and opportunities; older children, teens, and young adults have increasingly greater choices with regard to their educational experiences (choosing more or less challenging courses of study, more or less academically oriented peer groups, and so on). Thus, older children have more opportunities than younger children to follow their own (genetically mediated) preferences for academic pursuits.

An additional frequently misunderstood point is that *high heritability does not imply immutability.* The fact that a trait is highly heritable does not mean that there is little point in trying to improve the course of development related to that trait. Thus, for example, the fact that the heritability estimate for IQ is relatively high does not mean that the intellectual performance of young children living in poverty cannot be improved by appropriate intervention efforts (see Chapter 8).

Finally, studies of heritability to date primarily include samples of WEIRD (White, Educated, Industrialized, Rich, and Democratic) participants. This sampling bias limits generalizability and is a major issue across most areas of psychological science. Lack of diversity in a subfield that is explicitly oriented around discovering genetic and environmental contributions to individual differences is particularly problematic, given that the generalizations being drawn are intended to account for the heritability of human traits irrespective of culture. The large sample sizes (often including thousands of individuals) that are characteristic of the molecular genetics designs described in the next section represent one approach to solving this problem. Other approaches involve the inclusion of a broader range of participants who are more representative of human experiences around the world, as well as appreciating differences in culture and context as they influence the generalizability of findings (e.g., Hruschka et al., 2018).

Molecular Genetics Research Designs

A basic tenet of behaviour genetics is that DNA variation (and protein coding based on DNA transcription) renders behavioural variation. Molecular behaviour geneticists examine specific DNA sequences to identify mechanisms that link genes and behaviour. Innovations in molecular genetic techniques are providing new approaches to the study of heritability that may address some of the shortcomings of classic behaviour genetics studies. While heritability estimates used to be limited to within-family comparisons (as illustrated in Table 3.1), DNA-based methods permit the analysis of genetic influences in large samples of unrelated individuals. These methods are particularly helpful for understanding genetically based developmental disabilities, which are often sufficiently rare that studies of unrelated individuals are necessary (see Box 3.2).

As discussed earlier in this chapter, most traits that are of particular interest to developmental scientists—intelligence, temperament, aggression, autism, and the like—are polygenic, that is, are affected by the combination of many genes. For this reason, *genome-wide association studies* (GWAS) are used in attempts to link multiple DNA segments (single-nucleotide polymorphisms, SNPs) with particular traits. On their own, individual regions of chromosomes do not correlate with traits; it takes a combination of many genes, each with a small effect, to render a heritable trait. For example, one recent study involving almost 80,000 adults identified 18 different genomic regions (mostly those expressed in brain tissue) implicated in individual differences in intelligence (Sniekers et al., 2017).

Another method, known as *genome-wide complex trait analysis* (GCTA), takes advantage of actual genetic resemblance across large groups of individuals, making it possible to tease apart aspects of genes and environment that are confounded within families. For instance, socioeconomic status (SES) is difficult to integrate into traditional measures of heritability because it is shared by twins within families. One study used GCTA to determine whether the effects of family SES on school achievement are genetically mediated—a question that could not be answered using traditional twin-based behaviour genetics methods (Krapohl & Plomin, 2016). Using a large representative sample of unrelated British schoolchildren, the researchers found that genetic factors explained a substantial portion of the variance in school achievement. More surprisingly, genetic factors accounted for fully half of the correlation between school achievement scores and family SES. Children's educational attainments and social advantage appear to share some of the same genetic roots.

GCTA has also allowed researchers to determine whether the same genes are implicated in measures of a particular trait across development. For example, recall from our earlier discussion that the heritability of intelligence tends to increase over age. Since this discovery was first made, researchers have wondered whether this change is due to gene–environment correlations, as discussed previously—namely, that with increasing age and independence, children can select their own

BOX 3.2 INDIVIDUAL DIFFERENCES Genetically Transmitted Developmental Disorders

Thousands of human disorders have genetic origins. These conditions follow the various inheritance patterns described earlier in this chapter, and they have been studied using both quantitative and molecular genetics methods.

Dominant–Recessive Patterns

Many genetic disorders are caused by a single gene and can occur when an individual has two recessive alleles for the condition (for example, PKU discussed on page 85) or one dominant gene, as in cases of Huntington disease (a fatal degenerative condition of the brain) and neurofibromatosis (a disorder in which nerve fibres develop tumors). A combination of severe speech, language, and motor difficulties that was first discovered in a particular family in England was traced to a single gene mutation (FOXP2) that acts in a dominant fashion (Graham & Fisher, 2015).

In some cases, a single gene can have both harmful and beneficial effects. Sickle-cell disease (described in Box 3.1), which affects millions of people throughout the world, is a painful recessive-gene disorder affecting individuals who are homozygous for this trait (inheriting two sickle-cell genes, one from each parent). Individuals who are heterozygous for this trait (carrying one normal and one sickle-cell gene) have some abnormality in their blood cells but usually experience no negative effects. Yet the presence of sickle cell in an individual's blood confers resistance to malaria, a benefit for those who live in regions of the world where malaria is common, like West Africa. Several recent studies have yielded promising results for gene therapy treatments to cure this devastating disease (Kolata, 2019).

Note that even when the root cause of a disorder is a single gene, it does not mean that one gene is responsible for all manifestations of the disorder. The gene starts a cascade of events, turning on and off multiple genes with effects on many different aspects of development.

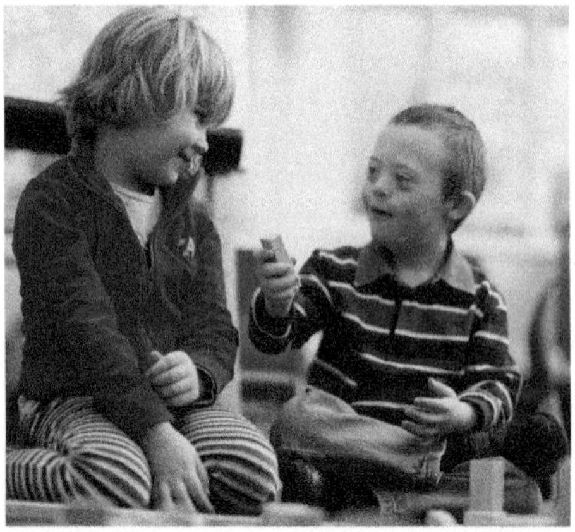

LAUREN SHEAR / SCIENCE SOURCE

One of the most common identifiable causes of intellectual disability is Down syndrome, which occurs in about 1 of every 750 live births in Canada. The risk increases dramatically with the age of the parents, especially the mother; the offspring of a 45-year-old expectant mother has a 1 in 30 chance of a Down syndrome diagnosis.

Sex-Linked Inheritance

Some single-gene conditions are carried on the X chromosome and are much more common in genetic males. (Genetic females inherit such conditions only if they inherit the culprit recessive alleles on both of their X chromosomes.) Sex-linked disorders range from relatively minor, such as male-pattern baldness and red–green colour blindness, to very serious, including hemophilia and Duchenne muscular dystrophy. Another sex-linked disorder is fragile-X syndrome, which involves mutations in the X chromosome and is the most common inherited form of intellectual disability.

Polygenic Inheritance

In contrast to single gene disorders, which require the presence of a single gene, many other disorders result from interactions between multiple genes, often in conjunction with environmental factors. Among the many diseases in this category are some forms of cancer and heart disease, type 1 and type 2 diabetes, and asthma. Psychiatric disorders (such as schizophrenia) and behaviour disorders (such as attention-deficit hyperactivity disorder and dyslexia) also involve numerous genes. Molecular genetics studies suggest that each gene has just a small effect on its own.

Chromosomal Anomalies

Some genetic disorders originate with errors in germ-cell division that result in a zygote with either more or fewer than the normal complement of chromosomes (*aneuploidy*). Down syndrome most commonly originates when the mother's egg cells do not divide properly, and an egg that is fertilized contains an extra copy of chromosome 21. The child pictured on the right in the accompanying photo shows some of the facial features common to individuals with Down syndrome, which is also marked by intellectual disability (ranging from mild to severe), a number of physical problems, and an easy temperament.

Gene Anomalies

Genetic disorders also result from extra, missing, or abnormal genes. One intriguing instance is Williams syndrome, which involves a variety of cognitive impairments, most noticeably in spatial and visual skills, and, to a lesser degree, in language ability. Individuals with Williams syndrome are also typically characterized by outgoing personalities and friendliness paired with anxiety and phobias. This condition has been traced to the deletion of a small section of approximately 25 genes on chromosome 7. Individuals with a smaller deletion show less impairment, suggesting a relationship between the number of deleted genes and the resulting phenotype (Karmiloff-Smith et al., 2012).

Unidentified Genetic Basis

For many developmental disorders, inheritance patterns clearly reveal genetic origins, though the specific genetic causes have yet to be identified. For example, consider *autism spectrum disorder* (ASD). A diagnosis of ASD is based on major impairments in social interaction and communication skills, as well as a limited set of interests or repetitive behaviours. ASD is highly heritable: identical twins are more than twice as likely as fraternal twins to share an autism diagnosis (Ronald & Hoekstra, 2011). Currently, there are between 500 and 1,000 candidate genes associated with ASD (Huguet, Benabou, & Bourgeron, 2016), and new genes continue to be identified through molecular genetics techniques (Yuen et al., 2017). Because autism is a complex and heterogeneous phenotype, differing greatly across individuals who share the same diagnosis, it is not surprising that its genetic roots are equally complex.

environments—or whether, instead, different genes affect intelligence at different times in development. By analyzing the DNA of a large sample of children from 7 to 12 years of age, researchers were able to uncover evidence of genetic stability: the same genes are implicated in heritable aspects of intelligence across this age span, with increasing effects of heritability across age (Trzaskowski et al., 2014).

In some cases, quantitative genetics and molecular genetics render divergent estimates of genetic contributions to individual differences. For example, GWAS and GCTA studies of traits such as reading ability suggest lower heritability than classic twin studies (Bishop, 2015). This puzzle of "missing heritability" suggests either that the twin studies overestimated heritability or that the molecular genetics studies underestimate it. Notably, the molecular genetics studies have vastly larger sample sizes than the twin studies. They also include more diverse participants by virtue of their larger sample sizes. Finally, twins may be particularly unrepresentative because, as discussed in Chapter 2, rates of twin births have increased due to the use of reproductive technologies like IVF, which are far more available to WEIRD families than to the rest of the globe. Future studies that include more representative samples may provide a deeper understanding of the degree to which individual differences in traits are heritable.

Environmental Effects

Every examination of genetic contributions to behaviour and development is also necessarily a study of environmental influences: estimating heritability automatically estimates the proportion of variance not attributable to genes. The most obvious source of shared environment is growing up in the same family. For example, substantial shared-environmental influence has been inferred for positive emotion in infancy because fraternal and identical twins were equally similar in measures of positive affect (Planalp et al., 2017).

Importantly, though, children in the same family do not necessarily share the same environment (Plomin et al., 2016). This may be due to aspects of the family structure. For instance, birth order may result in quite different experiences for siblings. The oldest child in a large family may have been reared by young, energetic, but inexperienced parents, whereas that child's much younger sibling will be parented by older and more sedentary, but more knowledgeable, individuals who are likely to have more resources available than they did as first-time parents. In addition, as discussed in Chapter 1, siblings may experience their parents' behaviour toward them differently (the "Mom always loved you best" syndrome).

Outside the family, siblings can also have highly divergent experiences. Highly active siblings who both like physical challenges and thrills will have very different experiences if one takes up rock climbing while the other hangs out with delinquent peers. Idiosyncratic life events—suffering a serious accident, having an inspiring teacher, being bullied on the playground—can contribute further to the development of individual differences among siblings. Much like the action of polygenic inheritance patterns, in which many genes of small effect work together to influence development, the effects of the environment are likely due to many experiences of small effect working together.

A final observation is that environments are much harder for researchers to measure than genes. Complex phenotypes of interest to developmental scientists (cognitive abilities, personality, psychopathology) are also notoriously difficult to assess in the context of large-scale experiments. In the next section, we will see how a better understanding of brain development is helping to answer some of these questions.

neurons cells that are specialized for sending and receiving messages between the brain and all parts of the body, as well as within the brain itself

cell body a component of the neuron that contains the basic biological material that keeps the neuron functioning

REVIEW QUESTIONS

A number of factors hinder our ability to study and understand the heritability of a given trait, including the fact that heritability is affected by the context in which it is measured. What are some other factors, and how do molecular genetics studies, such as GWAS and GCTA, address them? What limitations do these studies face? ■

Brain Development

The collaboration between nature and nurture takes centre stage in the development of the brain and nervous system.

The Neuron

The basic units of the brain's remarkably powerful informational system are its more than 100 billion **neurons** (depicted in Figure 3.6), which constitute the gray matter of the brain. Each neuron has three main components: (1) a **cell body,**

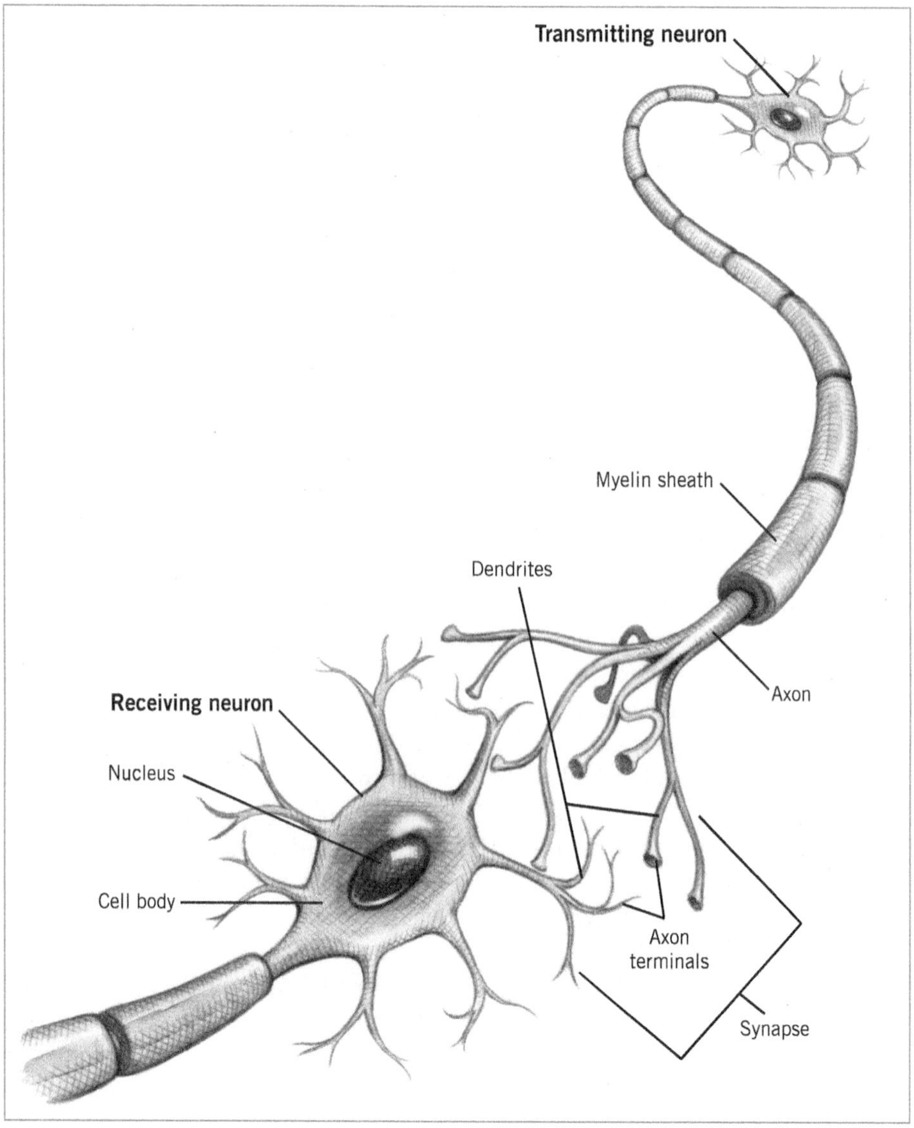

FIGURE 3.6 The neuron The cell body manufactures proteins and enzymes, which support cell functioning, as well as the chemical substances called neurotransmitters, which facilitate communication among neurons. The axon is the long shaft that conducts electrical impulses away from the cell body. Many axons are covered with a myelin sheath, which enhances the speed and efficiency with which signals travel along the axon. Branches at the end of the axon have terminals that release neurotransmitters into the synapses—the small spaces between the axon terminals of one neuron and the dendrites or cell body of another. The dendrites conduct impulses toward the cell body. An axon can have synapses with thousands of other neurons.

which contains the basic biological material that keeps the neuron functioning; (2) **dendrites**, fibres that receive input from other cells and conduct it toward the cell body in the form of electrical impulses; and (3) an **axon**, a fibre (anywhere from a few micrometres to more than a metre in length) that conducts electrical signals away from the cell body to connections with other neurons.

Neurons communicate at **synapses**, microscopic junctions between the axon terminal of one neuron and the dendritic branches of another. Electrical and chemical messages cross the synapses and cause the receiving neurons either to fire, sending a signal on to other neurons, or to be inhibited from firing. There are hundreds of trillions of synapses in the human brain, with some neurons having as many as 15,000 synaptic connections with other neurons.

Glial cells are another essential component of the brain, equal in numbers to neurons (von Bartheld, Bahney, & Herculano-Houzel, 2016). Glial cells perform a variety of critical functions, including the formation of a **myelin sheath** around axons, which increases the speed and efficiency of information transmission. Glial cells also function as neural stem and progenitor cells during prenatal brain development, and some glial cells continue to do so into adulthood. When the brain is injured, some glial cells react by rapidly increasing in numbers, protecting the brain and potentially aiding in regeneration.

dendrites neural fibres that receive input from other cells and conduct it toward the cell body in the form of electrical impulses

axons neural fibres that conduct electrical signals away from the cell body to connections with other neurons

synapses microscopic junctions between the axon terminal of one neuron and the dendritic branches or cell body of another

glial cells cells in the brain that provide a variety of critical supportive functions

myelin sheath a fatty sheath that forms around certain axons in the body and increases the speed and efficiency of information transmission

cerebral cortex the "gray matter" of the brain, consisting of four distinct lobes

The Cortex

The **cerebral cortex** constitutes 80% of the human brain, a much greater proportion than in other species. The folds and fissures visible in Figure 3.7 form as the brain grows within the confined space of the skull; these convolutions make it possible to pack more cortex into the limited space. The parts of the human cortex that are most enlarged compared with other species are also those that grow the most as children develop.

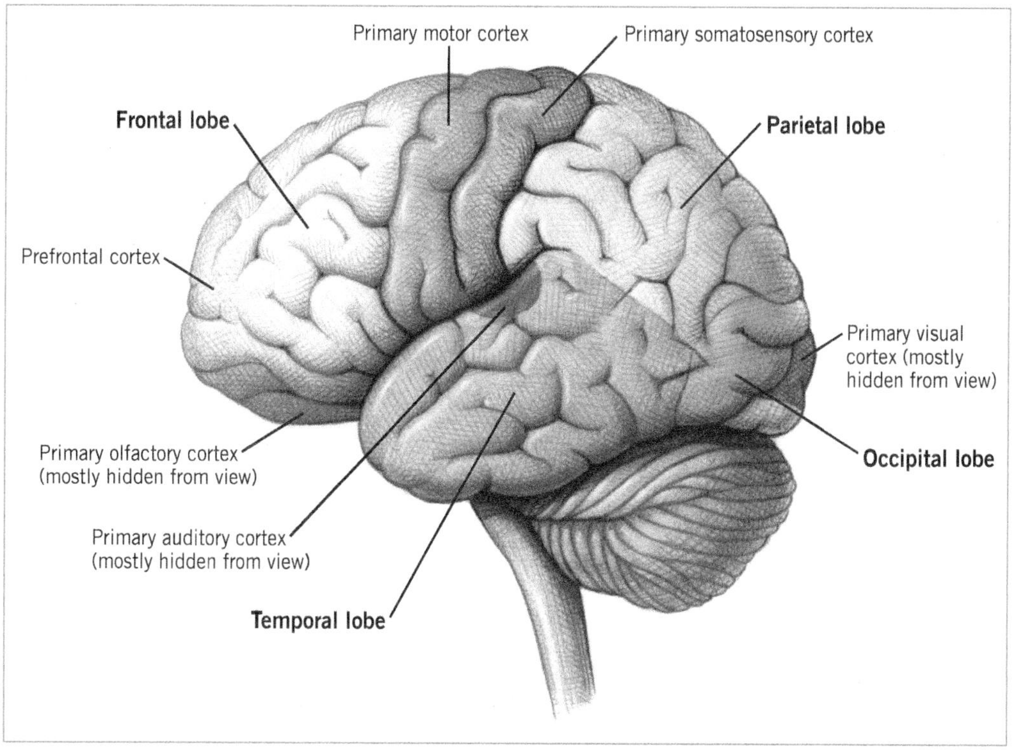

FIGURE 3.7 The human cerebral cortex This view of the left hemisphere of an adult brain shows the four major cortical regions—known as the lobes—which are divided from one another by deep fissures. Each of the primary sensory areas receives information from a particular sensory system, and the primary motor cortex controls the body's muscles. Information from multiple sensory areas is processed in association areas.

occipital lobe major area of the cortex that is primarily involved in processing visual information

temporal lobe major area of the cortex that is associated with speech and language, music, and emotional information

parietal lobe major area of the cortex that is associated with spatial processing and sensory information integration

frontal lobe major area of the cortex that is associated with working memory and cognitive control

association areas parts of the brain that lie between the major sensory and motor areas and that process and integrate input from those areas

cerebral hemispheres the two halves of the cortex

corpus callosum a dense tract of nerve fibres that enable the two hemispheres of the brain to communicate

cerebral lateralization the specialization of the hemispheres of the brain for different modes of processing

neurogenesis the proliferation of neurons through cell division

The cortex includes four lobes, each associated with a specific set of behavioural characteristics. Starting at the back of the brain, the **occipital lobe** is primarily involved in processing visual information. The **temporal lobe** is associated with speech and language, and the processing of emotion and auditory information. The **parietal lobe** engages in spatial processing and is also involved in the integration of information from different sensory modalities. The **frontal lobe**, the brain's "executive," is involved in cognitive control, including working memory, planning, decision making, and inhibitory control. Information from multiple sensory systems is processed and integrated in the **association areas** that lie in between the major sensory and motor areas. Complex mental functions are mediated by multiple areas of the brain, with an extraordinary degree of interactivity both within and across brain regions. (Box 3.3 examines some of the techniques that developmental scientists use to study brain functioning.)

The cortex is divided into two **cerebral hemispheres**. For the most part, sensory input from one side of the body goes to the opposite side of the brain, and the motor areas of the cortex control movements of the opposite side of the body. The hemispheres communicate with each other primarily by way of the **corpus callosum**, a dense tract of connective nerve fibres between the two hemispheres.

The hemispheres are specialized for different modes of processing, a phenomenon referred to as **cerebral lateralization**. Lateralization emerges early in human development. For example, young infants use their right hemispheres more than their left hemispheres to process faces (Adibpour, Dubois, & Dehaene-Lambertz, 2018), and their left hemispheres more than their right hemispheres to process most aspects of speech (e.g., Dehaene-Lambertz, 2017). However, contrary to popular belief, people are not left brained or right brained; individuals do not tend to have a general preference to use one hemisphere over the other (e.g., Nielsen et al., 2013).

Brain Development: Prenatal, Infants, and Toddlers

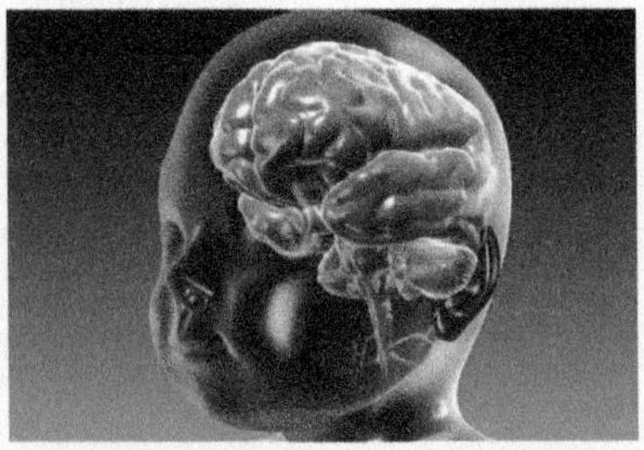

Developmental Processes

How does the incredibly complex structure of the human brain develop? Once again, we see a rich partnership between nature and nurture.

Neurogenesis and Neuron Development

Neurogenesis, the proliferation of neurons through cell division, begins 42 days after conception (in humans) and is virtually complete by the midway point of gestation (Stiles & Jernigan, 2010). Thus, most of the roughly 100 billion neurons you currently possess have been with you since before you were born. Notably, however, humans do continue to generate new neurons throughout life, particularly in the hippocampus—a brain area that is heavily involved in memory processes (Kempermann et al., 2018). Adult neurogenesis is affected by environmental factors: it increases under rewarding conditions and decreases in threatening environments (e.g., Opendak & Gould, 2015). As you will see, this is one of several ways in which experiences sculpt the brain.

After their "birth," neurons migrate to their ultimate destinations—typically outwards from the centre of the brain toward the developing neocortex. Some neurons are pushed along passively by the newer cells formed after them, whereas others actively propel themselves toward their ultimate location. Early in gestation, the brain is very small, so the distances travelled are quite short. But as the brain grows, neurons require guides. This is one of the many functions of glial cells, some of which provide scaffolding for neurons as they find their destinations.

BOX 3.3 A CLOSER LOOK Mapping the Mind

Developmental scientists employ a variety of techniques to investigate the relationships between brain areas and specific behaviours, thoughts, and feelings, as well as how brain functions change with age. Here, we provide examples of some of the techniques most often used to map the mind and its workings in children.

Electrophysiological Recording

Electrical recordings obtained through the scalp are noninvasive and can be used successfully even with very young infants. *Electroencephalographic* (EEG) recordings of electrical activity generated by neurons are used to study the time course of neural events and brain/behaviour relationships. *Event-related potentials* (ERPs) detect changes in the brain's electrical activity that occur in response to the presentation of a particular stimulus. *Magnetoencephalography* (MEG) detects magnetic fields generated by electrical currents in the brain. Unlike EEG, MEG can be used to localize the origin of the electrical signals within the brain, as well as their time course. In a recent MEG study, researchers recorded electrical signals from 7-month-olds as they were touched on either the hand or foot, and as they watched someone else being touched on the hand or foot (Meltzoff et al., 2018). The corresponding areas of somatosensory cortex were activated both when infants were touched and when they observed touch, suggesting that the developing brain already links tactile stimulation and visual perception.

Functional Magnetic Resonance Imaging (fMRI)

fMRI studies use a powerful electromagnet to detect fluctuations in cerebral blood flow in different areas of the brain. (fMRI is distinct from structural MRI, which essentially takes a snapshot of the brain.) Participants must be able to tolerate the noise and close confinement of an MRI machine and must also be able to remain very still. Thus, researchers often include practice sessions in a mock scanner to help young children acclimate to the MRI environment, as illustrated in the accompanying photograph. When fMRI studies involve infant participants, the infants usually need to be asleep (otherwise they move too much), which limits the kinds of research questions that can be investigated with this method (Ellis & Turk-Browne, 2018). However, one recent study did successfully use fMRI to test awake infants on a visual processing task (Deen et al., 2017).

Two applications of fMRI that have become increasingly prominent in developmental studies are *diffusion tensor imaging* (DTI) and *resting-state functional magnetic resonance imaging* (rs-fMRI). These methods allow researchers to study how brain networks develop. DTI is a variant of conventional MRI that uses the rate of water diffusion to model 3-D spatial location. This technique has been used to model white-matter development and myelination over the course of early postnatal development. DTI is also being used to investigate atypical patterns of brain connectivity in populations including preterm infants and autistic toddlers (Dimond et al., 2019; Fingher et al., 2017; Qiu, Mori, & Miller, 2015). Resting-state fMRI measures brain activity in the absence of any external stimuli or tasks, and it is appropriate for use with sleeping infants. Resting-state networks emerge early in development—some sensory networks are evident in full-term newborns, and others emerge over the first year of postnatal life (e.g., Gilmore, Knickmeyer, & Gao, 2018).

▶ Event-Related Potential Research

Near-infrared spectroscopy

Near-infrared spectroscopy (NIRS) is an optical imaging technique that measures neural activity by detecting metabolic changes that lead to differential absorption of infrared light in brain tissue. The infrared light is transmitted to the brain, and its absorption is detected by means of an optical-fibre skullcap or headband. Because NIRS is silent, noninvasive, and does not require head stabilization, it is particularly promising for research with infants and young children. One exciting use of this technology involved simultaneous recording from adult–infant pairs to examine coupling of their brain responses, as shown in the photo (Piazza et al., 2019). The results revealed that the brain responses of the infant and adult were correlated when the two were playing together, and the responses were uncorrelated when participants were each interacting with other adults (in the same room). This study takes a major step forward in its use of brain imaging to understand naturalistic interactions between adults and infants.

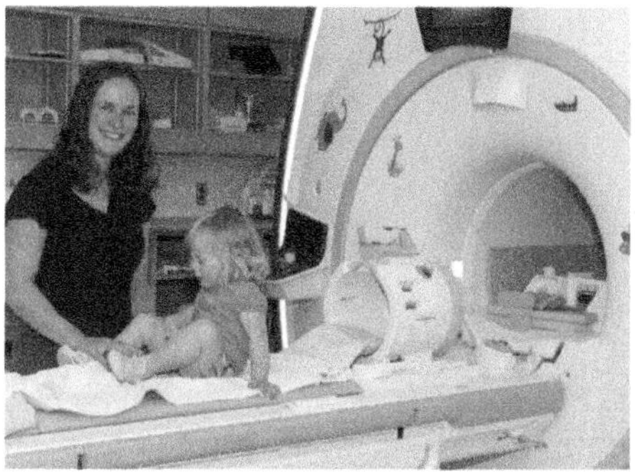

CATHERINE LEBEL

After a few practice sessions using a mock scanner, this young child is now ready for an actual MRI scan at the Alberta Children's Hospital.

Once neurons reach their destination, they first grow an axon and then a "bush" of dendrites (refer back to Figure 3.6). Thereafter, they take on the specific structural and functional characteristics of the different structures of the brain. Axons elongate as they grow toward their targets. The main change in dendrites is **arborization**—an enormous increase in the size and complexity of the dendritic "tree" that results from growth, branching, and the formation of **spines** on the branches. Arborization increases the dendrites' capacity to form connections with other neurons, as illustrated in Figure 3.8. As arborization allows neurons to grow in complexity over the first several years of postnatal life, the cortex grows in surface area and the layers of the cortex become thicker (e.g., Gilmore, Knickmeyer, & Gao, 2018).

Myelination, the formation of the insulating myelin sheath around some axons, begins prenatally and continues into early adulthood. The myelinated portions of

arborization formation of new dendritic trees and branches

spines formations on the dendrites of neurons that increase the dendrites' capacity to form connections with other neurons

myelination the formation of myelin (a fatty sheath) around the axons of neurons that speeds and increases information-processing abilities

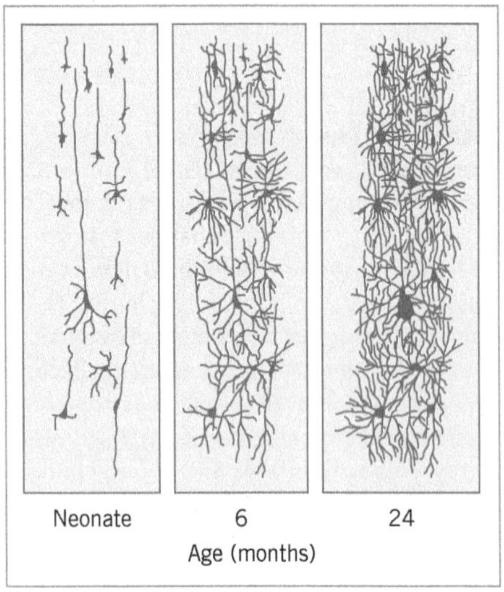

FIGURE 3.8 **Arborization** Arborization increases significantly in the first months and years of postnatal life, as shown in these images that illustrate the dendritic growth and branching from birth through 24 months. (Information from Gilmore, Knickmeyer, & Gao, 2018)

Brain Development: Myelination

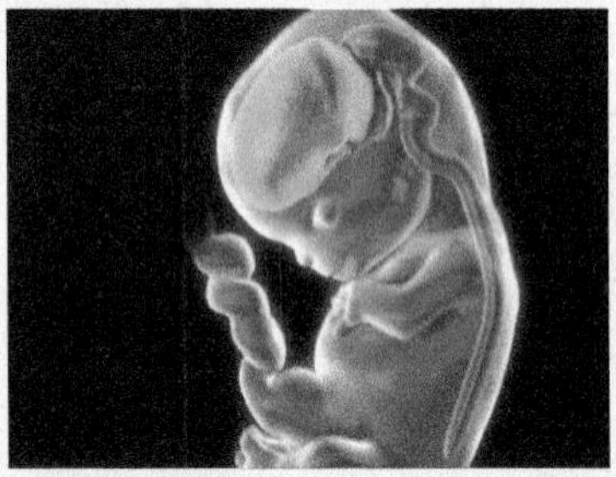

axons are white, leading to the term *white matter*, and lie below the *gray matter* (cell bodies) at the surface of the cortex. Myelination begins deep in the brain and moves upward and outward into the cortex. This process occurs rapidly for the first few months after birth, slows somewhat during toddlerhood, and continues slowly into young adulthood (e.g., Dubois et al., 2014). The various cortical areas become myelinated at very different rates, contributing to the different rates of maturation of different brain areas; for example, the sensory areas in the back of the brain mature much sooner than the executive function areas in the front of the brain, as shown in Figure 3.9.

Synaptogenesis

The extraordinary growth of axonal and dendritic fibres results in a wildly exuberant generation of neuronal connections. Each neuron forms synapses with thousands of others in a process called **synaptogenesis**, resulting in the formation of the trillions of connections referred to earlier. Figure 3.10 shows the course of synaptogenesis in the cortex over time. As you can see, it begins prenatally and proceeds very rapidly both before birth and for some time afterward. Note that both the timing and rate of synapse production vary for different cortical areas; synapse generation is complete much earlier in sensorimotor cortex, for example, than in the frontal area. As with myelination, the differential timing of synapse generation across areas of the brain likely contributes to the developmental timing of the onset of various abilities and behaviours.

Synapse Elimination

The explosive generation of neurons and synapses during synaptogenesis results in many more neural connections than any one brain can use. This overabundance of synapses includes an excess of connections between different parts of the brain. Approximately 40% of this great synaptic superfluity is eliminated through **synaptic pruning**, which occurs at different times in different areas of the brain, as shown in Figure 3.10.

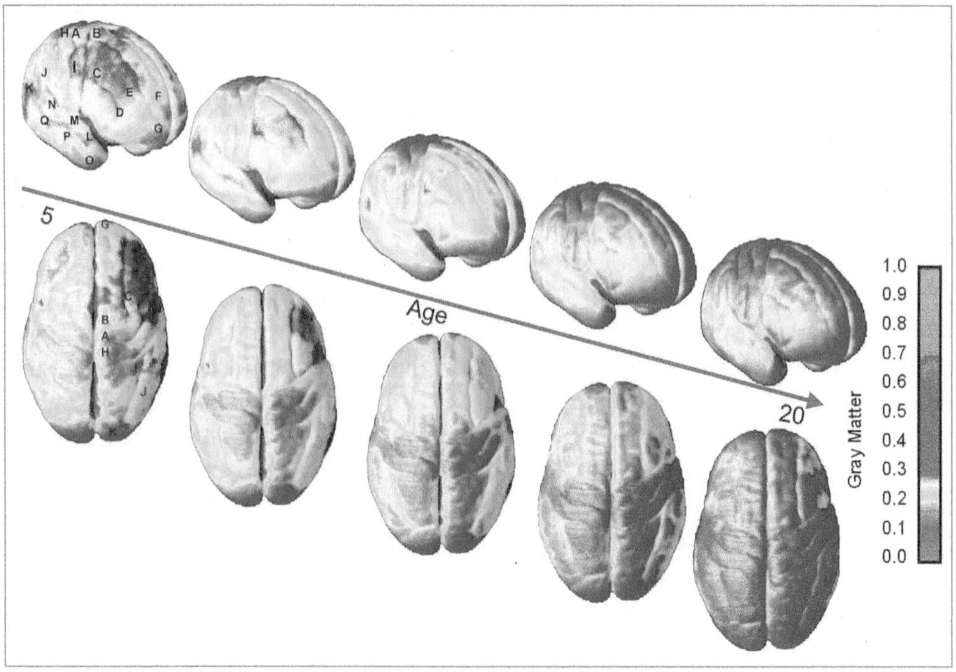

FIGURE 3.9 **Brain maturation** These views of the right side and top of the brain of 5- to 20-year-olds illustrate maturation over the surface of the cortex. The averaged MRI images come from participants whose brains were scanned repeatedly at 2-year intervals. The bluer the image, the more mature that part of the cortex is (i.e., the more gray matter has been replaced with white matter). Notice that the parts of the cortex associated with more basic functions (i.e., the sensory and motor areas toward the back) mature earlier than the areas involved in higher functions (i.e., attention, executive functioning). Notice particularly that the frontal areas, involved in executive functioning, approach maturity only in early adulthood. [Gogtay et al. (2004) "Dynamic Mapping of human cortical development during childhood and early adulthood," PNAS 101(21): 8174–8179. Copyright 2004 National Academy of Sciences, U.S.A.]

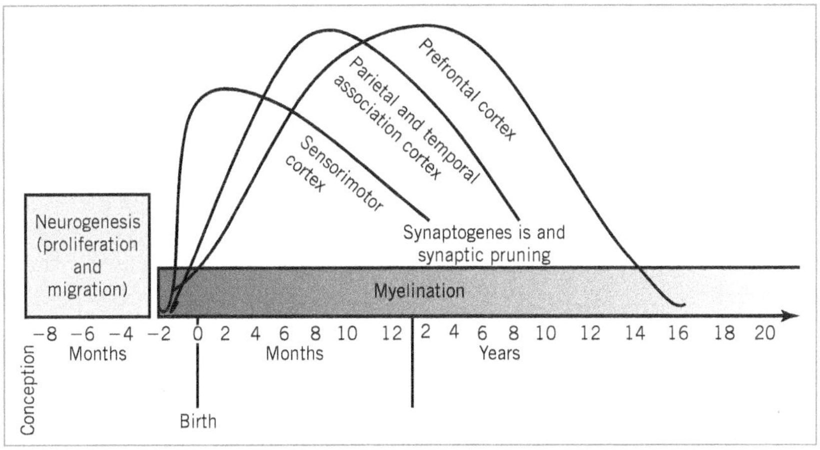

FIGURE 3.10 Neurogenesis and synapse production and elimination Synaptogenesis begins prior to birth and continues at a rapid pace for several years after, during which time myelination also occurs. Synaptogenesis (indicated by the rising curve) and synaptic pruning (indicated by the falling curve) take place at different rates and times for the various brain regions, influenced by post-natal experience. (Information from Casey et al., 2005)

The brain undergoes waves of synaptogenesis and synaptic pruning in the first months and years of life, but the brain also undergoes substantial changes during adolescence (Giedd et al., 1999; Gogtay, Giedd et al., 2004). This dramatic change is evident from measures of cortical thickness, which suggest that the outer layers of the cortex shrink at a faster rate during adolescence than during either childhood or early adulthood (Whitaker et al., 2016). The last area of the cortex to mature is the dorsolateral prefrontal cortex, which is vital for regulating attention, controlling impulses, foreseeing consequences, setting priorities, and other executive functions (refer back to Figure 3.9). It does not reach adult dimensions until after the age of 20, and synaptic pruning continues until individuals are in their 30s (Petanjek et al., 2011).

synaptogenesis the process by which neurons form synapses with other neurons, resulting in trillions of connections

synaptic pruning the normal developmental process through which synapses that are rarely activated are eliminated

Atypical patterns of pruning have been implicated in two developmental disorders: autism spectrum disorder (ASD) and schizophrenia. Young children with ASD have larger brains than do children with typical development, and studies suggest that children and adults with ASD have greater synaptic densities in some areas of their brains (e.g., Neniskyte & Gross, 2017). There is also evidence for increased cortical thickness in autistic children relative to neurotypical children, possibly indicating reduced or delayed rates of synaptic pruning (Khundrakpam et al., 2017).

Wiring abnormalities in schizophrenia follow a different trajectory and suggest excessive pruning in adolescence (Neniskyte & Gross, 2017; Sekar et al., 2016). As discussed earlier, there is typically a burst of synaptic pruning around adolescence, especially around the prefrontal cortex. The timing of the onset of schizophrenic symptoms in adolescence and young adulthood may be linked to aberrant pruning around puberty.

The Importance of Experience

What factors determine which of the brain's excess synapses will be pruned and which maintained? Experience plays a central role in what is essentially a case of "use it or lose it." The more often a synapse is activated, the stronger the connection between the neurons involved: in short, neurons that fire together wire together (Hebb, 1949). Conversely, when a synapse is rarely active, it is likely to disappear: the axon of one neuron withdraws and the dendritic spine of the other is pruned away.

BRIAN M. SMITH

Canadian psychologist Donald O. Hebb is considered the father of neuropsychology. Hebb's groundbreaking work more than 70 years ago continues to guide our understanding of neural networks today.

The process of massive overproduction of synapses, followed by selective pruning, is the brain's answer to a fundamental tension between rigidity and

plasticity the capacity of the brain to be affected by experience

experience-expectant plasticity the process through which the normal wiring of the brain occurs in part as a result of species-typical experiences

flexibility. Because of the brain's capacity to be molded or changed by experience, referred to as **plasticity**, less information needs to be encoded in the genes. This evolutionary economizing may, in fact, be a necessity: the number of genes involved in the formation and functioning of the human nervous system is enough to specify only a very small fraction of the normal complement of neurons and neural connections. In addition, if brain structures were entirely hard-wired, organisms would be unable to adapt to their environments.

The plastic brain can recover from some forms of injury because other brain areas can take over the function that would have been performed by the damaged area. Because children's brains are more plastic than adults' brains, children who suffer from brain damage have a better chance of recovering lost function than do adults who suffer similar damage. For example, young children who suffer damage to the language areas of the cortex generally recover most, if not all, of their language functions because other areas of the immature brain can take over those functions. In contrast, adults who sustain the same type of brain damage undergo minimal reorganization of language functions and may have a permanent loss in the ability to comprehend or produce speech.

The collaboration between nature and nurture in building the brain occurs differently for two kinds of plasticity. *Experience-expectant plasticity* involves the general experiences that almost all infants have just by virtue of being human. *Experience-dependent plasticity* involves specific, idiosyncratic experiences that children have as a result of their particular life circumstances—such as growing up in Canada or in the Amazon rain forest, experiencing frequent cuddling or abuse, and so on.

Experience-Expectant Processes

The role of species-typical experience in shaping brain development is known as **experience-expectant plasticity** (Greenough, Black, & Wallace, 1987). Each species evolves in a particular environmental niche, with a predictable array of experiences available to all typically developing members of that species. The specific circumstances and experiences under which a species evolves impacts how their brain development unfolds. For example, throughout human evolution, infants experienced patterned visual stimulation, voices and other sounds, movement and manipulation, and so forth. The human brain can thus "expect" that input from these reliable experiences will be available to fine-tune its circuitry—hence the term "experience-expectant" plasticity.

The benefit of experience-expectant plasticity is that, because experience helps shape the brain, fewer genes need to be dedicated to normal development. That is, less information needs to be pre-installed in the brain. The downside is heightened *vulnerability.* If for some reason the experience that the developing brain "expects" does not occur, due to inadequate stimulation or impaired sensory receptors, development may be compromised. This phenomenon is exemplified by the classic work of Hubel & Wiesel, who deprived kittens of light exposure in one of their eyes (Hubel & Wiesel, 1962, 1970; Wiesel & Hubel, 1963). When the eye was later reopened, it was functionally blind; the cells that would have normally responded to it reorganized, responding instead to the eye that had continued to receive visual input.

A human analogy to Hubel & Wiesel's kittens experiment comes from children who are born with cataracts that obscure their vision in both eyes. Research carried out at McMaster University in Hamilton demonstrated that the longer a cataract remains in place after birth, the more impaired the child's visual acuity will be once it is removed. Dramatic improvement typically follows early removal of the cataracts, although some aspects of visual processing (especially of faces) remain affected even into adulthood (de Heering & Maurer, 2014). Rather remarkably, these impairments appear to be due to recruitment of areas of visual cortex for use by the auditory system (Collignon et al., 2015). Deprived of visual input, the visual cortices of young infants with cataracts reorganize to process auditory information instead.

Similar evidence comes from research at McGill University focused on people who are born deaf, for whom brain regions typically linked to auditory processing are co-opted by visual processing (e.g., Shiell, Champoux, & Zatorre, 2016; Shiell & Zatorre, 2016). *Cross-modal reorganization* thus operates in both directions: individuals with early cataracts (or who are born blind) experience auditory takeover of brain areas that are typically part of the visual system, whereas individuals who are born deaf experience visual takeover of brain areas that are typically part of the auditory system. Reiterating the concept of experience-expectant plasticity, areas of the brain that typically specialize in auditory or visual information behave in an experience-expectant manner. Absent the experiences that are species-typical (visual and/or auditory input), the brain reorganizes.

Sensitive periods As in many other developmental processes, timing is a key element in experience-expectant plasticity. During sensitive periods, the human brain is especially sensitive to specific external stimuli. It is as though a window were temporarily opened, inviting environmental input to help organize the brain. Gradually, the window closes. The neural organization that occurs (or does not occur) during sensitive periods is typically irreversible.

Hubel and Wiesel's work with kittens provides an example of sensitive periods for vision. When adult cats are deprived of visual input in one eye, there are no long-term effects on the brain, unlike the effects on kittens. This finding suggests a sensitive period for the organization of the visual system in the brain. Sensitive periods are not limited to perceptual development. As discussed in Box 1.1, the extreme deprivation that the Romanian orphans suffered early in life, when children normally experience a wealth of social and other environmental stimulation, is considered by some to be an example of a sensitive-period effect. Adolescence, a time of rapid changes in the brain, may be a sensitive period for a range of cognitive and social processes (Blakemore & Mills, 2014; Fuhrmann, Knoll, & Blakemore, 2015). In Chapter 6, we will discuss another sensitive period in detail: the timing for optimal language learning.

Experience-Dependent Processes

The brain is also sculpted by the specific experiences that each individual has, distinct from those shared by the rest of the species. This process is referred to as **experience-dependent plasticity**. Neural connections are created and reorganized constantly, throughout an individual's life, as a function of that individual's idiosyncratic experiences.

Research on experience-dependent plasticity has largely focused on nonhuman animals because their environments can be readily manipulated. One such method involves comparisons between animals reared in complex environments full of objects to explore versus animals reared in bare laboratory cages. The brains of rats (and cats and monkeys) that grow up in richer environments have more dendritic spines on their cortical neurons, more synapses per neuron, and more synapses overall, as well as a generally thicker cortex and more of the supportive tissues (e.g., blood vessels and glial cells) that maximize neuronal and synaptic function. All this

experience-dependent plasticity the process through which neural connections are created and reorganized throughout life as a function of an individual's experiences

SHAWNA LAUFER, THE RAT WHISPERER (WWW.RATWHISPERER.NET)

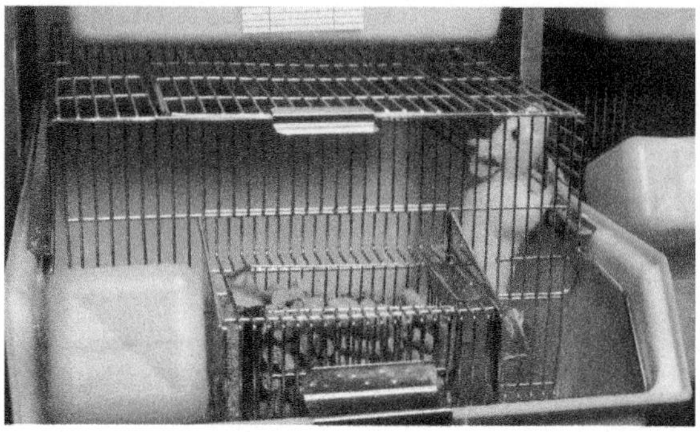

ENVIRONMENT IMAGES/UIG/GETTY IMAGES

As a result of growing up in a complex environment full of stimulating objects to explore and challenges to master, the brains of the rats in the photo on the left will contain more synapses than if they had been reared in unstimulating laboratory cages (right photo).

extra hardware seems to have a payoff: rats (and other animals) reared in a complex environment (which is more akin to their natural environment) perform better in a variety of learning tasks than do their counterparts raised in bare cages (e.g., Sale, Berardi, & Maffei, 2009). We see an analogy with human brain development in the effects of poverty on the brain, as discussed in Box 3.4 in the next section.

Training studies reveal how highly specific experiences can shape the brain. Research with musicians provides a "natural experiment" in which some body parts are trained more intensely than others. The resulting evidence of plasticity mirrors nonhuman animal studies. For example, adults who play wind instruments (such as trumpets and French horns) have thicker lip-related cortical areas than adults who do not play wind instruments (Choi et al., 2015). After years of practice, more cortical cells were devoted to controlling the lips of these skilled instrumentalists.

REVIEW QUESTION

The brain is shaped by experience-expectant plasticity and experience-dependent plasticity. How might the existence of sensitive periods, which require certain experiences for normal brain development, influence research and programs aimed at promoting child welfare? ■

The Body: Physical Growth and Development

Everything we think, feel, say, and do involves our physical selves, and changes in the body lead to changes in brain and behaviour. In this section, we overview key aspects of physical growth. Nutritional behaviour, a vital aspect of physical development, is featured as we consider the regulation of eating. We concentrate particularly on one of the consequences of poor regulation—obesity. Finally, we focus on the opposite problem—undernutrition. We end with a discussion of vaccines and their role in healthy development.

Physical Development in Infancy and Toddlerhood

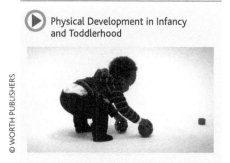

© WORTH PUBLISHERS

Growth and Maturation

Between birth and age 20, humans become 15 to 20 times heavier and 3 times taller. The proportion of body fat is highest in infancy, gradually declining thereafter until about 6 to 8 years of age. Body growth is uneven over time, most rapid in the first 2 years and in early adolescence. Growth is also uneven across the body. Following the principle of cephalocaudal development described in Chapter 2, the head region is initially relatively large—fully 50% of body length at 2 months of age, but only 10% of body length in adulthood.

Infants' large heads, high foreheads, and large eyes are characteristic not just of baby humans, but of infants across species, as shown in the photo. The ethologist Konrad Lorenz argued that these "cuteness" traits exist to increase parents' motivation to care for their offspring (Lorenz, 1971). And indeed, studies suggest that the reward circuitry in human adults' brains is activated by infant cuteness traits (Glocker et al., 2009).

MIGUEL SANZ/GETTY IMAGES

Across species, infants display disproportionately large heads, high foreheads, and large eyes, as seen in this photo of a human infant and puppy.

Variability

There is great variability across individuals in all aspects of physical development, due to both genetic and environmental factors. Genes affect growth and sexual maturation in large part by influencing the production of hormones, especially growth hormone (secreted by the pituitary gland) and thyroxine (released by the thyroid gland). The influence of environmental factors is particularly evident in **secular trends**, marked changes in physical development that have occurred over generations. In contemporary industrialized nations, adults are several inches taller than their great-grandparents were. This change is assumed to have resulted primarily from improvements in nutrition and general health. Conversely, children raised in institutions have a higher risk of growth impairment, likely due to both stress and poor nutrition (Johnson & Gunnar, 2011). For example, when children from Romanian orphanages arrived in their adoptive homes in Canada, their average weight was below the 4th percentile. About 8 years after adoption into their Canadian homes, these children had caught up considerably in growth. At 10½ years of age, the Romanian adoptees' average weight was around the 60th percentile and was no longer significantly different from that of Canadian-born, never-adopted children (Le Mare & Audet, 2006).

secular trends marked changes in physical development that have occurred over generations

Another secular trend that has emerged over the past few decades is that girls, on average, begin menstruating a few years earlier than their ancestors. This is particularly true of girls growing up in low-SES families. For example, a recent British study found that 11-year-old girls living in poverty were twice as likely as their peers in wealthy households to have begun menstruating (Kelly et al., 2017). Obesity and stress are both predictors of early menstruation.

Nutritional Behaviour

The health of our bodies depends on what we put into them. The development of nutritional behaviour is a crucial aspect of child development from infancy onward.

Infant Feeding

Throughout nearly the entire history of the human species, the only or primary source of nourishment for infants was breast milk. It is naturally free of bacteria, strengthens the infant's immune system, and contains the mother's antibodies against infectious agents the baby is likely to encounter. Breast-feeding is also good for mothers' health. Among other benefits, women who breast-feed their babies have lower risks of breast and ovarian cancer.

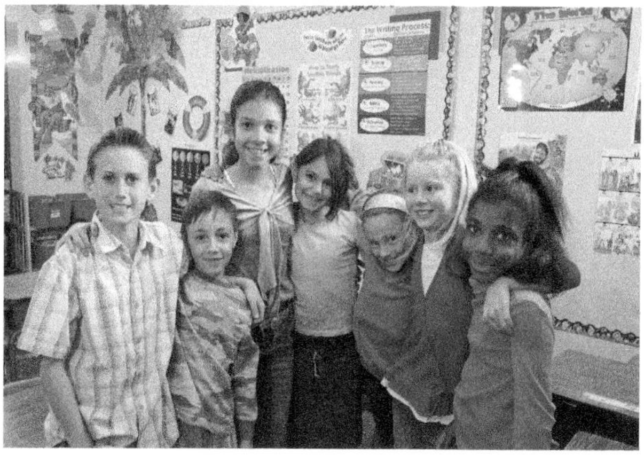

MYRLEEN PEARSON/ALAMY

A variety of genetic and environmental factors contribute to the wide variety of heights among these children, despite the fact that they are roughly the same age.

There have also been suggestions in the literature that the fatty acids in breast milk have a positive effect on cognitive development. A number of studies indicate higher IQ scores for children and adults who were breast-fed as infants, even after controlling for parental IQ (for review, see Kanazawa, 2015; Nisbett et al., 2012). These effects may be mediated by increased myelination in breast-fed infants, which, as discussed earlier in this chapter, increases efficiency of information transmission in the nervous system (Deoni et al., 2018). Other studies suggest that while there are long-term cognitive benefits of breast-feeding, they are relatively minor (e.g., Boutwell, Young, & Meldrum, 2018). Research findings in this area can be difficult to interpret because breast-feeding is linked with SES and household food insecurity in Canada (Orr et al., 2018), and SES is also correlated with IQ.

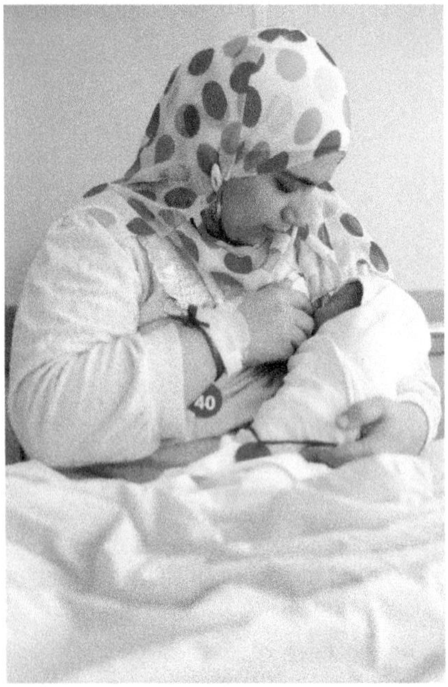

ZOUZOU/SHUTTERSTOCK

By breast-feeding her infant, this mother is providing her baby with many benefits that are not available in formula.

In spite of the well-established nutritional superiority of breast milk, as well as the fact that it is free, many infants around the world are formula-fed. Public health efforts focus on educating parents about the benefits of breast milk and encouraging employers to provide private space for working mothers to pump breast milk. Since these efforts were initiated, the number of Canadian newborns who are fed breast milk has increased annually and, by 2017, had risen to 90% of neonates (Statistics Canada, n.d.a). However, this good nutritional start is difficult for parents to maintain; by 6 months of age, only 32% of infants in Canada are exclusively breast-fed.

These rates are high relative to some other wealthy countries like Great Britain, where only 43% of 1-month-olds were breast-fed in 2017 (Public Health England, 2018). But they are low in comparison to poorer countries in sub-Saharan Africa, South America, and Southeast Asia, where the majority of infants are breast-fed until at least 1 year of age (Victora et al., 2016). In the absence of breast-feeding, infant formula is often mixed with polluted water in unsanitary containers. Breast-feeding is thus especially important in promoting positive health outcomes in countries with unsafe drinking water and fewer public health resources.

Development of Food Preferences

Food preferences impact what we eat throughout life, and some of these preferences are innate. Infants display some of the same reflexive facial expressions that older children and adults display in response to basic tastes: sweet, umami (savoury), bitter, sour, and salty (e.g., Ventura & Worobey, 2013). The first two flavours produce positive responses: a hint of a smile, lip smacking, sucking. Bitter flavours elicit negative responses, including frowning and nose wrinkling. Sour flavours elicit varied responses: some infants respond negatively while others respond positively. Salty flavours do not elicit much of a reaction until after 4 months of age, when a preference for salt emerges.

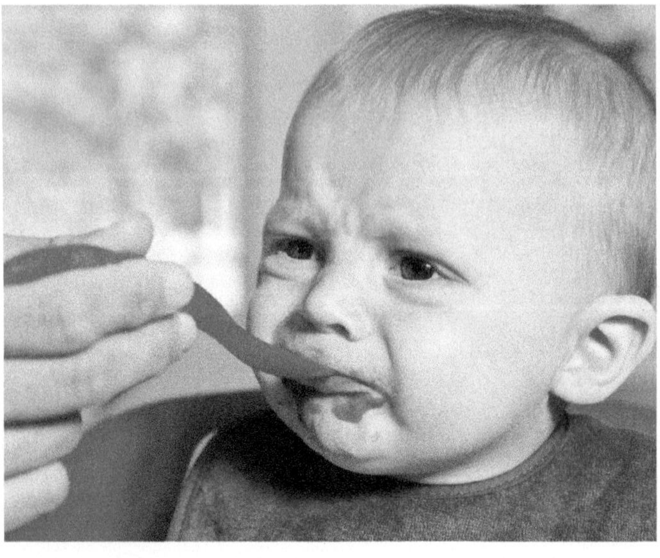

SDOMINICK/GETTY IMAGES

This infant is displaying the characteristic negative response to bitter flavour: frown and wrinkled nose.

Newborns' strong preference for sweetness is reflected both in their positive response to sweet flavours and in the fact that they will drink larger quantities of sweetened water than plain water. These preferences may have an evolutionary origin, because poisonous substances are often bitter or sour but almost never sweet. At the same time, recall from Chapter 2 that taste preferences can also be influenced by the prenatal environment, suggesting an important role for experience even in the earliest flavour preferences. Breast milk also takes on some of the flavours of the foods that mothers eat.

The rapid transition out of a primarily liquid diet brings a variety of opportunities and challenges. Most young children demonstrate *food neophobia:* an unwillingness to eat unfamiliar foods. Avoidance of unknown foods likely evolved as an adaptive response, helping to keep children safe (especially important given infants' and toddlers' propensity to put everything they find in their mouths). Research suggests that the best way to overcome children's conservative eating tendencies is to repeatedly introduce new foods, ideally between 6 and 15 times over the course of a few weeks (Ventura & Worobey, 2013). This exposure should include tasting; just seeing a novel food is insufficient to override children's wariness.

Pressuring children to try new foods, or bribing them ("If you have two bites of broccoli, you can have dessert"), is likely to backfire. By pairing foods in this fashion, parents send the message that broccoli is punishment while dessert is the reward. Parents also inadvertently increase the value of foods by restricting them. When access to certain foods is limited, children will tend to overindulge when they have the opportunity to do so (e.g., Ventura & Worobey, 2013). More generally, parental use of food as a way to control children's behaviours and emotions is a predictor of larger body mass indices (BMI) and other risk factors for obesity (e.g., Larsen et al., 2015).

Eating is an inherently social act, and much of what children learn about food comes from observing others (in Chapter 9, we will discuss the role of observational learning in social development more generally). Toddlers are more likely to accept novel foods from a caregiver than from a stranger. They are also more likely to choose foods endorsed by others who are similar to them along key social dimensions, including gender and native language (Shutts, Kinzler, & DeJesus, 2013). Indeed, infants expect individuals from their social group to share food preferences—but not preferences for non-food items such as novel objects, suggesting that even infants understand that food choices reflect social conventions (Liberman, Woodward, Sullivan, & Kinzler, 2016).

Associative learning, which we will discuss in Chapter 5, also influences children's food choices. Foods marketed to young children are often branded with popular cartoon characters (e.g., those from Sesame Street) and mascots (e.g., Tony the Tiger). Furthermore, as shown in a recent Canadian study, these foods tend to be of poor nutritional quality (Elliott & Scime, 2019). This branding strategy makes a difference: children are more likely to select, and rate more highly, foods that are branded with familiar characters (e.g., Kraak & Story, 2015). Nowhere is this strategy more evident than in the toys that fast-food restaurants offer to their youngest customers, leading to nearly a billion child-targeted meals served annually (Longacre et al., 2016). Child-targeted marketing of unhealthy foods, including the pairing of unhealthy foods with enticing toys, is one contributor to the obesity epidemic. Indeed, merely telling 5- and 6-year-olds that a food is popular with other children leads them to consume more of it (DeJesus, Shutts, & Kinzler, 2018)! In response to concerns about food marketing to children, Health Canada is working to restrict the marketing of unhealthy foods and drinks to children as part of their healthy eating strategy (Health Canada, n.d.).

Associative learning via branding can also be used to encourage healthy choices. One study used branding to market the salad bars in elementary school cafeterias in a large urban school district (Hanks, Just, & Brumberg, 2016). By simply fastening to the salad bar a banner that showed cartoon vegetable characters, the number of students who chose vegetables doubled. When the banner was paired with television advertisements featuring the vegetable characters, the number of students who chose vegetables tripled. Thus, advocates of healthy eating should consider taking advantage of the marketing tools that have so long predominated in the advertising of rather less healthy options.

Branding can be used to encourage unhealthy eating habits, as in the case of fast-food meals targeted at children, or healthy ones, as seen here in this elementary school's cafeteria salad bar.

COURTESY COVINA-VALLEY UNIFIED SCHOOL DISTRICT

Obesity

The most common dietary problems in Canada are related to overeating and its many consequences. While the rates of overweight and obesity in children in Canada have levelled off in the past few years, and even declined for children ages 2 to 11, around 6% of children aged 2 to 11 years and 11% of 12- to 17-year-olds were considered obese in 2015 (Statistics Canada, n.d.b).

Childhood obesity is a global problem, with 380 million overweight and obese children and adolescents worldwide (World Health Organization, 2018b). The majority of these children live in developing countries, which have shown a particularly steep rate of increase in obesity, as can be seen in Figure 3.11. For example, the number of children under the age of 5 in Africa who are overweight or obese has nearly doubled since 1990 (World Health Organization, 2018b). This situation exists largely because societies all over the world are increasingly adopting a "Western diet" of foods and drinks high in fat and sugar and low in fibre, paired with less physical activity in an increasingly urbanized world.

Two important questions need to be addressed: Why do some people but not others become overweight, and why is there an epidemic of obesity? Again, both genetic and environmental factors play roles. Genetic factors are reflected in the findings that (1) the weight of adopted children is more strongly correlated with that of their biological parents than with that of their adoptive parents, and (2) identical twins, including those reared apart, are more similar in weight than fraternal twins are (Plomin et al., 2012). Research on dogs has revealed a specific genetic deletion (POMC), occurring in breeds with high rates of obesity, associated with weight and appetite that causes these dogs to be hungrier than others (Raffan et al., 2016). The POMC gene is present in humans also, and, in rare cases, deficiencies lead to human obesity. However, GWAS studies suggest that, like most other complex traits, human obesity risk is polygenic (Tung et al., 2014). While no single gene predicts obesity, genes affect individuals' susceptibility to gaining weight and how much food they eat in the first place.

Genetic factors also influence an individual's temperament, which relates to self-regulation and impulse control. Childhood impulsivity is linked to overweight and obesity, and, in fact, young children with difficult temperaments tend to gain weight

FIGURE 3.11 Overweight Children by Region (1975–2016) These graphs show the steady rise over the last few decades in the number of overweight children (as measured by BMI) for various regions across the globe. (Information from NCD Risk Factor Collaboration, 2017)

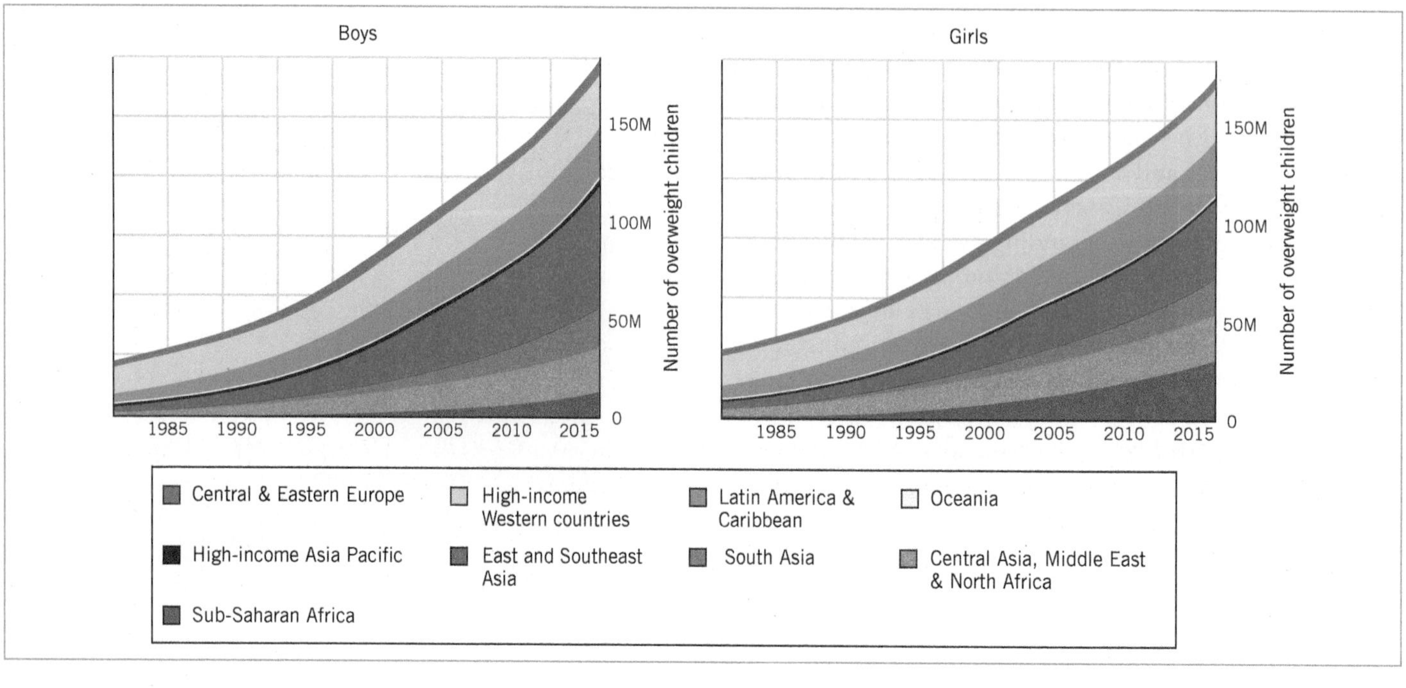

faster, have higher BMIs, and choose foods that tend to lead to obesity (Larsen et al., 2015; Thamotharan et al., 2013). Temperament influences children's self-control when confronted with large portions and sweet treats, both staples of the contemporary diet. (The Marshmallow Test described in Chapter 10, which also includes a detailed discussion of temperament, presents a striking demonstration of childhood impulsivity.)

A host of environmental factors fuel the ever-expanding waistlines of today's children. Schools provide cafeteria lunches consisting of high-fat foods and drinks. Canadian children today also spend far less time playing outside, and they are less likely to walk or bike to school than their counterparts in previous generations. Children spend increasingly more hours per day with screens (a trend that we will discuss in Chapter 9), and screen time is more highly predictive of obesity than amount of physical activity (Maher et al., 2012). Children who get less sleep are more prone to obesity, as are children with screens in their rooms (which may also detract from sleep duration) (Appelhans et al., 2014; Wethington, Pan, & Sherry, 2013). Finally, unhealthy foods are often cheaper and more readily available than healthier foods, especially in inner-city and rural areas that lack full-service supermarkets. In such areas, known as "food deserts," residents often must rely on convenience stores that stock primarily high-calorie prepackaged foods, making it difficult for parents to provide healthy foods for their children.

Obesity puts children and adolescents at risk for a wide variety of serious health problems, including heart disease and diabetes. In addition, many obese youth suffer the consequences of negative stereotypes and discrimination in a variety of areas. As early as 1st grade, children who are obese are more likely to be withdrawn and depressed (Harrist et al., 2016). According to child, peer, and teacher reports, these children are also more likely to struggle with friendships and are generally poorly treated by their peers, with teasing and rejection especially common for severely obese children (those with a BMI above the 99th percentile). Indeed, body size stigmatization appears to begin in preschool. Three- to 5-year-old girls were tested with a Barbie-like doll that was manipulated to be thin, average, or fat (Worobey & Worobey, 2014). The girls attributed more positive traits to the thin and average dolls ("smart," "pretty") and more negative traits to the fat doll ("sad," "tired"). While the roots of these negative attributions remain uncertain, it is clear that children who are obese have a very challenging road ahead, both physically and psychologically.

There is, unfortunately, no easy cure for obesity in children nor a clear means of prevention. Some of the techniques often thought to prevent obesity, such as breast-feeding in lieu of formula feeding or delaying the introduction of solid foods, do not have strong evidence-based support (Lumeng et al., 2015). However, some hope for the general obesity problem comes from the fact that public awareness is now focused on the severity of the problem and the variety of factors that contribute to it. Many schools have begun serving more nutritious, less caloric foods, including those available in vending machines, and fast-food chains have begun to include low-calorie options and calorie counts on their menus.

Many provinces have made daily physical activity mandatory in schools. In Alberta, for example, all students in Grades 1 to 9 must be physically active for 30 minutes a day through school activities. In another positive development, key Canadian health and scientific organizations have recently called on the federal government to restrict the marketing of unhealthy foods targeted to young children. As noted previously, Health Canada is currently working on such a plan.

Finally, promising obesity prevention programs are currently underway. One such program, called HomeStyles, was developed by nutrition scientists as an 18-month intervention focused on educating parents of preschool children about many of the topics presented in this section, including family meals, sleep duration, physical activity,

Health in Infancy and Toddlerhood

ARIEL SKELLEY/GETTY IMAGES

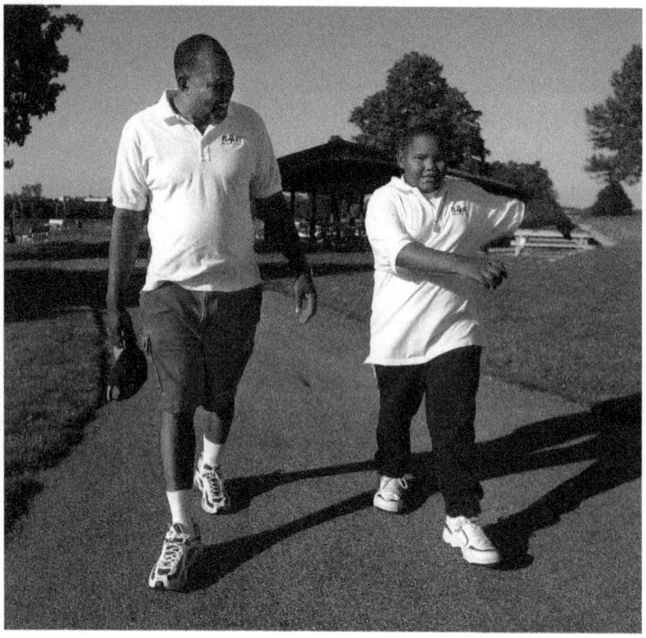

By exercising together, this parent and child may be taking one of the most effective steps they can toward weight control.

screen time, and dealing with picky eaters (Byrd-Bredbenner et al., 2018). An innovative strategy of HomeStyles is to nudge parents every few days (via SMS, email, or voicemail) to motivate them to work with their child toward positive health behaviours: "Move to the music and get active"; "Unplug the TV and talk to each other about your day." The results of this program suggest a range of improvements in obesity-preventative behaviours, including greater physical activity and less screen time in the intervention group compared to a control group.

Undernutrition

At the same time that many people are overeating their way to poor health, food insecurity plagues many communities globally. Undernutrition contributes to nearly half of all deaths of children under the age of 5 worldwide (World Health Organization, 2018a). Undernutrition impairs children's health by increasing their risk of succumbing to infections. For example, a child who is severely underweight is almost 10 times more likely to die of diarrhea than a child who is not underweight (UNICEF, 2013). These childhood illnesses, in turn, may decrease children's ability to take in nutrients, leading to a vicious cycle between infection and undernutrition.

Undernutrition and malnutrition are virtually always associated with poverty and myriad related factors, ranging from limited access to healthcare (a primary cause in the United States) to warfare, famine, and natural disasters. As we discuss in Box 3.4, the interaction of malnutrition with poverty and other forms of deprivation adversely affects all aspects of development, from brain development and physical growth to downstream effects on cognition, social development, educational attainment, and eventual economic productivity and quality of life. Strategies to counter undernutrition worldwide include improvements in maternal health, breast-feeding supports, access to supplementation of key nutrients (e.g., iodized salt, iron, vitamin A), improved water sanitation, and community-based interventions. In the United States, parental access to food stamps during pregnancy and early childhood is associated with positive outcomes in adulthood, ranging from lower rates of heart disease to higher rates of high school completion (Hoynes, Schanzenbach, & Almond, 2016).

Though most lack extensive health-care training, female community health-care workers in Nepal have played an important role in bringing treatment and medicine to a population that otherwise would not have access to basic health services. Their work may provide a model for improving the outcomes of women and children in impoverished communities.

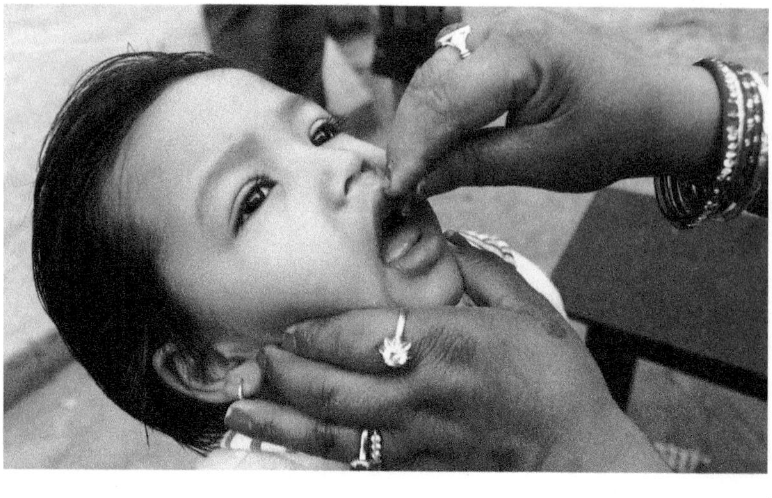

One noteworthy intervention is currently being used in Nepal, where most people live without access to routine healthcare. To begin to address this problem, Nepal developed a system of interventions delivered by female community health volunteers (UNICEF, 2013). Nearly 50,000 women travel the country to deliver basic healthcare, treating common childhood infections such as diarrhea and pneumonia. With their help, Nepal became the first country to deliver vitamin A supplements every 6 months to children nationwide. And because the volunteers are spread throughout the country, they are able to intervene rapidly. When women give birth in rural Nepal, volunteers arrive within the hour, prepared to detect and help manage low-birthweight neonates (Amano et al., 2014). While this program faces challenges—many of the volunteers are illiterate, requiring them to depend on memory about treatments and family histories, and the long walks between villages can hamper opportunities for training—it represents an important step toward improving children's nutritional and physical health in developing countries.

BOX 3.4 A CLOSER LOOK Poverty and Health Disparities

Poverty-related health disparities emerge early in life. In Canada, infants living in families with low socioeconomic status (SES) are more likely than other infants to die at birth or to die from SIDS (Gilbert et al., 2013).

Poverty also impacts brain development. As shown in the accompanying figure, brain growth is slowed in infants and toddlers growing up in poverty (e.g., Hanson et al., 2013). Importantly, infants' brains do not start out differently sized as a function of parental SES, as one might expect if differences in brain development were due to prenatal nutrition, preterm birth, or genetic differences that covary with SES (e.g., if the genes that affect brain size also influence parents' educational and occupational attainment). Instead, gray matter is roughly the same in very young infants across SES groups. But by 12 months of age, gray-matter volume has already begun to diverge as a function of SES; and by 24 months, there are substantial differences in gray matter in toddlers as a function of SES, a finding consistent with studies of older children and adults (e.g., Mackey et al., 2015; Noble et al., 2015).

As yet, it is unclear why these SES-related differences in brain size emerge. Possible reasons include the level of stress in the home, the richness of the environment (recall the earlier discussion of experience-dependent plasticity), toxins in the environment, or any number of other factors correlated with SES.

Children living in poverty are at heightened risk for a number of health problems. As noted previously, they are more likely than their peers to be overweight or obese, due to diet as well as their bodies' response to chronic stress. Poverty-related chronic stress also contributes to increased rates of diseases, including cardiovascular disease, immune system disorders, and psychiatric illnesses. Heightened rates of illness may be due, in part, to lack of access to good healthcare. But even when studies control for access to healthcare, effects of poverty remain.

One recent study examined rates of relapse for children with leukemia who were all treated at the same medical centre in New York City (Bona et al., 2016). Despite having access to the same treatments at the same hospital, children with leukemia living in low-income neighbourhoods were more likely to relapse after treatment than were children living in high-income neighbourhoods. Thus, family SES influenced cancer outcomes even when children received the same treatment protocols. This may be due to the presence of other underlying health problems, differences in adherence to therapies, or differences in family belief systems related to positive child development outcomes.

In Canada, which has a universal health care system, children living in poor neighbourhoods also have poorer physical health and well-being, as shown by research using the Early Development Inventory (EDI). The EDI was developed at McMaster University and is used across Canada for monitoring children's developmental health at school entry (Janus & Reid-Westoby, 2016). Research using the EDI has shown that children's physical health (as well as other aspects of developmental health) varies with neighbourhood socioeconomic status, with poorer children being more disadvantaged (Cushon et al., 2011; Janus & Duku, 2007). These health disparities impact children's readiness to learn. There is some good news, however: The number of children living in poverty in Canada has declined steadily from a peak of 15% in 2012 to 9% in 2017 (Statistics Canada, 2019).

As the developmental consequences of child poverty become increasingly apparent, healthcare professionals, developmental scientists, economists, and public policy experts have called on the government of Canada to take action. Fortunately, these calls have been heard and in 2018, the government launched Canada's first ever poverty reduction strategy (Opportunity for All, 2018). This strategy lays out poverty reduction targets, new legislation around poverty reductions, and a national advisory committee.

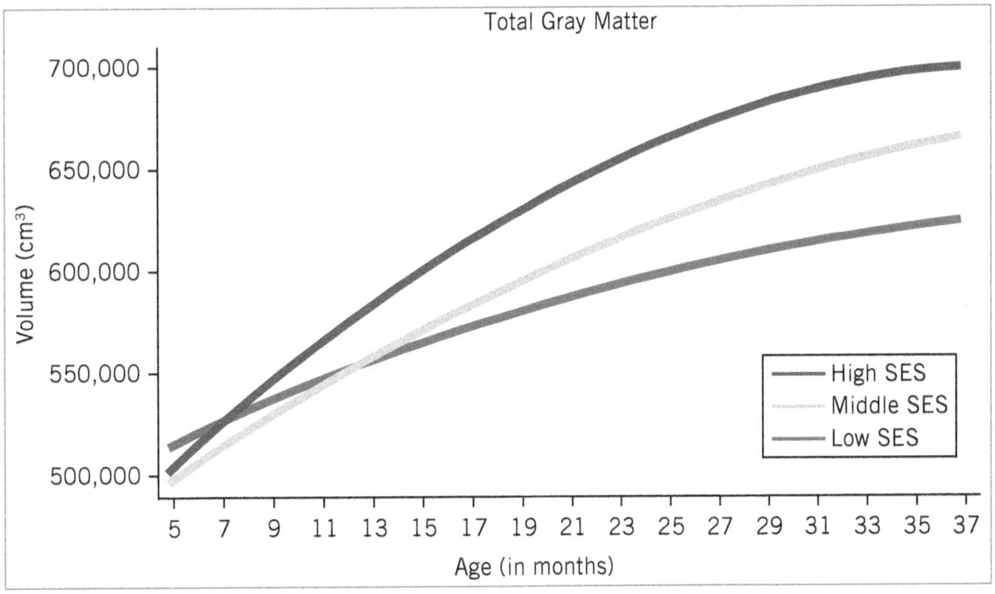

(Data from Hanson et al., 2013)

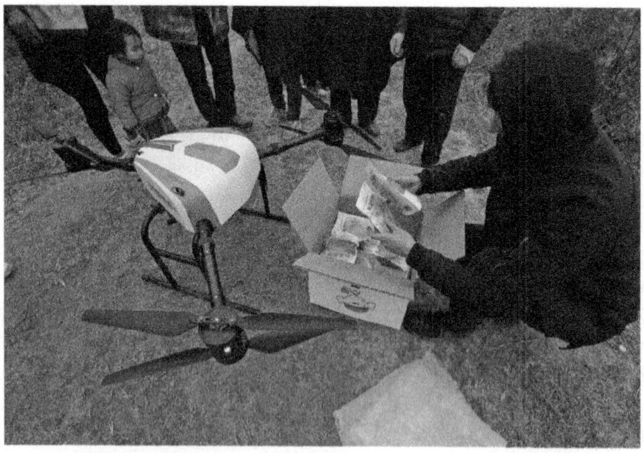

IMAGINE CHINA/NEWSCOM

Innovative strategies, such as the use of drone technology, for delivering vaccines and other medicines have the potential to dramatically improve health outcomes for people living in remote locations, such as a mountain village in China's Sichuan Province, pictured here.

Vaccines

Vaccines are another important factor in healthy physical development. They deliver a weak version of a disease to the body, prompting the body to produce antibodies to attack it. These antibodies provide protection against subsequent encounters with the disease. Vaccines are delivered on a specific schedule, often with multiple doses of each vaccine required for full immunization. The World Health Organization estimates that the use of vaccines prevents 2 to 3 million deaths worldwide each year from diseases including polio and measles. Other diseases, like smallpox, have been entirely eradicated due to vaccines.

Unfortunately, some parents believe that vaccines will harm their children. In a highly publicized study in the 1990s, a British physician claimed that autism is caused by the MMR vaccine routinely given to young children to prevent measles, mumps, and rubella (Wakefield et al., 1998). It was subsequently discovered that this paper was fraudulent, and it has since been retracted by the journal that published it (Godlee, Smith, & Marcovitch, 2011). Subsequent research has found no link between vaccines and autism (Hviid et al., 2019; Jain et al., 2015; McMahon et al., 2008; Price et al., 2010). For example, a recent longitudinal study, which followed more than 650,000 children in Denmark over 10 years, showed unequivocally that vaccination does not increase the risk for autism, even in those children who are at increased risk for autism (Hviid et al., 2019).

The decision by some parents to refuse MMR and other important vaccines creates a risk for both their children and others in the community. Because vaccines operate based on *herd immunity*, a certain percentage of the population must be immunized in order to protect the population. In Canada, vaccination is mandatory for enrollment in public school only in New Brunswick and Ontario, and parents in these provinces can exempt their children for religious or philosophical reasons. By voluntarily removing their children from the vaccinated population, parents risk dropping vaccine rates below the level needed for herd immunity, a particular problem for those children who cannot be vaccinated due to age or medical conditions (for example, cancer patients who are immune-compromised). These actions can have serious consequences, as in the case of the measles outbreak in Vancouver in 2019. The family at the centre of the outbreak did not vaccinate their children due to fears of autism.

According to the World Health Organization, 10% of infants worldwide did not receive vaccinations in 2016. In some parts of the world, vaccination is hampered by cost and logistical challenges. For example, vaccines need to be kept cold, which poses a problem in communities with irregular access to electricity. One innovative approach is being implemented in Vanuatu, a nation made up of 83 small islands in the South Pacific. About 20% of the children in Vanuatu do not receive all of their vaccinations due to the remoteness of villages and lack of electricity. To address this problem, UNICEF funded a program to deliver vaccines by drone. Each drone can hold a 5-pound pack of vaccines packaged in ice and can fly 30 miles to villages that are difficult to reach by road or sea. This program represents a clever use of modern technology to delivery life-saving vaccines.

REVIEW QUESTION

A number of factors related to nutrition and physical health can impact growth and maturation from infancy through childhood. Consider your own community. What steps could be taken to promote healthy habits and counteract unhealthy ones? ■

CHAPTER SUMMARY

Nature and Nurture

- The starting point for development is the genotype—the genes inherited at conception from one's parents. Only some of those genes are expressed in the phenotype, one's observable characteristics. Whether some genes are expressed at all is a function of dominance patterns. Most traits studied by developmental scientists are influenced by multiple genes.
- The eventual outcome of a given genotype is always contingent on the environment in which it develops. Parents and their behaviour toward their children—which is influenced by the parents' own genotypes—are a salient part of the children's environment. Similarly, the child's development is influenced by the aspects of the environment he or she seeks out and the different responses the child's characteristics and behaviour evoke from other people.
- Epigenetic effects—the switching on and off of genes—underlies many aspects of development and individual differences. This process is affected by experience via methylation.

Behaviour Genetics

- Behaviour genetics is concerned with the joint influence of genetic and environmental factors on behaviour. Quantitative behaviour geneticists use a variety of family-study designs to generate heritability estimates, examining the relative contributions of heredity and environment for individual differences for a range of traits and behaviours in a population. Molecular behaviour genetics approaches permit the field to move beyond family designs to investigate patterns of genes across large groups of people.

Brain Development

- Neurons, the basic units of the brain's informational system, transmit information between the brain and body via electrical signals. The brain's cortex is composed of several major areas, or lobes, specialized for different functions.
- Brain development involves several processes, beginning with neurogenesis and differentiation of neurons. In synaptogenesis, an enormous profusion of connections among neurons is generated, starting prenatally and continuing for the first few years after birth. Through synaptic pruning, excess connections among neurons are eliminated. Myelination, another important process for neural processing, begins before birth and continues through adulthood.
- Experience plays a crucial role in the strengthening or elimination of synapses and hence in the normal wiring of the brain. The fine-tuning of the brain involves experience-expectant processes, in which existing synapses are preserved as a function of stimulation that virtually every human encounters, and experience-dependent processes, in which new connections are formed as a function of experience and learning.
- Plasticity makes it possible in certain circumstances for the brain to rewire itself in response to damage. It also makes the developing brain vulnerable to the absence of stimulation at sensitive periods in development. The ability of the brain to recover from injury depends on the age of the child.

The Body: Physical Growth and Development

- Humans undergo a particularly prolonged period of physical growth, during which growth is uneven, proceeding more rapidly early in life and in adolescence. Secular trends have been observed in increases in average weight and height.
- Food preferences begin with innate responses by newborns to basic tastes, but additional preferences develop as a result of experience. Problems with the regulation of eating are evident in Canada, where obesity is clearly related to both environmental and genetic factors.
- Inadequate nutrition is closely associated with poverty, and it leads to a variety of behavioural and physical problems in virtually every aspect of the child's life. Prevention of undernutrition is needed to enable millions of children to develop normal brains and bodies.
- Vaccines help to protect vulnerable infants and children from a range of diseases. Highly publicized claims about links between autism and vaccines are based on falsified data; vaccines do not cause autism.

Test Yourself

1. The genetic material an individual inherits is called the
   a. chromosome.
   b. genome.
   c. phenotype.
   d. genotype.

2. Jiyeon has red hair, green eyes, and freckles. He is very active but shy. These characteristics are a reflection of Marcus's
   a. dominant genes.
   b. recessive genes.
   c. genotype.
   d. phenotype.

3. An individual's genetic sex is determined by
a. whether the mother has a Y chromosome.
b. the random interaction of the sex chromosomes of the mother and father.
c. the sex chromosomes contributed by the mother.
d. the sex chromosomes contributed by the father.

4. The continual switching on or off of specific genes at specific times throughout development is the result of a chain of genetic events primarily controlled by
a. alleles.
b. regulator genes.
c. glial cells.
d. synaptogenesis.

5. Traits such as aggression and shyness are the result of the contributions of a complex combination of genes. These traits are examples of which process?
a. Polygenetic inheritance
b. Experience-expectant plasticity
c. Mendelian inheritance
d. Experience-dependent plasticity

6. A twin-study design project reveals that the correlation between identical (MZ) twins on a given trait is substantially higher than that between fraternal (DZ) twins. Which of the following statements offers the most plausible explanation for the difference in how this trait is correlated in MZ twins compared with DZ twins?
a. Environmental factors are substantially responsible for the difference in correlation.
b. Genetic factors are substantially responsible for the difference in correlation.
c. Environmental and genetic factors are equally responsible for the difference in correlation.
d. No assumption can be made as to the contributions of environmental or genetic factors for the difference.

7. Which of the following responses would be consistent with the statement "High heritability does not imply immutability"?
a. The concept of inheritance plays a very small role in dictating an individual's phenotype.
b. Highly heritable traits affect all individuals in the same way.
c. Intervention efforts can successfully influence the course of development related to an inherited trait.
d. There is little point in trying to improve the course of development related to an inherited trait.

8. The points at which neurons communicate with one another are called
a. synapses.
b. glial cells.
c. dendrites.
d. myelin sheaths.

9. The process of synaptogenesis
a. involves the formation of connections between neurons.
b. causes the elimination of excess neurons.
c. is basically complete before birth.
d. is the proliferation of neurons through cell division.

10. The capacity of the brain to be molded or changed by experience is referred to as
a. synaptogenesis.
b. associative learning.
c. plasticity.
d. neurogenesis.

11. Rats that are raised in cages with toys develop more dendritic spines and more synapses per neuron than rats raised in cages without this stimulation. The different responses in the brains of these two groups of rats provide an example of which biological process?
a. Sensitive periods
b. Experience-expectant plasticity
c. Experience-dependent plasticity
d. Neurogenesis

12. Average at-birth length has increased in some industrialized nations over the course of the past few generations, possibly due to improvements in health and nutrition for pregnant women. This development is an example of
a. experience-expectant plasticity.
b. secular trends.
c. obesity.
d. genotype–environment interactions.

13. Belle is 3 years old. She loves bananas and other yellow foods, but when her father places a piece of broccoli, which she has never eaten, on her plate, she closes her mouth and refuses to open it. Belle is demonstrating
a. undernutrition.
b. associative learning.
c. experience-expectant plasticity.
d. food neophobia.

14. Epigenetic effects have been demonstrated in studies with rats in which the absence of specific grooming behaviours from the mother results in reduced levels of glucocorticoid receptor gene activity in her pups. This processing of gene expression silencing is known as
a. experience-expectant plasticity.
b. myelination.
c. synaptic pruning.
d. methylation.

15. Which of the following is *not* a function of glial cells?
a. Conduct electrical signals away from one neuron and to another.
b. Guide neurons to their final destinations within the growing brain.
c. Aid in the regeneration of neurons following injury.
d. Support the formation of myelin sheaths around axons.

Critical Thinking Questions

1. A major focus of this chapter was the interaction of nature and nurture. Consider yourself and your family (regardless of whether you were raised by your biological parents). Identify some aspect of who you are that illustrates each of the five relations depicted in Figure 3.1 and answer these questions: (a) How and when was your sex determined? (b) What are some alleles you are certain or relatively confident you share with other members of your family? (c) What might be an example of a gene–environment interaction in your parents' behaviour toward you? (d) What would be an example of your active selection of your own environment that might have influenced your subsequent development? (e) What aspects of your own environment might have had epigenetic effects on your gene expression?
2. "Fifty percent of a person's IQ is due to heredity and fifty percent to environment." Discuss what is wrong with this statement, describing what heritability estimates mean as well as what they do not mean.
3. Relate the developmental processes of synaptogenesis and synapse elimination to the concepts of experience-expectant plasticity and experience-dependent plasticity.
4. What aspects of brain development do researchers think may be related to the traits and behaviours of adolescents?
5. Many aspects of children's health are shaped by the world they live in, ranging from broad national differences (e.g., economic stability) to family factors (e.g., socioeconomic status, parental behaviour). What are some of the ways in which a child's health can be influenced by the environment? If you were a parent, what reasonable, long-lasting steps could you take to improve your child's health outcomes and eating habits?

Key Terms

Answers to Test Yourself

1. d, **2.** d, **3.** d, **4.** b, **5.** a, **6.** b, **7.** c, **8.** a, **9.** a, **10.** c, **11.** c, **12.** b, **13.** d, **14.** d, **15.** a

CHAPTER

4 Theories of Cognitive Development

DIEGO RIVERA, *Sweet Home—Singing the Corrido* (mural, 1925)

Piaget's Theory | **Information-Processing Theories**

Core-Knowledge Theories | **Sociocultural Theories** | **Dynamic-Systems Theories**

THEMES

NATURE AND NURTURE ■ THE ACTIVE CHILD ■ CONTINUITY/DISCONTINUITY ■ MECHANISMS OF CHANGE
THE SOCIOCULTURAL CONTEXT ■ INDIVIDUAL DIFFERENCES ■ RESEARCH AND CHILDREN'S WELFARE

A 7-month-old boy, sitting on his father's lap, becomes intrigued with the father's glasses, grabs one side of the frame, and yanks it. The father says, "Ow!" and his son lets go, but then reaches up and yanks the frame again. The father readjusts the glasses, but his son again grasps them and yanks. How, the father wonders, can he prevent the boy from continuing this annoying routine without causing him to start screaming?

Fortunately, the father, a developmental psychologist, soon realizes that Jean Piaget's theory of cognitive development suggests a simple solution: Put the glasses behind his back. According to Piaget's theory, removing an object from a young infant's sight should lead the infant to act as if the object never existed. The strategy works perfectly; after the father puts the glasses behind his back, his son turns his attention elsewhere. The father looks skyward and thinks, "Thank you, Piaget."

This experience, which one of the authors of this textbook actually had, illustrates in a small way how understanding theories of child development can yield practical benefits. It also illustrates three broader advantages of knowing about such theories:

1. *Developmental theories provide a framework for understanding important phenomena.* Theories help to reveal the significance of what we observe about children, both in research studies and in everyday life. Someone who witnessed the glasses incident but who did not know about Piaget's theory might have found the experience amusing but insignificant. Seen in terms of Piaget's theory, however, this passing event exemplifies a general and profoundly important developmental phenomenon: infants younger than 8 months react to the disappearance of an object as though the object has ceased to exist. In this way, theories of child development place particular experiences and observations in a larger context and deepen our understanding of their meaning.

2. *Developmental theories raise crucial questions about human nature.* Piaget's theory about young infants' reactions to disappearing objects was based on his informal experiments with infants younger than 8 months. Piaget would cover one of their favourite playthings with a cloth or otherwise put it out of sight and then wait to see whether the infants tried to retrieve the object. They rarely did, leading Piaget to conclude that before the age of 8 months, infants do not realize that hidden objects still exist. Other researchers have challenged this explanation. They argue that infants younger than 8 months do in fact understand that hidden objects continue to exist but lack the memory or problem-solving skills necessary for using that understanding to retrieve hidden objects (Baillargeon, 1993). Despite these disagreements about how best to interpret young infants' failure to retrieve hidden objects, researchers agree that Piaget's theory raises a crucial question about human nature: Do infants realize from the first days of life that objects continue to exist when out of sight, or is this something that they only learn later? Do they fear that Mom no longer exists when she disappears from sight?

The author whose son loved to grab his glasses is not the only one who has encountered this problem. Had the mom in this picture been lucky enough to read this textbook, she may have solved the problem in the same way.

ELIZABETH CREWS

3. *Developmental theories lead to a better understanding of children.* Theories also stimulate new research that may support the theories' claims, fail to support them, or require refinements of them, thereby improving our understanding of children. For example, Piaget's ideas led Yuko Munakata and her colleagues (1997) to test whether 7-month-olds' failure to reach for hidden objects was due to their lacking the motivation or the reaching skill to retrieve them. To find out, the researchers created a situation similar to Piaget's object-permanence experiment, except that they placed the object, an attractive toy, under a transparent cover rather than under an opaque one. In this situation, infants quickly removed the cover and regained the toy. This finding seemed to support Piaget's original interpretation by showing that neither lack of motivation nor lack of ability to reach for the toy explained the infants' usual failure to retrieve it.

In contrast, an experiment conducted by Adele Diamond (1985) indicated a need to revise Piaget's theory. Using an opaque covering, as Piaget did, Diamond varied the amount of time between when the toy was hidden and when the infant was allowed to reach for it. She found that even 6-month-olds could locate the toy if allowed to reach immediately, that 7-month-olds could wait as long as 2 seconds and still succeed, and that 8-month-olds could wait as long as 4 seconds and still succeed. Diamond's findings indicated that memory for the location of hidden objects, as well as the understanding that they continue to exist, is crucial to success on the task. In sum, theories of child development are useful because they provide frameworks for understanding important phenomena, raise fundamental questions about human nature, and motivate new research that increases our understanding of children.

Because child development is such a complex and varied subject, no single theory accounts for all of it. The most informative current theories focus primarily on either cognitive development or social development. Providing a good theoretical account of development in even one of these areas is an immense challenge, because each of them spans a huge range of topics. Cognitive development includes the growth of such diverse capabilities as perception, attention, language, problem solving, reasoning, memory, conceptual understanding, and intelligence. Social development includes the growth of equally diverse areas: emotions, personality, relationships with peers and family members, self-understanding, aggression, and moral behaviour. Given this immense range of developmental domains, it is easy to understand why no one theory has captured the entirety of child development.

Therefore, we present cognitive and social theories in separate chapters. We consider theories of cognitive development in this chapter, just before the chapters on specific areas of cognitive development, and consider theories of social development in Chapter 9, just before the chapters on specific areas of social development. The goal is to help you understand the theories that address fundamental questions about cognitive and social development. These theories provide much of the motivation behind the studies, presented here and in later chapters, that address those fundamental questions in specific contexts (such as language development and conceptual development).

This chapter examines five theories of cognitive development that are particularly influential: Piagetian, information-processing, core-knowledge, sociocultural, and dynamic-systems. We consider each theory's fundamental assumptions about children's nature, the central developmental issues on which the theory focuses, and practical examples of the theory's usefulness for educating children.

These five theories are influential in large part because they provide important insights into the basic developmental themes described in Chapter 1. Each one addresses all the themes to some extent, but each emphasizes different ones. For example, Piaget's theory focuses on *nature and nurture, continuity/discontinuity,* and the *active child,* whereas information-processing theories focus on *nature and nurture* and *mechanisms of change* (Table 4.1). Together, the five theories allow a broader appreciation of cognitive development than any one of them alone.

TABLE 4.1 Enduring Themes Addressed by Theories of Cognitive Development

Theory	Main Questions Addressed
Piagetian	Nature and nurture, continuity/discontinuity, the active child
Information-processing	Nature and nurture, how change occurs
Core-knowledge	Nature and nurture, continuity/discontinuity
Sociocultural	Nature and nurture, influence of the sociocultural context, how change occurs
Dynamic-systems	Nature and nurture, the active child, how change occurs

Piaget's Theory

Jean Piaget's studies of cognitive development are a testament to how much one person can contribute to a scientific field. Before his work began to appear in the early 1920s, there was no recognizable field of cognitive development. Nearly a century later, **Piaget's theory** remains the best-known cognitive developmental theory. What accounts for its longevity?

Piaget's theory the theory of Swiss psychologist Jean Piaget, which posits that cognitive development involves a sequence of four stages—the sensorimotor, preoperational, concrete operational, and formal operational stages—that are constructed through the processes of assimilation, accommodation, and equilibration

One reason is that Piaget's observations and descriptions vividly convey the texture of children's thinking at different ages. They remind parents, teachers, nurses, and child-care employees of their own experiences with children of different ages. Another reason is the exceptional breadth of the theory. It extends from infancy through adolescence and examines topics as diverse as conceptualization of time, space, distance, and number; language use; memory; understanding of other people's perspectives; problem solving; and scientific reasoning. A third source of its longevity is that it offers an intuitively plausible depiction of the interaction of nature and nurture in cognitive development, as well as of the continuities and discontinuities that characterize intellectual growth.

View of Children's Nature

Piaget's fundamental assumption about children was that they are mentally active from the moment of birth and that their mental and physical activity both contribute greatly to their development. His approach to understanding cognitive development is often labelled *constructivist,* because it depicts children as constructing knowledge for themselves in response to their experiences. According to Piaget, three of the most important of children's constructive processes are generating hypotheses, performing experiments, and drawing conclusions from their observations. If this description reminds you of scientific problem solving, you are not alone: the "child as scientist" is the dominant metaphor in Piaget's theory. Consider this description of his infant son:

> Laurent is lying on his back. . . . He grasps in succession a celluloid swan, a box, etc., stretches out his arm and lets them fall. He distinctly varies the position of the fall. When the object falls in a new position (for example, on his pillow), he lets it fall two or three more times on the same place, as though to study the spatial relation.
>
> (Piaget, 1952b, pp. 268–269)

Jean Piaget, whose work has had a profound influence on developmental psychology, is seen here interviewing a child to learn about his thinking.

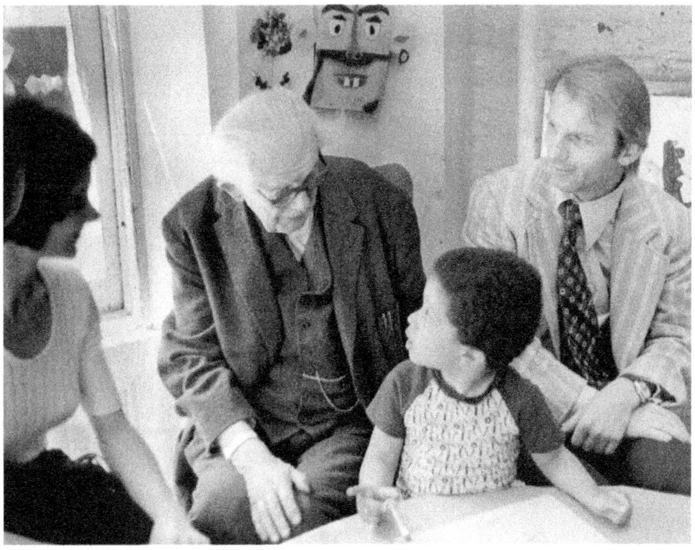

PHOTO RESEARCHERS / GETTY IMAGES

assimilation the process by which people translate incoming information into a form that fits concepts they already understand

accommodation the process by which people adapt current knowledge structures in response to new experiences

equilibration the process by which children (or other people) balance assimilation and accommodation to create stable understanding

In simple activities such as Laurent's game of "drop the toy from different places and see what happens," Piaget perceived the beginning of scientific experimentation. This example also illustrates a second basic Piagetian assumption: children learn many important lessons on their own, rather than depending on instruction from others. To further illuminate this point, Piaget cited a friend's recollection from childhood:

> [H]e put [the pebbles] in a row and he counted them one, two, three up to 10. Then he . . . started to count them in the other direction. . . . and once again he found that he had 10. He found this marvelous. . . .
>
> (Piaget, 1964, p. 12)

This incident also highlights a third basic assumption of Piaget's: children are intrinsically motivated to learn and do not need rewards from other people to do so.

Central Developmental Issues

In addition to his view that children actively shape their own development, Piaget offered important insights regarding the roles of *nature and nurture* and of *continuity/discontinuity* in development.

Nature and Nurture

Piaget believed that nature and nurture interact to produce cognitive development. In his view, nurture includes not just the nurturing provided by parents and other caregivers but every experience children encounter. Nature includes children's maturing brain and body; their ability to perceive, act, and learn from experience; and their tendency to integrate particular observations into coherent knowledge. As this description suggests, a vital part of children's nature is how they respond to nurture.

Sources of Continuity

Piaget depicted development as involving both continuities and discontinuities. The main sources of continuity are three processes—*assimilation, accommodation,* and *equilibration*—that work together from birth to propel development forward.

Assimilation is the process by which people incorporate incoming information into concepts they already understand. To illustrate, when one of our children was 2 years old, he saw a man who was bald on top of his head and had long frizzy hair on the sides. To his father's great embarrassment, the toddler gleefully shouted, "Clown! Clown!" (Actually, it sounded more like "Kown! Kown!") The man apparently looked enough like a "kown" that the boy could assimilate him to his clown concept.

Accommodation is the process by which people improve their current understanding in response to new experiences. In the "kown" incident, the boy's father explained to his son that the man was not a clown and that even though his hair looked like a clown's, he was not wearing a funny costume and was not doing silly things to make people laugh. With this new information, the boy was able to accommodate his clown concept to the standard one, allowing other men with bald pates and long side hair to proceed in peace.

Equilibration is the process by which people balance assimilation and accommodation to create stable understanding. Equilibration includes three phases. First, people are satisfied with their understanding of a particular phenomenon; Piaget labelled this a state of *equilibrium,* because people do not see any discrepancies between their observations and their understanding of the phenomenon. Then, new information leads them to perceive that their understanding is inadequate. Piaget said that this realization puts people in a state of *disequilibrium;* they recognize

Perhaps hearing toddlers yelling "Kown, kown!" set Larry, a member of The Three Stooges, on his career path.

EVERETT COLLECTION, INC.

shortcomings in their understanding of the phenomenon, but they cannot generate a superior alternative. Put more simply, they are confused. Finally, they develop a more sophisticated understanding that eliminates at least some of the shortcomings of the old one, creating a more advanced equilibrium within which a broader range of observations can be understood. Through innumerable equilibrations, children learn about the world around them.

Sources of Discontinuity

Although Piaget placed some emphasis on continuous aspects of cognitive development, the most famous part of his theory concerns discontinuous aspects, which he depicted as distinct *stages* of cognitive development. Piaget viewed these stages as products of the basic human tendency to organize knowledge into coherent structures. Each stage represents a unified way of understanding one's experience, and each transition between stages represents a discontinuous intellectual leap from one coherent way of understanding the world to the next, higher one. The following are the central properties of Piaget's stage theory:

1. *Qualitative change.* Piaget believed that children of different ages think in qualitatively different ways. For example, he proposed that children in the early stages of cognitive development conceive of morality in terms of the *consequences* of behaviour, whereas children in later stages conceive of it in terms of *intent.* Thus, a 5-year-old would judge someone who accidentally broke a whole jar of cookies as having been naughtier than someone who deliberately stole a single cookie; an 8-year-old would reach the opposite conclusion. This difference represents a *qualitative change* because the two children are basing their moral judgments on entirely different criteria.
2. *Broad applicability.* The type of thinking characteristic of each stage influences children's thinking across diverse topics and contexts.
3. *Brief transitions.* Before entering a new stage, children pass through a brief transitional period in which they fluctuate between the type of thinking characteristic of the new, more advanced stage and the type of thinking characteristic of the old, less advanced one.
4. *Invariant sequence.* Everyone progresses through the stages in the same order without skipping any of them.

Piaget hypothesized four stages of cognitive development: the *sensorimotor* stage, the *preoperational* stage, the *concrete operational* stage, and the *formal operational* stage. In each stage, children exhibit new abilities that enable them to understand the world in qualitatively different ways than they had previously.

1. In the **sensorimotor stage** (birth to age 2 years), infants' intelligence is expressed through their sensory and motor abilities, which they use to perceive and explore the world around them. These abilities allow them to learn about objects and people and to construct rudimentary forms of fundamental concepts such as time, space, and causality. Throughout the sensorimotor period, infants live largely in the here and now: their intelligence is bound to their immediate perceptions and actions.
2. In the **preoperational stage** (ages 2 to 7 years), toddlers and preschoolers become able to represent their experiences in language and mental imagery. This ability allows them to remember the experiences for longer periods and to form more sophisticated concepts. However, as suggested by the term *preoperational,* Piaget's theory emphasizes young children's inability to

sensorimotor stage the period (birth to 2 years) within Piaget's theory in which intelligence is expressed through sensory and motor abilities

preoperational stage the period (2 to 7 years) within Piaget's theory in which children become able to represent their experiences in language, mental imagery, and symbolic thought

concrete operational stage the period (7 to 12 years) within Piaget's theory in which children become able to reason logically about concrete objects and events

formal operational stage the period (12 years and beyond) within Piaget's theory in which people become able to think about abstractions and hypothetical situations

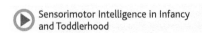

perform certain *mental operations,* such as considering multiple dimensions simultaneously. This leads to children's being unable to form certain ideas, such as the idea that pouring all the water from a short, wide glass into a taller, narrower glass does not change the total amount of water, even though the column of water is higher in the second glass. In other words, they do not recognize that the increased height of the liquid column in the second glass is compensated for by its being narrower.

3. In the **concrete operational stage** (ages 7 to 12 years), children can reason logically about concrete objects and events; for example, they understand that pouring water from one glass to a taller, narrower one leaves the amount of water unchanged. However, concrete operational reasoners cannot think in purely abstract terms or generate systematic scientific experiments to test their beliefs.
4. In the final stage of cognitive development, the **formal operational stage** (age 12 years and beyond), adolescents and adults can think deeply not only about concrete events but also about abstractions and purely hypothetical situations. They can also perform systematic scientific experiments and draw appropriate conclusions from them, even when the conclusions differ from their prior beliefs.

Sensorimotor Intelligence in Infancy and Toddlerhood

WORTH PUBLISHERS

With this overview of Piaget's theory, we can consider in greater depth major changes that take place within each stage and from one stage to another.

The Sensorimotor Stage (Birth to Age 2 Years)

One of Piaget's most profound insights was his realization that the roots of adult intelligence are present in infants' earliest behaviours, such as their seemingly aimless sucking, flailing, and grasping. He recognized that these behaviours are not random but instead reflect an early type of intelligence involving sensory (perceptual) and motor activity. Indeed, many of the clearest examples of the *active child* theme come from Piaget's descriptions of the development of what he called "sensorimotor intelligence."

Over the course of their first 2 years, infants' sensorimotor intelligence develops tremendously. The sheer amount of change may at first seem astonishing. However, when we consider the innumerable new experiences that infants encounter during this period, and the tripling of brain weight between birth and age 3 (with weight being an index of brain development), the huge increase in infants' cognitive abilities is understandable.

Infants are born with many reflexes. When objects move in front of their eyes, they visually track them; when objects are placed in their mouths, they suck them; when objects come into contact with their hands, they grasp them; when they hear noises, they turn toward them; and so on.

ROBERT SIEGLER

Piaget proposed that when infants suck on objects, they gain not only pleasure but also knowledge about the world beyond their bodies.

Even during their first month, infants begin to modify their reflexes to make them more adaptive. At birth, for example, they suck in a similar way regardless of what they are sucking. Within a few weeks, however, they adjust their sucking according to the object in their mouth. Thus, they suck on a milk-yielding nipple in a way that enhances the efficiency of their feeding and that is different from the way they suck on a finger or pacifier. As this example illustrates, from the first days out of the womb, infants accommodate their actions to the parts of the environment with which they interact.

Over the first few months, infants begin to organize separate reflexes into larger behaviours, most of them centred on their own bodies. For example, instead of

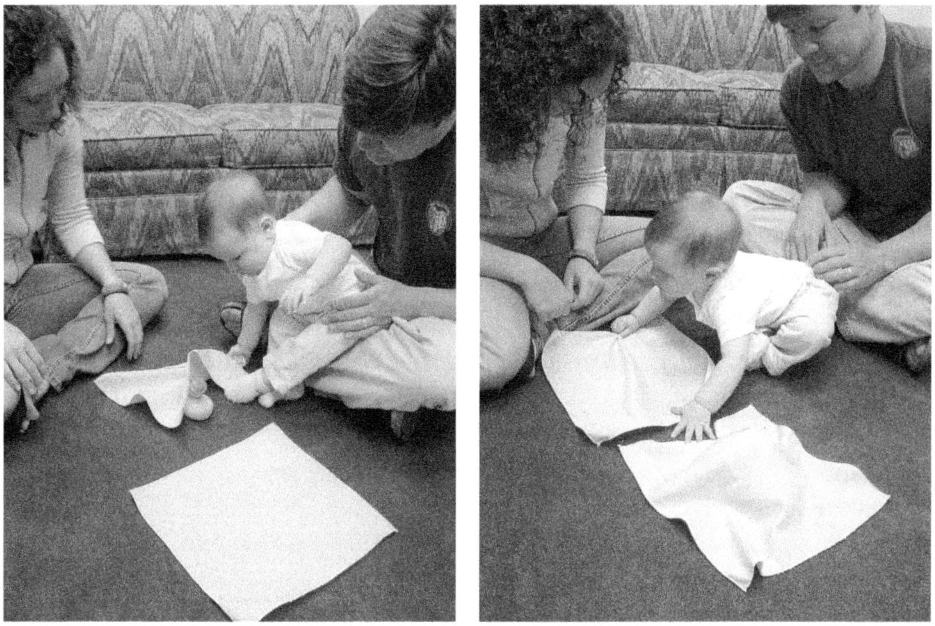

BEN CLORE

FIGURE 4.1 **Piaget's A-not-B task** A child looks for and finds a toy under the cloth where it was hidden (left frame). After several such experiences, the toy is hidden in a different location (right frame). The child continues to look where he found the toy previously, rather than where it is hidden now. The child's ignoring the visible protrusion of the toy under the cloth in the right frame illustrates the strength of the inclination to look in the previous hiding place.

being limited to exercising their grasping and sucking reflexes separately, they can integrate them: when an object touches their palm, they can grasp it, bring it to their mouth, and suck on it. Thus, their reflexes serve as components of more complex behaviours.

In the middle of their first year, infants become increasingly interested in the world around them—people, animals, toys, and other objects and events beyond their own bodies. A hallmark of this shift is repetition of actions that produce pleasurable or interesting results, such as repeatedly banging a rattle or squeezing a rubber duck again and again to make it squeak.

Along with this increasing interest in other people and objects, infants late in their first year begin to search for objects of interest that have disappeared from sight, a capability known as **object permanence**. Thus, the trick of hiding the glasses described at the beginning of this chapter probably would not work with a 1-year-old. Piaget hypothesized that this searching reflects the development of mental representations of objects that endure even when the objects are not visible.

However, Piaget also hypothesized that these initial representations of objects are fragile, as reflected in the **A-not-B error.** In this error, once 8- to 12-month-olds have reached for and found a hidden object several times in one place (location A), they tend to reach there again even when they have observed the object being hidden in a different place (location B) and are prevented from immediately reaching for it (see Figure 4.1). Not until around their 1st birthday do infants consistently search first at the object's current location.

At around 1 year of age, infants begin to actively and avidly explore the potential ways in which objects can be used. The "child as scientist" example presented earlier, in which Piaget's son Laurent varied the positions from which he dropped different objects to see what would happen, provides one instance of this emerging competency. Similar examples occur in every family with an infant. Few parents forget their 1-year-old sitting in a high chair, banging various objects against the chair's tray—first a spoon, then a plate, then a cup—seemingly fascinated by the different sounds.

In the last half-year of the sensorimotor stage (ages 18 to 24 months), according to Piaget, infants become able to form enduring mental representations. The first

object permanence the knowledge that objects continue to exist even when they are out of view

A-not-B error the tendency to reach for a hidden object where it was last found rather than in the new location where it was last hidden

Problem Solving and the A-not-B Error

WORTH PUBLISHERS

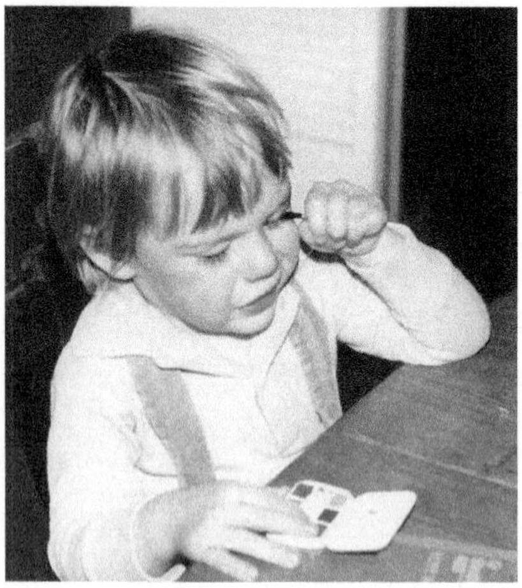

COURTESY OF JUDY DELOACHE

This toddler's techniques for applying eye makeup may not exactly mirror those he has seen his mother use, but they are close enough to provide a compelling illustration of deferred imitation, a skill that children gain during their second year.

sign of this new capability is **deferred imitation,** that is, the repetition of other people's behaviour minutes, hours, or even days after it occurred. Piaget provided the example of his daughter seeing a playmate stamp his feet during a tantrum and then doing the same thing herself, a day later, having never done anything like that previously.

When we consider Piaget's account of cognitive development during infancy, several notable trends are evident.

- At first, infants' activities centre on their own bodies; later, their activities include the world around them.
- Early goals are concrete (shaking a rattle and listening to the sound it makes); later goals often are more abstract (varying the heights from which objects are dropped and observing how the effects vary).
- Infants become increasingly able to form mental representations, moving from "out of sight, out of mind" to remembering a playmate's actions from days earlier. Such enduring mental representations make possible the next stage, which Piaget called preoperational thinking.

The Preoperational Stage (Ages 2 to 7)

Piaget viewed the preoperational period as including striking cognitive acquisitions and equally striking limitations. Perhaps the foremost acquisition is *symbolic representations;* among the most notable weaknesses are *egocentrism* and *centration.*

deferred imitation the repetition of other people's behaviour a substantial time after it originally occurred

symbolic representation the use of one object to stand for another

egocentrism the tendency to perceive the world solely from one's own point of view

Development of symbolic representations Have you ever seen preschoolers use two sticks to represent a gun or use a playing card to represent an iPhone? Forming such personal symbols is common among 3- to 5-year-olds. It is one of the ways in which they exercise their emerging capacity for **symbolic representation**—the use of one object, word, or thought to stand for another. Typically, objects that toddlers and preschoolers use as personal symbols physically resemble the objects they represent. The shapes of the sticks and playing card resemble those of a gun and an iPhone.

As children develop, they rely less on self-generated symbols and more on conventional ones. For example, when 5-year-olds play games involving pirates, they might wear a patch over one eye and a bandanna over their head because that is how pirates are commonly depicted. Heightened symbolic capabilities during the preoperational period are also evident in the growth of drawing. Children's drawings between ages 3 and 5 make increasing use of symbolic conventions, such as representing the leaves of flowers as Vs (Figure 4.2).

ILLUSTRATION BY VIVIAN HOXSEY

FIGURE 4.2 A 4-year-old's drawing of a summer day Note the use of simple artistic conventions, such as the V-shaped leaves on the flowers.

Egocentrism Piaget proposed that an important limitation of preoperational thinking is **egocentrism,** perceiving the world solely from one's own point of view. An example of this limitation involves preschoolers' difficulty in taking other people's spatial perspectives. Piaget and Inhelder (1956/1977) demonstrated this difficulty by having 4-year-olds sit at a table in front of a model of three mountains of different sizes (Figure 4.3). The children were asked to identify which of several photographs depicted what a doll would see if it were sitting on chairs at various locations around the table. Solving this problem required children to recognize that their own perspective was not the only one possible and to imagine the view from another location. Most 4-year-olds, according to Piaget, cannot do this.

The same difficulty in taking other people's perspectives is seen in quite different contexts—for example, in communication. As illustrated in Figure 4.4,

FIGURE 4.3 **Piaget's three-mountains task** When asked to choose the picture that shows what the doll sitting in the seat across the table would see, most children younger than 6 years choose the picture showing how the scene looks to them, illustrating their difficulty in separating their own perspective from that of others.

FIGURE 4.4 **Egocentrism** An example of young children's egocentric conversations.

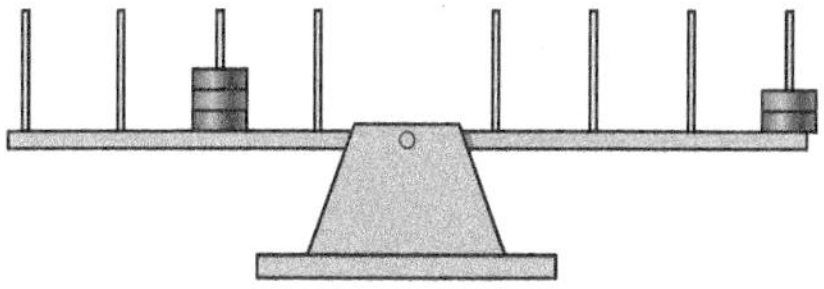

FIGURE 4.5 **The balance scale** When asked to predict which side of a balance scale, like the one shown here, would go down if the arm were allowed to move, 5- and 6-year-olds almost always centre their attention on the amount of weight and ignore the distances of the weights from the fulcrum. Thus, they would predict that the left side would go down, even though it is the right side that would actually drop.

preschoolers often talk right past each other, focused only on what they themselves are saying, seemingly oblivious to other people's comments.

Over the course of the preoperational period, egocentric speech becomes less common. An early sign of progress is children's verbal quarrels, which become increasingly frequent during this period. The fact that a child's statements elicit a playmate's objection indicates that the playmate is at least paying attention to the differing perspective that the other child's comment implies. Children also become better able to envision spatial perspectives other than their own during the preoperational period. We all remain somewhat egocentric throughout our lives—our own perspectives almost always seem more compelling than those of other people—but most of us do become less egocentric with age and experience.

The Balance-Scale Problem

MACMILLAN LEARNING

Centration Young children often focus on a single, perceptually striking feature of an object or event to the exclusion of other relevant features, a process that Piaget labelled **centration**. Their approaches to balance-scale problems provide a good example of centration. If presented with a balance scale like that in Figure 4.5 and asked which side will go down if a support were released, 5- and 6-year-olds centre on the amount of weight on each side, ignore the distance of the weights from the fulcrum, and say that whichever side has more weight will go down (Inhelder & Piaget, 1958).

Another good example of centration comes from Piaget's research on children's understanding of conservation. The idea of the **conservation concept** is that changing the appearance or arrangement of objects does not necessarily change other key properties, such as the quantity of material. Three variants of the concept that are commonly studied in 5- to 8-year-olds are *conservation of liquid quantity*, *conservation of solid quantity*, and *conservation of number* (Piaget, 1952a). In all three cases, the tasks used to measure children's understanding employ a three-phase procedure (Figure 4.6). First, as in the figure, children are shown two objects (e.g., two glasses of orange drink, two clay sausages) that are identical in quantity, or two sets of objects (e.g., two rows of pennies) that are identical in number. Once children agree that the dimension of interest (e.g., the amount of orange drink or the number of pennies) is equal in the two objects or sets, they observe a second phase in which the experimenter transforms one object or set in a way that makes it look different but does not change the dimension of interest. Orange drink might be poured into a taller, narrower glass; a short, thick clay sausage might be

centration the tendency to focus on a single, perceptually striking feature of an object or event

conservation concept the idea that merely changing the appearance of objects does not necessarily change the objects' other key properties

Piaget's Conservation-of-Liquid Task

WORTH PUBLISHERS

Piaget's Conservation-of-Number Task

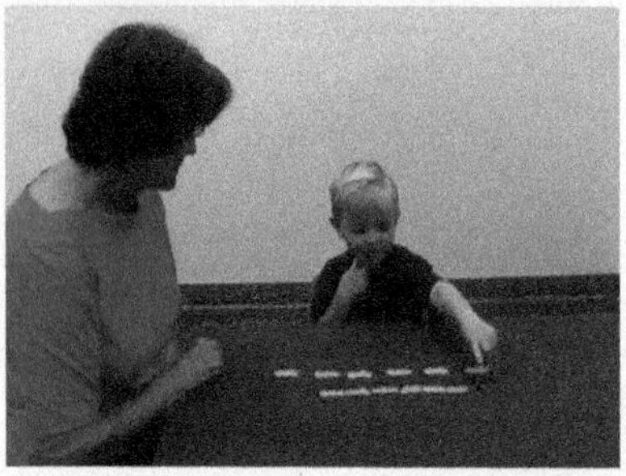

WORTH PUBLISHERS

molded into a long, thin sausage; or a row of pennies might be spread out. Finally, in the third phase, children are asked whether the dimension of interest, which they earlier had said was equal for the two objects or sets of objects, remains equal.

The large majority of 4- and 5-year-olds answer "no." On conservation-of-liquid-quantity problems, they claim that the taller, narrower glass has more orange drink; on conservation-of-solid-quantity problems, they claim that the long, thin sausage has more clay than the short, thick one; and so on. Children of this age make similar errors in everyday contexts; for example, they often think that if a child has one fewer cookie than another child, a fair solution is to break one of the short-changed child's cookies into two pieces, so that he or she will have as many cookies as the other child (Miller, 1984).

In the next period of cognitive development, the concrete operational stage, children considerably reduce their egocentrism and centration, which allows them to solve these and many other problems.

The Concrete Operational Stage (Ages 7 to 12)

At around age 7, according to Piaget, children begin to reason logically about concrete features of the world. For example, although few 5-year-olds solve any of the three conservation tasks described in the previous section, most 8-year-olds solve all of them. The same progress allows children in the concrete operational stage to solve many other problems that require attention to multiple dimensions. Thus, on the balance-scale problem, they consider distance from the fulcrum as well as weight on the two sides.

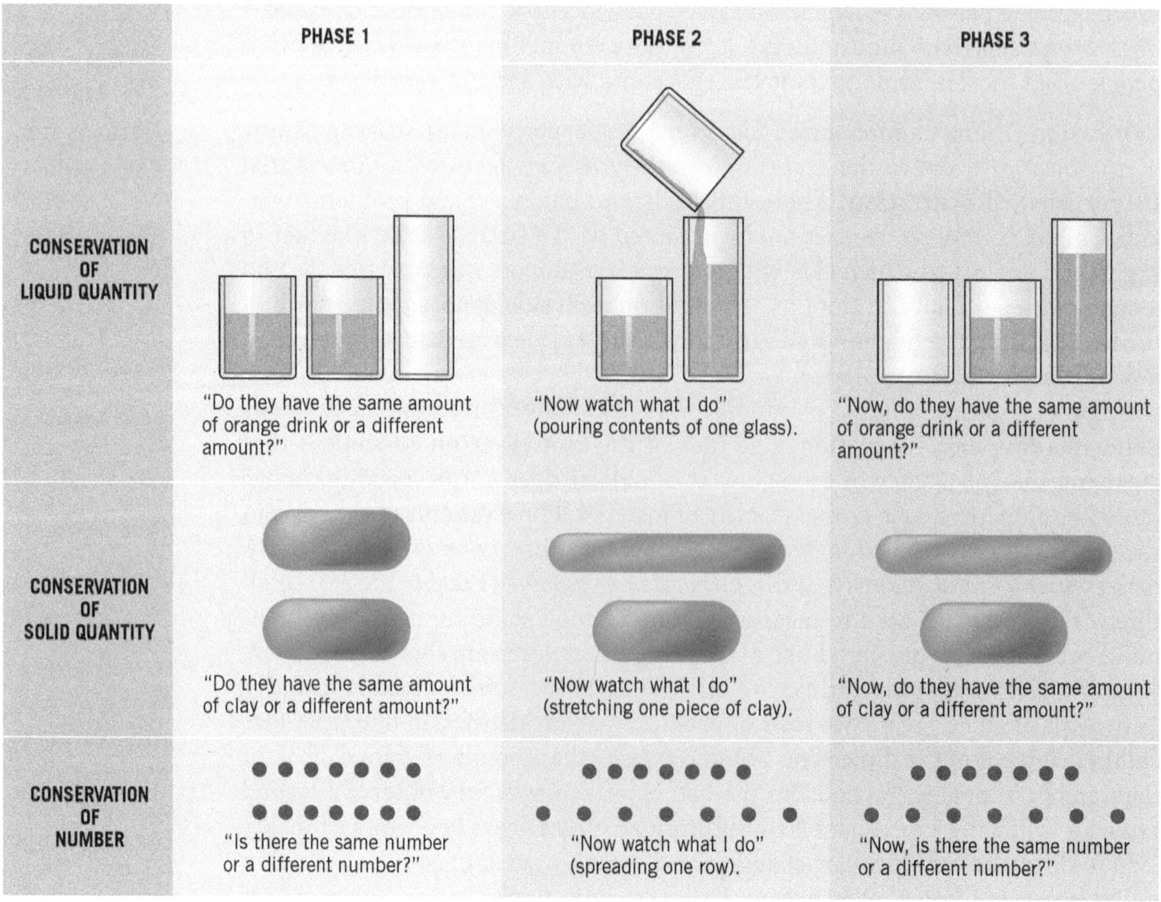
PHASE 1
PHASE 2
PHASE 3
CONSERVATION OF LIQUID QUANTITY
"Do they have the same amount of orange drink or a different amount?"
"Now watch what I do" (pouring contents of one glass).
"Now, do they have the same amount of orange drink or a different amount?"
CONSERVATION OF SOLID QUANTITY
"Do they have the same amount of clay or a different amount?"
"Now watch what I do" (stretching one piece of clay).
"Now, do they have the same amount of clay or a different amount?"
CONSERVATION OF NUMBER
"Is there the same number or a different number?"
"Now watch what I do" (spreading one row).
"Now, is there the same number or a different number?"

FIGURE 4.6 **Procedures used to test conservation of liquid quantity, solid quantity, and number** Most 4- and 5-year-olds say that the taller liquid column has more liquid, the longer sausage has more clay, and the longer row has more objects.

However, this relatively advanced reasoning is, according to Piaget, limited to concrete situations. Thinking systematically remains very difficult, as does reasoning about hypothetical situations. These limitations are evident in the types of experiments that concrete operational children perform to solve the pendulum problem (Figure 4.7; Inhelder & Piaget, 1958). In this problem, children are presented a pendulum frame, a set of strings of varying lengths with a loop at each end, and a set of metal weights of varying weights, any of which can be attached to any string. When the loop at one end of the string is attached to a weight, and the loop at the other end is attached to the frame of the pendulum, the string can be swung. The task is to perform experiments that indicate which factor or factors influence the amount of time it takes the pendulum to swing through a complete arc. Is it the length of the string, the heaviness of the weight, the height from which the weight is dropped, or some combination of these factors?

Most concrete operational children, like most adolescents and adults, begin their experiments believing that the relative heaviness of the weights being dropped is the most important factor, perhaps the only important one. What distinguishes the children's reasoning from that of older individuals is how they test their beliefs. Concrete operational children design biased experiments from which no valid conclusion can be drawn. For example, they might compare the travel time of a heavy weight on a short string dropped from a high position to the travel time of a light weight on a long string dropped from a lower position. When the first string goes faster, they conclude that, just as they thought, heavy weights go faster. This premature conclusion, however, reflects their limited ability to think systematically or to imagine all possible combinations of variables. They fail to imagine that the faster motion might be related to the length of the string or the height from which the string was dropped, rather than the weight of the object.

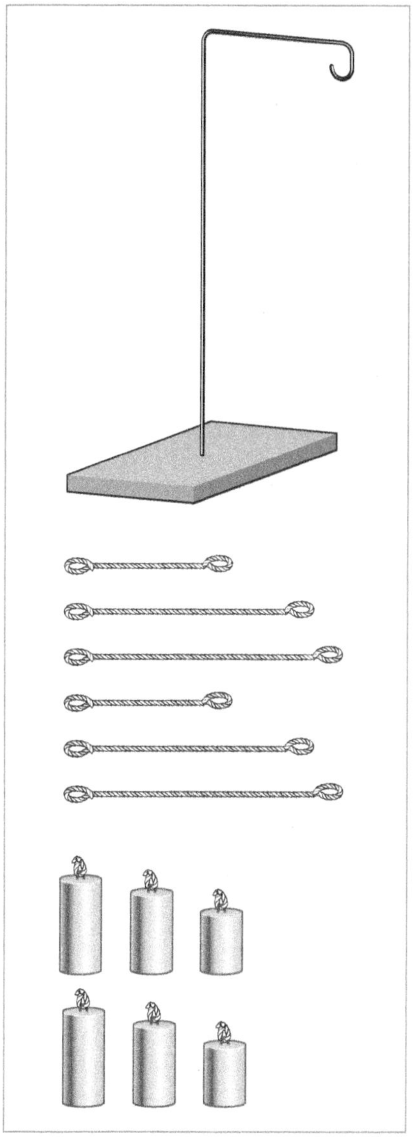

FIGURE 4.7 Inhelder and Piaget's pendulum problem The task is to determine the influence of weight, string length, and dropping point on the time it takes for the pendulum to swing back and forth. Unbiased experiments require varying one and only one variable at a time—for example, comparing a heavier weight to a lighter weight when both are attached to strings of the same length and dropped from the same point. Children younger than 12 usually perform unsystematic experiments and draw incorrect conclusions.

The Formal Operational Stage (Age 12 and Beyond)

Formal operational thinking, which includes the ability to think abstractly and to reason hypothetically, is the pinnacle of Piaget's stage progression. The difference between reasoning in this stage and in the previous one is clearly illustrated by formal operational reasoners' approach to the pendulum problem. Framing the problem more abstractly than do children in the concrete operational stage, formal operational reasoners see that any of the variables—weight, string length, and dropping point—might influence the time it takes for the pendulum to swing through an arc, and that it is therefore necessary to test the effect of each variable systematically. For example, to test the effect of weight, they compare times to complete an arc for a heavier weight and a lighter weight, attached to strings of equal length dropped from the same position. To test the effect of string length, they compare the travel times of a long and a short string, with equal weight dropped from the same position. Such systematic experiments allow the formal operational thinker to determine that the only factor that influences the pendulum's travel time is the length of the string.

Piaget believed that unlike the previous three stages, the formal operational stage is not universal: not all adolescents (or adults) reach it. For those adolescents who do reach it, however, formal operational thinking greatly expands and enriches their intellectual universe. Such thinking makes it possible for them to see the particular reality in which they live as only one of an infinite number of possible realities. This insight leads them to think about alternative ways that the world could be and to ponder deep questions concerning truth, justice, and morality. It no doubt also helps account for the fact that many people first acquire a taste

BOX 4.1 APPLICATIONS Educational Applications of Piaget's Theory

Piaget's view of children's cognitive development holds a number of general implications for how children should be educated (Case, 1998; Piaget, 1972). Among the most important is that children learn best by interacting with the environment, both mentally and physically. One research demonstration of this principle involved promoting children's understanding of the concept of speed (Levin, Siegler, & Druyan, 1990). The investigation focused on problems of a type beloved by physics teachers: "When a race horse travels around a circular track, do its right and left sides move at the same speed?" It appears obvious that they do, but, in fact, they do not. The side toward the outside of the track is covering a slightly greater distance in the same amount of time as the side toward the inside and therefore is moving slightly faster.

Iris Levin and her colleagues devised a procedure that allowed children to actively experience how different parts of a single object can move at different speeds. They attached one end of a 7-foot-long metal bar to a pivot that was mounted on the floor. One by one, 6th-graders and an experimenter took four walks around the pivot while holding onto the bar. On two of the walks, the child held the bar near the pivot and the experimenter held it at the far end; on the other two walks, they switched positions (see figure). After each walk, children were asked whether the inner or outer part of the bar had moved faster.

The child and adult are holding onto a bar as they walk around a circle four times. On the first two trips around, the child holds the bar near the pivot; on the second two trips, the child holds it at its end. The much faster pace needed to keep up with the bar when holding onto its end leads the child to realize that the end was moving faster than the inner portion (Levin et al., 1990).

The difference between the speeds required for walking while holding the inner and the outer parts of the metal bar was so dramatic that the children generalized their new understanding to other problems involving circular motion, such as cars moving around circular tracks on a computer screen. Physically experiencing the concept accomplished what years of formal science instruction usually fail to do. As one boy put it, "Before, I hadn't experienced it. I didn't think about it. Now that I have had that experience, I know that when I was on the outer circle, I had to walk faster to be at the same place as you" (Levin et al., 1990). Clearly, relevant physical activities, accompanied by questions that call attention to the lessons of the activities, can foster children's learning.

for science fiction during adolescence. The alternative worlds depicted in science-fiction stories appeal to adolescents' emerging capacity to think about the world they know as just one of many possibilities and to wonder whether a better world is possible.

The attainment of formal operational thinking does not mean that adolescents will always reason in advanced ways, but it does, according to Piaget, mark the point at which adolescents attain the reasoning powers of intelligent adults. (Some ways in which Piaget's theory has been applied to improving education are discussed in Box 4.1.)

MARK RICHARDS / PHOTOEDIT

Teenagers' emerging ability to understand that their reality is only one of many possible realities may cause teens to develop a taste for science fiction.

Piaget's Legacy

Although Piaget's theory was formulated many years ago, it remains a very influential approach to understanding cognitive development and includes many valuable insights (summarized in Table 4.2). However, it also has some crucial weaknesses (Miller, 2011):

1. *Piaget's theory is vague about the mechanisms that give rise to children's thinking and that produce cognitive growth.* Piaget's theory provides any number of excellent descriptions of children's thinking. It is less revealing, however, about the processes that lead children to think in a particular way and that produce changes in their thinking. Assimilation, accommodation, and equilibration have an air of plausibility, but how they operate is unclear.
2. *Infants and young children are more cognitively competent than Piaget recognized.* Piaget employed fairly difficult tests to assess most of the concepts he studied. This led him to miss infants' and young children's earliest knowledge of these concepts. For example, Piaget's test of object

TABLE 4.2 Piaget's Stages of Cognitive Development

Stage	Approximate Age	New Ways of Knowing
Sensorimotor	Birth to 2 years	Infants know the world through their senses and through their actions. For example, they learn what dogs look like and what petting them feels like.
Preoperational	2–7 years	Toddlers and young children acquire the ability to internally represent the world through language and mental imagery. They also begin to see the world from other people's perspectives, not just from their own.
Concrete operational	7–12 years	Children become able to think logically, not just intuitively. They now can understand that events are often influenced by multiple factors, not just one.
Formal operational	12 years and beyond	Adolescents can think systematically and reason about what might be, as well as what is. This allows them to understand politics, ethics, and science fiction about alternative political and ethical systems, as well as to engage in scientific reasoning.

permanence required children to reach for the hidden object after a delay; Piaget claimed that children do not do this until about 8 months of age. However, alternative tests of object permanence, which analyze where infants *look* immediately after the object has disappeared from view, indicate that by 3 months of age, infants at least suspect that objects continue to exist (Baillargeon, 1987a, b; 1993).

3. *Piaget's theory understates the contribution of the social world to cognitive development.* Piaget's theory focuses on how children come to understand the world through their own efforts. From the day that children emerge from the womb, however, they live in an environment of adults, older children, and cultural institutions and values that shape their cognitive development in countless ways. A child's cognitive development reflects the contributions of other people, and of the broader culture, to a far greater degree than Piaget's theory acknowledges.
4. *The stage model depicts children's thinking as being more consistent than it is.* According to Piaget, once children enter a given stage, their thinking consistently shows the characteristics of that stage across diverse concepts. Subsequent research, however, has shown that children's thinking is far more variable than this depiction suggests. For example, most children succeed on conservation-of-number problems by age 6, whereas most do not succeed on conservation-of-solid-quantity until about age 8 (Field, 1987).

These weaknesses of Piaget's theory do not negate the magnitude of his achievement: it remains one of the major intellectual accomplishments of the past century. However, appreciating the weaknesses as well as the strengths of his theory is necessary for understanding why alternative theories of cognitive development have become increasingly prominent.

In the remainder of this chapter, we consider the four most prominent alternative theories of cognitive development: information-processing, core-knowledge, sociocultural, and dynamic-systems. Each can be seen as an attempt to overcome a major weakness of Piaget's approach. *Information-processing theories* emphasize precise characterizations of the mechanisms that give rise to children's thinking and that produce cognitive growth. *Core-knowledge theories* focus on the surprisingly early knowledge and skills that infants and young children show in areas thought to be of evolutionary importance. *Sociocultural theories* emphasize the ways in which children's interactions with other people and with the products of their culture guide cognitive development. *Dynamic-systems theories* highlight the variability of children's thinking, even from moment to moment.

REVIEW QUESTIONS

Piaget proposed four primary stages of development, the last of which is reached in adolescence or later (if at all). Consider your own experience. How, if at all, does your thinking process reflect the characteristics of the formal operational stage? When do you think you began reasoning in this advanced way? ■

Information-Processing Theories

SCENE: DAUGHTER AND FATHER IN THEIR YARD.
A PLAYMATE RIDES IN ON A BIKE.

Child: Daddy, would you unlock the basement door?
Father: Why?
Child: 'Cause I want to ride my bike.
Father: Your bike is in the garage.
Child: But my socks are in the dryer.

(Klahr, 1978, pp. 181–182)

What reasoning could have produced this 5-year-old's enigmatic comment, "But my socks are in the dryer"? David Klahr, an eminent information-processing theorist (and the father in the conversation) formulated the following model of the thought process that led to it:

Top goal: I want to ride my bike.
  Bias: I need shoes to ride comfortably.
  Fact: I'm barefoot.
Subgoal 1: Get my sneakers.
  Fact: The sneakers are in the yard.
  Fact: They're uncomfortable on bare feet.
Subgoal 2: Get my socks.
  Fact: The sock drawer was empty this morning.
  Inference: The socks probably are in the dryer.
Subgoal 3: Get them from the dryer.
  Fact: The dryer is in the basement.
Subgoal 4: Go to the basement.
  Fact: It's quicker to go through the yard entrance.
  Fact: The yard entrance is always locked.
Subgoal 5: Unlock the door to the basement.
  Fact: Daddies have the keys to everything.
Subgoal 6: Ask Daddy to unlock the door.

Klahr's analysis of his daughter's thinking illustrates two notable characteristics of **information-processing theories.**[1] One is the precise specification of the surprisingly complex processes involved in children's thinking. To help specify these processes,

information-processing theories a class of theories that focus on the structure of the cognitive system and the mental activities used to deploy attention and memory to solve problems

[1] Here and throughout this section, we use the plural term "information-processing *theories*" rather than the singular "information-processing *theory*" because information-processing theories consist of a family of related approaches rather than a single theory. For the same reason, in subsequent sections we refer to "core-knowledge theories," "sociocultural theories," and "dynamic-systems theories."

Klahr used **task analysis**—that is, identification of goals needed to perform the task, obstacles that prevent immediate realization of the goals, prior knowledge relevant to achieving the goals, and potential strategies for reaching the desired outcome.

Task analysis helps information-processing researchers understand and predict children's behaviour and rigorously test precise hypotheses regarding how development occurs. In some cases, it also allows them to formulate a **computer simulation,** a type of mathematical model that expresses ideas about mental processes in precise ways. For example, Simon and Klahr (1995) created computer simulations of the knowledge and mental processes that led young children to fail on conservation problems and of the somewhat different knowledge and mental processes that allowed older children to succeed on them. Comparing the two simulations allowed the researchers to identify processes that produced the change from failure to success. Computer simulations have been used to model many other aspects of development as well, including object permanence (Munakata & McClelland, 2003), word learning (McMurray, Horst, & Samuelson, 2012), working memory (Buss & Spencer, 2014), reading (Seidenberg, 2005), and problem solving (Siegler & Araya, 2005).

A second distinctive feature of information-processing theories is an emphasis on thinking as a process that occurs over time. Often, a single simple behaviour, such as the initial request of Klahr's daughter that he open the basement door, reflects an extended sequence of fast, unconscious mental operations. Information-processing analyses identify what those mental operations are, the order in which they are executed, and how increasing speed and accuracy of mental operations lead to cognitive growth.

task analysis the research technique of specifying the goals, obstacles to their realization, and potential solution strategies involved in problem solving

computer simulation a type of mathematical model that expresses ideas about mental processes in precise ways

problem solving the process of attaining a goal by using a strategy to overcome an obstacle

View of Children's Nature

Information-processing theorists see cognitive development as occurring continuously, in small increments that happen at different ages on different tasks. This depiction differs fundamentally from Piaget's belief that children progress through qualitatively distinct, broadly applicable stages at similar ages.

The Child as a Limited-Capacity Processing System

In the information-processing view, cognitive development arises from children gradually surmounting their processing limitations, in particular their limited working memory capacity, processing speed, and knowledge of useful strategies and content. Through learning and maturation of brain structures, children expand the amounts of information they can process at one time, process information faster, and acquire new strategies and knowledge. Together, these changes yield improvement in problem solving, memory, and other cognitive functions.

The Child as Problem Solver

Also central to the view of human nature held by information-processing theories is the assumption that children are *active problem solvers.* As suggested by Klahr's analysis of his daughter's reasoning, **problem solving** involves strategies for overcoming obstacles and attaining goals. A description of a younger child's problem solving reveals the same combination of goal, obstacle, and strategy:

> Georgie (a 2-year-old) wants to throw rocks out the kitchen window. . . . Dad says that Georgie can't throw rocks out the window, because he'll break the lawnmower. . . . Georgie . . . goes outside, brings in some green peaches that he had been playing with, and says: "They won't break the lawnmower."
>
> (Waters, 1989, p. 7)

In addition to illustrating the typical goal–obstacle–strategy sequence, this example highlights another basic tenet of information-processing approaches: children's cognitive flexibility helps them attain their goals. Even young children show great ingenuity in surmounting the obstacles imposed by their parents, the physical environment, and their own lack of knowledge.

Central Developmental Issues

One distinctive characteristic of information-processing theories is their emphasis on precise descriptions of change mechanisms. The way in which information-processing theories address how change occurs can be seen particularly clearly in their accounts of the development of memory and problem solving.

The Development of Memory

Memory is crucial to everything we do. The skills we use on everyday tasks, the language we employ when writing or speaking, the emotions we feel on a given occasion—all depend on our memories of past experiences and the knowledge acquired through them. Information-processing theories distinguish among three types of memory processes: *working memory, long-term memory,* and *executive functioning.*

Working memory **Working memory** involves actively attending to, maintaining, and processing information (Cowan, 2016). For example, if a child was asked to read a story about birds and told that they would be asked questions about the story afterward, the child would use working memory processes to attend to and maintain information from the story, draw inferences from that information, retrieve relevant prior knowledge, and combine the information to construct a reasonable answer. All of this processing might occur in less than a second, thus illustrating the rapidity of working memory processes.

Working memory is limited in both its capacity (the amount of information that can be actively attended to at one time) and in the length of time for which it can maintain information in an active state without updating. For example, a child might be able to remember a sequence of five but not six digits, and might remember them for 10 seconds but not 15 without repeating them. The exact capacity and duration vary with age, the task, and the type of information being processed (Cowan, 2016).

The capacity and speed of working memory increase greatly during infancy, childhood, and adolescence (Barrouillet & Camos, 2015). These changes occur because of increasing knowledge of the content on which working memory operates and because of brain maturation (Nelson, Thomas, & de Haan, 2006; see Figure 4.8).

Long-term memory In contrast to the short-term nature of working memory, **long-term memory** consists of the knowledge that people accumulate over their lifetime. It includes factual knowledge (e.g., knowing the capitals of different countries or the team that won the Stanley Cup last year), conceptual knowledge (e.g., the concepts of justice and equality), procedural knowledge (e.g., knowing how to shoot a hockey puck or play a specific video game), attitudes (e.g., likes and dislikes regarding politicians or foods), and so on. Long-term memory thus is the totality of one's knowledge, whereas working memory is the subset of that knowledge attended to at a given time (Cowan, 2016).

In contrast to the strict limits on the capacity and duration of working memory, long-term memory can retain an unlimited amount of information

working memory memory system that involves actively attending to, maintaining, and processing information

long-term memory information retained on an enduring basis

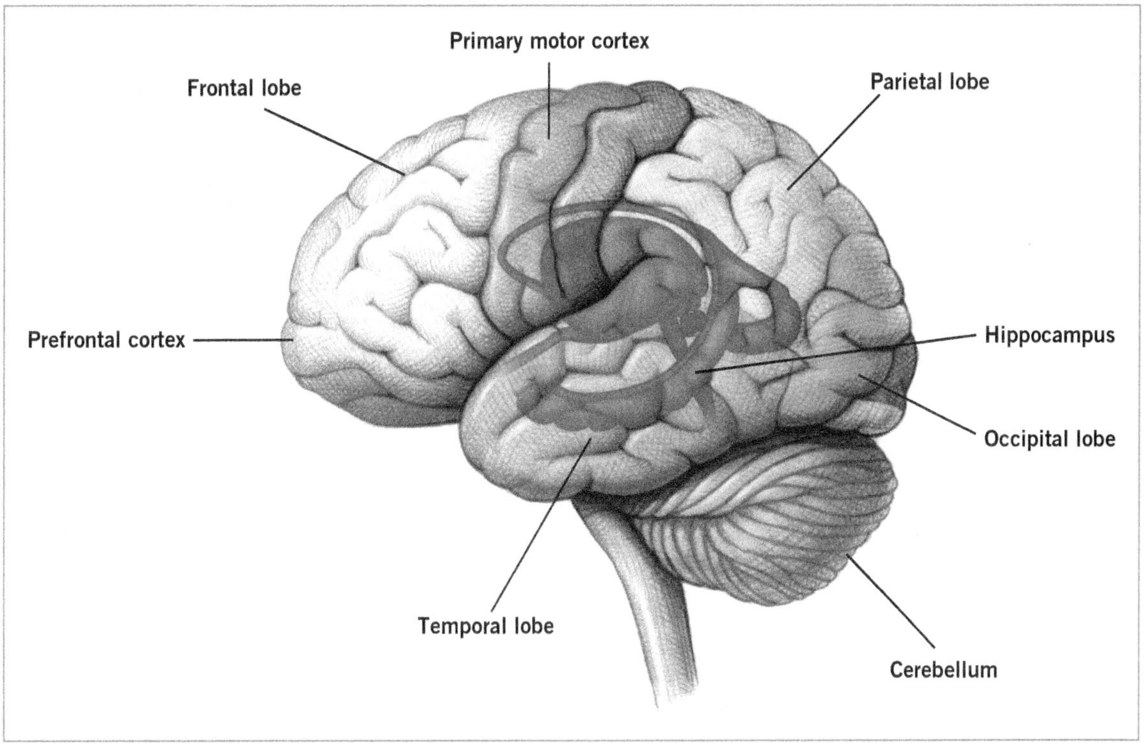

FIGURE 4.8 Major areas of the cortex All the major areas of the cortex shown here continue to mature after birth. Brain maturation continues for a particularly long time, at least into one's 20s, in the prefrontal cortex, an area that is especially involved in planning, inhibiting inappropriate behaviour, and adopting new goals in response to changing situations.

for unlimited periods of time. To cite one notable example, people who studied Spanish or algebra in high school often retain a substantial amount of what they learned 50 years later, despite their not having used the information in the interim (Bahrick & Phelps, 1987).

Executive functioning Executive functions control behaviour and thought processes. The prefrontal cortex (Figure 4.8) plays a particularly important role in this cognitive control. Three key executive functions are *inhibition,* as when resisting the temptation to play with one's phone when an important test looms; *enhancement of working memory* through use of strategies, such as selectively attending to the most important information; and *cognitive flexibility,* such as imagining someone else's perspective in an argument despite that perspective differing from one's own (Blair, 2016; Diamond, 2013).

The ability of executive functions to control thinking and action—enabling the individual to respond appropriately rather than acting impulsively or out of habit—increases greatly during the preschool and early elementary school years. One type of improvement is increased flexibility in shifting goals. For instance, when 3-year-olds are asked to sort toys by colour, then to sort the same toys by shape, then to sort them by colour again, and so on, most have difficulty switching their sorting goals. In contrast, 5-year-olds do so easily (Baker, Friedman, & Leslie, 2010; Zelazo & Carlson, 2012).

The ability to inhibit habitual responses becomes apparent slightly later and is evident in everyday games such as "Simon Says." The appeal of this game for preschoolers is the challenge, for them, of inhibiting the impulse to quickly respond to commands that are not preceded by the words "Simon says." Early elementary school children, in contrast, find inhibiting the impulse to act immediately much easier, which reduces the game's appeal for them (Best & Miller, 2010; Sabbagh et al., 2006).

basic processes the simplest and most frequently used mental activities

encoding the process of representing in memory information that draws attention or is considered important

The quality of executive functioning during early childhood predicts many important later outcomes, including high school academic achievement, college enrollment, and adult income and occupational prestige (Blair & Raver, 2015; Cantin et al., 2016). Executive functioning is also related to the benefits that children derive from instruction intended to help them gain other skills. For example, Canadian preschoolers with strong executive functioning skills learn more than peers from instruction intended to improve their understanding of other people's thinking (Benson et al., 2013).

Explanations of memory development Information-processing theorists try to explain both the processes that make memory as good as it is at each age and the limitations that prevent it from being better. These efforts have focused on three types of capabilities: *basic processes, strategies,* and *content knowledge.*

BASIC PROCESSES The simplest and most frequently used mental activities are known as **basic processes.** They include *associating* events with one another, *recognizing* objects as familiar, *recalling* facts and procedures, and *generalizing* from one instance to another. Another basic process, which is key to all the others, is **encoding**—the representation in memory of specific features of objects and events. With development, children execute basic processes more efficiently, enhancing their memory and learning for all kinds of materials.

Most of these basic processes are familiar and their importance obvious. However, *encoding* may be less familiar. Appreciating its significance requires some understanding of the way in which memory works. People often think of memory as something akin to an unedited movie of experiences, but memory is actually far more selective. People encode information that draws their attention or that they consider important, but they fail to encode a great deal of other information. If information is not encoded, it is not remembered later. Failure to encode information is probably evident in your own memory of the Canadian loonie; although you have seen this coin many times, you most likely have not encoded whether the loon faces to the right or to the left.

Studies of how children learn to solve balance-scale problems illustrate the importance of encoding for learning, memory, and problem solving. As discussed on page 125, most 5-year-olds predict that the side of the scale with more weight will go down, regardless of the distance of the weights from the fulcrum. Five-year-olds generally have difficulty learning more advanced approaches to solving balance-scale problems that take into account distance as well as weight, because they do not encode information about the distances of the weights from the fulcrum. To assess encoding of balance-scale configurations, children are shown a balance scale with varying arrangements of weights on pegs; the scale is then hidden behind an opaque barrier, and the children are asked to reproduce the arrangement on an identical but empty balance scale.

Five-year-olds generally reproduce the correct number of weights on each side but rarely put them the correct distance from the fulcrum (Siegler, 1976). Teaching a randomly chosen group of 5-year-olds to encode distance by telling them that both weight and distance are important and then showing them which side went down on several problems enabled them to learn more advanced balance-scale rules; peers who were not taught to encode distance failed to learn from the same problems.

Like improved encoding, improved speed of processing plays a key role in the development of memory, problem solving, and learning. As shown in Figure 4.9, processing speed increases most rapidly at young ages

"Mirror, mirror, on the wall, who's the fairest of the mall?"

Misencoding common sayings can lead to memorable confusions.

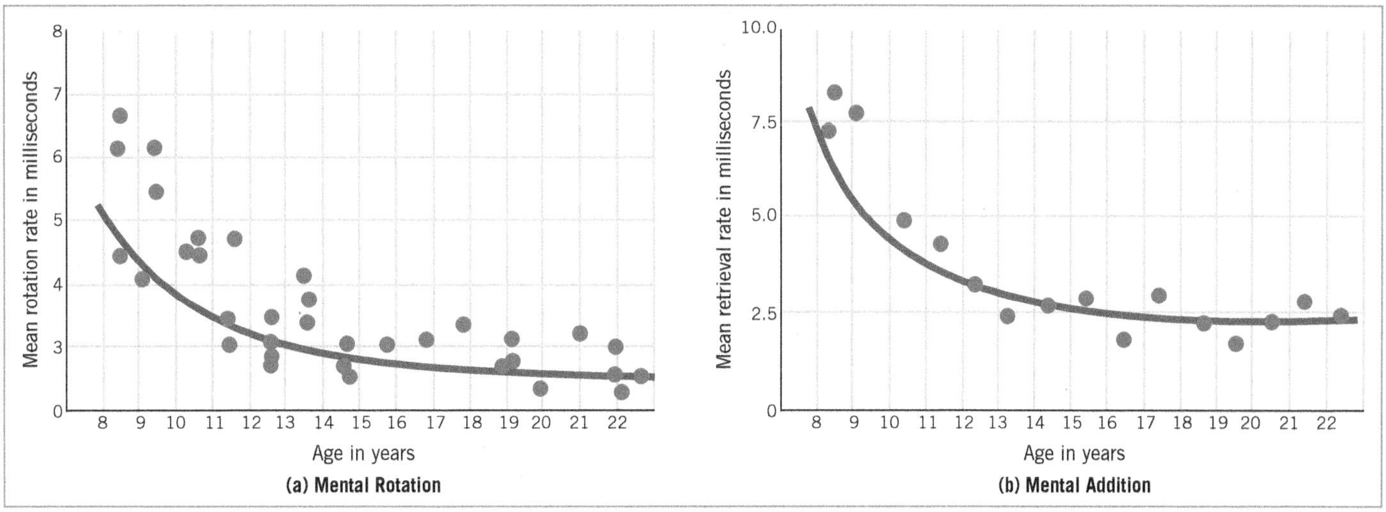

FIGURE 4.9 Increase with age in speed of processing on two tasks Note that the increase is rapid in the early years and more gradual later. (Data from Kail, 1991)

but continues to increase for many years thereafter (Kail, 1991; Kail, Lervåg, & Hulme, 2016).

Two biological processes that contribute to faster speed of processing are myelination and increased connectivity among brain regions (Johnson, 2011; Luna et al., 2004). As discussed in Chapter 3, from the prenatal period through adolescence, increasing numbers of axons become covered with myelin, the insulating substance that promotes faster and more reliable transmission of electrical impulses in the brain (Paus, 2010). Greater connectivity among brain regions also increases processing speed by allowing more direct transmission of information across brain areas.

Overcoming Attentional Inertia

STRATEGIES Information-processing theories point to the acquisition and growth of strategies as another major source of memory development. Between ages 5 and 8 years, children begin to use a number of broadly useful memory strategies, among them the strategy of **rehearsal,** the repeating of information multiple times in order to remember it. The following excerpt from a newspaper article illustrates the usefulness of rehearsal for remembering information verbatim:

> A 9-year-old boy memorized the license plate number of a getaway car following an armed robbery, a court was told Monday. . . . The boy and his friend . . . looked in the drug store window and saw a man grab a 14-year-old cashier's neck. . . . After the robbery, the boys mentally repeated the license number until they gave it to police.
>
> (*Edmonton Journal,* Jan. 13, 1981, cited in Kail, 1984)

Had the boys witnessed the same event when they were 5-year-olds, they probably would not have rehearsed the numbers and would have forgotten the license number before the police arrived.

Another widely used memory strategy that becomes increasingly prevalent in the preschool and early elementary school years is **selective attention,** the process of intentionally focusing on the information that is most relevant to the current goal (Hanania & Smith, 2010). If 7- and 8-year-olds are shown objects from two different categories (e.g., several toy animals and several tools) and are told that they later will need to remember the objects in only one category (e.g., "You'll need to remember the animals"), they focus their attention on the objects in the specified category and remember more of them. In contrast, given the

rehearsal the process of repeating information multiple times to aid memory of it

selective attention the process of intentionally focusing on the information that is most relevant to the current goal

overlapping waves theory an information-processing approach that emphasizes the variability of children's thinking

same instructions, 4-year-olds pay roughly equal attention to the objects in both categories, which reduces their memory for the objects they need to remember (DeMarie-Dreblow & Miller, 1988).

CONTENT KNOWLEDGE With age and experience, children's knowledge about almost everything increases. This increased knowledge improves recall of new material by making it easier to integrate the new material with existing understanding (Schneider & Ornstein, 2015). The importance of content knowledge to memory is illustrated by the fact that when children know more than adults about a topic, they often remember more new information about the topic than adults do. For example, when children and adults are provided new information about children's TV programs and books, the children generally remember more of the new information than do the adults (Lindberg, 1991). Similarly, children who know a lot about soccer learn more from reading new soccer stories than do children who are older and have higher IQs but who know less about soccer (Schneider, Körkel, & Weinert, 1989).

Prior content knowledge improves memory for new information in several different ways. One is through improving encoding. In tests of memory of various arrangements of chess pieces on a board, child chess experts remember far more than do adult novices (Chi & Ceci, 1987). The reason is that greater knowledge of chess leads these children to encode the positions of several pieces relative to one another rather than encoding the location of each piece separately (Lane & Chang, 2018).

Content knowledge also improves memory by providing useful associations. A child who is knowledgeable about birds knows that type of beak and type of diet are associated, so remembering either one increases memory for the other (Johnson & Mervis, 1994). In addition, content knowledge indicates what is and is not possible and therefore guides memory in useful directions. For example, when people familiar with baseball are asked to recall a particular inning of a game that they watched, and they can remember only two outs in that inning, they recognize that there must have been a third out and search their memories for it; people who lack baseball knowledge do not do this (Walker, 1987).

The Development of Problem Solving

Information-processing theories depict children as active problem solvers whose use of strategies often allows them to overcome limitations of knowledge and processing capacity. In this section, we present one prominent information-processing perspective on the development of problem solving—overlapping waves theory.

Piaget's theory depicted children of a given age as using a particular strategy to solve a particular class of problems. For example, he described 5-year-olds as solving conservation-of-number problems (see Figure 4.6) by choosing the longer row of objects, and 7-year-olds as solving the same problems by reasoning that if nothing was added or subtracted, the number of objects must remain the same. According to **overlapping waves theory,** however, individual children usually use a variety of approaches to solve such problems (Siegler, 1996). For instance, examining 5-year-olds' reasoning on repeated trials of the conservation-of-number problem reveals that most children use at least three different strategies (Siegler, 1995). The same child who on one

Through repeated experiences engaging in activities such as chess, children gain content knowledge that improves their memory for and reasoning about subsequent, similar events.

RONNIE KAUFMAN/LARRY HIRSHOWITZ/GETTY IMAGES

trial incorrectly reasons that the longer row must have more objects will on other trials correctly reason that spreading a row does not change the number of objects; on yet other trials, the child will count the number of objects in the two rows to see which has more.

Figure 4.10 presents the typical pattern of development envisioned by the overlapping waves approach, with Strategy 1 representing the simplest strategy and Strategy 5 as the most advanced. At the youngest age depicted, children usually use Strategy 1, but they sometimes use Strategy 2 or 4. With age and experience, the strategies that produce more successful performances become more prevalent; new strategies also are generated and, if they are more effective than previous approaches, are used increasingly. Thus, by the middle of the age range in Figure 4.10, children have added Strategies 3 and 5 to the original group and have almost stopped using Strategy 1.

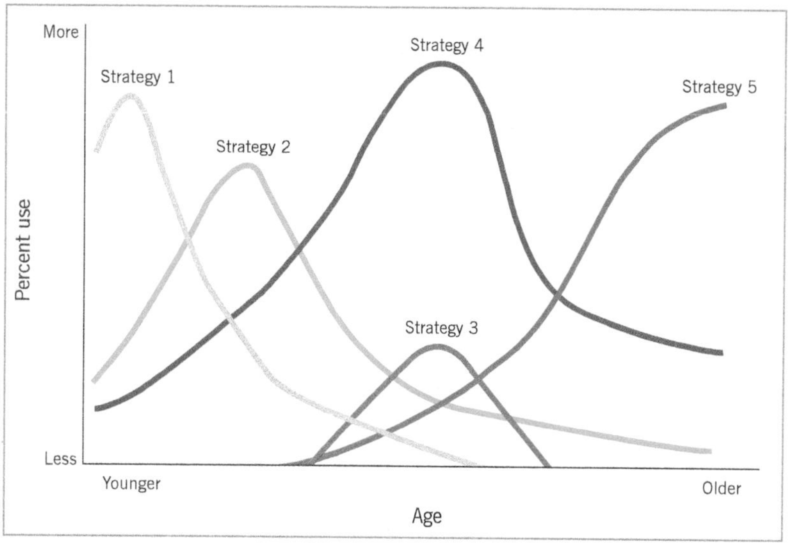

FIGURE 4.10 The overlapping waves model The overlapping waves model proposes that, at any one age, children use multiple strategies; that with age and experience, they rely increasingly on more advanced strategies (the ones with the higher numbers); and that development involves changes in the frequency of use of existing strategies as well as discovery of new approaches.

Overlapping waves theory has been shown to accurately characterize children's problem solving in a wide range of contexts, including arithmetic, time-telling, reading, spelling, scientific experimentation, biological understanding, tool use, and recall from memory (Siegler, 2006; Van der Ven et al., 2012). The theory also specifies several ways in which problem solving improves over the course of development. Children discover new strategies that are more effective than their previous ones, they learn to execute all strategies more efficiently, and they choose strategies that are more appropriate to the particular problem and situation (Lemaire & Brun, 2016).

All these sources of cognitive growth are evident in learning single-digit addition. During kindergarten and the first few years of elementary school, children's knowledge of these arithmetic problems improves greatly. One reason is that children discover new strategies, such as counting-on (e.g., solving 2 + 9 by thinking "9, 10, 11"). Another source of improvement is faster and more accurate execution of all the strategies that children know (e.g., retrieval of answers from memory, counting from one, and counting-on). A third source of improvement is that children choose among strategies increasingly adaptively (e.g., using counting-on most often on problems with a large difference between the addends, such as 2 + 9, but retrieving the answer on easy problems such as 2 + 2; Geary, 2006). (Box 4.2 provides an example of how information-processing analyses can improve education.)

Planning

Problem solving is often more successful if people plan before acting. Children benefit from planning the fastest route to friends' houses, how to get their way with parents, and how to break bad news to others in ways that are least likely to trigger angry reactions (Hudson, Sosa, & Shapiro, 1997). Despite the advantages of planning, however, children often fail to plan in situations in which it would help their problem solving (Berg et al., 1997). The question is why.

Information-processing analyses suggest that one reason planning is difficult for children is that it requires inhibiting the desire to solve the problem immediately in favour of first trying to choose the best strategy. Starting to work on an assigned paper without planning what will be written in the paper is one familiar example.

BOX 4.2 APPLICATIONS Educational Applications of Information-Processing Theories

Children's knowledge of numbers when they begin kindergarten predicts their mathematics achievement years later—in elementary school, middle school, and even high school (Watts et al., 2015). It is especially unfortunate, then, that children from low-income families are already far behind middle-income peers in such knowledge when they start kindergarten.

What might account for these early differences in numerical knowledge among children from different economic backgrounds? An information-processing analysis suggested that experience playing numerical board games such as Snakes and Ladders (known as Chutes and Ladders in some countries) might be one important factor. In Snakes and Ladders, players must move a token across 100 consecutively numbered squares, advancing on each of their turns by the number of spaces determined by a spinner or dice. A task analysis of the game indicated that the higher the number of the square on which a child's token rests at any given point in the game, the greater the number of number names the child will have spoken and heard during the game, the greater the distance the child will have moved the token from the first square, the greater the time the child will have been playing the game, and the greater the number of discrete hand movements with the token the child will have made. These verbal, spatial, temporal (time-based), and motor cues provide a broadly based, multisensory foundation for knowledge of numerical magnitudes (the quantities indicated by number words), a type of knowledge that is closely related to overall mathematics achievement (Siegler, 2016).

Ramani and Siegler (2008) applied this information-processing analysis to improving the numerical understanding of preschoolers from low-income families. The researchers randomly assigned 4- and 5-year-olds from impoverished families to either an experimental number-board condition or a control colour-board condition. The number-board condition was virtually identical to the first row of the Snakes and Ladders board; it included 10 squares numbered consecutively from left to right. On each turn, the child spun a spinner that yielded a 1 or a 2 and moved his or her token the corresponding number of squares on the board, stating the number on each square in the process. Children in the colour-board condition played the same game, except that their board had no numbers and the players would say the name of the colour of each square as they advanced their token. Players in both conditions played the game for four sessions, were helped by the experimenter if they did not know the numbers or colours in the squares, were given a pretest that examined their knowledge of numbers before playing the game, and were given a posttest that examined their knowledge of numbers just after the final game-playing session and again 9 weeks later.

On the posttest, children who played the number board game showed improved knowledge of the numbers 1 through 10 on all four tasks that were presented—counting, reading numbers, comparing magnitudes (e.g., "Which is bigger, 8 or 3?"), and estimating the locations of numbers on a number line. Significantly, all the gains were maintained on the follow-up test, 9 weeks later, thus demonstrating that the learning had lasting effects. In contrast, children who played the colour board game showed no improvement in any aspect of number knowledge.

Subsequent studies demonstrated that playing the 1–10 board game also improves preschoolers' ability to learn the answers to arithmetic problems, such as 2 + 4 = 6 (Siegler & Ramani, 2009), and that a 0–100 version of the board game improves kindergartners' knowledge of those larger numbers (Laski & Siegler, 2014). Thus, playing numerical board games can represent a quick, effective, and inexpensive means of improving the numerical knowledge of low-income preschoolers and kindergartners.

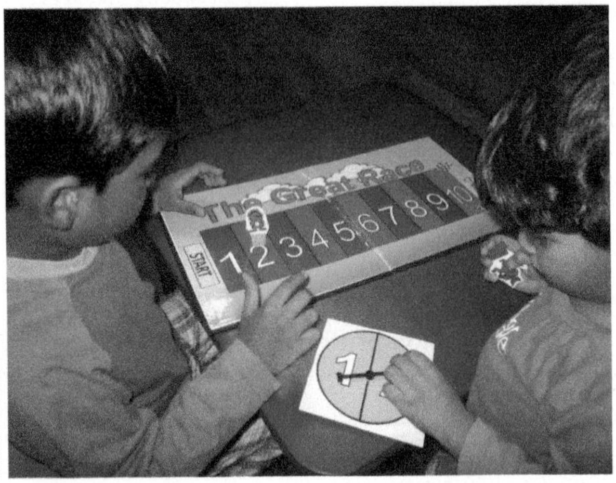

ROBERT SIEGLER

Playing this number board game improves preschoolers' numerical knowledge.

A second reason why planning is difficult for young children is that they tend to be overly optimistic about their abilities and believe they can solve problems without planning. Such overoptimism sometimes leads them to act rashly. For instance, 6-year-olds who overestimate their physical abilities have more accidents than peers who evaluate their abilities more realistically, presumably because their overconfidence leads to them not planning how to avoid potential dangers (Plumert & Kearney, 2018).

Over time, maturation of the prefrontal cortex, a part of the brain that is especially important for planning, along with experiences that reduce over-optimism or demonstrate the value of planning, lead to increases in the frequency and quality of planning, which improves problem solving (Chalmers & Lawrence, 1993).

Improvements in the planning process take a long time to become routine, however; in dangerous situations, 12-year-olds remain more likely than adults not to plan and to take risks (O'Neal et al., 2018).

REVIEW QUESTION

How does the overlapping wave model explain why children sometimes fail to plan when it would be useful, even though they plan effectively at other times?

COURTESY OF JODIE PLUMERT

Young children's overoptimism sometimes leads them to engage in dangerous activities. This particular plan worked out fine, but not all do.

Core-Knowledge Theories

I didn't break the lamp, and I won't do it again.

—*3-year-old, speaking to her mother (cited in Vasek, 1986)*

Although transparent from an adult's perspective, this 3-year-old girl's cover-up reflects rather sophisticated reasoning. She realizes that her mother does not know all that she herself knows about how the lamp was broken, so she attempts to deny responsibility. At the same time, she knows that her mother may not believe her, so she hedges her bets by promising not to do it again. The effort to deceive actually reflects a kind of progress in the child's reasoning; research by University of Toronto psychologist Kang Lee shows that, when placed in a situation where they are likely to transgress, the percentage of children who lie about the transgression steadily increases from age 2 to age 7, presumably due to increasing ability to imagine potential tells and generate ways of avoiding them (see Figure 4.11) (K. Lee, 2013).

Such studies of deception illustrate two characteristic features of research inspired by **core-knowledge theories.** First, this research focuses on types of knowledge that have been important throughout human evolution, not only understanding and manipulating other people's thinking to achieve one's goals, but also recognizing people's faces, finding one's way through space, understanding causes and effects, and learning language.

Deception research also reflects a second feature of core-knowledge theories: the assumption that in certain areas of probable importance in human evolution, infants and young children think in ways that are considerably more advanced than Piaget suggested were possible. If preschoolers were completely egocentric, they would assume that other people's knowledge is the same as their own; there would be no point in lying because the other person would know the lies are false. However, preschoolers' attempts to deceive indicate that they have non-egocentric understandings of other people's minds. The question is how children come to have such sophisticated knowledge so early in life.

View of Children's Nature

Core-knowledge theories depict children as active learners. For example, research from the core-knowledge perspective shows that 3-year-olds understand deception much better when they are actively involved in perpetrating the deceit than when they merely witness the same deception being perpetrated by others (Carlson, Moses, & Hix, 1998; Sullivan & Winner, 1993). In this respect, the core-knowledge perspective on children's nature resembles that of Piagetian and information-processing theories.

core-knowledge theories approaches that view children as having some innate knowledge in domains of special evolutionary importance and domain-specific learning mechanisms for rapidly and effortlessly acquiring additional information in those domains

However, core-knowledge theories differ dramatically from Piagetian and information-processing theories in their view of children's innate capabilities.

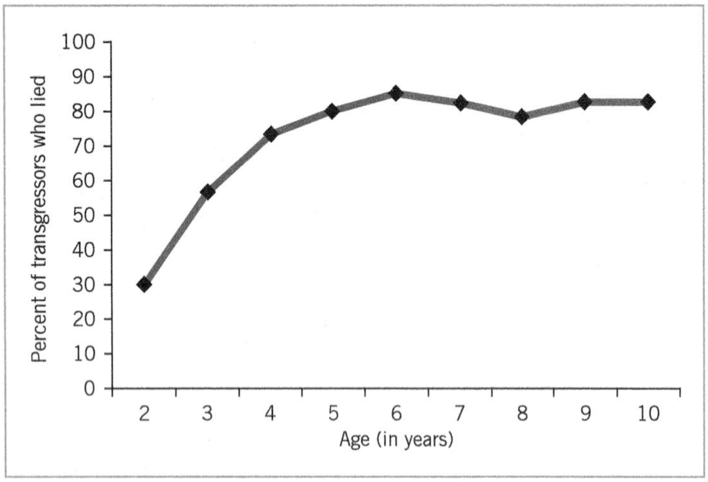

FIGURE 4.11 Children who lie about transgressions by age The percentage of children who lie to cover up transgressions increases substantially with age, perhaps because older children are more imaginative in generating plausible cover-ups. (Data from Lee, 2013)

Piagetian and information-processing theorists propose that children enter the world equipped with only general learning abilities that allow them to gradually increase their understanding of all types of content. By contrast, core-knowledge theorists view children as entering the world equipped not only with general learning abilities but also with specialized learning mechanisms, or mental structures, that allow them to quickly and effortlessly acquire information of evolutionary importance. Where the central metaphors within Piagetian and information-processing theories are, respectively, the child as scientist and the child as general-purpose problem solver, the central metaphor in the core-knowledge approach is the child as well-adapted product of evolution. This metaphor is strikingly apparent in the following statement:

> The brain is no less a product of natural selection than the rest of the body's structures and functions. . . . Hearts evolved to support the process of blood circulation, livers evolved to carry out the process of toxin extraction, and mental structures evolved to enable the learning of certain types of information necessary for adaptive behavior.
>
> (R. Gelman & Williams, 1998, p. 600)

The basic understandings proposed by core-knowledge theorists are assumed to be **domain specific,** that is, limited to a particular area. Domain-specific understandings in these areas allow children to distinguish between living and nonliving things; to anticipate that inanimate objects they encounter for the first time will remain stationary unless an external force is applied to them; to anticipate that animals they encounter for the first time might well move on their own; and to learn especially quickly in these and other areas of evolutionary importance. Different mechanisms are believed to produce development in each domain. For example, a kind of mechanism that has been labelled a *theory of mind module* (TOMM) is believed to produce learning about one's own and other people's minds, but different specialized mechanisms are believed to produce learning about faces, language, living things, and other important domains (Leslie, Friedman, & German, 2004; Mahy, Moses, & Pfeifer, 2014).

domain specific information about a particular content area

nativism the theory that infants have substantial innate knowledge of evolutionarily important domains

Central Developmental Issue: Nativism Versus Constructivism

Although core-knowledge theorists are united in believing that development reflects the operation of domain-specific as well as general learning mechanisms, they disagree regarding how much knowledge is inborn. Researchers who emphasize innate knowledge are labelled *nativists*; those who emphasize the generation of increasingly sophisticated domain-specific theories on top of the innate foundation are labelled *constructivists.*

Some transgressions are difficult to cover up; sometimes confessing, apologizing, and seeking the judge's mercy works better.

MEL YATES/GETTY IMAGES

Nativism

The belief that infants are born with substantial knowledge of evolutionarily important domains, as well as the ability to quickly and easily acquire more knowledge in these domains, is called **nativism.** Elizabeth Spelke proposed the most prominent nativist theory, which she labelled "core-knowledge theory" (e.g., Spelke, 2004; Spelke & Kinzler, 2007). She hypothesized that infants begin life with four core-knowledge systems, each of which includes understanding of a particularly important domain. One system represents inanimate objects and their mechanical interactions; a second system represents the minds of people and other animals capable of goal-directed actions; a third system represents numbers, such as numbers of objects and events; and a fourth system represents spatial layouts and geometric relations. Each system has its own principles. For instance, infants' understanding of physics includes the knowledge that all objects occupy space, move in continuous ways through it, and cannot simultaneously occupy the same space as another object. Consistent with this hypothesis, numerous studies have documented that infants indeed possess these basic understandings (e.g., Baillargeon, 2004; Hespos & vanMarle, 2012).

Language is another domain in which core-knowledge theorists propose that children have innate knowledge and a specialized learning mechanism, sometimes labelled the *language acquisition device* (e.g., Chomsky, 1988). Theorists hypothesize that this specialized learning mechanism enables young children to rapidly master the complicated systems of grammatical rules that are present in all human languages. One type of evidence for such specialized mechanisms is the universality of language acquisition. Virtually all children in all societies master the basic grammar of their native language quickly and effortlessly, even though adults almost never directly instruct them about grammar. In contrast, mastery of other complex rule systems—such as those in algebra, formal logic, and kinship relations (e.g., second cousin, twice removed)—is not universal and requires direct instruction from adults and considerable effort from children. Universality of acquisitions early in life, without apparent effort, and without instruction from other people, is characteristic of the domains that are viewed as particularly important by core-knowledge theorists.

Constructivism

As the term is used by core-knowledge theorists, **constructivism** blends elements of nativism, Piagetian theory, and information-processing theories. Like nativists, but unlike Piagetian and information-processing theorists, core-knowledge constructivists theorize that infants possess specialized learning abilities that allow them to quickly and effortlessly begin to understand domains of special evolutionary importance. However, unlike nativists, core-knowledge constructivists also emphasize that infants' initial knowledge in these domains is rudimentary and that construction of more advanced knowledge reflects specific learning experiences within the domain, such as observing the types of deceptions that go undetected.

Several core-knowledge constructivists have proposed that young children actively organize their understanding of the most important domains into informal theories (Gelman & Noles, 2011; Gopnik & Wellman, 2012). They hypothesize that children form naive theories of physics (knowledge of objects), psychology (knowledge of people), and biology (knowledge of plants and animals). Though much simpler, these theories share three important characteristics with formal scientific theories:

1. They identify fundamental units for dividing relevant objects and events into a few basic categories.
2. They explain many phenomena in terms of a few fundamental principles.
3. They explain events in terms of unobservable causes.

Each of these characteristics is evident in understanding of biology (Legare & Gelman, 2014). Consistent with the first characteristic, infants and young children divide all objects into three categories: people, other animals, and nonliving things. Consistent with the second characteristic, preschoolers understand broadly

constructivism the theory that infants build increasingly advanced understanding by combining rudimentary innate knowledge with subsequent experiences

BOX 4.3 APPLICATIONS Educational Applications of Core-Knowledge Theories

Although core-knowledge theorists emphasize what infants and young children understand about certain fundamental concepts, they also recognize that many other fundamental concepts are not mastered until much later. One such late-developing concept is natural selection, a key part of biological evolution, but one that even many adults struggle to understand (Gregory, 2009). Core-knowledge theorists, such as Gelman (2003), have hypothesized that one reason for the difficulty is that young children are *essentialists*. They believe that members of a species have a fixed inner essence that makes them what they are—that is, dogs have a "dogness," cats a "catness," and so on.

Essentialist thinking has important advantages for drawing valid inferences. For example, it enables preschoolers to reason that if they learn that one dog has a spleen, other dogs also do, and that even if a sheep is raised among goats, it remains a sheep. However, essentialism interferes with learning about natural selection because having a fixed essence would seem to preclude new species evolving from existing ones. Indeed, even extended instruction often leads to only modest improvement in understanding natural selection (Ferrari & Chi, 1998).

Deborah Kelemen, Patricia Ganea, and their colleagues (Kelemen et al., 2014) applied core-knowledge ideas, in particular the emphasis on causal explanations and on young children's ability to understand relatively advanced biological concepts, to help 5- to 8-year-olds learn about natural selection. To do so, they created storybooks about fictitious animals called "pilosas," who were suddenly dying off due to extreme climate change, which caused the insects they ate to burrow further underground. The effects of these changes depended on the pilosas' trunks, which they used to get the insects. Some of the pilosas had thin trunks that allowed them to reach into the narrow burrows where the insects had retreated, but other pilosas had trunks too wide to fit into the burrows. These circumstances led to the pilosas with thick trunks starving before they could reproduce and the pilosas with thin trunks surviving to have babies, most of whom had thin trunks like those of their parents. Over generations, the pilosas with thin trunks became the main type of pilosa.

Hearing and seeing the storybook led to children not only learning what they had been told, but also generalizing the logic of natural selection to questions about a different hypothetical species faced with a different environmental challenge. Consistent with core-knowledge theories, storybooks with more information about the causal mechanisms that produced the population-level change led to greater learning than did books with less information about causes. The children's increased understanding of natural selection remained evident 3 months later. These impressive results demonstrated the usefulness of applying core-knowledge theories to educationally important concepts.

applicable biological principles, such as that a desire for food and water underlies many behaviours of animals. Consistent with the third characteristic, preschoolers know that vital activities of animals, such as reproduction and movement, are caused by internal processes, rather than the external forces that determine the motions of inanimate objects.

At the same time, core-knowledge constructivists emphasize that children's initial simple theories grow considerably more complex with age and experience. For example, the prominent core-knowledge constructivists Henry Wellman and Susan Gelman (1998) suggested that the first theory of psychology emerges at about 18 months of age and is organized around the understanding that other people's actions, not just one's own, reflect their goals and desires. For example, 2-year-olds realize that another person will want to eat if he or she is hungry, regardless of whether the children themselves are hungry. The first theory of biology emerges at about 3 years and is organized around the realization that people and other animals are living things, different from nonliving things. For example, 3- and 4-year-olds realize that people and animals, but not manufactured objects, can heal themselves (Gelman, 2003).

More advanced theories follow. For instance, by age 7 years, children believe that the category of living things includes plants as well as animals (Inagaki & Hatano, 2008). Similarly, by age 3 or 4 years, children recognize the role of beliefs as well as desires in influencing their own and other people's actions (Wellman, Cross, & Watson, 2001). Research generated by advocates of the core-knowledge approach is examined in greater depth in Chapter 7. We close this section's overview of core-knowledge theories by examining an intriguing educational application of the approach (Box 4.3).

REVIEW QUESTION

What are the fundamental differences between the core knowledge approach and Piaget's stage theory of development? ■

Sociocultural Theories

A mother and her 4-year-old daughter, Sadie, assemble a toy, using a diagram to guide them:

> *Mother:* Now you need another one like this on the other side. Mmmmm . . . there you go, just like that.
> *Sadie:* Then I need this one to go like this? Hold on, hold on. Let it go. There. Get that out. Oops.
> *M:* I'll hold it while you turn it. *(Watches Sadie work on toy)* Now you make the end.
> *S:* This one?
> *M:* No, look at the picture. Right here *(points to diagram)*. That piece.
> *S:* Like this?
> *M:* Yeah.
>
> (Gauvain, 2001, p. 32)

This interaction probably strikes you as completely unexceptional—and it is. From the perspective of **sociocultural theories,** however, it and thousands of other similarly unexceptional interactions are of the utmost importance because they are what shapes development.

From the sociocultural perspective, a noteworthy feature of the vignette is that Sadie is learning to assemble the toy in an interpersonal context. Sociocultural theorists emphasize that much of cognitive development takes place through interactions between children and other people who want to help children acquire the skills, knowledge, beliefs, and attitudes valued by their culture. Whereas Piagetian, information-processing, and core-knowledge theories emphasize children's own efforts to understand the world, sociocultural theories emphasize the importance of children's interactions with others.

The interaction between Sadie and her mother is also noteworthy because it exemplifies **guided participation,** a process emphasized in sociocultural research in which more knowledgeable individuals organize activities in ways that allow less knowledgeable people to perform the activity at a higher level than they could manage on their own (Rogoff, 2003). Sadie's mother, for example, holds one part of the toy so that Sadie can screw in another part. On her own, Sadie would be unable to screw the two parts together and therefore could not improve her assembly skills. Similarly, Sadie's mother points to the relevant part of the diagram, enabling Sadie to encode key information, decide what to do next, and learn how diagrams convey information. As this episode illustrates, guided participation often occurs in situations in which the explicit purpose is to achieve a practical goal (such as assembling a particular toy), but in which learning more general skills, in this case assembling objects and learning about diagrams, occurs as a by-product of the activity.

A particularly important type of guided participation, **social scaffolding** is a process through which adults and others with greater expertise organize the physical and social environment to help children learn. The term is based on a

sociocultural theories approaches that emphasize that other people and the surrounding culture contribute greatly to children's development

guided participation a process in which more knowledgeable individuals organize activities in ways that allow less knowledgeable people to learn

social scaffolding a process in which more competent people provide a temporary framework that supports children's thinking at a higher level than children could manage on their own

IMAGE SOURCE PLUS / ALAMY

Through guided participation, parents can help children not only accomplish immediate goals but also learn skills, such as how to use written instructions and diagrams to assemble objects.

SIMON MARCUS/GETTY IMAGES

By providing their children with social scaffolding, parents enable them to play with toys and other objects in more advanced ways than would otherwise be possible, which helps the children learn.

construction metaphor. When putting up tall buildings, construction workers use metal frameworks called *scaffolds* that allow them to work high above the ground. Once a building's main structure is in place, that structure can support further work, thus allowing the scaffolding to be removed. In an analogous fashion, children's learning is aided by social scaffolding, in which more competent people provide a temporary framework that supports children's thinking at a higher level than children could manage on their own (Wood, Bruner, & Ross, 1976).

Ideally, supplying this framework includes choosing a task that is beyond children's current level but that they might be able to do with help, explaining the goal of the task, demonstrating how the task can be done, and helping learners accomplish the most difficult parts. This, in fact, is the way parents and teachers tend to instruct children (Bibok, Carpendale, & Müller, 2009; Simons & Klein, 2007). Moreover, the higher the quality of the scaffolding—that is, the more that it focuses at, but not beyond, the upper end of the child's capabilities—the greater that child's learning tends to be (Conner, Knight, & Cross, 1997; Gauvain, 2001).

Another noteworthy characteristic of the interaction between Sadie and her mother is that it occurs in a broader cultural context. This context includes not only other people but also the innumerable products of human ingenuity that sociocultural theorists refer to as **cultural tools**—symbol systems, manufactured objects, skills, values, and the many other ways in which culture influences our thinking. Without the symbol systems of printed diagrams and spoken language, Sadie and her mother would find the task of assembling the toy's pieces difficult if not impossible; without techniques for manufacturing toys, there would be no pieces to fasten; without skills such as Sadie's mother holding pieces of the toy in a way that allowed Sadie to fasten them together, Sadie could not have assembled the toy; without cultural values that encourage girls to learn mechanical skills, this interaction between Sadie and her mother would not have happened; and so on. Thus, sociocultural theories help us appreciate the many aspects of culture, embodied in even the most commonplace interactions, that shape development.

View of Children's Nature: Vygotsky's Theory

The giant of the sociocultural approach to cognitive development was the Russian psychologist Lev Vygotsky. Although Vygotsky and Piaget were contemporaries, Vygotsky's view of children's nature was very different from Piaget's. Whereas Piaget's theory emphasizes children's efforts to understand the world on their own, Vygotsky and subsequent sociocultural theorists portray children as social learners, intertwined with other people who help them gain skills and understanding. Whereas Piaget viewed children as intent on mastering physical, mathematical, and logical concepts that are the same in all times and places, Vygotsky viewed children as intent on participating in activities that are prevalent in the specific time and place in which they live. Whereas Piaget emphasized abrupt qualitative changes in children's thinking, Vygotsky emphasized gradual continuous changes. These Vygotskian views gave rise to the central metaphor of sociocultural theories: children as social learners, who gradually become full participants in their culture through interactions with other people and with the broader social environment of institutions, skills, attitudes, and values.

Vygotsky's emphasis on children as social learners is evident in his perspective on the relation between language and thought. Whereas Piaget viewed the two as largely independent, Vygotsky (1934/1962) viewed them as intertwined. In particular, he believed that thought is internalized speech originating in statements that other people make to children.

cultural tools the innumerable products of human ingenuity that enhance thinking

To illustrate the process of internalizing speech, Vygotsky described three phases in the growth of children's ability to regulate their own behaviour. At first, children's behaviour is controlled by other people's statements (as in the example of Sadie's mother telling her "Now you need another one like this on the other side"). Then, children's behaviour is controlled by their own **private speech,** in which they tell themselves aloud what to do, much as their parents might have done earlier. Finally, their behaviour is controlled by internalized private speech (thought), in which they silently tell themselves what to do. The transition between the second and third phases often involves whispers or silent lip movements; in Vygotsky's terms, the speech "goes underground" and becomes thought. Private speech is most evident between ages 4 and 6 years, although older children and adults also use it on challenging tasks, such as assembling furniture or operating unfamiliar devices (Díaz & Berk, 2014; Winsler et al., 2003).

HERITAGE IMAGE PARTNERSHIP LTD / ALAMY

The Russian psychologist Lev Vygotsky, founder of the sociocultural approach to child development.

private speech the second phase of Vygotsky's internalization-of-thought process, in which children develop self-regulation and problem-solving abilities by telling themselves aloud what to do, much as their parents did in the first stage

Children as Teachers and Learners

Contemporary sociocultural theorists, such as Michael Tomasello (2014), have extended Vygotsky's insights about human nature. Tomasello proposed that the human species has two unique characteristics that are crucial to our ability to create complex cultures. One is the inclination to teach others of our species; the other is the inclination to attend to and learn from such teaching. In every human society, adults communicate facts, skills, values, and traditions to their young. This is what makes culture possible; it enables the new generation to stand on the shoulders of the old and thus see farther. The inclination to teach emerges very early: even 1-year-olds spontaneously point to and name objects to call other people's attention to what they themselves find interesting, even when they have no desire to obtain the object. Only humans engage in such intentional teaching that is not tied to tangible goals.

Children as Products of Their Culture

Sociocultural theorists believe that many of the *processes* that produce development, such as guided participation, are the same in all societies. However, the *content* that children learn—the particular symbol systems, artifacts, skills, and values—vary greatly from culture to culture and shape thinking accordingly.

One example of how culturally specific content can impact thinking comes from a study of analogical problem solving, a process in which experience with previously encountered problems is applied to new ones. Chen, Mo, and Honomichl (2004) asked students attending universities in the United States and China to solve two problems. One problem required a solution analogous to leaving a trail of white pebbles to follow home, a strategy used in the fairy tale "Hansel and Gretel," which was well known to the U.S. students but unknown to those in China. The American college students were far more successful than their Chinese peers in solving that problem; many of them alluded to the fairy tale, even though they had not heard it in many years. The other problem required a solution analogous to that in a fairy tale well known to the students in China but not to those in the United States. College students in China were vastly superior in solving that problem, and many alluded to the relevant fairy tale in explaining their strategy.

The inclination to teach and the ability to learn from teaching are among the most distinctly human characteristics.

DANITA DELIMONT / GETTY IMAGES

Central Developmental Issues

Vygotsky and contemporary sociocultural theorists have proposed a number of specific ideas about *how change occurs* through social interaction. Two of these ideas—guided participation and social scaffolding—have already been discussed. In this section, we examine a third concept that plays a prominent role in sociocultural analyses of change: *intersubjectivity*.

Sociocultural theorists believe that the foundation of human cognitive development is our ability to establish **intersubjectivity,** the mutual understanding that people share during communication (Rochat, 2009). The idea behind this imposing term is both simple and profound: effective communication requires participants to focus on the same topic, as well as on each other's reaction to the information being communicated. Such a "meeting of the minds" is indispensable for effective teaching and learning.

KIANKHOON / GETTY IMAGES

As illustrated by this photo of an East Asian mother teaching her child to use an abacus, the tools available in a culture shape the learning of children within that culture.

intersubjectivity the mutual understanding that people share during communication

joint attention a process in which social partners intentionally focus on a common referent in the external environment

The roots of intersubjectivity are evident early in infancy. By age 6 months, infants can learn novel behaviours by attending to another person's behaviour (Collie & Hayne, 1999). This and related developments in early infancy set the stage for the emergence of a process that is at the heart of intersubjectivity—**joint attention.** In this process, infants and their social partners intentionally focus on a common referent in the external environment. The emergence of joint attention is evident in numerous ways. Around their first birthday, infants increasingly look toward objects that are the targets of their social partners' gaze, even if the partner is not acting on the objects. Around the same age, infants begin to actively direct a partner's attention toward objects that they themselves find interesting (Akhtar & Gernsbacher, 2008; Woodward, 2005).

Joint attention greatly increases children's ability to learn from other people. Consider language learning. When an adult tells a child the name of an object, the adult usually looks or points at it; children who are looking at the same object are in a better position to learn what the word means than ones who are not (Baldwin, 1991). Indeed, the degree to which infants follow other people's gaze when the other person is teaching them a new word predicts their later vocabulary development (Brooks & Meltzoff, 2008) and language development in general (Carpenter, Nagell, & Tomasello, 1998).

Joint attention also enables infants to evaluate the competence of other people and to use those evaluations to decide whom to imitate. Infants between 8 and 18 months of age more often attend to, imitate, and learn new labels for objects from adults whom they see pursuing goals competently than from adults they see acting incompetently (Brooker & Poulin-Dubois, 2013; Poulin-Dubois & Brosseau-Liard, 2016; Stenberg, 2013; Tummeltshammer et al., 2014).

Intersubjectivity continues to develop well beyond infancy, as children become increasingly able to take the perspectives of other people. For example, older preschoolers and elementary school-age children are more likely than younger ones to reach agreement with peers on the rules of a game they are about to play and the roles that each child will assume in it (Baines & Blatchford, 2011; Pellegrini, 2009). The continuing development of such perspective-taking abilities also leads to school-age children's increasing ability to teach and learn from one another (Gauvain, 2001). As discussed in Box 4.4, concepts from sociocultural theories also have proved useful for improving education in classrooms.

PHOTODISC / GETTY IMAGES

Joint attention, the process through which social partners focus on the same external object, underlies the human capacity to teach and to learn from teaching.

REVIEW QUESTION

Imagine that you have a classroom full of students from different backgrounds. How might sociocultural theory inform your approach to teaching your students? ■

BOX 4.4 APPLICATIONS Educational Applications of Sociocultural Theories

For some time, the educational systems in Canada and the United States have been criticized for promoting rote memorization of facts rather than deep understanding, for promoting competition rather than cooperation among students, and for generally failing to create enthusiasm for learning (National Association for the Education of Young Children, 2011). The emphasis of sociocultural theories on the role of culture in cognitive development implies that one way to improve schooling is to change the culture of schools. The culture should be one in which instruction is aimed at helping children gain deep understanding, in which learning is a cooperative activity, and in which learning a little creates a desire to learn more.

One impressive attempt to meet these goals is Ann Brown's (1997) *community-of-learners* program, which has focused on 6- to 12-year-olds, most of them African American children attending inner-city schools in Boston, Massachusetts, and Oakland, California. The main curriculum consists of projects that require research on some large topic, such as interdependence between animals and their habitats. The class divides into small groups, each of which focuses on a particular aspect of the topic. With the topic of the interdependence between animals and habitats, for example, one group might study predator–prey relations; another, reproductive strategies; another, protection from the elements; and so on.

At the end of roughly 10 weeks, new groups are formed, each including one child from each original group. Children in the new groups are asked to solve a problem whose solution incorporates parts of all the topics previously studied. For instance, children might be tasked with designing an "animal of the future" that would be particularly well adapted to its habitat. Because each child's participation in the previous group has resulted in the child's gaining expertise on the aspect of the problem studied by that group, and because no other child in the new group has that expertise, all the children's contributions are essential for the new group to succeed. This technique is sometimes called the *jigsaw approach* because, as in a jigsaw puzzle, all pieces are necessary for the solution.

Participating in communities of learners yielded both cognitive and motivational benefits (Brown, 1997). It helped children become increasingly adept at constructing high-quality solutions to the problems they tried to solve. It also helped them learn such general skills as identifying key questions and comparing alternative solutions to a problem. Finally, because success depended on everyone's contributions, the community-of-learners approach encouraged mutual respect and responsibility. In short, the approach created a culture of learning.

Dynamic-Systems Theories

Like all biological processes, thinking serves an adaptive purpose: it helps people and other animals solve problems and attain their goals. Attaining one's goals, however, requires action as well as thought; without the ability to act, thinking would be pointless (see Figure 4.12). Despite this inherent connection between thinking and acting, most theories of cognitive development have ignored the development of the skilled actions that allow children to enjoy the fruits of their mental labour.

dynamic-systems theories a class of theories that focus on how change occurs over time in complex systems

Infant Problem Solving

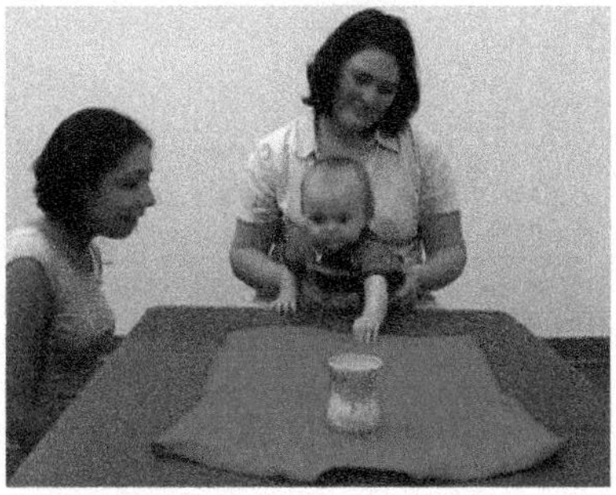

WORTH PUBLISHERS

One exception to this generalization is **dynamic-systems theories,** which emphasize the development of actions in complex systems over varying time periods—fractions of seconds, seconds, minutes, hours, days, months, and years. Consistent with the dynamic-systems perspective, detailed analyses of the development of infants' actions, such as crawling, walking, reaching, and grasping, have yielded impressive insights into how cognitive development occurs. For example, dynamic-systems research has shown that improved reaching allows infants to categorize objects in more advanced ways (Spencer et al., 2006; Thelen & Corbetta, 1994). Dynamic-systems research also has shown that the onset of crawling changes infants' relationships with family members, who may be thrilled to see their baby attain this milestone but less thrilled about the increased vigilance and rearrangement of living spaces needed to avoid harm to one's child and one's possessions (Campos, Kermoian, & Zumbahlen, 1992).

Esther Thelen and colleagues (1993) conducted a classic study that illustrates what dynamic systems theorists mean by "dynamic" and "systems." Thelen, who along with Linda Smith founded the dynamic-systems approach to cognitive development, repeatedly observed the reaching efforts of four infants during their

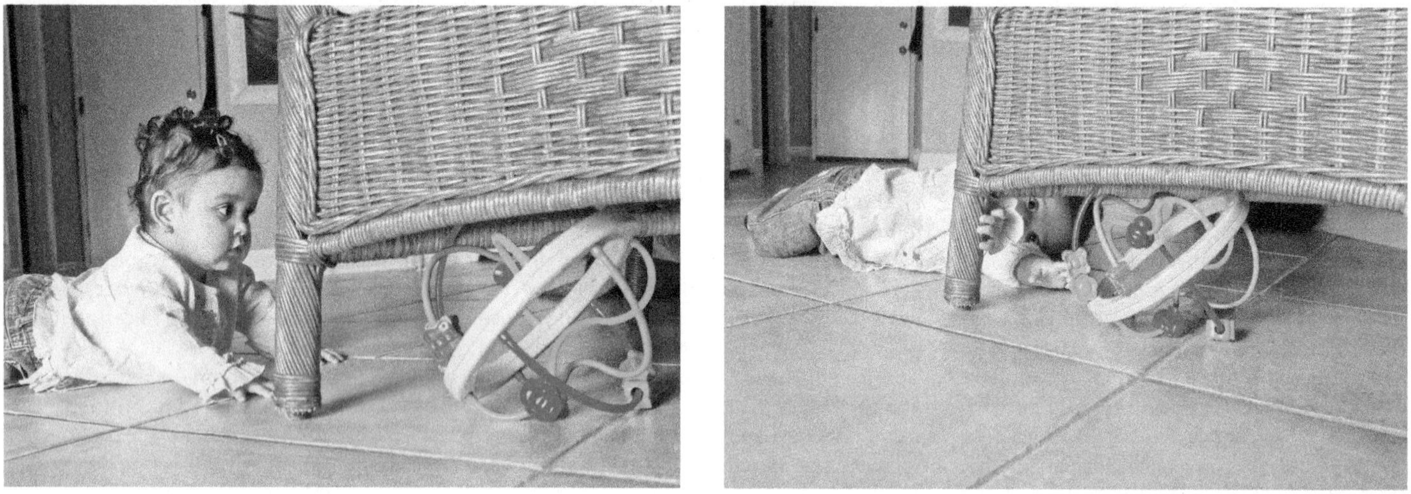

MYRLEEN PEARSON / ALAMY

FIGURE 4.12 **Problem solving often requires motor skills** A major insight of dynamic-systems theories is that thinking would be pointless without motor capabilities. In these photos, a 9-month-old surveys the barrier in the way of a desired toy (left frame). She then contorts her body, reaching under the barrier to retrieve the toy (right frame). If the infant lacked the motor ability to twist her body and reach her arm under the chair, her problem-solving processes would have been fruitless.

first year. Her team found that because of individual differences in the infants' physiology, activity level, arousal, motivation, and experience, each child faced different challenges in mastering the skill of reaching. One discovery was that the onset of adept reaching varies greatly among infants. For example, Nathan began to reach skillfully at 12 weeks, but Hannah and Justin did not accomplish this goal until 20 weeks. Another discovery was that, for each infant, the development of reaching showed periods of rapid change, periods without much change, and even regressions in performance. Some infants showed abrupt, discontinuous improvements in reaching; other infants' improvements were gradual and continuous (Thelen & Smith, 1998). The types of changes required for each infant to reach skillfully also varied; some infants needed to damp down overly vigorous movements; others needed to reach more vigorously (Thelen, 2001).

These descriptions help convey what is meant by the label "dynamic-systems." As suggested by the term *dynamic* (which in this context means "continuously changing"), dynamic-systems theories depict development as a process of constant change. Where Piaget hypothesized that development entails long periods of relatively stable stages separated by relatively brief transition periods, dynamic-systems theories propose that at all points in development, thought and action change from moment to moment in response to the current situation, the child's immediate past history, and the child's longer-term history in similar situations.

As suggested by *systems,* the second term in the label, dynamic-systems theories depict each child as a well-integrated system, in which many subsystems—perception, action, attention, memory, language, and social interaction—work together to determine behaviour. For example, dynamic-systems theorists argue that success on tasks viewed as measures of conceptual understanding, such as object permanence, is influenced by perception, attention, motor skills, and a host of other factors (Smith et al., 1999).

View of Children's Nature

Dynamic-systems theories are the newest of the five types of theories discussed in this chapter, and their view of children's nature incorporates influences from each of the other types. Like Piaget's theory, dynamic-systems theories emphasize children's innate motivation to explore the environment; like information-processing theories, they emphasize precise analyses of problem-solving activity; like core-knowledge theories, they focus on infants' and toddlers' surprising early competence; and like sociocultural theories, they emphasize the formative influence of other people. These similarities to other theories, as well as some notable differences from them, are evident in dynamic-systems theories' emphasis on motivation and action.

PHOTO © KLAUS LIBERTUS

Reaching with Velcro-covered mittens for Velcro-covered objects improved infants' later ability to grab and explore ordinary objects without the mittens (Libertus & Needham, 2010).

Motivators of Development

To a greater extent than any of the other theories except Piaget's, dynamic-systems theories emphasize that from infancy onward, children are internally motivated to learn about the world around them and to explore and expand their own capabilities (von Hofsten, 2007). This motivation to explore and learn is apparent in the fact that children persist in practicing new skills even when they possess well-practiced skills that are more efficient. Thus, 1-year-olds try to walk down ramps, despite the fact that crawling would get them down more quickly and without the risk of falling (Adolph & Berger, 2015).

Like sociocultural approaches, dynamic-systems theories also emphasize infants' interest in the social world as a crucial motivator of development. As noted in our discussion of the *active child* in Chapter 1, even newborns prefer attending to the sounds, movements, and features of the human face over almost any alternative. By 10 to 12 months of age, infants are motivated to direct the attention of others to objects and events they themselves find interesting (Deák, 2015). Dynamic-systems theorists have emphasized that observing other people, imitating their actions, and attracting their attention are all potent motivators of development (Fischer & Bidell, 2006).

The Centrality of Action

As noted previously, dynamic-systems theories are unique in their pervasive emphasis on how children's actions shape their development. Piaget's theory asserts the role of actions during infancy, but dynamic-systems theories emphasize that actions contribute to development throughout life. This focus on the developmental role of action has led to a number of non-intuitive discoveries. For example, infants' own reaching for objects helps them infer the goals of other people's reaches; infants who can skillfully reach are more likely to look at the probable target of another person's reaching just after the other person's reach begins (von Hofsten, 2007).

Sticky Mittens Training

COURTESY KLAUS LIBERTUS

Another example of infants' learning from actions comes from research in which infants were outfitted with Velcro mittens that enabled them to "grab" and explore Velcro-covered objects that they otherwise could not have picked up. After 2 weeks of successfully grabbing the Velcro-covered objects with the Velcro-covered mittens, infants showed greater ability to grab and explore ordinary objects without the mittens than did other infants of the same ages (Needham, 2016).

The ways in which actions shape development extend well beyond reaching and grasping in infancy. Actions influence categorization: in one study, encouraging children to move an object up and down led to their categorizing it as one of a group of objects that were easiest to move in that way, whereas encouraging children to move the same object from side to side led them to categorize it as one of a group of objects that were easiest to move in that way (Smith, 2005). Actions also affect vocabulary acquisition and generalization (Samuelson &

Horst, 2008): for instance, experimental manipulations that lead children to state an incorrect name for an object impair their future attempts to learn the object's correct name. In addition, actions shape memory, as demonstrated by research in which children's past attempts to locate and dig up objects they had seen being hidden in a sandbox altered their recall of the objects' new location after they saw them being re-hidden (Schutte, Spencer, & Schöner, 2003). Thus, just as thinking shapes actions, actions shape thinking.

Central Developmental Issues

Two developmental issues that are especially prominent in dynamic-systems theories are how the cognitive system organizes itself and how it changes. These issues exemplify our themes of the *active child* and *mechanisms of change.*

Self-Organization

Dynamic-systems theories view development as a process of self-organization that involves integrating attention, memory, emotions, and actions as needed to adapt to a continuously changing environment. The organizational process is sometimes called *soft assembly* because the components and their organization change from moment to moment and situation to situation, rather than being governed by rigid stages or rules that are consistently applied across time and situations.

The types of research to which this perspective leads are well illustrated by studies of the A-not-B error that 8- to 12-month-olds typically make in Piaget's classic object-permanence task. As noted earlier, this error involves infants' searching for a toy where they previously found it (location A), rather than where they last saw it hidden (location B). Piaget (1954) explained the A-not-B error by hypothesizing that before their 1st birthday, infants lack a clear concept of the permanent existence of objects.

In contrast, viewing the A-not-B error from a dynamic-systems perspective suggested that many factors other than conceptual understanding influence performance on the object permanence task. In particular, Smith and colleagues (1999) hypothesized that babies' previous reaches toward location A produce a habit of reaching there, which influences their behaviour when the object is subsequently hidden at location B. On the basis of this premise, the researchers made several predictions that were later borne out. One was that the more often babies had found an object by reaching to one location, the more likely they would be to reach there again when the object was hidden at a different location. Also supported was the prediction that increasing the memory demands of the task by not allowing infants to search for the object for 3 seconds after it was hidden at the B location would increase the likelihood of infants' reaching to location A (Clearfield et al., 2009). The reasoning here was that the strength of the new memory, which was based on viewing a single action, would fade rapidly relative to the fading of the habit of reaching to the previous hiding place, which was based on several actions.

The dynamic-systems perspective also suggested that infants' attention would influence their object-permanence performance. Consistent with this view, manipulating infants' attention by tapping one of the locations just as the infants were about to reach usually resulted in their reaching to the tapped location, regardless of where the object was actually hidden. Thus, rather than providing a pure measure of conceptual understanding, infants' performance on the object-permanence task appears to reflect the combined influence of the strength of the habit of reaching to location A, the memory demands of the current task, and the infant's current focus of attention.

Mechanism of Change

Dynamic-systems theories posit that changes occur through mechanisms of variation and selection that are analogous to those that produce biological evolution (Fischer & Bidell, 2006; Steenbeek & van Geert, 2008). In this context, *variation* refers to the use of different behaviours to pursue the same goal. For example, to descend a ramp, a 1-year-old will sometimes walk; sometimes crawl; sometimes do a belly slide; sometimes do a sitting, feet-first slide; and so on (Adolph & Berger, 2015). *Selection* involves increasingly frequent choice of behaviours that are effective in meeting goals and decreasing use of less effective behaviours. For instance, when children first learn to walk, they often are too optimistic about being able to walk down ramps and frequently fall; but after a few months of walking experience, they more accurately judge the steepness of ramps and whether they can walk down them, leading the infants to use another descent strategy if the ramp is too steep (Adolph & Hoch, 2019).

Children's selection among alternative approaches reflects several influences. Most important is the *relative success* of each approach in meeting a particular goal: as children gain experience, they increasingly rely on approaches that produce desired outcomes. Another important consideration is *efficiency*: children increasingly choose approaches that meet goals more quickly or with less effort than do other approaches. A third consideration is *novelty*, the lure of trying something new. Children sometimes choose new approaches that are no more efficient, or even less efficient, than an established alternative but that have the potential to become more efficient (Wittmann et al., 2008). As discussed in Box 4.5, the insights of dynamic-systems theories have led to useful applications as well as theoretical progress.

BOX 4.5 APPLICATIONS Educational Applications of Dynamic-Systems Theories

As noted in Chapter 2, children born prematurely with low birth weight are more likely than other children to encounter developmental difficulties, among them slower emergence of reaching (Fallang et al., 2003). These delays in reaching reduce the rate of development of brain areas involved in reaching, limiting infants' ability to explore and learn about objects (Lobo, Galloway, & Savelsbergh, 2004).

To help preterm infants improve their reaching, Heathcock, Lobo, and Galloway (2008) applied two findings from dynamic-systems research: (1) some infants' slowness to initiate arm activity impedes their development of reaching (Thelen et al., 1993), and (2) providing young infants with experience reaching for and grabbing Velcro-patched objects while wearing Velcro-covered mittens improves their later ability to reach for and grab ordinary objects barehanded (Needham, Barrett, & Peterman, 2002).

The investigators began their intervention by asking caregivers of preterm infants in an experimental group to provide the infants with special movement experiences. This experience involved the caregivers encouraging infants' arm movements by (1) tying a bell to the infants' wrists so that arm movements would make it ring, presumably motivating further arm movements, and (2) placing Velcro mittens on the infants' hands to allow them to reach for and grab Velcro-patched toys held in front of them. The caregivers were asked to do this at home as well as in a lab. Caregivers of preterm infants in a control group were asked to provide their infants with special social experiences that included singing to and talking with the infants on the same schedule as that of children in the experimental group. Periodically, infants in both groups were brought to the lab to allow project personnel to observe their reaching and exploration under controlled circumstances and during free play.

As might be expected, the reaching of preterm infants in both groups improved over the 8 weeks of the study. However, the infants in the experimental group improved more. They more often touched toys that were held in front of them, and more often did so with the inside rather than the outside of their hand, as is needed to grasp objects. Given connections between development of actions and brain activity (Koutsandréou et al., 2016), such interventions may facilitate brain development as well as motor development.

REVIEW QUESTION

Among the theories reviewed in this chapter, dynamic-systems theories are unique in their emphasis on the central role that children's actions play in their own development. Contrast this approach to the active child with those suggested by the other theories. ■

CHAPTER SUMMARY

Theories of development are important because they provide a framework for understanding important phenomena, raise major issues regarding human nature, and motivate new research. Five major theories of cognitive development are Piagetian, information-processing, core-knowledge, sociocultural, and dynamic-systems.

Piaget's Theory

- Among the reasons for the longevity of Piaget's theory are that it vividly conveys the flavour of children's thinking at different ages, extends across a broad range of ages and content areas, and provides many fascinating and surprising observations of children's thinking.
- Piaget's theory is often labelled constructivist because it depicts children as actively constructing knowledge for themselves in response to their experience. The theory posits that children learn through two processes that are present from birth—assimilation and accommodation—and that the contribution of these processes is balanced through a third process, equilibration. These processes produce continuities across development.
- Piaget's theory divides cognitive development into four broad stages: the sensorimotor stage (birth to age 2), the preoperational stage (ages 2 to 7), the concrete operational stage (ages 7 to 12), and the formal operational stage (age 12 and beyond). These stages reflect discontinuities in development.
- In the sensorimotor stage, infants' intelligence is expressed primarily through motor interactions with the environment. During this period, infants gain understanding of concepts such as object permanence and become capable of deferred imitation.
- In the preoperational stage, children become able to represent their experiences in language, mental imagery, and thought; but because of cognitive limitations such as egocentrism and centration, they have difficulty solving many problems, including Piaget's various tests of conservation and egocentrism.
- In the concrete operational stage, children become able to reason logically about concrete objects and events but have difficulty reasoning in purely abstract terms and in succeeding on tasks requiring hypothetical thinking, such as the pendulum problem.
- In the formal operational stage, children become able to think systematically, test hypotheses in valid ways, and reason about hypothetical situations.
- Four weaknesses of Piaget's theory are (1) it only vaguely describes the mechanisms that give rise to thinking and cognitive growth; (2) it underestimates infants' and young children's cognitive competence; (3) it understates the contribution of the social world to cognitive development; and (4) it depicts children's thinking as being more consistent than it is. Each shortcoming has motivated a theory intended in large part to address it.

Information-Processing Theories

- Information-processing theories focus on the specific mental processes that underlie children's thinking. Even in infancy, children are seen as actively pursuing goals; encountering physical, social, and processing limits; and devising strategies that allow them to surmount those limits and attain their goals.
- The memory system includes working memory, long-term memory, and executive functioning.
- Working memory is a system for actively attending to, gathering, maintaining, briefly storing, and processing information.
- Long-term memory is the enduring knowledge accumulated over a lifetime.
- Executive functioning is crucial for inhibiting inadvisable actions, enhancing working memory, and flexibly adapting to changing situations. It develops greatly during the preschool and early elementary school years and is related to later academic achievement and occupational success.
- The development of memory, problem solving, and learning reflects improvements in basic processes, strategies, and content knowledge.
- Basic cognitive processes allow infants to learn and remember from birth onward. Among the most important basic processes are association, recognition, recall, generalization, and encoding.
- Acquisition of strategies and content knowledge enhances learning, memory, and problem solving beyond the level that basic processes alone could provide.
- Important contributors to the growth of problem solving include the development of planning and encoding.

- Overlapping waves theory characterizes development of problem solving as involving acquisition of new strategies, increasingly efficient execution of existing strategies, and increasingly frequent choice of strategies that fit particular situations.

Core-Knowledge Theories

- Core-knowledge theories are based on the view that children begin life with a wide range of specific cognitive competencies.
- Core-knowledge approaches also hypothesize that children are especially adept at acquiring evolutionarily important information, such as language, spatial and numerical information, understanding of other people's thinking, and face recognition.
- These approaches further posit that from early ages, children organize information about the most important areas into domain-specific knowledge structures.
- Nativism is a type of core-knowledge approach that posits that infants are born with substantial knowledge of evolutionarily important domains.
- Core-knowledge constructivism proposes that children generate increasingly advanced theories of areas such as physics, psychology, and biology by combining basic innate knowledge with subsequent learning produced by both domain-general and domain-specific mechanisms.

Sociocultural Theories

- Starting with Vygotsky, sociocultural theorists have focused on how the social world molds development. These theories emphasize that development is shaped not only by interactions with other people and the skills learned from them, but also by the artifacts with which children interact and the beliefs, values, and traditions of the larger society.
- Sociocultural theories view humans as differing from other animals in their propensity to teach and their ability to learn from teaching.
- Sociocultural theories describe people as learning through guided participation and social scaffolding, in which others who are more knowledgeable support the learner's efforts.
- Establishing intersubjectivity between people through joint attention is essential to learning.

Dynamic-Systems Theories

- Dynamic-systems theories view change as the one constant in development. Rather than depicting development as being organized into long periods of stability and brief periods of dramatic change, these theories propose that there is no period in which substantial change is not occurring.
- These theories view each person as a unified system that, in order to meet goals, integrates perception, action, categorization, motivation, memory, language, and knowledge of the physical and social worlds.
- Dynamic-systems theories view development as a self-organizing process that brings together components as needed to adapt to a continuously changing environment, a process known as soft assembly.
- Attaining goals requires action as well as thought. Thought shapes action, but action also shapes thought.
- Just as variation and selection produce biological evolution, they also produce cognitive development.

Test Yourself

1. According to Piaget, development is both continuous and discontinuous. Which of the following aspects of Piagetian theory would be considered a source of discontinuity?
   a. Assimilation
   b. Accommodation
   c. Equilibration
   d. Invariant stages

2. Piaget's theory of cognitive development is comprised of four invariant stages from birth to adolescence. Which of the following is the correct chronology of these stages?
   a. Formal operational, preoperational, sensorimotor, and concrete operational
   b. Sensorimotor, preoperational, concrete operational, and formal operational
   c. Sensorimotor, concrete operational, formal operational, and preoperational
   d. Preoperational, concrete operational, formal operational, and sensorimotor

3. A noted accomplishment during Piaget's sensorimotor stage is ____________.
   a. symbolic representation
   b. object permanence
   c. conservation
   d. egocentrism

4. Thinking that does not factor in the viewpoints of others is known as ____________.
   a. symbolic representation
   b. centration
   c. egocentrism
   d. intersubjectivity

5. According to information-processing theories, the ability to encode, store, and retrieve information is referred to as ____________.
   a. memory
   b. rehearsal
   c. metacognition
   d. retrieval

6. Information-processing theories note several limits on children's thinking. Which of the following is *not* one of these limits?
   a. Memory capacity
   b. Implementation of task analysis
   c. Speed of processing information
   d. Ability to utilize problem-solving strategies
7. Overlapping waves theory explains children's ability to
   a. selectively attend to the most relevant aspect of a problem.
   b. identify the obstacles in achieving a goal.
   c. effectively process mental operations.
   d. discover new strategies that lead to more efficient problem solving.
8. Core-knowledge theories argue that ____________ play(s) a role in cognitive development.
   a. evolution
   b. memory strategies
   c. cultural tools
   d. biomechanical actions
9. According to core-knowledge theorists, children possess naive theories in what three major domains?
   a. Mathematics, psychology, and the arts
   b. Biology, sociology, and psychology
   c. Biology, physics, and psychology
   d. Sociology, physics, and psychology
10. Sociocultural theories emphasize the child's
   a. individual action in his or her environment.
   b. ability to self-regulate his or her learning.
   c. direct interactions with others.
   d. automatization of basic skills to promote new learning.
11. Five-year-old Marcus is learning gymnastics. He's having trouble on the balance beam, so his teacher assists by holding his hand as he walks across. This interaction can be described as ____________.
   a. guided participation
   b. discovery learning
   c. intersubjectivity
   d. the jigsaw approach
12. Jamal is walking with his mother. He taps her on the arm, points to an animal, and says, "Doggie!" This is an example of ____________.
   a. social scaffolding
   b. joint attention
   c. cultural tools
   d. directed learning
13. According to Vygotsky's sociocultural theory, young children will often talk aloud to themselves as a means of controlling their behaviour. This is referred to as ____________ speech.
   a. external
   b. egocentric
   c. directional
   d. private
14. Although Piaget argues that infants younger than 8 months fail the A-not-B error test due to a lack of object permanence, proponents of dynamic-systems theories argue their failure is
   a. due to a combination of habit, memory demands, and focus of attention.
   b. influenced by the infant's motor abilities.
   c. caused by an infant's fragile attachment to the hidden object.
   d. influenced by infant fatigue.
15. Although 15-month-old Lena has been walking unassisted for several months, on recent trips to the park her father has noticed Lena walking on some areas of the playground but crawling on others. Lena's regression from walking to crawling in this example is best explained by which theory?
   a. Constructivist theory
   b. Overlapping waves theory
   c. Sociocultural theories
   d. Information-processing theories

Critical Thinking Questions

1. Piaget's theory has been prominent for almost 100 years. Do you think it will continue to be prominent in the coming years as well? Why or why not?
2. Information-processing analyses tend to be more specific about cognitive processes than are analyses generated by other theories. Do you see this specificity as an advantage or a disadvantage? Why?
3. Of the two types of core-knowledge theories, nativist and constructivist, which do you think better explains children's early-developing capabilities? Why?

4. Imagine that you are trying to help a 6-year-old learn a skill that you possess. Using the sociocultural ideas of guided participation and social scaffolding, describe how you might go about this task.

5. Dynamic-systems theories have application beyond child development and have been used to enhance physical therapy and rehabilitation. How would the concepts of dynamic-systems apply to re-training an adult to walk after serious injury?

Key Terms

A-not-B error, p. 123
accommodation, p. 120
assimilation, p. 120
basic processes, p. 134
centration, p. 125
computer simulation, p. 131
concrete operational stage, p. 122
conservation concept, p. 125
constructivism, p. 141
core-knowledge theories, p. 139
cultural tools, p. 144
deferred imitation, p. 124
domain specific, p. 140
dynamic-systems theories, p. 147
egocentrism, p. 124
encoding, p. 134
equilibration, p. 120
formal operational stage, p. 122
guided participation, p. 143
information-processing theories, p. 130
intersubjectivity, p. 146
joint attention, p. 146
long-term memory, p. 132
nativism, p. 140
object permanence, p. 123
overlapping waves theory, p. 136
Piaget's theory, p. 119
preoperational stage, p. 121
private speech, p. 145
problem solving, p. 131
rehearsal, p. 135
selective attention, p. 135
sensorimotor stage, p. 121
social scaffolding, p. 143
sociocultural theories, p. 143
symbolic representation, p. 124
task analysis, p. 131
working memory, p. 132

Answers to Test Yourself

1. d, **2.** b, **3.** b, **4.** c, **5.** a, **6.** b, **7.** d, **8.** a, **9.** c, **10.** c, **11.** a, **12.** b, **13.** d, **14.** a, **15.** b

CHAPTER

5 Perception, Action, and Learning in Infancy

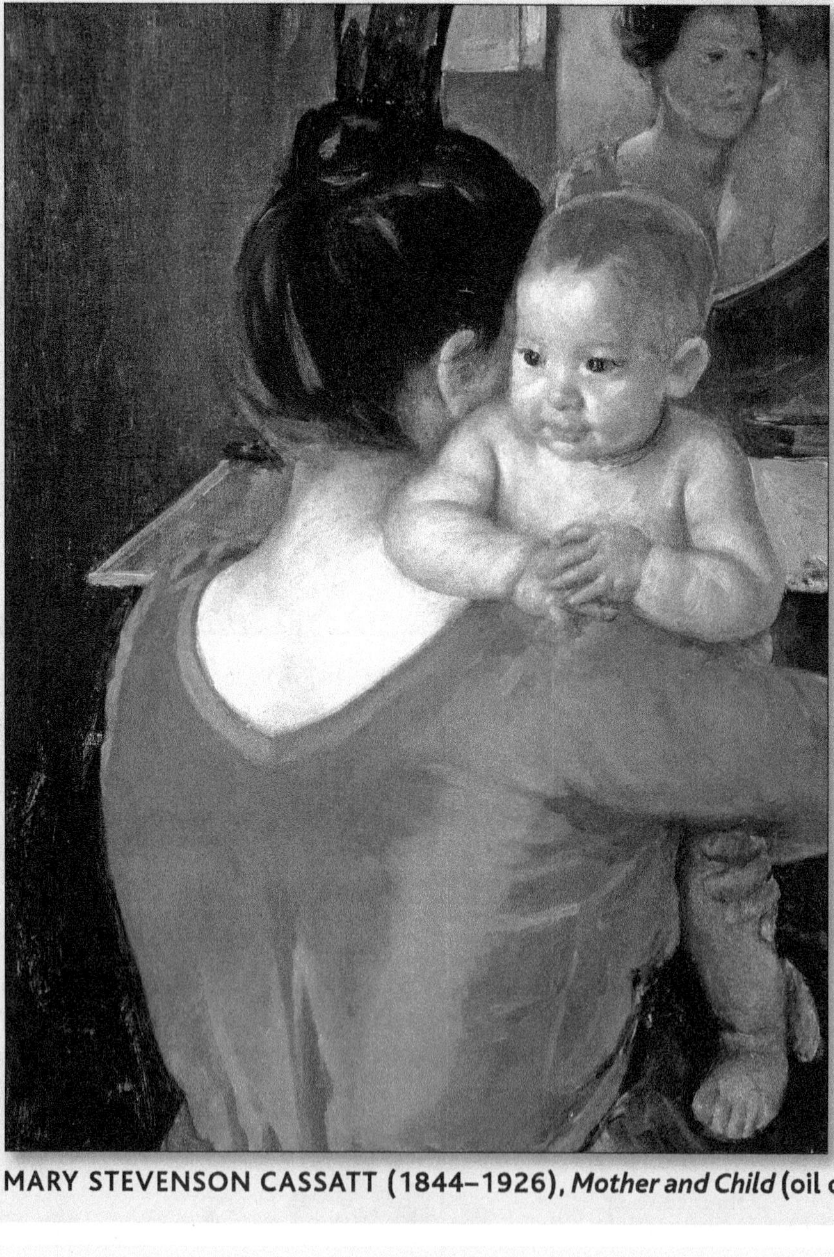

BROOKLYN MUSEUM OF ART/BROOKLYN MUSEUM OF ART, NEW YORK, USA/BRIDGEMAN IMAGES

MARY STEVENSON CASSATT (1844–1926), *Mother and Child* (oil on canvas, 1900)

Perception

Motor Development

Learning and Memory

THEMES

NATURE AND NURTURE ■ THE ACTIVE CHILD ■ CONTINUITY/DISCONTINUITY

MECHANISMS OF CHANGE ■ THE SOCIOCULTURAL CONTEXT ■ INDIVIDUAL DIFFERENCES

Four-month-old Benjamin, perched on the kitchen counter in his infant seat, is watching his parents wash the dinner dishes. What he observes is two people who move on their own, as well as a variety of glass, ceramic, and metal objects of differing sizes and shapes that move only when picked up and manipulated by the people. Other elements of the scene, like the sink and table, never move. Distinctive sounds emanate from his parents' moving lips, and different sounds occur as they deposit cutlery, skillets, and glasses on the counter. He sees objects disappear as they are moved behind other objects, or placed into the sink, but he never sees one object pass through another. The objects that are placed on the counter stay put, until Benjamin's father precariously places a crystal goblet on the edge of the counter. The crashing sound that follows startles all three people in the room, and Benjamin is further startled when the two adults begin emitting sharp, loud sounds toward one another. When Benjamin begins crying in response, the adults rush to him, patting him and making especially pleasant sounds.

This everyday example illustrates the enormous amount of information that is available for infants to perceive and learn from. Like most infants, Benjamin avidly explores everything and everyone around him, using every tool at his disposal: looking, listening, tasting, smelling, and touching. His explorations will gradually expand as he becomes capable first of reaching for objects, then manipulating them. Never will Benjamin explore so voraciously or learn so rapidly as in the first few years of his young life.

In this chapter, we discuss development in three closely related areas: perception, action, and learning. We concentrate on infancy because extremely rapid change occurs in all of these areas during the first two years of a child's life. A second reason is the fact that development in these domains is particularly intertwined: the minirevolutions that transform infants' behaviour and experience in one domain lead to minirevolutions in others. For example, when Benjamin starts to crawl and then walk, even more of the world will become available for him to perceive and learn about, including things his parents would prefer that he not investigate—such as electrical outlets and kitty litter.

This chapter features the *active child* theme, vividly embodied by infants' eager exploration of their environment. *Continuity/discontinuity* arises repeatedly in research that addresses the relation between behaviour in infancy and subsequent development. The *mechanisms of change* theme is also prominent, especially as we consider learning and memory. We will examine contributions made by the *sociocultural context*, most prominently in the area of motor development. Finally, the theme of *nature and nurture* has motivated an enormous amount of infancy research. Infants have less experience than older children and adults, suggesting the possibility of teasing apart the roles of experience-independent and experience-dependent factors. That said, even young babies

Like Benjamin, this infant will take in a great deal of perceptual information just observing his mother preparing food.

YELLOW DOG PRODUCTIONS/GETTY IMAGES

sensation the processing of basic information from the external world via receptors in the sense organs (eyes, ears, skin, etc.) and brain

perception the process of organizing and interpreting sensory information

preferential-looking technique a method for studying visual attention in infants that involves showing infants two images simultaneously to see if the infants prefer one over the other (indexed by longer looking)

visual acuity the sharpness and clarity of vision

amass a remarkable amount of experience rapidly, especially in the domains of sensation and perception. And, as you will see, infants are exceptional learners who excel at harnessing their early experiences.

Perception

Parents cannot help wondering what their babies experience—how much they can see, how well they can hear, and so on. William James, one of the first psychologists, believed that the newborn's world is a "big blooming, buzzing confusion." However, modern research has shown that infants come into the world with all their sensory systems functioning to some degree and that subsequent development occurs rapidly. **Sensation** refers to the processing of basic information from the external world by receptors in the sense organs (eyes, ears, skin, and so forth) and the brain. **Perception** is the process of organizing and interpreting sensory information about the objects, events, and spatial layout of the world around us.

Vision

Although newborns do not see as clearly as adults do, their vision improves extremely rapidly in their first months. And despite their immature visual systems, even newborns have some surprisingly sophisticated visual abilities.

Because infants cannot understand or respond to instructions, researchers who want to study infant perception must devise clever methods that are quite different from those used with older children and adults. The first breakthrough was achieved with the **preferential-looking technique** (Fantz, 1961). In this technique, two different visual stimuli are displayed side by side. If an infant looks longer at one of the two stimuli, the researcher can infer that (a) the baby can discriminate between them, and (b) the infant prefers one over the other. Fantz established that newborns, just like everyone else, would rather look at something than at nothing. When a pattern of any sort—black and white stripes, a bull's-eye, a face—was paired with a plain surface, the infants looked longer at the pattern.

Modern versions of preferential looking often involve the use of automatic eye trackers. By using a camera that measures eye movements via infrared light reflection, researchers can detect where on a screen infants are looking. Researchers also use head-mounted infant-eye trackers that show where infants are looking as they move their eyes freely around the room.

Another method used to study sensory and perceptual development is *habituation*, which you encountered in Chapter 2 in studies of fetal development. This procedure involves repeatedly presenting an infant with a particular stimulus until the infant habituates, that is, until their response declines. At this point, a novel stimulus is presented. If the infant dishabituates (i.e., the response increases) in response to the novel stimulus, the researcher infers that the baby can discriminate between the old and new stimuli. Despite their simplicity, habituation and preferential-looking procedures have turned out to be enormously powerful tools for studying infants' perception and understanding of the world.

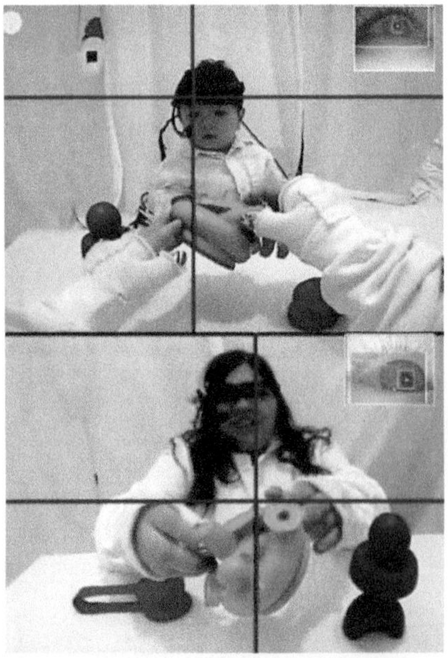

COURTESY OF CHEN YU

This infant and caregiver are each wearing a head-mounted eye tracker. The intersection of the purple lines shows where the viewer is looking. The top panel indicates that the caregiver's gaze is focused on the infant's face. The lower panel indicates that the infant's gaze is focused on the green object.

Visual Acuity and Colour Perception

The preferential-looking method enables researchers (and eye-care professionals) to assess **visual acuity**, that is, to determine how sharply or clearly infants can see. In adults and children, acuity is measured using eye charts, typically with letters and numbers. For obvious reasons, infants cannot be tested with eye charts!

COURTESY OF GOOD-LITE COMPANY

FIGURE 5.1 Testing visual acuity Paddles like the ones depicted here are used to assess young infants' visual acuity. Two paddles are shown to the infant simultaneously, one with stripes and one plain. If the infant can detect the contrast difference between the black and white stripes, the infant's gaze should be drawn toward the striped paddle. The ophthalmologist or researcher presents the infant a succession of paddles with increasingly narrow stripes, with increasingly narrow gaps between them, until the infant can no longer distinguish between the striped paddle and the plain one. The thickness of the stripes on the last paddle discriminated provides an indication of the infant's visual acuity.

Infant visual acuity measures take advantage of the observation that infants who can see the difference between a simple pattern and a solid grey field prefer to look at the pattern (Figure 5.1). By varying the patterns and assessing infants' preferences, researchers have learned a great deal about infants' early visual abilities. For example, young infants generally prefer to look at patterns of high visual contrast—such as a black-and-white checkerboard (Banks & Dannemiller, 1987). This is because young infants have poor **contrast sensitivity**: they can detect a pattern only when it is composed of highly contrasting elements.

One reason for infants' poor contrast sensitivity is the immaturity of their **cone cells**, the light-sensitive neurons that are highly concentrated in the *fovea* (the central region of the retina) and are involved in seeing fine detail and colour. Newborns' cones are spaced 4 times farther apart than adults' cones, and they catch only about 2% of the light striking the fovea, compared with 65% for adults (for review, see Arterberry & Kellman, 2016). This is partly why in their first month, babies have only about 20/120 vision (a level of acuity that would enable an adult to read only the large E at the top of a standard eye chart). Subsequently, visual acuity develops so rapidly that by 8 months of age, infants' acuity approaches that of adults. This progression from low to high levels of acuity is demonstrated in Figure 5.2.

For the first month or so, newborns do not appear to perceive differences between white and colour. However, by 2 months of age, infants' colour vision is similar to that of adults. They prefer colours that are unique hues, like blue, over colours that combine hues, like blue-green (Arterberry & Kellman, 2016).

Research on infant colour perception has been used to address a long-standing debate concerning the origin of colour categories. While humans can discriminate between thousands of different colours, languages use only a small number of terms to distinguish broad colour categories, and these categories differ across languages. To what extent is colour perception affected by language? This question was tested in a study of colour perception in infants who do not yet have words for colours (Yang et al., 2016). The researchers used fNIRS (discussed in Box 3.3) to determine whether 5-month-old infants categorize colours the same way adults do. Like adults, infants' brains responded to a change from a colour in one

contrast sensitivity the ability to detect differences in light and dark areas in a visual pattern

cone cells light-sensitive neurons that are highly concentrated in the fovea (the central region of the retina)

FIGURE 5.2 Visual acuity in infancy The blurred image on the left is roughly what a 1-month-old infant would perceive from about six inches away. The infant's relatively low level of visual acuity leads some features of the image to pop out—those with higher contrast (e.g., the woman's eyes and hairline). The series of images that follows shows the progression over the next few months as acuity improves. By 8 months of age, the infant's vision is similar to that of an adult (far right).

MANGOSTAR/SHUTTERSTOCK

smooth pursuit eye movements visual behaviour in which the viewer's gaze shifts at the same rate and angle as a moving object

perceptual constancy the perception of objects as being of constant size, shape, colour, etc., in spite of physical differences in the retinal image of the object

category to a new colour in a different category, but not to a new colour in the same category. These findings suggest that infants' brains represent at least some colour categories prior to learning the labels for colours.

Visual Scanning

Newborns start scanning the environment right away and are especially attracted to moving stimuli. However, they have trouble tracking these stimuli because their eye movements are jerky. Not until 4 months of age are infants able to track slow-moving objects smoothly (Rosander, 2007). To do so, infants must develop the use of **smooth pursuit eye movements**, in which the viewer's gaze shifts at the same speed and angle as a moving object, thereby keeping it in view. This developmental achievement appears to be less a function of visual experience than of maturation: preterm infants, whose neural and perceptual systems are immature, develop smooth visual tracking later than full-term infants do (Strand-Brodd et al., 2011).

Visual scanning is one of the few ways that infants have active control over what they observe and learn. When presented with a simple figure like a triangle, infants younger than 2 months old look almost exclusively at one corner. With more complex shapes, like faces, they tend to scan only the outer edges (Haith, Bergman, & Moore, 1977; Milewski, 1976). Thus, as Figure 5.3 shows, when 1-month-olds look at a line drawing of a face, they tend to fixate on the perimeter—on the hairline or chin, where there is relatively high contrast with the background. By 2 months of age, infants scan much more broadly, enabling them to pay attention to both overall shape and inner details. Indeed, as discussed in Box 5.1, faces are among the most prominent aspects of infants' visual environments.

Talking faces are a particularly important source of information for infant learners. At 4 months of age, before the onset of productive speech, infants primarily fixate on the eyes of the talking face (Lewkowicz & Hansen-Tift, 2012). However, after infants begin babbling, they primarily fixate on the speaker's mouth, supporting the view that attention to a talking mouth may be related to infants' development of spoken language. Interestingly, bilingual infants show this shift in visual scanning—preferring the mouth, not the eyes, of a talking face—earlier than do monolingual infants, which suggests that infants acquiring multiple languages take advantage of the information provided in the mouth earlier than do infants acquiring just a single language (Pons, Bosch, & Lewkowicz, 2015; though see Morin-Lessard and colleagues [2019] for conflicting results with Canadian French–English bilingual children). Bilingual infants learning two similar-sounding languages, like Spanish and Catalan—a particularly difficult task—pay even more attention to the talker's mouth than do bilingual infants learning two different-sounding languages, like Spanish and English (Birulés et al., 2018). We will learn more about how infants accomplish the impressive feat of learning multiple languages in Chapter 6.

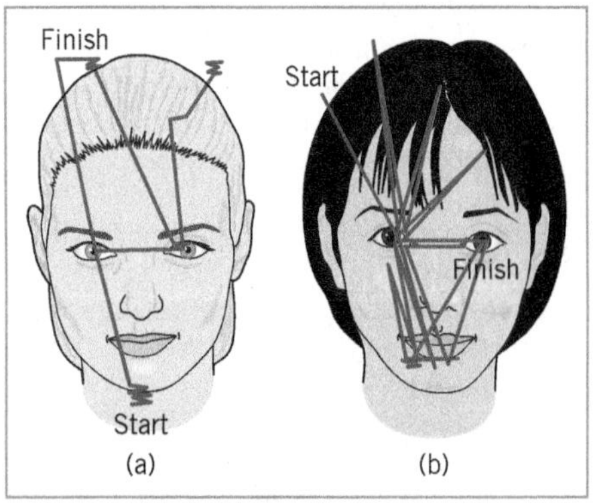

FIGURE 5.3 Visual scanning The lines superimposed on these face pictures show age differences in where two babies fixated on the images. (a) A 1-month-old looked primarily at the outer contour of the face and head, with a few fixations of the eyes. (b) A 2-month-old fixated primarily on the internal features of the face, especially the eyes and mouth. (Information from Maurer & Salapatek, 1976)

Object Perception

One of the most remarkable things about visual perception is how stable the world appears to be. When a person approaches or moves away from us, our retinal image of the person changes in size and shape, but we do not have the impression that the person changes in size and shape. Instead, we perceive a constant shape and size, a phenomenon known as **perceptual constancy**.

Perceptual constancy is evident early in life. In one study of this phenomenon, newborns were repeatedly shown either a large or a small cube at varying distances (Slater, Mattock, & Brown, 1990). While the cube's actual size remained the same, the size of the retinal image projected by the cube changed from one trial to the next (see Figure 5.4). The question was whether the newborns would perceive these events as multiple presentations of the same object or as presentations of similar objects of different sizes. To find out, the researchers subsequently presented the newborns with the original cube and a second one that was identical except that it was twice as large. The crucial factor was that the second cube was located twice as far away as the original one, so it produced the same-size retinal image as the original. The infants looked longer at the second cube, indicating that they saw it as different in size from the original one. This result revealed that the newborns perceived the multiple presentations of the original cube as a single object of a constant size, even though its retinal size varied.

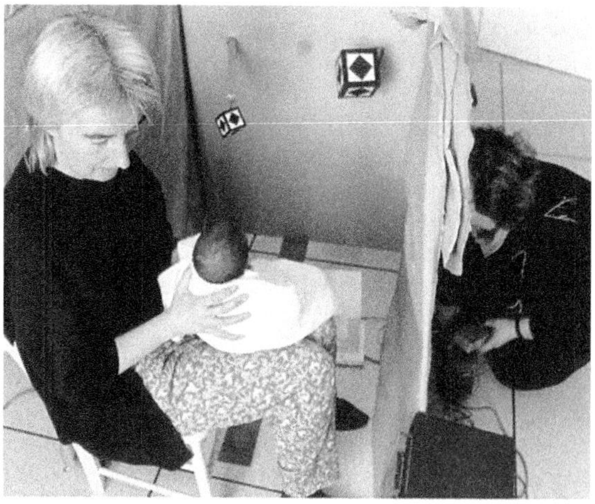

COURTESY OF ALAN SLATER

FIGURE 5.4 If this infant looks longer at the larger but farther-away cube, researchers will conclude that the child has size constancy.

Another crucial perceptual ability is **object segregation**, the perception of the boundaries between objects. To appreciate the importance of this ability, look at the room around you. How can you tell where one object ends and another begins? If the objects are separated by a visible gap, their boundaries are obvious. But what if there are no gaps? Suppose, for example, that as baby Benjamin watches his parents washing dishes, he sees a cup sitting on a saucer. An adult would perceive this arrangement as two distinct objects, but will Benjamin? Lacking experience with dishes, Benjamin may be unsure: the difference in shape suggests two objects, but the common texture suggests only one. Now suppose that Benjamin's parent picks up the cup, leaving the saucer on the table. Will he still be uncertain? No, because even infants treat the independent motion of cup and saucer (or any object) as a signal that they are separate entities.

object segregation the identification of separate objects in a visual array

The importance of motion as a cue indicating the boundaries between objects was initially demonstrated in a classic experiment by Kellman and Spelke (1983). First, 4-month-olds were presented with the display shown in Figure 5.5a. This display could be perceived either as two pieces of a rod moving on each end of a block of wood or as a single rod moving behind the block. Importantly, adults perceive displays of this type as a single rod. After habituating to the display, the infants were shown the two test displays in Figure 5.5b: a whole rod and a rod broken into two pieces. If the infants, like adults, assumed that there was a single intact rod moving behind the block during habituation, they should look longer at the broken rod because that display would be relatively novel. And that is exactly what the babies did.

What caused the infants to perceive the two rod segments presented during habituation as parts of a single object? The answer is *common movement*, that is, the fact that the two segments always moved together in the same direction and at the same speed. Four-month-olds who saw the same display as the one in Figure 5.5a, except that the rod was stationary, looked equally long at the two test displays. In other words, in the absence of common movement, the display was ambiguous.

Common movement is such a powerful cue that it leads infants to perceive disparate elements moving together as parts of a unitary object. It does not matter if the two parts of the object differ in colour, texture, and shape. Strikingly, however, even this seemingly very basic feature of visual perception must be learned. Newborn infants do not appear to make use of common motion as a cue to object identity (Slater et al., 1990, 1996); this ability emerges around 2 months of age (Johnson & Aslin, 1995). Thus, as powerful a cue as common motion may be, infants must learn to exploit it.

Older infants use additional sources of information for object segregation (Needham, 1997; Needham & Baillargeon, 1997). Consider the displays shown

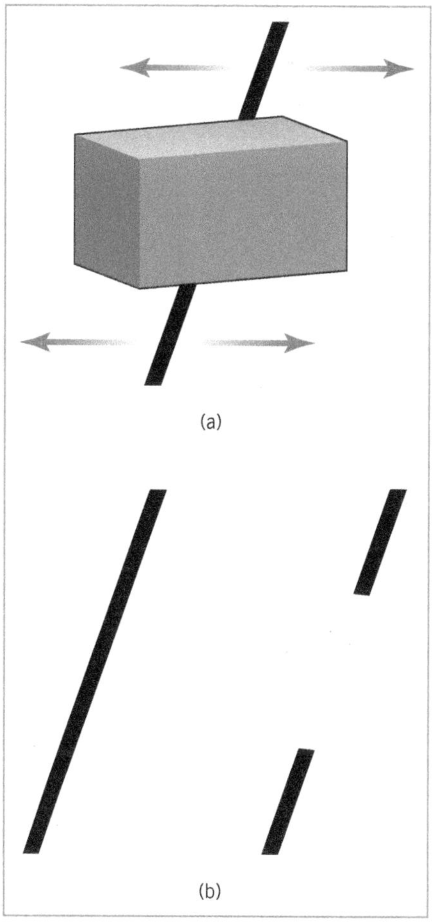

FIGURE 5.5 Object segregation Infants who see the combination of elements in (a) perceive two separate objects, a rod moving behind a block. After habituating to the display, they look longer at two rod segments than at a single rod (b), indicating that they find the single rod familiar but the two segments novel. If they first see a display with no movement, they look equally long at the two test displays. This result reveals the importance of movement for object segregation. (Information from Kellman & Spelke, 1983)

BOX 5.1 A CLOSER LOOK Infants' Face Perception

From birth (and possibly before, as discussed in Chapter 2), infants are drawn to facelike shapes. They are attracted by configurations with more elements in the upper half than in the lower half—something that characterizes all human faces (see the images on the left in the series below) (Macchi Cassia, Turati, & Simion, 2004). Additional evidence in support of a general bias to attend to facelike stimuli comes from studies showing that newborn humans are equally interested in human faces and monkey faces—as long as they are presented right-side up (Di Giorgio et al., 2012).

Newborns quickly learn to recognize and prefer their own caregivers' faces. After exposure to their mother over the first few days after birth, infants look longer at her face than at the face of another woman, even when controlling for olfactory cues (a necessary step because, as discussed in Chapter 2, newborns are highly attuned to their birth mother's scent) (Bushnell, Sai, & Mullin, 2011). Over the ensuing months, infants develop a preference for faces depicting the gender of the caregiver they see most often (Quinn et al., 2002).

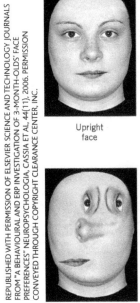

Studies using infant head cameras—imagine a baby version of a GoPro—have documented the ubiquity of faces. For their first few months, infants view faces for one-fourth of the time they are awake (Jayaraman, Fausey, & Smith, 2015; Sugden, Mohamed-Ali, & Moulson, 2014). Researchers at Ryerson University in Toronto found that these faces are mostly female (70%) and of the same race as the infant (96%) (Sugden et al., 2014). Similar facial statistics were observed for infants living in Hangzhou, China, suggesting cross-cultural similarities in the kinds of faces that infants are most likely to see (Liu, Xiao et al., 2015). This heavy focus on faces decreases with age, dropping to about 5 minutes of every hour by the end of the first year. At that point, infants are more focused on hands (and the objects they manipulate) than on faces (Fausey, Jayaraman, & Smith, 2016).

Face perception is shaped via experience by a process known as *perceptual narrowing*: infants become face specialists, better at discriminating amongst the kinds of faces that are frequently experienced in their environments. Evidence to support perceptual narrowing comes from an intriguing study of infants' and adults' ability to discriminate between individual human faces and individual monkey faces. Adults, 9-month-olds, and 6-month-olds could all readily discriminate between two human faces. However, only the 6-month-olds could discriminate between the monkey faces (Pascalis, de Haan, & Nelson, 2002). These data suggest that while 6-month-olds are still generalists, equally good at perceiving human and monkey faces, 9-month-olds have become specialists, no longer readily perceiving the dimensions that matter for discriminating between monkey faces.

Another source of evidence suggesting that perceptual narrowing shapes face perception comes from research on the perception of faces from different races. The *other-race effect (ORE)* is a well-established finding, initially observed in adults, in which individuals find it easier to distinguish between faces of individuals from their own racial group than between faces from other racial groups. An international team of researchers, including Kang Lee at the University of Toronto, demonstrated that the ORE emerges in infancy. Whereas newborns show no preference for own-race faces over other-race faces, 3-month-old White, African, and Chinese infants prefer own-race faces (Kelly, Liu et al., 2007; Kelly et al., 2005). Over the second half of the first year, infants' face processing continues to become more specialized, as shown by the emergence of the ORE. By 9 months of age, infants have more difficulty discriminating between other-race faces than between own-race faces (Kelly, Quinn et al., 2007; Kelly et al., 2009). Infants also appear to learn more in experimental tasks where the information is provided by an own-race face than by an other-race face (Pickron, Fava, & Scott, 2017; Xiao, Wu et al., 2018).

What drives these effects is not the infant's own race but, rather, the faces of individuals that the infant sees regularly (for a recent review, see Quinn, Lee, & Pascalis, 2019). For example, 3-month-old African emigrants to Israel who were exposed to both African and White caregivers showed equal

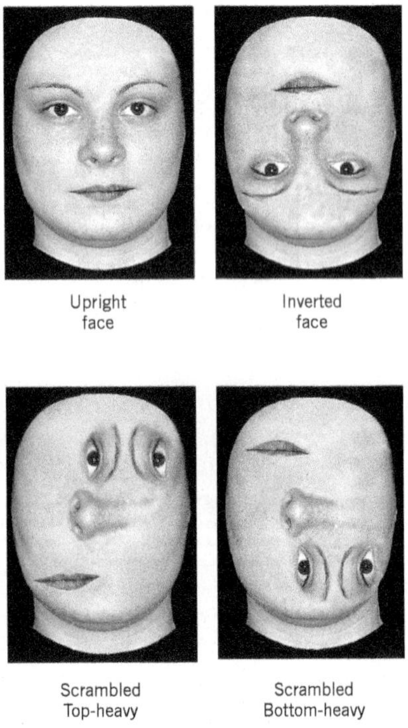

When presented with these pairs of stimuli, infants look longer at the images on the left, revealing a general preference for top-heavy stimuli that contributes to their preference for human faces (Macchi Cassia et al., 2004; Simion et al., 2002). Notice that this simple preference is all that is needed to result in newborns spending more time looking at their mother's face than at anything else. By 3 months of age, however, evidence suggest that infants' visual attention is no longer guided by a general top-heavy bias (Macchi Cassia et al., 2006).

in Figure 5.6 (on page 164). The differences in colour, shape, and texture between the box and the tube in Figure 5.6a suggest that there are two separate objects, although you cannot really be sure. However, your knowledge that objects cannot float in midair tells you that Figure 5.6b has to be a single object; that is, the tube must be attached to the box. Like you, 8-month-olds interpret these two displays differently. When they see a hand reach in and pull on the tube in Figure 5.6a, they look longer if the box and tube move together than if the tube comes apart from the box. This pattern of results is interpreted as surprise: if infants

COURTESY OF OLIVIER PASCALIS

Do the photos show the same person or different people? How about the two monkey photos? As an adult human, you no doubt can tell the two humans apart quite easily, but you probably can't tell whether the two monkey photos are of different individuals. (They are.)

interest in African and White faces (Bar-Haim et al., 2006). Further evidence of effects of visual experience on face perception comes from a study suggesting that the facial-scanning abilities of biracial infants—who are exposed to the facial features characteristic of two races in the home—are more mature than those of monoracial infants (Gaither, Pauker, & Johnson, 2012). Experiments have also shown that manipulations of experience—via picture books or videos providing additional other-race experience—can alter or even reverse these perceptual narrowing effects (Anzures et al., 2012; Heron-Delaney et al., 2011).

One of the most intriguing aspects of infants' facial preferences is that they prefer to look at faces judged by adults to be attractive (Langlois et al., 1991; Langlois et al., 1987; Rubenstein, Kalakanis, & Langlois, 1999; Slater et al., 1998, 2000). This preference also impacts infants' behaviour toward real people. This was demonstrated in a study in which 12-month-olds interacted with an experimenter whose face was either very attractive or very unattractive (Langlois, Roggman, & Rieser-Danner, 1990). The first key feature of this study was that the attractive experimenter and the unattractive experimenter were one and the same—the difference in appearance was achieved with the use of professional masks which conformed to what adults judge to be a very attractive face and a relatively unattractive one.

When interacting with the experimenter, infant participants behaved differently as a function of which mask she was wearing. They were more positive and playful when she was wearing the attractive mask than when she had on the unattractive one. This study was particularly well designed because the experimenter never knew on any given day which mask she had on. Thus, the infants' behaviour could not have been cued by the experimenter's behaviour.

Face perception may provide important hints about atypical development. Children and adults with autism spectrum disorders (ASD) show different patterns of visual attention to faces than do neurotypical individuals (see Frazier et al., 2017, for a recent meta-analysis). Researchers have proposed that infant preferences for non-faces—in particular, geometric shapes—may provide an early indication that the infant will eventually be diagnosed with ASD. One eye-tracking study found that autistic toddlers preferred a display of geometric shapes over a display of dynamic human images, whereas typically-developing toddlers showed the opposite pattern of preference (Pierce et al., 2016). Interestingly, autistic toddlers who most strongly preferred the geometric images had poorer language, cognitive, and social abilities than other autistic toddlers.

Another study in which toddlers' eyes were tracked while watching videos of naturalistic interactions found that autistic toddlers looked at faces half as often as did typically-developing toddlers, and they looked at objects twice as much as typically-developing toddlers did (Constantino et al., 2017). Infants with less interest in faces may have fewer opportunities to learn about the many types of information carried by faces, from speech sounds to social cues.

Finally, although infants are face specialists, face perception continues to develop well beyond infancy, as demonstrated by Daphne Maurer of McMaster University and Catherine Mondloch of Brock University. These researchers and their colleagues have shown that sensitivity to differences in the spacing of features, which helps people recognize individual faces, continues to develop throughout childhood (Laurence & Mondloch, 2016; Maurer, LeGrand, & Mondloch, 2002).

perceived the display as two separate objects, they should show interest when it moves like a single object. However, the opposite pattern occurs in Figure 5.6b: now the infants look longer if the tube alone moves, indicating that they perceive a single object. Experience with specific objects has been shown to help infants understand their physical properties. Younger infants (4½-month-olds) who have been previously familiarized with the objects in Figure 5.6 also exhibit the adultlike interpretation of these displays (Needham & Baillargeon, 1998). We will return to this idea later in this chapter when we discuss the impact of

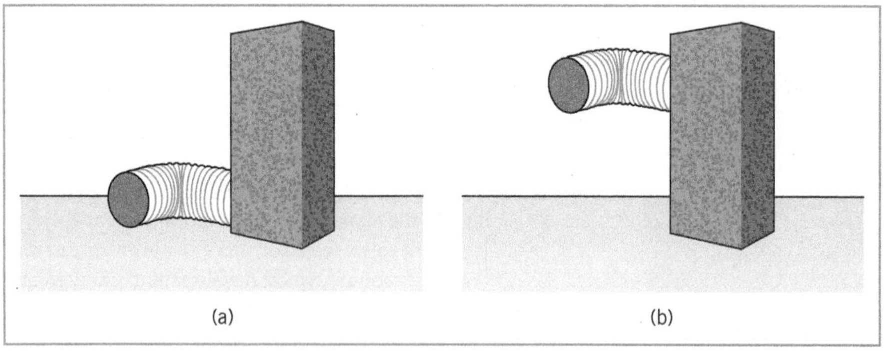

FIGURE 5.6 Knowledge and object segregation (a) It is impossible to know for sure whether what you see here is one object or two. (b) Because of your knowledge about gravity and support, you can be sure that this figure is a single (albeit very odd) object. (Information from Needham, 1997)

motor development (particularly reaching behaviour) on infants' object knowledge.

The culture within which infants develop—another form of experience—also influences their attention to the visual world. Decades of research in cultural psychology have documented different patterns of visual attention in different cultures. For example, when processing facial expressions, White Western adults are more likely to attend to the mouth, whereas East Asian adults are more likely to attend to the eyes (Jack et al., 2012). These cultural differences, which must be learned, influence face perception in the latter half of an infant's first year. In an eye-tracking study, researchers found that 7-month-old White infants growing up in the United Kingdom were more likely to focus on mouths, whereas East Asian infants growing up in Japan were more likely to focus on eyes (Geangu et al., 2016).

Cultural differences are also found in scene perception. Western adults tend to fixate on the focal objects in a scene, whereas East Asian adults tend to fixate on the actions and background contexts of the scene (e.g., Nisbett & Miyamoto, 2005). And indeed, when viewing dynamic scenes, American 2-year-olds pay more attention to objects, whereas Chinese 2-year-olds pay more attention to actions (Waxman et al., 2016). These effects may be due to cultural differences in what parents are paying attention to, which influences what their infants are paying attention to. Also, as we will see in Chapter 6, parents in East Asian countries are more likely than parents in the United States to label actions, which may heighten their salience for young children.

Development of Object Permanence in Infancy and Toddlerhood

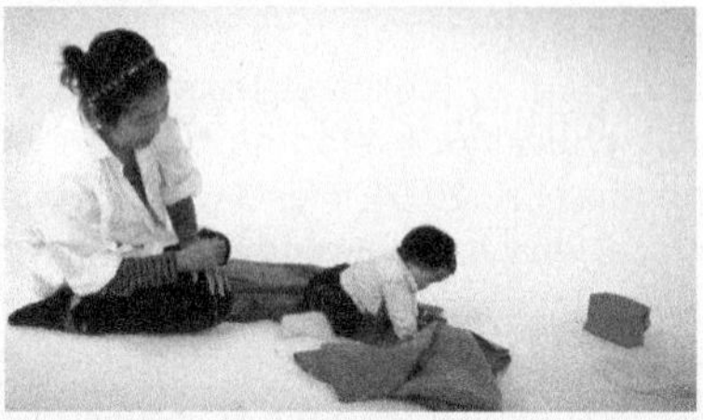

WORTH PUBLISHERS

Object Permanence: Reaching in the Dark

USED WITH PERMISSION FROM RACHEL KEEN, UNIVERSITY OF VIRGINIA

Object Knowledge

As we discussed in Chapter 4, Piaget believed that young infants' understanding of the world is severely limited by an inability to mentally represent and think about anything that they cannot currently see, hear, touch, or otherwise experience. Piaget based his theory in part on his tests of *object permanence,* which led him to infer that when an infant fails to search for an object that has disappeared from sight, it is because the object has also disappeared from the infant's mind. However, as also noted in Chapter 4, skepticism gradually arose about Piaget's explanation of this fascinating phenomenon. A number of clever studies since Piaget's time have established that out of sight is not out of mind, even for young infants.

The simplest evidence suggesting that young infants continue to represent an object that has vanished from sight is the fact that they will reach for objects in the dark. When young infants are shown an attractive object and the room is then plunged into darkness, most reach to where they last saw the object, indicating that they expect it to still be there (Perris & Clifton, 1988; Stack et al., 1989). Young infants even seem able to think about the size of invisible objects (Clifton et al., 1991). When 6-month-olds sitting in the dark heard the sound of a familiar large object, they reached toward it with both hands; but they reached with only one hand when the sound was that of a familiar small object.

Other studies have used the **violation-of-expectancy** procedure to study infants' object knowledge. The basic assumption is that if infants observe an event that is inconsistent with what they know about the world, they will be surprised—or at least interested. Thus, an unexpected event should evoke a greater response (such as longer looking or a change in heart rate) than an unsurprising event.

violation-of-expectancy a procedure used to study infant cognition in which infants are shown an event that should evoke surprise or interest if it goes against something the infant knows

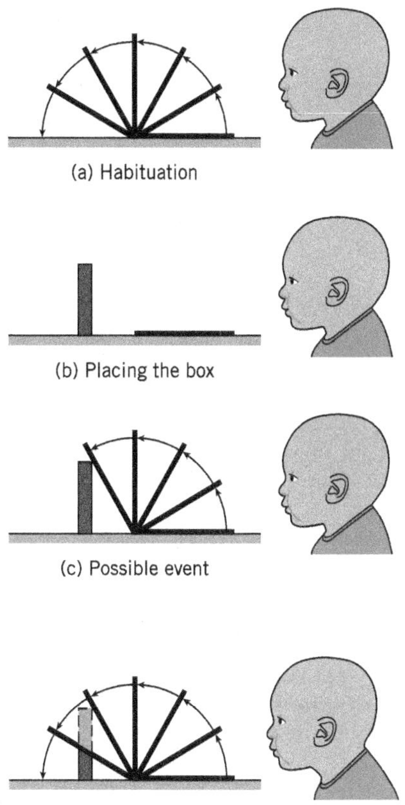

FIGURE 5.7 **Possible versus impossible events** In a classic series of tests of object permanence, Renée Baillargeon first habituated young infants to the sight of a screen rotating through 180 degrees. Then a box was placed in the path of the screen. In the possible event, the screen rotated up, occluding the box, and stopped when it reached the top of the box. In the impossible event, the screen rotated up, occluding the box, but then continued on through 180 degrees, appearing to pass through the space where the box was. Infants looked longer at the impossible event, showing that they mentally represented the presence of the invisible box. (Information from Baillargeon, 1987a)

The violation-of-expectancy technique was first used in a classic series of studies investigating infants' representations of non-visible objects (Baillargeon, Spelke, & Wasserman, 1985). Infants were habituated to the sight of a solid screen rotating back and forth through a 180-degree arc (see Figure 5.7). Then a box was placed in the screen's path, and the infants saw two test events. In the *possible event,* the screen rotated upward, occluding the box as it did so, and stopped when it contacted the box. In the *impossible event,* the screen continued to rotate a full 180 degrees, appearing to pass through the space occupied by the box.

Infants as young as 3½ months of age looked longer on trials depicting the impossible event than on trials depicting the possible one. The researchers reasoned that the full rotation of the screen (to which the infants had previously been habituated) would be more interesting or surprising than the partial rotation *only* if the infants had expected the screen to stop when it reached the box. This could only occur if they had expected the box to still be present, even though they could not see it. Note, however, that other researchers have raised concerns about the interpretation of studies using violation-of-expectation procedures, on the grounds that they require a "rich" view of infant knowledge, encompassing conceptual understanding of objects and the ability to reason about them. They suggest instead that there may be perceptual information in the visual displays that leads to infant preferences in this and other violation-of-expectation tasks (for one such alternative view, see Sirois & Jackson, 2012).

Controversy aside, research using two very different assessments—reaching in the dark and visual attention—provides converging evidence that infants who do not yet search for hidden objects nevertheless can represent their continued existence. Note that this is a very different view of infant cognition than that offered by Piaget and discussed in Chapter 4. In Piaget's sensorimotor period, objects do not exist for infants when they are not visible; out of sight is out of mind. Studies by Baillargeon and her colleagues paint a very different picture. While young infants still have much to learn about the properties of objects, they do expect objects to persist when they are out of sight. We will consider more complex aspects of object-related cognition in Chapter 7.

Baillargeon and the Impossible Event

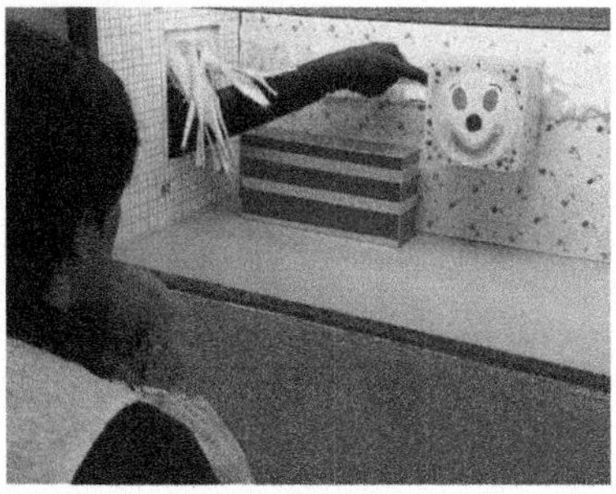

CHEDD-ANGIER PRODUCTION COMPANY

Depth Perception

Infants show early sensitivity to a variety of depth and distance cues. For example, as Benjamin increases his interactions with the world, he will use many sorts of cues to tell him whether he can reach the sippy cup on the table, and, eventually, whether the approaching car is far enough away that he can safely cross in front of it.

One depth perception cue that infants can exploit is **optical expansion**, in which the visual image of an object increases in size as it comes toward us, occluding more and more of the background. When the image of an approaching object expands symmetrically, we know that the object is headed right for us, and a sensible response is to duck. Infants cannot duck, but they can blink.

optical expansion a depth cue in which an object occludes increasingly more of the background, indicating that the object is approaching

CHICCODODIFC/GETTY IMAGES

As objects approach, they appear to grow in size. Optical expansion is a basic cue for depth perception.

Timing this blinking response is critical; if infants blink too soon or too late, they risk having the oncoming object hit their open eye. If you think about it, though, it's not at all obvious how infants would know how to correctly time a blink. Doing so requires infants to rapidly exploit information present in the visual image looming before them, including how rapidly the image is expanding and how much of the visual field is taken up by the image. Rather remarkably, infants as young as 1 month old blink defensively at an expanding image that appears to be an object heading toward them (Náñez, 1988). Preterm infants show a delayed developmental pattern of blinks to looming objects, suggesting that brain maturation, and not solely postnatal visual experience, is crucial for this developmental achievement (e.g., Agyei, van der Weel, & van der Meer, 2016).

The simple fact that we have two eyes also aids in the early development of depth perception. Because of the distance between our eyes, the retinal image of an object is never quite the same in both eyes. Consequently, the eyes never send exactly the same signal to the brain—a phenomenon known as **binocular disparity**. The closer the object, the greater the disparity between the two images; the farther away the object, the less the disparity. In a process known as **stereopsis**, the visual cortex computes the degree of disparity between the eyes' differing neural signals and produces the perception of depth. This form of depth perception emerges at around 4 months of age and is generally complete within a few weeks (Held, Birch, & Gwiazda, 1980).

The development of stereopsis is a classic example of the experience-expectant plasticity discussed in Chapter 3. Given the type of visual experience that infants normally receive, the development of binocular vision—both eyes working together to compute depth cues and other aspects of the visual scene—is a natural outcome of brain maturation. However, if infants are deprived of normal visual input, they may fail to develop normal binocular vision and will have difficulty making use of stereopsis and other binocular depth cues. There is a sensitive period for this aspect of visual development, which was first discovered in the research with cats discussed in Chapter 3: kittens deprived of vision in one eye before about 3 months of age fail to develop normal binocular vision when vision is restored (Hubel & Wiesel, 1962). The human analogue is a form of visual disruption known as *strabismus*, a disorder in which the two eyes do not line up in the same direction. Children whose strabismus is not treated (usually by corrective surgery) before the age of 3 years are at risk for pervasive lifelong challenges in binocular vision (Banks, Aslin, & Letson, 1975).

At about 6 or 7 months of age, infants become sensitive to a variety of **monocular depth cues** (which require just one eye) (Yonas, Elieff, & Arterberry, 2002). These cues are also known as **pictorial cues** because they can be used to portray depth in pictures. Three of them, including relative size, are presented in Figure 5.8. In a classic study, Yonas, Cleaves, and Pettersen (1978) capitalized on the fact that infants will reach toward whichever of two objects is nearer. Five- and 7-month-olds wore a patch over one eye (so binocular depth information would not be available) while viewing a trapezoidal window with one side considerably longer than the other (Figure 5.9). (When viewed by an adult with one eye closed, the window appears to be a standard rectangular window sitting at an angle with one side closer to the viewer.) The 7-month-olds (but not the 5-month-olds) reached toward the longer side, indicating that, like you, they perceived it as being nearer, providing evidence that they used relative size as a cue to depth. (Box 5.2 reviews research on infants' perception of pictures.)

binocular disparity the difference between the retinal image of an object in each eye that results in two slightly different signals being sent to the brain

stereopsis the process by which the visual cortex combines the differing neural signals caused by binocular disparity, resulting in the perception of depth

monocular depth (or pictorial) cues the perceptual cues of depth (such as relative size and interposition) that can be perceived by one eye alone

EMPEROR AUGUSTUS AND THE SIBYL, 1535, BORDONE, PARIS (1500–71)/ PUSHKIN MUSEUM, MOSCOW, RUSSIA/BRIDGEMAN IMAGES

FIGURE 5.8 Pictorial cues This Renaissance painting contains multiple examples of pictorial cues. One is interposition—nearer objects occlude ones that are farther away. The convergence of lines in the distance is another example. To appreciate the effectiveness of a third cue—relative size—compare the actual size of the man on the steps in the foreground to the actual size of the woman in the blue dress.

Auditory Perception

Sound is another rich source of infants' information about the world. As discussed in Chapter 2, fetuses can hear sufficiently well to learn basic features of their auditory environment (their mother's heartbeat, the rhythmic patterns of her native language, and so forth). At birth, the human auditory system is well developed relative to the visual system. That said, there are vast improvements in sound conduction from the outer and middle ear to the inner ear over the course of infancy. Similarly, over the first year, auditory pathways in the brain mature significantly. These developments in the ear and in the brain greatly improve the infant's ability to respond to, and learn from, sound.

auditory localization perception of the location in space of a sound source

Other factors add to infants' improvement in auditory perception. One example involves **auditory localization**, the perception of the spatial location of a sound source. When newborns hear a sound, they tend to turn toward it. However, they are far worse at determining the location of a sound than are older infants and toddlers. To localize a sound, listeners rely on differences in the sounds that arrive at both of their ears: a sound played to their right will arrive at their right ear before reaching their left ear and will be louder at their right ear than at their left ear, signaling the direction the sound is coming from. Young infants may have more difficulty using this information because their heads are small; the differences in timing and loudness in information arriving at an infant's ears are smaller than for toddlers and children with larger heads. Another reason why this

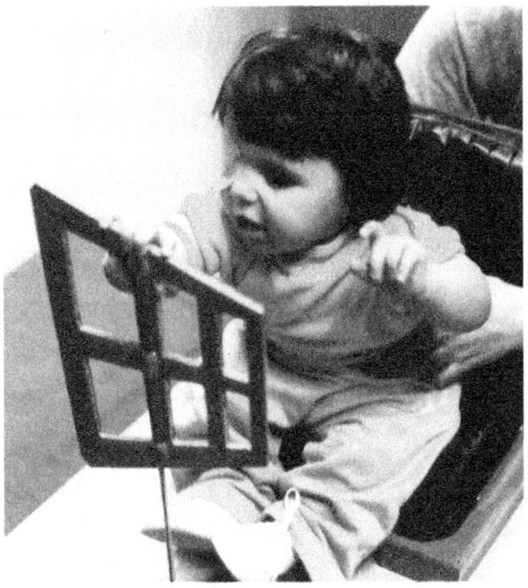

DR. ALBERT YONAS

FIGURE 5.9 Monocular depth cues This 7-month-old infant is using the monocular depth cue of relative size. Wearing an eye patch to take away binocular depth information, he is reaching to the longer side of a trapezoidal window. This behaviour indicates that the baby sees it as the nearer, and hence more readily reachable, side of a regular rectangular window (Yonas et al., 1978).

BOX 5.2 A CLOSER LOOK Picture Perception

Paintings, drawings, and photographs are ubiquitous in modern societies, and we acquire an enormous amount of information through them. When do we begin to perceive and understand these important cultural artefacts?

Even young infants perceive pictures in much the same way that you do. In one case study, Hochberg and Brooks (1962) raised their baby with no exposure to pictures: no art, picture books, or patterns on sheets, clothing, or toys. They even removed the labels from canned foods. Nevertheless, when tested at 18 months, the child readily identified people and objects in photographs and line drawings. Later research established that infants as young as 5 months old can recognize people and objects in photographs and drawings (e.g., DeLoache, Strauss, & Maynard, 1979; Dirks & Gibson, 1977), and even newborns can recognize two-dimensional versions of three-dimensional objects (Slater, Morison, & Rose, 1984).

Yet despite their precocious perception of pictures, infants do not fully understand their nature. The 9-month-olds shown here—two from the United States and two from a rural village in West Africa—are all manually exploring images of objects. Because they do not yet understand what two-dimensionality means, they attempt to treat pictured objects as if they were real objects—with an inevitable lack of success.

One source of evidence suggesting that infants do not fully understand the nature of 2-D images is that they sometimes attempt to pick up pictured objects, suggesting that they think the objects are real. Infants are more likely to attempt to grasp images that look real (like photographs) than images that do not (like line drawings; Pierroutsakos & DeLoache, 2003; Ziemer, Plumert, & Pick, 2012). They do, however, attempt more grasps at actual objects than pictured objects, suggesting that they have at least some rudimentary understanding of the distinction between 2-D and 3-D images. They also appear to understand the correspondence between 2-D and 3-D versions of the same object. Researchers at the University of Toronto demonstrated that 9-month-olds who were habituated to a 3-D object did not dishabituate when shown a 2-D image of the same object (Jowkar-Baniani & Schmuckler, 2011). This finding may reflect confusion on the part of infants, who are treating the 2-D and 3-D objects as the same thing. Alternatively, it may reflect infants' recognition of the correspondence between 2-D and 3-D representations of objects.

By 19 months of age and after substantial experience with pictures, American infants no longer manually investigate pictures, apparently having learned that pictures are to look at and talk about, but not to feel, pick up, or eat (DeLoache et al., 1998; Pierroutsakos & DeLoache, 2003). In short, they have come to understand the symbolic nature of pictures and appreciate that a depicted object stands for a real object (Uttal & Yuan, 2014). We will discuss the development of symbols further in Chapter 6.

Fascinating cross-cultural research suggests that infants who grow up in homes and communities without pictured objects do not show the same trajectory of understanding that pictures are representations of real objects. In one study, Canadian toddlers and preschoolers performed better than their peers from rural India and Peru in matching line drawings of objects to toy objects (Callaghan et al., 2011). Similarly, toddlers from rural Tanzania, who had no prior exposure to pictures, had greater difficulty

information may be difficult for infants to exploit is that the development of an auditory spatial map (i.e., a mental representation of how sounds are organized in physical space—right versus left, up versus down) requires multimodal experiences, through which infants become able to integrate information from what they hear with information from what they see and touch. We will discuss multimodal perception later in this chapter.

Infants are adept at perceiving patterns in the streams of sound they hear. They are remarkably proficient, for example, at detecting subtle differences in speech sounds—an ability we will review in detail in Chapter 6. Here, we focus on another realm in which infants display an impressive degree of sensitivity: music.

Music Perception

Caregivers around the world sing to their infants. In Canada, for example, 72% of mothers and 26% of fathers sing to their infants frequently (Trehub et al., 1997). They do so in a characteristic fashion which tends to be slower and higher-pitched, and to suggest more positive affect (similar to infant-directed speech, which we will discuss in Chapter 6), than does singing that is directed toward adult listeners. Perhaps because of these characteristics, infants prefer infant-directed singing over adult-directed singing (Masataka, 1999; Trainor, 1996). Interestingly, University of Toronto researcher Sandra Trehub and her colleagues have shown that infants enjoy listening to infant-directed singing even more than listening to infant-directed speech, possibly because mothers smile

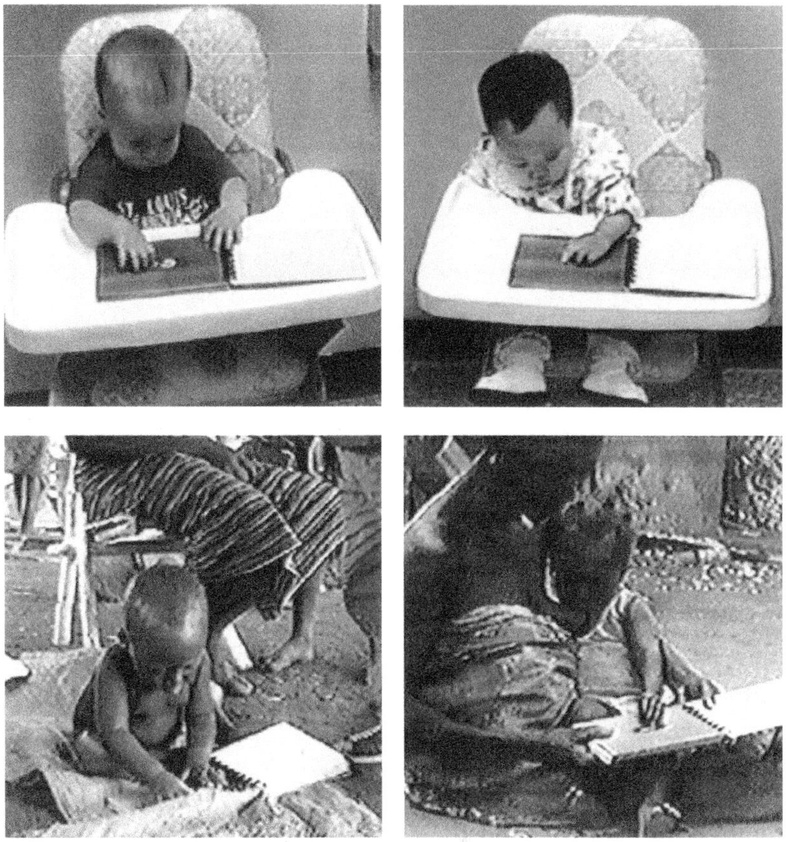

ALL COURTESY JUDY DELOACHE, PIERROUSTAKOS, UTTAL, ROSENGREN, AND GOTTLIEB

These 9-month-old infants—two from the United States (top row) and two from West Africa (bottom row)—are responding to pictures of objects as if they were real objects. They do not yet know the true nature of pictures.

than did North American toddlers in generalizing the names of objects in colour photographs to the objects themselves (Walker, Walker, & Ganea, 2013). These studies suggest that understanding the relationship between 2-D images and 3-D objects requires experience with pictorial media.

Many infants today have increased access to another form of 2-D images—moving images presented via screens, especially on handheld media devices. How do infants come to understand that Grandma on Skype is the same as "real" Grandma? By age 2 years, toddlers are as good at learning labels for objects via video chat as they are from in-person interactions, probably because both of these sources of information provide contingent interactions (Roseberry, Hirsh Pasek, & Golinkoff, 2014). When toddlers are given the same information via noncontingent interactions—as they would if they were watching a television show—they do not learn as well (Myers et al., 2017). Thus, it may be the case that 2-D images that interact contingently with infants are more readily understood as representing real people. We will return to questions about what leads infants to interpret objects as animate in Chapter 7.

Cognitive Development in Infancy: Manual Exploration of Pictures

more while singing than speaking (Corbeil, Trehub, & Peretz, 2015; Trehub, Plantinga, & Russo, 2015).

In many ways, infant music perception is adultlike. One well-studied example is the preference for consonant intervals (e.g., octaves, or perfect fifths like the opening notes of the ABCs song) over dissonant intervals (e.g., augmented fourths like the opening of the theme song from the TV show *The Simpsons*, or minor seconds like the theme from the film *Jaws*). From Pythagoras to Galileo to the present day, many scientists have argued that consonant tones are inherently pleasing to human ears, whereas dissonant tones are unpleasant. To see if infants agree, researchers employ a simple but reliable procedure. They draw infants' attention toward an audio speaker by using a visually interesting stimulus (e.g., a flashing light) and then play music through the speaker. The length of time infants spend looking at the speaker (actually, at the visual stimulus located by the speaker) serves as a measure of their interest in, or preference for, the music emanating from the speaker.

Using this method, researchers have shown that infants pay more attention to a consonant version of a piece of music than to a dissonant one (Trainor & Heinmiller, 1998; Zentner & Kagan, 1996, 1998). Even 2-day-old infants show this pattern of preference (Masataka, 2006). Notably, this study was conducted with hearing infants whose mothers were deaf, making it unlikely that the infants had prenatal exposure to singing. The results suggest that infant preferences for consonant music do not require musical experience.

In other aspects of music perception, infants diverge markedly from adult listeners. One example comes from *melodic perception,* in which infants can make perceptual discriminations that adults cannot. After hearing a repeated melody that follows the rules of Western music composition, Canadian adults and 8-month-olds were tested on the same melody with one note changed. On some trials, the changed note was in the same key as the melody; on others, it fell outside the key. Both infants and adults noticed changes that violated the key of the melody, but only infants noticed the changes that stayed within the key of the melody (Trainor & Trehub, 1992). Does this mean that infants are more musically attuned than adults? Probably not. The results reflect the infants' relative lack of implicit knowledge about Western music. For the adults in this study, who grew up immersed in Western culture, years of hearing music makes it very difficult to detect note changes that stay within a key.

Infants are also more "sensitive" to aspects of musical rhythm than are adults. Hannon and Trehub (2005a, 2005b) tested adults and 6-month-olds on their ability to detect meter-disrupting changes in simple rhythms versus complex rhythms. Some of the adult participants lived in the Balkans, where the local music contains complex rhythmic patterns; others lived in North America, where popular music is characterized by simpler rhythmic patterns. Although all groups detected changes in the simple rhythms, only the North American infants and the Balkan adults detected changes in the complex rhythms. Thus, North American 6-month-olds outperformed North American adults on this task. A follow-up study asked whether North American 12-month-olds and adults could be trained to detect such changes in the complex rhythms. After 2 weeks of exposure to the Balkan rhythms, the 12-month-olds were able to detect changes in complex rhythms, but the adults still failed to do so.

These examples suggest that, with experience, there is a process of **perceptual narrowing**. Infants, who are relatively inexperienced with music, can detect differences between musical stimuli that adults cannot. We find developmental changes in which experience fine-tunes the perceptual system across numerous domains. Indeed, you saw this process of perceptual narrowing in our discussion of face perception in Box 5.1, and you will see the same pattern of development when we examine intermodal perception (pages 172–174) and when we discuss speech perception in Chapter 6. Across all these examples, experience in a particular domain leads infants to become less sensitive to distinctions that they could make at earlier points in development. Perceptual narrowing permits the developing child to become attuned to patterns in biological and social stimuli that are important in their environment.

As discussed in Chapter 3, adult musicians' brains are shaped by the instruments that they play, demonstrating substantial plasticity. More generally, musicians are better than nonmusicians at processing aspects of pitch and rhythm in both speech and music (e.g., Kraus & Chandrasekaran, 2010; Wong et al., 2007). This finding raises a chicken and egg problem: Which comes first, enhanced auditory processing or musical training? That is, perhaps those individuals who persist in musical training are those who started out with unusually good auditory skills. Alternatively, infants may be similar in their auditory abilities, and musical training leads to enhanced auditory perception in those who receive it.

To address this question, researchers assigned 9-month-olds to one of two conditions, a musical intervention (12 sessions of musical exposure/play activities, akin to an infant music class) or a control condition consisting of nonmusical social play (Zhao & Kuhl, 2016). The researchers found that after the intervention,

perceptual narrowing developmental changes in which experience fine-tunes the perceptual system those infants who received additional musical experience were better able to process and detect altered patterns in both music and speech. These data support the view that experience plays a key role in supporting the development of musical abilities and suggest potential relationships between early musical experience and the development of language and literacy (e.g., Hannon, Nave-Blodgett, & Nave, 2018).

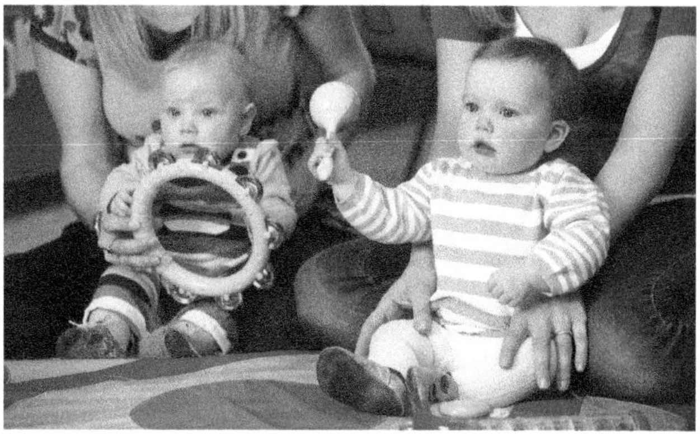

SPEEDKINGZ/SHUTTERSTOCK

These infants are engaging in musical activities as part of an infant music class, which is both enjoyable and provides potential benefits for perceptual development.

Taste and Smell

As you learned in Chapter 2, sensitivity to taste and smell develops before birth. Infants vary in the types of tastes they are exposed to early in life as a function of maternal diet (if they are breast-fed) and choice of formula (if they are formula fed). Some of those early experiences have long-lasting consequences. Early exposure to bitter flavours—before the age of 6 months—increases the likelihood of a later preference for those flavours (Nehring et al., 2015). However, the data regarding the long-term effects of early exposure to sweet and salty flavours is mixed, with some studies showing effects and others not. The timing of early exposure can also influence later taste preferences. For example, prenatal exposure to garlic increased children's intake of garlic-flavoured foods at age 8–9 years, whereas exposure to garlic in breast milk did not predict children's later preferences for garlic flavours.

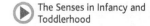

The Senses in Infancy and Toddlerhood

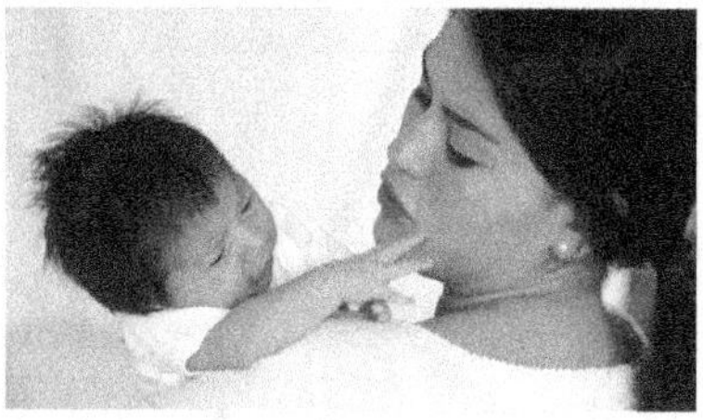

ARIEL SKELLEY/GETTY IMAGES

Preferences for smells are also present very early in life. Newborns prefer the smell of the natural food source for human infants—breast milk (Marlier & Schaal, 2005). Smell plays a powerful role in how a variety of infant mammals learn to recognize their mothers. It probably does the same for humans, as shown by studies in which infants chose between the scent of their own mother and that of another woman. In one such study, a pad that an infant's mother had worn next to her armpit was placed on one side of the infant's head and a pad worn by a different woman was placed on the other side. Two-day-old infants spent almost twice as long oriented to the pad infused with their mother's unique scent (Marin, Rapisardi, & Tani, 2015).

Smell and taste are an important component of the nutritional behaviours discussed in Chapter 3. One such behaviour is *food neophobia*, wherein children avoid unfamiliar foods. Researchers were interested in whether individual differences in the strength of toddlers' reactions to different tastes and smells could explain their degree of food neophobia (Monnery-Patris et al., 2015). Interestingly, toddlers' degree of reactivity to food odours, but not food tastes, predicted their degree of food neophobia. Thus, children's negative reaction to novel foods may be more strongly influenced by smell than by taste—a result that is consistent with many parents' frustration that their children regularly reject new foods before tasting them.

Touch

Infants also learn about their environment through active touch. Oral exploration dominates for the first few months, as infants mouth and suck on their own fingers and toes, as well as virtually any object they come into contact with. Through their ardent oral exploration, babies presumably learn about their own bodies (or at least the parts they can get their mouths on), as well as about the texture, taste, and other properties of the objects they encounter.

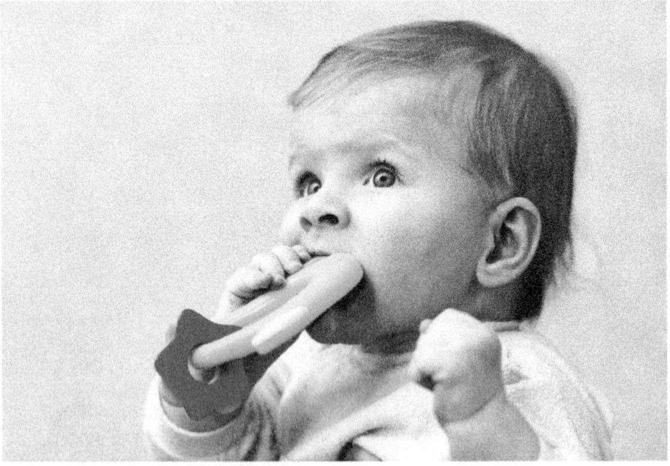

SERGEJS NESCERECKIS/ALAMY

GARETH BROWN/GETTY IMAGES

Initially, every object that a baby can pick up gets directed to his or her mouth for oral exploration—whether or not it will fit. Later, infants are more inclined to explore objects visually and manually, thereby showing an interest in the object itself.

From around the age of 4 months, as infants gain greater control over their hand and arm movements, manual exploration increases and gradually takes precedence over oral exploration. Infants actively rub, probe, and bang objects, and their actions become increasingly specific to the properties of the objects. For example, they tend to rub textured objects and bang rigid ones. They also begin to develop mental maps of their own bodies, relating the sensation of being touched to the locations on their bodies that are being touched (Ali, Spence, & Bremner, 2015). And, as we saw in Box 3.3, the brains of 7-month-old infants process the locations at which other people are touched (hands versus feet) using the corresponding areas of their own somatosensory cortex (Meltzoff, Ramírez et al., 2018). Important developments occur as infants become more adept at reaching, as we will discuss later in this chapter.

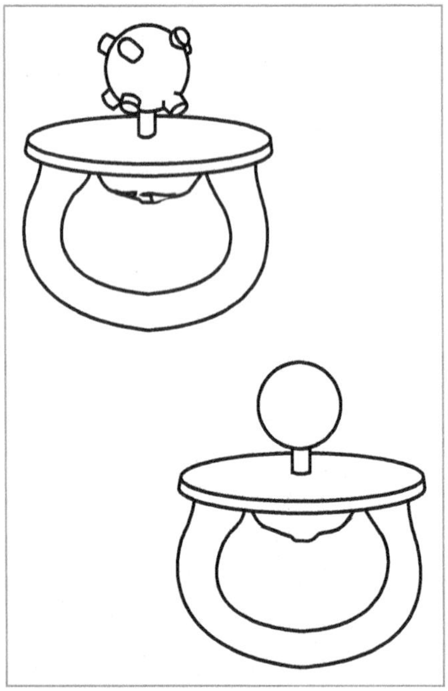

FIGURE 5.10 Bumpy and smooth pacifiers Studies with bumpy and smooth pacifiers demonstrate that infants can integrate visual and oral experiences (Meltzoff, 1990).

Intermodal Perception

Most events involve simultaneous stimulation through multiple sensory modalities. In the scenario described at the opening of this chapter, the shattering glass provided both visual and auditory stimulation. Via **intermodal perception**, the combining of information from two or more sensory systems, Benjamin's parents perceived the auditory and visual stimulation as a unitary, coherent event. It is likely that 4-month-old Benjamin did, too.

From very early on, infants integrate information from different senses. In studies with newborns (Kaye & Bower, 1994) and 1-month-olds (Meltzoff & Borton, 1979), infants sucked on a pacifier that they were prevented from seeing. They were then shown a picture of the pacifier that had been in their mouth and a picture of a novel pacifier of a different shape or texture (see Figure 5.10). The infants looked longer at the picture of the pacifier they had sucked on. Thus, these infants could visually recognize an object they had experienced only through oral exploration.

intermodal perception the combining of information from two or more sensory systems

To study auditory–visual intermodal perception, infants simultaneously view two different videos side by side, while listening to a soundtrack that is synchronized with one of the videos but not the other. If an infant looks more to the video that matches the soundtrack, this suggests that the infant detects the common structure in the auditory and visual information. Another way to think about these phenomena is that infants prefer to attend to multisensory events that can be perceived as emanating from a single object (Murray et al., 2016).

In a classic study of cross-modal matching using this procedure, Spelke (1976) showed 4-month-olds two videos: a person playing peekaboo, and a hand beating a drumstick against a block. When the infants heard a voice saying "Peekaboo," they looked more at the person, but when they heard a beating sound, they looked longer at the hand. In subsequent studies, infants showed finer discriminations. For instance, 4-month-olds viewing a pair of videos of a "hopping" toy animal looked more at a video in which the sounds of impact coincided with the animal's landing on a surface than they did at a video in which the impact sounds occurred while the animal was in midair (Spelke, 1979). Infants can also draw more abstract connections between sights and sounds. For example, 3- to 4-month-olds look longer at visual displays in which dimensions in each modality are congruent, such as a ball rising and falling at the same rate as a whistle rising and falling in pitch (Walker et al., 2010; though see Lewkowicz & Minar, 2014, for conflicting results).

Intermodal tasks can be used to examine relatively complex cross-modal associations. In one such study, researchers asked whether Chinese infants associate own- and other-race faces with emotional cues present in music (Xiao, Quinn et al., 2018). Young infants (3- and 6-month-olds) did not show a preference for a specific face when paired with happy versus sad music. However, 9-month-olds looked longer at own-race faces paired with happy music than at own-race faces paired with sad music, and vice versa for other-race faces. These results extend the findings about face preferences shown in Box 5.1 to include associations with emotional states, and they raise questions about early roots of social categories and preferences (a topic we will return to in Chapters 7 and 11).

One of the most dramatic demonstrations of auditory–visual intermodal perception is an illusion known as the *McGurk effect* (McGurk & MacDonald, 1976). To elicit this illusion, the auditory syllable *ba* is dubbed onto a video of a person speaking the syllable *ga*. Someone watching this display will hear the syllable *da*, which is intermediate between *ba* and *ga*. To experience this illusion, the perceiver must be able to integrate auditory and visual information together. And indeed, 4½-month-olds are able to experience this illusion: they treat the *da* sound as familiar after familiarization with the McGurk stimulus, even though they did not actually ever hear *da* (Burnham & Dodd, 2004; Kushnerenko et al., 2008).

The McGurk Effect

TIM REVELL

The processes of perceptual narrowing noted earlier also occur in intermodal perception. Young infants can detect correspondences between speech sounds and facial movements for speech sounds not present in their native language, but older infants cannot (Pons et al., 2009). Similarly, young infants can detect the correspondence between monkey facial movements and monkey vocalizations, but older infants cannot (Lewkowicz & Ghazanfar, 2006). Experience thus fine-tunes the types of intermodal correspondences that infants detect.

How does intermodal perception develop when one sense is absent early in life? This intriguing question has been the target of investigation in India, a nation with an unusually large population of blind individuals. In most of these cases, blindness is due to cataracts, which can be easily removed surgically, restoring sight. In one study, researchers asked whether newly

This child is a participant in a project focused on restoring sight to blind children and adults in India and studying their subsequent perceptual development.

PAWAN SINHA/PROJECT PRAKASH

reflexes fixed patterns of action that occur in response to particular stimulation

sighted adults could match an object that they felt via touch with an object that they saw (Held et al., 2011). Immediately after regaining sight, formerly blind adults could not match a visual shape with a tactile shape. However, after just 5 days of visual experience, the adults successfully performed this visual–tactile intermodal matching task. These results suggest that experience is indeed necessary in order to help previously blind learners discover the links between modalities.

TABLE 5.1 Common Neonatal Reflexes

Reflex	Description
Rooting 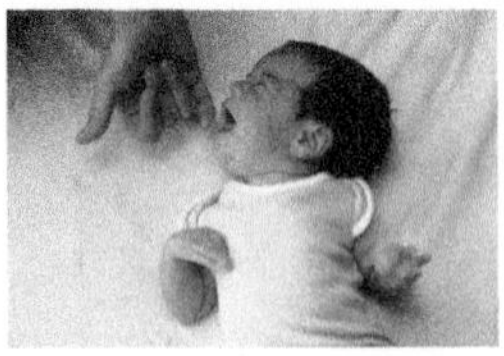	Turning of the head and opening of the mouth in the direction of a touch.
Sucking and swallowing 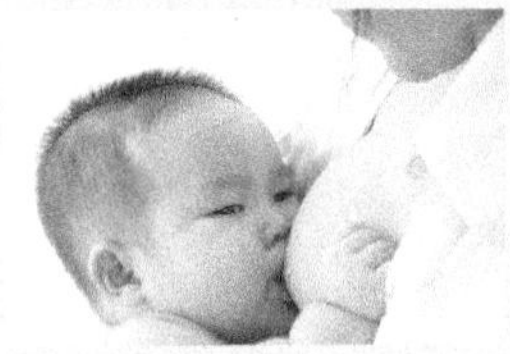	Oral response when the roof of the mouth is stimulated.
Tonic neck 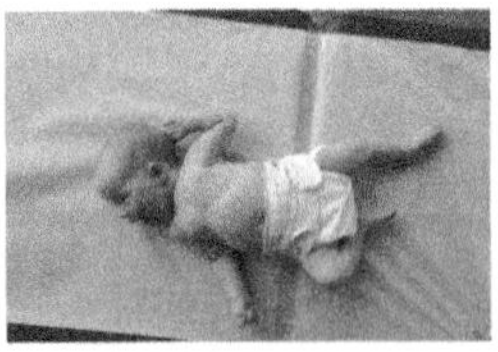	When the head turns or is positioned to one side, the arms on that side of the body extends, while the arm and knee on the other side flex.
Moro (startle) 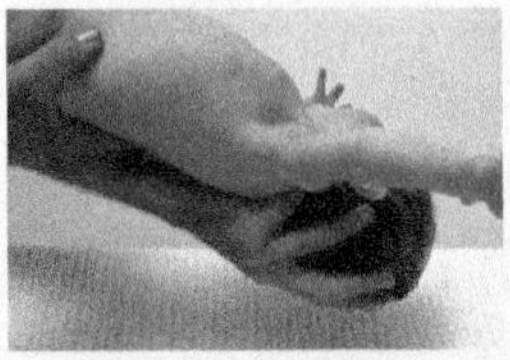	Throwing back the head and extending the arms, then rapidly drawing them in, in response to a loud, sound, or sudden movement.
Grasping 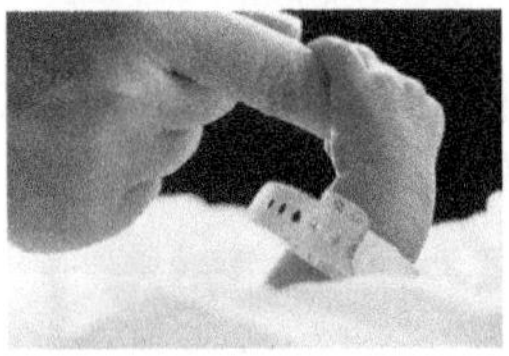	Closing the fingers around an object that is pressed to the palm.
Stepping 	Stepping or dancing with the feet when being held upright with feet touching a solid surface.

Photo credits from top to bottom:
ELIZABETH CREWS/THE IMAGE WORKS; WONG SZE YUEN/SHUTTERSTOCK; CUSTOM MEDICAL STOCK PHOTO/ALAMY; PETIT FORMAT/SCIENCE SOURCE; CHRISTOPHER BRISCOE/SCIENCE SOURCE; PHANIE/ALAMY

REVIEW QUESTION

Piaget's stage theory of development suggests that in the sensorimotor stage, infants' understanding of the world is bound by their immediate perceptions and actions—by what they are able to see and do in the here and now. How do the studies discussed in this section confirm or conflict with this theory? ■

Motor Development

As you learned in Chapter 2, human movement starts well before birth, as the fetus floats weightlessly in amniotic fluid. After birth, the newborn's movements are jerky and relatively uncoordinated, in part because of physical and neurological immaturity and in part because the baby is experiencing the full effects of gravity for the first time. As you will see in this section, the story of how the uncoordinated newborn, a prisoner of gravity, becomes a competent toddler confidently exploring the environment is remarkably complicated. The infant must acquire motor skills during a time of rapid bodily changes, including long-term alterations in weight, mass, height, and muscular strength, as well as hour-to-hour alterations in clothing and footwear and moment-to-moment alterations in body posture and position (Adolph & Hoch, 2019). The infant's motoric achievements have cascading effects on many other aspects of development, especially in the realms of visual perception and social behaviour.

Reflexes

Newborns start off with tightly organized patterns of action known as **reflexes**. Some reflexes have clear adaptive value; others have no known adaptive significance. Table 5.1 describes some of the major newborn reflexes. In the *grasping* reflex, newborns close their fingers around anything that presses against the palm of their hand. When stroked on the cheek, infants exhibit the *rooting* reflex, turning their head in the direction of the touch and opening their mouth. Thus, when their cheek comes into contact with their mother's breast, they turn toward the breast, opening their mouth as they do. Oral contact with the nipple then sets off a *sucking* reflex, followed by the *swallowing* reflex, both of which increase the baby's chance of getting nourishment and ultimately of surviving.

These reflexes are not *fully* automatic; for example, rooting is more likely to occur when an infant is hungry. No benefit is known to be associated with certain other reflexes, such as the *tonic neck* reflex; in this case, when an infant's head turns or is turned to one side, the arm on that side of the body extends while the arm and knee on the other side flex. Most of the neonatal reflexes disappear on a regular schedule, although some—including coughing, sneezing, blinking, and withdrawing from pain—remain throughout life.

Motor Milestones

Infants progress quickly in acquiring basic movement patterns, shown in Figure 5.11. Consistent with the dynamic systems approach described in Chapter 4, infants' acquisition of new ways to interact with the world provides them with new things to learn and new ways to think about the world.

The average ages indicated in Figure 5.11 are primarily based on research with North American infants. Importantly, there are tremendous individual and cultural differences in the ages at which these milestones are achieved. Because most developmental research still focuses on participants from WEIRD (Western, educated, industrialized, rich, and democratic) cultures, the causes and consequences of these cultural differences are not well-characterized (e.g., Kline, Shamsudheen, & Broesch, 2018). But when cultural differences in the development of specific motor skills have been studied, their impact has been vast and fascinating.

For example, the range for sitting shown in Figure 5.11 is roughly 5 to 7 months of age. However, in a study of the development of sitting, conducted in seven different countries, the percentage of 5-month-olds who could sit independently ranged from 0% (in Italy) to 92% (in Cameroon), with the United States falling below average at 17% (Karasik et al., 2015). As these data make clear, using Western children as the sole yardstick to measure development is both inaccurate and misleading.

Differences in the course of motor development reflect the contexts in which infants are developing. In countries where infants tend to sit independently earlier, they also tend to be placed in locations that offer less postural support, such as on the ground (in Kenya) and on adult furniture (in Cameroon). In countries where sitting tends to emerge later, such as Italy and the United States, infants spend more time in child furniture (infant carriers, swings, etc.) or being held.

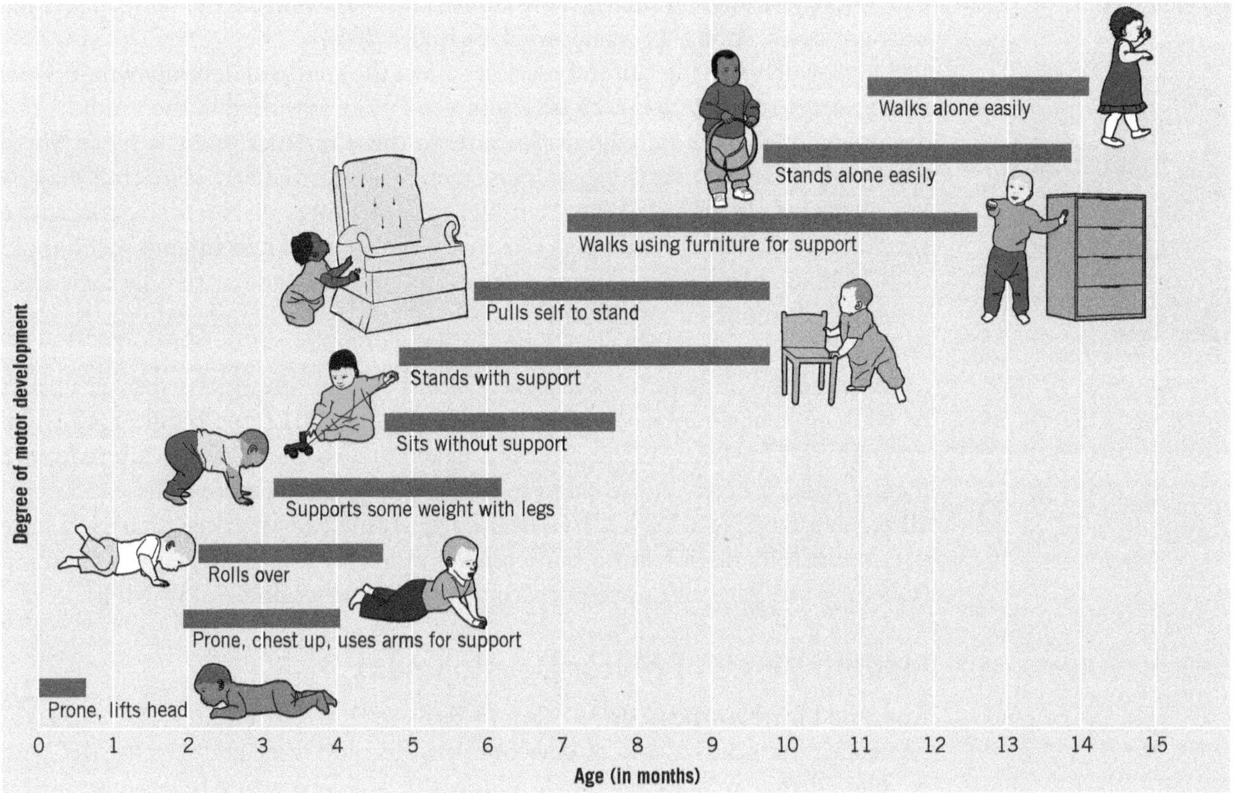

FIGURE 5.11 The major milestones of motor development in infancy Shown here are the average age and range of ages at which North American infants achieve each milestone. Note that these age norms are based on research with North American infants and do not reflect cross-cultural variation.

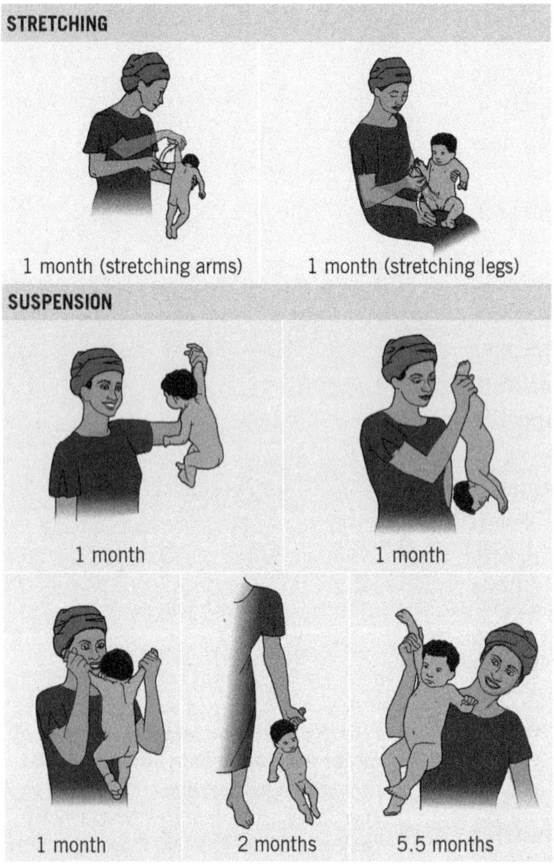

FIGURE 5.12 Promoting motor development in West Africa Caregivers in Mali believe it is important to exercise their infants to promote their physical and motor development. The maneuvers shown here hasten their early motor skills. (Information from Bril & Sabatier, 1986)

Because their posture is supported for more of the time, these infants have less opportunity to learn how to cope with gravity in order to keep from toppling over.

The degree to which motor skills are encouraged also varies from one culture to another. Caregivers in some cultures actively *discourage* early locomotion. In urban China, for example, infants are often restricted from crawling due to hygienic concerns (He, Walle, & Campos, 2015). These restrictions make it difficult for infants to develop the muscle strength required to support their upper trunk, which is necessary for crawling. Among the Aché, a nomadic people who live in the rain forest of Paraguay, infants spend almost all of their first 3 years of life being carried or kept very close to caregivers because of safety concerns. These infants thus get relatively little opportunity to exercise their locomotor skills (Kaplan & Dove, 1987).

In direct contrast, caregivers in other cultures actively encourage motor development. Exercises—including massage, limb manipulation, and other forms of motor stimulation—are a widespread parenting practice in many cultures in sub-Saharan Africa, including the Kipsigis, Kung San, Gusii, Wolof, and Bambora communities. These activities, shown in Figure 5.12, are often accompanied by singing, rhythmic bouncing, and high positive affect from the caregiver, and they are chosen intentionally to promote the infants' motor development. As described by one mother, "stretching the legs, the hands, and everything of the body makes the baby physically strong" (Carra, Lavelli, & Keller, 2014).

West African Exercise Routine

These widely varying cultural practices affect the course of development. Infants who undergo massage and exercise regimes are more advanced in their motor-skill development than those who don't undergo these regimes, such as most North American infants. Infants whose movements are particularly restricted may be less advanced. In one striking example, some families in Northern China use sandbags instead of cloth diapers due to water scarcity. Their infants spend more than 16 hours per day lying inside a bag filled with fine sand, with only their arms unrestricted, and show significant delays in sitting and walking (Adolph, Karasik, & Tamis-LeMonda, 2010).

Even the use of diapers—a relatively recent cultural invention—has an impact on walking behaviour (Cole, Lingeman, & Adolph, 2012; see Figure 5.13). The same group of infants was tested both naked and diapered and exhibited more mature walking behaviour when tested naked, despite the fact that these infants—all residents of New York City—were accustomed to wearing diapers. These data beautifully demonstrate that cultural practices undertaken in one domain (toileting) can have unforeseen consequences in another domain (walking).

Modern Views of Motor Development

Impressed by the orderly acquisition of skills reflected in Figure 5.11, two early pioneers in the study of motor development, Arnold Gesell and Myrtle McGraw, concluded that infants' motor development is governed by brain maturation

(Gesell & Thompson, 1938; McGraw, 1943). In contrast, current theorists emphasize that early motor development results from a confluence of numerous factors that include developing neural mechanisms, increases in infants' strength, posture control, balance, and perceptual skills, as well as changes in body proportions and motivation. (Box 5.3 offers a detailed account of a research program exemplifying this approach.)

A particularly important aspect of motor development is the infant's discovery of **affordances**—that is, the possibilities for action offered, or afforded, by objects and situations (Gibson, 1988). They discover, for example, that small objects—but not large ones—afford the possibility of being picked up; that solid, flat surfaces afford stable walking whereas squishy, slick, or steeply sloping ones do not; that chairs of a certain size afford the possibility of being sat on; and so forth. Infants discover affordances by figuring out the relations between their own bodies and abilities and the things around them.

Every milestone in infants' transition from newborns unable to lift their heads to toddlers who walk independently is fueled by what they can perceive of the external world and their motivation to experience more of it. The vital role of motivation is especially clear in infants' determined efforts to attempt to walk when they can get around much more efficiently by crawling. Most parents—and many researchers—have the impression that infants derive pleasure from pushing the envelope of their motor skills. And motor development pays off, as we will see in the next section; infants' increasing ability to explore and manipulate the world around them facilitates learning about the world. Indeed, individual differences in motor maturity at 5 months of age—as indexed by motor control and exploratory behaviour—predict children's academic achievement at 14 years of age (Bornstein, Hahn, & Suwalsky, 2013). This research suggests that infants who are better able to interact with their environment—by reaching for and manipulating objects, changing their body position, and so on—may have an advantage in perceptual and cognitive development by being better able to seek out new opportunities for learning.

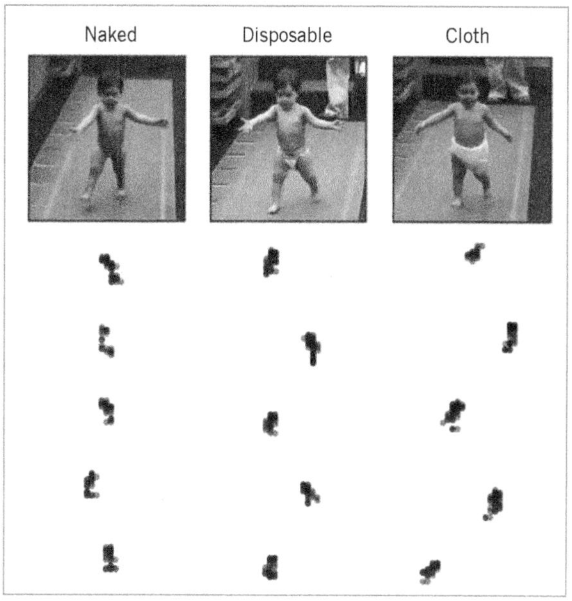

FIGURE 5.13 These images depict the footprint paths for a single infant participant who was tested walking naked, wearing lightweight disposable diapers, and wearing bulkier cloth diapers. The most mature walking behaviour was seen in the left-most path, in the absence of diapers (Cole et al., 2012).

Infants' Exploration of Objects

The Expanding World of the Infant

Infants' mastery of each of the milestones shown in Figure 5.11 greatly expands their world: there is more to see when they can sit up, more to explore when they can reach for things themselves, and even more to discover when they can locomote. In this section, we consider some of the ways that motor development affects infants' experience of the world.

Reaching

The development of reaching sets off a minirevolution in the infant's life: "once infants can reach for and grasp objects, they no longer have to wait for the world to come to them" (Bertenthal & Clifton, 1998). However, reaching takes time to develop. That is because, as discussed in Chapter 4, this seemingly simple behaviour actually involves a complex interaction of multiple independent components, including muscle development, postural control, and development of various perceptual and motor skills.

affordances the possibilities for action offered, or afforded, by objects and situations

BOX 5.3 A CLOSER LOOK "The Case of the Disappearing Reflex"

One of the primary proponents of the dynamic-systems point of view we discussed in Chapter 4 was Esther Thelen. Early research by Thelen and her colleagues provides an excellent example of this approach to investigating motor development. In one study, they held infants under the arms and submerged them waist-deep in water. As you read the following paragraphs, see how soon you can figure out the rationale for this somewhat strange-sounding but, in fact, extremely informative, experiment.

This particular study was one in a series of investigations that Thelen (1995) referred to as "the case of the disappearing reflex." The **stepping reflex** can be elicited by holding a newborn under the arms with the feet touching a surface. The baby will reflexively step, lifting first one leg and then the other (as in walking). The reflex typically disappears at about 2 months of age.

It was long assumed that the stepping reflex disappears from the infant's motor repertoire as a result of cortical maturation. However, 2-month-old infants given extra practice exercising their stepping reflex continued to show the reflex long after it would otherwise have disappeared (Zelazo, Zelazo, & Kolb, 1972). Furthermore, when 7-month-olds (who neither walk nor typically show the stepping reflex) are supported on a moving treadmill, they step smartly (Thelen, 1986). If the stepping reflex can be prolonged or elicited long after it is supposedly scheduled to disappear, cortical maturation cannot account for it vanishing. Why then does it normally disappear?

A clue was provided by the observation that, generally, the more body mass a baby has, the later that baby begins walking (and crawling). Thelen reasoned that infants' very rapid weight gain in the first few weeks after birth may cause their legs to get heavier faster than they get stronger. More strength is needed to lift a chubby leg than a thin one. Thus, Thelen hypothesized that the solution to the mystery might have more to do with brawn than with brains.

In one test of this hypothesis, the researchers put weights on the ankles of very young infants who still had a stepping reflex. The amount of weight was roughly equivalent to the amount of fat typically gained in the first few months. When the weight was added, the babies suddenly stopped stepping. In another study, older infants who no longer showed a stepping reflex were suspended waist-deep in a tank of water. As predicted, the babies resumed stepping when the buoyancy of the water supported their weight. Thus, the scientific detective work of these investigators established that the disappearance of the stepping reflex is not caused by cortical maturation. Rather, the movement pattern (and its neural basis) remains but is masked by the changing ratio of leg weight to strength. Only by considering multiple variables simultaneously was it possible to solve the mystery of the disappearing reflex.

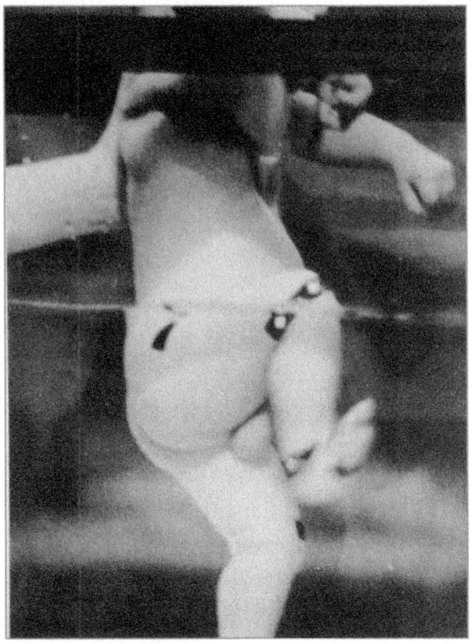
ESTHER THELEN

This infant, who no longer shows a stepping reflex on dry land, does show it when suspended in water.

Esther Thelen: Motor Development

Initially, infants are limited to **pre-reaching movements**—clumsy swiping in the general vicinity of objects. At about 3 to 4 months of age, they begin successfully reaching for objects, although their movements are initially somewhat jerky and poorly controlled, and their grabs fail more often than not.

Infants' achievements in motor development pave the way for new experiences and opportunities to learn. A particularly compelling example comes from studies (described in Chapter 4) in which pre-reaching infants were given Velcro-patched mittens and Velcro-patched toys that allowed them to pick up objects (Needham, Barrett, & Peterman, 2002). The manual exploration of objects made possible by these "sticky mittens" led to the infants' increased interest in objects and the earlier emergence of their ability to reach independently for them. Months later, these infants showed more sophisticated patterns of object exploration than did infants who had not experienced the sticky mittens intervention (Libertus, Joh, & Needham, 2015; Wiesen, Watkins, & Needham, 2016).

The achievement of stable sitting and smooth reaching at about 7 months enables infants to enlarge their sphere of action, because they can now lean forward to capture objects previously out of reach. Increased opportunities for

stepping reflex a neonatal reflex in which an infant lifts first one leg and then the other in a coordinated pattern like walking

pre-reaching movements clumsy swiping movements by young infants toward objects they see object exploration have ramifications for visual perception. For example, consider the difficulty of perceiving 3-D objects in their entirety. By their very nature, the front portions of 3-D objects block perception of their back portions. Having more experience manipulating objects—via better sitting and reaching skills—helps infants to become better at this process of 3-D object completion (Soska, Adolph, & Johnson, 2010). This form of self-directed visual experience also helps infants learn labels for objects; infants who gather more variable visual information about objects by manipulating them show larger increases in their vocabularies over the ensuing months (Slone, Smith, & Yu, 2019).

This right-handed 14-month-old—a participant in research by Rachel Keen and colleagues—is having a hard time getting the applesauce he has been offered into his mouth. As the photo on the left shows, he has been presented the spoon with its handle to his left, but he has grabbed it with his dominant right hand, which makes it extremely difficult to keep the spoon upright on its way to his mouth. A spill ensued.

These sources of evidence suggest a great deal of interaction between visual development and motor development. Infants can also use other types of sensory information to succeed on motor tasks in the absence of vision. For example, infants in a completely dark room can successfully nab an invisible object that is making a sound (Clifton et al., 1991).

Reaching behaviour interacts with infants' growing understanding of the world around them. For example, 8-month-olds are more likely to reach toward a distant object when an adult is present than when they are alone (Ramenzoni & Liszkowski, 2016). These data suggest that reaching behaviour has a social component; infants perceive adults as able to help them accomplish goals when they can't manage on their own.

Self-Locomotion

At about 8 months of age, infants become capable of **self-locomotion**, that is, of moving around in the environment on their own. No longer limited to being only where someone else carries or puts them, their world must seem vastly larger to them. Self-locomotion also alters other aspects of infants' perceptual experience. Babies who are lying down or sitting can easily seek out their caregivers' faces, but crawling babies cannot see a standing caregiver's face, no matter how hard they crane their necks (Franchak, Kretch, & Adolph, 2018). Thus, advances in self-locomotion may help to explain a result described earlier in this chapter: younger infants spend much more time looking at faces than older infants do.

self-locomotion the ability to move oneself around in the environment

Van Gogh's painting *First Steps* may have been inspired by the joy that most parents feel at seeing their baby walk alone for the first time and the joy the baby feels taking those first steps.

Infants' first success at moving forward under their own power typically takes the form of crawling. Many (perhaps most) infants begin by belly crawling or using other idiosyncratic patterns of self-propulsion, referred to as the "inchworm belly-flop" style (Adolph, Vereijken, & Denny, 1998). Most belly crawlers then shift to hands-and-knees crawling, which is less effortful and faster. Other styles of crawling also have colourful names: bear crawls, crab crawls, spider crawls, commando crawls, and bum shuffles (Adolph & Robinson, 2013). The broader point is that infants are remarkably good at finding ways to get around prior to their being able to walk.

When infants first begin walking independently, at about 11 to 12 months, they keep their feet relatively wide apart, which increases their base of support; they flex slightly at the hip and

BOX 5.4 A CLOSER LOOK "Gangway—I'm Coming Down"

The interdependence of different developmental domains is beautifully illustrated by a rich and fascinating series of experiments conducted over six decades. This work started with a landmark study by Eleanor Gibson and Richard Walk (1960) that addressed the question of whether infants can perceive depth. It has culminated in research linking depth perception, locomotion, cognitive abilities, emotion, and the social context of development.

To answer the depth-perception question, Gibson and Walk used an apparatus known as the "visual cliff." As the photo shows, the visual cliff consists of a thick sheet of Plexiglas. A platform across the middle divides the apparatus into two sides. A checked pattern right under the glass on one side makes it look like a solid, safe surface. On the other side, the same pattern is far beneath the glass, and the contrast in the apparent size of the checks makes it look as though there is a dangerous drop-off—a "cliff"—between the two sides.

Gibson and Walk reported that 6- to 14-month-old infants would readily cross the shallow, safe-looking side of the visual cliff. They would not, however, cross the deep side, even when a parent was beckoning to them to come across it. The infants were apparently unwilling to venture over what looked like a precipice—strong evidence that they perceived and understood the significance of the depth cue of relative size, and used this visual information to make judgments about safe motor behaviour.

Karen Adolph, who was a student of Gibson, has conducted extensive research on the relation between perception and action in infancy. Adolph and her colleagues have discovered surprising discontinuities in infants' learning what they can and cannot accomplish with their developing locomotor and postural skills (for a recent review, see Adolph & Hoch, 2019). The investigators asked parents to try to entice their infants to lean over or crawl across gaps of varying widths in an elevated surface or to crawl or walk down sloping walkways that varied in how steep they were. Some of these tasks were possible for a given infant; the infant would have no trouble, for example, negotiating a slope of a particular steepness. Other tasks, however, were impossible for that infant. Would the infants identify which tasks were which?

The accompanying photos show how infants behaved on slopes when beckoned by an adult (usually their parent). In their first weeks of crawling, infants (averaging about 8½ months in age) unhesitatingly and competently went down shallow slopes. Confronted with slopes that were too steep to crawl down, the infants typically paused for a moment, but then launched themselves headfirst anyway (requiring the experimenter to catch them). With weeks of crawling practice, the infants got better at judging when a slope was simply too steep and should be avoided. Infants learned to use both visual and tactile information to determine when it was safe to climb a steep slope or cross a narrow bridge. They also improved at devising strategies to get down somewhat steep slopes, such as turning around and cautiously inching backward down the slope.

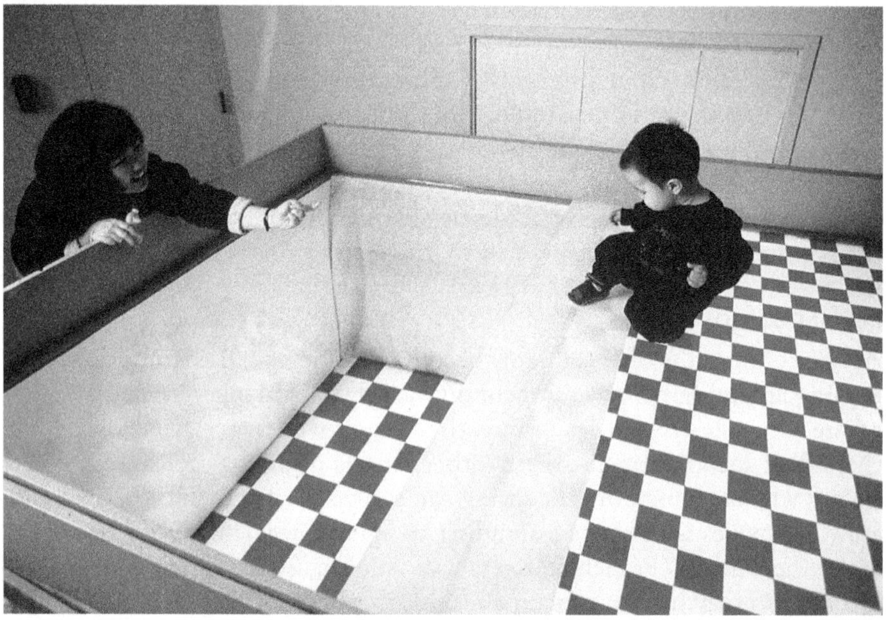

COURTESY OF PROFESSOR JOSEPH J. CAMPOS, UNIVERSITY OF CALIFORNIA, BERKELEY

This infant is refusing to cross the deep side of the visual cliff, even though his mother is calling and beckoning to him from the other side.

knee, thereby lowering their centre of gravity; they keep their hands in the air to facilitate balance; and they have both feet on the ground 60% of the time (as opposed to only 20% for adults) (Bertenthal & Clifton, 1998). As they grow stronger and gain experience, their steps become longer, straighter, and more consistent. Just as with other motor activities, like learning to play a sport or a musical instrument, practice is vital to infants' gradual mastery over their initially weak muscles and precarious balance. And practice they do: Adolph and colleagues (2012) found that their sample of 12- to 19-month-olds in New York City averaged 2368 steps—about the length of eight American football fields—and 17 falls per hour! This practice pays off: infants' proficiency at motor tasks is predicted by the number of days since they first began to engage in that behaviour (Adolph & Robinson, 2015).

COURTESY OF KAREN ADOLPH

Integrating perceptual information with new motor skills Researcher Karen Adolph will need to rescue the newly crawling young infant on the left, who does not realize that this slope is too steep for her current level of crawling expertise. In contrast, the experienced walker on the right is judiciously deciding that the slope is too steep for him to walk down.

However, when the infants started walking, they again misjudged which slopes they could get down, trying to walk down slopes that were too steep. They failed to transfer what they had learned about crawling down slopes to walking down them. Infants must learn how to integrate perceptual information with each new motor behaviour they develop. And this makes sense; because the bodily systems involved in each motor behaviour differ, the infant has to relearn as new motor behaviours emerge. For this reason, Adolph and Hoch (2019) describe motor development as "learning to learn to move," rather than learning to move.

Infants' decisions also depend on social information. Infants who are close to being able to make it down a relatively steep walkway can be discouraged by a parent telling them, "No! Stop!" Conversely, enthusiastic encouragement can lead an inexperienced crawler or walker to attempt a currently too-steep slope. Thus, the child uses both perceptual and social information in deciding what to do. In this case, the information is obtained through *social referencing*, the child's use of another person's emotional response to a situation to decide how to behave (see Chapter 10). With experience, infants learn to heed advice only in uncertain situations where the perceptual information about risk is ambiguous, ignoring adult input when the situation is either extremely risky or extremely safe (for review, see Adolph & Hoch, 2019). This developmental accomplishment shows the exquisite interplay between the infant's locomotor development, perceptual abilities, and social acumen.

▶ The Visual Cliff Experiment

The everyday life of the newly mobile crawler or walker is replete with challenges—slippery floors, spongy carpets, paths cluttered with obstacles, stairs, slopes, and so on. Infants must constantly evaluate whether their developing skills are adequate to enable them to travel from one point to another. Eleanor Gibson and her colleagues found that infants adjust their mode of locomotion according to their perception of the properties of the surface they want to traverse (Gibson et al., 1987; Gibson & Schmuckler, 1989). For example, an infant who had promptly walked across a rigid plywood walkway would prudently revert to crawling in order to get across a waterbed. Box 5.4 summarizes a program of research on the development of locomotion and other forms of motor behaviour in infancy, focusing specifically on the integration of perception and locomotion.

JUDY DELOACHE

FIGURE 5.14 Scale errors These three children are making scale errors, treating a miniature object as if it were a much larger one. The girl on the left has just fallen off the toy slide she was trying to go down; the boy in the middle is persistently trying to get into a very small car; and the boy on the right is attempting to sit in a miniature chair. (From DeLoache et al., 2004)

Scale Errors

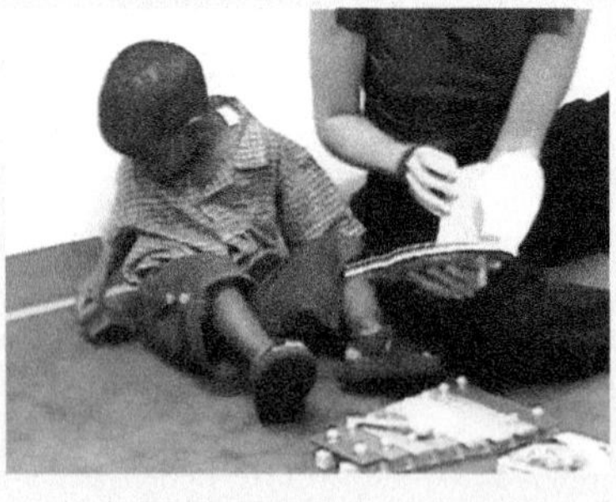

COURTESY OF DR. JUDY DELOACHE

Challenges in integrating perceptual information with motor behaviour can result in quite surprising behaviours. A particularly dramatic example is provided by **scale errors** (Brownell, Zerwas, & Ramani, 2007; DeLoache, Uttal, & Rosengren, 2004; Ware et al., 2006). In this kind of error, young children try to do something with a miniature replica object that is far too small for the action to be possible. For instance, toddlers will attempt, in all seriousness, to sit in a tiny, dollhouse-sized chair or to get into a small toy car (see Figure 5.14). In committing a scale error, the child momentarily, and sometimes repeatedly, fails to take into account the mismatch between body size and object size. Other types of errors that result from a mismatch between perception and action include *grasp errors,* in which the child tries to pick up an object from a 2-D representation (like a photograph, as discussed earlier in this chapter), and *media errors,* in which a child using interactive technology tries to pass or receive an object through a screen (Jiang & Rosengren, 2018).

REVIEW QUESTION

This section describes several studies that show how culture influences the timing of certain motor development milestones. What examples from your personal experience demonstrate the influence of culture on the development of these motor skills? ■

Learning and Memory

Who do you think learned more today—you or a 10-month-old infant? We'd bet on the baby, because there is so much that is new to an infant. Think back to Benjamin in the kitchen with his parents. A wealth of learning opportunities are embedded in that everyday scene. Benjamin was gaining experience with the differences between animate and inanimate entities, with the sights and sounds that co-occur in events, with the consequences of objects' losing support, and so on. He also experienced consequences of his own behaviour, such as his parents' response to his crying.

In this section, we review seven different types of learning through which infants acquire knowledge about their world, as well as the memory systems that support learning. These learning abilities are implicated in developmental achievements

scale error the attempt by a young child to perform an action on a miniature object that is impossible due to the large discrepancy in the relative sizes of the child and the object across every domain of human functioning, from vision to language to emotion to social skills. It is impossible to think about developmental change without considering the learning mechanisms that support it. We will explore learning in childhood and adolescence, as it pertains to the acquisition of knowledge ranging from language to math to emotions to gender, throughout the rest of the book.

Habituation

The simplest form of learning is to recognize that something has been experienced before. As discussed in Chapter 2 and again earlier in this chapter, babies—like everybody else—tend to respond relatively less to stimuli they have previously experienced and relatively more to novel stimuli. The occurrence of ***habituation***—a decrease in response after repeated stimulation—reveals that learning has taken place; the infant has formed a memory representation of the repeated, and now familiar, stimulus (see Figure 5.15). Habituation is highly adaptive: diminished attention to what is familiar enables infants to pay attention to, and learn about, what is new.

The speed with which an infant habituates is believed to reflect the general efficiency of the infant's processing of information. Related measures of attention, including duration of looking and degree of novelty preference, also indicate speed and efficiency of processing. Differences in habituation speed among infants appear to be related to aspects of general cognitive ability. Infants who habituate relatively rapidly, who take relatively short looks at visual stimuli, and/or who show a greater preference for novelty tend to have higher IQs when tested as many as 18 years later (Bornstein, Hahn, & Wolke, 2013; Colombo et al., 2004; Rose & Feldman, 1997).

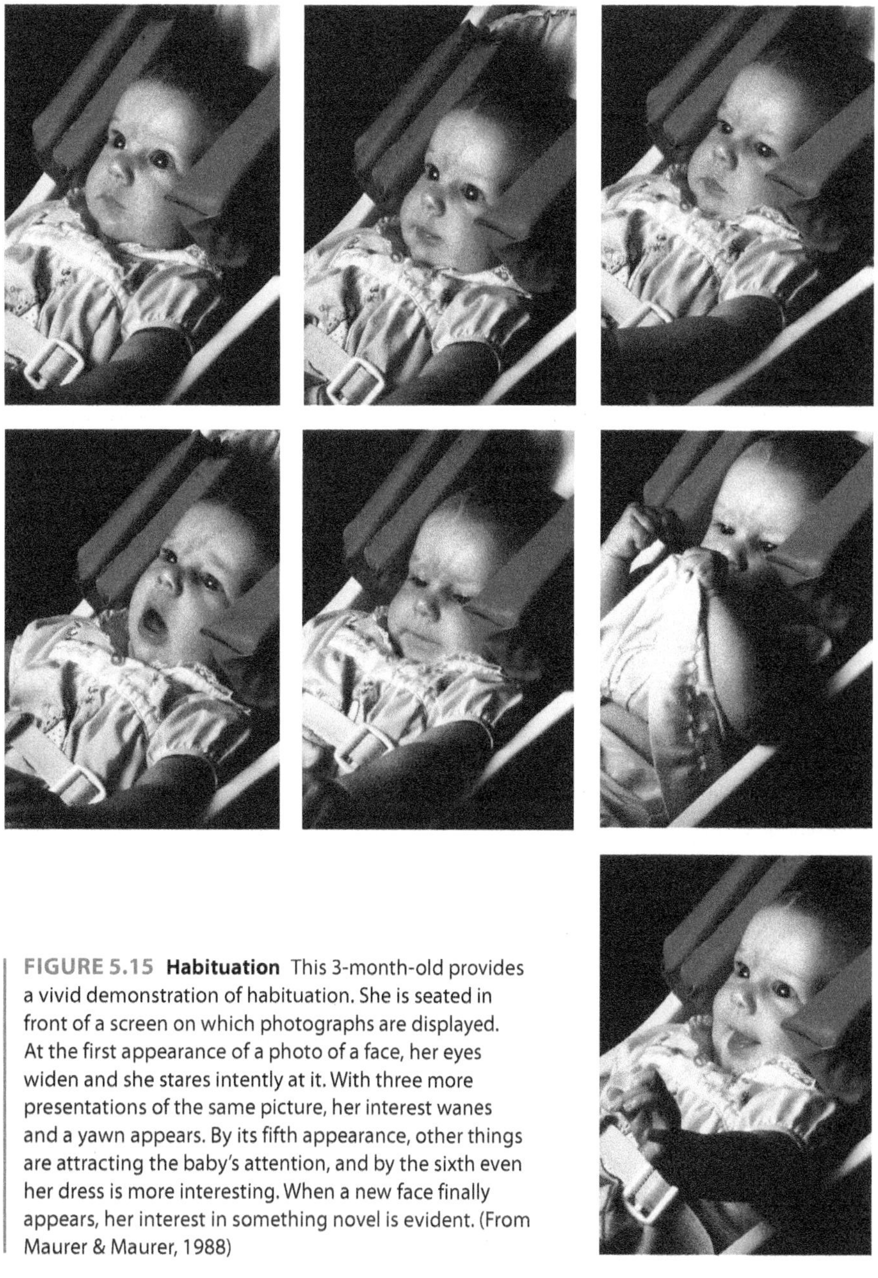

FIGURE 5.15 Habituation This 3-month-old provides a vivid demonstration of habituation. She is seated in front of a screen on which photographs are displayed. At the first appearance of a photo of a face, her eyes widen and she stares intently at it. With three more presentations of the same picture, her interest wanes and a yawn appears. By its fifth appearance, other things are attracting the baby's attention, and by the sixth even her dress is more interesting. When a new face finally appears, her interest in something novel is evident. (From Maurer & Maurer, 1988)

Statistical Learning

A related type of learning involves detecting statistical patterns. The environment contains a high degree of regularity and redundancy: certain events occur in a predictable order, certain objects appear at the same time and place, and so on. A common example for a baby is the regularity with which the sound of Mom's voice is accompanied by her face.

Infants are highly sensitive to the regularity with which one event follows another. In one study, 2- to 8-month-olds were habituated to six simple visual shapes that were presented one after another with specified levels of probability (Kirkham,

classical conditioning a form of learning that consists of associating an initially neutral stimulus with a stimulus that always evokes a particular reflexive response

unconditioned stimulus (UCS) a stimulus that evokes a reflexive response

unconditioned response (UCR) a reflexive response that is elicited by the unconditioned stimulus

conditioned stimulus (CS) the neutral stimulus that is repeatedly paired with the unconditioned stimulus

conditioned response (CR) the originally reflexive response that comes to be elicited by the conditioned stimulus

Slemmer, & Johnson, 2002). In a test, the order of appearance of one or more of the shapes was changed. The infants looked longer when the structure inherent in the initial set was violated, suggesting that they had learned the order of the shapes presented during the habituation phase.

Statistical learning abilities have been measured across numerous domains, including music, action, and speech (Saffran & Kirkham, 2018). Even newborn infants track statistical regularities in these domains, suggesting that statistical learning mechanisms are available at birth if not before (Bulf, Johnson, & Valenza, 2011; Fló et al., 2019; Kudo et al., 2011; Teinonen et al., 2009). Statistical learning has been proposed to play an important role in language learning, as we will discuss in Chapter 6.

Infants prefer to attend to certain types of statistical patterns over others. In particular, they appear to prefer patterns that have some variability over patterns that are perfectly predictable or very complex (random) (Gerken, Balcomb, & Minton, 2011; Kidd, Piantadosi, & Aslin, 2012, 2014). This "Goldilocks effect"—avoiding patterns that are either too easy or too hard—suggests that infants preferentially attend to the patterns that are most informative given their learning abilities.

Classical Conditioning

Classical conditioning was discovered by Ivan Pavlov in his famous research with dogs (who learned an association between the sound of a bell and the arrival of food, eventually salivating at the sound of the bell alone). Classical conditioning plays a role in infants' learning about the relations between significant environmental events. Consider young babies' mealtimes, which occur frequently and have a predictable structure. A breast or bottle contacts the infant's mouth, eliciting the sucking reflex. The sucking causes milk to flow into the infant's mouth, and the infant experiences the pleasurable sensations of a delicious taste and the satisfaction of nourishment. Classical conditioning is revealed when an infant's sucking motions begin to occur at the mere sight of the bottle or breast.

The nipple in the infant's mouth is an **unconditioned stimulus (UCS)** that reliably elicits an unlearned response—in this case, the sucking reflex—called the **unconditioned response (UCR)**. Learning occurs when an initially neutral stimulus—the breast or bottle, which is the **conditioned stimulus (CS)**—repeatedly occurs just before the unconditioned stimulus (the baby sees the breast or bottle before receiving the nipple). Gradually, the originally reflexive response becomes a learned behaviour, or **conditioned response (CR)**, triggered by exposure to the CS (anticipatory sucking movements now begin as soon as the baby sees the breast or bottle). In other words, the sight of the bottle or breast has become a signal of what will follow. Gradually, the infant may also come to associate caregivers with the entire sequence, including the pleasurable feelings that result from feeding.

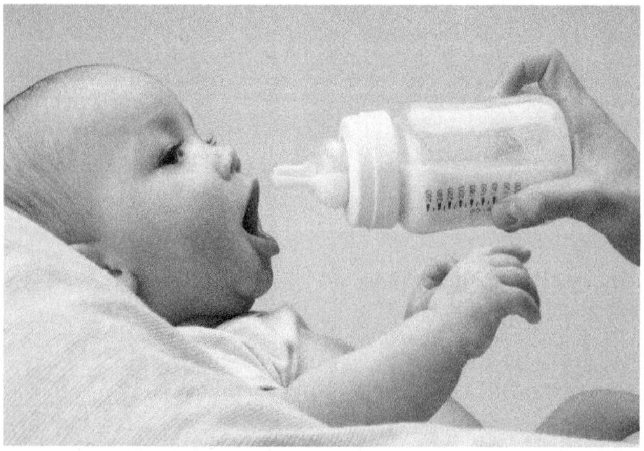

OJO IMAGES/GETTY IMAGES

Infants typically display the classically conditioned response of opening their mouths in anticipation when triggered by the appearance of a bottle or breast.

Classical conditioning is displayed by newborn infants. In eye-blink conditioning, a tone (CS) is paired with a puff of air (UCS) to the eye, eliciting an eye-blink (UCR). After exposure to the paired tone and air puff, infants begin to blink in response to the tone alone (CR). Even sleeping newborns learn this response, supporting the view that classical conditioning is a potent form of learning early in postnatal life (Fifer et al., 2010).

Instrumental Conditioning

A key form of learning is to discover consequences of one's own behaviour. Infants learn that shaking a rattle produces an interesting sound, that cooing at your parents gets them to coo back, and that exploring the dirt in a potted plant leads to a parental reprimand. **Instrumental conditioning** (or *operant conditioning*) involves learning the relationship between a behaviour and its consequences. Most research on instrumental conditioning in infants involves **positive reinforcement**, a reward that reliably follows a behaviour and increases the likelihood that the behaviour will be repeated. A *contingency* relation exists between the behaviour and the reward: if the infant performs the target behaviour, *then* the infant receives the reinforcement.

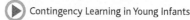

Contingency Learning in Young Infants

COURTESY OF CAROLYN ROVEE-COLLIER

instrumental (or operant) conditioning learning the relation between one's own behaviour and the consequences that result from it

positive reinforcement a reward that reliably follows a behaviour and increases the likelihood that the behaviour will be repeated

Carolyn Rovee-Collier (1997) used a particularly clever instrumental-conditioning procedure for studying learning and memory. A ribbon is attached to the baby's ankle and connected to a mobile hanging above the infant's crib (Figure 5.16). In the course of naturally kicking their legs, infants as young as 2 months of age quickly learn the relation between their leg movements and the enjoyable sight of the jiggling mobile. They then increase their rate of kicking. The mobile movement thus serves as reinforcement for the kicking. This task has been used extensively to investigate age-related changes in how long, and under what circumstances, infants continue to remember the contingency between kicking and mobile movement (e.g., Rovee-Collier, 1999). Among the findings: (1) 3-month-olds remember the kicking response for about 1 week, whereas 6-month-olds remember it for 2 weeks; (2) infants younger than about 6 months of age remember the kicking response only when the test mobile is identical to the training mobile, whereas older infants remember it with novel mobiles; (3) a brief reminder, in the form of simply observing the moving mobile, increases the duration of infants' retention of the kicking response.

Infants' intense motivation to explore and master their environment, which we have emphasized in our *active child* theme, shows up in instrumental-learning situations: infants work hard at learning to predict and control their experience, and they display positive emotions during peaks in performance (Angulo-Barroso et al., 2017). Infants may also learn that there are situations over which they have little or no control. For example, infants of depressed mothers tend to smile less than infants whose mothers are not depressed. In part, this may be because their smiles are not consistently rewarded by their preoccupied parent; mothers struggling with postpartum depression are more likely to be negative and/or disengaged (e.g., Brummelte & Galea, 2016). More generally, instrumental learning helps infants learn about the relation between themselves and their environment and the extent to which they can have an impact on it.

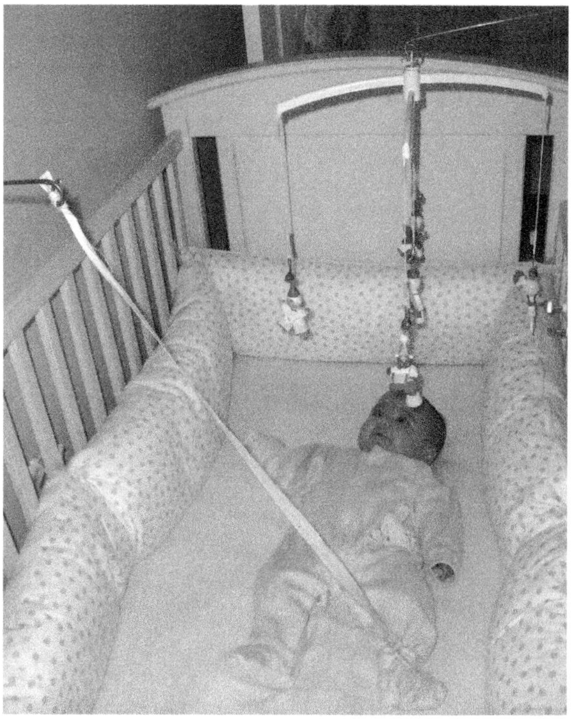

CAROLYN ROVEE-COLLIER

FIGURE 5.16 Contingency This young infant learned within minutes that kicking her leg would cause the mobile to move in an interesting way; she learned the contingency between her own behaviour and an external event.

Observational Learning/Imitation

A particularly potent source of infants' learning is their observation of other people's behaviours. Imitation is a form of observational learning, though exactly when in infancy this ability emerges is a matter of scientific debate. Meltzoff and Moore (1977, 1983) found that after newborns watch an adult model slowly and repeatedly stick out their tongue, the newborns often stick out their own tongues. However, subsequent studies found mixed results for neonatal imitation (for review, see Simpson et al., 2014). Of particular note is a recent large-scale study that failed to replicate Meltzoff and Moore's influential finding, calling the existence of newborn imitation into question (Oostenbroek et al., 2016)—though see the rebuttal by Meltzoff, Murray, and colleagues (2018), who point out methodological flaws in the Oostenbroek study, and the subsequent back-and-forth (Meltzoff et al., 2019; Oostenbroek et al., 2018).

By the second half of the first year, infants begin to imitate more complex actions. In one study, infants observed an experimenter performing unusual behaviours with objects, such as touching a box with their head, causing the box to light up. The infants were later presented with the same objects the experimenter had acted on. Infants as young as 6 to 9 months imitated some of the novel actions they witnessed, even after a delay of 24 hours (for review, see Meltzoff & Marshall, 2018). Fourteen-month-olds imitated such actions a full week after first seeing them (Meltzoff, 1988b). Studies like these suggest that imitation is an important component of cultural transmission.

In choosing to imitate a model, infants seem to analyze the reason for the person's behaviour. If infants see a model lean over and touch a box with her forehead, they later do the same. If, however, the model remarks that she's cold and tightly clutches a shawl around her body as she leans over and touches a box with her forehead, infants reach out and touch the box with their hand instead of their head (Gergely, Bekkering, & Kiraly, 2002). They apparently reason that the model wanted to touch the box and would have done so in a standard way if her hands had been free. Their imitation is thus based on their analysis of the person's intentions.

Further evidence of infants' attention to intention comes from research in which 18-month-olds observed an adult attempting, but failing, to pull apart a small dumbbell toy (Meltzoff, 1995a). The adult pulled on the two ends, but his hand "slipped off," and the dumbbell remained in one piece (Figure 5.17a). When the infants were subsequently given the toy, they pulled the two ends apart, imitating what the adult had *intended* to do, not what he had actually done. This research also established that infants' imitative actions are limited to human acts. A different group of 18-month-olds watched a mechanical device with pincers grasp the two ends of the dumbbell. The pincers either pulled apart the dumbbell or slipped off the ends (Figure 5.17b). Regardless of what the infants had seen the mechanical device do, they rarely attempted to pull apart the dumbbell themselves. Thus, infants attempt to reproduce the behaviour and intentions of other people but not of inanimate objects.

Not only do infants analyze the reason for a person's behaviour, but they also pay attention to the credibility of the person. In one study, Concordia University researchers first had an adult behave in either a reliable way (i.e., the adult looked happy when looking inside a container that held a toy) or in an unreliable way (i.e., the adult looked happy when looking inside an empty container). The researchers

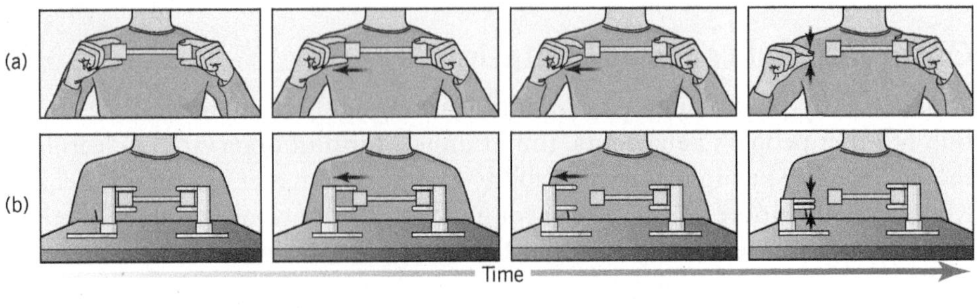

FIGURE 5.17 Imitating intentions
(a) When 18-month-olds see a person apparently try but fail to pull the ends off a dumbbell, they imitate pulling the ends off—the action the person intended to do, not what the person actually did. (b) They do not imitate a mechanical device at all. (Information from Meltzoff, 1995a)

then tested whether 14-month-olds would imitate the adult's unusual behaviour of switching on a light by touching her forehead to it. As can be seen in Figure 5.18, babies are skeptics; they were more likely to imitate the head touch behaviour of the reliable experimenter but not of the unreliable experimenter. In the latter case, they tended to turn on the lights in the more usual way, using their hands (Poulin-Dubois, Brooker, & Polonia, 2011)!

The neural underpinnings of imitative learning have received a great deal of attention. *Mirror neurons* were discovered when neuroscientists who were monitoring the brain activity of a monkey noticed that when the monkey happened to see a lab assistant raising an ice cream cone to his mouth, neurons in the monkey's premotor cortex began firing as though the monkey itself were about to eat the ice cream cone (Gallese et al., 1996). Similarly, EEG studies in which newborn macaque monkeys observe adult humans making facial gestures reveal a pattern of brain activation, known as the *mu rhythm*, that is characteristic of the mirror neuron system (Ferrari et al., 2012). This pattern of brain electrical activity is evoked by viewing actions like facial movements but not by movements of inanimate objects.

The degree to which the same system is present in infants remains unclear. Patterns of infant brain activity are consistent with the hypothesis that mirror neurons are present—the aforementioned mu rhythm—when infants are observing an action that is similar to those they display when they are performing the same action (see Figure 5.19; Marshall & Meltzoff, 2014). These brain patterns have consequences: 7-month-olds whose brains showed greater mu rhythm while observing an experimenter produce a goal-directed action were later more likely to reproduce the action (Filippi et al., 2016). To date, however, it remains unknown how early these brain patterns emerge in development and whether they are at the root of human imitation.

Observational learning is not limited to motor acts. Infants also learn about more abstract concepts, such as how hard to try at a given task—a quality described as "grit." This idea that a characteristic like grit can be learned via observation was investigated in a clever study by Leonard, Lee, & Schulz (2017). First, 15-month-olds watched as an adult experimenter completed two simple tasks (removing a lid from a container and removing a toy from a keychain). In one condition, the experimenter struggled to complete the tasks, visibly exerting effort while persisting. Other infants saw an experimenter who quickly and effortlessly completed both goals. The infants were then given a new, difficult task

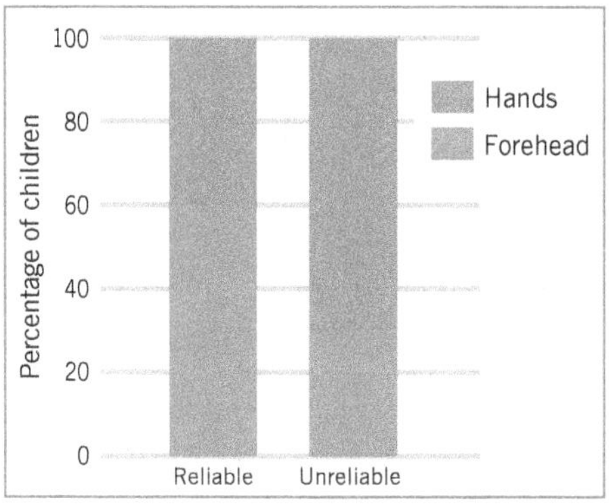

FIGURE 5.18 Skeptical babies Babies are highly selective in terms of whom they imitate. Babies were more likely to imitate the experimenter who switched on a light with her head, when her earlier emotional response made sense. When the experimenter's earlier responses did not make sense, babies were more likely to use their hands to switch on the light. (Data from Poulin-Dubois, Brooker, & Polonia, 2011)

FIGURE 5.19 Mu rhythms The patterns of EEG recordings taken when 14-month-old infants observed the act of pressing a button (right) were similar to the patterns when they executed the action themselves (left).

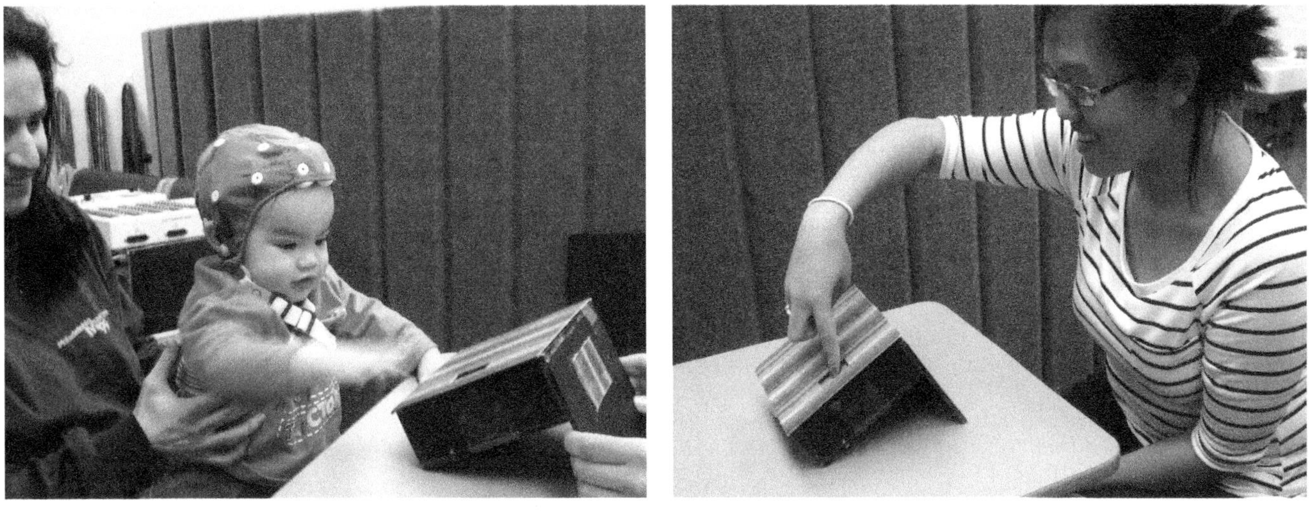

rational learning the ability to use prior experiences to predict what will occur in the future

to complete (pushing a hidden button to make a toy play music). Those infants who had seen the persistent experimenter tried harder, and longer, to get the toy to play music than those infants who had not. By observing adults expending effort to accomplish their goals, infants may learn to persist at their own goals. That is, they may learn that persistence pays off.

Rational Learning

As adults, we have many beliefs about the world, and we are surprised when the world violates our expectations based on those beliefs. We then adjust our expectations based on the new information we have just received. For example, you can infer from prior meals at your favourite Chinese restaurant that it will be serving Chinese food the next time you go there, and your expectations would be violated if the restaurant served Mexican food on your next visit. You would likely update your expectations about the nature of the cuisine at that establishment. Indeed, scientific reasoning is based on precisely this sort of inference from prior data—for instance, using data drawn from a sample to make predictions about a population. Infants, too, use prior experience to generate expectations about what will happen next. This is called **rational learning** because it involves integrating the learner's prior beliefs and biases with what actually occurs in the environment (Xu & Kushnir, 2013).

In an elegant study, Xu & Garcia (2008) demonstrated that 8-month-old Canadian infants could make predictions about simple events. Infants were shown a box containing 75 Ping-Pong balls; 70 were red and 5 were white (see Figure 5.20). The infants then observed an experimenter close her eyes (to suggest a random selection) and draw 5 balls from the box—either 4 red and 1 white or 4 white and 1 red—and put them on display. The infants looked longer at the display with the 4 white balls, indicating that they were surprised the experimenter drew mostly white balls from a box that was mostly filled with red balls. (Recall from earlier in this chapter the discussion of *violation-of-expectation* paradigms, which use infants' "surprise" at unexpected outcomes to draw inferences about their expectations.) It is important to note that the infants showed no such surprise when it was clear that the displayed balls did not come from the box (as when the

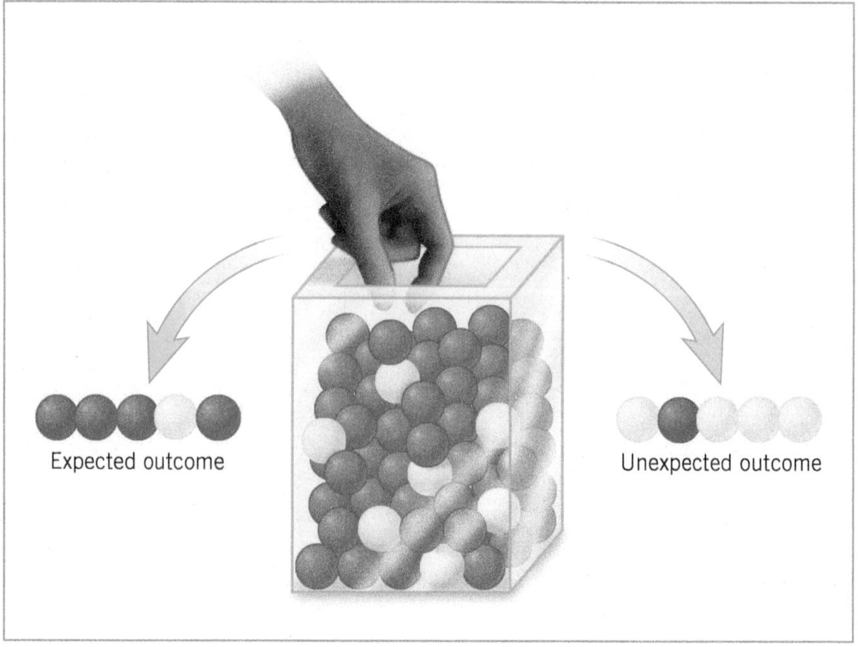

FIGURE 5.20 Rational learning After viewing a container dominated by red Ping-Pong balls, 8-month-olds are surprised when they observe the experimenter extract mostly white Ping-Pong balls (the unexpected outcome) (Xu & Garcia, 2008).

experimenter took them from her pocket) or when they could see that the red balls were stuck to the box and could not be removed (Denison & Xu, 2010; Teglas et al., 2007; Teglas et al., 2011; Xu & Denison, 2009; Denison, Reed, & Xu, 2013).

Similar findings are emerging across a number of domains, all suggesting that infants generate inferences about the future based on prior data and use new experiences to adjust incorrect inferences (e.g., Schulz, 2012; Xu & Kushnir, 2013). For example, 16-month-olds confronted with a toy that doesn't work use prior experience to interpret their failure (Gweon & Schulz, 2011). If the infants had previously seen other people fail to operate the toy, they interpreted the toy's malfunction as a property of the toy (and chose a new toy to play with). However, if the infants had previously seen other people successfully operate the toy, the infants interpreted the malfunction to be caused by themselves and passed the toy to their caregivers to operate. This study suggests sophisticated reasoning in the context of a simple toy-based interaction: When the problem appeared to be with the toy, infants explored new toys instead; but when the problem appeared to lie in the infants' ability to operate the toy, infants sought help.

active learning learning by engaging with the world, rather than passively observing objects and events

Active Learning

We often think of learning as a passive process: information-to-be-learned is presented to us by a teacher or some other expert. However, ever since Piaget's groundbreaking studies, we have known that infants learn by acting on the world—that is, via **active learning**.

This perspective—that we learn by doing and that we can learn more when we are actively engaged—has been supported by a number of experiments. In one such study, 16-month-olds were shown pairs of objects and asked to choose one of them by pointing (Begus, Gliga, & Southgate, 2014). The experimenter then showed the infants the function of one of the objects in the pair: either the chosen object or the unchosen object. The researchers found that infants learned more about the object when they had chosen it themselves during the pointing task. Similarly, 2-year-olds given a computerized learning task learn more about object locations when they are required to actively engage with a touchscreen than when they passively observe the screen (Choi & Kirkorian, 2016). Studies like these suggest that active engagement facilitates learning.

What prompts active exploration of the environment? One hypothesis is that surprise is a driving factor in active learning. When something unexpected happens, infants may be more likely to seek out explanations for what has just occurred. A particularly compelling example comes from a study in which 11-month-old infants observed events that violated physical laws: balls passing through walls, or toys magically hanging in the air (Stahl & Feigenson, 2015). As the infants watched these surprising events, they heard sounds paired with the objects. The researchers found that infants learned more about the sound–object pairs when the objects did unexpected things. The infants also appeared to test hypotheses about how the surprising objects worked. For instance, if the infants had seen a toy hanging in the air, they were more likely to explore it by dropping it than if they'd seen the same toy passing through a wall. These infants acted on the world in an attempt to better understand the strange occurrences that they had just observed (Stahl & Feigenson, 2018).

Note that the various forms of learning we have discussed work together. For example, infants kicking to operate a mobile in an instrumental-conditioning procedure are engaging in active learning, trying to figure out how the mobile works. Rational learning depends on infants' ability to track statistics about their environment, such as the distribution of colours in a box of Ping-Pong balls. One reason why infants are such exceptional learners is their ability to integrate multiple types of learning toward the common goal of figuring out how their world works.

Memory

Most adults report little or no memory of their experiences during infancy and early childhood. But for learning to occur, memory systems must be present in the brain. And given that even fetuses can learn, it is evident that memory systems are available early in life. In Chapter 4, we presented two forms of memory—working memory and long-term memory—established through studies with kindergarten and elementary-aged children. But the methods that are used to study memory in older children, such as repeating back sequences of digits, are not feasible with infants.

A recurring theme of this chapter is that infancy researchers have developed clever methods to investigate the minds of their young participants. We have already seen one such method used to explore the domain of memory: Rovee-Collier's use of operant conditioning with mobiles to investigate infants' long-term memory for the association between kicking and mobile reinforcement. Her data suggest that infants retain this information over weeks or months, depending on their age, and that long-term memory strengthens with age.

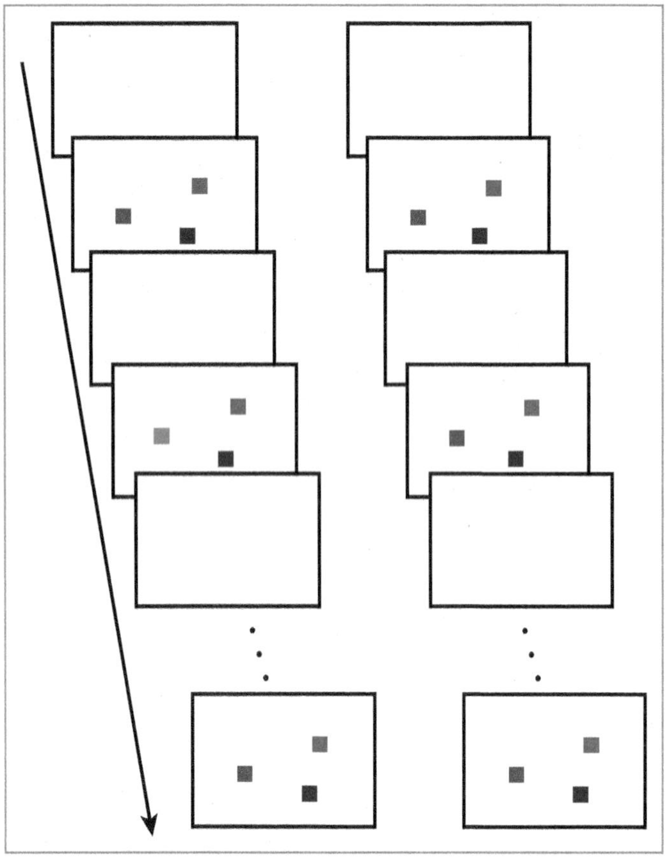

FIGURE 5.21 Change-detection task In this version of the change-detection task, infants are shown two arrays that vanish and reappear continuously. While one array remains unchanged (right), the other undergoes a slight alteration (left). Using preferential-looking techniques, researchers can determine whether infants can remember the items in the array based on the time spent looking at the altered array. (Information from Kibbe, 2015)

Researchers have been similarly clever in their studies of the development of working memory. One method employs a change-detection task that relies on the same logic as the preferential-looking studies with which we began this chapter. Infants view displays on two screens simultaneously (see Figure 5.21; Kibbe, 2015). One of the displays repeats the same image, while the other display introduces a change in the image between repetitions. If infants notice the change, they should find that display more interesting. By manipulating the type of change and the amount of time between repetitions, it is possible for researchers to assess what infants encode about the displays. Results from these studies suggest rapid changes over the first year. For example, 6-month-olds detect changes in only a single item's colour or location, whereas 12-month-olds can maintain up to four items in working memory (e.g., Ross-Sheehy, Oakes, & Luck, 2003; Oakes et al., 2011).

Another method for studying memory takes advantage of infants' propensity to reach for desirable objects, even when the objects are hidden. In one such study, 10- and 12-month-olds watched as an experimenter placed different numbers of crackers into two different buckets (Feigenson, Carey, & Hauser, 2002). The infants were then permitted to crawl to the bucket of their choice and retrieve the crackers. When one bucket held one cracker and the other held two, infants chose the bucket holding the larger number of crackers (infants also selected a bucket holding three crackers over a bucket holding two crackers, but failed as numbers reached four and higher). Similarly, when crackers were of different sizes, infants made their selections based on the difference in cracker volume. These data provide evidence that infants retained the contents of the containers in working memory, at least for small numbers of objects; we will explore infants' representation of number in Chapter 7.

REVIEW QUESTION

Chapter 4 outlined five overarching theories for cognitive development. How would these theories explain the different forms of learning described in this section?

CHAPTER SUMMARY

Perception

- Newborns' visual systems are relatively immature, with poor acuity, low contrast sensitivity, and minimal colour vision. They begin visually scanning the world minutes after birth and show preferences for strongly contrasted patterns, including faces.
- Some visual abilities, including perception of constant size and shape, are present at birth; others develop rapidly over the first year. Binocular vision emerges at about 4 months of age, and the ability to identify object boundaries (i.e., object segregation) is also present at that age. By 7 months, infants are sensitive to a variety of monocular, or pictorial, depth cues.
- Contrary to Piaget's beliefs about object permanence, experiments suggest that young infants can remember objects that are no longer visible.
- The auditory system is comparatively well developed at birth, and newborns will turn their heads to localize a sound. Young infants' remarkable proficiency at perceiving pattern in auditory stimulation underlies their sensitivity to musical structure.
- Through active touching, using both mouth and hands, infants explore and learn about themselves and their environment.
- Research on intermodal perception has revealed that from very early on, infants integrate information from different senses.

Motor Development

- Motor development proceeds rapidly in infancy through a series of "motor milestones," starting with newborn reflexes. Some aspects of motor development vary across cultures.
- Each new motor achievement, from reaching to self-locomotion, expands the infant's experience of the world but also presents new challenges. Infants adopt a variety of strategies to move around in the world. In the process, they make some surprising mistakes.

Learning and Memory

- Multiple forms of learning are present in infancy. Infants habituate to repeated stimuli, thereafter preferring novel stimuli. Through active exploration, they engage in perceptual learning. They also learn through classical conditioning, which involves forming associations between natural and neutral stimuli, as well as through instrumental conditioning, which involves learning about the contingency between one's own behaviour and some outcome. They can track statistical patterns in their environment and make use of prior experiences to generate expectations about the future. Observational learning—watching and imitating the behaviour of other people—is an important source of social information. By acting on the world, infants have the opportunity to make their own choices about what to learn.
- Infants' memory abilities support learning even before birth and develop rapidly over the course of the first postnatal year.

Test Yourself

1. A researcher presents an infant with two objects. To determine whether the infant is able to discriminate between the objects and favors one over the other, the researcher measures the amount of time the infant spends looking at each object. Which experimental technique is this researcher using?
   a. Contrast sensitivity technique
   b. Visual acuity method
   c. Preferential-looking technique
   d. Active learning method
2. The understanding that two objects are separate, even when they are touching, is referred to as ____________.
   a. object segregation
   b. object permanence
   c. perceptual narrowing
   d. perceptual constancy
3. One-month-old Bella is shown a small cube that is close to her. Next she is shown a larger cube that is farther away from her. Because the two cubes are at different distances from Bella, they appear to be the same size. Bella's actions indicate

that she recognizes that the second cube is larger, signifying that she has ____________.

a. perceptual constancy
b. intermodal perception
c. perceptual narrowing
d. optical expansion

4. An infant's ability to follow the path of a moving object is a demonstration of
a. visual acuity.
b. object segregation.
c. smooth pursuit eye movement.
d. binocular disparity.

5. Which of the following is a possible explanation for why young infants tend to have more trouble with auditory localization than older infants and children do?
a. Young infants are not adept at perceiving patterns, particularly sound patterns.
b. Young infants do not yet understand that sound can come from a variety of sources.
c. Children's ears do not fully develop until they are close to 1 year old.
d. Young infants have smaller heads, which makes it more difficult for them to perceive whether a sound is closer to one ear or the other.

6. The tendency of an infant to look longer at a smiling face that is paired with a happy voice is an indication of that infant's ____________.
a. dishabituation
b. classical conditioning
c. intermodal perception
d. optical expansion

7. Five-week-old Johnny is touched on the cheek and promptly turns his head to the side that was touched. Johnny is displaying ____________.
a. intermodal perception
b. contrast sensitivity
c. the rooting reflex
d. the tonic neck reflex

8. Jane is a 2-month-old infant. She wants to get her hands on the rattle that is lying next to her; however, all she can do is make very clumsy swiping movements in the general vicinity of the toy. Jane's movements are known as ____________.
a. self-locomotion
b. rooting reflex
c. optical expansion
d. pre-reaching motions

9. Seven-month-old Trevor has learned that small round objects can be rolled across a flat surface. Trevor's discovery is an example of which developmental learning process?
a. Affordances
b. Continuity
c. Differentiation
d. Unconditioned stimulus

10. Five-month-old Kenji is lying in his crib. His mother hides out of view, then pops out above him and yells, "Boo!" Kenji squeals with delight, but after his mother repeats her actions a few times, his excitement dissipates and his attention wanders to the mobile hanging overhead. Kenji's response is an example of ____________.
a. instrumental conditioning
b. differentiation
c. habituation
d. observational learning

11. The violation-of-expectancy procedure provides evidence of what basic assumption about infants' understanding of their world?
a. Infants will repeat actions if they receive positive reinforcement from those actions.
b. Infants' imitative actions are limited to the actions of other humans.
c. Infants will look longer at a seemingly impossible event than at a possible event.
d. Infants' attention will diminish after repeated exposure to the same stimuli.

12. Two-year-old Jayden attempts to put her foot inside of a toy car that is clearly too small for her. She is making which type of error?
a. Violation-of-expectation error
b. Scale error
c. Grasp error
d. Intermodal error

13. Researchers design an experiment in which 8- to 10-month-old infants are placed in a highchair with a string attached to one of their arms. When they lift their arms, the string tips a small cup that spills cereal onto the table in front of them. A few weeks later, these same infants are placed in a different chair but outfitted with a similar string and cup mechanism. The fact that these infants will remember that lifting their arms will result in cereal being dispensed is an example of ____________.
a. instrumental conditioning
b. social referencing
c. object permanence
d. intermodal perception

14. How does the element of surprise aid in the process of active learning in infants?
a. Surprise instills fear, which prompts the child to seek out less risky situations.
b. Infants are more likely to search for explanations to unexpected events.
c. Parents can explain unexpected events to their children, thus helping them learn.
d. Infants are more likely to seek out situations that conform to their understanding.

15. Which of the following is an example of perceptual narrowing?
    a. Compared to older children and adults, infants are better able to distinguish between different individual monkeys.
    b. Infants display a preference for top-heavy, upright faces.
    c. Older infants will more likely attempt to grasp an object in a realistic photograph than the same object displayed in a line drawing.
    d. As infants gain more experience, they become more adept at devising strategies for crawling down a steep slope.

LaunchPad
macmillan learning

DON'T STOP NOW! Research shows that testing yourself is a powerful learning tool. Visit LaunchPad to access the LearningCurve adaptive quizzing system, which gives you a personalized study plan to help build your mastery of the chapter material through videos, activities, and more. **Go to launchpadworks.com.**

Critical Thinking Questions

1. A major theme throughout this chapter is nature and nurture. Consider the following research findings discussed herein: infants' preference for consonance (versus dissonance) in music, their preference for faces that adults consider attractive, and their ability to represent the existence of objects that are not visible. To what extent do you think these preferences and abilities rest on innate factors, and to what extent might they be the result of experience?
2. As you have seen from this chapter, researchers have learned a substantial amount about infants in the recent past. Were you surprised at some of what has been learned? Describe to a friend something from each of the main sections of the chapter that you would never have suspected an infant could do or would know. Similarly, tell your friend a few things that you were surprised to learn infants do not know or that they fail to do.
3. Studying infants' perceptual and cognitive abilities is especially tricky given their limited abilities to respond in a study—they can't respond verbally or even with a reliable reach or point. Consider some of the methods described in this chapter (preferential looking/eye-tracking, conditioning, habituation, violation of expectation, imitation, EEG/ERP, and so on). What kinds of questions are best suited to each method?
4. What is perceptual narrowing? Describe some of the evidence suggesting that perceptual narrowing plays an important role in perceptual development. Of the types of learning discussed in this chapter, which of them might underlie perceptual narrowing, and why?

Key Terms

active learning, p. 189
affordances, p. 177
auditory localization, p. 167
binocular disparity, p. 166
classical conditioning, p. 184
conditioned response (CR), p. 184
conditioned stimulus (CS), p. 184
cone cells, p. 159
contrast sensitivity, p. 159
instrumental (or operant) conditioning, p. 185
intermodal perception, p. 172
monocular depth (or pictorial) cues, p. 166
optical expansion, p. 165
object segregation, p. 161
perception, p. 158
perceptual constancy, p. 160
perceptual narrowing, p. 170
positive reinforcement, p. 185
preferential-looking technique, p. 158
pre-reaching movements, p. 178
rational learning, p. 188
reflexes, p. 174
scale error, p. 182
self-locomotion, p. 179
sensation, p. 158
smooth pursuit eye movements, p. 160
stepping reflex, p. 178
stereopsis, p. 166
unconditioned response (UCR), p. 184
unconditioned stimulus (UCS), p. 184
violation-of-expectancy, p. 164
visual acuity, p. 158

Answers to Test Yourself

1. c, **2.** a, **3.** a, **4.** c, **5.** d, **6.** c, **7.** c, **8.** d, **9.** a, **10.** c, **11.** c, **12.** b, **13.** a, **14.** b, **15.** a

CHAPTER

6 Development of Language and Symbol Use

NICOLA BEALING, *Lucas Talking to a Dog* (oil on board, 2006)

Language Development | The Process of Language Acquisition

Theoretical Issues in Language Development | Nonlinguistic Symbols and Development

THEMES

NATURE AND NURTURE ■ THE ACTIVE CHILD

THE SOCIOCULTURAL CONTEXT ■ INDIVIDUAL DIFFERENCES

"Woof." (age 11 months, referring to neighbour's dog)
"Hot." (age 14 months, referring to stove, matches, candles, light reflecting off shiny surfaces, and so forth)
"Read me." (age 21 months, requesting a story)
"Why I don't have a dog?" (age 27 months)
"If you give me some candy, I'll be your best friend. I'll be your two best friends." (age 48 months)
"Granna, we went to Cagoshin [Chicago]." (age 65 months)
"It was, like, ya know, totally awesome, dude." (age 192 months)

Each of these utterances, produced by a single child acquiring English (Clore, 1981), reflects the capacity that most sets humans apart from other species: the creative and flexible use of **symbols**. We use symbols to represent our thoughts, feelings, and knowledge, and to communicate them to others. Our ability to use symbols frees us from the present, enabling us to learn from the generations of people who preceded us and to contemplate the future. In this chapter, we will focus primarily on the acquisition of the preeminent human symbol system: language. We will then discuss children's understanding and creation of nonlinguistic symbols, such as pictures and models.

The dominant theme will once again be the relative contributions of *nature and nurture*. The *sociocultural context* is another prominent theme as we examine language acquisition across cultures and communities. A third recurring theme is *individual differences*, both in terms of the range of typical language development and as we consider developmental language disorders. The *active child* theme also puts in repeated appearances, as infants and young children learn to use symbols to communicate.

symbols systems for representing our thoughts, feelings, and knowledge, and for communicating them to other people

language comprehension understanding what others say (or sign or write)

language production the process of speaking (or signing or writing)

These children are intent on mastering one of the many important symbol systems in the modern world.

STUART PEARCE/AGE FOTOSTOCK

Language Development

What is the average kindergartner almost as good at as you are? Not much, with one important exception: using language. By 5 years of age, most children have mastered the basic structure of their native language or languages (the possibility of bilingualism is to be assumed whenever we refer to "native language"), whether spoken or manually signed. Although their vocabulary and powers of expression are less sophisticated than yours, their sentences tend to be as grammatically correct as the ones that adults produce. This is a remarkable achievement.

Language use requires **comprehension**, which refers to understanding what others say (or sign or write), and **production**, which refers to speaking (or signing or writing). As we have observed for other areas of development, infants and young children understand much more than they can say.

The Components of Language

generative a system in which a finite set of words can be combined to generate an infinite number of sentences

phonemes the smallest units of meaningful sound

morphemes the smallest units of meaning in a language

syntax rules specifying how words from different categories (nouns, verbs, adjectives, etc.) can be combined

All languages share overarching similarities. Pieces combine at different levels to form a hierarchy: sounds become words, words become sentences, and sentences become stories and conversations. The enormous benefit that emerges from this combinatorial process is a system that is **generative**; using a finite set of words and our knowledge of the systematic ways in which those words can be combined, we can generate an infinite number of sentences, expressing an infinite number of ideas. We can understand sentences we have never heard or read before; although most of the sentences in this book are new to you, you understand them because they make use of familiar words and grammatical structures. As English speakers, we know that the plural of *wug* is *wugs*, even if we have never heard the word *wug* before.

The generative power of language carries a cost for young learners, who are faced with a massively complex task. To appreciate the challenge facing children, imagine yourself as a stranger in a strange land. Someone walks up to you and says, "*Jusczyk daxly blickets Nthlakapmx.*" You would have absolutely no idea what this person had just said. Why?

First, you would probably have difficulty perceiving some of the sounds. Speech is composed of units of sound, called **phonemes**; a change in phoneme changes the meaning of a word. While "rake" and "lake" differ by only one phoneme (/r/ versus /l/), the two words have quite different English meanings. Different languages employ different sets of phonemes; English uses just 45 of the roughly 200 sounds found across the world's languages. The phonemes that distinguish meaning differ across languages. For example, /r/ and /l/ are a single phoneme in Japanese and do not carry different meanings. Furthermore, combinations of sounds that are common in one language may never occur in others. When you read *Nthlakapmx* in the last paragraph, you probably had no idea how to pronounce it because some of its sound combinations do not occur in English (though they do occur in the Nthlakapmx language, which is an indigenous language spoken in Western Canada).

Another reason you would not know what the stranger had said to you is that you would have no idea what the sounds mean. The smallest units of meaning are called **morphemes**. Morphemes, alone or in combination, constitute words. The word *dog*, for example, contains one morpheme. The word *dogs* contains two morphemes, one designating a familiar furry entity (*dog*) and the second indicating the plural (*-s*).

Even if you knew the meaning of each word, you would still not have understood the utterance unless you knew how words are combined in the stranger's language. **Syntax** refers to the permissible combinations of words from different categories (nouns, verbs, adjectives, etc.). In English, for example, the *order* in which words can appear in a sentence is crucial: "Lila ate the lobster" does not mean the same thing as "The lobster ate Lila." Other languages indicate which noun did the eating and which noun was eaten by adding morphemes, such as suffixes, to the nouns. For example, a Russian noun ending in "a" is likely to refer to the entity doing the eating, while the same noun ending in "u" is likely to refer to the thing that was eaten.

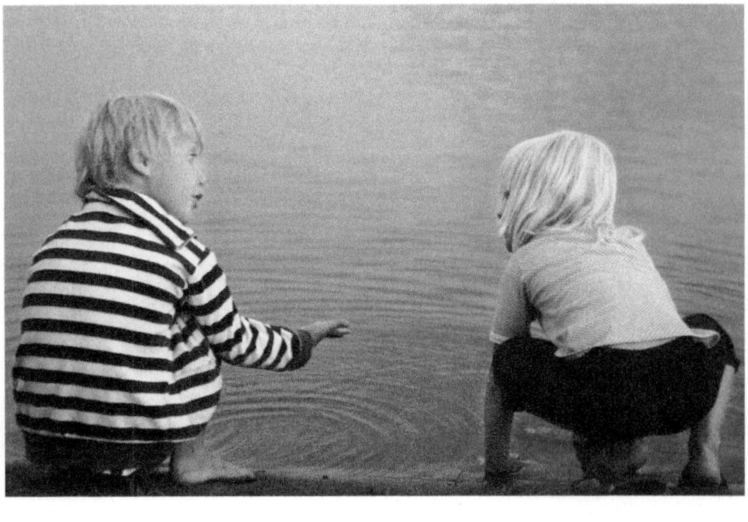

ESTA/SUPERSTOCK

By the age of 5, children can generate novel sentences that are correct in terms of the phonology, semantics, and syntax of their native language. They are also able to make appropriate pragmatic inferences regarding the content of their partner's utterances.

Finally, a full understanding of the interaction with the stranger would necessitate knowledge of the cultural rules and contextual variations for using language. In some societies, for example, it would be quite bizarre to be addressed by a stranger. You would also need to know how to go beyond the words to understand what the speaker was really trying to communicate—using the context and emotional tone to read between the lines. **Pragmatics** refers to the understanding of how language is typically used in a specific cultural context.

pragmatics knowledge about how language is used

All of these same factors are involved in learning a sign language, in which the basic linguistic elements are hand shapes and motions rather than sounds. In Canada, the two sign languages used most commonly are American Sign Language (ASL) and Langue des Signes Québécoise (LSQ). Around the world, there are more than 200 sign languages. These signed languages, which are based on both manual and facial gestures, are true languages in every sense and are as different from one another as spoken languages. The course of acquisition of a sign language is remarkably similar to that of a spoken language (e.g., Newport & Meier, 1985).

What Is Required for Language?

What does it take to be able to learn a language? Full-fledged language acquisition is achieved only by humans, so, obviously, one requirement is the human brain. But a single human, isolated from all sources of linguistic experience, could never learn a language; exposure is a crucial ingredient for successful language development.

A Human Brain

The key to language development lies in the human brain. Language is a *species-specific* behaviour: only humans acquire language in the normal course of development. Furthermore, it is *species-universal:* language learning is achieved by typically developing children across the globe.

In contrast, no other animals naturally develop anything approaching the complexity or generativity of human language, even though they can communicate with one another. In one of the complex examples of nonhuman animal communication, vervet monkeys reveal the presence and identity of predators through specific calls, telling their listeners whether they should look down to avoid a snake or look up to avoid an eagle (Seyfarth & Cheney, 1993). As sophisticated as this system is, compared with other nonhuman communication systems, it is very limited in scope.

Kanzi, a bonobo ape, and his caretakers communicate with one another using a specially designed set of symbols for a variety of objects, people, and actions.

LAURENTIU GAROFEANU/BARCROFT USA/BARCOFT MEDIA/GETTY IMAGES

Researchers have had limited success in training nonhuman primates to use human communicative systems. Washoe, a chimpanzee, and Koko, a gorilla, became famous for their ability to communicate with their human trainers and caretakers using manual signs (Gardner & Gardner, 1969; Patterson & Linden, 1981). Washoe could label a variety of objects and could make requests ("more fruit," "please tickle"). However, their simple utterances lacked syntactic structure (Terrace et al., 1979; Wallman, 1992).

The most successful sign-learning nonhuman is Kanzi, a great ape of the bonobo species. Kanzi's sign-learning began when he observed researchers trying to teach his mother to communicate using a lexigram board, a panel composed of graphic symbols representing specific objects and actions ("give," "eat," "banana," etc.) (Savage-Rumbaugh et al., 1993). Over the years, Kanzi's lexigram vocabulary grew to more than 350 words. He is adept at using his lexigram board to answer questions, to make requests, and even to offer comments. He often combines symbols, but whether they can be considered syntactically structured sentences is not clear.

There are also several well-documented cases of nonprimate animals that have learned to respond to spoken language. Rico, a border collie, knew more than 200 words and could learn and remember new words using some of the

MANUELA HARTLING/REUTERS/NEWSCOM

This photo shows Rico demonstrating his language comprehension by fetching specific toys on request.

same kinds of processes that toddlers use (though with important limitations; Kaminski, Call, & Fischer, 2004; Tempelmann, Kaminski, & Tomasello, 2014; van der Zee, Zulch, & Mills, 2012). Alex, an African-gray parrot, learned to produce and understand basic English utterances, although his skills remained at a toddler level (Pepperberg, 1999).

Unlike nonhuman animals, who require a great deal of concentrated training to learn rudimentary aspects of human languages, human children learn language with little explicit teaching. Furthermore, while the most advanced nonhuman communicators do combine symbols, their utterances show limited evidence of syntactic structure (Tomasello, 1994). In short, only the human brain is capable of acquiring a communicative system with the complexity, structure, and generativity of language. Correspondingly, we humans are notoriously poor at learning the communicative systems of other species (Harry Potter's ability to speak Parseltongue with snakes aside).

Brain–language lateralization There are hemispheric differences in language functioning (as discussed in Chapter 3). For the 90% of people who are right-handed, language is primarily represented and controlled by the left hemisphere. Left-hemisphere specialization for most aspects of language emerges very early in life (Bortfeld, Fava, & Boas, 2009; Dehaene-Lambertz, Dehaene, & Hertz-Pannier, 2002; Pena et al., 2003). Using PET scans, a brain-imaging technique discussed in Chapter 3, researchers at McGill University found similar patterns of brain activation in the left hemisphere for hearing speakers of English and deaf signers of ASL and LSQ, when performing similar language tasks (Petitto et al., 2000).

Although it is evident that the left hemisphere predominantly processes linguistic stimuli from early in life, the reasons for this are not yet known. One possibility is that the left hemisphere is innately predisposed to process language but not other types of stimuli. However, lifelong signers process sign languages in left-lateralized language centres in the brain, whereas non-signers do not, illustrating the type of experience-dependent plasticity discussed in Chapter 5 (e.g., Newman et al., 2015). This observation suggests that left-hemisphere brain regions are not solely specialized for spoken language but are used for signed languages as well.

Sensitive period for language development If you were to survey your peers about their language-learning experiences, we predict you would discover that those who learned a second language in adolescence or adulthood found it much more challenging than did those who learned a second language in early childhood. A considerable body of evidence suggests that the early years constitute a sensitive period during which languages are learned relatively easily. After this period (which ends sometime between age 5 and puberty), language acquisition outcomes become more variable and, on average, less successful.

The most famous sources of evidence relevant to this hypothesis come from reports of children who were deprived of early linguistic experience. The best known case in modern times is Genie, who was discovered in appalling conditions in Los Angeles in 1970. From the age of approximately 18 months until she was rescued at age 13 years, Genie's parents kept her tied up and locked alone in a room. During her imprisonment, no one spoke to her. At the time of her rescue, Genie's development was stunted—physically, motorically, and emotionally—and she could barely speak. With intensive training, she made some progress, but her language ability never developed much beyond the level of a toddler's: "Father take piece wood. Hit. Cry" (Curtiss, 1977, 1989; Rymer, 1993).

Does this extraordinary case support the sensitive-period hypothesis? Possibly, but it is difficult to know for sure. Genie's failure to develop full, rich, language after her discovery might have resulted as much from the bizarre and inhumane treatment she suffered as from linguistic deprivation.

Other areas of research provide much stronger evidence for the sensitive-period hypothesis. As noted in Chapter 3, adults are more likely to suffer permanent language impairment from brain damage than are children, presumably because other areas of the young brain (but not the older brain) are able to take over language functions. Moreover, adults who learned a second language after puberty use different neural mechanisms to process that language than do adults who learned their second language from infancy (e.g., Kim et al., 1997; Pakulak & Neville, 2011). The same is true for rare cases of individuals who were not exposed to their first language until after puberty—typically, deaf individuals who did not receive signed language input early in life (e.g., Mayberry et al., 2018). In one study at McGill University, researchers tested two different groups of adults: deaf adults who had no exposure to language during early childhood and deaf adults who had learned a spoken language during childhood (both groups were born hearing but later became profoundly deaf) (Mayberry, Lock, & Kazmi, 2002). Both groups began learning ASL at school between the ages of 9 and 15 years. As can be seen in Figure 6.1, those adults who had exposure to a language during infancy, even though it was in a different modality, performed much better on the ASL task than adults who had received minimal language input during early childhood. These results strongly suggest that the neural circuitry supporting language learning operates differently (and better) during the early years.

In an important behavioural study, Johnson and Newport (1989) tested the English knowledge of Chinese and Korean immigrants to the United States who had begun learning English at different ages. The results, shown in Figure 6.2, reveal that comprehension of key aspects of English grammar was related to the age at which these individuals began learning English, but not to the length of their exposure to the language. The most proficient were those who had begun learning English before the age of 7.

A recent large-scale study of almost 700,000 adult English learners tested via an online grammar quiz also revealed a drop-off in proficiency, but one that starts later, toward the end of adolescence (Hartshorne, Tenenbaum, & Pinker, 2018). The differing patterns of results between these two studies may be due to a range of factors, including the testing procedures (a controlled laboratory experiment versus an online quiz spread "virally"), use of a listening-based task versus a reading-based task, the large differences in sample sizes, and the different native languages spoken by participants (limited to Chinese and Korean versus fully inclusive).

A similar pattern has been described for first-language acquisition in the Deaf community: individuals who acquired ASL as a first language when they were children

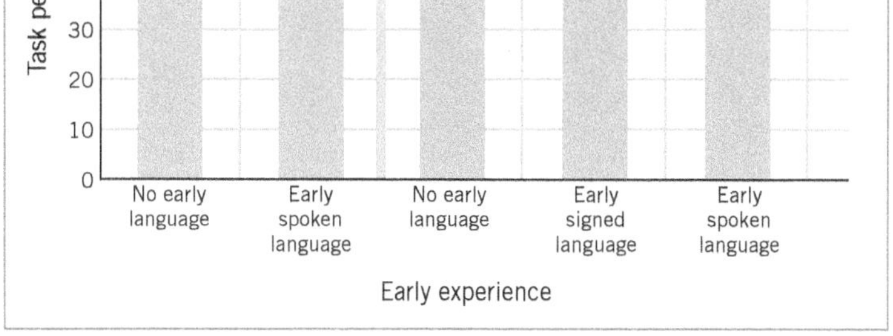

FIGURE 6.1 The importance of early language experience on later language performance (a) The ASL performance of deaf adults who did not experience language in early life is significantly poorer than that of deaf adults who had experienced spoken language in development. (b) Results show that judgments of complex written English sentences are particularly difficult for deaf adults who had no early life language experience. In contrast, the performance of deaf adults who had experience with ASL in infancy and that of hearing adults who had experienced spoken languages other than English in infancy did not differ. (Data from Mayberry et al., 2002)

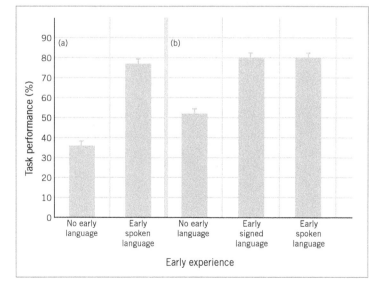

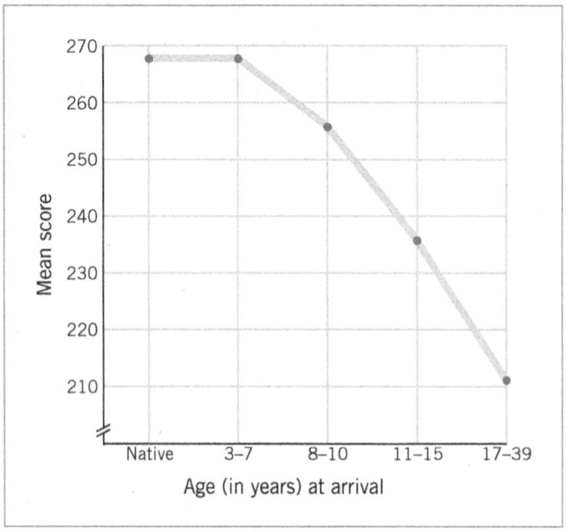

FIGURE 6.2 Test of sensitive-period hypothesis Performance on a test of English grammar by adults originally from Korea and China was related to the age at which they came to the United States and were first exposed to English. The scores of adults who emigrated before the age of 7 were indistinguishable from those of native speakers of English. (Data from Johnson & Newport, 1989)

develop a better understanding of the grammar of ASL than do individuals who acquired ASL as a first language as teens or adults (Newport, 1990). There is also a great deal of variability among "late learners"—language learners beyond puberty. As in the findings we predicted for your survey of classmates, some individuals achieved skills commensurate with native learners, whereas the language outcomes for others were quite poor.

The reasons for a sensitive period for language remain unknown. Theories suggest developmental changes in the plasticity of language-related regions of the brain and motivational differences across ages (for additional discussion, see Mayberry & Kluender, 2018). One account suggests that children's native language knowledge increasingly impinges on second language learning (Seidenberg & Zevin, 2006). In this view, as children learn more about their first language, that knowledge begins to interfere with the fragile knowledge that is acquired during second language learning. Note, however, that this theory cannot explain the presence of sensitive period effects for first language learning, as in the case of language acquisition in the Deaf community described earlier. Another intriguing hypothesis suggests that children's poorer working memory abilities lead them to extract and store smaller chunks of the language than adults do (Newport, 1990). Because the crucial building blocks of language (the meaning-carrying morphemes) tend to be quite small, young learners' limited cognitive abilities may, paradoxically, actually facilitate language learning.

The evidence for a sensitive period in language acquisition has clear practical implications. For one thing, deaf children should be exposed to sign language as early as possible to ensure access to a native language during the sensitive period. For another, foreign-language exposure at school, discussed in Box 6.1, should begin as early as possible to maximize children's opportunity to achieve native-level skills.

A Human Environment

Possession of a human brain is not enough for language to develop. Children must also be exposed to other people using language—any language, signed or spoken. Adequate linguistic experience is readily available in the environment of almost all children around the world.

Infants identify speech as something important very early on. When given the choice, newborns prefer listening to speech rather than to artificial sounds (Vouloumanos et al., 2010). Intriguingly, newborns also prefer nonhuman primate (rhesus macaque) vocalizations to other nonspeech sounds, and show no preference for speech over macaque vocalizations until 3 months of age (Vouloumanos et al., 2010). These results suggest that infants' auditory preferences are fine-tuned through experience with human language.

Infant-directed speech

Imagine yourself on a bus listening to a stranger who is seated behind you and speaking to someone. Could you guess whether the stranger was addressing an infant or an adult? We have no doubt that you could, even if the stranger was speaking an unfamiliar language. The reason is that in virtually all cultures, adults adopt a distinctive mode of speech when talking to babies and toddlers, known as **infant-directed speech (IDS)**.

infant-directed speech (IDS) the distinctive mode of speech used when speaking to infants and toddlers

bilingualism fluency in two languages

CHARACTERISTICS OF INFANT-DIRECTED SPEECH When communicating with infants and young children, adults tend to speak with greater pitch variability, slower speech, shorter utterances, more word repetition, and more questions (Fernald et al., 1989; Snow, 1972; Soderstrom et al., 2008). They even enhance the clarity

BOX 6.1 APPLICATIONS Two Languages Are Better Than One

Bilingualism, or fluency in two languages, has attracted substantial attention in recent years. In Canada, approximately 17% of the population is bilingual, meaning that individuals can carry on conversations in both official languages (French and English) (Statistics Canada, 2017). Another 20% of the population reports speaking a first language other than French or English (Statistics Canada, 2017). The bilingual population is much larger in multilingual countries like Singapore; a 2015 survey revealed that 73% of the Singapore population was literate in at least two languages (Department of Statistics Singapore, 2016). Remarkably, despite the fact that bilingual children have twice as much to learn as monolingual children, they show little confusion and language delay. In fact, there is evidence to suggest that being bilingual improves aspects of cognitive functioning in childhood and beyond.

Bilingual learning can begin in the womb. Researchers in Vancouver showed that newborns born to bilingual English/Tagalog mothers prefer listening to these two languages over other languages. Furthermore, a second study demonstrated that newborns can discriminate between the two languages spoken by their mother, setting the stage for their acquisition of both languages (Byers-Heinlein, Burns, & Werker, 2010). Bilingual infants discriminate the speech sounds of their two languages at roughly the same pace that monolingual infants distinguish the sounds of their one language (e.g., Albareda-Castellot, Pons, & Sebastián-Gallés, 2011; Sundara, Polka, & Molnar, 2008). How might this be, given that bilingual infants have twice as much to learn? One possibility is that bilingual infants' attention to speech cues is heightened relative to monolingual infants. For example, bilingual infants are better than monolingual infants at using purely visual information (a silent talking face) to discriminate between unfamiliar languages (Sebastián-Gallés et al., 2012).

For the most part, children who are acquiring two languages do not seem to confuse them; indeed, they appear to build two separate linguistic systems. Canadian research shows that even when bilingual children produce only two words at a time, they show differentiated use of their two languages—for example, they adjust their language to their conversational partner (Genesee, Boivin, & Nicoladis, 1996; Nicoladis & Genesee, 1996). Language mixing, also known as code mixing or code switching, is a phenomenon in which bilingual speakers conversing in one language insert words or phrases from their other language. This practice is a normal aspect of bilingual development and does not reflect confusion. When language mixing occurs, it often reflects a gap of knowledge in one language that the child is trying to fill in with the other. It can also reflect the fact that bilingual parents frequently code switch (Bail, Morini, & Newman, 2015). One study of bilingual families in Montreal, Canada, found that more than 90% of parents mixed their languages in speech to their infants (Byers-Heinlein, 2013). It is thus not at all surprising that most bilingual children engage in language mixing as well.

At a broad level, both the course and the rate of language development are generally very similar for bilingual and monolingual children in Canada (see Genesee & Nicoladis, 2007; Smithson, Paradis, & Nicoladis, 2014): bilingual children produce their first words around the same time as monolingual children, have similar vocabulary sizes (as long as one considers both languages), and use the same types of words. Furthermore, bilingual toddlers are just as fast as their monolingual peers at recognizing familiar words (DeAnda et al., 2016).

Evidence indicates that there are cognitive benefits to bilingualism, both for the young and the old, as demonstrated by York University professor Ellen Bialystok and Concordia University professor Diane Poulin-Dubois. Children who are competent in two languages perform better on a variety of measures of executive function and cognitive control than do monolingual children (Bialystok, 2009; Bialystok & Craik, 2010; Costa, Hernandez, & Sebastián-Gallés, 2008). Results reveal that these effects emerge very early. Bilingual infants and toddlers show greater cognitive flexibility in learning tasks (Kovács & Mehler, 2009a, b; Poulin-Dubois et al., 2011). Finally, being bilingual seems to delay the onset of symptoms in individuals with Alzheimer's disease (Craik, Bialystok, & Freedman, 2010).

The link between bilingualism and improved cognitive flexibility likely lies in the fact that bilingual individuals must rapidly switch between languages, both in comprehension and production. Indeed, even bilingual infants exhibit cognitive effort when listening to speakers who switch from one language to another (Byers-Heinlein, Morin-Lessard, & Lew-Williams, 2017). Bilingual infants also outperform monolingual infants on word-learning tasks in new languages that require them to make use of unfamiliar sound patterns, suggesting increased openness to non-native languages (Antovich & Graf Estes, 2018; Graf Estes & Hay, 2015; Singh, 2018).

BSIP/GETTY IMAGES

Canadian research on bilingualism reveals a variety of benefits of proficiency in multiple languages. However, the issue of bilingualism in the classroom has been a topic of intense debate in other parts of the world—for example, in the United States, which, unlike Canada, has only one official language.

Countries with multiple large language communities, like Canada, have widely embraced bilingual education. French immersion programs, where English-speaking children receive anywhere from 50% to 100% of their instruction in French, were introduced into Canadian schools in the 1970s, with the goal of encouraging bilingualism across the country. Since that time, other types of second-language immersion programs have been introduced in Canadian public schools, including Mandarin, Spanish, and First Nations languages.

Despite the success of multilingual programs, some countries, including many regions of the United States, have not embraced multilingual schooling, despite the presence of large numbers of English-as-a-second-language learners. The debate is tied up with a host of political and social issues. One side advocates for total English immersion, with the goal of rapid proficiency for English language learners, often at the expense of their native language. The other side recommends an approach that initially provides children with instruction in basic subjects in their native language and gradually increases the amount of instruction provided in English (Castro et al., 2011).

In support of the latter view, there is evidence that bilingual children are more successful in learning both of their languages when the school environment provides support for both languages (e.g., McCabe et al., 2013). This research has led the Society for Research in Child Development to endorse policies aimed at broadening children's access to bilingual educational opportunities.

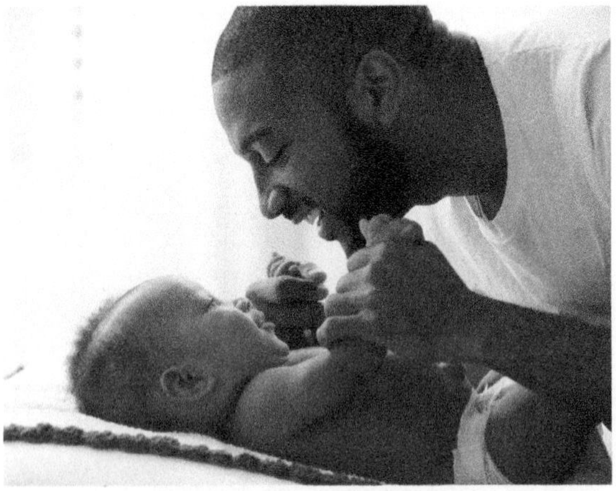

SELECTSTOCK/GETTY IMAGES

The infant-directed talk used by this father grabs and holds his baby's attention.

of vowels and adjust the sound of their voices (Kuhl et al., 1997; Piazza, Iordan, & Lew-Williams, 2017). Their exaggerated speech is accompanied by exaggerated facial expressions. These characteristics have been noted in adults speaking such languages as Arabic, French, Italian, Japanese, Mandarin, and Spanish (de Boysson-Bardies, 1996/1999), as well as signed languages (Masataka, 1992).

Caregivers use IDS to share important information even when infants don't know the meaning of the words. For example, a word uttered with sharply falling pitch communicates disapproval, whereas a cooed warm sound indicates approval. These pitch patterns serve the same function in language communities ranging from English and Italian to Japanese (Fernald et al., 1989). Interestingly, infants exhibit appropriate facial emotion when listening to these pitch patterns, even when the language is unfamiliar (Fernald, 1993).

IDS draws infants' attention to speech, likely because of its exaggerated pitch contours. Indeed, infants prefer IDS to adult-directed speech (ADS), even when the IDS is in a language other than their own (Cooper & Aslin, 1994; Pegg, Werker, & McLeod, 1992). Infants' preference for IDS over ADS was recently confirmed in the largest infant study to date—a sample of over 2000 babies, tested in 67 labs around the world (The ManyBabies Consortium, 2019).

Some studies suggest that infants' preference for IDS may emerge because it is "happy speech"; when speakers' affect is held constant, the preference disappears (Singh, Morgan, & Best, 2002). Perhaps because they pay greater attention to IDS, infants learn and recognize words better when the words are presented in IDS than when they are presented in ADS (Ma et al., 2011; Singh et al., 2009; Thiessen, Hill, & Saffran, 2005). For instance, Laurel Trainor at McMaster University found that IDS helps young infants discriminate vowel sounds (Trainor & Desjardins, 2002). These behavioural effects are mirrored by the reactions of infant brains, which show greater activation when hearing IDS than ADS (e.g., Naoi et al., 2012).

Around the world, parents in some cultures talk directly to their babies, whereas parents in other cultures, such as this Kwara'ae mother, do not.

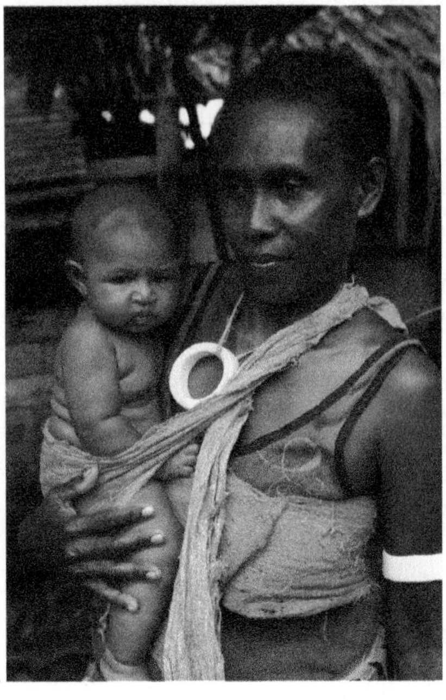

JOHN BORTHWICK/GETTY IMAGES

Although IDS is very common throughout the world, it is not universal. In some cultures, such as the Kwara'ae of the Solomon Islands, the Ifaluk of Micronesia, and the Kaluli of Papua New Guinea, it is believed that because infants cannot understand what is said to them, there is no reason for caregivers to speak to them (Le, 2000; Schieffelin & Ochs, 1987; Watson-Gegeo, & Gegeo, 1986). For example, young Kaluli infants are carried facing outward so that they can engage with other members of the group (but not with their caregiver), and if they are spoken to by older siblings, the mother will speak for them (Schieffelin & Ochs, 1987). Thus, even if they are not addressed directly by their caregivers, these infants are still immersed in language. In other cultures, such as the Tsimane of Bolivia (a rural foraging-farming group), adults rarely address infants; babies hear less than 1 minute of speech directed to them per daylight hour (Cristia et al., 2017). Thus, like so many other aspects of early development, cultural context is an important variable to consider.

That infants begin life equipped with the two basic necessities for acquiring language—a human brain and a human environment—is only the beginning of the story. Of all the things we learn as humans, languages are arguably the most complex; so complex, in fact, that scientists have yet to program computer systems to acquire a human language. How, then, do children manage to acquire their native language with such astounding success? We turn next to the many steps through which that remarkable accomplishment proceeds.

REVIEW QUESTION

Considering the importance of exposure and environment in language development, especially during sensitive periods, what interventions can you think of to ensure adequate opportunities for experience? ■

The Process of Language Acquisition

Infants start out paying attention to what people say or sign, and they know a great deal about language long before their first linguistic productions.

Speech Perception

The first step in language learning is figuring out the sounds of one's native language. As you saw in Chapter 2, the task usually begins in the womb, as fetuses develop a preference for their mother's voice and the language they hear her speak. The basis for this very early learning is **prosody**, the characteristic rhythmic and intonation patterns with which a language is spoken. Differences in prosody are in large part responsible for why languages—from Japanese to French to Swahili—sound so different from one another.

Speech perception also involves determining which differences between speech sounds are important and which can be ignored. Perhaps surprisingly, young infants perceive speech in very much the same way that adults do.

Categorical Perception of Speech Sounds

Both adults and infants perceive speech sounds as belonging to categories. This phenomenon, referred to as **categorical perception**, has been established by studying people's response to speech sounds. In this research, listeners hear a speech sound that gradually changes from one phoneme, such as /b/, into a related one, such as /p/. These two phonemes are produced in exactly the same way except for one crucial difference—the length of time between when air passes through the lips and when the vocal cords start vibrating. This lag, referred to as **voice onset time (VOT)**, is shorter for /b/ (less than 25 milliseconds [ms]) than for /p/ (greater than 25 ms). (Try saying "ba" and "pa" alternately several times, with your hand on your throat, and you will likely experience this difference in VOT.)

To study the perception of VOT, researchers create recordings of speech sounds that vary along this VOT continuum, so that each successive sound is slightly different from the one before, with /ba/ gradually changing into /pa/. Adults do not perceive the continuous change in this series of sounds. Instead, all the sounds in this continuum that have a VOT of less than 25 ms are perceived as /b/, and all those that have a VOT greater than 25 ms are perceived as /p/. Thus, adults automatically divide the continuous signal into two categories—/b/ and /p/. This perception of a continuum as two categories is very useful because it focuses listeners on sound differences that are linguistically meaningful (the difference between /b/ and /p/), while ignoring meaningless differences (like the difference between a 10 ms VOT /b/ versus a 20 ms VOT /b/).

Young infants draw the same sharp distinctions between speech sounds. In the original, classic study of this phenomenon, 1- and 4-month-olds sucked on a pacifier hooked up to a computer (Eimas et al., 1971). The harder they sucked, the more often they heard repetitions of a single syllable. After hearing

prosody the characteristic rhythm and intonational patterns with which a language is spoken

categorical perception the perception of phonemes as belonging to discrete categories

voice onset time (VOT) the length of time between when air passes through the lips and when the vocal cords start vibrating

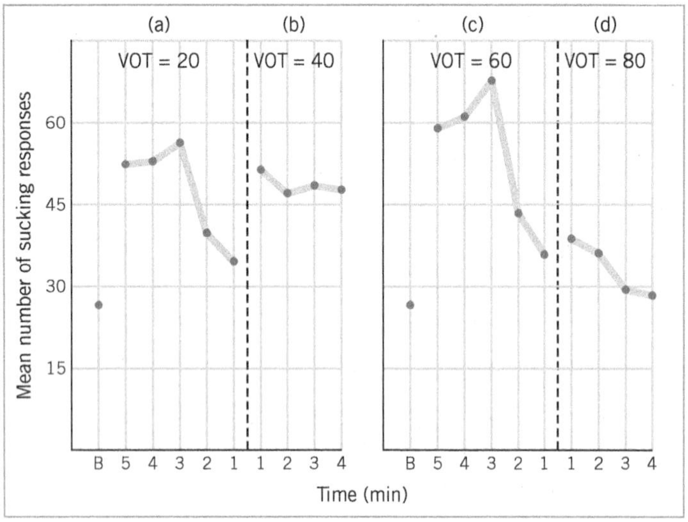

FIGURE 6.3 Categorical perception of speech sounds One- and 4-month-olds were habituated to speech sounds. (a) One group repeatedly heard a /ba/ with a VOT of 20 ms, and they gradually habituated. (b) When the sound changed to /pa/, with a VOT of 40 ms, they dishabituated, indicating that they perceived the difference between the two sounds, just as adults do. (c) A different group was habituated to a /pa/ sound with a VOT of 60 ms. (d) When the sound changed to another /pa/ with a VOT of 80 ms, the infants remained habituated, suggesting that, like adults, they did not discriminate between these two sounds. (Data from Eimas et al., 1971)

the same syllable repeatedly, the babies gradually sucked less enthusiastically (*habituation*). Then a new syllable was played. If the infants' sucking rate increased, the researchers inferred that the infants discriminated the new syllable from the old syllable (*dishabituation*).

The crucial factor in this study was the relation between the new and old sounds—specifically, whether they were from the same or different phonemic categories. For one group of infants, the new sound was from a different category; thus, after habituation to a series of sounds that adults perceive as /ba/, sucking now produced a sound that adults identify as /pa/. For the second group, the new sound was within the same category as the old one (i.e., adults perceive them both as /ba/). A critical feature of the study is that for both groups, the new and old sounds differed *equally* in terms of VOT.

As Figure 6.3 shows, after habituating to /b/, the infants increased their rate of sucking when the new sound came from a different phonemic category (/p/ instead of /b/). Habituation continued, however, when the new sound was within the same category as the original one. Since this classic study, researchers have established that infants show categorical perception of numerous speech sounds from languages around the world.

A fascinating outcome of this research is the discovery that young infants actually make *more* distinctions than adults do. Any given language uses only a subset of the large variety of phonemes that exist. As noted earlier, the sounds /r/ and /l/ make a difference in English, but not in Japanese. Similarly, speakers of Arabic, but not of English, perceive a difference between the /k/ sounds in "keep" and "cool." Adults simply do not perceive differences in speech sounds that are not important in their native language, which partly accounts for why it is so difficult for adults to become fluent in a second language.

In contrast, infants can distinguish between phonemic contrasts made in all the languages of the world—about 600 consonants and 200 vowels. Japanese-learning infants, unlike Japanese adults, can discriminate between /r/ and /l/. English-learning infants can discriminate non-English distinctions made in languages ranging from German and Spanish to Thai, Hindi, and Zulu.

This research reveals an early-emerging ability that is experience-independent: infants can discriminate between speech sounds they have never heard before. Infants are primed to start learning whichever of the world's languages they happen to hear around them.

Research of Janet Werker on Infant Speech Perception

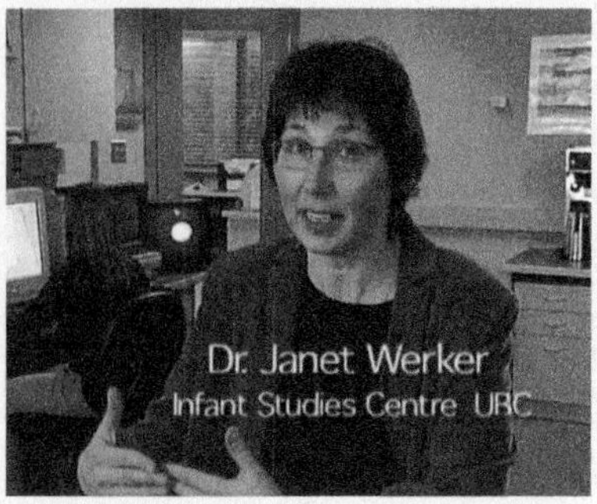

COURTESY OF JANET WERKER

Developmental Changes in Speech Perception

Recall the concept of perceptual narrowing, introduced in Chapter 5 to describe infants' increasing specialization, including poorer discrimination of non-native faces and music at later ages. The same type of process unfolds for speech perception. Infants increasingly home in on the speech sounds of their native language, and by 12 months of age, they become less sensitive to the differences between non-native speech sounds. This shift was first demonstrated by Janet Werker at the University of British Columbia and her colleagues (Werker & Lalonde, 1988; Werker & Tees, 1984), who tested Canadian English-speaking infants on their ability to discriminate speech contrasts that are not used in English but that are important in two other languages—Hindi and Nthlakapmx (a language

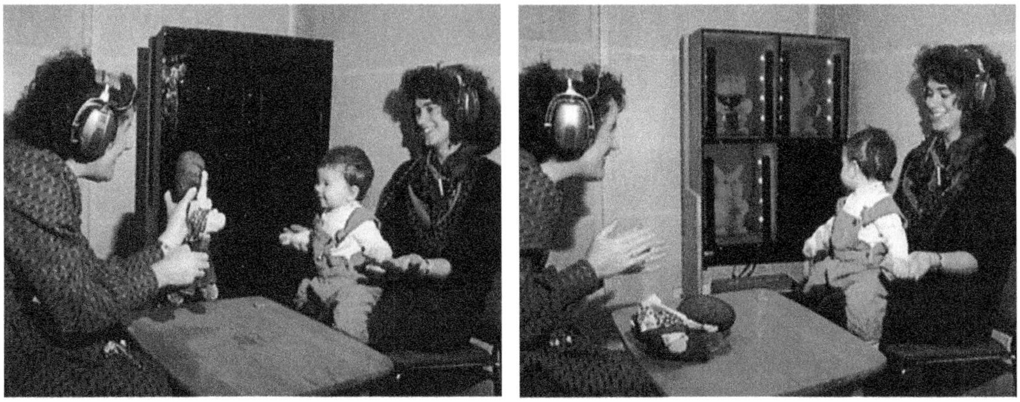

PHOTOS COURTESY OF PETER MCLEOD, ACADIA UNIVERSITY.

FIGURE 6.4 **Speech perception** This infant is participating in a study of speech perception in the laboratory of Janet Werker at the University of British Columbia. The baby has learned to turn his head to the sound source whenever he hears a change from one sound to another. A correct head turn is rewarded by an exciting visual display, as well as by the applause and praise of the experimenter. To make sure that neither the parent nor the experimenter can influence the child's behaviour, they are both wearing headphones that prevent them from hearing what the baby hears. (Information from Werker, 1989)

spoken by indigenous First Nations peoples in south central British Columbia). The researchers used a simple conditioning procedure, shown in Figure 6.4. The infants learned that if they turned their head toward the sound source when they heard a change in the sounds they were listening to, they would be rewarded by an interesting visual display. If the infants turned their heads immediately following a sound change, the researchers inferred that they had detected the change.

Figure 6.5 shows that at 6 to 8 months of age, Canadian English-learning infants readily discriminated between non-English phonemes; they could tell one Hindi syllable from another, and one Nthlakapmx syllable from another. At 10 to 12 months of age, however, the infants no longer perceived the differences they had detected a few months before. A similar change occurs (slightly earlier) for the discrimination of vowels (Kuhl et al., 1992; Polka & Werker, 1994).

Interestingly, perceptual narrowing does not appear to be an entirely passive process. Kuhl, Tsao, and Liu (2003) found that infants learned more about the phonetic structure of Mandarin from a live interaction with a Mandarin speaker than from watching a video of one. This is an example of the benefits of active learning, as discussed in Chapter 5. In an interesting twist, a follow-up study found that infant learners were more successful at learning Mandarin phonemes from the screen when they did so along with a peer (another 9-month-old) than when they were alone (see the photos on the next page; Lytle, Garcia-Sierra, & Kuhl, 2018).

Word Segmentation

As infants tune into the sounds of their language, they also begin to discover another crucial feature of speech: words. This is no easy feat. Unlike written language, there are no spaces between words in speech "*Lookattheprettybaby*! *Haveyoueverseensuchaprettybaby*?" Infants have to figure out where the spoken words start and end. They begin this process of **word segmentation** during the second half of the first year.

The first demonstration of infant word segmentation focused on 7-month-old infants (Jusczyk & Aslin, 1995). First, the babies listened to passages in which a particular word recurred—for example, "The *cup* was bright and shiny. A clown

word segmentation discovering where words begin and end in fluent speech

FIGURE 6.5 **Percent of infants able to discriminate foreign-language speech sounds** Infants' ability to discriminate between speech sounds that are not in their native language declines between 6 and 12 months of age. Most 6-month-olds from English-speaking families readily discriminate between syllables in Hindi (blue bars) and Nthlakapmx (green bars), but most 10- to 12-month-olds do not. (Data from Werker, 1989)

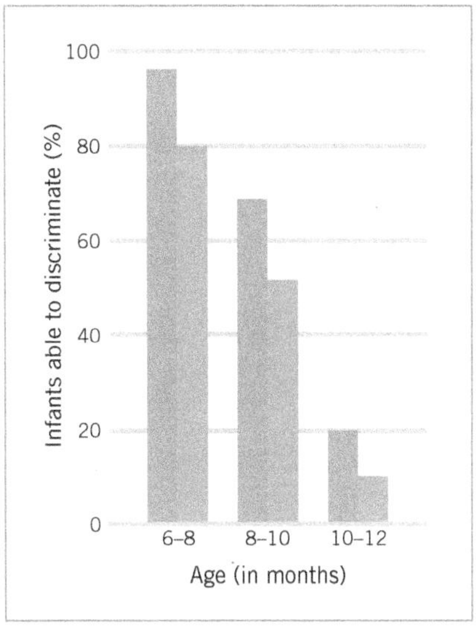

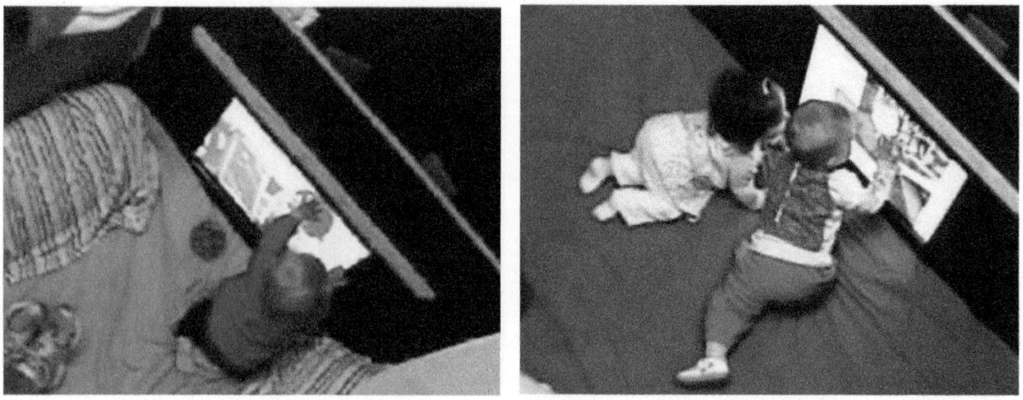

TWO ARE BETTER THAN ONE: INFANT LANGUAGE LEARNING FROM VIDEO IMPROVES IN THE PRESENCE OF PEERS. SARAH ROSEBERRY LYTLE, ADRIAN GARCIA-SIERRA, AND PATRICIA K. KUHL. PNAS OCTOBER 2, 2018, 115 (40) PHOTO COURTESY SARAH LYTLE

In their study of Mandarin phoneme learning, Lytle and colleagues (2018) found that two is better than one: The peers on the right will be more successful at language learning from a screen than the solitary infant on the left.

drank from the red *cup*. His *cup* was filled with milk." They were then tested using a head-turn preferential looking procedure to see whether they recognized the words that had been repeated in the sentences. In this method, flashing lights mounted near two loudspeakers located on either side of an infant are used to draw the infant's attention to one side or the other. When the infant turns to look at the light, sounds are played through the speaker on that side, continuing as long as the infant is looking in that direction. The length of time the infant spends looking at the light—and hence listening to the sound—provides a measure of the degree to which the infant is attracted to that sound.

Infants in this study were tested on repetitions of words that had been presented in the sentences (such as *cup*) or words that had not (such as *bike*). The researchers found that infants listened longer to words that they had heard in the passages of fluent speech, as compared with words that never occurred in the passages. This result indicates that the infants were able to pull the words out of the stream of speech—a task so difficult that even sophisticated speech-recognition computer software often fails at it.

distributional properties of speech in any language, certain sounds are more likely to occur together than are others

How do infants find words in pause-free speech? They appear to be remarkably good at picking up regularities in their native language that help them to find word boundaries. One example is stress patterning, an element of prosody. In English, the first syllable in two-syllable words is much more likely to be stressed than the second syllable (as in "English," "often," and "second"). By 8 months of age, English-learning infants expect stressed syllables to begin words and can use this information to pull words out of fluent speech (Curtin, Mintz, & Christiansen, 2005; Johnson & Jusczyk, 2001; Thiessen & Saffran, 2003). In contrast, to find words in fluent speech, Canadian French-learning infants in Québec rely on a pattern in which stress falls at the end of a phrase—a pattern that is typical in their native language (Polka & Sundara, 2012).

How quickly could you pick out a word from a stream of speech like the one shown here? It takes 8-month-old infants only 2 minutes of listening.

Another regularity to which infants are surprisingly sensitive concerns the **distributional properties** of the speech they hear. As discussed in Chapter 5, infants are skilled at statistical learning. Sounds that are part of the same word are more likely to occur together than are others. Sensitivity to such regularities in the speech stream was demonstrated in a series of statistical learning experiments (Saffran, Aslin, & Newport, 1996). The infants listened to a 2-minute recording of four different three-syllable "words" (e.g., *tupiro, golabu, bidaku, padoti*) repeated in random order with no pauses between the "words." Then, on a series of test trials, the babies were presented with the "words" they had heard (e.g., *bidaku, padoti*) or with sequences that were not words (e.g., *kupado,* made up from the end of *bidaku* and the beginning of *padoti*).

Using the same kind of preferential-listening test described for the Juscyzk & Aslin (1995) study, the researchers found that infants discriminated between the words and the sequences that were not words. To do so, the babies must have registered that certain syllables often occurred together in the sample of speech they heard. Thus, the infants used predictable sound patterns to fish words out of the passing stream of speech. This ability appears to be available at the youngest age tested, just days after birth (Fló et al., 2019).

Probably the most salient regularity for infants is their own name. Infants as young as 4½ months will listen longer to repetitions of their own name than to repetitions of a different name (Mandel, Jusczyk, & Pisoni, 1995). Just a few weeks later, they can pick their own name out of background conversations (Newman, 2005). This ability helps them to find new words in the speech stream. After hearing "It's Jerry's cup!" a number of times, 6-month-old Jerry is more likely to learn the word *cup* than if he had not heard it right after his name (Bortfeld et al., 2005). Over time, infants recognize more and more familiar words, making it easier to pluck new ones out of the speech that they hear.

Infants are exceptional in their ability to identify patterns in the speech surrounding them. They start out with the ability to make crucial distinctions among speech sounds but then narrow their focus to the sounds and sound patterns that make a difference in their native language. This process lays the groundwork for their becoming not just native listeners but also native speakers.

Preparation for Production

Newborns' repertoire of sounds is extremely limited: they cry, sneeze, sigh, burp, and smack their lips. At about 6 to 8 weeks of age, infants begin to coo—producing drawn-out vowel sounds, such as "ooohh" or "aaahh." They click, smack, blow raspberries, squeal—all with apparent fascination and delight. Through this practice, infants gain motor control over their vocalizations. While their sound repertoire is expanding, infants become increasingly aware that their vocalizations elicit responses from others, and they begin to engage in dialogues of reciprocal cooing with their caregivers. Indeed, infants with more responsive caregivers are more likely to use more mature vocalization patterns (Miller, 2014).

Babbling

Babies begin **babbling** between 6 and 10 months of age (on average at around 7 months). They produce strings of consonant-vowel syllables ("papapa"; "babababa") drawn from a fairly limited set of sounds, some of which are not part of their native language (de Boysson-Bardies, 1996/1999). For instance, a longitudinal study of Canadian-English and Parisian-French infants found highly similar patterns in the babble of the two groups of infants (Blake & de Boysson-Bardies, 1992).

babbling repetitive consonant–vowel sequences ("bababa . . .") or hand movements (for learners of sign languages)

Language exposure is a key component in the development of babbling. Research at McGill University showed that deaf infants who are regularly exposed to signed languages like ASL babble with their hands! They produce repetitive hand movements made up of pieces of full ASL signs, just as vocally babbled sounds are made up of pieces of spoken words (Petitto & Marentette, 1991). Thus, like infants learning spoken languages, infants learning sign languages seem to experiment with the elements that will eventually become the words of their native language (Figure 6.6).

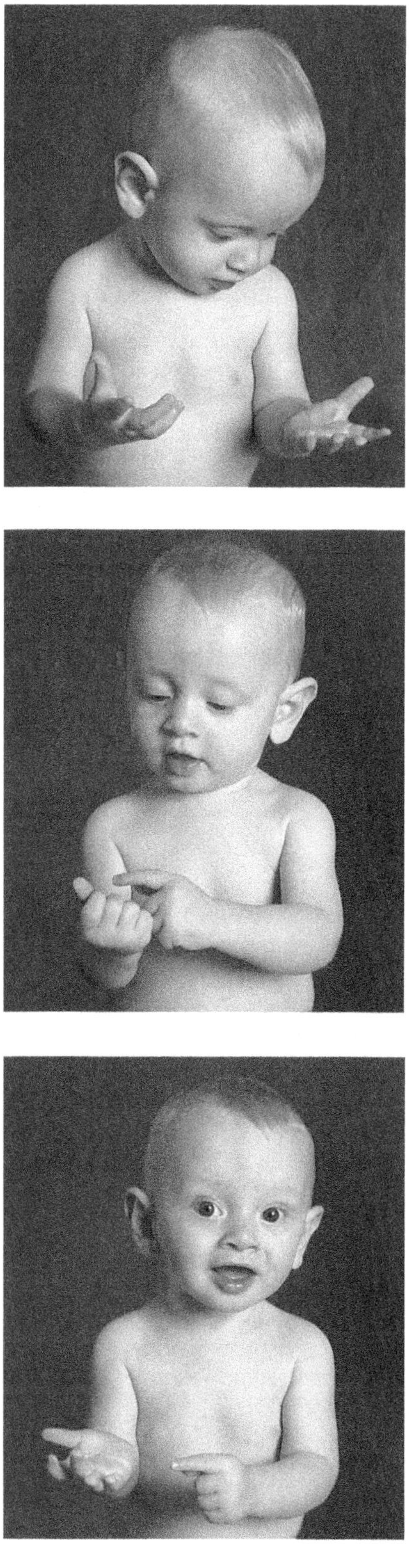

JEFFREY DEBELLE / DR. LAURA-ANN PETITO

FIGURE 6.6 Manual babbling Babies who are exposed to the sign language of their deaf parents babble with their hands. A subset of their hand movements differs from those of infants exposed to spoken language and corresponds to the rhythmic patterning of adult signs. (Information from Petitto et al., 2001)

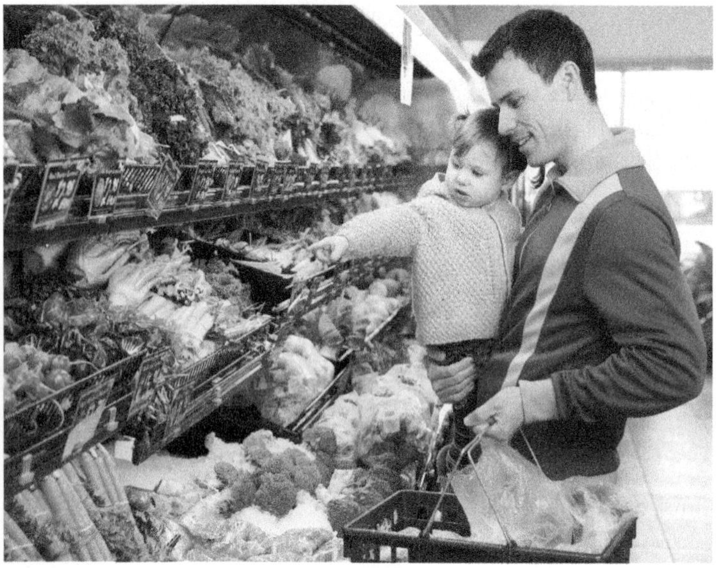
PAUL BURNS/GETTY IMAGES

This toddler is pointing to get her father to share her attention—to achieve intersubjectivity. Once the father identifies the focus of his daughter's attention, he may even decide to add it to the shopping basket.

Infants' babbling gradually takes on the sounds, rhythm, and intonational patterns of the language infants hear (or see) daily. However, it is still very difficult to tell what language an infant is learning just by listening to their babbling. In one study of English-learning and Chinese-learning 12-month-olds, adult listeners were unable to tell from their babbles alone which language the infants were learning (Lee et al., 2016).

Early interactions

In a conversation, mature participants alternate between speaking and listening. Learning to take turns in social interactions is facilitated by parent–infant games, such as peekaboo and "give and take," in which caregiver and baby take turns giving and receiving objects (Bruner, 1977; Ratner & Bruner, 1978). In these "dialogues," the infant has the opportunity to alternate between an active and a passive role, as in a conversation, giving infants practice in bidirectional communication. Caregivers' responses to babbling may serve a similar function. Consistent with our active learning theme, infant babbling evokes a range of parental responses that in turn may help the infant learn (Albert, Schwade, & Goldstein, 2018). Babbling also provides a signal that the infant is attentive and ready to learn. When an adult labels an object for an infant just after the infant babbles, the infant learns more than when the labelling occurs in the absence of babbling (Goldstein et al., 2010).

As discussed in Chapter 4, successful communication also requires *intersubjectivity,* in which two interacting partners share a mutual understanding. The foundation of intersubjectivity is *joint attention,* in which the caregiver follows the baby's lead, looking at and commenting on whatever the infant is looking at. By 12 months of age, infants have begun to understand the communicative nature of pointing, with many infants also able to point themselves (Behne et al., 2012).

First Words

To learn words, infants must map sounds (or signs) onto meanings. How do they figure out what words mean? Take the word "bunny." Even if the child hears this new word in the presence of a rabbit, how does the child know whether it refers to the rabbit itself, to its fuzzy tail, to its colour, or to the twitching of its nose (Quine, 1960)?

FIGURE 6.7 Eye-tracking studies When this infant hears the word *mouth,* will she look at the mouth or the apple? The speed and accuracy of her response provide a measure of her vocabulary knowledge.

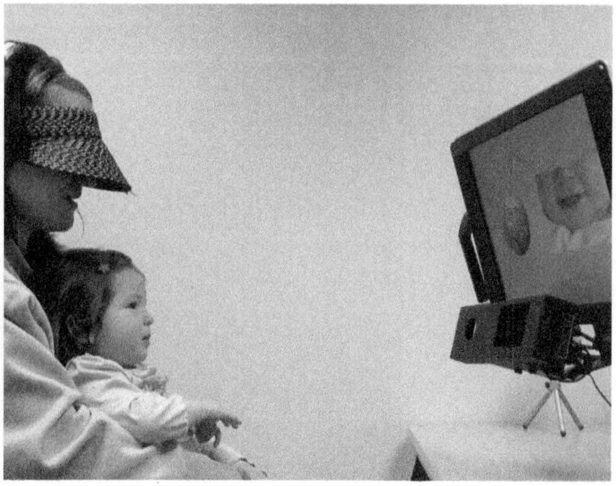
PHOTO BY ELIKA BERGELSON

Early Word Recognition

Infants begin to understand highly frequent words surprisingly early on. When 6-month-olds hear either "Mommy" or "Daddy," they look toward an image of the appropriate person (Tincoff & Jusczyk, 1999). Bergelson and Swingley (2012) showed infants pairs of pictures of common foods and body parts and tracked the infants' eye gaze when one of the pictures was named (see Figure 6.7). Even 6-month-olds looked to the correct picture significantly more often than would be expected by chance. Strikingly, most of their parents reported that the infants did not know the meanings of these words. So not only do infants understand far more words than they can produce; they also understand far more words than even their caregivers realize. The same phenomenon occurs for autistic toddlers, who tend to have delayed language abilities (as we will discuss in Box 6.5): parents think that their autistic toddlers understand fewer words than they actually do, as measured by sensitive eye-tracking tasks (Venker et al., 2016).

With linguistic experience, infants become skilled at rapid word comprehension. In studies where infants were presented a pair of objects and hear one of them labelled, 15-month-olds waited until they had heard the whole word to look at the target object, but 24-month-olds looked at the correct object after hearing only the first part of its label, just as adults do (e.g., Fernald, Perfors, & Marchman, 2006). Older children can also use context to help them recognize words. For example, toddlers who are learning a language that has a grammatical gender system (like Spanish or French) can use the gender of the article preceding the noun (*la* versus *el* in Spanish; *la* versus *le* in French) to speed their recognition of the noun itself (Lew-Williams & Fernald, 2007; Van Heugten & Shi, 2009).

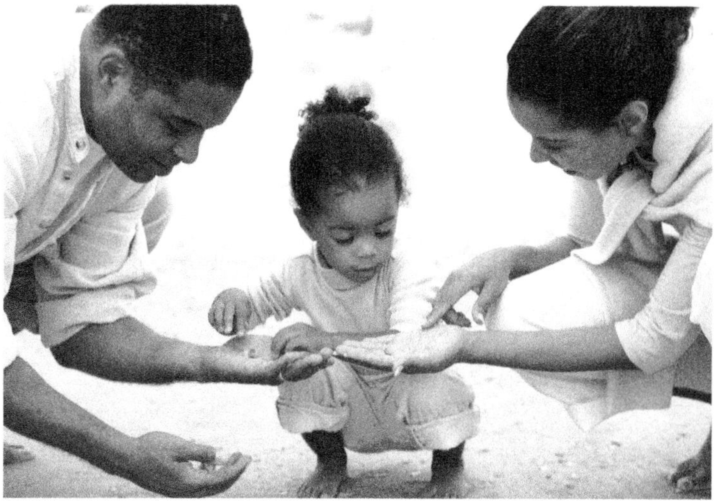

PURESTOCK/AGE FOTOSTOCK

A classic problem posed by philosopher Willard Quine was how someone who does not know the word *bunny* could figure out exactly what those sounds refer to. These parents are helping their daughter learn a new word by labelling the referent while it is the focus of their child's attention.

Early Word Production

What counts as an infant's first word? It can be any specific utterance consistently used to refer to or express a meaning. Even with this loose criterion, identification of an infant's earliest few words can be problematic. For one thing, babbling can sound word-like. For another, early words may differ from their corresponding adult forms. For example, *Woof* was one of the first words spoken by the boy whose linguistic progress was illustrated at the beginning of this chapter. It was used to refer to the dog next door—both to excitedly name the animal when it appeared in the neighbours' yard and to wistfully request the dog's presence when it was absent.

On average, infants produce their first words between 10 and 15 months of age, but these early words are mispronounced in a variety of predictable ways. Infants leave out the difficult bits of words, turning *banana* into "nana," or they substitute easier sounds for hard-to-say ones—"bubba" for *brother*, "wabbit" for *rabbit*. Sometimes they reorder parts of words to put an easier sound at the beginning of the word, as in the common "pisketti" (for *spaghetti*) or the more idiosyncratic "Cagoshin" (the way the child quoted at the beginning of the chapter pronounced *Chicago*).

Language Development in Infancy and Toddlerhood

Early words often refer to family members, pets, and important objects such as cookies, juice, and balls. Frequent routines are also labelled—"up," "bye-bye," "night-night." Important modifiers are also used—"mine," "hot," "all gone." Table 6.1 reveals substantial cross-linguistic similarities in the content of the most common first 10 words of children in the United States, Beijing, and Hong Kong. Many of infants' first words referred to specific people or were sound effects (Tardif et al., 2008). Indeed, early words across a range of cultures are similar in their meanings, suggesting that infants around the world have similar interests and priorities (Mayor & Plunkett, 2014).

Initially, infants express their thoughts with one-word utterances. But what they want to talk about quickly outstrips their limited vocabularies. This dilemma results in **overextension**—using a word in a broader context than is appropriate, as when children use *dog* for any four-legged animal, *moon* for a dishwasher dial, or *hot* for

overextension an overly broad interpretation of the meaning of a word

TABLE 6.1 Rank-Ordered List of Earliest Words in Three Languages*

English	Putonghua (Mandarin)	Cantonese
Daddy	**Daddy**	**Mommy**
Mommy	Aah	**Daddy**
BaaBaa	**Mommy**	*Grandma (paternal)*
Bye	*YumYum*	*Grandpa (paternal)*
Hi	*Sister (older)*	**Hello?/Wei?**
UhOh	**UhOh** (Aiyou)	*Hit*
Grr	*Hit*	Uncle (paternal)
Bottle	**Hello/Wei**	Grab/grasp
YumYum	Milk	*Auntie (maternal)*
Dog	Naughty	**Bye**
No	*Brother (older)*	**UhOh** (Aiyou)
WoofWoof	*Grandma (maternal)*	*Ya/Wow*

*Words in boldface were common across all three languages; those in italics were common for two of the languages. Information from Tardif et al. (2008).

underextension an overly narrow interpretation of the meaning of a word

any reflective metal. Young children also exhibit **underextension**—using a word in a more limited context than appropriate, such as believing that *dog* refers only to their dog, but not the neighbour's dog. Both overextensions and underextensions represent efforts to communicate given the child's limited vocabulary. They may also reflect incorrect mappings between words and meanings that will have to be revised as language learning continues.

Word Learning

After producing their first words, children typically plod ahead slowly, reaching a productive vocabulary of 50 or so words by about 18 months of age. At this point, the rate of learning appears to accelerate, leading to what appears to be a "vocabulary spurt" (e.g., Bloom, 1973; McMurray, 2007). Although scholars disagree about whether learning actually speeds up for all or even most children (Bloom, 2000), it is clear that children's communicative abilities are growing rapidly (Figure 6.8).

FIGURE 6.8 Language achievement On average, North American children say their first word at about 13 months, experience a vocabulary spurt at about 19 months, and begin to produce simple sentences at about 24 months. The error bars indicate substantial variability. (Data from Bloom, 1998)

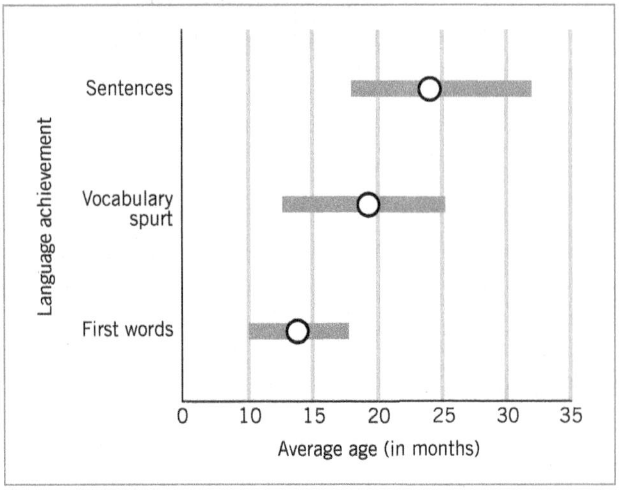

Adult influences on word learning The most important way that caregivers influence word learning is by talking to their children. As we discuss in Box 6.2 on page 212, the amount and quality of talking that children hear predicts how many words they learn. In addition to using IDS, which makes word learning easier for infants, adults facilitate word learning by stressing or repeating new words. They also play naming games, asking the child to point to a series of named items—"Where's your nose?" "Where's your ear?" "Where's your tummy?" Adults can also enhance word learning by choosing optimal naming moments. For example, toddlers show better word learning when the object being labelled is centred in their visual field rather than in the periphery (see Figure 6.9; Pereira, Smith, & Yu, 2014).

Early word learning is also influenced by the contexts in which words are used. New words that are used in very distinct contexts (like kitchens or bathrooms) are produced earlier than words that are used across a range of contexts (Roy et al., 2015). These contexts can be quite specific. For example, while toddlers are generally better at learning the names for solid substances than non-solid substances, toddlers do better at learning the names for non-solids when seated in a high-chair—a context where they frequently encounter non-solid food items (Perry, Samuelson, & Burdinie, 2014).

Caregivers may also facilitate word learning by maintaining spatial consistency with the objects they are labelling. For instance, infants learn the names of objects more readily when the objects are presented in predictable locations (Benitez & Saffran, 2018; Benitez & Smith, 2012; Samuelson et al., 2011). Presumably, consistency in the visual environment helps children map words onto objects and events.

This young Inuit child is playing a naming game; her mother has just asked her to point to her nose.

Children's contributions to word learning When confronted with new words, children exploit the context in which the word was used in order to infer its meaning. Theorists have proposed that children are guided by a number of assumptions about the possible meanings of a new word. For example, children expect that a given entity will have only one name, an assumption referred to as *mutual exclusivity.* Early evidence for this assumption came from a study in which 3-year-olds saw pairs of objects—a familiar object for which the children had a name and an unfamiliar one for which they had no name. When the experimenter said, "Show me the blicket," the children mapped the novel label to the novel object, the one for which they had no name (see Figure 6.10a on page 214; Markman & Wachtel, 1988). Interestingly, bilingual and trilingual infants, who are accustomed to hearing more than one name for a given object, are less likely to follow the mutual exclusivity assumption in word learning (Byers-Heinlein & Werker, 2009) and, unlike monolingual infants, are unsurprised when an object has more than one name (Byers-Heinlein, 2017).

Another useful constraint on word learning is known as the *whole-object* assumption: children expect a novel word to refer to a whole object rather than to a part, property, action, or other aspect of the object (Markman, 1989). Thus, in the case of Quine's rabbit problem (see page 208), the whole-object assumption leads children to map the label "bunny" to the whole animal, not just to its tail or the twitching of its nose.

Children also exploit a variety of **pragmatic cues** to word meaning by paying attention to the *social contexts* in which the words are used. For example, children use an adult's focus of attention as a cue to word meaning. In a study by Baldwin (1993),

pragmatic cues aspects of the social context used for word learning

FIGURE 6.9 **Visual information in word learning** These images are taken from the infant's perspective; the infant is wearing a head-mounted eye tracker. The infant is more likely to learn the name for the green object when it is centred in the visual field (left panel) than when it is less prominent (right panel) at the moment it is labelled (Pereira, Smith, & Yu, 2014).

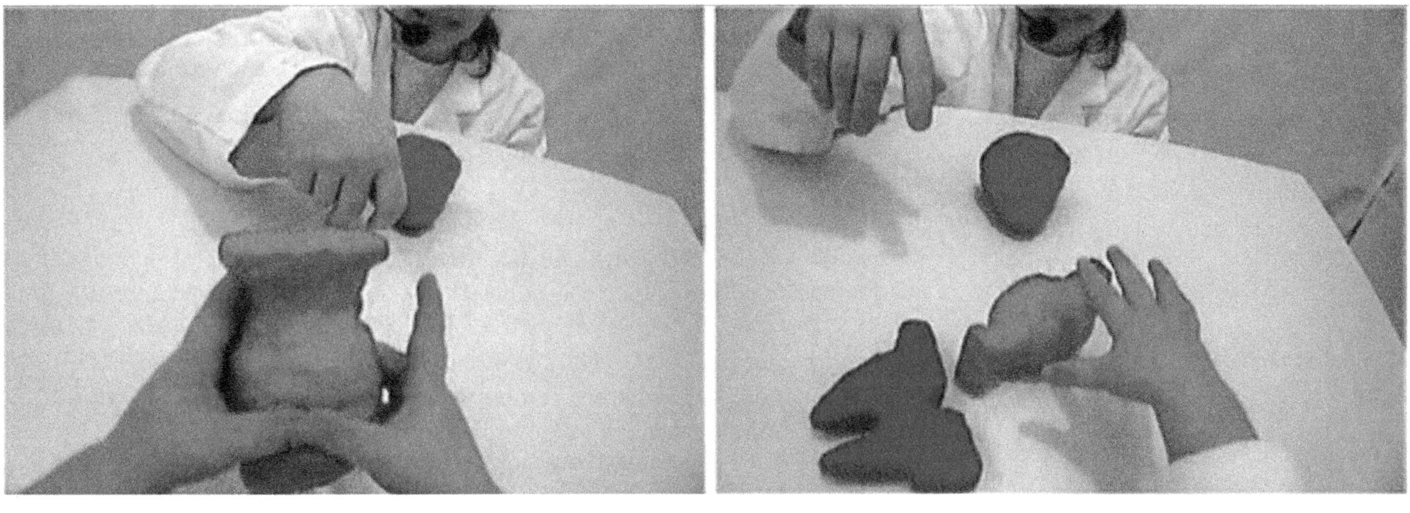

BOX 6.2 INDIVIDUAL DIFFERENCES Language Development and Socioeconomic Status

Parents often notice linguistic differences among their own children. These differences are greatly magnified across a community. In a single kindergarten classroom, there may be a tenfold difference in the number of words used by different children. What accounts for these differences?

The number of words children know is intimately related to the number of words they hear, which is linked to their caregivers' vocabularies. One of the key determinants of the language children hear is the socioeconomic status of their parents. In a seminal study, Hart and Risley (1995) recorded the speech that 42 parents used with their infants over the course of 2½ years. Some of the parents were upper-middle class, others were working class, and others were on welfare. The results were astonishing: the average child whose parents were on welfare received half as much linguistic experience (616 words per hour) as did the average working-class parents' child (1251 words per hour) and less than one-third that of the average child in a professional family (2153 words per hour). The researchers did the math and suggested that after 4 years, an average child with upper-middle-class parents would have heard 45 million words, compared with 26 million for an average child in a working-class family and 13 million for an average child with parents on welfare.

The researchers noted differences in how parents talked to their children as well, with more questions and conversations initiated in the higher-income families. More recent research suggests that these estimated differences in the amount of input may be exaggerated because they discount speech that is not directed to the child via a primary caregiver (Sperry, Sperry, & Miller, 2018). Nevertheless, this body of research has brought a great deal of attention to income disparities in language input.

Why are researchers and policy makers so worried about the amount of language input that children receive? One reason is that the number of words that children hear predicts the number of words they learn. On average, children from higher-SES families have larger vocabularies than children from lower-SES families. Differences in the amount of language input also affect how quickly toddlers recognize familiar words: children whose mothers talked more to them at 18 months of age were faster at recognizing words at 24 months than were children whose mothers provided less input (Hurtado, Marchman, & Fernald, 2008).

It is important to note that SES-related differences are average differences, subsuming a range of income brackets and parenting behaviours. In any given study, some parents from lower-SES backgrounds provide more input than some parents from higher-SES backgrounds (Rowe, 2018). And within groups of parents of similar SES, there is a great deal of variability in the amount of input parents provide. One study of low-income Spanish-speaking families in California found that 19-month-old infants who heard more speech had larger vocabularies and were faster at processing words 6 months later (Weisleder & Fernald, 2013). Thus, early differences in language input appear to have cascading effects on language development, potentially contributing to achievement gaps between wealthier and poorer children (e.g., Duncan & Murnane, 2011).

Input quality also impacts language learning, perhaps even more than input quantity. In one study of low-income toddlers in the United States, researchers found that the richness of the communicative context, as assessed by such variables as joint engagement, routines and rituals, and fluency, predicted children's language attainment a year later (Hirsh-Pasek, Adamson et al., 2015). Indeed, these indicators of quality were a better predictor of language development than the amount of speech the children heard. And notably, children who experienced higher-quality language input—in particular, a greater number of conversational back-and-forths—showed greater activation in language areas of the brain (Romeo et al., 2018), as well as increased cortical surface area in left-hemisphere language regions (Merz et al., 2019).

The physical environments in which children learn language also influence the quality of language input. For example, toddlers have more difficulty learning new words in noisy environments (Dombroski & Newman, 2014; McMillan & Saffran, 2016). Children living in poverty are more likely to experience crowded and noisy home environments and to be exposed to street sounds and other sources of noise pollution that may make it more difficult for them to process language input.

Similar issues—of both quantity and quality in language input—emerge in the school context. When preschool children with low language skills are placed in classrooms with peers who also have low language skills, they show less language growth than do their counterparts who are placed with classmates who have high language skills (Justice et al., 2011). These peer effects have important implications for programs like Head Start (discussed fully in Chapter 8), which are designed to enhance language development and early literacy for children living in poverty. Congregating children from lower-SES families together in the same preschool classrooms may limit their ability to "catch up." However, negative peer effects may be offset by positive teacher effects. For example, one study found that children whose preschool teachers used a rich vocabulary showed better reading comprehension in 4th grade than did children whose preschool teachers used a more limited vocabulary (Dickinson & Porche, 2011).

---

an experimenter showed 18-month-olds two novel objects and then concealed them in separate containers. Next, the experimenter peeked into one of the containers and commented, "There's a modi in here." The adult then removed and gave both objects to the child. When asked for the "modi," the children picked the object that the experimenter had been looking at when saying the label (see Figure 6.10b).

Infants can even use an adult's emotional response to infer the name of a novel object that they cannot see (Tomasello, Strosberg, & Akhtar, 1996). In a study establishing this fact, an adult announced her intention to "find the gazzer." She then picked up one of two objects and showed obvious disappointment with it.

Signs with messages like these were placed around grocery stores in low-income neighbourhoods to encourage caregivers to engage in more conversational interactions with their young children—and they worked!

One promising intervention to provide rich language exposure to children in low-SES environments lies in increased access to children's books, which often include words that parents don't typically use in conversation with their infants (Montag, Jones, & Smith, 2015). Reach Out and Read is an intervention program originated in the United States that provides books during pediatrician visits, building on studies that suggest that primary care physicians can influence language outcomes by modeling and promoting reading to young children (High et al., 2014). Providing parents in Reach Out and Read programs with bookmarks that include age-specific advice about reading to children further increases family literacy-related behaviours (Obus et al., 2017).

This program was recently implemented in Toronto through the public library system and St. Michael's Hospital. Another early intervention program that has Canadian roots, Parent–Child Mother Goose, helps parents learn to use rhymes, songs, and stories with their young infants. This program is available in many different settings across Canada and internationally. One evaluation of this program in Australia showed that children showed significant improvement in their language skills after participating in it (Terrett, White, & Spreckley, 2012).

Other interventions focus on increasing the amount of time that lower-SES parents spend speaking to their children. In one such intervention, signs were placed in supermarkets in low and middle-SES neighbourhoods, encouraging parents to converse with their children about foods they saw in the market (Ridge et al., 2015). In the low-SES neighbourhood where the signs were present, parents increased both the quality and quantity of talk to their children while shopping (a similar effect was not found in the middle-SES neighbourhood). Other interventions provide parents with individualized coaching about both quality and quantity of interactions; results suggest both enhanced parental input and larger child vocabularies (Ferjan Ramírez et al., 2018).

Larger-scale interventions—like the Thirty Million Words Initiative in Chicago—aim to do something similar by providing parents with recording devices that track how much they speak to their baby so that they can monitor and increase their amount of speech. These interventions are motivated by research suggesting that educating parents about their own role has a positive effect on language development outcomes (M. L. Rowe, 2008; Suskind et al., 2015). Finally, enhancing teacher training and support in low-income school settings is another promising route for intervention (Dickinson, 2011; Hindman, Wasik, & Snell, 2016). Regardless of the source, what goes in is what comes out: we can only learn words and grammatical structures that we hear (or see or read) in the language surrounding us.

When she gleefully seized the second object, the infants inferred that it was a "gazzer." (Figure 6.10c–d depicts another instance in which a child infers the name of an unseen object from an adult's emotional expression.)

If an adult's labelling of an object conflicts with a child's knowledge of that object, they will nevertheless accept the label if the adult clearly used it intentionally (for a recent review, see Harris et al., 2018). When an experimenter simply used the label "dog" in referring to a picture of a catlike animal, preschool children were reluctant to extend the label to other catlike stimuli, or to learn a new word from this "untrustworthy" adult. However, they were much more willing to do so when

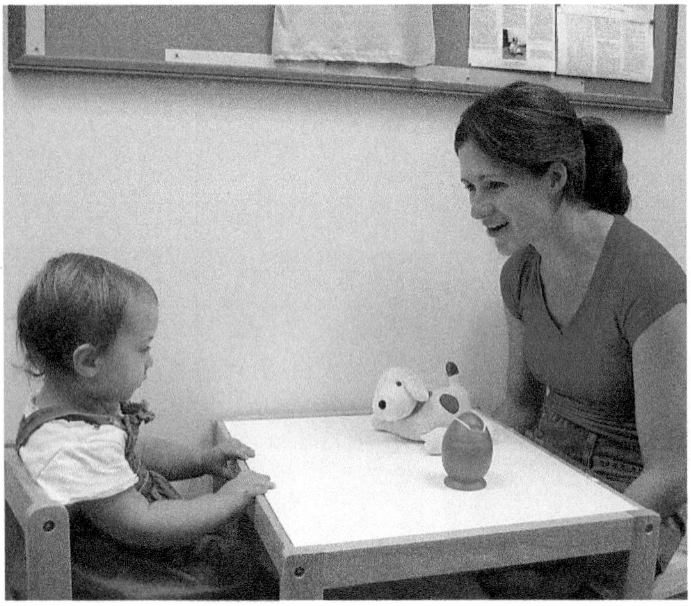

FIGURE 6.10 Cues for word learning (a) Mutual exclusivity: Because this child already knows the name of the familiar object, she will pick up the novel object when the adult requests "the blicket."

(b) Pragmatic cues: This child will assume that when the experimenter says a novel word, it refers to the novel object the experimenter is looking at, even though the child cannot see the object and is looking at a different novel object.

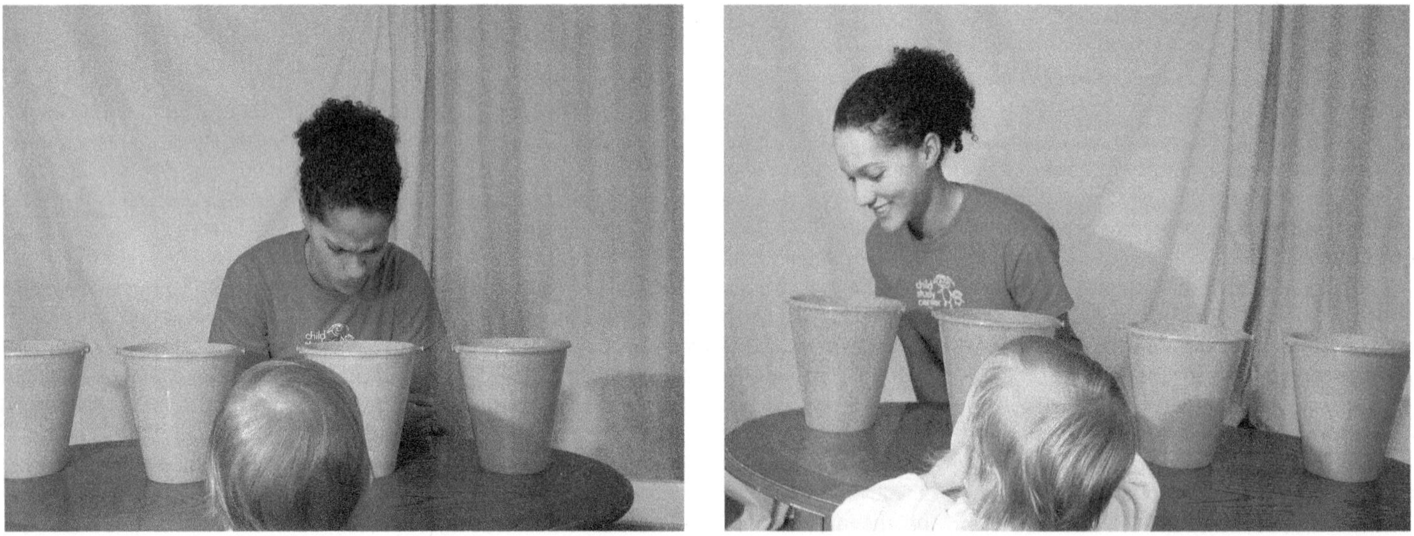

COURTESY OF JUDY DELOACHE

(c–d) Pragmatic cues: This child will learn "gazzer" as the name of the novel object that the adult smiles at triumphantly after she had previously announced that she wanted to find "the gazzer."

the experimenter made it clear that he really intended his use of the unexpected label by saying, "You're not going to believe this, but this is actually a dog."

Young children also use the linguistic context in which a novel word occurs to infer its meaning. In one of the first experiments on language acquisition, Roger Brown (1957) established that the grammatical form of a novel word influences how children interpret its meaning. He showed preschool children a picture of a pair of hands kneading a mass of material in a container (Figure 6.11). The picture was described to one group of children as "sibbing," to another as "a sib," and to a third as "some sib." The children subsequently interpreted *sib* as referring to the action, the container, or the material, depending on which form (verb, count noun, or mass noun) of the

FIGURE 6.11 Linguistic context When Roger Brown, a pioneer in the study of language development, described a drawing like this as "sibbing," "a sib," or "some sib," preschool children made different assumptions about the meaning of "sib."

word they had heard. Even infants and toddlers can draw on some of these links to interpret the meaning of novel words (e.g., Ferguson, Graf, & Waxman, 2018).

Object shape is another useful tool in word learning, possibly because shape is a good cue to category membership. Children readily extend a novel noun to novel objects of the same shape, even when those objects differ dramatically in size, colour, and texture (Graham & Poulin-Dubois, 1999; Landau, Smith, & Jones, 1988). Thus, a child who hears a U-shaped wooden block called "a dax" will assume that *dax* also refers to a U-shaped object covered in blue fur or to a U-shaped piece of red wire—but not to a wooden block of a different shape (Figure 6.12). This attention to the shared shape of objects is evident in categorization tasks before infants have acquired many productive words (Graham & Diesendruck, 2010). Attention to shape is also evident in toddlers' recognition of familiar words. When confronted with known objects with the wrong colours, like a pink cow paired with a black-and-white patched pig, toddlers still look at the cow when they hear "cow," though they are slower to do so than for correctly coloured objects (Perry & Saffran, 2017).

Another potentially useful cue to word meaning is the repeated correspondence between words the child hears and objects the child observes in the world. Any single scene is ambiguous. For example, if the child hears "dax" in the presence of multiple novel objects, the child has no way of knowing which object is the dax. But across experiences, the child might observe that whenever "dax" is said, one of those objects is always present, and thus that object is probably the dax. Through this process of **cross-situational word learning,** even infants can narrow down the possible meanings of new words (e.g., Smith & Yu, 2008; Vouloumanos & Werker, 2009).

Children also figure out the meanings of new words by using the grammatical structure of the sentences in which those words occur—a strategy referred to as **syntactic bootstrapping** (Fisher, 1999; Fisher, Gleitman, & Gleitman, 1991; Yuan & Fisher, 2009). An early demonstration of this phenomenon involved showing 2-year-olds a video of a duck using its left hand to push a rabbit down into a squatting position while both animals waved their right arms in circles (see Figure 6.13 on page 217) (Naigles, 1990). As they watched, some children heard "The duck is kradding the rabbit"; others heard "The rabbit and the duck are kradding." The children then saw two videos side by side, one showing the duck pushing on the rabbit and the other showing both animals waving their arms in circles. Instructed to "Find kradding," the two groups looked at the event that matched the syntax they had heard while watching the initial video. Those who had heard the first sentence took "kradding" to mean what the duck had been doing to the rabbit, whereas those who had heard the second sentence thought it meant what both animals had been doing. Thus, the children had arrived at different interpretations for a novel verb based on the *structure* of the sentence in which it occurred.

In Box 6.3, we discuss the popularity of digital tools to help with early word learning, and the evidence for how effective these tools actually are.

Word Learning

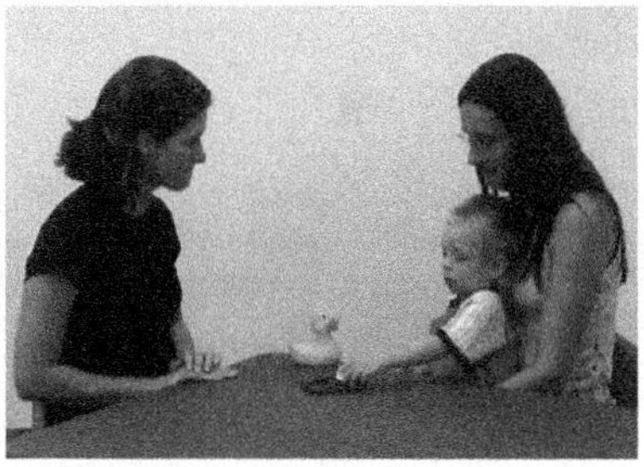

cross-situational word learning determining word meanings by tracking the correlations between labels and meanings across scenes and contexts

syntactic bootstrapping the strategy of using grammatical structure to infer the meaning of a new word

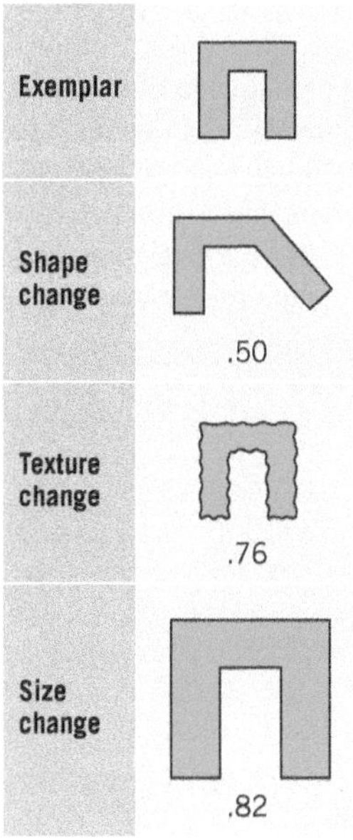

FIGURE 6.12 Shape bias In one of many studies of the shape bias, children were shown the exemplar at the top of this figure and told that it was a "dax" (or some other nonsense word). Then they were asked which of the objects below the exemplar was also a "dax." The numbers under the objects indicate the proportion of children who thought each object was a "dax." As you can see, they most often thought that the word referred to the object that was of the same shape as the exemplar, even if the surface texture or size was different. (Information from Landau, Smith, & Jones, 1988)

BOX 6.3 APPLICATIONS iBabies: Technology and Language Learning

Like you, most infants are immersed in technology. Businesses market all manner of digital toys, apps, and videos claiming to enhance babies' intellectual growth. Some of these claims have been negated by developmental research—so much so that the companies producing these products (e.g., "Baby Einstein") were forced to stop promoting their "educational" value. However, there is still concern over technology marketed for infants and toddlers, and questions about screen time are ubiquitous among parents in industrialized cultures.

In one of the most rigorous studies to date, DeLoache and colleagues (2010) used random assignment to determine whether a best-selling "educational" DVD had an impact on infant language development. The researchers randomly assigned 12- to 18-month-olds into four groups. Infants in the *video-with-interaction* group watched the video repeatedly while interacting with a parent. Infants in the *video-without-interaction* group received the same amount of exposure but without a parent watching along with them. Infants in the *parent-teaching* group did not watch the video at all. Instead, their parents were given a list of 25 words featured on the video and asked to teach the infants those words in whatever way felt most natural to them. Finally, infants in the *control* group received no intervention, serving as a baseline for typical vocabulary development.

At the beginning and end of the study, the infants were tested on a subset of the words featured on the DVD. The infants in the parent-teaching group showed the greatest vocabulary development. Infants in the DVD-viewing conditions learned no more than the infants in the control group. Interestingly, the performance of infants in the DVD-viewing conditions was unrelated to how much parents thought their infant had learned from the DVD. However, there was a correlation between how much the parents liked the DVD themselves and how much they thought their infant had learned: the more parents liked the DVD, the more likely they were to overestimate its positive effects.

While passive viewing does not appear to support learning, infants do seem able to learn when they can actively engage with another human, even via screens. As discussed in Chapter 5, when infants are given the opportunity to learn from live video interactions (e.g., Skype or FaceTime), they do better than when learning from prerecorded versions of the same interactions (e.g., Myers et al., 2016; Roseberry, Hirsh-Pasek, & Golinkoff, 2014). Live video maintains social contingencies between the infant and the teacher in a way that recorded video does not. And indeed, the most recent screen time recommendations from the American Academy of Pediatrics note that live video chat is the only acceptable use of technology for infants younger than 2 years of age (AAP Council on Communications and Media, 2016a).

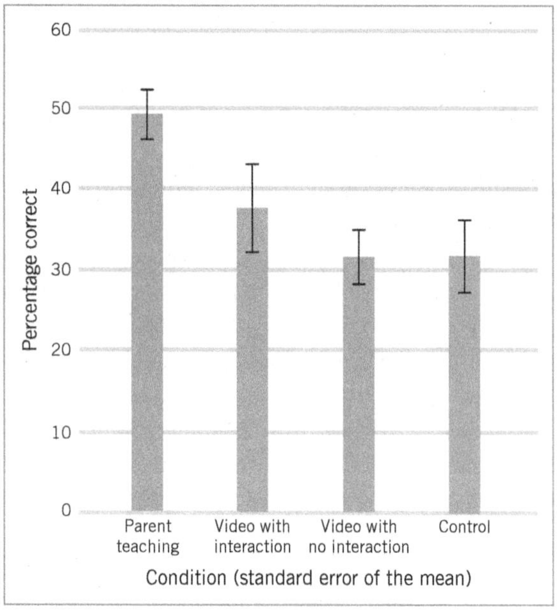

As shown in this figure from DeLoache et al. (2010), the infants who learned from parents (shown in the first column) performed best on the study's measure of word learning. Infants in the two video-learning conditions (middle two columns) did not perform significantly better than the control group (last column).

Questions about electronic media for infants are only going to increase, given the delight with which young children, and even infants, have embraced the apps on their parents' smartphones and tablets. Although the number of educational apps intended for young children continues to grow, their effect on children's development remains largely unknown (Hirsh-Pasek, Zosh et al., 2015). As with any type of activity, a little here and there probably doesn't hurt. But it is important to approach any claims of "educational value" with a great deal of skepticism.

Caregivers should also be cautious about their own use of technology around their children. Device usage can detract from adults' responsiveness to children's needs and from opportunities to provide learning opportunities. In a clever study, researchers tested the hypothesis that something as ubiquitous as a parent responding to a phone call could impact toddlers' word learning (Reed, Hirsh-Pasek, & Golinkoff, 2017). Parents were asked to teach two new words to their 2-year-olds. During the learning session for one of the two words, the parent was interrupted by a cell phone call. The results revealed better learning for the word that was taught without phone interruption—despite the fact that both words were heard the same number of times during the learning phase of the study—suggesting that interruptions in interactions, which are increased by the prevalence of mobile technology, can hinder children's opportunities to learn.

Putting Words Together

A major landmark is achieved when children start combining words into sentences, enabling them to express increasingly complex ideas. This ability is what most distinguishes children's emerging language abilities from the communication systems of nonhuman animals.

First Sentences

Most children begin to combine words into simple sentences by the end of their second year. However, in another example of comprehension preceding production, young children understand word combinations much earlier than when they can produce them. In one of the first studies to show early sensitivity to word order, 17-month-olds viewed a pair of videos presented simultaneously—one showing Cookie Monster tickling Big Bird, and the other showing Big Bird tickling Cookie Monster (Hirsh-Pasek & Golinkoff, 1996). When they heard a sentence like "Where is Cookie Monster tickling Big Bird?" they looked at the appropriate scene, suggesting that they could use the order of the words to interpret the meaning of the sentence. This finding is remarkable given that these infants were still months away from producing sentences themselves.

Children's two-word utterances have been described as **telegraphic speech** because, just as in telegrams (where senders paid by the word), nonessential elements are left out. Consider the following two-word utterances: "Read me," "Mommy tea," "Ride Daddy," "Hurt knee," "All wet," "More boy," "Key door," "Andrew sleep" (Braine, 1976). They lack a number of elements that would appear in adult utterances. Children's early sentences possess this telegraphic quality in languages as diverse as English, Finnish, Dholuo (Kenya), and Kaluli (Papua New Guinea) (de Boysson-Bardies, 1996/1999).

LETITIA R. NAIGLES, UNIVERSITY OF CONNECTICUT

FIGURE 6.13 Syntactic bootstrapping When children in Naigles's (1990) study heard an adult describe this video as "The duck is kradding the rabbit," they used the syntactic structure of the sentence to infer that kradding is what the duck is doing to the rabbit.

telegraphic speech short utterances that leave out non-essential words

Many children continue to produce short utterances for some time, whereas others quickly move on to sentences consisting of three or more words. Figure 6.14 shows the rapid increase in the mean length of utterances of three children who were studied longitudinally (Brown, 1973). As you can see from the figure, Eve's sentences increased in length much earlier than for the other two children. The length of children's utterances increases in part because they begin to systematically incorporate some of the elements that were missing from their telegraphic speech.

Grammar: A Tool for Building New Words and Sentences

As noted at the beginning of this chapter, human languages are *generative:* through the use of the finite set of words and morphemes, individuals can create an infinite number of sentences and express an infinite number of ideas. Each language has a particular set of rules (and exceptions) that governs how linguistic elements can be combined. The power of language derives from the mastery of these regularities, which allows individuals to produce and understand language beyond the specific words and sentences to which they have been exposed. How does this mastery come about?

Much of the research on this topic has focused on morphemes that are added to nouns and verbs. In English, nouns are made plural by adding *s,* and verbs

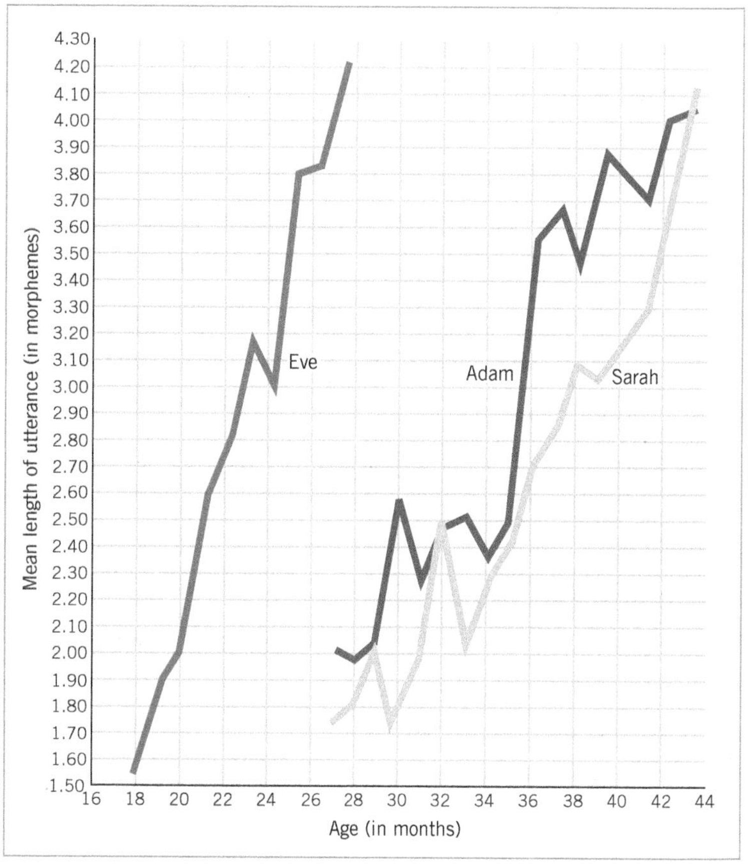

FIGURE 6.14 Length of utterance This graph shows the relation between age and the mean length of utterance for the three children—Eve, Adam, and Sarah—studied by Roger Brown. (Data from Brown, 1973)

are put into the past tense by adding *ed,* with notable exceptions (e.g., *men, went*). Young children recognize these patterns and are able to generalize them to novel words. In a classic experiment by Jean Berko (1958), preschoolers were shown a picture of a made-up animal, which the experimenter referred to as "a wug." Then the children saw a picture of two of the creatures, and the experimenter said, "Here are two of them; what are they?" (See Figure 6.15.) Children as young as 4 readily answered "wugs." Since the children had never heard the word *wugs* before, their ability to produce the correct plural form can't be attributed to imitation. Instead, these results provide evidence that the participants had learned the English plural, generalizing beyond words they had previously heard.

This is a Wug.
Now there is another one.
There are two of them.
There are two _____.

JEAN BERKO GLEASON

FIGURE 6.15 Evidence of learning morphology If a child responds to the final query with "Wugs," this is evidence that she understands how to create the English plural (by adding *–s* to the end of the word). The child must be generalizing from prior experience, since she has never heard "wugs" before (Berko, 1958).

Evidence for generalization also comes from the way children treat irregular cases. Consider the plural of *man* and the past tense of *go.* Children initially use the correct irregular forms of these words, saying "men" for the plural of *man* and "went" for the past tense of *go.* They then start making occasional **overregularization** errors, in which they treat irregular forms as if they were regular. For instance, a child who previously said "men" and "went" may begin producing novel forms such as "mans" and "goed," as well as "foots," "feets," "breaked," "broked," and even "branged" and "walkeded." The following dialogue with a 2½-year-old illustrates this kind of error, as well as the difficulty of correcting it:

> *Child:* I used to wear diapers. When I growed up (*pause*)
> *Father:* When you grew up?
> *Child:* When I grewed up, I wore underpants.
>
> (Clark, 1993)

Parents play a role in their children's grammatical development, although a more limited one than you might expect. Clearly, they provide a model of grammatically correct speech. In addition, they frequently fill in missing parts of their children's incomplete utterances, as when a parent responds to "No bed" by saying, "You really don't want to go to bed right now, do you?"

One might think that parents also contribute to their children's language development by correcting their grammatical errors. In fact, parents generally ignore even wildly ungrammatical mistakes, accepting sentences such as "I magicked it," "Me no want go," or "I want dessert in front of dinner" (Brown & Hanlon, 1970; Bryant & Polkosky, 2001). And, as the parent who tried to correct his child's use of "growed" discovered, such efforts are largely futile anyway. In general, parents are more likely to correct factual errors than grammatical errors.

Given this lack of correction, how do infants learn the syntax of their native language? One approach to answering this question involves creating miniature languages—known as artificial grammars—and determining which types of linguistic patterns infants are able to learn. After a brief exposure in the lab, infants as young as 8 months can learn new grammatical patterns, generalizing beyond the specific items they have heard (e.g., Gerken, Wilson, & Lewis, 2005; Gómez, 2002; Saffran et al., 2008). For example, infants who have heard a list of three-word sequences in which the second word is repeated, such as "le di di, wi je je, de li li . . ." recognize the pattern when it is presented in new syllables, such as "ko ga ga" (Marcus et al., 1999).

Language Development in Early Childhood

Overregularization
The over-application of grammar rules

© WORTH PUBLISHERS

Conversational Skills

Although young children are eager to participate in conversations, their conversational skills lag well behind their burgeoning language skills. For one thing, their speech is often directed to themselves, rather than to another person. Vygotsky

overregularization speech errors in which children treat irregular forms of words as if they were regular

(1934/1962) believed that young children's *private speech* serves as a strategy to organize their actions. Gradually, private speech is internalized as thought, and children become capable of mentally organizing their behaviour, so they no longer need to talk out loud to themselves.

collective monologue conversation between children that involves a series of non sequiturs

narratives story-like structured descriptions of past events

As noted in Chapter 4, when young children converse with other children, their conversations tend to be egocentric. Piaget (1923/1926) labelled young children's talk with their peers as **collective monologues.** Their conversations tend to be a series of non sequiturs, with the content of each child's turn having little or nothing to do with what the other child has just said. The following conversation between two preschoolers is a good example of what Piaget observed:

> *Jenny:* My bunny slippers . . . are brown and red and sort of yellow and white. And they have eyes and ears and these noses that wiggle sideways when they kiss.
> *Chris:* I have a piece of sugar in a red piece of paper. I'm gonna eat it but maybe it's for a horse.
> *Jenny:* We bought them. My mommy did. We couldn't find the old ones. These are like the old ones. They were not in the trunk.
> *Chris:* Can't eat the piece of sugar, not unless you take the paper off.
> (Stone & Church, 1957, pp. 146–147)

Gradually, children's capacity for sustained conversation increases, and they become better able to stick to the same topic as their conversational partners. They also become better able to talk about the past. Three-year-olds' conversations include occasional brief references to past events (if any). In contrast, 5-year-olds produce **narratives**—descriptions of past events that have the form of a story (with a beginning, middle, and end organized coherently).

Parents actively assist their children in developing the ability to produce coherent accounts of past events by *scaffolding* (discussed in Chapter 4) their children's narratives. Consider this exchange between 27-month-old Harriet and her mother. Harriet does not actually say much, but the parent's questions help her think about the event, and the parent also provides a conversational model:

> *Harriet:* I got [*unintelligible*] my pants fall, fall down.
> *Mother:* You got wee-wees in your pants and you fell down. Is that what you said? . . . Did Helen look after you when you were sick?
> *Harriet:* Yeah.
> *Mother:* . . . Did you fall asleep?
> *Harriet:* I can't close my eyes.
> (McCabe & Peterson, 1991, p. 238)

Parents help young children learn to talk about past events.

STATICNAK1983/GETTY IMAGES

A crucial aspect of becoming a good conversational partner is the *pragmatic development* that allows children to understand how language is used to communicate. Such understanding allows listeners to go beyond the words they are hearing to grasp their actual meaning—as in instances of rhetorical questioning, sarcasm, irony, and the use of hyperbole or understatement to make a point. Over the course of the preschool years, children learn to take the perspective of their conversational partner, something that is clearly lacking in the example of the "conversation" between preschoolers Jenny and Chris, quoted earlier. Kindergarten-age listeners are able to make use of a conversational partner's perspective (e.g., by considering what information relevant to the conversation the partner does or doesn't have) to figure out what the partner means, and to provide a pertinent response (Nilsen & Graham, 2009).

They also learn to use information other than words to read between the lines in a conversation. For example, older preschoolers can exploit the vocal affect of an ambiguous statement to figure out a speaker's intention (Berman, Chambers, & Graham, 2010). When presented with two dolls—one intact, the other broken—and directed to "Look at the doll," Canadian English-speaking 4-year-olds (but not 3-year-olds) looked at the intact doll when the instruction was given with positive affect, and at the broken doll when the instruction was given with negative affect. In a more difficult task, in which children's emotional responses in a game conflicted with adults' emotional responses, Canadian English-speaking 4-year-olds were nevertheless able to make use of the adults' perspective to adjust their strategies in the game (Khu, Chambers, & Graham, 2018).

The development of conversational perspective-taking ability is related to children's level of executive function; as children become more able to control their tendency to assume their own perspective, it becomes easier for them to take the perspective of a conversational partner (Nilsen & Graham, 2009). Several recent studies suggest that children's own experiences with language influence their ability to take other people's perspective in communication settings. In tasks that require participants to take the experimenter's perspective, infants and young children who are monolingual perform worse than those who are bilingual—and also worse than those who, while not bilingual themselves, live in multilingual environments (Fan et al., 2015; Liberman et al., 2017). Bilingual children are also better at adapting to the needs of their communication partner than monolingual children (Gampe, Wermelinger, & Daum, 2019). Living in a diverse linguistic environment may attune children to the challenges of communication—and the need to take others' perspective in order to effectively communicate—in a way that monolingual environments do not.

Later Development

While children continue to develop their language skills beyond the ages of 5 or 6 years, this later development is less dramatic than in the early years of life. For example, the ability to sustain a conversation, which grows so dramatically in the preschool years, continues to improve into adulthood. School-age children become increasingly capable of reflecting upon and analyzing language, and they master more complex grammatical structures, such as the use of passive constructions in languages like English.

One consequence of schoolchildren's more reflective language skills is their increasing appreciation of the multiple meanings of words, which is responsible for the emergence of the endless series of puns, riddles, and jokes with which they delight themselves and torture their parents. They also are able to learn the meaning of new words by hearing them defined, a factor that helps their comprehension vocabulary expand—from the 10,000 words that the average 6-year-old knows to the 40,000 words estimated for 5th-graders (Anglin, 1993) to the average college-student vocabulary that has been estimated to be as high as 150,000 words (Miller & Gildea, 1987).

REVIEW QUESTION

How do the steps in perceptual and motor development described in Chapter 5 relate to the process of language development described in this section? ■

Theoretical Issues in Language Development

Universal Grammar a proposed set of highly abstract structures that are common to all languages

As you have seen throughout this chapter, there is ample evidence for both nature (the human brain) and nurture (language experience) in the process of language development. Despite the obvious interaction between the two, the nature–nurture debate continues to rage fiercely in the area of language development. Why?

Chomsky and the Nativist View

The modern study of language development emerged from a theoretical debate. In the 1950s, B. F. Skinner proposed a behaviourist theory of language development (Skinner, 1957). *Behaviourists* believed that development is a function of learning through reinforcement and punishment of overt behaviour. Skinner argued that parents teach children to speak by means of the same kinds of reinforcement techniques that are used to train animals to perform novel behaviours.

In what was probably the most influential book review ever published, Noam Chomsky (1959) countered Skinner by pointing out some of the reasons why language cannot be learned via reinforcement and punishment. One key reason was noted earlier in this chapter: we can understand and produce sentences that we have never heard before (generativity). If language-learning proceeds by means of reinforcement and punishment, how could we know that a sentence like "Colourless green ideas sleep furiously" is a grammatical English sentence, whereas "Green sleep colourless furiously ideas" is not (Chomsky, 1957)? Similarly, how could children produce words they have never heard before, like *wented* or *mouses*? Children appear to know details about the structure of our native language that we have not been taught—facts that are unobservable and thus impossible to reinforce—contrary to Skinner's proposal.

Chomsky proposed that humans are born with a **Universal Grammar**, a hard-wired set of principles and rules that govern grammar in all languages. Chomsky's account is consistent with the fact that, despite many surface differences, the world's languages are fundamentally similar. His strongly *nativist* account also provides an explanation for why most children learn language with exceptional rapidity, while nonhumans (who presumably lack a Universal Grammar) do not. (The Universal Grammar hypothesis is highly relevant to investigations of emerging languages like Nicaraguan Sign Language discussed in Box 6.4.)

Ongoing Debates in Language Development

Current theories of language development all acknowledge Chomsky's crucial observations, such as the fact that human languages share many characteristics. Theories must also explain how language users are able to generalize beyond the

According to theorist Noam Chomsky, all these children rely on the same innate linguistic structures in acquiring their various languages.

GERARD SIOEN/GAMMA-RAPHO VIA GETTY IMAGES

GLORIASALGADO/GETTY IMAGES

SUTIPORN SOMNAM/GETTY IMAGES

BOX 6.4 A CLOSER LOOK "I Just Can't Talk Without My Hands": What Gestures Tell Us About Language

People around the world gesture while they speak. The naturalness of gesturing is revealed by the fact that blind people gesture as they speak just as much as sighted individuals do, even when they know their listener is also blind (Iverson & Goldin-Meadow, 1998).

Infants often produce recognizable, meaningful gestures before they speak recognizable words. According to Acredolo and Goodwyn (1990), many "baby signs" are invented by infants themselves. One infant in their research signed "alligator" by putting her hands together and opening and closing them to imitate snapping jaws; another signalled "flower" by sniffing. Infants gain earlier motor control of their hands than of their vocal apparatus, facilitating the use of signs during the first year.

Interestingly, there is a relation between infants' use of gestures and later vocabulary size: infants who gesture more have larger vocabularies when measured months or even years later (e.g., Rowe, Ozcaliskan, & Goldin-Meadow, 2008; Salo, Rowe, & Reeb-Sutherland, 2018). Differences in the amount of gesturing by high- and low-SES families are one factor that influences the SES effects discussed in Box 6.2 (Rowe & Goldin-Meadow, 2009).

Especially dramatic evidence of intimate connections between gesture and language comes from remarkable research on children who have *created* their own gesture-based languages. Goldin-Meadow and colleagues studied congenitally deaf children whose hearing parents had little or no proficiency in any formal sign language (for review, see Brentari & Goldin-Meadow, 2017). These children and their parents created "homesigns" in order to communicate with one another, and the children's gesture vocabulary quickly outstripped that of their parents.

More important, the children in this study (but not the parents) *spontaneously* imposed a structure—a rudimentary grammar—on their gestures. Both groups of children used a grammatical structure that occurs in some languages but not those of their parents. As a result, the sign systems of the children were more similar to one another than to those of their own parents. The children's signs were also more complex than those of their parents.

The most extensive and extraordinary example of language creation by children comes from the invention of Nicaraguan Sign Language (NSL), a completely new language that has been evolving over the past 40 years.

SUSAN GOODWYN

This young participant in the research of Acredolo and Goodwyn is producing her idiosyncratic "baby sign" for pig.

Research on Infant Gestures from Linda Acredolo and Susan Goodwyn

COURTESY LINDA ACREDOLO AND SUSAN GOODWYN

specific words and sentences they have been exposed to, providing an explanation for findings like the "wug" study described earlier (Berko, 1958). But the ways in which various accounts handle these facts differ along two key dimensions. The first dimension is the degree to which these explanations lie within the child (*nature*) versus within the environment (*nurture*). The second dimension pertains to the child's contributions: Did the cognitive and neural mechanisms underlying language learning evolve solely to support language learning (*domain specific*), or are they used for learning many different kinds of things (*domain general*)?

With respect to the first dimension, theorists have countered Chomsky's argument about the universality of language structure by pointing out that there are also universals in children's environments. Parents all over the world need to communicate about certain things with their children, and these things are likely to be reflected in the language that children learn. For example, recall Table 6.1, which shows the remarkable overlap in the earliest words acquired across three diverse cultures (Tardif et al., 2008). These similarities reflect what parents and infants want to communicate about.

Indeed, accounts that are focused on social interaction maintain that virtually everything about language development is influenced by its communicative function. Children are motivated to interact with others, to communicate their own thoughts and feelings, and to understand what other people are trying to communicate to them. According to this position, children learn by paying close attention to the

structure and the environmental input and attempt to determine what is crucial when simulating children's language acquisition. One influential perspective is **connectionism**, a type of computational model that emphasizes the simultaneous activity of numerous interconnected processing units. Connectionist researchers simulate various aspects of cognitive development, including language acquisition. The model learns from experience, gradually strengthening certain connections among units in ways that mimic children's developmental progress. Connectionist accounts have achieved impressive success with respect to modeling specific aspects of language development, including children's acquisition of the past tense in English and the development of the shape bias for word learning (e.g., Rumelhart & McClelland, 1986; Samuelson, 2002). However, connectionist models are open to criticism regarding the features that were built into the models in the first place (e.g., do they have the same "innate" constraints as infants?) and how well the input provided to them matches the input received by real children.

connectionism a computational modeling approach that emphasizes the simultaneous activity of numerous interconnected processing units

dual representation treating a symbolic artefact both as a real object and as a symbol for something other than itself

REVIEW QUESTION

How do your own experiences with language development—yours or someone else's which you observed—align with the various theories described in this section? ■

Nonlinguistic Symbols and Development

Although language is our preeminent symbol system, humans have invented a wealth of other symbols for communication. Virtually anything can serve as a symbol so long as it stands for something other than itself. We regularly encounter symbols ranging from the printed words, numbers, graphs, photographs, and drawings in your textbooks to thousands of everyday items such as app icons, maps, and clocks.

Symbolic proficiency involves both the mastery of the symbolic creations of others and the creation of new symbolic representations; we will consider the development of each of these functions in turn. In Chapter 7, we will consider children's creation of symbolic relations in pretend play, and in Chapter 8, we will examine older children's development of two of the most important of all symbolic activities—reading and mathematics.

Using Symbols as Information

The primary function of many symbols is to provide useful information. For example, a map—whether a crude sketch or a Google map—can be crucial for locating a particular place. Using a symbolic artefact such as a map requires **dual representation**; that is, the artefact must be represented mentally in two ways at the same time, as a real object and as a symbol for something other than itself.

Young children have substantial difficulty with dual representation, finding it challenging to treat an object both as itself and as a representation of something else. Their difficulties are reminiscent of Piaget's preoperational stage, in which children have difficulty considering multiple dimensions of objects simultaneously (as in conservation tasks). Challenges with dual representation limit toddlers' ability to exploit symbolic artefacts. A classic demonstration uses scale models to symbolize full-size rooms. In this method, a young child watches as an experimenter hides a miniature toy in a scale model of the regular-sized room next

FIGURE 6.16 Scale-model task In a test of young children's ability to use a symbol as a source of information, a 3-year-old child watches as the experimenter (Judy DeLoache) hides a miniature troll doll under a pillow in a scale model of an adjacent room. The child searches successfully for a larger troll doll hidden in the corresponding place in the actual room, indicating that she appreciates the relation between the model and room.

door (Figure 6.16) (DeLoache, 1987). The child is then asked to find a larger version of the toy that the child is told "is hiding in the same place in the big room." Three-year-olds readily use their knowledge of the location of the miniature toy in the model to figure out where the large toy is in the adjacent room. In contrast, most 2½-year-old children fail to find the large toy; they seem to have no idea that the model refers to the full-size room. Because the model is so interesting in and of itself, young children fail to notice the symbolic relation between the model and the room it stands for. Lacking a firm grasp of dual representation, they do not treat the model as both an object and as a representation of the large room.

This interpretation received strong support in a study with 2½-year-old children in which reasoning between a model and a larger space was not necessary (DeLoache, Miller, & Rosengren, 1997). An experimenter showed each child a "shrinking machine" (really an oscilloscope with lots of dials and lights) and explained that the machine could "make things get little." The child watched as a troll doll was hidden in a movable tentlike room (approximately 8 feet by 6 feet) and the shrinking machine was "turned on." Then the child and experimenter waited in another room while the shrinking machine did its job. When they returned, a small-scale model of the tentlike room stood in place of the original. (Assistants had, of course, removed the original tent and replaced it with the scale model.) When asked to find the troll, the children succeeded.

Why should the idea of a shrinking machine enable these 2½-year-olds to perform the task? The answer is that if a child believes the experimenter's claims about the shrinking machine, then in the child's mind the model simply *is* the room. Hence, there is no symbolic relation between the two spaces and no need for dual representation.

Another example where symbolic representations may lead to challenges comes from forensic psychology. Investigators often use anatomically detailed dolls to interview young children in cases of suspected sexual abuse, assuming that the relation between the doll and themselves would be obvious. However, children younger than 5 years often fail to make any connection between themselves and the doll, so the use of a doll does not improve their memory reports and may even make them less reliable (e.g., DeLoache & Marzolf, 1995). Young children have particular difficulty with self-symbols—symbols intended to represent themselves—even when the symbols are the same size as the child (Herold & Akhtar, 2014). For this reason, current practice in child forensics discourages the use of interview props with young children and focuses instead on building rapport, asking open-ended questions, and encouraging children to draw as a way to comfort themselves during stressful interviews (e.g., Johnson et al., 2016; Katz, Barnetz, & Hershkowitz, 2014).

Increasing ability to achieve dual representation—to immediately interpret a symbol in terms of what it stands for—enables children to discover the abstract nature of various symbolic artefacts. For example, unlike younger children, school-age children realize that the red line on a road map does not mean that the real road would be red (Liben & Myers, 2007). This developing ability is affected by children's experiences. Cross-cultural studies reveal that in cultures where pictures are ubiquitous, as in most parts of Canada, younger children are more likely to understand that pictures can serve a symbolic function than in cultures where children are rarely exposed to pictures, such as rural villages in India and Peru (Callaghan, Rochat, & Corbit, 2012).

Indeed, the advances in picture perception that we discussed in Box 5.2 provide evidence for early forms of symbolic understanding. Canadian infants as young as 13 months of age understand that properties of objects presented in pictures can be extended to real objects (Keates, Graham, & Ganea, 2014). These findings suggest that even at this early age, infants are able to detect links between images of objects and actual objects. By age 4, children interpret images of scenes using the same geometric abilities that guide their navigation in the real world (Dillon & Spelke, 2015). Thus, with experience comes the ability to engage in the kinds of abstractions necessary to understand dual representations like maps and mathematical manipulatives. Increased understanding of dual representation may also help children to avoid the types of action errors shown in Figure 5.14, such as when children attempt to climb into a doll-sized car or sit on a tiny chair (Jiang & Rosengren, 2018). By coming to understand that the tiny car and chair are symbols for their real-life counterparts, children become better able to inhibit the motor behaviours typically associated with climbing into cars and sitting on chairs.

Drawing and Writing

When young children first start making marks on paper, their focus is almost exclusively on the activity per se, with no attempt to produce recognizable images. At about 3 or 4 years of age, most children begin trying to draw pictures *of* something; they try to produce representational art (Callaghan, 1999). Exposure to representational symbols affects the age at which children begin to produce them. One cross-cultural study (Callaghan et al., 2011) found that children from homes filled with pictorial images (a rural Nova Scotian sample) produce such images earlier and more often than children from homes with few such images (rural Indian and Peruvian samples).

Initially, children's artistic impulses outstrip their motor and planning capabilities. Figure 6.17 shows what at first appears simply to be a classic scribble. However, the 2½-year-old artist was narrating as he drew, making it possible to ascertain his intentions. While he represented the individual elements of his picture reasonably well, he was unable to coordinate them spatially.

Just as infants who are first beginning to speak simplify their first words, young children simplify their drawings, as shown in Figure 6.18. Even for these very crude shapes, the child must plan the drawing and must spatially coordinate the individual elements; the "tadpole" people do have the legs on the bottom and the arms on the side—although often emerging from the head.

Figure 6.19 reveals some of the strategies children use to produce more complex pictures. The drawing depicts the route from the artist's home to the local grocery store. The child relied on a well-practiced formula for representing houses: a rectangle with a door and a roofline. Another strategy is to coordinate the placement of each house with respect to the road, at the cost of the overall coordination among the houses.

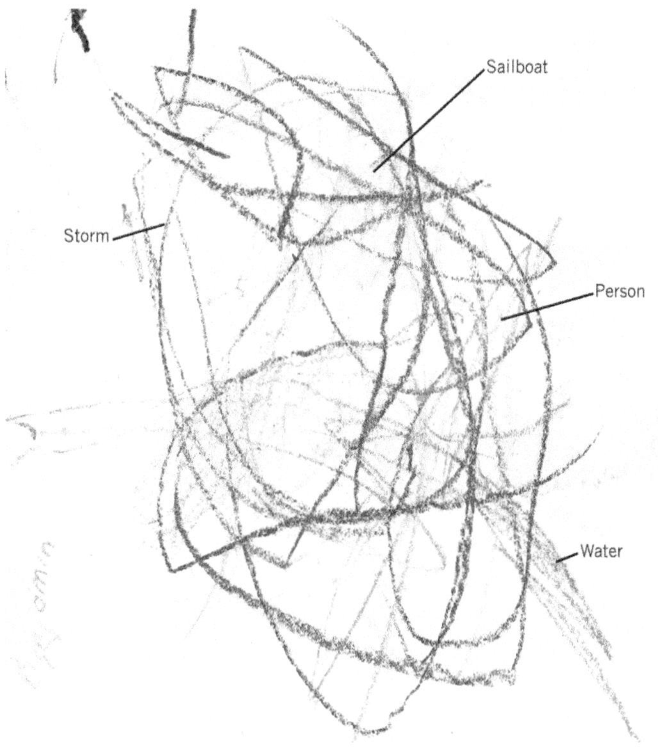

FIGURE 6.17 Early drawing This is not random scribbling, as shown by the 2½-year-old artist's verbal commentary. As he drew a roughly triangular shape, he said it was a "sailboat." A set of wavy lines was labelled "water." Some scribbled lines under the "sailboat" were denoted as the "person driving the boat." Finally, the wild scribbles all over the rest were "a storm." Thus, each element was representational to some degree, even though the picture as a whole did not appear as such.

FIGURE 6.18 **Tadpole drawings**
Young children's early drawings of people typically take a "tadpole" form.

Children's scribbles also reflect their emerging understanding of writing. Even in their earliest scribbles, before age 3, children produce different types of scribbles when writing versus drawing (D. W. Rowe, 2008). This finding is also true for preschoolers growing up with writing systems like Chinese, with characters that more closely resemble drawings (Treiman & Yin, 2011). By age 4, children understand a key difference between writing and drawing, namely that written words correspond to specific spoken words, whereas a drawing can correspond to many different words (Treiman et al., 2016). As with the development of dual representation described earlier, children initially depend on perceptual similarity between the symbol and what it is intended to represent; for example, longer words may be "written" with longer scribbles (e.g., Uttal & Yuan, 2014).

FIGURE 6.19 **More complex drawings** This child's drawing relies on some well-practiced strategies, but the child has not yet worked out how to represent complex spatial relationships.

REVIEW QUESTIONS

How does the development of symbol use relate to the development of language? What steps do these two processes share? ■

CHAPTER SUMMARY

A critical feature of what it means to be human is the creative and flexible use of one or more of a variety of languages and other symbols. The enormous power of language comes from the fact that this system is generative—a finite set of words can be used to generate an infinite number of sentences.

Language Development

- Acquiring a language involves learning the complex systems of phonology, semantics, syntax, and pragmatics that govern its sounds, meaning, grammar, and use.
- Language ability is species-specific. The first prerequisite for its full-fledged development is a human brain. Nonhuman animals do not learn full-fledged human languages.
- The early years constitute a sensitive period for language acquisition; many aspects of language are more difficult to acquire thereafter.
- A second prerequisite for language development is exposure to language. Much of the language babies hear takes the form of infant-directed speech (IDS).

The Process of Language Acquisition

- Infants have remarkable speech-perception abilities. Like adults, they exhibit categorical perception of speech sounds, perceiving physically similar sounds as belonging to discrete categories. As they learn the sounds that are important in their language(s), infants' ability to distinguish between non-native sounds declines.
- Infants are remarkably sensitive to the distributional properties of language and use them to segment words from fluent speech.
- Infants begin to babble at around 7 months of age, either repeating syllables ("bababa") or, if exposed to sign language, using repetitive hand movements.
- During the second half of the first year, infants learn how to communicate with other people, including developing the ability to establish joint attention.
- Infants begin to recognize highly familiar words at about 6 months of age, and they begin to produce words at about 1 year of age. Infants use a variety of strategies to figure out what new words mean.
- By the end of their second year, most toddlers produce short sentences. The length and complexity of their utterances gradually increase.
- In the early preschool years, children exhibit generalization, extending such patterns as "add *-s* to make plural" to novel nouns, and making overregularization errors.
- Children develop their burgeoning language skills as they go from collective monologues to sustained conversation.

Theoretical Issues in Language Development

- All current theories agree that there is an interaction between innate factors and experience.
- Nativists such as the influential linguist Noam Chomsky posit an innate knowledge of Universal Grammar, the set of highly abstract rules common to all languages.
- Theorists focused on social interaction emphasize the communicative context of language development and use.
- Other perspectives argue that language learning requires powerful general-purpose cognitive mechanisms.

Nonlinguistic Symbols and Development

- Symbolic artefacts like maps or models require dual representation. To use them, children must represent both the object itself and its symbolic relation to what it stands for.
- Drawing and writing are popular symbolic activities. Young children's early scribbling quickly gives way to the intention to draw pictures *of* something. Early attempts at writing, while illegible, contain some characteristics of mature writing systems.

Test Yourself

1. Language ____________ refers to the understanding of what others say; language ____________ refers to the process of speaking.
   a. comprehension; production
   b. development; generativity
   c. pragmatics; semantics
   d. perception; distribution

2. The smallest units of meaning in a language, such as the English words *dog* or *mom,* are called ____________.
   a. morphemes
   b. syntactic patterns
   c. phonemes
   d. semantics

3. The understanding of the cultural contexts of language—including shifts in tone and body language, which allow two strangers who speak the same language to successfully communicate—is known as ___________ knowledge.
   a. semantic
   b. syntactic
   c. pragmatic
   d. phonological
4. Between 6 and 12 months of age, infants typically experience a linguistic perceptual narrowing. What effect does this change have on their language development?
   a. They become increasingly more sensitive to non-native speech sounds.
   b. They focus more on the words they hear most frequently.
   c. They become increasingly less sensitive to non-native speech sounds.
   d. Their ability to distinguish between speech and other environmental sounds diminishes.
5. Emily is given two pictures: one shows a flower, a word she already knows, and the other shows a unicorn, which is new to her. When asked to point to the "unicorn," Emily points to the unknown image, which is of a unicorn. Which assumption is Emily making in order to learn this new word?
   a. Social contexts
   b. Intentionality
   c. Mutual exclusivity
   d. Grammatical categorization
6. Which of the following statements is *not* true of infant-directed speech (IDS)?
   a. The exaggerated tone and pitch of IDS is often accompanied by exaggerated facial expressions.
   b. Infants tend to prefer infant-directed speech to adult-directed speech.
   c. Evidence suggests that IDS is a universal practice across all cultures.
   d. Infant-directed signing has similar attributes to infant-directed speech but in the visual modality.
7. The tendency of specific sounds to frequently recur in a language is known as ___________.
   a. distributional properties
   b. overregularization
   c. syntactic bootstrapping
   d. prosody
8. Thirteen-month-old Christian calls all men "Dad." This is an example of ___________.
   a. pragmatic learning
   b. syntactic bootstrapping
   c. mapping
   d. overextension
9. Six- to 8-month-old infants are better able to distinguish between phonemes spoken in a non-native language than are infants who are just a few years older. This phenomenon is explained by ___________.
   a. prosody
   b. perceptual narrowing
   c. underextension
   d. overextension
10. Two-year-old Ravi goes to the zoo with his mother. Even though he has never heard of a giraffe or seen one before, when his mother points to an animal and calls it a "giraffe," Ravi then calls that animal a giraffe. This exchange demonstrates Ravi's use of ___________.
    a. pragmatic cues
    b. cross-situational word learning
    c. language mixing
    d. telegraphic speech
11. Using the structure of a sentence to derive the meaning of a novel word is known as ___________.
    a. telegraphic speech
    b. Universal Grammar
    c. syntactic bootstrapping
    d. pragmatics
12. Preschoolers Ahmed and Max are talking together. Ahmed says that his father is old. Max says that he likes cars. Ahmed says that his father is probably more than 10 years old. Max says that he likes blue cars the best. According to Piaget, Ahmed and Max are engaging in ___________.
    a. babbling
    b. private speech
    c. dual representation
    d. collective monologues
13. Chomsky's proposition that humans are born with an understanding of the basic principles and rules that govern all language is known as ___________.
    a. mutual exclusivity theory
    b. the behaviourist theory of language development
    c. Universal Grammar
    d. the connectionist model
14. ___________, a computational modeling approach that has been applied to language development, emphasizes the simultaneous activity of numerous interconnected processing units.
    a. Generative theory
    b. The distributional perspective
    c. Dual representation theory
    d. Connectionism
15. *Dual representation* refers to one's ability to ___________.
    a. communicate both verbally and nonverbally
    b. understand a symbolic artefact as both a real object and as a symbol for something else
    c. understand that a single word may have more than one meaning
    d. distinguish between the words that someone uses and the intention behind those words

LaunchPad
macmillan learning

DON'T STOP NOW! Research shows that testing yourself is a powerful learning tool. Visit LaunchPad to access the LearningCurve adaptive quizzing system, which gives you a personalized study plan to help build your mastery of the chapter material through videos, activities, and more. **Go to launchpadworks.com.**

Critical Thinking Questions

1. Drawing on the many parental behaviours that were discussed in this chapter, give some examples of how parents influence their children's language development.
2. Language development is a particularly complex aspect of child development, and no single theory successfully accounts for all that is known about how children acquire language. Would you weight the child's contributions (nature) or the environment's contributions (nurture) more strongly?
3. What are overregularization errors, and why do they offer strong evidence for the acquisition of grammatical structures by children?
4. Many parallels were drawn between the process of language acquisition in children learning spoken language and in those learning sign language. What do these similarities tell us about the basis for human language?

Key Terms

babbling, p. 207
bilingualism, p. 201
categorical perception, p. 203
collective monologues, p. 219
comprehension, p. 195
connectionism, p. 225
cross-situational word learning, p. 215
distributional properties, p. 206
dual representation, p. 225
generative, p. 196
infant-directed speech (IDS), p. 200
morphemes, p. 196
narratives, p. 219
overextension, p. 209
overregularization, p. 218
phonemes, p. 196
pragmatic cues, p. 211
pragmatics, p. 197
production, p. 195
prosody, p. 203
symbols, p. 195
syntactic bootstrapping, p. 215
syntax, p. 196
telegraphic speech, p. 217
underextension, p. 210
Universal Grammar, p. 221
voice onset time (VOT), p. 203
word segmentation, p. 205

Answers to Test Yourself

1. a, **2.** a, **3.** c, **4.** c, **5.** c, **6.** c, **7.** a, **8.** d, **9.** b, **10.** a, **11.** c, **12.** d, **13.** c, **14.** d, **15.** b

CHAPTER

7 Conceptual Development

CHRISTIES IMAGES/PRIVATE COLLECTION/BRIDGEMAN IMAGES

JOHN GEORGE BROWN (1813–1913), *The Little Joker* (oil on canvas)

Understanding Who or What

Understanding Why, Where, When, and How Many

THEMES

NATURE AND NURTURE ■ THE ACTIVE CHILD

MECHANISMS OF CHANGE ■ THE SOCIOCULTURAL CONTEXT

Shawna, an 8-month-old, crawls into her 7-year-old brother's bedroom. The room contains many objects, among them a bed, a dresser, a dog, a puck, a hockey stick, books, magazines, shoes, and dirty socks. To her older brother, the room includes furniture, clothing, reading material, and sports equipment. But what does the room look like to Shawna?

Infants lack concepts of furniture, reading material, and sports equipment. They also lack more specific concepts such as hockey sticks and books. Thus, Shawna does not understand the scene in the same way as her older brother. However, without knowledge of child development research, an observer would not know whether a baby as young as Shawna has formed other concepts relevant to understanding the scene. Has she formed concepts of living and nonliving things that help her understand why the dog runs around but the books never do? Has she formed concepts of heavier and lighter that allow her to understand why she could pick up a sock but not a dresser? Has she formed concepts of before and after that allow her to understand that her brother always puts on his socks before his shoes rather than in the opposite order? Or is it all a jumble to her?

As this imaginary scene indicates, concepts are crucial for people to make sense of the world. But what exactly are concepts, and how do they help us understand the world?

Concepts are general ideas that organize objects, events, qualities, or relations on the basis of some similarity. There are infinite possible concepts because there are infinite ways in which objects or events can be similar. For example, objects can have similar shapes (all soccer fields are rectangular), materials (all diamonds are made of compressed carbon), sizes (all skyscrapers are tall), tastes (all lemons are sour), colours (all colas are brown), functions (all knives are for cutting), and so on.

Concepts help us understand the world and act effectively in it by allowing us to generalize from prior experience. If we like the taste of one carrot, we probably will like the taste of others. Concepts also tell us how to react emotionally to new experiences, as when we fear all dogs after being bitten by one. Life without concepts would be unthinkable: every situation would be new, and we would have no idea what past experience would be relevant in a new situation.

concepts general ideas or understandings that can be used to group together objects, events, qualities, or abstractions that are similar in some way

Several themes are especially prominent in research on conceptual development. One is *nature and nurture:* children's concepts reflect the interaction between their specific experiences and their biological predispositions to process information in particular ways. Another recurring theme is the *active child:* from infancy onward, many of children's concepts reflect their active attempts to make sense of the world. A third major theme is *how change occurs:* researchers who study conceptual development attempt to understand not only what concepts children form but also the processes by which they form them. A fourth is the *sociocultural context:* the concepts we form are influenced by the society in which we live.

What does this infant see when he looks at this room?

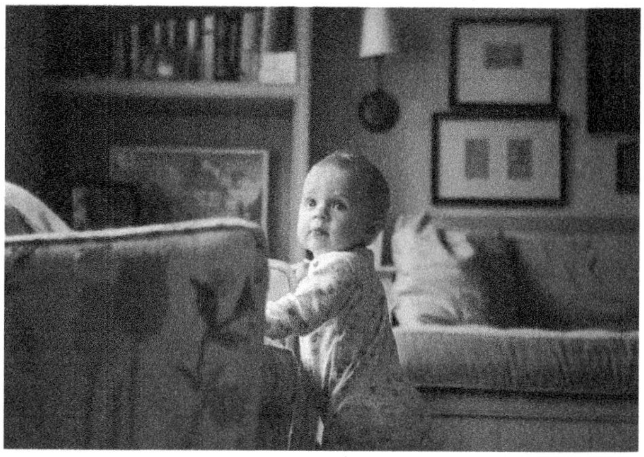

CAVAN IMAGES/GETTY IMAGES

Although there is widespread agreement that conceptual development reflects the interaction of nature and nurture, the particulars of this interaction are hotly debated. The controversy parallels the nativist/empiricist controversies described previously in the context of theories of cognitive development (Chapter 4), perceptual development (Chapter 5), and language development (Chapter 6). In the context of conceptual development, nativists, such as Liz Spelke (2011), Alan Leslie (Scholl & Leslie, 2001), and Karen Wynn (2008), believe that innate understanding of basic concepts plays a central role in development. They argue that infants are born with some sense of fundamental concepts, such as time, space, number, causality, and the human mind, or with specialized learning mechanisms that allow them to acquire rudimentary understanding of these concepts unusually quickly and easily. Within the nativist perspective, nurture plays an important role in helping children move beyond this initial level of conceptual understanding, but not in forming the basic understanding.

By contrast, empiricists, such as Vladimir Sloutsky (2010), Scott Johnson (2010), Lisa Oakes (Baumgartner & Oakes, 2013), and Marianella Casasola (2008), argue that nature endows infants with only general learning mechanisms, such as the ability to perceive, attend, associate, generalize, and remember. Within the empiricist perspective, the rapid and universal formation of fundamental concepts such as time, space, number, causality, and mind arises from infants' massive exposure to experiences that are relevant to these concepts. Empiricists also maintain that the data on which many nativist arguments are based—such as data involving infants' looking times in habituation studies—are not sufficient to support the nativists' conclusions that infants understand the concepts in question (Campos et al., 2008; Kagan, 2008). The continuing debate between nativists and empiricists reflects a fundamental, unresolved question about human nature: Do children form all concepts through the same learning mechanisms, or do they also possess special mechanisms for forming a few particularly important concepts?

This chapter focuses on the development of fundamental concepts—those that are useful in the greatest number of situations. These concepts fall into two groups. One group of fundamental concepts is used to categorize the kinds of things that exist in the world—human beings, living things in general, and inanimate objects—and their properties. The other group of fundamental concepts involves dimensions used to represent our experiences: space (where the experience occurred), time (when it occurred), number (how many times it occurred), and causality (why it occurred).

You may have noticed that these fundamental concepts correspond closely to the questions that every news story should answer: Who or what? Where? When? Why? How? The similarity between the concepts that are most fundamental for children and those that are most important in news stories is no accident. Knowing who or what, where, when, how many, and why is essential for understanding any event.

Because early conceptual development is so crucial, this chapter focuses on development in the first 5 years. This does not mean that conceptual growth ends at age 5. Beyond this age, children form vast numbers of more specialized concepts, and their understanding of all types of concepts deepens for many years thereafter. Rather, the focus on early conceptual development reflects the fact that this is the period in which children acquire a basic understanding of the most crucial concepts—those that are universal, that allow children to understand their own and other people's experiences, and that provide the foundations for subsequent conceptual growth.

Understanding Who or What

How can infants and young children make sense of the innumerable objects they encounter? What they seem to do is adopt a kind of divide-and-conquer strategy, in which they quickly divide the objects into three general categories: inanimate objects, people, and other animals (they are unsure for many years whether plants are more like animals or more like inanimate objects) (Gelman & Kalish, 2006).

Dividing Objects into Categories

Forming broad divisions for inanimate objects, people, and other animals is crucial because different types of concepts apply to different types of objects (Keil, 1979). Some concepts apply to anything—all things, living and nonliving, have height, weight, colour, size, texture, and so on. Other concepts apply only to living things—only living things eat, drink, grow, and breathe, for example. Yet other concepts, such as reading, shopping, pondering, and gossiping, apply only to people. Forming these general categories of objects allows children to draw accurate inferences about unfamiliar entities. For instance, when told that a platypus is a kind of animal, children know immediately that a platypus can move, eat, grow, reproduce, and so on.

In addition to dividing objects into these very general categories, children form innumerable more specific categories: vehicles, tools, furniture, sports equipment, and endless others. Children tend to organize these categories of objects into **category hierarchies**—that is, categories organized according to set–subset relations. These category hierarchies help them make finer distinctions among the objects within each level. The furniture/chair/La-Z-Boy hierarchy shown in Table 7.1 is one example. The category "furniture" includes all chairs; the category "chair" includes all La-Z-Boys. Forming such category hierarchies greatly simplifies the world for children by allowing them to draw accurate inferences. Knowing that a La-Z-Boy recliner is a kind of chair allows children to use their general knowledge of chairs to infer that people sit on La-Z-Boys and that La-Z-Boys are neither lazy nor boys.

category hierarchy a category that is organized by set–subset relations, such as animal/dog/poodle

Of course, infants are not born knowing about La-Z-Boys and chairs, nor are they born knowing the other categories shown in Table 7.1. How do infants and older children form categories that apply to all kinds of objects, living and nonliving?

Categorization of Objects in Infancy

Even in the first months of life, infants form categories of objects. Quinn and Eimas (1996), for example, found that when 3- and 4-month-olds were shown a series of photographs of cats, they habituated to the general category of cats; that is, they looked at novel cat photographs for less and less time. However, when the infants were subsequently shown a picture of a dog, lion, or other animal, they dishabituated; that is, their looking time increased. Their habituation to the cat photographs suggests that the infants saw all the cats, despite their differences in colour, size, striping, and so on, as members of a single category; the infants'

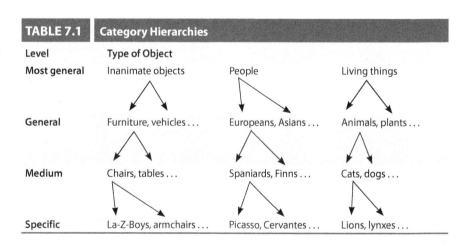

TABLE 7.1 Category Hierarchies

Level	Type of Object		
Most general	Inanimate objects	People	Living things
General	Furniture, vehicles . . .	Europeans, Asians . . .	Animals, plants . . .
Medium	Chairs, tables . . .	Spaniards, Finns . . .	Cats, dogs . . .
Specific	La-Z-Boys, armchairs . . .	Picasso, Cervantes . . .	Lions, lynxes . . .

perceptual categorization the grouping together of objects that have similar appearances

superordinate level the general level within a category hierarchy, such as "animal" in the animal/dog/poodle example

subordinate level the most specific level within a category hierarchy, such as "poodle" in the animal/dog/poodle example

basic level the middle level, and often the first level learned, within a category hierarchy, such as "dog" in the animal/dog/poodle example

subsequent dishabituation to the photo of the dog or other kind of animal suggests that they saw those creatures as members of categories other than cats.

Infants also form categories more general than "cats." Behl-Chadha (1996) found that 6-month-olds habituated after repeatedly being shown pictures of different types of mammals (dogs, zebras, elephants, and so forth) and then dishabituated when they were shown a picture of a bird or a fish. The infants apparently perceived similarities among the mammals that led to their eventually losing interest in them, and perceived differences between the mammals and the bird or fish that led them to show renewed interest.

As suggested by this example, infants frequently use **perceptual categorization**, the grouping together of objects that have somewhat similar appearances (Cohen & Cashon, 2006; Madole & Oakes, 1999). Prior to participating in the Behl-Chadha (1996) study, few if any of the infants would have seen zebras or elephants. Thus, the distinctions the infants made between the mammals on one hand and the birds and fish on the other had to be made on the basis of their appearance.

Infants categorize objects along many perceptual dimensions, including colour, size, and movement. Sometimes their categorization is largely based on specific parts of an object rather than on the object as a whole; for example, infants younger than 18 months rely heavily on the presence of legs to categorize objects as animals, and they rely heavily on the presence of wheels to categorize objects as vehicles (Rakison & Lupyan, 2008a).

One of the key dimensions that infants use to categorize objects is overall shape. This is a useful assumption because, for many objects, shape indeed is similar for different members of a category. If we see a silhouette of a cat, hammer, or chair, we can use the shape to identify the object. However, we rarely can do the same if we know only the object's colour or size. This reliance on shape for categorization emerges early in development. For example, when 15-month-old Canadian infants were shown an unfamiliar object with a specific property (e.g., it makes a sound when squeezed), they assumed that other objects of the same shape also share that property even when the objects differ from one another in size and colour (Graham & Diesendruck, 2010).

Categorization of Objects Beyond Infancy

As children move beyond infancy, they increasingly grasp not only individual categories but also hierarchical and causal relations among categories.

Category hierarchies The category hierarchies that young children form often include three of the levels in Table 7.1: the general one, which is called the **superordinate level**; the very specific one, called the **subordinate level**; and the medium or in-between one, called the **basic level** (Rosch et al., 1976). As its name suggests, the basic level is the one that children usually learn first. Thus, they typically form categories of medium generality, such as "tree," before they form more general categories such as "plant" or more specific ones such as "oak."

It is not surprising that children tend to form basic-level categories first. A basic-level category such as "tree" has a number of consistent characteristics: bark, branches, relatively large size, and so on. In contrast, the more general category "plant" has fewer consistent characteristics: plants come in a wide range of shapes, sizes, and colours (consider an oak, a rose, and a house plant). Subordinate-level categories have the same consistent characteristics as the basic-level category, and some additional ones—all maples, but not all trees, have rough bark and pointed leaves, for example. However, it is relatively difficult to discriminate among different subordinate categories within the same basic-level category (maples versus oaks, for example).

Very young children's basic categories do not always match those of adults. For example, rather than forming separate categories of cars, motorcycles, and buses, young children seem to group these objects together into a category of "objects with wheels" (Mandler & McDonough, 1998). Even in such cases, however, the initial categories are less general than such categories as "moving things" and more general than ones such as "Toyotas."

Having formed basic-level categories, how do children go on to form superordinate and subordinate categories? Part of the answer is that parents and others use the child's basic-level categories as a foundation for explaining more specific and more general categories (Gelman et al., 1998). When parents teach children superordinate categories such as furniture, they typically illustrate properties of the relevant terms with basic-level examples that the child already knows (Callanan, 1990). They might say, "Furniture includes things, like chairs, tables, and sofas that people have inside their houses and that make living there more comfortable."

Parents also refer to basic-level categories to teach children subordinate-level terms (Callanan & Sabbagh, 2004; Waxman & Senghas, 1992). For example, a parent might say, "Belugas are a kind of whale." Preschoolers are sensitive to the nuances of such statements; for instance, they generalize more widely from categorical statements such as "Belugas are a kind of whale" than from statements about specific objects, such as "This beluga is a whale" (Chambers, Graham, & Turner, 2008; Cimpian & Scott, 2012). Sensitivity to the differences between these kinds of statements emerges early in development. One study found that 30-month-olds learning Canadian-English were more likely to generalize properties of unfamiliar objects when they heard categorical-type statements (e.g., "Wugs drink milk") versus when they heard more specific sentences (e.g., "These wugs drink milk") (Graham, Nayer, & Gelman, 2011). Thus, statements that specify relations among categories of objects allow children to use what they already know about basic-level categories to form superordinate- and subordinate-level categories.

Although parents' explanations clearly enhance children's conceptual understanding, the learning path sometimes involves amusing detours. In one such case, Susan Gelman (2003) gave her 2-year-old son a spoon and a container filled with bite-size pieces of fruit and said, "This is a fruit cup." The boy responded to her description by picking up the "cup" and attempting to drink the fruit in it. After all, that's what you do with cups.

Causal understanding and categorization Even in their first months, infants have a rudimentary understanding of causal interactions among objects, such as interactions involving gravity, inertia, and support, an understanding that gradually increases during their first year. At 3 months of age, infants look longer if a box that is released in midair remains suspended (as in Figure 7.1a) rather than falling (Baillargeon, Needham, & DeVos, 1992; Needham & Baillargeon, 1993). However, as long as there is any contact at all between the box and the support, 3-month-olds do not react when the box remains stationary (as in Figures 7.1b and 7.1c).

By approximately 5 months of age, infants appreciate the relevance of the type of contact involved in support. They now know that the box will be stable only if it is released on top of the support, so they would be surprised by the display in Figure 7.1b. Roughly a month later, they recognize the importance of the amount of contact, looking longer when the box in Figure 7.1c stays put with only a small portion of its bottom surface on the support. Shortly after their 1st birthday, infants also take into account the shape of the object and hence are surprised if an asymmetrical object like that shown in Figure 7.1d remains stable.

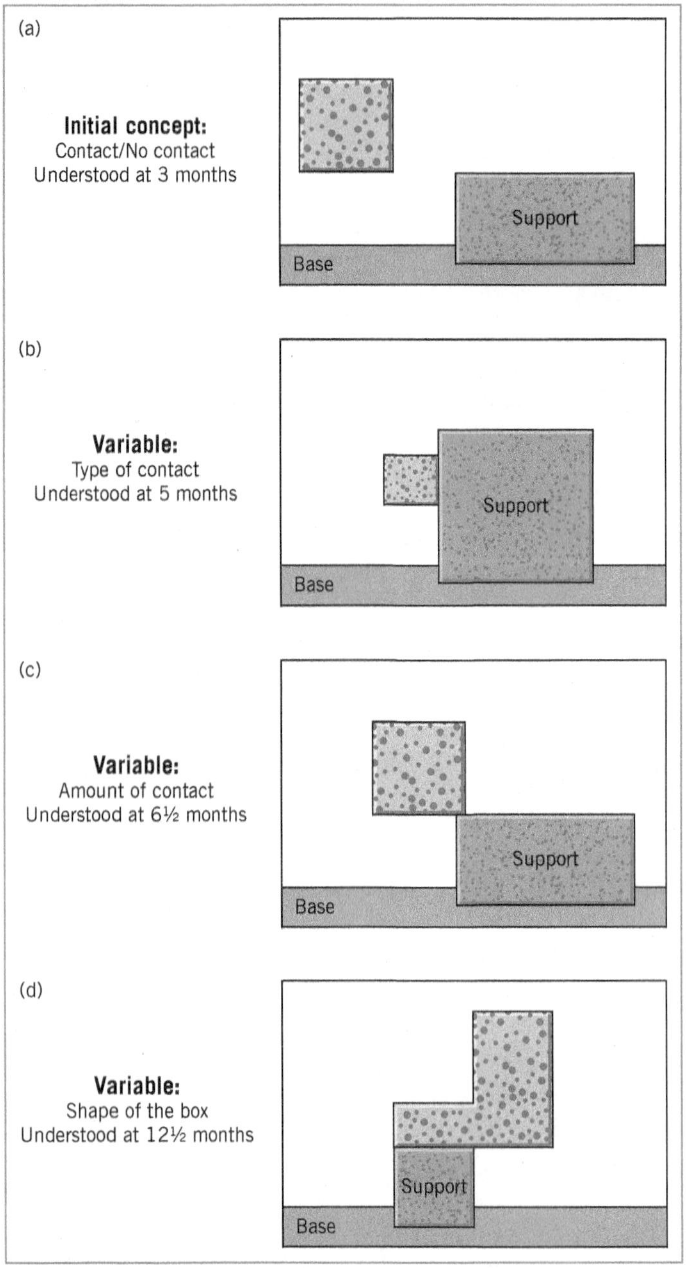

FIGURE 7.1 Infants' developing understanding of support relations In all four parts of the figure, the relation of interest is that between a grey support, which is resting on a brown base (such as a table top), and a pink object, which varies in its location relative to the grey support. (a) 3-month-olds show surprise (through longer looking times) when the pink object is not in contact with the support and does not fall; (b) by 5 months of age, infants also show surprise when the pink object is in contact with the side of the support but does not fall; (c) by 6½ months of age, infants also show surprise when the pink object does not fall, despite only a small part of it being above and in contact with the support; (d) by 12½ months of age, infants also show surprise when the pink object does not fall despite a substantial part, but not most of it, being above and in contact with the support. (Information from Baillargeon, 1998)

This causal understanding extends to moving as well as stationary objects. Five-month-olds look longer at an object that travels more slowly as it rolls down a slope than at one that picks up speed as it descends (Kim & Spelke, 1992). They also seem to know that an object cannot pass through a grid with openings smaller than the object, though liquids can (Hespos et al., 2016).

Development of understanding of causal relations, of course, continues long after infancy. One reason is that young children actively seek knowledge about causes. Toddlers and preschoolers are notorious for their endless questions about causes and reasons. "Why do dogs bark?" "How does the phone know where to call?" "Where does rain come from?" Parents are often exasperated by such questions, but respecting and answering children in informative ways can help them learn (Chouinard, 2007).

Understanding causal relations is crucial in forming many categories. How could children form the category of "light switches," for example, if they did not understand that flipping or pushing certain objects causes lights to go on and off? To study how an understanding of causes and effects influences category formation, Krascum and Andrews (1998) told 4- and 5-year-olds about two categories of imaginary animals: wugs and gillies. Some of the preschoolers were provided only physical descriptions of the animals: they were told that wugs usually have claws on their feet, spikes on the end of their tails, horns on their heads, and armor on their backs; gillies were described as usually having wings, big ears, long tails, and long toes. Other children were provided the same physical descriptions, plus a simple causal story that explained why wugs and gillies are the way they are. These children were told that wugs have claws, spikes, horns, and armor because they like to fight. Gillies, in contrast, do not like to fight; instead, they hide in trees. Their big ears let them hear approaching wugs, their wings let them fly away to treetops, and so on. After the children in both groups were given the information about these animals, they were shown the pictures in Figure 7.2 and asked which animal was a wug and which animal was a gilly.

The children who were told why wugs and gillies have the physical features they do were better at classifying the pictures into the appropriate categories. When tested the next day, those children also remembered the categories better than did the children who were given the physical descriptions without explanations. Thus, understanding cause–effect relations helps children learn and remember.

Understanding Oneself and Other People

Although understanding of oneself and others varies greatly among people, just about everybody has a commonsense level of psychological understanding. This **naïve psychology** is crucial to normal human functioning and is a major part of what makes us human. Adult chimpanzees are the equal of human 2½-year-olds on a wide range of tasks that require physical reasoning, such as how to use tools to obtain food, but they fall far short of toddlers on tasks requiring social reasoning, such as inferring intentions from behaviour (Herrmann et al., 2007; Tomasello, 2008).

At the centre of naïve psychology are three concepts that we all use to understand human behaviour: desires, beliefs, and actions (Gopnik & Wellman, 2012). We apply these concepts almost every time we think about why someone did something. For example, why did Billy go to Abdul's house? He *wanted* to play with Abdul (a desire), he *expected* that Abdul would be at home (a belief), so he *went* to Abdul's house (an action). Why did Riya turn the TV to Channel 5 at 8:00 A.M. on Saturday? She was *interested in* watching *Team Umizoomi* (a desire), she *thought* the program was on Channel 5 at 8 in the morning (a belief), so she *selected* that channel at that time (an action).

FIGURE 7.2 Cause–effect relations Hearing that wugs are well prepared to fight and gillies prefer to flee helped preschoolers categorize novel pictures like these as wugs or gillies (Krascum & Andrews, 1998). In general, understanding cause–effect relations helps people of all ages learn and remember.

Three properties of naïve psychological concepts are especially noteworthy. First, many refer to invisible mental states. No one can see a desire or a belief or other psychological concepts such as a perception or a memory. We, of course, can see actions related to invisible psychological concepts, such as Billy ringing Abdul's doorbell, but we can only infer the underlying mental state, such as Billy's desire to see Abdul. Second, psychological concepts are linked to one another in cause–effect relations. Billy, for instance, might become annoyed if Abdul isn't home, despite saying that he would be, which could negatively affect Billy's mood, causing him to be mean to his younger brother. The third noteworthy property of these naïve psychological concepts is that they develop surprisingly early in life, though how early, and the process through which the capability occurs, remains a subject of heated debate.

naïve psychology a commonsense level of understanding of other people and oneself

Naïve Psychology in Infancy

Sharp disagreements have arisen between nativists and empiricists regarding the source of early psychological understanding. Nativists (e.g., Leslie, 2000) argue that the early understanding is possible only because children are born with a basic understanding of human psychology. By contrast, empiricists (e.g., Frye et al., 1996; Ruffman, Slade, & Crowe, 2002) argue that experiences with other people and general information-processing capacities are the key sources of the early understanding of other people. There is evidence to support each view.

The emergence of self-consciousness Infants seem to be born with a kind of implicit self-consciousness, a rudimentary understanding that they are separate from other people and can act in ways that accomplish their goals (Rochat, 2018). Reflecting this implicit self-consciousness, if another person touches an infant's cheek, the infant is likely to turn in the direction of the touch; but if infants touch their own cheek, they rarely turn in that direction. By age four months, infants show basic understanding of what they can and cannot do; they reach for small objects within their grasp, but not for larger or more distant objects (Rochat, 2011). By age 18 to 24 months, they try to wipe smudges off their faces when they see them in mirrors and make efforts to look good to other people, reflecting a more explicit kind of self-consciousness (Botto & Rochat, 2018).

"Mommy, how much grape juice would be bad for the rug?"

Indirect ways of breaking bad news are a specialty of young children and reflect their understanding that other people's reactions might not be the same as their own.

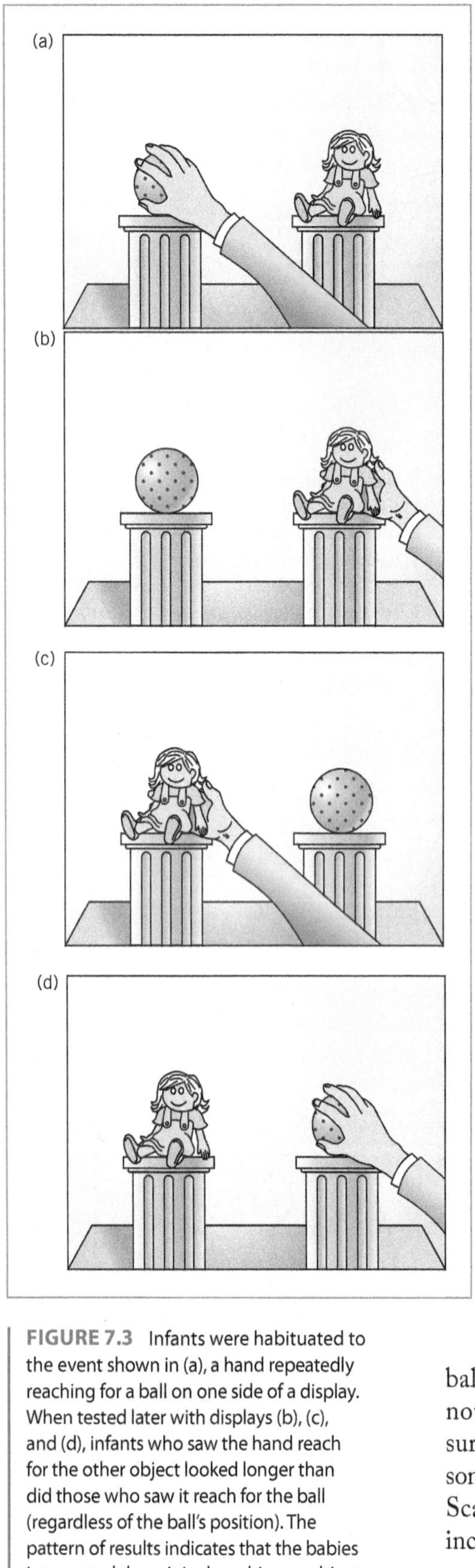

FIGURE 7.3 Infants were habituated to the event shown in (a), a hand repeatedly reaching for a ball on one side of a display. When tested later with displays (b), (c), and (d), infants who saw the hand reach for the other object looked longer than did those who saw it reach for the ball (regardless of the ball's position). The pattern of results indicates that the babies interpreted the original reaching as object-directed. (Information from Woodward, 1998)

Understanding other people As we saw in Chapter 5, infants in their first year find other people interesting, pay careful attention to them, and learn an impressive amount about them. They prefer to look at people's faces rather than at other objects and imitate other people's facial movements, such as sticking out their tongue, more often than they imitate similar looking motions of inanimate objects. And it is not just faces that interest infants; they also prefer to watch the movements of cartoons of human bodies over cartoons showing the same parts arranged haphazardly but with equal amounts of movement (Bertenthal, 1993). By imitating other people and forming emotional bonds with them, infants encourage more interaction, creating additional opportunities for the infants to acquire psychological understanding. These interactions help infants learn both about people in general and about differences between individuals.

Infants learn quite early that other people's behaviours, like those of the infants themselves, have purpose and are goal-directed. In research by Amanda Woodward (1998), 6-month-olds saw a hand repeatedly reach toward one of two objects sitting side by side in a display (see Figure 7.3). Then, the position of the two objects was reversed, and the hand reached again. The question was whether the infants interpreted the reaching as directed toward a particular object. They did, as shown by their looking longer (thus indicating surprise) when the hand went to the object they had not reached for previously. Thus, the infants apparently interpreted the reaching as directed toward a specific object rather than toward a specific location. Infants even move their eyes to the goal object before the hand gets there (Cannon & Woodward, 2012; Kim & Song, 2015). However, this is true only when a human hand does the reaching; infants do not react the same way when a mechanical claw moves toward an object, suggesting that they understand that the motion of nonliving things does not reflect the nonliving things' intentions.

Under some conditions, however, such as cartoons, infants do seem to attribute intentions to nonliving things. Cartoon clips are often used to study infants' reactions to human-like actions, because such cartoons avoid the possibility that specific characteristics of individual people could influence the infants' reactions. In one study using cartoons, Hamlin, Wynn, and Bloom (2007) presented 10-month-olds with a video showing a ball, a cube, and a pyramid, all with "googly" eyes. To adults, at least, the ball appeared to be trying repeatedly to reach the top of a hill, each time falling back to the bottom. Then, the ball either appeared to be helped toward the crest by the pyramid "pushing" it upward or hindered from reaching the peak by the cube "pushing" it downward. Soon after, infants were shown all three objects and observed the ball either approach the previously "helpful" pyramid or the previously "unhelpful" cube. Infants looked longer when the ball approached the cube that had hindered its progress, presumably indicating not only their understanding of the "intentions" of the objects but also their surprise that the ball seemed to prefer the "hinderer" to the "helper." Although some investigators have been unable to replicate this effect (Salvadori et al., 2015; Scarf et al., 2012), a recent meta-analysis indicated that it does replicate but is inconsistent (Margoni & Surian, 2018).

Understanding differences between people Infants understand individual differences among people, as reflected by the fact that their preferences for specific people vary based on those people's actions and characteristics. For instance,

10-month-olds are more likely to choose a food offered by a speaker of their language than by a speaker of another language (Shutts et al., 2009). They also are more likely to select a toy that was previously held by someone who speaks their language than a toy held by someone who speaks a different language (Kinzler, Dupoux, & Spelke, 2007). By age 12 months, most infants accept one cracker from a puppet whom they observed acting nicely rather than accept two crackers from a puppet they observed being mean (Tasimi & Wynn, 2016). This preference for niceness has its limits, though; when the "mean puppet" offered eight crackers and the "nice puppet" only one, most babies took the eight crackers.

Naïve Psychology Beyond the First Year

As noted in previous chapters, several important aspects of psychological understanding emerge in the second year: (1) a sense of self, in which children more explicitly realize that they are individuals distinct from other people; (2) joint attention, in which two or more people focus intentionally on the same referent; (3) intersubjectivity, the mutual understanding that people share during communication. This emerging understanding of other people during the second year also includes some insight into their emotions. Consider Michael, a 15-month-old who

> is struggling with his friend Paul over a toy. Paul starts to cry. Michael appears concerned and lets go of the toy, so Paul has it. Paul continues crying. . . . Michael pauses again, runs to the next room, gets Paul's security blanket, and gives it to him. Paul stops crying.
>
> (Hoffman, 1976, pp. 129–130)

Although interpreting anecdotes is always tricky, it seems likely that Michael understood that giving Paul something that he liked might make him feel better. Michael's leaving the room, getting Paul's security blanket, and bringing it back to him suggests that Michael had the further insight that Paul's blanket might be useful for soothing his hurt feelings. This interpretation is consistent with a variety of evidence suggesting that 1-year-olds fairly often offer both physical comfort (hugs, kisses, pats) and comforting comments ("You be okay") to unhappy playmates. Presumably, experiences with their own emotions and what soothes them when they are upset is the basis for such insights (Harris, 2006).

Theory of Mind

In the first few years, children build on their early-emerging psychological understanding to develop an understanding of differences as well as similarities between their own and other people's thinking. This process yields what is often referred to as a theory of mind.

The growth of a theory of mind Infants' and preschoolers' naïve psychology, together with their strong interest in other people, provides the foundation for a **theory of mind**, an organized understanding of how mental processes such as intentions, desires, beliefs, perceptions, and emotions influence behaviour. Preschoolers' theory of mind includes, for example, knowledge that beliefs often originate in perceptions, such as seeing an event or hearing someone describe it; that desires can originate either from physiological states, such as hunger or pain, or from psychological states, such as wanting to see a friend; that desires and beliefs produce actions; and that differences in people's beliefs lead to differences in their actions (Miller, 2012).

One important component of such a theory of mind—understanding the connection between other people's desires and their actions—emerges by the end

theory of mind an organized understanding of how mental processes such as intentions, desires, beliefs, perceptions, and emotions influence behaviour

FIGURE 7.4 Testing children's theory of mind The Smarties task is frequently used to study preschoolers' understanding of false beliefs. Most 3-year-olds answer the way the child in this cartoon does, which suggests a lack of understanding that people's actions are based on their own beliefs, even when those beliefs deviate from what the child knows to be true.

false-belief problems tasks that test a child's understanding that other people will act in accord with their own beliefs even when the child knows that those beliefs are incorrect

of the first year. In a study by Phillips, Wellman, and Spelke (2002), 12-month-olds saw an experimenter look at one of two stuffed kittens and say in a joyful voice, "Ooh, look at the kitty!" Then a screen descended, and when it was raised 2 seconds later, the experimenter was holding either the kitty that she had just gushed over or the other one. The 12-month-olds looked longer when the experimenter was holding the other kitty, suggesting that they expected the experimenter to want to hold the kitty that had excited her so much and were surprised that she was holding the other one.

In contrast, when presented the same experience, 8-month-olds looked for similar amounts of time regardless of which kitty the experimenter held, suggesting that the understanding that people's desires guide their actions develops toward the end of the first year (Phillips et al., 2002). Consistent with this conclusion, 10-month-olds can use information about a person's earlier desires to predict that person's later desires, but only if the earlier and later circumstances are virtually identical (Sommerville & Crane, 2009).

The understanding that desires lead to actions is firmly established by age 2 years. Children of this age, for instance, predict that characters in stories will act in accord with their own desires, even when those desires differ from the child's preferences (Gopnik & Slaughter, 1991; Lillard & Flavell, 1992). Thus, if 2-year-olds who would rather play with trucks than with dolls are told that a character in a story would rather play with dolls than with trucks, they predict that, given the choice, the character in the story will choose in accord with the character's own preference, rather than the child's preference.

By age 3 years, children show some understanding of the relation between beliefs and actions. For example, they answer questions such as "Why is Billy looking for his dog?" by referring to beliefs ("He thinks the dog ran away") as well as to desires ("He wants it") (Bartsch & Wellman, 1995). Most 3-year-olds also have some knowledge of how beliefs originate and why people's beliefs differ. They know, for example, that seeing an event produces beliefs about it, whereas simply being next to someone who sees the event does not (Pillow, 1988).

At the same time, 3-year-olds' understanding of the relation between people's beliefs and their actions is limited in important ways. These limitations are evident when children are presented with **false-belief problems**, in which another person believes something to be true that the child knows is false. The question is whether the child thinks that the other person will act in accord with his or her own false belief or in accord with the child's correct understanding of the situation. Studying such situations reveals whether children understand that other people's actions are determined by the contents of their own minds rather than by the objective truth of the situation.

In one widely studied false-belief problem, preschoolers are shown a box (Figure 7.4) that ordinarily has Smarties (the candy) inside it. The experimenter then asks the preschoolers what is inside the box. Logically enough, they say "Smarties." Next, the experimenter opens the box, revealing that it actually contains pencils. Most 5-year-olds laugh or smile and admit their surprise. When asked what another child would say if shown the closed box and asked to guess its contents, they say the child would answer "Smarties," just as they had. Not 3-year-olds! One study at the University of Toronto showed that a large majority of 3-year-olds claim they always knew what was in the box, and they predict that if another child were shown the box, that child would also believe that the box contained pencils (Gopnik & Astington, 1988). The 3-year-olds' responses show they have difficulty understanding that other people act on their own beliefs, even when those beliefs are false, and that other people do not necessarily know what the child knows.

This finding is extremely robust. A review of 178 studies of children's understanding of false beliefs showed that similar results emerged with different forms of the problem, different questions, and different societies (Wellman, Cross, & Watson, 2001). In one noteworthy cross-cultural study, false-belief problems were presented to children attending preschools in Canada, India, Peru, Thailand, and Samoa (Callaghan et al., 2005). Performance improved greatly between ages 3 and 5 years in all five societies; averaged across them, accuracy increased from 14% correct for 3-year-olds to 85% correct for 5-year-olds. Especially striking was the consistency of performance across these very different societies: in no country did 3-year-olds answer more than 25% of problems correctly, and in no country did 5-year-olds answer less than 72% correctly.

Although 3-year-olds generally err on false-belief problems when the problems are presented in the standard way, quite a few children of this age succeed if the task is presented in a manner that facilitates understanding. For example, if an experimenter tells a 3-year-old that the two of them are going to play a trick on another child by hiding pencils in a Smarties box and enlists the child's help in filling the box with pencils, most 3-year-olds correctly predict that the other child will say that the box contains Smarties (Sullivan & Winner, 1993). Presumably, assuming the role of deceiver by hiding the pencils in the candy box helps 3-year-olds see the situation from the other child's perspective. Nonetheless, it is striking just how difficult 3-year-olds find standard false-belief problems. To date, no set of conditions has enabled the majority of 3-year-olds to consistently solve standard false-belief questions correctly.

Children's theories of mind continue to develop far beyond this early period, with at least some of the development dependent on specific experiences. For example, 14-year-olds who gained experience acting in plays over the course of a school year showed greater understanding of other people's thinking at the end of the year than before their acting experience (Goldstein & Winner, 2011). In contrast, peers who received other types of arts education (music or visual arts) over the same period did not show comparable improvements in understanding other people's thinking.

theory of mind module (TOMM) a hypothesized brain mechanism devoted to understanding other human beings

Explaining the development of theory of mind People's lives clearly would be very different without a reasonably sophisticated theory of mind. However, findings on improvements in a typical child's theory of mind between ages 3 and 5 do not tell us what causes the improvement. This question has generated enormous controversy, and currently there is great disagreement about how to answer it.

Consistent with the perspective described at the beginning of this section, investigators who take a nativist position have proposed the existence of a **theory of mind module (TOMM)**, a hypothesized brain mechanism devoted to understanding other human beings (Baron-Cohen, 1995; Leslie, 2000). Advocates of this position argue that among typical children exposed to a typical environment, the TOMM matures over the first 5 years, producing an increasingly sophisticated understanding of people's minds. These investigators cite evidence from brain-imaging studies showing that certain

Despite leading very different lives, Pygmy children in Africa and same-age peers in industrialized North American and European societies respond to the false-belief task in the same way.

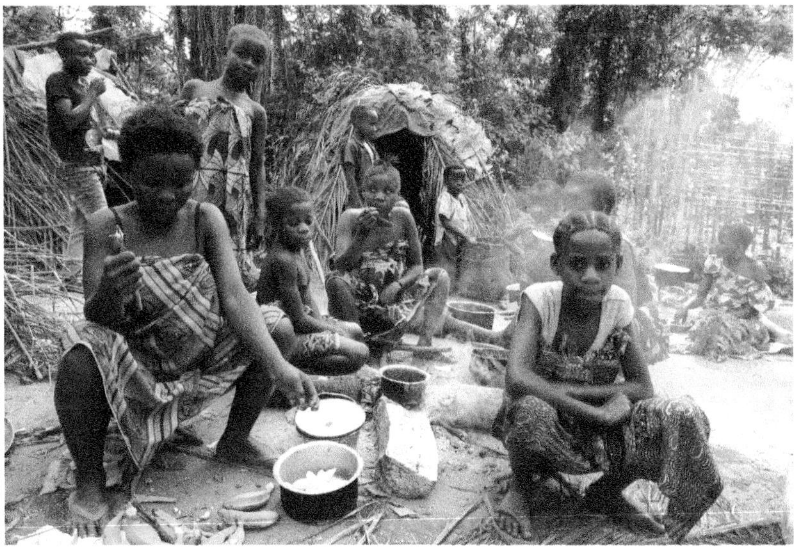

FRIEDRICH VON HÖRSTEN/ALAMY

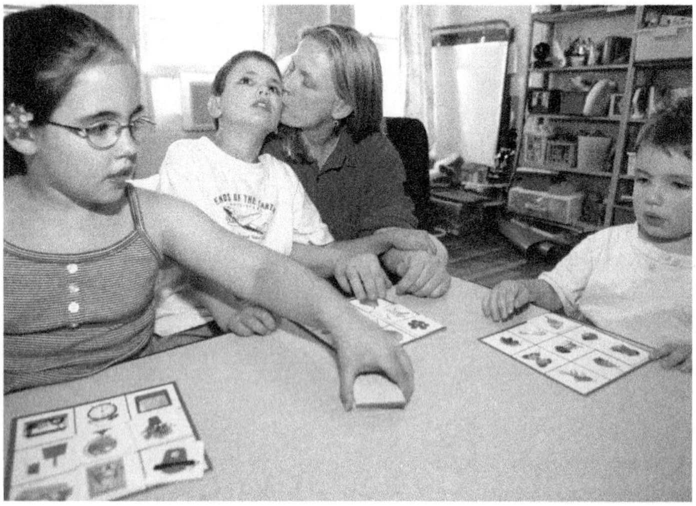

JAN SONNENMAIR/CAVAN IMAGES

The child sitting in his mother's lap seems to show a lack of interest in her affection, behaviour that can be common among children with autism spectrum disorders and which may be related to their poorer performance on tasks that require an understanding of other people's minds.

areas of the brain are consistently active in representing beliefs across different tasks, and that the areas are different from those involved in other complex cognitive processes, such as understanding grammar (Saxe & Powell, 2006).

Studies of children with autism spectrum disorders (ASD) are often cited to support the idea of the TOMM. As discussed in Box 7.1, these children have great difficulty with false-belief problems, as well as with understanding people more generally. Consistent with the idea of a TOMM, one reason for these difficulties in understanding the social world appears to be a typical sizes and activity of certain brain areas that are crucial for understanding people (Amaral, Schumann, & Nordahl, 2008; Dinstein et al., 2012).

Theorists who take an empiricist stance suggest different explanations for the emergence of theory of mind. Some emphasize the role of learning from experiences with physical situations and with other people. For example, although many infants follow the gaze of adults wearing blindfolds, experience with wearing the blindfolds themselves reduces 12-month-olds' frequency of following the gaze of blindfolded adults (Meltzoff & Brooks, 2008). Other empiricist research emphasizes interactions with other people (Doherty, 2008; Ruffman, Slade, & Crowe, 2002). For example, on false-belief tasks, preschoolers who have siblings outperform peers who do not (Doherty, 2008). This finding appears to be strongest when the siblings are older or of the opposite gender, presumably because interacting with people whose interests, desires, and motives are different from their own broadens children's understanding of other people and how they differ from themselves (Jenkins & Astington, 1996; Miller, 2012).

Moreover, repeated exposure to other people acting on false beliefs has been found to produce substantial improvements among 3-year-olds who had relatively advanced understanding before the experiences, though not on peers with less advanced understanding (Rhodes & Wellman, 2013). From this perspective, the tendency of autistic children not to interact much with other people seems likely to be a major contributor to their difficulty in understanding others.

Other investigators who take an empiricist stance emphasize the growth of general information-processing skills as essential to understanding other people's minds (e.g., Austin, Groppe, & Elsner, 2014). They cite evidence that children's understanding of false-belief problems is substantially correlated with their ability to reason about complex counterfactual statements (German & Nichols, 2003) and with their ability to inhibit their own behavioural propensities when necessary (Carlson, Mandell, & Williams, 2004). The ability to reason about counterfactual statements is important because false-belief problems require children to predict what a person would do on the basis of a counterfactual belief (e.g., the belief that the Smarties box contained Smarties). The ability to inhibit behavioural propensities is important because false-belief problems also require children to suppress the assumption that the person would act on the truth of the situation as the child understands it. Investigators in this camp argue that typical children younger than 4 years and some autistic children lack the information-processing skills needed to understand others' minds, whereas typical older children can engage in such processing.

All of these explanations have merit. Normal development of brain regions relevant to understanding other people, specific experiences that build understanding of perception and cognition, interactions with other people,

BOX 7.1 INDIVIDUAL DIFFERENCES Children with Autism Spectrum Disorders (ASD)

Although most children readily handle false-belief problems by the age of 5 years, one group continues to find them very difficult even when they are teenagers: children with autism spectrum disorders (ASD). As discussed in Chapter 3, this syndrome—which affects roughly 1 in 66 children in Canada, most of them male (Ofner et al., 2018)—involves difficulties in social interaction, communication, and other intellectual and emotional functions.

Although there is a great deal of variability in severity of symptoms and behaviours, children with ASD can engage in solitary, repetitive behaviours, such as continually rocking back and forth or endlessly skipping around a room. Some interact minimally with other children and adults, rarely form close relationships, produce little or no language, and tend to be more interested in objects than in people (Willis, 2009). These problems, among others, have led many researchers to speculate that a failure to understand other people underlies these children's limited engagement in the social world.

Research supports this hypothesis. Autistic children tend to have trouble establishing joint attention with other people (Klin et al., 2004). Compared with typical children, as well as children who have abnormally low IQs, autistic children show less concern when other people appear distressed (Sigman & Ruskin, 1999) or experience circumstances that would lead most people to be distressed (Hobson et al., 2009). These children also tend to have poor language skills (Tager-Flusberg & Joseph, 2005), which both reflects their lack of attention to other people and limits their opportunities to learn about people's thoughts and feelings through conversation. In line with these patterns, some autistic children struggle with false-belief questions (Baron-Cohen, 1991). For example, fewer than half of autistic 6- to 14-year-olds solve false-belief problems that are easy for typical 4- and 5-year-olds (Peterson, Wellman, & Liu, 2005). Autistic children have some understanding of how desire affects behaviour, but the ways in which beliefs influence behaviour largely elude them (Harris, 2006; Tager-Flusberg, 2007).

Impaired theory-of-mind mechanisms are not the only source of the difficulty that autistic children encounter in understanding other people. More general deficits in planning, adapting to changing situations, and controlling working memory also contribute (Ozonoff et al., 2004). Nonetheless, impaired theory of mind is a source of particular difficulty, especially in understanding situations in which people's beliefs differ from reality (Baron-Cohen, 1993; Tager-Flusberg, 2007), and is particularly related to issues in social communication and repetitive behaviours (Jones et al., 2018).

Fortunately, many problems caused by ASD can be mitigated by intense and prolonged early treatment. Dawson and colleagues (2010) randomly assigned autistic 1- and 2-year-olds to receive either Early Start Denver Model (ESDM) treatment or community-based treatment (the control condition). The ESDM treatment included roughly 15 hours per week of sessions with trained therapists, during which time the therapists and children practiced everyday activities, such as eating and playing, and used operant conditioning techniques to promote desired behaviours. These desired behaviours were chosen by the children's parents, who also were taught how to use the approach and were encouraged to use it with their child during common activities such as playing and bathing. The parents reported using the approach for an average of 16 hours per week, beyond the formal ESDM sessions. The effects of ESDM were compared with those of the community-based treatment, which included comprehensive diagnostic evaluations, the provision of resource manuals and reading materials, and referrals for other types of treatment.

After 2 years, children who received the ESDM treatment showed considerably greater gains in IQ score, language, and daily living skills than did peers who received the community-based treatment. This study and others (e.g., Voos et al., 2013) suggest that early, intensive treatment of ASD can yield large benefits. Applications of the ESDM approach to even younger children (7- to 15-month-olds) have also yielded promising preliminary results (Rogers et al., 2014), which suggest that the ESDM program may be even more effective during infancy than during the toddler period in helping autistic children.

▶ Autism Spectrum Disorder

and improved information-processing capacity all contribute to the growth of psychological understanding during the preschool years. Together, they allow almost all children to achieve a basic, but useful, theory of mind by age 5.

The Growth of Play

One way in which children learn about other people's thinking, as well as about many other aspects of the world, is through play. *Play* refers to activities that are pursued for their own sake, with no motivation other than the enjoyment they bring. The earliest play occurs in the first year and includes behaviours such as banging spoons on high-chair trays and repeatedly throwing food on the floor.

One early milestone in the development of play is the emergence, between 12 and 18 months of age, of **pretend play**, make-believe activities in which children create new symbolic relations (Lillard, 2017). When engaged in pretend play, children act as if they are in a different situation than their actual one. They often engage in **object substitution**, ignoring many of a play object's characteristics

pretend play make-believe activities in which children create new symbolic relations, acting as if they were in a situation different from their actual one

object substitution a form of pretense in which an object is used as something other than itself, for example, using a broom to represent a horse

BETH SIEGLER RETCHLESS

Object substitution enables children to pursue play activities they enjoy, even when they do not have the exact objects for those activities. These twins' costumes were imitations of their father's outfit when he bicycled to work. The fire trucks were their bikes, the hats were their helmets, and the glasses were their goggles. Thanks to their mother (the daughter of one of the authors) for explaining the symbolism.

so that they can pretend that it is something else. Typical examples of object substitution are a child's treating a cylindrical wooden block as a bottle and pretending to drink from it or treating a plastic soap dish as a boat and floating it on the water while taking a bath.

Such early pretend play often emerges in interactions between infants and their parents in those societies that emphasize such interactions (Nakamichi, 2015). For example, when a mother pretends to bite into a plastic cookie and says "yum," her infant might do the same. Through signals such as strong eye contact, oddly timed movements, and smiles just after a completed action, parents convey to infants that such actions are not to be taken seriously; infants' reciprocal behaviours indicate that infants and parents both understand the message that this activity is pretend (Lillard, 2017).

Over the next few years, children's pretend play becomes more complex and involves a greater number of other people. Toddlers begin to engage in **sociodramatic play**, a kind of pretend play in which they enact miniature dramas with other children or adults, such as "mother comforting baby" or "doctor helping sick child" (Lillard et al., 2013). Consider, for example, "tea party" rituals, in which a child and parent "pour tea" for each other from an imaginary teapot, daintily "sip" it, "eat" imaginary cookies, and comment on how delicious the cookies are.

sociodramatic play activities in which children enact miniature dramas with other children or adults, such as "mother comforting baby"

Young children's sociodramatic play is typically more sophisticated when playing with a parent or older sibling who can scaffold the play sequence than when they are pretending with a peer (Bornstein, 2007; Lillard, 2007). Such scaffolding during play provides children with opportunities for learning, in particular for improving their storytelling skills (Nicolopoulou, 2007). Consider one mother's comments as her 2-year-old played with two action figures:

> Oh look, Lantern Man is chasing Spider Man. Oh no, he is pushing him down. Spider Man says, "Help, Lantern Man is grabbing me." Look, Spider Man is getting away.
>
> (Kavanaugh & Engel, 1998, p. 88)

Such adult elaboration of implicit storylines in children's play provides a useful model for children to follow in later pretend play with peers or by themselves.

By the elementary school years, play becomes even more complex and social. It begins to include activities such as sports and board games, which have conventional rules that participants must follow. The frequent quarrels that arise among young elementary school students regarding who is obeying the rules and playing fair attest to the cognitive and emotional challenges posed by these games (Rubin, Fein, & Vandenberg, 1983).

Children often enjoy having a parent join them in sociodramatic play, which tends to be richer and more informative with a parent's participation because the parent usually provides scaffolding for the play episode. Along with helping to structure the tea-time conversation, the father in this scenario may also be providing his daughter with tips on party etiquette.

MARK HALL/GETTY IMAGES

Pretend play is often thought of as limited to early childhood, but it actually continues far beyond that time. In a survey of college students, the majority reported that they had engaged in pretend play at least weekly when they were 10 or 11 years old, and most reported doing so at least monthly when they were 12 or 13 years old (Smith & Lillard, 2012). Boys and only children tended to report engaging in pretend play at older ages more than did girls and children with siblings.

In addition to being fun, pretend play may expand children's understanding of the social world. Children who engage in greater amounts of pretend play tend to show greater understanding of other people's thinking and emotions (Lillard, 2015). The type of pretend play in which children engage also matters: social pretend play is more strongly related to understanding other people's thinking than is nonsocial pretend play (Harris, 2000). Preschoolers also learn from watching others' pretend play (Sutherland & Friedman, 2012). Such evidence has led some experts in the area to conclude that high levels of pretend play are causally related to increased social understanding (e.g., Hirsh-Pasek et al., 2009; Tomlinson, 2009).

However, a comprehensive review of studies of pretend play found limited evidence for such a causal relation (Lillard et al., 2013). Instead, both frequent pretend play and high levels of social understanding may be caused by parents who promote both. Moreover, some children with high social skills simply enjoy engaging in pretend play and thinking about other people (an example of how children shape their own development through their activities). The jury remains out on whether pretend play is a cause of improved social understanding, but it is clear that such play is not harmful and that it enriches many children's lives.

Children's interest in social play is so strong that many of them do not let the absence of playmates prevent them from engaging in it. On such occasions, and even sometimes when playmates are available, these children turn to imaginary companions (Box 7.2).

Knowledge of Living Things

Children are fascinated by living things, especially animals. One sign of their fascination is how often they talk about them. In a study of the first 50 words used by children, the two terms other than "mama" and "dada" that were used by the greatest number of children were "dog" and "cat" (and variants such as "doggie" and "kitty") (Nelson, 1973). "Duck," "horse," "bear," "bird," and "cow" also were common early terms. A more recent study of the earliest words spoken by 8- to 16-month-olds in the United States and two regions of China showed similar word choices 35 years later across very different cultures (Tardif et al., 2008).

By the time children are 4 or 5 years old, their fascination with living things translates into impressive knowledge, including knowledge about growth, inheritance, illness, and healing (Gelman, 2003). Coexisting with this relatively advanced knowledge, however, are a variety of immature beliefs and types of reasoning. For example, children often fail to understand the difference between artifacts, such as chairs and cars (which are built by people for specific purposes), and living things, such as monkeys (which are not created by people for any purpose). Thus, when Kelemen and DiYanni (2005) asked 6- to 10-year-olds why the first monkey came to exist, the children often referred to how monkeys serve human purposes, such as "The manager of the zoo-place wanted some" and "So then we had somebody to climb trees."

Another weakness in young children's biological knowledge is their incorrect beliefs about which things are living and which are not (as discussed in Chapter 4). For instance, most 5-year-olds believe that plants are not alive, and some believe that the moon and mountains are alive (Inagaki & Hatano, 2002). Such erroneous notions have led some investigators to conclude that children have only a shallow and fragmented understanding of living things until they are 7 to 10 years old (Carey, 1999; Slaughter, Jaakkola, & Carey, 1999). In contrast, other investigators believe that by age 5 years, children understand the essential characteristics of living things and what separates them from nonliving things but are just confused on a few points (Gelman, 2003). A third view is that young children simultaneously possess both mature and immature biological understanding (Inagaki & Hatano,

BOX 7.2 INDIVIDUAL DIFFERENCES Imaginary Companions

Many children have an imaginary companion. Hearing one's child talk about an invisible friend sometimes leads parents to worry about the child's sanity, but children's creation of such characters is entirely normal.

Children around the world have imaginary companions. A recent multi-country study showed that an average of 21% of children in Kenya, Nepal, Malawi, and the Dominican Republic reported having an imaginary companion (Wigger, 2018). In the United States, research conducted by Marjorie Taylor (1999) indicates that the majority of children have an imaginary friend at one time or another. She found that 63% of children whom she interviewed at age 3 or 4 years and again at age 7 or 8 years reported having imaginary companions at one or both times. In another study, Taylor and colleagues (2004) found that as many 6- and 7-year-olds as 3- and 4-year-olds said that they had imaginary companions—31% of older children and 28% of younger ones (most children had an imaginary friend at one age but not the other).

Most of the imaginary playmates described by the children in Taylor's studies were ordinary boys and girls who happened to be invisible. Others were more colourful. They included Derek, a 91-year-old man who was said to be only 2 feet tall but able to hit bears; "The Girl," a 4-year-old who always wore pink and was "a beautiful person"; Joshua, a possum who lived in San Francisco; and Nobby, a 160-year-old businessman. Other imaginary companions were modelled after specific people: two examples were MacKenzie, an imaginary playmate who resembled the child's cousin MacKenzie, and "Fake Rachel," who resembled the child's friend Rachel.

As with real friends, children have a variety of complaints about their imaginary companions. In a study of 36 preschoolers with imaginary companions, only one child had no complaints; the other 35 children griped that their imaginary companions argued with them, refused to share, failed to come when invited, and failed to leave when no longer welcome (Taylor & Mannering, 2007). In this independence from their creator, the imaginary companions resemble characters invented by novelists, many of whom report that their characters at times seem to act independently, including arguing with and criticizing their creator.

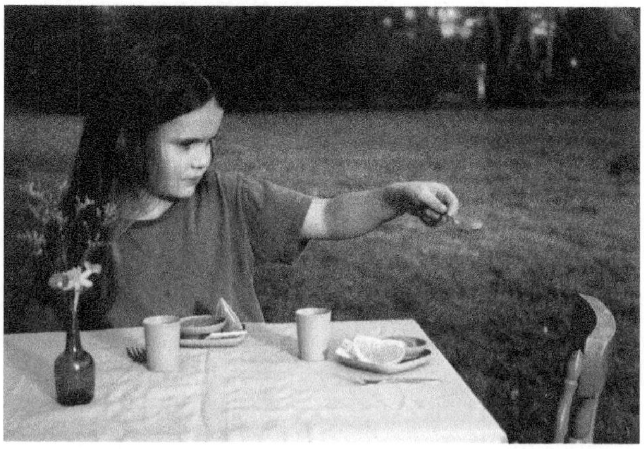

Although the sight of their child feeding someone who isn't there might worry some parents, the creation of imaginary friends is entirely normal, and the majority of children enjoy the company of such characters at some time in early childhood.

Contrary to popular speculation, Taylor (1999) found that, in terms of broad characteristics such as personality, intelligence, and creativity, children who invent imaginary playmates are no different from children who do not. This finding is true even for the relatively small number of children who report having imaginary friends in middle school (about 9% of children; Pearson et al., 2001). Although these children tend not to be especially popular among peers during middle school, by the end of high school, they are as well-adjusted as their peers (Taylor, Hulette, & Dishion, 2010).

Taylor and her colleagues identified a few relatively specific differences between children with and without imaginary companions. Children who created imaginary playmates were more likely (1) to be firstborn or only children; (2) to watch relatively little television; (3) to be verbally skillful; and (4) to have advanced theories of mind (Carlson et al., 2003). These relations make sense. Being without siblings may motivate some firstborn and only children to invent friends to keep them company; not watching much television frees time for imaginative play; and being verbally skilled and having an advanced theory of mind may enable children to imagine especially interesting companions and especially interesting adventures with them.

Companionship, entertainment, and enjoyment of fantasy are not the only reasons why children invent imaginary companions. Children also use them to deflect blame ("I didn't do it; Blebbi Ussi did"); to vent anger ("I hate you, Blebbi Ussi"); and to convey information that the child is reluctant to state directly ("Blebbi Ussi is scared of falling into the potty"). Many young children also report that when they are sad, their imaginary companions comfort them (Sadeh, Hen-Gal, & Tikotzky, 2008). As Taylor (1999) noted, "Imaginary companions love you when you feel rejected by others, listen when you need to talk to someone, and can be trusted not to repeat what you say" (p. 63). No wonder so many children invent them.

▶ Imaginary Companions: The Research of Marjorie Taylor

2008). With this dispute in mind, we will now consider what young children do and do not know about living things and how they acquire knowledge about them.

Distinguishing Living from Nonliving Things

As noted previously, infants in their first year already are interested in people and distinguish them from nonliving things (Figure 7.5). Other animals also attract infants' interest, though infants act differently toward them than they do toward people. For example, researchers in Montreal have shown that 9-month-olds pay more attention to rabbits than they do to inanimate objects, but they smile less at rabbits than they do at people (Poulin-Dubois, 1999; Ricard & Allard, 1993).

These behavioural reactions indicate that infants in their first year distinguish people from other animals and that they distinguish both from inanimate objects. However, the reactions do not indicate when children construct a general category of living things that includes plants as well as animals or when they recognize humans as a type of animal. It is difficult to assess knowledge of these and many other properties of living and nonliving things until the age of 3 or 4 years, when children can comprehend and answer questions about these categories. By this age, they clearly know quite a bit about the similarities among all living creatures and about the differences between living creatures and inanimate objects. This knowledge of living things is not limited to visible properties such as having legs, moving, and making distinctive noises. It also extends to biological processes such as digestion and heredity (S. Gelman, 2003). At least through age 5 or 6, however, many children deny that people are animals (Carey, 1985).

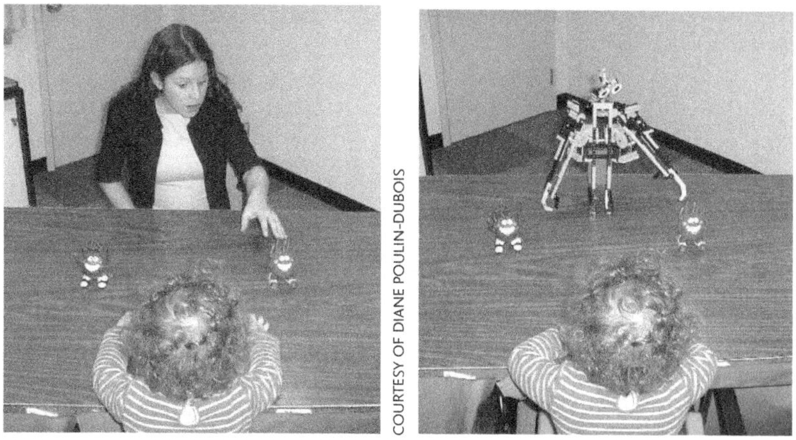

(a) COURTESY OF DIANE POULIN-DUBOIS

(b) COURTESY OF DIANE POULIN-DUBOIS

FIGURE 7.5 Distinguishing people from nonliving things These photos show a task used by Diane Poulin-Dubois (1999) from Concordia University in Montréal to study infants' reactions when they see people and inanimate objects (in this case, a robot) engaging in the same action. Both 9- and 12-month-olds show surprise when they see inanimate objects move on their own, suggesting that they understand that self-produced motion is a distinctive characteristic of people and other animals.

Understanding the life status of plants also presents a challenge to young children. On one hand, most preschoolers know that plants, like animals but unlike inanimate objects, grow (Hickling & Gelman, 1995; Inagaki & Hatano, 1996), heal themselves (Backscheider, Shatz, & Gelman, 1993), and die (Springer, Nguyen, & Samaniego, 1996). On the other hand, most preschoolers believe that plants are not alive; in fact, it is not until age 7 to 9 years that a clear majority of children realize that plants are living things (Hatano et al., 1993). Part of the reason is that children often equate being alive with being able to move in adaptive ways that promote survival; plants do move in this way, but their adaptive movements, such as bending toward sunlight, occur too slowly to observe under ordinary circumstances (Opfer & Gelman, 2001). Consistent with this interpretation, letting 5-year-olds know that plants bend toward sunlight and that their roots grow toward water leads the children to conclude that plants, like animals, are living things (Opfer & Siegler, 2004).

More generally, culture and direct experience influence the age at which children understand that plants are, in fact, alive. For example, children growing up in rural areas realize that plants are living things at younger ages than do children growing up in cities or suburbs (Coley, 2000; Ross et al., 2003).

Understanding Biological Processes

Preschoolers understand that biological processes, such as growth, digestion, and healing, differ from psychological ones (Wellman & Gelman, 1998). For instance, while 3- and 4-year-olds recognize that desires influence what people do, they also recognize that some biological processes are independent of one's desires. Distinguishing between biological and psychological processes, for example, leads preschoolers to predict that people who overeat but wish to lose weight will not get their wish (Schult & Wellman, 1997).

Preschoolers also recognize that properties of living things often serve important functions for the organism, whereas properties of inanimate objects do not. Thus, 5-year-olds recognize that the green colour of plants is crucial for

Children are interested in living things, plants as well as animals—especially when part of the plant tastes good.

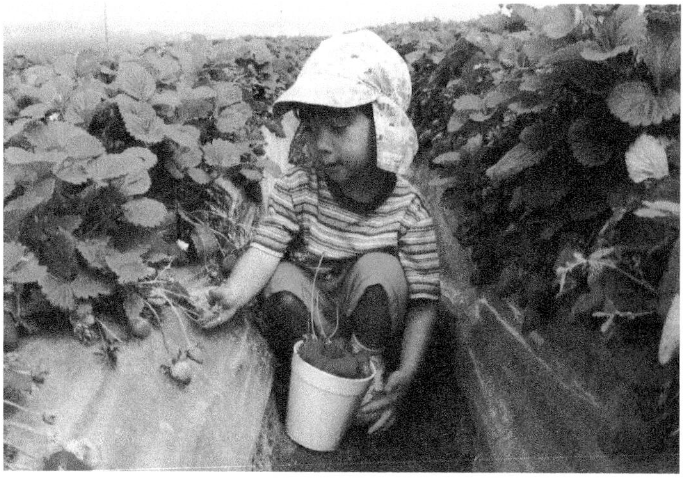

COURTESY OF SUWANNA & DAVID SIEGLER

essentialism the view that living things have an essence inside them that makes them what they are

them to make food, whereas the green colour of emeralds has no function for the emerald (Keil, 1992). The extent of preschoolers' understanding of biological processes can be understood more fully by examining their specific ideas about inheritance, growth, and illness.

Inheritance Although 3- and 4-year-olds obviously know nothing about DNA or the mechanisms of heredity, they do know that physical characteristics tend to be passed on from parent to offspring. If told, for example, that Mr. and Mrs. Bull have hearts of an unusual colour, they predict that Baby Bull also will have a heart of that colour (Springer & Keil, 1991). Similarly, they predict that a baby mouse will eventually have hair of the same colour as its parents, even if it is presently hairless.

Older preschoolers also know that certain aspects of development are determined by heredity rather than by environment. For instance, 5-year-olds realize that an animal of one species raised by parents of another species will become an adult of its own species (Johnson & Solomon, 1997).

Coexisting with this understanding are numerous misguided beliefs about inheritance. Many preschoolers believe that mothers' desires can play a role in their children's inheritance of physical qualities, such as having blue eyes (Weissman & Kalish, 1999). Many preschoolers also believe that adopted children are at least as likely to look like their adoptive parents as like their birth parents (Solomon et al., 1996). In other situations, preschoolers' belief in heredity is too strong, leading them to deny that the environment has any influence. For example, preschoolers tend to believe that differences between boys and girls in play preferences are due totally to heredity (Taylor, 1993).

Related to this general belief in the importance of heredity is one of the most basic aspects of children's biological beliefs—**essentialism**, the view that living things have an essence inside them that makes them what they are (Gelman, 2003). Thus, most preschoolers (as well as most older children and adults) believe that puppies have a certain "dogness" inside them, kittens have a certain "catness," roses have a certain "roseness," and so on. From this perspective, their essence is what makes all living things in a given category similar to one another and different from members of other categories; for instance, their inner "dogness" leads to dogs' barking, chasing cats, and liking to be petted. This essence is viewed as being inherited from one's parents and being maintained throughout the organism's life. Thinking in terms of such essences seems to make it difficult, both for children and for many adults, to understand and accept biological evolution (Evans, 2008; Kelemen et al., 2014). If animals inherit an unchanging essence from their parents, how, they may wonder, would it be possible, say, for mice and whales to have common ancestors? (Recall, though, that carefully designed and informative storybooks can help children understand natural selection; see Box 4.3).

A fanciful representation of the inner essence that children believe makes a dog a dog, a cat a cat, and so on.

"I've been getting in touch with the puppy in me."

Growth, illness, and healing Preschoolers realize that growth, like inheritance, is a product of internal processes. They recognize, for example, that plants and animals become bigger and more complex over time because of something going on inside them (again, preschoolers are not sure what; Rosengren et al., 1991). Three- and 4-year-olds also recognize that the growth of living things generally proceeds in only one direction (smaller to larger) at least until old age, whereas inanimate objects such as balloons can become either smaller or larger at any point in time.

Preschoolers also show a basic understanding of illness. Three-year-olds have heard of germs and have a general sense of how they operate. They know that eating food that is contaminated with germs can make a person sick, even if the person is unaware of the germs' presence (Kalish, 1997). Conversely, they realize that psychological processes, such as being aware of germs in one's food, do not cause illness.

Finally, preschoolers know that plants and animals, unlike inanimate objects, have internal processes that often allow them to regain prior states or attributes. For example, 4-year-olds realize that a tomato plant that is scratched can heal itself and that an animal's hair can grow back after being cut but that a scratched chair cannot heal itself and that a doll's hair cannot grow back (Backscheider et al., 1993). Preschoolers also recognize the limits of living things' recuperative processes: they understand that both illness and old age can cause death, from which no recuperation is possible (Nguyen & Gelman, 2002).

STEPHEN WILKES/GETTY IMAGES

The feelings of awe experienced by many children (and adults) upon seeing remains of great animals of the past and present, such as dinosaurs, elephants, and whales, were a major reason for the founding of natural history museums. Despite all the depictions of monsters and superheroes on television, in movies, and in video games, these fossils and models inspire the same sense of wonder in children growing up today.

How Do Children Acquire Biological Knowledge?

As with other aspects of conceptual development, nativists and empiricists have very different ideas regarding how children acquire biological understanding. Nativists propose that humans are born with a "biology module" much like the theory of mind module described earlier in the chapter. This brain structure or mechanism helps children learn quickly about living things (Atran, 1990, 2002). Nativists use three main arguments to support the idea that people have a biology module.

- During earlier periods of our evolution, it was crucial for human survival that children learn quickly about animals and plants.
- Children throughout the world are fascinated by plants and animals and learn about them quickly and easily.
- Children throughout the world organize information about plants and animals in very similar ways (in terms of growth, reproduction, inheritance, illness, and healing).

Empiricists, by contrast, maintain that children's biological understanding comes from their personal observations and from information they receive from parents, teachers, and the general culture (Callanan, 1990). When mothers read to their 1- and 2-year-olds about animals, for example, many of the mothers' comments suggest that animals have intentions and goals, that different members of the same species have a lot in common, and that animals differ greatly from inanimate objects (Gelman et al., 1998). Such teaching is often elicited by children's questions: when 3- to 5-year-olds encounter unfamiliar objects, they ask a higher percentage of questions about the functions of objects that appear to be humanmade but ask a higher percentage of questions about the biological properties of objects that look like animals or plants (Margett & Witherington, 2011). Such questions reflect children's biological knowledge and can increase it.

Empiricists also note that children's biological understanding reflects the views of their culture. For example, 5-year-olds in Japan are more likely than their peers in the United States and Israel to believe that nonliving things and plants are able to feel physical sensations, such as pain and cold (Hatano et al., 1993). This tendency of Japanese children echoes the Buddhist tradition, still influential in Japanese society, which views all objects as having certain psychological properties.

As with the parallel arguments regarding the sources of psychological understanding, both nature and nurture seem certain to play important roles in the acquisition of biological understanding. Young children are innately fascinated by animals and learn about them much more quickly than about aspects of their environment that they find less interesting. At the same time, the particulars of what children learn obviously are influenced by the information, beliefs, and values conveyed to them by their parents and their society. And, as always, nurture responds to nature, as when parents provide informative answers to their children's many questions about living things, which in turn reflect, and sometimes increase, the children's interest in those things.

REVIEW QUESTIONS

Do you find the nativist or empiricist arguments more persuasive? Why? ■

Understanding Why, Where, When, and How Many

Making sense of our experiences requires accurately representing not only who or what was involved in an event but also why, where, when, and how often the event occurred. Development of all these concepts begins in infancy, but major improvements continue throughout childhood and adolescence.

Causality

The great eighteenth-century Scottish philosopher David Hume described causality as "the cement of the universe." His point was that causal connections unite discrete events into coherent wholes. Consistent with Hume's view, from early in development, children rely heavily on their understanding of causal mechanisms to infer why physical and psychological events occur. When children take apart toys to find out how they work, ask how flipping a switch makes a light go on, or wonder why Mommy is upset, they are trying to understand causal connections. We discussed the development of understanding of psychological causes earlier in this chapter; we now focus on the development of understanding of physical causes.

You will not be surprised to learn that nativists and empiricists disagree about the origins of understanding of physical causes. The difficulty of making sense of the world without some basic causal understanding and the fact that children show some such understanding early in infancy have led nativists to propose that infants possess an innate causal module or core theory that allows them to extract causal relations from the events they observe (e.g., Leslie, 1986; Spelke, 2003). Empiricists, however, have proposed that infants' causal understanding arises from their observations of innumerable events in the environment (e.g., Cohen & Cashon, 2006; Rogers & McClelland, 2004) and of the causal effects of their own actions (Rakison & Krogh, 2012). One fact both sides agree on is that children show impressive causal reasoning from infancy onward.

Causal Reasoning in Infancy

By 6 months of age, infants perceive causal connections among some physical events (Cohen & Cashon, 2006). In a typical experiment demonstrating infants' ability to perceive such relations, Oakes and Cohen (1995) presented 6- to 10-month-olds a

(a) (b) (c) (d)

ALL: COURTESY OF PATRICIA BAUER

FIGURE 7.6 Imitating sequences of events Understanding the actions they are imitating helps toddlers perform the actions in the correct order. In this illustration of the procedure used by Bauer (1995) to demonstrate this point, a toddler imitates a previously observed three-step sequence to build a rattle. The child (a) picks up a small block; (b) puts it into the bottom half of the container; (c) pushes the top half of the container onto the bottom, thus completing the rattle; and (d) shakes it.

series of video clips in which a moving object collided with a stationary object and the stationary object immediately moved in the way one would expect. Different moving and stationary objects were used in each clip, but the basic "plot" remained the same. After seeing a few of these video clips, infants habituated to the collisions. Then the infants were shown a slightly different clip in which the stationary object started moving shortly before it was struck. Infants looked at this event for a longer time than they had looked during the preceding trials, presumably because the new video clip violated their sense that inanimate objects do not move without an external force.

Infants' and toddlers' understandings of physical causality influence not only their expectations about inanimate objects but also their ability to remember and imitate sequences of actions. When 9- to 11-month-olds are shown actions that are causally related (e.g., making a rattle by putting a small object inside two cups that can be pushed together to form a single container), they usually can reproduce the actions (Figure 7.6 shows a toddler performing this procedure; Bauer, 1995). In contrast, when similar but causally unrelated actions are shown, children do not reliably reproduce them until a year later, at age 20 to 22 months (Bauer, 2007).

By the end of their second year, and by some measures even earlier, children can infer the causal impact of one variable based on indirectly relevant information about another. Sobel and Kirkham (2006), for instance, presented 19- and 24-month-olds a box called a "blicket detector" that, the experimenter explained, played music when a type of object called a blicket was placed on it. Then the experimenter simultaneously placed two objects, A and B, on the blicket detector,

The Development of Purposive Reasoning

DEB KELEMEN

FIGURE 7.7 Toddlers' problem solving In the task used by Chen and Siegler (2000) to examine toddlers' causal reasoning and problem solving, choosing the right tool for getting the toy turtle required children to understand the importance of both the length of the shaft and the angle of the head relative to the shaft. Compared with younger toddlers, older toddlers had greater understanding of these causal relations, which led them to more often use tools, rather than just reaching for the toy, and to more often choose the right tool for the task.

and the music played. When the experimenter then placed object A alone on the blicket detector, the music did not play. Finally, the children were asked to turn on the blicket detector. The 24-month-olds consistently chose object B, suggesting that seeing the ineffectiveness of object A led them to infer that object B must be the blicket. In contrast, the 19-month-olds chose object A as often as object B, suggesting that they did not draw this inference.

Another illustration of this growing understanding of causality comes from a study of 1- and 2-year-olds' tool use (Chen & Siegler, 2000). The toddlers were presented an attractive toy that was sitting on a table beyond their reach. Between the child and the toy were six potential tools that varied in length and in the type of head at the end of the shaft (Figure 7.7). To obtain the toy, the toddlers needed to understand the causal relations that would make one tool more effective than the others, in particular, that a sufficiently long shaft and a head at right angles to the shaft were essential.

The 2-year-olds succeeded considerably more often than the 1-year-olds did in obtaining the toy, both in their initial efforts to get it on their own and after being shown by the experimenter how they could use the optimal tool to obtain it. One reason for the older toddlers' greater success was that they more often used a tool to try to get the toy, as opposed to reaching for it with their hands or seeking their mother's help. Another reason was that the older toddlers chose the optimal tool in a greater percentage of trials in which they used some tool. A third reason was that the older toddlers more often generalized what they had learned on the first problem to new, superficially different problems involving tools and toys with different shapes, colours, and decorations. All these findings indicate that the older toddlers had a deeper understanding of the causal relations between a tool's features and its usefulness for pulling in the toy, and that they had learned more from observing other people's actions.

Causal Reasoning During the Preschool Period

Causal reasoning continues to develop in the preschool period. Preschoolers seem to expect that if a variable causes an effect, it should do so consistently (Schulz & Sommerville, 2006). When 4-year-olds see a potential cause produce an effect inconsistently, they infer that some variable that they cannot see must cause the effect; when the same effect occurs consistently, they do not infer that a hidden variable was important. For example, if 4-year-olds saw some dogs respond to petting by eagerly wagging their tails and other dogs respond to petting by growling, they might infer that some variable other than the petting, such as breed, caused the effect. But if all the dogs they had seen looked happy when petted, they would not infer that the dogs' breed was relevant.

Toddler's Use of Tools

ROBERT SIEGLER

Preschoolers' emerging understanding that events must have causes also seems to influence their reactions to magic tricks. Most 3- and 4-year-olds fail to see the point of such tricks; they grasp that something strange has happened but do not find the "magic" humorous or actively try to figure out what caused the strange outcome (Rosengren & Hickling, 2000). By age 5, however, children become fascinated with magic tricks precisely because no obvious causal mechanism could produce the effect (Box 7.3). Many want to search the magician's hat or other apparatus to see how such a stunt was possible. This increasing appreciation that even astonishing events must have causes, along with an increasing understanding

BOX 7.3 A CLOSER LOOK Magical Thinking and Fantasy

Lest you conclude that by age 5, children's causal reasoning is as advanced as that of adults, consider the following conversation between two kindergartners and their teacher:

> *Lisa:* Do plants wish for baby plants?
> *Deana:* I think only people can make wishes. But God could put a wish inside a plant. . . .
> *Teacher:* I always think of people as having ideas.
> *Deana:* It's just the same. God puts a little idea in the plant to tell it what to be.
> *Lisa:* My mother wished for me and I came when it was my birthday.
> (Paley, 1981, pp. 79–80)

This is not a conversation that would have occurred among 10-year-olds and their teacher. Rather, as noted by Jacqui Woolley, a psychologist who studies preschoolers' fantasies, it reflects one of the most charming aspects of early childhood: Preschoolers and young elementary school children "live in a world in which fantasy and reality are more intertwined than they are for adults" (Woolley, 1997).

Young children's belief in fantasy and magic, as well as in normal causes, is evident in many ways. Most 4- to 6-year-olds believe that they can influence other people by wishing them into doing something, such as buying a particular present for their birthday (Vikan & Clausen, 1993). They believe that effective wishing takes a great deal of skill, and perhaps magic, but that it can be done. In related fashion, many believe that getting in good with Santa Claus can make their hopes come true. The fantasies can have a dark side as well, such as when children fear that monsters might hurt them (Woolley, 1997).

Research has shown that young children not only believe in magic; they sometimes also act on their belief. In one experiment, preschoolers were told that a certain box was magical and that if they placed a drawing into it and said magical words, the object depicted in the drawing would appear. Then the experimenter left the children alone with the box and a number of drawings. The children put drawings of the most attractive items into the box, said the "magical words," and were visibly disappointed when they opened the box and found only the drawings (Subbotsky, 1993, 1994).

How can we reconcile preschoolers' understanding of physical causes and effects with their belief in magic, wishing, and Santa Claus? The key is to recognize that here, as in many situations, children simultaneously believe a variety of somewhat contradictory ideas (Evans, Legare, & Rosengren, 2011; Harris & Giménez, 2005; Legare & Gelman, 2008; Woolley, Cornelius, & Lacy, 2011). They may think that magic or the power of their imagination can cause things to happen but do not depend on it when doing so could be embarrassing.

In one demonstration of this limited belief in magic and the power of the imagination (Woolley & Phelps, 1994), an experimenter showed preschoolers an empty box, closed it, and then asked them to imagine a pencil inside it. The experimenter next asked the children whether there was now a pencil in the box. Many said "yes." Then an adult came into the room and said that she needed a pencil to do her work. Very few of the preschoolers opened the box or handed it to her. Thus, it appeared that many children said the box contained a pencil when no consequences would follow if they were wrong, but they did not believe in magic strongly enough to act in a way that might look foolish.

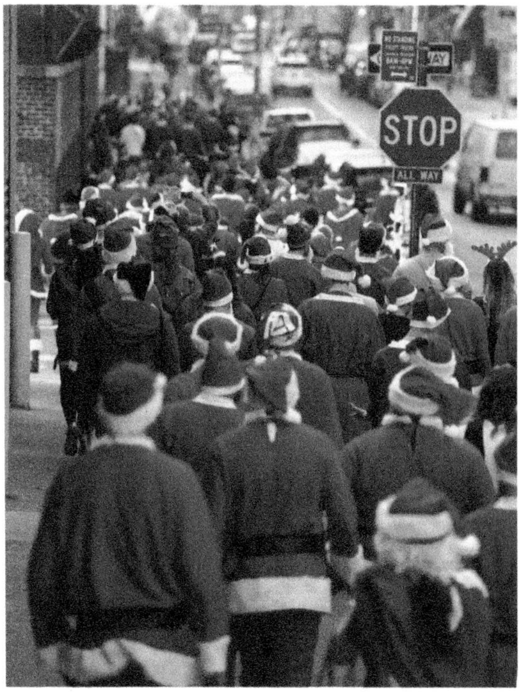

TIMOTHY A. CLARY/GETTY IMAGES

Personal experience, such as seeing a large group of Santas walking down the street, can help children move beyond magical thinking. Of course, the belief in magic might persist if, for example, the child reasons that these Santas are all imposters.

How do children move beyond their belief in magic? One way is learning more about real causes: the more children know about the true causes of events, the less likely they are to explain them in magical terms (Woolley, 1997). Another influence is personal experiences that undermine the child's magical beliefs, such as hearing peers pooh-pooh the idea of Santa Claus or seeing multiple Santa Clauses on the same street. Sometimes, however, children salvage their hopes by distinguishing between flawed manifestations of the magical being and the magical being itself. They may, for example, fervently distinguish between the real Santa Claus and imposters who dress up to look like him.

Although this world of the imagination is most striking between ages 3 and 6, aspects of it remain evident for years thereafter. In one study that demonstrated the persistence of magical thinking, many 9-year-olds and some adults reverted to magical explanations when confronted with a trick that was difficult to explain in physical terms (Subbotsky, 2005). In polls of representative samples, about 30% of Canadian and American adults report that they believe in ghosts (Angus Reid Institute, 2016; Rasmussen, 2011). These beliefs in the supernatural cannot be written off as simply reflecting a lack of education. Subbotsky (2005) found that 0 of 17 American college-student participants were willing to allow someone who was said to be a witch to cast an evil spell on their lives. Innumerable other adults indulge superstitions such as not walking under ladders, avoiding cracks in sidewalks, and knocking on wood. In explaining certain improbable events, adults actually generate supernatural explanations more often than children (Woolley et al., 2011). Apparently, we never entirely outgrow magical thinking.

Magical Thinking

IMAGES-USA/ALAMY

Most 5-year-olds find magic tricks thrilling, even though they would have been uninterested in them a year or two earlier.

of the mechanisms that connect causes and their effects, are important parts of the growth of causal reasoning.

Space

The nativist/empiricist debate has also been vigorous with regard to spatial thinking. Nativists argue that children possess an innate module that is specialized for representing and learning about space and that processes spatial information separately from other types of information (Hespos & Spelke, 2004; Spelke, Lee, & Izard, 2010). Empiricists argue that children acquire spatial representations through the same types of learning mechanisms and experiences as those that produce cognitive growth in general, that children adaptively combine numerous types of spatial and nonspatial information to reach their goals, and that experience with locomotion, language, and cultural tools such as jigsaw puzzles shapes spatial development (Jirout & Newcombe, 2015; Newcombe, Levine, & Mix, 2015).

Nativists and empiricists agree on some issues. For example, from early in infancy, children show impressive understanding of some spatial concepts, such as *above, below, left of,* and *right of* (Casasola, 2008; Quinn, 2005). Another common conclusion is that self-produced movement around the environment stimulates processing of spatial information. A third shared belief is that certain parts of the brain are specialized for coding particular types of spatial information; for instance, development of the hippocampus appears to produce improvements in place learning—the ability to encode information about the location and position of objects or events (Sutton, Joanisse, & Newcombe, 2010). A fourth common conclusion is that geometric information—information about lengths, angles, and directions—is important in spatial processing. When toddlers and preschoolers are given clues to an object's location, through pointing or language (such as, "a little to the left of the tree") they often weigh such geometric information more strongly than seemingly simpler non-geometric cues, such as the object's being in front of the one blue wall in the room (Newcombe, 2019).

Effective spatial thinking requires coding space relative to oneself and relative to the external environment. Next, we consider each of these types of spatial coding.

Representing Space Relative to Oneself

From early in infancy, children code the locations of objects in relation to their own bodies. As noted in Chapter 5, when young infants are presented with two objects, they tend to reach for the closer one (van Wermeskerken et al., 2013). This shows that they recognize which object is closer and that they know the direction of that object relative to themselves.

Over the ensuing months, infants' representations of spatial locations become increasingly durable, enabling them to find objects they observed being hidden some seconds earlier. For example, 7-month-olds reach to the correct location for objects that were hidden 2 seconds earlier under one of two identical opaque covers, but not for objects hidden 4 seconds earlier; yet most 12-month-olds accurately reach for objects hidden 10 seconds earlier (Diamond, 1985). In part, these increasingly enduring object representations reflect brain maturation, particularly of the dorsolateral prefrontal cortex, an area in the frontal lobe that is involved in the formation and maintenance of plans and in the integration of new and previously learned information (Diamond & Goldman-Rakic, 1989; Nelson, 2005). However, the improved object representations reflect learning as well: infants who are provided a learning experience with a hidden object in one situation show improved location of hidden objects in other situations (Johnson, Amso, & Slemmer, 2003).

Note that the preceding examples of infants' ability to code space involve infants remaining in a single location and coding locations relative to their bodies. Piaget (1954/1971) proposed that this is the one kind of spatial coding that infants can do. The reason, according to his theory, is that during the sensorimotor period, infants can form only **egocentric spatial representations**, in which the locations of objects are coded relative to the infants' position at the time of the coding. As evidence, Piaget reported experiments showing that if infants repeatedly found a toy located to their right, they would continue to turn right to find it, even if they were repositioned so that the hidden object was now on their left. Subsequent investigators replicated this finding (e.g., Bremner, 1978).

Egocentric spatial representation during infancy is not absolute, however. If toys are hidden adjacent to a distinctive landmark, such as a tower, infants usually find the toy despite changes in their own position (Lew, 2011). Still, the question remains: How do young children become able to find objects when their own position has changed and when no landmarks are available to guide their search?

A major factor in helping infants acquire a sense of space independent of their own location appears to be self-locomotion. Infants who crawl or have had experience propelling themselves in walkers more often remember the locations of objects on the object permanence task (Chapter 4) than do infants of the same age without such locomotor experience (Bertenthal, Campos, & Kermoian, 1994; Campos et al., 2000). Similarly, compared with infants who have not yet moved across rooms on their own, those infants who have done so show an earlier understanding of depth and drop-offs on the surfaces they travel; this is evidenced by acceleration in their heart rate as they approach the visual cliff in the procedure described in Chapter 5.

egocentric spatial representations coding of spatial locations relative to one's own body, without regard to the surroundings

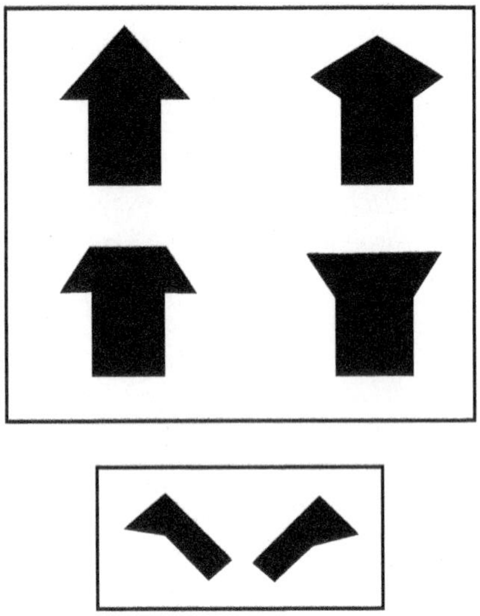

SUSAN LEVINE

FIGURE 7.8 Measuring early spatial reasoning These are the shapes used by Levine and colleagues (2012) to examine the effects of playing with puzzles on preschoolers' spatial skills. The task was to identify which shape in the top panel could be constructed from the pair of shapes in the bottom panel.

The reasons why self-locomotion enhances infants' representation of space should be familiar to anyone who has both driven a car and been a passenger in one. Just as driving requires continuous updating of information about the surroundings, so does crawling or walking. In contrast, just as being a passenger in a car does not usually lead to such continuous updating of one's location relative to the overall route, neither does being carried.

As would be expected from this analysis, self-locomotion also enhances older children's spatial coding. Striking evidence for this conclusion emerged from a study in which kindergarteners were tested in the kitchens of their own homes (Rieser, Garing, & Young, 1994). Some kindergartners were asked to stand in place and imagine themselves walking from their seat in the classroom to the teacher's chair, and then turning around to face the class. Next, they were asked to point from this imagined position in the classroom to the locations of various objects within it—the fishbowl, the alphabet chart, the coatroom door, and so on. Under these conditions, the 5-year-olds' pointing was inaccurate.

Other kindergartners went through the same procedure, except that they were instructed to actually walk through their kitchen and turn around as they imagined themselves walking to the teacher's chair and then turning to face the class. Under these conditions, the children's pointing to the imagined objects in their imagined classroom was far more accurate. This result, like those described above with infants, highlights the interconnectedness of the system that produces self-generated motion and the system that produces mental representations of space (Adolph & Robinson, 2015).

Another type of experience that contributes to spatial development beyond infancy is assembling puzzles. Children who played with puzzles more often than their peers between their 1st and 4th birthdays were more successful as 4½-year-olds on the spatial transformation task shown in Figure 7.8 (Levine et al., 2012). The relation between puzzle play and subsequent spatial reasoning occurred regardless of parents' education, income, and use of spatial terms while interacting with their children. This relation between puzzle play and spatial reasoning makes sense. Putting together puzzles requires identifying appropriate pieces for specific locations and physically rotating them into the proper orientation. Mentally rotating pieces to identify plausible candidates for filling empty locations allows more efficient solutions than would otherwise be possible. Such practice in mental rotation seems likely to build spatial-reasoning skills that can be used in future situations.

You might be wondering about blind children—do they represent space? As discussed in Box 7.4, they do.

Representing Spatial Relations in the External Environment

As we have noted, infants as young as 6 months can use landmarks to code the location of objects they observe being hidden (Lew, 2011). However, for such young infants to use a landmark successfully, it must be the only obvious landmark in the environment and must be located right next to the hidden object.

With development, infants become increasingly able to choose among alternative potential landmarks. When 12-month-olds are presented a single yellow cushion, a single green cushion, and a large number of blue cushions, they have little trouble finding an object hidden under either the yellow or the green cushion (Bushnell et al., 1995). At 22 months, but not at 16 months, the presence of a landmark improves children's ability to locate an object that is not hidden immediately adjacent to the landmark but that is fairly close to it (Newcombe et al., 1998). By

BOX 7.4 INDIVIDUAL DIFFERENCES Development of Spatial Concepts in Blind and Visually Impaired People

People often equate spatial thinking with vision; the underlying assumption is that we can think spatially only about layouts that we have seen. Even in infancy, however, spatial representations can be based on senses other than vision. Thus, when 3-month-olds are brought into a totally dark room in which nothing can be seen, they use sounds emitted by nearby objects to identify the objects' spatial locations and reach for them (Keen & Berthier, 2004).

Although infants can use their auditory sense, as well as other senses, to form spatial representations, visual experience during infancy does play an important role in spatial development. Evidence for this conclusion comes from cases in which surgery restored sight to people who were born either blind (Carlson, Hyvärinen, & Raninen, 1986) or with severely impaired vision due to cataracts that prevented patterned stimulation from reaching the retina (Le Grand et al., 2001, 2003). The surgery was performed early—on average at 4 months of age—and those who underwent it subsequently had between 9 and 21 years of postsurgical visual experience before being tested. Despite their extensive visual experience after the corrective surgery, most of these people could not use visual information to represent space as well as most people.

Problems remained even 20 years after the surgery (and thus after 20 years of visual experience). The deficits extended to aspects of visual processing that might not immediately be viewed as spatial, such as face perception. Young adults with central eye cataracts that prevented any vision until they were removed during their first year (on average, at age 4 months) showed reduced brain activity in areas involved in face processing and reduced connectivity among neurons in these areas (Grady et al., 2014).

These findings do not mean that children who are born blind cannot represent space. They actually tend to have a surprisingly good sense of space. On tasks involving the representation of very small spaces, such as being guided in drawing two sides of a triangle on a piece of paper and then being asked to complete the triangle by drawing the third side themselves, children who are born blind perform as well as sighted children who are blindfolded (Thinus-Blanc & Gaunet, 1997). On tasks involving representation of large spaces, such as those formed by exploring unfamiliar rooms, the spatial representations of people born blind also are surprisingly good, about as good as those formed by sighted people who were blindfolded during the exploration period. A study by Ann Bigelow at San Francis Xavier University in Nova Scotia found that blind children's mastery of spatial tasks was somewhat slower relative to that of sighted children, but it followed the same sequence, suggesting similar underlying processes (Bigelow, 1996). Thus, although some spatial skills, especially face perception, require early visual experience, many blind people develop impressive senses of space without ever seeing the world.

SCOTT T. BAXTER/GETTY IMAGES

Blind adolescents and adults, even those blind from birth, tend to have a quite accurate sense of space, which helps them move around the environment skillfully.

age 5 years, children can also represent an object's position in relation to multiple landmarks, such as when it is midway between a tree and a street lamp (Newcombe, Uttal, & Souter, 2013).

Children, like adults, have more difficulty forming a spatial representation when they move around in an environment without distinctive landmarks or when the only landmarks are far from the target location. To understand the challenge of such tasks, imagine walking in a forest without cleared paths and not being able to remember exactly how you arrived at your current location. How easily could you find your way back to your starting point?

Even toddlers show some degree of navigational ability—good enough to lead them in the right general direction (Loomis et al., 1993). In one experiment, 1- and 2-year-olds first saw a small toy hidden in a long, rectangular sandbox and then saw a curtain descend around the sandbox, thus hiding the toy. The toddlers then walked to a different location, after which they were asked to find the toy. Despite no landmarks being present, the toddlers kept track of the hidden toy's location well enough to show better than chance accuracy in their searches (Newcombe et al., 1998).

PENNY TWEEDIE/PANOS PICTURES

Spatial skills tend to be especially well developed in cultures in which they are crucial for survival.

Precisely coding locations in the absence of straightforward landmarks continues to be difficult for people well beyond 2 years of age. Six- to 8-year-olds are not very good at it (Broadbent, Farran, & Tolmie, 2014; Bullens et al., 2010); 12-year-olds are better (Lingwood et al., 2018), but even adults vary tremendously in their abilities to form this type of spatial representation (Newcombe, 2019). For example, when adults are asked to walk around the perimeter of an unfamiliar college campus and then to walk straight back to the starting point, some are quite accurate, but many choose routes that take them nowhere near the original location (Cornell et al., 1996).

The degree to which people develop spatial skills is strongly influenced by the importance of such skills in their culture. To demonstrate this point, Kearins (1981) compared the spatial abilities of seminomadic aboriginal children growing up in the Australian desert with those of White peers growing up in Australian cities. Spatial ability is essential within aboriginal culture, because much of life within this culture consists of long treks between distant water holes that vary in when they have water. Needless to say, the aboriginal people cannot rely on road signs or maps; they must rely on their sense of space to get to the water. Consistent with the importance of spatial skills in their everyday lives, aboriginal children are superior to their city-dwelling peers in memory for spatial location, even in board games, a context that is more familiar to the urban children (Kearins, 1981). Thus, consistent with the general importance of the sociocultural context, use of spatial thinking in everyday activity greatly influences the quality of spatial thinking.

Time

What then is time? I know well enough what it is, provided nobody asks me; but if I am asked and try to explain, I am baffled.

—Saint Augustine, 398 C.E. (2002)

As this quotation suggests, even the deepest thinkers—from Saint Augustine who wrote in the fourth century to Albert Einstein who wrote in the twentieth—have been mystified by the nature of time. Yet even infants in their first half-year have a rudimentary sense of time, including perception of the order and duration of events (Friedman, 2008).

Experiencing Time

Probably the most basic sense of time involves knowledge of temporal order—that is, knowing what happened first, what happened next, and so on. Not surprisingly, given how mystifying life would be without such a basic sense of time, infants know the order in which events occur from as early as the capability can be effectively measured. In one study, 3-month-olds were presented a series of interesting photos, first on their left, then on their right, then on their left, and so on. Within 20 seconds, they began to look to the side where each new photo was to appear even before the photo was presented (Adler et al., 2008; Haith, Wentworth, & Canfield, 1993). This looking pattern indicated that the 3-month-olds detected the repetitive order of events over time and used the information to form expectations of where the next photo would appear (note that the concept "next" assumes a representation of time). The same conclusion has arisen using other experimental methods; for example, 4-month-olds who were habituated to three objects falling in a constant order dishabituated when the order changed (Lewkowicz, 2004).

Infants also have an approximate sense of the duration of events. In one study, 4-month-olds saw periods of light and darkness alternate every 5 seconds for eight cycles, at which point the pattern was broken by the light's failing to appear. Within half a second of the break, infants' heart rates decelerated, a change that is characteristic of increased attention. In this case, the heart-rate deceleration suggested that the infants had a rough sense of the 5-second interval, expected the light to go on at the end of the interval, and increased their attention when it did not appear (Colombo & Richman, 2002).

Infants can also discriminate between longer and shorter durations. The ratio of the durations, rather than differences in their absolute length, is critical for noticing the differences (Brannon, Suanda, & Libertus, 2007). For instance, 6-month-olds discriminate between two durations when their ratio is 2:1 (1 second versus 0.5 second or 3 seconds versus 1.5 seconds), but not when the ratio is 1.5:1 (1.5 seconds versus 1 second or 4.5 seconds versus 3 seconds). Over the course of the first year, the precision of these discriminations increases. Thus, 10-month-olds, unlike 6-month-olds, discriminate when the ratio of the durations is 1.5:1.

What about longer periods, such as weeks, months, or years? It is unknown whether infants have a sense of such long periods, but preschoolers do possess some knowledge regarding them. For example, when asked which of two past events occurred more recently, most 4-year-olds knew that a specific event that happened a week before the experiment (Valentine's Day) happened more recently than an event that happened 7 weeks earlier (Christmas) (Friedman, 1991). However, preschoolers correctly answer such questions only when the more recent event is quite close in time and much closer than the less recent one. Ability to distinguish more precisely among the timing of past events develops slowly during middle childhood (Friedman, 2003). For example, when children who had been presented a distinctive classroom experience were asked 3 months later to recall the month in which the experience occurred, correct recall increased from 20% among 5-year-olds to 46% among 7-year-olds to 64% among 9-year-olds (Friedman & Lyon, 2005).

Understanding of the timing of future events also increases during this age range (Friedman, 2000, 2003). Preschoolers often confuse past and future. For example, 5-year-olds predict a week after Valentine's Day that the next Valentine's Day will come sooner than the next Halloween or Christmas; they also predict that their next lunch is the same amount of time in the future regardless of whether they are tested just before lunch or just after it. Six-year-olds, by contrast, generally predict correctly in both cases. The improvement in children's sense of future time between the ages of 5 and 6 years is probably influenced by their experience in kindergarten classrooms, where the cycle of seasons, holidays, and daily routines is often emphasized, as well as by increases in language abilities (DeNigris & Brooks 2018).

Children, like adults, are subject to certain illusions about time, in part because of the role attention plays in time perception. When 8-year-olds' attention is focused on the passage of time (e.g., when they expect a prize at the end of a 2-minute wait), they perceive the duration as longer than the same interval when they are not anticipating a prize. Conversely, when they have little to do, they perceive the duration as longer than when they are very busy (Zakay, 1992, 1993). Thus, the adage "A watched pot never boils" has psychological merit.

Reasoning About Time

During middle childhood, children become increasingly proficient at reasoning about time. In particular, they become able to infer that if two events started at the same time, but one event ended later than the other, then the event that ended later lasted longer.

Children as young as 5 years can sometimes make such logical inferences about time, but only in simple, straightforward situations. For instance, when told that two dolls fell asleep at the same time and that one doll awoke before the other, 5-year-olds reason correctly that the doll that awoke later also slept longer (Levin, 1982). However, when 5-year-olds see two toy trains travel in the same direction on parallel tracks, and one train stops farther down the track, they usually say that the train that stopped farther down the track travelled for a longer time, even if the trains started moving from corresponding positions on the tracks and started and stopped at the same time (Acredolo & Schmid, 1981). The problem is that the 5-year-olds' attention is captured by the one train being farther down the track, which leads them to focus on the spatial positions of the trains rather than on their relative starting and stopping times. If this observation reminds you of Piaget's idea of centration (Chapter 4), there is good reason: Piaget's (1969) observations of performance on this task were part of what led him to conclude that children in the preoperational stage often centre on a single dimension and ignore other, more relevant ones.

Preoperational and Concrete Operational Thought

Number

Like causality, space, and time, number is a central dimension of human experience. It is hard to imagine how the world would appear if we did not have at least a crude sense of number—we would not know how many fingers, family members, or shoes we have, for example.

Unsurprisingly, the nativist/empiricist debate has extended to number. Nativists argue that children are born with a core concept of number that includes special mechanisms for representing and learning about the relative numbers of objects in sets, counting, and approximate addition and subtraction (Feigenson, Dehaene, & Spelke, 2004). As evidence, they note that specific brain areas, particularly the intraparietal sulcus, are heavily involved in representing numerical magnitudes (Ansari, 2008; Nieder & Dehaene, 2009) and that specific neurons respond most strongly when particular numbers of objects (e.g., 5 objects) are displayed (Nieder, 2012).

In contrast, empiricists argue that children learn about numbers through the same types of experiences and learning mechanisms that help them acquire other concepts and that infants' numerical competence is not as great as nativists claim (Clearfield,

2006; Lyons & Ansari, 2015). They also note the existence of large differences in numerical understanding among children from different cultures and document the contributions of instruction, language, and cultural values to these differences (Bailey et al., 2015). In this section, we review current evidence regarding numerical development as well as nativist and empiricist perspectives on the evidence.

numerical equality the realization that all sets of *N* objects have something in common

Numerical Equality

Perhaps the most basic understanding of numbers involves **numerical equality**, the idea that all sets of *N* objects have something in common. For example, understanding numerical equality implies recognizing that two dogs, two cups, two balls, and two shoes share the property of "twoness."

Newborns already have some sense of numerical equality in a nonlinguistic (often called "nonsymbolic") sense. One example of this nonsymbolic sense is that after repeatedly hearing sets of four identical syllables, with adjacent sets separated by pauses (e.g., "tu, tu, tu, tu," pause, "tu, tu, tu, tu"), they look more at four objects than at 12; in contrast, after hearing sets of 12 identical syllables, separated by pauses, they look more at the 12 objects (Izard et al., 2009). Although newborns do not know the words "four" or "twelve," they already have a rough concept of these set sizes.

As with discriminations among temporal durations, infants' discriminations between numerical sets depend in large part on the ratio of the number of entities in them. In the study by Izard and colleagues (2009), newborns showed the same tendency to discriminate between 6 and 18 syllables and objects, but not with 4 versus 8, suggesting that they could discriminate the 3:1 ratio but not the 2:1 ratio.

Discrimination among numbers becomes increasingly more precise during the first year and beyond. By 6 months of age, infants discriminate between sets with 2:1 ratios (e.g., 16 versus 8 dots or sounds), but they still cannot discriminate between sets with ratios of 3:2 (e.g., 12 versus 8 dots or sounds) (Libertus & Brannon, 2010; Lipton & Spelke, 2003). By 9 months, infants discriminate ratios of 3:2 but not 4:3 ratios (Cordes & Brannon, 2008). By adulthood, many people are able to reliably discriminate 8:7 ratios (Halberda & Feigenson, 2008).

One exception to the ratio dependence of nonsymbolic number discrimination is that discrimination between very small sets (1 to 4 objects or events) is more accurate, faster, and less variable than would be expected from the ratios alone. For example, infants discriminate two objects from one object and three objects from two objects before they can discriminate larger sets with the same ratio (Piazza, 2011). This phenomenon, which is also apparent in species as varied as guppies, chickens, and monkeys (Agrillo, Piffer, & Bisazza, 2011), indicates that there are at least two different mechanisms for processing the numbers of sights and sounds: one that is used to process very small sets and is based on the specific numbers of objects or events, and one that is based on the ratios of objects or events and is applicable to all numbers of them.

Infants' Arithmetic

In addition to representing nonsymbolic numerical magnitudes, infants can also perform approximate arithmetic on these representations. Four- to 5-month-olds dishabituate when it appears (through trickery) that adding one or two objects to an initial set of one or two objects has produced more or fewer objects than the correct number; infants of the same age also dishabituate when shown unexpected subtractive outcomes with similarly small sets of objects (Wynn, 1992). Older infants dishabituate to surprising addition and subtraction outcomes on larger sets (5 to 10) of objects (McCrink & Wynn, 2004).

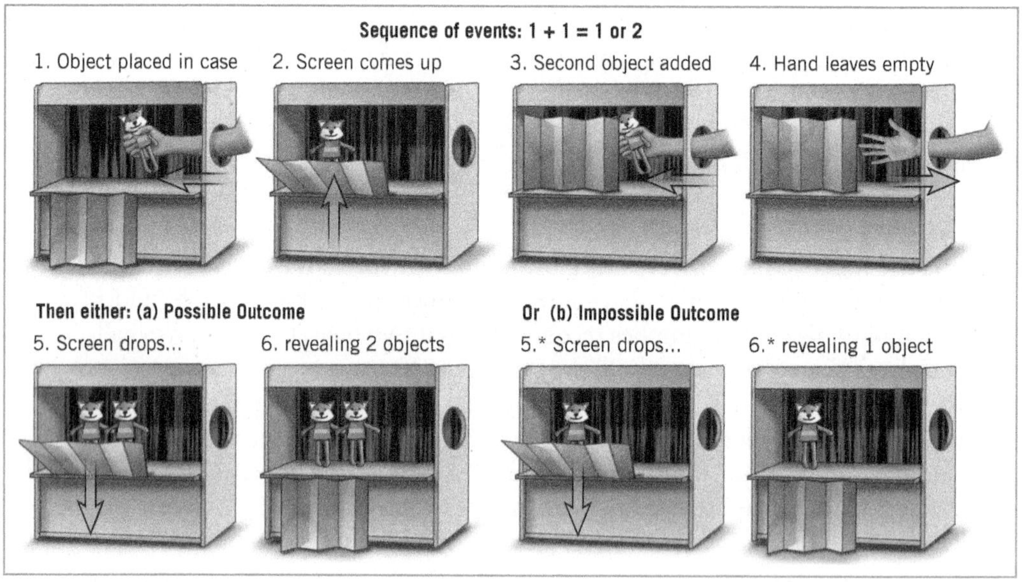
Sequence of events: 1 + 1 = 1 or 2
1. Object placed in case
2. Screen comes up
3. Second object added
4. Hand leaves empty
Then either: (a) Possible Outcome
5. Screen drops...
6. revealing 2 objects
Or (b) Impossible Outcome
5.* Screen drops...
6.* revealing 1 object

FIGURE 7.9 Infants' understanding of addition On the task used by Wynn (1992) to examine whether infants have a rudimentary grasp of addition, 5-month-olds saw (1) a single doll placed on a stage, (2) a screen raised to hide the doll, (3) a hand with a doll in it move toward and then behind the screen, and (4) the hand return empty after having been behind the screen. Then the screen dropped, revealing either the possible event of two dolls on the stage (5 and 6) or the seemingly impossible event of one doll on the stage (5* and 6*). Infants younger than 6 months looked for a longer time at the seemingly impossible event, suggesting their surprise at seeing one doll rather than two.

Figure 7.9 illustrates the experiment used by Wynn to produce this evidence for infant knowledge of arithmetic. A 5-month-old sees a doll on a stage. A screen comes up, hiding the doll from the infant's sight. Next, the infant sees a hand place a second doll behind the screen and then sees the hand emerge from behind the screen without the doll, thus seeming to have left the second doll with the first one. Finally, the screen drops down, revealing either one doll or two. Most 5-month-olds look longer when there is only one doll, suggesting that they expected that 1 + 1 should equal 2 and that they were surprised when they saw only a single object. Similar results are seen with subtraction: 5-month-olds look longer when the apparent removal of one of two objects results in two objects being present than when the removal results in one object being there (Wynn, 1992).

Counting

Many children begin to count verbally at 2 years of age, but their initial understanding of what they are doing is severely limited. After counting flawlessly from 1 to 10, many 2-year-olds have no idea whether 3 is bigger than 5 or 5 is bigger than 3 (Le Corre & Carey, 2007). Toddlers' initial counting resembles singing a song in an unfamiliar foreign language.

Learning the meaning of the counting words at first occurs number by number. Toddlers associate the word "one" with 1 object; a month or two later, they associate "two" with 2 objects; and a month or two later, they associate "three" with 3 objects. After this slow early acquisition period, toddlers seem to realize that these counting words indicate differing quantities, and they subsequently learn the link between number words and the quantities they represent more quickly (Le Corre & Carey, 2007; Le Corre et al., 2006).

In addition to learning counting procedures, preschoolers also acquire understanding of five principles underlying counting (Gelman & Gallistel, 1978):

1. *One–one correspondence:* Each object must be labelled by a single number word.
2. *Stable order:* The numbers should always be recited in the same order.
3. *Cardinality:* The number of objects in the set corresponds to the last number stated.

4. *Order irrelevance:* Objects can be counted left to right, right to left, or in any other order.
5. *Abstraction:* Any set of discrete objects or events can be counted.

Much of the evidence that preschoolers understand these principles comes from their judgments when observing two types of counting procedures: incorrect counts and unusual but correct counts. When 4- or 5-year-olds see a puppet counting in a way that violates the one–one correspondence principle—for example, by labelling a single object with two number words (Figure 7.10a)—they consistently say that the counting is incorrect (Frye et al., 1989; Gelman, Meck, & Merkin, 1986). In contrast, when they see the puppet count in ways that are unusual but that do not violate any principle—for example, by starting in the middle of a row but counting all the objects once and only once (Figure 7.10b)—many (though far from all) 4- and 5-year-olds judge the counting to be correct, even though they say they would not count that way themselves (Briars & Siegler, 1984). The preschoolers' realization that procedures they themselves would not use are nonetheless correct shows that they understand the principles that distinguish correct from incorrect counting.

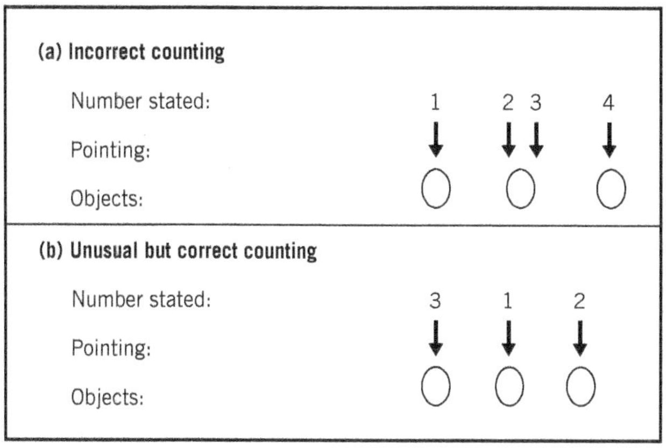

FIGURE 7.10 Counting procedures Counting procedures similar to those used by Frye and colleagues (1989) and Gelman, Meck, and Merkin (1986): (a) an incorrect counting procedure; (b) an unusual but correct procedure.

Although children all over the world learn number words, the rate at which they do so is affected by the specifics of the number system used in their culture. As Kevin Miller and his colleagues (1995) note, for example, most 5-year-olds in China can count to 100 or more, whereas most 5-year-olds in the United States cannot count nearly as high. Part of the reason for this difference in counting proficiency seems to be the greater regularity of the Chinese number system, particularly with respect to numbers in the teens. In both Chinese and English, the words for numbers greater than 20 follow a regular rule: decade name first, digit name second (e.g., twenty-one, twenty-two, and so forth). In Chinese, the words for numbers between 11 and 19 follow the same rule (equivalent to ten-one, ten-two, and so on). In English, however, no simple rule indicates the numbers between 11 and 19; each term has to be learned separately.

Figure 7.11 charts the apparent impact of this cultural difference in number systems. Three-year-olds in the United States and China are comparable in their ability to recite the numbers 1 through 10, which do not follow any rule either in English or Chinese. However, Chinese 4-year-olds quickly learn the numbers in the teens and succeeding decades, whereas their U.S. peers experience prolonged difficulty with the teens. The difference in language is not the only reason that the counting skill of U.S. children lags behind that of children in China. Chinese culture places a much greater emphasis on mathematical skill than U.S. culture does, and Chinese preschoolers are consequently more advanced than their U.S. peers in numerical skills generally, including arithmetic and number line estimation (Siegler & Mu, 2008). Still, the greater simplicity of the Chinese system for naming numbers in the teens seems to contribute to Chinese children's greater counting proficiency.

FIGURE 7.11 Counting level Although 3-year-olds in China and the United States can count to about the same point, 4- and 5-year-olds in China can count much higher than their U.S. peers. One reason for the faster development of Chinese children's counting ability appears to be that the Chinese words for numbers in the teens follow a consistent, easily learned pattern, whereas the English words for numbers in the teens must be memorized one by one. (Data from Miller et al., 1995)

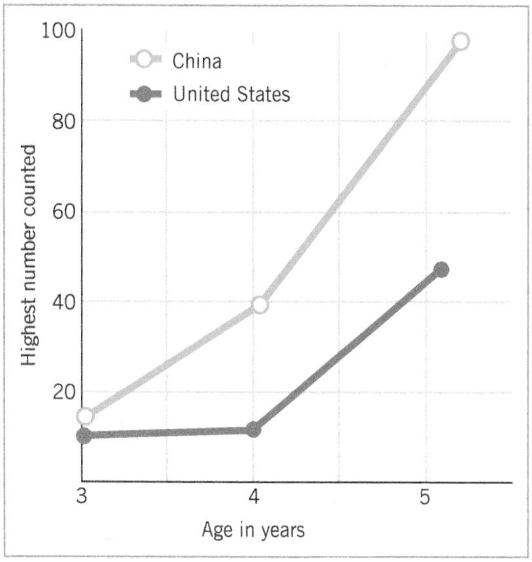

Relations Among Understanding of Space, Time, and Number

Piaget (1952a) hypothesized that infants possess only a general, undifferentiated concept of magnitude, and lack specific concepts of space, time, and number. That is, he thought that infants have a concept of "bigness" but do not distinguish among larger size, longer time, and greater number. Subsequent research has shown that infants *can* distinguish among size, duration, and number. For example, after habituating to different displays with the same number of objects, infants dishabituate when the number of objects changes, even though the space occupied by the new objects and the time for which they are displayed is the same as previously (Xu & Arriaga, 2007; Xu & Spelke, 2000).

However, the fact that infants possess specific concepts of space (including sizes of objects), time, and number does not mean that they lack the type of undifferentiated magnitude concept that Piaget suggested. Indeed, Lourenco and Longo (2010) found that 9-month-olds have a general sense of magnitude that extends to space, number, and time. The infants in their study were initially habituated to the type of display shown at the top of Figure 7.12, in which a particular decoration (e.g., black with white stripes) consistently accompanied the larger of two stimuli on one of the three dimensions (size of objects, number of objects, or duration of display of the objects). Then the infants were presented displays in which the link between decoration and relative magnitude *on a different dimension* either was maintained or changed. For example, infants who had habituated to a link between black with white stripes and larger size might now see that decoration accompanying either the more numerous set (bottom left in Figure 7.12) or the less numerous one (bottom right in Figure 7.12).

Lourenco and Longo found that the infants dishabituated when the decoration that had accompanied the larger size stimulus now accompanied the stimulus that was smaller on another dimension (number), but not when that decoration

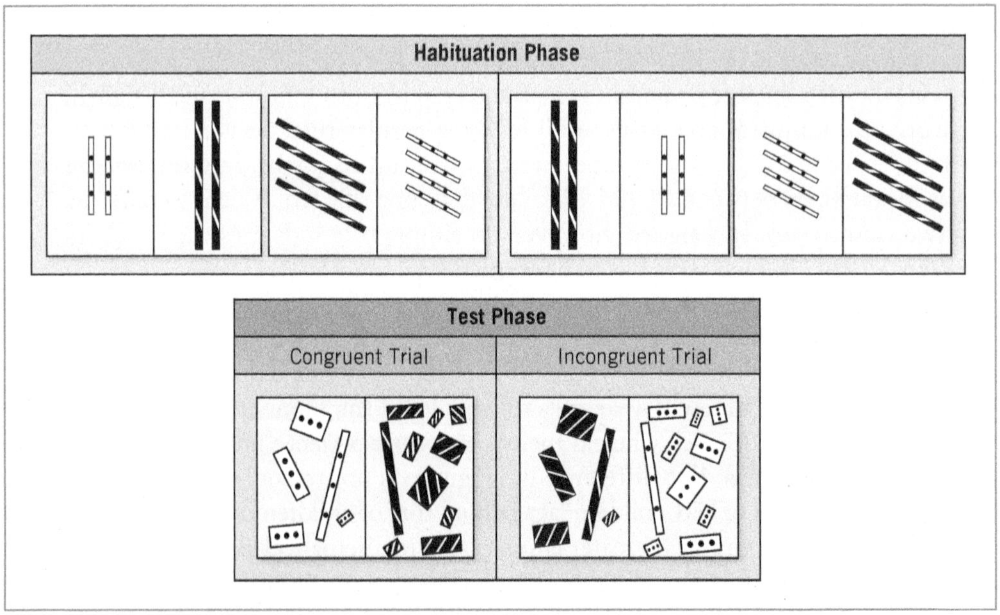

COURTESY OF STELLA LOURENCO

FIGURE 7.12 Infants' general magnitude representations To test whether infants possess a general sense of magnitude, Lourenco and Longo (2010) first presented pairs of figures, such as those in the top panel, in which one decoration (here, black with white stripes) was associated with the larger value of one quantitative dimension (here, larger size). After this habituation phase, the infants were shown in the test phase either congruent trials (bottom left), in which the same decoration accompanied the choice with the greater quantitative value (here, the greater number of objects), or incongruent trials (bottom right), in which that decoration accompanied the choice with the smaller quantitative value (here, the smaller number of objects). Regardless of the particular pair of quantitative dimensions used during the habituation and test phases, children looked longer during incongruent trials, indicating that they expected that particular decoration to continue to accompany the choice with the larger value on whichever quantitative dimension varied.

accompanied the stimulus that was larger on that other dimension. Similar results were obtained regardless of whether the habituated dimension was size, number, or time and regardless of whether the dimension that subsequently varied was size, number, or time.

Other research suggests the same conclusion (de Hevia & Spelke, 2010; Srinivasan & Carey, 2010). For instance, the ratios required for infants of a given age to discriminate between two stimuli are similar regardless of whether the discrimination involves time, space, or number (Brannon, Lutz, & Cordes, 2006; Brannon, Suanda, & Libertus, 2007). Moreover, overlapping brain areas in the intraparietal sulcus are involved in representing all three dimensions (Dehaene & Brannon, 2011). Thus, infants appear to have both the general, undifferentiated concept of magnitude that Piaget hypothesized they have, as well as the more specific concepts of time, space, and number that he hypothesized they lack.

REVIEW QUESTION

How would you construct a study of the understanding of space, number, or time among infants and young children? ■

CHAPTER SUMMARY

To understand their experiences, children must learn that the world includes several types of objects: people, other living things, and inanimate objects. Children also need a basic understanding of causality, space, time, and number, so that they will be able to code their experiences in terms of why, where, when, and how often events occurred.

Understanding Who or What

- Early categories of objects are based in large part on perceptual similarity, especially similarity in the shapes of the objects.
- By age 2 or 3 years, children form category hierarchies: animal/dog/poodle, furniture/chair/La-Z-Boy, and so on.
- From infancy onward, children differentiate people from other animals and inanimate objects. For example, infants smile more at people than at either rabbits or robots.
- By age 4 or 5 years, preschoolers develop a rudimentary but well-organized theory of mind for understanding people's behaviour. A key assumption of this theory of mind is that desires and beliefs motivate specific actions.
- Understanding that other people will act on their beliefs, even when the beliefs are false, is very difficult for 3-year-olds; many children do not gain this understanding until age 5.
- Animals and plants, especially animals, are of great interest to young children. When animals are present, infants and toddlers pay careful attention to them.
- By age 4 years, children develop an elaborate understanding of living things, including coherent ideas about invisible processes such as growth, inheritance, illness, and healing. Both their natural fascination with living things and the input they receive from the environment contribute to their knowledge about plants and animals.

Understanding Why, Where, When, and How Many

- Debates between nativists and empiricists have increased our understanding of infants' impressive understanding of fundamental concepts regarding cause–effect relations, the human mind, space, time, and number, as well as the experiences and learning mechanisms that contribute to subsequent development of these concepts.
- The development of causal reasoning about physical events begins in infancy. By 6 to 12 months, infants understand the likely consequences of objects colliding. Understanding causal relations among actions helps 1-year-olds remember them.
- By 4 or 5 years, children seem to realize that causes are necessary for events to occur. When no cause is obvious, they search for one. However, many preschoolers believe in magic as well as physical cause–effect relations.
- People, like other animals, are biologically prepared to code space. Early in infancy, they code locations of other objects in

relation to their own location and to landmarks. As they gain the ability to move around on their own, children gain a sense of locations relative to the overall environment as well as to their own body's current location.

- Children who are born blind have surprisingly good representations of space, though some aspects of their spatial processing, especially processing of faces, remain poor even if corrective surgery is performed during infancy.
- Just as infants are born with an ability to code some aspects of space, so they are born with an ability to code some aspects of time. Even 3-month-olds code the order in which events occur. Infants of that age can also use consistent sequences of past events to anticipate future events.
- By age 5 years, children can reason about time, in the sense of inferring that if two events started at the same time, and one stopped later than the other, the event that stopped later took longer. However, they can do this only when there are no interfering perceptual cues.
- Infants discriminate differences between the numbers of objects, sounds, or events when the ratio of the numbers is large. During their first year, they become able to discriminate smaller ratios of objects and events, a trend that continues to adulthood. From infancy onward, representations of small sets, those with 1 to 4 items, is more precise than those with larger sets.
- By age 3 years, most children learn to count 10 objects. Their counting seems to reflect understanding of certain principles, such as that each object should be labelled by a single number word. Children's subsequent rate of learning about numbers reflects their culture's number system and the degree to which their culture values numerical knowledge.
- From infancy onward, children also possess a general representation of magnitude that extends to space, time, and number.

Test Yourself

1. The belief that infants are born with some sense of fundamental concepts, such as time, space, and number, is a basic component of
   a. naïve psychology.
   b. theory of mind.
   c. nativism.
   d. empiricism.
2. In Krascum and Andrews' experiments, young children were better able to classify wugs and gillies after being told stories explaining each creature's unique appearance. Their findings support the importance of
   a. naïve psychology.
   b. causal relationships.
   c. magical thinking.
   d. false beliefs.
3. Research by Gelman and Kalish (2006) suggests that infants tend to divide objects into three general categories. Which of the following is *not* one of the general categories as identified by their research?
   a. Food
   b. Inanimate objects
   c. People
   d. Other animals
4. Which of the following represents the most typical organization of superordinate, subordinate, and basic category levels that young children tend to form?
   a. Animals/dogs/poodles
   b. Objects/plants/animals
   c. Parents/siblings/grandparents
   d. Dogs/animals/poodles
5. Which category level do children tend to form first?
   a. Superordinate
   b. Subordinate
   c. Basic
   d. Primary
6. The proposed existence of a theory of mind module, which is the brain mechanism devoted to understanding other human beings, is most closely associated with advocates of which position?
   a. Empiricism
   b. Existentialism
   c. Essentialism
   d. Nativism
7. What is the significance of the false-belief problem?
   a. It illustrates that very young children do not understand that other people act on their own beliefs, even when those beliefs are false.
   b. It presents evidence that young children do not fully understand causal relationships.
   c. It proves that there are certain false beliefs that an individual will maintain from early childhood into adolescence.
   d. It supports the view that the age at which a child can understand other people's intentions varies by culture.
8. Which of the following is an example of sociodramatic play?
   a. Ezra is making car noises while pushing a toy car.
   b. Tanya is using her water bottle as a microphone.
   c. Laila is pretending that she is in school and her friend Tosha is the teacher.
   d. LeDonna is flying a kite with her father.

9. Ted believes that the reason his dog barks, wags her tail, and likes to go outside is because the dog has an inner "dogness." Ted's belief is an example of
   a. false belief.
   b. essentialism.
   c. nativism.
   d. perceptual categorization.
10. A mother magically produces a coin from behind her 6-year-old son's ear. Which of the following scenarios describes the response of a typical 6-year-old?
    a. The son searches his mother's hands, up her sleeves, and behind his ear to try to make sense of the event.
    b. The son does not react to this unusual event.
    c. The son does not find the trick funny and storms out of the room.
    d. The son realizes immediately that the mother has hidden the coin in her hand.
11. Nativists and empiricists have intense debates about the development of spatial thinking, but on which of the following points do these two groups tend to agree?
    a. Infants show little to no understanding of spatial concepts.
    b. Self-movement does not appear to aid in the development of spatial learning.
    c. Children are unable to use geometric information in locating objects.
    d. The development of the hippocampus is related to improvements in spatial learning.
12. According to Piaget, children's coding of locations of objects relative to their own bodies is referred to as ____________ representations.
    a. landmark
    b. allocentric spatial
    c. egocentric spatial
    d. directional
13. In front of Sue are three balls, three teddy bears, three pencils, and three apples. Sue studies the groups of objects and realizes that they all share the property of "threeness." Sue is demonstrating an understanding of what concept?
    a. Stable order
    b. Order irrelevance
    c. Numerical equality
    d. Abstraction
14. Kamar is happily counting all of his holiday candy, reciting a number as he touches each piece: "One, two, three, four, five, six, seven, eight, nine." He holds up the final piece and states, "I have seven pieces of candy!" Kamar's counting skills suggests he lacks an understanding of
    a. stable order.
    b. cardinality.
    c. one–one correspondence.
    d. abstraction.
15. Which of the following statements describes the counting principle of abstraction?
    a. Any set of discrete objects or events can be counted.
    b. Objects can be counted in any order.
    c. Each object must be labelled by a single number word.
    d. The numbers should always be recited in the same order.

LaunchPad
macmillan learning

DON'T STOP NOW! Research shows that testing yourself is a powerful learning tool. Visit LaunchPad to access the LearningCurve adaptive quizzing system, which gives you a personalized study plan to help build your mastery of the chapter material through videos, activities, and more. **Go to launchpadworks.com.**

Critical Thinking Questions

1. Why is it useful for people to organize categories into hierarchies, such as animal/dog/poodle or vehicle/car/Tesla?
2. Did you have an imaginary companion as a child or know someone who did? What functions did the invisible friend serve, and why do you think you or the other person later stopped imagining the companion?
3. Why do you think 5-year-olds are so much better at false-belief problems than 3-year-olds are?
4. Self-produced movement enhances children's representation of space. What evolutionary purpose might this serve?
5. Describe the thoughts that might go through a 5-year-old's mind when the child sees two Santa Clauses walking past each other.
6. Do infants possess a basic understanding of arithmetic? Why or why not?
7. Why might it be useful for children to have a general representation of quantity, as well as specific representations of space, time, and number?
8. After reading this chapter, do you lean more toward a nativist or an empiricist approach to conceptual development? What reasons led to your conclusion?

Key Terms

basic level, p. 236
category hierarchy, p. 235
concepts, p. 233
egocentric spatial representations, p. 257
essentialism, p. 250
false-belief problems, p. 242
naïve psychology, p. 238
numerical equality, p. 263
object substitution, p. 245
perceptual categorization, p. 236
pretend play, p. 245
sociodramatic play, p. 246
subordinate level, p. 236
superordinate level, p. 236
theory of mind, p. 241
theory of mind module (TOMM), p. 243

Answers to Test Yourself

1. c, **2.** b, **3.** a, **4.** d, **5.** c, **6.** d, **7.** a, **8.** c, **9.** b, **10.** a, **11.** d, **12.** c, **13.** c, **14.** b, **15.** a

CHAPTER

8

Intelligence and Academic Achievement

HERITAGE IMAGES/GETTY IMAGES

CHARLES HAIGH-WOOD (1856–1927), *Story Time* (oil on canvas, 1893)

THEMES

NATURE AND NURTURE ■ THE ACTIVE CHILD ■ CONTINUITY/DISCONTINUITY

MECHANISMS OF CHANGE ■ THE SOCIOCULTURAL CONTEXT

INDIVIDUAL DIFFERENCES ■ RESEARCH AND CHILDREN'S WELFARE

In 1904, the minister of education of France faced a problem. France, like other western European and North American countries, had recently introduced universal public education, and it was apparent that some children were not learning well. Therefore, the minister wanted a means of identifying children who would have difficulty succeeding in standard classrooms, so that they could be given special education. His problem was how to identify such children.

One obvious solution was to ask teachers to indicate which of their students were encountering difficulty. However, the minister worried that teachers' assessments might be biased. In particular, he was concerned that some teachers would be prejudiced against poor children and would claim that those children were unable to learn, even if they actually could. He therefore asked Alfred Binet, a French psychologist who studied intelligence, to develop an easy-to-administer objective test of intelligence.

The prevailing view at the time was that intelligence is based on simple skills, such as associating objects with the sounds they make (e.g., ducks with quacking, bells with ringing), responding quickly to stimuli, and recognizing whether two objects are identical or subtly different. According to this view, children who are more adept than their peers at such simple skills learn more quickly and thus become more intelligent. The theory was plausible—but wrong. Differences in simple skills among children proved only modestly related to differences among them in broader, everyday indicators of intelligence, such as school performance.

Binet's theory differed from the prevailing wisdom of his time. He believed that the key components of intelligence were high-level abilities, such as problem solving, reasoning, and judgment, and he maintained that intelligence tests should assess such abilities directly. Therefore, on the test that he and his colleague Théophile Simon devised—the *Binet–Simon Intelligence Test*—children were asked (among other things) to interpret proverbs, solve puzzles, define words, and sequence cartoon panels so that the jokes made sense.

Binet's approach was successful in identifying children who would have difficulty learning from classroom instruction; they were the children who rarely could interpret the proverbs, solve the puzzles, define the words, and so on. More generally, children's performance on the Binet–Simon Intelligence Test correlated highly not only with their school grades at the time of testing but also with their grades years later. The test was also reasonably successful in meeting a goal of intelligence testing that has been pursued ever since—to provide an objective measure of scholastic aptitude that would allow fairer decisions about children's schooling, including which children should be in honors classes and which need special education.

In addition to the practical impact of his test, Binet's theoretical approach to intelligence has continued to influence research on the topic to this day. In most areas of cognitive development—perception, language, conceptual understanding, and so forth—the emphasis is on age-related changes: the ways in which younger children differ from older ones. Following Binet's lead, however, research on intelligence has focused on *individual differences*—that is, on how and why children of the same age differ from one another and on the amount of continuity of such individual differences over time.

Questions regarding the development of intelligence excite strong passions, and for good reason. Research in this area raises many of the most basic issues about human nature: the roles of heredity and environment, the influence of ethnic and racial differences, the effects of wealth and poverty, and the possibility of improvement. Almost everyone has opinions, often heartfelt ones, about why some people are more intelligent than others.

Intelligence research has added greatly to understanding all the major themes emphasized in this book: the nature and origins of *individual differences*, the contributions of the *active child* and of the *sociocultural context*, the way in which *nature and nurture* together shape development, the degree of *continuity* in a key human trait, the *mechanisms* that produce changes, and the relation between *research and children's welfare*. Before examining what is known about the development of intelligence, however, we must examine a question that sounds simple but actually is very complex: What *is* intelligence?

What Is Intelligence?

Intelligence is notoriously difficult to define, but this has not kept people from trying. Part of the difficulty is that intelligence can reasonably be described at three levels of analysis: as one thing, as a few things, or as many things (Carroll, 1993).

Intelligence as a Single Trait

Some researchers view intelligence as a single trait that influences all aspects of cognitive functioning. Supporting this idea is the fact that performance on all intellectual tasks is positively correlated: children who do well on one task usually do well on others (Geary, 2005). These positive correlations occur even among dissimilar intellectual tasks—for example, remembering lists of numbers, knowing word meanings, and folding pieces of paper to reproduce printed designs. Such omnipresent positive correlations have led to the hypothesis that each of us possesses a certain amount of ***g***, or **general intelligence**, and that *g* influences our ability to think and learn on all intellectual tasks (Carroll, 2005; Spearman, 1927).

Numerous findings attest to the usefulness of viewing intelligence as a single trait. Measures of *g*, such as overall scores on intelligence tests, correlate positively with school grades and achievement test performance (Gottfredson, 2011). At the level of cognitive and brain mechanisms, *g* correlates with information processing speed (Coyle et al., 2011; Deary, 2012), speed of neural transmission (Vernon et al., 2000), and brain volume (McDaniel, 2005). Measures of *g* also correlate strongly with people's general information about the world (Lubinski & Humphreys, 1997). Such evidence supports the view of intelligence as a single trait that involves the ability to think and learn.

Intelligence as a Few Basic Abilities

There are also good arguments for viewing intelligence as more than a single general trait. The simplest such view holds that there are two types of intelligence: *fluid intelligence* and *crystallized intelligence* (Geary, 2005):

- **Fluid intelligence** involves the ability to think on the spot—for example, by drawing inferences and understanding relations between concepts that have not been encountered previously. It is closely related to adaptation to novel tasks, speed of information processing, working-memory functioning, and ability to control attention (Geary, 2005).

***g* (general intelligence)** cognitive processes that influence the ability to think and learn on all intellectual tasks

fluid intelligence ability to think on the spot to solve novel problems

crystallized intelligence factual knowledge about the world

primary mental abilities seven abilities proposed by Thurstone as crucial to intelligence

three-stratum theory of intelligence Carroll's model that places *g* at the top of the intelligence hierarchy, eight moderately general abilities in the middle, and many specific processes at the bottom

- **Crystallized intelligence** is factual knowledge, such as knowledge of word meanings, state capitals, answers to arithmetic problems, and so on. It reflects long-term memory for prior experiences and is closely related to verbal ability.

The distinction between fluid and crystallized intelligence is supported by the fact that tests of each type of intelligence correlate more highly with tests of the same type than they do with tests of the other type (Horn & McArdle, 2007). Thus, a child's performance relative to peers on one test of fluid intelligence tends to more closely resemble the child's performance on other tests of fluid intelligence than it does the child's relative performance on tests of crystallized intelligence. Similarly, children's relative performance on different tests of crystallized intelligence tend to be more similar than their performance on one test of crystallized and one test of fluid intelligence.

The two types of intelligence also have different developmental courses. Crystallized intelligence increases steadily from early in life to old age, whereas fluid intelligence peaks around age 20 and slowly declines thereafter (Salthouse, 2009). The brain areas most active in the two types of intelligence differ, too: the prefrontal cortex usually is highly active on measures of fluid intelligence but tends to be less active on measures of crystallized intelligence (Jung & Haier, 2007).

A somewhat more differentiated view of intelligence proposes that the human intellect is composed of seven **primary mental abilities**: word fluency, verbal meaning, reasoning, spatial visualization, numbering, rote memory, and perceptual speed (Thurstone, 1938). The key evidence for the usefulness of dividing intelligence into these seven abilities is similar to that for the distinction between fluid and crystallized intelligence. Scores on various tests of a single ability tend to correlate more strongly with one another than do scores on tests of different abilities. For example, although both spatial visualization and perceptual speed are measures of fluid intelligence, children tend to perform more similarly on two tests of spatial visualization than they do on a test of spatial visualization and a test of perceptual speed. The trade-off between these two views of intelligence is between the simplicity of the crystallized/fluid distinction and the greater precision of the seven primary mental abilities.

Intelligence as Numerous Cognitive Processes

A third view envisions intelligence as comprising numerous, distinct *processes*. Information-processing analyses of how people solve intelligence test items and how they perform everyday intellectual tasks such as reading, writing, and arithmetic reveal that a great many processes are involved. These processes include remembering, perceiving, attending, comprehending, encoding, associating, generalizing, planning, reasoning, forming concepts, solving problems, generating and applying strategies, and so on. Viewing intelligence as "many processes" allows yet more precise specification of the mechanisms involved in intelligent behaviour than do approaches that view it as "a single trait" or as "several abilities."

A Proposed Resolution

How can these competing perspectives on intelligence be reconciled? After studying intelligence for more than half a century, John B. Carroll (1993, 2005) proposed a grand synthesis: the **three-stratum theory of intelligence** (Figure 8.1). At the top of the hierarchy is *g*; in the middle are several moderately general abilities (which include fluid and crystallized intelligence and other competencies similar

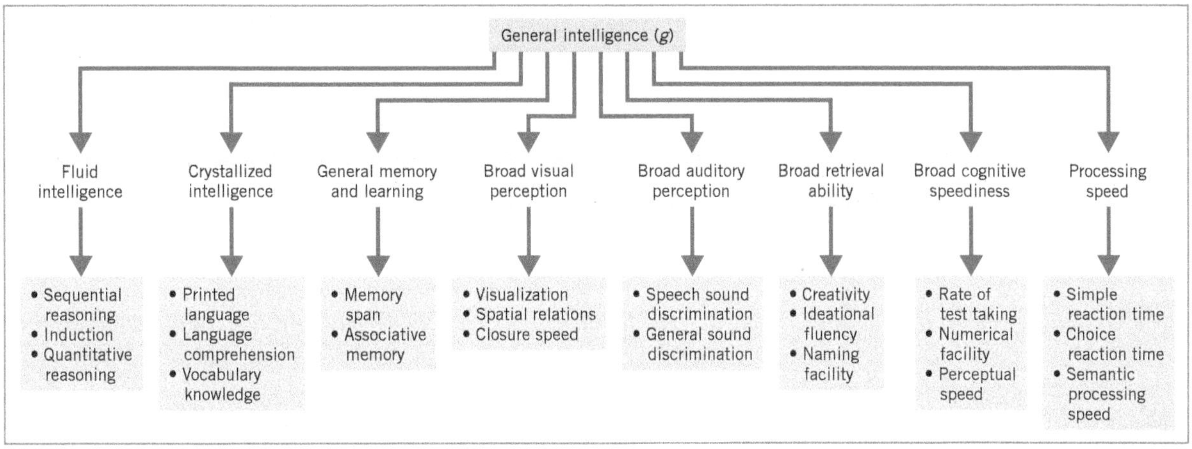

FIGURE 8.1 **Carroll's three-stratum theory of intelligence** In Carroll's hierarchy, general intelligence (*g*) influences several intermediate-level abilities, and each intermediate-level ability influences a variety of specific processes. As this model suggests, intelligence can be usefully viewed as a single entity, as a small set of abilities, or as a very large number of particular processes.

to Thurstone's seven primary mental abilities); at the bottom are many specific processes. General intelligence influences all moderately general abilities, and both general intelligence and the moderately general abilities influence the specific processes. For instance, knowing someone's general intelligence allows for fairly reliable prediction of the person's general memory skills; knowing both general intelligence and general memory skills allows quite reliable prediction of the person's memory span; and knowing all three allows very accurate prediction of the person's memory span for a particular type of material, such as words, letters, or numbers. Thus, for the question "Is intelligence a single trait, a few abilities, or many processes?" the correct answer seems to be "All of the above."

REVIEW QUESTIONS

How would you have defined intelligence prior to reading this section? Which elements of the various theories of intelligence, including Carroll's three-stratum theory, align with your previous conception of intelligence, and which do not? ■

Measuring Intelligence

Although intelligence is usually viewed as an invisible *capacity* to think and learn, any measure of it must be based on *observable behaviour*. Thus, when we say that a person is intelligent, we mean that the person acts in intelligent ways. One of Binet's profound insights was that the best way to measure intelligence is by observing people's actions on tasks that require varied types of intelligence: problem solving, memory, language comprehension, spatial reasoning, and so on. Modern intelligence tests continue to sample these and other aspects of intelligence.

Intelligence testing is highly controversial. Critics such as Ceci (1996) and Sternberg (2008) argue that measuring a quality as complex and multifaceted as intelligence requires assessing a much broader range of abilities than are assessed by current intelligence tests; that current intelligence tests are culturally biased; and that reducing a person's intelligence to a number (the IQ score) is simplistic and ethically questionable. In contrast, advocates (e.g., Gottfredson, 1997; Horn & McArdle, 2007) argue that intelligence tests are better than any alternative method for predicting important outcomes such as school grades, achievement test scores, and occupational success; that they are valuable for making decisions such as which children should be given special education; and that alternative methods for making educational decisions, such as evaluations by teachers or psychologists, are subject to greater bias. Knowing the facts about intelligence tests and understanding the issues surrounding their use is crucial to generating informed opinions about these issues.

The Contents of Intelligence Tests

Intelligence is manifested in different abilities at different ages. For example, language ability is not a part of intelligence at 4 months of age because infants this young neither produce nor understand words, but it is obviously a vital part of intelligence at 4 years of age. The items on tests developed to measure intelligence at different ages reflect these changing contributions. For instance, on the Stanford–Binet intelligence test (a descendant of the original Binet–Simon test), 2-year-olds are asked to identify the objects depicted in line drawings (a test of object recognition), to find an object that they earlier saw someone hide (a test of learning and memory), and to place each of three objects in a hole of the proper shape (a test of perceptual skill and motor coordination). The version of the Stanford–Binet presented to 10-year-olds asks them to define words (a test of verbal ability), to explain why certain social institutions exist (a test of general information and verbal reasoning), and to count the blocks in a picture in which the existence of some blocks must be inferred (a test of problem solving and spatial reasoning).

Intelligence tests have had their greatest success and widest application with children who are at least 5 or 6 years old. The exact abilities examined, and the items used to examine them, vary somewhat from test to test, but there is considerable similarity among the leading tests.

The most widely used intelligence test for children 6 years and older is the **Wechsler Intelligence Scale for Children (WISC)**. In Canada, the WISC-V-Canadian is used (Cormier, Kennedy, & Aquilina, 2016). This version of the test relies on the same test items as the WISC-IV but is normed on a Canadian sample of children. Thus, it captures the abilities of the current population of children in Canada rather than relying on comparisons to samples of American children.

The conception of intelligence underlying the WISC-V is consistent with Carroll's three-stratum framework, proposing that intelligence includes general ability (*g*), several moderately general abilities, and a large number of specific processes. The test yields not only an overall score but also separate scores on five moderately general abilities — verbal comprehension, visual-spatial processing, working memory, fluid reasoning, and processing speed. The WISC-V measures these abilities because they reflect skills that are important within information-processing theories, correlate positively with other aspects of intelligence, and are related to important outcomes, notably school grades and later occupational success. Figure 8.2 illustrates several types of items that appear on the WISC-V (the actual items are protected by copyrights and thus cannot be reprinted).

Wechsler Intelligence Scale for Children (WISC) widely used test designed to measure the intelligence of children 6 years and older

IQ (intelligence quotient) a quantitative measure of a child's intelligence relative to that of other children of the same age

The Intelligence Quotient (IQ)

Intelligence tests such as the WISC and the Stanford–Binet provide an overall quantitative measure of a child's intelligence relative to that of other children of the same age. This summary measure is referred to as the child's **IQ (intelligence quotient)**.

Typical Verbal Comprehension Items

Vocabulary "What is a helicopter?"

Similarities "How are a mountain and a river alike?"

Typical Visual-Spatial Processing Items

Block design "Put these nine blocks together so that they look exactly like the picture."

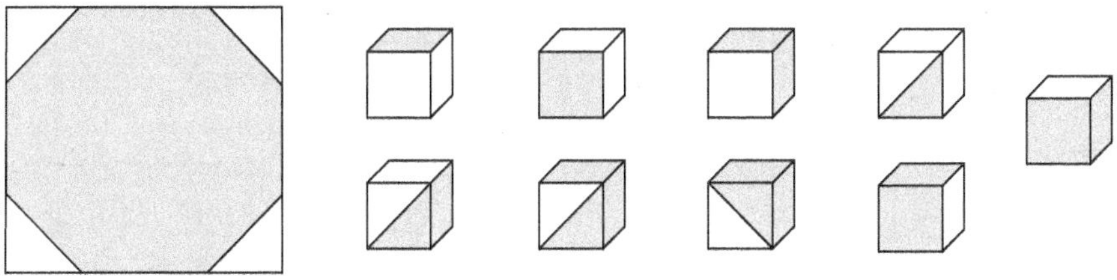

Typical Fluid Reasoning Items

Picture concepts "Pick an object from each pair to make a group of objects that go together"

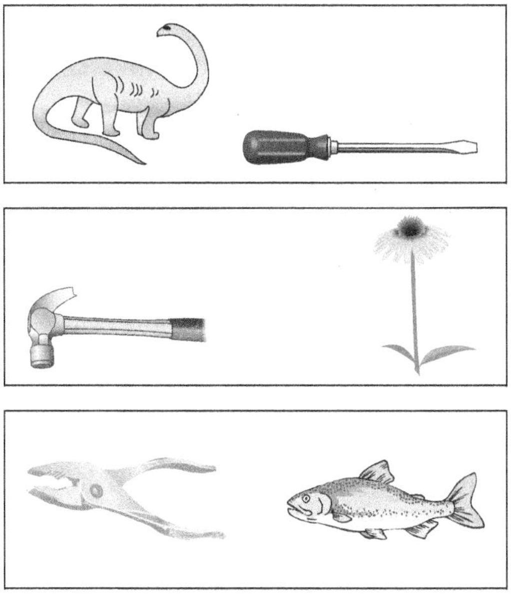

Typical Working Memory Items

Digit span "Repeat the following numbers in order when I'm finished: 5, 3, 7, 4, 9." "Now say these numbers from last to first: 2, 9, 5, 7, 3."

Letter-number sequencing "Repeat the numbers from smallest to biggest, then repeat the letters from earliest to latest in the alphabet: 4, D, 2, G, 7."

Typical Processing Speed Items

Coding "Under each square, put a plus; under each circle, put a minus; under each triangle, put an X."

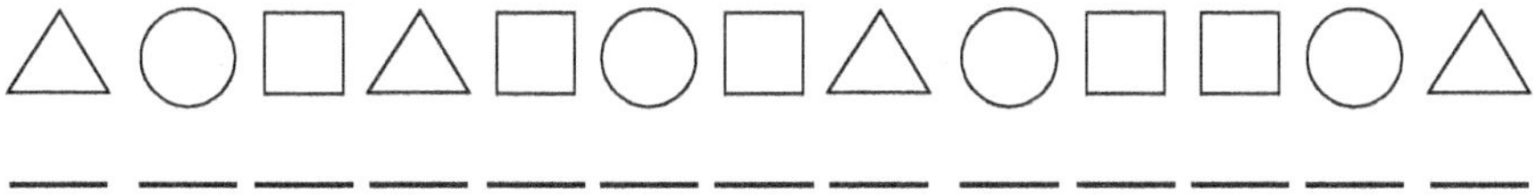

Symbol search "Does the figure to the left of the vertical line also appear to the right of the line?"

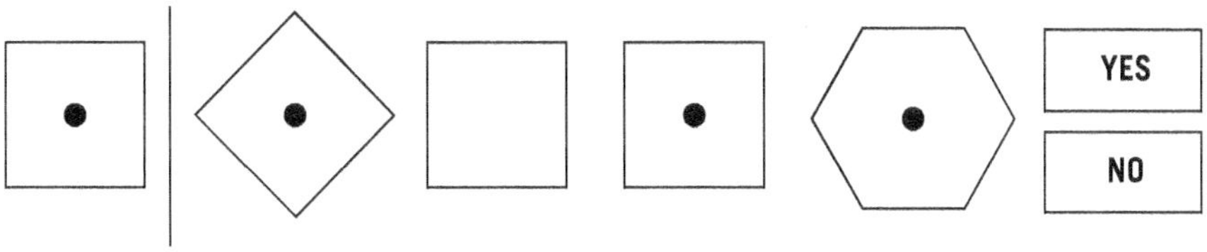

FIGURE 8.2 Four abilities tested by WISC-V This figure shows examples of the types of items used on the WISC-V to measure four aspects of children's intelligence. On most subtests, the measure of performance is simply whether answers are correct, but on some subtests, such as "perceptual speed," the measure of performance is the number of correct answers that are generated in a limited time. These are not actual items from the test but rather are of the same type; copyright restrictions prevent the reproduction of the actual items.

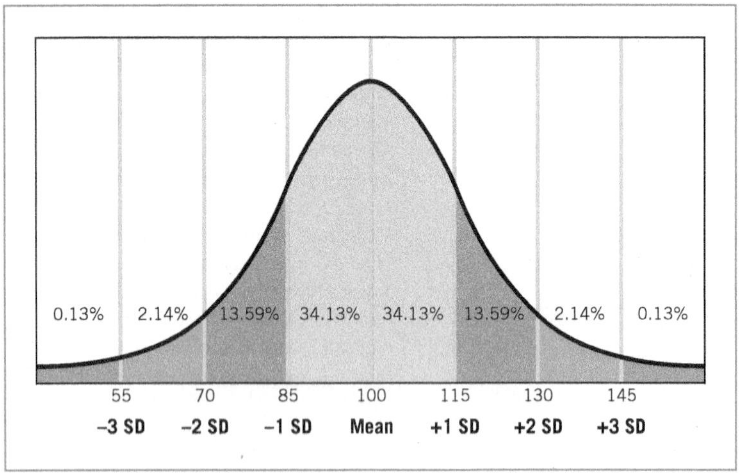

FIGURE 8.3 A normal distribution of IQ scores IQ scores fall into a normal distribution, with a mean of 100 and a standard deviation of 15. Here, the numbers along the base of the graph correspond to IQ scores. The number just below each IQ score indicates how many standard deviation units that score is below or above the mean. Thus, an IQ score of 55 is 3 standard deviations below the mean. The percentages in each interval indicate the percentage of children whose scores fall within that interval; for example, less than 1% of children have IQ scores below 55 and slightly more than 2% score between 55 and 70.

Early researchers on intelligence decided that the mean IQ score would be 100, a convention that has continued ever since.

Understanding how IQ scores are computed, and why they are computed in this way, requires a little background. Early psychologists observed that many human characteristics, such as men's heights, women's heights, men's weights, and women's weights, fall into a **normal distribution**. As shown in Figure 8.3, normal distributions are symmetrical around a mean (average) value, with most scores falling near the mean. The farther a score is from the mean, the smaller the percent of people who obtain it. For example, the mean height of adult males in Canada is approximately 1.74 metres. Many men are 1.72 metres or 1.76 metres, but few men are 1.6 metres or 1.9 metres. The farther from the mean a height falls, the smaller the number of men of that height. IQ scores reflect not only the mean for the test but also its **standard deviation (SD)**, a measure of the variability of scores within a distribution. By definition, in a normal distribution, 68% of scores fall between 1 SD below the mean and 1 SD above it, and 95% of scores fall between 2 SDs below the mean and 2 SDs above it.

On most IQ tests, the standard deviation is about 15 points. Thus, as shown in Figure 8.3, a child scoring 1 SD above the mean for his or her age (a score higher than 84% of children) receives a score of 115 (the mean of 100 plus the 15-point SD), and a child scoring 1 SD below the mean (a score higher than only 16% of children) receives a score of 85 (the mean of 100 minus the SD of 15).

An advantage of this scoring system is that IQ scores at different ages are easy to compare, despite the great increases in knowledge that accompany development in all children. A score of 130 at age 5 means that a child's performance exceeded that of 98% of age peers; a score of 130 at age 10 or 20 means exactly the same thing. This property has facilitated analysis of the stability of individuals' IQ scores over time, a topic to which we turn next.

Intelligence and Testing in Middle Childhood

Continuity of IQ Scores

If IQ is a consistent property of a person, then the IQ scores that people obtain at different ages should be highly correlated. Longitudinal studies that have measured the same children's IQ scores at different ages have, in fact, shown impressive continuity from age 5 onward. For example, one study indicated that the same children's IQ scores at ages 5 and 15 correlated 0.67 (Humphreys, 1989). This is a remarkable degree of continuity over a 10-year period. (Recall from Chapter 1 that a correlation of 1.00 indicates that two variables are perfectly correlated; a correlation of 0.67 is considered strong.) Indeed, the IQ score may be the most stable of all psychological traits (Brody, 1992).

Several variables influence the degree of stability of IQ scores over time. As might be expected, the closer in time that IQ tests are given, the more stability is found. Thus, the same study that found that IQ scores at ages 5 and 15 correlated 0.67 also found that scores at ages 5 and 9 correlated 0.79, and that scores at ages

normal distribution pattern of data in which scores fall symmetrically around a mean value, with most scores falling close to the mean and fewer and fewer scores farther from it

standard deviation (SD) measure of the variability of scores in a distribution; in a normal distribution, 68% of scores fall within 1 SD of the mean, and 95% of scores fall within 2 SDs of the mean

5 and 6 correlated 0.87. In addition, for any given length of time between tests, scores are more stable at older ages. For instance, in one study, IQ scores of 4- and 5-year-olds correlated 0.80, those of 6- and 7-year-olds correlated 0.87, and those of 8- and 9-year-olds correlated 0.90 (Brody, 1992).

Although a person's IQ scores at different ages tend to be similar, the scores are rarely identical. Children who take an IQ test at age 4 and again at age 17 show an average change, up or down, of 13 points; those who take the test at ages 8 and 17 show an average change of 9 points; and those who take it at ages 12 and 17 show an average change of 7 points (Brody, 1992). These changes in the same child's score from one age to another are due at least in part to random variation in factors such as the child's alertness and mood on the test days. Changes in the child's environment, such as those associated with parental divorce or remarriage or moving to a better or worse neighbourhood, also can produce changes in IQ score; the greater similarity of children's environments over shorter periods of time contributes to the greater similarity of scores over shorter periods (Sameroff et al., 1993).

BLEND IMAGES/ALAMY

The IQ scores of children whose parents take an interest in their academic success tend to increase over time.

REVIEW QUESTION

Describe some of the potential limitations of intelligence tests at capturing an accurate measure of a child's intelligence. ■

IQ Scores as Predictors of Important Outcomes

IQ scores are a strong predictor of academic, economic, and occupational success (Nisbett et al., 2012; Sackett, Borneman, & Connelly, 2008). They correlate quite strongly with school grades and achievement test scores, both at the time of the test and years later (Ritchie, 2016). Substantial relations between IQ score and performance in intellectually demanding occupations are present not only when the person is hired but for at least 10 years after (Sackett et al., 2008).

In part, the positive relation between IQ score and occupational and economic success stems from the fact that standardized test scores serve as gatekeepers, determining which students gain access to the training and credentials required for entry into lucrative professions. Even among people who initially have the same job, however, those with higher IQ scores tend to perform better, earn more money, and receive better promotions (Schmidt & Hunter, 2004).

A child's IQ score is more closely related to the child's later occupational success than is the socioeconomic status of the child's family, the school the child attends, or any other variable that has been studied (Ganzach et al., 2013). These relations hold even at the top of the test score distribution. Although popular books

PETER BECK/GETTY IMAGES

Exceptionally early readers, such as this 3½-year-old, often continue to be excellent readers throughout life.

self-discipline ability to inhibit actions, follow rules, and avoid impulsive reactions

such as *Outliers* (Gladwell, 2008) claim that people with *fairly* high test scores achieve grades and occupational success equivalent to those of people with *very* high scores, empirical research indicates that even at the top of the distribution, the higher the test score, the higher that subsequent achievement is likely to be (Lubinski, Benbow, & Kell, 2014).

Consider a long-term study of 320 children who took the SAT, a standardized test for college admission in the United States, by age 13 as part of a national talent search and who scored in the top 0.01% (1 in 10,000) in verbal or math ability. Among their accomplishments by age 23 were adapting Pink Floyd's *The Wall* into a multimedia rock opera, developing one of the most popular video games in the United States, and inventing a navigation system that was used to land a rocket on Mars (Lubinski et al., 2001). As a group, they had published 11 articles in scientific and medical journals and won numerous major awards in areas ranging from physics to creative writing. By age 38, more than half of the original sample had received a PhD, MD, or JD (Kell, Lubinski, & Benbow, 2013). Their rate of PhDs was more than 50 times higher than that for the general population, and their rate of patents was 11 times that in the general population. Even within this elite sample, higher initial SAT mathematics scores predicted higher achievement. For example, the higher the score on the SAT math test at age 13, the greater the number of patents and publications in scholarly journals—especially those in science, engineering, and mathematics—at age 38.

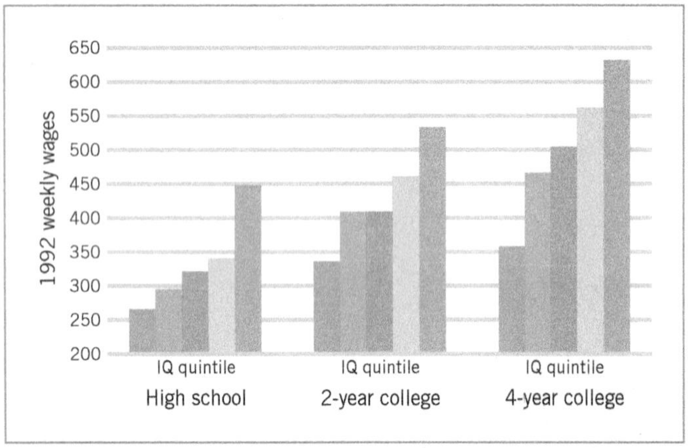

FIGURE 8.4 Effects of intelligence and education on income Intelligence influences income, but so do other factors, such as education. These data indicate the average income of people who received different levels of education and who scored in different quintiles (fifths) of the IQ distribution. Within any given educational level, people with higher IQ scores earned more. Thus, among people with only a high school education, those who scored in the bottom 20% on an IQ test (the blue bar) averaged only about half as much in weekly salary as those who scored in the top 20% (the purple bar). Even among people in the top 20% in IQ score, those whose most advanced educational attainment was completing high school earned only about two-thirds as much as those with a four-year college education. (Data from Ceci, 1996)

Other Predictors of Success

As strong a predictor of academic, economic, and occupational success as IQ score is, it is far from the only influence. A child's other characteristics, such as motivation to succeed, conscientiousness, intellectual curiosity, persistence in the face of obstacles, creativity, physical and mental health, and social skills, are also very important (Makel et al., 2016; Ritchie, 2016). For instance, **self-discipline**—the ability to inhibit actions, follow rules, and avoid impulsive reactions—is more predictive of changes in report card grades between 5th and 9th grades than is IQ score, though IQ score is more predictive of changes in achievement test scores over the same period (Duckworth, Quinn, & Tsukayama, 2012). Similarly, "practical intelligence"—skills useful in everyday life but not measured by traditional intelligence tests, such as accurately reading other people's intentions and motivating others to work effectively as a team—predict occupational success beyond the influence of IQ score (Cianciolo et al., 2006; Sternberg, 2003). Moreover, IQ tests measure motivation to succeed on the test as well as intellect (Duckworth et al., 2011).

As these studies demonstrate, the same data set can provide evidence for the impact of IQ and of other factors on educational, economic, and occupational success. Consider the data in Figure 8.4. Consistent with the importance of IQ, the figure shows that among people with the same level of education, those with higher IQ scores have higher incomes. Consistent with the importance of other factors, the figure shows that among people with comparable IQ scores, those who complete more years of education have higher incomes. Thus, while IQ is a key contributor to educational, occupational, and economic success, motivational and environmental factors are also crucial.

REVIEW QUESTION

How would you construct a study to investigate the relationship between IQ score and other factors, such as motivation, SES, or level of educational attainment, in predicting an individual's future success? ■

Genes, Environment, and the Development of Intelligence

No issue in psychology has produced more acrimonious debate than the issue of how heredity and environment influence intelligence. Even people who recognize that intelligence, like all human qualities, is constructed through the continuous interaction of genes and environment often forget this fact and take extreme positions that are based more on emotion and ideology than on logic and evidence.

A useful starting point for thinking about genetic and environmental influences on intelligence is Bronfenbrenner's (1993) bioecological model of development. This model, which is discussed in more depth in Chapter 9, envisions children's lives as embedded within a series of increasingly encompassing environments. The child, with a unique set of qualities, including his or her genetic endowment and personal experiences, is at the centre. Surrounding the child is the immediate environment, especially the people and institutions with which the child interacts directly: family, school, classmates, teachers, neighbours, and so on. Surrounding the immediate environment are more distant, and less tangible, forces that also influence development: cultural attitudes, the social and economic system, mass media, the government, and so on. We now examine how qualities of the child, the child's immediate environment, and the broader society influence the development of intelligence.

Qualities of the Child

Children contribute greatly to their own intellectual development through their genetic endowment, the reactions they elicit from other people, and their choice of environments.

Genetic Contributions to Intelligence

As noted in Chapter 3, the genome substantially influences intelligence. This genetic influence varies with age (Figure 8.5): it is moderate in early childhood and becomes large by adolescence and adulthood (Plomin & Deary, 2015). Reflecting the same trend, IQ scores of adopted children and their biological parents become increasingly correlated as the children develop, even without contact between them, but the scores of adopted children and their adoptive parents become less correlated over the course of development (Plomin et al., 1997).

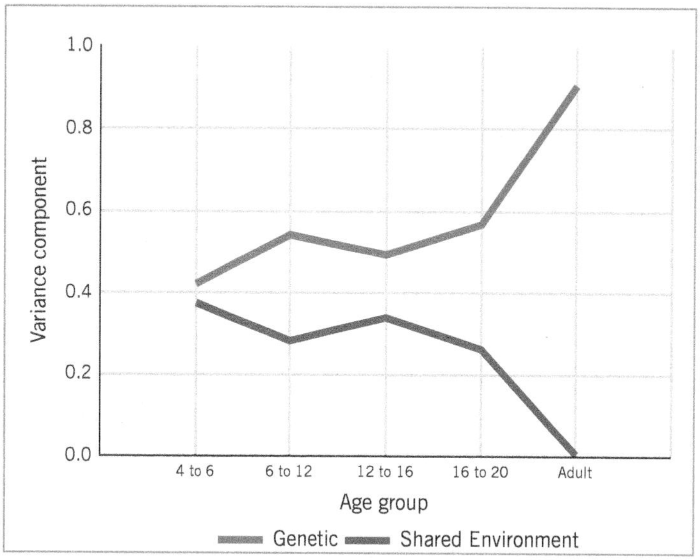

FIGURE 8.5 Changes with age in factors influencing intelligence As children grow into adults, the influence of genetics on individual differences in intelligence increases, whereas the influence of shared aspects of family environment decreases. (Data from McGue et al., 1993)

One reason for this increasing genetic influence is that some genetic processes do not exert their effects until late childhood or adolescence. For example, some types of

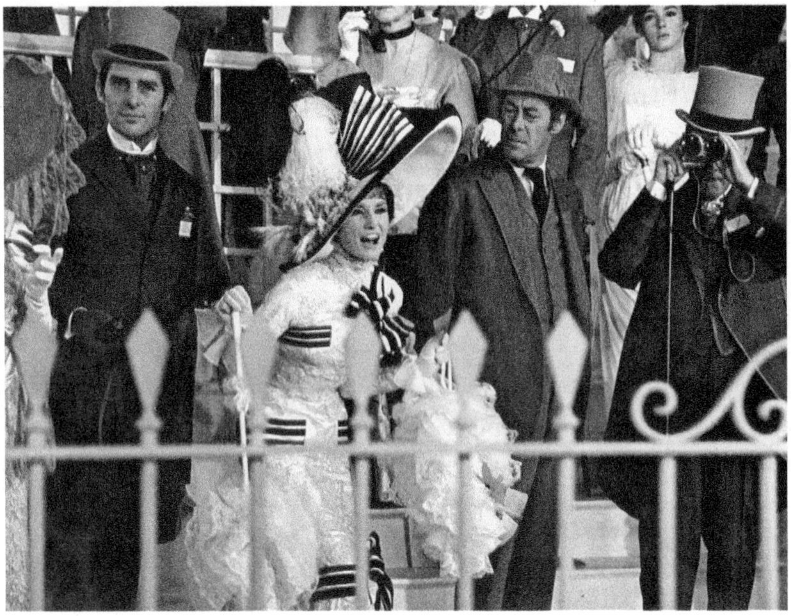

WARNER BROS/REX/SHUTTERSTOCK

In the movie *My Fair Lady,* Eliza Doolittle found it easier to don the clothing of an upper-class lady than to adopt the haughty reserve viewed as appropriate by that class at that time. This scene of opening day at the Ascot Racecourse, as well as the movie as a whole, makes the argument that differences that might be attributed to nature are actually the product of nurture.

synchronization of activities of distant brain areas are not evident until adolescence or early adulthood, and the extent of such synchronization, which influences a variety of cognitive activities, reflects genetic influences (Uhlhaas et al., 2010). Another reason is that children's increasing independence with age allows them greater freedom to choose environments that are compatible with their own genetically based preferences but not necessarily with those of the parents who are raising them (McAdams & Olson, 2010).

Advances in genetics have inspired research aimed at identifying genes that explain individual differences in intelligence. These efforts have led to identification of a large number of genes that are associated with mental retardation (Inlow & Restifo, 2004) and a large number of other genes that are consistently related to normal variation in intelligence (Trzaskowski et al., 2014). However, all known correlations between individual alleles of genes and IQ are very small. These findings suggest that genetic influences on intelligence reflect small contributions from many different genes, as well as complex interactions among them, rather than one or a small number of master genes (Chabris et al., 2015; Mukherjee, 2016; Nisbett et al., 2012). Simply put, there is no "intelligence gene" or even a small group of "intelligence genes."

Genotype–Environment Relations

As noted in Chapter 3, the environments children encounter are influenced by the children's and their parents' genotypes. Sandra Scarr (1992) proposed that gene–environment relations involve three types of processes: passive, evocative, and active.

- *Passive effects* of the genotype arise when children are raised by their biological parents. These effects occur not because of anything the children do but because of the overlap between their parents' genes and their own. Thus, children whose genotypes predispose them to enjoy reading are likely to grow up in homes with plentiful access to reading matter because their parents also like to read. The passive effects of the genotype help explain why some correlations between biological parents' and their children's IQ scores are higher when the children live with their biological parents than when they live with adoptive parents.
- *Evocative effects* of the genotype emerge through children influencing other people's behaviour. For example, even if a child's parents are not avid readers, they will read more bedtime stories to a child who is interested in the stories than to one who is uninterested.
- *Active effects* of the genotype involve children's choosing environments that they enjoy. A high school student who loves reading will read a great deal, regardless of whether he or she was read to when young.

The evocative and active effects of the genotype help explain how children's IQ scores become more closely related over time to those of their biological parents, even if the children are adopted and never see their biological parents.

Influence of the Immediate Environment

The influence of nurture on the development of intelligence begins with a child's immediate environment of family and schools.

BLEND IMAGES - KIDSTOCK/GETTY IMAGES

Children influence their own development: these children's positive reactions to their father's reading ensure that he will want to read to them in the future.

Family Influences

If asked to identify the most important environmental influence on their intelligence, most people probably would say, "My family." Testing the influence of the family environment on children's intelligence, however, requires some means of assessing that environment. How can something as complex and multifaceted as a family environment be measured, especially when it differs for different children in the same family (e.g., if parents favour one child over another, the family environment can be very different for the two children)?

Bradley and Caldwell (1979) tackled this problem by devising a measure known as the HOME (Home Observation for Measurement of the Environment). The HOME samples various aspects of children's home life, including organization and safety of living space; intellectual stimulation offered by parents; whether children have books of their own; amount of parent–child interaction; parents' emotional support of the child; and so on. Table 8.1 shows the items and subscales used in the original HOME, which was designed to assess the family environments of children from birth to age 3 years. Subsequent versions of the HOME have been developed for application with preschoolers, school-age children, and adolescents (Totsika & Sylva, 2004).

Throughout childhood, children's IQ scores, as well as their math and reading achievement scores, are positively correlated with scores on the HOME (Bradley et al., 2001). A large multi-site study, which included a group of children from Hamilton, Ontario, found that HOME scores of 12-month-olds correlated positively with the IQ scores of the same children at 3 years of age (Bradley et al., 1989). Similarly, HOME scores of 2-year-olds correlate positively with IQ scores and school achievement of the same children at age 11 years (Olson, Bates, & Kaskie, 1992). When HOME scores are relatively stable over time, IQ scores also tend to be stable; when HOME scores change, IQ scores also tend to change in the same direction (Totsika & Sylva, 2004). Thus, assessing varied aspects of a child's family environment allows prediction of the child's IQ score.

Given this evidence, it is tempting to conclude that better-quality home environments cause children to have higher IQ scores. Whether that is actually the case, however, is unknown. The uncertainty reflects two factors. First, the intellectual environment that parents establish in the home is almost certainly influenced by their genetic makeup. Second, almost all studies using the HOME have focused on families in which children live with their biological parents.

Stimulating home environments, especially those in which adults and children undertake challenging tasks together, are associated with high IQ scores and high achievement in school.

OCEAN/CORBIS

TABLE 8.1 Sample Items and Subscales on the HOME (Infant Version)

I.	Emotional and Verbal Responsivity of Mother
	1. Mother spontaneously vocalizes to child at least twice during visit (excluding scolding).
	2. Mother responds to child's vocalizations with a verbal response.
	3. Mother tells child the name of some object during visit or says name of person or object in a "teaching" style.
II.	Avoidance of Restriction and Punishment
	4. Mother does not shout at child during visit.
	5. Mother does not express overt annoyance with or hostility toward child.
	6. Mother does not interfere with child's actions or restrict child's movements more than three times during visit.
III.	Organization of Physical and Temporal Environment
	7. When mother is away, care is provided by one of three regular substitutes.
	8. Child is taken regularly to doctor's office or clinic.
	9. Child has a special place in which to keep his or her toys and "treasures."
IV.	Provision of Appropriate Play Materials
	10. Child has push or pull toy.
	11. Child has stroller or walker, kiddie car, scooter, or tricycle.
	12. Child has learning equipment appropriate to age—cuddly toy or role-playing toys.
V.	Maternal Involvement with Child
	13. Mother tends to keep child within visual range and to look at him or her often.
	14. Mother "talks" to child while doing her work.
	15. Mother structures child's play periods.
VI.	Opportunities for Variety of Daily Stimulation
	16. Mother reads stories at least three times weekly.
	17. Child eats at least one meal per day with mother and father.
	18. Child has three or more books of his or her own.

Information from Bradley & Caldwell (1984).

These two considerations may mean that parents' genes influence both the intellectual quality of the home environment and children's IQ scores; thus, the home intellectual environment as such may not cause children to have higher or lower IQ. Consistent with this possibility, in the few studies in which the HOME has been used to study adoptive families, the correlations between it and children's IQ scores are lower than in studies of children living with their biological parents (Plomin et al., 1997). Thus, although scores on the HOME correlate with children's IQ scores, whether causal relations exist between the two remains uncertain.

Shared and non-shared family environments The phrase "family intellectual environment" is often taken to mean characteristics that are the same for all children within the family: how much the parents value education, the number of books in the house, the frequency of intellectual discussions around the dinner table, and so on. As discussed in Chapter 3, however, each child within a given family also encounters unique, non-shared environments. In any family, only one child can be the firstborn and receive the intense, undivided parental attention early in life that this status tends to bring (for better and worse). Similarly, a child whose interests or personality characteristics mirror those of one or both parents may receive more positive attention than other children in the family. If homes that are extremely lacking in intellectual stimulation are excluded from consideration, such within-family variations in children's environment may have a greater impact on the development of intelligence than do between-family variations (Petrill et al., 2004). In addition, the influence of the non-shared environment increases with age, and the influence of the shared environment decreases with age, as children become increasingly able to choose their own friends and activities (Plomin & Daniels, 2011; Segal et al., 2007).

The relative influence of shared environments and genetics varies with family income. Among children and adolescents from low-income families in the United States, the shared environment accounts for more of the variance in IQ scores and academic achievement than genetics does. In contrast, among children and adolescents from middle- and high-income families in the United States, the relative influence of shared environment and genetics is reversed (Nisbett, et al., 2012; Turkheimer et al., 2003). These differing patterns are found as early as age 2 years (Tucker-Drob et al., 2011). Interestingly, the differing relations between shared environments and genetics among richer and poorer families have not been found in Great Britain, Germany, Sweden, the Netherlands, or Australia (Tucker-Drob & Bates, 2016). This may be because those countries ensure access to quality education regardless of family income, thus making the children's intellectual development less dependent on the family in which they grow up.

DARREN MODRICKER/AGE FOTOSTOCK

With age, children increasingly shape their own environments in ways that reflect their personalities and tastes.

Influences of Schooling

Attending school makes children smarter. Evidence for this conclusion came from a study that examined IQ scores of older and younger Israeli children within the 4th, 5th, and 6th grades (Cahan & Cohen, 1989). As indicated by the gradual upward trends in the graphs in Figure 8.6, older children within each grade did somewhat better than younger children within that grade on each part of the test. However, the jumps in the graphs between grades indicate that children who were only slightly older, but who had a year more schooling, did much better than the slightly younger children in the grade below them. For example, on the verbal-oddities subtest (which involves indicating which word in a series does not belong with the others), the results show a small gap between 123- and 124-month-old 4th-graders but a large gap between both of them and 125-month-old 5th-graders. A meta-analysis of studies on the relation between IQ and total number of years of formal education indicated that an extra year attending school increases IQ scores by 1 to 5 points (Ritchie & Tucker-Drob, 2018).

Another type of evidence indicating that going to school makes children smarter is that average IQ and achievement test scores rise during the school year but not during summer vacation (Huttenlocher, Levine, & Vevea, 1998). The details of the pattern are especially telling. Children from families of

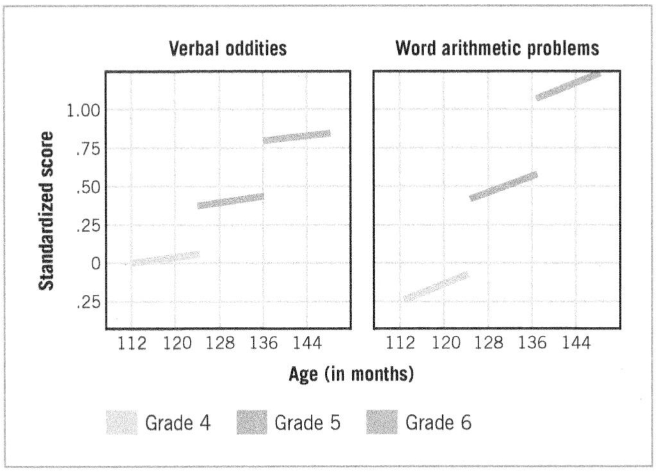

FIGURE 8.6 Relations of age and grade to performance on two parts of an IQ test The jumps between grade levels indicate that schooling exerts an effect on intelligence test performance beyond that of the child's age. (Data from Cahan & Cohen, 1989)

Early Childhood Education

low socioeconomic status and those from families of high socioeconomic status make comparable gains in school achievement during the school year. However, over the summer, the achievement test scores of low-SES children tend to stay constant or drop, whereas the scores of high-SES children tend to rise (Alexander, Entwisle, & Olson, 2007). The likely explanation is that during the academic year, schools provide children of all backgrounds with relatively stimulating intellectual environments, but when school is not in session, fewer children from low-SES families have experiences that increase their academic achievement.

Influence of Society

Intellectual development is influenced not only by characteristics of children and their local environments but also by broader characteristics of the societies within which they develop. One reflection of societal influences is that in many countries throughout the world, average IQ scores have consistently risen over the past 80 years; this phenomenon has been labelled the **Flynn effect** in honor of James Flynn, the researcher who discovered the trend (Flynn, 1987, 2009). For example, in the United States, the gains have been roughly 10 points (Flynn & Weiss, 2007). Given that the gene pool has not changed appreciably over this period, the increase in IQ scores must be due to changes in society.

The specific source of the Flynn effect remains controversial. Some researchers argue that the key factors are improvements in the lives of low-income families, such as improved nutrition (Lynn, 2009) and health (Eppig, Fincher, & Thornhill, 2010). These researchers point to evidence that in some countries, the increase in IQ scores has been greatest among those in the lower part of the IQ score and income distributions, who previously had received poor nutrition and health care. For example, among Danes born from 1942 to 1980, there was no change in the scores of people in the top 10% of the IQ distribution, but there was a large change among those in the bottom 10% (Geary, 2005). IQ score changes in some other countries, including Spain and Norway, show a similar pattern. However, gains in other countries, including the United States, France, and Britain, have been comparable throughout the IQ score and income distributions (Nisbett et al., 2012).

Education in Middle Childhood

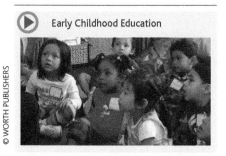

An alternative explanation for the rise in IQ scores is increased societal emphasis on abstract problem solving and reasoning (Flynn, 2009). Supporting this interpretation, scores on tests of fluid intelligence, which reflect abstract problem solving and reasoning, have increased roughly twice as much as scores on tests of crystallized intelligence, which measure previously acquired knowledge (Nisbett et al., 2012; Pietschnig & Voracek, 2015).

One source of these increases in fluid intelligence might be experience with new technologies, such as video games. Playing video games has been found to improve a variety of cognitive processes: executive functioning (e.g., Flynn & Richert, 2018), selective attention (e.g., Glass, Maddox, & Love, 2013), problem solving (Blumberg & Randall, 2013), and even processes that improve learning of reading (Franceschini et al., 2017) and math (Deater-Deckard et al., 2014). Some studies have not found such positive effects of playing video games (e.g, Powers et al., 2013; Unsworth et al., 2015), but the literature as a whole seems to support the hypothesis that playing video games contributes to increases in fluid intelligence (Blumberg et al., 2019).

Flynn effect consistent rise in average IQ scores that has occurred over the past 80 years in many countries

Although many conclusions about intelligence remain controversial, one conclusion that sparks little controversy is that poverty hinders intellectual development. In the following sections, we consider how poverty affects children's development in different societies and how it contributes to differences in IQ scores and school achievement. We will also consider risk factors associated with poverty that adversely affect intelligence, as well as programs that can enhance poor children's intellectual development.

Effects of Poverty

The negative effects of poverty on children's IQ scores are indisputable. Even after taking into account the mother's education, whether both parents live with the child, and the child's race, the adequacy of family income for meeting family needs is related to children's IQ scores (Duncan & Murnane, 2014). Further, the more years children spend in poverty, the lower their scores tend to be (Korenman, Miller, & Sjaastad, 1995).

Poverty can exert negative effects on intellectual development in numerous ways. Chronic inadequate diet early in life can disrupt brain development; missing meals on a given day (e.g., achievement test day) can impair intellectual functioning on that day; reduced access to health services can result in more absences from school; conflicts between adults in the household can produce emotional turmoil that interferes with learning; insufficient intellectual stimulation can lead to a lack of background knowledge needed to understand new material; and so on. Poverty does not guarantee that these adverse influences will affect any individual child—some children from impoverished families receive adequate diets and health services, do not encounter unusual amounts of emotional turmoil, receive considerable intellectual stimulation, and so on—but poverty makes the presence of adverse influences more likely.

Consistent with this analysis, in all countries that have been studied, children from wealthier homes tend to score higher on IQ and achievement tests than do children from poorer homes (Ganzach et al., 2013). Large mean differences between children from less and more affluent backgrounds are already present in measures of reading and math knowledge when children enter kindergarten (see Figure 8.7; Larson et al., 2015), and the differences grow even larger over the course of schooling (Goodman, Gregg, & Washbrook, 2011).

More telling, in those developed countries where the income gap between rich and poor is widest, such as the United States, the difference between the intellectual achievement of children from rich and poor homes is much larger than in countries in which the income gap is smaller, such as the Scandinavian countries and, to a lesser degree, Canada, Germany, and Great Britain. As shown

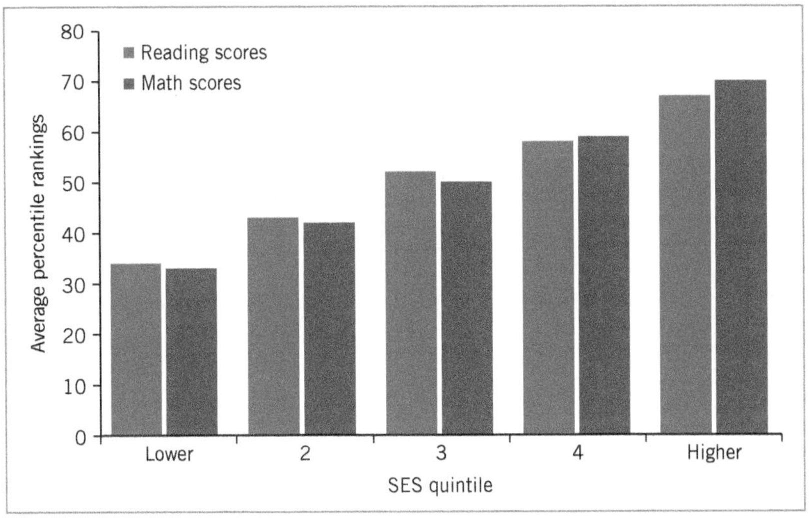

FIGURE 8.7 Reading and math scores upon entering kindergarten, by SES Even at the beginning of kindergarten, children from families with lower incomes and education lag far behind peers from more affluent and educated backgrounds. (Data from Larson et al., 2015)

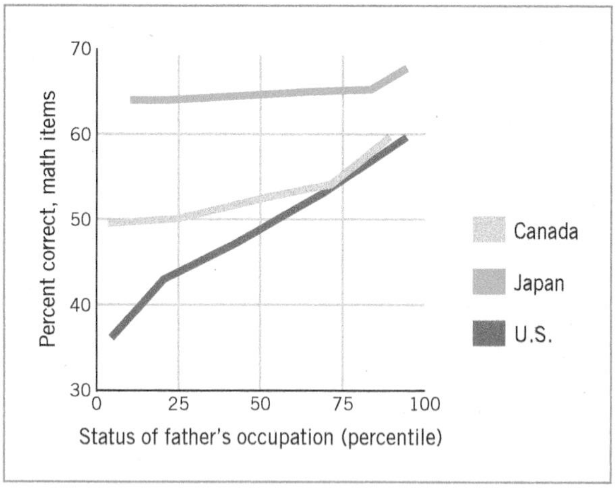

FIGURE 8.8 Relation in three countries between fathers' occupational status and children's math achievement As research by Robbie Case at the University of Toronto has demonstrated, Canadian and Japanese children whose fathers hold low-status jobs perform, on average, far better on math achievement tests than do children whose fathers hold comparable jobs in the United States. In contrast, Canadian children whose fathers have high-status jobs perform, on average, as well as children whose fathers hold comparable jobs in the United States and almost as well as children from similar backgrounds in Japan. (Data from Case et al., 1999)

in Figure 8.8, children from affluent U.S. families score, on average, about the same on mathematics achievement tests as children from affluent families in some comparison countries with greater income equality, including Canada and Japan. In contrast, children from poor U.S. families score far below children from poor families in those same comparison countries.

The key difference is that poor U.S. families are much poorer, relative to others in their society, than their counterparts in many other developed countries. Thus, as shown in Figure 8.9, in 2015–2016, more than 15% of U.S. children lived in families with lower than 50% of the median family income; as can be seen in this figure, the percent of families this poor relative to others in their country was far lower in many other countries (OECD, 2018).

Risk Factors and Intellectual Development

In the popular media, reports on how to help all children reach their intellectual potential often focus on a single factor—the need to eliminate poverty, or the need to eliminate racism, or the need to preserve two-parent families, or the need for high-quality day care, or the need for universal preschool education, and so on. However, no single factor, nor even any small group of factors, is *the* key. Instead, many factors contribute to poor intellectual development.

To capture the impact of these multiple influences, Arnold Sameroff and his colleagues developed an *environmental risk scale* (Sameroff et al., 1993) based on a number of features of the environment that put children at risk for low IQ scores (e.g., head of household being unemployed or working in a low-status occupation, mother who did not complete high school, no father or stepfather in the home, a large number of stressful life events in recent years, maternal mental health problems, and negative mother–child interactions). Each child's risk score is a simple count of the number of major risks facing the child.

Sameroff and his colleagues measured the IQ scores and environmental risks of more than 100 children when they were 4-year-olds and again when they were

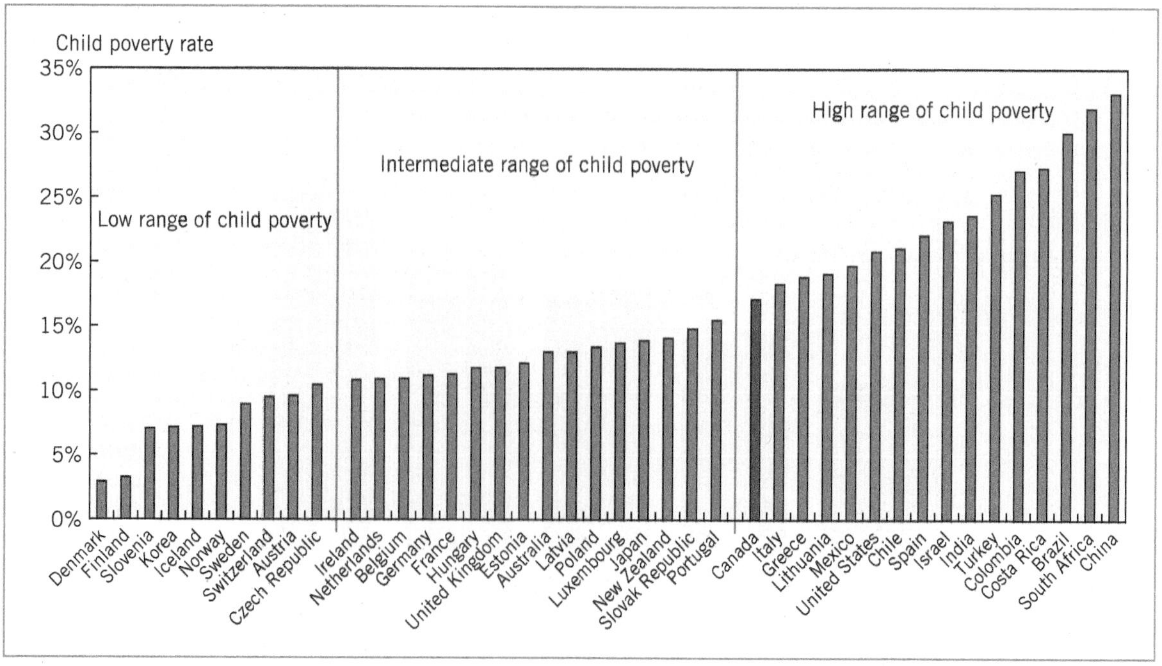

FIGURE 8.9 Child poverty rates by country Canada has a high rate of child poverty, relative to most other developed countries. (Data from OECD, 2018)

13-year-olds. They found that the more risks in a child's environment, the lower the child's IQ score tended to be. As shown in Figure 8.10, the effect was large. The average IQ score of children whose environments did not include any of the risk factors was around 115; the average score of children whose environments included six or more risks was around 85. The sheer number of risks in the child's environment was a better predictor of the child's IQ score than the presence of any particular risk. Subsequent studies demonstrated similarly strong relations between number of risk factors and school grades (Gutman, Sameroff, & Cole, 2003).

The Sameroff (1993) study also provided an interesting perspective on why children's IQ scores are highly stable. It is not just that children's genes remain constant; over time, their environment tends to remain fairly constant as well. The study revealed that there was just as much stability in the number of risk factors in children's environments at ages 4 and 13 years as in their IQ scores over that period.

Although Sameroff and his colleagues described their measure as a "risk index," it is as much a measure of the quality of a child's environment as of its potential for harm. High IQ scores are associated with favourable environments as much as low scores are associated with adverse ones. This is true for children from low-income families as well as for children in general. Low-income parents who are responsive to their children and provide them with safe play areas and varied learning materials have children with higher IQ scores (Bradley et al., 1994). Thus, high-quality parenting can help offset the risks imposed by poverty.

Programs for Helping Poor Children

Beginning in the early 1960s, it became clear that children from economically disadvantaged families were at risk for poor outcomes. Child development research contributed to this consensus by demonstrating that children's environments had significant effects on their cognitive growth (Dennis & Najarian, 1957; Hunt, 1961). As a consequence, over the next decade, many intervention programs were initiated to enhance the intellectual development of preschoolers from impoverished families.

In a comprehensive analysis of 11 of the most prominent early-intervention programs—all of which focused on 2- to 5-year-old African American children from low-income families—Lazar and colleagues (1982) found a consistent pattern. Participation in the programs, most of which lasted a year or two, initially increased children's IQ scores substantially—by 10 to 15 points. However, over the next 2 or 3 years, the gains decreased, and by the fourth year after the end of the programs, no differences were apparent between the IQ scores of participants and those of nonparticipants from the same neighbourhoods and backgrounds. Similar effects have been found subsequently for math and reading achievement—initial gains fade all too quickly (Bailey et al., 2016). One reason is that children in the programs forget what they learned earlier; a bigger reason is that children who weren't in the programs catch up by learning the skills and concepts that children in the programs learned earlier (Kang et al., 2019).

Fortunately, other effects of these experimental programs aimed at helping preschoolers from low-income backgrounds are more enduring. Program participants are more likely to later graduate from high school than preschoolers from low-income backgrounds who do not participate, and they are less likely to be assigned to special education classes, held back in school, or be arrested by age 18 (Reynolds, Temple, & Ou, 2010).

FIGURE 8.10 Risk factors and IQ score For both younger and older children, the more risk factors in the environment, the lower the average IQ score. (Data from Sameroff et al., 1993)

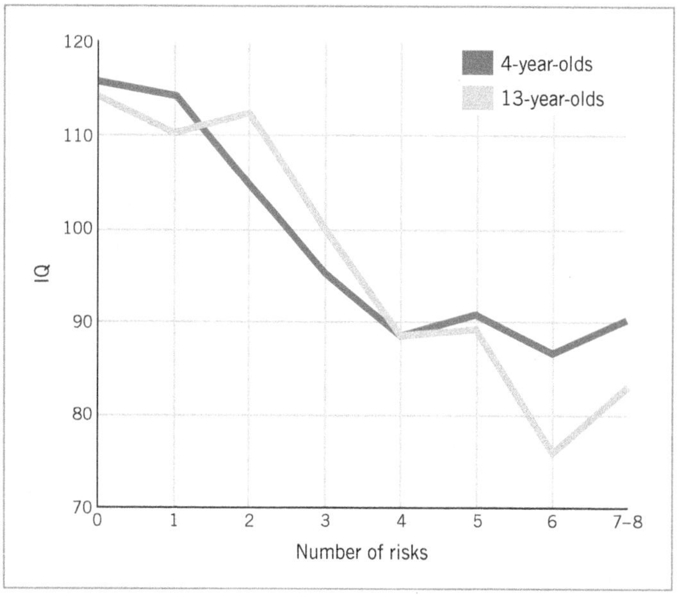

BOX 8.1 APPLICATIONS Highly Successful Early Interventions: Better Beginnings, Better Futures (BBBF) and the Carolina Abecedarian Project

The difficulty of producing enduring gains in poor children's IQ and achievement test scores led some early evaluators to conclude that intelligence is unalterable (Jensen, 1973; Westinghouse Learning Corporation, 1969). However, the same findings motivated other researchers to find out if interventions that started in infancy, continued for a number of years, and attempted to improve many aspects of children's lives might produce enduring increases in IQ. Two such projects, the **Better Beginnings, Better Futures (BBBF)** project and the Carolina Abecedarian Project, clearly demonstrate that enduring changes can be achieved.

BBBF began in 1991 as a 25-year longitudinal prevention project, in response to the results of the 1983 Ontario Child Health Study. This study indicated that 1 in 6 children had an emotional or behavioural problem and that children from socioeconomically disadvantaged homes were at higher risk for these problems (Peters et al., 2010).

BBBF was based on a universal prevention approach. That is, rather than identifying particular children and families who were at risk for adverse outcomes, the project focused on communities in Ontario that were defined as "at risk." These communities were considered economically disadvantaged: they had high numbers of families living below the low-income line, high levels of unemployment, high numbers of children on social assistance, and high numbers of children living in subsidized housing. In addition, factors existed that were considered indicators for poor child development: infant mortality, low birth weight, lone-parent families, adolescent pregnancy, low maternal educational achievement, high rates of high school dropout, and immigration (see Peters et al., 2010 for further details). The three Ontario sites chosen for participation in BBBF were Cornwall, Highfield (in the greater Toronto area), and Sudbury. Following selection of the BBBF sites, two comparison sites with similar characteristics were selected: Ottawa-Vanier and Etobicoke (in Toronto).

All children between the ages of 4 and 8 who were living in one of the selected neighbourhoods could participate in the program, as could the children's families. Drawing on the ecological model of development advanced by Bronfenbrenner (detailed in Chapter 9), the project targeted child development in a variety of areas, including physical, social, and cognitive development, as well as mental health. Furthermore, in keeping with the ecological model, family, school, and neighbourhoods were targeted for change. The specific programming delivered at each site varied; it was developed within the specific communities, with extensive consultation from community members. The accompanying table provides a list of programs that were offered at all three sites, for a total of 4 years.

The impact of programming was measured at grades 3, 6, and 9. For the purposes of this chapter, we will focus on school functioning and academic achievement, which were assessed at grades 6 and 9. At grade 6, children from the BBBF sites had higher math achievement and fewer school suspensions than did those from the comparison sites. At grade 9, children in the BBBF programs required fewer special education services, were less likely to repeat grades, and were rated by teachers as better prepared to learn and to have greater potential to go further in school (Peters et al., 2010). A follow-up

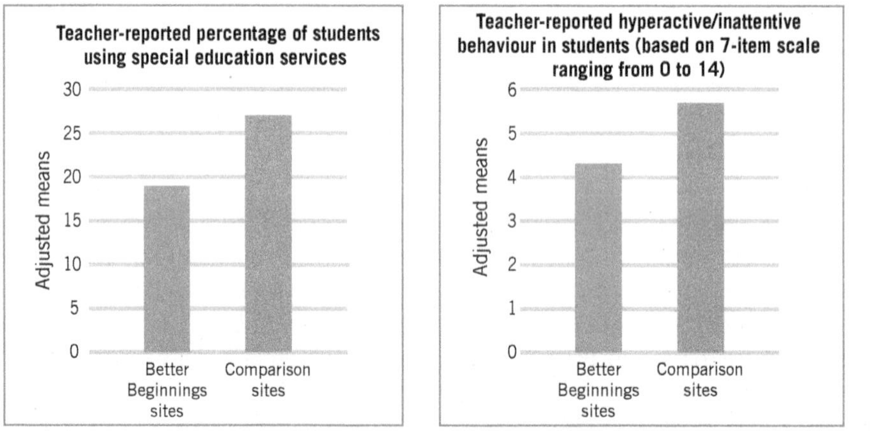

As illustrated in these graphs, at grade 9, children who had taken part in BBBF were less likely to use special education services (left) and to display hyperactive/inattentive behaviours in class (right) than were children from comparably disadvantaged backgrounds from the comparison sites. The benefits of participating in BBBF remained evident 6 years after the end of the program. (Data from Roche, Petrunka, & Peters, 2008)

This combination of findings may seem puzzling. If the intervention programs did not result in lasting increases in IQ or achievement test scores, why would they have led to fewer children being assigned to special-education classes or being held back in school? A likely reason is that the interventions had long-term effects on children's motivation and conduct. These effects would help children do well enough in the classroom to be promoted with their classmates, which in turn might make them less likely to drop out of high school and less likely to turn to criminal activity. In Box 8.1, we discuss one prevention program in

Better Beginnings, Better Futures (BBBF) Ontario-based prevention project designed for young children who have multiple risks for poorer child development of children at grade 12 indicated that the positive effects continued, with children from BBBF sites requiring fewer special education services (Peters et al., 2016).

Not only did the BBBF program yield long-term benefits to the children enrolled, this program yielded economic benefits as well. A recent analysis showed that those children who were enrolled in BBBF programs used fewer government programs from ages 4 to 18, leading to savings of $2.50 for every $1.00 invested by the government (Peters et al., 2016).

A similarly successful early intervention program in the United States was the **Carolina Abecedarian Project,** which operated at one North Carolina site from 1972 to 1985. In the Abecedarian (pronounced "a-bee-cee-darian") program, children who were at high risk for poor outcomes due to low family income, the absence of a father in the home, low maternal IQ score and education, and other factors began attending a special daycare centre by the time they were 6-month-olds and continued to do so through the age of 5 years. Children aged 3 years and younger underwent a program that emphasized general social, cognitive, and motor development; for 4- and 5-year-olds, the program also provided systematic instruction in math, science, reading, and music. At all ages, the program emphasized language development and ensured extensive verbal communication between teachers and children.

Program personnel also worked with the children's mothers outside the daycare centre to improve their understanding of child development. Families of children in the experimental program were provided with nutritional supplements and access to high-quality health care. Families of children in a comparison group received similar nutritional and health benefits, but the children did not attend the daycare centre.

This well-planned, multifaceted program proved to have lasting positive effects on the IQ scores and achievement levels of children in the experimental group. At the age of 21 years, 15 years after the program had ended, these children had mean IQ scores 5 points higher than the children in the control group: 90 versus 85 (Campbell et al., 2001). Participants' achievement test scores in math and reading were also higher. As with less encompassing intervention programs, fewer participants were ever held back in school or placed in special education classes. At age 30, a higher percentage of children in the experimental group than in the control group had graduated from college: 23% versus 6% (Campbell et al., 2012). A replication of the program demonstrated that the lower the mother's educational level, the greater the difference the program made (Ramey & Ramey, 2004).

Better Beginnings, Better Futures Programs Common to the Three Sites

Program type	Program Description
Child-focused	In-class and in-school programs
	Childcare enhancements
	Before- and after-school activities
	School "breakfast club"
	Recreation programs
Parent-focused	Home visitors
	Parent support groups
	Parenting workshops
	One-on-one support
	Child care for parent relief
Family- and community-focused	Community leadership development
	Special community events and celebrations
	Safety initiatives in neighbourhood
	Community field trips
	Adult education
	Family camps
	Outreach to families

Source: Peters et al., 2010

What lessons can be drawn from these early intervention projects? One important lesson is the benefit of starting interventions early and continuing them for substantial periods. A version of the Abecedarian program that ended at age 3 did not produce long-term effects on intelligence, nor did a program that provided educational support from kindergarten through grade 2 (Burchinal et al., 1997; Ramey et al., 2000). A more recent study demonstrated that two years, as opposed to just one year, of enhanced preschool programming led to greater improvements in the early literacy and numeracy skills of economically disadvantaged children (Domitrovich et al., 2010). A second crucial lesson is that the gains produced by successful early-intervention programs are likely due at least as much to improvements in children's self-control and perseverance as to changes in children's IQ scores (Heckman, 2011; Knudsen et al., 2006). Probably the most important lesson is the most basic: it is possible to design interventions that have substantial, lasting, positive effects on economically disadvantaged children's intellectual development.

Canada—Better Beginnings, Better Futures (BBBF)—and one in the United States—the Carolina Abecedarian Project—that have shown the possibility of producing enduring gains in both IQ scores and school achievement.

Project Head Start In the 1960s, the U.S. government initiated a large-scale intervention program: Project Head Start. In the past 50 years, this program has provided a wide range of services to more than 36 million children in the United States (U.S. Department of Health and Human Services [DHHS], 2019).

Carolina Abecedarian Project comprehensive and successful enrichment program in the United States for children from low-income families

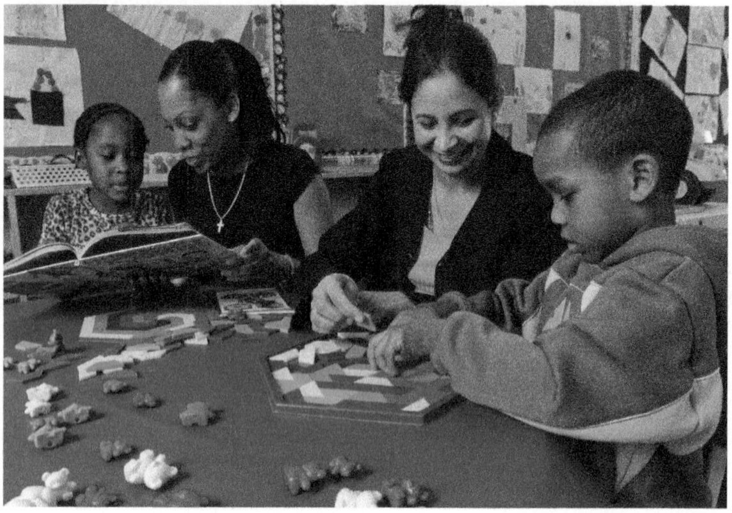
MICHAEL STUPARYK/GETTY IMAGES

Children who participate in Head Start programs, like the youngsters pictured here, are in later years less likely to be held back in the same grade and more likely to graduate from high school than are children from similar backgrounds who do not participate in these programs.

Consistent with the findings of the smaller experimental intervention programs, participation in Head Start produces higher IQ and achievement test scores at the end of the program and briefly thereafter. The strongest evidence for this conclusion comes from the Head Start Impact Study (U.S. DHHS, 2010), which included 5000 children, aged 3 and 4 years old, from low-income families who were on waiting lists to participate in a Head Start program. Half the children were randomly assigned to participate in Head Start; the other half followed another path of their parents' choosing. The children comprised a nationally representative sample of the low-income population, and the Head Start centres in which the children enrolled were representative in terms of their quality. Children who participated in Head Start showed better pre-reading and pre-writing skills at the end of one year in the program (U.S. DHHS, 2006), but their intellectual outcomes did not differ from those of nonparticipants by the end of 1st grade (U.S. DHHS, 2010) or 3rd grade (Puma et al., 2012).

On the other hand, participation in Head Start produces a number of positive effects that do endure: greater likelihood of graduating from high school and enrolling in college, better health and social skills, and lower frequency of later being held back in school, using drugs, and delinquency (Love, Chazan-Cohen, & Raikes, 2007; Zigler & Styfco, 2004). These important gains have contributed to the enduring popularity of Head Start.

In Canada, the federal government launched a version of the Head Start program called the Aboriginal Head Start Program in Urban and Northern Communities (AHSUNC). Initially, AHSUNC was provided to off-reserve Aboriginal families in urban communities and the northern region, but it was expanded in 1998 to on-reserve communities (Health Canada, 1998). The program provides funding for early intervention for children under the age of 6 and their families, with programs designed and delivered by First Nations communities. AHSUNC focuses on six aspects: education; health promotion; culture and language; nutrition; social support; and parental/family involvement (Nguyen, 2011). The program reaches between 4600 and 4800 children annually (Public Health Agency of Canada, 2017). An evaluation study showed that AHSUNC has effectively increased First Nations children's school readiness, including better language, motor, and academic skills. Furthermore, children and families report that exposure to Indigenous culture and language programming offered by sites yields long-term benefits (Public Health Agency of Canada, 2012, 2017).

REVIEW QUESTION

Why does children's likelihood of attending college increase if they attended Head Start, despite neither their math nor reading achievement showing gains beyond early elementary school? ■

Alternative Perspectives on Intelligence

Although the traditional theories of intelligence described in this chapter remain very influential, several contemporary theorists, notably Howard Gardner and Robert Sternberg, have argued that these conceptions are too narrow. This has led these theorists to formulate new conceptions of intelligence that incorporate a broader range of capabilities than previously included.

multiple intelligences theory Gardner's theory of intellect, based on the view that people possess at least eight types of intelligence

theory of successful intelligence Sternberg's theory of intellect, based on the view that intelligence is the ability to achieve success in life

Gardner's Theory

Gardner's (1993; 1999) **multiple intelligences theory** proposes that people possess at least eight kinds of intelligence: linguistic, logical-mathematical, spatial, musical, naturalistic, bodily-kinesthetic, intrapersonal, and interpersonal (Table 8.2). Although the first three are central in traditional theories of intelligence, the other five are unique to his theory.

Gardner used several types of evidence to arrive at this set of intelligences. One involved deficits shown by people with brain damage. For example, some brain-damaged patients function well in most respects but have no understanding of other people (Damasio, 1999). This phenomenon suggested to Gardner that interpersonal intelligence was distinct from other types of intelligence. Another type of evidence that Gardner noted was the existence of prodigies, people who from early in life show exceptional ability in one area but not in others. Wolfgang Amadeus Mozart displayed musical genius while still a child but was unexceptional in many other ways. The existence of highly specialized musical talents such as Mozart's provides evidence for viewing musical ability as a separate intelligence.

Although Gardner's theory of multiple intelligences is backed by much less supporting evidence than traditional theories of intelligence, its optimistic message—that children have a variety of strengths on which parents and teachers can build—has led to its having a large influence on education.

TABLE 8.2 Gardner's Theory of Multiple Intelligences

Type of Intelligence	Description	Professions that Require this Type of Intelligence
Linguistic intelligence	Sensitivity to the meanings and sounds of words; mastery of syntax; appreciation of the ways language can be used	Poet, political speaker, teacher
Logical-mathematical intelligence	Understanding of objects and symbols, of the actions that can be performed on them, and of the relations between these actions; ability for abstraction; ability to identify problems and seek explanations	Mathematician, scientist
Spatial intelligence	Capacity to perceive the visual world accurately, to perform transformations upon perceptions, and to re-create aspects of visual experience in the absence of physical stimuli; sensitivity to tension, balance, and composition; ability to detect similar patterns	Artist, engineer, chess master
Musical intelligence	Sensitivity to individual tones and phrases of music; an understanding of ways to combine tones and phrases into larger musical rhythms and structures; awareness of emotional aspects of music	Musician, composer
Naturalistic intelligence	Sensitivity to, and understanding of, plants, animals, and other aspects of nature	Biologist, farmer, conservationist
Bodily-kinesthetic intelligence	Use of one's body in highly skilled ways for expressive or goal-directed purposes; capacity to handle objects skillfully	Dancer, athlete, actor
Intrapersonal intelligence	Access to one's own feeling life; ability to draw on one's emotions to guide and understand one's behaviour	Novelist, therapist, parent
Interpersonal intelligence	Ability to notice and make distinctions among the moods, temperaments, motivations, and intentions of other people and potentially to act on this knowledge	Political leader, religious leader, parent, teacher, therapist

Information from H. Gardner (1993).

Sternberg's Theory

Sternberg's (1999; 2007) **theory of successful intelligence** envisions intelligence as "the ability to achieve success in life, given one's personal standards, within one's sociocultural context" (Sternberg, 1999, p. 4). In his view, success in life reflects people's ability to build on their strengths, compensate for their weaknesses, and select environments in which they can succeed. When people choose a job, for instance, their understanding of whether it will motivate them can be crucial to their success.

Sternberg proposed that success in life depends on three types of abilities: analytic, practical, and creative. *Analytic abilities* involve the linguistic, mathematical, and spatial skills measured by traditional intelligence tests. *Practical abilities* involve reasoning about everyday problems, such as how to resolve conflicts with other people. *Creative abilities* involve intellectual flexibility and innovation that allow adaptation to novel circumstances.

As indicated in Gardner's and Sternberg's theories, success in life involves a much broader range of capabilities than those measured by traditional IQ tests. Assessing broader ranges of capabilities may allow more encompassing theories of intelligence. There is not now, nor will there ever be, a single correct theory of intelligence, nor a single best measure of it. What is possible is a variety of theories and measures that together reveal the varied ways in which people can be intelligent.

FINE ART/GETTY IMAGES

Mozart's musical genius was evident from early in childhood, leading some of the greatest musicians of his day to play music with him when he was still a child, as illustrated in this portrait by Louis Carrogis Carmontelle, painted when Mozart was 7 years old.

REVIEW QUESTION

In what ways has your educational experience reflected the influence of Gardner's Theory of Multiple Intelligences or Sternberg's Theory of Successful Intelligence? ■

Acquisition of Academic Skills: Reading, Writing, and Mathematics

One important goal to which children apply their intelligence is learning the skills and concepts taught at school. Because these skills and concepts are central to success in adulthood, and because they can be difficult to learn, children spend more than 2000 days in school from 1st through 12th grade, much of the time devoted to acquiring proficiency in reading, writing, and mathematics. In this section, we focus on how children learn these subjects, why some children have difficulty mastering them, and how children's learning can be improved.

Reading

Many children learn to read effortlessly, but others do not. You probably can remember the painful times classmates—and perhaps you, yourself—seemed to take forever to read aloud simple sentences, even in 2nd and 3rd grade. Why is it that some children learn to read so easily, whereas others experience such great difficulty? To answer this question, we must examine the typical path of reading development, as well as how and why children deviate from it.

Chall (1979) described five stages of reading development. These stages provide a good overview of the typical path to mastery:

1. *Stage 0* (birth until the beginning of 1st grade): During this time, many children acquire key prerequisites for reading. These include knowing the letters of the alphabet and gaining **phonemic awareness**, that is, recognition of the individual sounds within words.
2. *Stage 1* (1st and 2nd grades): Children acquire **phonological recoding skills**, the ability to translate letters into sounds and to blend the sounds into words (informally referred to as "sounding out").
3. *Stage 2* (2nd and 3rd grades): Children gain fluency in reading simple material.

phonemic awareness ability to identify component sounds within words

phonological recoding skills ability to translate letters into sounds and to blend sounds into words; informally called *sounding out*

4. *Stage 3* (4th through 8th grades): Children become able to acquire reasonably complex, new information from written text. To quote Chall, "In the primary grades, children learn to read; in the higher grades, they read to learn" (1983, p. 24).
5. *Stage 4* (8th through 12th grades): Adolescents acquire skill not only in understanding information presented from a single perspective but also in coordinating multiple perspectives. This ability enables them to appreciate the subtleties in sophisticated novels and plays, which almost always include multiple viewpoints.

This description of developmental stages provides a general sense of the reading acquisition process and a framework for understanding how particular developments fit into the broader picture.

Pre-reading Skills

Preschoolers acquire certain basic information about reading just from their parents reading to them as they look at the pages. They learn how text is oriented on the page: for example, children immersed in English and other European languages learn that text is read from left to right; that after they reach the right end of a line, the text continues at the extreme left of the line below; and that words are separated by small spaces.

Having books in the home and being read to, however, are not enough. As Carleton University researchers Monique Sénéchal and Jo-Anne LeFevre have demonstrated, these activities alone are not directly related to eventual reading outcomes (Sénéchal & LeFevre, 2002). For example, in one comprehensive Ontario study, general reading activities at home did not predict kindergarten children's early literacy skills (Evans, Shaw, & Bell, 2000). Instead, the frequency with which parents taught their young children letters and sounds of letters, as well as engaged in printing activities, predicted how much children knew about letter names and sounds—key ingredients for later literacy.

Although kindergartners' mastery of letter names is positively correlated with their later reading achievement through at least grade 7 (Sénéchal & LeFevre, 2002; Vellutino & Scanlon, 1987), there does not appear to be a causal relation between the two: teaching the *names* of the letters to randomly chosen preschoolers does not increase their subsequent reading achievement (Piasta & Wagner, 2010). Instead, it appears that other variables, such as children's interest in books and parents' interest in and expectations about their children's reading, stimulate both early knowledge of the alphabet and later high reading achievement (Martini & Sénéchal, 2012).

Phonemic awareness, on the other hand, is correlated with later reading achievement and also is a cause of it. To measure awareness of the component sounds within words, researchers ask children to decide whether two words start with the same sound, to identify component sounds within a word, and to indicate what would remain if a given sound were removed from a word (e.g., if we started with "dish" and removed the "duh" sound, what would be left?).

Kindergartners' performance on these measures of phonemic awareness is the strongest known predictor of their ability to sound out and spell words in the early grades—stronger even than IQ score or social-class background (Nation, 2008). Phonemic awareness continues to be related to reading achievement as many as 11 years later, above and beyond the influence of the child's social-class background (MacDonald & Cornwall, 1995).

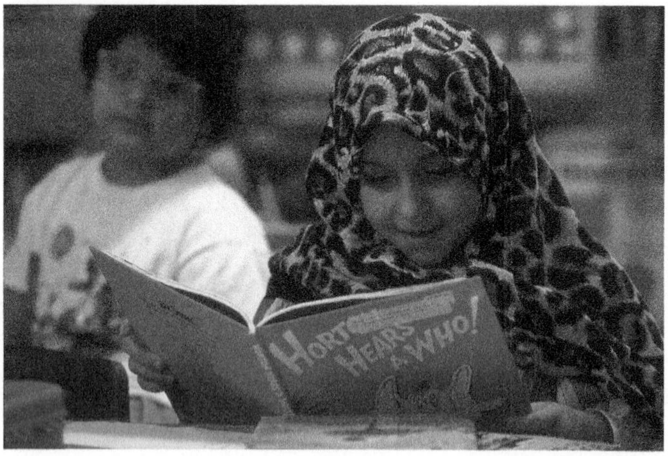
STEVE LISS/GETTY IMAGES

The appeal of nursery rhymes to young children has always been obvious, but only recently have the benefits of such rhymes for phonemic awareness and reading acquisition become known.

Even more impressive, a review of 52 well-controlled experimental studies indicated that teaching phonemic-awareness skills to 4- and 5-year-olds causes them to become better readers and spellers, with the effects enduring for years after the training (Lonigan, 2015). Instructing young children to break words into their component sounds and then writing the letter that best matches each successive sound causes especially large gains in spelling (Levin & Aram, 2013).

Although explicit training can help foster phonemic awareness, most children do not receive such training. Where, then, does phonemic awareness come from in the natural environment? One source is nursery rhymes. Many nursery rhymes highlight the contribution of individual sounds to differences among words (e.g., "I do not like green eggs and *ham;* I do not like them, *Sam* I *am*"). Consistent with this hypothesis, 3-year-olds' knowledge of nursery rhymes correlates positively with their later phonemic awareness, above and beyond their IQ scores and their mother's educational level (Maclean, Bryant, & Bradley, 1987). Other factors that contribute to the development of phonemic awareness include growth of working memory, increasingly efficient processing of oral language, and, especially, reading itself (Foorman et al., 2016; McBride-Chang, 2004). Children with greater phonemic awareness read more and read better, which, in turn, leads to further increases in their phonemic awareness and in the quantity and quality of their reading.

Word Identification

Rapid, effortless word identification is crucial not only to reading comprehension but also to reading enjoyment. One remarkable finding makes the point: 40% of 4th-graders with poor word identification skills said they would rather clean their rooms than read (Juel, 1988). One child went so far as to volunteer, "I'd rather clean the mold around the bathtub than read." Not only does poor word identification make reading slow and labourious, it also leads children to read no more than is absolutely necessary, which, in turn, limits improvement in reading skills.

Words can be identified in two main ways: *phonological recoding* and *visually based retrieval.* As previously indicated, phonological recoding involves converting the visual form of a word into a speech-like form and using the speech-like form to determine the word's meaning. **Visually based retrieval** involves processing a word's meaning directly from its visual form.

Most young children use both approaches and choose adaptively between them from 1st grade onward (Share, 2004). They employ a **strategy–choice process**, in which they choose the fastest approach that is likely to allow correct word identification. In the context of reading, this means that on easy words, children rely heavily on the fast but not always accurate approach of visually based retrieval; on hard words, they resort to the slower but surer strategy of phonological recoding. As shown in Figure 8.11, 1st-graders are very skillful in adjusting their strategies to the difficulty of a particular word.

visually based retrieval proceeding directly from the visual form of a word to its meaning

strategy–choice process procedure for selecting among alternative ways to solve a problem

The mechanisms underlying this adaptive strategy choice involve a form of associative learning in which children's past behaviour shapes their future behaviour (Siegler, 1996). Beginning readers rely heavily on phonological recoding because the associations between words' visual forms and their sounds are too weak to allow much use of retrieval. Correct use of phonological recoding increases the associations between words' visual forms and their sounds, which in

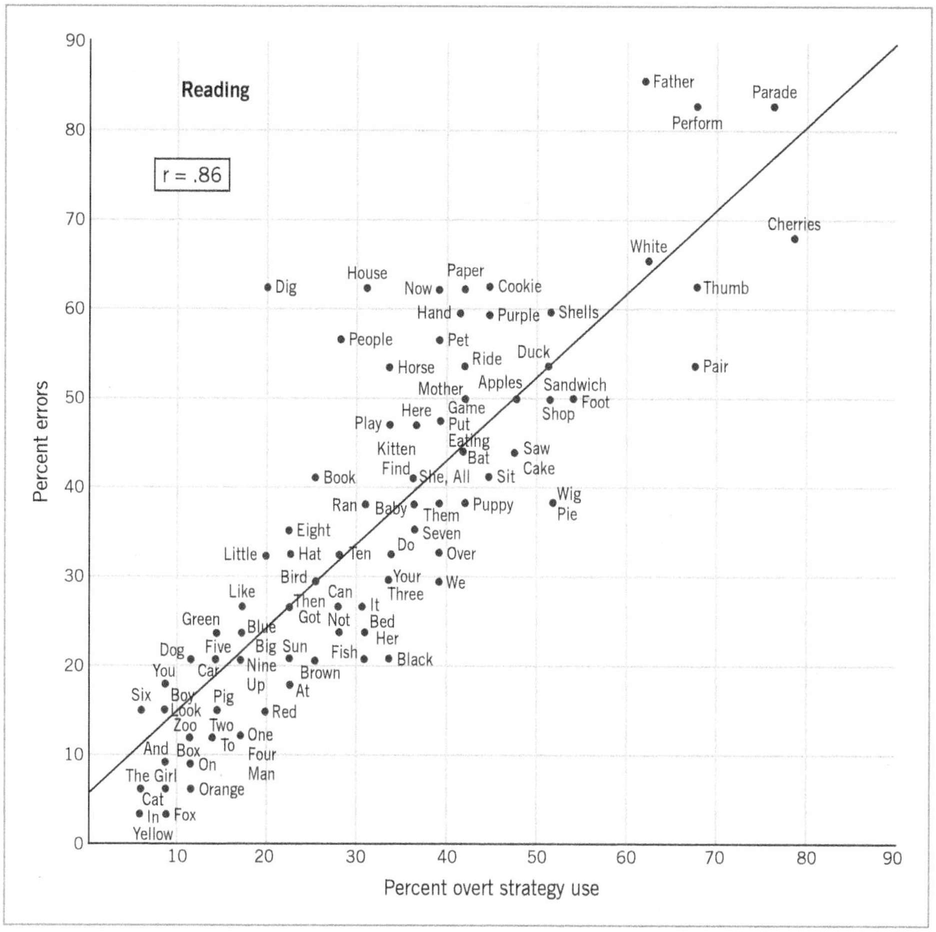

FIGURE 8.11 Young children's strategy choices in reading A strong positive correlation exists between the difficulty of a word, as defined by the percentage of errors children make when reading it, and the frequency of young children's use of an overt strategy, such as audible phonological recoding, to read it. Thus, on words that 1st-graders find easy, such as "in," they generally retrieve the word's pronunciation, but on words they find difficult, such as "parade," they often fall back on overt strategies such as sounding out. (Data from Siegler, 1986)

turn allows greater use of visually based retrieval. Consistent with this view, the shift to retrieval occurs earliest for words on which children most often execute phonological recoding correctly—words such as "dog" that are short, frequent, and have typical letter–sound relations. Also consistent with this view, children who are better at phonological recoding stop using that approach sooner because their past success with it enables them to shift more rapidly to visually based retrieval. A third correct implication is that reading instruction that emphasizes phonics, and the strategy of phonological recoding, increases the speed and accuracy of word identification (Foorman et al., 2016).

With age and experience, vocabulary knowledge becomes an increasingly important influence on word identification (Quinn et al., 2015). This is seen in the positive effect of teaching relevant vocabulary on children's subsequent comprehension of passages that include those terms (Apthorp et al., 2012). However, phonological recoding skill also continues to be important, even for adults when they encounter unfamiliar words. Box 8.2 discusses the relation between poor phonological recoding skills and the reading disability known as *dyslexia.*

Comprehension

Identifying individual words is essential for readers to comprehend the texts in which the words appear. Indeed, the **simple view of reading**, which posits that reading comprehension depends solely on decoding skill and comprehension of oral language, has proven very useful for understanding and predicting reading ability (Lervåg, Hulme, & Melby-Lervåg, 2018). Skillful decoding (translation of

simple view of reading perspective that comprehension depends solely on decoding skill and comprehension of oral language

BOX 8.2 INDIVIDUAL DIFFERENCES Dyslexia

Some children whose parents encourage reading nonetheless read very poorly. Such poor reading, despite typical intelligence levels, is referred to as **dyslexia**, a condition that affects 5% to 10% of children (Compton et al., 2014). The causes of dyslexia are not well understood, but genetics are clearly part of the story. If one of a pair of monozygotic twins is diagnosed as dyslexic, the probability of the other twin receiving a similar diagnosis is 84%, whereas if the twins are dizygotic, the corresponding probability is 48% (Kovas & Plomin, 2007; Oliver, Dale, & Plomin, 2004). The extent of genetic influences varies with parental educational level: as with IQ score, the relative influence of genetics on dyslexia are larger with children of highly educated parents than with children of less educated parents, perhaps because the intellectual environment provided by less educated parents varies more (Olson et al., 2014).

At a cognitive level of analysis, dyslexia stems primarily from poor phonemic awareness, limited vocabulary for spoken words, and weak decoding skills (Perry, Zorzi, & Ziegler, 2019). Determining the sounds that go with vowels is especially difficult for children with dyslexia, at least in English, where a single vowel can be pronounced in many ways (consider the sounds that accompany the letter "a" in *ha, hat, haul,* and *hate*). Because of these weaknesses, dyslexic children have great difficulty mastering the letter–sound correspondences used in phonological recoding, especially in languages, such as English, with irregular sound–symbol correspondences (Peterson, Pennington, & Olson, 2013).

For instance, as shown in the figure, when asked to read pseudowords such as *parding,* dyslexic 13- and 14-year-olds perform at the same level as typical 7- and 8-year-olds (Siegel, 1993). As would be expected from the strategy–choice model described on page 296, this difficulty with phonological processing causes most dyslexic children to be poor at visually based retrieval, as well as at phonological recoding (Compton et al., 2014).

The problem is often a lasting one: most individuals who have poor phonological processing skills in early elementary school remain poor readers as adults (Ehri, 2014). Indeed, 5th-graders with poor decoding skills showed almost no progress in comprehension skill over the next three years (Wang et al., 2019). These effects are especially strong for children who are from disadvantaged backgrounds and attend poorer quality schools: children with dyslexia who come from more advantaged family backgrounds and attend better schools more often show substantial improvements (Shaywitz, Mody, & Shaywitz, 2006).

Studies of brain functioning support the view that poor phonological processing is at the heart of dyslexia. When dyslexic children read, two areas of their brains are less active than the corresponding areas in typical children reading the same words (Schlaggar & Church, 2009; Tanaka et al., 2011). One such area is directly involved in discriminating phonemes; the other area is involved in integrating visual and auditory data (in this case, integrating letters seen on the page with accompanying sounds).

How can dyslexic children be helped? One tempting idea is that because these children have difficulty learning phonics, they would learn better through an approach that de-emphasizes letter–sound relations and instead emphasizes either visually based retrieval or reliance on context to make educated guesses about the word.

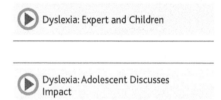

▶ Dyslexia: Expert and Children

▶ Dyslexia: Adolescent Discusses Impact

---

printed words into their meanings) is the best predictor of text comprehension in the early grades; after 4th grade, listening comprehension becomes an even better predictor, though decoding skill continues to predict reading comprehension as well (Castles, Rastle, & Nation, 2018).

Reading comprehension involves forming an initial **situation model** to represent the situation or idea being depicted in the text, then continuously updating the model as new information appears (Perfetti & Stafura, 2014). In forming situation models, readers bring together information explicitly stated in the text, prior knowledge relevant to the topics discussed in the text, and inferences based on the text and prior knowledge. Reading comprehension reflects the types of mental operations that influence cognitive development in general—basic processes, strategies, metacognition (knowledge about people's thinking), and content knowledge.

Basic processes such as encoding (identification of key features of an object or event) and automatization (executing a process with minimal demands on cognitive resources) are crucial to reading comprehension. The reason is simple: children who identify the key features of stories will understand the story better, and children who automatically identify the key features of words will have more cognitive resources available to comprehend the text. Fast, accurate word identification correlates positively with reading comprehension at all points from 1st grade through adulthood (Foorman et al., 2016).

dyslexia inability to read and spell well despite having normal intelligence

situation model cognitive processes used to represent a situation or sequence of events

These alternative methods work poorly, however (Compton et al., 2014). Instead, teaching children with dyslexia to use strategies that enhance their decoding appears to be at least somewhat helpful. Effective strategies include drawing analogies to known words with similar spellings; generating alternative pronunciations of vowels when the first attempt at sounding out does not yield a known word; and, with long words, "peeling off" prefixes and suffixes and then trying to identify the rest of the word.

Another promising strategy involves drawing upon children's *invented spelling:* their early, often unconventional, attempts to spell words (e.g., "prpul" for "purple"). A recent study found that kindergarteners in Ottawa who were at risk for poor reading achievement benefitted significantly from an 8-week program that capitalized on this invented spelling, offering individualized feedback to make the spelling more phonologically sensitive (Sénéchal, 2016; Sénéchal et al., 2012). For example, a child who spelled the word "lady" as "ledi" would be shown a spelling with one change at a time (e.g., replacing the "e" in "ledi" with an "a" and then, on another occasion, replacing the "i" with a "y").

After reviewing interventions that used such strategic approaches, however, Compton and colleagues concluded that "unfortunately, our best attempts at developing potent interventions . . . can best be described as producing limited successes" (2014, p. 56). The improvements in word identification produced by teaching word-identification strategies have not yielded large gains in reading comprehension (Solis et al., 2012). These researchers and others (e.g., Perfetti & Stafura, 2014) argue that the only way to substantially improve the reading comprehension of dyslexic children is to greatly increase their vocabulary and general information about the world. Pursuing this path poses daunting challenges because of the vast amount of vocabulary and general information to be learned, but substantially improving reading comprehension of dyslexic children probably requires it.

This chart shows the number of pseudowords identified correctly by 7- to 14-year-olds with and without reading disabilities. Note that 13- and 14-year-olds with reading disabilities correctly identified no more items than did typical 7- and 8-year-olds. The poor phonological recoding skills of children with reading disabilities lead them to have special difficulty with pseudowords that, because they are totally unfamiliar, can be pronounced only by using phonological recoding. (Data from Siegel, 1993)

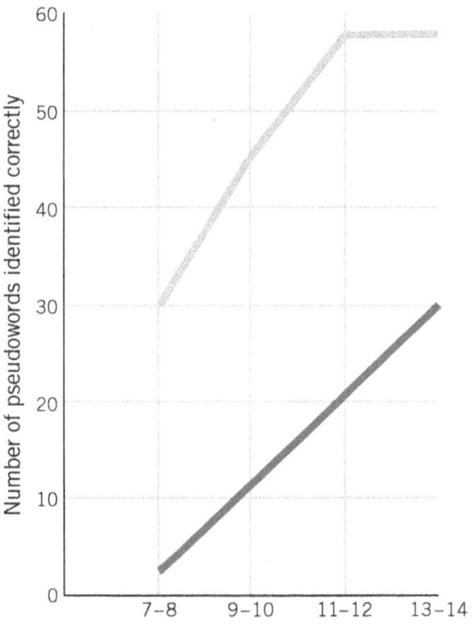

Development of reading comprehension is also aided by acquisition of reading strategies. For example, good readers proceed slowly when they need to master written material in depth and speed up when they need only a rough sense of it (Pressley & Hilden, 2006). Proficiency in making such adjustments develops surprisingly late. Even when 10-year-olds are told that some material in a passage is crucial and other material is not, they tend to read all the material at the same speed. In contrast, 14-year-olds skim the nonessential parts and spend more time on the important ones (Kobasigawa, Ransom, & Holland, 1980).

Increasing metacognitive knowledge also enhances reading comprehension. With age and experience, readers increasingly monitor their ongoing understanding and reread passages they do not understand (Nicholson, 1999). Such **comprehension monitoring** differentiates good readers from poor ones at all ages from 1st grade through adulthood. Instructional approaches that focus on comprehension monitoring and other metacognitive skills, such as anticipating questions that a teacher might ask about the material, have been shown to improve reading comprehension (Palincsar & Magnusson, 2001).

Perhaps the most powerful influence on the development of reading comprehension is increasing content knowledge. This content knowledge includes understanding vocabulary terms, possessing general information about the subject, and grasping idioms (Castles et al., 2018). Grasping idioms can be especially problematic for non-native speakers (Smith & Murphy, 2015); interpreting

Reading and Reading Disorders

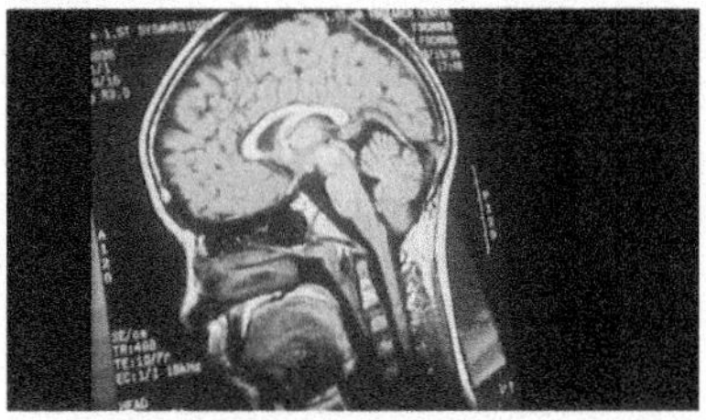

BBC/CBS/PRINCESTON ACADEMIC RESOURCES

comprehension monitoring process of keeping track of one's understanding of a verbal description or text expressions such as "broke the ice" or "kicked the bucket" requires knowledge beyond that of the individual words in the expression. Possessing such content knowledge frees cognitive resources to focus on new or complex material in the text and allows readers to draw reasonable inferences about information left unstated. Thus, when reading the headline "Blue Jays Maul Giants," readers knowledgeable about baseball realize that the headline concerns a baseball game; it is unclear how readers who lack baseball knowledge would interpret such a headline.

The path to strong or weak reading comprehension begins even before children start school. Hearing stories told or read by their parents helps preschoolers learn how stories tend to go, facilitating their understanding of new stories once they learn to read. It also enhances their general level of language development (Foorman et al., 2016). The amount that parents read to their children during the preschool years also partially accounts for differences between the reading comprehension skills of children from middle- and low-income families. For example, a study conducted in Israel showed that in an affluent school district with high reading-achievement scores, 96% of parents of preschoolers read to them daily. The same was true of only 15% of parents of preschoolers in a poor district with low achievement test scores (Feitelson & Goldstein, 1986).

The straightforward implication of these findings is that if preschoolers from poor families were read to daily, they too would become better readers. The evidence is consistent with this inference. Encouraging low-income parents to also actively engage their children in the reading process, such as by asking them to relate what is being read to their own experiences or to explain the characters' goals and motivations, helps even more (Zevenbergen & Whitehurst, 2003). Persuading low-income parents to read to their children on a continuing basis is not easy, because of demands on the parents' time and, often, the pressures of being a single parent, but when parents do so, their children's reading comprehension benefits (Whitehurst et al., 1999).

Once children enter school, the amount of material they read has a large effect on their reading comprehension. However, children vary tremendously in the amount they read. For instance, U.S. 5th-graders whose reading-achievement test scores are in the 90th percentile for their grade report roughly 200 times as much discretionary reading as peers who score in the 10th percentile (Anderson, Wilson, & Fielding, 1988). Higher reading proficiency leads children to read more; reading more, in turn, leads to higher reading proficiency (Willingham, 2017). Thus, early reading skill is important not only in itself but also because it motivates children to read more and become better readers.

Individual Differences

Individual differences in reading proficiency tend to be stable over time. Children who have relatively advanced reading skills when they enter kindergarten tend to be better readers throughout elementary school, and better readers at the end of elementary school tend to be better readers in high school (Duncan et al., 2007; Hulslander et al., 2011). Studies of adoptive and non-adoptive siblings, as well as of monozygotic and dizygotic twins, indicate that these continuities of individual differences reflect both shared genes and shared environments (Petrill et al., 2007). As we have noted, genetic and environmental influences are mutually reinforcing: parents who are good and frequent readers are likely to provide both genes and environments that make it likely that their children will be relatively good readers when they are young, which makes it more likely that the children will read more as they get older, which will further improve their reading, and so on.

Writing

Much less is known about the development of children's writing than about the development of their reading, but what is known shows interesting parallels between the two.

FIGURE 8.12 A 3½-year-old's effort at writing The child's symbols, although unconventional, indicate an understanding that words require separate symbols.

Pre-writing Skills

The development of writing, like the development of reading, begins before children receive formal schooling. Figure 8.12 displays writing efforts typical of a 3½-year-old. The marks are not conventional letters of the alphabet, but they look vaguely like them and are arranged along a roughly horizontal line. By age 4, children's "writing" is sufficiently advanced that adults have no trouble distinguishing it from the figures they produce when asked to draw a flower or a house (Tolchnisky, 2003).

Preschoolers' "writing" indicates that they expect meaning to be reflected in print. They use more marks to represent words that signify many objects, such as "forest," than to represent words that signify a single object, such as "tree" (Levin & Korat, 1993). Similarly, when asked to guess which of several words is the name for a particular object, they generally choose longer words for larger objects (Bialystok, 2000). Although written language does not work this way, the children's guess seems reasonable.

script typical sequence of actions used to organize and interpret repeated events, such as eating at restaurants, going to doctors' appointments, and writing reports

Generating Written Text

Learning to write, in the sense of composing an essay or story, is more difficult than learning to read. This is not surprising, because writing requires focusing simultaneously on numerous goals, both low level and high level (Bouwer, Koster, & van den Bergh, 2018). The low-level goals include forming letters, spelling words, using correct capitalization and punctuation, and adhering to grammatical rules. The high-level goals include making arguments comprehensible without the intonations and gestures that help us communicate when we speak, organizing arguments into a coherent framework, and providing the background information that readers need to understand the writing. The difficulties children have in meeting low-level and high-level goals simultaneously result in the type of flat story illustrated in Figure 8.13.

FIGURE 8.13 A 4th-grader's story The intended title of this story was "The Kid Who Lost Things." See if you can figure out the rest.

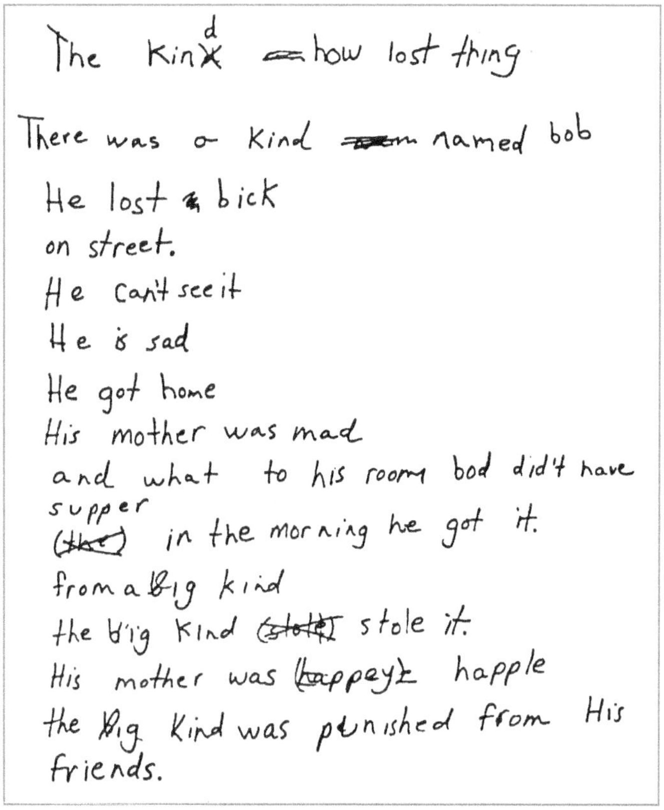

As with development of reading comprehension, growth of writing proficiency reflects improvements in basic processes, strategies, metacognition, and content knowledge. Automatizing low-level skills, such as spelling and punctuation, aids writing not only because correct spelling and punctuation make writing easier to understand but also because automatizing the low-level skills frees cognitive resources for pursuing the higher-level communicative goals of writing. Consistent with this conclusion, children's proficiency at low-level skills such as punctuation correlates positively with the quality of their essays (McCutchen, 2011).

Acquisition of strategies also contributes to improvements in writing. One common strategy is to sequence high-level goals in a standard organization, or **script**, a set of actions

TABLE 8.3 Stories Written at Beginning, Middle, and End of Year for Class News Assignment

SEPTEMBER 24, 1956	Today is Monday, September 24, 1956. It is a rainy day. We hope the sun will shine. We got new spelling books. We had our pictures taken. We sang Happy Birthday to Barbara.
JANUARY 22, 1957	Today is Tuesday, January 22, 1957. It is a foggy day. We must be careful crossing the road. This morning, we had music. We learned a new song. Linda is absent. We hope she comes back soon. We had arithmetic. We made believe that we were buying candy. We had fun. We work in our English books. We learned when to use is and are.
MAY 27, 1957	Today is Monday, May 27, 1957. It is a warm, cloudy day. We hope the sun comes out. This afternoon, we had music. We enjoyed it. We went out to play. Carole is absent. We hope she comes back soon. We had a spelling lesson, we learned about a dozen. Tomorrow we shall have show and tell. Some of us have spelling sentences to do for homework. Danny brought in a cocoon. It will turn into a butterfly.

Information from H. S. Waters (1980).

or events that occur repeatedly. Harriet Waters, a psychologist whose proud mother saved all her daughter's "class news" assignments from 2nd grade, was one child who employed such an approach (Waters, 1980). As shown in Table 8.3, in each class news essay, Waters first noted the date, then described the weather, and then discussed events of the school day—a strategy that greatly simplified her writing task. For older children, formulating outlines serves a similar purpose of dividing the task of writing into manageable parts: first figure out what you want to say, then figure out the best order for making your main points, then figure out how to make each point.

Metacognitive understanding plays several crucial roles in writing. Perhaps the most basic type of metacognitive understanding is recognizing that readers may not have the same knowledge as the writer and that the writing therefore needs to provide readers the information they need to grasp what is being said. Good writers consistently exhibit such understanding by high school; poor writers rarely do (Berninger & Richards, 2002b). A second crucial type of metacognitive knowledge involves understanding the need to plan before writing, rather than just jumping in and starting to write. Good writers spend much more time than do poor writers planning what they will say before they begin writing—making notes, constructing outlines, and so on (Graham et al., 2012). Understanding the need for revision is a third key type of metacognitive knowledge. Good writers spend more time revising their already relatively good first drafts than poor writers spend revising their poorer ones (Fitzgerald, 1992).

Fortunately, instruction aimed at inculcating metacognitive understanding can enhance writing skills (Graham et al., 2012). In particular, the writing of both typical and learning-disabled children improves when they are shown models of how good writing is generated, taught to revise their own and other children's work, and encouraged to ask themselves several basic questions: What are your goals in writing this piece? Who is the audience? What do readers need to know to understand what you're writing? What revisions are necessary to improve the initial draft? A large-scale study in the Netherlands found that an 8-week intervention that taught such strategies improved the writing of 4th-, 5th-, and 6th-graders, with the gains continuing for at least 8 weeks beyond the end of the intervention (Bouwer et al., 2018).

Finally, as in reading, content knowledge plays a crucial role in writing. Children generally write better when they are familiar with the topic than when they are not (Graham et al., 2012). Children can gain content knowledge through reading, which is one reason why children who are skillful readers and read more than most peers also tend to be good writers (Graham et al., 2012).

Mathematics

In Chapter 7, we examined infants' early-developing nonverbal number sense and the emergence of counting between ages 2 and 4 years. Here we examine mathematical development, including development of arithmetic, that occurs beyond this base.

Arithmetic

People often think of arithmetic learning as a process of rote memorization of facts and procedures, but it is actually far more complex and interesting. How well children learn arithmetic depends on the strategies they use, the precision of their representations of numerical magnitudes, and their understanding of mathematical concepts and principles.

Strategies From about age 5 years, when most children begin to learn arithmetic, they use a variety of problem-solving strategies. The most common initial strategies are counting from 1 (e.g., solving 2 + 2 by putting up two fingers on each hand and counting "1, 2, 3, 4") and retrieval (recalling answers from memory). At first, children can use these strategies to answer only a few simple problems, such as 1 + 2 and 2 + 2, but they gradually expand use of the strategies to a wider range of single-digit problems (Geary, 2006).

When children begin to do arithmetic daily, usually in 1st grade, they add several new strategies. One is *counting from the larger addend* (e.g., solving 3 + 9 by counting, "9, 10, 11, 12"). Another strategy is *decomposition,* which involves dividing a problem into two easier ones (e.g., solving 3 + 9 by thinking "3 + 10 = 13; 13 − 1 = 12"). Children continue to use the earlier developing strategies as well; most 1st-graders use three or more strategies to add single-digit numbers (Siegler, 1987).

"Maybe it's not a wrong answer—maybe it's just a different answer."

BARBARA SMALLER THE NEW YORKER COLLECTION/THE CARTOON BANK

Learning arithmetic is harder than it looks.

Children use similarly varied strategies on all four arithmetic operations. For example, one study of Canadian schoolchildren demonstrated that they used a variety of strategies to solve a multiplication problem such as 3 × 4; they sometimes write three 4s and add them, sometimes make three bundles of four hatch marks and count them, and sometimes retrieve 12 from memory (Mabbott & Bisanz, 2003). Use of these arithmetic strategies is surprisingly enduring: even Canadian university students use strategies other than retrieval on 15% to 30% of single-digit problems (LeFevre et al., 1996).

Just as children's choices among word-identification strategies are highly adaptive, so are their choices among arithmetic strategies (Siegler, 1996). Even 4-year-olds choose in sensible ways, usually solving easy problems such as 2 + 2 quickly and accurately by using retrieval and usually solving harder problems such as 5 + 2 less quickly but still accurately by counting from 1. As children gain experience with the answers to single-digit arithmetic problems, their strategy choices shift increasingly toward using retrieval of those answers. The learning process seems to be the same as with the corresponding shift from phonological recoding toward visually based retrieval in reading. The more often children generate the correct answer to a problem, regardless of the strategy they use to generate it, the more often they will be able to retrieve that answer, thereby avoiding the need to use slower strategies.

Arithmetic Strategies: The Research of Robert Siegler

COURTESY OF ROBERT SIEGLER

Understanding numerical magnitudes **Numerical magnitude representations** are mental models of the way quantities are ordered along a less-to-more dimension. Regardless of whether "7" refers to a distance (7 inches), a weight (7 pounds),

numerical magnitude representations mental models of the sizes of numbers, ordered along a less-to-more dimension a duration (7 hours), or a set size (7 people), the magnitude represented by "7" is larger than that indicated by "6"— and smaller than that indicated by "8"—of the same unit.

The idea that symbolically expressed numbers represent magnitudes might seem obvious, but accurately linking such numbers and the magnitudes they represent actually constitutes a challenge for children over a prolonged period of development. For example, many preschoolers who can count flawlessly from 1 to 10 do not know whether 4 or 8 indicates the greater number of objects (Le Corre & Carey, 2007); many elementary school children estimate the location of 150 as being near the midpoint of a number line with 0 and 1000 at the two ends (Laski & Yu, 2014); and many adolescents and adults have no idea whether 3/5 is larger or smaller than 5/11 (Fazio, DeWolf, & Siegler, 2016). What is lacking in all these cases is accurate representation of numerical magnitudes.

Although the learning process takes a prolonged period, the range of numbers whose magnitudes children represent reasonably precisely, as indicated by the accuracy of their magnitude comparisons and number-line estimates, increases greatly with age and experience (Figure 8.14). Accuracy of magnitude representations of the numbers 1–10 increases greatly between ages 3 and 6 (Berteletti et al., 2010); that of numbers 1–100, between ages 6 and 8 (Geary et al., 2007); that of numbers 1–1000, between ages 8 and 12 (Thompson & Opfer, 2010); and so on. These ages reflect when children first gain substantial experience with each numerical range: most children learn to count from 1–10 in the preschool period; they learn to count, add, and subtract numbers from 1–100 in early elementary school, and so on.

Children of any given age differ considerably in their knowledge of numerical magnitudes. These differences are related to the children's overall mathematical knowledge. During elementary school, children who more accurately estimate whole-number magnitudes on number lines have higher math achievement. During middle school, the same is true for children who accurately estimate fraction magnitudes (Jordan et al., 2013).

Part of the reason for this relation is that more accurate magnitude representations help children learn arithmetic. The more precisely a child understands numerical

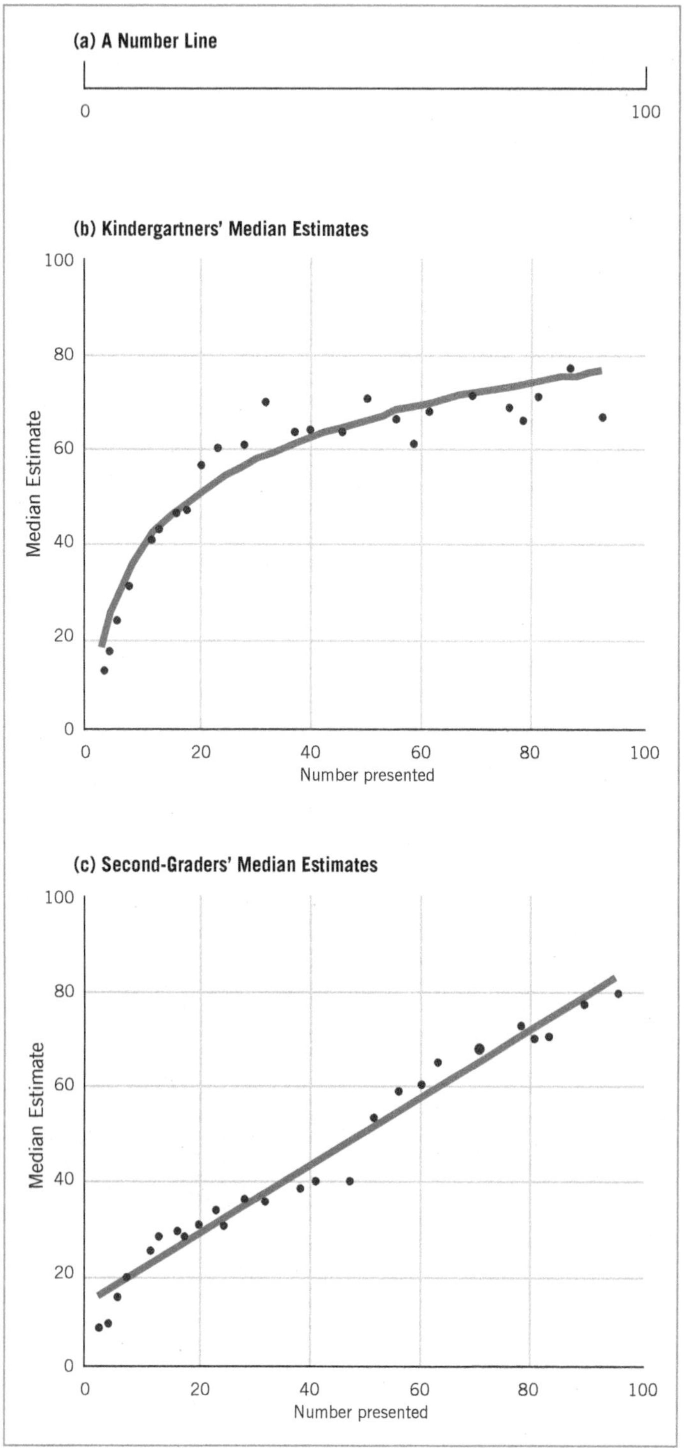

FIGURE 8.14 The number-line task and typical developmental changes on it (a) On each trial with a 0–100 number line, children need to estimate a different number's location on the line. (b) Kindergartners' median estimates for each number on the 0–100 number-line task increased with the number being estimated, but in a way that involved overestimates of relatively small numbers and underestimates of large ones. (c) 2nd-graders' median estimates for each number on the same task increased linearly with the size of the number being estimated, and were quite accurate. (Data from Siegler & Booth, 2004)

magnitudes, as measured by the child's accuracy in estimating the position of numbers on a number line, the greater the child's arithmetic proficiency with both whole numbers and fractions (Schneider et al., 2018). Moreover, instruction that improves the accuracy of children's symbolic numerical magnitude representations also improves their subsequent learning of arithmetic, again with both whole numbers and fractions (Fuchs et al., 2013; Siegler & Ramani, 2009). Accurate magnitude representations may enhance arithmetic learning by suggesting plausible answers and eliminating implausible ones from consideration. A child who understands fraction magnitudes will know that 12/13 + 7/8 equals a little less than 2; the fact that most U.S. middle school students claim that the answer is about 19 or 21 reveals the serious difficulties that they have with fractions (Lortie-Forgues, Tian, & Siegler, 2015).

mathematical equality concept that the values on each side of the equal sign must be equivalent

gesture–speech mismatches phenomenon in which hand movements and verbal statements convey different ideas

Conceptual understanding of arithmetic Understanding why some arithmetic procedures are appropriate and others inappropriate poses a major challenge for many children, even those who have memorized the correct procedure. Some simple types of conceptual understanding of arithmetic appear during the preschool period; for example, many 4-year-olds understand the *commutative law of addition,* the principle that adding a + b is the same as adding b + a (Canobi, Reeve, & Pattison, 2002). Not until years later, however, do they master more advanced arithmetic concepts, such as **mathematical equality**—the idea that the values on the two sides of the equal sign must balance. On almost all problems in which young children encounter the equal sign, numbers appear only to the left of it (e.g., 3 + 4 + 5 = __). For purposes of solving such problems, children can interpret the equal sign merely as a signal to start adding.

Eventually, however, children encounter arithmetic problems with numbers on both sides of the equal sign, such as 3 + 4 + 5 = __ + 5. As late as 4th grade, most children in the United States answer such problems incorrectly (Goldin-Meadow, Cook, & Mitchell, 2009). The most common incorrect approach is to add all numbers to the left of the equal sign, which in the above problem sum to 12, and to assume that this sum is the answer to the problem. Such errors reflect interference from children's extensive practice solving typical addition problems, which have no number following the equal sign (McNeil et al., 2011), as well as a lack of understanding that the equal sign means that the values on both sides of it are equivalent.

In many cases, children's hand gestures reveal that they have somewhat better understanding of mathematical equality than is revealed by their answers or explanations. For example, on the problem 3 + 4 + 5 = __ + 5, children often answer "12" and explain that they solved the problem by adding 3 + 4 + 5, but during their explanation, they point to all four numbers rather than just to the three preceding the equal sign. This pointing suggests an implicit recognition that the fourth number might be important, even though the child did not include it in the calculation (Alibali et al., 2011). Children who initially show such **gesture–speech mismatches**, in which their gesturing conveys more information than their verbal statements, learn more from instruction on mathematical equality problems than do peers whose gesturing and speech before the instruction were consistent (i.e., those who said "12" and pointed only to the three numbers that they added).

Interview with Susan Goldin-Meadow

WORTH PUBLISHERS

The gestures play a causal role in learning as well: children who are encouraged to gesture appropriately while explaining answers to mathematical equality problems learn more than children who are asked not to gesture (Goldin-Meadow et al., 2009). The positive relation between gesture–speech mismatches and subsequent learning has emerged on number conservation and physics problems as well as on mathematical equality problems. These findings illustrate a widespread phenomenon: variability of thought and action (e.g., generating gestures that differ from one's speech, or advancing multiple explanations of a phenomenon rather than just one) often indicates heightened readiness to learn (Church, 1999; Thelen & Smith, 2006).

Cultural influences Children's knowledge of arithmetic varies greatly among countries. Those in China, Japan, South Korea, and other East Asian countries acquire far greater proficiency than those in even high-achieving European and North American countries (e.g., Finland, the Netherlands, and Canada), who in turn tend to know more than peers in other European and North American countries, including the United States, Spain, and Italy (Bailey et al., 2015). The differences start even before children enter formal schooling (Siegler & Mu, 2008) and seem to be related to cultural emphasis (or lack of emphasis) on math, quality of math teachers and textbooks, and time spent on math in classrooms and homes (Leung et al., 2015).

Mathematics Anxiety

Many children experience *mathematics anxiety,* a negative emotional state that leads to fear and avoidance of math (Ashcraft & Ridley, 2005). Such anxiety can be evident as early as 1st grade (Ramirez et al., 2012) and for many people, it presents a lifelong problem; 25% of students at four-year colleges and as many as 80% of students at community colleges report moderate to high math anxiety (Beilock & Willingham, 2014). Math evokes more anxiety than other school subjects, probably because of the unambiguous right/wrong status of answers to mathematics problems, the widespread belief that mathematics is closely linked to intelligence, and the frustrating periods with no apparent progress that mathematics learning often entails.

Although mean math achievement of boys and girls is almost identical (Halpern et al., 2007), mathematics anxiety is considerably more prevalent in girls than in boys (Devine et al., 2012). Not surprising, it is more common among people who do poorly in math, though some people experience it despite having high mathematics achievement and not suffering from high anxiety in general (Moore & Ashcraft, 2013). The dread that math can inspire contributes to the negative outcomes that are feared; a likely reason is that the anxiety reduces the working memory resources needed to solve many math problems (Beilock & Willingham, 2014). Consistent with this interpretation, when presented with mathematics tasks, people with math anxiety show both unusually great activity on the right side of the amygdala, a part of the brain involved in processing negative emotions, and depressed activity in brain areas crucial to working memory (Young, Wu, & Menon, 2012).

Why do some children become anxious about math? One contributor appears to be the views of adults who are important in the children's lives. Parents and teachers who are themselves anxious about mathematics tend to convey their beliefs and feelings to their children. Thus, 1st-graders' math learning is negatively related to the math anxiety of their parents (Berkowitz et al., 2015) and teachers (Beilock et al., 2010). Strikingly, among parents with high math anxiety, providing more help with homework is associated with their 1st- and 2nd-grade children learning *less* than the children of parents with equally high math anxiety who

BOX 8.3 APPLICATIONS Mathematics Disabilities

Between 5% and 8% of children perform so poorly in math that they are classified as having a mathematics disability (Shalev, 2007). These children have IQ scores in the normal range (85 or higher) but perform extremely poorly in mathematics. In the first few grades, they tend to be slow in learning to count and to accurately solve single-digit arithmetic problems (Jordan, 2007). Their performance improves with experience, but even in later grades and adulthood, most continue to be slow at single-digit arithmetic and to have difficulty with the many math skills that build on it, such as multi-digit arithmetic, fractions, and algebra (Geary et al., 2012).

Although people often think of mathematics as a type of knowledge necessary for school but not afterward, the experience of adults with mathematics disabilities illustrates the lifelong debilitating effects of this problem:

> I worked for Nabisco. As a mixer, you had to know the correct scale and formulas. I kept messing up. I lost my job.
>
> (Curry, Schmitt, & Waldron, 1996, p. 63)

> Dairy Queen wouldn't hire me because I couldn't make change in my head.
>
> (Curry, Schmitt, & Waldron, 1996, p. 63)

> For as long as I can remember, numbers have not been my friend.
>
> (Blackburn, cited in M. McCloskey, 2007, p. 415)

Several specific problems contribute to mathematics disabilities (Geary et al., 2012). In severe cases, damage to one or more brain areas that are central to numerical processing, such as the intraparietal sulcus, is often the cause (Simon & Rivera, 2007). In less severe cases, minimal exposure to numbers prior to beginning school often contributes. Children who as preschoolers lack knowledge of the key mathematical concepts and skills that their peers possess tend to lag far behind throughout school (Watts et al., 2014). Other variables that are associated with, and might cause, mathematics disabilities are poor working memory for numbers, poor executive functioning, slow processing of numerical information, and mathematics anxiety (Cragg & Gilmore, 2014; Lyons & Beilock, 2012).

A variety of programs have been designed to improve the mathematics knowledge of children with mathematics disabilities. One particularly successful program (Fuchs et al., 2013) emphasized learning of fraction magnitudes through instruction in magnitude comparison (e.g., "Which is larger: 1/2 or 1/5?") and number-line estimation (e.g., "Where would 1/5 go on this number line?"). The instruction, which was implemented with 9- and 10-year-olds, not only improved the children's learning of these capabilities but also improved their learning of fraction arithmetic, relative to that of children who received more fraction arithmetic instruction in the classroom but less instruction in understanding fraction magnitudes. Such findings indicate that effective instruction can reduce the problems associated with mathematics disabilities.

provide less homework help. This negative relation between homework help and math learning is not seen among children of parents who are not high in math anxiety (Maloney et al., 2015).

The negative impact of anxiety on mathematics learning has prompted efforts to find ways of reducing the anxiety. One promising intervention is surprisingly simple: have students write a brief description of their emotions just before taking a test. Such expressive writing reduces anxiety and boosts performance in a variety of areas in which negative emotions interfere with learning and performance, including mathematics (Ramirez & Beilock, 2011). Putting the negative thoughts on paper might help students think about the situation more objectively and thus allow them to concentrate on the math problems.

Even among children with mathematics anxiety, most learn the basics reasonably well. However, as noted in Box 8.3, the process of learning math goes seriously awry with certain children who suffer from *mathematics disability*, the general difficulty in thinking about numbers.

REVIEW QUESTION

What parallels do you see in the process of acquiring reading, writing, and mathematics skills described in this section and your own experience? ■

CHAPTER SUMMARY

- Alfred Binet and his colleague Théophile Simon developed the first widely used intelligence test. Its purpose was to identify children who were unlikely to benefit from standard instruction in the classroom. Modern intelligence tests are descendants of the Binet–Simon test.
- One of Binet's key insights was that intelligence includes diverse high-level capabilities that need to be assessed in order to measure intelligence accurately.

What Is Intelligence?

- Intelligence can be viewed as a single trait, such as *g*; as a few separate abilities, such as Thurstone's primary mental abilities; or as a very large number of specific processes, such as those described in information-processing analyses.
- Intelligence is often measured through use of IQ tests, such as the Stanford–Binet and the WISC. These tests examine general information, vocabulary, arithmetic, language comprehension, spatial reasoning, and a variety of other intellectual abilities.

Measuring Intelligence

- A person's overall score on an intelligence test, the IQ score, is a measure of general intelligence. It reflects the individual's intellectual ability relative to age peers.
- Most children's IQ scores are quite stable over periods of years, though scores do vary somewhat over time.

IQ Scores as Predictors of Important Outcomes

- IQ scores correlate positively with long-term educational and occupational success.
- Other factors, such as social understanding, creativity, and motivation also influence success in life.

Genes, Environment, and the Development of Intelligence

- Development of intelligence is influenced by the child's own qualities, by the immediate environment, and by the broader societal context.
- Genetic inheritance is one important influence on IQ score. This influence tends to increase with age, in part due to some genes not expressing themselves until late childhood or adolescence, and in part due to genes influencing children's choices of environments.
- A child's family environment, as measured by the HOME, is related to the child's IQ score. The relation reflects within-family influences, such as parents' intellectual and emotional support for the particular child, as well as between-family influences, such as differences in parental wealth and education.
- Schooling positively influences IQ score and school achievement.
- Broader societal factors, such as poverty and discrimination against racial and ethnic minorities, also influence children's IQ scores.
- To alleviate the harmful effects of poverty, the United States has undertaken both small-scale preschool intervention programs and the much larger Project Head Start. Both have initial positive effects on intelligence and school achievement, though the effects fade over time. On the other hand, the programs have enduring positive effects on the likelihood of not being held back in a grade and the likelihood of completing high school and enrolling in college.
- Intensive intervention programs, such as the Carolina Abecedarian Project, that begin in the child's first year and provide optimal childcare circumstances and structured academic curricula have produced increases in intelligence that continue into adolescence and adulthood.

Alternative Perspectives on Intelligence

- Novel approaches to intelligence, such as Gardner's multiple intelligences theory and Sternberg's theory of successful intelligence, attempt to broaden traditional conceptions of intelligence.

Acquisition of Academic Skills: Reading, Writing, and Mathematics

- Many children learn letter names and gain phonemic awareness before they start school. Both skills correlate with later reading achievement, and phonemic awareness also is causally related to it.
- Word identification is achieved by two main strategies: phonological recoding and visually based retrieval.
- Reading comprehension benefits from automatization of word identification because it frees cognitive resources for understanding the text. Use of strategies, metacognitive understanding, and content knowledge also influence reading comprehension, as does the amount that parents read to their children and the amount that children themselves read.
- Although many children begin to write during the preschool period, writing well remains difficult for many years. Much of the difficulty comes from the fact that writing well requires children to attend simultaneously to low-level processes, such as punctuation and spelling, and to high-level processes, such as anticipating what readers will and will not know.

- As with reading, automatization of basic processes, use of strategies, metacognitive understanding, and content knowledge influence development of writing.
- Most children use several strategies to learn arithmetic, such as adding by counting from 1, counting from the larger addend, and retrieving answers from memory. Children typically choose in adaptive ways, using more time-consuming and effortful strategies only on the more difficult problems where such approaches are needed to generate correct answers.
- Precise representations of numerical magnitudes facilitate learning arithmetic and other mathematical skills.
- As children encounter more advanced math, conceptual understanding becomes increasingly important. Understanding mathematical equality, for example, is essential for grasping advanced arithmetic and algebra problems.
- Mathematics anxiety can interfere with performance and learning because the heightened emotions reduce working-memory resources.

Test Yourself

1. Who developed the first objective intelligence test that directly assessed specific high-level abilities identified as key components of intelligence?
   a. Spearman
   b. Wechsler
   c. Gardner
   d. Binet
2. Chris is an elementary school student who is good at putting together puzzles, identifying which object doesn't belong to a given set, and thinking on the spot. Chris's proficiency in these various intellectual tasks is an indication of his level of ___________ intelligence.
   a. crystallized
   b. fluid
   c. emotional
   d. processing
3. Which of the following best describes Carroll's three-stratum theory of intelligence?
   a. Intelligence is best measured by reading, writing, and mathematics concepts.
   b. Each individual can be categorized into one of three levels of intelligence.
   c. Successful intelligence involves analytic, practical, and creative abilities.
   d. General intelligence influences intermediate abilities, which influence specific processes.
4. The summary measure that is the result of an intelligence test is referred to as a person's ___________.
   a. normal distribution
   b. intelligence quotient
   c. general intelligence
   d. individual quantitative measure
5. As an individual moves from early childhood into adolescence and adulthood, the influence of genetic factors on intelligence ___________.
   a. increases
   b. fluctuates
   c. remains stable
   d. decreases
6. Six-year-old Aliya loves to read. Her parents aren't particularly engaged in reading themselves, but because of Aliya's evident interest, they surround her with books and read to her. According to Sandra Scarr, the relationship between Aliya's interests and her parents' actions is an example of ___________.
   a. passive effects
   b. active effects
   c. evocative effects
   d. mental modeling
7. The HOME was developed to measure the complex influences of family environment on a child's intelligence. Though this measure can be used to predict a child's IQ score, why are researchers not able to conclude that better home environment causes higher scores?
   a. Children's IQ scores tend to fluctuate widely with age.
   b. This measure does not account for the influence of parents' genes on the home environment and the child's intelligence.
   c. Children's IQ scores are not normally distributed and therefore cannot be used to draw causal relationships.
   d. Subsequent measures have shown that home environment has little influence on intelligence.
8. Which of the following statements is true regarding the relation between environmental risk and intelligence, according to the environmental risk scale?
   a. Parental education level is the key factor in predicting a child's intellectual development.
   b. The impact of additional risks diminishes greatly after the presence of three risk factors.
   c. The total number of risks is a better predictor of IQ than the presence of any single risk.
   d. Though IQ score remains stable over time, the number of risk factors in a child's environment is highly variable.
9. The fact that certain types of brain damage can lead to deficiencies in specific areas (e.g., interpersonal skills) and that prodigies show remarkable ability in specific areas (e.g., musical intelligence) but not in others led to the development of which theory?
   a. Sternberg's theory of successful intelligence
   b. The Flynn effect

   c. Gardner's theory of multiple intelligences
   d. Thurston's theory of primary mental abilities
10. What are the three components of Sternberg's theory of successful intelligence?
   a. Analytic abilities, practical abilities, and creative abilities
   b. Linguistic intelligence, logical-mathematical intelligence, and spatial intelligence
   c. Passive effects, evocative effects, and active effects
   d. General intelligence, intermediate-level abilities, and specific processes
11. Performance on measures of ____________ is the strongest predictor of a kindergartner's later ability to sound out and spell words.
   a. phonemic awareness
   b. letter name mastery
   c. IQ
   d. phonological recoding skills
12. Comprehension monitoring describes an individual's ability to
   a. process a word's meaning from its visual form.
   b. translate letters into sounds and blend those sounds into words.
   c. keep track of one's ongoing understanding of a text.
   d. recognize that readers may not have the same knowledge as the writer.
13. Which high-level writing strategy involves the repetition of a certain sequence of actions, such as determining a thesis, outlining the main points, and figuring out how to support those points?
   a. Following a script
   b. Comprehension monitoring
   c. Planning
   d. Strategy–choice processing
14. The knowledge that the number 5 represents a unit that falls between the numbers 4 and 6, regardless of whether one is referring to distance, weight, set size, or some other measurement, is known as ____________.
   a. mathematical equality
   b. decomposition
   c. numerical magnitude representations
   d. mental modeling
15. When asked to solve the problem $2 + 3 + 4 = \_\_ + 4$, 10-year-old Nevin gives the incorrect answer 9, but explains his answer by pointing to all four numbers, rather than just the three that come before the equal sign. Nevin's behaviour illustrates ____________.
   a. mathematical inequality
   b. gesture–speech mismatch
   c. decomposition
   d. visual retrieval error

Critical Thinking Questions

1. Intelligence can be viewed as a single ability, several abilities, or many processes. List the characteristics that you think are the most important components of intelligence and explain their relevance.
2. Individual differences in intelligence are more stable than individual differences in other areas of psychological functioning such as emotional regulation or aggression. Why do you think this is so?
3. Among children from middle- and upper-income families, genetics are more influential than the shared environment on individual differences in intelligence, but among children from low-income families, the opposite is the case. Why do you think that is?
4. Participation in Head Start does not lead to higher IQ or achievement test scores by the end of high school, but it does lead to lower rates of dropping out or being placed in special-education classes. Why do you think this is the case?
5. Explain Chall's (1979) statement: "In the primary grades, children learn to read; in the higher grades, they read to learn."
6. The development of reading, writing, and mathematics shows a number of similarities. What are these similarities, and why do you think development occurs in similar ways in the three areas?

Key Terms

Better Beginnings, Better Futures (BBBF), p. 290
Carolina Abecedarian Project, p. 291
comprehension monitoring, p. 299
crystallized intelligence, p. 274
dyslexia, p. 298
fluid intelligence, p. 273
Flynn effect, p. 286
g (general intelligence), p. 273
gesture–speech mismatches, p. 305
IQ (intelligence quotient), p. 276
mathematical equality, p. 305
multiple intelligences theory, p. 293
normal distribution, p. 278
numerical magnitude representations, p. 303
phonemic awareness, p. 294
phonological recoding skills, p. 294
primary mental abilities, p. 274
script, p. 301
self-discipline, p. 280
simple view of reading, p. 297
situation model, p. 298
standard deviation (SD), p. 278
strategy–choice process, p. 296
theory of successful intelligence, p. 293
three-stratum theory of intelligence, p. 274
visually based retrieval, p. 296
Wechsler Intelligence Scale for Children (WISC), p. 276

Answers to Test Yourself

1. d, **2.** b, **3.** d, **4.** b, **5.** a, **6.** c, **7.** b, **8.** c, **9.** c, **10.** a, **11.** a, **12.** c, **13.** a, **14.** c, **15.** b

CHAPTER

9 Theories of Social Development

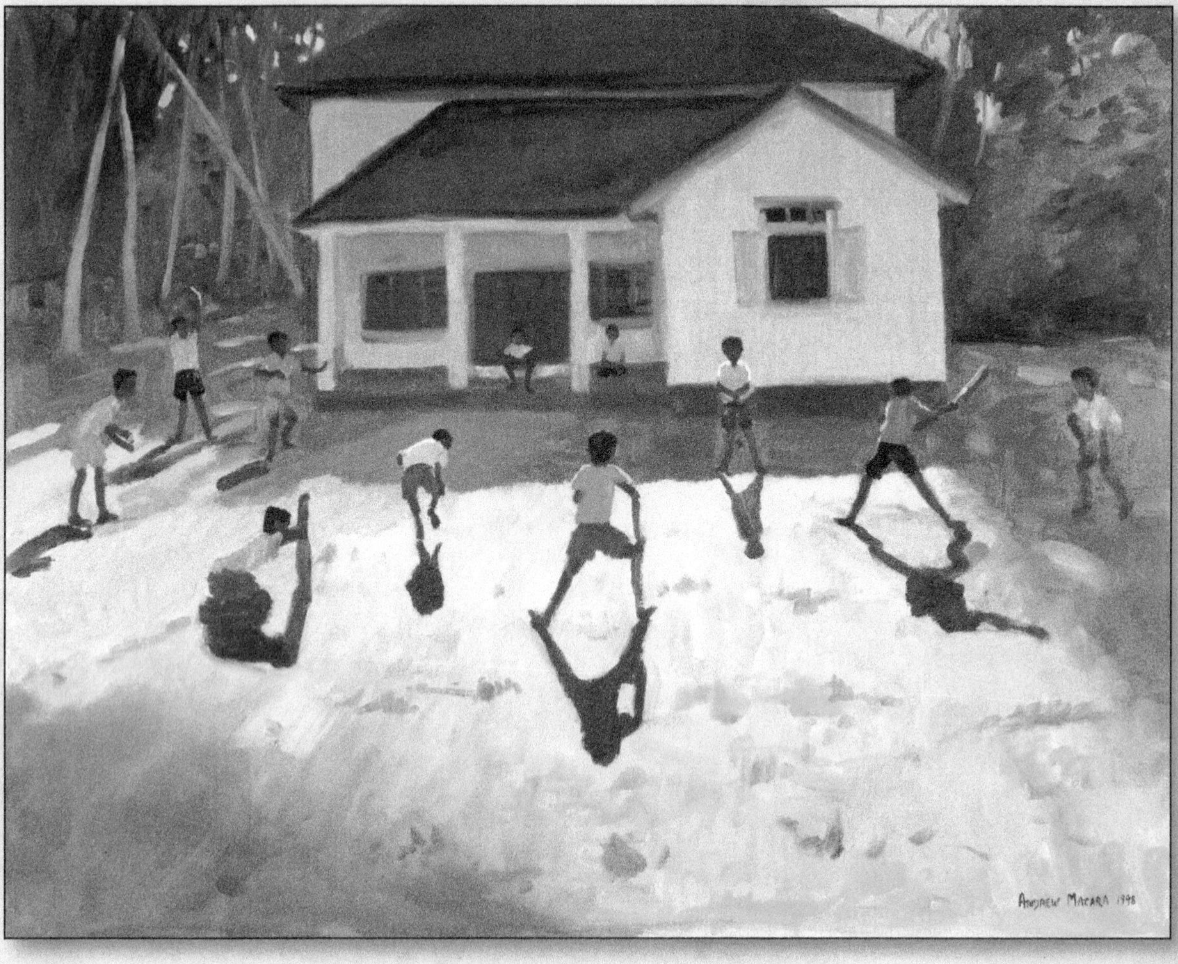

ANDREW/ANDREW MACARA/PRIVATE COLLECTION/BRIDGEMAN IMAGES

ANDREW MACARA, *Cricket, Sri Lanka* (oil on canvas, 1998)

Psychoanalytic Theories | Learning Theories
Theories of Social Cognition | Ecological Theories

THEMES

NATURE AND NURTURE ■ THE ACTIVE CHILD ■ CONTINUITY/DISCONTINUITY
MECHANISMS OF CHANGE ■ THE SOCIOCULTURAL CONTEXT ■ INDIVIDUAL DIFFERENCES ■ RESEARCH AND CHILDREN'S WELFARE

Imagine yourself interacting face-to-face with an infant. What is it like? You naturally smile and speak in an affectionate tone of voice, and the infant probably smiles and makes happy sounds back at you. If for some reason you speak in a loud, harsh voice, the baby becomes quiet and wary. If you look away, the infant follows your gaze, as though there is something interesting to see in that direction. Of course, the baby does not just respond to what you do; the baby also engages in independent behaviours, examining objects or events in the room or fussing for no obvious reason. Your interaction with the baby evokes emotions in you—joy, affection, frustration, and so on. Over time, through repeated interactions, you and the infant learn about each other and smile and vocalize more readily to each other than to someone else.

Now imagine that you are asked to interact with Kismet, the robot pictured below, just as you would with a human infant. Although the request might seem strange, Kismet's facelike features make you willing to give it a try. So you smile and speak in an affectionate tone—"Hi, Kismet, how are you?" Kismet smiles back at you and gurgles happily. You speak harshly, "Kismet, stop that right now." The robot looks surprised—even a bit frightened—and makes a whimpering sound. You find yourself spontaneously attempting to console Kismet: "I'm sorry; I didn't mean it." After just a few moments, you have lost your feeling of self-consciousness and find the interaction with your new metallic friend remarkably natural. You may even start to feel fond of Kismet.

Kismet was one of the world's first "social robots." Unlike robots that are programmed to perform specific tasks (like a vacuuming Roomba), social robots

PETER MENZEL/SCIENCE SOURCE

Like interactions between a parent and infant, a face-to-face interaction between Kismet and its designer involves talking, cooing back and forth, and responding to each other's facial expressions.

are programmed to learn from their interactions with humans, just as infants do. Accordingly, Kismet was designed as a sociable, "cute" robot that could elicit "nurturing" from humans. Kismet's behaviour is readily interpretable in human terms, and the robot even seems to have internal mental and emotional states and a personality. Kismet learns from its interactions with people—from their instructions and from their reactions to its behaviour. Through these interactions, Kismet figures out how to interpret facial expressions, how to communicate, what behaviours are acceptable, and so on (Breazeal, 1998). Thus, Kismet develops over time as a function of the interaction between the "innate" structure built into it and its subsequent socially mediated experience. Just like a baby!

The challenge for Kismet's designers was in many ways like the task of developmental scientists trying to understand how children's development is shaped through their interactions with other people. Any successful account of social development must include the many ways we influence one another, starting with the simple fact that no human infant can survive without intensive, long-term care by other people. We learn how to behave based on how others respond to our behaviour; we learn how to interpret ourselves according to how others treat us; and we interpret other people by analogy to ourselves—all in the context of social interaction. Pioneers in robotics have continued to use machines as a way to better understand the role of social dynamics from infancy onward. In one recent application of robotics to social development, researchers modeled the development of infant smiling by having undergraduate students interact with a baby-faced robot named Diego-San, programmed to both perceive and produce smiling behaviour (Ruvolo, Messinger, & Movellan, 2015). The researchers found that by carefully timing Diego-San's smiles, it elicited the maximum amount of adult smiling.

In this chapter, we review some of the most important and influential general theories of social development. These theories attempt to account for many important aspects of development, including emotion, motivation, personality, attachment, self, peer relationships, morality, and gender. We will describe four types of theories that address these topics, reflecting, in turn, the psychoanalytic, learning, social cognitive, and ecological perspectives. We will discuss the basic tenets of each theory and examine some of the relevant evidence.

Advances in artificial intelligence have allowed researchers to test theories of social development in unique ways. Diego-San, pictured here, is being used to study the motivation and timing of parent and infant smiles.

All of our seven themes appear in this chapter, with three of them being particularly prominent. The most pervasive theme is *individual differences,* as we examine how the social world affects children's development. The theme of *nature and nurture* helps us distinguish between the theories, because they vary in the degree to which they emphasize biological and environmental factors. The *active child* theme is also a major focus: some theories emphasize children's active participation in, and effect on, their own socialization, whereas others view children's development as shaped primarily by external forces.

Psychoanalytic Theories

No psychological theory has had a greater impact on Western culture and on thinking about personality and social development than the psychoanalytic theory of Sigmund Freud (1856–1939). The life-span developmental theory of Erik Erikson (1902–1994), a successor to Freud's theory, has also been quite influential. In both Freud's and Erikson's theories, development is largely driven by biological maturation. For Freud, behaviour is motivated by the need to satisfy basic drives. In Erikson's theory, development is driven by a series of developmental crises related to age and biological maturation.

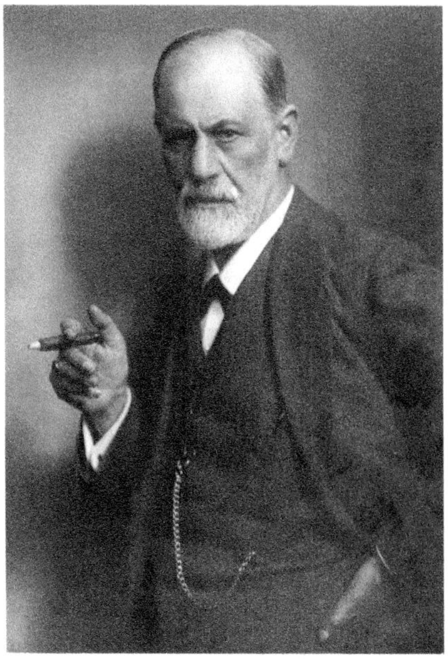

Sigmund Freud, the father of psychoanalysis, has had a lasting influence on developmental psychology through his emphasis on the lifelong impact of early relationships.

Freud's Theory of Psychosexual Development

Freud made fundamental, lasting contributions to developmental psychology; however, as we will discuss later in this chapter, his current influence is limited to broad psychological concepts, not the specifics of his theory of *psychosexual* development. Freud thought that even very young children have a sexual nature that motivates their behaviour and influences their relationships. He proposed that children pass through a series of universal developmental stages. In each successive stage, children encounter conflicts related to a particular **erogenous zone,** that is, areas of the body that are erotically sensitive (e.g., mouth, anus, and genitals). He maintained that children's success or failure in resolving these conflicts affects their development throughout life.

The Developmental Process

In Freud's view, development starts with a helpless infant beset by instinctual drives, foremost among them hunger. The distress associated with hunger is expressed through crying, prompting the mother to breast-feed the baby. The resulting satisfaction of the infant's hunger, as well as the experience of nursing, is a source of intense pleasure for the infant. The instinctual drives with which the infant is born constitute the unconscious **id**—the earliest and most primitive of three personality structures posited by Freud. The id is ruled by the *pleasure principle*—the goal of achieving maximal gratification as quickly as possible. Whether the gratification involves eating, drinking, eliminating, or physical comfort, the id wants it *now*. Throughout one's life, the id is most apparent in selfish or impulsive behaviour in which immediate gratification is sought with little regard for consequences. During the first year of life, the infant is in Freud's first stage of psychosexual development, the **oral stage,** so called because the primary source of gratification and pleasure is oral activity, such as sucking and eating.

Later in the first year, the next personality structure, the rational **ego,** arises out of the need to resolve conflicts between the id's demands for immediate gratification and the restraints imposed by the external world. Whereas "the id stands for the untamed passions," the ego "stands for reason and good sense" (Freud, 1933/1964a). Over time, as it continually seeks resolution between the demands of the id and those of the real world, the ego begins to develop into the individual's sense of self. Nevertheless, the ego is never fully in control.

During the infant's second year, maturation facilitates the development of control over some bodily processes, including urination and defecation. At this point, the infant enters Freud's second stage, the **anal stage,** which lasts until roughly age 3. In this stage, the child's erotic interests focus on the pleasurable relief of tension derived from defecation. Conflict ensues when, for the first time, the parents begin to make specific demands on the infant, most notably their insistence on toilet training.

Freud's third stage, the **phallic stage,** spans the ages of 3 to 6. In this stage, the focus of sexual pleasure again migrates as children become interested in their own genitalia and curious about those of parents and playmates. Freud believed that during the phallic stage, children identify with same-sex caregivers, giving rise to

erogenous zones in Freud's theory, areas of the body that become erotically sensitive in successive stages of development

id in psychoanalytic theory, the earliest and most primitive personality structure. It is unconscious and operates with the goal of seeking pleasure

oral stage the first stage in Freud's theory, occurring in the first year, in which the primary source of satisfaction and pleasure is oral activity

ego in psychoanalytic theory, the second personality structure to develop. It is the rational, logical, problem-solving component of personality

anal stage the second stage in Freud's theory, lasting from the second year through the third year, in which the primary source of pleasure comes from defecation

phallic stage the third stage in Freud's theory, lasting from age 3 to age 6, in which sexual pleasure is focused on the genitalia

IMAGE SOURCE/ALAMY

Through identifying with his father, this young boy should, according to Freud's theory, develop a strong superego.

gender differences in attitudes and behaviour. Freud also believed that young children experience intense sexual desires during the phallic stage, and he proposed that their efforts to cope with them leads to the emergence of the third personality structure, the **superego.** The superego is essentially what we think of as conscience and is based on the child's adoption of their parents' standards for acceptable behaviour. The superego guides the child to avoid actions that would result in guilt, which the child experiences when violating these internalized standards.

The fourth developmental stage, the **latency period,** lasts from about age 6 to age 12. It is, as its name implies, a time of relative calm, with sexual desires hidden away in the unconscious. The fifth and final stage, the **genital stage,** begins with the advent of sexual maturation. The sexual energy that had been kept in check for several years reasserts itself with full force, directed toward peers.

According to Freud, if fundamental needs are not met during any of the stages of psychosexual development, children may become *fixated* on those needs, continually attempting to satisfy them and to resolve associated conflicts. In Freud's view, these unsatisfied needs are unconscious and are expressed in indirect or symbolic ways. For example, if an infant's needs for oral gratification are not adequately satisfied during the oral stage, later in life the individual may repeatedly engage in substitute oral activities, such as excessive eating, nail-biting, smoking, and so on. Similarly, if toddlers are subjected to very harsh toilet training during the anal stage, they may remain preoccupied with issues related to cleanliness, becoming either compulsively tidy and psychologically rigid or extremely sloppy and lax. Thus, in Freud's view, the child's passage through the stages of psychosexual development shapes the individual's personality for life.

superego in psychoanalytic theory, the third personality structure, consisting of internalized moral standards

latency period the fourth stage in Freud's theory, lasting from age 6 to age 12, in which sexual energy gets channeled into socially acceptable activities

genital stage the final stage in Freud's theory, beginning in adolescence, in which sexual maturation is complete

Erikson's Theory of Psychosocial Development

Of the many followers of Freud, none has had greater influence in developmental psychology than Erik Erikson. Erikson accepted the basic elements of Freud's theory but incorporated social factors into it, including cultural influences and contemporary issues, such as juvenile delinquency, changing sexual roles, and the generation gap. Consequently, his theory is regarded as a theory of *psychosocial* development.

TED STRESHINSKY PHOTOGRAPHIC ARCHIVE/GETTY IMAGES

Erik Erikson was hired as an art instructor in a school run by Anna Freud, Sigmund Freud's daughter, and became an analyst. He immigrated to the United States in the early 1930s, when fascism was on the rise in Germany.

The Developmental Process

Erikson proposed eight age-related stages of development that span infancy to old age. Each stage is characterized by a specific *crisis,* or set of developmental issues, that the individual must resolve. If the dominant issue of a given stage is not successfully resolved before the onset of the next stage, the person will continue to struggle with it. In the following summary, we discuss only the first five stages, which cover infancy through adolescence.

1. *Basic Trust Versus Mistrust (the 1st year).* The crucial issue for the infant is developing a sense of trust in caregivers. If the ability to trust others when it is appropriate to do so does not develop, the person will have difficulty forming intimate relationships later in life.
2. *Autonomy Versus Shame and Doubt (ages 1 to 3½).* The challenge for the child is to achieve a strong sense of autonomy while adjusting to increasing social demands. Going well beyond Freud's focus on toilet training,

Erikson pointed out that during this period, the dramatic increases that occur in every realm of children's real-world competence—including motor skills, cognitive abilities, and language—foster children's desires to make their own choices. Infants' newfound ability to explore the environment on their own (as discussed in Chapter 5) changes the family dynamics, initiating a long-running battle of wills with caregivers. In a supportive atmosphere that allows children to achieve self-control without the loss of self-esteem, children gain a sense of autonomy. In contrast, if children are subjected to severe punishment or ridicule, they may come to doubt their abilities.

3. *Initiative Versus Guilt (ages 4 to 6).* Like Freud, Erikson saw this period as the time during which children come to identify with, and learn from, their parents. Like Freud, Erikson also believed that a crucial attainment is the development of conscience. The challenge for the child is to achieve a balance between initiative and guilt.
4. *Industry Versus Inferiority (age 6 to puberty).* This stage is crucial for ego development. Children master cognitive and social skills that are important in their culture, and they learn to work industriously and to cooperate with peers. Successful experiences give the child a sense of competence, but failure can lead to excessive feelings of inadequacy or inferiority.
5. *Identity Versus Role Confusion (adolescence to early adulthood).* Erikson accorded great importance to adolescence, seeing it as critical for the achievement of a core sense of *identity*. The dramatic physical changes of puberty and the emergence of strong sexual urges are accompanied by new social pressures, including a need to make educational and occupational decisions. Caught between their past identity as a child and the many options and uncertainties of their future, adolescents must resolve the question of who they really are or live in confusion about what roles they should play as adults.

Theories of Emotional Development in Infancy and Toddlerhood

Theories of Middle Childhood Development

Current Perspectives

Freud's emphasis on the importance of early experience and close relationships has been especially influential in setting the foundation for modern-day attachment theory and research (which you will read about in Chapter 11). The research in this area strongly suggests that the nature of infants' relationships with their parents not only affects behaviour in infancy but also has important long-term effects on close relationships throughout life. In addition, Freud's remarkable insight that much of our mental life occurs outside the realm of consciousness is fundamental to modern cognitive science and neuroscience. Erikson's emphasis on the quest for identity in adolescence has had a lasting impact, providing the foundation for a wealth of research on this aspect of adolescence. The signal weakness of both theories is that their major claims are too vague to be testable, and many of their specific elements, particularly in Freud's theory, are generally regarded as highly questionable. Regardless, both of these theories have been enormously influential.

The vast abundance of cartoons about Freud and psychoanalysis testify to his enormous impact on society.

"You're born, you deconstruct your childhood, and then you die."

How might psychoanalytic theories be useful to Kismet's designers? They have already tried to make Kismet as sociable as possible. Probably the most important further step they can take, based on Freud's and Erikson's theories, is to program Kismet to form a few very close relationships, to ensure a sense of security and well-being. Those relationships should have a lasting effect on Kismet's internal organization so that they continue to influence the robot throughout its "life."

REVIEW QUESTIONS

What are some examples of the ways in which the influence of the psychoanalytic theories of Freud and Erikson manifest in our culture? What aspects of these theories do they accurately reflect? ■

Learning Theories

I imagine the minds of children as easily turned this or that way, as water itself.
—John Locke, from his essay "Some Thoughts Concerning Education"

As you may recall from Chapter 1, the empiricist philosopher John Locke believed that experience shapes the nature of the human mind. His intellectual descendants also consider learning to be the primary factor in social and personality development. In contrast to Freud's emphasis on the role of internal forces and subjective experience, learning theorists emphasize the role of external factors in shaping social behaviour.

The primary developmental question on which learning theories take a unanimous stand is whether they demonstrate *continuity* or *discontinuity:* they all emphasize continuity. Because the same principles control learning and behaviour throughout life, there are no qualitatively different stages in development. Like information-processing theorists, learning theorists focus on the role of specific *mechanisms of change*—which, in their view, involve learning principles, such as reinforcement and observational learning. Children become different from one another primarily because they have different histories of reinforcement and learning opportunities. The theme of *research and children's welfare* is also relevant: approaches based on learning principles have been widely applied to a range of issues in child rearing.

Watson's Behaviourism

John B. Watson (1878–1958), the founder of behaviourism, believed that development is determined by the child's environment, via learning through conditioning (see Chapter 5). He believed that psychologists should study visible behaviour, not the "mind." The extent of Watson's (1924) faith in the power of conditioning is clear in his famous boast:

> Give me a dozen healthy infants, well-formed, and my own specified world to bring them up in, and I'll guarantee to take any one at random and train him to become any type of specialist I might select—doctor, lawyer, artist, merchant-chief, and yes, even beggar man and thief, regardless of his talents, penchants, tendencies, abilities, vocations, and race of his ancestors.
>
> (p. 104)

On a much less ambitious scale, Watson demonstrated the power of classical conditioning in a famous—and famously unethical—experiment with a

9-month-old infant referred to as "Little Albert" (Watson & Rayner, 1920). Watson first exposed Little Albert to a perfectly nice white rat in the laboratory. Initially, Albert reacted positively to the rat. On subsequent exposures, however, the researchers repeatedly paired the presentation of the rat with a loud noise that frightened Albert. After a number of such pairings, Albert became afraid of the rat itself.

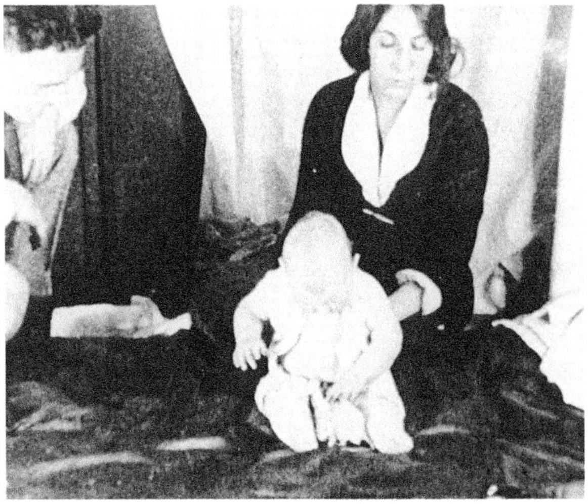
THE DRS. NICHOLAS AND DOROTHY CUMMINGS CENTER FOR THE HISTORY OF PSYCHOLOGY, THE UNIVERSITY OF AKRON

To demonstrate the power of conditioning, John B. Watson and his assistant Rosemary Raynor conditioned "Little Albert" to fear a white rat.

Our everyday lives are filled with examples of conditioned responses. Young children, for example, often show fear at the sight of a doctor or nurse in a white lab coat, based on their previous association between people wearing white coats and painful injections. (To counteract this problem, healthcare professionals wear street clothes or brightly coloured scrubs, hoping to avoid this association.)

Believing that he had established the power of learning in development, Watson placed the responsibility for guiding children's development squarely on their parents' shoulders. In his child-rearing manual, *Psychological Care of Infant and Child* (1928), he offered parents stern advice for fulfilling this responsibility. One particular piece of advice that was widely adopted in Canada and the United States was to put infants on a strict feeding schedule. The idea was that the baby would become conditioned to expect a feeding at regular intervals and therefore would not cry in between. To help implement this strict regimen, Watson advised parents to achieve distance and objectivity in their relations with their children (just as he exhorted psychologists to be objective in their research):

> Treat them as though they were young adults. Dress them, bathe them with care and circumspection. Let your behavior always be objective and kindly firm. Never hug and kiss them, never let them sit on your lap. If you must, kiss them once on the forehead when they say good night. Shake hands with them in the morning. Give them a pat on the head if they have made an extraordinarily good job on a difficult task. Try it out. In a week's time you will find how easy it is to be perfectly objective with your child and at the same time kindly. You will be utterly ashamed of the mawkish, sentimental way you have been handling it.
>
> (pp. 81–82)

Watson's overly strict child-rearing advice gradually fell out of favour with the publication and widespread success of Dr. Benjamin Spock's *The Common Sense Guide to Baby and Child Care,* first published in 1946 (Spock's thinking about early development and child rearing was very strongly influenced by Freud). However, Watson's emphasis on the environment as the key factor in determining behaviour persisted in the work of B. F. Skinner.

B. F. Skinner, who once appeared in 40th place in a popular magazine's list of the 100 most important people who ever lived (Miller, 2002), believed that children's development is primarily a matter of their reinforcement history.

NINA LEEN/GETTY IMAGES

Skinner's Operant Conditioning

B. F. Skinner (1904–1990) was just as forceful as Watson in proposing that behaviour is under environmental control, once claiming that "a person does not act upon the world, the world acts upon him" (Skinner, 1971, p. 211). As described in Chapter 5, a major tenet of Skinner's theory of operant conditioning is that we tend to repeat behaviours that lead to favourable outcomes—that is, reinforcement—and suppress those that result in unfavourable outcomes—that is, punishment. Skinner believed that everything we do in life is an operant response influenced by the outcomes of past behaviour.

Skinner's research on the nature and function of reinforcement led to many discoveries, including two that are of particular interest to parents and teachers.

intermittent reinforcement inconsistent response to a behaviour; for example, sometimes punishing unacceptable behaviours, and other times ignoring it

behaviour modification a form of therapy based on principles of operant conditioning in which reinforcement contingencies are changed to encourage more adaptive behaviour

One is the fact that *attention* can by itself serve as a powerful reinforcer: children often do things "just to get attention" (Skinner, 1953, p. 78). The popular behaviour-management strategy of *time-out,* or temporary isolation, involves systematically withdrawing attention and thereby removing the reinforcement for inappropriate behaviour, with the goal of extinguishing it.

When the toddler son of one of the authors first graduated to a "big-boy bed," he repeatedly got up after having been put to bed, using one pretext after another to join his parents. This undesirable behaviour was extinguished in just a few nights by his father, who sat in a chair outside the bedroom door. Every time the child appeared, his father gently, but firmly and silently, put him back in his bed. The key to this successful intervention was the fact that there was no reinforcement for getting out of bed—no talking, no yelling, no drink of water, no interaction of any sort—in short, none of the potent reinforcers that parental attention provides.

A second important discovery was the difficulty of extinguishing behaviour that has been *intermittently reinforced,* that is, that has sometimes been followed by reward and sometimes not. As Skinner discovered in his research with animals, **intermittent reinforcement** makes behaviours resistant to extinction. If a behaviour is only occasionally rewarded, an animal is likely to maintain the expectation that the next performance of the behaviour may produce the reward, leading to persistence of the behaviour even in the absence of reward. Inadvertently, parents often encourage unwanted behaviour by applying intermittent reinforcement. We try not to reward children's whiny or aggressive demands, but—being human—we sometimes give in. Such intermittent reinforcement is very powerful: if a parent who had occasionally given in to whining never did so again, the child would nevertheless continue to resort to whining, assuming that because it worked in the past, it might work again in the future.

Skinner's work on reinforcement led to a form of therapy known as **behaviour modification.** A simple example of this approach involved a preschool child who frequently chose solitary activities. Observers noticed that the boy's teachers were unintentionally reinforcing his withdrawn behaviour: they comforted him when he was alone but tended to ignore him when he played with other children. The boy's withdrawal was modified by reversing the reinforcement contingencies: the teachers began paying attention to the boy whenever he joined a group but ignored him whenever he withdrew. Soon the child was spending most of his time playing with his classmates (Harris, Wolf, & Baer, 1967).

Although scolding is intended to discourage a behaviour, the fact that it is also a form of paying attention to a child may actually reinforce undesirable behaviours and cause them to persist.

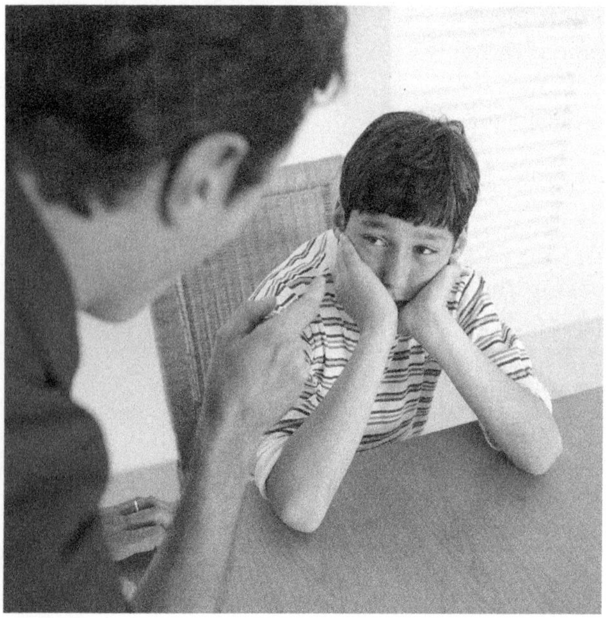

STOCKBYTE/GETTY IMAGES

Social-Learning Theory

Social-learning theory, like other learning-oriented theories, attempts to account for social development in terms of learning mechanisms. However, unlike Skinner's focus on reinforcement, social-learning theory emphasizes observation and imitation. Albert Bandura (1977, 1986), for example, has argued that most human learning is inherently *social* in nature and is based on observation of the behaviour of other people. Children learn rapidly and efficiently simply from watching what other people do and then imitating them. They can also learn from indirect models, that is, from reading books and viewing screens, in the absence of any direct reinforcement for their behaviour (see Box 9.1). These ideas connect to the discussion of infant imitation and observational learning in Chapter 5.

Over time, Bandura increasingly emphasized the cognitive aspects of observational learning, eventually renaming his view "social cognitive theory." Observational learning clearly depends on basic cognitive processes of *attention* to others' behaviour, *encoding* what is observed, *storing* the information in memory, and *retrieving* it at some later time in order to reproduce the behaviour observed earlier. Thanks to observational learning, many young children know quite a bit about adult activities—such as driving a car (you insert and turn the ignition key, press on the accelerator, turn the steering wheel)—long before being allowed to engage in them themselves.

Unlike earlier learning theorists like Watson and Skinner, Bandura emphasized the active role of children in their own development, describing development as a **reciprocal determinism** between children and their social environment. The basic idea of this concept is that children have characteristics that lead them to seek particular kinds of interactions with the external world. These interactions influence children's future environments. For example, a child who enjoys playing violent video games (a topic we will address later in this chapter) may encourage peers to begin playing violent games together. The child may then seek out these peers above others; as their skill level in the games mounts, the members of the group may become desensitized to violence in games, encourage each other to behave more aggressively, and be rejected by other peers, thereby becoming even more committed to their social group (e.g., Anderson & Bushman, 2001).

JON BRENNEIS/GETTY IMAGES

Albert Bandura was born in Mudare, a small town in central Alberta. He completed his undergraduate degree at the University of British Columbia and then moved to the University of Iowa for his graduate training. Bandura has been described as the "greatest living psychologist" in recognition of the impact his social cognitive theory has had on psychology.

Current Perspectives

In contrast to psychoanalytic theories, learning theories are based on principles derived from experiments. As a result, they allow explicit predictions that can be empirically tested. Partly for this reason, they have inspired an enormous amount of research concerning parental socialization practices and how children learn social behaviours. They have also led to important practical applications, including behaviour modification. The primary weakness of the learning approach is that because it is focused on behaviour, not brains or minds, it lacks attention to biological influences and largely minimizes the impact of perceptual, motor, cognitive, and language development.

Kismet's designers took learning theories seriously by giving the robot the crucial capacity to learn from humans. Kismet can acquire new behaviours by modeling what it "sees" and "hears" humans do. Kismet's ability to learn from people is a crucial aspect of what makes it seem sociable. But to what extent can Kismet learn via reciprocal determinism, shaping its own environment? Contemporary social robots, like the baby-faced smiling robot discussed earlier in the chapter (Ruvolo et al., 2015), do have the capacity to shape their environment and to learn how to control the behaviour of those around it. This innovation may be one of the most important "social" developments in artificial intelligence.

REVIEW QUESTION

Based on the learning theories described in this section, what advice would you give to parents who are potty-training their 3-year-old? ■

reciprocal determinism child–environment influences operate in both directions; children are both affected by and influence aspects of their environment

BOX 9.1 A CLOSER LOOK Bandura and Bobo

A series of classic studies by Albert Bandura and his colleagues (Bandura, 1965; Bandura, Ross, & Ross, 1963) will give you a good sense of the kind of questions and methods that typify social-learning-theory research. The investigators began by having preschool children individually watch a short film in which an adult model performed highly aggressive actions on a Bobo doll (an inflatable toy, with a weight in the bottom so it pops back up as soon as it is knocked down). The model punched the doll, hit it with a mallet while shouting "Sockeroo," threw balls at it while shouting "Bang bang," and so on.

In one study, three groups of children observed the adult model receive different consequences for these aggressive behaviours. One group saw the model receive rewards and praise. Another group saw the model punished (scolded). The third group saw the model experience no consequences. The question was whether **vicarious reinforcement**—observing someone else receive a reward or a punishment—would affect the children's subsequent reproduction of the behaviour. After viewing the film, each child was left alone in a playroom with a Bobo doll, and hidden observers recorded children's behaviour. Later, whether or not they had imitated the model, the children were offered an incentive (juice and prizes) to reproduce as many of the model's actions as they could remember.

The results are shown in the figure. The children who had seen the model punished imitated the behaviour less than did those in the other two groups. However, the children in all conditions had *learned* from observing the model's behaviour and remembered what they had seen; when offered rewards to reproduce the aggressive actions, they did so, even if they had not spontaneously performed them in the initial test.

One particularly interesting feature of this research is the gender differences that emerged: boys were more physically aggressive toward the Bobo doll than girls were. However, the girls had learned as much about the modeled behaviours as the boys had, as shown by their increased level of imitation when offered a reward. Presumably, boys and girls inhibit behaviours they believe to be inappropriate for their own gender, even though they learn about a wide range of behaviours.

This classic research thus demonstrates that children can quickly acquire new behaviours simply as a result of observing others, that their tendency to

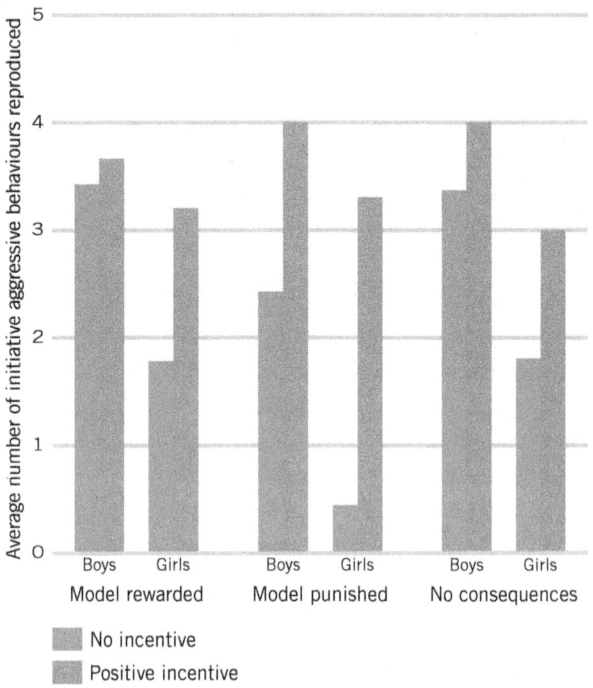

This graph shows the average number of aggressive behaviours children imitated after seeing a model rewarded, punished, or receiving no consequences for aggressive behaviour. In the no-incentive test, the children were simply left alone in the room with the Bobo doll and were given no instructions. In the positive-incentive test, they were offered a reward to do what they had seen the model do. The results clearly show that the children had learned from what they observed and that they had learned more than they initially showed. (Data from Bandura, 1965)

vicarious reinforcement observing someone else receive a reward or punishment

Theories of Social Cognition

How do children come to understand their own and other people's thoughts, feelings, motives, and behaviours? Like adults, children are active processors of social information. They pay attention to what other people do and say, and they are constantly drawing inferences, forming interpretations, constructing explanations, or making attributions regarding what they observe. They process information about their own behaviour and experiences in the same way. The complexity of children's thinking and reasoning about the social world is related to, and limited by, the complexity of their thought processes in general. After all, the same mind that solves arithmetic and conservation problems also solves problems having to do with making friends and resolving moral dilemmas. With advances in cognitive development, the way that children think about themselves and other people deepens and becomes more abstract.

Social cognitive theories provide a sharp contrast to the emphasis that psychoanalytic and learning theories place on external forces as the primary

These photographs show an adult performing a series of aggressive actions on a Bobo doll. The boy who had observed the adult's behaviour subsequently imitated it when left alone in the room with the Bobo doll. The girl, who did not initially reproduce the model's aggressive actions, did imitate the model's behaviour when offered a reward to do so.

reproduce what they have learned depends on whether the person whose actions they observed was rewarded or punished, and that what children learn from watching others is not necessarily evident in their behaviour.

Observation Learning of Aggression: Bandura's Bobo Doll Study

source of development. Instead, social cognitive theories emphasize the process of **self-socialization**—children's active shaping of their own development. According to this view, children's knowledge and beliefs about themselves and other people lead them to adopt particular goals and standards to guide their own behaviour.

The central theme of most relevance to social cognitive theories is the *active child.* Another prominent theme is *individual differences,* particularly in the comparisons that are often drawn between the thinking and behaviour of males and females, aggressive and nonaggressive children, and so on. The theme of *continuity/discontinuity* distinguishes different theories. Prominent stage theories emphasize discontinuity: age-related qualitative changes in how children think about the social world. Information-processing theories, on the other hand, stress continuity in the processes involved in social reasoning. In the following discussions, we will consider these two types of social cognitive theories. The first type is represented by Selman's stage theory of role taking; the second type is represented by Dodge's information-processing theory of social problem solving and by Dweck's attributional account of academic achievement.

self-socialization the idea that children play a very active role in their own socialization through their activity preferences, friendship choices, and so on

role taking being aware of the perspective of another person

Selman's Stage Theory of Role Taking

In formulating his theory of social cognition, Robert Selman (1980; Yeates & Selman, 1989) focused on the development of **role taking**—the ability to think about something from another's point of view. He proposed that adopting the perspective of another person is essential to understanding others' thoughts, feelings, and motives.

According to Selman, young children's social cognition is limited by their inability to engage in role-taking behaviour. Indeed, Selman, like Piaget, suggested that before the age of 6 years, children are virtually unaware that there is any perspective other than their own. (Note though, that as discussed in Chapter 7, more sensitive tasks reveal perspective taking and theory-of-mind abilities at younger ages).

Selman proposed that children go through four increasingly complex and abstract stages in their thinking about other people. In stage 1 (roughly ages 6 to 8), children learn that someone else can have a perspective different from their own, but they assume that the different perspective is merely due to that person's not possessing the same information they do. In stage 2 (ages 8 to 10), children not only realize that someone else can have a different view, but they also are able to think about the other person's point of view. However, it is not until stage 3 (ages 10 to 12) that children can systematically compare their own point of view with another person's. In stage 4 (age 12 and older), adolescents attempt to understand another's perspective by comparing it with that of a "generalized other," assessing whether the person's view is the same as that of most people in their social group.

Notice that in Selman's stages of role taking, as children become less egocentric, they become increasingly capable of considering multiple perspectives simultaneously (e.g., their own, another person's, and "most people's"). This growth in social cognition mirrors the changes identified by Piaget (and discussed in Chapter 4).

Many of young children's arguments with others stem from their difficulty appreciating that another person can have a point of view different from their own.

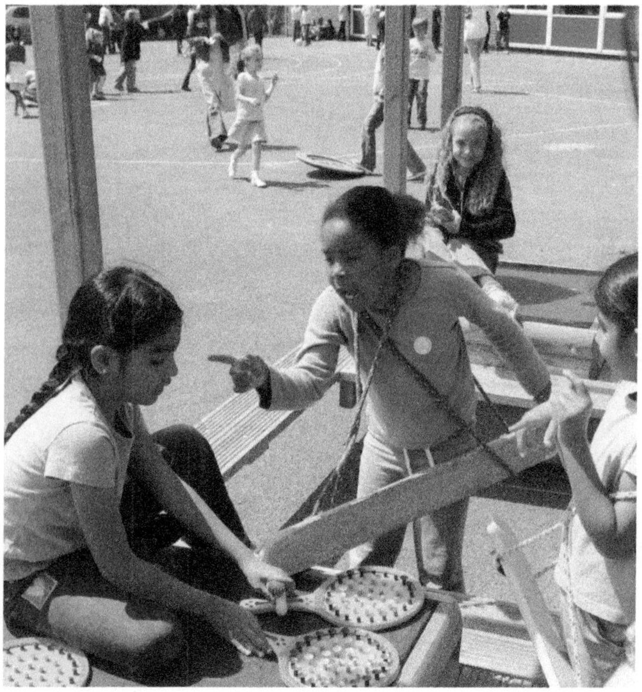

JOHN BIRDSALL/AGE FOTOSTOCK

Dodge's Information-Processing Theory of Social Problem Solving

The information-processing approach also emphasizes the role of cognition in social behaviour. This approach is exemplified by Dodge's analysis of children's use of aggression as a problem-solving strategy (Dodge, 1986; Dodge, Dishion, & Lansford, 2006). In the research that motivated Dodge's theory, elementary-school-age children were presented with stories that involved a child who suffers because of another child's actions, the intentions of which are ambiguous. For example, in one story, as a child is working hard to assemble a puzzle, a peer bumps into the table, scattering the puzzle pieces, and says "Oops." The children were then asked to imagine themselves as the victim in this scenario and to describe how they would respond and why. Some children interpreted the other child's knocking into the table as an accident and said that they would simply ignore the event. Others concluded that the peer bumped the table on purpose, and they reported that they would find a way to get even (many thought that punching the offender would be a good way to achieve that goal).

Some children have a **hostile attributional bias:** a general expectation that others are antagonistic to them (Crick & Dodge, 1994; Graham & Hudley, 1994). This bias leads such children to search for evidence of hostile intent on the part of the peer in the above scenario and to attribute to the peer a desire to harm them. They are likely to conclude that retaliation is the appropriate response to the peer's behaviour. Hostile attributional biases become self-fulfilling prophecies: a child's aggressive retaliation to the presumed hostile act of a peer elicits counterattacks and rejection by peers, further fueling the child's belief in the hostility of others. The development of hostile attributional biases does not appear to be specific to a particular cultural group or gender. A large-scale study including a wide range of locations (including cities and towns in China, Colombia, Jordan, Kenya, and Sweden) observed the same pattern: children with hostile attributional biases asserted that they would react aggressively to a provocation (Dodge et al., 2015).

hostile attributional bias in Dodge's theory, the tendency to assume that other people's ambiguous actions stem from hostile intent

Why might children begin to attribute hostile intent to those around them? Early harsh parenting predicts social information-processing biases that persist into early adulthood (Pettit et al., 2010). Children who have been physically abused are particularly likely to attribute anger to others, even in neutral situations (Pollak et al., 2000). The experience of physical abuse may heighten children's sensitivity to anger cues. For example, physically abused children are better at recognizing angry facial expressions than are children who have not experienced abuse, and the speed with which they do so is related to the degree of anger and hostility to which they have been subjected (as reported by their parent) (Pollak et al., 2009).

Physically abused children also have difficulty reasoning about negative emotions. In one study, abused children had difficulty determining which situations might trigger anger in parents, endorsing both positive and negative events as potential causes of parental anger (Perlman, Kalish, & Pollak, 2008). For instance, when presented hypothetical stories about child–parent situations, the abused children saw anger as a plausible response to positive events, such as a child's winning a prize at school or helping around the house. A tendency to assume anger in others (even when it is not present), paired with difficulty understanding what might provoke anger in others, is likely to result in a hostile attributional bias. (We will examine child maltreatment in more detail in Chapter 12.)

School systems have particular problems in dealing with children who have a hostile attributional bias. One strategy is to put them into special classrooms in which they can be more closely supervised (Dodge, Lansford, & Dishion, 2006). However, grouping children with hostile attributional biases together has other negative consequences. They may be more likely to react to one another in a hostile fashion, supporting their expectation of hostility from others and reinforcing one another's aggressive tendencies. Furthermore, by segregating children at risk, they lose the opportunity to learn more effective social strategies from well-adjusted peers.

An alternative intervention strategy targets social cognitive processes themselves. Fast Track is a multiyear preventive intervention program focused on aggression, targeting high-risk kindergartners with small-group activities, parent training, peer coaching, and other programming (e.g., Conduct Problems Prevention Research Group, 2002). This program has shown long-term benefits of decreased aggression through improved social cognitive processing. Children in the program were more likely to assume benign intent on the part of others, responded more competently to social challenges, and viewed aggression as detrimental (Dodge, Godwin, & Conduct Problems Prevention Research Group, 2013). These alterations in social information processing meant that participants were less likely to engage in delinquent and criminal behaviours as adults

(Sorensen, Dodge, & Conduct Problems Prevention Research Group, 2016). Thus, by directly targeting children's thinking about social behaviour—both their own and others—it may be possible to decrease the likelihood of later antisocial behaviour.

Dweck's Theory of Self-Attributions and Achievement Motivation

Imagine two grade-school children, Amara and Mia, both hard at work trying to solve math problems and both initially failing. Coming to the realization that the problems are quite difficult, Amara feels excited about meeting the challenge and works persistently to get the answers. Mia, in contrast, feels anxious and makes only a half-hearted effort to solve the problems. What explains this difference in the children's reaction to failure?

According to Carol Dweck's social cognition perspective (2006), the difference in their reaction is attributable to a difference in their **achievement motivation**—that is, in whether they are motivated by *learning goals,* seeking to improve their competence and master new material, or by *performance goals,* seeking to receive positive assessments of their competence or to avoid negative assessments. From this perspective, Amara has an *incremental* view of intelligence, the belief that intelligence can be developed through effort. She is motivated by a desire for mastery—on meeting challenges and overcoming failures, and she generally expects her efforts to be successful. Indeed, her increased effort and persistence following failure will in all likelihood improve her subsequent performance.

Mia, on the other hand, has an *entity* view of intelligence, the belief that her intelligence is fixed. Her goal is to be successful, and as long as she is succeeding, all is well. However, when she fails at something, she feels "helpless." Not succeeding leads her to feel bad and doubt her abilities and self-worth.

Underlying these two patterns of achievement motivation are differences in the attributions children make about themselves, particularly with regard to their sense of self-worth. Children with an **entity/helpless orientation** tend to base their sense of self-worth on the approval they receive (or do not receive) from other people about their personal qualities. To feel good about themselves, they seek out situations in which they can be assured of success and receive praise, and they avoid situations in which they might be criticized. In contrast, the self-esteem of children with an **incremental/mastery orientation** is based more on their own effort and learning and not on how others evaluate them. Because they do not equate failure on a task with a personal flaw, they can enjoy the challenge of a hard problem and persist in the attempt to solve it.

These different motivation patterns are evident as early as preschool (Smiley & Dweck, 1994). Given a choice of working on a puzzle they have already solved or on one they had previously failed to solve, some 4- and 5-year-old children strongly prefer the one they already know how to do, whereas others want to continue working on the one they had failed to solve.

Older children's views of themselves involve more complex concepts and reasoning than those of younger children. Some have what Dweck and her colleagues refer to as an **entity theory** of intelligence (Cain & Dweck, 1995; Dweck, 1999; Dweck & Leggett, 1988). This way of thinking about oneself, like Mia's view of her own intelligence, is rooted in the idea that intelligence is fixed and unchangeable. Over time, this theory comes to include the belief that success or failure in academic situations depends on how smart one is. When evaluating their own performance, children with an entity theory of intelligence focus on

achievement motivation refers to whether children are motivated by mastery or by others' views of their success

entity/helpless orientation a tendency to attribute success and failure to enduring aspects of the self and to give up in the face of failure

incremental/mastery orientation a general tendency to attribute success and failure to the amount of effort expended and to persist in the face of failure

entity theory a theory that a person's level of intelligence is fixed and unchangeable outcomes—success or failure—not on effort or learning from mistakes. Thus, when they experience failure (as everyone does some of the time), they think they are not very smart and that there is nothing they can do about it. They feel helpless.

Other children subscribe to an **incremental theory** of intelligence. This theory, like Amara's view of her own intelligence, is rooted in the idea that intelligence can grow as a function of experience. Children who hold an incremental theory of intelligence believe that academic success is achievable through effort and persistence. When evaluating their performance, they focus on what they have learned, even when they have failed, and they believe they can do better in the future by trying harder. They feel hopeful.

BLUE JEAN IMAGES/ALAMY

A teacher's comments could be either beneficial or detrimental, depending on whether they focus on the student's intelligence or effort.

Given what you have just read, what kind of praise and criticism do you think would reinforce these two patterns? An incremental/mastery pattern is reinforced by focusing on children's effort, praising them for a good effort ("I like the way you kept at it") and criticizing them for an inadequate one ("I think you can do better if you try harder"). In contrast, an entity/helpless pattern is reinforced by both praise and criticism focused on children's enduring traits ("You're very smart at these problems," "You just can't do math").

Do these two different types of internal theories have real-world ramifications? As you read in Chapter 1, Dweck and her colleagues have demonstrated that the answer is yes. They found that 7th-graders with an incremental theory of intelligence showed an upward trajectory in math scores over the next 2 years, while the scores of 7th-graders with an entity theory of intelligence remained flat (Blackwell, Trzesniewski, & Dweck, 2007). The investigators then provided an 8-session intervention to a new group of 7th-graders who had an entity theory of intelligence. Students in this group were taught an incremental theory of intelligence based on some of the same neuroscience concepts you read about in Chapter 3: the brain is plastic and always changing; learning forges new connections among synapses; and so on. A control group received training in basic study skills. Remarkably, the children who received the intervention showed a positive change in motivation as well as improvements in grades, while the children in the control group showed a decline in grades.

Do these two types of internal views—entity theories and incremental theories—have implications for children's development in domains beyond academic achievement? Again, the answer appears to be yes. For example, recall the hostile attributional bias discussed in the previous section. Adolescents who maintain an entity theory about personality traits are more likely to demonstrate a hostile attributional bias than are adolescents who endorse an incremental theory (Yeager et al., 2013). In other words, if they hold the view that people's behaviours are due to fixed personality traits (some people are good, others are bad), rather than due to situations or circumstances, they are more likely to interpret other people's harmful behaviour as hostile rather than as accidental or situational. If this is the case, then learning to take a more incremental view should diminish their tendency to make hostile attributions. And indeed, when adolescents received an intervention about neuroscience concepts (as described in the previous paragraph)

incremental theory a theory that a person's intelligence can grow as a function of experience designed to shift their perspectives away from the fixed-entity view and closer to the incremental view, there was a reduction in participants' hostile attributions. Thus, internal theories about traits of self and others have important implications for diverse aspects of development.

Where do these individual differences in internal theories come from? One obvious source is parents, who often try very hard to enhance their child's self-esteem. Unfortunately, doing something that might seem purely positive—praising a child for being good at something—can actually undermine the child's motivation for improvement. When parents instead praise their toddlers' effort, the children are more likely to have an incremental perspective in elementary school (Gunderson et al., 2013, 2018). Another obvious source is teachers. The way teachers comfort poor-performing students when the teacher has an entity perspective (as seen in comments like "It's okay; not everyone can be good at math") can undermine their students' motivation and self-expectations (Rattan, Good, & Dweck, 2012). Parents and teachers alike should be aware that some kinds of praise and comfort are beneficial, whereas others are not.

Current Perspectives

Social cognitive theorists have made many important contributions to the study of social development. One is their emphasis on children as active seekers of information about the social world. Another contribution is the insight that the effect of children's social experience depends on their interpretation of those experiences. Thus, children who make different attributions about a given social event (such as someone's causing them harm) or an academic event (such as doing poorly on a test) will respond differently to that event. In addition, a large amount of research has supported the social cognitive position. Although these theories have provided a very healthy antidote to social theories that left children's cognition out of the picture, they too provide an incomplete account. Most notably, social cognitive theories, like learning theories, have very little to say about biological factors in social development. However, this is beginning to change. As discussed in Box 9.2, current research efforts are taking advantage of cognitive neuroscience methods to begin to uncover the neural processes underlying social development.

Kismet is designed to shape its own development through its understanding of the behaviour of humans toward it—a form of self-socialization emphasized by social cognition theorists. What would it take for Kismet to draw inferences about others' cognitions, feelings, and motivations? For example, will it ever be possible for Kismet to make different attributions about a given behaviour, based on subtle aspects of the social context of its history with a person? Will Kismet come to know that people can hold points of view different from one another and from its own? Finally, can Kismet develop some sense of self-worth that will affect its attributions about itself? These questions about Kismet's potential to mimic social cognition highlight the vast complexity of human social development and the challenge faced by theorists trying to understand it.

REVIEW QUESTION

How does the role of the child as described in the social cognition theories differ from the role described in the psychoanalytic and learning theories presented earlier in this chapter? ■

BOX 9.2 A CLOSER LOOK Developmental Social Neuroscience

How does the social environment affect the developing brain? What neural mechanisms underlie the development of social behaviour? These are the types of questions being asked in the emerging field of developmental social neuroscience.

While many of the theories of social development we discuss in this chapter invoke biological mechanisms, from instincts to imprinting to genetic adaptation, they largely avoid invoking brain systems. A number of contemporary accounts, however, take their inspiration from neuroscience. One such approach emerged from the literature on caregiving in nonhuman animals. For example, as we discussed in Chapter 3, hormonal systems appear to be disrupted by adverse experience early in the lives of nonhuman animals. In particular, the development of the hypothalamic–pituitary–adrenal (HPA) axis, which regulates hormones that are critically involved in the body's response to stress, is impacted by adverse rearing conditions (e.g., Meaney, 2001; Parker & Maestripieri, 2011).

Taking their lead from these studies, developmental social neuroscientists have investigated unfortunate situations in which human children are exposed to adverse rearing conditions. One such group are children who were raised in orphanages abroad, in settings that lacked consistent emotional and physical contact from caregivers, prior to being internationally adopted. Like the nonhuman animals that received aberrant early care, these children show atypical hormonal responses in social situations (Wismer Fries et al., 2005; Wismer Fries, Shirtcliff, & Pollak, 2008). By examining the neural consequences of early social stress, it is possible to begin to understand why some children, such as those reared in institutions, show pervasive social challenges, including difficulties with attachment to their adoptive families.

Developmental social neuroscience methods have also been used to investigate interventions that may be effective in improving the outcomes of children growing up in adverse conditions. One such intervention was used in Bucharest, Romania, to ameliorate the negative impacts of orphanage-rearing discussed in Chapter 1. The Bucharest Early Intervention Project randomly selected a group of institutionalized children to move into foster homes, while their peers remained behind in orphanages (Nelson et al., 2007). The results of a structural MRI study several years later showed that the children who had left the orphanage had more white matter in their brains than did the children still living in the orphanage (Sheridan et al., 2012), suggesting improvements in neural information transmission. Remarkably, the brains of the children who had transitioned to foster care were indistinguishable from other Romanian children who had grown up at home with their families. These results illustrate *resilience;* leaving the stark orphanage setting for foster care had a palliative effect on these children's brains. But the news is not all good; even years later, as adolescents, the children who had been moved to foster care showed residual negative effects on cognitive functioning as compared to peers who grew up at home with their families, suggesting lingering negative effects of early institutional care (Wade et al., 2019).

Research in adult social and affective neuroscience also inspires new approaches to studying development. One current example lies in the potentially beneficial effects of mindfulness meditation on the brain. Over the past decade, the emerging field of contemplative neuroscience has provided evidence that at least for adults, there are numerous benefits of meditation, ranging from effects on the immune system to those parts of the brain associated with attention. Neuroimaging studies suggest that the brain bases of these effects reside largely in the prefrontal cortex, in areas that are responsible for such behaviours as emotion regulation, selective attention, and empathy (e.g., Davidson et al., 2012). These findings have led to a great deal of interest in the potential use of meditation and other contemplative practices with children and teens, especially given the fact that developing brains are more plastic than adult brains.

In one study, researchers used a mediation-based (mindfulness) Kindness Curriculum in a preschool setting. After 12 weeks, they observed improvements in the children's social competence and measures of executive function relative to a wait-list control group (Flook et al., 2015). Another study focused on low-income middle-schoolers living in high-stress

DAVID TAYLOR/ALAMY

urban environments. Researchers used a randomized-control trial method to assign children to a mindfulness-based stress reduction curriculum (Sibinga et al., 2016). Results revealed beneficial effects on a range of outcomes, including decreased levels of depression and negative affect.

To date, however, no developmental studies have gone beyond behavioural measures to demonstrate neural changes as a function of meditation. And, despite a great deal of interest in developing meditation-based interventions for a range of developmental disorders, including ADHD and autism, it is important to be cautious about the cause of any observed positive effects. For example, one study focused on rumination behaviour—a tendency to focus on one's negative emotions, which, as you'll see in Chapter 10, is a risk factor for adolescent depression. The results suggested that distraction—that is, purposely directing one's attention to happier thoughts or activities—was just as effective as meditation in reducing rumination (Hilt & Pollak, 2012). Thus, while mindfulness is a promising route to healthier minds, brains, and bodies, it may not be the only, or even the best, route to positive outcomes.

ethology the study of the evolutionary bases of behaviour

imprinting a form of learning in which the newborns of some species become attached to and follow adult members of the species

Ecological Theories

We now turn to a set of theories united by the fact that they take a very broad view of the context of social development. Virtually all theories emphasize the role of the environment in the development of individual children. However, the "environment" in many of these theories is narrowly construed as immediate contexts—family, peers, schools. The first two ecological approaches discussed here—ethological and evolutionary psychology views—relate children's development to the context of the evolutionary history of our species. These theories view children as inheritors of genetically based abilities and predispositions, and thus focus on aspects of behaviour that serve, or once served, an adaptive function.

The third approach—the bioecological model—considers how multiple levels of environmental influence simultaneously affect development. This type of theory stresses the effects of context on development, but it also emphasizes the child's active role in selecting and influencing those contexts. Children's personal characteristics—temperament, intellectual ability, athletic skill, and so on—lead them to choose certain environments over others and also influence the people around them. This last point is reminiscent of Bandura's concept of *reciprocal determinism,* discussed earlier in the chapter.

The developmental issue that is front and centre in ecological theories is the interaction of *nature and nurture,* given their focus on the evolutionary history of the organism under study. The importance of the *sociocultural context* and the *continuity* of development are implicitly emphasized in all these theories. Another central focus is the *active role* children play in their own development.

This famous photograph shows Konrad Lorenz (1952) and a gaggle of goslings that were imprinted on him and followed him all over his farm. Lorenz discovered that mallard ducklings are more discriminating: they would imprint on him only if he squatted low and dragged himself around, quacking all the while, for hours on end. He was a very dedicated scientist.

THOMAS D. MCAVOY/GETTY IMAGES

Ethological and Evolutionary Theories

Ethological and evolutionary theories are concerned with understanding development in terms of a given animal's evolutionary heritage. Of particular interest are species-specific behaviours—behaviours that are common to members of a particular species (such as humans) but not typically observed in other species.

Ethology

Ethology, the study of behaviour within an evolutionary context, attempts to understand behaviour in terms of its adaptive or survival value. According to ethologists, a variety of behaviour patterns in animals were shaped by evolution just as surely as their physical characteristics were. The best-known example of an ethological approach to a developmental topic is the study of imprinting made famous by Konrad Lorenz (1935, 1952). **Imprinting** is a process by which newborn birds and mammals of some species become attached to their mother at first sight and follow her everywhere, a behaviour that ensures that the baby will stay near a source of protection and food. For imprinting to occur, the infant has to encounter its mother during a specific *sensitive period* very early in life.

The basis for imprinting is not actually the baby's mother per se; rather, the infants of some species are genetically predisposed to follow the first moving object with particular characteristics that they see after birth or hatching. Which particular object the individual will dutifully trail after is thus a matter of experience-expectant processes (discussed in Chapter 3). Usually, the first moving object any chick sees *is* its mother, so everything works out just fine.

Although humans do not "imprint," they do have strong tendencies that draw them to members of their own species. Examples noted in Chapter 5 include an early-emerging visual preference for faces, which seems to result from an attraction to a face shape with more "stuff" in the top half. Even though this attraction is not based on a specific human face template, it gets the infant to pay attention to other humans in the environment. Also, like other mammals, human newborns orient to sounds, tastes, and smells familiar from their experience in the womb—a predisposition that inclines them toward their own mother (see Chapter 2).

One of the most influential applications of ethology to human development, which we discuss in Chapter 11, is Bowlby's (1969) extension of the concept of imprinting to the process by which infants form emotional attachments to their mother. According to Bowlby, attachment is essentially an emotional version of imprinting, an adaptive relationship that increases the helpless infant's chances of survival by creating reciprocal emotional ties between caregiver and infant. When the attachment relationship is positive, the infant has a secure base from which to begin exploring the world.

Evolutionary Psychology

Closely related to ethology, evolutionary psychology applies the Darwinian concepts of natural selection and adaptation to human behaviour. The basic idea is that in the evolutionary history of our species, certain genes predisposed individuals to behave in ways that solved the adaptive challenges they faced (obtaining food, avoiding predators, establishing social bonds). These individuals were more likely to survive, mate, and reproduce, passing along their genes to their offspring. These adaptive genes became increasingly common and were passed down to modern humans; thus, many of the ways we behave today are a legacy of the demands on our prehistoric ancestors (Geary, 2009).

One of the most important adaptive features of the human species—that clearly distinguishes us from other species—is the large size of our brains (relative to body size). The trade-off is that humans experience a prolonged period of immaturity and dependence. We are "a slow-developing, big-brained species" (Bjorklund & Pellegrini, 2002), as illustrated in Figure 9.1. In Chapter 2, we discussed how the size of the human brain at birth is limited by the size of the female pelvis. As humans evolved, enlargement of our brains was made possible by birth occurring earlier in development than other mammals. These evolutionary changes were made possible by increased social complexity, which is necessary for successful caregiving of helpless offspring. A related consequence of our large brains and slow development is the high level of neural plasticity that supports our unrivaled capacity for learning from experience. As Bjorklund (1997) points out, in addition to its adaptive benefits, this extended immaturity is a necessity for humans who

> must survive by their wits; human communities are more complex and diverse than those of any other species, and this requires that they have not only a flexible intelligence to learn the conventions of their societies but also *a long time to learn them.*
>
> (p. 153, emphasis added)

Evolutionary psychology theorists have suggested that *play,* which is one of the most salient forms of behaviour during the period of immaturity of most mammals, is an evolved platform for learning (Bjorklund & Pellegrini, 2002). Children develop motor skills by racing and wrestling with one another, throwing toy spears, or kicking a ball. They try out and practice a variety of social roles (as mentioned in Chapter 7), enacting what they know about being, say, a parent or a

FIGURE 9.1 Brain sizes of various primates and humans The larger the brain size of various primates, the longer their developmental period. (Data from Bonner, 1988)

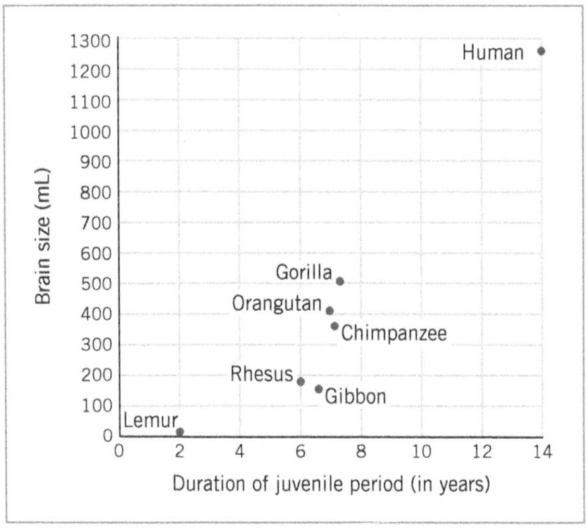

parental-investment theory a theory that stresses the evolutionary basis of many aspects of parental behaviour that benefit their offspring

police officer. One of the main virtues of play is that children can experiment in a situation with minimal consequences; no one gets hurt if a baby doll is accidentally dropped on its head.

To benefit from their protracted immature status, children must survive it. Their survival and development require parents to expend an enormous amount of time, energy, and resources. Why are parents willing to sacrifice so much for the benefit of their offspring? According to **parental-investment theory** (Trivers, 1972), parents are motivated by the drive to perpetuate their genes, which can happen only if their offspring survive long enough to pass those genes to the next generation.

Parental-investment theory also points to a potential dark side of the evolutionary picture—the so-called Cinderella effect—which refers to the fact that rates of child maltreatment are considerably higher for stepparents than for biological parents. McMaster University psychologists Martin Daly and Margo Wilson have provided some of the most detailed examinations of the Cinderella effect. As Figure 9.2 shows, estimates of murders committed by stepfathers against children residing with them is hundreds of times higher than the rate for fathers and their biological children. Furthermore, in families in which both natural and stepchildren reside, abusive parents typically target their abuse toward their stepchildren (Daly & Wilson, 1996). Notably, this pattern is not just present in Canada, where the original Daly and Wilson study was conducted, but more recent studies have observed this pattern in countries ranging from Australia to South Korea to Colombia (Archer, 2013).

Similar findings suggest that unintended child fatalities (e.g., accidental drowning) are also more likely to occur in homes with a resident stepparent than in homes with no stepparent, suggesting that there is less commitment to protecting children in stepparent homes (Tooley et al., 2006). Of note, however, the risks of fatal assaults by stepfathers relative to genetic fathers diminish after the age of 4, suggesting that Cinderella effects are disproportionately higher for infants and young children (Nobes, Panagiotaki, & Jonsson, 2019).

These findings are consistent with parent-investment theory; because parenting is so costly, it is not, from an evolutionary point of view, worth investing in children who cannot contribute to the perpetuation of one's own genes. However, it is also possible that there are contextual differences that contribute to these effects. For example, a large longitudinal study in Australia found that while there were indeed more injuries to children living in stepfamilies, this pattern can be explained by

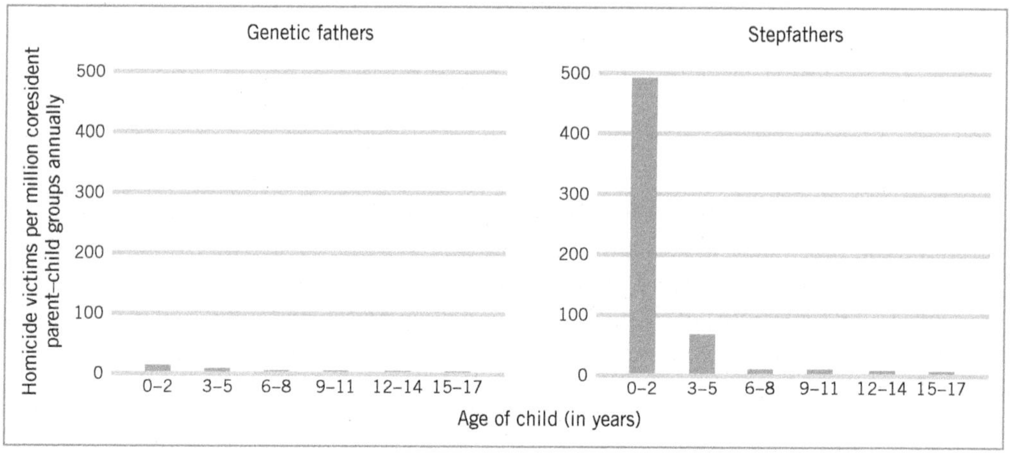

FIGURE 9.2 Estimated rates of child homicide committed by genetic fathers versus stepfathers in Canada from 1974 to 1990 As is shockingly clear, stepchildren, especially very young ones, are much more likely to be murdered by a stepfather than other children are likely to be murdered by their biological fathers. (Data from Daly & Wilson, 1996)

other risk factors correlated with family structure, including maternal alcohol use and child behaviour problems (Malvaso et al., 2015). The age of the stepfather also matters; younger stepfathers are more likely to fatally assault their stepchildren than older stepfathers, again suggesting that there are other family and individual variables that impact behaviour beyond genetic relatedness (Nobes et al., 2018). The next section focuses on approaches to social development that are squarely focused on the effects of the contexts in which children develop.

The Bioecological Model

The most encompassing model of the general context of development is Urie Bronfenbrenner's bioecological model (Bronfenbrenner, 1979; Bronfenbrenner & Morris, 1998). This perspective treats the child's environment as "a set of nested structures, each inside the next, like a set of Russian dolls" (1979, p. 22). Each structure represents a different level of influence on development (Figure 9.3). The child is at the centre, with a particular constellation of characteristics (genes, gender, age, temperament, health, intelligence, and so on).

Over the course of development, the child's characteristics interact with the environmental forces present at each level. The different levels vary in how immediate their effects are, but Bronfenbrenner emphasizes that *every* level, from the intimate context of a child's home to the culture in which the family lives, impacts that child's development. Note that each of the levels depicted in Figure 9.3 is labelled as a "system," emphasizing the complexity and interconnectedness of what goes on in each level. This theory is ecological in the sense that, just as in the study of the ecology of other living things, it considers how multiple levels of context influence outcomes. It just happens that instead of the soil and rainfall that might be the relevant ecological contexts for plants, the ecological systems influencing children range from families to neighbourhoods to governments. The ecological levels in which children develop range from quite narrow (microsystem) to extremely broad (macrosystem).

The first level in which the child is embedded is the **microsystem** — the activities and relationships in which the child *directly* participates. The child's family is a crucial component of the microsystem, and its influence is predominant in infancy and early childhood. The microsystem becomes richer and more complex as the child grows older and interacts increasingly often with peers, teachers, and others in settings such as school, neighbourhood, organized sports, arts, clubs, religious activities, and so on. Children have some influence on their microsystem through their choices of peers, activities, and technology. Other aspects are heavily influenced by family expectations and resources. Bronfenbrenner stresses the *bidirectional* nature of all relationships within the microsystem. For example, the parents' marital relationship may affect how they treat their child, and their child's behaviour may, in turn, have an impact on the marital relationship.

The next two levels in Bronfenbrenner's model extend into the child's community. The **mesosystem** encompasses the *interconnections* amongst microsystems, such as family, peers, and schools. Supportive relations amongst these contexts can benefit the child. For instance, a child's academic success is facilitated when parents and peers value scholastic endeavours. The **exosystem** comprises settings that the child may not directly be a part of but that can still influence development. Parental workplaces, for example, can affect the child in many ways, including policies about parental leave, flexible work hours, and on-site childcare.

microsystem the immediate environment that an individual child personally experiences and participates in

mesosystem the interconnections among immediate, or microsystem, settings

exosystem environmental settings that a child does not directly experience but that can affect the child indirectly

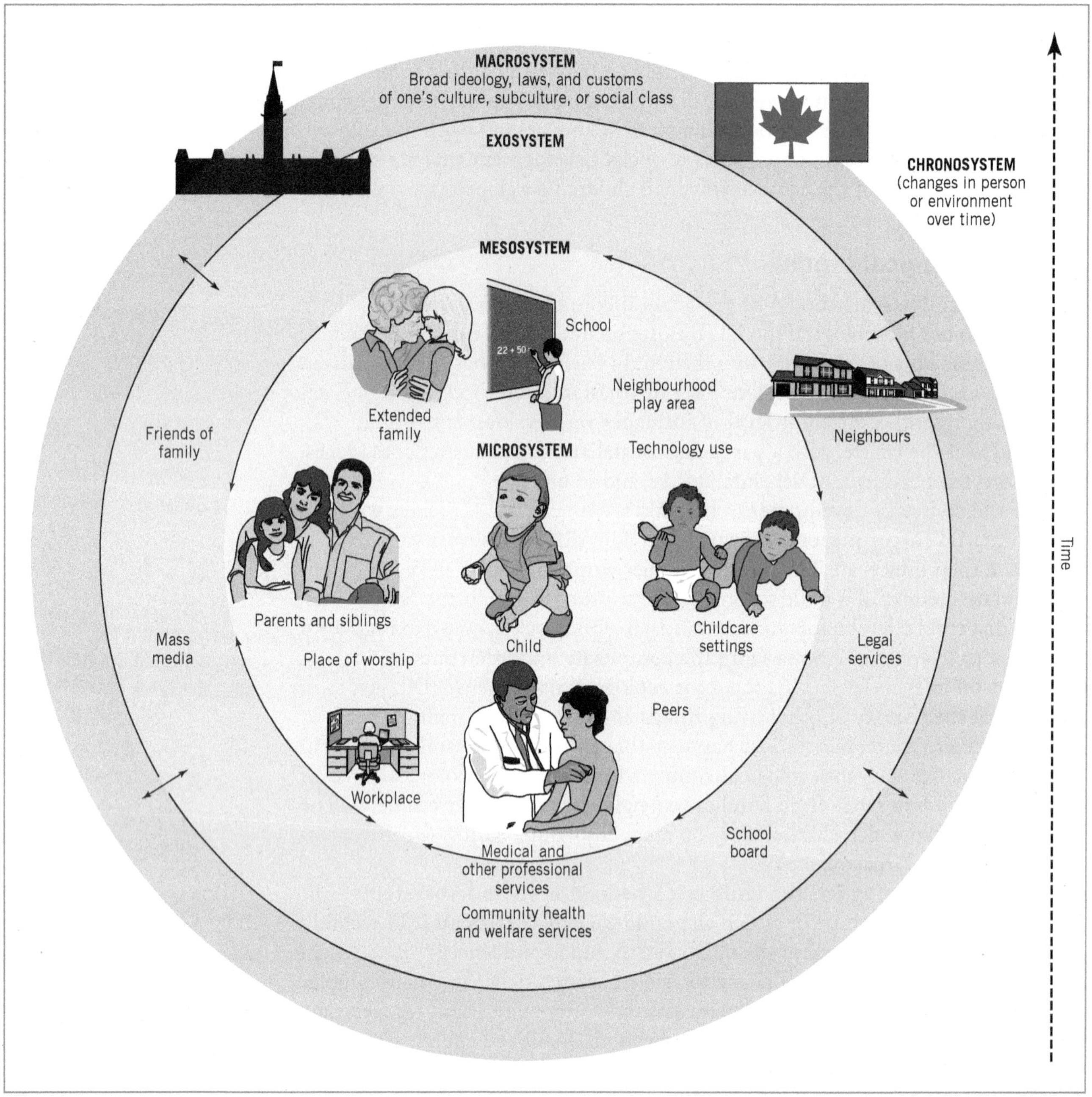

FIGURE 9.3 The bioecological model The child's environment is composed of nested structures, including the microsystem (the immediate environment), the mesosystem (interconnections among microsystems), the exosystem (social settings that the child is not a part of but that nevertheless affect the child's development), and the macrosystem (the general cultural context in which all the other systems are embedded). These systems all exist within the chronosystem, which describes the changes to the elements of the system, including the individual, that occur over time. This figure illustrates the environment of a child living in Canada. (Information from Bronfenbrenner, 1979)

The outer level of Bronfenbrenner's model is the **macrosystem,** which consists of the general beliefs, values, customs, and laws of the larger society in which all the other levels are embedded. Cultural and class differences permeate almost every aspect of a child's life, including differences in beliefs about what qualities should be fostered in children and how best to foster them. National laws can also have a major impact on child development. For example, consider paid parental-leave policies around the world. The United States is the only developed country out of the 38 surveyed by the OECD that currently does not mandate paid maternity leave (see Figure 9.4; Organisation for Economic Co-operation and Development, n.d.).

macrosystem the larger cultural and social context within which the other systems are embedded

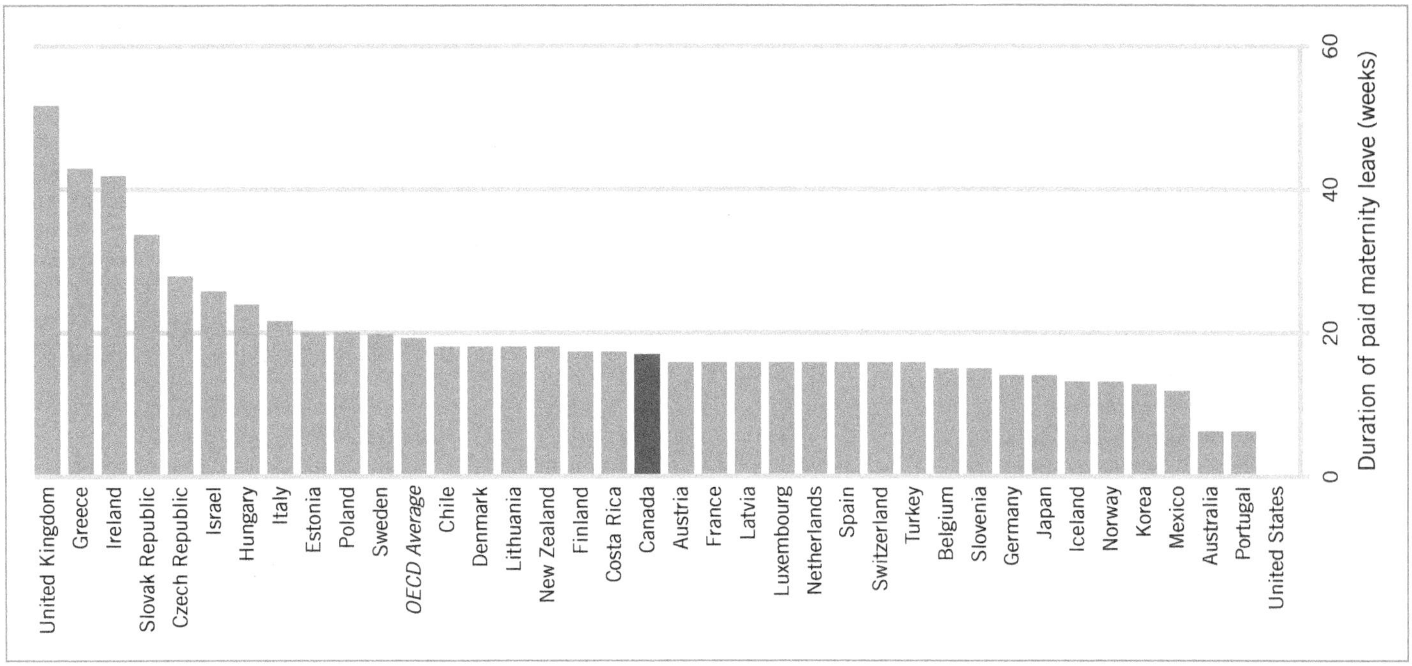

FIGURE 9.4 Length of paid maternity leave, 2016 National laws and policies are part of what form a child's macrosystem. For example, the United States is alone among the developed countries surveyed in not mandating some length of paid maternity leave, a policy which significantly impacts child-rearing practices. In comparison, Canada allows up to 15 weeks of paid maternity leave, along with an additional 40 weeks of paid parental leave to be distributed to both parents, and an extended 69 weeks of paid parental leave. (Data from Organisation for Economic Co-Operation and Development, n.d.)

The average paid leave across these nations is just over 19 weeks; Canada offers 15 weeks of paid maternity leave, along with an additional 35 to 61 weeks for parental leave, which can be used by either parent. In fact, the majority of these countries also mandate paid leave for new fathers (though for a shorter duration of time, averaging 8 weeks). There are also huge national differences in the duration of parental leave, paid or unpaid (a year or more in many countries, like Canada, but only 12 weeks in the United States), and in other policies that influence child-rearing practices. For example, some countries, including Peru and the Philippines, provide nursing mothers with paid breast-feeding breaks at their workplaces. National policies and priorities can render stark differences in the options available to parents.

Finally, Bronfenbrenner's model has a temporal dimension, the **chronosystem.** Beliefs, values, customs, family structure and dynamics, and technologies change over time, with consequences for the child's development. For instance, as we discuss later in this chapter, children today have access to a vast realm of digital information and entertainment unimaginable to previous generations, impacting their relationships with parents, peers, community, and the broader culture. Another important aspect of the temporal dimension, which we have noted on several occasions, is the fact that as children become older, they take an increasingly active role in their own development, making their own decisions about their friends, activities, and environments. As Box 9.3 on attention-deficit hyperactivity disorder suggests, the chronosystem can even be a factor in developmental disorders.

chronosystem historical changes that influence the other systems

To provide a better sense of how these contextual levels influence children's development, we discuss a large-scale U.S. survey from the Pew Research Center (December 17, 2015) that contrasts parents from different economic brackets with respect to the experiences of their children and their attitudes about parenting. This research gives an intriguing glimpse into the very different contexts in which children living in the same country are growing up.

Beginning with the microsystem, the Pew survey gives us a sense of how parental education and income influence some of the ways that children spend their time.

Community Support Groups in Asia, Africa, and South America

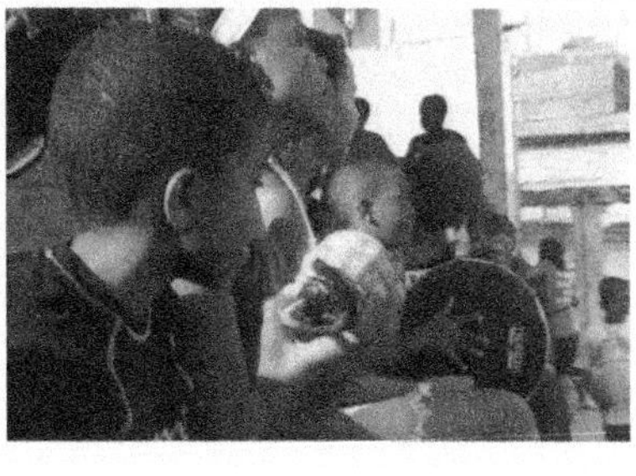

COURTESY OF UNICEF

BOX 9.3 INDIVIDUAL DIFFERENCES Attention-Deficit Hyperactivity Disorder

Many developmental disorders can be profitably examined with the different levels of the bioecological model in mind. Influences and interventions from different levels can make it easier or harder for children to manage the challenges they face. A good case in point is **attention-deficit hyperactivity disorder (ADHD).** Children with ADHD tend to be of normal intelligence and do not typically show serious emotional disturbances. However, they have difficulty sticking to plans, following rules and regulations, and persevering on tasks that require sustained attention (especially ones they find uninteresting). Many are hyperactive, constantly fidgeting, drumming on their desks, and moving around. Academic skills such as reading and writing can be difficult to acquire, since they require prolonged periods of focused attention. Many also have problems suppressing aggressive reactions when they are frustrated. All these symptoms seem to reflect an underlying difficulty in inhibiting impulses to act, especially when interesting distractors are present. Thus, the core challenges facing children with ADHD span the domains of cognition, behaviour, and emotion (see Hinshaw, 2018, for a detailed review).

A recent analysis of healthcare data in Canada indicated that approximately 4% of children under age 17 receive a diagnosis of ADHD, with the prevalence being about three times greater in boys than in girls (Vasiliadis et al., 2017). Notably, ADHD diagnoses appear to be somewhat subjective and linked to comparisons with peers. One recent study compared the oldest children in a grade (those with birthdays closest to the school entry-age cutoff) to the youngest children in a grade (those with birthdays farthest from the school entry-age cutoff) and found that ADHD diagnoses were 34% higher for the youngest birthday group in each grade (Layton et al., 2018). That is, the children who were younger than most of their classmates were one-third more likely to be diagnosed with ADHD than the children who were older than most of their classmates. These data suggest that parents of younger children and teachers may be biased by comparisons with older peers, who are likely to be more neurodevelopmentally mature.

The causes of ADHD are quite varied. Genetic factors clearly play a role. Heritability estimates from twin studies fall in the 70% to 90% range (Chang et al., 2013; Larsson et al., 2014). Indeed, heritability for ADHD is greater than any other developmental disorder, with the possible exception of autism spectrum disorder. Complicating the picture is the likelihood of vicious cycles between genes and environment. For example, a child's behavioural challenges may frustrate parents, who react harshly rather than providing the extra support the child needs (Hinshaw & Arnold, 2015). In such a case, the child's genes (a predisposition for ADHD) may elicit an environment (hostile parenting) that is particularly conducive to the development of the disorder.

Environmental factors in the microsystem also influence the development of ADHD. As discussed in Chapter 2, prenatal exposure to alcohol and tobacco smoke affects brain development, and both have been linked to the development of ADHD (Han et al., 2015). Synthetic food additives, including artificial colours, have also been implicated as a potential cause, and restriction diets that avoid these elements may benefit some children with ADHD (Nigg et al., 2012). More research, however, is needed (Pelsser et al., 2017). Social factors that have been associated with the development of ADHD include low SES, high levels of parent–child conflict, and severe early deprivation (Thapar et al., 2013).

Note, however, that while all these factors have been associated with ADHD, it is very difficult to establish causality. For example, mothers who smoke while pregnant may also pass genetic risk for ADHD to their offspring. Indeed, recent studies examining the effects of paternal smoking during pregnancy have also shown enhanced risk of ADHD, suggesting that at least some of the risk factors associated with tobacco may lie in other genetic or household factors, rather than solely exposure in the uterus via the mother (Langley et al., 2012; Zhu et al., 2014).

Current treatment for ADHD involves agents in the microsystem (the family doctor), the exosystem (the pharmaceutical industry), and the macrosystem (the government). The most common approach taken by physicians

attention-deficit hyperactivity disorder (ADHD) a syndrome that involves difficulty in sustaining attention

For example, 71% of parents with a bachelor's degree report reading to their young children every day; this number drops to 33% for parents with a high school diploma or less. Similarly, 84% of higher-income parents (earning over $75K/year) report that their child participated in sports in the past year; this number drops to 59% for lower-income parents (earning under $30K/year). The Pew survey also reveals mesosystem-level influences that are mediated by parental income. While 78% of higher-income families rated their neighbourhood as an excellent/very good place to raise their children, only 42% of lower-income families endorsed a positive view of their neighbourhood.

An aspect of the exosystem that has a major influence on child development is mass media, especially electronic media. According to the Pew survey, 80% of kids younger than 6, and 90% of kids older than 6, have daily screen time; these statistics suggest ample opportunities for children to be influenced by media, including social media for older children. Later in this chapter, we will discuss some of the ways in which electronic media impact child development.

is to prescribe stimulant medications, such as Ritalin. Although it seems paradoxical that stimulants could help children who are already overly active, they improve symptoms in 70% to 90% of children for whom they are prescribed. The reason is that their brain systems are actually underaroused; children's restless and sometimes disruptive behaviour is actually an attempt to wake the brain up. Appropriate medication, which stimulates neurotransmitter systems, allows children with ADHD to focus their attention better and to be less distractible.

As with many medications, there are numerous potential side effects associated with medication used to treat ADHD, including loss of appetite, disrupted sleep patterns, and high blood pressure. Because of these and other concerns, many parents who choose stimulants for their children limit use to school days. As it's become possible to follow children over decades of treatment, important concerns about prolonged use of medication have been alleviated. For example, stimulant treatment over many years had no negative effects on height, despite long-standing worries about stunted growth (Harstad et al., 2014).

It is important to realize, however, that the benefits of Ritalin continue only as long as children take the medication. Longer-lasting gains require not only medication but also behavioural treatments. Behavioural interventions can target youth directly, or they target parents and teachers, providing tools to help promote the child's self-regulation. Combination treatments, integrating both medication and psychosocial interventions, are particularly effective, especially when parents are also able to reduce their negative or ineffective disciplinary practices (Hinshaw & Arnold, 2015). Developmental social neuroscience may offer new ways to think about treatment, such as the mindfulness meditation approach discussed in Box 9.2.

BEN GARVIN/THE NEW YORK TIMES/REDUX

Standing desks, such as the one used by this elementary school student, might help children who have trouble sitting quietly for long periods of time.

The availability of medications helpful to those with ADHD is a function of the exosystem; in order to research and develop medications, pharmaceutical companies must perceive that they can profit from ADHD medications. It also depends on the medication's receiving a favourable evaluation from the FDA, based on research to determine the drug's efficacy and potential side effects. Thus, the fate of children in need of medication could be quite different, depending on factors far outside the influence of their families.

But would any intervention be necessary in the first place if it were not the case that school-age children are expected to spend a substantial amount of time on most days sitting quietly at a desk, concentrating on tasks that they may have little interest in? Pointing to the highest level of the bioecological model—the chronosystem—many experts have suggested that ADHD may have emerged as a serious problem only since the advent of compulsory schooling. Before then, an individual who had attentional difficulties that would have posed problems in a classroom might very well have been able to function successfully in an environment where such difficulties were inconsequential, even unnoticed.

Finally, the Pew survey reveals broad cultural differences in parents' aspirations for their children, showing the influence of the macrosystem. For example, African American and Hispanic parents in the United States are almost twice as likely as White parents to say it is extremely important to them that their children earn a college degree. Parental concerns are also influenced by cultural differences. Twice as many White parents than African American parents report fears that their child may eventually have problems with drugs or alcohol, whereas twice as many African American parents than White parents report fears that their child may get shot. This last finding is likely a result of recent and widespread fatal police shootings that raise significant concerns about racial profiling, suggesting an effect of the chronosystem.

Children and the Media: The Good, the Bad, and the Awful

To further illustrate the richness of the bioecological model for thinking about and investigating child development, we will consider an example in which the

HULTON ARCHIVE/GETTY IMAGES

BETTMANN/GETTY IMAGES

RICHARD HUTCHINGS/PHOTOEDIT

What different experiences were available to these girls born in different historical times? How did their educational and employment opportunities differ?

interactions among multiple levels of the model are particularly clear and relevant: children and electronic media. Media are situated in the exosystem, but they are subject to influences from the chronosystem (which determines which consumer technologies and media are available to households over time); from the macrosystem (including cultural values and government policies); from other elements in the exosystem (such as economic pressures); and from the microsystem (such as parental monitoring).

A recent economic study demonstrates how the introduction of educational television, in the form of *Sesame Street,* had positive long-term effects on those children who had access to it (Kearney & Levine, 2015). When *Sesame Street* was introduced in 1969, its content was designed to enhance school readiness, and roughly one-third of American children between the ages of 2 and 5 watched it regularly. But because the show was aired on broadcast television, there were disparities in the quality of the signal that families' TV antennae received. Kearney and Levine (2015) used differences in the chronosystem (cohorts of children before and after *Sesame Street* began airing) and the macrosystem (whether or not households were located in counties with good television reception) to investigate the long-term effects of *Sesame Street* viewing using census data. The researchers found that quality of television reception did not affect educational outcomes (as measured by age at grade level) before *Sesame Street* started broadcasting. However, after *Sesame Street* began airing, children living in counties with better television reception were 14% more likely not to fall behind appropriate grade level. The authors of the study describe *Sesame Street* as the first MOOC (Massive Open Online Course), and their results are consistent with numerous smaller-scale findings of social and cognitive benefits from *Sesame Street* viewing around the world (Mares & Pan, 2013).

Researchers found that broadcast quality for programming like *Sesame Street* had an impact on educational outcomes. Would researchers find similar results for access and speed of Internet service?

CHILDREN'S TELEVISION WORKSHOP/STRINGER/GETTY IMAGES

As screens have become ever more pervasive, moving from living rooms to bedrooms to children's pockets, and as streaming video and social media have become commonplace, concerns about screen time have mounted. In a position statement, the Canadian Pediatric Society recommends no screen time for children under 2 years of age, and no more than 1 hour daily for children 2 to 5 years of age (Canadian Pediatric Society, 2017). Parents of older children are advised to develop and follow a family media-use plan designed to place appropriate limits on media use (Canadian Pediatric Society, 2019). But consider the following statistics from a large-scale study of children in Alberta: 2-year-olds had an average of 2.44 hours per day of screen time and 3-year-olds averaged 3.5 hours per day (Madigan et al., 2019). Canada-wide data from 2015 showed that almost 69% of 12- to 17-year-olds spend more than 2 hours per day on screens (see Figure 9.5; Statistics Canada, 2015).

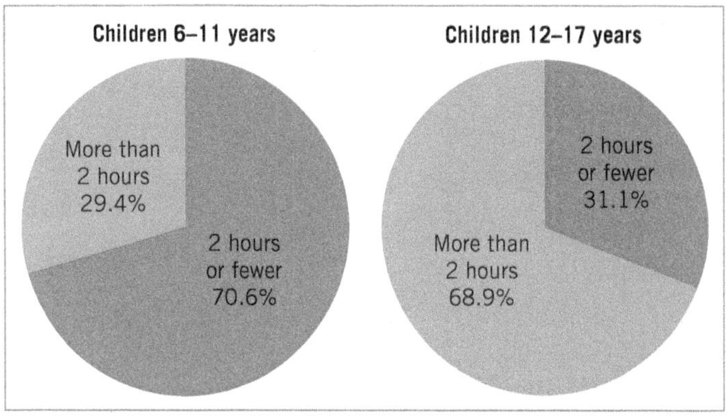

FIGURE 9.5 Children's screen time per day, 2015 As this figure shows, one-third of 6- to 11-year-olds and two-thirds of 12- to 17-year-olds spend over 2 hours per day on screens. (Data from Statistics Canada, 2015)

While relatively little is known about the impacts of digital screen time on well-being, one large study in the United Kingdom, with more than 120,000 adolescent participants, suggests that moderate use—as defined by the middle range of time spent on the various electronic devices in this sample—does not increase risks to mental health, though high use does confer a measurable risk (Przybylski & Weinstein, 2017). Many adolescents do express concern that spending time online is a problem; 60% of American teens in a recent survey reported that spending too much time online is a major problem for people their age, and more than half believed that they themselves spend too much time on their cell phones (Jiang, 2018). Two-thirds of the parents in this survey expressed concerns about their teenagers' amount of screen time. Interestingly, both teens and their parents note that their parents/children are frequently distracted by their phones during conversations, suggesting that the impacts of technology on social relationships can also be driven by parental engagement in media.

Very young children are increasingly active participants in this media immersion. In a 2015 study of children under age 4 in a low-income area of Philadelphia, almost all the participants had used mobile devices for media content delivery (97%), and fully three-fourths of the 4-year-olds had their own mobile device (Kabali et al., 2015). In a national U.S. study, parents of 2- to 10-year-olds reported that they participate in their children's media usage about one-third of the time (watching videos together or playing games together), and that nearly 50% of their children's time is spent on shows and apps that they consider to be educational (though parents may have quite divergent views about what is educational for their child; over 10% of parents rated *Angry Birds* and *SpongeBob* to be at least somewhat educational; Rideout, 2014). Three-quarters of the parents surveyed by Kabali and colleagues (2015) reported that they used the mobile device to keep their child calm in public or to distract their child so they could complete chores, and one-quarter of the parents used the device to help their child fall asleep.

Thus, parents appear to have many motivations for engaging their children in digital media, from educational aspirations to behaviour management. Though more research is needed to better understand the effects of media exposure on children, findings from the research available suggests benefits to media exposure and use in learning, cognition, relationships, and other areas of development, depending on the content (Society for Research in Child Development, 2019).

Concerns about children's exposure to media Children's media exposure has aroused a variety of concerns, ranging from the possible effects of media violence and pornography to those of isolation and inactivity. Notably, these concerns are not

DAVID J. GREEN - LIFESTYLE/ALAMY

Some researchers have concluded that viewing media violence increases the incidence of aggression and violent behaviour, though the degree and nature of this relationship remains a topic of debate.

limited to affluent Western nations. A recent survey of parents living in countries with emerging economies (including Kenya, Jordan, Vietnam, and Mexico) found that 79% of adults said that people should be very concerned about children being exposed to harmful or immoral content, and more than half agreed that mobile media and the Internet have had a bad influence on children in their country (Anderson & Silver, 2019).

MEDIA VIOLENCE Concerns about media violence initially focused on television viewing. A comprehensive study reported that 61% of TV programs between 1994 and 1997 contained episodes of violence (Wilson et al., 1997). Somewhat more recent estimates suggest that 90% of movies include depictions of violence, as do 68% of video games, 60% of TV shows, and 15% of music videos (Wilson, 2008). In one example of the increased degree to which children are regularly exposed to media violence, portrayals of gun violence in the top grossing PG-13 movies since 2012 has exceeded similar portrayals in R-rated movies, and this form of violence in PG-13 movies typically occurs without visible consequences, such as blood (The Annenberg Public Policy Center, 2017). The fictionalized form of aggression typically seen in screen media is particularly concerning because it tends to be both glamorized and trivialized.

Extensive reviews of the vast amount of research on this issue have led many researchers to conclude that media violence increases aggression and violence and is therefore a risk factor for positive youth development. However, as discussed in Chapter 1, a recent meta-analysis by Ferguson (2015) suggests that video games in particular may have only minimal effect on children's and adolescents' aggression. This paper was published alongside a number of rebuttals by other scientists, who argue that the Ferguson (2015) analysis suffers from methodological weaknesses and underestimates the negative effects of video games (e.g., Boxer, Groves, & Docherty, 2015; Gentile, 2015; Rothstein & Bushman, 2015; Valkenburg, 2015). The presence of such heated debate in the pages of a major scientific journal clearly demonstrates the high stakes on both sides of the issue, as well as the societal importance of better understanding the effects of media violence on children.

Exposure to media violence may have an impact in four different ways. First, seeing actors engage in aggression teaches aggressive behaviours and inspires imitation of them, as you saw in Box 9.1. Second, viewing aggression activates the viewer's own aggressive thoughts, feelings, and tendencies. This heightened aggressive mindset makes it more likely that the individual will interpret new interactions and events as involving aggression and will respond aggressively. Furthermore, when aggression-related thoughts are frequently activated, they may become part of the individual's normal internal state. These factors may lead to a hostile attributional bias, as described by Dodge and discussed earlier in this chapter.

Third, media violence is exciting and arousing for most youth, and their heightened physiological arousal makes them more likely to react violently to provocations right after watching violent films. Finally, frequent long-term exposure to media violence gradually leads to emotional desensitization—a reduction in the level of unpleasant physiological arousal most people experience when observing violence. Because this arousal normally helps inhibit violent behaviour, emotional desensitization can render violent thoughts and behaviours more likely. These factors, taken together, can help to explain disturbing findings like those from a longitudinal study in New Zealand: individuals who watched more television during childhood were more likely to engage in antisocial behaviours later in their lives, including criminal convictions, and receive diagnoses of antisocial personality disorders (Robertson, McAnally, & Hancox, 2013).

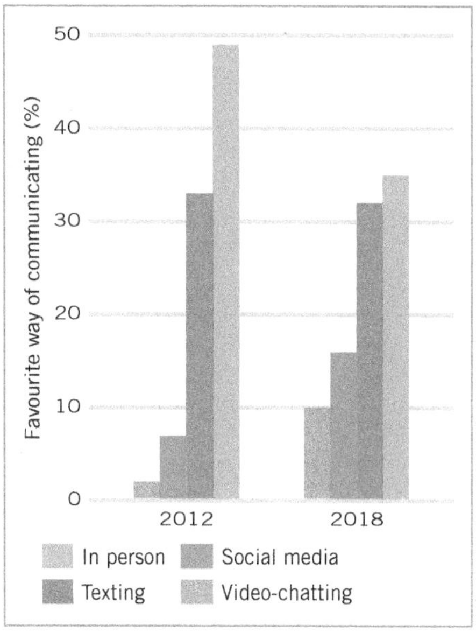

FIGURE 9.6 Changes in adolescent communication preferences In recent years, social media technology has influenced teens' preferred methods of communication, with texting now topping in-person communication as the favoured method. (Data from Common Sense, 2018)

SOCIAL MEDIA The vast majority (96%) of all Canadian youth use social networking sites (Statistics Canada, 2018). Access to social media has fundamentally altered Canadian teens' communication with friends after school, with the majority of grade 10 boys and girls (50% and 69%, respectively) reporting that they contact their friends daily through text (Coe, Chan, & Freeman, 2016). As shown in Figure 9.6, there has been a significant shift in recent years in American teens' preference for texting and social media over face-to-face interaction (Common Sense, 2018). For most teens, social media enhances their sense of connectedness with their peers; 81% of American teens in a recent study reported that social media helped them feel connected, and 68% said that social media helped them feel as though they could rely on people who will support them in tough times (Anderson & Jiang, 2018). According to this same study, two-thirds of teens say that social media helps them broaden their networks and diversify their perspectives. Although equivalent tracking of Canadian teens' social media habits does not exist, evidence suggests that trends among Canadians are similar.

The majority of U.S. teens reported that they had made at least one new friend online, and one-third reported online flirting with a potential partner (Lenhart, 2015a; Lenhart, Smith, & Anderson, 2015). Unfortunately, this behaviour is not always welcome; one-quarter of all teens reported that they had unfriended or blocked someone on social media whose flirting made them uncomfortable. And after relationships end, 13% of teen daters report that partners spread rumors about them on social media. Furthermore, while social media may depict less in the way of physical violence than other forms of media, hate speech is prevalent on social media; one in four teen social-media users say that they "often" encounter racist, sexist, or homophobic comments online (Rideout, 2012). As one teen wrote: "Once you read it, it can be deleted from the computer but not from your head" (Smahel & Wright, 2014). Cyberbullying, bullying perpetrated via social media technology, continues to be highly prevalent amongst teens (as we will discuss in Chapter 13): in a recent survey, 15% of Canadian youth aged 15 to 34 years reported being harassed or bullied online (Statistics Canada, 2018).

With increased use of social media platforms, concerns have emerged about potential negative effects on mental health, particularly for teens. For example, Twenge and colleagues (2018) used a large representative sample of over 500,000 American adolescents to examine relationships between depressive symptoms/suicide-related outcomes and time spent with new media (including social media and on devices such as smartphones). The results suggest that teens who spend more time with new media were more likely to report mental health issues, whereas teens who spent more time with non-screen activities were less likely to do so. Other researchers have pointed out that the use of cross-sectional data rather than longitudinal data make these correlations difficult to interpret. Indeed, in a recent longitudinal study, Heffer and colleagues (2019) found that, amongst adolescent girls, depressive symptoms reported in childhood and early adolescence predicted more frequent social media use. No relationship was observed for boys. The results of this latter study suggest a different direction of influence: rather than social media leading to increased mental health concerns, pre-existing mental health concerns led to increased social media use. The contrast between these two studies underscores how important it is to consider study design when attempting to draw conclusions.

Research in this area highlights another methodological problem: the use of self-reporting to gauge activities such as screen usage. Studies of screen time typically include retrospective reports, whereby participants provide an estimate of their weekly device use. These estimates are often unreliable. A recent study including more than 17,000 participants from the United States, UK, and Ireland used a more detailed and contemporaneous measure of screen use—daily diaries broken into 10-minute intervals—to assess relationships between screen use and adolescent well-being (Orben & Przbylski, 2019). The results revealed little, if any, effect of screen use on well-being, including time spent before bed. This study provides another example of the importance of methodology in deriving accurate estimates of human behaviour. Indeed, researchers have called on social media companies to collaborate with scientists by providing the kinds of detailed data that would permit researchers to address and hopefully resolve these pressing questions (Orben, Dienlin, & Przbylski, 2019).

PHYSICAL INACTIVITY Another concern with media usage has to do with the fact that a child who is glued to a screen is not outside playing or otherwise engaging in robust physical activity. The sedentary nature of screen time, combined with the onslaught of commercials encouraging the consumption of sweet, fatty foods, have been linked to the recent increase in childhood obesity discussed in Chapter 3. More generally, there is a negative relationship between screen time and physical activity in the tween and teen years, such that heavy users of screen media are less likely to be physically active on a daily basis (Rideout, 2015). And when a child both exceeds screen time recommendations and has a TV in their bedroom—as do more than half of 8- to 18-year-olds (Rideout, 2015)—the child is at heightened risk of becoming obese (Wethington, Pan, & Sherry, 2013). These observations are not limited to North American children. For example, in a recent study in China, where rates of childhood obesity are rising rapidly—especially for boys—high levels of screen viewing predicted increased obesity in grade-school-aged children, as did high levels of after-school homework and inadequate sleep (Ren et al., 2017). In response to these concerns, the World Health Organization recently issued guidelines suggesting that children under 5 years of age should engage in no more than 1 hour of sedentary screen time per day; for children under 2 years of age, the recommendation is no sedentary screen time (World Health Organization, 2019).

EFFECTS ON ACADEMIC ACHIEVEMENT According to a study by the Kaiser Family Foundation, there is a strong relationship between media use and school grades (Rideout, Foehr, & Roberts, 2010). For example, children who are categorized as heavy users of screen media (more than 16 hours per day) are far more likely to report fair/poor grades (Cs or below) than are those who are moderate users (3 to 16 hours per day) or light users (fewer than 3 hours per day). Specific aspects of electronic media usage may be particularly problematic; for instance, teen girls who feel a compulsive need to text have worse grades and perceived academic competence than their peers (Lister-Landman, Domoff, & Dubow, 2015). A similar negative correlation has been found between screen time and achievement of developmental milestones in preschool children in Alberta (Madigan et al., 2019). Of course, there are many other confounding factors that might account for links between media usage and grades, such as low parental supervision, or a family culture (parents included) that deemphasizes reading and other academic pursuits in favour of screen time.

However, one cleverly designed study was able to draw causal conclusions about the relation between video games and school achievement (Weis & Cerankosky, 2010). Boys in the 1st through 3rd grades who did not already own a video game console were randomly assigned to an experimental group, whose members were given a console at the beginning of the study, or to a comparison group, whose members were, in the name of fairness, given a console after the study was completed. The boys who received the game console at the beginning of the study subsequently spent less time on after-school academic pursuits than did the boys in the comparison group. Four months into the study, they performed more poorly on measures of literacy and had a higher rate of teacher-reported academic problems than did the comparison group. Boys who spent the most time with the games showed the poorest academic outcomes.

PORNOGRAPHY A serious concern for many parents is children's exposure to pornography on television and the Internet, whether inadvertent or intentional. And their children are worried, too; in a large 2014 sample of European children and teens, pornography was the most frequent concern that participants voiced about their own online activities (Smahel & Wright, 2014). An analysis by one Internet security company revealed that 10% of visitors to porn sites are less than 10 years of age, despite the fact that website users are required to confirm that they are over 18 (Muresan, 2016). Exposure to pornography can make children and teens more tolerant of aggression toward women, as well as more accepting of premarital and extramarital sex (Greenfield, 2004).

Of special concern is pornography featuring children. Child pornography is a multibillion-dollar industry that has increased dramatically since the advent of the Internet and other digital technologies. Today, pedophiles commonly use the Web, including chat rooms, to share illegal photographs of children and to lure children into sexual relationships.

The most effective weapons against the various negative effects of media on children operate at the microsystem level, with parents exercising control over their children's access to undesirable media. As children get older, parents become less vigilant; a recent study found that while 68% of parents of 13- to 14-year-olds check their child's Web-browsing history, this number drops to 56% for 15- to 17-year-olds (Pew Research Centre, 2016). The burden of online safety clearly shifts from parent to child over the course of development. There are also impacts at the macrosystem level, with legal controls and government programs designed to minimize the negative features of the media with which children interact. Effective control is complicated, however, by concerns about freedom of speech and, in the case of Internet pornography, the global nature of the problem.

This extended discussion of media exposure provides just one example of the multiple levels considered by the bioecological model of child development. Another example is child maltreatment, which encompasses neglect and abuse. Such maltreatment can impact the child at multiple levels, including the microsystem (e.g., parental substance dependency), mesosystem (e.g., unemployment), exosystem (e.g., community violence), macrosystem (e.g., a lack of policies or agencies responsive to signs of maltreatment), and chronosystem (e.g., the current opioid epidemic, which has led to a massive increase in foster care placements for children whose parents who have overdosed or are struggling with addiction; Collier, 2018).

Current Perspectives

The three theoretical positions discussed in this section have all made valuable contributions to developmental science by placing individual development in a much broader context than is typically done in mainstream psychology. All of them challenge researchers to look beyond the lab—far beyond it.

The primary contribution of ethology and evolutionary psychology comes from the emphasis on children's biological nature, including genetic tendencies grounded in evolution. Evolutionary psychology has provided fascinating insights into human development, but it has also come under serious criticism. One frequent complaint is that, like psychoanalytic theories, many of the claims of evolutionary psychologists are impossible to test. Often, a behavioural pattern that is consistent with an evolutionary account is at least equally consistent with social learning or some other perspective. Finally, evolutionary psychology theories tend to overlook one of the most remarkable features of human beings, a feature strongly emphasized by Bronfenbrenner—our capacity to transform our environments and ourselves.

Bronfenbrenner's bioecological model has made an important contribution to our thinking about development. His emphasis on the broad context of development and the many different interactions among factors at various levels has highlighted how complex the development of every child is. The main criticism of this model is its lack of emphasis on biological factors. Genetics, epigenetics, brain development, plasticity, hormones, and other key biological determinants of behavioural development do not have a place in the levels of this model. That is not to say that they could not be accommodated, but clearly, environmental factors were most prominent in Bronfenbrenner's thinking.

What is the relevance of ecological theories to Kismet's design? Evolution is basically irrelevant to it. Evolutionary change does not apply to individual development, and, without the possibility for reproduction, it simply cannot occur.

With respect to the bioecological model, Kismet developed in an extremely limited microsystem—a lab at the Massachusetts Institute of Technology—populated with a small number of people. It has no mesosystem at present, although that could change in the future. This fact makes Kismet's experience quite different from that of most human children. The development of social robots could be affected by the macrosystem at any time, if changes in research priorities of the federal government cut off funding for the project. In terms of the chronosystem, such a remarkable robot was unimaginable until recently, and even more remarkable ones are currently being developed to follow in Kismet's footsteps.

It is interesting that the most difficult parallels to draw between Kismet's development and that of children and theories of social development concern the larger context of human development. Part of what is unique about the human species is the fact that every individual is embedded in multiple layers of human interactions, institutions, traditions, and history.

REVIEW QUESTIONS

This section mentions several areas in which the Bronfenbrenner's bioecological model could be applied. Can you think of another example? How would this example be represented in the various levels of this model? ■

CHAPTER SUMMARY

Four major types of social development theories present contrasting views of the social world of children.

Psychoanalytic Theories

- Freud's psychoanalytic theory has had an enormous impact on developmental psychology, primarily through Freud's emphasis on the importance of early experience for personality and social development, his depiction of unconscious motivation and processes, and his emphasis on the importance of close relationships.
- Erikson extended Freud's theory by identifying eight stages of psychosocial development extending across the entire life span. Each stage is characterized by a developmental crisis that, if not successfully resolved, will continue to trouble the individual.

Learning Theories

- Watson believed strongly in the power of environmental factors, especially reinforcement, to influence children's development.
- Skinner held that all behaviour can be explained in terms of operant conditioning. He discovered the importance of intermittent reinforcement and the powerful reinforcing value of attention.
- Bandura's social-learning theory and his empirical research stresses the importance of observational learning and cognition in social learning.

Theories of Social Cognition

- Social cognitive theories assume that children's knowledge and beliefs are vitally important in social development.
- Selman's theory proposes that children go through four stages in the development of the ability to take the role or perspective of another person. They progress from the simple appreciation that someone can have a view different from their own to being able to think about the view of a "generalized other."
- The social information-processing approach emphasizes the importance of children's attributions regarding their own and others' behaviour. The role of such attribution is clearly reflected in the hostile attributional bias, described by Dodge, which leads children to assume hostile intent on the part of others and to respond aggressively in situations in which the intention of others is ambiguous.
- Dweck's theory of self-attribution focuses on how children's achievement motivation is influenced by their attributions about the reasons for their successes and failures. Children with an incremental/mastery orientation enjoy working on challenging problems and tend to be persistent in trying to solve them, whereas children with an entity/helpless orientation prefer situations in which they expect to succeed and tend to withdraw when they experience failure.

Ecological Theories of Development

- Ethological theories examine behaviour within the evolutionary context, trying to understand its adaptive or survival value. Lorenz's research on imprinting has been particularly relevant to certain theories of social development in children.
- Evolutionary psychologists apply Darwinian concepts of natural selection to human behaviour. Characteristic of their approach are parental-investment theory and the idea that the long period of immaturity and dependence in human infancy enables young children to learn and practice many of the skills needed later in life.
- Bronfenbrenner's bioecological model conceptualizes the environment as a set of nested contexts, with the child at the centre. These contexts range from the microsystem, which includes the activities, roles, and relationships—the environment—in which a child directly participates on a regular basis, to the chronosystem, the historical context that affects all the other systems.

Test Yourself

1. The first signs of superego development appear during which stage of Freud's psychoanalytic theory?
   a. The oral stage
   b. The anal stage
   c. The phallic stage
   d. The genital stage
2. Each of Erikson's stages is characterized by
   a. the intervention of a caregiver or mentor.
   b. a crisis that the individual must resolve.
   c. individual goal setting.
   d. mastery of social skills, however rudimentary.
3. Which of the following best describes a parenting style influenced by Watson's theories?
   a. Rigid and strict
   b. Overprotective
   c. Permissive
   d. Child-centred

4. According to Skinner, everything we do in life is an operant response influenced by
   a. the immediate sociocultural context.
   b. the outcomes of past behaviour.
   c. the behaviour of peers.
   d. behaviour modification.

5. Social learning theory emphasizes ___________ as the primary mechanism(s) of development.
   a. observation and imitation
   b. genetic encoding
   c. reinforcement
   d. social influences

6. Bandura's Bobo doll experiment demonstrated
   a. the pleasure principle.
   b. vicarious reinforcement.
   c. operant conditioning.
   d. basic trust versus mistrust.

7. Dodge's approach to social cognition centres on the use of ___________ as a problem-solving strategy.
   a. negotiation
   b. role-taking
   c. aggression
   d. the "generalized other"

8. According to Dweck, whether a child meets a new challenge with a sense of excitement or with a sense of anxiety depends on that child's
   a. skill level.
   b. achievement motivation.
   c. parental engagement.
   d. hostile attributional bias.

9. Though younger children realize that someone else can have a perspective different from theirs, it is not until adolescence that we are able to compare our perspective to a generalized other. This ability represents the fourth stage in Roger Selman's ___________ theory.
   a. psychosocial
   b. reciprocal determinism
   c. role-taking
   d. self-socialization

10. What is the term used to describe the study of behaviour within an evolutionary context?
   a. Ethology
   b. Biology
   c. Sociology
   d. Mesosystem

11. Parental-investment theory stresses the ___________ basis of many aspects of parental behaviour.
   a. evolutionary
   b. empirical
   c. behaviourist
   d. bioecological

12. Lisa's peers are picking on her at recess because she wears glasses. Which level of Bronfenbrenner's bioecological model is affecting Lisa?
   a. The macrosystem
   b. The exosystem
   c. The microsystem
   d. The mesosystem

13. Which level of Bronfenbrenner's model would account for how changes in a society's customs over time affect the development of a child?
   a. The macrosystem
   b. The exosystem
   c. The chronosystem
   d. The mesosystem

14. Media use and exposure can impact an individual on every level of the bioecological model. Which of the following would represent an intervention at the mesosystem?
   a. National policies directed at limiting access by young children to violent media
   b. The installation of educational video games within the classroom
   c. The development of increasingly effective security measures for digital devices
   d. Watching an R-rated movie

15. Of the four broad theoretical frameworks for social development presented in this chapter, which group places the most emphasis on the importance of the child's knowledge and beliefs?
   a. Psychoanalytic theories
   b. Learning theories
   c. Social cognition theories
   d. Ecological theories

LaunchPad
macmillan learning

DON'T STOP NOW! Research shows that testing yourself is a powerful learning tool. Visit LaunchPad to access the LearningCurve adaptive quizzing system, which gives you a personalized study plan to help build your mastery of the chapter material through videos, activities, and more. **Go to launchpadworks.com.**

Critical Thinking Questions

1. The concept of self-socialization plays a prominent role in social cognitive theories. Explain what is meant by this term. To what extent and in what ways do the other major theories reviewed in the chapter allow for the possibility of self-socialization?
2. Consider your behaviour when preparing for and taking tests and when receiving feedback on your academic performance. Do you see yourself as having primarily an incremental/mastery orientation or an entity/helpless orientation to academic achievement?
3. Imagine yourself raising a child. Identify one or two things from each of the four types of theories discussed in this chapter that you think might be helpful to you as a parent.
4. How could Bronfenbrenner's bioecological model be used to describe the experiences of the Romanian orphans discussed in Box 9.2 (as well as in Box 1.1)?

Key Terms

achievement motivation, p. 326
anal stage, p. 315
attention-deficit hyperactivity disorder (ADHD), p. 336
behaviour modification, p. 320
chronosystem, p. 335
ego, p. 315
entity theory, p. 326
entity/helpless orientation, p. 326
erogenous zones, p. 315
ethology, p. 330
exosystem, p. 333
genital stage, p. 316
hostile attributional bias, p. 325
id, p. 315
imprinting, p. 330
incremental theory, p. 327
incremental/mastery orientation, p. 326
intermittent reinforcement, p. 320
latency period, p. 316
macrosystem, p. 334
mesosystem, p. 333
microsystem, p. 333
oral stage, p. 315
parental-investment theory, p. 332
phallic stage, p. 315
reciprocal determinism, p. 321
role taking, p. 324
self-socialization, p. 323
superego, p. 316
vicarious reinforcement, p. 322

Answers to Test Yourself

1. c, **2.** b, **3.** a, **4.** b, **5.** a, **6.** b, **7.** c, **8.** b, **9.** c, **10.** a, **11.** a, **12.** c, **13.** c, **14.** c, **15.** c

CHAPTER

10 Emotional Development

CHRISTIES IMAGES/PRIVATE COLLECTION/BRIDGEMAN IMAGES

FREDERICK MORGAN (1856–1927), *Never Mind!* (oil on canvas, 1884)

The Development of Emotions | Understanding Emotions | Emotion Regulation
The Role of Family in Emotional Development | Temperament
Mental Health, Stress, and Internalizing Mental Disorders

THEMES

NATURE AND NURTURE ■ THE ACTIVE CHILD ■ CONTINUITY/DISCONTINUITY

THE SOCIOCULTURAL CONTEXT ■ INDIVIDUAL DIFFERENCES

Imagine the following situation: a young girl is taken to a room in her preschool where an experimenter shows her some tasty treats, such as Smarties, marshmallows, or pretzels. The experimenter tells the girl that he is going to leave the room "for a while" and that she has two choices: if she waits until he returns to the room, she can have two of the treats; or, if she wishes, she can ring a bell, and the experimenter will return immediately—but she will get only one treat. The child is then left alone for a considerable period, say 15 to 20 minutes, or until she rings the bell.

You may have heard of this famous experiment, commonly known as "the marshmallow test" (Mischel, 2015). Walter Mischel and his colleagues first used this procedure with a group of preschoolers in the 1960s to study their ability to delay immediate gratification in order to obtain larger rewards. The researchers were interested in whether or not the children would wait for the second treat, but they also wanted to observe the children's strategies for coping with the long wait. Videos showed them using a variety of strategies: some distracted themselves by talking, singing, trying to sleep, or making up games to play; others stared at the treats or at the bell; and some, of course, just rang the bell and ate the single treat right away, preferring one immediate but guaranteed treat to the possibility of more treats later.

Mischel believed that a child's ability to delay eating one marshmallow for the reward of eating two marshmallows later was an indicator of that child's self-control or willpower in the face of immediate pleasure or happiness (however fleeting). The ability to exhibit self-control early in life, he reasoned, predicted success later in life. After all, much of success in adulthood depends on working toward long-term goals, whether in matters related to higher education, professional career, or exercise and physical health. Success also entails resisting temptation and exercising self-restraint.

To test his theory, Mischel interviewed the children who participated in his original marshmallow test at regular intervals over the subsequent four decades. At every 10-year interval, those children who were able to wait the longest were found to be more intelligent, attentive, strategic, and self-reliant than those who

The marshmallow test was designed to determine how well children can delay gratification—in other words, how well they manage the frustration of waiting to eat one treat in order to get two treats in the future.

BILL ARON/PHOTOEDIT

Can Young Children Delay Gratification?

BBC MOTION GALLERY/PRINCETON ACADEMIC RESOURCES

displayed less patience (Mischel, 2015; Peake, Hebl, & Mischel, 2002). Once they got to high school, they earned higher SAT scores and scored higher on a behavioural measure requiring control of one's attention and behavioural responses on a computer task (Eigsti et al., 2006); and at about age 30, they had achieved a higher educational level, had higher self-esteem, and were reported to be better able to cope with stress (Ayduk et al., 2000). Furthermore, in computer-task assessments 40 years after the original experiment, those who scored low in delay of gratification in Mischel's study continued to exhibit greater difficulty in delaying responses to rewarding stimuli than did those who scored high in delay (Casey et al., 2011).

Emotions are a basic part of human experience, but how children learn to regulate them and their behaviour can have lifelong consequences. In this chapter, we examine the development of children's emotions, as well as the development of their ability to regulate their emotions and the behaviour associated with them. In addition, we consider links between children's temperaments and their behaviour, as well as links between emotional stress and mental health. In the course of our discussion, we will give particular emphasis to several of our themes. Key among them will be the theme of *individual differences,* as we examine differences among children in various aspects of their emotional functioning. We also discuss the origins of these differences, including heredity, parental socialization practices, cultural beliefs related to emotion, and how the child's behaviour in a given context affects his or her physiological reactions. Thus, the themes of *nature and nurture* and the *sociocultural context* will also be prominent. The theme of the *active child* is also touched upon with respect to children's attempts to regulate their own emotions and behaviour. Finally, the theme of *continuity versus discontinuity* is discussed briefly in regard to the emergence of self-conscious emotions.

The Development of Emotions

Most people equate emotions with "feelings." However, emotions are more complicated than simply sensations or reactions. Developmentalists working in this area attempt to explain why we experience emotions and why we express them outwardly on our faces or in our voices. They view **emotions** as a combination of physiological and cognitive responses to thoughts or experiences. Emotions have several components (Izard, 2010):

1. Neural responses
2. Physiological factors, including heart rate, breathing rate, and hormone levels
3. Subjective feelings
4. Emotional expressions
5. The desire to take action, including the desire to escape, approach, or change people or things in the environment

The following example illustrates how each of these components contributes to the experience of emotion. Imagine you are walking in your neighbourhood and come across a growling dog without a leash or an owner nearby. You stop suddenly, realize you may be trapped, and begin to feel a sense of dread that you label as fear (subjective feeling). You recognize that your heart is racing and your eyes are widening (physiological factors) and that your eyebrows are raised and your mouth is pulled back (emotional expression), all as you try to figure out how to get away

emotions neural and physiological responses to the environment, subjective feelings, cognitions related to those feelings, and the desire to take action from the dog and toward someplace safe (desire to take action). Although you cannot observe it directly, your brain is rapidly processing information about the dog and the environment around you, as well as about the likely odds of success of any action you might take, and signalling the production of hormones that will help you mobilize your muscles to flee from the terrorizing dog (neural responses). All of these responses happen in a split second—so fast, in fact, that it is hard to say which comes first.

The nearly simultaneous nature of these components has led researchers to consider whether emotion is mostly innate (*nature*) or mostly learned (*nurture*) (Izard, 2010; Lindquist et al., 2013). Do we experience the physiological reaction first and then learn to call it "fear"? Or do we cognitively assess a situation as one that is fear inducing and then experience the corresponding physiological reactions and facial expressions? In other words, what role does cognition play in our experience of emotion? Research on these questions is ongoing, yet, as with so many other topics in this book, there is evidence for the influence of both nature and nurture. This chapter will explore some of the possible explanations currently under investigation, as well as some of the aspects of emotion and emotional development about which some consensus has emerged.

Theories on the Nature and Emergence of Emotion

Determining whether emotions are innate or learned requires knowing whether humans are born with the ability to experience key emotions. Consequently, research on emotional development tends to focus on infants. One view, known as **discrete emotions theory,** argues that neurological and biological systems have evolved to allow humans, from infancy, to experience and then express a set of basic emotions through adaptation to our surroundings (Ekman & Cordaro, 2011; Izard, Woodburn, & Finlon, 2010). Given its emphasis on evolution and adaptation, it is not surprising that this theory was first put forward by Charles Darwin in his 1872 book *The Expression of the Emotions in Man and Animals.* Based on careful observation of facial, verbal, and gestural expressions, Darwin argued that the expressions for certain basic emotional states are innate to the species and therefore are similar across all peoples, including young babies. According to discrete emotions theory, emotional responses are largely automatic and not based on cognition.

Adherents to discrete emotions theory point to several aspects of emotional development to support the proposition that emotions are innate and evolved over the course of human evolution. Infants express a set of recognizable, discrete emotions well before they can be actively taught about them (Izard et al., 2010). Also, similar emotional facial expressions have been observed around the world, including in remote tribes, although cultures vary in how they label these expressions (Ekman & Cordaro, 2011). Vocalizations of basic emotions such as anger, joy, and sadness are recognizable across very different cultural groups, from individuals living in England to members of the seminomadic Himba tribe in Namibia (Sauter et al., 2010).

In contrast, the **functionalist perspective** argues that individuals experience emotions in order to manage the relationship between themselves and the environment (Campos et al., 1994; Saarni et al., 2006). According to this perspective, emotions are partly responses to how individuals appraise the environment and whether factors in the environment are promoting or hindering

discrete emotions theory a theory in which emotions are viewed as innate, and each emotion has a specific and distinctive set of bodily and facial reactions

functionalist perspective a theory which argues that the basic function of emotions is to promote action toward achieving a goal. In this view, emotions are not discrete from one another and vary somewhat based on the social environment.

TABLE 10.1 The Goals, Meanings, and Actions Associated with Particular Emotions

Emotion type	Goal connected with the emotion	Meaning regarding the self	Action tendency
Disgust	Avoiding contamination or illness	This stimulus may contaminate me or make me ill	Rejection of the thing causing disgust
Fear	Maintaining one's own physical and psychological integrity	This stimulus is threatening to me	Flight or withdrawal
Anger	Attaining the end state that the individual currently is invested in	There is an obstacle to my obtaining my goal	Forward movement, especially to eliminate obstacles to one's goal
Sadness	Attaining the end state that the individual currently is invested in	My goal is unattainable	Disengagement and withdrawal
Shame	Maintaining others' respect and affection; preserving self-esteem	I am bad (my self-esteem is damaged), and others notice how bad I am	Withdrawal; avoiding others, hiding oneself
Guilt	Meeting one's own internalized values	I have done something contrary to my values and perhaps hurt someone else	Movement to make reparation, to inform others, or to punish self

their well-being (Moors et al., 2013). Emotions and emotional expressions are thus goal driven: when children want something to stop, they cry, whereas when they want something to continue, they smile and laugh.

Table 10.1 provides some examples of goals and goal meanings, as well as the actions they may precipitate. These appraisal processes most often occur at the subconscious level in both children and adults. The exceptions occur when children realize that people can fake emotions and that faking emotions can be another way to reach their goals. For example, a 4-year-old may fake crying after a fight with his big sister to evoke sympathy from an unsuspecting mother. We will return to this idea of fake emotions later in the chapter.

The Emergence of Emotions

Most researchers agree that there are six basic emotions—happiness, fear, anger, sadness, surprise, and disgust—that are universal in all human cultures. Each of these basic emotions serves important survival and communication functions. These basic emotions appear very early in life, lending support to the idea that emotions may be partly innate and, thus, a result of *nature*. Box 10.1 describes the coding schemes researchers have developed for recognizing each of the following emotions in children and adults.

Happiness

The first clear sign of happiness that infants express is a smile. During the first month, they exhibit fleeting smiles primarily during the REM phase of sleep; after the first month, they sometimes smile when they are stroked gently. These early smiles may be reflexive and seem to be evoked by some biological state rather than by social interaction (Sullivan & Lewis, 2003), although there is some evidence that even newborns less than a day old smile when they are being touched (see Cecchini et al., 2011).

Between the 3rd and 8th weeks of life, infants begin to smile in reaction to external stimuli, including touching, high-pitched voices, and other stimuli that engage their attention (Sullivan & Lewis, 2003). By the third month of life, and sometimes as early as 6 or 7 weeks of age, babies also begin to exhibit **social smiles,** that is, smiles directed toward people (Wörmann, Holodynski, Kärtner, & Keller, 2012). After about 3 or 4 months of age, infants laugh during a variety of activities that give them pleasure. For example, they are likely to laugh when a parent tickles them or blows on their tummy, bounces them on a knee or swings

social smiles smiles that are directed at people; they first emerge around the third month of life

BOX 10.1 A CLOSER LOOK Basic Emotional Expressions in Infants

To make their own interpretations of infants' emotions more objective, researchers have devised highly elaborate systems for identifying the emotional meaning of infants' facial expressions. These systems involve coding dozens of facial cues—whether an infant's eyebrows are raised or knitted together; whether the eyes are wide open, tightly closed, or narrowed; whether the lips are pursed, softly rounded, or retracted straight back; and so on—and then analyzing the combinations in which these cues are present.

AFFEX is a prominent system for coding emotions in infants that links particular facial expressions and facial muscle movements with particular emotions (Izard & Dougherty, 1980). Researchers first watch training videos of infants' facial expressions and compare what they see on screen to the official set of AFFEX facial codes; when they consistently agree with the official set, they have established interrater reliability (see Chapter 1). They can then watch videos of infants' and older children's faces and make note of which facial and muscle movements they see. The videos are played in slow motion to adequately capture expressions that sometimes last a second or less.

The following table provides brief descriptions and photographs of the combinations of muscle and facial movements that result in the recognition of six basic emotions.

The AFFEX system has been used to demonstrate links between children's emotional expressions and their emotion regulation skills and social behaviours. In one study conducted with 3- to 5-year-old children attending a Head Start centre in the United States, the more the children expressed anger and sadness in a laboratory task, the more they displayed mental health and behaviour problems in their classrooms 6 months later (Morgan, Izard, & Hyde, 2014).

Happiness: smiling, either with a closed mouth or with an open upturned mouth; raised cheeks, which in turn make the eyes squint a bit

ROSS WHITAKER/GETTY IMAGES

Sadness: downturned corners of the mouth, lips pushed together and possibly trembling, slightly furrowed brow

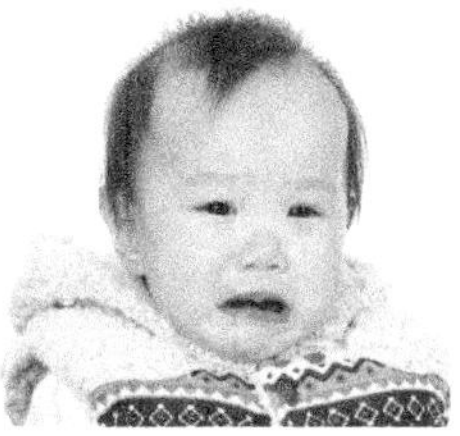

LEUNGCHOPAN/GETTY IMAGES

Anger: strongly furrowed brow that comes down in the centre, almost making an X of the brow muscles; open square-shaped mouth, sometimes baring teeth; flared nostrils

HEATHER PERRY/GETTY IMAGES

Fear: eyes wide open; brows raised in the middle, making a triangle shape; corners of mouth pulled back into a grimace, with mouth either open or closed

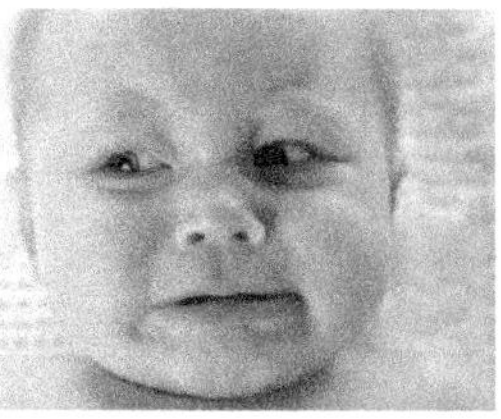

BELYNDA WEBB/SUPERSTOCK

Surprise: eyes wide open; eyebrows raised into arches; mouth open in round O shape

MILLA1974/GETTY IMAGES

Disgust: nose crinkled and nostrils flared; mouth open wide with lips pulled back and possibly with tongue sticking out

ANATOLS/GETTY IMAGES

them around in the air, or shares with them a favourite activity such as bathing. Studies across cultures (including ethnic Nso in Cameroon and middle-class parents in Münster, Germany) have found that social smiles frequently occur during interactions with parents and tend to elicit the adult's delight, interest, and affection, which in turn inspires more social smiling from the infant (Wörmann et al., 2012). Thus, the infant's early social smiles likely promote care from parents and other adults and strengthen the infant's relationships with other people.

Children's expressions of happiness increase across the first year of life (Rothbart & Bates, 2006), perhaps because they are able to understand and respond to more interesting and positive events and stimuli. Beginning at 5 months, they laugh

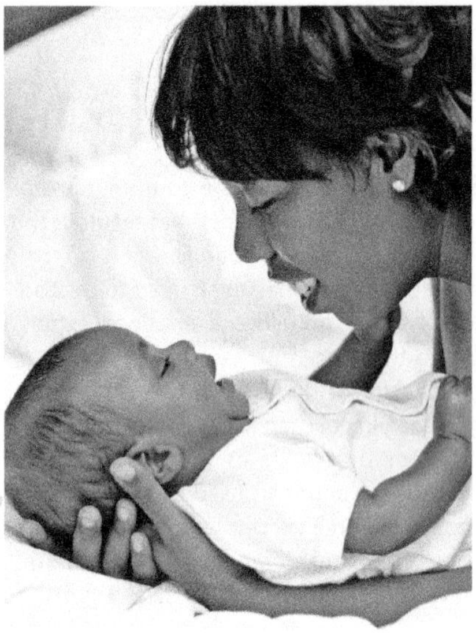

FUSE/GETTY IMAGES

Social smiles directed toward people typically first appear around the infant's second or third month.

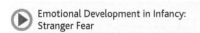

when they find something funny, such as a parent blowing air raspberries, and especially when their parents provide humour cues, such as laughing (Mireault et al., 2015). As their language skills develop along with their understanding of people and events, children in the preschool years begin to find humour and enjoyment in words, including jokes. One study in Italy found that children as young as 3 years of age understood jokes, including ones based on irony, such a puppet saying "Well done!" to another puppet that failed to score a basket (Angeleri & Airenti, 2014).

Fear

Although there is little firm evidence of distinct fear reactions in infants during the first months of life (Witherington et al., 2010), by the age of 7 months, initial signs of fear begin to appear (Camras, Malatesta, & Izard, 1991), as does the ability to recognize fear in the faces of other people (Leppänen & Nelson, 2012).

One form of fear that infants show early on—and one that is clearly adaptive—is fear of strangers. Because babies often do not have the ability to escape from potentially dangerous situations on their own, they must rely on their parents to protect them, and expressions of fear and distress are powerful tools for bringing help and support when they are needed. Individual differences in the decline in this kind of fear seem to be related to the quality of children's relationships with their mothers and how effectively their mothers deal with their children's expressions of fear (Buss & Kiel, 2011; Kochanska, 2001).

Emotional Development in Infancy: Stranger Fear

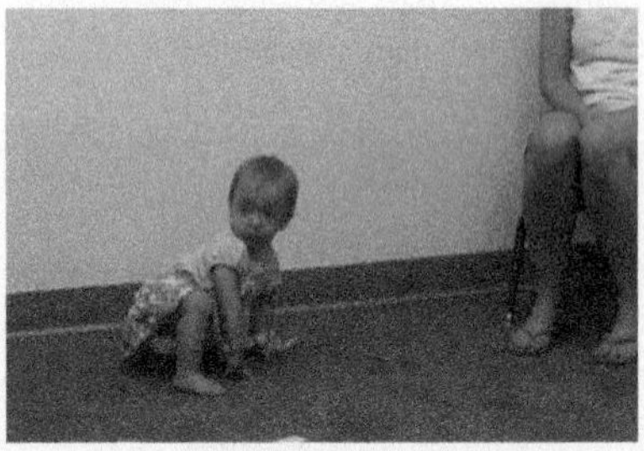

© WORTH PUBLISHERS

To determine when this fear of strangers develops in infants, one team of researchers repeated the same procedure with infants every 4 months from age 4 months to age 16 months (Braungart-Rieker, Hill-Soderlund, & Karrass, 2010). An experimenter, a stranger to the infant, slowly approached the infant while the mother sat close by; the stranger talked to the infant and picked him or her up. Observers rated the infants' facial expressions of fear using the AFFEX code described in Box 10.1 on a scale from 0 (no evidence of fear) to 4 (strong evidence of fear); they also rated the amount of distress in the infants' vocalizations. Infants displayed no fear of the approaching stranger at 4 months but experienced a steep increase in expressions of fear such that the fear of strangers was clearly in place by 8 months. There was little change in how much fear was expressed between 8 and 16 months, suggesting that after 8 months infants have more experience with novel situations and thus maintain some wariness but do not become increasingly distressed in fear-inducing situations (Braungart-Rieker et al., 2010).

Emotional Development in Infancy: Separation Anxiety

© WORTH PUBLISHERS

separation anxiety feelings of distress that children, especially infants and toddlers, experience when they are separated, or expect to be separated, from individuals to whom they are emotionally attached

A particularly salient type of fear that emerges at about 8 months of age is **separation anxiety**—distress due to separation from the parent who is the child's primary caregiver. When infants experience separation anxiety, they typically whine, cry, or otherwise express fear and upset. Separation anxiety tends to appear around 8 months and then begins to decline around 15 months (Kagan, 1976). This pattern of separation anxiety occurs across many cultures, displayed by infants reared in environments as disparate as the U.S. middle class, Israeli kibbutzim (communal farming communities), and !Kung San hunting-and-gathering groups in the Kalahari Desert in Africa (Kagan, 1976). Some amount of separation anxiety is both typical and adaptive, as it encourages infants to stay in close proximity to adults who can protect them and provide for their needs.

In the preschool years, as their cognitive ability to represent imaginary phenomena develops, children are prone to magical thinking and often fear imaginary creatures such as ghosts or monsters (see Chapter 7 for a more detailed discussion). As they approach school age (i.e., age 5 or 6), children learn to differentiate between real and imaginary fears (Zisenwine et al., 2013) and tend to be afraid of animals and darkness (Gullone, 2000). School-age children's anxieties and fears tend to be related to real-life issues, such as challenges at school (tests and grades, being called on in class, and pleasing teachers), health (their parents' and their own), and personal harm (being robbed, mugged, or shot; Gullone, 2000).

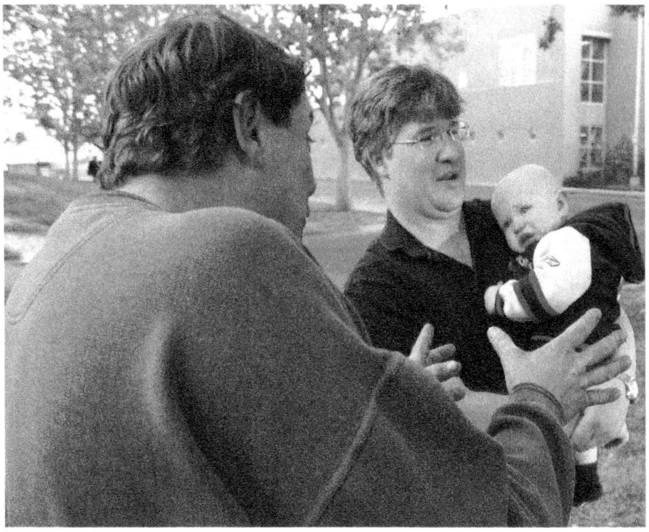

CHRISTINA KENNEDY

Young children who were not afraid of strangers at 6 months of age often suddenly show fear of them at 7 or 8 months of age.

Anger

Anger is a child's response to a frustrating or threatening situation and is largely an interpersonal experience. It is also an adaptive emotion because it helps humans marshal self-defense mechanisms and can motivate humans to work more diligently toward their goals (Harmon-Jones & Harmon-Jones, 2016). Research suggests that children are more likely to be angry with another person than an object and are more likely to be angry in certain contexts than in others (Sears et al., 2014).

Infants rarely express anger as a single emotion; rather, they often express anger blended with sadness, which suggests that infants tend to express a general state of distress and that they are unable to differentiate whether a stimulus is making them sad or angry (Sullivan & Lewis, 2003). By their 1st birthday, however, infants clearly and frequently express anger (Lemerise & Dodge, 2008). In the same experiment described earlier, in which fear was induced by the actions of a stranger, anger was elicited by having the mother gently hold the infant's arms while an attractive toy was put on the table in front of them (Braungart-Rieker et al., 2010). This was clearly a frustrating experience for infants who at 4 months have just developed the ability to reach for objects (see Chapter 5). Infants' expressions were coded using the AFFEX system (see Box 10.1). Infants displayed moderate anger at 4 months, and it steadily increased in intensity over the subsequent year (Braungart-Rieker et al., 2010).

Children's tendency to react to a situation with anger appears to peak around 18 to 24 months of age (Cole et al., 2011), and from age 3 to 6 years, children show less negative emotion on structured laboratory tasks designed to elicit it (Durbin, 2010). The general decline in children's expressions of anger is likely due to their increasing ability to express themselves with language (Kopp, 1992) and to regulate their emotions, which will be discussed later in this chapter.

The causes of anger also change as children develop a better understanding of others' intentions and motives. For example, in the early preschool years, a child is likely to feel anger when harmed by a peer, whether or not the harm was intentional. In contrast, young school-age children are less likely to be angered if they believe that harm done to them was unintentional or that the motive for some harmful action was benign rather than malicious (Lemerise & Dodge, 2008). As they grow older, children tend to express more anger at home with their families, although their anger is typically low in intensity (Sears et al., 2014), perhaps in conjunction with their developing identities as individuals separate from their parents (see Chapter 11).

Sadness

Infants often exhibit sadness in the same types of situations in which they show anger, such as after a painful event and when they cannot control outcomes in their environment. By the time children reach the preschool years, their displays of sadness appear to be somewhat less frequent than displays of anger (Rothbart et al., 2001). Young children also exhibit intense and prolonged displays of sadness when they are separated from their parents for extended periods and are not given sensitive care during this period (Bowlby, 1973). Like fear, sadness is clearly an adaptive emotion because it can draw in the attention and support from a caregiver who can help the child regulate her emotion with a calming touch and soft words.

Surprise

Surprise is an emotional reaction to a sudden, unexpected event. It is more than just the physical reaction to being startled by something like a loud noise, which, as we saw in Chapter 5, infants display from birth, but rather involves a cognitive understanding that something is not as it usually is. Most infants begin to express surprise by age 6 months (Sullivan & Lewis, 2003). Expressions of surprise tend to be brief, and they usually transform into another emotional expression, such as happiness (Sullivan & Lewis, 2003). The experience of surprise indicates to children when the world is working contrary to expectations, and thus surprise is thought to be important to early learning (Feigenson, 2016; see the discussion of violation-of-expectancy experiments in Chapter 5).

The extent to which infants express surprise to novel events is influenced by the emotional environment provided by their parents. In one study conducted in Scotland, infants whose mothers had symptoms of depression expressed less surprise in reaction to a jack-in-the-box than did infants of mothers without depressive symptoms (Reissland & Shepherd, 2006). This same study also found that mothers with depressive symptoms themselves expressed lower intensity of surprise in reaction to the jack-in-the-box, which suggests that how infants express emotions is influenced by how strongly their caregivers express emotions (Reissland & Shepherd, 2006).

Disgust

The emotional experience of disgust—which involves opening the mouth and sticking out the tongue—is thought to have an evolutionary basis, as it helps humans avoid potential poisons or disease-causing bacteria (Rozin, Haidt, & McCauley, 2016). Children learn, at least in part, from the behaviours of adults what they should react to with disgust, such as how their caregivers react to particular foods (Widen & Russell, 2013). For example, eating insects is a normal practice in some countries, such as Thailand, but it is considered unacceptable and disgusting by most cultures in the United States, Canada, and Europe. Of course, most children younger than 3 or 4 years of age do not know the words "disgust" or "disgusting," or their equivalents in other languages; however, even at such a young age, children are able to express feelings of disgust using other words to convey that something is *yucky* or *gross* (Widen & Russell, 2013). For young children, these feelings are mostly directed at food, but older children and adults eventually come to view some behaviours and moral transgressions with disgust as well (Rozin et al., 2016).

The Self-Conscious Emotions

The emotions discussed above are thought to be innate and to occur well before children are able to communicate with others. Some other emotions are considered **self-conscious emotions** because they require that children have a sense of themselves as separate from other people (Lewis, 2016)—an ability that is not fully developed until children are nearly 2 years old, as will be discussed in greater detail in Chapter 11. The expression of these emotions is an example of *discontinuous*

self-conscious emotions emotions such as guilt, shame, embarrassment, and pride that relate to our sense of self and our consciousness of others' reactions to us *growth:* there is an abrupt, qualitative change in children's abilities to experience self-conscious emotions that is linked to the emergence of a sense of self (Lewis, 2016). The emergence of self-conscious emotions is also fostered by children's growing sense of what adults and society expect of them and their acceptance of these external standards (Lagattuta & Thompson, 2007). The set of self-conscious emotions includes guilt, shame, jealousy, empathy, pride, and embarrassment. For brevity, the discussion that follows is limited to the development of guilt and shame; however, all of the self-conscious emotions develop in a similar fashion.

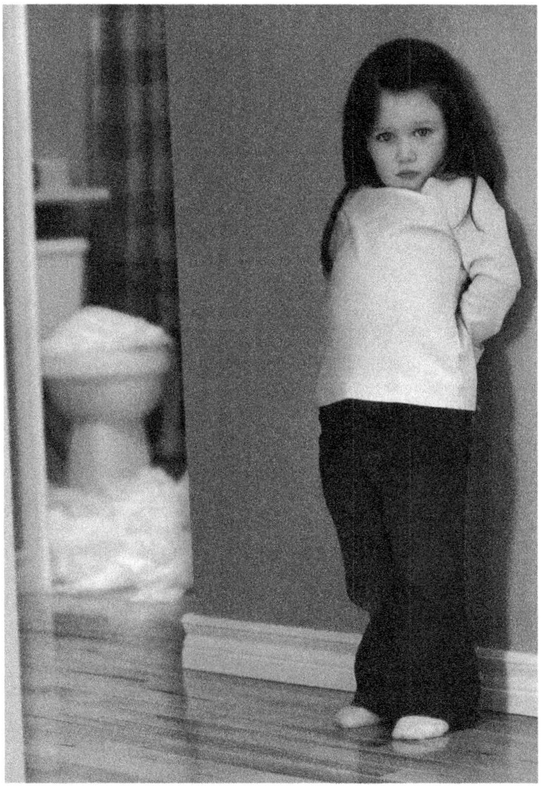

DESIGN PICS/MISTY BEDWELL/GETTY IMAGES

Children in the preschool years often exhibit shame or guilt when they do something they know they are not supposed to do.

Guilt and shame are sometimes mistakenly thought of as equivalent, but they are actually quite distinct. Guilt is associated with empathy for others and involves feelings of remorse and regret about one's behaviour, as well as the desire to undo the consequences of that behaviour (Lewis, 2016). In contrast, shame does not seem to be related to concern about others. When children feel shame, their focus is on themselves and the acceptance of a personal failure; they feel that they are exposed, and they often feel like hiding (Lewis, 2016; Tangney, Stuewig, & Mashek, 2007). In short, people may feel guilt associated with a specific behaviour they have undertaken, but feelings of shame are associated with their self-worth.

Shame and guilt can be distinguished fairly early, as documented by a study in which researchers arranged for 2-year-olds to play with a doll that had been rigged so that one leg would fall off during play while the experimenter was out of the room. When the "accident" occurred, some toddlers displayed a pattern of behaviour that seemed to reflect shame: they avoided the adult when she returned to the room and delayed telling her about the mishap. Other children showed a pattern of behaviour that seemed to reflect guilt: they repaired the doll quickly, told the adult about the mishap shortly after she returned to the room, and showed relatively little avoidance of her (Barrett, Zahn-Waxler, & Cole, 1993). In general, the degree of association of guilt feelings with bad or hurtful behaviour increases in the second to third year (Aksan & Kochanska, 2005), and the individual differences in children's guilt observed at 22 months of age remain relatively stable across the early preschool years (Kochanska et al., 2002).

In everyday life as well, the same situation often elicits shame in some individuals and guilt in others. Which emotion children experience partly depends on parental practices. Studies of North American children have found that they are more likely to experience guilt than shame if, when they have done something wrong, their parents emphasize the "badness" of the behaviour ("You did a bad thing") rather than of the child ("You're a bad boy"). In addition, children are more likely to feel guilt rather than shame if their parents help them understand the consequences their actions have for others, teach them the need to repair the harm they have done, avoid publicly humiliating them, and communicate respect and love for their children even when disciplining them (Hoffman, 2000; Tangney & Dearing, 2002).

The situations likely to induce self-conscious emotions in children vary across cultures, as does the frequency with which specific self-conscious emotions are likely to be experienced (Cole, Tamang, & Shrestha, 2006). For instance, among many First Nations people in Canada, humility is encouraged and accepted as an indication of respect for others rather than a lack of pride in oneself, one's family, and one's community (Blackstock, 2003). Similarly, the Japanese culture frowns upon bestowing praise on the individual because to do so would encourage a focus on the self rather than on the needs of the larger social group. Japanese children are thus less likely to report experiencing pride as a consequence of personal success than are American children (Furukawa, Tangney, & Higashibara, 2012). This cultural influence is also powerful in Chinese children: because they are reluctant to demonstrate personal pride, they rate lying about doing good deeds more positively than do Canadian children (K. Lee et al., 1997).

In many Asian or Southeast Asian cultures that emphasize the welfare of the group rather than the individual, not living up to social or familial obligations is likely to evoke shame or guilt (Mascolo, Fischer, & Li, 2003), and children in these cultures report experiencing guilt and shame more than do children in the United States (Furukawa et al., 2012). In such cultures, parents' efforts to elicit shame from their young children are often direct and disparaging (e.g., "You made your mother lose face," "I've never seen any 3-year-old who behaves like you") (Fung & Chen, 2001, pp. 424–425). This kind of explicit belittling appears to have a more positive effect on children in these Asian cultures than it does on children in Western cultures. Indeed, a longitudinal study in the United States found that children who were more prone to feelings of guilt when they were 5th-graders were less likely to engage in risky behaviours, such as using illegal drugs and having many sexual partners, once they turned 18, whereas those who experienced more shame as 5th-graders engaged in more risky behaviours later in life (Stuewig et al., 2015).

REVIEW QUESTIONS

Which theory — the discrete emotions theory or the functionalist perspective — best describes the purpose of emotions? Why? ■

Understanding Emotions

In addition to the development of children's capacity to *feel* emotions, another key influence on children's emotional reactions and regulation is their *understanding* of emotion — that is, their understanding of how to identify emotions, as well as their understanding of what emotions mean, their social functions, and what factors affect emotional experience. Because an understanding of emotion affects social behaviour, it is critical to the development of social competence. Children's understanding of emotions is primitive in infancy but develops rapidly over the course of childhood.

Identifying the Emotions of Others

The first step for children to develop an understanding of emotion is to recognize different emotions in others. By 3 months of age, infants can distinguish facial expressions of happiness, surprise, and anger (Grossmann, 2010). This ability is determined through the use of the habituation paradigm, which was first discussed in Chapter 5. Three- or 4-month-olds who were first habituated to pictures of happy faces before being presented with a picture of a face depicting surprise showed renewed interest by looking longer at the new picture. By 7 months of age, infants appear to discriminate a number of additional expressions, such as fear, sadness, and interest (Grossmann, 2010). For example, 7-month-olds exhibit different patterns of brain waves when they observe fearful and angry facial expressions, a finding that suggests some ability to discriminate these emotions (Kobiella et al., 2008).

One experiment compared a group of 12- to 14-month-olds with a second group of 16- to 18-month-olds to determine when infants develop the ability to relate facial expressions of emotion and emotional tones of voice to events in the environment (Martin et al., 2014). Individually, the children were shown an object and a video of a facial expression at the same time; specific toys were associated with each of six different emotional expressions—anger, fear, sadness, surprise, happiness, and a neutral expression. The children were then presented with both an emotion-paired toy and a neutral toy that had not been paired with an emotion; experimenters observed which toy the children reached for. As seen in Figure 10.1, an age difference clearly emerged. The 12- to 14-month-olds did not differentiate between objects that had been associated with each emotion; they reached for all of them at about the same rates. However, infants just a few months older, at 16 to 18 months, strongly preferred the toys associated with surprise and happy faces and strongly avoided toys that had been associated with anger or fear (Martin et al., 2014).

Such skills are evident in children's **social referencing**—that is, their use of a parent's or other adult's facial expression or vocal cues to decide how to deal with novel, ambiguous, or possibly threatening situations. In laboratory studies of this phenomenon, infants are typically exposed to novel people or toys while their mother, at the experimenter's direction, shows a happy, fearful, or neutral facial expression. In studies of this type, 12-month-olds tend to stay near their mother when she shows fear, to move toward the novel person or object if she expresses positive emotion, and to move partway toward the person or object if she shows no emotion (Carver & Vaccaro, 2007). By 14 months of age, the emotion-related information obtained through social referencing has an effect on children's touching of the object even an hour later (Hertenstein & Campos, 2004). Children seem to be better at social referencing if they receive both vocal and facial cues of emotion from the adult, and the use of vocal cues seems to be more effective than just the use of visual cues alone (Vaillant-Molina & Bahrick, 2012; Vaish & Striano, 2004).

By age 3, children in laboratory studies demonstrate a rudimentary ability to label a fairly narrow range of emotional expressions displayed in pictures or on puppets' faces (Denham, 1986). Young children—even 2-year-olds—are skilled at labelling happiness (usually by pointing to pictures of faces that reflect happiness; Michalson & Lewis, 1985). The ability to label anger, fear, and sadness emerges and increases in the next 1 or 2 years, and the ability to label surprise and disgust gradually appears in the late preschool and early school years (Widen & Russell, 2003, 2010a). Most children cannot label the self-conscious emotions pride, shame, and guilt until early to middle elementary school (Saarni et al., 2006), but the scope and accuracy of their emotion labelling improve thereafter into adolescence (Montirosso et al., 2010).

Children's facility for reading others' emotions can also be determined by their environments. Children who grow up in environments with violence or without adults they can trust may develop heightened awareness to emotional cues of conflict. A study of homeless orphaned children in Sierra Leone found that they were much more likely than children living in homes with families to detect anger in facial expressions

social referencing the use of a parent's or another adult's facial expression or vocal cues to decide how to deal with novel, ambiguous, or possibly threatening situations

FIGURE 10.1 Developmental change in ability to associate emotions with objects Differences by age group in proportion of time spent touching a toy that had been associated with each facial emotion. (Data from Martin et al., 2014)

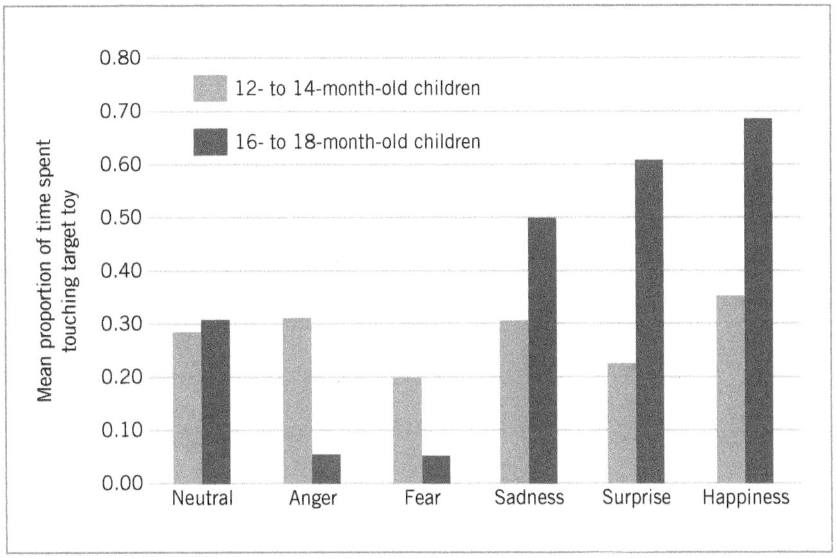

ISTOCK/GETTY IMAGES

The ability to read peers' facial expressions provides children with information about a peer's motives, which helps children respond appropriately in a potential conflict situation.

and less likely to detect sadness (Ardizzi et al., 2015). These tendencies, sadly, are likely important aspects of self-preservation for living on the streets.

Children's ability to recognize the facial expression of disgust in others develops over time; very few children of preschool age recognize disgust, but one-third of 12- to 14-year-olds recognize it, and three-quarters of 15- to 17-year-olds do (Widen & Russell, 2013). There are cultural differences as well: cross-cultural comparisons have found that school-age French children are more likely to correctly match a disgust face to a story about a disgusting event than are American children, who in turn do so more readily than Palestinian children (Widen & Russell, 2013). The exact reason for such cultural differences is not clear, although it may be affected by the languages spoken in each culture and whether terms like "disgust" have literal translations across them.

Children's inability to recognize emotions in others has been linked with the development of mental health problems: one study found that 1st-grade children who were low in emotion recognition ability had high levels of loneliness, perhaps because they misinterpreted others' emotional cues and thus had difficulties in relationships (Castro et al., 2018). Box 10.2 describes emotional intelligence and some related interventions to help children better understand their emotions and those of others.

Understanding Real and False Emotions

An important component in the development of emotional understanding is the realization that the emotions people express do not necessarily reflect their true feelings. The beginnings of this realization are seen in 3-year-olds' occasional (and usually transparent) attempts to mask their negative emotions when they receive a disappointing gift or prize (Cole, 1986). By age 5, children's understanding of false emotion has improved considerably; in one study, a group of 3- to 5-year-olds were presented with stories that involved children feeling emotions, such as the following:

> Michelle is sleeping over at her cousin Johnny's house today. Michelle forgot her favourite teddy bear at home. Michelle is really sad. . . . But, she doesn't want Johnny to see how sad she is because Johnny will call her a baby. So, Michelle tries to hide how she feels.
>
> (Banerjee, 1997)

After the children were questioned to ensure that they understood each story, they were presented with illustrations of various emotional expressions and given instructions such as "Show me the picture for how Michelle really feels" and "Show me the picture for how Michelle will try to look on her face." Although only half of 3- and 4-year-olds chose the appropriate pictures for four or more of the stories, more than 80% of 5-year-olds chose correctly (Banerjee, 1997). These findings suggest that the younger children did not appreciate that someone could express one emotion while feeling another, whereas the older children did. Studies with both Japanese and Western children also confirm that between 4 and 6 years of age, children increasingly understand that people can be misled by others' facial expressions (Gardner et al., 1988; Gross & Harris, 1988).

display rules a social group's informal norms about when, where, and how much one should show emotions and when and where displays of emotion should be suppressed or masked by displays of other emotions

Part of the improvement in understanding false emotion involves a growing understanding of **display rules,** which are a social or cultural group's informal

BOX 10.2 A CLOSER LOOK Emotional Intelligence

Cognitive intelligence, as discussed in Chapter 8, refers to the ability to reason about, learn from, and remember verbal or visual information. **Emotional intelligence** refers to individuals' ability to cognitively process information about emotions and to use that information to guide both their thoughts and behaviours (Mayer, Roberts, & Barsade, 2008). Importantly, emotional intelligence involves the ability to understand one's own emotions as well as the emotions of others, as perceived through their facial expressions, body movements, and verbal tone.

To measure emotional intelligence in children and adolescents, researchers typically ask participants to respond to direct statements about themselves and their abilities. For example, one commonly used measure, known as the Trait Emotional Intelligence Questionnaire, asks adolescents to rate the truth of statements such as "I can control my anger when I want to" and "I'm good at getting along with my classmates" (Petrides et al., 2006).

Emotional intelligence has been linked to a range of positive outcomes in both childhood and adolescence. Children high in emotional intelligence are better able to manage their own emotions and are less likely to engage in aggressive behaviour than are children with lower emotional intelligence (Lomas et al., 2012). A review of studies conducted in a diverse set of countries (Australia, China, Spain, Trinidad, the United Kingdom, and the United States) found that children high in emotional intelligence in adolescence have fewer mental health problems, lower risk behaviours, and better strategies for coping with stress than do children low in emotional intelligence (Resurrección, Salguero, & Ruiz-Aranda, 2014). Emotional intelligence also appears to predict these positive outcomes over and above other related factors such as self-esteem, personality, and cognitive intelligence (Resurrección et al., 2014).

Such findings have led researchers to develop interventions to promote emotional intelligence as a way of reducing aggressive and antisocial behaviour. One notable program is Roots of Empathy (ROE), targeted at children in kindergarten through grade 8 (Gordon, 2009). This program began as a small project in Toronto in 1996 but is now delivered in every province in Canada, in rural, urban, and remote communities, including Indigenous communities. The program, which lasts for the school year, is built around monthly class visits by an infant–parent pair who are "adopted" by the class. During each monthly visit, children learn about the baby's development through interaction and observation. A ROE program instructor, who visits the classroom three times each month—before, during, and after the parent–infant visit—provides lessons that focus on emotional understanding, empathy, problem solving, perspective taking, effective parenting, infant development, and caring for others. The lessons and activities vary with the age of the baby and the developmental level of the students in the classroom. Apart from the instructor visits, classroom teachers incorporate information and ideas from the ROE lessons into their regular lessons (Schonert-Reichl et al., 2012).

An evaluation of the program, which studied 585 children from grades 4 to 7 and included reports from peers and teachers, yielded promising results. Children who participated in ROE demonstrated a greater understanding of why infants cry. Peer reports indicated increases in prosocial behaviour, and teacher reports pointed to more proactive behaviour and less relational aggression. Children's own reports of empathy and perspective taking did not show significant changes (Schonert-Reichl et al., 2012).

Another intervention for middle and high school students in Spain focuses on enhancing aspects of emotional intelligence, such as perceiving emotions in others and being aware of how emotions influence thought processes. For example, one activity uses emotionally laden music, poems, and short stories as a springboard for a discussion of the role and usefulness of emotion in daily life (Castillo et al., 2013). In an experimental evaluation, students who participated in the intervention engaged in less verbal and physical aggression and reported fewer mental health problems than did students who were not in the program (Castillo et al., 2013; Salguero, Palomera, & Fernández-Berrocal, 2012).

As this research shows, emotional intelligence is a helpful concept for understanding how emotion-related skills affect children's interactions with others and provides a useful target for interventions aimed at improving children's social-emotional skills and mental health.

---

norms about when, where, and how much one should show emotions, as well as when and where displays of emotion should be suppressed or masked by displays of other emotions (Cole & Jacobs, 2018; Saarni, 1979). Display rules sometimes require that children express an emotion that is not matched with their felt emotion. The two main strategies for engaging in display rules are simulating an emotion, typically in order to be nice to someone else (such as pretending to love an aunt's cooking), and masking an emotion as a self-protective measure (such as pretending not to be afraid of an approaching bully). Displaying context-appropriate emotion and avoiding uncontrolled emotions are key to successful social interactions (Saarni et al., 2006).

Children as young as 1½ years of age can recognize exaggerated and fake emotional displays (Walle & Campos, 2014). Over the preschool and elementary school years, children develop a more refined understanding of when and why display rules are used (Wu, Wang, & Liu, 2017). With age, children also better understand that people tend to break eye contact and avert their gaze when lying, and they are increasingly able to use this knowledge to conceal their own deception (McCarthy & Lee, 2009).

emotional intelligence the ability to cognitively process information about emotions and to use that information to guide both thought and behaviour

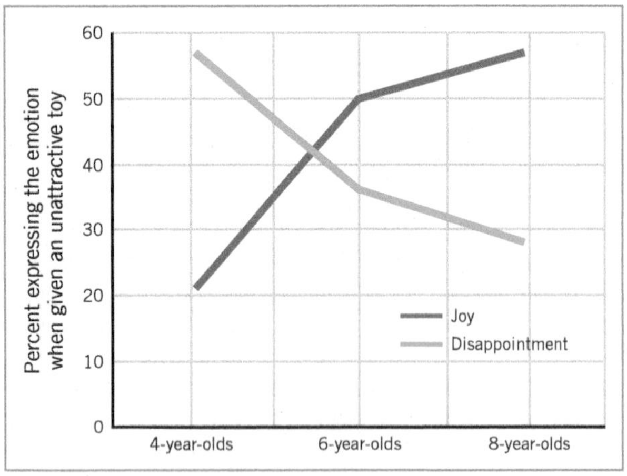

FIGURE 10.2 Development of display rules Percent of children simulating joy to deceive an experimenter about an unattractive gift (successful use of display rule) and percent of children expressing their actual disappointment in the unattractive gift (a failure to mask their emotion), by age of the child. (Data from Kromm et al., 2015)

In order to determine how display rules develop, researchers conducting a study of 4-, 6-, and 8-year-olds in Germany devised a scenario to encourage children to fake emotions in order to win a prize (Kromm, Färber, & Holodynski, 2015). The children were shown three boxes with lids. One box had an attractive gift (e.g., a glitter tattoo), one had an unattractive gift (e.g., a broken pencil), and the third had no gift at all. The children were instructed to look in each box and then try to trick the experimenter into thinking one of the boxes *without* the attractive toy was in fact the box *with* the attractive toy; if they succeeded in tricking the experimenter, they could keep the attractive toy. In fact, the experimenter always "guessed" incorrectly, and so all children got to take home the preferred toy, but the experimenters video recorded the children's facial expressions during the task. They found that the 4-year-olds were not successful in following display rules; they were unable to mask their disappointment, and they were unable to simulate joy to trick the experimenter. Yet, as Figure 10.2 shows, children became increasingly better at these two aspects of emotion display rules with age, such that nearly 60% of 8-year-olds could simulate joy to trick the experimenter and only 28% failed to mask their disappointment with the unattractive toy (Kromm et al., 2015). This study provides clear evidence that children experience a steep increase in their understanding and implementation of display rules in middle childhood.

These age-related advances in children's understanding of real versus false emotion and display rules are linked to increases in children's cognitive capacities (Flavell, 1986; Harris, 2000). However, social factors also seem to affect children's understanding of display rules. For example, 10-year-olds in Iran are more likely to report using display rules around happiness, fear, and sadness than are 10-year-olds in the Netherlands (Novin et al., 2009). In many cultures, display rules are somewhat different for males and females and reflect societal beliefs about how males and females should feel and behave (Ruble, Martin, & Berenbaum, 2006; Van Beek, Van Dolderen, & Demon Dubas, 2006). This is especially true for girls from cultures such as India, where females are expected to be deferential and to express only socially appropriate emotions (Joshi & MacLean, 1994). Differences are also found in the United States, where elementary school girls are more likely than boys to feel that openly expressing emotions such as pain is acceptable (Zeman & Garber, 1996).

emotion regulation a set of both conscious and unconscious processes used to both monitor and modulate emotional experiences and expressions

REVIEW QUESTIONS

In what ways does your own emotional development in early childhood and elementary school map onto the pattern described in this section? What display rules did you learn as part of your emotional development? ■

Developing Self-Control in Early Childhood

Emotion Regulation

Throughout life, being able to regulate one's emotions is crucial to successful development across domains, including cognitive and behavioural. **Emotion regulation** is a set of conscious and unconscious processes used to both monitor and modulate emotional experiences and expressions. Emotion regulation develops gradually over the course of childhood and paves the way for success in social interactions as well as in academic settings.

The Development of Emotion Regulation

NORBERT SCHAEFER/GETTY IMAGES

Parents often help young children regulate themselves by physically calming them or distracting them with an object.

When young infants are distressed, frustrated, or frightened, there is little they can do to fix the situation. Their parents typically try to help them regulate their emotional arousal by attempting to soothe or distract them (Gianino & Tronick, 1988). For example, mothers tend to use caressing and other affectionate behaviour to calm a crying 2-month-old. Over the next few months, they increasingly include vocalizations (e.g., talking, singing, "shushing") in their calming efforts, as well as in their attempts to divert the infant's attention. Holding or rocking upset young infants while talking soothingly to them seems to be the most reliable approach, and feeding them if they are not highly upset is also effective (Jahromi, Putnam, & Stifter, 2004). Thus, the emotional states of young infants are externally controlled by a process known as **co-regulation,** in which a caregiver provides the needed comfort or distraction to help the child reduce his or her distress.

As children develop in their abilities to control their own bodies and to understand their environments, they are gradually able to take control of regulating their own emotions. By 5 months of age, infants show signs of rudimentary emotion regulation in aversively arousing or uncertain situations. One strategy that infants use is known as **self-comforting behaviours,** which are repetitive actions that regulate arousal by providing a mildly positive physical sensation; examples include sucking fingers and rubbing hands together (Planalp & Braungart-Rieker, 2015). Another strategy infants use is **self-distraction,** which involves looking away from the upsetting stimulus in order to regulate their level of arousal (Ekas, Lickenbrock, & Braungart-Rieker, 2013); for instance, an infant may turn his head away from an older sibling jangling a set of keys in front of his face. Over the course of the first year of life, infants decrease their use of self-comforting behaviours in stressful situations and increase their use of self-distraction (Planalp & Braungart-Rieker, 2015).

co-regulation the process by which a caregiver provides the needed comfort or distraction to help a child reduce his or her distress

self-comforting behaviours repetitive actions that regulate arousal by providing a mildly positive physical sensation

self-distraction looking away from an upsetting stimulus in order to regulate one's level of arousal

These changes in children's self-regulation are at least partly due to the increasing maturation of the neurological systems—including portions of the frontal lobe that are central to managing attention and inhibiting thought and behaviours (Berger, 2011; Smith et al., 2016). They are also partly due to changes in what adults expect of children. As children age, adults increasingly expect them to manage their own emotional arousal and behaviour. Once children are capable of crawling, for example, they are viewed as being more responsible for their behaviour and for complying with parental expectations (Campos, Kermoian, & Zumbahlen, 1992). At about 9 to 12 months of age, children start to show awareness of adults' demands and begin to regulate themselves accordingly (Kopp, 1989). Their compliance grows rapidly in the second year of life (Kaler & Kopp, 1990), and they are increasingly likely to heed simple instructions, such as to not touch dangerous objects.

Over the course of the early years, children develop and improve their ability to distract themselves from distress by playing on their own. They also become less likely to seek comfort from their parents when they are upset (Bridges & Grolnick, 1995). And because of their growing ability to use language, when they are upset by parental demands, they are more likely to discuss and negotiate the situation with a parent than to engage in an emotional outburst (Campos, Frankel, & Camras, 2004; Klimes-Dougan & Kopp, 1999; Kopp, 1992). For example, if preschoolers are unhappy when parents tell them to stop playing and instead clean up their rooms, the children may verbally protest and lobby for extra playtime or work out a timetable for cleaning up rather than throwing fits.

HELEN LIU/ALAMY

When distressed, many young children engage in self-soothing behaviours, such as rubbing their body, sucking a thumb, or clinging to well-loved objects such as a favourite blanket.

Developing Self-Control in Middle Childhood

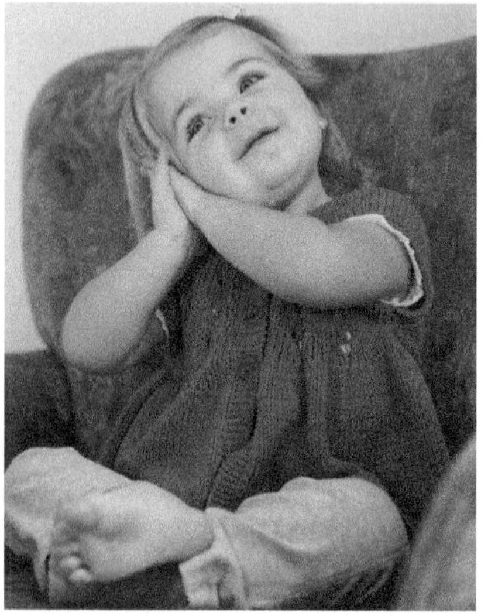

This little girl is using signs to communicate that she wants to take a nap. Children who can indicate their wants and needs with language or signs are less likely to get frustrated and to exhibit unregulated behaviour.

Children's ability to regulate their attention improves across the early years (Rueda, Posner, & Rothbart, 2011). As a result, children are increasingly able to conform to adults' expectations, such as not hurting others when angry and staying seated at school when they would much prefer to get up and talk or play with classmates. In adolescence, the neurological changes that occur in the cortex (see Chapter 3 for details) further contribute to self-regulation and other cognitive functioning. They also likely contribute to the decline in risk taking and the improvement in judgment that often occur in the transition from adolescence to young adulthood (Steinberg, 2010).

Whereas younger children regulate their emotional distress primarily by using behavioural strategies (e.g., distracting themselves with play), older children are also able to use cognitive strategies and problem solving to adjust to emotionally difficult situations (Zimmer-Gembeck & Skinner, 2011). Finding themselves caught in unpleasant or threatening circumstances, they may rethink their goals or the meaning of events so that they can adapt gracefully to the situation. This ability helps children avoid acting in ways that might be counterproductive. When older children are teased by peers, for instance, they may be able to defuse the situation by downplaying the importance of the teasing rather than reacting to it in a way that would provoke more teasing.

The Relation of Emotion Regulation to Social Competence and Adjustment

The development of emotion regulation has important consequences for children, especially with regard to their social competence. **Social competence** derives from a set of skills that helps individuals achieve their personal goals in social interactions while maintaining positive relationships with others (Rubin, Bukowski, & Parker, 1998). A variety of studies indicate that children who have the ability to inhibit inappropriate behaviours, delay gratification, and use cognitive methods of controlling their emotion and behaviour tend to be well adjusted and liked by their peers and by adults (Doan, Fuller-Rowell, & Evans, 2012; Olson et al., 2011).

Moreover, children and adolescents who are able to deal constructively with stressful situations—negotiating with others to settle conflicts, planning strategies to resolve upsetting situations, seeking social support, and so on—generally are better adjusted than are children who lack these skills, including those who avoid dealing with stressful situations altogether (Jaser et al., 2007). Children who are unable to successfully regulate their emotions are at higher risk of becoming victims of bullying compared with their peers who are better at emotion regulation (Morelen, Southam-Gerow, & Zeman, 2016). Well-regulated children also do better in school than their less regulated peers do, likely because they are better able to pay attention and are better behaved and better liked by teachers and peers, and, consequently, like school better (Denham et al., 2012; Duckworth, Quinn, & Tsukayama, 2012).

Children who exhibit positive affect and laughter tend to be well liked by peers.

social competence the ability to achieve personal goals in social interactions while simultaneously maintaining positive relationships with others

REVIEW QUESTIONS

Do you think there are some children who can have social competence without being high in self-regulation? Why or why not? ■

The Role of Family in Emotional Development

As children's primary environment during the early stages of emotional development, families in general and parents in particular have an important influence on how children interpret and respond to emotions in others, as well as on how they interpret and regulate their own emotions. Some of the ways that parents affect emotional development are indirect, such as through their own expressions of emotion to their children; others are more direct, such as parents' reactions to their children's emotions and their explicit coaching of emotion.

Parents' Expression of Emotion

Parents' expression of emotion provides children with a model of when and how to express emotion (Denham, Zoller, & Couchoud, 1994; Dunn & Brown, 1994). This modeling may affect children's understanding of what types of emotional expressions are appropriate and effective in interpersonal relations (Morris et al., 2007). In families in which parents tend not to express emotions, children may get the message that emotions are basically bad and should be avoided or inhibited (Gottman, Katz, & Hooven, 1997). In addition, the parental emotions to which children are exposed may affect their general level of distress and arousal in social interactions, in turn affecting their ability to process important information about the interactions (e.g., others' verbal and nonverbal cues) that would help them moderate their behaviour (Eisenberg, Cumberland, & Spinrad, 1998; Hoffman, 2000).

Whatever the underlying reason, it is clear that the consistent and open expression of emotions in the home is associated with children's emotional expressions as well as their behaviour. In a review of studies, Halberstadt and colleagues found that when positive emotions such as happiness are prevalent in the home, children tend to express happiness themselves. These children in turn are socially skilled, well adjusted, low in aggression, able to understand others' emotions, and typically high in self-esteem (Halberstadt & Eaton, 2003; see also Barry & Kochanska, 2010; Brophy-Herb et al., 2011; McCoy & Raver, 2011). In a more recent study in China, researchers found that the more often mothers expressed positive emotions to their children, the better their children were at understanding emotion display rules, a concept introduced earlier in this chapter (Wu et al., 2017).

In contrast, when negative emotions such as anger are prevalent in the home, especially when they are intense, children tend to exhibit low levels of social competence and to experience and express negative emotion themselves, including depression and anxiety (Raval & Martini, 2011; Stocker et al., 2007). Even when the conflict or anger in the home is not directed at the children, there is an increased likelihood that they will develop anger, behaviour problems, and deficits in social competence and self-regulation (Kouros, Cummings, & Davies, 2010; Rhoades et al., 2011). These outcomes are also more likely when children are exposed to high levels of parental depression (Blandon et al., 2008; Cicchetti & Toth, 2006), perhaps in part because children of depressed parents are especially attentive to expressions of sadness in others (Lopez-Duran et al., 2013).

Children who are exposed to relatively high levels of positive emotion in the family tend to express more positive emotion and are more socially skilled and better adjusted than children who are exposed to high levels of negative emotion.

JACK HOLLINGSWORTH/GETTY IMAGES

emotion socialization the process through which children acquire the values, standards, skills, knowledge, and behaviours that are regarded as appropriate for their present and future roles in their particular culture

Still-Face Experiment with Edward Tronick

LOVETT STORIES + STRATEGIES

Parents' failures to express emotion can also influence children's emotional development. In the 1970s, Edward Tronick and his colleagues developed an experimental procedure known as the Still-Face Paradigm (Tronick et al., 1978). For this procedure, mothers and their infants, usually around 4 months of age, are brought into the laboratory; the infants are strapped into highchairs, and each mother is seated 1½ feet away from her infant, where she can easily interact with the infant. Mothers in the control group are instructed by the experimenters to play with their children for 10 minutes. Mothers in the experimental group first are instructed to play normally for 2 minutes with their babies; then, they are told to sit back in their chairs, maintain a neutral expression, and not talk to, touch, or otherwise react to their babies—in other words, to keep a "still face." After 2 minutes, they again alternate another play episode with a still-face episode, before concluding with a final play episode.

What is remarkable about the findings from this research is how quickly the infants become distressed when their mothers do not express emotion or react to the infants' emotional expressions. The accompanying photos show the change in an infant's emotions and behaviour from a play episode to a still-face episode; remember that each episode is only 2 minutes long! Using data from a recent study (DiCorcia et al., 2015), Figure 10.3 compares the amount of time in each episode the infants looked at their mothers or expressed distress; infants show a steep decrease in the time spent looking at their mothers during the still-face episodes, which is a clear example of infants using the self-distraction method. The infants' emotional distress increases during the still-face episodes, and a more intense distress reaction occurs in the second still-face episode. These results illustrate that even at a few months of age, infants are attuned to their mothers' emotional expressions and behaviours and experience distress when their mothers do not react as they have come to expect.

LOVETT STORIES + STRATEGIES

LOVETT STORIES + STRATEGIES

Parents' Socialization of Children's Emotional Responses

In addition to being affected by parents' displays of emotion, children's emotional development is influenced by parents' **emotion socialization** of their children—that is, the direct and indirect influence that parents have on their children's standards, values, and ways of thinking and feeling.

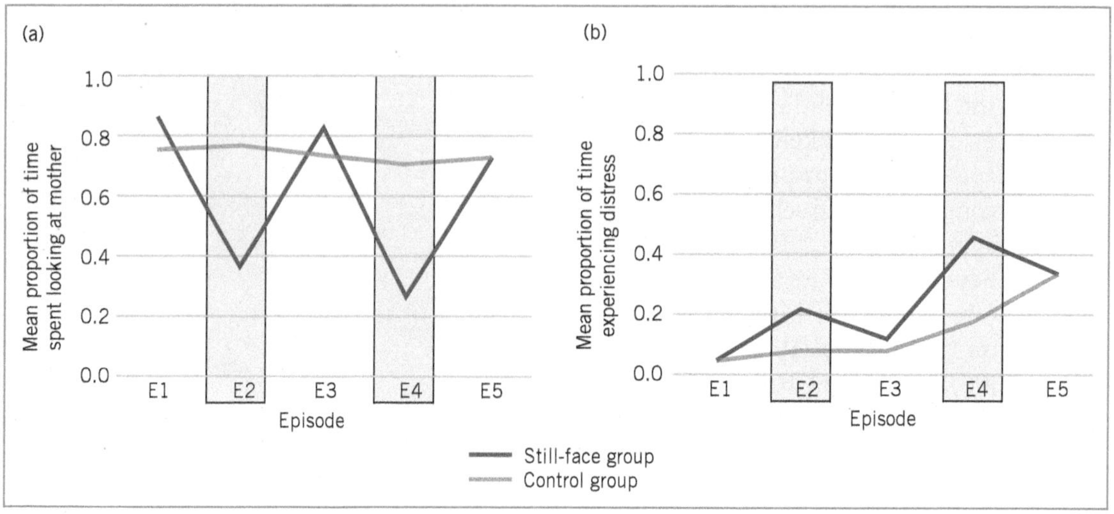

FIGURE 10.3 Children's reactions to mothers' still faces An infant happily interacting with her mother (top panel of photo series) quickly becomes distressed when the mother keeps a still face and does not interact with the infant (bottom panel). The two graphs highlight the episodes when mothers kept a still face in the experimental condition; mothers in the control condition continued to play with their babies normally across all episodes. Infants significantly reduce the time they spend looking at their mothers during still-face episodes and increase their expressions of negative affect. (Data from DiCorcia et al., 2015)

Parents socialize their children's emotional development through their reactions to their children's expression of emotion and through the discussions they have with their children about emotion and emotion regulation. These avenues of socialization, which are often interrelated, can affect not only children's emotional development but also their social competence (Baker, Fenning, & Crnic, 2011; Thompson, 2015).

Culture plays a significant role in influencing which emotional expressions are encouraged or discouraged by parents. When asked about norms for emotional expression, adults from 48 countries (3 in North America including Canada, 4 in South America, 17 in Europe, 7 in Africa, 16 in Asia, and Australia) varied widely in the extent to which they believed children should display happiness, fearfulness, or anger (Diener & Lucas, 2004). Because parents are typically responsible for guiding their children in social norms, these cultural differences are often reflected in parents' emotion socialization (Friedlmeier, Corapci, & Cole, 2011).

Numerous studies have explored cultural differences related to emotion socialization. American mothers appear to be more likely than Japanese mothers to encourage their children to express their emotions (Zahn-Waxler et al., 1996). This tendency is in keeping with the high value European American culture places on independence, self-assertion, and individual expression (Zahn-Waxler et al., 1996). In contrast, Japanese culture emphasizes interdependence, the subordination of oneself to the group, and, correspondingly, the importance of maintaining harmonious interpersonal relationships. A similar contrast is found in other East Asian cultures, such as in China, where mothers often discourage their children from expressing anger (Matsumoto, 1996; Mesquita & Frijda, 1992). As a consequence, children in these societies learn not to express their anger or frustration (Raval & Martini, 2009). Similarly, the degree to which mothers in different Nepali subcultures report teaching their children to manage emotions predicts whether Nepali children report masking certain emotions (Cole & Tamang, 1998).

Parents' Reactions to Children's Emotions

Parents' reactions to their children's emotions directly influence the children's own tendencies to express emotions, as well as their social competence and adjustment. Parents who dismiss or criticize their children's expressions of sadness and anxiety communicate to their children that their feelings are not valid. Parents send similar messages when they react to their children's anger with threats, belligerence, or dismissive comments. In turn, their children are likely to be less emotionally and socially competent than are children whose parents are emotionally supportive. They tend, for example, to be lower in sympathy for others, less skilled at coping with stress, and more prone to express anger and to engage in problem behaviours such as aggression (Engle & McElwain, 2011; Luebbe, Kiel, & Buss, 2011).

In contrast, parents who are supportive when their children are upset help their children regulate their emotional arousal and find ways to express their emotions constructively. This process can start early in a child's development. In the !Kung San hunter-gatherer community of Botswana, mothers keep their infants close by for the first years of their lives and respond very quickly (within 10 seconds) to their infants' cries (Kruger & Konner, 2010)—a clear example of the co-regulation of emotions discussed above. As a result, even at the peak age for crying (1–12 weeks), !Kung infants cry for the equivalent of 1 minute per hour, with only 6% of all observed crying bouts lasting longer than 30 seconds; compare this tendency with Western newborns who, as we learned in Chapter 2, cry for approximately 2 hours per day.

PAMELA COLE

Interviews with children in remote villages in Nepal allowed Pamela Cole and her colleagues to examine how Buddhist and Hindu values contribute to children's understanding of emotion.

Although not all parents can be as quick to respond as !Kung mothers, the more mothers acknowledge and respond contingently to their children's emotions, the more their children feel validated. In turn, these children tend to be better adjusted and more competent with their peers and to perform better in school (Raval & Martini, 2011). Supportive parental reactions may be especially helpful in reducing problem behaviours for children who have difficulty regulating their physiological responses to challenges (Hastings & De, 2008).

Another striking example of cultural influences in emotional socialization is provided by the Tamang in rural Nepal. The Tamang are Buddhists who place great value on keeping one's *sem* (mind–heart) calm and clear of emotion, and they believe that people should not express anger because it has disruptive effects on interpersonal relationships. Consequently, although Tamang parents are responsive to the distress of infants, they often ignore or scold children older than age 2 when those children express anger, and they seldom offer explanations or support to reduce children's anger. Such parental reactions are not typical of all Nepali groups, however; for instance, parents of Brahman Nepali children respond to children's anger with reasoning and yielding (Cole et al., 2006).

Of particular interest is the fact that although nonsupportive parental behaviour comparable to that of the Tamang has been associated with low social competence in U.S. children, it does not seem to have a negative effect on the social competence of Tamang children. Because of the value placed on controlling the expression of emotion in Tamang culture, parental behaviours that would seem dismissive and punitive to U.S. parents likely take on a different meaning for Tamang parents and children and probably have different consequences (Cole & Dennis, 1998; Cole et al., 2006).

When children from Western backgrounds do experience shame or sadness, their mothers seem to be most concerned with helping them feel better about themselves. In contrast, Chinese mothers more often than Western mothers use such situations as opportunities to teach proper conduct and help their child understand how to conform to social expectations and norms—for example, asking "Isn't it wrong for you to get mad at Papa?" (Cheah & Rubin, 2004; Friedlmeier et al., 2011; Wang & Fivush, 2005). When teaching about emotion, Chinese immigrant parents living in the United States are more likely to focus on behaviours that can cause, or resolve, emotional states, whereas European American parents are more likely to talk about internal emotional states (Doan & Wang, 2010).

Parents' Discussion of Emotion

Family conversations about emotion are an important aspect of children's emotional socialization. By discussing emotions with their children, parents teach them about the meanings of emotions, the circumstances in which they should and should not be expressed, and the consequences of expressing or not expressing them (LaBounty et al., 2008; Thompson, 2006). An additional help in emotional socialization is **emotion coaching,** in which parents not only discuss emotions with their children but also help them learn ways to cope with their emotions and express them appropriately (Power, 2004). Children who receive this type of guidance tend to display better emotional understanding than children who do not.

A longitudinal study by Judy Dunn and her colleagues found, for example, that the degree to which children are exposed to, and participate in, discussions of emotions with family members at ages 2 and 3 predicts their understanding of others' emotions until at least age 6 (Brown & Dunn, 1996; Dunn, Brown, & Beardsall, 1991; Dunn, Brown et al., 1991). In two similar studies, mothers' references to their children's desires at 15 months of age predicted their children's understanding

emotion coaching the use of discussion and other forms of instruction to teach children how to cope with and properly express emotions of emotions and use of emotion language at 24 months. In fact, mothers' verbal references to others' thoughts and knowledge when describing a series of pictures to their children at 24 months of age predicted children's use of emotion language and understanding of emotion at 33 months of age (Taumoepeau & Ruffman, 2006, 2008). Indeed, in these same two studies, as well as in another (Ensor & Hughes, 2008), mothers' references to others' mental states predicted children's emotion understanding better than did mothers' references to emotions themselves, perhaps because references to mental states help children understand the thoughts that accompany and motivate emotional states.

JGI/JAMIE GRILL/GETTY IMAGES

Parents actively teach children about emotions through emotion coaching.

Researchers have also found that children whose parents use emotion coaching are more socially competent with peers, more empathic, and less likely to exhibit problem behaviours or depression than are children who do not receive such guidance (Brophy-Herb et al., 2011; Katz, Maliken, & Stettler, 2012; Stocker et al., 2007). Of course, children's own characteristics—such as their ability to sustain attention and their initial understanding of emotions—may affect the degree to which adults talk about emotion with them. For instance, in one study, parents engaged in more conversations about emotional past events with their 5- and 6-year-olds if the children were relatively well regulated and if their expression of negative emotions such as anger, sadness, or fear was consistent with what their parents expected from a child of their age (Bird, Reese, & Tripp, 2006). In another study, researchers at Mount Saint Vincent University in Halifax found that parents' emotional style (i.e., whether they took more of a coaching approach versus a dismissive approach) and children's temperament together predicted children's coping styles (Lagacé-Séguin & Gionet, 2009).

REVIEW QUESTION

In what ways did emotion coaching and emotion socialization influence your early emotional development? ■

Temperament

Although the overall development of emotions and emotion regulation capabilities is roughly similar for most children, there are also very large individual differences in children's emotional functioning. Some infants and children are relatively mellow: they do not become upset easily, and they usually do not have difficulty calming down when they are upset. Other children are quite emotional: they get upset quickly and intensely, and their negative emotion persists for a long time. Moreover, children differ in their timidity, in their expression of emotions, and in the ways they deal with their emotions. Compare these two 3-year-old children, Maria and Bruce, as they react to Teri, an adult female stranger:

> When Teri walks over to Maria and starts to talk with her, Maria smiles and is eager to show Teri what she is doing. When Teri asks Maria if she would like to go down the hall to the play room (where experiments are conducted), Maria jumps up and takes Teri's hand.
>
> In contrast, when Teri walks over to Bruce, Bruce turns away. He doesn't talk to her and averts his eyes. When Teri asks him if he wants to play a game, Bruce moves away, looks timid, and softly says "no."
>
> (N. Eisenberg, laboratory observations)

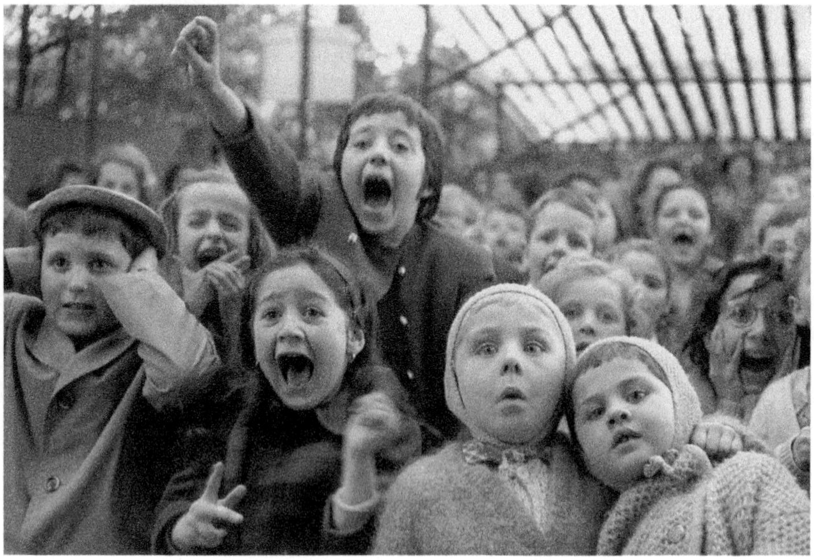

Due partly to variations in temperament, children often show very different reactions to the same situation.

Temperament in Infancy and Toddlerhood

Such differences in how individual children react to similar situations led researchers to develop the concept of temperament. **Temperament** refers to individual differences in emotion, activity level, and attention that are exhibited across contexts and that are present from infancy; thus, they are thought to be genetically based (Bornstein et al., 2015). As we will see later, the temperament of any given child is influenced both by his or her genes and by the environment in which he or she lives; therefore, the construct of temperament is highly relevant to our themes of *individual differences* and the role of *nature and nurture* in development.

Alexander Thomas and Stella Chess are pioneers of temperament research (Thomas & Chess, 1977; Thomas, Chess, & Birch, 1968). They began by interviewing a sample of parents, repeatedly and in depth, about their infants' specific behaviours. To reduce the possibility of bias in the parents' reports, the researchers asked that instead of giving interpretive characterizations, such as "he's often cranky" or "she's interested in everything," the parents provide detailed descriptions of their infants' specific behaviours. On the basis of those interviews, nine characteristics of children were identified, including their mood, adaptability, activity level, attention span, and persistence. Further analyzing the interview results in terms of these characteristics, the researchers classified the infants into three groups:

1. *Easy babies* adjusted readily to new situations, quickly established daily routines such as sleeping and eating, and generally were cheerful in mood and easy to calm.
2. *Difficult babies* were slow to adjust to new experiences, tended to react negatively and intensely to novel stimuli and events, and were irregular in their daily routines and bodily functions.
3. *Slow-to-warm-up babies* were somewhat difficult at first but became easier over time as they had repeated contact with new objects, people, and situations.

In the initial study, 40% of the infants were classified as easy, 10% as difficult, and 15% as slow to warm up. The rest did not fit into any single category but rather displayed characteristics of more than one category. Of particular importance, some dimensions of temperament showed relative stability within children over time; temperament in infancy predicted how children were doing years later. For example, "difficult" infants tended to have problems with adjustment at home and at school, whereas few of the "easy" children had such problems.

Measuring Temperament

temperament individual differences in emotion, activity level, and attention that are exhibited across contexts and that are present from infancy and thus thought to be genetically based

Since the groundbreaking efforts of Thomas and Chess, researchers studying temperament no longer group children into categories such as easy, difficult, or slow to warm up, which reflects what is known as a *between-person* approach to understanding development. Rather, researchers now characterize every child along the same set of dimensions of temperament—a *within-person* approach to understanding development. According to this newer approach, every child has some level of each dimension of temperament. Not all researchers agree on exactly how many dimensions of temperament there are; however, one of the leading experts in this area, Mary Rothbart, has identified five key dimensions of temperament: fear, distress/anger/frustration, attention span, activity level, and smiling and laughter (Gartstein & Rothbart, 2003; Rothbart et al., 2001). She has created measures of temperament in both infancy (the Infant Behaviour Questionnaire) and early childhood (the Child Behaviour Questionnaire) that ask parents, teachers, or observers to rate each child along several dimensions of temperament (Gartstein & Rothbart, 2003; Rothbart et al., 2001).

These measures ask parents, teachers, or observers to indicate how well a range of statements describes the target child. The participants are then asked to respond to several items about each dimension of temperament; next, their responses are averaged together so that each child gets a score reflecting how high or low he or she rates on that dimension. Table 10.2 presents examples of these items for each of these two measures of temperament. Ratings of temperament tend to be fairly stable over time and tend to predict later development in areas such as behavioural problems, anxiety disorders, and social competence (Berger, 2011; Rothbart, 2011; Rothbart & Bates, 2006).

In addition to measuring temperament through the use of rating scales, researchers also use physiological measures of emotional reactions to laboratory situations to assess temperament. For example, researchers have found that children with different temperaments exhibit differences in the variability of their heart rates (Kagan & Fox, 2006). Heart-rate variability—how much an individual's heart rate normally fluctuates—is believed to reflect, in part, the way the central nervous system responds to novel situations and the individual's ability to regulate emotion (Porges, 2007). Another commonly used physiological measure of temperament is electroencephalographic recordings (see Chapter 3) of frontal-lobe activity. Activation of the left frontal lobe of the cortex as measured with an electroencephalogram (EEG) has been associated with approach behaviour, positive affect, exploration, and sociability.

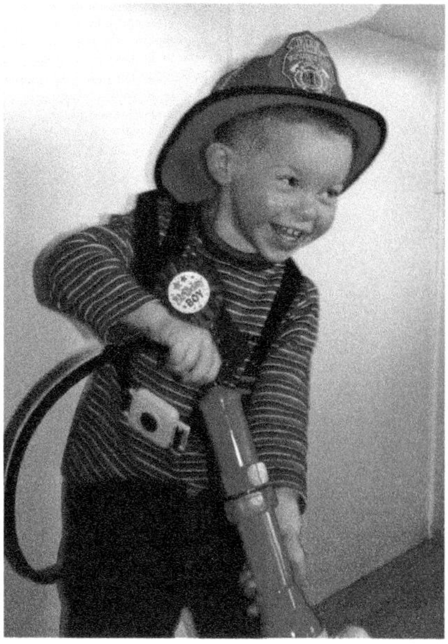

SUSAN GRAHAM

Who could resist this toddler? Children whose temperaments are happy and agreeable are likely to elicit more positive reactions from adults than children who are highly irritable.

TABLE 10.2 Measuring Infant and Child Temperament: The Infant Behaviour Questionnaire and the Child Behaviour Questionnaire

		Infant Behaviour Questionnaire (for ages 0 to 12 months)	Child Behaviour Questionnaire (for ages 3 to 7)
Temperament dimension	**Description**	**Sample items in measure for infants (aged 0 to 12 months), rated from 1 (never) to 7 (always)**	**Sample items in measure for children (aged 3 to 7), rated from 1 (extremely untrue of your child) to 7 (extremely true of your child)**
Fear	Tendency to experience unease, worry, or nervousness to novel or potentially threatening situations	"How often during the last week did the baby startle to a sudden or loud noise?"	"My child is not afraid of large dogs and/or other animals" (reversed for scoring).
Distress at limitations (infant) or anger/frustration (in childhood)	Negative emotional response related to having ongoing task interrupted or blocked	"When placed on his/her back, how often did the baby fuss or protest?"	"My child has temper tantrums when s/he doesn't get what s/he wants."
Attention span	Attention to an object or task for an extended period of time	"How often during the last week did the baby stare at a mobile, crib bumper, or picture for 5 minutes or longer?"	"When picking up toys or other jobs, my child usually keeps at the task until it's done."
Activity level	Rate and extent of gross motor body movements	"When put into the bath water, how often did the baby splash or kick?"	"My child seems always in a big hurry to get from one place to another."
Smiling and laughter	Positive emotional response to a change in the intensity, complexity, or incongruity of a stimulus	"How often during the last week did the baby smile or laugh when given a toy?"	"My child laughs a lot at jokes and silly happenings."

Information from the Revised Infant Behaviour Questionnaire (Gartstein & Rothbart, 2003) and the Child Behaviour Questionnaire (Rothbart et al., 2001).

In contrast, activation of the right frontal lobe has been linked to withdrawal, a state of uncertainty, fear, and anxiety (Kagan & Fox, 2006). When confronted with novel stimuli, situations, or challenges, infants and children who show greater right frontal activation on the EEG are more likely to react with anxiety and avoidance (Kagan & Fox, 2006), whereas individuals who show left frontal activation are more likely to exhibit a relaxed, often happy mood and an eagerness to engage in new experiences or challenges (Kagan & Fox, 2006; White et al., 2012).

The key advantage of parents' reports of temperament is that parents have extensive knowledge of their children's behaviour in many different situations. One important disadvantage of this method is that parents may not always be objective in their observations, as suggested by the fact that their reports sometimes do not correspond with what is found using laboratory measures (Rothbart & Bates, 2006). Another disadvantage is that many parents do not have wide knowledge of other children's behaviour to use as a basis for comparison when reporting on their own children; what is irritability to some parents, for example, may be near-placidness to others.

In contrast, the key advantage of laboratory observational data is that such data are less likely to be biased than is an adult's personal view of the child. A key disadvantage is that children's behaviour usually is observed in only a limited set of circumstances, and thus lab-based measures of temperament may not have external validity (see Chapter 1). Consequently, laboratory observational measures may reflect a child's mood or behaviour at a given moment, in a particular context, rather than the totality of the child's temperament. No measure of temperament is perfect, and it is prudent to assess temperament using a variety of different methods (Rothbart & Bates, 2006).

Temperament is considered to be relatively consistent across time and across situations. Using parents' ratings on the Infant Behaviour Questionnaire, one study found that an infant's level on each dimension of temperament is considerably stable across the first year of life but that there is some evidence of change over time as well (Bornstein et al., 2015). Across early childhood, children who are prone to more anger and distress than their peers at age 3 tend to be more angry and distressed than their peers at ages 6 and 8 (Rothbart, Derryberry, & Hershey, 2000); those prone to display happiness remain relatively happy across the same age range (Durbin et al., 2007; Sallquist et al., 2009). But this is not to say that temperament is entirely immutable; it can and does change over time. Children aged 3 to 6 have much more stable temperaments than do children aged 0 to 3 (Roberts & DelVecchio, 2000). There is now evidence that some aspects of temperament may not emerge until childhood or adolescence and may change considerably at different ages (Saudino & Wang, 2012; Shiner et al., 2012). As we discussed in Chapter 3, genes switch on and off throughout development, and this process impacts when and how temperament and the behaviours that relate to it are expressed (Saudino & Wang, 2012).

Determinants of Temperament

Temperament is believed to have a strong basis in biology and genetics (Saudino & Wang, 2012). Evidence for a genetic component to temperament comes from dozens of studies. For example, identical twins are more similar to each other in these aspects of their emotion and regulation than are fraternal twins (Rasbash et al., 2011; Saudino & Wang, 2012). Recent studies have shown connections between an individual's genes and aspects of temperament such as self-regulatory capacity (Depue & Fu, 2012; Goldsmith, Pollak, & Davidson, 2008; Saudino & Wang, 2012). For example, genes related to the functioning of dopamine and other neurotransmitters that affect voluntary attentional processes (executive attention) appear to be especially relevant for self-regulation (Posner, Rothbart, & Sheese, 2007).

Although genes are clearly important for temperament, the environment plays a role as well, even from before birth. In Chapter 2, we learned about teratogens, which are external agents that can cause birth defects in a fetus. Teratogens such as nutritional deficiencies, exposure to cocaine, or maternal stress and anxiety during pregnancy have each been found to predict infants' and young children's temperament-based abilities to regulate their attention and behaviour (Dennis et al., 2006; Huizink, 2008, 2012).

As children age, the behaviours of their parents become a strong influence on temperament. Children who grow up in home environments that are harsh or unstable tend to have problems with self-regulation and the expression of emotion (Lewis et al., 2007). Warm and responsive parenting can have the opposite effect; in a twin study, the twin who received more warm and responsive parenting had fewer emotional problems and exhibited more positive affect and more prosocial behaviours than the twin sibling (Deater-Deckard et al., 2001).

Yet, as suggested by the *active child* theme, children's temperamental characteristics can affect their environments and particularly their parents' behaviours (Belsky, Bakermans-Kranenburg, & van IJzendoorn, 2007; E. H. Lee et al., 2013). For example, parents of angry, unregulated children may eventually become less patient and more punitive with their children; in turn, this intensification of discipline may cause their children to become even more angry and unregulated. Alternatively, children who are high in regulation and in sociability may elicit more warmth from parents, which in turn predicts continued regulation and sociability in children. Thus, temperament plays a role in the development of children's social and psychological adjustment, but that role is complex and varies as a function of the child's social environment and the degree to which a child represents a challenge to the parent (Ganiban et al., 2011).

To determine whether genes or the environment have more influence over temperament, a group of researchers (Lemery-Chalfant et al., 2013) used a twin study, which is a research design we learned about in Chapter 3. In this study, parents of 807 pairs of twins (301 MZ [monozygotic, or identical], 263 same-sex DZ [dizygotic, or fraternal], and 243 opposite-sex DZ) reported on both of their children's temperaments, and then statistical analyses were used to determine how similar the twins were. If MZ twins in the same home environment were more similar than DZ twins who shared the same home environment, then they would conclude that temperament is more determined by genes than the environment.

Indeed, that is what they found: a large portion of the variance in three aspects of temperament (effortful control, negative affectivity, and extraversion) was explained by heritability (Lemery-Chalfant et al., 2013). They also found that key aspects of the home environments — namely how chaotic and unsafe they were — had a heritable component as well: parents' temperaments affected children both directly through genetic transmission and indirectly through the home environment they created (Lemery-Chalfant et al., 2013). This latter contribution of genes to children's temperament is referred to as

goodness of fit the degree to which an individual's temperament is compatible with the demands and expectations of his or her social environment

differential susceptibility a circumstance in which the same temperament characteristic that puts some children at high risk for negative outcomes when exposed to a harsh home environment also causes them to blossom when their home environment is positive

a passive gene–environment correlation, a concept discussed in Chapter 8 with regard to the heritability of intelligence. Undoubtedly, a combination of genetic and environmental factors jointly contributes to individual differences in children's emotions and related behaviours (Rasbash et al., 2011; Saudino & Wang, 2012).

How Temperament Fits with Environment

Children with different temperaments will have different reactions to the same situation, and thus some situations are better suited for certain temperaments. Imagine two 4-year-old boys who arrive at a loud and chaotic birthday party. The child who has a high activity level will immediately join in, whereas the child high in fearfulness will observe from the perimeter before finding a way to play with the other children. The high-activity child is in his element; the high-fearfulness child is decidedly not. How well a child's temperament matches the demands of a particular context is called **goodness of fit.**

The family provides arguably the most important context for issues related to goodness of fit. Research indicates that children who are impulsive or low in emotion regulation seem to have more problems and are less sympathetic to others if exposed to hostile, intrusive, and/or negative parenting rather than to supportive parenting (Hastings & De, 2008; Kiff, Lengua, & Zalewski, 2011; Lengua et al., 2008). Similarly, children prone to emotions such as anger are more likely to have behavioural problems such as aggression if exposed to hostile parenting or low levels of positive parenting (Bates, Schermerhorn, & Petersen, 2012). A Canadian study found that children whose parents rated them as high in shyness had fewer problems with peers and fewer emotional problems if their mothers were high in warmth (Coplan, Arbeau, & Armer, 2008).

It is important to note, however, that some children's temperaments make them highly reactive to both positive and negative family environments. These children exhibit a characteristic known as **differential susceptibility,** which means that the same temperament characteristic that puts some children at high risk for negative outcomes when exposed to a harsh home environment also leads them to blossom when their home environments are positive (Belsky & Pluess, 2009). For example, children with impulsive temperaments have been found to exhibit high levels of behaviour problems in adolescence if they are raised in harsh family environments; but if raised in positive family environments, they exhibit low levels of behaviour problems (Rioux et al., 2016b).

Children with such susceptible, or highly responsive, temperaments have been described as "orchids" who thrive when conditions are good but wither when they are bad. In contrast, children who are less sensitive to their environments and do well in all but the most high-risk environments are thought of as "dandelions" (Boyce & Ellis, 2005). Although evidence for differential susceptibility has been found in several longitudinal studies, including the Québec Longitudinal Study of Child Development (Rioux et al., 2016a), it is also the case that all children benefit from positive parenting environments, regardless of whether their genetic and temperamental characteristics make them likely to be reactive to their environments (Belsky et al., 2015).

Some children are highly reactive to their environments, such that the same temperament characteristics that lead to behavioural issues for a child exposed to a negative family environment might flourish in a supportive, positive one.

PHOTO AND CO/GETTY IMAGES

REVIEW QUESTION

The interplay of nature and nurture in the expression of temperament is evident when considering concepts like goodness of fit and differential susceptibility. How might these concepts inform interventions designed to improve self-regulation and adjustment? ■

mental health children's sense of well-being both internally, such as in their emotions and stress levels, and externally, such as in their relationships with family members and peers

stress a physiological reaction to some change or threat in the environment

Mental Health, Stress, and Internalizing Mental Disorders

Mental health is an important component of emotional development. It reflects children's sense of well-being both internally, such as in their emotions and stress levels, and externally, such as in their relationships with family members and peers. Mental health is a continuum, and children (or adults, of course) can be at the high end one day but at the low end another. An individual's mental health becomes a source of concern if one spends many days on the low end of the continuum. Mental health is promoted when children have safe and healthy environments as well as supportive and nurturing caregivers. The absence of one or both of these factors increases the risk of the development of stress and related mental health disorders, as do certain genetic predispositions.

Stress

When children are in situations or environments that they perceive to be frightening, threatening, or overwhelming, they can experience **stress**—a physiological reaction to some change or threat in the environment. The stress response involves increased heart rate, secretion of stress hormones, increased flow of blood to the brain, and a heightened feeling of vigilance and fear (Shonkoff, Boyce, & McEwen, 2009). Each of these physiological reactions underlies the body's "fight or flight" response to a threat in the environment. In reaction to a challenging situation, the adrenal cortex secretes steroid hormones such as cortisol, which helps to activate energy reserves (Danese & McEwen, 2012).

Stress can be a common experience in childhood and adolescence, when the pressures of school, extracurricular activities, family obligations, and peer relationships may be overwhelming at times. In most cases, periodic stress serves the beneficial and adaptive function of mobilizing the child to take actions to reduce or manage exposure to the stimulus in the environment that is provoking the anxiety. For example, a stress response can prompt a child to flee a dangerous situation or to focus and work hard for an important test. Children can learn how to cope with the periodic stress if stress is not constant or if they have an adult who can provide support and help them manage the stress. Stress can become problematic when children experience it repeatedly. (See Box 10.3 for a more in-depth discussion of toxic stress.)

Sometimes a single major negative event can trigger a form of stress known as *traumatic stress,* which is severe stress brought on by a sudden catastrophic event. Children and adolescents who are directly exposed to such events, such as hurricanes or terrorist attacks, tend to experience unusually high levels of emotions such as fear and anxiety and to experience mood disorders such as depression and posttraumatic stress disorder (Gershoff, Aber et al., 2010; Weems et al., 2010).

Although some stress can be adaptive, too much stress can interfere with children's daily activities and relationships.

LEAH-ANNE THOMPSON/SHUTTERSTOCK

BOX 10.3 APPLICATIONS Toxic Stress and Adverse Childhood Experiences

Children who experience chronic high levels of stress and who lack supportive adults to help mitigate the effects are said to experience **toxic stress** (Shonkoff et al., 2012). When a child's stress response system is overworked by toxic stress, regions of the brain that regulate fear (e.g., amygdala, hippocampus) become overloaded and suffer atrophying of neuron dendrites and shrinkage (Danese & McEwen, 2012). Some changes are permanent and may lead to long-term changes both in responses to stress and in stress-related chronic disease in adulthood (Shonkoff et al., 2012).

A landmark study known as the Adverse Childhood Experiences Study has linked potential sources of toxic stress in childhood—including physical or emotional abuse, neglect, poverty and material deprivation, parental divorce, exposure to substance abuse, exposure to violence, and death of a parent—to later mental and physical health in adulthood. In this study, more than 17,000 adult participants indicated their exposure to various **adverse childhood experiences** (or ACEs), which were summed to give each participant an ACE score. Nearly 64% of the participants had at least one ACE, and 12.5% had an ACE score of 4 or higher (Anda et al., 2006). Physical abuse was the most common ACE (28%), followed by having a household member with a substance abuse problem (27%) and having parents who separated or divorced (23%; see the table). Other ACE categories in this study include sexual abuse (21%), household member with mental illness (19%), exposure to violence against the mother (13%), emotional abuse (11%), and household member who was incarcerated (5%).

An important finding of the study was that the more ACEs the participants had experienced, the greater their risk of having high levels of stress, depression, anxiety, severe obesity, smoking, and alcoholism. As shown in the figure, the relationship between ACEs and problems in adulthood followed a clear and consistent pattern: as the number of ACEs increased, the likelihood of experiencing a mental or physical health problem increased. This pattern is consistent regardless of the participant's gender, race, or level of education. The fact that ACEs are linked with increased high stress in adulthood suggests that experiences of toxic stress in childhood may prime children to experience high levels of stress in adulthood as well, which in turn lead to physical health problems such as severe obesity. Recent Canadian research shows ACEs can influence the next generation as well: a large study of 1994 women in Alberta showed that mothers who reported three or more ACEs had children with more anxiety and behaviour problems at age 3 (McDonald et al., 2019).

There is some evidence that exposure to non-stressful environments and treatment can reverse some of the harmful effects of toxic stress. For example, children who had been maltreated by their families but were removed to foster-care homes that provided consistent discipline and positive reinforcement showed normalization of levels of the stress hormone cortisol and reduction in behaviour problems (Fisher et al., 2000). Trauma-focused mental health interventions such as cognitive behavioural therapy, play therapy, multisystemic therapy, and parent–child interaction therapy are also effective in helping victims of maltreatment (Saunders, Berliner, & Hanson, 2004).

Of course, public health research is also focused on preventing the events or circumstances that trigger toxic stress in the first place. The American Academy of Pediatrics (AAP) has called for public policies and community-based programs aimed at reducing toxic stress exposure in children's lives (Shonkoff et al., 2012). Maltreatment ACEs in particular could be prevented through individual and community-wide parenting education and alternatives to harsh parenting (Prinz et al., 2009). The AAP's Early Brain and Child Development initiative seeks to focus the attention of pediatricians and other public health workers on understanding, recognizing, and preventing toxic stress (American Academy of Pediatrics, 2016). In Canada, the Alberta Family Wellness Initiative, a program funded by the Palix Foundation, brings together researchers, policymakers, healthcare professionals, and members of the community to help integrate research on the lifelong effects of early experiences and toxic stress on mental health, addiction, and other health outcomes with practice and policy. Research on toxic stress is just beginning, and as more interventions are tested, experts will know more about how to treat and prevent toxic stress.

Adverse Childhood Experience (ACE) Categories, Definitions, and Prevalence in a Sample of 17,337 Adults

Category	Prevalence
Emotional abuse	11%
Physical abuse	28%
Sexual abuse	21%
Someone in household engaged in substance abuse	27%
Someone in household had mental illness	19%
Mother was treated violently	13%
Someone in household was incarcerated	5%
Parents were separated or divorced	23%

Source: Data from Table 1 of Anda et al. (2006).

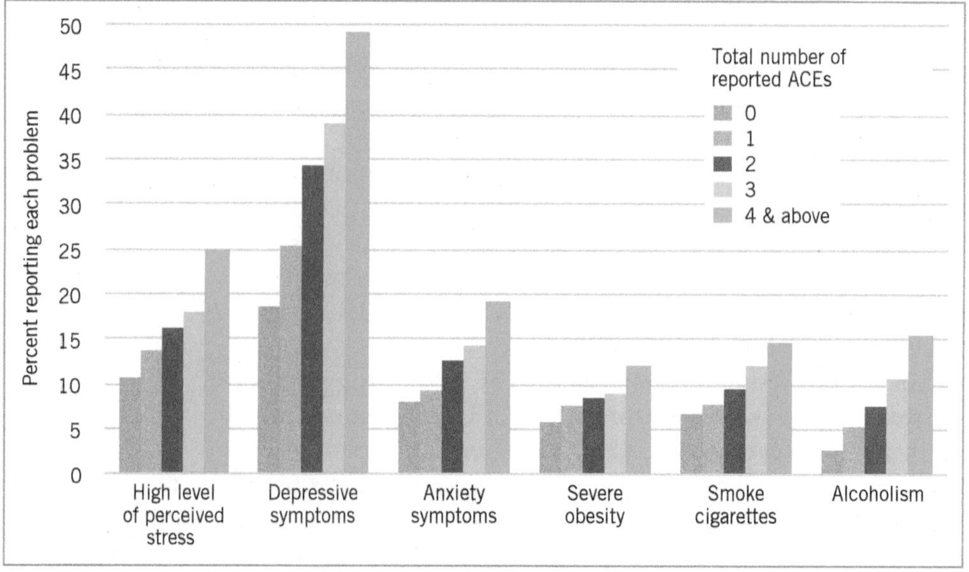

ACEs and adult health The more ACEs adults recall from their childhoods, the more mental, physical, and behavioural health problems they report. (Data from Anda et al., 2006)

Internalizing Mental Disorders

Exposure in childhood to repeated or traumatic stress can lead to the development of **mental disorders,** which are chronic, negative emotional reactions to aspects of the environment or to social relationships that affect daily life and may persist throughout childhood and into adulthood (Perou et al., 2013). Psychologists have identified several categories of mental disorders, including psychotic disorders, eating disorders, personality disorders, and behaviour disorders. In this section, we will focus on internalizing mental disorders, which include depression and anxiety disorders. Because they involve internal emotional states, internalizing mental health disorders are often difficult to identify and diagnose compared with behaviour disorders (also called externalizing disorders), which manifest in disruptive or aggressive actions. (Behaviour disorders will be discussed in Chapter 14.)

As we will see, there is no single pathway to a disorder; rather, the prediction of disorders follows a concept known as **equifinality,** which means that various factors (e.g., genetic predisposition, a chaotic home environment, a traumatic event) can each lead to the same mental disorder. Yet disorders can also exhibit a quality known as **multifinality,** which refers to the fact that certain risk factors do not always lead to a disorder (Hinshaw, 2015; Masten & Cicchetti, 2010). For example, although children who have been maltreated are twice as likely as non-maltreated children to develop depression or anxiety in adolescence or young adulthood (Scott, Smith, & Ellis, 2010), not every maltreated child develops a disorder.

toxic stress the experience of overwhelming levels of stress without support from adults to help mitigate the effects of that stress

adverse childhood experiences (ACEs) traumatic childhood experiences, such as abuse, neglect, violence exposure, or death of a parent, that are linked to mental and physical health problems later in life

mental disorder a state of having problems with emotional reactions to the environment and with social relationships in ways that affect daily life

equifinality the concept that various causes can lead to the same mental disorder

multifinality the concept that certain risk factors do not always lead to a mental disorder

depression a mental disorder that involves a sad or irritable mood along with physical and cognitive changes that interfere with daily life

Depression

According to the *Diagnostic and Statistical Manual of Mental Disorders* (DSM-5), the definitive clinical guide for diagnosing mental disorders, **depression** is a mental disorder that involves a sad or irritable mood along with physical and cognitive changes that affect the child's or adolescent's ability to behave and interact in a normal way (American Psychiatric Association, 2013). In order to be diagnosed with depression, a child or an adolescent must report feeling, or be observed by their parents to feel, sad or irritable for a period of 2 weeks, and the individual must exhibit physical and cognitive symptoms such as difficulties sleeping (either too much or too little), significant changes in weight (either loss or gain), inability to concentrate, or loss of interest in activities (American Psychiatric Association, 2013). Some children and adolescents with depression also think about or even attempt suicide.

A review of research conducted in 27 different countries (including Canada) determined that 3% of children and adolescents meet criteria for depression (Polanczyk et al., 2015). In 2017, in Canada specifically, 4.5% of children aged 12 to 19 years reported having been diagnosed with a mood disorder (which includes major depression, bipolar disorder, or dysthymia, a milder form of depression; Statistics Canada, 2019). Risk of depression increases as children develop into adolescence, and a second uptick in risk occurs when they age into young adulthood (Avenevoli et al., 2015; Costello, Copeland, & Angold, 2011). Girls are 2 to 3 times as likely as boys to develop depression (Avenevoli et al., 2015), a fact that is discussed in depth in Box 10.4.

Psychological Disorders in Adolescence

AILA IMAGES/SHUTTERSTOCK

Both *nature* and *nurture* influence whether a child experiences depression. On the side of nature, children and adolescents with depression tend to have elevated levels of the stress hormone cortisol and to exhibit differences in brain structure and function, compared with their peers who are not depressed (Klein et al., 2013). Depression also has a genetic component: it often runs in families. The heritability

BOX 10.4 INDIVIDUAL DIFFERENCES Gender Differences in Adolescent Depression

One of the most striking features of adolescent depression is the gender-related differences in its occurrence (Costello et al., 2008; Twenge & Nolen-Hoeksema, 2002). Although the chance of depression at some point in their lifetime increases across adolescence for both boys and girls in the United States, the increase is twice as fast for girls (Hankin et al., 2015; see the figure). Similar gender differences in the patterns of adolescent depression have been found in Canada, Great Britain, and New Zealand (Galambos, Leadbeater, & Barker, 2004; Hankin et al., 1998; Wade, Cairney, & Pevalin, 2002).

One reason for these gender differences is that girls tend to express more internalizing emotions, such as sadness and anxiety, than do boys (Chaplin & Aldao, 2013). Another reason is that the biological changes brought on by puberty tend to be more difficult for girls and may contribute to girls' vulnerability (Hilt & Nolen-Hoeksema, 2009). Girls are more affected by chronic stress from social interactions with peers (e.g., lack of friendships or conflict with friends), which in turn predicts depressive symptoms (Hankin et al., 2015). In addition, adolescent girls in North America also tend to report greater dissatisfaction with their bodies than boys report with theirs. This dissatisfaction, fueled by a cultural obsession with an "ideal" body type attainable by only a few, seems to contribute substantially to low self-esteem and depression in adolescent girls (Compian, Gowen, & Hayward, 2004; Hankin & Abramson, 1999; Harter, 2006; Wichstrom, 1999).

Also appearing to contribute to the higher rates of depression for adolescent girls is the fact that they, more than their male peers, are prone to repeatedly focus on causes, consequences, and symptoms of their sadness or frustration ("I'm so fat" or "I'm so tired") and on the meaning of their distress ("What's wrong with my life?") without engaging in efforts to remedy their situation (Hankin, Stone, & Wright, 2010). The more adolescents engage in such thinking about stress events, called **rumination,** the more likely they are to be depressed; girls are more likely to engage in rumination in response to stress than boys (Abela et al., 2012; Nolen-Hoeksema, 2012). Moreover, **co-rumination**—that is, extensively and almost exclusively discussing and self-disclosing emotional problems with another person, usually a peer (Rose, 2002)—is more common for girls and accounts for much of the gender difference in depression (Hankin et al., 2010; Schwartz-Mette & Rose, 2012; Stone et al., 2011).

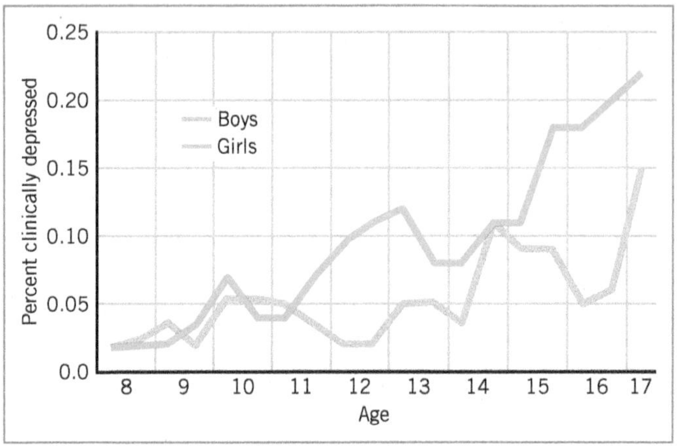

Gender differences in adolescent depression Beginning around age 11, boys and girls diverge dramatically in their risk for becoming clinically depressed. (Data from Hankin et al., 2015)

rumination the act of focusing on one's own negative emotions and negative self-appraisals and on their causes and consequences, without engaging in efforts to improve one's situation

co-rumination extensively discussing and self-disclosing emotional problems with another person

of depression is 40%; that is, an individual's genetic makeup explains 40% of the likelihood that he or she will experience depression (American Psychiatric Association, 2013; see Chapter 3 for a more detailed discussion of heritability).

On the nurture side, a variety of family factors likely also contribute to depression in youth. In particular, low levels of parental sensitivity, support, or acceptance and high levels of parental negativity have each been linked with higher levels of depressive symptoms in children (Auerbach et al., 2011; Schwartz et al., 2012). Depressed parents are more likely than nondepressed parents to be insensitive and disengaged, yielding an environmental pathway through which parent depression increases the likelihood of child depression (Belsky, Schlomer, & Ellis, 2012; Garber & Cole, 2010). Adverse childhood experiences, such as those discussed in Box 10.3, are also risk factors for depression, as are stressful life events (American Psychiatric Association, 2013).

Depression also has a cognitive component. Depressed children and adolescents tend to have unrealistic expectations about social relationships and see themselves, rather than external or chance events, as causing negative events (Klein et al., 2013). Depressed individuals also tend to ruminate extensively about negative events in their lives (Abela et al., 2012; Nolen-Hoeksema, 2012; see Box 10.4). Research to date has not yet been able to determine whether these cognitive factors precede depression or are consequences of it.

Depressed children and adolescents tend to have problems in their relationships with their peers, but there is evidence that such problems are both a cause and an outcome of depression. For example, the more children are victimized by their peers, the more likely they are to develop depression (Witvliet, Olthof et al., 2010), but it is also true that children with depression are more likely to be victimized by their peers (Kochel, Ladd, & Rudolph, 2012; Tran, Cole, & Weiss, 2012). Taken together, these findings suggest a vicious cycle whereby the presence of either depression or victimization increases the chances that the other will occur.

anxiety disorders a set of mental disorders that involve the inability to regulate fear and worry

Anxiety Disorders

Anxiety disorders involve the inability to regulate the emotions fear and worry (Weems & Silverman, 2013) such that the individual experiences excessive and uncontrollable fear of real or perceived threats and worries about future threats (American Psychiatric Association, 2013). Unlike the temporary fear or anxiety that an individual may feel in response to a threat in the environment, anxiety disorders manifest as intense fear or anxiety that lasts days or even months and impairs the individual's ability to interact with others or to concentrate on tasks (Weems & Silverman, 2013). Anxiety disorders are believed to involve overactivation of areas of the brain associated with reaction to threat, including the amygdala and hippocampus brain structures, as well as the sympathetic nervous system (Weems & Silverman, 2013).

In young children, the most common anxiety disorder is separation anxiety disorder, which involves persistent fear about being separated from a caregiver or about a caregiver being in danger (American Psychiatric Association, 2013). As noted earlier in this chapter, some separation anxiety is normative in young children and, as will be discussed in Chapter 11, is often seen in the positive development of secure attachment with caregivers. However, if the separation anxiety becomes severe and persistent and interferes with behaviour, then it is considered a disorder. Children with anxiety disorder may be described by adults as intrusive and demanding of constant attention (American Psychiatric Association, 2013). Children and adolescents with anxiety disorder may also suffer from panic attacks, which are sudden and intense surges of fear and discomfort, or from phobias about certain animals or certain social situations (American Psychiatric Association, 2013).

Around the world, 7% of children and adolescents meet criteria for anxiety disorder (Polanczyk et al., 2015). Over the course of development from childhood to adolescence and into young adulthood, there is an increase in several types of anxiety disorder, namely panic disorder and agoraphobia (the fear of open or public spaces), but a decrease in separation anxiety disorder and in other phobias (Costello et al., 2011). Anxiety disorder typically develops in childhood and can persist into adulthood if not treated (American Psychiatric Association, 2013).

Like depression, both genetic (*nature*) and environmental (*nurture*) factors contribute to the onset of anxiety disorder. About one-third of the variance in anxiety is thought to be heritable, with some of that heritability coming from temperament: children who have fearful or inhibited temperaments are more likely than those without such temperaments to experience problems with anxiety (Weems & Silverman, 2013). Yet the environment also plays an important role. Children can come to associate certain people or events with fear and anxiety, even when fear and anxiety are not warranted. Such association may come about either through conditioning (e.g., a child is bitten by a dog and develops a strong fear of dogs), through observation (e.g., a child's mother is afraid of dogs, and the child adopts that same fear), or through instruction (e.g., hearing about a rabid dog terrorizing a neighbourhood) (Weems & Silverman, 2013). Parenting behaviour has also been implicated as a precursor of children's anxiety disorders. Parents' overprotective, overinvolved, and controlling

KATARZYNABIALASIEWICZ/GETTY IMAGES

Children with internalizing mental disorders have been shown to benefit from psychotherapy. (Photo is being used for illustrative purposes only; person depicted in photo is a model.)

behaviours have been linked to increased anxiety in children (Möller et al., 2016). For example, a representative study of Québec children and their mothers found that overprotective behaviours combined with maternal depression predicted increased anxiety in children (Laurin et al., 2015).

Treatment of Internalizing Mental Disorders

Drug therapy is a common treatment for depression in children and adolescents. A recent report indicated that 7% of children and youth living in Western Canada were prescribed at least one medication for mood or anxiety disorders (Canadian Institute for Health Information, 2016). The drugs typically used to treat children and adolescents are serotonin reuptake inhibitors, or SRIs (Maughan, Collishaw, & Stringaris, 2013). Significant concerns have been raised about the possibility that antidepressants may increase the risk of suicidal thinking and suicidal behaviour among some adolescents (Calati et al., 2011).

A psychotherapeutic approach known as cognitive behavioural therapy (CBT) has been found to be very effective in treating both depression and anxiety in children. In CBT, children learn to recognize when they are having maladaptive thoughts and learn ways to actively modify those thoughts and their reactions to them (Hofmann et al., 2012). CBT has been found to be more effective at reducing anxiety symptoms than other forms of treatment (Hofmann et al., 2012; Silk et al., 2016). CBT is as effective at treating depression as drug therapy, and the combination of CBT and drug therapy can be particularly effective in reducing depressive symptoms (Hofmann et al., 2012).

Although effective therapies exist for both depression and anxiety, unfortunately many children and adolescents with these disorders do not receive treatment. In Canada, wait times to see mental health specialists are a significant barrier to treatment. For example, children in Ontario waited about three months to see a physician for mental health services (MHASEF Research Team, 2015). In British Columbia, waitlists of six months or more for assessments by psychiatry or child and youth mental health clinicians are common (Turpel-Lafond, 2013). In Canada and in the United States, children living in disadvantaged families are also less likely to receive services or treatment, despite having a higher rate of diagnosed mental disorders than their advantaged peers (MHASEF Research Team, 2015; Bringewatt & Gershoff, 2010). In addition, children in rural and remote areas of Canada have less access to mental healthcare in their communities and tend to rely on emergency department hospital services instead (Canadian Institute for Health Information, 2016).

The good news is that children and youth with mental health problems as a result of exposure to ACEs, but who receive services experience improvements in several domains, including decreases in their behaviour problems and internalizing problems, as well as improvements in school attendance and school performance (Substance Abuse and Mental Health Services Administration, 2018).

REVIEW QUESTION

Based on your understanding of the genetic, biological, and sociocultural factors influencing emotional development, how would you approach interventions and treatments to address some of the mental health issues discussed in this section? ■

CHAPTER SUMMARY

The Development of Emotions

- Discrete-emotions theorists believe that a set of biological and neurological reactions to the environment have evolved so that humans experience a core set of basic emotions that are universal across all human cultures. In contrast, proponents of the functionalist perspective believe that emotions reflect what individuals are trying to do in specific situations—that is, their concerns and goals at the moment—and that there is not a set of innate, discrete emotions but rather that there are many emotions based on people's many different interactions with the social world. As with several other aspects of development, there is evidence to support both the *nature* (discrete emotions) and *nurture* (functionalist) interpretations of emotion.
- Researchers have identified six basic emotions: happiness, fear, anger, sadness, surprise, and disgust. Each of these emotions can be reliably identified in infants, and each is thought to play an important role in both survival and social communication.
- Emotions undergo change in the early months and years of life. Smiles become social around the second month of life, and what makes children smile and laugh changes with cognitive development.
- Fear appears by 7 months of age, such as when infants become distressed in the presence of strangers. At around 8 months of age, infants display stranger anxiety and begin to exhibit separation anxiety when separated from their parents.
- Infants begin expressing anger and frustration by 4 months of age and peak in their likelihood of responding with anger by 24 months of age. As they age, children increasingly match their anger to the situation, getting angrier if an act was intentional than if it was unintentional.
- Sadness, surprise, and disgust each appear in the first year as well. How often and to what stimuli children express each of these emotions is closely tied to their home and cultural environment.
- The self-conscious emotions—guilt, shame, jealousy, empathy, pride, and embarrassment—emerge in the second year of life. Their emergence is tied in part to the development of a rudimentary sense of self and to an appreciation of others' reactions to the self.

Understanding Emotions

- An important aspect of emotional development is children's understanding of different types of emotion, what they mean, and what events cause them. These skills are important for interacting successfully with others in their environments. By 12 months of age, infants exhibit social referencing.
- By age 3, children demonstrate a rudimentary ability to use words to label facial expressions.
- Children's understanding of the situations that cause emotions, display rules, and the complexities of emotional experience increases in the preschool and elementary school years.

Emotion Regulation

- Emotion regulation involves a set of both conscious and unconscious processes used to both monitor and modulate emotional experiences and expressions. Emotion regulation develops gradually over the course of childhood and paves the way for success both in social interactions and in academic settings.
- Newborns are not able to regulate their own emotions and must rely on adults to manage their emotions through a process called co-regulation. However, beginning after the fifth month, infants can engage in self-comforting and self-distraction behaviours when they are in stressful situations. Improvements in children's regulatory capacities are based on increases in both their cognitive development and their ability to control their own bodies, as well as on changes in others' expectations of them.
- Emotion regulation is generally associated with high social competence and low problem behaviour.

The Role of Family in Emotional Development

- Children's emotional development is affected indirectly by the quality of their early social relationships and by their parents' own expressions of emotion.
- Infants have a strong negative reaction when their mothers do not react emotionally to them, as is demonstrated in still-face experiments.
- Parents engage in active emotion socialization to teach children about the appropriateness of emotion expression and about circumstances that require emotion regulation.
- Cultural factors have been shown to influence what emotions parents encourage their children to express, and certain emotions are more encouraged or discouraged in some cultures than others.

Temperament

- Temperament—individual differences in emotion, activity level, and attention exhibited across contexts—is relatively stable but can undergo some change over time.
- Temperament can be measured through laboratory assessments or through parent reports; both strategies have strengths and weaknesses.
- Temperament is thought to be determined by both genetic and environmental factors.
- Children do best when there is high goodness of fit between their temperament and their environments.
- Some children experience differential susceptibility, such that they do very poorly in harsh conditions but very well in enriched conditions.

Mental Health, Stress, and Internalizing Mental Disorders

- Mental health involves children's sense of well-being both internally, such as in their emotions and stress levels, and externally, such as in their relationships with family members and peers.
- Stress, although adaptive and beneficial in short doses as a means of organizing a response to a threatening event, can be problematic when experienced repeatedly over long periods or at toxic levels.
- Children who have difficulties with their emotional reactions to their environments are said to have a mental disorder. The same mental disorder can be caused by different risks across different people (equifinality); however, the presence of a risk factor does not always lead to a disorder (multifinality).
- Three percent of all children and adolescents around the world experience depression, which involves a combination of sad or irritable mood with physiological and cognitive changes affecting one's ability to conduct normal interactions. Depression appears to have both biological and environmental causes.
- Seven percent of all children have an anxiety disorder, which involves excessive and uncontrollable fear of or worry about real or perceived threats. Anxiety is typically manifested as separation anxiety disorder in early childhood and as panic disorder and agoraphobia in later childhood and adolescence.
- Both depression and anxiety disorders can be successfully treated through psychotherapy, drug treatment, or a combination of both.

Test Yourself

1. Which of the following statements best summarizes the findings by Mischel and his colleagues from their famous marshmallow test?
   a. The ability to exhibit self-control early in life can predict success later in life.
   b. The ability to experience and express emotion is a result of human evolution.
   c. Individuals experience emotions in order to manage their relationship to their environment.
   d. Infants across all cultures are born with the ability to express the six basic human emotions.
2. Tom is walking down the street and suddenly encounters a dog that is crouched and growling. Tom begins to perspire, his breathing quickens, and his heart rate increases. This reaction is an example of which component of emotion?
   a. Neural responses
   b. Physiological factors
   c. Subjective feelings
   d. The desire to take action
3. The notion that humans have evolved to experience a basic set of emotions through adaptation to their surroundings is central to which theory?
   a. Functionalist perspective theory
   b. The AFFEX approach
   c. Display rules theory
   d. Discrete emotions theory
4. How do self-conscious emotions differ from the set of basic emotions discussed in this chapter?
   a. Self-conscious emotions are thought to be innate.
   b. Self-conscious emotions tend to occur very early in infancy.
   c. Self-conscious emotions develop after the child has acquired a sense of himself as separate from others.
   d. Self-conscious emotions have a consistently negative effect on development.
5. Based on your understanding of the chapter, how would a 12-month-old respond to a novel stimulus in a given situation if his or her parent expressed positive emotion?
   a. The infant would be likely to stay near his or her parent.
   b. The infant would be likely to move closer to the novel stimulus.
   c. The infant would be likely to stay in between the parent and the novel stimulus.
   d. The infant would be likely to show a fear response and avoid the novel stimulus.
6. ____________ refer(s) to the social and cultural norms related to emotion expression.
   a. Emotion regulation
   b. Temperamental traits
   c. Display rules
   d. Emotional intelligence
7. An infant is startled by a loud noise and begins to cry. Her mother calms her by playing with her and speaking soothingly to her. This interaction is an example of ____________.
   a. co-regulation
   b. self-comforting
   c. emotion socialization
   d. co-rumination
8. A decreased reliance on self-comforting behaviours, an increased ability to inhibit motor behaviour, and an improved ability to distract oneself when distressed all result from developments in ____________.
   a. emotional intelligence
   b. emotion regulation
   c. temperament
   d. social competence

9. Which of the following is *not* one of the five key dimensions of temperament, according to research by Mary Rothbart?
   a. Disgust
   b. Smiling
   c. Attention span
   d. Fear
10. Twin studies conducted by Lemery-Chalfant and colleagues have led to which important conclusion regarding temperament?
    a. Temperament is most strongly affected by environmental factors.
    b. Temperament is completely determined by genetic factors.
    c. Temperament is determined more by genes than by environment.
    d. Genes and environment play equal roles in determining temperament.
11. Researchers conducting Tronick's famous Still-Face Paradigm found that during the distressing still-face episodes, infants spent very little time looking at their mothers. This response is an example of which of the following behaviours?
    a. Anxiety disorder
    b. Self-distraction
    c. Self-comforting
    d. Co-rumination
12. What are the two components of mental health?
    a. Genetics and environment
    b. Physical health and emotional stability
    c. Internal well-being and external relationships
    d. Parents and peers
13. Two 6-year-old boys, Cal and Sam, accompany their class to the library. Sam grabs a book from the shelf and sits quietly to read. Cal is unable to sit still and ends up disrupting other children. The different reactions that these two boys have to this situation illustrate ____________.
    a. emotion socialization
    b. goodness of fit
    c. personal preferences
    d. differential susceptibility
14. Chronic high-level stress that is experienced without the mitigating benefits of support or treatment is referred to as ____________ stress.
    a. inherent
    b. manageable
    c. ruminative
    d. toxic
15. The fact that a variety of factors can each lead to a given mental disorder is known as ____________.
    a. multifinality
    b. equifinality
    c. differential susceptibility
    d. rumination

LaunchPad
macmillan learning

DON'T STOP NOW! Research shows that testing yourself is a powerful learning tool. Visit LaunchPad to access the LearningCurve adaptive quizzing system, which gives you a personalized study plan to help build your mastery of the chapter material through videos, activities, and more. **Go to launchpadworks.com.**

Critical Thinking Questions

1. How might differences in children's cognitive abilities contribute to (a) the emotions they display and (b) their understanding of emotions? What other factors might contribute to children's understanding of their own and others' emotions?
2. List at least five aspects of children's temperament. What aspects of adults' personality might each predict?
3. Suppose that you wanted to assess changes with age in children's regulation of emotion. Think of five different tasks you could use to assess age-related changes. Which would be best to use in early childhood, and which would better reflect changes at older ages?
4. Recall from Chapter 7 the development of children's theory of mind. How might advances in children's understanding of theory of mind relate to their understanding of emotion? What aspects of understanding emotion might be mostly associated with an understanding of theory of mind?
5. Imagine that you are devising an intervention that will enhance children's emotional development in the preschool years. On what skills would you focus? On whom would you focus your efforts—the children, their parents, their teachers, or their peers?

Key Terms

Answers to Test Yourself

1. a, **2.** b, **3.** d, **4.** c, **5.** b, **6.** c, **7.** a, **8.** b, **9.** a, **10.** d, **11.** b, **12.** c, **13.** b, **14.** d, **15.** b

CHAPTER

11

Attachment to Others and Development of the Self

HECTOR MCDONNELL (BACS)/PRIVATE COLLECTION/BRIDGEMAN IMAGES

HECTOR MCDONNELL, *Refugee Mother and Baby, Goma* (oil on canvas, 1997)

The Caregiver–Child Attachment Relationship | The Self

THEMES

NATURE AND NURTURE ■ THE ACTIVE CHILD ■ THE SOCIOCULTURAL CONTEXT
INDIVIDUAL DIFFERENCES ■ RESEARCH AND CHILDREN'S WELFARE

Well into the twentieth century, many professionals working in orphanages and similar institutions believed that children could be raised in an environment that prioritized good physical care, including proper nourishment and health care, over the emotional dimensions of caregiving, and develop as expected. Yet studies of children who lost their parents during World War II demonstrated the opposite: no matter how hygienic and competently managed they may be, institutions like orphanages put babies and children at high risk because they do not provide the kind of caregiving that enables infants to form close socioemotional bonds (Bowlby, 1953). Foster care and adoption—the earlier, the better—came to be viewed as far better options.

Although we no longer put children into orphanages in Canada, there are other circumstances in which separation from parents can have significant implications for a child's development. These circumstances range from short-term separation, such as placement in a childcare centre or with a nonparent caregiver while parents are at work, to long-term separations, as when a parent is deployed overseas or when an abused or neglected child is removed from the home. How children adapt to these separations has become an important focus of developmental science. Indeed, those early studies of institutionalized children inspired systematic research into how the quality of parent–child interactions affects children's development in families, especially their development of emotional attachments to other people. This research, which continues today, has led to a much deeper understanding of the ways in which the early parent–child emotional bond likely influences children's interactions with others from infancy into adulthood. It has also provided new insight into the development of children's sense of self, as well as of their emotions, including their feelings of self-worth.

In this chapter, we will first explore how children develop **attachments**—close and enduring emotional bonds to parents or other primary caregivers. Then we will examine the ways in which the nature of these attachments to others seems to set the stage for the child's near- and long-term development. As you will see, the attachment process appears to be biologically based, yet it unfolds in different ways, depending on the familial and cultural context. Thus, the themes of *nature and nurture* and the *sociocultural context* will be important in our discussion of this topic. You will also see that although most children in typical social circumstances develop attachments to their parents, the quality of these attachments differs in important ways and has implications for each child's social and emotional development. The theme of *individual differences* will therefore figure prominently in our discussion as well. The theme of *research and children's welfare* is also relevant to our examination of experimental interventions designed to enhance the quality of mother–child attachment.

The second half of this chapter will examine a related issue—the development of children's sense of self, that is, their self-understanding, self-identity, and self-esteem. Although many factors influence these areas of development, the quality of children's early attachments lays the foundation for how children feel about themselves, including their sense of security and well-being. Over time, children's self-understanding, self-esteem, and self-identity are also shaped by how others

attachment an emotional bond with a specific person that is enduring across space and time perceive and treat them, by biologically based characteristics of the child, and by children's developing abilities to think about and interpret their social worlds. Thus, the themes of *nature and nurture, individual differences,* the *sociocultural context,* and the *active child* will be evident in our discussion of the development of self.

The Caregiver–Child Attachment Relationship

The research on children adopted from institutions in Romania (discussed in Chapter 1) demonstrates that emotional deprivation and a lack of meaningful relationships with caregivers in the first years of life hinder optimal social and cognitive development (Bick et al., 2015; McCall et al., 2011; Rutter et al., 2010). Although by the middle of the twentieth century there was agreement amongst researchers that children and their parents share a special bond, exactly why they share such a bond was initially a matter of debate. Proponents of *behaviourism* (see Chapter 9) argued that food, such as breast milk, is the basis for the bond. Infants link food to mothers through the process of classical conditioning, in which food is the *unconditioned stimulus* that causes the infant to experience pleasure and mothers are the *conditioned stimulus* linked with the food. From a behaviourist perspective, mothers evoke pleasure in the infant only because of this association (Dollard & Miller, 1950).

Psychologist Harry Harlow proposed another idea, based on his work with rhesus monkeys. Harlow had seen firsthand that infant monkeys reared in a laboratory setting away from their mothers were physically healthy but developed emotional and behavioural problems unless they were given some form of affection and something soft to cling to. Harlow decided to test whether the pleasure of food or the pleasure of comfort was most important to infant monkeys.

Harlow constructed two surrogate "mothers" made of wire and wood: one was covered in terrycloth over sponge rubber (the "cloth mother") and the other was left uncovered. Harlow then took infant monkeys from their mothers and put them in cages with these two surrogate mothers. He varied which of the two surrogates provided milk to the infant and watched how much time the infant monkeys spent on each one. Both groups of infants spent more time on the cloth mothers, though initially the group fed by the cloth mother spent more time with it than did the monkeys fed by the wire mother (see Figure 11.1). Interestingly,

HARLOW PRIMATE LABORATORY

This infant rhesus monkey prefers to be close to the cloth mother rather than the wire mother that feeds it.

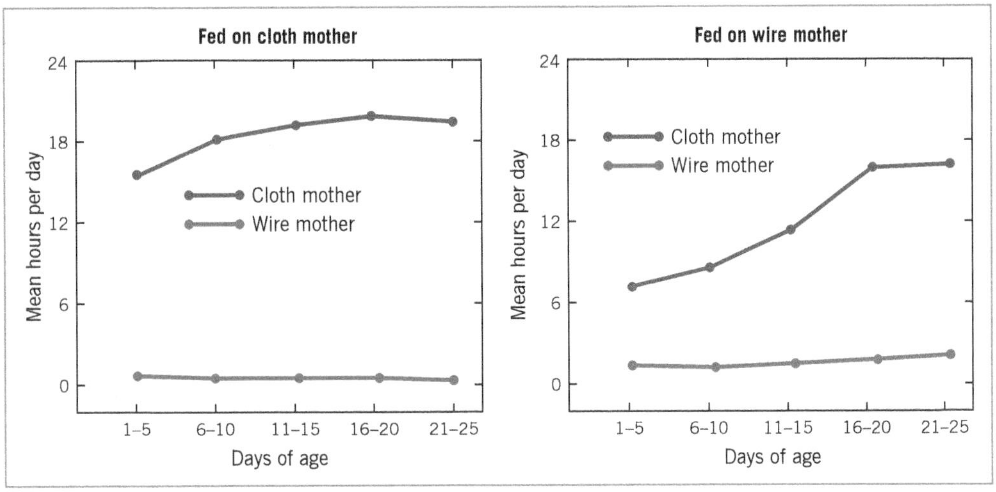

FIGURE 11.1 Time infant rhesus monkeys spent on the cloth and wire mothers in Harlow's famous experiment. (Data from Harlow, 1958)

the monkeys fed by the wire mothers increased the amount of time spent on the cloth mothers as they got older, such that eventually they spent as much time on the cloth mother as did the monkeys who were fed by the cloth mother (Harlow, 1958). These results provided Harlow with evidence that infant monkeys strongly preferred, and thus likely needed, the comfort provided by the cloth mother.

Harlow also found that when infant monkeys were put in an unfamiliar situation without a surrogate mother, they would cower and engage in self-comforting behaviours, such as rocking and thumb-sucking. Yet when the cloth surrogate mother was introduced, they would initially cling to it but then eventually explore the room, periodically returning to the cloth mother. Harlow concluded that the cloth mother functioned as "a source of security, a base of operations" and that it "provides its young with a sense of security . . . when mother and child are in a strange situation" (Harlow, 1958, pp. 678–679).

Harlow's experiments taught developmentalists about the importance of physical comfort for infant monkeys, but it did so at a severe cost. Many of the monkeys in Harlow's experiments were extremely disturbed and had difficulties in their later lives. His research has been criticized as unnecessarily cruel and unethical, but he established without a doubt that infants require more than their physical needs met to thrive in the world.

Attachment Theory

The findings from observations of children and monkeys separated from their parents were so dramatic that psychiatrists and psychologists were compelled to rethink their ideas about early development. Foremost in this effort were John Bowlby, who proposed **attachment theory,** and his colleague, Mary Ainsworth, who extended and tested Bowlby's ideas.

Bowlby's theory of attachment (1953) was initially influenced by several key tenets of Freud's theories, especially the idea that infants' earliest relationships with their mothers shape their later development. However, Bowlby replaced the psychoanalytic notion of a "needy, dependent infant" with the idea of a "competence-motivated infant" who uses his or her primary caregiver as a **secure base** (Cassidy, 2016). As with Harlow's use of the term with infant monkeys, the general idea of the secure base for infant humans is that the presence of a trusted caregiver provides them with a sense of security that allows them to explore the environment and hence to become generally knowledgeable and competent. In addition, the primary caregiver serves as a haven of safety when the infant feels threatened or insecure, and the child derives comfort and pleasure from being near the caregiver. Infants thus develop an attachment to their caregiver.

Attachment serves several important purposes. First, it enhances the infant's chance of survival by keeping the caregiver (who is also the source for food and protection) in close proximity. Second, attachment helps the child feel emotionally secure, which allows the child to explore the world without fear. Third, it serves as a form of *co-regulation* (see Chapter 10) that helps children manage their levels of arousal and their emotions. Bowlby was directly influenced by Harlow's work as well as by ethological theories, particularly the concept of *imprinting* identified by Konrad Lorenz (see Chapter 9). Bowlby proposed that the attachment process between infant and caregiver is rooted in evolution and increases the infant's chance of survival. Just like imprinting, this attachment process develops from the interaction between species-specific learning biases (such as infants' strong tendency to look at faces; see Chapter 5) and the infant's experience with his or

attachment theory theory based on John Bowlby's work that posits that children are biologically predisposed to develop attachments to caregivers as a means of increasing the chances of their own survival

secure base refers to the idea that the presence of a trusted caregiver provides an infant or toddler with a sense of security that makes it possible for the child to explore the environment her caregiver. Thus, the attachment process is viewed as having an innate basis, but the development and quality of infants' attachments are highly dependent on the nature of their experiences with caregivers.

Attachment is not only important for survival and emotional regulation. Through the process of attachment, the child develops an **internal working model of attachment,** a mental representation of the self, of attachment figures, and of relationships in general. This internal working model is based on young children's perception of the extent to which their caregivers can be depended on to satisfy their needs and provide a sense of security. Bowlby believed that this internal working model guides the individual's expectations about relationships throughout life. If caregivers are accessible and responsive, young children come to expect interpersonal relationships to be gratifying and they feel worthy of receiving care and love. As adults, they look for, and expect to find, satisfying and security-enhancing relationships similar to the ones they had with their attachment figures in childhood. If children's attachment figures are unavailable or unresponsive, children develop negative perceptions of relationships with other people and of themselves (Bowlby, 1973, 1980; Bretherton & Munholland, 2016). Thus, children's internal working models of attachment are believed to influence their overall adjustment, social behaviour, perceptions of others, and the development of their self-esteem and sense of self (Thompson, 2008).

COURTESY OF SIR RICHARD BOWLBY

John Bowlby, who laid the foundations of attachment theory, was influenced by psychoanalytic work and research on animals' social behaviour.

Measurement of Attachment Security

Attachment encompasses how a child thinks and feels about a caregiver. It is usually measured by observing children's behaviours with their caregivers or by interviewing parents and children about each other's behaviours and the quality of their relationship.

Ainsworth's Strange Situation Procedure

Mary Ainsworth, who began working with John Bowlby in 1950, provided empirical support for Bowlby's theory, extending it in important ways and further emphasizing the concept of the primary caregiver as a secure base. In research conducted in both Uganda (Ainsworth, 1967) and the United States (Ainsworth et al., 1978), Ainsworth studied mother–infant interactions during infants' explorations and separations from their mother. On the basis of her observations, she came to the conclusion that two key factors provide insight into the quality of the infant's attachment to the caregiver: (1) the extent to which an infant is able to use the primary caregiver as a secure base, and (2) how the infant reacts to brief separations from, and reunions with, the caregiver (Ainsworth, 1973; Ainsworth et al., 1978).

With these factors in mind, Ainsworth designed a laboratory test for assessing the security of an infant's attachment to his or her parent. This test is called the **Strange Situation** because it is conducted in a context that is unfamiliar to the child and likely to heighten the child's need for his or her parent (similar to Harlow's strange situation for the rhesus monkey infants). In this test, the child, accompanied by the parent, is placed in a laboratory playroom equipped with interesting toys. After the experimenter introduces the parent and child to the room, the child is exposed to seven episodes, including two separations from, and reunions with, the parent, as well as two interactions with a stranger—one when the parent is out of the room and one when the parent is present (see Table 11.1). Each episode lasts approximately 3 minutes unless the child becomes overly upset. Throughout

internal working model of attachment the child's mental representation of the self, of attachment figure(s), and of relationships in general that is constructed as a result of experiences with caregivers. The working model guides children's interactions with caregivers and other people in infancy and at older ages.

Strange Situation a procedure developed by Mary Ainsworth to assess infants' attachment to their primary caregiver

DR. PATRICIA CRITTENDEN

Mary Ainsworth, who completed her PhD at the University of Toronto, extended our understanding of attachment theory, which she developed with her colleague John Bowlby, through her groundbreaking Strange Situation experiments.

these episodes, observers rate the child's behaviours, including attempts to seek closeness and contact with the parent, resistance to or avoidance of the parent, interactions with the stranger, and interactions with the parent from a distance using language or gestures. Particularly important to determining a child's attachment is his or her reaction to the parent when that parent returns after the separation (Steps 5 and 8 in Table 11.1).

Through her use of the Strange Situation, Ainsworth and her colleagues (1978) discerned three distinct patterns of infants' behaviour that seemed to indicate the quality or security of their attachment bonds and that are associated with distinct patterns of parenting behaviour. These patterns have been replicated many times in research with mothers and fathers. On the basis of these patterns, Ainsworth identified three attachment categories. It is important to emphasize that these attachment categories characterize a child's relationship with a particular caregiver and is not a feature of the child; children can have different attachments with different caregivers (Granqvist et al., 2017).

The first attachment category—the one into which the majority of infants fall—is **secure attachment.** Infants in this category use their mother as a secure base during the initial part of the session, leaving her side to explore the many toys available in the room. As they play with the toys, these infants occasionally look back to check on their mother or bring a toy over to show her. They are usually, but by no means always, distressed to some degree when their mother leaves the room, especially when they are left totally alone. However, when their mother returns, they make it clear that they are glad to see her, either by simply greeting her with a happy smile or, if they have been upset during her absence, by going to her to be picked up and comforted. If they have been upset, their mother's presence comforts and calms them, often enabling them to explore the room again. Between 50% and 60% of children in Canada and the United States whose mothers are not clinically disturbed fall into this category (Chisholm, 1998; van IJzendoorn, Schuengel, & Bakermans-Kranenburg, 1999).

The other two attachment categories that Ainsworth originally identified involve children who are rated as insecurely attached, that is, who have less positive attachment to their caregivers than do securely attached children. One type of

TABLE 11.1 Episodes in Ainsworth's Strange Situation Procedure

Episode	Events	Aspect of Attachment Behaviour Assessed
1	Experimenter introduces caregiver and infant to the unfamiliar room; shows toys to baby; then leaves.	None
2	Caregiver and child are alone; caregiver is told not to initiate interaction but to respond to infant as appropriate.	Exploration and use of caregiver as a secure base
3	Stranger enters and is seated quietly for 1 minute; then talks to caregiver for 1 minute; then tries to interact with the infant for 1 minute.	Reaction to the stranger
4	Caregiver leaves child alone with the stranger, who lets the infant play but offers comfort if needed. Segment is shortened if the infant becomes too distressed.	Separation distress and reaction to stranger's comforting
5	Caregiver calls to the infant from outside door, enters the room, and pauses by the door. Stranger leaves. Caregiver lets the infant play or may comfort the infant if distressed.	Reaction to reunion with caregiver
6	Caregiver leaves infant alone in the room. Segment is ended if the infant is too distressed.	Separation distress
7	Stranger enters room, greets the infant, and pauses. She sits or comforts the infant if the infant is upset. Segment is ended if the infant is very upset.	Ability to be soothed by stranger
8	Caregiver calls from outside the door, enters and greets the infant and pauses. Caregiver sits if the infant is not upset but may provide comfort if the infant is distressed. Caregiver allows the infant to return to play if interested.	Reaction to reunion

Source: Ainsworth et al. (1978).

insecure attachment is **insecure/resistant.** Infants in this category are often clingy from the beginning of the Strange Situation, staying close to the mother instead of exploring the toys. When their mother leaves the room, they tend to get very upset, often crying intensely. In the reunion, the insecure/resistant infant typically reestablishes contact with the mother, only to then rebuff her efforts at offering comfort. For example, the infant may rush to the mother, crying and with outstretched arms, signalling the wish to be picked up—but then, as soon as he or she is picked up, arch away from the mother or begin squirming to get free from her embrace. About 9% of children in Canada and the United States fall into the insecure/resistant category (van IJzendoorn et al., 1999).

The other type of insecure attachment is **insecure/avoidant.** Children in this category tend to avoid their mother in the Strange Situation. For example, they often fail to greet her during the reunions and ignore her or turn away while she is in the room. Approximately 15% of children fall into the insecure/avoidant category (van IJzendoorn et al., 1999).

Subsequent to Ainsworth's original research, attachment investigators found that the reactions of a small percentage of children in the Strange Situation did not fit well into any of Ainsworth's three categories (Duschinsky, 2015). These children seem to have no consistent way of coping with the stress of the Strange Situation. Their behaviour is often confused or even contradictory. For example, they may exhibit fearful smiles and look away while approaching their mother, or they may seem quite calm and contented and then suddenly display angry distress. They also frequently appear dazed or disoriented and may freeze in their behaviour and remain still for a substantial period of time. These infants, characterized as having a **disorganized/disoriented** attachment to their caregiver, seem to have an unsolvable problem: they want to approach their caregiver, but they also seem to regard her as a source of fear from which they want to withdraw (Main & Solomon, 1990; Granqvist et al., 2017). About 15% of infants in Canada and the United States fall into this category. However, this percentage may be considerably higher amongst maltreated infants, amongst infants whose parents are having serious difficulties with their own working models of attachment, and amongst preschoolers from lower socioeconomic backgrounds (Granqvist et al., 2017).

Development of Attachment in Infancy and Toddlerhood

A key question, of course, is whether there is some similarity between infants' behaviour in the Strange Situation and their behaviour at home. The answer is: Yes (Solomon & George, 1999). For example, Western University researchers David Pederson and Greg Moran (1996) found that 12-month-olds who are securely attached exhibit more enjoyment of physical contact, are less fussy or difficult, and are better able to use their mothers as a secure base for exploration at home, compared with infants who are insecurely attached (Pederson & Moran, 1996). Thus, they are more likely to learn about their environments and to enjoy doing so. In addition, children's behaviour in the Strange Situation correlates with attachment scores derived from observing their interactions with their mother over several hours (van IJzendoorn et al., 2004).

The Strange Situation remains the standard means of measuring infants' attachment security, but it has been criticized on several fronts. First, the Strange Situation requires substantial resources; it must be conducted in a laboratory with video-recording equipment and an extensively trained staff (Tryphonopoulos, Letourneau, & Ditommaso, 2014). Second, some psychologists argue that, rather than falling into categories, the attachment security of parent–child relationships

secure attachment a pattern of attachment in which infants or young children have a positive and trusting relationship with their attachment figure. In the Strange Situation, a securely attached infant may be upset when the caregiver leaves but may be happy to see the caregiver return, recovering quickly from any distress. When children are securely attached, they can use caregivers as a secure base for exploration.

insecure/resistant attachment a type of insecure attachment in which infants or young children are clingy and stay close to their caregiver rather than exploring their environment. In the Strange Situation, insecure/resistant infants tend to become very upset when the caregiver leaves them alone in the room. When their caregiver returns, they are not easily comforted and both seek comfort and resist efforts by the caregiver to comfort them.

insecure/avoidant attachment a type of insecure attachment in which infants or young children seem somewhat indifferent toward their caregiver and may even avoid the caregiver. If the infant gets upset when left alone, he or she is as easily comforted by a stranger as by a parent.

disorganized/disoriented attachment a type of insecure attachment in which infants or young children have no consistent way of coping with the stress of the Strange Situation. Their behaviour is confused or even contradictory, and they often appear dazed or disoriented.

BOX 11.1 A CLOSER LOOK Does Childcare Interfere with Attachment?

Attachment develops in the first year of life, but many parents work out of the home during their child's first year. This predicament has led researchers and parents to wonder if time away from primary caregivers, particularly mothers, and in the care of non-parental caregivers might interfere with children's ability to form secure attachments with their parents.

Growing interest in the effects of childcare on infants and toddlers prompted the National Institute of Child Health and Human Development (NICHD) to fund a large, longitudinal study of children and families from 10 cities around the United States. Started in 1991, the Study of Early Child Care and Youth Development (SECCYD) studied the development of 1364 children from birth to adolescence and kept careful track of their various childcare arrangements in their early years. The study measured (1) characteristics of children's families and their childcare settings, (2) children's attachment to their mothers using the Strange Situation procedure, (3) the quality of their mothers' interactions with them, and (4) their social behaviour, cognitive development, and health status. The SECCYD has provided the strongest examination into potential links between childcare and attachment to date.

The first important finding was that 15-month-olds in childcare were just as likely to be securely attached to their mothers as were children not in childcare (NICHD Early Child Care Research Network, 1997). The same pattern was found with children at 36 months of age: the number of hours in childcare, the type of childcare, the number of childcare arrangements, the age the child entered childcare, and the quality of childcare did not predict children's security of attachment (NICHD Early Child Care Research Network, 2001).

Second, the SECCYD found that maternal sensitivity was a very strong predictor of children's attachment security, even when aspects of the children's childcare arrangements and other aspects of the family (income, mother education, mother depressive symptoms) were accounted for (NICHD Early Child Care Research Network, 1997, 2001). Aspects of childcare were related to attachment security when children experienced risks in both the childcare and home contexts, namely poor-quality care in the childcare setting *and* insensitive or unresponsive parenting in the home setting (NICHD Early Child Care Research Network, 1997).

Additionally, the study found evidence that high-quality childcare can serve a compensatory function. Specifically, children who had insensitive and unresponsive mothers were more likely to be securely attached to those mothers if they experienced high-quality childcare than if they experienced low-quality childcare (NICHD Early Child Care Research Network, 1997). This finding demonstrates that, in addition to not undermining parent–child attachment security, under some circumstances childcare can actually promote attachment security in the parent–child relationship.

Other studies have replicated these findings. A study in Chile found that children who attended childcare were not more likely to have insecure attachments or to experience less sensitive parenting than children who did not attend childcare (Cárcamo et al., 2016). Similarly, a meta-analysis of studies comparing links between maternal and nonmaternal care and children's development found no evidence that children in childcare are less securely attached than other children or that they display less positive behaviour in interactions with their mothers (Erel, Oberman, & Yirmiya, 2000). As with the SECCYD findings, the only time that childcare appears to interfere with attachment is when the care is of low quality (e.g., frequent turnover in caregivers or a high ratio of infants per caregiver) (Sagi et al., 2002).

should be measured along multiple continuous dimensions. This possibility was demonstrated in a sample of several thousand children: security dimensions provided a better explanation of children's observed attachment behaviours than did categories (Fraley & Spieker, 2003). Despite these findings, researchers continue to overwhelmingly prefer attachment categories.

A third critique of the Strange Situation is that it is no longer so "strange" in a world where 61% of children under the age of 5 are cared for by someone other than their mothers on a daily basis (Laughlin, 2013). However, a study of children's behaviour toward their parents at drop-off and pickup from childcare found that 67% were classified as secure, 9% were insecure/avoidant, 14% were insecure/resistant, and 10% were disorganized/disoriented (Bick, Dozier, & Perkins, 2012)—numbers similar to those found by the Strange Situation measure. This study also found that children's behaviour in these childcare settings matched their behaviour during the laboratory-based Strange Situation (Bick et al., 2012). See Box 11.1 for more information about the connection between childcare and attachment security.

Sources of Individual Differences in Attachment Styles

If children are biologically disposed to form attachments to their caregivers, why are some children securely attached and some insecurely attached? Three main sources for these individual differences are parental sensitivity, genetic predispositions, and culture.

Parenting and Attachment Styles

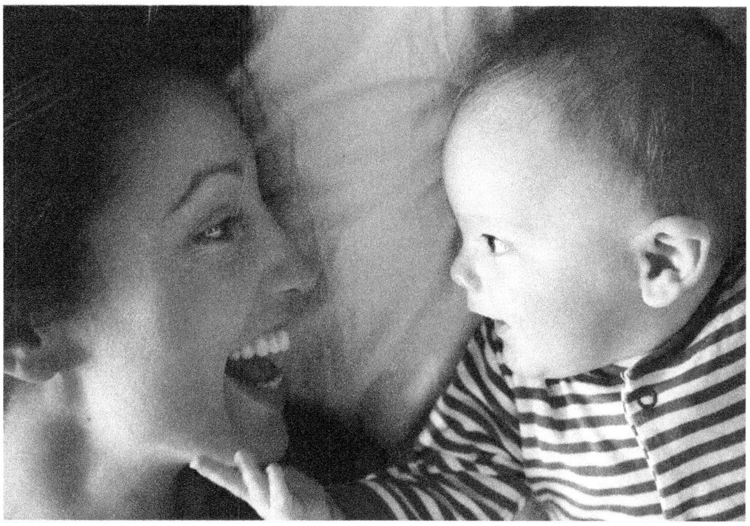

The mothers of securely attached infants generally respond warmly to their offspring and are sensitive to their needs.

Given that attachment security is a marker of the quality of the relationship between a parent and child, it makes sense that parental behaviour should be a strong predictor of children's attachment styles. Indeed, after developing the Strange Situation procedure, Ainsworth and her colleagues (1978) checked the validity of their measure by observing whether mothers' behaviour in the home was linked with their children's attachment classifications. They found that it was, and several subsequent studies have found similar relationships across the three original classifications as well as the disorganized/disoriented classification (see Table 11.2 for a summary of behaviours associated with each classification).

One key aspect of parenting that has been consistently linked with attachment styles is **parental sensitivity,** which is caregiving behaviour that involves the expression of warmth as well as contingent and consistent responsiveness to children's needs. The mothers of securely attached 1-year-olds tend to read their babies' signals accurately, responding quickly to the needs of a crying baby and smiling back at a beaming one. Positive exchanges between mother and child, such as mutual smiling and laughing, making sounds at each other, or engaging in coordinated play, are a characteristic of sensitive parenting that may be particularly important in promoting secure attachment (Bigelow et al., 2010; Cassidy, 2016). An association between fathers' sensitivity and the security of their children's attachment has also been found, though it is somewhat weaker than that for mothers (Brown, Mangelsdorf, & Neff, 2012; Lucassen et al., 2011).

In contrast, the mothers of insecure/resistant infants tend to be inconsistent in their early caregiving: they sometimes respond promptly to their infants' distress, but sometimes they do not. These mothers often seem highly anxious and overwhelmed by the demands of caregiving. Mothers of insecure/avoidant infants tend to be indifferent and emotionally unavailable, sometimes rejecting their baby's attempts at physical closeness (Leerkes, Parade, & Gudmundson, 2011). Mothers of disorganized/disoriented infants sometimes exhibit abusive,

parental sensitivity caregiving behaviour that involves the expression of warmth and contingent responsiveness to children, such as when they require assistance or are in distress

TABLE 11.2 Patterns of Child and Parent Behaviour Characteristic of the Four Styles of Attachment

Style of Attachment	Child's Behaviours During Strange Situation Procedure	Parent's Behaviours Toward Child at Home
Secure	Uses parent as secure base; is upset at separation; seeks parent at reunion and is easily soothed by the parent	Is responsive and sensitive to the child's signals; is affectionate and expressive; initiates frequent close contact with the child
Insecure/Avoidant	Readily separates to explore; avoids or ignores the parent; does not prefer the parent to the stranger	Is insensitive to the child's signals; avoids close contact and rejects child's bids for contact; may be angry, irritable, or impatient
Insecure/Resistant	Does not separate to explore; is wary of the stranger even when the parent is present; is extremely upset at separation; is not soothed by the parent and resists the parent's attempts to soothe	Is inconsistent or awkward in reacting to child's distress; seems overwhelmed with tasks of caregiving
Disorganized/Disoriented	Goes to parent reluctantly, perhaps looking away from parent; may express fear when with parent; may seem to "freeze" their behaviour and expressions for short periods	Is intrusive; is emotionally unavailable; may dissociate or be in a trance-like state; confuses or frightens the child; may be harsh or abusive

Sources: Ainsworth et al. (1978); Hesse & Main (2006); Isabella (1993); Leerkes, Parade, & Gudmundson (2011); Main & Solomon (1990).

frightening, or disoriented behaviour and may be dealing with unresolved loss or trauma (Granqvist et al., 2017). Particularly striking is the finding that infants whose mothers are insensitive show only a 38% rate of secure attachment, which is considerably less than the typical 50% to 60% (van IJzendoorn & Sagi, 1999). Madigan and colleagues found that Canadian adolescent mothers with unresolved attachment were more likely to exhibit disrupted behaviour with their infants (e.g., not soothing their infant when distressed, using a loud voice, removing an interesting toy from the infant) than mothers with organized attachment patterns (Madigan, Moran, & Pederson, 2006).

The association between maternal sensitivity and the quality of infants' and children's attachment has been demonstrated in studies involving over 26 different cultural groups (Mesman, van IJzendoorn, & Sagi-Schwarz, 2016; Posada et al., 2016). That said, what constitutes sensitive and responsive parenting differs by cultural group. In some cultures, parents may be likely to respond to a child's attempts to talk with a smile, some with a touch, and some by repeating the sound made by the child (Mesman et al., 2016). What is the same across cultures is that caregivers respond in a soothing and encouraging manner to the child when he or she seeks their attention.

Evidence that parental sensitivity does in fact have a causal effect on infants' attachment has been provided by short-term experimental interventions designed to enhance the sensitivity of mothers' caregiving. These interventions, discussed in Box 11.2, have been found to increase not only mothers' sensitivity with their infants but also the security of their infants' attachment (Bakermans-Kranenburg, van IJzendoorn, & Juffer, 2003; van IJzendoorn, Juffer, & Duyvesteyn, 1995). Moreover, in twin studies of infants' attachment, nearly all the variation in attachments was due to environmental factors (Bokhorst et al., 2003; Roisman & Fraley, 2006).

Although secure attachments are more likely when parents display sensitivity, children can still develop secure attachments to their parents even when they are not consistently sensitive. In a study of preschoolers, half of whom were involved in the child protective system because their mothers had maltreated them, the maltreated preschoolers were indeed more likely to be insecure or disorganized than the non-maltreated children. However, 23% of the maltreated children had secure attachments to the mothers who had maltreated them (Stronach et al., 2011). Though surprising, this finding likely derives from the fact that abusive parents can also be loving and sensitive at times, factors that promote children's attachment. The findings also demonstrate that the biological drive to be securely attached to a caregiver is powerful enough to overcome frightening and painful parental behaviour.

Genetic Influences

Over the last 20 years, researchers have sought out genetic explanations for why some children develop secure attachments and others do not. In part, these efforts are an attempt to determine how much of the underlying mechanisms are universal and how much are influenced by the child's environment, including culture. However, the search for a genetic explanation has been largely unsuccessful. Twin studies have provided no evidence that attachment styles are heritable (Bakermans-Kranenburg & van IJzendoorn, 2016). However, several studies have shown that epigenetic effects play a role in the expression of attachment behaviour, including support for the differential susceptibility hypothesis introduced in Chapter 10.

BOX 11.2 APPLICATIONS Interventions to Improve Attachment

Clinicians who work with families have developed programs to intervene in parent–child relationships in order to promote attachment security. A meta-analysis carried out by Canadian researchers examined 10 attachment interventions for families at risk for insecure attachments. This analysis found that infants were nearly 3 times as likely to have a secure attachment classification if they and their parents participated in an attachment intervention, compared with infants and parents who did not (Letourneau et al., 2015). The interventions were most effective if they occurred early (when children were between 3 and 9 months of age) and if the family had a history of maltreatment. Some of these efforts are directed entirely at parenting behaviour but others are directed at both parents and children.

One commonly used intervention targeted at parenting behaviour is called the Circle of Security (Powell et al., 2014). Parents are encouraged to reflect on their own mental representations of how parents and children should interact and then are guided by trained therapists to change any maladaptive representations, such as assuming the child should automatically know what the parent wants or that the role of the child is to comfort the parent rather than vice versa. A study in Australia evaluated the effectiveness of the Circle of Security intervention with a sample of young children with documented behaviour problems and their caregivers. After 20 weeks, the caregivers developed more positive representations and the number of children with a disorganized/disoriented attachment style decreased (Huber, McMahon, & Sweller, 2015).

Another intervention, known as the Attachment and Biobehavioural Catch-Up (ABC), was developed specifically for mothers identified as at risk for maltreating their children (Dozier & Bernard, 2017). ABC focuses on changing parents' behaviours, rather than changing mental representations. Trainers teach parents to achieve three goals: provide nurturance to the child, follow the child's lead, and avoid frightening behaviours. Trainers observe parent–child interactions and give the parents immediate positive feedback and concrete suggestions to implement in the moment. ABC also includes structured parent–child activities (such as preparing a simple snack) to help parents practice their new skills.

The ABC intervention has been found to be very effective at changing both parents' behaviours and children's security. Maltreated children who participated in the ABC intervention with their parents were more likely to have secure attachments, compared with maltreated children who were not in the intervention (52% versus 33%), and they were less likely to have disorganized attachments (43% versus 57%; Bernard et al., 2012). The ABC intervention shows promise for changing such insensitive behaviour; maltreating mothers who participated in ABC showed improvement in their attention to and processing of infant emotional expressions (Dozier & Bernard, 2017).

Other interventions that used similar techniques have also succeeded in reducing the rate of disorganized attachment and increasing the rate of secure attachment. For example, in one study, parents in Montréal who had been reported for maltreatment were provided with a short-term home visiting intervention focused on improving parental sensitivity (Moss et al., 2011). The 8-week intervention was successful in improving both parental sensitivity and child attachment security. As we saw in Chapter 10, contingent and appropriate responses to children's emotions are key to promoting children's own positive emotional and social development.

These interventions together demonstrate that even very problematic parent–child relationships can be improved, with clear benefits for children's attachment security.

One recent study focused on the possible influence that allelic variants of the serotonin transporter gene, SLC6A4 (formerly named 5HTT), might have on behaviour in the Strange Situation. The participants were Ukrainian preschoolers, some of whom had been raised in institutions and some of whom had been raised in their biological families. Those participants who had an SLC6A4 variant, frequently associated with vulnerability in the face of stress, exhibited less attachment security and more attachment disorganization if they grew up in an institution than did preschoolers with the same variant who lived with their families. In contrast, participants who were raised in an institution but who had a different SLC6A4 genotype, one that is frequently associated with less reactivity and less vulnerability, did not exhibit adverse attachment behaviour (Bakermans-Kranenburg, Dobrova-Krol, & van IJzendoorn, 2012).

Similarly, there is some research indicating that certain genes, such as DRD4 (which is involved in the dopamine system), are associated with disorganized/disoriented attachment when an infant is in a stressful environment (as when the mother is suffering from trauma or loss) but are associated with greater attachment security in a less stressful context (Bakermans-Kranenburg & van IJzendoorn, 2007; Wazana et al., 2015). Such studies highlight the concept of *differential susceptibility* described in Chapter 10. That is, they suggest that certain genes result in children being differentially susceptible to the quality of their rearing environment, such that those with the "reactive" genes benefit more from having

STEVENSONPHOTOGRAPHY.COM

Studies suggest that attachment security is universal across cultures.

a secure attachment (e.g., are better adjusted and more prosocial than their peers) but do more poorly if they have an insecure attachment (Bakermans-Kranenburg & van IJzendoorn, 2007, 2011; Kochanska, Philibert, & Barry, 2009).

The links between attachment security and genetic makeup have been found to last into adulthood. One longitudinal study followed children from infancy, when attachment was assessed with the Strange Situation, all the way to age 26, when attachment was assessed with the Adult Attachment Interview. Researchers found that the continuity in individuals' attachment security depended on which variant of an oxytocin receptor gene OXTR they had, although not on variations in DRD4 (Raby et al., 2013). Taken together, these studies indicate that individuals' genetic makeup affects both the way in which environmental forces influence their attachment security in childhood and the continuity of attachment security into adulthood.

Cultural Variations in Attachment Styles

Because human infants are believed to be biologically predisposed to form attachments with their caregivers, one might expect attachment behaviours to be similar in different cultures. In fact, in large measure, infants' behaviours in the Strange Situation are similar across numerous cultures, including those of Africa, East Asia, Latin America, and Europe. In all these cultures, there are securely attached, insecure/resistant, and insecure/avoidant infants, with the average percentages approximating those established in Canada and the United States (Mesman et al., 2016). One study that compared mothers and their young children across nine countries (Canada, Colombia, France, Italy, Japan, Peru, Portugal, Taiwan, and the United States) found that, in all countries, children used their mothers as a secure base when exploring new surroundings (Posada et al., 2013). This finding supports the notion that attachment security is a universal phenomenon. However, this study also revealed some behavioural differences: Children in Colombia and Peru were least likely to remain in close physical proximity to their mothers, whereas children in Italy and Portugal were much more likely than children in other countries to maintain physical contact with their mothers (Posada et al., 2013).

Attachment and Social-Emotional Development

Children's attachment status, both in infancy and later in childhood, has been found to predict their later social-emotional development, with securely attached infants experiencing better adjustment and more social skills than insecurely attached children. One explanation for this may be that children with a secure attachment are more likely to develop positive and constructive internal working models of attachment. (Recall that children's working models of attachment are believed to shape their adjustment and social behaviour, their self-perceptions and sense of self, and their expectations about other people; there is also some direct evidence for this belief [e.g., Johnson & Chen, 2011; Johnson, Dweck, & Chen, 2007].) In addition, children who experience the sensitive, supportive parenting that is associated with secure attachment are likely to learn that it is acceptable to express emotions in an appropriate way and that emotional communication with others is important (Cassidy, 1994; Kerns et al., 2007; Riva Crugnola et al., 2011). In contrast, insecure/avoidant children, whose parents tend to be nonresponsive to their signals of need and distress, are likely to learn to inhibit emotional expressiveness and to not seek comfort from other people (Bridges & Grolnick, 1995).

Consistent with these patterns, children who were securely attached in infancy seem to have closer, more harmonious relationships with peers later in childhood than do children who were insecurely attached (McElwain, Booth-LaForce, &

Interview with Gilda Morelli

WORTH PUBLISHERS

Wu, 2011; Pallini et al., 2014). For example, securely attached children are higher in self-regulation, sociability, and social competence with peers than are insecurely attached children (Drake, Belsky, & Fearon, 2014; Panfile & Laible, 2012). Correspondingly, they are less anxious, depressed, or socially withdrawn (Brumariu & Kerns, 2010; Madigan et al., 2016)—especially compared with children who had insecure/resistant attachments (Groh et al., 2012)—as well as less aggressive and delinquent (Fearon et al., 2010; Groh et al., 2012; Hoeve et al., 2012; Madigan et al., 2016; NICHD Early Child Care Research Network, 2006).

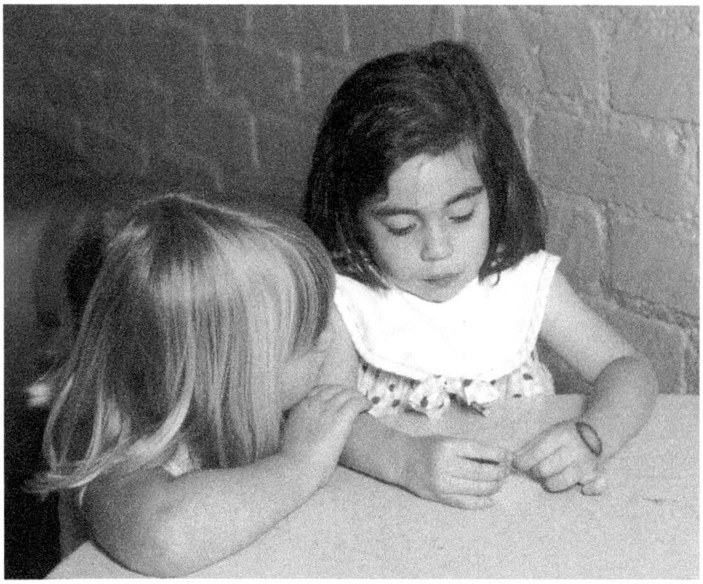

MARY KATE DENNY/PHOTOEDIT

Toddlers who were securely attached as infants are more likely to engage in prosocial behaviour, such as trying to comfort someone who is sad, than are those who were insecurely attached as infants.

Securely attached children are also better able to understand others' emotions (Steele, Steele, & Croft, 2008; Thompson, 2008) and display more helping, sharing, and concern for peers (Eisenberg, Fabes, & Spinrad, 2006; Kestenbaum, Farber, & Sroufe, 1989; Panfile & Laible, 2012). A meta-analysis of 165 studies concluded that children with a secure attachment to a caregiver were 2.5 times less likely to develop mental health problems, such as anxiety or depression, or behaviour problems than were children with an insecure attachment to their caregivers (Madigan et al., 2016).

Securely attached children are also more likely to report positive emotion and to exhibit normal rather than abnormal patterns of reactivity to stress (Bernard & Dozier, 2010; Borelli et al., 2010; Luijk et al., 2010). Secure attachment in infancy predicts positive peer and romantic relationships and emotional health in adolescence (Carlson, Sroufe, & Egeland, 2004; Collins et al., 1997) and early adulthood (Englund et al., 2011), as well as physical health in adulthood (Puig et al., 2013). Finally, attachment also predicts academic performance. A study of French-Canadian children demonstrated that securely attached children scored higher on measures of communication, mastery motivation, and engagement in problem solving than did their insecure peers (Moss & St-Laurent, 2001).

Although there are only a few studies in which infants' attachments to both parents were assessed, a recent Canadian study showed that an insecure father–child attachment was more strongly correlated with child conduct problems than an insecure mother–child attachment, highlighting the importance of considering both mother–child and father–child attachments (Bureau et al., 2017). It does appear that children may be most at risk if they have insecure attachments to both their mother and their father. In a study in which attachment was assessed at 15 months of age, children with insecure attachments to both parents were especially prone to problem behaviours such as aggression and defiance in elementary school. Having secure attachment(s) with one or both parents was associated with low levels of problem behaviours (Kochanska & Kim, 2013). It is not clear yet if having one secure attachment buffers against other types of negative outcomes, such as internalizing problems (e.g., anxiety, depression) or problems in interpersonal relations.

REVIEW QUESTIONS

How would you characterize your own style of attachment to parents, guardians, caregivers, or mentors in your life, based on the styles described in this section? Does your style of attachment vary across these different relationships? ■

self-concept a conceptual system made up of one's thoughts and attitudes about oneself

The Self

Who are you? The answer could involve a description of physical characteristics; personality traits; personal preferences; social and familial relationships; or details of ethnicity, culture, or national origin. The self is in fact all of these things and, over the course of development, children assimilate each of them into a sense of who they are. This section will focus on three main aspects of the self and how each develops across childhood: self-concept, self-esteem, and identity. Self-concept describes how individuals view themselves, whereas self-esteem refers to how they evaluate and feel about themselves. Self-concept and self-esteem are thus internal to the individual (Baumeister, 2005).

In contrast, identity involves descriptions or categories that are often externally imposed, such as through membership or participation in a family, religion, race/ethnic group, or school (Baumeister, 2005). To understand the difference between self-concept and identity, think of a newborn baby; the baby does not have a conscious self-concept but does have an identity because the baby has a name and is part of a family, which in turn is part of a larger community (Baumeister, 2005). As we will see below, children and adolescents can—and do—have multiple identities based on various facets of their lives, including ethnic identity and sexual identity.

Self-Concept

Self-concept refers to a system made up of one's thoughts and attitudes about oneself. This conceptual system can include thoughts about one's own physical being (e.g., body, possessions), social characteristics (e.g., relationships, personality, social roles), and internal characteristics (e.g., thoughts, psychological functioning). It is also an understanding of how the self changes or remains the same over time, of beliefs about one's own role in shaping these processes, and even of reflections on one's own consciousness of selfhood (Damon & Hart, 1988). The development of the self is important because individuals' self-conceptions, including the ways they view and feel about themselves, influence their overall feelings of well-being and self-confidence when faced with external criticism (Harter, 2012a). As we will see, children's self-concept develops primarily through interactions with people in their environments.

Self-Concept in Infancy

Self-concept starts as an appreciation of one's physical self. Infants must first differentiate themselves from the environment, which they do by developing the sense that they are physical beings (Oyserman, Elmore, & Smith, 2012). Infants do this in part by realizing that some things are always present, such as their hands, while other things come and go, such as their parents or toys. Eventually, infants understand that the things that are always present are part of their own bodies (Baumeister, 2005).

In their theories of cognitive development, both Piaget and Vygotsky argue that children learn by interacting with their environments (see Chapter 4). One important lesson infants learn through experience is that they can affect their environments. For example, over the first few months of life, infants learn that if they cry, a parent will come and provide comfort and that if they grab a toy, they can bring it closer to play with or suck on. Through such interactions, infants gradually appreciate that they are separate from the people and objects in their environments and that they can influence these people and objects to meet their own needs.

There is compelling evidence that infants have a rudimentary self-concept in the first months of life. As noted in Chapter 5, by 2 to 4 months of age, infants have a sense of their ability to control objects outside themselves. In one study, infants clearly demonstrated a sense of self in the enthusiasm they displayed when making a mobile move by pulling a string attached to their arm and in the anger displayed when their efforts no longer have an effect (Lewis, Alessandri, & Sullivan, 1990). Infants also seem to have some understanding of their own bodily movements. Self-concept becomes much more distinct at about 8 months of age. According to attachment theory, this is the age when infants react with separation distress if kept apart from a parent, suggesting that they recognize that they and their mother are separate entities. Thus, the development of self-concept is the first necessary step in the development of attachment to a caregiver.

ROOM THE AGENCY/ALAMY

This boy recognizes that the child in the mirror with a spot on his cheek is himself.

As discussed in Chapter 4, around their 1st birthday, infants begin to show joint attention with respect to objects in the environment. For example, they will visually follow a caregiver's pointing finger to find the object that the caregiver is calling attention to, and then turn back to the caregiver to confirm that they are indeed looking at the intended object (Stern, 1985). They sometimes will also give objects to an adult in an apparent effort to engage the adult in their activities (West & Rheingold, 1978). By around 15 months of age, most children are able to distinguish themselves and others by both gender and age (Damon & Hart, 1988).

An emerging recognition of the self becomes more directly apparent by 18 to 20 months of age, when many children can look into a mirror and recognize themselves (Nielsen, Suddendorf, & Slaughter, 2006), which requires that they have memories of their appearance that they can match to the image in the mirror (Oyserman et al., 2012). A commonly used test of this ability is the mirror self-recognition test or "rouge test," in which an experimenter surreptitiously puts a dot of rouge on a child's face, places the child in front of a mirror, and observes the child's reaction (Lewis & Brooks-Gunn, 1979). Children younger than 18 months old typically respond by either trying to touch the image in the mirror or doing nothing, suggesting that they do not recognize the image as themselves. Most children between 18 and 24 months old will touch the rouge on their own face, indicating that they recognize themselves in the mirror (Courage, Edison, & Howe, 2004), although children with autism spectrum disorder (ASD) can have significant difficulties in this regard (see Box 11.3).

Self-Awareness and the Rouge Test

© WORTH PUBLISHERS

The rouge test was developed in the United States, and when it has been tried in developing countries, even children much older than 2 years of age often fail to recognize themselves in the mirror (Broesch et al., 2010). Researchers wondered whether these children really had less self-recognition or whether differences in autonomy due to cultural factors accounted for the different test results. For instance, children in interdependent cultures may ignore the mark because they assume the experimenter put it there on purpose, while children in independent cultures are more disposed to explore the mark on their own (Ross et al., 2016).

To examine this idea, researchers administered the mirror self-recognition test to infants in Scotland, Turkey, and Zambia, along with a second test known as the "body-as-obstacle" task. In this task, children are made to stand on a mat that is attached to a toy cart and are then encouraged to push the cart to their mothers. Children who realize they must step off the mat in order to push the cart are considered to have a sense of self-concept. In this three-country study, children from Scotland did best on the mirror self-recognition test, whereas children from Zambia did best on the body-as-obstacle task (see Figure 11.2).

FIGURE 11.2 Percent of children in three countries who show self-awareness in two different tasks Children in the more interdependent country (Zambia) did best on the task that required meeting a social goal, namely pushing a toy to their mothers. (Data from Ross et al., 2016)

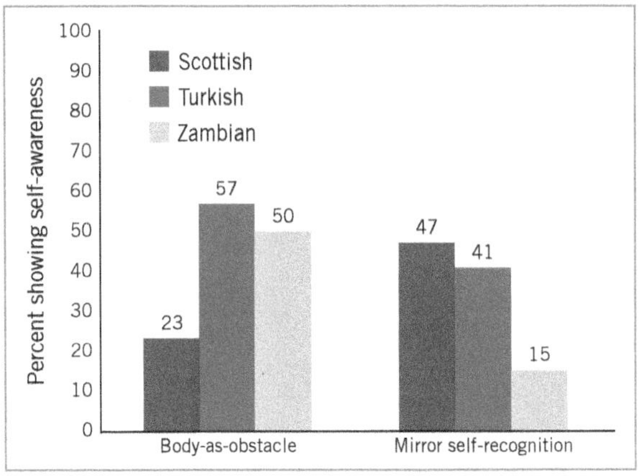

BOX 11.3 INDIVIDUAL DIFFERENCES Development of Self-Awareness Amongst Autistic Children

Children with autism spectrum disorder (ASD) have a variety of cognitive and emotional difficulties, including impairments in the development of a theory of mind and in their ability to identify with others (American Psychiatric Association, 2013; also see Boxes 3.2 and 7.1). Researchers have wondered whether the difficulties autistic children have in interacting with other people, as well as in behaviours such as maintaining personal hygiene, derive in part from the fact that they have an impaired sense of self-awareness (Duff & Flattery, 2014).

Researchers have found that autistic children typically refer to themselves in the third person (Duff & Flattery, 2014). In addition, autistic children have difficulties differentiating themselves from other people—difficulties that they may be aware of. Take, for example, this quote from a high-functioning young adult with ASD:

> I really didn't know there were people until I was seven years old. I then suddenly realized there were people. But not like you do. I still have to remind myself that there are people . . . I never could have a friend. I really don't know what to do with other people.
>
> (Cohen, 1980, p. 388)

Therapists and teachers have designed interventions to improve these children's self-awareness, with the hope that they will develop the skills to function independently. One such intervention promotes self-awareness amongst autistic adolescents through joint attention activities, which involve attracting the attention of another person in order to share interest in an object or event (e.g., "Look at that pretty butterfly!"). Participants are first taught about reflected mirror images using joint attention. This ability is then generalized over time such that eventually the participants can recognize themselves in the mirror. Participation in these activities did in fact lead to greater self-awareness in the participants who did not already have it (Duff & Flattery, 2014), indicating that autistic children can be guided into having greater self-awareness.

Another intervention goes a step further by focusing on this disorder as an identity. PsychoEducational Groups for Autism Spectrum Understanding and Support (known as PEGASUS) teaches high-functioning autistic children about their diagnosis in order to foster ASD-related self-awareness (Gordon et al., 2015). Participants experienced significant gains in self-awareness and, importantly, did not experience an accompanying decrease in self-esteem (Gordon et al., 2015). Although PEGASUS can only be helpful to high-functioning autistic children, such as those who can speak and understand a language, it does illustrate that self-awareness can be fostered through direct instruction. This intervention thus points to a potentially valuable strategy for working with the two-thirds of autistic children who do not also have intellectual disability (Baio et al., 2018).

These findings make clear that cultural contexts can influence how children think about themselves and their environments.

By age 2, many children can recognize themselves in photographs. A study of 18-month-olds found that they showed more brain activity when shown their own face than when they were shown faces of familiar or unfamiliar children and adults (Stapel et al., 2017). During their third year, children's self-awareness becomes quite clear in other ways as well. Similar to how memory aids in self-recognition, young children use language to store memories of their own experiences and behaviours, which they then use to construct narratives of their own "life story" and develop more enduring self-concepts (Harter, 2012a). As we saw in Chapter 10, 2-year-olds exhibit embarrassment and shame—emotions that require a self-concept (Lewis, 1998). The strength of 2-year-olds' awareness of self is even more evident in their notorious self-assertion, which has led to the period between ages 2 and 3 being called the "terrible twos." During this time, children begin to act independently of, and often in direct opposition to, what their parents (and other adults) want them to do (Calkins & Williford, 2009).

Self-Concept in Childhood

As children progress through childhood, their self-concept becomes increasingly complex. Susan Harter, a leading researcher on children's emerging sense of self, argues that sense of self is largely a social construction based on the observations and evaluations of others, particularly of caregivers (Harter, 2012a). These evaluations can be both direct and indirect. For instance, if a teacher tells a child that she is doing very well on her math tests, the child will internalize that she is a person who is good at math; the teacher has directly influenced the child's sense of self. Indirect influences come from how children are treated by others. As seen in the discussion of attachment, a child who is nurtured, loved, and supported develops an internal working model of herself as a lovable, worthy person. In contrast, a child who is treated in a punitive and rejecting manner can develop an internal working model that she is incompetent and unworthy of love (Harter, 2012a).

Combining statements made by a wide array of children in a number of empirical studies, Harter has constructed composite examples of children's typical self-descriptive statements at different ages. The following is a composite example of how 3- to 4-year-olds describe themselves:

> I'm 3 years old, I'm a boy, and my name is Jason. I live with my mommy and daddy who really love me. My mommy makes me yummy spaghetti! I am going to get my own baby sister for Christmas! I have blue eyes and a kitty that is orange and a television in my own room, it's all mine! I know all of my ABC's, listen: A, B, C, D, E, F, G, H, J, L, K, O, P, Q, R, X, Y, Z. I can run real fast, faster than when I was 2. And I can kick a soccer ball real far, all the way from one end of the field to the other. . . . I can climb to the top of the jungle gym, I'm not scared! I'm never scared! I'm always happy. I'm really strong. I can lift this chair, watch me!
>
> (Harter, 2012a, p. 28)

PURESTOCK/GETTY IMAGES

In describing themselves, young children often make reference to their preferences and possessions such as a family pet.

As this composite self-description demonstrates, at age 3 to 4, children understand themselves in terms of concrete, observable characteristics related to physical attributes ("I have blue eyes"), physical activities and abilities ("I can run real fast"), and psychological traits ("I'm not scared! I'm never scared!"). For example, even when the child made a general statement about himself ("I'm really strong"), this statement was closely tied to actual behaviour (lifting a chair). Young children also describe themselves in terms of their preferences ("yummy spaghetti") and possessions ("I have . . . a kitty . . . and a television").

The composite example reflects another characteristic typical of children's self-concept during the preschool years: their self-appraisals are unrealistically confident (Trzesniewski, Kinal, & Donnellan, 2010). These overly positive views of themselves are not attempts to lie or brag but rather are a result of cognitive limitations; rather, young children seem to think that they are really like what they want to be (Harter, 2012a).

Children begin to refine their conceptions of self in elementary school, in part because they increasingly engage in **social comparison,** comparing themselves with others in terms of their characteristics, behaviours, and possessions ("He is bigger than me"). At the same time, they increasingly pay attention to discrepancies between their own and others' performance on tasks ("She got an A on the test and I only got a C") (Chayer & Bouffard, 2010).

By middle to late elementary school, children's conceptions of self are becoming integrated and more broadly encompassing, as is illustrated by the following composite self-description that would be typical of a child between the ages of 8 and 11:

> I'm in fourth grade this year. It's a little tougher than when I was younger, in the "baby" grades. I'm pretty popular, at least with the girls who I spend time with, but not with the super-popular girls who think they are cooler than everybody else. With my friends, I know what it takes to be liked, so I'm nice to people and helpful and can keep secrets. . . . At school, I'm feeling pretty smart in certain subjects like language arts and social studies, someday I will probably get a job that depends on having good English skills. . . . But I'm feeling pretty dumb in math and science, especially when I see how well a lot of the other kids are doing. . . . At school, I try not to act like I'm better than other people. But some kids are show-offs and they make fun of others in class who aren't doing as well as they are. . . . If you ask me, they are just acting like they're totally awesome but I think they really aren't that sure of themselves.
>
> (Harter, 2012a, p. 59)

social comparison the process of comparing aspects of one's own psychological, behavioural, or physical functioning to that of others in order to evaluate oneself

PAUL RADENFELD/GETTY IMAGES

In middle childhood, children start to refine their sense of self by comparing their own attributes and behaviour with those of their peers. This process of social comparison involves a variety of areas, ranging from physical abilities and academic achievement to material well-being.

The developmental changes in older children's self-concept reflect cognitive advances in their ability to use higher-order concepts that integrate more specific behavioural features of the self. For example, the child in the preceding self-description was able to relate being "popular" to several behaviours, such as being "nice to others" and being able to "keep secrets." In addition, older children can coordinate opposing self-representations ("smart" and "dumb") that, at a younger age, they would have considered mutually exclusive (Harter, 2012a). This new cognitive capacity to form higher-order conceptions of the self allows older children to construct more global views of themselves and to evaluate themselves as a person overall. These abilities result in a more balanced and realistic assessment of the self, although they also can result in feelings of inferiority and helplessness (see the discussion of achievement motivation in Chapter 9).

The preceding self-description also reflects the fact that schoolchildren's self-concepts are increasingly based on others' evaluations of them, especially those of their peers. Consequently, their self-descriptions often contain a pronounced social element and focus on characteristics that may influence their place in their social networks, as reflected in the following interview:

> *Interviewer:* What are you like?
> *Child:* I am friendly.
> *Interviewer:* Why is that important?
> *Child:* Other kids won't like you if you aren't.
>
> (Damon & Hart, 1988, p. 60)

Because older school-age children's conceptions of self are strongly influenced by the opinions of others, children at this age are vulnerable to low self-esteem if others view them negatively or as less competent than their peers (Harter, 2006).

Self-Concept in Adolescence

Children's self-concept changes in fundamental ways across adolescence, due in part to the emergence of abstract thinking during this stage of life (see Chapter 4). The ability to use this kind of thinking allows adolescents to conceive of themselves in terms of abstract characteristics that encompass a variety of concrete traits and behaviours. Adolescents typically develop multiple selves (Harter, 2012a)—the self they are with their parents is different from the self they are with their friends, and both of these are different from the self they are in school or at a job. Initially, adolescents may lack the ability to integrate these different selves into a coherent whole, resulting in feelings of uncertainty and internal conflict. However, as they develop, adolescents are able to appreciate that they can act differently in different situations and still be the same person, thereby resolving this sense of confusion (Harter, 2012a). Consider the following composite self-description of a young adolescent, 11 to 13 years old:

> I'm an extrovert with my friends: I'm talkative, cheerful, and funny. My friends really like me. So I like myself a lot when I'm around my friends but not so much when I'm with my mom and dad. . . . I spend a lot of time worrying about what other people think of me. . . . In school, it seems like I'm pretty intelligent, because I feel smart and sometimes creative. . . . Socially, I can be a real introvert around

people I don't know well. . . . I shouldn't be phony and act like I'm somebody else. But sometimes you have to because it's very important to seem as if you really like yourself, it's a big deal to show that you have high self-esteem.

(Harter, 2012a, pp. 74–75)

ANSGAR PHOTOGRAPHY/GETTY IMAGES

Egocentric tendencies in adolescence manifest in the form of personal fables and a preoccupation with imaginary audiences.

As is evident in this composite example, young people's concern over their social competence and their social acceptance, especially by peers, intensifies in early adolescence (Damon & Hart, 1988). The example also illustrates young adolescents' ability to arrive at higher-level, abstract self-descriptions such as "extrovert" based on personal traits such as "talkative," "cheerful," and "funny." Particularly notable is the fact that adolescents can conceive of themselves in terms of a variety of selves, depending on the context. The adolescent in the composite, for instance, describes himself/herself as a somewhat different person with friends and with parents, as well as with familiar and unfamiliar people.

Thinking about the self in early adolescence is characterized by a form of egocentrism called the **personal fable,** in which adolescents overly differentiate their feelings from those of others and come to regard themselves, and especially their feelings, as unique and special (Alberts, Elkind, & Ginsberg, 2007; Elkind, 1967). They may believe that only they can experience whatever misery or rapture or confusion they are currently feeling. This belief is typified in the adolescent assertions "But you don't know how it feels!" and "My parents don't understand me, what do *they* know about what it's like to be a teenager?" (Harter, 2012a, p. 95). The tendency to exhibit this type of egocentrism is often still evident in late adolescence (Schwartz, Maynard, & Uzelac, 2008).

The kind of egocentrism that underlies adolescents' personal fables also causes many adolescents to be preoccupied with what others think of them (Harter, 2012a). This preoccupation is called having an **imaginary audience** (Alberts et al., 2007; Elkind, 1967); in practice, it means that because adolescents are so concerned with their own appearance and behaviour, they assume that everyone else is, too. Wherever they are, whatever they are doing, they think that all eyes are on them, scrutinizing their every blemish or social misstep. This dimension of adolescent egocentrism, like the personal fable, has been found to become stronger across adolescence for boys but not girls (Schwartz et al., 2008).

In their middle teens, adolescents often begin to agonize over the contradictions in their behaviour and characteristics. They tend to become introspective and concerned with the question "Who am I?" (Harter, 2012a). Their concern with this question is reflected in the following composite self-description of a 15-year-old:

What am I like as a person? You're probably not going to understand. I'm complicated! With my really *close* friends, I am very tolerant, I mean I'm understanding and caring. With a *group* of friends I'm rowdier. I'm also usually friendly and cheerful, but I can be pretty obnoxious and intolerant if I don't like how they're acting. . . . I really don't understand how I can switch so fast from being cheerful with my friends, then coming home and feeling anxious, and then getting frustrated and sarcastic with my parents. Which one is the *real* me?

(Harter, 2012a, p. 94)

Although adolescents in their middle teens can identify contradictions in themselves, such as being different with friends than with parents, and often feel conflicted about these inconsistencies, most still do not have the cognitive

personal fable a form of adolescent egocentrism that involves beliefs in the uniqueness of one's own feelings and thoughts

imaginary audience the belief, stemming from adolescent egocentrism, that everyone else is focused on the adolescent's appearance and behaviour skills needed to integrate their recognition of these contradictions into a coherent self-concept. As a consequence, adolescents of this age often feel confused and concerned about who they really are. As one teen put it, "It's not right, it should all fit together in one piece!" (Harter, 2012a, p. 100).

In late adolescence and early adulthood, the individual's conception of self becomes both more integrated and less determined by what others think. Both of these shifts are captured by Harter's composite representation of a high school senior:

> I'd like to be an ethical person who treats other people fairly; that's why I want to be a lawyer. Basically, I like who I am. . . . Being athletic isn't that high on my own list of what is important, even though it is for a lot of the kids in our school. But I don't really care what they think anymore, at least I try to convince myself that I don't. I try to believe that what *I* think is what counts. After all, I have to live with myself as a person and to respect that person, which I do now, more than a few years ago.
>
> (Harter, 2012a, p. 118)

As in the case of this prototypical senior, older adolescents' conceptions of self frequently reflect internalized personal values, beliefs, and standards. Many of these were instilled by others in the child's life but are now accepted and generated by adolescents as their own. Thus, older adolescents place less emphasis on what other people think than they did at younger ages and are more concerned with meeting their own standards and with their future self—what they are becoming or who they are going to be (Harter, 2012a).

Older adolescents are also more likely to have the cognitive capacity to integrate opposites or contradictions in the self that occur in different contexts or at different times (Higgins, 1991). They may explain contradictory characteristics in terms of the need to be flexible, and they may view variations in their behaviour with different people as "adaptive" because one cannot act the same with everyone. Similarly, they may integrate changes in emotion under the characteristic "moody." Moreover, they are likely to view their contradictions and inconsistencies as a normal part of being human, which likely reduces feelings of conflict and upset.

Whether older adolescents are able to successfully integrate contradictions in themselves likely depends not only on their own cognitive capacities but also on the help they receive from parents, teachers, and others in understanding the complexity of personalities. The support and tutelage of others in this regard allow adolescents to internalize values, beliefs, and standards that they feel committed to and to feel comfortable with who they are (Harter, 1999, 2012a).

Self-Esteem

Self-esteem incorporates a child's overall subjective evaluation of his or her worth and the feelings he or she has about that evaluation (Orth & Robins, 2014). Self-esteem does not emerge until children reach age 8 or so (Harter, 2012a). To measure children's self-esteem, researchers ask children, verbally or by questionnaire, about their perceptions of such things as their own physical attractiveness, athletic competence, social acceptance, scholastic ability, and the appropriateness of their behaviour. In addition, researchers typically ask children about their global self-worth—how they feel about themselves in general.

self-esteem an individual's overall subjective evaluation of his or her worth and the feelings he or she has about that evaluation

Individuals with high self-esteem tend to feel good about themselves and hopeful in general, whereas individuals with low self-esteem tend to feel worthless and hopeless (Harter, 2012a). In particular, low self-esteem in childhood and adolescence is associated with problems such as anxiety, depression, and bullying, both as perpetrator and victim (Modecki, Barber, & Vernon, 2013; Rieger et al., 2016; Sowislo & Orth, 2013).

It should also be noted that high self-esteem, especially if not based on positive self-attributes, may have costs for children and adolescents (Lee & Lee, 2012). For example, high self-esteem in aggressive children is associated with their increasingly valuing the rewards that they derive from their aggression and their belittlement of victims (Menon et al., 2007). The combination of high self-esteem and narcissism—grandiose views of the self, inflated feelings of superiority and entitlement, and exploitative interpersonal attitudes—has been associated with especially high levels of aggression in young adolescents (Thomaes et al., 2008).

Sources of Self-Esteem

There are several sources of individual differences in self-esteem. One is age: an individual's self-esteem is not constant and varies by developmental stage. Self-esteem tends to be high in childhood before declining in adolescence and then rebounding in adulthood (Orth & Robins, 2014). Physical attributes, such as attractiveness, also are linked with self-esteem. In childhood and adolescence, attractive individuals are much more likely to report high self-esteem than are those who are less attractive (Harter, 2012a), possibly because attractive people are viewed more positively by others and receive better treatment than people who are considered less attractive.

Gender is another source of individual differences in self-esteem. Studies in 48 countries, including Canada, have established that boys tend to have higher overall self-esteem than girls, and that this tendency persists across the life span (Bleidorn et al., 2016; Orth & Robins, 2014). Although this gender difference has been found for overall self-esteem, it may be that females have higher self-esteem than males in certain domains. A meta-analysis of studies examining domain-specific self-esteem found that males have higher self-esteem than females in the domains of athletics, personal appearance, and self-satisfaction, whereas females were higher in the domains of behavioural conduct (perceiving themselves as well-behaved) and moral-ethical self-esteem (see Figure 11.3; Gentile et al., 2009). No gender differences were found in self-esteem related to academic performance, which suggests that although girls may have lower self-esteem in some domains, this does not prevent them from seeing themselves as able to do well in school (Gentile et al., 2009).

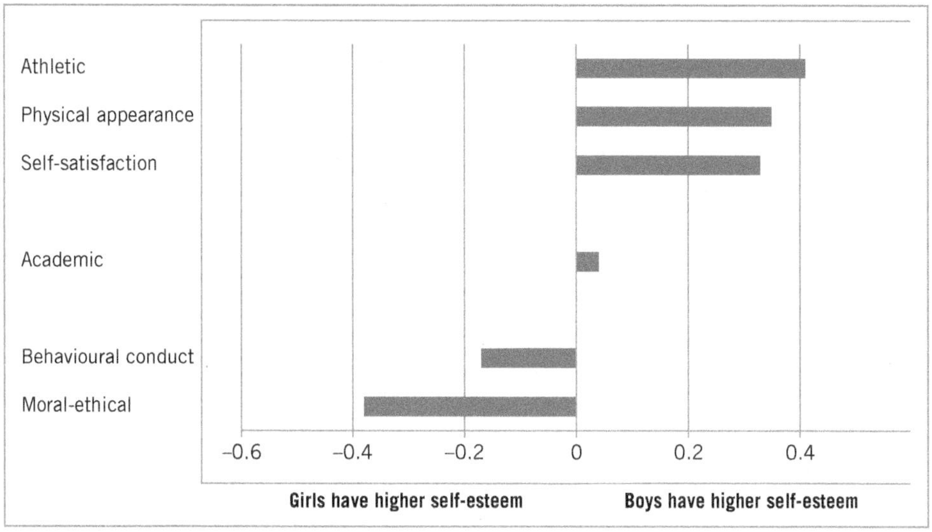

FIGURE 11.3 Gender differences in self-esteem by domain Boys are higher in self-esteem in terms of athletics, personal appearance, and self-satisfaction. Girls have higher self-esteem when it comes to behavioural conduct and moral-ethical behaviour. There is no gender difference in academic self-esteem. (Data from Gentile et al., 2009)

SEIYA KAWAMOTO/THINKSTOCK

Although far from being the only factors in shaping a child's self-esteem, the quality and nature of interactions with parents and other caregivers are amongst the more important influences.

Perhaps the most important influence on children's self-esteem is the approval and support they receive from others, particularly their parents. Early theories viewed self-esteem as the internalization of the views of ourselves held by important people in our lives. In this view, self-esteem is a reflection of what others think of us, or our "looking glass self" (Cooley, 1902). Similar ideas were proposed by Erikson (1950) and Bowlby (1969), who argued that children's self-esteem is grounded in the quality of their relationships with their parents. If children feel loved when young, they come to believe that they are lovable and worthy of others' love; if they feel unloved when young, they come to believe the opposite. Indeed, securely attached children with sensitive and responsive parents tend to have higher self-esteem (Boden, Fergusson, & Horwood, 2008; Cassidy et al., 2003).

Parents' behaviour with and discipline of their children affect the children's self-esteem. Parents who are accepting of and involved with their children and who use supportive yet firm child-rearing practices tend to have children and adolescents with high self-esteem (Behnke et al., 2011; Cooper & McLoyd, 2011). In contrast, parents who regularly react to their children's unacceptable behaviour with belittlement or rejection—in effect, condemning the child rather than the behaviour—are likely to instill in their children a sense of worthlessness and of being loved only to the extent that they meet parental standards (Harter, 2006; Heaven & Ciarrochi, 2008). Parents can also undermine children's self-esteem by constantly relying on social comparison as a means of motivating children (e.g., "Why can't you be helpful like your sister?"). They can also give children unrealistically high self-esteem by praising too often (see Box 11.4).

Over the course of childhood, children's self-esteem is increasingly affected by peer acceptance (Harter, 1999). Indeed, in late childhood, children's feelings of competence about their appearance, athletic ability, and likability may be affected more by their peers' evaluations than by their parents'. This tendency to evaluate the self on the basis of peers' perceptions has been associated with a preoccupation with approval, fluctuations in self-esteem, lower levels of peer approval, and lower self-esteem (Harter, 2012a). At the same time, children's self-esteem likely affects how peers respond to them. Youth who see themselves as competent in their peer relationships tend to be well liked (Caldwell et al., 2004), perhaps because their behaviour is confident and socially engaging.

MARY KATE DENNY/PHOTOEDIT

Children who do poorly in school tend to have lower self-esteem than do their more successful peers. However, children's perceptions of their academic competence tend to be less important to their overall self-esteem than are their perceptions of their appearance.

Children's and adolescents' self-esteem can also be affected by their school and neighbourhood environments. The effect of the school environment is most apparent in the decline in self-esteem that is associated with the transition from elementary school to junior high or middle school (Eccles et al., 1989). The junior high/middle school environment often is not a good developmental match for 11- and 12-year-olds because many children of that age are distressed by the switch from having one teacher whom they know well and who is well acquainted with their skills and weaknesses to having many teachers who know little about them.

In addition, the transition to junior high or middle school forces students to enter a new group of peers and to go from the top of one school's pecking order to the bottom of another's. Especially in poor, overcrowded, urban schools, young adolescents often do not receive the attention, support, and friendship they need to do well and to feel good about themselves (Wigfield et al., 2006). At the same time, junior high and middle schools are more competitive environments than elementary schools, and those older students are subjected to repeated social comparisons (Harter, 2012a). But there is a bright spot—support from teachers does promote higher self-esteem in adolescents (Sterrett et al., 2011).

BOX 11.4 A CLOSER LOOK Is Too Much Praise Bad for Self-Esteem?

The vast majority (87%) of adults in Western society believe that children need to be praised in order to have a positive view of themselves (Brummelman, Crocker, & Bushman, 2016). Such beliefs have led to the recent trend of rewarding participation rather than achievement (the "everybody gets a trophy" phenomenon). Researchers have become concerned with one particular kind of praise known as *inflated praise,* which involves exaggerated language (e.g., "Wow! Your drawing is amazing!" or "You are the best at building sandcastles!"). Adults have been observed using inflated praise twice as often with children who have low self-esteem than with children who have high self-esteem (Brummelman et al., 2014), suggesting that adults think such language will be especially effective with children who are not feeling good about themselves.

To test how inflated praise affects children's behaviour, researchers in the Netherlands did an experiment with 240 children ages 8 to 12 who were visiting a science museum (Brummelman et al., 2014). The children were first asked to draw a copy of a famous painting (Van Gogh's *Wild Roses*) and were told that a professional painter working in another room would judge their painting (this was a ruse—there was no "professional painter"). For one group of children, the experimenter brought a note back from the "painter" that said, "You made an *incredibly* beautiful drawing!"—this was the inflated praise condition. For a second group of children, the message said, "You made a beautiful drawing!"—this constituted the non-inflated praise condition. The last group was the no-praise condition; these children did not receive any communication from the painter.

SUSAN CHIANG/GETTY IMAGES

Although many adults think giving everyone a medal for participation is good for self-esteem, research suggests otherwise.

In the second half of the experiment, each child was given the option of two pictures to copy: one easy and one difficult. The data revealed that inflated praise in the first part of the experiment decreased children's challenge-seeking behaviour in the second part, but only amongst children who rated themselves as having low self-esteem before the experiment started (Brummelman et al., 2014). Yet when children with low self-esteem were given non-inflated praise, they sought out the more challenging drawing task. In other words, inflated praise was backfiring — it was most harmful to the children whom adults think most need it. Instead, only children who started the experiment with high self-esteem were more likely to accept the challenge of the difficult drawings if they were given inflated praise for their initial drawing.

Why does inflated praise undermine the effort of children with low self-esteem? The researchers surmised that inflated praise sets high standards (e.g., you must be "perfect" or "the best" at something to get praise), which in turn leads these children to avoid activities where they might fail, as a form of self-protection (Brummelman et al., 2014). So, what is a well-meaning parent or teacher to do? Praising children for their *effort* rather than for their ability or for the products of their effort is one way to encourage children to persist in the face of challenges. Another important take-away is that, contrary to their instincts, adults should avoid using inflated praise with children who have low self-esteem. Instead, they should target such praise at children with high self-esteem. Of course, if you don't know the level of a child's self-esteem, then it may be best to avoid inflated praise in the first place. And you may want to rethink giving everyone trophies.

Aspects of the neighbourhoods in which adolescents live have also been linked with self-esteem in some countries and cultures. Living in impoverished and violent neighbourhoods is associated with lower self-esteem amongst adolescents in the United States (Behnke et al., 2011). This may be due to high levels of stress that undermine the quality of parenting, prejudice from more affluent peers and adults, and inadequate material and psychological resources (Behnke et al., 2011). Interestingly, this relation between poverty and self-esteem does not hold in Canada and Britain, perhaps due to universal health care and social services (Fagg et al., 2013).

Culture and Self-Esteem

In various cultures, the sources, form, and function of self-esteem may be different, and the criteria that children use to evaluate themselves may vary accordingly. Between Asian and Western cultures, for example, there are fundamental differences that appear to affect the very meaning of self-esteem. In Western

THE CANADIAN PRESS/PRINCE ALBERT DAILY HERALD-KAREN LONGWELL

Cultures differ in the skills they value. Children learn what abilities are valued in their group through participation in the family and larger community and evaluate their own competence accordingly.

cultures, self-esteem is related to individual accomplishments and self-promotion. By contrast, in Asian societies such as Japan and China, which traditionally have had a collectivist (or group) orientation, self-esteem is believed to be more related to contributing to the welfare of the larger group and affirming the norms of social interdependence. In this cultural context, self-criticism and efforts at self-improvement may be viewed as evidence of commitment to the group (Heine et al., 1999). But in terms of measures of self-esteem used by North American researchers, this motivation toward self-criticism is reflected as lower self-evaluation; in fact, in Western industrialized cultures, where an autonomous, relatively stable self is valued, adolescents who base their self-evaluations on others' standards and approval are at risk for psychological problems (Harter, 2012a; Higgins, 1991).

It is not surprising, then, that scores on measures of self-esteem vary considerably across cultures. Self-esteem scores tend to be lower in China, Japan, and Korea than in the United States, Canada, Australia, and some parts of Europe (Harter, 2012a). These differences seem to be partly due to the greater emphasis that the Asian cultures place on modesty and self-effacement—which results in less positive self-descriptions (Cai et al., 2007; Suzuki, Davis, & Greenfield, 2008). Indeed, European American and African American adolescents tend to be more comfortable with being praised and with events that make them look good and cause them to stand out than are Asian American and Latino adolescents (Suzuki et al., 2008); this could affect the degree to which they report high self-esteem, and hence could account for the pattern of ethnic differences in self-esteem (Harter, 2012a).

In some Asian societies, people tend to be more comfortable acknowledging discrepancies in themselves—for example, the existence of both good and bad personal characteristics—than are people in Western cultures; this tendency results in reports of lower self-esteem in late adolescence and early adulthood (Hamamura, Heine, & Paulhus, 2008; Spencer-Rodgers et al., 2004). The same types of cultural influences may affect measures of self-esteem in U.S. subcultures that have maintained traditional non-Western ideas about the self and its relation to other people.

Surprisingly, studies have shown that culture does not appear to be a factor in gender differences related to self-esteem. A large study of 1 million adolescents and adults in 48 countries (including Argentina, Canada, China, Egypt, India, Japan, Malaysia, South Africa, Thailand, and the United States) confirmed that males have higher self-esteem on average than females, and that while self-esteem increases from age 16 on for both genders, females' self-esteem on average never reaches that of males (Bleidorn et al., 2016). Why is there such a stark gender difference in self-esteem across countries and cultures? The reasons are not entirely clear, though they may derive from gender roles and stereotypes. However, this same study found that the gender differences in self-esteem were largest in countries that were wealthy, individualistic, and egalitarian, where women officially have the same freedoms as men, rather than in highly patriarchal countries where gender roles are traditionally more restrictive (Bleidorn et al., 2016).

Identity

identity a description of the self that is often externally imposed, such as through membership in a group

An **identity** is a definition of the self. Importantly, each of us has multiple identities that are more salient than others at certain times or in certain situations. If you are on a university campus, you might say you are a student. If you are at a family reunion, you could say you are a son, daughter, or grandchild. You can be a friend, a coworker, a teammate, a member of a religious group.

Adolescence is the period at which children appreciate their multiple identities and begin to forge new identities that may be distinct from those of their family and childhood friends. The earliest theory of identity formation was proposed by Erik Erikson, as briefly described in Chapter 9. Erikson argued that all adolescents experience an identity crisis, in part as a means of separating from their parents (Erikson, 1968). In his view, the challenge is as follows: "From among all possible and imaginable relations, [the person] must make a series of ever-narrowing selections of personal, occupational, sexual, and ideological commitments" (1968, p. 245). Successful resolution of this crisis results in **identity achievement**—that is, an integration of various aspects of the self into a coherent whole that is stable over time and across events.

In the decades after Erikson published his theory, researchers rejected the idea that all individuals must go through an identity crisis (Baumeister, 2005). Psychologist James Marcia (1980), who spent most of his career at Simon Fraser University, developed an alternate way of describing adolescents' identity development by considering where an individual falls on the dimensions of identity exploration and identity commitment. On the basis of an adolescent's responses in a structured interview, that individual is classified into one of four categories of identity status: identity achievement, moratorium, identity foreclosure, and identity diffusion (see Table 11.3).

The modern conception of identity achievement aligns with Erikson's original description: the individual has explored potential identities and has decided on a coherent and consolidated identity. Identity achievement represents the ideal endpoint of identity development for adolescents and young adults. The other three states represent individuals who have not yet reached identity achievement but could. Individuals in a state of **moratorium** are exploring possible commitments to identities but have not committed to one. Some may explore potential identities with breadth, trying out a variety of candidate identities before choosing one. For example, a person might consider being a musician, a lawyer, or a historian. Others may make an initial commitment and explore it in depth, through continuous monitoring of current commitments in order to make them more conscious (Meeus et al., 2010). Thus, they may try out various types of art (painting, sculpture) before committing to being an artist.

The state of **identity foreclosure** refers to individuals who have committed early to an identity before engaging in any real exploration. A typical example would be an adolescent who has been told all their life that they will be a doctor, and who therefore commits to the identity of being a doctor without exploring other potential careers and identities. The fourth identity status, **identity diffusion**, involves individuals who have neither committed to an identity nor explored potential identities; they are not concerned about their identity and thus make no concrete steps toward recognizing their identity.

In the course of adolescence and early adulthood, individuals generally progress slowly toward identity achievement

identity achievement an integration of various aspects of the self into a coherent whole that is stable over time and across events

moratorium period in which the individual is exploring various occupational and ideological choices and has not yet made a clear commitment to them

identity foreclosure period in which the individual has not engaged in any identity experimentation and has established a vocational or ideological identity based on the choices or values of others

identity diffusion period in which the individual does not have firm commitments regarding the issues in question and is not making progress toward developing them

Identity Development in Adolescence

BRAD S. ZERIVITZ - FOOTAGE/ GETTY IMAGES

TABLE 11.3 The Four Groups of Identity Status Developed by Marcia (1980)

	Exploration	No Exploration
Commitment	**Identity achievement** The individual has explored potential identities and has committed to one.	**Identity foreclosure** The individual has not explored potential identities and has chosen an identity based on the choices or values of others.
No commitment	**Moratorium** The individual is exploring various identities and has not yet made a clear commitment to any.	**Identity diffusion** The individual is not making progress toward exploring or committing to an identity.

JOHN WARBURTON-LEE PHOTOGRAPHY/ALAMY

In some traditional cultures, adolescents have few role options and, consequently, know from a young age what their adult identity will be.

(Kroger, Martinussen, & Marcia, 2010; Meeus, 2011). The most typical sequences of change appear to be from diffusion → foreclosure → achievement, or from diffusion → moratorium → foreclosure → achievement (Meeus, 2011). There is little evidence that many adolescents have the kind of sustained identity confusion that Erikson maintained could lead to severe psychological disturbance (Meeus, 2011).

Researchers generally have found that, at least in modern Western societies, the identity status of adolescents and young adults is related to their adjustment, social behaviour, and personality, with identity achievement being most closely associated with mental health and positive social outcomes (Crocetti, 2017). Those who have made a commitment, whether through foreclosure or identity achievement, tend to be low in depression and anxiety, and high in personality characteristics of extroversion and agreeableness (Morsunbul et al., 2016). Young adults who explore possible commitments more in depth than in breadth tend to be extroverted, agreeable, and conscientious (reliable, regulated), whereas those who explore more in breadth tend to be prone to negative emotionality but open to experience (Luyckx, Soenens, & Goossens, 2006).

A number of factors influence adolescents' identity formation. One key factor is the approach parents take with their offspring. Adolescents who experience warmth and support from parents tend to have a more mature identity and less identity confusion (Meeus, 2011; Morsunbul et al., 2016). In addition, parents tend to react with support when young university students explore in depth and make identity commitments (Beyers & Goossens, 2008), and this support may reinforce their children's choices. Youths who are subject to parental psychological control tend to explore in breadth and are lower in making commitment to an identity (Luyckx et al., 2007). Identity formation is also influenced by both the larger social context and the historical context (Bosma & Kunnen, 2001). Until a few decades ago, for instance, most adolescent girls focused their search for identity on the goal of marriage and family. Even in developed societies, few career opportunities were available to women. Today, women in many cultures are more likely to base their identity on both family and career. Thus, familial, individual, socioeconomic, historical, and cultural factors all contribute to identity development.

LAINDIAPIAROA/GETTY IMAGES

Trying out various "looks" can be an aspect of the self-discovery that occurs amongst many adolescents.

Ethnic and Racial Identity

Ethnic and racial identity is especially salient in adolescence. An **ethnic and racial identity** encompasses the beliefs and attitudes an individual has about the ethnic or racial groups to which they belong (Umaña-Taylor et al., 2014). Ethnicity refers to the relationships and experiences a child has that are linked with their cultural or ethnic ancestry, religion, or native language, whereas race typically refers to physical characteristics, most commonly skin colour (Umaña-Taylor et al., 2014). It is important to emphasize at the outset that race is a social construct—there is no genetic basis for there being separate "races" (Kolbert, 2018).

Children have different understandings of their ethnic and racial identity at different points of their development. Preschool children do not really understand the significance of being a member of an ethnic group, although they may be able to label themselves as belonging to an ethnic group or race (e.g., Indo-Canadian, Cree). Even if they engage in behaviours that characterize their ethnic or racial group and have some simple knowledge about the group, they do not understand that ethnicity and race are lasting features of the self.

ethnic and racial identity the beliefs and attitudes an individual has about the ethnic or racial groups to which they belong

acculturation the process of adjusting to a new culture while retaining some aspects of one's culture of origin

By the early school years, children know the common characteristics of their ethnic or racial group, start to have feelings about being members of the group, and may have begun to form ethnically based preferences regarding foods, traditional holiday activities, language use, and so forth (Ocampo, Bernal, & Knight, 1993). Children tend to identify themselves according to their ethnic or racial group between the ages of 5 and 8. However, a study of African American, White, and mixed race 9-year-olds in the United States found that each group viewed gender as a more essential part of their identities than race (Rogers & Meltzoff, 2017). By late elementary school, minority children in the United States often have a very positive view of their ethnic or racial group (Hughes, Way, & Rivas-Drake, 2011).

The family and the larger social environment play a major role in the development of children's ethnic and racial identity. Parents and other family members and adults can be instrumental in teaching their children about the strengths and unique features of their ethnic culture or race and instilling them with pride (Evans et al., 2012). Such instruction can be especially important for the development of a positive ethnic identity when the child's racial or ethnic group is the object of prejudice and discrimination in the larger society (Gaylord-Harden, Burrow, & Cunningham, 2012; Spencer & Markstrom-Adams, 1990).

The issue of ethnic or racial identity often becomes more central in adolescence, as young people begin actively exploring their multiple identities. Minority-group members in particular may be faced with difficult decisions as they try to decide the degree to which they will adopt the values of their ethnic group or those of the dominant culture. This dilemma is especially difficult for children of immigrants, who must adjust the behaviours and values they learned from their origin culture as they take on some of the behaviours and values of their new culture, a process known as **acculturation.** Children and parents can acculturate at different rates to their new culture, sometimes resulting in acculturation gaps between them, which can in turn be a source of conflict. For example, in a study of Latino youth born in the United States to foreign-born parents, parent–youth acculturation gaps were related to increased parent–youth conflict, which negatively affected academic performance amongst the youth (Nair, Roche, & White, 2018). Similarly, a study of Arab Canadian youth transitioning to adulthood found that acculturation gaps were linked with more youth–parent conflict, but mostly when the relationship was low in trust and communication (Rasmi, Chuang, & Hennig, 2015).

Research suggests that higher levels of ethnic and racial identity are generally associated with high self-esteem, well-being, and low levels of emotional and behavioural problems (Neblett, Rivas-Drake, & Umaña-Taylor, 2012; Rivas-Drake et al., 2014). For example, youth from immigrant Chinese families in British Columbia who had higher levels of ethnic identity were less likely to show symptoms of depression, performed better in school, and had higher self-esteem (Costigan et al., 2010). Similarly, First Nations children in Canada who identified with their group had higher self-esteem than children with lower levels of identification (Corenblum, 2014). Furthermore, adolescents with a positive ethnic and racial identity appear to be buffered from the negative effects of discrimination, as illustrated by a recent meta-analysis of 51 studies from countries around the world, including Canada (Yip et al., 2019).

Establishing a clear ethnic identification may be more difficult and less consistent for some adolescents, such as multi-ethnic or multi-racial youth, who could develop identifications with more than one ethnic or racial group (Marks, Patton, & Garcia Coll,

Much of young children's learning about their ethnic group takes place in the family. Parents teach their children the specific practices associated with their group and can instill in them pride in their ethnic heritage.

SERGEI BACHLAKOV/SHUTTERSTOCK

2011; Nishina et al., 2010). However, when ethnic- or racial-minority parents actively socialize their children by teaching about their culture and instilling pride, children tend to have a more positive ethnic and racial identity (Neblett et al., 2012; Umaña-Taylor & Guimond, 2010) and are less susceptible to the negative effects of discrimination (Neblett et al., 2008; Wang & Huguley, 2012).

In some cases, ethnic- and racial-minority youth develop a *bicultural identity* that includes a comfortable identification with both the majority culture and their own ethnic culture. Although trying to straddle two cultures can be stressful, it is not always so, and for some minority youths it can provide certain benefits, such as positive perceptions of opportunities in the majority society (Kiang, Yip, & Fuligni, 2008). However, research on adolescents in traditional cultures, such as Canadian First Nations, has found that a bicultural identity can be associated with lower levels of some strengths that are part of successful identity development, such as certain traditional values, as well as fidelity (loyalty and commitment) and wisdom (Gfellner & Armstrong, 2012).

The study of racial and ethnic identities has almost entirely focused on children in racial or ethnic minority families. However, researchers also recognize that children growing up in White families in the United States also experience socialization from parents that helps shape their beliefs about their own race and ethnic identity (Burton et al., 2010). Research indicates White parents often do not discuss race with their children or do not think they have a "race" and that some White parents actively teach their children to be "colourblind" (Hagerman, 2017). This is an emerging area of research.

Ethnic and racial identities are also linked with adolescents' self-esteem. Despite the fact that African American children and adolescents experience discrimination and stereotyping, they have higher self-esteem on average than their White American peers (Gray-Little & Hafdahl, 2000). This may be the case because ethnic and racial identity is an important aspect of self-concept for many African Americans, and the emphasis by parents and other adults in the community on the positive features of being African American may enhance African American children's and adolescents' self-esteem (Gray-Little & Hafdahl, 2000; Herman,

FRESH YOUTH INITIATIVES

Engaging in activities that promote the welfare of others in their ethnic or racial group may contribute to adolescents' having a positive sense of ethnic identity. The adolescents shown here are members of a youth-development group that carries out community projects ranging from cleaning parks and painting neighbourhood murals to tending community gardens and working in a food pantry for the needy.

2004). Although discrimination can have a negative effect on adolescents' self-esteem, how ethnic minority children and adolescents think about themselves is influenced much more strongly by acceptance from their family, neighbours, and friends than by reactions from strangers and the society at large (Galliher, Jones, & Dahl, 2011; Seaton, Yip, & Sellers, 2009). Thus, minority-group parents can help their children develop high self-esteem and a sense of well-being by instilling them with pride in their culture and by being generally supportive (Bámaca et al., 2005; Berkel et al., 2009; Cooper & McLoyd, 2011).

Sexual Identity

In childhood and especially adolescence, an individual's identity includes his or her **sexual identity**, which refers to one's sense of oneself as a sexual being. Sexual identity includes **sexual orientation**—an individual's romantic or erotic attractions to people of the opposite gender, same gender, both, or neither. Sexual identity is thus separate from gender identity, which is an individual's awareness of himself or herself as a male, as a female, or as transgendered and will be discussed in Chapter 15.

Puberty, during which there are large rises in gonadal hormones, is the most common time for youth to begin experiencing feelings of sexual attraction to others (Diamond, Bonner, & Dickenson, 2015). Studies using a variety of methodologies, including twin and adoption studies as well as epigenetic studies, indicate that a person's sexual orientation is at least partly hereditary; identical twins, for example, are more likely to exhibit similar sexual orientations than are fraternal twins (Ngun & Vilain, 2014).

The majority of adolescents, like the majority of adults, are heterosexual—they are attracted to members of the opposite biological sex. In Canada and the United States, 88.8% of high school students reported a heterosexual identity, with 2% to 10% identifying themselves as gay, lesbian, or bisexual (Cénat et al., 2015; Kann et al., 2016). The minority status of non-heterosexual youth has led to concern—as well as significant research—about the well-being of **sexual-minority youth,** namely adolescents who are attracted to people from their same biological sex or from both sexes, sometimes collectively called lesbian, gay, and bisexual (LGB) youth. Although sexual-minority youth are often grouped with transgender and questioning individuals, the latter are more accurately described as gender-minority youth (discussed in detail in Chapter 15). In the discussion that follows, we focus on sexual-minority, or LGB, youth.

Sexual-minority youth (and adults) face discrimination both in law and in practice and are frequent targets for harassment and violence. Even with the growing acceptance of sexual-minority people in Western society, and with the legality of same-sex marriage in Canada, the United States, and several other countries, hate crimes against sexual-minority individuals are still prevalent, making up 16% of all hate crimes in the United States in 2017 (Federal Bureau of Investigation, 2018). Sexual orientation was the motivation for 10% of all hate crimes in Canada in 2017 (Statistics Canada, 2018).

Throughout childhood and adolescence, sexual-minority youth often feel "different" (Savin-Williams & Cohen, 2007), and some even display cross-gender behaviours from a relatively early age—for example, in their preferences for toys, clothes, or leisure activities (Drummond et al., 2008). However, these youth may take a long time to recognize that they are lesbian, gay, or bisexual. This process begins with the *first recognition*—an initial realization that one is somewhat different from others, accompanied by feelings of alienation from oneself and others. At this point, the individual is generally aware that same-sex attractions may be the relevant issue but does not reveal this to others.

sexual identity one's sense of oneself as a sexual being

sexual orientation a person's preference in regard to males or females as objects of erotic feelings

sexual-minority youth young people who experience same-sex attractions

Figure 11.4 displays data from a study of sexual-minority adults who recalled the development of their sexual identities and recognition of their sexual orientation. Across genders, sexual identities, and age, most participants reported experiencing their first same-sex attraction between ages 10 and 15 but did not identify themselves as lesbian, gay, or bisexual until after age 15 (Martos, Nezhad, & Meyer, 2015). On average, disclosure of their sexual orientation did not occur until after age 20, though there was considerable variation by age cohort: young adults (18 to 29) reported disclosing their sexual orientation before age 20, whereas adults aged 45 to 59 did not disclose until age 25 (Martos et al., 2015). This finding likely reflects the growing acceptance of homosexual and bisexual identities in Western society; identifying as homosexual had more negative consequences for the older generation than for the younger generation.

One factor that complicates the study of sexual identity is the fact that, especially for females, there is considerable instability in adolescents' and young adults' reports of same-sex attraction or sexual behaviour (Savin-Williams & Ream, 2007). By university age, for example, a notable number of young women identify themselves as "mostly straight"—that is, mostly heterosexual but somewhat attracted to females (Diamond et al., 2015). One longitudinal study that followed 79 lesbian, bisexual, and unlabelled (those with some same-sex involvement who were unwilling to attach a label to their sexuality) women ages 18 to 25 found that, over a 10-year period, two-thirds changed the identity labels they had claimed at the beginning of the study and one-third changed labels two or more times (Diamond, 2008). Overall, females are more likely to describe themselves as bisexual or "mostly heterosexual" than are males (Saewyc, 2011). Male youth who have engaged in same-sex sexual experiences show an increasing preference for males from adolescence to early adulthood (Smiler, Frankel, & Savin-Williams, 2011).

When they do "come out," or publicly self-identify as lesbian, gay, or bisexual, sexual-minority youths usually disclose to a best friend (typically a sexual-minority friend), to a peer to whom they are attracted, or to a sibling, and they do not tell

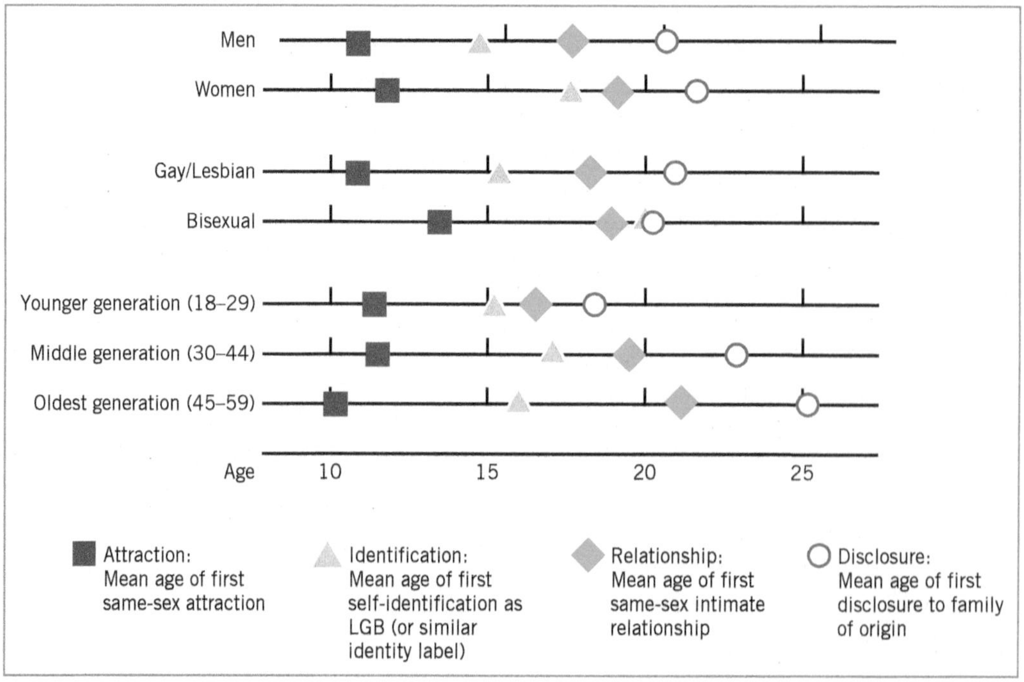

FIGURE 11.4 Milestones of sexual identity and behaviour recalled by LGB adults The younger generation (18–29) experienced milestones earlier and with smaller gaps than did the oldest generation (45–59) in the study, reflecting the differences in the social standing of LGB individuals across generations. (Data from Martos, Nezhad, & Meyer, 2015)

their parents until a year or more later, if at all (Savin-Williams, 1998b). If they do reveal their sexual orientation to their parents, they usually tell their mothers before telling their fathers, often because the mother asked or because they wanted to share that aspect of their lives with their mother (Savin-Williams & Ream, 2003).

Although many parents react in a supportive or only slightly negative manner to their children's coming out, it is sadly not unusual for parents to initially respond to such a disclosure with anger, disappointment, and especially denial (Heatherington & Lavner, 2008; Savin-Williams & Ream, 2003). Unfortunately, some parents respond with threats, insults, or physical violence (M. S. Friedman et al., 2011). Likely as a result of such reactions, sexual-minority youth are at greater risk for suicidal behaviour than their heterosexual peers (Kann et al., 2016). For example, a large British Columbia study showed that lesbian and bisexual girls were 4 times more likely to show suicidal behaviours than were heterosexual girls (Peter et al., 2017).

Victimization and harassment by peers and others in the community are also commonly experienced by sexual-minority youth (M. S. Friedman et al., 2011; Martin-Storey & Crosnoe, 2012). Sexual-minority youth are more likely than heterosexual youth to be involved or injured in a physical fight and to be the victim of dating violence or sexual assault (Kann et al., 2016; see Figure 11.5). Three-quarters of sexual-minority youth report having been verbally threatened because of their sexual orientation (Human Rights Campaign, 2018). Fear of being harassed or rejected outside the home is one reason many sexual-minority youth hide their sexual orientation from heterosexual peers. These high rates of victimization may also explain why sexual-minority youth are more likely to engage in truancy (Kann et al., 2016).

In one survey, the top three most important life problems listed by sexual-minority youth were non-accepting families, bullying at school, and fear of being open about their sexual identity; in contrast, the top three problems listed by heterosexual youth were grades, university, and financial pressures (Human Rights Campaign, 2012). Clearly, the lives of sexual-minority youth are strongly affected by their sexual identities, and related concerns may prevent them from focusing on the day-to-day issues that concern most adolescents. A more recent survey, which also included transgender and gender questioning individuals, found that only 27% of LGBTQ youth feel they can be themselves as an LGBTQ person in school; in addition, only 19 states have enacted anti-bullying laws that protect LGBTQ students (Human Rights Campaign, 2018). The daily struggles of sexual-minority youth lead them to be twice as likely as heterosexual youth to say they will need to move to another town to feel that they are accepted (Human Rights Campaign, 2012).

Given these levels of harassment and violence, it is not surprising that sexual-minority youth are vulnerable to a number of social and psychological problems. In Canadian studies, sexual-minority adolescents reported experiencing more symptoms of depression,

FIGURE 11.5 Exposure to violence and internalizing mental health problems by sexual orientation Sexual-minority youth report more of all forms of violence than heterosexual youth, and they report higher sadness and likelihood to attempt suicide. (Data from Kann et al., 2016)

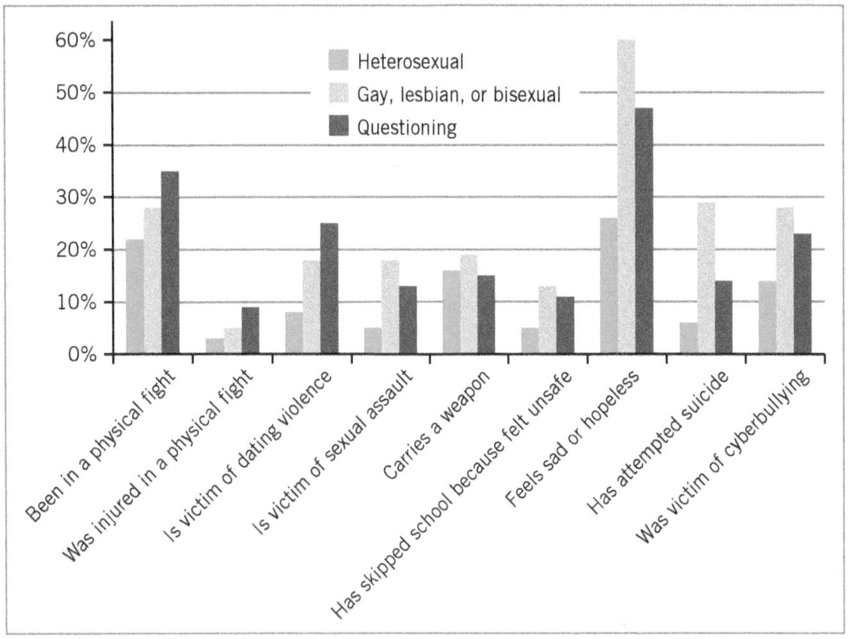

AP PHOTO/JIM MONE

Sexual-minority youth deal with many of the same family and identity issues as do other adolescents, and they are generally equally as adjusted as other teens. However, they face special challenges if their peers and family do not accept their sexual identity. In what may be a sign of changing attitudes, these two Minnesota high school seniors, who were amongst the students elected to their school's ceremonial "royal court," filed a civil suit to gain the right to walk together as a couple in the royal court's opening procession. Their legal victory and their appearance together in the procession brought cheers from many of their schoolmates.

more acting-out behaviours, more bullying, more sexual harassment, and less connection with their closest friends than did heterosexual adolescents (Cénat et al., 2015; Peter, Taylor, & Chamberland, 2015; Williams et al., 2005; Watson et al., 2018). They also report higher levels of tobacco, alcohol, and drug use than do other youth (Kann et al., 2016). They are also more likely to be homeless or in foster care, frequently because they have run away from, or have been kicked out of, their home (Coker, Austin, & Schuster, 2010; Fish et al., 2019).

High rates of suicide amongst sexual- and gender-minority youth led to the creation of the It Gets Better Project (www.itgetsbetter.org) in 2010. More than 60,000 videos, in which sexual-minority individuals and their allies share their personal stories, have been uploaded across six continents (It Gets Better Project, n.d.). Such efforts seem to be having an impact; a survey of sexual-minority youth in 2012 found that 77% said that they knew their lives would get better (Human Rights Campaign, 2012). Connecting with each other through social media may help sexual- and gender-minority adolescents cope with the stress of their lives; 73% of sexual-minority youth say they are more honest about themselves online, compared with only 43% of heterosexual youth (Human Rights Campaign, 2012).

Sexual-minority youth who are also of minority race or ethnic status are a special source of concern, given that they may experience discrimination on two fronts. One survey of adolescents in British Columbia found that sexual-minority Asian youth experienced more harassment and discrimination than did heterosexual youth—although social support helped buffer the psychological distress from this discrimination (Poon, Saewyc, & Chen, 2011). However, a study of more than 1000 sexual- and gender-minority young women found that LGBTQ women found no difference in the ranges of mental health problems (depression, anxiety) and health-related behaviours (alcohol consumption, smoking) across African American, Latino American, Asian American, and White American groups (Balsam et al., 2015).

Despite the heightened risks, it is important to emphasize that in most ways, sexual-minority children and adolescents are developmentally indistinguishable from their heterosexual peers: they deal with many of the same family and identity issues in adolescence and generally function just as well. Three-quarters of youth now say that they hear positive messages about sexual-minority identities online and in the media, at school, or by elected leaders (Human Rights Campaign, 2012). Many schools across Canada have implemented Gay Straight Alliances (GSAs), which are social clubs to support LGBTQ student inclusion and well-being. A recent study in British Columbia found that GSAs have a positive effect on school climate, with LGB students reporting that they feel safer in school (Saewyc et al., 2019). The increasing positive portrayals of sexual-minority people in the media, as well as increasing social equality and cultural acceptance of sexual minorities, may also contribute to this positive trend (Diamond et al., 2015).

REVIEW QUESTION

Many of the studies cited in this text, and in this field, describe participants in terms of various identities. How does an understanding of identity affect the way these studies are interpreted? ■

CHAPTER SUMMARY

The Caregiver–Child Attachment Relationship

- Harlow demonstrated through studies with monkeys that infants need and prefer a "cloth mother" over a wire one that provides food, and they use the cloth mothers as a secure base for exploration.
- According to Bowlby's theory, attachment is a biologically based process, rooted in evolution, that increases the helpless infant's chance of survival. A secure attachment provides children with a secure base for exploration. Children's early relationships with their parents and other caregivers provide children with internal working models of relationships.
- Ainsworth's Strange Situation can be used to categorize the quality of a child's attachment to his or her primary caregiver as securely attached, insecurely attached (insecure/resistant, insecure/avoidant), or disorganized/disoriented. Children are more likely to be securely attached if their caregivers are sensitive and responsive to their needs.
- There are similarities in children's attachments across many cultures, although the percentages of children in different attachment categories sometimes vary across cultures or subcultures.
- Intervention programs demonstrate that parents can be trained to be more sensitive, attentive, and stimulating in their parenting. These changes are associated with increases in infants' sociability, exploration, ability to soothe themselves, and security of attachment.

The Self

- Young children's conceptions of themselves are concrete—based on physical characteristics and overt behaviour—and usually positive. As children age, their self-concepts are increasingly based on internal qualities and the quality of relationships with others; they also become more realistic, integrated, abstract, and complex.
- Because young adolescents focus on what others think of them, they think about an "imaginary audience" and develop "personal fables."
- Children's self-esteem is affected by many factors, including genetic predispositions, the quality of parent–child and peer relationships, physical attractiveness, academic competence, and various social factors.
- Concepts of how a person should think and behave differ across cultures, and therefore self-evaluations and self-esteem scores also differ.
- The development of an ethnic and racial identity involves identifying oneself as a member of an ethnic or racial group, developing an understanding of group constancy, engaging in ethnic-role behaviours, acquiring knowledge about one's group, and developing a sense of belonging to the group. Family and community influence these aspects of development.
- Minority adolescents often start to explore the meaning of their ethnicity or race and its role in their identity. Many youth initially tend to be diffused or foreclosed in regard to their identities, and then become increasingly interested in exploring their ethnicity or race (search/moratorium). Some come to embrace their ethnicity or race; others gravitate toward the majority culture; still others become bicultural.
- Sexual-minority (lesbian, gay, or bisexual) youth are similar to others in their development of identity and self, although they can face special difficulties. Many have some awareness of their same-sex attractions by late childhood. The process of self-identification and disclosure amongst sexual-minority youth may involve several phases: first recognition, test and exploration, identity acceptance, and identity integration. However, not all sexual-minority individuals go through all these stages, or go through them in the same order, and some have difficulty accepting and revealing their sexual-minority identity.

Test Yourself

1. Critical to an infant's growth is the development of a positive emotional connection to a primary caregiver, such as a parent. This enduring emotional bond is known as ___________.
   a. co-regulation
   b. attachment
   c. co-dependency
   d. imprinting
2. Harlow's work with infant rhesus monkeys found that the monkeys spent more time with the cloth "mothers" that did not feed them than the wire "mothers" that did feed them. What is the main implication of this finding?
   a. The monkeys were not motivated by food.
   b. The monkeys were drawn to food more than to physical comfort.
   c. The monkeys were drawn to physical comfort more than to food.
   d. The monkeys' choices were explained by behaviourism.
3. Three attachment types were initially identified in research by Mary Ainsworth. Which attachment type was later added to categorize those that did not fit well into Ainsworth's initial three categories?
   a. Securely attached
   b. Disorganized/disoriented
   c. Insecure/resistant
   d. Insecure/avoidant

4. A father who responds quickly to the needs of his child and shows emotional warmth by smiling, laughing, and communicating positively to his child is demonstrating
   a. caregiver responsibility.
   b. paternal instinct.
   c. parental security.
   d. parental sensitivity.
5. Which of the following best describes a typical individual's experience with attachment?
   a. Once a child develops an attachment style, that style remains consistent for all relationships in their lives.
   b. Children are born with an internal working model of attachment, pre-programmed in their genes.
   c. A child's attachment may vary from person to person.
   d. Attachment is only relevant in strange situations.
6. Studies have shown that the link between attachment security and genetic make-up
   a. disappears by adulthood.
   b. can be differentially impacted by the quality of the child's environment.
   c. can be changed by altering the levels of oxytocin in the brain.
   d. is proof that genetic markers cause specific attachment security types.
7. A couple who have just become parents need to continue working outside the home but are concerned that putting their child in a childcare centre will interfere with the infant's development. How can you best reassure them?
   a. Childcare doesn't really matter because children spend more time with their parents.
   b. Childcare primarily has negative effects if it is of low quality, so paying attention to quality is important.
   c. High quality home environments are more important that childcare environments.
   d. Both b and c.
8. ____________ involves a person's overall subjective evaluation of oneself and the feelings associated with that evaluation.
   a. Self-esteem
   b. Self concept
   c. Self-reflection
   d. Self-measure
9. Two-year-old Lani walks by a mirror and notices chocolate around her mouth. She uses the bottom of her shirt to carefully wipe it off. Lani is displaying ____________.
   a. self-recognition
   b. self-consciousness
   c. self-determination
   d. self-esteem
10. As children's cognitive abilities increase, their self-concepts shift from focusing on ____________ characteristics to ____________ qualities.
    a. psychological; physical
    b. active; passive
    c. physical; psychological
    d. flattering; unflattering
11. Self-concept in adolescence is characterized by a reemergence of a form of egocentrism, exemplified by the individual overly differentiating his or her feelings from those of others. This type of egocentrism is called the
    a. looking-glass self.
    b. personal fable.
    c. imaginary audience.
    d. introspective mirror.
12. According to James Marcia's theory of identity development, which stage is noted by the exploration of identity status?
    a. Identify diffusion
    b. Identity foreclosure
    c. Confusion
    d. Moratorium
13. The process of adjusting to a new culture while retaining some aspects of one's culture of origin is called ____________.
    a. enculturation
    b. ethnic identification
    c. acculturation
    d. identity blending
14. Which of the following statements is *not* true about racial and ethnic identity during adolescence?
    a. The more an adolescent identifies with his or her ethnic and racial identity, the lower his or her self-esteem.
    b. Minority-group members can face challenges in adopting the values of their ethnic group or those of the dominant culture.
    c. Because they may have had early experiences with discrimination, ethnic- and racial-minority adolescents may feel ambivalent about their own ethnic status.
    d. Development of a bicultural identity can lead to positive benefits for some minority youth and can lead to challenges for others.
15. For sexual-minority youth, the process of *first recognition* is noted by
    a. feelings of alienation resulting from the realization that they are different from others.
    b. a preference for social interaction with other sexual-minority individuals.
    c. an individual's first experience with same-sex sexual activities.
    d. an individual's initial disclosure about his/her sexual identity.

LaunchPad
macmillan learning

DON'T STOP NOW! Research shows that testing yourself is a powerful learning tool. Visit LaunchPad to access the LearningCurve adaptive quizzing system, which gives you a personalized study plan to help build your mastery of the chapter material through videos, activities, and more. **Go to launchpadworks.com.**

Critical Thinking Questions

1. Some theorists believe that early attachment relationships have enduring long-term effects. Others think that such effects depend on the quality of the ongoing parent–child relationship, which tends to be correlated with the security of children's early attachment to parents. How do you think researchers might go about examining this issue?
2. Based on what you have read about attachment and the development of the self, what negative effects might children experience as a result of being placed in a series of different foster-care homes? How might these effects vary with the age of the child?
3. Self concept, self-esteem, and identity are related but distinct constructs. What kinds of questions could you ask of adolescents to get at each aspect of themselves?
4. What are some of the practical and conceptual difficulties of determining when children first recognize that they are physically attracted to same-sex or other-sex individuals?

Key Terms

acculturation, p. 411
attachment, p. 386
attachment theory, p. 388
disorganized/disoriented attachment, p. 391
ethnic and racial identity, p. 410
identity, p. 408
identity achievement, p. 409
identity diffusion, p. 409
identity foreclosure, p. 409
imaginary audience, p. 403
insecure/avoidant attachment, p. 391
insecure/resistant attachment, p. 391
internal working model of attachment, p. 389
moratorium, p. 409
parental sensitivity, p. 393
personal fable, p. 403
secure attachment, p. 390
secure base, p. 388
self-concept, p. 398
self-esteem, p. 404
sexual identity, p. 413
sexual orientation, p. 413
sexual-minority youth, p. 413
social comparison, p. 401
Strange Situation, p. 389

Answers to Test Yourself

1. b, **2.** c, **3.** b, **4.** d, **5.** c, **6.** b, **7.** d, **8.** a, **9.** a, **10.** c, **11.** b, **12.** d, **13.** c, **14.** a, **15.** a

CHAPTER

12 The Family

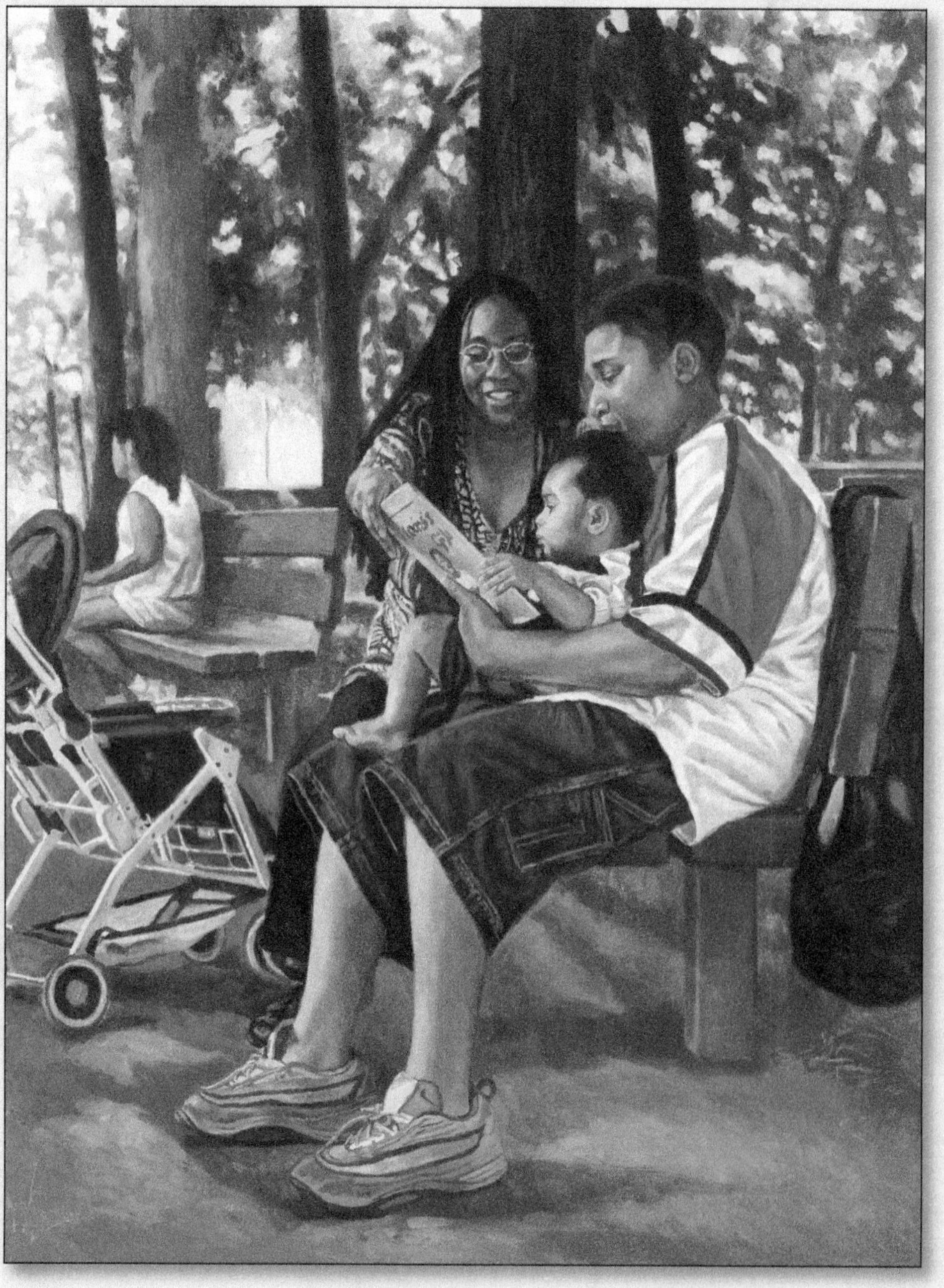

COLIN BOOTMAN, *Family in the Park* (oil on canvas, 1999)

THEMES

NATURE AND NURTURE ▪ THE ACTIVE CHILD ▪ THE SOCIOCULTURAL CONTEXT
INDIVIDUAL DIFFERENCES ▪ RESEARCH AND CHILDREN'S WELFARE

Each of us defines family differently. For some, a family might be just those individuals who live under the same roof, and for others it may include extended family and even non-related community members. Major life events such as marriage, divorce, remarriage, and childbirth can expand the number of families to which an individual might belong. An official definition of "family" comes from Statistics Canada (2015), which defines the family very broadly to include children (of any age, so long as they are not living with a partner or their own children) living in the same household with married couples, common-law couples, lone parents of any marital status, or grandparents (in those cases in which no parents are present). Couples can be of the same or opposite gender. As broad as this definition is, it excludes family members who do not live in the same household but who may play an important role in children's lives, such as grandparents, aunts, uncles, and cousins. If we expand our understanding of family beyond the Statistics Canada definition, there are biological families, extended kin families, in-law families, adoptive families, and foster families.

For this chapter, we define "family" from the perspective of the child. Thus, a **family** is a group that involves at least one adult who is related to the child by birth, marriage, adoption, or foster status and who is responsible for providing basic necessities as well as love, support, safety, stability, and opportunities for learning. Multiple adults can contribute to these responsibilities and there can be multiple children in the family as well.

family a group that involves at least one adult who is related to the child by birth, marriage, adoption, or foster status and who is responsible for providing basic necessities as well as love, support, safety, stability, and opportunities for learning

Families are crucial to the development of children. According to Bronfenbrenner's bioecological model (discussed in Chapter 9), family is central to a child's microsystem, providing direct support for the child's development. For example, families tend to be smaller today than in the past, many more mothers work outside the home, more people are choosing to have children outside of marriage, and same-sex parenting is increasingly common and accepted. Such changes in the makeup of a child's family can affect the resources available to the child, as well as the parents' child-rearing practices and behaviour.

In this chapter, we examine many developmental aspects of family interaction. We begin by considering how family functioning and children's development may have been affected by certain social changes that have occurred in Canada over the past several decades—from the increased age of first-time parents to increased rates of divorce, remarriage, and maternal employment. We then discuss the ways in which parents' approach to parenting can influence their children's development, the ways in which children can influence their parents' parenting, and the ways in which siblings may influence one another. Finally, we explore the impact that factors such as poverty and culture may have on developmental outcomes.

As you will see, the theme of *nature and nurture* is central to the study of the role of the family because a child's heredity and rearing influence each other and jointly affect the

Some family forms, such as families headed by same-sex parents, are more common and accepted now than in the past.

SARAHWOLFEPHOTOGRAPHY/GETTY IMAGES

family structure the number of and relationships amongst the people living in a household

child's development. In addition, the theme of the *active child* is evident in our discussion of how children influence the way their parents socialize them. The theme of *sociocultural context* is also key, in that parenting practices are strongly influenced by cultural beliefs, biases, and goals and are related to different outcomes for children in different cultures. Furthermore, the issue of *individual differences* is a major theme in this chapter because different parenting styles, child-rearing practices, and family structures are associated with differences in children's social and emotional functioning. Finally, because parenting influences the quality of children's day-to-day experience, as well as children's beliefs and behaviours, understanding patterns of family functioning has relevance for our theme of *research and children's welfare.*

Family Structure

Family structure refers to the number of and relationships amongst the people living in a household. Alterations in the family structure due to births, deaths, divorce, remarriage, or other factors can also influence interactions amongst family members and may affect family routines and norms, as well as children's emotional well-being (Brown, Manning, & Stykes, 2015; Lee & McLanahan, 2015). In many cases, the effects of such shifts in family dynamics tend to be gradual. However, a single event such as a traumatic divorce or the death of a parent may cause a fairly dramatic change in a child's behaviour and emotional adjustment. In this section, we will first consider recent societal changes in family structure before reviewing in depth what is known about three specific family structures about which there has been some concern and much debate: same-sex parents, divorced parents, and stepparents.

Family Structure and Function in Middle Childhood

WORTH PUBLISHERS

Changes in Family Structure in Canada

Family structure has changed in several significant ways over the past 60 or more years. Let's explore some of the shifts that are most important for understanding child development and family life.

More Children Live with Lone or Unmarried Parents

If asked to describe the typical family structure, many Canadians would list a mother and a father who are married to each other and one or more children. In 1961, that characterization described the vast majority of children (Bohnert, Milan, & Lathe, 2014). According to the 2016 census data, however, only 70% of children in Canada were living with both of their biological or adoptive parents and without step- or half-siblings (Statistics Canada, 2017a). Furthermore, nearly 20% of children (0–14 years) were living in a lone-parent household, a percentage that has been slowly increasing in recent years, particularly in situations where the father is the lone parent. As displayed in Figure 12.1, the likelihood of living in a lone-parent or stepfamily household increases steadily with age (Statistics Canada, 2017a).

These changes in average family structure obscure some important qualifications; for example, the likelihood that a child in Canada will live with a lone parent, stepfamily, or without parents varies according to the province in which they live. As can be seen in Figure 12.2, the proportions of children aged 0–14 years living in one of these three situations was the highest in the territories (38.6%) and Nova Scotia (38.7%) and was the lowest in British Columbia (28.2%), Alberta (27.1%) and Ontario (28.5%; Statistics Canada, 2017a). There are undoubtedly many reasons for these cross-country

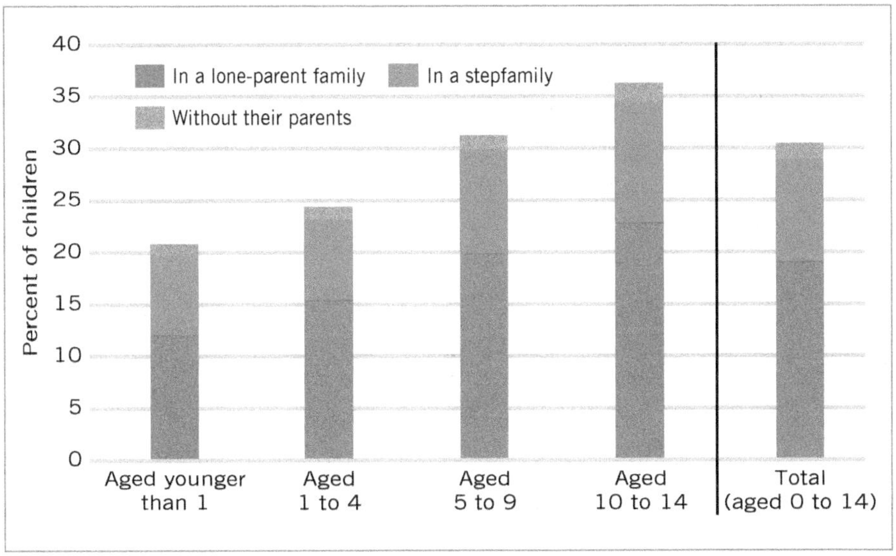

FIGURE 12.1 **Proportion of children (0–14 years) living with a lone parent or stepfamily, 2016** More than 30% of children aged 0–14 years live in either a lone-parent or stepfamily household or do not live with their parents. These proportions increase steadily as the child gets older. (Data from Statistics Canada, 2017a)

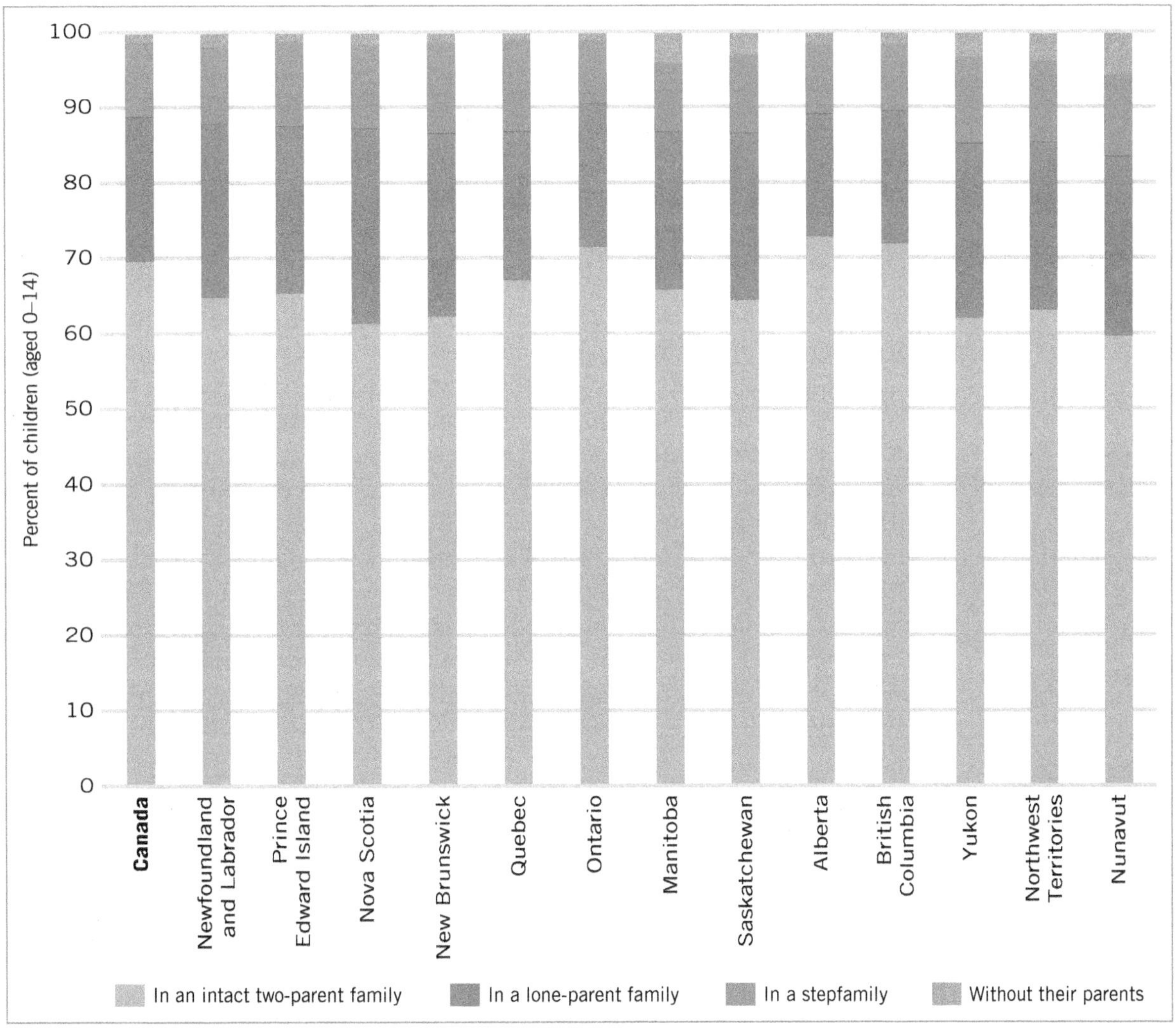

FIGURE 12.2 **Family situation for children aged 0–14 years, by province/territory, 2016** (Data from Statistics Canada, 2017a)

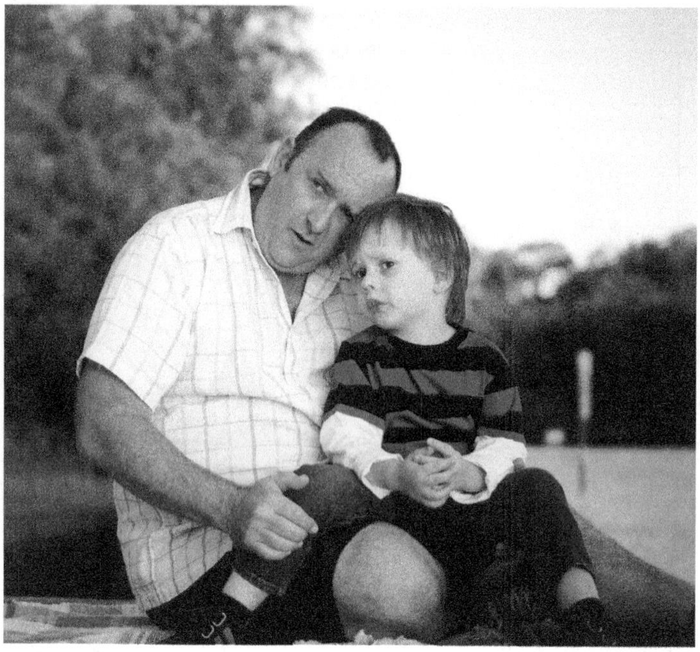

LYN WALKERDEN PHOTOGRAPHY/GETTY IMAGES

On average, older fathers engage in more verbal interactions with their preschool-age children than do younger fathers.

differences, but one potential contributing factor may come from the fact that Ontario, Alberta, and British Columbia have had more immigration than other areas of Canada. Although varying by country of origin, immigrants to Canada may be less likely to be divorced or have children when not married (Lee & Edmonston, 2013; Statistics Canada, 2017a).

Family structure has big implications for family income. Twenty-seven percent of children living with a female lone parent live below the poverty line in Canada, compared with 6.9% of children living with two married parents (Statistics Canada, 2019a). Another major implication of living with a lone parent is that the parent has less time to spend with each child because they must do all the household tasks alone and often must have more than one job in order to support the family. As a result, lone parents are much less likely than married parents to read to their children, although they are not less likely to eat breakfast with their children (Laughlin, 2014).

First-Time Parents Are Older than in the Past

The average age at which Canadian women have their first child has increased over the past two decades, from 27 years in 2001 to 29 years in 2016 (Provencher et al., 2018). This average has increased both because women are delaying when they have children and because the teen birth rate has been decreasing. See Box 12.1 for a more detailed discussion of teen parenting.

Having children at a later age has definite parenting advantages. Older first-time parents tend to have more education, higher-status occupations, and higher incomes than younger parents do. Older parents are also more likely to have planned the births of their children and to have fewer children overall. Thus, they have more financial resources for raising a family. They are also less likely to get divorced within 10 years if they are married (Bramlett & Mosher, 2002). In addition, older parents tend to be more positive in their parenting of infants than younger parents are. For example, one study found that, compared with people who became parents between the ages of 18 and 25, older mothers and fathers had lower rates of observed harsh parenting with their 2-year-olds, which, in turn, predicted fewer problem behaviours a year later (Scaramella et al., 2008). Furthermore, men who delay parenting until approximately age 30 or later are likewise more positive about the parenting role and tend to be more responsive, affectionate, and cognitively and verbally stimulating with their infants than are younger fathers (NICHD Early Child Care Research Network, 2000a).

Grandparents as Parents

WORTH PUBLISHERS

More Children Live with Grandparents

About 9% of children in Canada under 14 years old live with a grandparent, either with or without their own parents (Statistics Canada, 2019b). Most of these households are multigenerational—that is, children live with their parent(s) and at least one grandparent. A small minority of children (0.6%) live in *skip-generation* families—families where the grandparents act as their primary caregivers and no parents are present. The highest rate of skip-generation families in Canada is in Nunavut (2.7%; Statistics Canada, 2017a).

BOX 12.1 INDIVIDUAL DIFFERENCES Teenagers as Parents

The rate of teen pregnancies has dropped dramatically over the past several decades: births to teen girls in Canada between ages 15 and 19 have declined from a rate of 59.9 births per 1000 teens in 1959 to 8.4 births per 1000 teens in 2016, the lowest rate on record (Provencher et al., 2018). This decline is likely due in large part to better sex education and to greater availability of birth control and abortion services. However, teen pregnancy remains an issue that poses unique challenges for teenage parents and their children.

A number of factors increase the risk that a teen will become a parent. Growing up in a disadvantaged household, doing poorly in or being suspended from school, having low expectations of attending university, and having sexual intercourse for the first time before age 14 are all predictive of both boys and girls becoming parents as teenagers (Smith, 2018). In Canada, Indigenous women are more likely to have given birth before 20 years of age than non-Indigenous women (Boulet & Badets, 2017). Conversely, factors like living with both biological parents and being involved in school activities and religious organizations reduce the risk of teen childbearing (Ellis et al., 2003; Moore et al., 1998).

SANDRA TEDDY/GETTY IMAGES

Parenting classes for teen parents, such as the one shown here, can improve outcomes for both the babies and the teen parents themselves.

Having a child in adolescence is associated with many negative consequences for the teen parent, including a higher risk of living in poverty and receiving welfare benefits, a greater likelihood of being a single parent, and a reduced likelihood of graduating from high school or university (Diaz & Fiel, 2016; Mollborn & Dennis, 2012). The effects persist even after the teen parent becomes an adult: a study that followed teen mothers and fathers up to age 32 found that teen parents are more likely than their peers to either not attend or drop out of university, to live in poverty, to receive welfare benefits, and to be unemployed (Assini-Meytin & Green, 2015).

The children of teen parents also have a higher risk for negative outcomes than their peers, including school readiness, language ability, and academic achievement (Baudry et al., 2017). A study of Ontario teen parents showed that they tend to have less education, income, and life satisfaction as young adults (Lipman, Georgiades, & Boyle, 2011). Teen parents spend less time interacting with and reading to their children and more time speaking and behaving harshly with them, and these factors are linked with lower achievement and more behaviour problems in children (Mollborn & Dennis, 2012). One explanation for these findings is that teen mothers tend to have had high levels of exposure to adverse childhood experiences (ACEs) in their own childhoods (see Chapter 10), which in turn leads to greater parenting stress and a stronger reliance on physical punishment, both of which predict their children's behaviour problems (Yoon et al., 2019). The good news is that intervention programs that teach teens how to be responsive parents have been found to be effective at improving their parenting skills and in turn improving their children's cognitive development (Baudry et al., 2017).

One promising strategy being used by pediatric clinics in the United States is the implementation of "teen–tot" programs. These programs allow teen parents and their children to be seen by the same doctor and also provide an array of other services, including child development education, parenting education, safety education, family planning, and financial planning (Cox et al., 2019). A randomized experiment involving a teen–tot program in Boston found that teen mothers in the program were higher in caretaking skills, higher in self-esteem, and lower in rates of repeat pregnancy than teen mothers in the control group (Cox et al., 2019). However, the intervention did not reduce teen mothers' depressive symptoms or their risk for maltreating their children. It is clear that teen parents need a variety of services and supports to overcome the challenges of raising a child while still being one themselves.

Grandparent-headed families tend to be poorer than households not headed by grandparents, as grandparents have the added cost of caring for children on what may be fixed retirement incomes (Ganong, Coleman, & Russell, 2015). It is also difficult for grandparents raising grandchildren to maintain a social support network, as friends their age are often not struggling with raising a new generation of children, and they are not of the same generation as the parents of their grandchildren's friends (Ganong et al., 2015). Unfortunately, children raised by grandparents are more likely to experience a range of emotional and behavioural problems (Fergusson, Maughan, & Golding, 2008), although it is impossible to know if the difficulties result from grandparenting, poor parenting from their biological parents, or the trauma of separation from their biological parents (Strong, Bean, & Feinauer, 2010).

Families Are Smaller

Families are smaller now than in the past, which can be attributed to women delaying pregnancies because they have careers, as well as to increased access to birth control. In 1961, the fertility rate (number of children per woman) in Canada was around 4. By 2016, that number had decreased to 1.54 (Provencher et al., 2018). This change, of course, means that fewer children have multiple, if any, siblings.

Family Structures Are More Fluid

A commonly repeated statistic is that 50% of marriages end in divorce. That was the case in 1987 when the divorce rate in Canada reached a high of 50.6%. Since that time, the divorce rate has remained relatively stable, fluctuating between 35% and 42% (Kelly, 2012). This high rate of divorce means that a substantial proportion of children experience some, and sometimes repeated, changes in family structure through the entrance or exit of a parent or parent's cohabitating partner. Nearly one-fifth of all children experience a change in family structure as a result of separation, divorce, remarriage, cohabitation, or parental death over a 3-year period (Laughlin, 2014). The more family structure transitions a child undergoes, the more instability the child experiences, which can lead to the development of behaviour problems (Cavanagh & Huston, 2006; Osborne & McLanahan, 2007).

Next, we look at several specific family structures and how they influence child development: same-sex parents, divorced parents, and stepparents.

A growing body of research suggests that the development of children of gay and lesbian parents does not differ from that of children of heterosexual parents.

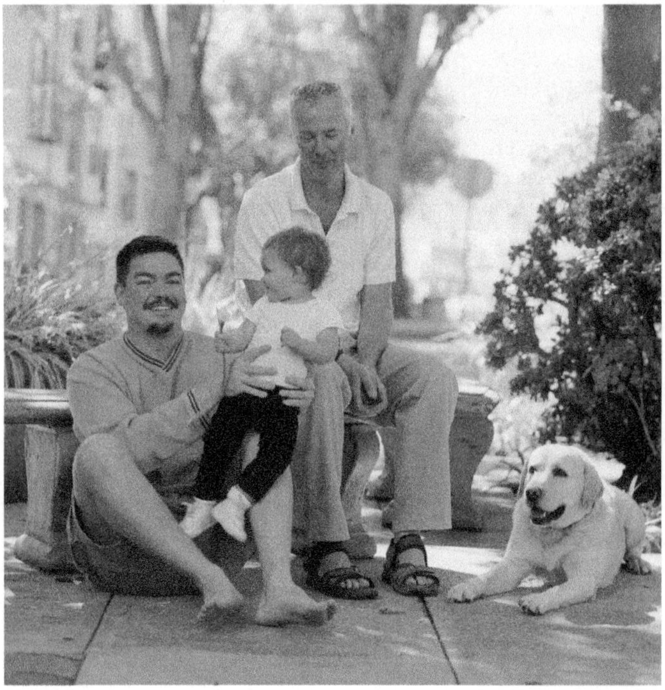
JAMIE CHOMAS/GETTY IMAGES

Same-Sex Parents

In Canada, the number of same-sex couples reporting that they are raising children, either biological or adopted, has risen steadily over the past 15 years from 8.6% in 2001 to 12% in 2016 (Statistics Canada, 2017b).

Although many legal barriers have been weakened or removed, same-sex couples face obvious practical barriers to becoming parents. Some lesbian women turn to artificial insemination, and some gay men seek out surrogate mothers who will donate their eggs or carry the gay couple's baby. The non-biological parent can adopt the same-sex spouse's biological child in a process known as second-parent adoption. Other same-sex parents choose to become foster or adoptive parents, although several states still have legal barriers to such adoptions.

Same-sex couples have likely been raising children for hundreds of years, but the lack of social acceptance of same-sex relationships meant that these instances were largely hidden. With the increasing acceptance of same-sex couples and same-sex parenting, more and more same-sex couples have become parents. At the same time, some members of the public have voiced concerns about the capability of same-sex couples to be "good" parents. Many researchers have examined whether same-sex parents are any different from different-sex parents and whether the children of same-sex parents experience different outcomes from the children of different-sex parents. A growing body of research in the United States and in Europe has consistently shown that children with same-sex parents are not different from children of different-sex parents in terms of mental health, behaviour, and academic achievement (Bos, Kuyper, & Gartrell, 2018; Bos et al., 2016; Farr, 2017; Fedewa, Black, & Ahn, 2015; Potter, 2012).

In addition, these children are similar to their peers of different-sex parents in their sexual orientation, in their gender identity, and in the degree to which their behaviour is gender typed (Farr et al., 2018; Fedewa et al., 2015), as well as in their romantic involvements and sexual behaviour as adolescents (Wainright, Russell, & Patterson, 2004). As in families with heterosexual parents, the adjustment of children with lesbian and gay parents seems to depend on family dynamics, including the closeness of the parent–child relationship (Wainright & Patterson, 2008), how well the parents get along, parental supportiveness, regulated discipline, and the degree of stress parents experience in their parenting (Farr, Forssell, & Patterson, 2010; Farr & Patterson, 2013).

Divorced Parents

Most divorced people re-partner, either by marrying again or entering into a common-law relationship. In 2016, 9.8% of children in Canada lived in a stepfamily (Statistics Canada, 2017a). Given the number of children in these situations, the effects of divorce and remarriage on children have been the subjects of extensive research (Amato, 2010).

Divorce precipitates a number of changes in a child's life (Amato, 2010). For example, the parents separate and live in different residences, and a family court helps decide whether one parent retains custody or whether both parents share joint legal custody; such agreements cover almost two-thirds (65.4%) of divorced families in Canada (Canadian Department of Justice, 2017). As a result of the stress associated with such changes, the parenting style of newly divorced parents, compared with that of parents in two-parent families, often tends to be characterized by more irritability and coercion and by less warmth, emotional availability, consistency, and supervision of children (Hetherington, Bridges, & Insabella, 1998; Sutherland, Altenhofen, & Biringen, 2012). This outcome is unfortunate because children tend to adjust best during and after the divorce if their custodial parent is supportive and emotionally available (Altenhofen, Sutherland, & Biringen, 2010; Bastaits & Mortelmans, 2016).

Divorce can thus disrupt children's routines and social networks. Sometimes as a result of the financial hardship that accompanies being a lone parent, and sometimes for other practical reasons, the custodial parent (or both parents, if they have joint custody) may move the children to a new neighbourhood and a new school; children then must go through an often wrenching transition to a new home, neighbourhood, school, and peer group at the same time that they are adjusting to a new family structure (Braver, Ellman, & Fabricius, 2003; Fabricius & Braver, 2006). All of these potentially stressful life changes during and after divorce can affect children's mental health directly (Sun & Li, 2011) but

TATIANA GLADSKIKH/GETTY IMAGES

Because ongoing marital conflict poses a variety of risks for children, research suggests that staying together "for the sake of the children" may be more harmful than divorce in highly conflictual marriages.

can also affect children indirectly by undermining positive parenting and enjoyable family interactions (Ge, Natsuaki, & Conger, 2006).

Most experts agree that children of divorce are at greater risk for a variety of short-term and long-term problems than are children who live with both biological parents. Compared with their peers in intact families, for instance, children of divorce are more likely to experience depression and sadness, have lower self-esteem, and be less socially responsible and competent (Amato, 2010; Ge et al., 2006). In addition, children of divorce, especially boys, are prone to externalizing problem behaviours such as aggression and antisocial behaviour, both soon after the divorce and years later (Burt et al., 2008; Hartman, Magalhães, & Mandich, 2011). Problems such as these may contribute to the drop in academic achievement that children of divorce often exhibit (Potter, 2010). Adolescents whose parents divorce exhibit a greater tendency to drop out of school, engage in delinquent activities and substance abuse, and have children outside of marriage (Hetherington et al., 1998; Song, Benin, & Glick, 2012).

Divorce can also lead to an exacerbation of conflict between parents about finances or parenting decisions. This ongoing conflict is especially likely to have negative effects on children if they feel caught in the middle—for example, if they are forced to act as intermediaries between their parents or to inform one parent of the other's activities. Similar pressures may arise if children feel the need to hide from one parent information about, or their loyalty to, the other parent—or if the parents inappropriately disclose to them sensitive information about the divorce and each other. Adolescents who feel caught up in their divorced parents' conflict are at increased risk for having mental health problems and behaviour problems (Afifi, Afifi, & Coho, 2009; Afifi & McManus, 2010; Elam et al., 2016).

Most children whose parents divorce do not suffer significant, enduring problems as a consequence (Amato, 2010). Although divorce can usually be a very painful experience for children, the differences between children from divorced families and children from intact families in terms of their psychological and social functioning are small overall (Burt et al., 2008). In fact, divorce may also result in positive outcomes, particularly if the parents were engaged in high levels of conflict while married. Parental conflict has been linked to increased emotional problems as well as increased behavioural problems in children and adolescents (Buehler, Lange, & Franck, 2007; Davies, Cummings, & Winter, 2004; Grych, Harold, & Miles, 2003). Indeed, among children raised in high-conflict families, those whose parents divorced were better adjusted than those whose parents stayed together (Amato, Loomis, & Booth, 1995). High levels of warmth from either parent can also buffer children from the effects of conflict during the divorce transition (Sandler, Wheeler, & Braver, 2013). Thus, for children from high-conflict families, divorce is a positive change if it can disrupt that conflict.

Stepparents

In Canada, 567,270 children currently live in households with stepparents (Statistics Canada, 2017a). Stepfamilies can have a variety of structures, including *simple* stepfamily households, in which a new stepparent joins another parent and his or her children, or *complex* or *blended* stepfamilies, which involve both a new stepparent and stepsiblings (Ganong et al., 2015). The majority of stepfamilies are formed through divorce and remarriage, but some are formed after the death of one of a child's biological parents.

The introduction of a stepparent can affect a child in a number of ways. A parent's remarriage often leads to less frequent contact with the noncustodial parent, which can be stressful to the child and can lead to difficulties adjusting to the stepparent (Ganong et al., 2015). A custodial parent's remarriage can have a positive effect on family income, although if a stepparent is supporting his or her own biological children from a previous marriage, that impact will be diminished (Ganong et al., 2015). A child who bonds with the stepparent also gains another trusted adult in his or her life, which can have positive benefits for emotional and behavioural health (Ganong, Coleman, & Jamison, 2011). Importantly, positive relationships with each parent—the custodial biological parent, the noncustodial biological parent, and the stepparent—can have independent positive benefits on children, including reduced stress (Jensen, Shafer, & Holmes, 2017).

BRAUNS/GETTY IMAGES

Children of divorce benefit from interaction with noncustodial fathers, particularly if that interaction is of high quality.

Both the benefits and challenges in stepfamilies may differ somewhat for families with stepfathers and those with stepmothers. Conflict between stepfathers and stepchildren tends to be greater than that between fathers and their biological offspring (Bray & Berger, 1993; Hakvoort et al., 2011; Hetherington et al., 1999), perhaps in part because stepfathers are more likely to see the children as burdens than their biological fathers are (O'Connor & Boag, 2010). Similarly, stepmothers generally have more difficulty with their stepchildren than do stepfathers (Gosselin & David, 2007), possibly because the biological fathers expect stepmothers to take an active role in parenting, and children frequently resent and reject the stepmothers' role as disciplinarian. This may help explain why stepmothers are more likely than biological mothers to feel resentment toward their children and view them as a burden (O'Connor & Boag, 2010). Children of both sexes are most adjusted in stepfamilies when the stepparent is warm and involved and supports the custodial parent's decisions rather than trying to exert control over the children independently (Bray & Berger, 1993; Hetherington et al., 1998).

An additional factor in children's adjustment in stepfamilies is the attitude of the noncustodial biological parent toward the stepparent and the level of conflict between the two (Wallerstein & Lewis, 2007). If the noncustodial parent has hostile feelings toward the new stepparent and communicates these feelings to the child, the child is likely to feel caught in the middle, increasing his or her adjustment problems (Buchanan, Maccoby, & Dornbusch, 1991). The noncustodial parent's hostile feelings may also encourage the child to behave in a hostile or distant manner with the stepparent. Not surprisingly, children in stepfamilies fare best when the relations between the noncustodial parent and the stepparent are supportive and the relations between the biological parents are cordial (Golish, 2003). Thus, the success or failure of stepfamilies is affected by the behaviour and attitudes of all involved parties.

REVIEW QUESTIONS

How do you define "family"? Which individuals or groups constitute family in your life? How does this description of family match the one provided in this section? ■

Family Dynamics

Families fulfill several vital functions, including ensuring the survival of children to maturity, providing the means for children to acquire skills needed to be economically productive, and teaching children the basic values of the culture (LeVine, 1988). How well a family fulfills these basic child-rearing functions obviously depends on a great many factors. Not the least of these is **family dynamics**—that is, how family members interact through various relationships: mother with each child, father with each child, mother with father, and siblings with one another. In subsequent sections, we discuss the ways in which individual family members contribute to a child's development. However, it is important to frame these discussions with a clear appreciation of the overall impact of family dynamics. Families are complex social units whose members are all interdependent and reciprocally influence one another.

Parenting

Socialization is the process through which children acquire the values, standards, skills, knowledge, and behaviours that are regarded as appropriate for their present and future roles in their particular culture (Maccoby, 2015). When asked about the characteristics they want their children to possess, a majority of Canadian parents say they want their children to make values-based decisions (88%), to have the self-assurance to follow their dreams (85%), and to be generous and giving toward others (66%) (Boys and Girls Club [BGCBIGS], 2014). With these long-term goals in mind, parents engage in a variety of socialization behaviours that they hope will foster these characteristics in their children. We will focus on two key aspects of parenting that are particularly important for children's development: parents' use of discipline and their overall parenting style.

Discipline

Discipline is the set of strategies and behaviours parents use to teach children how to behave appropriately. Parental discipline is effective when the child stops engaging in an undesirable misbehaviour (e.g., hitting a sibling to get a toy) and, ideally, engages in a preferred behaviour (e.g., taking turns to share a toy). Discipline is considered to be most effective if it leads to a permanent change in the child's behaviour because the child has learned and accepted the reasons for the desired behaviour; this process is called **internalization** (Grusec & Goodnow, 1994).

Reasoning focused on the effects of a behaviour on other people, referred to as *other-oriented induction*, is particularly effective at promoting internalization. For example, if a parent emphasizes that being hit hurts the other child's body and feelings, the child will begin to understand why it is better not to engage in the original misbehaviour. The use of other-oriented induction has the added benefit of teaching children empathy for others, which is a foundational skill for acting prosocially toward others. Indeed, reasoning and other-oriented induction have been linked with greater social competence in children (Hastings, Miller, & Troxel, 2015). Thankfully, reasoning is the most common form of discipline, and three-quarters of American parents report that they use reasoning on a regular basis (Pew Research Center, 2015).

Internalization occurs best when parents apply the right amount of psychological pressure on children. If they apply too little, the children will discount the parents' message and do what they want. If parents apply too much pressure, the children

family dynamics the way in which family members interact through various relationships: mother with each child, father with each child, mother with father, and siblings with one another

socialization the process through which children acquire the values, standards, skills, knowledge, and behaviours that are regarded as appropriate for their present and future roles in their particular culture

discipline the set of strategies and behaviours parents use to teach children how to behave appropriately

internalization the process by which children learn and accept the reasons for desired behaviour may comply but only because they feel they are being forced to do so; children then attribute their compliance to an external force (i.e., their parents) rather than internalizing the reason for complying (Maccoby & Martin, 1983). Children in this situation will likely act in desirable ways only when they know there is a risk that they will get caught by their parents if they don't comply.

Discipline techniques that apply too much psychological or even physical pressure on children are not effective at promoting internalization. Most punishments fall into this category. **Punishment** is a negative stimulus that follows a behaviour to reduce the likelihood that the behaviour will occur again (Hineline & Rosales-Ruiz, 2012). Punishments, such as time-out or taking away privileges, make clear that the parent disapproves of the misbehaviour, but on their own they do not teach the child how to behave in the future. While mild punishments, such as those listed above, can provide the minimally sufficient pressure needed for internalization, it is important to remember that a parent's slightly raised voice or disapproving look are often all the pressure that is needed to get a child to comply.

A large body of research indicates that spanking, a form of physical punishment, is not effective at teaching children how to behave and is linked with a range of unintended negative consequences for children (Gershoff & Grogan-Kaylor, 2016a; see Box 12.2). Other forms of punishment, such as yelling, time-out, taking away privileges, and love withdrawal (withholding affection from a child because of his or her behaviour), have also been found to be ineffective and linked with negative outcomes for children (Gershoff et al., 2010), despite the fact that between 20% and 40% of parents report using each of these methods (Pew Research Center, 2015).

Parenting Styles

Although specific parenting behaviours can influence child development, parents' overall style of interacting with their children can also govern the parent–child relationship and children's developmental outcomes (Darling & Steinberg, 1993). **Parenting style** is the constellation of parenting behaviours and attitudes that set the emotional climate of parent–child interactions.

In trying to understand the impact that parents can have on children's development, researchers have identified two dimensions of parenting style that are particularly important: (1) the degree of parental warmth and responsiveness, and (2) the degree of parenting control and demandingness (Maccoby & Martin, 1983). Parents who exhibit warmth are affectionate with their children and enjoy being with them. Parental responsiveness refers to how quickly and appropriately parents respond to children's needs, requests for assistance, or distress. Parental control, on the other hand, is the extent to which parents monitor and manage their children's behaviour through rules and consequences, and demandingness refers to an expectation of conformance to parents' desires and a low tolerance for children's own interests and desires.

A pioneering research study on parenting style was conducted by Diana Baumrind (1973), who differentiated among four styles of parenting related to the dimensions of support and control. These styles, diagrammed in Figure 12.3 on page 433, are referred to as *authoritative, authoritarian, permissive,* and *uninvolved* (Baumrind, 1973, 1991b).

According to Baumrind, **authoritative parenting** is a style that tends to be demanding but also warm and responsive. Authoritative parents set clear standards and limits for their children, monitor their children's behaviour, and are firm about enforcing important limits. However, they allow their children considerable

punishment a negative stimulus that follows a behaviour to reduce the likelihood that the behaviour will occur again

parenting style parenting behaviours and attitudes that set the emotional climate in regard to parent–child interactions, such as parental responsiveness and demandingness

authoritative parenting a parenting style that is high in demandingness and supportiveness. Authoritative parents set clear standards and limits for their children and are firm about enforcing them; at the same time, they allow their children considerable autonomy within those limits, are attentive and responsive to their children's concerns and needs, and respect and consider their children's perspective

Parenting in Middle Childhood

ARIEL SKELLEY/GETTY IMAGES

Parenting in Adolescence

VIKRAM RAGHUVANSHI/GETTY IMAGES

BOX 12.2 APPLICATIONS Should Parents Spank Their Children?

Spanking typically involves striking a child on the bottom with an open hand, although some parents also use objects, such as a wooden spoon. The percentage of parents who spank their children has dropped significantly over the past several decades in both the United States (Zolotor et al., 2011) and Canada (Clément & Chamberland, 2014). However, the majority of parents still spank their children at some point (Gershoff et al., 2012). Spanking has been the subject of hundreds of research studies and debates among experts, and a number of conclusions are now clear.

Spanking does not improve children's behaviour. A meta-analysis of the research on spanking determined that spanking does not increase children's immediate compliance (Gershoff & Grogan-Kaylor, 2016a). Spanking also does not improve children's behaviour in the long term; the more children are spanked, the less likely they are to behave appropriately in the future, and the more likely they are to behave aggressively or to engage in antisocial behaviour (Gershoff & Grogan-Kaylor, 2016a). This finding holds even when the initial tendency for children's aggression or antisocial behaviour to elicit more spanking from parents has been taken into account through longitudinal research designs (Berlin et al., 2009; Gershoff et al., 2012; Lee, Altschul, & Gershoff, 2013).

Spanking increases children's risk for a range of negative outcomes. In addition to not improving children's behaviour, spanking has been linked with a range of negative, unintended outcomes that can be thought of as negative "side effects." The more children are spanked, the more mental health problems they have, the more problems they have in their relationships with their parents, the lower their self-esteem, and the lower their cognitive ability (Gershoff, 2013; Gershoff & Grogan-Kaylor, 2016a).

The most serious outcome linked with spanking is physical abuse. The more frequently parents spank, the greater the likelihood they will use harsher methods that can injure children (Zolotor et al., 2011). Parents who spanked their children at age 1 had a 33% greater likelihood of being suspected of physically abusing their children by the time they were age 5 (Lee, Grogan-Kaylor, & Berger, 2014). A review of child maltreatment cases in Canada revealed that a majority of physical abuse cases started out as physical punishment (Durrant et al., 2006).

Spanking is linked with negative outcomes equally across cultural groups. As discussed in this chapter, culture can determine which parenting practices are seen as both normal and advisable. Cultural groups, particularly those defined by race or ethnicity, differ in how often they use spanking (Gershoff et al., 2012). However, the extent to which spanking is linked with negative outcomes, such as increased aggression, does not vary across racial and ethnic groups: spanking is linked with more aggression and more externalizing behaviour problems across all racial and ethnic groups (Berlin et al., 2009; Gershoff et al., 2012; Gershoff & Grogan-Kaylor, 2016b) and even across countries with differing levels of spanking use (Gershoff et al., 2010).

For these reasons, among others, the United Nations has declared that spanking and physical punishment are forms of violence against children that violate their human rights to protection from violence (United Nations, Committee on the Rights of the Child, 2006). In response to this growing body of evidence linking spanking with harm to children, 54 countries have banned all physical punishment of children, including that by parents (Global Initiative to End All Corporal Punishment of Children, 2019).

In Canada, physical punishment by parents is allowed for children aged 2 to 12, but the Canadian Paediatric Society (2016) and the Canadian Psychological Association (2004) have called on Canadian parents to abandon spanking. In addition, the Centers for Disease Control and Prevention in the United States (Fortson et al., 2016) have identified reducing the use of spanking and other forms of physical punishment as a key step toward ending physical abuse.

autonomy within those limits, are not restrictive or intrusive, and are able to engage in calm conversation and reasoning with their children. They are attentive to their children's concerns and needs and communicate openly with their children about them. They are also measured and consistent, rather than harsh or arbitrary, in disciplining them. Authoritative parents usually want their children to be socially responsible, assertive, and self-controlled.

Baumrind found that children of authoritative parents tend to be competent, self-assured, and popular with peers. They are also able to behave in accordance with adults' expectations and are low in antisocial behaviour. In a Canadian study, mothers and fathers who have authoritative parenting styles are more likely to have toddlers with higher levels of adaptive skills, including social skills and functional communication (Rinaldi & Howe, 2012). Children with authoritative parents seem to accept their parents' socialization efforts; for example, in one study children with authoritative parents were more likely to share and take turns with an unfamiliar peer than were children of authoritarian parents (Hastings et al., 2007). As adolescents, children from authoritative families tend to be relatively high in social and academic competence, self-reliance, and coping skills and relatively low in drug use and other problem behaviour (Baumrind, 1991a; Driscoll, Russell, & Crockett, 2008; Hoeve et al., 2011; Lamborn et al., 1991).

Authoritarian parenting is a style that tends to be cold and unresponsive to children's needs. Authoritarian parents are high in control and demandingness and expect their children to comply without question. Authoritarian parents tend to enforce their demands through the exercise of parental power, especially the use of threats and punishment and psychological control. Examples include parents interrupting children when they want to express themselves, threatening to withdraw love and attention if they do not behave as expected, exploiting children's sense of guilt, belittling their worth, and discounting or misinterpreting their feelings. Such behaviours on behalf of authoritarian parents engender hostility in children and a refusal to accept parents' attempts at socialization (Hastings et al., 2015).

Children of authoritarian parents tend to be relatively low in social and academic competence, unhappy and unfriendly, and low in self-confidence, with boys being more negatively affected than girls in early childhood (Baumrind, 1991b). Authoritarian parenting has also been linked with children's inability to cope with everyday stressors (Zhou et al., 2008) and with high levels of depression, aggression, delinquency, and alcohol problems (Bolkan et al., 2010; Driscoll et al., 2008; Kerr, Stattin, & Özdemir, 2012; Rinaldi & Howe, 2012).

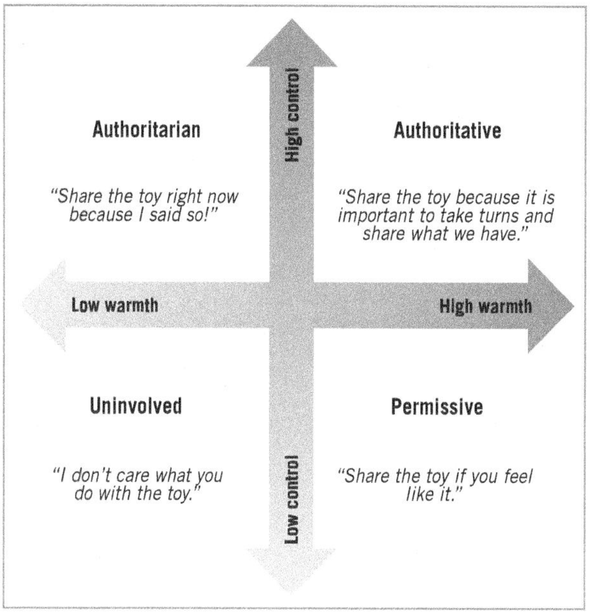

FIGURE 12.3 **Parental control and warmth** In Baumrind's typology of parenting styles, every parent falls somewhere on the dimensions of warmth and control. Baumrind grouped parents into one of four potential parenting styles. This figure shows the four potential responses of parents reacting to a child who will not share a toy. (Information from Baumrind, 1973)

Permissive parenting is a style that is responsive to children's needs and wishes but so much so that parents are overly lenient with them. Permissive parents do not require their children to regulate themselves or act in appropriate ways. The children of permissive parents tend to be impulsive, low in self-regulation, high in externalizing problems, and low in school achievement (Baumrind, 1973, 1991a, 1991b; Rinaldi & Howe, 2012). As adolescents, they engage in more school misconduct and drug or alcohol use than do peers with authoritative parents (Driscoll et al., 2008).

Uninvolved parenting is a style that is low in both demandingness and responsiveness to children; in other words, uninvolved parents are generally disengaged. They do not set limits for children or monitor their behaviour and are not supportive of them. Sometimes they are rejecting or neglectful of their children altogether. These parents are focused on their own needs rather than their children's. Children who have uninvolved parents tend to have disturbed attachment relationships when they are infants or toddlers and to have problems with peer relationships as older children (Parke & Buriel, 1998; Thompson, 1998). In adolescence, they tend to exhibit a wide range of problems, from antisocial behaviour and low academic competence to internalizing problems (e.g., depression, social withdrawal), substance abuse, and risky or promiscuous sexual behaviour (Baumrind, 1991a, 1991b; Driscoll et al., 2008; Hoeve et al., 2011). The negative effects of this type of parenting appear to continue to accumulate and worsen over the course of adolescence (Steinberg et al., 1994).

Although parenting style appears to have an effect on children's adjustment, it is important to keep in mind that children's behaviour sometimes shapes parents' typical parenting style as well. For example, adolescents' reports of relatively high levels of externalizing problems (e.g., delinquency, loitering, intoxication) and internalizing problems (e.g., low self-esteem, depressive symptoms) predicted a decline in parents' authoritative parenting styles (as reported by the youths) 2 years later, whereas an increase or decline in authoritative parenting over the same 2 years did not predict a change in the adolescents' adjustment (Kerr et al., 2012).

authoritarian parenting a parenting style that is high in demandingness and low in responsiveness. Authoritarian parents are nonresponsive to their children's needs and tend to enforce their demands through the exercise of parental power and the use of threats and punishment. They are oriented toward obedience and authority and expect their children to comply with their demands without question or explanation.

permissive parenting a parenting style that is high in responsiveness but low in demandingness. Permissive parents are responsive to their children's needs and do not require their children to regulate themselves or act in appropriate or mature ways.

uninvolved parenting a parenting style that is low in both demandingness and responsiveness to their children; in other words, this style describes parents who are generally disengaged

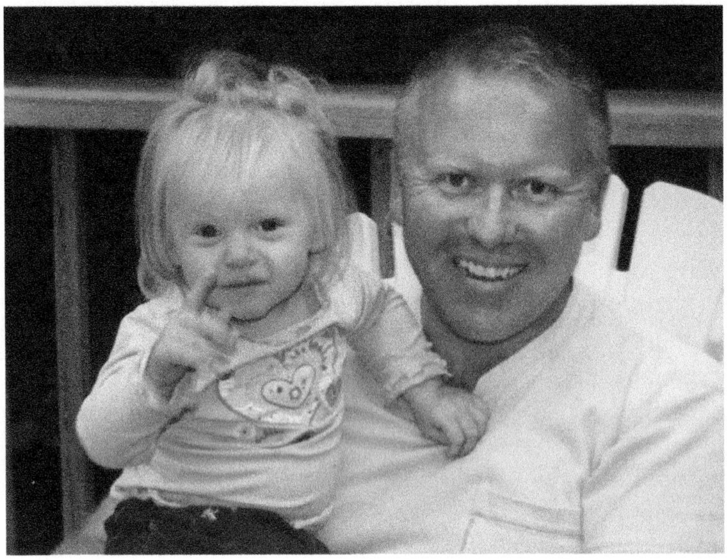

SUSAN GRAHAM

Positive social and academic outcomes are more likely when levels of parental warmth and control are both high.

Interview with Jay Belsky

WORTH PUBLISHERS

More recent research has moved away from the idea that parents have a single style or that parents can be easily placed into one of Baumrind's four categories (Hastings et al., 2015). Rather, whether parents exhibit, for example, an authoritative or authoritarian style at any given moment depends on contextual factors, such as whether the child's misbehaviour is dangerous, whether the parent and child are running late for an appointment, or whether the parent and child are in a good mood (Maccoby, 2015).

Differences in Mothers' and Fathers' Interactions with Their Children

Although fathers are engaged in child rearing more now than in the past, differences remain in mothers' and fathers' child-rearing behaviours. For example, there is a major difference in the amounts of time mothers and fathers spend caring for their children. Although in most Western cultures today, spouses share childcare responsibilities to some degree, in the majority of families, mothers—including those who work outside the home—still spend an average of an hour and a half more with their children each day than fathers do (Biehle & Mickelson, 2012; Yavorsky, Kamp Dush, & Schoppe-Sullivan, 2015).

There is also a difference in what types of child-rearing behaviours mothers and fathers engage in. Mothers are more likely to provide physical care and emotional support than are fathers (Moon & Hoffman, 2008); for instance, in a sample of families in the Netherlands, mothers were warmer and more responsive to their children than were fathers (Hallers-Haalboom et al., 2014). In contrast, fathers in modern industrialized cultures spend a greater proportion of their available time playing with their children, both in infancy and childhood, than do mothers, and they engage in more physical and rough-and-tumble play than do mothers (Parke & Buriel, 1998). In the United States, mothers are more likely than fathers to say that they are overprotective and that they praise their children too much, whereas fathers are more likely than mothers to have coached their children's sports teams (Pew Research Center, 2015).

The degree of maternal and paternal involvement in parenting and the nature of parents' interactions with children vary somewhat as a function of cultural practices and factors such as the amount of time parents work away from home and the amount of time children spend at home. In some countries, such as Estonia, Finland, Russia, South Korea, and the United States, mothers play more with their young children than do fathers, while in other countries, including Brazil and Malaysia, there are no differences in amount of play between mothers and fathers (Roopnarine & Davidson, 2015). Regardless of which partner spends more time with their children, both mothers and fathers in countries around the world spend significant amounts of their non-work time playing with their children (Roopnarine & Davidson, 2015).

Despite these distinctions in amount and type, however, the effects of mothers' and fathers' parenting on child development are the same. A meta-analysis of studies from 22 countries found that both mothers' and fathers' acceptance of and warmth toward their children were linked with children's positive psychological adjustment (Khaleque & Rohner, 2012); in other words, parenting from mothers and parenting from fathers were equally important for children's mental health, and this has been found to be true across a range of countries, including Bangladesh, Colombia, Egypt, Mexico, Nigeria, Sweden, Turkey, and the United States (Khaleque & Rohner, 2012). Similarly, a study of 12 cultural groups in 9 countries found that, within each culture, both maternal and paternal warmth were linked with children's positive adjustment (Lansford et al., 2018). Thus, warm and responsive parenting, whether from mothers or fathers, is universally beneficial for children.

PAVEL LOSEVSKY/GETTY IMAGES

Fathers tend to engage in more physical play with their children than do mothers.

The Child's Influence on Parenting

Among the strongest influences on both parental discipline and on parenting style is children's own behaviour. Thus, *individual differences* in children contribute to the parenting they receive. Consistent with the theme of the *active child,* children also actively shape the parenting process through their behaviour and expressions of temperament. Children who are disobedient, angry, or challenging, for example, make it more difficult for parents to use authoritative parenting than do children who are compliant and positive in their behaviour (Kerr et al., 2012).

How children behave with their parents—including the degree to which they express anger, low self-regulation, or disobedience—can be due to a number of factors. The most prominent of these are genetic factors related to temperament (Saudino & Wang, 2012). In line with our discussion of *differential susceptibility* in Chapter 10, some children may be more reactive to the quality of parenting they receive than are others. For instance, children with anxious temperaments tend to become fearful and immobilized in response to harsh and demanding parenting; in contrast, these same children are eager to please and comply with warm and responsive parents (Beach et al., 2012; Kiff, Lengua, & Zalewski, 2011; Pluess & Belsky, 2010). At the genetic level, some children have an allele of the serotonin transporter gene SLC6A4 that makes them especially responsive to their rearing environment, whether it be warm and responsive parenting or controlling and demanding parenting (Kochanska et al., 2011).

Children's noncompliance and externalizing problems offer further insight into the complex ways in which children can affect their parents' behaviour toward them. In resisting their parents' demands, for example, children may become so whiny or aggressive that their parents back down; the parents' behaviour has been affected by the children's behaviour, and the children's behaviour has been reinforced by the parents' behaviour. As these parents become frustrated, they may escalate their negative behaviours (e.g., yelling, spanking), which evoke even more negative behaviour from children. Such patterns have been called *coercive cycles* (Patterson, 1982). By adolescence, such patterns appear to be influenced more by the child than the parent: youths who are noncompliant and antisocial, in part due to their heredity, evoke harsh parenting from their parents to a greater degree than their parents' harshness leads to the youths' externalizing problems (Marceau et al., 2013).

Over time, the mutual influence, or **bidirectionality,** of interactions between a parent and child reinforces and perpetuates their behaviour (Combs-Ronto et al., 2009; Morelen & Suveg, 2012). Bidirectionality is a key factor in parent–child relationships that exhibit a pattern of cooperation, positive affect, harmonious communication, and coordinated behaviour, with the positive behaviour of each partner eliciting analogous positive behaviour from the other (Aksan, Kochanska, &

bidirectionality of parent–child interactions the idea that parents and their children are mutually affected by one another's characteristics and behaviours

Ortmann, 2006; Altschul, Lee, & Gershoff, 2016; Denissen, van Aken, & Dubas, 2009). For example, as we saw in Chapter 10, when babies begin displaying social smiles, parents may get excited and smile back, which then will lead babies to smile again. Bidirectionality can also occur with negative behaviours: parents' use of spanking at age 1 predicts greater child aggression at age 3, which in turn predicts more parental spanking at age 5 (Altschul et al., 2016); in addition, parents' hostile and inconsistent behaviours toward their adolescents are often rewarded with similar hostile, insensitive, disruptive, and inflexible behaviours from the adolescents (Roche et al., 2011; Scaramella et al., 2008).

Sibling Relationships

Siblings influence one another's development and the functioning of the larger family system in many ways, both positive and negative. Siblings serve not only as playmates for one another but also as sources of support, instruction, security, assistance, and caregiving (Gamble, Yu, & Kuehn, 2011; Gass, Jenkins, & Dunn, 2007). The sibling relationship is unique. Sibling relationships are often similar to peer relationships; like peers, siblings who are close in age interact in ways characterized by sharing and reciprocity (Dirks et al., 2015). However, in other cases, sibling relationships are more like parent–child relationships, in which one (the older) sibling has more power and influence over the other (younger) sibling (Dirks et al., 2015). Indeed, the more frequently older siblings engage in positive and prosocial behaviour, the more likely their younger siblings are to engage in such behaviour years later; however, the younger sibling's behaviour does not impact the older sibling's behaviour (Pike & Oliver, 2017). Children in the middle of sibling groups may thus have both types of sibling relationships.

Siblings, of course, also can be rivals and sources of mutual conflict and irritation; they live in close proximity to one another and are often in competition for resources, from toys to parents' time. The quality of the sibling relationship plays a key role in the influence that siblings have on one another. For example, researchers at Concordia University in Montreal have demonstrated that siblings with a positive relationship are more likely to compromise with one another when resolving a conflict than are siblings who have a less positive relationship (Howe et al., 2001; Karavasilis Karos, Howe, & Aquan-Assee, 2008; Recchia & Howe, 2009). In some cases, sibling conflict can contribute to the development of undesirable behaviours, such as disobedience, delinquency, and drinking (Dirks et al., 2015), as well as depression, anxiety, and social withdrawal (Morgan, Shaw, & Olino, 2012). In addition, high levels of sibling aggression and conflict predict low self-regulation (Padilla-Walker, Harper, & Jensen, 2010) and risky sexual behaviour in one or both siblings (McHale, Bissell, & Kim, 2009). Sibling conflict can also be a crucible for learning important life skills: research with families in Ontario, Canada, has found that when parents are taught how to mediate sibling conflicts, siblings successfully learn constructive means of conflict resolution (Ross & Lazinski, 2014).

Siblings' relationships tend to be less hostile and more supportive when their parents are

The quality of sibling relationships is intertwined with the quality of parents' relationships with each sibling.

HERO IMAGES/GETTY IMAGES

warm and accepting of them (Grych, Raynor, & Fosco, 2004; Kim et al., 2006). Siblings also have closer, more positive relationships with each other if their parents treat them similarly. If parents favour one child over another, the sibling relationship may suffer, and the less favoured child may experience distress, depression, and other problems with adjustment, especially if the child does not have a positive relationship with his or her parents (Meunier et al., 2013; Shanahan et al., 2008; Solmeyer et al., 2011). When children view differential treatment by parents as justified, they report more positive relationships with their sibling and their parents than when they feel that differential parental treatment is unfair (Kowal, Krull, & Kramer, 2004).

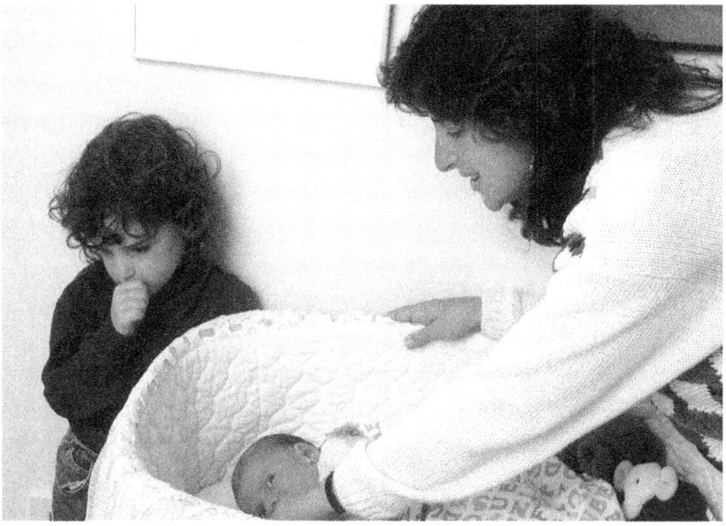
LAURA DWIGHT

Young children are more likely than older children to respond poorly when they perceive that an infant sibling receives more attention than they themselves do.

Cultural values may also play a role in children's evaluations of, and reactions to, differential parental treatment. For example, in a study of Mexican American families, older siblings who embraced the cultural value of *familism*, which emphasizes interdependence, mutual support, and loyalty among family members, were not put at risk of higher levels of depressive symptoms or risky behaviours by their parents' preferential treatment of younger siblings (McHale et al., 2005). A study that compared a sample of Moroccan siblings to a sample of Dutch siblings found that the children from the collectivist Moroccan culture had less conflict than the siblings from the individualistic culture of the Netherlands. However, for the children from both cultures, when sibling conflict was present, mental health and behaviour problems were also found (Buist et al., 2014).

Another factor that can affect the quality of siblings' interactions is the nature of the parents' relationship with each other. Siblings get along better if their parents get along with each other (Erel, Margolin, & John, 1998; McGuire, McHale, & Updegraff, 1996). In contrast, siblings whose parents fight with each other are likely to have more hostile interactions because their parents not only model negative behaviour for their children but also may be less sensitive and appropriate in their efforts to manage their children's interactions with one another (Howe et al., 2001).

Rivalry and conflict between siblings tend to be higher in divorced families and in remarried families than in non-divorced families, even between biological siblings. Although some siblings turn to one another for support when their parents divorce or remarry (Jenkins, 1992), they may also compete for parental affection and attention, which often are scarce in those situations. Relationships between half-siblings can be especially emotionally charged, perhaps because the older half-sibling may resent the younger half-sibling who is born to both parents in the new marital relationship (Hetherington, 1999). In general, the more a child in a blended family perceives a parent's treatment of a sibling—whether a full sibling or a half-sibling—to be preferential, the worse the child's relationship is with that sibling (Baham et al., 2008).

Thus, the quality of sibling relationships differs across families depending on the ways that parents interact with each child and with each other and children's perceptions of their treatment by other family members. Such differences highlight the fact that families are complex, dynamic social systems and that all members contribute to one another's functioning.

REVIEW QUESTIONS

Imagine the following familiar situation: a child is throwing a tantrum because he or she does not want to leave the playground. What response would you expect from each of the different parenting styles shown in Figure 12.3? What might be the child's response in each of these scenarios? ■

Child Maltreatment

One of the most serious threats to children's development is **child maltreatment.** Maltreatment has been defined as an action or a failure to act by an adult that either results in physical or emotional harm to a child or puts the child at risk of serious harm (Public Health Agency of Canada, 2012). It is important to note that this definition includes both action, such as physical abuse, and inaction, such as leaving a young child unattended for long periods of time, and it includes exposure to family violence. The definition also stipulates that the perpetrator of maltreatment can include a parent, sibling, relative, teacher, caregiver, or guardian.

Canada has not tracked national maltreatment rates since 2008, but some individual provinces track these figures. The most recent data on child maltreatment in Canada comes from the 2013 Ontario Incidence Study of Reported Abuse and Neglect. In 2013, roughly 43,067 children were confirmed to be victims of child maltreatment, with 59% of those cases involving multiple incidents of maltreatment (Fallon et al., 2015). The victims included nearly equal numbers of girls (18.85 per 1000) and boys (17.70 per 1000), but the highest rates of substantiated maltreatment were for 7-year-old girls (27.19 per 1000). When you consider the statistics above, bear in the mind that they include only cases that were investigated by child welfare agencies; therefore, the numbers might be an underestimate of the overall prevalence of child maltreatment. Indeed, when you ask adults about their experiences of child maltreatment, 33% of Canadians reported that they experienced some form of maltreatment before the age of 15 (Statistics Canada, 2017a).

When most people think of child maltreatment, they think of physical abuse, but most authorities identify five main types of maltreatment (Public Health Agency of Canada, 2012):

- *Neglect* refers to the failure of a caregiver to provide the physical and psychological necessities of life to a child (e.g., failure to supervise and medical neglect).
- *Physical abuse* is the application of unreasonable force to a child (e.g., harsh physical discipline, use of restraints, and hitting).
- *Emotional harm* involves a pattern of behaviour in which a caregiver demeans, rejects, repeatedly criticizes, or withholds love from a child or otherwise communicates to a child that they are worthless, unloved, or unwanted.
- *Sexual abuse* involves sexual acts or sexual exploitation involving children; it includes both inappropriate touching of a child and exposure to sexual content such as pornography.
- *Exposure to family violence* involves a child being exposed to violence occurring between a parent/caregiver and other family members.

child maltreatment action or failure to act on the part of a parent or caretaker that results in physical or emotional harm to a child or a risk of serious harm

As shown in Figure 12.4, the most common forms of maltreatment were exposure to intimate partner violence, neglect, and physical abuse. These five types of maltreatment also do not occur in isolation; many abused children experience more than one form of maltreatment, an occurrence known as **polyvictimization.**

Risks for Maltreatment

Certain characteristics increase the risk for maltreatment, such as parents' lack of knowledge about their children's needs and abilities or strong negative reaction to stress, or the family's low income, inadequate housing and material resources, or social isolation (Centers for Disease Control and Prevention, 2019). Parental alcohol and other drug dependence also increase the probability of maltreatment, as does whether a parent is in an abusive romantic relationship (U.S. Department of Health and Human Services Children's Bureau, 2019).

Parents with a history of being maltreated themselves are twice as likely (29%) as parents without a maltreatment history (15%) to maltreat their own children (Centers for Disease Control and Prevention, 2019; Widom, Czaja, & DuMont, 2015). However, it is important to note that not all adults who were maltreated in childhood become abusers themselves; 71% of these adults do *not* maltreat their own children (Widom et al., 2015).

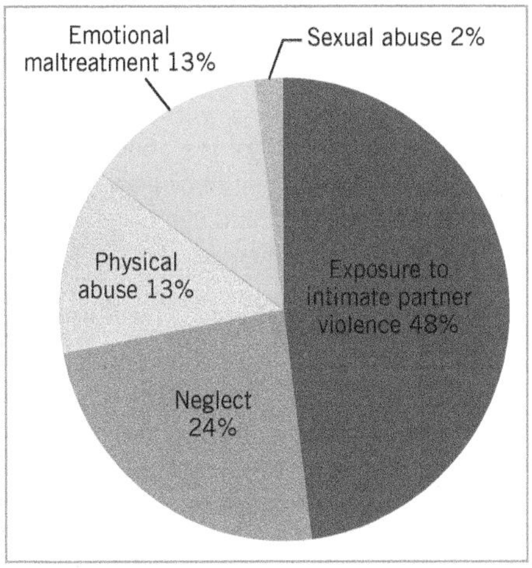

FIGURE 12.4 **Primary categories of child maltreatment in Canada in 2013** Neglect and exposure to intimate partner violence are the most common forms of substantiated child maltreatment in Canada, followed by physical, emotional, and sexual abuse. (Data from Fallon et al., 2015)

Consequences of Maltreatment

Children who are maltreated experience a range of immediate outcomes that can include physical pain and injury (from physical or sexual abuse); hunger, cold, or other physical discomfort (from neglect); and fear or anxiety (from any type of maltreatment, but particularly from emotional abuse). The effects emerge early: 3-month-old infants who have been physically abused show increased rates of fearfulness, anger, and sadness while interacting with their mother (Cicchetti & Ng, 2014). In later infancy, maltreated infants are at risk of developing an unusual attachment pattern to their caregivers, known as the disorganized/disoriented attachment pattern, discussed in Chapter 11 (Cyr et al., 2010). Children who are victims of maltreatment are at increased risk of developing cognitive delays and antisocial behaviours and of engaging in risky behaviours in adolescence and into adulthood (Fortson et al., 2016; Jaffee & Christian, 2014). Like other ACEs, maltreatment increases the likelihood that a child will be diagnosed with a psychiatric disorder in adolescence or adulthood and that these disorders will be more severe and less amenable to treatment (McCrory & Viding, 2015).

Children who are victims of physical abuse show a heightened response to anger cues that manifests in increased aggressive behaviour, changes in brain functioning and other physiological responses that are typical responses to threats (e.g., heart rate, skin conductance), and increased negative emotion, as measured via facial musculature (McCrory et al., 2013; Shackman & Pollak, 2014; Teicher et al., 2016). Such responses might be highly adaptive for the survival of children growing up in homes marked by threat and danger, but these same adaptations can lead to later mental health and behaviour problems (Teicher et al., 2016) and likely to physical health problems as well.

The more chronic the abuse, the worse the outcomes for a child later in life, including higher rates of substance abuse, violent delinquency, and suicide attempts (Jonson-Reid, Kohl, & Drake, 2012). Child maltreatment also leads to significant health consequences, ranging from negative effects on the immune system in childhood to increased rates of coronary heart disease and other biological risk factors in adulthood (Friedman et al., 2015; Miller, Chen, & Parker, 2011; Shirtcliff, Coe, & Pollak, 2009). Of particular concern is the fact that the

polyvictimization the co-occurrence of multiple forms of maltreatment

BOX 12.3 APPLICATIONS Preventing Child Maltreatment

The vast majority of the public considers child maltreatment to be a serious public health problem and views finding ways to prevent maltreatment as a public priority (Research America, 2018). In the United States, the Centers for Disease Control and Prevention (CDC) has identified five general strategies to prevent both child abuse and neglect (Fortson et al., 2016). These strategies are targeted to multiple ecological models (see Chapter 9) that include families, schools, communities, and federal and state governments:

In the United States, the CDC recommends several strategies for preventing child maltreatment, including parental education and the promotion of an enriching environment.

1. **Strengthen the economic situation of families.** It is not surprising that poverty is the root cause of much child neglect. Government efforts to ensure that families can make ends meet and that parents have secure jobs with family-friendly policies can go a long way toward preventing maltreatment.
2. **Change social norms to promote positive parenting.** The CDC notes that the best way to prevent physical abuse is to reduce acceptance of spanking and other forms of physical punishment (see Box 12.2). It recommends public campaigns and potentially legislation to affect change in these attitudes.
3. **Provide quality early education to children.** Ensuring that all children have safe, supervised, and enriched environments from an early age can reduce rates of abuse and neglect and can help compensate for negative or inadequate home environments.
4. **Enhance parenting skills.** Babies do not come with guidebooks, and thus most parents learn on the job. Numerous research studies have shown that parental education programs, including home visits from childcare professionals, that teach child development basics and healthy parenting behaviours reduce maltreatment.
5. **Intervene to help children and prevent recurrence of maltreatment.** Children who have been maltreated clearly need care and protection. Parent perpetrators of maltreatment also need help to ensure that they do not harm their children again. Individual counseling and group parenting sessions have been successful in reducing recurrence of maltreatment.

association between physical abuse in childhood and negative health outcomes in adulthood persists decades after the abuse has occurred and is not accounted for by the victim's adult SES or health behaviours. (See Box 10.3 for more on the consequences of adverse childhood experiences.)

Thankfully, most children survive maltreatment and go on to have healthy and productive lives. Such positive outcomes are more likely if abused children have sources of resilience in their lives, such as positive relationships with other adults (including aunts, uncles, grandparents, or teachers), if physical needs are being met, if their parents are otherwise nurturing, if their parents have a stable relationship with each other, and if they have access to medical care and social services (Centers for Disease Control and Prevention, 2019). Of course, the ideal situation would be if society could find a way to prevent child maltreatment altogether. Box 12.3 explores several strategies for making this happen.

REVIEW QUESTION

Why do you think children under 1 year of age are the most common victims of maltreatment? ■

Family Socioeconomic Context

According to Bronfenbrenner's bioecological model (see Chapter 9), children's development is affected by a variety of contexts that are nested into a set of hierarchical systems. The family is the child's most proximal context and thus the one that has the most direct influence on development. Yet the family itself is affected by the contexts in which it is embedded, including cultural contexts, economic contexts, and work contexts.

To see how these various contexts relate to one another, consider the diverse ways in which family members affect one another in the following scenario. A man loses his job because of company downsizing, and the ensuing stress causes him to become very irritable with his partner and children. His partner, in turn, has to work extra hours to make ends meet, and the increasing fatigue leaves his partner less patient with the children and more likely to fight with him. A mother's increased workload also means that a couple's 8-year-old daughter is expected to do more of the household chores. This makes the daughter angry because her 6-year-old brother is not required to help her out. Soon the daughter becomes hostile to both her parents and her brother. Not surprisingly, the brother starts to fight with his sister, further upsetting the parents. Over time, tension and conflict among all family members increase, adding to the stress created by the family's economic situation.

As is clear from this example, a change from outside the family (e.g., the father's workplace) creates a cascading series of events that alter the various relationships within the family. In the sections that follow, we will consider how cultural contexts, economic contexts, and work contexts affect family life, particularly parenting behaviours, and child development.

Cultural Contexts

Parents' beliefs about what constitutes optimal child development, as well as their decisions about how to behave with and discipline their children, have a strong basis in their culture (Rogoff, 2003). Culture reflects the beliefs and practices that are linked with a family's country, religion, ethnic group, race, or similar group or affiliation. In Canada and the United States, much cross-cultural research on families has been focused on cultural similarities and differences between ethnic and racial groups. Internationally, research has focused on similarities and differences across countries. In this section, we briefly review research from each of these categories.

Research into cultural influences on child development has tended to look at two aspects of parenting: the degree to which parents in different cultures engage in specific disciplinary practices, and the degree to which similar parental behaviours affect child outcomes across different cultures. Some studies have looked at differences across racial and ethnic groups within Canada and the United States. For example, European-Canadian mothers tend to be more authoritative and sensitive and more responsive to their children during play than East Asian immigrant mothers (Chan et al., 2010). In the United States, several studies have found that African American parents spank their children more often than European American, Latino American, and Asian American parents do (Gershoff et al., 2012), and in some surveys African American parents are twice as likely as European American and Latino American parents to say they spank their children regularly (Pew Research Center, 2015).

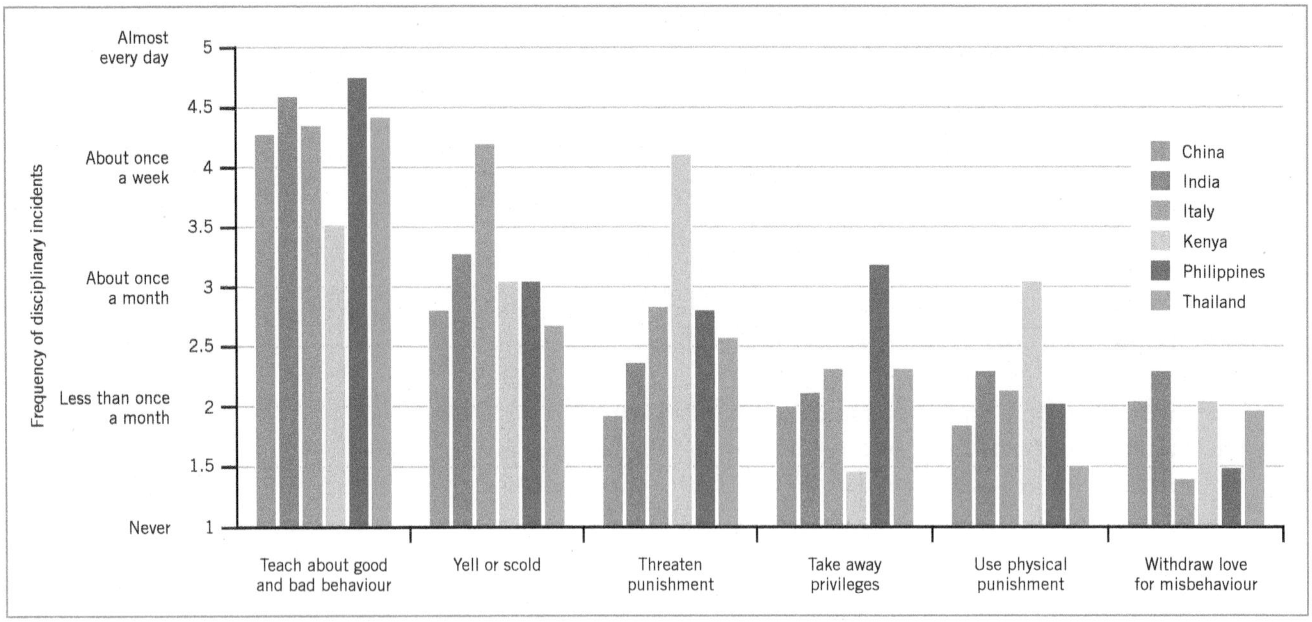

FIGURE 12.5 Differences in the frequency with which mothers reported each of six discipline techniques across six countries Mothers across all countries reported high rates of teaching about good and bad behaviour and low rates of love withdrawal. However, some clear country-level differences are seen in how often parents reported yelling or scolding, threatening punishment, taking away privileges, and using physical punishment. (Data from Gershoff et al., 2010)

Several studies have investigated whether parents around the world use similar methods of discipline with their children. A study of families in eight countries (Colombia, Italy, Jordan, Kenya, Philippines, Sweden, Thailand, and the United States) found that mothers and children in each of the countries reported high levels of positive discipline, such as inductive reasoning, and of parental warmth (Pastorelli et al., 2016). This finding suggests that both positive discipline and warm parenting were favoured by parents across cultures.

A separate study in some of the same countries and two others (China, India, Italy, Kenya, the Philippines, and Thailand) found both cross-country similarities and differences in how often mothers reported using a variety of discipline techniques (Gershoff et al., 2010; see Figure 12.5). Mothers in all six countries reported teaching children about good and bad behaviour very often, with most averaging between once a week and almost every day. The mothers in this international sample were also similar in the method they used least often—that is, love withdrawal—with mothers in Italy and the Philippines saying they rarely used this method of discipline. For the four types of punishment in the middle of Figure 12.5, there was more variation: mothers in Italy were much more likely to yell or scold than were mothers from other countries; mothers from Kenya were much more likely to threaten punishment and to use physical punishment; and mothers from the Philippines were more likely to say they would take away privileges (something the Kenyan mothers said they almost never do).

Given these differences in the frequency with which parents use different discipline techniques, the next question is whether they matter: Are certain techniques more effective in some cultures than others? Differences in the effectiveness of a particular technique could arise from the different parenting beliefs and values held by different cultures. Some researchers have argued that the extent to which a disciplinary technique predicts negative or positive outcomes in children depends on how normative it is in their wider culture (Deater-Deckard & Dodge, 1997). As you might expect, there are some similarities and some differences across cultures in how parenting behaviours predict children's development.

For instance, in European American families, authoritative parenting, as noted above, seems to be associated with a close relationship between parent and child and with children's positive psychological adjustment and academic success. Although a somewhat similar relation between authoritative parenting and adjustment has been found in China, it tends to be weaker (Chang et al., 2004; Cheah et al., 2009; Nelson, Thomas, & de Haan, 2006; Zhou et al., 2004, 2008). In fact, some features of parenting that are considered appropriate in traditional Chinese culture are more characteristic of authoritarian parenting than of authoritative parenting. Compared with American mothers, for example, Chinese American mothers are more likely to believe that children owe unquestioning obedience to their parents and thus use scolding, shame, and guilt to control them (Chao, 1994). Although such a pattern of parental control generally fits the category of authoritarian parenting, it appears to have few negative effects for Chinese American and Chinese children, at least prior to adolescence. Rather, for younger Chinese children, physical punishment is the primary type of punishment related to negative outcomes (Eisenberg, Chang et al., 2009; Zhou et al., 2004, 2008).

The Pastorelli study described earlier also found similarity across all eight countries in the extent to which children who were high in prosocial behaviour elicited more positive discipline and warmth from their parents over time (Pastorelli et al., 2016). This study focused on children 9 and 10 years of age, and it may be that positive parenting plays its strongest role in promoting prosocial behaviour before that age (Newton et al., 2014), such that the parental effect is evident before adolescence, and then the effect of the child's prosocial behaviour on positive parenting comes later.

Taken together, the results of the research to date suggest that while there are cultural—and often cross-country—differences in which parenting behaviours are preferred by parents, there is strong evidence that for any given parenting behaviour, strong cross-cultural similarities exist in the implications of those behaviours for children's development.

Economic Contexts

Raising a child is expensive. It has been estimated that the average Canadian family will spend close to $13,000 per child per year, reaching a total of $243,660 per child by the time they reach 18 years of age (Cornell, 2011). Yet one can imagine that there is considerable variation around that average, depending on income level. High-income parents can buy more and better-quality goods (e.g., books, electronics) and experiences (e.g., music lessons, sports team memberships) for their children than low-income parents can (Pew Research Center, 2015). Lower-income parents also have a harder time paying for basic necessities like food, clothing, medicine, and shelter. Low-income children thus experience a range of material hardships that the majority of high-income children will never personally experience.

In addition to influencing what families can buy, income influences the amount and quality of time parents spend with their children. Low-income parents may need to work multiple jobs or jobs with irregular or night hours; such jobs make it difficult for parents to spend time helping their children with homework or taking them to extracurricular activities—in other words, to "invest" in their children (Yoshikawa, Aber, & Beardslee, 2012). Having difficulty making ends meet and experiencing material hardships also create stress for low-income parents, and that stress can

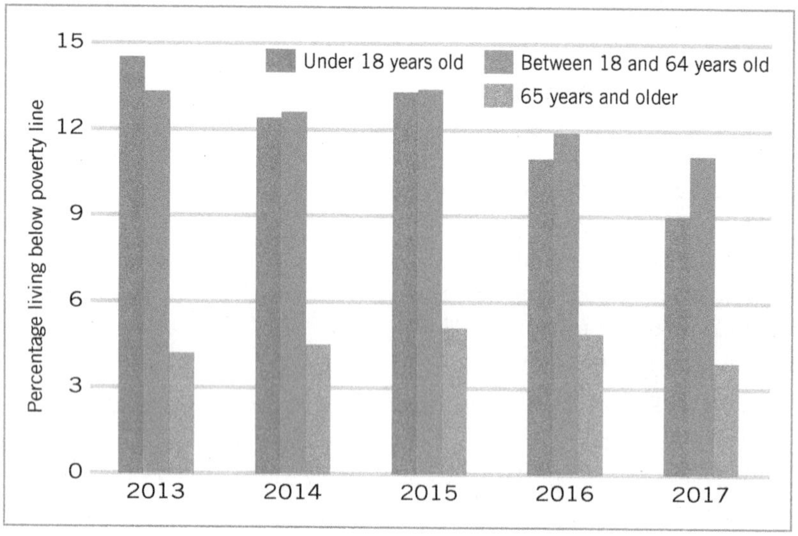

FIGURE 12.6 Percentage of people in Canada living below the poverty line, 2017 Children are somewhat less likely to be living in poverty, compared to adults, as the result of recent reductions in child poverty rates. (Data from Statistics Canada, 2019a)

lead to depression, irritability, harsh parenting, and marital conflict (Benner & Kim, 2010; Gershoff et al., 2007). Adequate family income thus matters to parents and children, both for what it can buy and for the stress it can alleviate.

Sadly, many children live in poor and low-income families, both in Canada and elsewhere around the world. In 2017, 9% of children in Canada lived below the poverty line, down from 15% in 2012 (Statistics Canada, 2019a). In the United States, one in five children lives in poverty; this rate has been steady for the past 40 years (Fontenot, Semega, & Kollar, 2018) and is the second highest among the world's 35 richest nations (UNICEF Innocenti Research Centre, 2012). Around the world, children make up one-third of the world's population but constitute half of the people living in extreme poverty, defined as living on less than $1.25 per day (Partners United in the Fight Against Poverty, 2015). As seen in Figure 12.6, Canada is an exception to that rule, due to recent reductions in child poverty rates.

Because living in poverty can mean living without food, medical care, adequate shelter, or safe schools and neighbourhoods, poor children suffer in their development across a range of domains. It is not surprising that children in poverty have lower academic achievement, more mental health problems, more behavioural problems, and more health problems than their higher-income peers (Benner & Kim, 2010; Doan, Fuller-Rowell, & Evans, 2012; Yoshikawa et al., 2012). Poor families are also at risk of becoming homeless, a crisis state that of course exacerbates all the stressors the parents and children experience (see Box 12.4).

Low-income parents are twice as likely as high-income parents to be afraid their child will get shot or will get in trouble with the law (Pew Research Center, 2015). All parents, regardless of income, worry that their child will be bullied and will have alcohol or drug problems, but low-income parents are more likely to also be afraid that their child will be physically assaulted. These fears likely stem from the qualities of the neighbourhoods in which they live; low-income parents are 3 times as likely as high-income parents to view their neighbourhoods as not being good places to raise children (Pew Research Center, 2015).

Clearly, having a higher income makes parenting and raising children easier, at least from a practical point of view. However, if parents have to spend long hours out of the home and away from their children in order to earn that income, or if high-achieving parents put extra pressure on their children and adolescents, the psychological costs may diminish the material benefits. A growing body of research has found that children living in high-income families, and thus not traditionally considered at risk for behaviour problems and delinquency, actually manifest comparable or higher rates of drug use, delinquent behaviour, and mental health problems compared with their low-income peers (Luthar, Barkin, & Crossman, 2013). These findings are not intended to equate the experiences and difficulties of children from poor and high-income families. Children in

BOX 12.4 A CLOSER LOOK Homelessness

It is impossible to know the precise number of homeless children and families in Canada, much less in the world. One way to estimate the number of homeless people is to examine the use of homeless shelters. In Canada, it is estimated that 35,000 people are homeless on any given night and that more than 235,000 individuals experience homelessness in a year (Gaetz, Gulliver, & Richter, 2014). Although the majority of shelter clients are males over the age of 16, a growing number of children in Canada are using shelters. Between 2005 and 2009, the number of children in shelters increased from 6205 to 9459, a change of over 50% (Segaert, 2012).

Homelessness is considered an adverse childhood experience (ACE; see Chapter 10) that puts children at risk in a variety of ways (Masten et al., 2014). At the most basic level, homeless children lack a regular routine and often lack adequate food and medical care. They may move frequently, which results in chronic absences from school, if they attend school at all. They also frequently change schools, which has been shown to undermine academic achievement (National Research Council, 2010). As a result of these risks, homeless children suffer a range of negative outcomes. For example, they score lower on math and reading tests than their peers (Masten et al., 2014). In addition, compared with poor children who are not homeless, homeless children experience more internalizing problems, such as depression, social withdrawal, and low self-esteem (Buckner et al., 1999; DiBiase & Waddell, 1995; Rafferty & Shinn, 1991), and they suffer more from both health and behavioural problems (Tobin & Murphy, 2013).

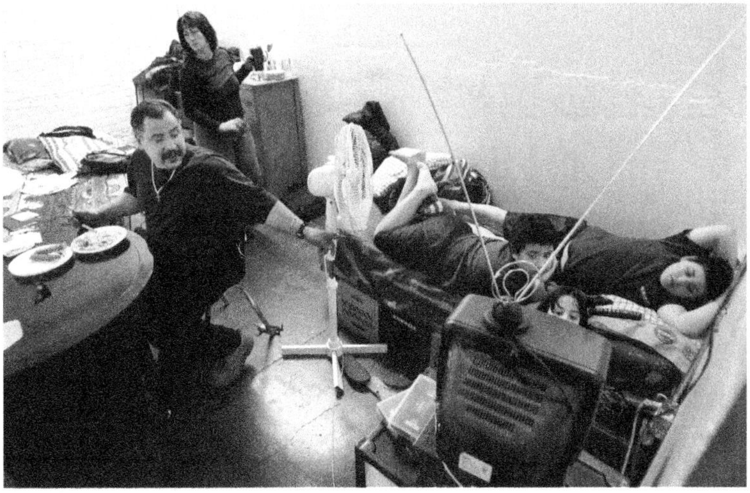

AMY SANCETTA/AP IMAGES

Children in homeless families, including those living in shelters, are at risk for depression, behavioural problems, and academic failure.

One particularly at-risk group are homeless youth living on their own, either because they have been kicked out of or have run away from their homes. Youth between 16 and 24 years of age account for about 20% of the homeless population in Canada (Segaert, 2012). Runaway youth report a range of ACEs that preceded their being without a home. A study conducted in the United States found that amongst a sample of homeless youth in Los Angeles, 59% had suffered emotional abuse, 51% had been physically abused, and 33% had been sexually abused; 40% had been removed from their homes by child protective services because of such maltreatment. In addition, 27% had been in juvenile detention, 83% were racial or ethnic minorities, and 42% had minority sexual orientations. While homeless, 37% had been victims of physical assault, and 13% had been victims of sexual assault (Wong, Clark, & Marlotte, 2016). Both the adverse experiences before homelessness and the assaults experienced while homeless predicted greater depression, self-injury, and posttraumatic stress disorder (Wong et al., 2016).

Worldwide, there are between 10 million and 15 million homeless children, sometimes referred to as "street children" (Naterer & Lavrič, 2016). In some underdeveloped countries, homeless children often have been orphaned because of AIDS or military conflicts; have been abandoned because their families cannot feed or care for them; or have fled to escape sexual, mental, or physical abuse at home (Aptekar & Ciano-Federoff, 1999). In some cases, children living on the streets do so in order to earn money for their very poor families and reside at least part of the time with a parent or another relative (Aptekar & Stoecklin, 2014). Street children are at risk of being coerced into prostitution or sexual slavery or into organized crime (Aptekar & Stoecklin, 2014). However, many street children form family-like groups to substitute for the traditional families they lack (Naterer & Godina, 2011).

Various intervention strategies have been attempted to help homeless and street children. Given that these children are at immediate physical risk and often already suffer from mental health and drug problems, deciding which problem to tackle first is a serious challenge for those working with them. An organization known as the Canadian Homelessness Research Network has compiled several examples of successful strategies, including providing mental health care, providing substance abuse treatment, providing job training, and reconnecting them with family members (Gaetz et al., 2013). Homelessness is a complex population, and helping homeless children requires a multipronged approach, whether they are in the United States, Canada, or elsewhere.

high-income families do not experience the stress of survival that low-income children and adolescents do. What these studies do make clear, however, is that there is more than a single pathway to certain maladaptive outcomes; this phenomenon, known as *equifinality*, is discussed in detail in Chapter 10 (Cicchetti & Rogosch, 1996).

Consistent with Bronfenbrenner's bioecological model, economic and educational factors at the country level also seem to be related to the degree to which mothers engage in various caregiving activities. In a study of mothers in 28 developing countries who had children younger than 5, mothers in countries that had higher average levels of educational attainment and a higher gross national product were more likely to engage in caregiving activities that are cognitively stimulating (e.g., reading books, counting, naming objects) and were less likely to leave their children alone or in the care of a child younger than 10. It is likely that cultural differences in the importance placed on literacy and cognitive growth account for these differences in mothers' caregiving activities (Bornstein & Putnick, 2012).

Parents' Work Contexts

In families throughout the world, one or both parents have to work outside the home in order to support their children. The workplace environment can provide parents with a sense of accomplishment and a social network, both of which can enhance their mental health and, in turn, the quality of their parenting. However, work can also cause stress, and many parents, wittingly or not, bring home that stress.

Two studies in Australia provide insight into the effect of work on family life and child development. In the first study, nearly 3000 employed parents of 4- and 5-year-olds were asked about their work life and family life (Strazdins et al., 2013). Most parents reported that they found work rewarding, but one-third also admitted that they experienced family difficulties and conflicts as a result of working. The extent to which a family experienced work–family conflict was in turn related to higher levels of emotional and behavioural problems in their children; this finding was true even when family income was accounted for, suggesting that the harm of conflict from a stressful job was not outweighed by the benefits of higher income (Strazdins et al., 2013). The second Australian study hinted at potential mechanisms for these findings. In this survey of 2151 mothers of young children, work–family conflict was linked with more parent irritability and less parental warmth, whereas work–family reward was associated with more warmth and more consistency (Cooklin et al., 2015).

The fact that many more mothers work now than in past generations means that many more families may be susceptible to work–family conflict. In Canada in 1976, only 39% of mothers with children younger than 16 were employed outside the home (Ferrao, 2010). In 2015, about 70% of mothers with children under 6 years of age, 78% of mothers with children aged 6 to 11 years old, and 81% of mothers with children aged 12 to 17 worked outside the home (Moyser, 2017). These changes in the rates of maternal employment reflect a variety of factors, including greater acceptance of mothers working outside the home, more workplace opportunities for women, and an increase in women who obtain university and graduate degrees, most of whom work.

The dramatic rise in the number of mothers working outside the home raised a variety of concerns. Some experts predicted that maternal employment, especially in an infant's first year, would seriously diminish the quality of maternal caregiving and that the mother–child relationship would suffer accordingly. Others worried that "latchkey" children who were left to their own devices after school would get into serious trouble, academically and socially. Over the past two decades, much research has been devoted to addressing such concerns. For the most part, the findings have been reassuring.

Taken as a whole, the research does not support the idea that maternal employment has negative effects on children's development. Even in the area of greatest debate — the effects of maternal employment on infants in their first year of life — when negative relations between maternal work and children's cognitive or social behaviour have been found, the results have not been consistent across studies, ethnic groups, or the type of analyses applied to the data (Berger et al., 2008; Brooks-Gunn, Han, & Waldfogel, 2010; Burchinal & Clarke-Stewart, 2007). For example, some research suggests that early maternal employment is associated with better adjustment at age 7 for children in low-income African American families, whereas no such effect was found for those in a study of low-income Latino American families (Coley & Lombardi, 2013).

LWA/DANN TARDIF/CORBIS

Over the past 30 years, there has been a dramatic rise in the number of mothers in paid employment, working either from home or outside the home. Although change led to worries about the impact that maternal employment would have on children's development, research suggests that there is no cause for concern.

Studies of maternal employment extending beyond infancy also reveal contextual variation in the effects that maternal employment can have on children's development. For instance, a study of 3- to 5-year-olds found that those whose mother worked a night shift (starting at 9:00 P.M. or later) tended to exhibit more aggressive behaviour, anxiety, and depressive symptoms than did the children whose mothers worked a typical daytime schedule (Dunifon et al., 2013). In another study, researchers found that mothers who worked more often at night (starting at 9:00 P.M. or later) spent less time with their adolescents and that their adolescents had a lower-quality home environment (in terms of the quality of mother–child interactions, the cleanliness and safety of the home, and so on), which in turn predicted higher levels of risky behaviours among the adolescents. However, similar negative effects were not found in the case of mothers who worked evening shifts that ended by midnight or who had other nonstandard work schedules (e.g., those with varying hours) that allowed them greater knowledge of their children's whereabouts (Han, Miller, & Waldfogel, 2010).

One aspect of work life that is invaluable to working families in Canada is the paid family-leave policy, which we explore in depth in Box 12.5.

Childcare Contexts

Because so many mothers work outside the home, a large number of infants and young children receive care on a regular basis from someone besides their parents. In Canada, about 60% of children under 5 years of age receive some type of childcare (Statistics Canada, 2019c). Of those children, around 52% are in centre-based childcare, 25% are cared for by a nonrelative in a home environment (e.g., babysitter, family day-care provider, nanny), and 25% are cared for by a relative other than a parent (see Figure 12.7; Statistics Canada, 2019d).

FIGURE 12.7 **Childcare in Canada, 2019** In Canada, 60% of children under the age of 5 receive formal or informal childcare. About half (51.9%) of these children are in care provided by childcare centres. (Data from Statistics Canada, 2019e)

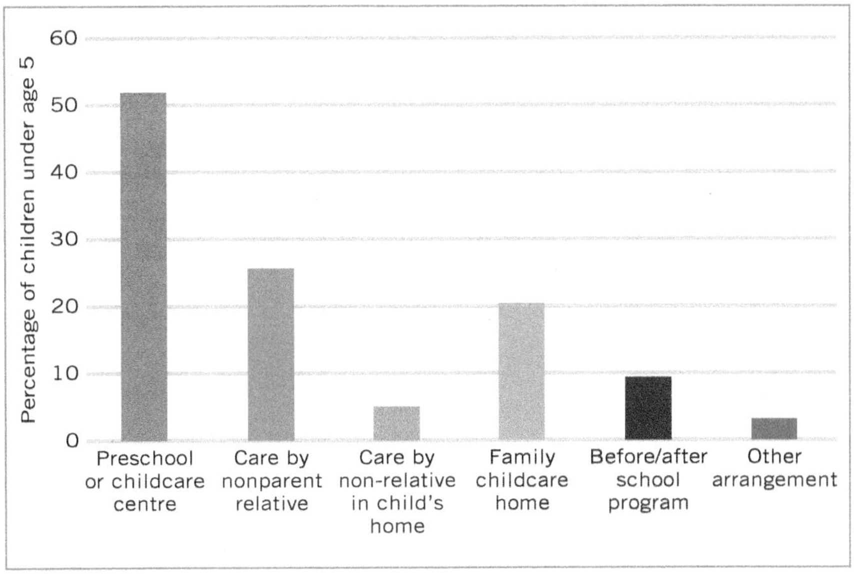

The increase in the number of children in Canada in nonparental childcare began in the 1970s. Initially, the greatest concern among researchers studying this trend was that it might undermine the early mother–child

BOX 12.5 APPLICATIONS Family-Leave Policies

Caring for a new baby, whether because of a birth or an adoption, takes both time and energy on the part of parents. As we learned in Chapter 2, infants wake up often and eat often, meaning that one or both parents have to get up repeatedly to take care of them. We also learned in Chapter 11 that the early months of life are an important time for establishing attachment bonds that will form the basis of the parent–child relationship.

For much of human history, the bulk of the responsibility of caring for young children fell to mothers. However, as the number of women in the workforce has increased, women are increasingly unable to stay home to care for their children. This fact has necessitated family-leave policies that allow one or both parents to take an extended absence from work without worry of losing their jobs. In Canada, job-protected maternity leave was first introduced in 1921 in British Columbia. It was only in 1971, however, that the federal government introduced paid maternity leave through the employment insurance benefits plan. The plan at that time only included 15 weeks of paid leave. In 1994, the federal government added 10 weeks of paid parental leave (i.e., leave that could be taken by mothers or fathers) to the maternity leave benefit. The last change to the federal legislation occurred in 2017, when the parental leave benefit was expanded to 69 weeks.

Today, parents can therefore take up to 21 months of leave after the birth of their child (up to 15 weeks maternity leave plus up to 69 weeks paid parental leave) or 61 weeks following the adoption of their child. These leave periods are paid through employment insurance (EI), and employers must guarantee that a parent's job will be there for them, following their return to work. The only stipulation is that parents must have accumulated a minimum of 600 hours and paid employment insurance premiums. In addition to the EI benefits, 1 in 5 women receive supplementary top-up pay during their leave from their employer (Marshall, 2010).

A large-scale study done in 2011 indicated that just about 70% of mothers worked in the 12 months before the birth or adoption of their child. Of those mothers, 90% took leave, with 83% of women taking a paid leave of around 40 weeks (the number is slightly higher in Quebec, which has its own employment insurance program). Those mothers who did not take any leave were more likely to be lone parents, have less education, and earn a lower income compared to those who did take leave (Findlay & Kohen, 2012). Although fathers are eligible for parental leave, this same study showed that only 26% of fathers outside of Quebec (versus 76% in Quebec) took leave following the birth or adoption of a child—the average length of leave was around 2 weeks (around 5 weeks in Quebec).

The majority of industrialized countries in the world are like Canada and provide at least one year of paid leave to parents (OECD Family Database, 2019). In contrast, the United States is the only industrialized country that does not provide paid family leave for new parents, despite the fact that a large majority (84%) of Americans support a paid family and medical leave policy for all working individuals (National Partnership for Women & Families, 2018). (Figure 9.4 shows the number of weeks of paid maternity leave offered by industrialized countries.)

Paid parental leave allows women to recover from pregnancy and childbirth and to care for their newborns. It also allows both parents, including adoptive parents, time to bond with their babies. Paid family leave has been linked with a range of important child outcomes, including a decrease in infant mortality, an increase in breast-feeding, an increase in vaccination rates, and a reduction in child maltreatment (Raub et al., 2018).

relationship (Belsky, 1986). For example, on the basis of attachment theory (see Chapter 11), it has been argued that young children who are frequently separated from their mothers are more likely to develop insecure attachments to their mothers than are children whose daily care is provided by their mothers. Yet as we saw in Box 11.1, that concern was unfounded. Several other outcomes have been linked with children's experiences in childcare—some of them to the children's benefit and some not.

Adjustment and Social Behaviour

Much research has considered whether children in childcare centres are more aggressive than children not in childcare centres because they compete for resources (e.g., crayons, toy cars, the time of their teachers). The findings have been mixed and sometimes depend on the specific mode of analysis (e.g., Crosby et al., 2010) and the country where the research was conducted. A number of investigators have found that children who are in childcare do not differ in problem behaviour from those cared for at home (Barnes, Beaver, & Miller, 2010; Erel, Oberman, & Yirmiya, 2000). Indeed, in two recent large studies in Norway, a country in which the quality of childcare is uniformly high, researchers found little consistent relation between amount of time in childcare and children's externalizing problems, such as aggression and noncompliance, or social competence (Solheim et al., 2013; Zachrisson et al., 2013).

These findings are in notable contrast to those from a longitudinal NICHD study in the United States, where the quality of childcare is more variable. (See Box 11.1 for a discussion of this study in the context of attachment.) The NICHD study indicates that the number of hours per day that a child is in care or the number of changes in caregivers the child experiences in the first 2 years of life predicted lower social competence and more noncompliance with adults at age 2 (NICHD Early Child Care Research Network, 1998a). At 4½ years of age, children in extensive childcare were viewed by care providers (but not by mothers) as exhibiting more problem behaviours, such as aggression, noncompliance, and anxiety/depression (NICHD Early Child Care Research Network, 2006). The relation between more hours in centre care and teacher-reported externalizing problems (e.g., aggression, defiance) was also found in the elementary school years but generally was not significant by 6th grade (Belsky, Bakermans-Kranenburg, & van IJzendoorn, 2007). However, more hours of nonrelative care predicted greater risk-taking and impulsivity at age 15 (Vandell et al., 2010).

JUPITERIMAGES/SUPERSTOCK

In Canada, more than half of children between the ages of 6 months and 5 years are in some form of nonparental care.

Significantly, the finding that greater time in childcare is related to increased risk for adjustment problems appears not to apply to children from very low-income, high-risk families (Côté et al., 2008). In fact, longer time in childcare has been found to be positively related to the better adjustment of such children, unless the quality of care is very low (Votruba-Drzal, Coley, & Chase-Lansdale, 2004). Similarly, a large study of children from high-risk families in Canada found physical aggression to be less common among children who were in group childcare than among those who were looked after by their own families (Borge et al., 2004). High-quality childcare that involves programs designed to promote children's later success at school may be especially beneficial for disadvantaged children. As in the case of Project Head Start, discussed in Chapter 8, children who experience these programs show improvements in their social competence and declines in conduct problems (Keys et al., 2013; Lamb, 1998; Peisner-Feinberg et al., 2001; Webster-Stratton, 1998; Zhai, Brooks-Gunn, & Waldfogel, 2011).

In addition, it must be remembered that the background characteristics (e.g., family income, parental education, parental personality) of children who are in childcare for long hours likely differ in a variety of ways from those of children in childcare for fewer hours. Therefore, cause-and-effect relations cannot be assumed, even when the effects of some of these factors are taken into account (Bolger & Scarr, 1995; NICHD Early Child Care Research Network, 1997). Furthermore, the number of hours spent in childcare is less relevant than the quality of childcare provided: no matter what their SES background, children in high-quality childcare programs tend to be well adjusted and to develop social competencies (Love et al., 2003; NICHD Early Child Care Research Network, 2003; Votruba-Drzal et al., 2004).

Cognitive and Language Development

The possible effects of childcare on children's cognitive and language performance are of particular concern to educators as well as to parents. Research suggests that high-quality childcare can have a modest, positive effect on these aspects of children's functioning (Keys et al., 2013), although the effects sometimes weaken over time (Côté et al., 2013). The NICHD study found that, overall, the number of hours in childcare did not correlate with cognitive or language development when demographic variables such as family income were taken into account. However, higher-quality childcare that included specific efforts to stimulate children's language development was linked to better cognitive and language development in the first 3 years of life (NICHD Early Child Care Research Network, 2000b). Children in higher-quality childcare (especially centre care) scored higher on tests of pre-academic cognitive skills, language abilities, and attention than did those in lower-quality care (NICHD Early Child Care Research Network, 2002, 2006; NICHD Early Child Care Research Network & Duncan, 2003).

In addition, children from low-income families who spend long hours in childcare, compared with those who spend fewer hours, tend to show increases in quantitative skills (Votruba-Drzal et al., 2004). It is likely that childcare, unless it is of low quality, provides greater cognitive stimulation than is available in some low-income homes.

Availability and Quality of Childcare

It is not surprising that the quality of care children receive outside the home is related to some aspects of their development. In Canada, each province regulates childcare centres and sets minimum standards for care. For example, by law, a childcare centre in Alberta must meet the following minimum standards to be licensed by the provincial government:

- A caregiver-to-child ratio of 1:3 for children aged 12 months or younger; 1:4 for 12- to 19-month-olds; 1:6 for 19-month-olds to 3-year-olds, 1:8 for 3- to 4½-year-olds, and 1:10 for 4½ years and older
- Maximum group sizes of six for 12-months-olds and younger; eight for 13- to 19-month-olds; twelve for 19-month-olds to 3-year-olds; sixteen for 4½-year-olds; and twenty for 4½ years and older
- Formal training for caregivers, with lead teachers having a bachelor's degree in early childhood education, school-age care, child development, social work, nursing, or other child-related field or an associate's degree in early childhood education and currently working toward a bachelor's degree
- Specific guidelines for the physical space, outdoor equipment, record-keeping, and other health and safety matters

In addition, Alberta is the only province to develop an accreditation process for childcare programs to measure and promote excellence in childcare (see Table 12.1). Furthermore, organizations like the Canadian Child Care Federation provide resources for parents seeking high-quality childcare. Studies from Canada, the United States, Chile, and Sweden have demonstrated that the quality of childcare influences children's development (Broberg et al., 1997; Herrera et al., 2005; NICHD Early Child Care Research Network, 1998b). For example, a recent study in Quebec found that quality childcare was related to better cognitive development in preschoolers. Interestingly, the best predictor of overall childcare quality in this study was the type of language stimulation that teachers and caregivers used—that is, whether they responded to children's vocalizations, praised children, asked questions, and were positive in the language they directed to children (Côté et al., 2013).

TABLE 12.1 Alberta Child Care Accreditation Standards

Experts in early childhood education recommend that parents assess childcare programs before selecting one for their children. Following are the Alberta Child Care Accreditation Standards; Alberta is the only province to develop an accreditation process for childcare programs. These standards apply to licensed daycare centres, approved family day homes, and licensed out-of-school care. The standards are divided into four categories: outcomes for children, for families, for staff, and for the community. (Note that these standards are more stringent than the basic provincial/territorial regulatory requirements.)

Outcomes for Children

Standard 1: Positive, supportive relationships and enriched physical and emotional environments foster children's well-being and development.

1.1 Childcare programs promote and nurture children's positive sense of self and belonging through supportive relationships.

1.2 Childcare programs demonstrate respectful, positive interactions and communications with children.

1.3 Childcare programs incorporate well-designed physical indoor learning environments to foster the optimal development in children.

1.4 Children's development is supported through outdoor environments with active play spaces and opportunities to experience and learn about the natural world.

Standard 2: Program planning and practices support every child's optimal development in an inclusive early learning and care environment that incorporates the value and importance of play.

2.1 Childcare programs incorporate inclusive approaches that respect children's diversity and value children's individual needs and backgrounds.

2.2 Childcare programs promote physical wellness in all children and incorporate physical literacy in everyday programming.

2.3 Childcare programs promote competence, active exploration, and learning through play.

2.4 Childcare programs use observation, recording, and documentation to plan the program based on the needs, abilities, and interests of children and their experiences with families and communities.

Outcomes for Families

Standard 3: Relationships with families are supportive and respectful.

3.1 Childcare programs work in partnership with families and respect their beliefs and expertise in their child-rearing role as primary caregivers.

3.2 Childcare programs implement clear, simple practices that promote regular exchange of information with families.

3.3 Childcare programs support families through parental involvement, sharing of resources, and providing information regarding additional supports for their children.

Outcomes for Staff

Standard 4: Childcare programs create a supportive work environment to maintain a qualified team of childcare professionals and assist them in providing high quality childcare services through its philosophy, policies, procedures, and practices.

4.1 Childcare programs have clear and current statements of program philosophy, policies, goals, and strategies in place to assist childcare professionals in providing quality care.

4.2 Childcare programs have well-defined human resources and management practices to support a qualified team of childcare professionals and maintain a positive work environment.

4.3 Childcare programs demonstrate a positive workplace environment and organizational culture that support the well-being and educational development of childcare professionals.

Outcomes for Community

Standard 5: Childcare programs collaborate with community organizations and services to respond to the needs of children and families they serve.

5.1 Childcare programs are responsive to the diverse needs of the children and families they serve.

5.2 Childcare programs establish working relationships with organizations and services within the community.

5.3 Childcare programs have a clearly defined process for involving community stakeholders.

Standard 6: Continuous quality improvement is demonstrated through ongoing self-monitoring and evaluation processes.

6.1 Childcare programs engage in ongoing monitoring and evaluation processes involving administrative staff, families, childcare professionals, and other stakeholders to support continuous quality improvement.

6.2 Childcare programs use a Quality Enhancement Plan to set program goals annually.

6.3 Childcare programs have sound administrative policies and procedures in place to support quality services.

Information from Association for the Accreditation of Early Learning and Care Services, Alberta Human Services (2013).

ELKE VAN DE VELDE/GETTY IMAGES

The positive academic outcomes associated with high-quality childcare have been found to persist into elementary grades.

One major issue for working parents is the cost of childcare, which varies widely across Canada. In some regions of the country, keeping a child in a licensed childcare centre requires more than 35% of a woman's income, making it cost-prohibitive and effectively reducing women's participation in the labour force (Macdonald & Friendly, 2014). It is thus not surprising that parents and policymakers have each cited childcare affordability as an issue in need of urgent policy attention.

Countries are increasingly recognizing that public funding for preschool programs can both help promote children's development and help working families. As of 2018, in the United States, 44 states had state-funded preschool programs that enrolled 43% of 4-year-olds and 17% of 3-year-olds (Friedman-Krauss et al., 2019). In Canada in 2016, public preschool programs in provinces and territories enrolled 40% of 4-year-olds (Akbari & McCuaig, 2017). Neither the United States nor Canada provides universal access to free preschool, and thus both countries are lagging behind many other countries around the world that offer universal access; for example, universal free preschool begins at age 1 year in Germany, Kazakhstan, Norway, Slovenia, and Sweden and *at birth* in Finland (Organisation for Economic Co-operation and Development, 2017). The United States and Canada have much work to do to guarantee all of their children and families access to free preschool.

REVIEW QUESTION

Considering what you have learned about the role that socioeconomic context—including culture, income, parental work situations, neighbourhood, and childcare options—plays in development, what public policies or programs would provide the most support for parents and best outcomes for their children? ■

CHAPTER SUMMARY

Family Structure

- Family structure has changed in Canada over the past few decades: first-time parents are older, more children are being born to single mothers, families are smaller, and divorce and remarriage are common occurrences.
- A disproportionate number of adolescent parents come from impoverished backgrounds. Adolescent mothers tend to be less effective at parenting than older mothers, and their children are at risk for behavioural and academic problems, delinquency, and early sexual activity. Children of adolescent mothers fare better if their mothers have more knowledge about parenting and if the children themselves have a warm, involved relationship with their fathers.
- There is no evidence that children raised by lesbian or gay parents differ from children of heterosexual parents in their sexual orientation or in their cognitive and social adjustment.
- Although most children adjust well after parental divorce, some children experience enduring negative outcomes. The major factor contributing to negative outcomes for children of divorce is the occurrence of hostile, dysfunctional family interactions, including continuing conflict between ex-spouses.
- Parents' remarriage can have both positive impacts on children, including greater resources and a new trusted adult in their lives, and negative impacts, such as increased conflict in the family. Children do best if all parents are supportive.

Family Dynamics

- Parents socialize their children's development through direct instruction; through their modeling of skills, attitudes, and behaviour; and through their managing of children's experiences and social lives.

- The use of discipline that emphasizes reasoning has been linked with better compliance and social competence. Punishments, such as spanking, have been linked with worse behaviour in children over time.
- Researchers have identified several types of parenting styles related to the dimensions of warmth and control. A style that balances both warmth and control, sometimes called an authoritative parenting style, is best for promoting children's social competence.
- The significance and effects of different parenting styles or practices may vary somewhat across cultures.
- Parenting styles and practices are affected by characteristics of the children, including their attractiveness, behaviour, and temperament.
- Economic stressors can undermine the quality of marital and parent–child interactions, increasing children's risk for depression, academic failure, disruptive behaviour, and drug use.
- Mothers typically interact with their children much more than fathers do. Fathers' play tends to be more physical than mothers' play. However, the nature of parent–child interactions differs across cultures.
- Siblings learn from one another, can be sources of support for one another, and sometimes engage in conflict with one another. Siblings get along better if they have good relationships with their parents and if they feel that their parents treat them equally well.

Child Maltreatment

- Children who experience maltreatment are at risk for developing cognitive delays, antisocial behaviours, and mental health problems.
- Evidence also indicates that maltreatment leads to long-term changes in brain structure and functioning. The most common form of child maltreatment is neglect.

Family Socioeconomic Context

- A family's culture affects the parents' choice of behaviours, such as discipline, but the effect of these behaviours on children is largely similar across cultures.
- Parenting behaviours and, in turn, children's development are affected by the family's economic resources. About 9% of children in Canada are from poor families, putting them at risk for a range of cognitive and behavioural problems.
- Children and mothers reap some benefits from maternal employment, and maternal employment has few negative effects on children if they are in childcare of acceptable quality and are supervised and monitored by adults. New parents are eligible for up to 21 months of paid parental leave.
- Children in high-quality care do better in their cognitive and language development than children in low-quality care. Whether childcare has positive or negative effects on children's functioning probably depends in part on the characteristics of the child, the child's relationship with his or her mother, and the quality of the childcare.

Test Yourself

1. A recent trend in family structure in Canada is the increasing ages of first-time parents. Which of the following is *not* true of these older parents compared with younger parents?
   a. Older parents tend to be more highly educated.
   b. Older parents tend to earn higher incomes.
   c. Older parents tend to use a harsher parenting style.
   d. Older parents are less likely to get divorced within 10 years of having a child.
2. Recent research has shown which of the following to be true of children of same-sex parents, compared with children of heterosexual parents?
   a. They exhibit more mental health disorders.
   b. They tend to perform better socially and academically.
   c. They are similar in their sexual orientation and degree of gender-typed behaviour.
   d. They report higher levels of parental aggression in adolescence.
3. Which of the following statements is *not* true of divorce?
   a. Young children tend to react more negatively to a parent's remarriage than do young adolescents.
   b. For children in high-conflict families, divorce may increase the likelihood of positive outcomes for their adjustment.
   c. Joint custody is the most common arrangement for parents and children after divorce.
   d. Most children do not suffer significant, enduring problems as a result of their parents' divorce.
4. The process through which children acquire the values, knowledge, and behaviours that are regarded as appropriate in their culture is known as ________.
   a. parenting style
   b. socialization
   c. behaviourism
   d. joint attention
5. Which of the following factors has *not* been shown to influence children's adjustment in stepfamilies?
   a. The amount of conflict between the custodial parent and the noncustodial parent
   b. The relationship between the noncustodial parent and stepparent
   c. The genders of the child and stepparent
   d. The age difference between the biological parent and stepparent

6. Which of the following descriptions best fits the definition of "other-oriented induction"?
   a. After a toddler has taken a toy from his friend, the toddler's mother scolds him and makes him apologize.
   b. A father spanks his toddler after that toddler has taken a toy from her friend.
   c. A mother puts her toddler in a time-out after he has taken a toy from his friend.
   d. A father explains to his toddler that by taking a toy from her friend, she has hurt her friend's feelings.
7. Internalization is best described as
   a. the feelings of guilt that a child may experience after his or her parents divorce.
   b. the process by which parent–child interactions reinforce and perpetuate the parent's and child's behaviour.
   c. the process through which a child learns and accepts a desired behaviour as a result of appropriate discipline.
   d. the negative impact harsh punishment can have on a child's sense of self-esteem.
8. Which of the following statements is an accurate description of punishment?
   a. Punishment is an effective form of discipline.
   b. Punishment, although more harsh than other forms of discipline, can teach the child how to behave.
   c. Punishments such as yelling and revoking privileges have been found to be successful at encouraging internalization.
   d. Punishments, when mild, provide minimally sufficient pressure for internalization.
9. Jayden wants to go to a party at a friend's house. When she asks her father for permission, he immediately says no. Jayden asks why, and her father angrily says, "Because I said so!" Jayden's father is displaying which parenting style?
   a. Permissive
   b. Authoritarian
   c. Authoritative
   d. Uninvolved
10. Eric and his friend are playing a game that could become dangerous. Eric's father tells them to stop. Eric pleads with him to let them continue. His father firmly restates his refusal and explains why he thinks their game is dangerous. He then suggests some alternative activities. Eric's father is displaying which parenting style?
    a. Permissive
    b. Authoritarian
    c. Authoritative
    d. Friendly
11. Which of the following is *not* an area in which mothers and fathers tend to differ in interactions with their children?
    a. The type of play they tend to engage in with their children
    b. The amount of time they spend with their children
    c. The effect that their parenting style has on their children's mental health
    d. The amount of physical care and emotional support they provide for their children
12. Six-year-old Trevor has a tendency to act aggressively in order to get his way. His parents react to this behaviour with harsh discipline, including spanking. Trevor's response, however, is to act out even more, which escalates his parents' reactions. This cycle of parent–child behaviour is an example of what concept?
    a. Bidirectionality
    b. Interdependence
    c. Equifinality
    d. Child effects only
13. Siblings get along best if
    a. their parents also get along.
    b. their parents treat each child similarly.
    c. they live in a collectivist community.
    d. all of the above.
14. Which of the following statements is true of the potential effect of socioeconomic context on child development?
    a. Poverty has little impact on children's academic achievement.
    b. Children living in high-income families tend to show lower rates of drug use, delinquency, and mental health problems than their low-income peers.
    c. Living in poverty has negative effects on multiple domains of development.
    d. Maternal employment tends to significantly diminish the quality of mothers' interactions with their children.
15. Which of the following has *not* been found to influence the positive or negative effects of childcare on a child's development?
    a. Number of hours per day the child spends in childcare
    b. Type of relationship the child has with his or her mother
    c. Quality of the childcare facility
    d. Number of siblings the child has

LaunchPad
macmillan learning

DON'T STOP NOW! Research shows that testing yourself is a powerful learning tool. Visit LaunchPad to access the LearningCurve adaptive quizzing system, which gives you a personalized study plan to help build your mastery of the chapter material through videos, activities, and more. **Go to launchpadworks.com.**

Critical Thinking Questions

1. It often is assumed that parental socialization of children's behaviour is a bidirectional process, with the parent affecting the child's behaviour and the child's behaviour also evoking some socialization practices or behaviours. Provide examples of bidirectional causality in regard to (a) the relation between spanking and children's aggression and (b) the relation between parental use of punitive control and children's self-regulation.
2. In some cultures, respect for parental authority is valued more than in many Western industrialized countries. How might this cultural variation affect interactions between parents and children and the relation of parenting styles to children's social and emotional development?
3. Think about the ways your parent or guardian interacted with you when you were a child. Based on Baumrind's categories of parenting style, which type of parenting did your parent or guardian display? What specific behaviours did you use to classify their parenting?
4. Make a list of the advantages and disadvantages of joint custody for children of divorce. How would the advantages and disadvantages vary for families in which the parents either (a) argue a lot or get along and (b) live 50 km apart or 5 km apart after the divorce?
5. In the past few decades, the number of children being cared for by nonparents or in childcare centres has increased dramatically. What are the potential benefits and costs to parents for putting their children in childcare or preschool? What are the benefits and costs to children? To society?

Key Terms

authoritarian parenting, p. 433
authoritative parenting, p. 431
bidirectionality of parent–child interactions, p. 435
child maltreatment, p. 438
discipline, p. 430
family, p. 421
family dynamics, p. 430
family structure, p. 422
internalization, p. 430
parenting style, p. 431
permissive parenting, p. 433
polyvictimization, p. 439
punishment, p. 431
socialization, p. 430
uninvolved parenting, p. 433

Answers to Test Yourself

1. c, **2.** c, **3.** a, **4.** b, **5.** d, **6.** d, **7.** c, **8.** d, **9.** b, **10.** c, **11.** c, **12.** a, **13.** d, **14.** c, **15.** d

CHAPTER

13 Peer Relationships

GEOFFREY CLEMENTS/GETTY IMAGES

HOMER WINSLOW (1836–1910), *Snap the Whip* (oil on canvas, 1872)

THEMES

NATURE AND NURTURE ■ THE ACTIVE CHILD

CONTINUITY/DISCONTINUITY ■ THE SOCIOCULTURAL CONTEXT

INDIVIDUAL DIFFERENCES ■ RESEARCH AND CHILDREN'S WELFARE

"Why did you do all this for me?" he asked. "I don't deserve it. I've never done anything for you."
"You have been my friend," replied Charlotte. "That in itself is a tremendous thing."

— *E. B. White,* Charlotte's Web

As this quote from E. B. White's classic work of children's literature suggests, friendships motivate many of our behaviours, actions, and beliefs. They influence the formation of our identities and provide powerful indications of who we are and who we might become. Friends—and peers in general—are an important part of our lives, whether they are from our workplace, our school, our community, or even our past. The Internet has made it much easier to connect with friends and associates, and texts and instant messaging have made keeping in touch quicker and easier than ever. Facebook even made "friend" into a verb—which of course was quickly followed by its antithetical verb, "unfriend."

In the digital era, peer relationships can span the globe and develop between individuals who have never met in person but who communicate in real-time through online video, messaging, or gaming applications. A survey of 13- to 17-year-olds in the United States revealed that 57% had made at least one friend online and 29% had met five or more friends online, but only 20% had actually met their online friend in person (Lenhart, Smith, & Anderson, 2015). Though comparable data is not readily available for Canadian adolescents, the patterns are likely similar. Parents or teachers likely have little influence over or knowledge about whom children meet and interact with online, meaning that children have more control than ever before over who constitutes their peer groups.

Clearly, the people in children's lives outside their families can have a strong influence on them, both for good and for bad. This influence becomes increasingly important as children become older and spend more time with their **peers**, who are children of their own age and status to whom they are not related (Rubin, Bukowski, & Bowker, 2015). And though children can have close and warm relationships with their siblings, the peers that a child considers to be friends are uniquely different from siblings because those friends are chosen by the child.

Many theorists throughout the years have argued that peer relationships provide special opportunities for children's development. Piaget (1932/1965) suggested that because children are relatively equal in social status, they tend to be more open and spontaneous when expressing their ideas and beliefs with peers than with adults. Similarly, Vygotsky (1978) observed that children learn new skills and develop their cognitive capacities in peer interactions; he emphasized the ways in which children's working together helps to build new skills and abilities, as well as to convey the knowledge and skills valued by the culture.

In this chapter, we consider the special nature of peer interactions and their implications for children's social development. First, we look at the nature of play, which is one of the most important methods through which children interact. Then we turn to friendships, the most intimate form of peer relationships, and consider

peers people of approximately the same age and status who are unrelated to one another

ANDREW MICHAEL/ALAMY

Theorists have emphasized both disagreement and cooperation within the context of peer relationships as important contributors to children's cognitive development. Even something as seemingly simple as establishing the ground rules for an informal game of hockey can hone children's skills in debate and compromise.

questions such as: How do children's interactions with friends differ from those with other peers? How do friendships change with age? What do children get out of friendships, and how do they think about them?

Next, we consider children's relationships in the larger peer group. These relationships are discussed separately from friendships because they appear to play a somewhat different role in children's development, particularly in regard to the provision of intimacy. We consider questions such as: What are the differences amongst children who are liked, disliked, or not noticed by their peers? Does children's acceptance or rejection by peers have long-term implications for their behaviour and psychological adjustment? Finally, we end by discussing both the direct and indirect ways that parents affect their children's peer relationships.

The discussion of children's relationships with their peers will incorporate the theme of *individual differences* and the ways in which differences in peer relationships may cause differences in development. In addition, we will focus on the influence that the *sociocultural context* has on peer relationships, the contributions that both *nature and nurture* make to the quality of children's peer relationships, and the role of the *active child* in choosing friends and activities with peers. We will also consider whether changes in children's thinking about friendships exhibit *continuity or discontinuity*. Finally, we will examine issues of *research and children's welfare* related to interventions to improve children's interactions with other children.

Play

One of the key ways that children interact with their peers is through play. As we saw in Chapter 7, **play** refers to activities that children pursue for their inherent enjoyment. Play is enjoyable, active, and voluntary—if children are rewarded for their behaviours or are indifferent about the activity, it is not play (Rubin, Fein, & Vandenberg, 1983). Although children can play by themselves, and typically do so early in development (see Box 13.1), the majority of children's play from age 4 onward is social and thus involves siblings, peers, and friends (Howe & Leach, 2018).

In addition to allowing children to interact with their peers, play can help with many other aspects of development (Howe & Leach, 2018). Social-emotional development may be the domain most affected by play; children learn how to cooperate, take turns, and try out social roles. Because play is inherently enjoyable, children will experience happiness through play. Play also provides a chance for children to learn and practice empathy and concern for others. Play helps foster cognitive development by giving children opportunities to practice problem solving, to strengthen their memory, and to express their creativity. Because the coordination of behaviours requires communication amongst participants, play can encourage language development. In addition, when children engage in active physical play, such as might occur outside or in an indoor gym, they are developing their gross motor skills as well as their coordination, balance, and strength. There is also evidence that active physical play promotes emotion regulation and increases positive emotions (Lindsey & Colwell, 2013).

play voluntary activities, particularly those of children, with no specific motivation beyond their inherent enjoyment

BOX 13.1 INDIVIDUAL DIFFERENCES The Development of Children's Social Play

In the 1930s, a researcher named Mildred Parten attempted to determine whether children's social play, or the extent to which they play with others, followed a developmental sequence. She observed 42 children enrolled at a preschool at the University of Minnesota over a period of 7 months (Parten, 1932). From her multiple observations of each classroom, she identified six types of play that increase in complexity of their social interactions. The least complex play is non-social—children choose and engage in activities by themselves. This type of play is observed more amongst the youngest children (below 2 years of age) who are in the process of learning language as well as social norms for interacting with peers. The most complex forms of play are social and are observed more amongst the oldest children (4 years old and older), who are able to engage in more advanced play as they master communication and self-regulatory skills.

Non-Social Types of Play Parten observed three types of play that do not involve the active participation of peers and thus are considered to be non-social:

- *Unoccupied play,* in which the child watches things in the environment, but only briefly. Nothing holds their interest for very long.
- *Onlooker play,* in which the child watches other children's play. The child may ask questions about the play but will not try to join in.
- *Solitary play,* in which the child is engrossed in his or her own activity and does not attend to the behaviour of others. All the preschool children were observed to engage in this type of play at some point, but some children engaged in it more than others.

Social Types of Play Parten also observed three types of play that involve social interactions between children:

- *Parallel play,* in which the child plays alongside, but not with, other children. They are typically engaged in similar activities but play independently.
- *Associative play,* in which the child plays with other children in a common activity. The child may share toys with a peer or comment on their behaviour, but the two do not have a shared goal; each child does what they want and they do not coordinate their play.
- *Cooperative play,* in which the child plays with peers in an organized activity with a goal, which involves playing a game (e.g., hockey), reaching an aim (e.g., building the tallest block tower), or enacting a dramatic situation from daily life (e.g., pretending to be staff and patrons at a restaurant). The activity typically involves a distinction in roles and children who do not conform to their assigned roles may be criticized by the other participants.

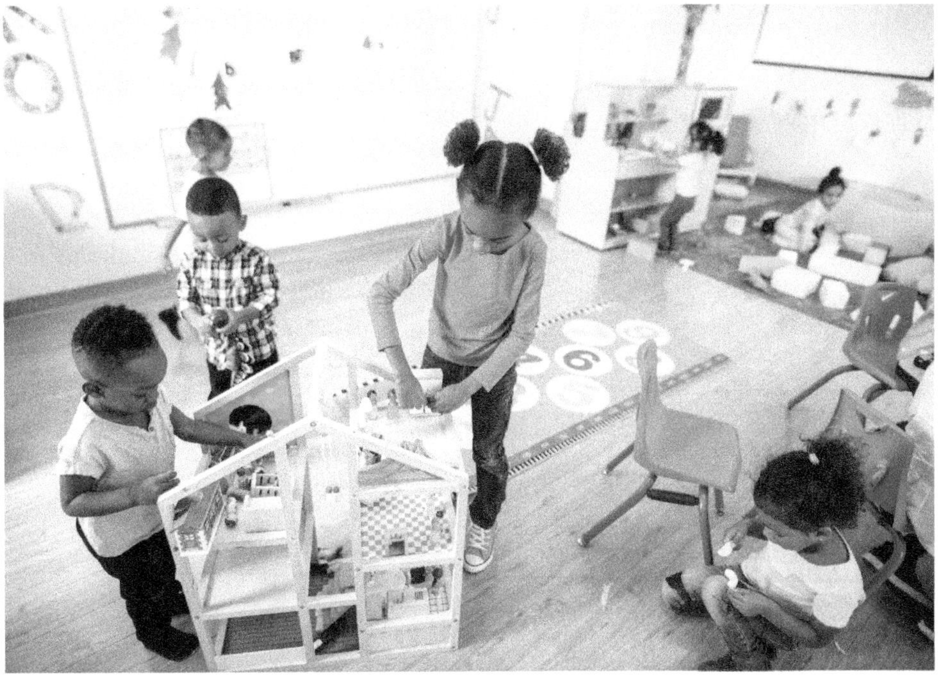

KATE_SEPT2004/GETTY IMAGES

Several of the types of play described by Parten can be observed simultaneously in the same preschool classroom.

Although these observations took place almost a century ago, Parten's classification of children's social play remains an important frame for understanding the development of play across early childhood (Xu, 2010). For example, a recent study observed 3- to 5-year-old children in their preschool classrooms and coded their behaviours into Parten's categories. The higher the children scored in situational emotion knowledge, which involves taking the perspective of another person, the more they engaged in social forms of play and the less they engaged in the non-social forms of play (Gal-Szabo et al., 2019).

Although adults may see children's play as frivolous, it is quite the opposite. Play is an essential part of child development, and indeed the United Nations Convention on the Rights of the Child (1989) explicitly recognizes a child's right "to engage in play and recreational activities appropriate to the age of the child" (Article 31, part 1). Education experts view play-based curricula, which guide children to learn through engaging in activities rather than through explicit instruction, as an essential developmentally appropriate practice in early childhood education (National Association for the Education of Young Children, 2018).

The Development of Play in Early Childhood

ARIEL SKELLEY/GETTY IMAGES

Play can also help children cope with difficult situations. A therapeutic technique known as child-centred play therapy (CCPT) encourages children to express their thoughts and emotions through free play (Ray, 2011). CCPT has been shown to be effective in reducing children's externalizing symptoms (such as aggression) and internalizing symptoms (such as anxiety), as well as improving their social skills (Lin & Bratton, 2015; Pester, Lenz, & Dell'Aquila, 2019).

Tragic natural experiments, such as that which took place in the Romanian orphanages described in Chapter 1, also illustrate the importance of play. In addition to being deprived of adult contact, children in orphanages are often deprived of toys and opportunities to play. Thankfully, interventions can reverse the harm that results from a lack of play. For example, Mother Teresa's orphanage in India introduced structured play to the children's daily routines and found that they experienced improvement in their mental abilities, motor skills, and social skills after only three months (Taneja et al., 2002).

REVIEW QUESTION

Think about the typical features of a preschool classroom: blocks, small toys (sometimes called "manipulatives"), a dramatic play area, art resources, and books. What types of play does each of these features promote? ■

Friendships

Most children, at every stage of development and across all cultures, have at least one peer whom they consider to be a friend (Rubin et al., 2015). Researchers generally agree that friends are people who like to spend time together and feel affection for one another. In addition, their interactions are characterized by *reciprocities;* that is, friends have mutual regard for one another, exhibit give-and-take in their behaviour (such as cooperation and negotiation), and benefit in comparable ways from their social exchanges (Bagwell & Bukowski, 2018; Bukowski, Newcomb, & Hartup, 1996). In brief, a **friend** is a peer with whom an individual has an intimate, reciprocated, and positive relationship.

Children's Choice of Friends

What factors influence a child's friendship decisions? Not surprisingly, children tend to be friends with peers who are friendly and who act prosocially toward others (Rubin et al., 2015). Another key determinant of friendship is similarity of interests and behaviour. Children tend to like peers who are similar to themselves in the cognitive maturity of their play (Rubin et al., 1994) and in the levels of their cooperativeness, antisocial behaviour, acceptance by peers, and shyness (Chen, Cen et al., 2005; Rose, Swenson, & Carlson, 2004). Friends in both childhood and adolescence are also more similar than nonfriends in their academic motivation and self-perceptions of competence (Altermatt & Pomerantz, 2003; Dijkstra, Cillessen, & Borch, 2013; Rubin et al., 2015). Friends also tend to share similar levels of negative emotions such as distress and depression (Haselager et al., 1998) and are similar in their tendencies to attribute hostile intentions to others (Halligan & Philips, 2010; see Chapter 9 for more on hostile attribution bias).

For young children, proximity is an obvious key factor—they tend to become friends with peers who are physically nearby, such as neighbours, playgroup members, or preschool classmates. However, as Box 13.2 points out, young children's access to peers can vary widely by culture. Although proximity becomes

friend a person with whom an individual has an intimate, reciprocated, positive relationship

BOX 13.2 INDIVIDUAL DIFFERENCES Culture and Children's Peer Experience

The patterns of peer development described in this chapter reflect trends averaged across groups of children and sometimes across cultures. These averages mask interesting cultural differences in the types and extent of children's relationships with their peers. One classic study of cross-cultural differences in peer relationships compared children from six countries, namely India, Japan, Kenya, Mexico, the Philippines, and the United States (Whiting & Edwards, 1988). They found that in some communities, such as in Okinawa, Japan, children were free to wander in the streets and public areas of town and had extensive contact with peers. By contrast, children in some regions of Kenya were confined primarily to the family yard and therefore had relatively little contact with peers other than their siblings.

A recent study of adolescents in 11 countries found that the greater the importance of traditional family values — defined as high feelings of family obligation, acceptance of children's duty to be obedient, and an orientation toward the family instead of a focus on autonomy and individualism — the less peer acceptance was related to adolescents' life satisfaction (Schwarz et al., 2012). Thus, in cultures with traditional family values, the peer group appears to be less important, and adolescents' well-being is less related to how well-liked they are by peers.

Cultural differences have also been found in how children interact with their peers. A major study across nine countries (China, Colombia, Italy, Jordan, Kenya, the Philippines, Sweden, Thailand, and the United States) asked children how often in the previous month they had engaged in physical aggression (e.g., "hitting or slapping other children") or in relational aggression (e.g., "trying to keep others from liking someone by saying mean things about that person") (Lansford et al., 2012). Children in China, Italy, and Thailand reported engaging in more relational than physical aggression, whereas children in Jordan and Kenya were more physically than relationally aggressive; children in the other countries engaged in both kinds of aggression at equal rates. There were cultural similarities in one key aspect of aggression: boys were more likely than girls to engage in physical aggression across all nine countries, but there were no consistent gender differences for relational aggression across the nine countries (Lansford et al., 2012). These findings suggest that not only are there different cultural norms about what type of aggression is more acceptable, but also that there is a shared norm that it is more acceptable for boys to be physically aggressive than girls.

Other studies have also identified cross-cultural similarities in some aspects of peer relationships. For example, one ambitious study followed children from ages 7 to 15 in four different countries: China, Iceland, Russia, and the former East Germany (Gummerum & Keller, 2008). Children were interviewed at four different ages about what makes someone a friend and why friends are important. Researchers coded their responses according to friendship complexity. Despite the differences in these cultures, the children followed a remarkably similar pattern of development in the complexity of their friendship descriptions across childhood (see the figure). Findings such as these provide evidence that some universal aspects of the development of peer and friend relationships exist across childhood and adolescence.

In some communities in Kenya, children are discouraged from forming relationships with peers who are not related. Thus, children interact primarily with siblings and adult relatives.

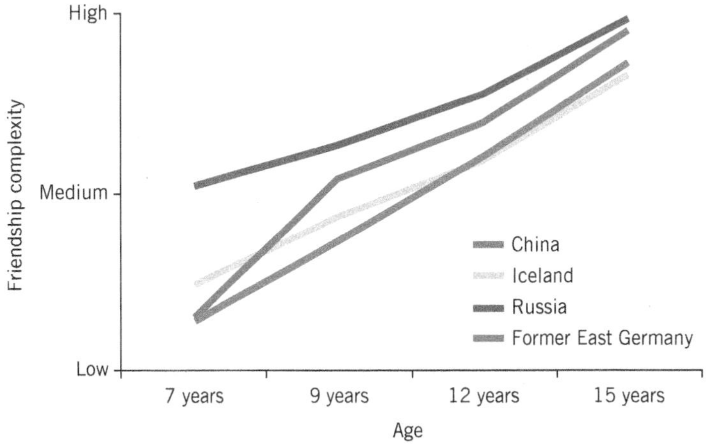

Change in complexity of friendship descriptions across childhood
From age 9 on, in the four different countries listed here, the complexity of children's friendship descriptions increased at the same rate, and all were nearly equal in their high ratings of complexity by age 15. (Data from Gummerum & Keller, 2008)

less important with age, it continues to play a role in individuals' choices of friends into adolescence (Clarke-McLean, 1996; Dishion, Andrews, & Crosby, 1995), in part because of involvement in similar activities at school (e.g., sports, academic activities, arts) which promote the development of new friendships. One study found that when two adolescents participated in the same activity, they

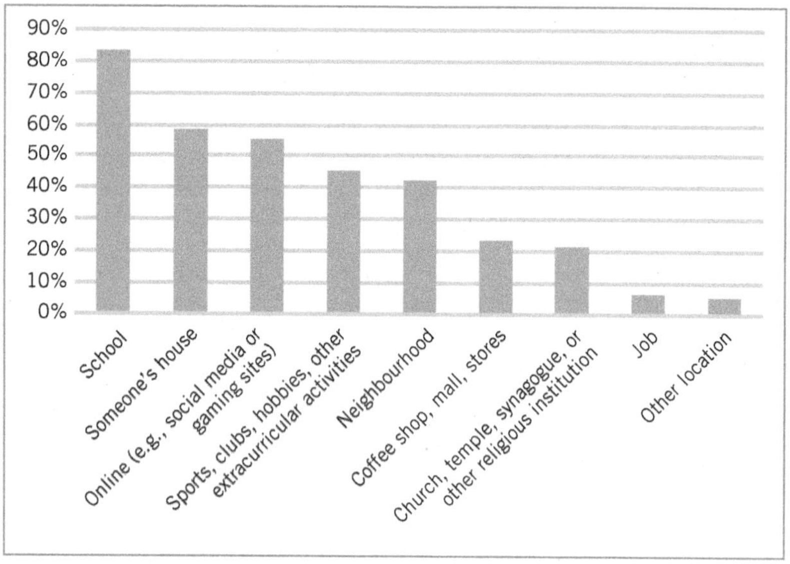

FIGURE 13.1 Main places adolescents say they hang out with close friends Physical proximity still plays a key role in both whom teens are friends with and where they spend time together, although online platforms are used by more than half of teens to spend time with their close friends. (Data from Lenhart, 2015)

were 2.3 times more likely to be friends than were adolescents who did not participate in the same activity (Schaefer et al., 2011).

As seen in Figure 13.1, the vast majority of adolescents in the United States (83%) report that school is the most common setting where they spend time with their close friends. Nearly half of the teens surveyed regularly spend time with friends while doing extracurricular activities (45%) or in their neighbourhoods (42%), and one-fifth spend time with friends who attended the same religious institution (21%). Of course, physical proximity is no longer necessary for children who have regular access to the Internet; 55% of adolescents regularly spend time with friends online, either through social media or gaming sites (Lenhart, 2015). These tendencies are similar for Canadian adolescents. We will discuss the role of technology in friendships more in depth later in this chapter.

In most industrialized countries, similarity in age is also a major factor in friendship, with most children tending to make friends with age-mates (Aboud & Mendelson, 1996; Dishion et al., 1995). In part, this may be due to the fact that in most industrialized societies, children are segregated by age in school: in societies where children do not attend school or otherwise are not segregated by age, they are more likely to develop friendships with children of different ages.

Another powerful factor in friend selection is a child's gender: girls tend to be friends with girls, and boys, with boys (Knecht et al., 2011; Martin et al., 2013; Rose & Rudolph, 2006). Cross-gender friendships, though not uncommon, tend to be more fragile (Lee, Howes, & Chamberlain, 2007; Maccoby, 2000; see Chapter 15). The preference for same-gender friends emerges in preschool and continues through childhood (Hartup, 1983) while the liking of other-gender peers increases over the course of childhood and into early adolescence (Poulin & Pedersen, 2007; Arndorfer & Stormshak, 2008). As seen in Figure 13.2, time in groups with only same-sex peers peaks around age 13 years, whereas time in groups that include opposite-sex peers increases steadily from age 10 years onward, although this increase is much steeper for girls than for boys (Lam, McHale, & Crouter, 2014).

To a lesser degree, children tend to be friends with peers of their own racial/ethnic group, although this tendency varies across groups and contexts (Knecht et al., 2011). For instance, a study that examined friendships in French–English integrated primary schools in Montreal demonstrated that most students had similar numbers of friends from each ethnolinguistic group (Aboud & Sankar, 2007). Similarly, in a study of inter-ethnic friendships in Toronto, students in grades 7 and 8 listed similar numbers of friends from both within and outside their

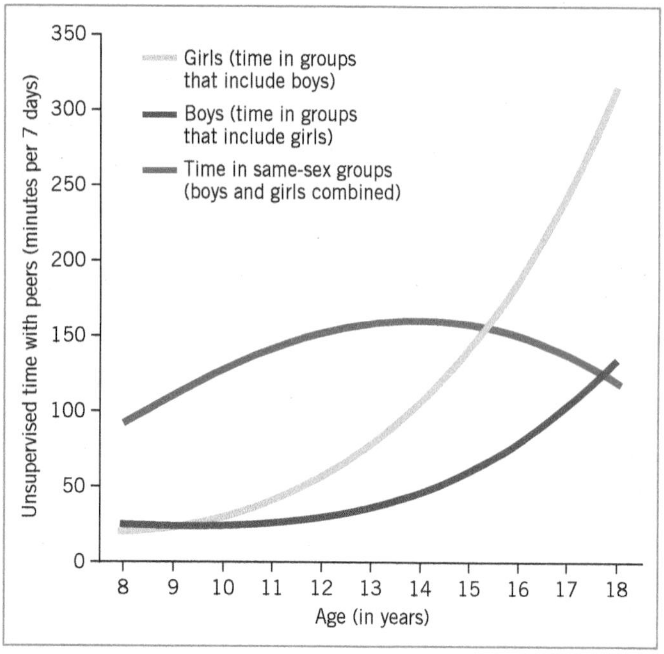

FIGURE 13.2 Change in the amount of unsupervised time children spend with same-sex and opposite-sex peers from age 8 to age 18 After age 13, time exclusively with same-sex peers decreases, while time with opposite-sex peers increases, although more so for girls than for boys. (Data from Lam, McHale, & Crouter, 2014)

ethnic groups, although there was a tendency for best friends to be from the same ethnic group (Smith & Schneider, 2000).

In general, efforts to establish friendships outside one's own racial/ethnic group are less likely to be reciprocated than are efforts within the group (Vaquera & Kao, 2008); and when they are reciprocated, they often are not as long lasting (Lee et al., 2007). A study of junior high students in Montreal and Toronto demonstrated that 70% of co-ethnic friendships lasted for at least six months versus 57% of inter-ethnic friendships (Schneider, Dixon, & Udvari, 2007). Youths who maintain cross-racial/ethnic friendships tend to be leaders and relatively inclusive in their social relationships (Kawabata & Crick, 2008), as well as socially competent and high in self-esteem (Eisenberg, Valiente et al., 2009; Fletcher, Rollins, & Nickerson, 2004; Kawabata & Crick, 2011).

A study of children in Germany and Turkey found that, for majority-group children, having cross-ethnic friendships is associated with positive attitudes toward people in other groups in the future (Feddes, Noack, & Rutland, 2009). However, cross-race friendships can have costs. For example, middle-school African American and Asian American youths whose best friends are all of a different race from their own tend to be lower in emotional well-being than those with best friends only from the same racial group, perhaps because their friends of different races are not subject to the same forms of racial discrimination and are less able to provide support when they are faced with it (McGill, Way, & Hughes, 2012).

The fact that friends tend to be similar on a number of dimensions underscores the difficulty of knowing whether friends actually affect one another's behaviour or whether children simply seek out peers who think, act, and feel as they do.

Social Developmental in Childhood: Developmental Trends in Children's Conception of Friendship

WORTH PUBLISHERS

Developmental Changes in Friendship

Children appear to have friends as early as their second year of life. Children as young as 12 to 18 months of age display a preference for some children over others by touching the preferred children, smiling at them, and engaging in positive interactions with them more than they do with other peers (Hay, Caplan, & Nash, 2018). University of Waterloo psychologist Hildy Ross and University of Guelph psychologist Susan Lollis (1989) note that starting at around 20 months of age, children increasingly initiate more interactions with some children than with others, and they contribute more when playing games with those children. By the time they reach 24 months of age, children have begun to develop skills that allow greater complexity in their social interactions, including imitating peers' social behaviours, engaging in cooperative problem solving, and trading roles during play (Brownell, Ramani, & Zerwas, 2006; Seehagen & Herbert, 2011).

By age 3 or 4, children can make and maintain friendships with peers (Dunn, 2004) and most have at least one friendship (Quinn & Hennessy, 2010). Even in these early years, children can identify their "best friends" and characterize their relationships with best friends as more positive than their relationships with other friends (Sebanc et al., 2007). During preschool, children begin to prefer playing with same-gender peers and this preference continues through middle childhood (Howe & Leach, 2018).

From about age 5 years on, children who are friends communicate more often with one another and cooperate and work together more effectively than do nonfriends (Hartup, 1996). Friends also fight

Children's friendships begin at about 2 years of age or even earlier.

ELIZABETH CREWS

HILL STREET STUDIOS/GETTY IMAGES

Adolescent friends are more likely to share confidences with one another than are younger friends.

with each other more often, but they are more likely to negotiate their way out of the conflict than are nonfriends (Laursen, Finkelstein, & Betts, 2001). Between ages 6 and 8, for example, children define friendship primarily on the basis of actual activities with their peers and tend to define "best" friends as peers with whom they play all the time and share everything (Gummerum & Keller, 2008).

Studies conducted in both Asian and Western countries (including Canada) have shown that, throughout middle childhood, children increasingly define their friendships in terms of characteristics such as companionship, similarity in attitudes/interests, acceptance, trust, genuineness, mutual admiration, and loyalty (Gummerum & Keller, 2008; McDougall & Hymel, 2007). At about 9 years of age, children seem to become more sensitive to the needs of others and to inequalities in the ways some groups of people are treated compared to other groups. For children at this age, friends are those peers who take care of one another's physical and material needs, provide general assistance and help with schoolwork, reduce loneliness, and share feelings.

The Importance of Peers in Middle Childhood

LEWKMILLER/GETTY IMAGES

During adolescence, friendships become an increasingly important source of intimacy and self-disclosure, as well as a source of honest feedback. Friendships also become more exclusive in adolescence, as adolescents begin to focus on having just a few close friends (Rubin et al., 2015). These changes may explain why adolescents perceive the quality of their friendships as improving from middle to late adolescence and why they value them so highly (Way & Greene, 2006). However, friendships in adolescence can also be less stable than they were in middle childhood; whereas 75% of friendships at age 10 persist for the entire school year, only half endure in adolescence (Rubin et al., 2015).

What accounts for the various age-related changes that occur in children's friendships, particularly with regard to their concept of friendship? Selman (1980) suggested that changes in children's reasoning about friendships are a consequence of age-related qualitative changes in their ability to take others' perspectives (see Chapter 9). In the view of Selman, as well as of Piaget and others, young children have limited awareness that others may feel or think about things differently than they themselves do. Consequently, their thinking about friendships is limited by the degree to which they consider issues beyond their own needs. As children begin to understand others' thoughts and feelings, they realize that friendships involve consideration of both parties' needs so that the relationship is mutually satisfying. Selman's descriptions of friendship development have been confirmed in research with children in North America and across Europe (Rubin et al., 2015).

The Role of Technology in Friendships

Social technologies, such as online social media, instant messaging, and texting, play an increasingly significant role in peer interactions of children and especially of adolescents. In a large survey of Canadian 11- to 15-year-olds, the majority said that texting is one of the three most common ways they contact their closest friends (Coe, Chan, & Freeman, 2016). As shown in Figure 13.3, there are gender and age differences regarding frequency of communication; girls are more likely than boys to contact their friends daily by text and social media, and the frequency with which both girls and boys contact their friends using technology increases between grades 6 and 10.

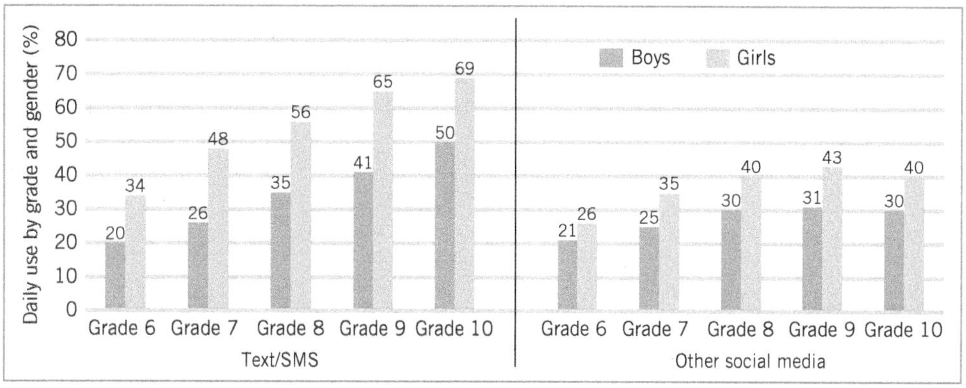

FIGURE 13.3 How adolescents stay in touch with their best friends Texting and social networks are common ways adolescents contact their friends on a daily basis, although girls are more likely than boys to use each of these modes of communication. Furthermore, the use of technology to facilitate contact with friends increases between grades 6 and 10. (Data from Coe, Chan, & Freeman, 2016)

Researchers have identified several key ways in which electronic communication facilitates the creation and maintenance of friendships amongst children (Schneider, 2016), including the following:

- *Greater anonymity* leads children and youth to reduce their social inhibitions, which, particularly for temperamentally shy children, could help them interact with others online. It goes without saying, however, that children can get carried away with this disinhibition.
- *Less emphasis on physical appearance* when conversation is conducted through typing or audio allows children and youth to connect with others based on their shared interests and their personalities rather than on their appearance. This tendency will be less true for video communication, of course.
- *More control over interactions,* because they can control when, how, and with whom they connect, leads children and youth to feel they are in charge of their social lives.
- *Finding similar peers* is much easier in the Internet age than in the past, which allows youth to connect with others who share their interests, thereby increasing their sense of belongingness and well-being.
- *24/7 access* means that children and youth can connect with friends and peers throughout their day. The downside is that such ubiquitous access can also interfere with school and sleep.
- *It's fun* to connect with friends online and to share thoughts, photos, videos, and game time online.

The potential for communication through technology to enhance friendships has been confirmed by research. A longitudinal study involving nearly 700 Dutch children ages 10 to 17 years found that the more they used instant messaging, the more comfortable they were introducing themselves to new people and suggesting to new friends that they hang out sometime (Koutamanis et al., 2013).

Given youths' tremendous use of digital technologies for their social interactions, social and behavioural scientists, as well as parents, have expressed concern about the effects that these modes of communication may have on social development — and especially on social relationships. Two major perspectives have guided research on this issue. One view is the *rich-get-richer hypothesis,* which proposes that those youths who already have good social skills benefit from the Internet and related forms of technology when it comes to developing friendships (Khan et al., 2016; Schneider, 2016). In support of the rich-get-richer hypothesis, a study of Palestinian youth found that individuals with lots of friends in their off-line lives tended to have large online social networks as well (Abbas & Mesch, 2018). Moreover, youths who were better adjusted at ages 13 to 14 use social networking more at ages 20 to 22 and exhibit a similarity in their online and offline social competence (e.g., in peer relationships, friendship quality, adjustment) (Mikami et al., 2010). By contrast, youth who are shy or withdrawn tend to inappropriately vent anger online, which impairs further interactions with peers (Laghi et al., 2013).

Thus, socially competent people may benefit most from the Internet because they are more likely to interact in appropriate and positive ways when engaged in social networking.

Yet there is also support for a competing hypothesis, namely the *social-compensation hypothesis,* which argues that social media may be especially beneficial for lonely, depressed, and socially anxious adolescents (McKenna & Bargh, 1998). Specifically, because they can take their time thinking about and revising what they say and reveal in their messages, these youths may be more likely to make personal disclosures online than offline, which eventually fosters the formation of new friendships. Lonely and socially anxious youths seem to prefer online communication over face-to-face communication (Pierce, 2009). Evidence also suggests that youths with high levels of depressive symptoms use online communication to make friends and to express their feelings (Hwang, Cheong, & Feeley, 2009), and that such use is associated with less depression for youths with low-quality best-friend relationships (Selfhout et al., 2009).

Internet-based communication technologies appear to facilitate communication amongst existing friends, allowing them to maintain and enhance the closeness of their relationships (Valkenburg & Peter, 2011). For example, Brock University researchers found that teenage girls who interacted with their friends online more often had better friendships than girls who did not often use the computer with their friends (Desjarlais & Willoughby, 2010). In existing friendships, online communication seems to foster self-disclosure, which enhances friendship quality. In fact, many adolescents tend to use social-networking sites to connect with people they know offline and to strengthen these preexisting relationships (Reich, Subrahmanyam, & Espinoza, 2012). Similarly, the use of instant messaging has been associated with an increase in the quality of adolescents' existing friendships over time (Valkenburg & Peter, 2009). In contrast, high levels of Internet use primarily for entertainment (e.g., playing games, surfing) or for communication with strangers can harm the quality of friendships (Punamäki et al., 2009) and predicts increases in anxiety and depression (Selfhout et al., 2009).

Effects of Friendships on Psychological Functioning and Behaviour

The most important benefits of friendship, noted by Piaget, Vygotsky, and others, are emotional support and the validation of one's own thoughts, feelings, and worth, as well as opportunities for the development of important social and cognitive skills.

Support and Validation

Friends can provide a source of emotional support and security, even at an early age. Children with best friends and with intimate, supportive friendships experience less loneliness than children who do not have a best friend or whose friends are less caring and intimate (Kingery, Erdley, & Marshall, 2011). Children who experience chronic friendlessness are more likely than children with friends to develop symptoms of depression and social withdrawal (Engle, McElwain, & Lasky, 2011; Palmen et al., 2011).

The support of friends can be particularly important during periods of transition. For example, young children have more positive initial attitudes toward school if they begin school with a large number of established friends as classmates (Ladd & Coleman, 1997; Ladd, Kochenderfer, & Coleman, 1996), likely because the presence of established friends in the early weeks of school reduces the strangeness of the new environment. Similarly, as children move into junior high or middle school, they are more likely to increase their levels of sociability and leadership if they have stable, high-quality, intimate friendships and have higher levels of academic achievement (Berndt, Hawkins, & Jiao, 1999; Ng-Knight et al., 2018).

Friendships may also serve as a buffer against unpleasant experiences, such as being yelled at by the teacher, being excluded or victimized by peers (Bukowski, Laursen, & Hoza, 2010; Waldrip, Malcolm, & Jensen-Campbell, 2008), or being socially isolated (i.e., having low levels of involvement with peers more generally; Laursen et al., 2007). This is especially true if friends provide intimacy, security, and help when needed (Kawabata, Crick, & Hamaguchi, 2010). In one Canadian study that demonstrated this effect, 10- and 11-year-olds reported on their negative experiences over a 4-day period, indicating shortly after each bad experience how they felt about themselves and whether or not a best friend had been present during each episode. The researchers also recorded the children's cortisol levels multiple times each day, as a measure of the children's stress reactions. The study showed that when a best friend was not present, the more negative children's everyday experiences were, the greater the increase in their cortisol levels and the greater the decline in their sense of self-worth following each experience (Adams, Santo, & Bukowski, 2011). In contrast, when a best friend was present, there was less change in cortisol response and in the child's self-worth due to negative experiences.

As noted previously, the degree to which friends provide caring and support generally increases from childhood into adolescence (De Goede, Branje, & Meeus, 2009). Around age 16, adolescents, especially girls, report that friends are more important confidantes and providers of support than their parents are (Bokhorst, Sumter, & Westenberg, 2010) (Figure 13.4).

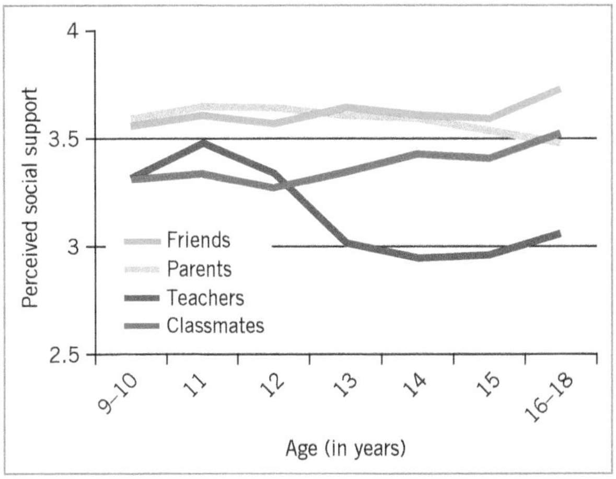

FIGURE 13.4 Age trends in social support from various sources Support from parents and support from friends are relatively stable across childhood and adolescence. Support from teachers drops dramatically once children enter adolescence, while at the same time support from nonfriend classmates increases slightly. (Data from Bokhorst, Sumter, & Westenberg, 2010)

The Development of Social and Cognitive Skills

Friendships provide a context for the development of social skills and knowledge that children need to form positive relationships with other people. Throughout childhood, positive behaviours such as cooperation and negotiation are all more common amongst friends than amongst nonfriends. In addition, young children who discuss emotions with their friends develop a better understanding of others' mental and emotional states than do children whose peer relationships are less close (Hughes & Dunn, 1998; Maguire & Dunn, 1997). Children can use these skills when helping their friends. In a study of 3rd- to 9th-graders over the course of the school year, those with high-quality friendships improved in the quality of their reported strategies for helping friends deal with social stressors. For example, they reported becoming more likely to be emotionally engaged in talking with their friend about a problem and less likely to act as though the problem did not exist (Glick & Rose, 2011).

Friendship provides other avenues to social and cognitive development as well. Through gossip with friends about other children, for example, children learn about peer norms, including how, why, and when to display or control the expression

Interactions with friends provide children with opportunities to get constructive feedback regarding their behaviour and ideas.

JUPITERIMAGES/GETTY IMAGES

of emotions and other behaviours (McDonald et al., 2007). As Piaget pointed out, friends are more likely than nonfriends to criticize and expand on one another's ideas and to elaborate and clarify their own ideas (Azmitia & Montgomery, 1993).

This kind of openness promotes cognitive skills and enhances performance on creative tasks (Miell & MacDonald, 2000; Rubin et al., 2015). One demonstration of this was provided by a study in which teams of 10-year-olds, half of them made up of friends and the other half made up of nonfriends, were assigned to write a story about rain forests. The teams consisting of friends engaged in more constructive conversations (e.g., they posed alternative approaches and provided elaborations more frequently) and were more focused on the task than were teams of nonfriends. In addition, the stories written by friends were of higher quality than those written by nonfriends (Hartup, 1996).

Because friendships fill important needs for children, it is not surprising that having friends enhances children's social and emotional health. In fact, having close, reciprocated friendships in elementary school has been linked to a variety of positive psychological and behavioural outcomes for children, not only during the school years but also years later in early adulthood. In a longitudinal study, researchers looked at children when they were 10 years of age and again when they were young adults. They found that children who had best friends were viewed by classmates as more mature and competent, less aggressive, and more socially prominent (e.g., they were liked by everyone or were picked for such positions as class president or team captain). Thirteen years later, individuals who had best friends at age 10 reported greater success in university and in their family and social lives than did individuals who had not had a best friend at age 10. They also reported higher levels of self-esteem, fewer legal problems, and less psychopathology (e.g., depression) (Bagwell, Newcomb, & Bukowski, 1998). Thus, having a best friend in preadolescence relates not only to positive social outcomes in middle childhood but also to self-perceived competence and adjustment in adulthood.

The Possible Costs of Friendships and Negative Peer Interactions

Not all peer interactions are positive, not even when those peers are considered to be a child's close friends. Peers can encourage negative behaviours, such as aggression or alcohol and substance use. They can also be a source of emotional and physical harm through bullying.

Aggression and disruptiveness There can be costs to having friends, if the friends engage in or encourage negative behaviours rather than positive ones (Simpkins, Eccles, & Becnel, 2008). Friends who have behavioural problems may exert a detrimental influence, contributing to the likelihood that a child or adolescent will engage in violence, drug use, or other negative behaviours. In the elementary school years and early adolescence, children who have antisocial and aggressive friends tend to exhibit antisocial, delinquent, and aggressive tendencies themselves (Snyder et al., 2008). However, the research in this area is correlational, so it is difficult to know if children pick friends who are like them, or if children become more like their friends over time.

Aggressive and disruptive children may gravitate toward peers who are similar to themselves in temperament, preferred activities, or attitudes, thereby taking an active role in creating their own peer group (Knecht et al., 2010). At the same time, friends appear to affect one another's behaviour: for example, a longitudinal study of children in northwestern Quebec demonstrated that friends affect one another's disruptive and deviant behaviour (Vitaro, Pedersen, & Brendgen, 2007). Through their talk and behaviour, youths who are antisocial may both model and reinforce aggression and deviance in one another by making these behaviours seem acceptable, a process known as *deviancy training* (Dishion & Tipsord, 2011). Deviancy training has been found to begin as early as age 5 and to predict antisocial and delinquent behaviours into adolescence (Snyder et al., 2012).

SOLSTOCK/GETTY IMAGES

A child's peers can encourage him to be aggressive, but it is also the case that aggressive children seek out peers who are similar to themselves.

Alcohol and substance abuse Adolescents tend to choose friends who are similar to themselves in terms of drinking and the use of drugs (Knecht et al., 2011). Youths who are highly susceptible to the influence of their close friends seem particularly vulnerable to any pressure from them to use drugs and alcohol (Allen, Porter, & McFarland, 2006), and, as in the case of aggression, this is especially the case if those friends have high status in the peer group (Allen et al., 2012). There is also evidence that adolescents' use of alcohol and drugs and their friends' alcohol and substance use mutually reinforce each other, often resulting in an escalation of use (Bray et al., 2003; Popp et al., 2008; Poulin et al., 2011).

Yet another factor in the association between adolescents' abuse of drugs and alcohol and that of their friends is their genetic makeup. Youths with similar genetically based temperamental characteristics such as risk-taking may be drawn both to one another and to alcohol or drugs (Dick et al., 2007; Hill et al., 2008). Thus, friends' alcohol and drug abuse may be correlated because of their similarity in genetically based characteristics as well as in their socialization experiences, although the effect of a group of friends on youths' drinking is not due solely to genetics (Cruz, Emery, & Turkheimer, 2012).

The extent to which friends' use of drugs and alcohol may put individuals at risk for use themselves seems to depend, in part, on the nature of the child–parent relationship. Adolescents with substance-using close friends are at risk primarily if those adolescents' parents are uninvolved—low in warmth and low in control and monitoring (Kiesner, Poulin, & Dishion, 2010; Mounts & Steinberg, 1995; Pilgrim et al., 1999). If the adolescents' parents are authoritative in their parenting—high in control but also high in warmth (see Chapter 12)—those adolescents are more likely to be protected against peer pressure to use drugs. If the adolescents' parents are more authoritarian—high in control but low in warmth—those adolescents are more susceptible to peers' drug use and thus to using drugs themselves (Mounts, 2002).

FIGURE 13.5 Percentage of children involved in bullying, by grade and gender Bullying occurs in all locations in and around schools. From grades 6 to 10, girls are more likely to be bullied than boys. (Data from Craig, Lambe, & McIver, 2016)

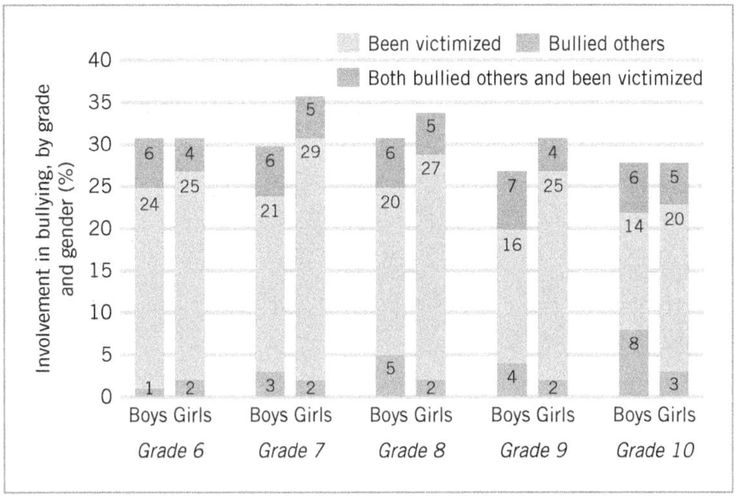

Bullying and victimization Bullying is unfortunately a relatively common experience in the lives of many children and adolescents. In a 2014 Canadian survey of students aged 11 to 15, around 22% reported that they had been bullied at school in the past two months (Craig, Lambe, & McIver, 2016). Girls are more likely than boys to be bullied across all ages (25% versus 19%) and there is a slight decline in being victimized across ages, as can be seen in Figure 13.5. Bullies are of course

BOX 13.3 A CLOSER LOOK Cyberbullying

Cyberbullying is the repeated and intentional harassment or mistreatment of someone through digital devices such as cell phones, computers, and tablets (Hinduja & Patchin, 2019). Cyberbullying can occur through texting, instant messaging, email, social media, blog posts, or a variety of other online platforms, and it has been on the rise in recent years.

According to a national survey of Canadian children aged 10 to 17 years, 14% of children had experienced cyberbullying once or more in the last month. Furthermore, twice as many children reported being a victim of cyberbullying as reported being a perpetrator (Beran et al., 2015). Recent data from Saskatchewan showed that girls (12%) were more likely to be victims of cyberbullying than boys (8%). Indigenous children (16.2%) were also more likely to be bullied than non-Indigenous children (9.4%; Mobin, Feng, Neudorf, 2017). The accompanying figure details the percentage of children who were victims of cyberbullying (including harassment via text, social media platforms, email, and websites), based on a Canadian national survey of students in grades 6 to 10.

Cyberbullies tend to believe aggression is an acceptable way to solve problems and to be high in moral disengagement (Kowalski et al., 2014). For example, a large study of more than 16,000 youth in Finland found that cyberbullying is more common in classrooms where students are accepting of bullying in general, agreeing with such statements as, "Kids who are weak are just asking for trouble" (Elledge et al., 2013, p. 702). Cybervictims, like offline bullying victims, tend to be high in social anxiety, psychological distress, and symptoms of depression, as well as to have aggressive tendencies, poor anger management, and problems at school (Kowalski et al., 2014; Valkenburg & Peter, 2011). However, many cybervictims are also cyberperpetrators, perhaps in retaliation or as self-protection (Kowalski et al., 2014).

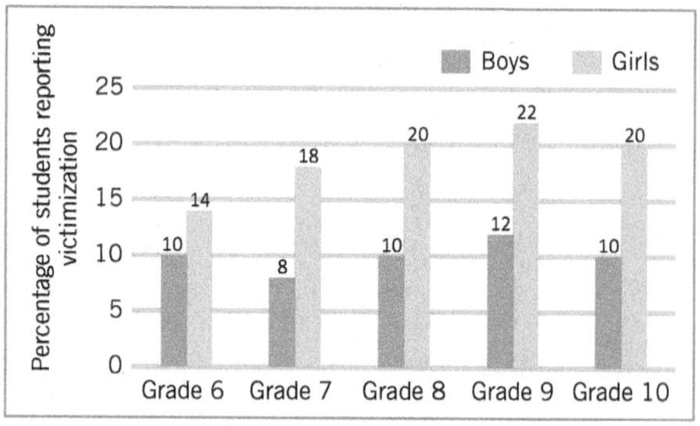

Girls are more likely to be "cyberbullied" than boys, as reported by a sample of 12- to 15-year-olds in Canada. (Data from Craig et al., 2016)

In response to concerns amongst parents, school personnel, and children all around the world, a variety of school-based interventions to reduce cyberbullying have been developed and shown to be effective. The No Trap! intervention in Italy, which uses peer educators to increase awareness amongst adolescents of the harms of cyberbullying, has succeeded in reducing both cyberbullying and cybervictimization (Palladino, Nocentini, & Menesini, 2016). A successful intervention implemented in Spain focuses on correcting children's beliefs that cyberbullying is normative by showing them that in fact only a small proportion of their peers engage in cyberbullying (Del Rey, Casas, & Ortega, 2016). In Germany, the Media Heroes program successfully reduces cyberbullying by increasing students' empathy for cybervictims (Schultze-Krumbholz et al., 2016). Schools in Australia that implemented the Cyber Friendly Schools program, which emphasizes appropriate and responsible online behaviour ("netiquette"), experienced a decrease in cyberbullying and cybervictimization (Cross et al., 2016). Each of these programs is promising, and together they illustrate that there are multiple effective strategies for reducing cyberbullying.

cyberbullying repeated and intentional harassment or mistreatment of an individual via digital devices such as cell phones, computers, and tablets

often themselves peers: 13% of the adolescents admitted to bullying others in the previous year (Huang & Cornell, 2015). Many of the tendencies of in-person bullying are mirrored in the context of cyberbullying, as detailed in Box 13.3.

Why do some children bully others? In the moment, children engage in bullying in order to seem powerful to their peers and to gain power and status (Rodkin, Espelage, & Hanish, 2015). Yet if we consider why some children are bullies and others are not, a complex picture emerges. Consistent with Bronfenbrenner's bioecological model (see Chapter 9), bullying behaviour is influenced by a range of individual, home, school, neighbourhood, and societal factors (Swearer & Hymel, 2015). Children who are bullies tend to be callous and antisocial, susceptible to peer pressure, and higher in social status (Swearer & Hymel, 2015) and tend to have harsh and insensitive parents (Rodkin et al., 2015).

Victims, on the other hand, are likely to be rejected by peers, feel depressed, and do poorly in school, although some are aggressive as well (Swearer & Hymel, 2015; Tom et al., 2010). In addition, hereditary factors associated with aggression appear to predict peer victimization, suggesting that temperamental or other personal characteristics may increase the likelihood of children becoming both aggressive and victimized (Brendgen et al., 2011). For example, low self-regulation is related to both aggression and peer victimization (Eisenberg, Sallquist et al., 2009; Iyer et al., 2010).

Of course, these same characteristics that elicit bullying may also be the result of bullying, and research suggests that there is a bidirectional relationship between aggression and victimization, with each leading to more of the other over time (Reijntjes et al., 2011; van Lier et al., 2012).

A small proportion of children (20% or less) are both perpetrators and victims of bullying and thus tend to be more aggressive, like bullies, yet are also more anxious, like victims (Lereya et al., 2015). Researchers speculate that these children may have developed hostile attributional biases as a result of being victims and that such biases make them more likely to act aggressively toward others in the future whom they suspect may harm them (Lereya et al., 2015). In one study in Ontario, Canada, that followed several hundred children from age 10 to age 14 (and thus included the transition into high school), about 6% of children started off as victims but transitioned into bullies themselves; these victims-to-bullies had rates of anxiety and depression that were as high as or higher than children who were just victims (Haltigan & Vaillancourt, 2014).

Although some children cope with bullies by ignoring or avoiding them, other children choose to stand up to bullies on behalf of victims. Research in Finland found that three-quarters of victims report having a classmate who defends them against bullies (Sainio et al., 2011) and that the children who defend others against bullies tend to have empathy for the victims and confidence that they will be successful (Peets et al., 2015). Importantly, when children stand up against bullies, they help protect the intended target in the immediate situation yet also help reduce bullying behaviour in the classroom in the long-term (Hawkins, Pepler, & Craig, 2001; Sainio et al., 2011).

Many children engage in social bullying behaviours that are known as **relational aggression**, such as excluding others from the group, withholding friendship to inflict harm, and spreading rumors to ruin a peer's reputation. Unlike physical aggression, which harms the victim physically and perhaps emotionally, relational aggression is aimed at damaging the victim's peer relationships. It is particularly common amongst high-status children, particularly high-status girls (Cillessen & Mayeux, 2004; Hoff et al., 2009; Prinstein & Cillessen, 2003). Youth who are perceived as having high status, especially if they are aware of this perception, tend to increasingly use both relational and physical aggression, perhaps because they tend to be arrogant and are allowed by their peers to get away with it (Cillessen & Mayeux, 2004; Mayeux & Cillessen, 2008; Rose, Swenson, & Waller, 2004). Yet they may also use either physical or relational aggression as a means of both securing and maintaining their status in the peer group (Rubin et al., 2015).

relational aggression a kind of aggression that involves excluding others from the social group and attempting to do harm to other people's relationships; it includes spreading rumors about peers, withholding friendship to inflict harm, and ignoring peers when angry or frustrated or trying to get one's own way

Understanding Bullying: An Interview with Robert Selman

Gender Differences in the Functions of Friendships

As children grow older, gender differences emerge in what girls and boys feel they want and get from their friendships. Girls are more likely than boys to desire closeness and dependency in friendships and also to worry about abandonment, loneliness, hurting others, peers' evaluations, and loss of relationships if they express anger (Rose & Rudolph, 2006). By age 12, girls, compared with boys, feel that their friendships are more intimate and provide more validation, caring, help, and guidance (Bauminger et al., 2008; Rose & Rudolph, 2006; Zarbatany, McDougall, & Hymel, 2000). For instance, girls are more likely than boys to report that they rely on their friends for advice or help with homework, that they and their friends share confidences and stick up for one another, and that their friends tell them that they are good at things and make them feel special.

Girls Bullying Girls

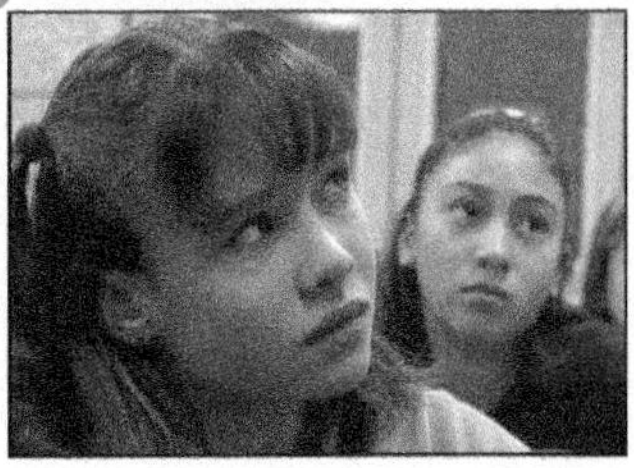

DAVIDGOLDMANPHOTO/GETTY IMAGES

As children age into middle childhood and adolescence, the willingness to lend support and help, including with homework, becomes an important dimension of friendship—however, girls tend to be more likely than boys to rely on this kind of support.

Probably as a consequence of this intimacy, girls also report getting more upset than do boys when friends betray them, are unreliable, or do not provide support and help (MacEvoy & Asher, 2012). Girls also report more friendship-related stress, such as when a friend breaks off a friendship or reveals their secrets or problems to other friends, and greater stress from dealing emotionally with stressors that their friends experience (Rose & Rudolph, 2006). Yet despite these differences in peer relationship stress, girls' relationships with peers are just as stable as are boys' relationships with peers (Meter & Card, 2016).

As discussed in Chapter 10, girls are also more likely than boys to *co-ruminate* with their close friends, that is, to extensively discuss problems and negative thoughts and feelings (Smith & Rose, 2011; see Box 10.4 on page 378). Compared with their male counterparts, girls who are socially anxious or depressed seem more susceptible to the anxiety or depression of their friends (Giletta et al., 2011; Van Zalk et al., 2010; Van Zalk et al., 2011). Unfortunately, while providing support, a co-ruminating anxious or depressed friend may also reinforce the other friend's anxiety or depression, especially in young adolescent girls (Rose, Carlson, & Waller, 2007; Schwartz-Mette & Rose, 2012).

Girls and boys are less likely to differ in the amount of conflict they experience in their best friendships (Rose & Rudolph, 2006). Boys' and girls' friendships also do not differ much in terms of the recreational opportunities they provide (e.g., doing things together, going to one another's house; Parker & Asher, 1993), although they often differ in the time spent together in various activities (e.g., sports versus shopping; Rose & Rudolph, 2006). For example, Canadian preadolescent girls tend to focus more heavily on socializing with their best friends than do preadolescent boys (Zarbatany et al., 2000).

REVIEW QUESTIONS

In what ways is technology, in the form of smartphones and social media, changing the dynamics of friendships? In what ways do these tools facilitate the same patterns in friendships that existed prior to their advent? ■

Status in the Peer Group

Children and adolescents are often extremely concerned with their peer status: being popular is of great importance, and peer rejection can be a devastating experience. Rejection by peers is associated with a range of developmental outcomes for children, such as dropping out of school and problem behaviours, and these relations can hold independent of any effects of having, or not having, close friends (Gest, Graham-Bermann, & Hartup, 2001).

Because of the central role that peer relations play in children's lives, developmental researchers have devoted a good deal of effort to studying the concurrent and long-term effects associated with peer status. In this section, we will examine children's status in the peer group, including how it is measured, its stability, the characteristics that determine it, and the long-term implications of being popular with, or being rejected by, peers.

Measurement of Peer Status

sociometric status a measurement that reflects the degree to which children are liked or disliked by their peers as a group

The most common method developmentalists use to assess peer status is to ask children to rate how much they like or dislike each of their classmates. Alternatively, they may ask children to nominate classmates whom they like the most or the least, or whom they do or don't like to play with. The information from these procedures is used to calculate each child's **sociometric status**—that is, the degree to which a child is liked or disliked by their peers. The most commonly used sociometric system classifies children into one of five groups: popular, rejected, neglected, average, or controversial (see Table 13.1; Bukowski, Cillessen, & Velasquez, 2012).

Do popular children always remain at the top of the social heap? Do rejected children sometimes become better liked? In other words, how stable is a child's sociometric status in the peer group? The answer depends in part on the particular time span and sociometric status that are in question.

Over relatively short periods such as weeks or a few months, children who are popular or rejected tend to remain so, whereas children who are neglected or controversial are likely to acquire a different status (Asher & Dodge, 1986; Chen, Rubin, & B. Li, 1995; Newcomb & Bukowski, 1984; Walker, 2009). Over longer periods, children's sociometric status is more likely to change. In one study in which children were rated by their peers in 5th grade and again 2 years later, only those children who had initially been rated average maintained their status overall, whereas nearly two-thirds of those who had been rated popular, rejected, or controversial received a different rating later on (Newcomb & Bukowski, 1984). Over time, sociometric stability for rejected children is generally higher than for popular, neglected, or controversial children (Harrist et al., 1997; Parke et al., 1997; Walker, 2009) and may increase with the age of the child (Coie & Dodge, 1983; Rubin, Bukowski, & Parker, 1998).

Why are some children liked better than others? One obvious factor is physical attractiveness. From early childhood through adolescence, children who are rated as objectively attractive by observers are much more likely to be popular, and are less likely to be victimized by peers, than are children who are considered unattractive (Langlois et al., 2000; Rosen, Underwood, & Beron, 2011; Vannatta et al., 2009). Athleticism is also related to high peer status, albeit more strongly for boys than for girls (Vannatta et al., 2009). Further affecting peer status is the status of one's friends: having popular friends appears to boost one's own popularity (Eder, 1985; Sabongui, Bukowski, & Newcomb, 1998). Beyond these simple determiners, sociometric status also seems to be affected by a variety of other factors, including

TABLE 13.1	Common Sociometric Categories for Peer Ratings
Popular	Children are designated as popular if they are rated by their peers as being highly liked and accepted and highly impactful.
Rejected	Children are designated as rejected if they are low in acceptance and preference and high in rejection but also high in impact.
Neglected	Children are designated as neglected if they are low in social impact—that is, if they receive few positive or negative ratings. These children are not especially liked or disliked by peers; they simply go unnoticed.
Average	Children are designated as average if they receive moderate ratings on both impact and preference.
Controversial	Children are designated as controversial if they are rated as very high in impact but average in preference. They are noticed by peers and are liked by quite a few children and disliked by quite a few others.

Source: Bukowski et al. (2012).

HILL STREET STUDIOS/AGE FOTOSTOCK

Physically attractive children and teens tend to be more popular than their less attractive peers.

children's social behaviour, personality, cognitions about others, and goals when interacting with peers.

Popular Children

Popular children are rated by peers as being both accepted and impactful and thus have high status in the peer group. Popular children tend to be skilled at initiating interaction with peers and at maintaining positive relationships with others (Rubin et al., 2015). Popular children are perceived by their peers, teachers, and adult observers as cooperative, friendly, sociable, helpful, and sensitive to others (Lansford et al., 2006; Rubin et al., 2015). They are also able to regulate their own emotions and behaviours (Kam, Greenberg et al., 2011) and tend to have a relatively high number of low-conflict reciprocated friendships (Litwack, Wargo Aikins, & Cillessen, 2012). Popular children tend to have more emotional and behavioural strengths compared to children in the other sociometric groups (Rytioja, Lappalainen, & Savolainen, 2019).

Popular children are not necessarily the most likable in their peer group; rather, they have other attributes, such as prestige, athletic ability, physical attractiveness, or wealth, that give them power over their peers (Prinstein et al., 2018). They also tend to be above average in aggression and to use their aggressiveness to obtain their goals (Cillessen, 2011; Kuryluk, Cohen, & Audley-Piotrowski, 2011). This association between aggression and perceived popularity has been observed amongst children as early as preschool (Vaughn et al., 2003); for example, preschool children rated by peers as being the leaders of their class are also observed to engage in more exclusion of other children, saying things like, "There are too many kids here right now; maybe you can play with us later" and "You hate her, right?" (Fanger, Frankel, & Hazen, 2012, p. 235). Popular children are thus able to control the interactions of their peers.

Rejected Children

Rejected children tend to differ from more popular children in their social motives and in the way they process information related to social situations (Lansford et al., 2010). For example, rejected children are more likely than better-liked peers to be motivated by goals such as "getting even" with others or "showing them up" (Crick & Dodge, 1994). Rejected children also have more trouble than other children do in finding constructive solutions to difficult social situations, such as wanting to take a turn on a swing when someone else is using it. When asked how they would deal with such situations, rejected children suggest fewer strategies than do their more popular peers, and the ones they suggest are more hostile, demanding, and threatening (Dodge et al., 2003). Rejected children also tend to be anxious and depressed and to be rated lowest by teachers in their behavioural competence compared to the other sociometric groups (Rytioja et al., 2019). (Box 13.4 discusses programs designed to help rejected children gain peer acceptance.)

Perhaps one reason rejected children are more likely to select inappropriate strategies is that their *theory of mind* (see Chapter 7) is less developed than that of their better-liked peers; they may therefore have greater difficulty understanding others' feelings and behaviours. In support of this idea, a longitudinal study of 5-year-olds in Italy found that children with lower theory of mind abilities had lower prosocial behaviour one year later and then higher rejection by their peers two years later (Caputi et al., 2012).

popular (peer status) children or adolescents who are viewed positively (liked) by many peers and are viewed negatively (disliked) by few peers

rejected (peer status) children or adolescents who are liked by few peers and disliked by many peers

BOX 13.4 APPLICATIONS Fostering Children's Peer Acceptance

Given the difficult and often painful outcomes commonly associated with a child's being rejected or having few friends, a number of interventions have been developed with the goal of improving children's peer interactions by helping children understand and communicate about their own and others' emotions, as well as regulate their own behaviour. As we saw in Chapter 10, emotion recognition and empathy are key skills children acquire as they develop. Thus, these interventions aim to improve children's relationships with their peers by enhancing aspects of their emotional development.

A notable example of this approach is the Promoting Alternative Thinking Strategies (PATHS) curriculum, in which children from 4 to 11 years of age learn to identify emotional expressions (using pictures, for example) and to think about the causes and consequences of different ways to express emotions (Domitrovich et al., 2007; Domitrovich et al., 2010). In addition, the program provides children with opportunities to develop conscious strategies for self-control through verbal mediation (self-talk) and practicing ways to self-regulate. The PATHS approach is illustrated by the Control Signals Poster (CSP), which, like the Turtle Technique discussed in Chapter 1, is designed to remind children how to deal with troubling social situations.

As with a traffic light, the CSP uses the colours red, yellow, and green to encourage calming behaviours. When confronted with a stressful social situation, red signals children to stop and calm down, which they can do by breathing deeply and calmly identifying the problem and their feelings about it. Next, yellow signals children to take it slow, consider potential solutions, and decide on a productive course of action. Finally, green signals children to go and try out their chosen solution. A final step in this process encourages reflection and evaluation of the results and the formulation of new plans if necessary (Riggs et al., 2006).

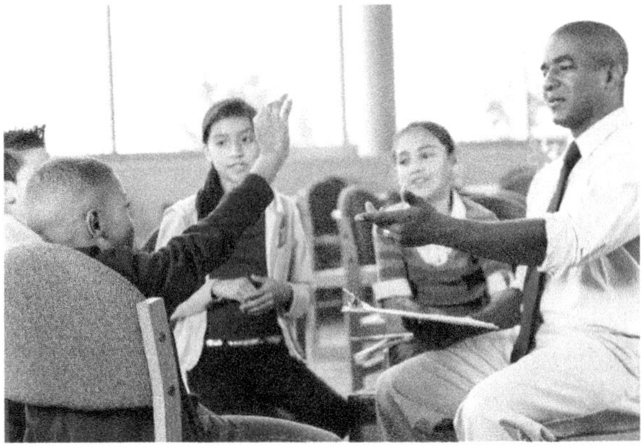
STEVE DEBENPORT/GETTY IMAGES

Programs such as PATHS can help young children learn self-regulation and problem-solving skills.

Programs like this one tend to succeed in fostering knowledge about emotions, self-regulation, prosocial behaviour, and social competence—and sometimes in reducing social withdrawal and aggression as well (e.g., Bierman et al., 2010; Domitrovich et al., 2007; Izard et al., 2008; Riggs et al., 2006). Such improvements have been found, especially for children with numerous problem behaviours and for children in disadvantaged schools (Bierman et al., 2010). The PATHS curriculum has been shown to be effective in randomized control trials in the United States (e.g., Crean & Johnson, 2013; Stanley, 2019) and has been successfully adapted for use in a number of countries, including China (Kam, Wong, & Fung, 2011) and Pakistan (Inam, Tariq, & Zaman, 2015). This program is also currently being used in schools in Alberta, Manitoba, and Nova Scotia. The increases in social competence that often result as a consequence of participation in such an intervention would be expected to promote children's social status, although this issue usually has not been specifically tested.

A majority of rejected children tend to fall into one of two categories: those who are overly aggressive and those who are withdrawn.

aggressive-rejected (peer status) children who are viewed by their peers as especially prone to physical aggression, disruptive behaviour, delinquency, and negative behaviour such as hostility and threatening others

Aggressive-rejected children According to reports from peers, teachers, and adult observers, 40% to 50% of rejected children tend to be aggressive. These **aggressive-rejected** children are especially prone to hostile and threatening behaviour, physical aggression, disruptive behaviour, and delinquency (Lansford et al., 2010; Pedersen et al., 2007; Rubin, Bukowski, & Parker, 2006). When they are angry or want their own way, many rejected children also engage in relational aggression (Cillessen & Mayeux, 2004). Aggressive-rejected children are at risk for becoming even more aggressive over time, and for engaging in delinquent behaviour and to exhibit symptoms of hyperactivity and attention-deficit disorder, conduct disorder, and substance abuse (Gooren et al., 2011; Lansford et al., 2010; Modin, Östberg, & Almquist, 2011; Sturaro et al., 2011).

The key question is whether peer rejection actually *causes* problems at school and in adjustment or whether children's maladaptive behaviour (e.g., aggression) leads to both peer rejection and problems in adjustment (Woodward & Fergusson, 1999). The links are likely cyclical, such that children who are aggressive may become rejected by their peers, which then leads them to be both lonely and angry, which they express through more aggression, as shown in a study with children in British Columbia (Leadbeater & Hoglund, 2009). Thus, it is likely that there are complex bidirectional relations amongst children's adjustment, social competencies,

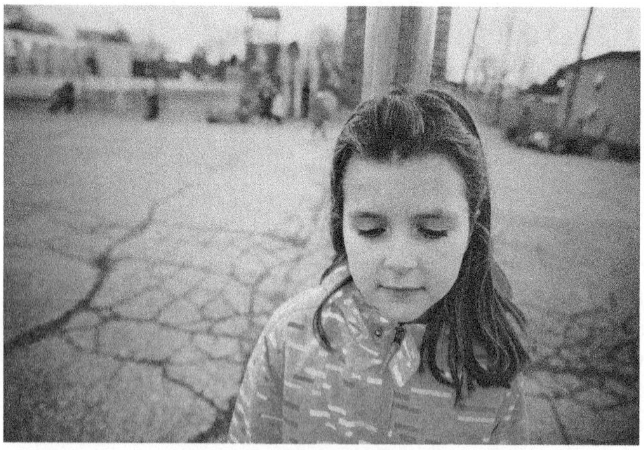
VITAPIX/GETTY IMAGES

Children who are initially withdrawn may be rejected by their peers, leading them to withdraw from interactions even more.

and peer acceptance (Lansford et al., 2010; Obradović & Hipwell, 2010; Sentse, Kretschmer, & Salmivalli, 2015).

Withdrawn-rejected children The second group of rejected children includes those who are **withdrawn-rejected.** These children, who make up 10% to 25% of the rejected category, are socially withdrawn, wary, timid, and socially anxious (Booth-LaForce et al., 2012). They frequently are victimized by peers, and many feel isolated, lonely, and depressed (Katz et al., 2011; Woodhouse, Dykas, & Cassidy, 2012). By the middle-to-late elementary school years, children who are highly withdrawn stand out, tend to be disliked, and appear to become increasingly alienated from the group over time (Rubin et al., 2018). Thus, as with aggression, social withdrawal may be part of a negative feedback loop: withdrawn children are rejected by their peers, which leads them to withdraw further to avoid peer rejection, a pattern that can repeat over and over (Rubin et al., 2018).

Neglected Children

Research suggests that children who are withdrawn with peers but are relatively socially competent tend to be merely **neglected**—that is, they are not nominated as either liked or disliked by peers (Booth-LaForce & Oxford, 2008). These children tend to be both less sociable and less disruptive than average children (Rytioja et al., 2019) and are likely to back away from peer interactions that involve aggression (Coie & Dodge, 1998). Children and adolescents who are simply not social and prefer solitary activities may not be especially prone to peer rejection (Bowker & Raja, 2011; Coplan & Armer, 2007). Neglected children perceive that they receive less support from peers (Walker, 2009), yet they are not particularly anxious about their social interactions (Rytioja et al., 2019). In fact, other than being less socially interactive, neglected children are rated by their teachers as being as socially competent as popular children (Rytioja et al., 2019). They appear to be neglected primarily because they are simply not noticed by their peers.

Controversial Children

In some ways, the most intriguing group of children are **controversial** children, who are liked by numerous peers and disliked by numerous others. Controversial children tend to have characteristics of both popular and rejected children (Rytioja et al., 2019). For example, they tend to be aggressive, disruptive, and prone to anger, but they also tend to be cooperative, sociable, good at sports, and humorous (Bukowski et al., 1993; Coie & Dodge, 1998). In addition, they are very socially active and tend to be group leaders (Coie et al., 1990). Although it may seem counterintuitive that aggressive children could also be popular, it is the case that aggressive children sometimes develop a network of aggressive friends and are accepted in their peer group (Xue & Meisels, 2004), and some elementary school and preadolescent children who start fights and get into trouble are viewed as "cool" and are central in their peer group (Hoff et al., 2009; Rodkin et al., 2000, 2006). At the same time, controversial children tend to be viewed by peers as arrogant and snobbish (Hatzichristou & Hopf, 1996), which could explain why they are disliked by some peers even if they are perceived as having high status in the peer group (Robertson et al., 2010).

withdrawn-rejected (peer status) rejected children who are socially withdrawn, wary, and often timid

neglected (peer status) children or adolescents who are infrequently mentioned as either liked or disliked; they simply are not noticed much by peers

controversial (peer status) children or adolescents who are liked by quite a few peers and are disliked by quite a few others

Cross-Cultural Similarities and Differences in Factors Related to Peer Status

Most of the research on behaviours associated with sociometric status has been conducted in Canada and the United States, but findings similar to those discussed here have been obtained in a wide array of cross-cultural research. Studies from Australia, Canada, China, Finland, Greece, Indonesia, Italy, Japan, and the Netherlands have found that socially rejected children tend to be aggressive and disruptive while popular children tend to be prosocial and to have leadership skills (Attili, Vermigli, & Schneider, 1997; Chung-Hall & Chen, 2010; French, Setiono, & Eddy, 1999; Gooren et al., 2011; Hatzichristou & Hopf, 1996; Kawabata et al., 2010; Schwartz et al., 2010; Tomada & Schneider, 1997; Walker, 2009; Xu et al., 2004).

Research in a variety of regions, including North America, China, and Indonesia, further indicates that rejected children, especially those who are aggressive, are more likely than their peers to have academic difficulties (Chen, Wang, & Cao, 2011; Chung-Hall & Chen, 2010; French et al., 1999; Véronneau et al., 2010; Wentzel, 2009). In particular, they have higher rates of school absenteeism (DeRosier, Kupersmidt, & Patterson, 1994) and lower grade-point averages (Wentzel & Caldwell, 1997). Those who are aggressive are especially likely to be uninterested in school and to be viewed by peers and teachers as poor students (Hymel, Bowker, & Woody, 1993; Wentzel & Asher, 1995). Longitudinal research, conducted mostly in the United States, indicates that students' classroom participation is lower during periods in which they are rejected by peers than during periods when they are not, and that the tendency of rejected children to do relatively poorly in school worsens across time (Ladd, Herald-Brown, & Reiser, 2008). Approximately 25% to 30% of rejected children drop out of school, compared with approximately 8% or less of other children (Rubin et al., 1998). Clearly, children who are rejected by peers are at risk for academic and adjustment problems.

Similar cross-cultural parallels have been found with regard to withdrawal and rejection. Various studies done in Germany, Italy, and Hong Kong, for example, have shown that, as in the United States, withdrawal becomes linked with peer rejection in preschool or elementary school (Asendorpf, 1990; Attili et al., 1997; Casiglia, Lo Coco, & Zappulla, 1998; Nelson et al., 2010; Schwartz et al., 2010).

Research has also demonstrated that there are certain cultural and historical differences in the characteristics associated with children's sociometric status. One notable example involving both types of differences is the status associated with shyness amongst Chinese children. In studies conducted in the 1990s, Chinese children who were shy, sensitive, and cautious or inhibited in their behaviour were—unlike their inhibited or shy Western counterparts—viewed by teachers as socially competent and as leaders, and they were liked by their peers (Chen, Rubin, & B. Li, 1995; Chen, Rubin, & Z.-y. Li, 1995; Chen et al., 1999; Chen, Rubin, & Sun, 1992). A probable explanation for this difference is that Chinese culture traditionally values self-effacing, withdrawn behaviour, and Chinese children are encouraged to behave accordingly (Ho, 1986).

Children who are well-liked tend to have similar characteristics in many cultures, as do children who are rejected by their peers.

DESIGN PICS INC/ALAMY

In contrast, because Western cultures place great value on independence and self-assertion, withdrawn children in these cultures are likely to be viewed as weak, needy, and socially incompetent. However, Chen found that since the early 1990s, shy, reserved behaviour in Chinese elementary school children has become increasingly associated with lower levels of peer acceptance, at least for urban children (Chen, Chang et al., 2005). Chen argues that the economic and political changes in China over the past several decades have been accompanied by an increased valuing of assertive, less inhibited behaviour. For children from rural areas who have had only limited exposure to the dramatic cultural changes in China in recent years, shyness is associated with high levels of both peer liking and disliking, albeit more to liking; thus, for groups somewhat less exposed to cultural changes, shyness is viewed with some ambivalence by peers (Chen et al., 2011; Chen, Wang, & Wang, 2009). In addition, for the rural children, being unsociable—that is, uninterested in social interaction—is associated with peer rejection (Chen et al., 2009), whereas amongst North American children it often is not, at least for younger children. Thus, culture and changes in culture appear to affect children's evaluations of what is desirable behaviour.

REVIEW QUESTION

Why might sociometric status for some categories, such as rejected or average, be more stable over time than for other categories, such as popular, neglected, or controversial? ■

The Role of Parents in Children's Peer Relationships

As we saw in Chapter 12, there is ample evidence that parents affect children's development in a multitude of ways. It is also true that parents affect children's peer relationships, both indirectly (through their interactions with their children) and directly (through monitoring and coaching; see Box 13.5). Attachment theorists (see Chapter 11) as well as social learning theorists (see Chapter 9) have asserted that early parent–child interactions are linked to children's peer interactions at an older age. We will explore some of these links next.

Relations Between Attachment and Competence with Peers

Attachment theory maintains that whether a child's attachment to the parent is secure or insecure affects the child's future social competence and the quality of the child's relationships with others, including peers. Attachment theorists have suggested that a secure attachment between parent and child promotes competence with peers in at least three ways (Elicker, Englund, & Sroufe, 1992). First, securely attached children develop positive social expectations and are thus inclined to interact readily with other children, expecting these interactions to be positive and rewarding. Second, because of their experience with a sensitive and responsive caregiver, they develop the foundation for understanding reciprocity in relationships. Consequently, they learn to give and take in relationships and to be empathic to others. Finally, securely attached children are likely to be self-regulated, confident, enthusiastic, and friendly—characteristics that are attractive to other children and that facilitate social interaction (Booth-LaForce & Groh, 2018).

BOX 13.5 A CLOSER LOOK Parents' Strategies for Shaping Peer Relationships

Parents can play a number of active roles in their children's competencies in peer relationships. Two of the more salient ones are in monitoring their children's social life and in coaching their children in social skills.

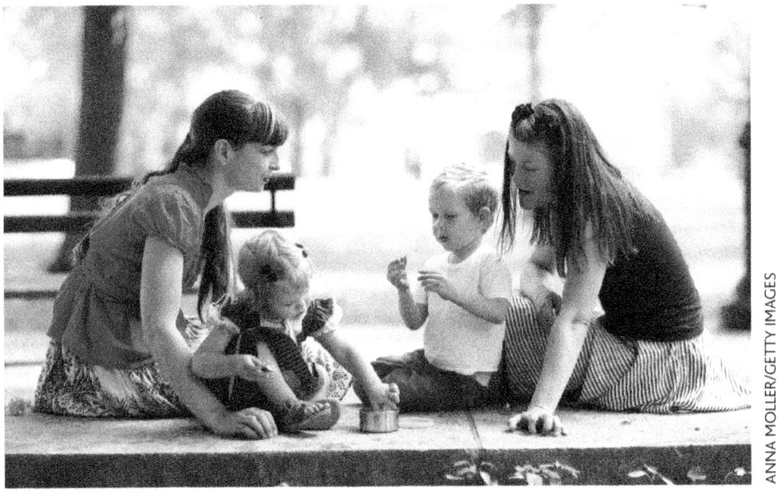

Parents may contribute to their children's development of social competence by arranging opportunities for their children to interact with peers.

Monitoring Parents, especially those of young children, typically spend considerable time orchestrating and monitoring their children's interactions with peers. Parents decide with whom the children interact and how much time they spend with peers doing various activities. However, some parents are more thoughtful and active in this role than are others (Mounts, 2002). Preschoolers whose parents arrange and oversee opportunities for them to interact with peers tend to be more positive and social with peers, have a larger and more stable set of play partners, and more easily initiate social interactions with peers than do other children — so long as their parents are not overly controlling (Ladd & Hart, 1992). Similarly, elementary school children whose parents allow them to engage in numerous social activities in the neighbourhood and extracurricular activities at school are more socially competent and liked by peers (McDowell & Parke, 2009).

When children reach adolescence, they spend more time out of the home and with peers, and increasingly in unsupervised situations (see Figure 13.1); thus, parental monitoring becomes especially important. Knowing where a child is and with whom at all times is important for his or her safety and well-being, and research has shown that it can reduce adolescents' engagement in risky behaviours in the future. A survey of more than 5000 children between 12 and 14 years of age asked them how much their parents knew about their social lives: who their best friends are, who the parents of their best friends are, whom they are with when they are not at home, who their teachers are, and how they are doing in school (Abar, Jackson, & Wood, 2014). Those children who reported high levels of parental knowledge were less likely to get involved in heavy drinking, marijuana use, and delinquency in the ensuing four years. In addition, the more children engaged in these risky behaviours early in adolescence, the more they perceived their parents as monitoring them (Abar et al., 2014). Adolescents are thus both affected by parents' monitoring behaviour and actively elicit monitoring through their own behaviour.

In adolescence, monitoring may be affected by parents' cultural orientation. For example, in Mexican American families, parents who had a stronger orientation toward Mexican culture and the traditional Mexican value of *familism* — which emphasizes closeness in the family, family obligations, and consideration of the family in making decisions — placed more restrictions on adolescents' peer relationships than did parents whose orientation was less traditional. Parents who strongly identified with Mexican culture were also more likely to restrict their adolescents' — especially a daughter's — contact with peers if the adolescent reported associating with deviant peers (Updegraff et al., 2010).

Coaching Preschool children tend to be more socially skilled and more likely to be accepted by peers if their parents effectively coach them on how to interact with unfamiliar peers (Laird et al., 1994; McDowell & Parke, 2009). Mothers of accepted children tend to teach their children group-oriented strategies for gaining entry into a group of peers; for instance, they may make suggestions about what to say when entering the group or they may discourage the child from disrupting the group's current activities. In contrast, mothers of children who are low in sociometric status often try to direct the group's activity themselves or urge their child to initiate activities that are inconsistent with what the group is currently doing (Finnie & Russell, 1988; Russell & Finnie, 1990).

Children may also benefit in their peer relations when their parents provide emotion coaching (see Chapter 10) — that is, explanations about the acceptability of emotions and how to appropriately deal with them (Katz, Maliken, & Stettler, 2012). Children whose parents use high levels of emotion coaching are, for example, more likely to use appropriate conflict-avoidance strategies (e.g., laughter) to deflect teasing, and they are less likely to display socially inappropriate behaviours when dealing with peers' provocations (Katz, Hunter, & Klowden, 2008). Some evidence suggests that a fairly high level of parental advice giving is sometimes associated with low levels of children's social competence and peer acceptance; but, in part, this may be because parents are more likely to try to help when their children are experiencing a high level of problems (McDowell & Parke, 2009).

It is likely that coaching needs to be provided in a sensitive, skilled manner to be effective; that is, it should convey clear, useful information about others' feelings and behaviour, along with strategies for dealing with them, and it should be presented in a way that does not overwhelm children or derogate them. For reasons that are not yet clear, mothers' coaching may be especially important for enhancing girls' social skills (Pettit et al., 1998).

Conversely, attachment theorists argue that an insecure attachment is likely to impair a child's competence with peers. Children with insecure attachments have difficulties regulating their emotions because their parents' inconsistent and rejecting behaviours have not taught these children how to handle their emotional reactions (Booth-LaForce & Groh, 2018). If parents are rejecting and hostile or neglectful, young children are likely to become hostile themselves and to expect negative behaviour from other people. They may be predisposed to perceive peers as hostile and, consequently, are likely to be aggressive toward them. These children may also expect rejection from other people and may try to avoid experiencing it by withdrawing from peer interaction instead (Furman et al., 2002; Renken et al., 1989).

There is a good deal of evidence to support these theoretical views. Children who are not securely attached do, in fact, tend to have difficulties with peer relationships. Toddlers and preschoolers who were insecurely attached as infants tend to be aggressive, whiny, socially withdrawn, and low in popularity in elementary school (Bohlin, Hagekull, & Rydell, 2000; Burgess et al., 2003; Erickson, Sroufe, & Egeland, 1985). Throughout childhood, these children, in comparison with securely attached children, express less happiness with peers, as well as less sympathy and prosocial behaviour, and they demonstrate poorer skills in resolving conflicts (Elicker et al., 1992; Fox & Calkins, 1993; Panfile & Laible, 2012; Raikes & Thompson, 2008). A meta-analysis of 80 different studies found that children with a secure attachment to their parents had higher social competence with their peers, while children with insecure attachments to their parents exhibited poor competence with peers, even when peer competence was assessed over 10 years after the initial studies (Groh et al., 2014).

Securely attached children tend to be generally happy and to have good social skills, as has been found in studies with children from Mexico, Peru, and the United States (Nóblega et al., 2019; Posada et al., 2019). It is thus not surprising that children with secure attachments tend to have high-quality friendships and to be relatively popular with peers—both as preschoolers (McElwain, Booth-LaForce, & Wu, 2011) and in elementary school and adolescence (Granot & Mayseless, 2001; Schneider, Atkinson, & Tardif, 2001; see Chapter 11). Even in late childhood and early adolescence, children with more and higher-quality (e.g., intimate and supportive) friendships tend to be those with a history of a secure attachment (Dwyer et al., 2010; Freitag et al., 1996; Schneider et al., 2001; Simpson et al., 2007). Some recent studies, including by Concordia University researchers, suggest that the security of attachment with fathers may be especially important for the quality of children's and adolescents' friendships (e.g., Doyle, Lawford, & Markiewicz, 2009; Veríssimo et al., 2011).

Children who have secure attachment relationships with their parents tend to develop better social skills than do their peers who are not securely attached.

PEATHEGEE INC/GETTY IMAGES

Thus, security of the parent–child relationship is linked with quality of peer relationships. This link probably arises from both the early and the continuing effect that parent–child attachment has on the quality of social behaviour, as well as children's working models of relationships (Shomaker & Furman, 2009). However, it is also possible that the individual characteristics of each child, such as sociability, influence both the quality of attachments and the quality of his or her relationships with peers.

Quality of Ongoing Parent–Child Interactions and Peer Relationships

Ongoing parent–child interactions are associated with peer relations in much the same way that attachment patterns are. For example, socially competent, popular children tend to have mothers who are warm in general; discuss feelings with them; and who use warm control, positive verbalizations, reasoning, and explanations in their approach to parenting (Kam, Greenberg et al., 2011; Updegraff et al., 2010). Research that has investigated ongoing father–child interactions has found that fathers, too, can play a role in children's peer relationships. For example, fathers' warmth and affection toward their children have been linked to the positivity of children's interactions with close friends in the preschool years (Kahen, Katz, & Gottman, 1994; Youngblade & Belsky, 1992) and to children's peer acceptance in elementary school (McDowell & Parke, 2009).

Overall, research in this area suggests that when the family is generally characterized by a warm, involved, and harmonious family style, young children tend to be sociable, socially skilled, liked by peers, and cooperative in childcare (Feldman & Masalha, 2010). These associations may occur because such parenting fosters children's self-regulation (Eiden et al., 2009; Eisenberg, Zhou et al., 2005; Kam, Greenberg et al., 2011). In contrast, parenting that is characterized by harsh, authoritarian discipline and low levels of child monitoring is often associated with children's being unpopular and victimized (Dishion, 1990; Duong et al., 2009; Hart, Ladd, & Burleson, 1990; Ladd, 1992).

In considering findings such as these, it is generally assumed that quality of parenting influences the degree to which children behave in socially competent ways, which in turn affects whether children are accepted by peers. But it is difficult to prove that quality of parenting actually has a causal influence on children's social behaviour with peers. As noted in Chapter 12, it may be that children who are aggressive and disruptive because of constitutional factors (e.g., heredity, prenatal influences) elicit both negative parenting and negative peer responses (Rubin et al., 1998); or it may be that both harsh parenting and the children's negative behaviour with peers are due to heredity. The most likely possibility is that the causal links are bidirectional—that parents' behaviour affects their children's social competence and vice versa.

Such bidirectionality was indeed demonstrated in a study of more than 9000 Dutch elementary school children who were studied over three data points across two years. Parents' warmth predicted less, and their rejection predicted more, bullying behaviour in their children several months later, while that bullying behaviour in turn elicited more rejection and less warmth from parents several more months later (Kaufman et al., 2019).

Parents can also serve as a buffer when their children's peer relationships are not going well. A longitudinal study of several hundred 7- to 9-year-olds found that children having difficulty with their peers were less likely to experience increases over time in depressive symptoms if they had positive, close relationships with their parents (see Figure 13.6; Hazel et al., 2014). Similarly, maternal supportiveness has been found to buffer the links between adolescents' romantic stress and their later depressive symptoms (Anderson, Salk, & Hyde, 2015). As with many aspects of children's lives, a risk factor in one relationship can be

FIGURE 13.6 **Associations amongst peer stress, parent support, and children's depressive symptoms** When children have high peer stress and low parent support, they report high levels of depressive symptoms. In contrast, children report the same level of depressive symptoms regardless of the amount of stress from their peers if they have supportive parents. (Data from Hazel et al., 2014)

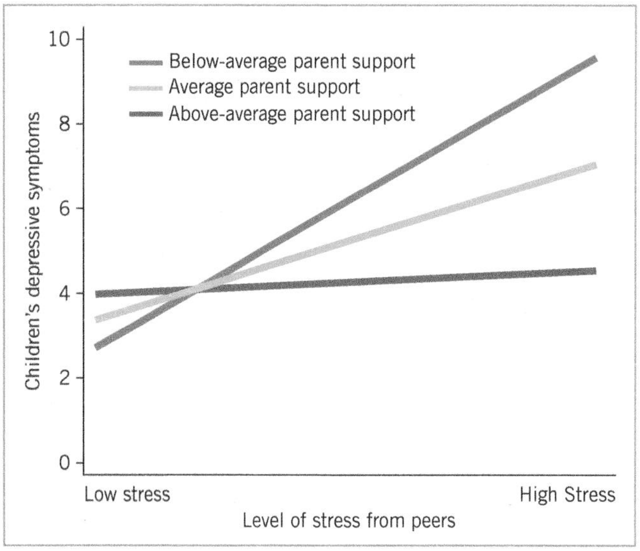

counteracted with a protective factor in another relationship. Parents do matter, even when it comes to children's relationships with their peers—and as displayed in Figure 13.6, relationships with parents may have a stronger link to mental health than peer relationships.

REVIEW QUESTION

How does the concept of bidirectionality explain the influence that parents have on their child's peer relationships? ■

CHAPTER SUMMARY

Play

- Play refers to voluntary activities that children engage in with no specific motivation beyond their inherent enjoyment. Play has been shown to benefit children's social, emotional, cognitive, and physical development. Children engage in increasingly complex forms of social play as they age.
- Play is the basis for interventions to help children dealing with mental health problems or trauma.

Friendships

- Children tend to become friends with peers who are similar in age, sex, and race and who are similar in behaviours such as aggression, sociability, and cooperativeness—although each of these factors matters less as children age into adolescence.
- Even very young children have friends whom they prefer over other children. Toddlers and preschoolers engage in more complex and cooperative play with friends than with nonfriends, although because they spend more time together, they also engage in more conflict.
- Children's conceptions of friends change with age. Young children define friendship primarily on the basis of actual activities with their peers. With age, issues such as loyalty, mutual understanding, trust, cooperative reciprocity, and self-disclosure become important components of friendship.
- As children age and especially when they reach adolescence, friendships are characterized by more self-disclosure and intimacy.
- Electronic communication facilitates both the creation and maintenance of friendships, largely because it is available all the time, gives children a feeling of control, is fun, and can be anonymous.
- Having friends is associated with positive developmental outcomes, such as social competence and adjustment. However, having friends who engage in problematic behaviours such as violence or substance abuse increases the risk that a child or adolescent will engage in such behaviours.
- The degree to which adults encourage children to play with unrelated peers varies greatly in different cultures, as does the degree to which parents expect their children to develop social skills with peers (e.g., negotiating, taking initiative, standing up for their rights). In addition, the hours children spend with unrelated peers varies considerably across cultures.
- In some circumstances, the peer group may contribute to the development of antisocial behaviour, alcohol consumption, and substance use, although youths may also actively seek out peers who engage in similar levels of these behaviours.
- Bullying is a relatively common experience amongst children and adolescents. Children who engage in bullying do so to gain power and status. Children who are the victims of bullying tend to suffer both behavioural and mental health problems.

Status in the Peer Group

- On the basis of their sociometric ratings, children typically have been classified as popular, rejected, neglected, average, or controversial, although these statuses can change over time.
- Children's status in the larger peer group varies as a function of their social behaviour and thinking about their social interactions, as well as their physical attractiveness.
- Popular children, who are well liked by their peers, tend to be high in social skills and in regulation of their emotions and behaviours, yet they also tend to be higher than average in aggression.
- Children who are rejected by their peers tend to be either aggressive or socially withdrawn. Aggressive-rejected children are low in social skills, tend to make hostile attributions about others' intentions, and have trouble coming up with constructive strategies for dealing with difficult social situations. Withdrawn-rejected children tend to feel isolated, lonely, and depressed over time.
- Neglected children—those who are not nominated by peers as either liked or disliked—tend to be less sociable, aggressive, and disruptive than average children. They display relatively few behaviours that differ greatly from those of average children and appear not to be noticed by other children.

- Controversial children tend to have characteristics of both popular and rejected children: they tend to be aggressive, disruptive, and prone to anger, as well as helpful, cooperative, sociable, good at sports, and humorous.
- Across numerous cultures, children who are popular or rejected share similar characteristics. However, reticent behaviour may be more valued in some East Asian cultures and has, at least until recently, been related in China to others' perceptions of a child's social competence.

The Role of Parents in Children's Peer Relationships

- Consistent with the predictions of attachment theorists, securely attached children tend to be more positive in their behaviour and affect, more socially skilled, and better liked than insecurely attached children.
- Parents of socially competent and popular children are more likely than parents of less competent children to use warm control, positive verbalizations, reasoning, and explanations in interactions with their children. They also hold more positive beliefs about their children's abilities. It is likely that the causal links between quality of parenting and children's social competence are bidirectional and that both environmental and biological factors play a role in the development of children's social competence with peers.
- Positive relationships with parents can buffer children against the potential negative effects of peer relationships.

Test Yourself

1. Which of the following is *not* a characteristic of play?
   a. Play is always enjoyable and active.
   b. Play is internally motivated.
   c. Play is an opportunity for children to work through frustrations.
   d. Play is aimed at achieving a set goal.
2. Yomna, Katie, and Julio are playing "house," in which Katie pretends to be the baby daughter, Julio pretends to be the daddy, Yomna pretends to be the mommy, and together the three eat an imaginary meal. These children are engaged in
   a. interactive play.
   b. cooperative play.
   c. associative play.
   d. parallel play.
3. Friendships emerge in early childhood as children become more capable of cooperation and coordinated interactions, and as they learn to trust those individuals whom they consider to be friends. Which of the following statements is not true of these early childhood friendships?
   a. Preschool friends are more likely than nonfriends to resume interactions with each other following a conflict.
   b. Preschool friends quarrel less with each other than they do with nonfriends.
   c. Preschool friends tend to resolve conflicts in an equitable manner.
   d. Pretend play occurs more often between friends than nonfriends.
4. Research indicates that friendships change in what significant respect as children grow older?
   a. Average duration of children's friendships lengthens.
   b. Level and importance of the intimacy increases.
   c. Children are more willing to display aggressive behaviours with their friends.
   d. The total number of close friends an individual reports increases.
5. Friendships in adolescence tend to be more ____________.
   a. stable
   b. co-dependent
   c. harmful
   d. exclusive
6. Tyler thinks of himself as socially awkward. He has a few close friends, but tends to be shy around most peers and adults. He is more comfortable on social media, where he tends to express his emotions more openly. Tyler's experience supports which perspective on the impact of social media on development?
   a. The rich-get-richer hypothesis
   b. The sociometric status perspective
   c. The social-compensation hypothesis
   d. Selman's perspective
7. What does the term *deviancy training* refer to?
   a. An intervention to discourage aggressive tendencies by encouraging supportive peer interactions
   b. Parental interactions that have the unintended consequence of increasing risky and aggressive behaviours in children
   c. The process through which antisocial youth reinforce aggressive and deviant tendencies in one another
   d. A school-based intervention to provide methods for teachers and other adults to maintain order amongst at-risk children

8. According to research, which of the following is true of relationships between girls in middle childhood and adolescence compared with those of boys of the same ages?
   a. Girls' friendships tend to last longer than those of boys.
   b. Girls are less likely than boys to discuss their problems and negative thoughts.
   c. Girls are more likely than boys to desire closeness and to worry about abandonment from their friends.
   d. Girls tend to engage in more conflict with their best friends than do boys.
9. Which of the following statements about cyberbullying is *not* true?
   a. Cyberbullying is more common in classrooms where students are accepting of bullying in general.
   b. There are more children who say they are perpetrators of cyberbullying than children who say they are victims of cyberbullying.
   c. Gay, lesbian, and bisexual students are twice as likely as heterosexual students to be cyberbullied.
   d. There are more children who say they are victims of cyberbullying than children who say they are perpetrators of cyberbullying.
10. Bullying and victimization are said to have a bidirectional relationship. Which of the following statements best describes that relationship?
    a. Bullying may lead to behavioural changes in victims (e.g., becoming withdrawn) that in turn elicit more bullying from the bullies.
    b. Both bullies and victims often have insecure attachments to their parents.
    c. Aggressors tend to choose as victims individuals who they feel may threaten them in the future.
    d. Both aggressive children and victimized children tend to befriend other children who share their status.
11. The degree to which a child is liked or disliked by peers is a measure of that child's ____________ .
    a. sociometric status
    b. relational aggression
    c. social-compensation level
    d. temperament
12. Vikram tends to be cooperative and sociable but also prone to outbursts and can be disruptive in class. Vikram is well liked by some classmates but disliked by others. Which of the following best describes Vikram's sociometric status?
    a. Confused
    b. Aggressive-rejected
    c. Controversial
    d. Popular-unpopular
13. Beth often ascribes negative motives to others when she doesn't get her way, and will lash out at other children if she perceives a slight. Rather than cooperate with other children, she is more apt to push another child out of the way. Other children tend to avoid her. Which of the following best describes Beth's sociometric status?
    a. Popular
    b. Rejected
    c. Neglected
    d. Controversial
14. Children who are neither liked nor disliked by their peers are considered to be ____________ .
    a. controversial
    b. neglected
    c. withdrawn-rejected
    d. aggressive-rejected
15. According to Box 13.5, the two main ways that parents structure children's peer interactions are through
    a. punishment and reward.
    b. gender stereotyping and coaching.
    c. teaching and modeling.
    d. coaching and monitoring.

Critical Thinking Questions

1. What are some of the ways in which same-age peer relationships and relationships with older or younger siblings might differ? On what dimensions are they typically the same?
2. What procedures and methods might someone use to assess which 2-year-old playmates in a group are close friends? How would these methods be the same or different if one were assessing close friendships at ages 6, 11, and 17?
3. What are the similarities and differences between popular and controversial children? Between aggressive-rejected and withdrawn-rejected children?
4. Given what you read about bullies in this chapter, design an intervention that can both reduce bullying behaviour and support the victims of bullying.
5. Consider a child who is growing up in an isolated area with few peers nearby and is being schooled at home. In what ways might his or her daily experience differ from that of children attending school? How might this affect his or her development, positively or negatively? What factors might mitigate or increase these effects?
6. Electronic communication, which includes texting, messaging, and social media, can be a great way for children and adolescents to connect with new and old friends, but it exposes them to potential cyberbullying. What are some ways that parents and schools can ensure children enjoy the benefits of electronic communication without its risks?

Key Terms

aggressive-rejected (peer status), p. 475
controversial (peer status), p. 476
cyberbullying, p. 470
friend, p. 460
neglected (peer status), p. 476
peers, p. 457
play, p. 458
popular (peer status), p. 474
rejected (peer status), p. 474
relational aggression, p. 471
sociometric status, p. 473
withdrawn-rejected (peer status), p. 476

Answers to Test Yourself

1. d, **2.** b, **3.** b, **4.** b, **5.** d, **6.** c, **7.** c, **8.** c, **9.** b, **10.** a, **11.** a, **12.** c, **13.** b, **14.** b, **15.** d

CHAPTER

14 Moral Development

FINE ART PHOTOGRAPHIC LIBRARY, LONDON/ART RESOURCE, NY

VICTOR GILBERT (1847–1933), *Make Believe*

THEMES

NATURE AND NURTURE ■ THE ACTIVE CHILD ■ CONTINUITY/DISCONTINUITY

MECHANISMS OF CHANGE ■ THE SOCIOCULTURAL CONTEXT

INDIVIDUAL DIFFERENCES ■ RESEARCH AND CHILDREN'S WELFARE

On October 22, 2014, Michael Zehaf-Bibeau shot and killed Corporal Nathan Cirillo, a Canadian soldier on ceremonial guard duty at the Canadian National War Memorial. Zehaf-Bibeau then entered the Centre Block of the Canadian Parliament and engaged in a shootout with security personnel. He was shot by the Parliamentary Sergeant-at-Arms, Kevin Vickers, and died at the scene. After the incident, it was discovered that Zehaf-Bibeau had left a video describing his motives, focusing on Canada's foreign policy in the Middle East. Further investigation brought to light other information about Zehaf-Bibeau, including his struggles with drugs, the law, and mental illness.

Two years prior to the Parliament Hill shootings, Malala Yousafzai, a young girl living in the Swat Valley of Pakistan, had been advocating for the education of girls, in defiance of local Taliban leaders who banned girls from attending school and even attacked some girls' schools. She gave speeches, wrote a blog for the BBC, and was the subject of a documentary by the *New York Times.* She was awarded the first National Peace Prize of Pakistan in 2011.

Then, in October 2012, when Malala was 15 years old, a Taliban gunman shot her point-blank in the head right after she boarded a bus to return home after school. She survived the assassination attempt and received extensive medical treatment in England. She was unable to return to Pakistan because the Taliban made clear that it still planned to kill her. She currently is living in exile with her family.

Despite these considerable obstacles, Malala remains undeterred from her main goal. She has continued to advocate for children's education in general and for girls' education in particular. She has given speeches to the United Nations, wrote a best-selling autobiography, and was the subject of a major 2015 documentary. Two million people signed a right-to-education petition started in her honor. She now heads the Malala Fund (www.malala.org), which works to support the education and empowerment of girls throughout the world.

In recognition of her efforts to promote access to education for all children, Malala was awarded the 2014 Nobel Peace Prize, which she shared with Kailash Satyarthi, an advocate for the rights of children in India. At 17, Malala was the youngest recipient of the prize in history.

Why do some children and adolescents act in moral and prosocial ways, like Malala, while others act in immoral and antisocial ways, like Zehaf-Bibeau? The starting point for answering this question lies in understanding the aspects of children's thinking and behaviour that contribute to morality. To act in moral ways on a regular basis, children must have an understanding of right and wrong and the reasons why certain actions are moral or immoral. In addition, they must have a conscience—that is, they must be concerned about acting in a moral manner and feel guilty when they do not.

When studying moral development, researchers have focused on a number of different questions related to these requirements. How do children think about

REUTERS/CORPORAL M'LANI GIRARD/THE CANADIAN ARMED FORCES/HANDOUT

Corporal Nathan Cirillo was on ceremonial guard duty at the Canadian National War Memorial when he was shot and killed by Michael Zehaf-Bibeau on October 22, 2014.

RICHARD STONEHOUSE/GETTY IMAGES

At age 15, Malala Yousafzai survived an assassination attempt by the Taliban for her advocacy of education for girls, and at age 17 she became the youngest recipient of the Nobel Peace Prize.

moral issues, and how does that thinking change as they age? Does children's reasoning about moral issues relate to their behaviour? How early do caring and sharing—or their opposites, aggression and cruelty—first appear in children? What factors contribute to differences amongst children in the degree to which they display helpful and caring behaviours or *antisocial behaviours*—namely, disruptive, hostile, or aggressive behaviours? Can steps be taken to help children develop caring and helpful behaviours and reduce the likelihood of their developing immoral or antisocial behaviours?

We start our discussion of moral development by examining children's moral judgment—that is, how children think about situations involving moral decisions. Then we examine findings on the early emergence of conscience and the development of *prosocial* behaviours—behaviours such as helping and sharing that benefit others. Next, we turn to aggression and other antisocial behaviours such as stealing. As you will see, children's moral development is influenced by advances in their social and cognitive capacities, as well as by both genetic factors and environmental factors (see Chapter 3), including family and culture. Therefore, the themes of *individual differences, nature and nurture,* and the *sociocultural context* will be prominent in our discussion of moral development. Theory and research on moral judgment grew out of Piaget's work in this area, which, like his theory of cognitive development (see Chapter 4), involves stages of development and assumes that children actively try to understand the world around them. Consequently, the themes of *continuity/discontinuity, mechanisms of change,* and the *active child* are evident in our consideration of the development of moral judgment as well. Also in play is the theme of *research and children's welfare,* as we survey intervention programs that are designed to promote prosocial thinking and behaviour and to prevent antisocial behaviour.

Moral Judgment

The morality of a given action is not always obvious. Consider a girl who steals food to feed her starving sister. Stealing is usually regarded as an immoral behaviour, but obviously the morality of this girl's behaviour is not so clear. Or consider an adolescent male who offers to help fix a friend's bike but does so because he wants to borrow it later, or perhaps because he wants to find out if the bike is worth stealing. Although this adolescent's behaviour may appear altruistic on the surface, it is morally ambiguous, at best, in the first instance and clearly immoral in the second. These examples illustrate that the morality of a behaviour is based partly on the thinking—including conscious intentions and goals—that underlies the behaviour.

Indeed, some psychologists (as well as philosophers and educators) argue that the reasoning behind a given behaviour is critical for determining whether that behaviour is moral or immoral, and they maintain that changes in moral reasoning form the basis of moral development (Turiel, 2014). As a consequence, much research on children's moral development has focused on how children think when they try to resolve moral conflicts and how their reasoning about moral issues changes with age. The most important contributors to current understanding of the development of children's moral reasoning are Jean Piaget and Lawrence Kohlberg, both of whom took a cognitive developmental approach to studying the development of morality.

Piaget's Theory of Moral Judgment

The ideas presented in Piaget's book *The Moral Judgment of the Child* (1932/1965) form the foundation of cognitive theories about the origin of morality. Piaget describes how children's moral reasoning changes from a rigid acceptance of the dictates and rules of authorities to an appreciation that moral rules are a product of social interaction and are therefore modifiable. Piaget believed that interactions with peers, more than adult influence, account for advances in children's moral reasoning.

Piaget initially studied children's moral reasoning by observing children playing games with their peers that often involve dealing with issues of rules and fairness. In addition, Piaget interviewed children to examine their thinking about questions such as what constitutes a transgression of a rule, what role a person's intentions plays in morality, whether certain punishments are just, and how goods can be distributed amongst individuals fairly. In these open-ended interviews, he typically presented children of various ages with pairs of short vignettes such as the following:

> A little boy who is called John is in his room. He is called to dinner. He goes into the dining room. But behind the door there was a chair, and on the chair there was a tray with fifteen cups on it. John couldn't have known that there was all this behind the door. He goes in, the door knocks against the tray, bang go the fifteen cups, and they all get broken!
>
> Once there was a little boy whose name was Henry. One day when his mother was out he tried to get some jam out of the cupboard. He climbed up onto a chair and stretched out his arm. But the jam was too high up and he couldn't reach it and have any. But while he was trying to get it he knocked over a cup. The cup fell down and broke.
>
> (Piaget, 1932/1965, p. 122)

After children heard these stories, they were asked which boy was naughtier and why. Partly on the basis of children's responses to such vignettes, Piaget concluded that there are two stages of development in children's moral reasoning—a first stage in which the outcome is more important than the intention and a second stage in which the intention is seen as paramount—as well as a transitional period between them.

Piaget's first stage of moral development, which he referred to as *heteronomous morality,* is most characteristic of children who have not achieved Piaget's stage of concrete operations—that is, children younger than 7 years who are in the preoperational stage (see Chapter 4). In response to the vignette above, these children would judge that the child who broke 15 cups was naughtier. This response is in contrast to the response of older children, who said that the child who was trying to sneak jam was naughtier, even though he broke only one cup. Children in the heteronomous morality stage regard rules and duties to others as unchangeable "givens." In their view, justice is whatever authorities (adults, rules, or laws) say is right, and authorities' punishments for noncompliance are always justified. In this stage, children believe that what determines whether an action is good or bad are the consequences of the action, not the motives or intentions behind it.

Piaget suggested that young children's belief that rules are unchangeable is due to two factors, one social and one cognitive. First, Piaget argued that parental control of children is coercive and unilateral, leading to children's unquestioning respect for rules set by adults. Second, children's cognitive immaturity causes them to believe that rules are "real" things, like chairs or gravity, that exist outside people and are not products of the human mind.

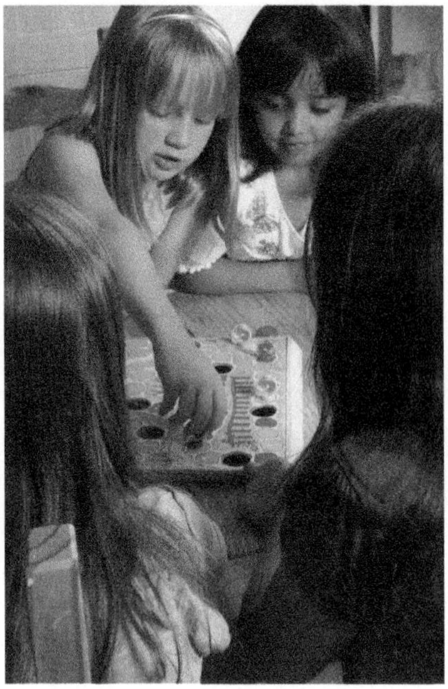

BEN MOLYNEUX PEOPLE/ALAMY

Piaget argued that through games, children learn that rules are a creation of human beings—that they are not absolute but rather interpreted and that they can be changed with the consensus of the peer group.

Moral Development in Early Childhood

WORTH PUBLISHERS

After this first stage, children enter a transition period in which interactions with their peers lead them to develop the ability to take one another's perspective and to develop beliefs about fairness. At around ages 11 or 12, children enter Piaget's second stage of *autonomous morality*. Piaget believed that children at this stage no longer accept blind obedience to authority as the basis of moral decisions. They fully understand that rules are the product of social agreement and can be changed if the majority of a group agrees to do so. In addition, they consider fairness and equality amongst people as important factors to consider when constructing rules. Children at this stage believe that punishments should "fit the crime" and that adults are not always fair in how they deliver punishment. They also consider individuals' motives and intentions when evaluating their behaviour; thus, they view breaking one cup while trying to sneak jam (as was done by Henry in the earlier vignette) as worse than accidentally breaking 15 cups (as was done by John in the vignette).

According to Piaget, children typically progress from the heteronomous morality of constraint to autonomous moral reasoning. Individual differences in the rates of children's progress are due to numerous factors, including differences in cognitive maturity, in opportunities for interactions with peers and for reciprocal role-taking, and in how authoritarian and punitive parents are with them.

Critique of Piaget's Theory

Piaget's theory of moral development has received some support from empirical research. Studies of children from many countries and various racial or ethnic groups have shown that as they age, boys and girls increasingly take motives and intentions into account when judging the morality of actions (Berg & Mussen, 1975; Lickona, 1976). In addition, parental punitiveness has been associated with less mature moral reasoning and moral behaviour, as Piaget predicted (Laible, Eye, & Carlo, 2008). Finally, consistent with Piaget's belief that cognitive development plays a role in the development of moral judgment, children's performances on tests of perspective-taking skills, Piagetian logical tasks, and IQ have all been associated with their level of moral judgment (Berg & Mussen, 1975; Lickona, 1976).

However, the body of research on this topic has led to an overall rejection of Piaget's theory of moral judgment. Piaget underestimated young children's ability to appreciate the role of intentionality in morality (Nobes, Panagiotaki, & Pawson, 2009). When Piagetian moral vignettes are presented in ways that make the individuals' intentions more obvious—such as by using video-recorded dramas—preschoolers and early elementary school children are more likely to recognize individuals with bad intentions (Grueneich, 1982; Rakoczy et al., 2015; Yuill & Perner, 1988). Most 4- and 5-year-olds understand that a person could not cause a negative outcome "on purpose" if the person did not know that outcome was a possible consequence of their action (Pellizzoni, Siegal, & Surian, 2009).

In contrast to Piaget's theory, even young children use knowledge of intentionality to evaluate others' behaviour. In one study, 3-year-olds who saw an adult intend (but fail) to hurt another adult were less likely to help that person than they were if the person's behaviour toward the other adult was neutral (intended to neither help nor hurt the other). In contrast, the 3-year-olds helped an adult who accidentally caused harm as much as they helped an adult whose behaviour was neutral (Vaish, Carpenter, & Tomasello, 2010). This ability to appreciate others' intentions is present in children younger than 2 years old: In a study conducted at

Queen's University, 21-month-olds were more likely to help an adult who had tried (but failed) to assist them in retrieving a toy than an adult who had been unwilling to assist them. They were also more likely to help an adult who had tried (but failed) to assist them than an adult whose intentions had been unclear (Dunfield & Kuhlmeier, 2013). Finally, as you will see later in the chapter, it is clear that young children do not believe that some actions, such as hurting others, are right even when adults say they are.

Despite its shortcomings, Piaget's theory provided clear and interesting arguments for subsequent research on the development of moral judgment to support or refute. The most notable example is the more complex theory of moral reasoning formulated by Kohlberg.

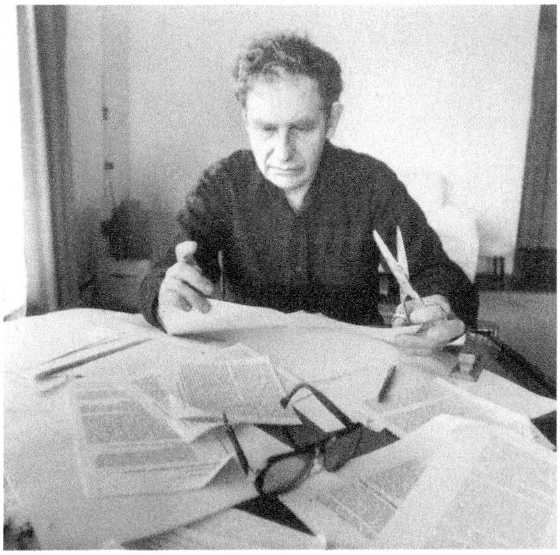
LEE LOCKWOOD/GETTY IMAGES

Kohlberg (pictured here), like Piaget, argued that stages of moral reasoning involve a qualitative change in reasoning and that each stage represents a new way of thinking that replaces the child's thinking at prior, lower levels.

Kohlberg's Theory of Moral Reasoning

Heavily influenced by the ideas of Piaget, Lawrence Kohlberg (1976; Colby & Kohlberg, 1987a, 1987b) was interested in the sequences through which children's moral reasoning develops over time. On the basis of a longitudinal study in which he first assessed the moral reasoning of three cohorts of boys (beginning at ages 10, 13, and 16, respectively), Kohlberg proposed that the development of moral reasoning proceeds through a specific series of stages that are discontinuous and hierarchical. That is, each new stage reflects a qualitatively different, more advanced way of thinking than the one before it.

Kohlberg assessed moral reasoning by presenting children with hypothetical moral dilemmas and then questioning them about the issues involved. The most famous of these is known as the Heinz dilemma:

> In Europe, a woman was near death from a special kind of cancer. There was one drug that the doctors thought might save her. It was a form of radium that a druggist in the same town had recently discovered. The drug was expensive to make, but the druggist was charging 10 times what it cost him to make. He paid $200 for the radium and charged $2,000 for a small dose of the drug. The sick woman's husband, Heinz, went to everyone he knew to borrow the money, but he could only get together about $1,000, which is half of what it cost. He told the druggist that his wife was dying, and asked him to sell it cheaper or let him pay later. But the druggist said, "No, I discovered the drug and I'm going to make money from it." So Heinz gets desperate and considers breaking into the man's store to steal the drug for his wife.
>
> (Colby et al., 1983, p. 77)

After relating this dilemma to an initial sample of boys aged 10 to 16, Kohlberg asked them questions such as: Should Heinz steal the drug? Would it be wrong or right if he did? Why? Is it a husband's duty to steal the drug for his wife if he can get it no other way? Kohlberg was not interested in whether the children said Heinz should or should not steal the drug; instead, he was interested in the moral reasoning behind their choices. For example, the response that "Heinz should steal the drug because he probably won't get caught and put in jail" was considered less advanced than "Heinz should steal the drug because a human life is more important than property or profits." Based on these interviews, Kohlberg proposed that there are three levels of moral reasoning—preconventional, conventional, and postconventional (principled)—each of which has two stages within it.

Moral Development: Kohlberg's Heinz Moral Dilemma

WORTH PUBLISHERS

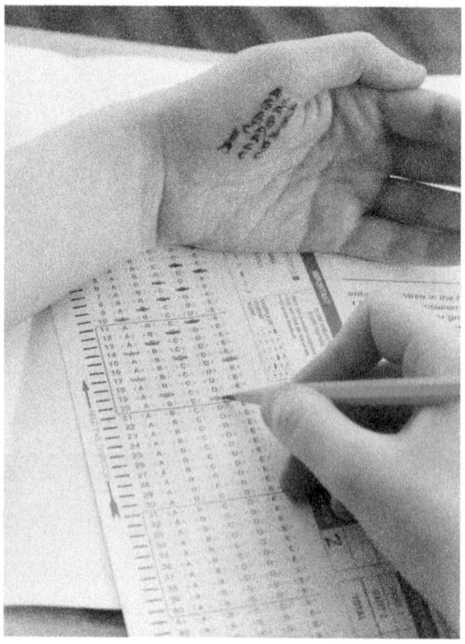

Most children and adolescents engage in only basic moral reasoning. Moreover, even if their reasoning is at a higher level, they sometimes act in ways that do not reflect their highest level of moral reasoning, such as the person in this photo, who knows cheating is immoral.

Preconventional Level

Preconventional moral reasoning is self-centred. A child at this level focuses on getting rewards and avoiding punishment.

Stage 1: Punishment and Obedience Orientation. At Stage 1, obedience to authorities is what is seen as right. A child's moral actions are motivated by avoidance of punishment. The child does not consider the interests of others or recognize that those interests might differ from his or her own.

Stage 2: Instrumental and Exchange Orientation. At Stage 2, what is right is what is in the child's own best interest or involves equal exchange between people (e.g., you hurt me, so I hurt you).

Conventional Level

Conventional moral reasoning is centred on social relationships. A child at this level focuses on compliance with social duties and laws.

Stage 3: Mutual Interpersonal Expectations, Relationships, and Interpersonal Conformity Orientation. In Stage 3, good behaviour is doing what is expected by people who are close to the person or what people generally expect of someone in a given role (e.g., "a son"). Being "a good girl" or a "good boy" is important and entails having good motives, showing concern about others, and maintaining good relationships with others.

Stage 4: Social System and Conscience Orientation. Moral behaviour in Stage 4 involves fulfilling one's duties, upholding laws, and contributing to society or one's group. The individual is motivated to keep the social system going and to avoid a breakdown in its functioning.

Postconventional or Principled Level

Postconventional moral reasoning is centred on ideals. A child at this level focuses on moral principles.

Stage 5: Social Contract or Individual Rights Orientation. At Stage 5, moral behaviour involves upholding rules that are in the best interest of the group ("the greatest good for the greatest number"), are impartial, or were mutually agreed upon by the group. An individual at this stage might reason that if society agrees that a law is not benefiting everyone, that law should be changed.

Stage 6: Universal Ethical Principles. Moral behaviour in Stage 6 is commitment to self-chosen ethical principles that reflect universal principles, such as life, liberty, basic human rights, and the dignity of each human being. Moral reasoning at this stage would assert that these principles must be upheld in any society, regardless of majority opinion. When laws violate these principles, the individual should act in accordance with these universal principles rather than with the law. It is worth noting that so few people ever attained Stage 6 of the postconventional level that Kohlberg (1978) eventually stopped scoring it as a separate stage, and many theorists consider it an elaboration of Stage 5 (Lapsley, 2006).

Kohlberg argued that people in all parts of the world move through his stages in the same order, although they differ in how quickly and how far they progress. As in Piaget's theory, age-related advances in cognitive skills, especially perspective taking, are believed to underlie the development of higher-level moral reasoning. Consistent with Kohlberg's theory, people who have higher-level cognitive and perspective-taking skills exhibit higher-level moral reasoning (Colby et al., 1983; Mason & Gibbs, 1993; Rest, 1983).

Critique of Kohlberg's Theory

Kohlberg's work is important because it demonstrated that children's moral reasoning changes in relatively systematic ways as they develop. In their longitudinal study, Kohlberg and his colleagues (Colby et al., 1983) followed 58 boys into adulthood and found that moral reasoning changed systematically with age (see Figure 14.1). When the boys were 10 years old, they used primarily Stage 1 reasoning (blind obedience to authority) and Stage 2 reasoning (self-interest). Thereafter, reasoning in these stages dropped off markedly. For most adolescents aged 14 and older, Stage 3 reasoning (being "good" to earn approval or maintain relationships) was the primary mode of reasoning, although some adolescents occasionally used Stage 4 reasoning (fulfilling duties and upholding laws to maintain social order). Only a small number of participants, even by age 36, ever achieved Stage 5 (upholding the best interests of the group while recognizing life and liberty as universal values). In addition, because an individual's levels of moral reasoning have been related to his or her moral behaviour, especially for people reasoning at higher levels (e.g., Kutnick, 1986; Underwood & Moore, 1982), Kohlberg's work has been useful in understanding how cognitive processes contribute to moral behaviour.

However, Kohlberg's theory and findings have also been criticized on several fronts. One criticism is that Kohlberg did not sufficiently differentiate between truly moral issues and issues of social convention (Nucci & Gingo, 2011; we examine this differentiation later in the chapter). Another criticism pertains to cultural differences. Although children in many non-Western, nonindustrialized cultures start out reasoning much the way Western children do in Kohlberg's scoring system, their moral reasoning within this system generally does not advance as far as that of their Western peers (e.g., Nisan & Kohlberg, 1982; Snarey, 1985). This may be because, in many non-Western societies, the goal of preserving group harmony is of critical importance, whereas issues of individual rights and civil liberties are not viewed as especially relevant. This finding has raised concern that assessment through the use of dilemmas, like Kohlberg's Heinz dilemma, is not valid across cultures (Snarey, 1985).

To address this concern, more than 75 studies have used a measure of moral development that instead asks the child concrete moral questions such as "How important is it for a person (without losing his or her own life) to save the life of a friend?" (Gibbs et al., 2007, p. 465). In these studies across a range of Western and

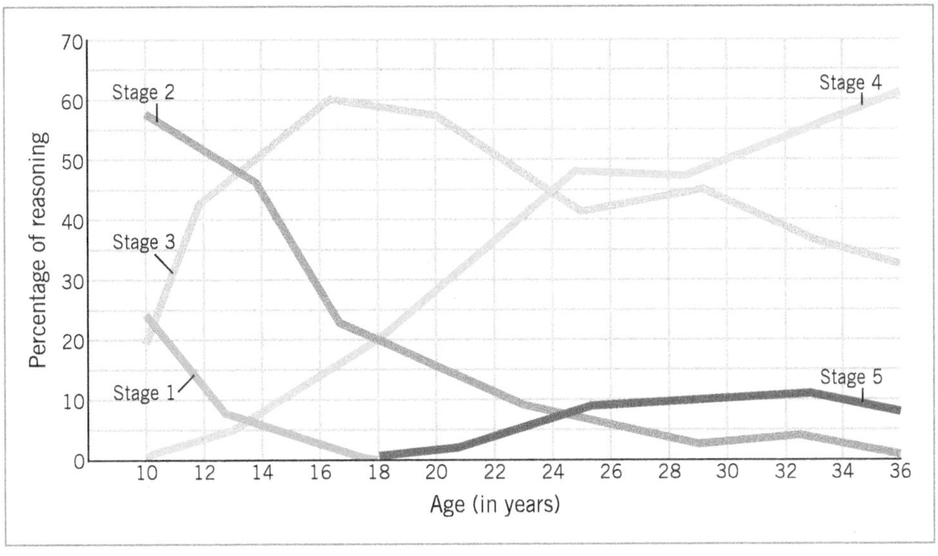

FIGURE 14.1 Mean percentage of moral reasoning at each stage for each age group This graph shows age trends in moral reasoning in Kohlberg's longitudinal sample. (Data from Colby et al., 1983)

non-Western countries—including Bahrain, Bosnia, Canada, China, Germany, Italy, Japan, Kenya, Russia, Sweden, and the United States—children shared a basic set of common values and showed the same stages of moral development, thus supporting the universality of Kohlberg's theory (Gibbs et al., 2007).

Another criticism has to do with Kohlberg's argument that change in moral reasoning is discontinuous. Kohlberg asserted that because each stage is more advanced than the previous one, once an individual attains a new stage, he or she seldom reasons at a lower stage. However, research has shown that children and adults alike often reason at different levels on different occasions—or even on the same occasion (Carpendale, 2000; Rest, 1979). As a consequence, it is not clear that the development of moral reasoning is qualitatively discontinuous. Rather, children and adolescents may gradually acquire the cognitive skills to use higher stages of moral reasoning but also may use lower stages when doing so is consistent with their goals, motives, or beliefs in a particular situation. For example, even an adolescent who is capable of using Stage 4 reasoning may well use Stage 2 reasoning to justify a decision to break the law for personal gain.

An issue regarding Kohlberg's theory that has been debated over the years is whether gender differences exist in moral reasoning. As noted previously, Kohlberg developed his conception of moral-reasoning stages on the basis of interviews with a sample of boys. Carol Gilligan (1982) argued that Kohlberg's classification of moral reasoning is biased against females because it does not adequately recognize differences in the way males and females reason morally. Gilligan suggested that because of the way they are socialized, males tend to value principles of justice and rights, whereas females value caring, responsibility for others, and avoidance of exploiting or hurting others (Gilligan & Attanucci, 1988). This difference in moral orientation, according to Gilligan, causes males to score higher on Kohlberg's dilemmas than females do.

Contrary to Gilligan's theory, there is little evidence that boys and girls, or men and women, score differently on Kohlberg's stages of moral reasoning (Turiel, 1998). However, consistent with Gilligan's arguments, during adolescence and adulthood, females focus somewhat more on issues of caring about other people in their moral judgments, whereas males tend to focus on issues of justice (Hyde, 2005; Jaffee & Hyde, 2000). Differences in males' and females' moral reasoning seem to be most evident when individuals report on moral dilemmas in their own lives (Jaffee & Hyde, 2000). Thus, while Gilligan's work has been very important in broadening the focus of research on moral reasoning to consider the potential for gender differences, there are many more gender similarities than there are differences (Hyde, 2005; we will explore gender similarities and differences in more depth in Chapter 15).

Social Domain Theory of Moral Development

In place of the stage models proposed by Piaget and Kohlberg, current thinking about children's moral development is largely driven by *social domain theory.* According to this theory, growth in moral reasoning occurs not through stage-like change but through gradual change based on the child's social interactions with peers and adults as well as through direct socialization from their parents (Smetana & Jambon, 2018; Turiel, 2014). Differences in children's moral judgments are understood to result from differences in the environments in which children live and the experiences they have within those environments. Parents are key in this process: parents transmit values to their children both explicitly (through teaching and discipline) and implicitly (by example). However, this relationship is understood to be bidirectional, such that children's moral judgments and related behaviours also affect their parents' behaviours. (See Chapter 12 for more on bidirectionality.)

Much like Piaget, social domain theory also emphasizes the role of peers as a strong influence on children's moral development. Peer relationships involve equal power (in contrast to the parent–child relationship), which allows children to have more agency in their behaviours in moral situations. Moreover, peer-to-peer interactions involve numerous settings in which children both observe and are forced to initiate moral behaviours.

Social domain theory argues that, in order to successfully negotiate their social worlds, children must understand principles in three different domains of social knowledge. The first is the **moral domain,** in which children understand that the universal concepts of right and wrong, fairness, justice, and individual rights apply across contexts and supersede rules or authority (Smetana & Jambon, 2018). Knowing that it is not acceptable to steal another child's toy would fall under the moral domain. Parents play an important role in this domain by teaching children how and why to cooperate with, take the perspective of, and help other children and adults (Dunn, 2014).

The second domain of social knowledge is the **societal domain,** which encompasses concepts regarding the rules and conventions through which societies maintain order. Choices about clothing (e.g., not wearing pajamas to school), manners (e.g., saying "Please" when making a request), and forms of greeting (e.g., calling adults by a formal name rather than by first name) all fall under the societal domain. Knowledge in this domain helps children negotiate interactions with peers and adults in their environments.

The **personal domain,** the third domain of social knowledge, pertains to actions in which individual preferences are the main consideration; there are no right or wrong choices. This domain covers decisions children might make about their appearance, how they spend their money, and their choice of friends. Decisions children make in this domain are central to the development of their sense of autonomy as well as their identity. (See Chapter 11 for a more detailed discussion of identity development.)

Support for the social domain theory has been growing over the past two decades. Children aged 4 to 9 years consistently rate moral transgressions, such as hitting, teasing, or unfairly distributing resources (e.g., crayons), as morally wrong, even when the transgression is perpetrated against a bully (Smetana & Ball, 2019). From an early age, children distinguish between moral and societal transgressions. By age 3, children generally believe that violations of moral rules are more wrong than violations of societal conventions. By age 4, they believe that moral transgressions, but not societal transgressions, are wrong even if an adult does not know about them or even if adult authorities have not said they are wrong (Smetana & Braeges, 1990). In another example of this distinction between reasoning in the moral and societal domains, a 5-year-old boy was told about a school in which students were allowed to hit each other; he was then asked if he thought it was right for the school to do that. The boy replied:

> No. It is not okay. . . . that is like making other people unhappy. You can hurt them that way. It hurts other people, hurting is not good.
>
> (Turiel, 1987, p. 101)

moral domain an area of social knowledge based on concepts of right and wrong, fairness, justice, and individual rights; these concepts apply across contexts and supersede rules or authority

societal domain an area of social knowledge that encompasses concepts regarding the rules and conventions through which societies maintain order

personal domain an area of social knowledge that pertains to actions in which individual preferences are the main consideration; there are no right or wrong choices

This boy is firm in his belief that hurting others is wrong, even if adults say it is acceptable. Children tend to justify their condemnation of moral violations by referring to violations of fairness and harm to others' welfare (Turiel, 2008). Compare that reasoning with the same boy's response to a question about the acceptability of a school policy that allows children to take off their clothes in hot weather:

> If that's what the boss wants to do, he can do that. . . . He is in charge of the school.
> (Turiel, 1987, p. 101)

In this latter case, the same boy who reasoned that hurting people was always wrong, even if adults give permission (the moral domain), argued that the adults' rules do matter in situations involving the societal domain, likely because he (rightly) sees adults as the ones making societal rules.

With regard to both moral and societal issues in the family, children—and to a lesser degree adolescents—believe that parents have authority (Smetana, 1988; Yau, Smetana, & Metzger, 2009), unless the parent gives commands that violate moral or societal principles (Yamada, 2009).

With respect to matters of personal judgment, however, even preschoolers tend to believe that they themselves should have control; older children and adolescents strongly believe that they should control choices in the personal domain at home and at school (Lagattuta, Nucci, & Bosacki, 2010; Nucci & Gingo, 2011). At the same time, parents usually feel that they should have some authority over their children's personal choices, even into adolescence, so parents and teenagers frequently do battle in this domain—and parents often lose these battles (Lins-Dyer & Nucci, 2007; Smetana, 1988; Smetana & Asquith, 1994).

Cultural and Socioeconomic Similarities and Differences

Cultures around the world share some characteristics when it comes to how their members make moral decisions. All human societies maintain social order through norms. The moral, societal, and personal judgments discussed above are found across cultures (Smetana, Jambon, & Ball, 2014), and children's ability to distinguish amongst the domains appears across a variety of cultures (Killen & Smetana, 2015). Moral judgments in particular, such as judgments about behaviours related to fairness and the welfare of others, are largely universal (Nucci, 2001). For example, a study of seven countries (Canada, India, Mexico, Peru, Senegal, Uganda, and the United States) found that children from all countries protested when they were at a disadvantage (had fewer treats) compared to another child (Blake et al., 2015). Thus, children across these societies all recognized unfairness when it happened to them. However, only children from Canada, the United States, and Uganda recognized unfairness when they were the one at an advantage (Blake et al., 2015).

Children in India are much more likely than children in the United States to say that helping other people is a moral obligation, not a matter of personal choice.

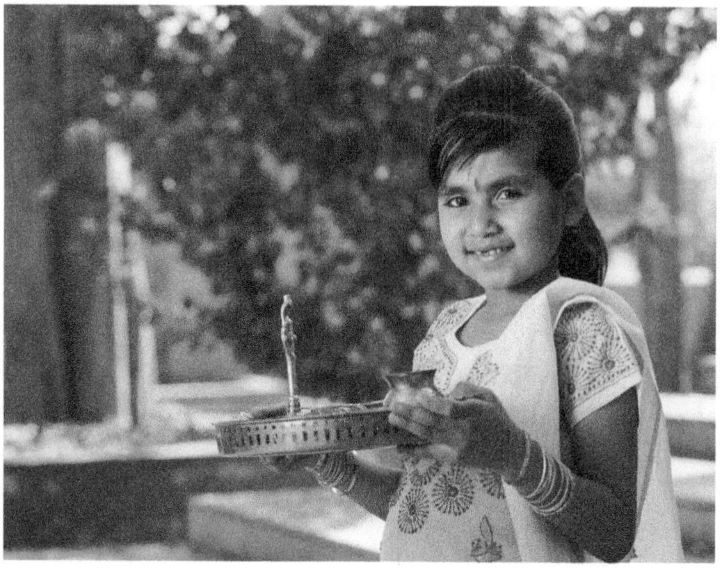

UNIQUELY INDIA/AGE FOTOSTOCK

What issues fall within the societal domain or the personal domain differ across cultures (Shweder, Mahapatra, & Miller, 1987). Take the question of one's obligation to attend to the needs of one's parents and to try to address the needs of friends or strangers. Children in India believe they have a clear moral obligation to attend to these needs, while children in the United States appear to consider it a matter of personal judgment or a combination of moral and personal judgments (Miller, Bersoff, & Harwood, 1990). A hint about the source of the differences between the behaviours of children in these two countries came from an experiment in which parents were asked to model giving a stingy or generous donation to unseen adults while their children watched (Blake et al., 2016). The children were then provided with 10 candies and given the opportunity to donate a portion to an unseen child. U.S. children in the generous parent model condition were no more generous with their own candies than were children in a control condition with no parent-modeled behaviour (Figure 14.2a). However, U.S. children did become more stingy than children in a control condition when they observed their parents being stingy.

In contrast, Indian children's behaviour was affected both when parents were generous and when they were stingy (Figure 14.2b). Overall, in the generous condition, 10% or fewer of U.S. children shared more than half of their candies at any of the ages studies (3–4 years, 5–6 years, or 7–8 years), while more than 20% of Indian 3- to 4-year-olds, 60% of Indian 5- to 6-year-olds, and 50% of 7- to 8-year-olds shared more than half of their candies (see Figure 14.3; Blake et al., 2016).

Even within a given society, religious beliefs may affect what is considered a moral judgment or a societal judgment (Turiel, 2006; Wainryb & Turiel, 1995). In Finland, for example, conservative religious adolescents are less likely to make a distinction between the moral and societal domains than are nonreligious youths. For the religious youths, the crucial factor for societal judgments is God's word as written in the Bible (i.e., whether or not the Bible says a particular social convention is wrong; Vainio, 2011).

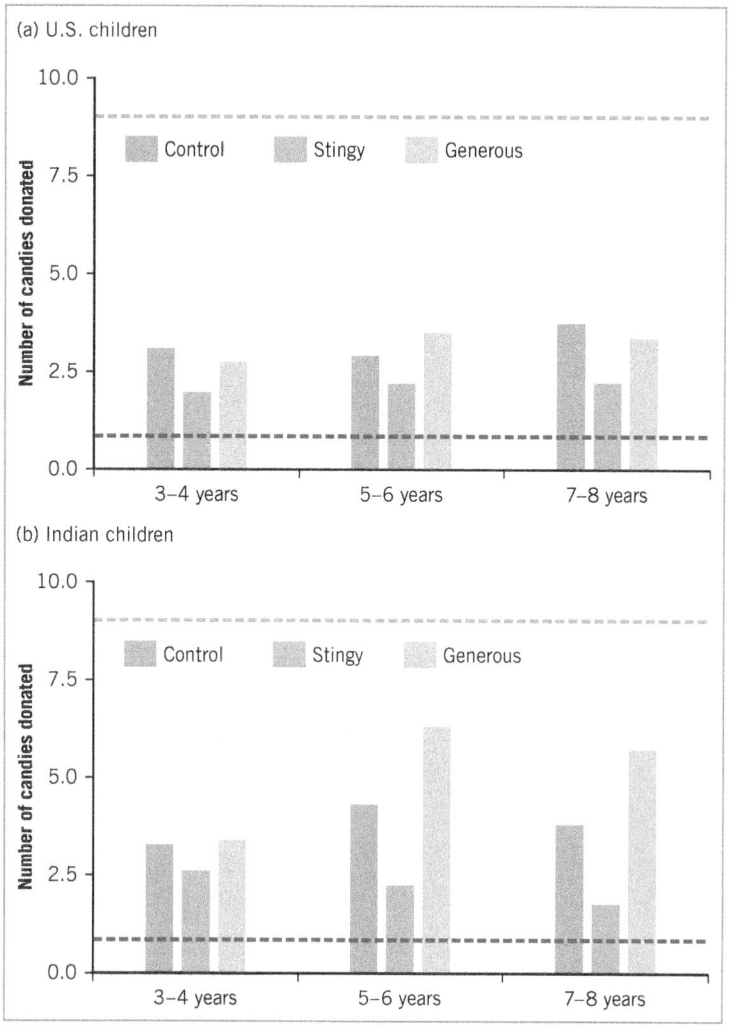

FIGURE 14.2 Children's donations by country, age, and condition (generous, stingy, or control) U.S. children are shown in panel (a) and Indian children in panel (b). The blue line in each graph indicates the number of candies parents in the generous condition were told to donate (9 candies), and the red line indicates the number of candies the parents in the stingy condition were told to donate (1 candy). U.S. children did not increase their level of donation when their parents modeled generous behaviour, but the Indian children did, with the two older groups giving away over half of their own candies. (Data from Blake et al., 2016)

Socioeconomic class can also influence the way children make such designations. Research in the United States and Brazil indicates that children of lower-income families are somewhat less likely than middle-class children to differentiate sharply between moral and societal actions and, prior to adolescence, are less likely to view personal judgments as a matter of choice. These differences may be due to the tendency of individuals of low socioeconomic status to place a greater emphasis on submission to authority and to allow children less autonomy (Nucci, 1997). This social-class difference in children's views may evaporate as youths approach adolescence, although Brazilian mothers of lower-income adolescents still claim more control over personal issues than do mothers of middle-income youths (Lins-Dyer & Nucci, 2007).

The Development of Conscience

One factor that may push a child toward making a moral judgment (whether in the moral, societal, or personal domain) is conscience. We are all familiar with the popular notion of conscience—that voice inside us that pushes us to behave

FIGURE 14.3 Percentage of children donating more than half of their candies by country, age, and condition (Data from Blake et al., 2016)

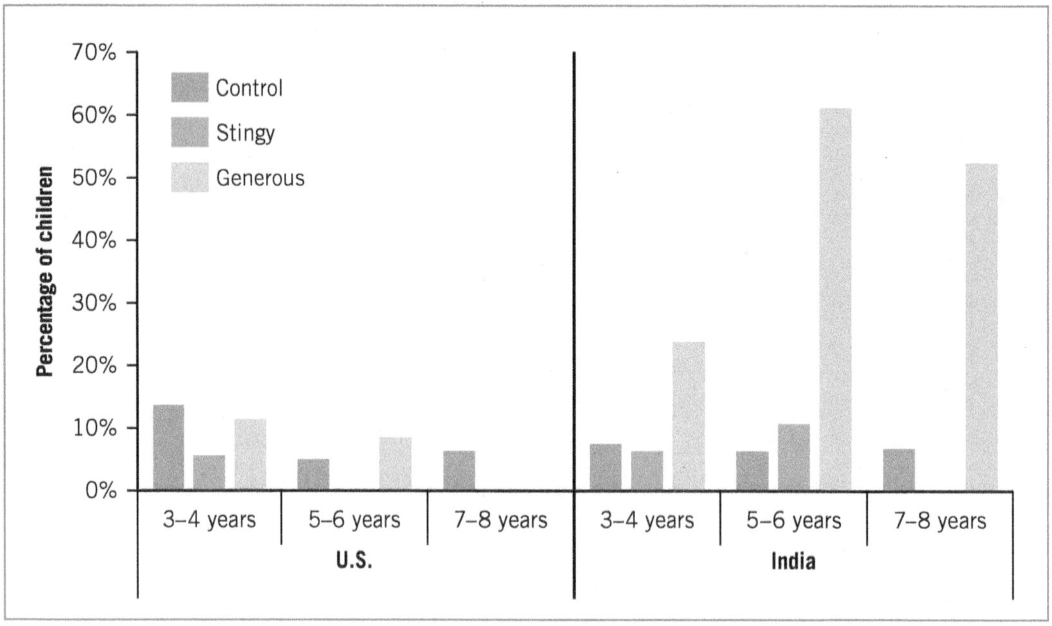

in appropriate ways and makes us feel guilty if we do not. Stated more formally, **conscience** is an internal regulatory mechanism that increases the individual's ability to conform to standards of conduct accepted in his or her culture. Conscience restrains antisocial behaviour or destructive impulses and promotes a child's compliance with adults' rules and standards, even when no one is monitoring the child's behaviour (Kochanska, 2002). Conscience can also promote prosocial behaviour by causing the child to feel guilty when engaging in uncaring behaviour or failing to live up to internalized values about helping others (Eisenberg, 2000; Hoffman, 1982).

Good Guys vs. Bad Guys: How Do Babies Know the Difference?

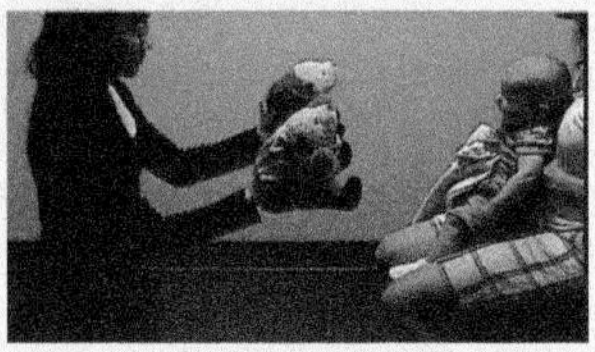

Because conscience is tied to cultural standards about right or wrong, psychologists long thought that morality was completely learned (i.e., *nurture*) and not at all innate (i.e., *nature*). However, recent evidence from studies with infants suggests that humans may have an innate drive to prefer actions that help others over ones that hinder them. In a study with 10-month-olds, a puppet in the shape of a red circle was shown on its own trying, but failing, to "climb" a hill. In one condition, a yellow triangle puppet (the "helper") appears and pushes the red circle up the hill. In a second condition, a blue square (the "hinderer") appears and pushes the red circle back down the hill (see Figure 14.4). When later shown the red circle approaching either the helper or the hinderer, the 10-month-olds showed more surprise when the red circle approached the hinderer, indicating that they expected the red circle to prefer the puppet that helped the circle rather than the one that hindered it.

This research team produced similar findings with even younger babies: when shown scenarios with puppets who helped another puppet in trouble or puppets who hindered another puppet needing help, infants as young as 4½ months preferred the helper puppet (Hamlin, 2013). These findings indicate that infants have the beginnings of a moral sense long before they can be taught one by their parents, which suggests some innate component to prosocial behaviour. These innate preferences for prosocial behaviour may provide the building blocks on which morality, learned from family and culture, is built.

conscience an internal regulatory mechanism that increases an individual's ability to conform to standards of conduct accepted in their culture

FIGURE 14.4 Helper/hinderer Viewers of the "climber" event described in the text — infants and adults alike — readily interpret it in terms of intentional action. First, they see the ball as "trying" to move up a hill but then rolling back down, thereby "failing" to achieve its goal of reaching the top. On some trials, after the ball starts to roll back down, a triangle appears below the ball and seems to "push" it upward, "helping" it get to the top. On other trials, a cube appears in front of the ball and "hinders" it by seeming to "push" it down the hill.

Children develop a conscience slowly over time. By age 2, toddlers start to recognize moral standards and rules and exhibit signs of guilt when they do something wrong (Kopp, 2001; Thompson & Newton, 2010). Individual differences in these two components of conscience — the desire to comply with rules and feelings of guilt when failing to do so — are quite stable in early development from 22 to 45 months of age (Aksan & Kochanska, 2005; Kochanska et al., 2002). Children's growing understanding of others' emotions and goals, and their increasing capacity for empathic concern, are likely contributors to the development of conscience (Thompson, 2012).

As they mature, children are more likely to take on their parents' moral values — and to exhibit guilt for violating those values — if their parents use disciplinary practices low in parental power and high in reasoning that help children understand and learn the parents' values (Kochanska & Aksan, 2006; Laible et al., 2008; Volling, Mahoney, & Rauer, 2009). Children's adoption of their parents' values is also facilitated by a secure, positive parent–child relationship, which inclines children to be open to, and eager to internalize, their parents' values (Kochanska et al., 2005; Kochanska et al., 2008).

Children with different temperaments may develop a conscience in different ways. Toddlers who are prone to fear unfamiliar people or situations tend to exhibit more guilt at a young age than do less fearful children (Kochanska et al., 2002). Moreover, for those infants who are prone to fear, the development of conscience seems to be promoted by the mother's use of gentle discipline that includes reasoning with the child and providing nonmaterial incentives for compliance (Kochanska & Aksan, 2006). When mothers use gentle discipline, fearful children do not become so anxious that they tune out their mother's messages about desired behaviour. Gentle discipline arouses fearful children just enough that they attend to and remember what their mother tells them (Kochanska, 1993).

In contrast, gentle discipline seems to be unrelated to the development of conscience in fearless young children, perhaps because it is insufficient to arouse their attention (Kochanska, Aksan, & Joy, 2007). What does seem to foster the development of conscience in fearless children is a parent–child relationship characterized by responsive parenting, mutual cooperation, and positive affect (Kochanska, Aksan, & Joy, 2007). Fearless children appear motivated more by the desire to please their

Young children often have not yet internalized some of their parents' prohibitions and values. The degree to which they do so appears to depend partly on the quality of the parenting they receive and partly on their temperament.

mother than by a fear of her (Kochanska, 1997). Little research on this topic has been conducted with fathers, but the one study that has done so did not find a similar match between children's fearfulness and fathers' parenting behaviours (Kochanska, Aksan, & Joy, 2007).

The effects of parenting on children's conscience also vary with the child's genes because genes affect children's temperaments. This can be seen in the dynamic between maternal responsiveness—the mother's acceptance of, and sensitivity to, the child—and the child's genotype for the serotonin transporter gene, SLC6A4. As discussed in Chapter 11, a particular allele variant of SLC6A4 is believed to make children especially reactive to their rearing environment. For children with this allele variant, high maternal responsiveness is associated with high levels of conscience at 15 to 52 months of age. Conversely, for children with this same variant, low maternal responsiveness is associated with low conscience. For children with a different allele for SLC6A4, their level of conscience is unrelated to their mother's responsiveness (Kochanska et al., 2011). This pattern is an example of *goodness of fit* between temperament and environment (see Chapter 10), whereby some children are more reactive than others to the quality of parenting they receive.

Early development of conscience undoubtedly contributes to whether children come to accept the moral values of their parents and society. Indeed, in a longitudinal assessment of children's behavioural and affective expressions of guilt (in which they were led to believe that they had broken a valuable object), the children's levels of guilt at 22 and 45 months of age predicted their morality at 54 months of age (e.g., their tendency to violate rules about touching prohibited toys, to cheat on tasks, and to express selfish and antisocial themes when discussing vignettes with morally relevant topics) (Kochanska et al., 2002). This, in turn, predicted whether they engaged in hurtful or problematic social behaviour at 67 months (Kochanska et al., 2008). In a related study, children's internalization of parental rules at 2 to 4 years of age predicted their self-perceptions as being moral at 67 months (Kochanska et al., 2010). Therefore, the nature of early parent–child disciplinary interactions sets the stage for children's subsequent moral development.

REVIEW QUESTION

How does social domain theory address the critiques of Piaget's and Kohlberg's stage theories of moral development? ■

Prosocial Behaviour

Malala, whose experiences and activism are described briefly at the beginning of this chapter, has lived a life driven by the desire to act prosocially; in other words, she engaged in **prosocial behaviour,** which is voluntary behaviour intended to benefit others, such as by helping, sharing with, or comforting them. While not all children (or even adults) are as selfless as Malala, all children are capable of prosocial behaviours. They vary, however, in how often they engage in these behaviours and in their reasons for doing so.

prosocial behaviour voluntary behaviour intended to benefit another, such as helping, sharing with, and comforting others

The Development of Prosocial Behaviour

The origins of prosocial behaviour are rooted in the capacity to feel empathy and sympathy. As discussed in Chapter 10, *empathy* is an emotional response to another's emotional state or condition (e.g., sadness, poverty) that reflects the other person's state or condition (Eisenberg, Spinrad, & Knafo-Noam, 2015). For example, if a child becomes sad upon observing another person's sadness or pain, the child is experiencing empathy. To experience empathy, children must be able to identify the emotions of others (at least to some degree) and understand that another person is feeling an emotion or is in some kind of need.

Sympathy is a feeling of concern for another in response to the other's emotional state or condition. Although sympathy often is an outcome of empathizing with another's negative emotion or negative situation, what distinguishes sympathy from empathy is the element of concern: people who experience sympathy for another person are not merely feeling the same emotion as the other person.

ELIZABETH CREWS

ANDY COX/GETTY IMAGES

Young children who view another child's distress sometimes respond with looks of concern or attempts to console or help the distressed peer. Recognizing others' emotions is necessary before children can feel empathy or act prosocially.

In order for children to express empathy or sympathy, they must be able to take the perspective of others. Although early theorists such as Piaget believed that children are unable to do this until age 6 or 7 (Piaget & Inhelder, 1956/1977), it is now clear that children have some ability to understand others' perspectives much earlier (Vaish, Carpenter, & Tomasello, 2009). By 14 months of age, children become emotionally distressed when they see other people who are upset (Knafo et al., 2008; Roth-Hanania, Davidov, & Zahn-Waxler, 2011) and express verbal and nonverbal concern for an adult who has been hurt (Hastings et al., 2014). These studies suggest that children feel empathy and sympathy by the second year of life.

By 18 to 25 months of age, toddlers in laboratory studies sometimes share a personal object with an adult whom they have seen being harmed by another (e.g., by having a piece of personal property taken away or destroyed). Research at Queen's University demonstrated that toddlers will sometimes comfort an adult who appears to be injured or distressed or help an adult retrieve a dropped object or obtain food (Dunfield et al., 2011; Vaish et al., 2009). Such behaviours are especially likely to occur if the adult explicitly and emotionally communicates his or her need (Brownell, Svetlova, & Nichols, 2009), but they sometimes occur even when the adult does not express an emotional reaction (Vaish et al., 2009).

In displaying empathy, children in the second year of life also are more likely to try to comfort someone who is upset than to become upset themselves, indicating that they know who it is that is suffering. For example, researchers in one study observed an 18-month-old girl who got visibly upset by a crying baby; she responded by bringing offerings of toys and cookies to the baby and by trying to get her own mother to help soothe the child (Radke-Yarrow & Zahn-Waxler, 1984).

In the second to fourth years of life, some types of prosocial behaviours increase, while others decrease. In one laboratory study, Canadian 2-, 3-, and 4-year-olds were equally likely to help an adult get something that was out of reach (Dunfield & Kuhlmeier, 2013; see Figure 14.5). There were no statistically significant age differences for sharing stickers or food with an adult who did not have any. However, 3- and 4-year-olds were much more likely than 2-year-olds

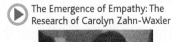

The Emergence of Empathy: The Research of Carolyn Zahn-Waxler

COURTESY CAROLYN ZAHN-WAXLER

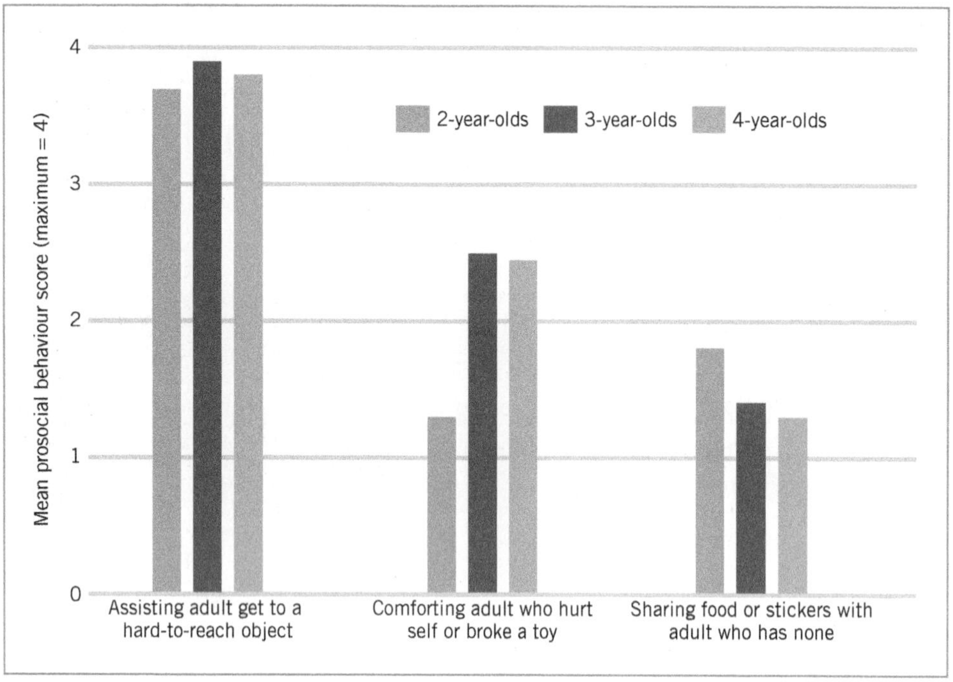

FIGURE 14.5 Observed prosocial behaviour by age in response to adults expressing three types of needs Performance of three types of prosocial behaviours by age researchers at Queen's University have demonstrated that different types of prosocial behaviour—responding to instrumental need, emotional distress, and material desire—emerge at different ages and develop differently over time. (Data from Dunfield & Kuhlmeier, 2013, p. 1772)

to provide assistance or verbal reassurance to adults who were emotionally distressed because they had broken a toy or hurt themselves. This finding suggests that young children may not be able to act on their feelings of sympathy when others are distressed until they reach age 3, in part because that is the age at which they begin to understand social norms (Tomasello & Vaish, 2013).

Cooperation is another form of prosocial behaviour, one that may be driven by sympathy but may also be driven by a child's sense of fairness. In a laboratory experiment, children as young as 14 months of age were able to cooperate with another child or an adult to reach a goal that would benefit them both, such as getting prizes (Warneken & Tomasello, 2007). In a display of a different type of cooperation, children also tended to divide prizes evenly if they were initially given to the children unevenly (Tomasello & Vaish, 2013). In contrast, when researchers repeated this division task with chimpanzees, the chimps' interactions were characterized by competition rather than cooperation. This finding lends support to the idea that cooperative prosocial behaviour may have evolved especially in humans (Tomasello & Vaish, 2013).

As children age through middle childhood and into adolescence, their increasingly higher levels of moral reasoning and of their perspective-taking ability lead to accompanying increases in how often they engage in prosocial behaviours such as helping, sharing, and donating (Knafo et al., 2008; Luengo Kanacri et al., 2013; Nantel-Vivier et al., 2009).

Children's ability to sympathize with others appears to increase with age in early and middle childhood. This group of students are participating in the World Partnership Walk in London, Ontario, in support of education, health, and economic development programs in Africa and Asia.

JONNY WHITE/ALAMY

The Origins of Individual Differences in Prosocial Behaviour

Although children's prosocial behaviours change with age, consistent with the theme of *individual differences,* there is great variation amongst children of the same age in their propensity to help, share with, and comfort others. To identify the origins of these individual differences, we must consider the themes of *nature and nurture* and *sociocultural context.*

Biological Factors

Many biologists and psychologists have proposed that humans are biologically predisposed to be prosocial (Hastings, Zahn-Waxler, & McShane, 2005). They believe that humans have evolved the capacity for prosocial behaviour because collaboration in foraging for food and in repelling enemies ensured survival (Tomasello & Vaish, 2013). According to this view, people who help others are more likely than less helpful people to be assisted when they themselves are in need and, thus, are more likely to survive and reproduce (Trivers, 1983). In addition, assisting those with whom they share genes increases the likelihood that those genes will be passed on to the next generation (Wilson, 1975).

In support of the view that humans have evolved to be prosocial, researchers at the University of British Columbia have shown that 2-year-olds are happier when giving treats to others than when taking treats for themselves (Aknin, Hamlin, & Dunn, 2012). Moreover, this tendency holds true across cultures: both adults and 2-year-olds living in a rural, isolated village in Vanuatu, a small island nation in the Pacific, were happier giving than receiving gifts (Aknin et al., 2015). Evolutionary explanations for prosocial behaviour, however, pertain to the human species as a whole and do not explain individual differences in empathy, sympathy, and prosocial behaviour.

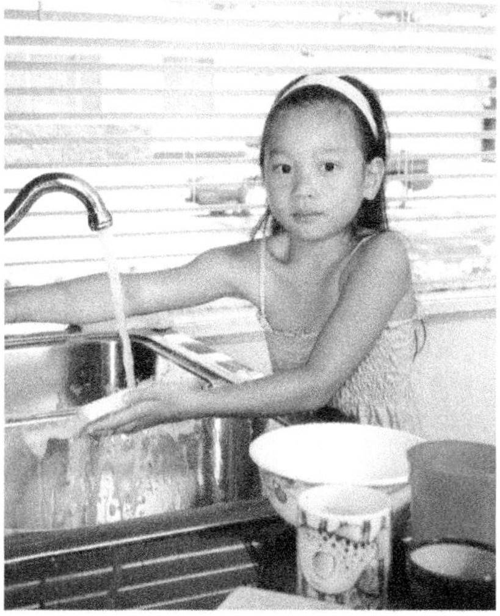
MEIKO ARQUILLOS/AGE FOTOSTOCK

From an early age, children display helping behaviours at home, often by doing chores.

Genetic factors do contribute to individual differences in these characteristics (e.g., Waldman et al., 2011). In studies with adults, twins' reports of their own empathy and prosocial behaviour are considerably more similar for identical twins than for fraternal twins (Gregory et al., 2009; Knafo & Israel, 2010). In one of the few twin studies of children's prosocial behaviours, researchers observed young twins' reactions to adults' simulations of distress in the home and in the laboratory and had the twins' mothers report on their everyday prosocial behaviour. On the basis of *heritability* estimates (see Chapter 3) derived from this study, it appears that the role of genetic factors in the children's prosocial concerns for others and in their prosocial behaviour increases with age (Knafo et al., 2008).

Researchers have identified specific genes that might contribute to individual differences in prosocial tendencies (Knafo & Israel, 2010). For example, certain genes are associated with individual differences in oxytocin, a hormone that plays a role in pair bonding and parenting and that has been associated with parental attachment, empathy, and prosocial behaviour (Eisenberg et al., 2015; Feldman, 2012; MacDonald & MacDonald, 2010; Striepens et al., 2011).

How else might genetic factors affect empathy, sympathy, and prosocial behaviour? One likely path is through differences in temperament. For instance, differences in children's ability to regulate emotion are related to their empathy and sympathy. Children who tend to experience emotion without getting overwhelmed by it are especially likely to experience sympathy and to act prosocially (Eisenberg et al., 2007; Trommsdorff, Friedlmeier, & Mayer, 2007). Moreover, children who are not responsive to others' emotions or who are too inhibited to help others may be relatively unlikely to act prosocially (Liew et al., 2011). For example, one recent Canadian study showed that preschoolers who were more socially-inhibited (very shy) were less likely to intervene to help an experimenter (Karasewich et al., 2019). Regulation is also related to children's theory of mind (see Chapter 7), and theory of mind predicts children's prosocial behaviour (Caputi et al., 2012). Thus, the effect of heredity on sympathy and prosocial behaviour might involve individual differences in social cognition as well as in temperament.

The Socialization of Prosocial Behaviour

A number of environmental factors contribute to sympathy and prosocial behaviour (Knafo & Plomin, 2006a, 2006b; Volbrecht et al., 2007). The primary environmental influence on children's development of prosocial behaviour is their socialization in the family. Researchers have identified three ways in which parents socialize prosocial behaviour in their children: (1) by modeling and teaching prosocial behaviour; (2) by arranging opportunities for their children to engage

BOX 14.1 A CLOSER LOOK Cultural Contributions to Children's Prosocial Tendencies

The amount of prosocial behaviour that children display can be influenced by the particular culture of which they are a part (Wainryb & Recchia, 2014). Studies have found that children from traditional communities and subcultures (e.g., Mexicans, Mexican Americans) are more likely to cooperate on laboratory tasks than are children from urban Westernized groups (Knight, Cota, & Bernal, 1993). Similar patterns have been found in observations of children interacting at home and in their neighbourhoods (Whiting & Edwards, 1988; Whiting & Whiting, 1975): children in traditional societies in Kenya, Mexico, and the Philippines helped, shared, and offered support to others in their families and communities more than did children in the United States, India, and Japan.

More recent studies, however, have found that disparities in prosocial behaviour are not as strong for children living in collectivist versus individualistic societies. A study of 5- to 12-year-old children in five countries found that age was a better predictor of generosity than culture: older children were more generous than younger children across all five countries (Cowell et al., 2017). There were some cultural differences: children from Canada, China, and the United States were more generous than children from South Africa or Turkey. This finding confounds past arguments that children from individualistic cultures (e.g., Canada, the United States) should share less than children from collectivist cultures, such as China (Cowell et al., 2017).

There may be cultural differences in the people toward whom children's caring behaviour is directed. In a study of children ranging from 3 to 11 years old (de Guzman, Carlo, & Edwards, 2008), children in the Philippines were more prosocial toward relatives than toward nonrelatives, whereas children in the United States were more prosocial toward nonrelatives than toward relatives. Children in both cultures were more prosocial toward infants and toddlers than toward older children and adults (de Guzman et al., 2008). In contrast to children in industrialized societies, children in traditional cultures may be socialized to help people with whom they have close ties but may be relatively disinclined to help people with whom they do not have a close connection.

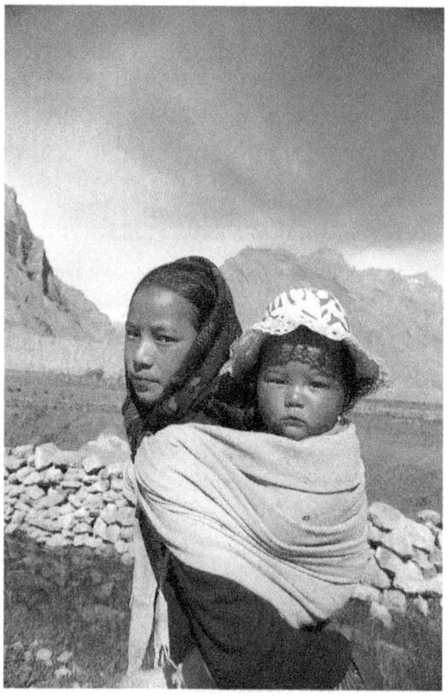

CATHERINE URSILLO/SCIENCE SOURCE

Cross-cultural research has shown that girls who live in societies in which they are expected to take care of younger children are more prosocial than are girls who live in societies that do not have this expectation.

Even in various industrial societies today, there are differences in cultural values regarding prosocial behaviour. For instance, Mexican American youths are more prosocial if they espouse the traditional Mexican value of *familism*—a set of norms that promotes emotional and economic interdependence within an extended network of kin—rather than mainstream U.S. norms of individualism (Armenta et al., 2011). Along similar lines, the incidence of children's sharing, helping, and comforting is higher in the traditionally collectivist cultures of Taiwan and Japan than it is in the United States (Rao & Stewart, 1999; Stevenson, 1991).

In contrast to the typically Western values of self and competition, Chinese and Japanese cultures traditionally place great emphasis on teaching children to share and to be responsible for the needs of others in the group (the family, class, or community). In Japan, there has traditionally been an emphasis on creating a "community of learners" in the elementary school classroom—that is, teaching children to respond supportively to one another's thoughts and feelings (Lewis, 1995). However, the traditional emphasis on prosocial behaviour in many Asian cultures seems to be eroding, perhaps due to increasing economic modernization and exposure to Western culture and values: Asian children have not been found to be more prosocial than Western children in several relatively recent studies (Kärtner, Keller, & Chaudhary, 2010; Trommsdorff et al., 2007).

in prosocial behaviour; and (3) by disciplining their children and eliciting prosocial behaviour from them. Parents also communicate and reinforce cultural beliefs about the value of prosocial behaviour (see Box 14.1).

Modeling and the communication of values Consistent with social-learning theory's emphasis on observation and imitation (see Chapter 9), children tend to imitate other people's helping and sharing behaviour, including even that of strangers (Eisenberg & Fabes, 1998). Children are especially likely to imitate the prosocial behaviour of adults with whom they have a positive relationship (Hart & Fegley, 1995). This may help explain the fact that parents and children tend to be similar in their levels of prosocial behaviour (Stukas, Switzer et al., 1999), although heredity may also contribute to the similarity between parent and child in sympathy and helpfulness.

In a particularly interesting study, individuals who had risked their lives to rescue Jews from the Nazis in Europe during World War II were interviewed many years later, along with "bystanders" from the same communities who had not been involved in rescue activities (Oliner & Oliner, 1988). As shown in Table 14.1, when recalling the values they had learned from their parents and other influential adults, 44% of the rescuers mentioned generosity and caring for others, whereas only 21% of bystanders mentioned the same values. Rescuers were 7 times more likely than bystanders to report that their parents taught them that values related to caring should be applied to everyone (28% of rescuers; 4% of bystanders), commenting:

TABLE 14.1 Percentage of Rescuers and Bystanders Who Reported Learning a Given Type of Value from Parents

Type of Value	Rescuers (%)	Bystanders (%)
Economic competence	19	34
Independence	6	8
Fairness/equity (including reciprocity)	44	48
Fairness/equity applied universally	14	10
Caring	44	21
Caring applied universally	28	4

Data from Oliner & Oliner (1988).

> *Rescuer 1:* They taught me to respect all human beings.
>
> *Rescuer 2:* He taught me to love my neighbor—to consider him my equal whatever his nationality or religion.
>
> (Oliner & Oliner, 1988, p. 165)

Bystanders also reported that their parents emphasized ethical obligations to family, community, church, and country, but they rarely reported that their parents emphasized their having such obligations to other people. Thus, the values parents convey to their children may influence not only *whether* children are prosocial but also *toward whom* they are prosocial.

One effective way for parents to teach their children prosocial values and behaviours is to have discussions with them that appeal to their ability to sympathize. In laboratory studies, when elementary school children heard adults explicitly point out the positive consequences of prosocial actions for others (e.g., "Poor children . . . would be so happy and excited if they could buy food and toys"), they were more likely to donate money anonymously to help other people (Eisenberg-Berg & Geisheker, 1979; Perry, Bussey, & Freiberg, 1981). Children were less likely to donate anonymously if adults simply said that helping is "good" or "nice" and did not provide sympathy-arousing rationales for helping or sharing (Eisenberg & Fabes, 1998).

Children are more likely to donate to charity if they see others donate and if adults explain to them how donating helps others. This group of schoolchildren are collecting money in support of those affected by the Fort McMurray wildfire that occurred in May 2016.

© SANDY LONG

Opportunities for prosocial activities Providing children with opportunities to engage in helpful activities can increase their willingness to take on prosocial tasks at a later time (Eisenberg et al., 1987). In the home, opportunities to help others include household tasks that are performed on a routine basis and benefit others (Richman et al., 1988; Whiting & Whiting, 1975). For example, a study of Australian and Canadian families found that performance of household tasks may foster prosocial actions directed primarily toward family members (Grusec, Goodnow, & Cohen, 1996). For adolescents, voluntary community service such as working in homeless shelters or other community agencies also can be a way of gaining experience in helping others and deepening feelings of

JIM WILKES/GETTY IMAGES

Volunteering helps children, such as these students at a food bank in Toronto, learn the value of giving back to their community, increases their self-esteem and sense of pride as they discover that they can make a difference, and gives them a broader perspective of the diverse ways in which people live.

prosocial commitment (Lawford et al., 2005; Pratt et al., 2003). Service learning, which is an educational strategy that integrates community service with instruction to promote learning, is increasingly common in middle and high schools. (Box 14.4 in the last section of this chapter examines positive youth development and service-learning programs.)

Participation in prosocial activities may also give children and adolescents opportunities to take others' perspectives, to increase their confidence that they are competent to assist others, and to experience emotional rewards for helping. A two-year longitudinal study of high school students in Ontario showed that those students who were involved in community-helping activities at age 17 subsequently placed more importance on holding prosocial values (Pratt et al., 2003). Even mandatory school-based service activities have been associated with future prosocial values (Hart et al., 2007), as well as with increased voluntary service at a later date for those high school youths who were not initially inclined to engage in such activities (Metz & Youniss, 2003). It should be noted, however, that forcing older adolescents or young adults into service activities can sometimes backfire and undermine their motivation to help (Stukas, Snyder, & Clary, 1999).

Discipline and parenting style High levels of prosocial behaviour and sympathy in children tend to be associated with constructive and supportive parenting, including authoritative parenting (Houltberg et al., 2014; Michalik et al., 2007). When parents are involved with and close to their children, the children are higher in sympathy and regulation, which in turn predicts higher levels of prosocial behaviour (Padilla-Walker & Christensen, 2011). For example, University of Toronto researchers found that the degree to which mothers were responsive to their children's distress predicted their children's empathy and prosocial behaviours toward others in distress (Davidov & Grusec, 2006). Parental support of and attachment to the child have been found to be especially predictive of prosocial behaviour for youths who are low in fearfulness (Padilla-Walker & Nelson, 2010).

It is important to note, however, that not only might supportive, authoritative parenting promote sympathy and prosocial behaviour, but prosocial, sympathetic children might also elicit more support from their parents (Miklikowska, Duriez, & Soenens 2011; Padilla-Walker et al., 2012). In contrast, a parenting style that involves physical punishment, threats, and an authoritarian approach (see Chapter 12) tends to be associated with a lack of sympathy and prosocial behaviour in children and adolescents (Houltberg et al., 2014; Laible et al., 2008).

The way in which parents attempt to directly elicit prosocial behaviour from their children is also important. If children are regularly punished for failing to engage in prosocial behaviour, they may start to believe that the reason for helping others is primarily to avoid punishment (Dix & Grusec, 1983; Hoffman, 1983). Similarly, if children are given material rewards for prosocial behaviours, they may come to believe that they helped solely for the rewards and, thus, may be less motivated to help when no rewards are offered (Warneken & Tomasello, 2008).

What does seem particularly likely to foster children's voluntary prosocial behaviour is discipline that involves reasoning (Carlo, Mestre et al., 2010).

This is especially true when the reasoning points out the consequences of the child's behaviour for others (Krevans & Gibbs, 1996) and encourages perspective taking (Farrant et al., 2012). Such reasoning also encourages sympathy for others and provides guidelines children can refer to in future situations (Henry, Sager, & Plunkett, 1996; Hoffman, 1983). Maternal use of reasoning oriented toward others (e.g., "Can you see that Tim is hurt?") seems to increase prosocial behaviour even for 1- to 2-year-olds, as long as mothers state their reasoning in an emotional tone of voice (Zahn-Waxler, Radke-Yarrow, & King, 1979). Emotion in the mother's voice likely catches her toddler's attention and communicates that she is very serious about what she is saying.

SKYNESHER/GETTY IMAGES

When adults point out the consequences of a child's transgressions against others, children are more likely to respond with sympathy and prosocial behaviour in other situations.

The combination of parental warmth and certain parenting practices—not parental warmth by itself—seems to be especially effective for fostering prosocial tendencies in children and adolescents. Therefore, children tend to be more prosocial when their parents are not only warm and supportive but also when they model prosocial behaviour, include reasoning and references to moral values and responsibilities in their discipline, and expose their children to prosocial models and activities (i.e., use authoritative parenting; Hastings et al., 2007; Janssens & Deković, 1997; Yarrow et al., 1973).

Peer influences Relationships with other children are another key way that children learn and practice moral principles, such as fairness, justice, reciprocity (e.g., sharing and taking turns), conflict resolution, and not hurting or taking advantage of others (Killen & Smetana, 2015; Turiel, 2014). This practice in moral reasoning within peer relationships translates into prosocial behaviour. A study of adolescents and their best friends found that those pairs that had the highest levels of moral reasoning also were most successful at resolving conflict (McDonald et al., 2014). Children are motivated to do nice things for their friends, both because they care about them and because doing so increases the likelihood that those friends will do nice things for them in return.

Interventions Because most of the research on the socialization of prosocial responding is correlational in design, it does not allow firm conclusions about cause-and-effect relations. However, some school interventions have been effective at promoting prosocial behaviour in children, so environmental factors must contribute to its development (see Box 14.2). The research underlying such interventions indicates that experience in helping and cooperating with others, exposure to prosocial values and behaviours, and adults' use of reasoning in discipline contribute to the development of prosocial behaviour.

REVIEW QUESTION

What is the relationship between the development of an individual's theory of mind and their tendency to engage in prosocial behaviours over the course of childhood? ■

BOX 14.2 APPLICATIONS School-Based Interventions for Promoting Prosocial Behaviour

Knowledge about the socialization of helping and sharing behaviour has been used to design school interventions aimed at fostering such behaviour. One popular approach used across Canada, as well as in Australia, New Zealand, and the United States, is Positive Behavioural Interventions and Supports (PBIS; Bradshaw, Waasdorp, & Leaf, 2012; McIntosh, 2014). PBIS is a school-wide intervention program that aims to change the overall school climate and thereby reduce negative behaviours and increase positive behaviours amongst staff and students (Sugai & Horner, 2006). PBIS is based on principles from learning theories (see Chapter 9), namely, that positive student behaviour can be increased by praising it when it does occur (i.e., behaviourism) and by having staff model such behaviour so that students will in turn imitate it (i.e., social-learning theory). To achieve these goals, some PBIS schools reward children who are "caught" behaving well; for example, children who are observed spontaneously picking up litter outside school or helping a teacher carry materials are given a voucher for a small prize, such as a treat at lunch. By paying special attention to positive behaviour rather than only noting negative behaviour, PBIS schools hope to increase the frequency of positive behaviour.

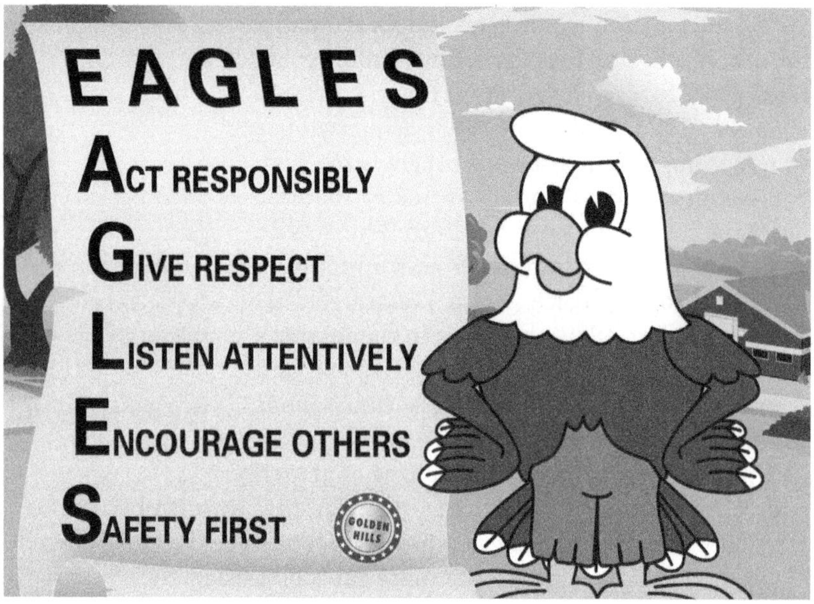

PBIS ROLL OUT KIT POSTER BY PBIS TEACHING TOOLS

Posters with positive behavioural messages are displayed throughout a school as part of the PBIS approach.

Research on prevention programs (which attempt to prevent a problem from occurring) and intervention programs (which aim to help children who already exhibit a problem) divides the programs into three levels: (1) primary prevention (targeting all children in a setting, e.g., school); (2) secondary prevention (targeting individuals at risk for developing a problem); and (3) tertiary intervention (targeting individuals who already exhibit a problem). The PBIS program uses all three levels of prevention and intervention:

1. **Primary prevention** is universal and thus aimed at all children and staff in a school. Posters that clearly state behavioural expectations are displayed around the school and are aimed directly at the students; an example of a common PBIS poster message is "Be Safe; Be Responsible; Be Respectful." School staff, including teachers, are trained to model appropriate behaviour and to praise children when they behave appropriately. This level of the intervention is aimed at preventing problem behaviours from occurring in the first place and increasing the likelihood that positive behaviours will be repeated (Sugai & Horner, 2006).
2. **Secondary prevention** is targeted toward children who are deemed at risk for problem behaviour. These children may exhibit

primary prevention a program targeting all individuals in a particular setting (e.g., a school) in order to prevent the occurrence of a problematic behaviour or condition

secondary prevention a program designed to help individuals at risk for developing a problem or condition, with the goal of preventing the problem or condition

antisocial behaviour disruptive, hostile, or aggressive behaviour that violates social norms or rules and that harms or takes advantage of others

aggression behaviour aimed at physically or emotionally harming or injuring others

Antisocial Behaviour

Pick up any newspaper or open any news site, and you are inevitably reminded of the **antisocial behaviour**—defined as disruptive, hostile, or aggressive behaviour that violates social norms or rules and that harms or takes advantage of others—from school shootings to everyday incidents of bullying and aggression. **Aggression** is a subcategory of antisocial behaviour that involves acts intended to physically or emotionally harm others (Eisner & Malti, 2015).

Why do some children and adolescents exhibit aggression and antisocial behaviour? Are youths who commit violent or antisocial acts already aggressive in childhood? How do levels of aggression change with development? What factors contribute to individual differences in children's antisocial behaviour? As we address these issues, the themes of *individual differences, nature and nurture,* the *sociocultural context,* and *research and children's welfare* will be particularly salient.

problems with attention, self-regulation, or peer interactions that the staff recognize as leading to potential behaviour problems. These children are given extra attention and monitoring from staff, who praise them when they engage in appropriate behaviour and provide reminders about expected behaviour when they do not. This level of intervention is projected to target about 15% of the student population, with the goal of reducing problem behaviour (Sugai & Horner, 2006).

3. **Tertiary intervention** is focused on children who consistently engage in inappropriate, aggressive, or antisocial behaviour. The school staff create an individualized plan for each student at this level of intervention; the plan may include interactions with school counselors, special education teachers, and other specialists. The goal at this level of intervention is to reduce the frequency and severity of problem behaviour (Sugai & Horner, 2006).

These three levels of prevention and intervention are typically thought of as a pyramid, with the largest number of children receiving primary prevention and the smallest number receiving tertiary intervention. Given that the programs and treatment involved at the level of tertiary intervention tend to be intensive and require specialized training to administer, they tend to be more expensive than primary prevention, even though they involve fewer children.

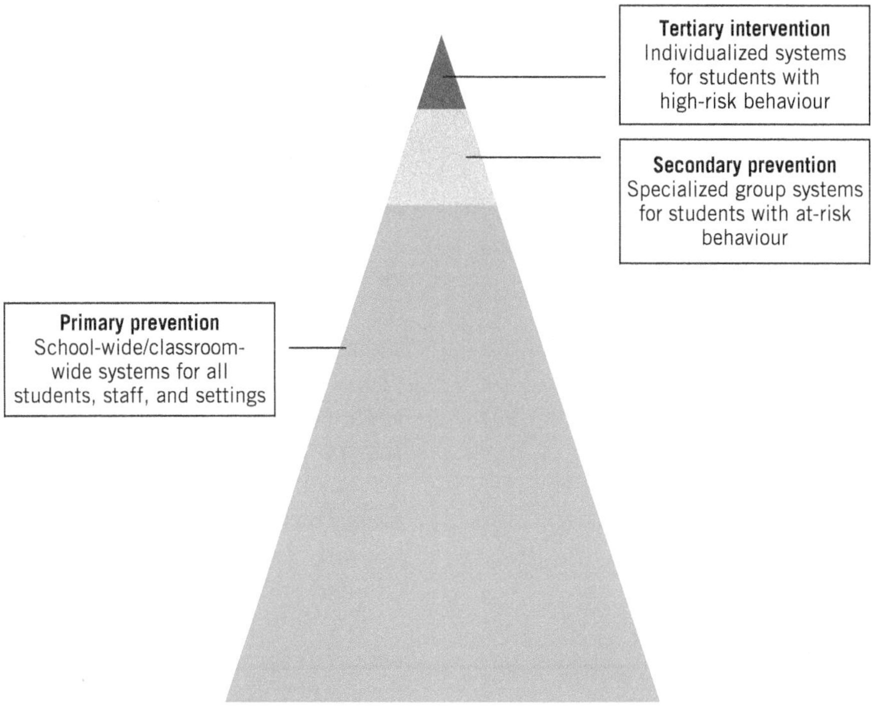

PBIS incorporates three levels of intervention to promote positive behaviour in schools. (Information from Sugai & Horner, 2006)

The effectiveness of PBIS has been evaluated systematically through research particularly in the United States. A study of PBIS in 37 elementary schools, in which schools were randomly assigned to implement PBIS or not, found that children in PBIS schools had significantly fewer attention or behaviour problems and improved prosocial behaviour up to 4 years later (Bradshaw et al., 2012). Another study of PBIS implemented in all 474 schools in the state of Maryland found that the more comprehensively a school implemented PBIS, the greater reductions it experienced in student truancy and student suspensions (Pas & Bradshaw, 2012). Importantly, PBIS was also associated in this study with significant improvements in children's math and reading achievement (Pas & Bradshaw, 2012), indicating that an intervention focused on improving student behaviour can impact student academic outcomes as well.

The Development of Antisocial Behaviours

Aggression emerges quite early. How early? Instances of aggression over possessing objects occur between infants before 12 months of age — especially behaviours such as trying to tug objects away from each other (Hay, Mundy et al., 2011) — but most do not involve bodily contact such as hitting (Coie & Dodge, 1998). Beginning around 18 months of age, physical aggression such as hitting and pushing — particularly over the possession of objects — is normative in development and increases in frequency until about age 2 or 3 (Alink et al., 2006; Hay, Hurst et al., 2011). Then, with the growth of language skills (see Chapter 6), physical aggression decreases in frequency. Results from the Quebec Newborn Twin Study suggest that physical aggression and vocabulary are negatively correlated in 19-month-olds: that is, those 19-month-olds with larger vocabularies were less likely to be physically aggressive (Dionne et al., 2003).

tertiary intervention a program designed to help individuals who already exhibit a problem or condition

instrumental aggression aggression motivated by the desire to obtain a concrete goal

As physical aggression decreases, verbal aggression, such as insults and taunting, increases (Bonica et al., 2003; Mesman et al., 2009; Miner & Clarke-Stewart, 2008).

Amongst the most frequent causes of aggression in the preschool years are conflicts between peers over possessions (Fabes & Eisenberg, 1992; Shantz, 1987) and conflict between siblings over almost anything (Abramovitch, Corter, & Lando, 1979). Conflict over possessions often is an example of **instrumental aggression,** that is, aggression motivated by the desire to obtain a concrete goal, such as gaining possession of a toy or getting a better place in line. Preschool children sometimes also use *relational aggression* (Crick, Casas, & Mosher, 1997), which, as explained in Chapter 13, is intended to harm others by damaging their peer relationships. Amongst preschoolers, this typically involves excluding peers from a play activity or a social group (Underwood, 2003). This relational aggression has been linked to theory of mind skills, particularly for children with low levels of prosocial skills (see Chapter 7 for more details on theory of mind). For instance, a longitudinal study of young children in Quebec demonstrated that theory of mind skills at age 5 predicted levels of relational aggression 1 year later, but only for children who were rated as low to average on prosocial behaviour (Renouf et al., 2010).

The drop in physical aggression in the preschool years is likely due not only to children's increasing ability to use verbal and relational aggression but also their developing ability to use language to resolve or pursue conflicts and to control their own emotions and actions (Coie & Dodge, 1998). Overt physical aggression continues to remain low or to decline in frequency for most children during elementary school, although a relatively small number of children—most of them boys (Moffitt & Caspi, 2001; NICHD Early Child Care Research Network, 2004)—develop frequent and serious problems with aggression and antisocial behaviour at this age (Campbell et al., 2010; Shaw et al., 2003) or in early adolescence (Xie, Drabick, & Chen, 2011). Whereas aggression in young children is usually instrumental (goal directed), aggression in elementary school children often is hostile, arising from the desire to hurt another person, or is motivated by the need to protect oneself against a perceived threat to self-esteem (Dodge, 1980; Hartup, 1974).

Aggressive conflicts over objects are very common amongst young children.

MYRLEEN PEARSON/PHOTOEDIT

Children who engage in physical aggression tend to also engage in relational aggression (Card et al., 2008). A study of more than 3000 Canadian children found that children between the ages of 4 and 11 years were consistent in the type of aggression they exhibited, be it physical or relational (Vaillancourt et al., 2003). Overall, the frequency of physical aggression decreases for most teenagers (Di Giunta et al., 2010; Loeber, 1982), at least after mid-adolescence (Karriker-Jaffe et al., 2008).

Despite this overall developmental trend toward less physical aggression, serious acts of violence increase markedly in mid-adolescence, as do property offences and status offences such as drinking and truancy (Lahey et al., 2000). As illustrated in Figure 14.6, adolescent violent crime peaks at age 17, when 29% of males and 12% of females report committing at least one serious violent offence. As the figure also shows,

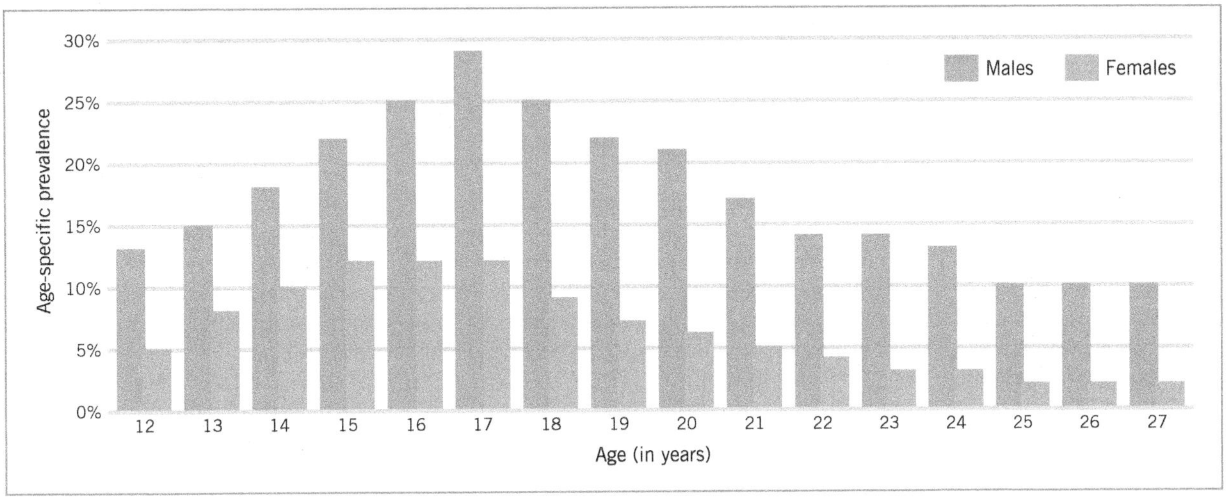

FIGURE 14.6 **Prevalence of self-reported violent crime for males and females at different ages** At all ages, males report engaging in more violent behaviour than do females. (Data from Coie & Dodge, 1998)

male adolescents and adults engage in much more violent behaviour and crime than do females (Coie & Dodge, 1998).

There is considerable consistency in individual differences in both girls' and boys' aggression across childhood and adolescence. Children who are the most aggressive and prone to antisocial behaviour such as stealing in middle childhood tend to be more aggressive and delinquent in adolescence than children who first develop conduct problems at a later age (Burt et al., 2011). This holds especially true for boys (Fontaine et al., 2009). In one classic study, children who had been identified as aggressive by their peers when they were 8 years old had more criminal convictions and engaged in more serious criminal behaviour at age 30 than did those who had not been identified as aggressive (see Figure 14.7) (Eron et al., 1987). More recently, in a 19-year longitudinal study of Quebec children, physical aggression during the early school years was the strongest predictor of criminal charges at 25 years of age (Pingault et al., 2013). Even in girls, relational aggression in childhood was related to subsequent *conduct disorders* (Keenan et al., 2010). (Conduct disorders are discussed in Box 14.3.)

Many children who are aggressive from early in life have neurological deficits (i.e., brain dysfunctions) that underlie problems such as hyperactivity and difficulty in paying attention (Eisner & Malti, 2015; Gatzke-Kopp et al., 2009). These deficits, which may become more marked with age (Aguilar et al., 2000), can result in troubled relations with parents, peers, and teachers that further fuel the child's aggressive, antisocial pattern of behaviour. Problems with attention are particularly likely to have this effect because they make it difficult for aggressive children to carefully consider all the relevant information in a social situation before deciding how to act; thus, their behaviour often is inappropriate for the situation. In addition, callous, unemotional traits, which often accompany aggression and conduct disorder (e.g., Keenan et al., 2010), appear to be associated with a delay in cortical maturation in brain areas involved in decision making, morality, and empathy (De Brito et al., 2009).

Youths who develop problem behaviours in adolescence typically stop engaging in antisocial behaviour later in adolescence or early adulthood (Moffitt, 1993a). However, some—especially those who have low impulse control, poor regulation

FIGURE 14.7 **The relation of peer-nominated aggression at age 8 to self-reported aggression at age 30** Boys and girls who were nominated as high in aggression at age 8 were higher in self-reported aggression at age 30 than were their peers who had been nominated as lower in aggression. (Data from Eron et al., 1987)

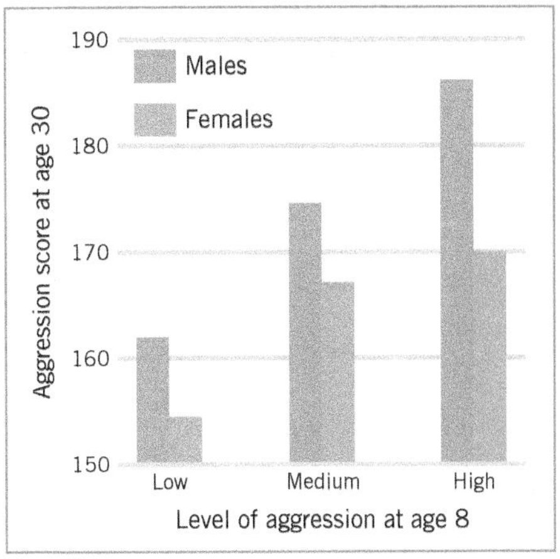

BOX 14.3 A CLOSER LOOK Oppositional Defiant Disorder and Conduct Disorder

If a child's problem behaviours become serious, the child is likely to be diagnosed by psychologists or psychiatrists as having a clinical disorder. Two such disorders that involve antisocial behaviour are *oppositional defiant disorder* and *conduct disorder*, both of which are defined in the *Diagnostic and Statistical Manual of Mental Disorders, 5th edition* (*DSM-V*: American Psychiatric Association, 2013). **Oppositional defiant disorder (ODD)** is characterized by angry, defiant behaviour that is age-inappropriate and persistent (lasting at least 6 months). Children with ODD typically lose their temper easily, arguing with adults and actively defying adults' requests or rules. They are also prone to blame others for their own mistakes or misbehaviour and are often spiteful or vindictive.

Conduct disorder (CD) includes more severe antisocial and aggressive behaviours that inflict pain on others (e.g., bullying, initiating fights, cruelty to animals) or that involve the destruction of property or the violation of the rights of others (e.g., stealing, robberies). Other diagnostic signs of CD include frequently running away from home, staying out all night before age 13 despite parental prohibitions, or being truant from school beginning prior to age 13. To warrant a diagnosis of ODD or CD, children must exhibit multiple persistent symptoms that are clearly impairing their social relationships and school performance, distinguishing them from children who display the designated behaviours on an infrequent or inconsistent basis (American Psychiatric Association, 2013).

Recent prevalence data from Ontario indicate that 7.52% of children aged 4 to 17 years have ODD and just over 1% have CD (Georgiades et al., 2019). Children and adolescents with CD often, but not always, develop ODD first (Loeber & Burke, 2011). In many instances, youth with ODD or CD also have been diagnosed with other disorders such as anxiety disorder or attention-deficit hyperactivity disorder (about half of youth with ODD or CD also have attention-deficit hyperactivity disorder) (Hinshaw & Lee, 2003). When a child is diagnosed with two distinct mental disorders, the disorders are said to be *comorbid*.

ODD and CD seem to differ somewhat in their prediction of later problem behaviours: CD has been found to predict primarily behavioural problems in early adulthood, including antisocial behaviour, whereas ODD shows stronger prediction of emotional disorders in early adulthood (Loeber & Burke, 2011; Rowe et al., 2010).

Several family- and child-level factors have been found to predict whether a child develops ODD, namely high levels of family conflict, high levels of family stress, parent depression, insecure attachment, and low self-regulation (Lavigne et al., 2019). Preschool predictors of later CD include high-intensity aggression to people and animals, destruction of property, deceitfulness, and problems with peers (Hong, Tillman, & Luby, 2015). For both disorders, it is likely that a variety of these factors jointly contribute to children's developing ODD or CD and that the most important factors vary according to the age of onset, the specific problem behaviours, and individual characteristics of the children, including their temperament and intelligence.

---

oppositional defiant disorder (ODD) a disorder characterized by age-inappropriate and persistent displays of angry, defiant, and irritable behaviours

conduct disorder (CD) a disorder that involves severe antisocial and aggressive behaviours that inflict pain on others or involve destruction of property or denial of the rights of others

of aggression, and a weak orientation toward the future (Monahan, Steinberg, Cauffman, & Mulvey, 2009)—continue to engage in troublesome behaviours and to have some problems with their mental health and substance dependence until at least their mid-20s (Moffitt et al., 2002).

The Origins of Aggression and Antisocial Behaviour

What are the causes of aggression and antisocial behaviour in children? Key contributors include genetics, socialization by family members, the influence of peers, and cultural factors.

Biological Factors

Biological factors undoubtedly contribute to individual differences in aggression, but their precise role is not very clear (Eisner & Malti, 2015). Twin studies suggest that antisocial behaviour runs in families and is partially due to genetics (Waldman et al., 2011). For example, results from the Quebec Newborn Twin study found that genetic factors accounted for the frequency and stability of physical aggression during the preschool years (Lacourse et al., 2014). In addition, heredity appears to play a stronger role in aggression in early childhood and adulthood than it does in adolescence, when environmental factors are a major contributor to it (Taylor, Iacono, & McGue, 2000). Heredity also contributes to both proactive and reactive aggression; but in terms of stability of individual differences in aggression and the association of aggression with psychopathic traits (e.g., callousness, lack of affect, including lack of remorse, and manipulativeness), the influence of heredity is greater for proactive aggression (Bezdjian et al., 2011; Tuvblad et al., 2009).

One genetically influenced contributor to aggression is difficult temperament. Children who develop problems with aggression and antisocial behaviour tend to exhibit a difficult temperament and a lack of self-regulatory skills from a very early age (Espy et al., 2011; Rothbart, 2012; Yaman et al., 2010). Similarly, preschoolers who exhibit lack of control, impulsivity, high activity level, irritability, and distractibility are prone to fighting, delinquency, and other antisocial behaviour at ages 9 through 15 years. They also are inclined toward aggression and criminal behaviour in late adolescence and, in the case of men, to violent crime in adulthood (Caspi et al., 1995; Caspi & Silva, 1995; Tremblay et al., 1994).

Some aggressive children and adolescents tend to exhibit callous personality traits, in that they feel neither guilt nor empathy nor sympathy for others (de Wied et al., 2012; Pardini & Byrd, 2012). They are often charming but insincere and insensitive. The combination of impulsivity, problems with attention, and callousness in childhood is especially likely to predict aggression, antisocial behaviour, and criminal behaviour in adolescence (Frick & Morris, 2004; Hastings et al., 2000).

Whatever their specific role, the biological correlates of aggression are most likely neither necessary nor sufficient to cause aggressive behaviour in most children. Genetic, neurological, or hormonal characteristics may put a child at risk for developing aggressive and antisocial behaviour, but whether the child becomes aggressive will depend on numerous factors, including experiences in the social world; in other words, nature and nurture both play a role.

Social Cognition

Children's aggressive behaviours are often in reaction to how they interpret social situations. As discussed in Chapter 9, aggressive children tend to interpret the world through an "aggressive" lens. They are more likely than nonaggressive children to attribute hostile motives to others in contexts in which the other person's motives and intentions are unclear; this process has been called the "hostile attributional bias" (Dodge, Lansford, & Dishion, 2006; Lansford et al., 2010; MacBrayer, Milich, & Hundley, 2003; Nelson, Mitchell, & Yang, 2008). Compared with nonaggressive peers, their goals in such social encounters are also more likely to be hostile and inappropriate to the situation, typically involving attempts to intimidate or get back at a peer (Crick & Dodge, 1994; Slaby & Guerra, 1988). For example, aggressive children are more likely to interpret an ambiguous situation—such as a child spilling a drink on them in the cafeteria—as intentional rather than accidental and to think they need to "get back at" that child (Dodge, Lansford, & Dishion, 2006). Correspondingly, when asked to come up with possible solutions to a negative social situation, aggressive children generate fewer options than do nonaggressive children, and those options are more likely to involve aggressive or disruptive behaviour (Deluty, 1985; Slaby & Guerra, 1988).

Most children are more likely to describe their own aggressive behaviour as a natural reaction to the behaviour of others than they are to describe their helping behaviours as such. For example, a study asked Canadian 7-, 11-, and 16-year-olds to describe their reasons behind a specific instance in which they hurt a friend and one in which they helped a friend. Each age group focused on their own perspective and on external constraints when explaining hurtful actions (e.g., "He crashed his sled into me"). However, each group focused on their friends' perspectives in describing the reasons behind their helpful behaviours (e.g., "He was cold without a jacket"; Recchia et al., 2015). In line with these tendencies, aggressive children and adolescents are also inclined to evaluate aggressive responses more favourably

ODILON DIMIER/AGE FOTOSTOCK

Proactive aggression (purposeful aggression not evoked by emotion) is used by children to bully others and to get what they want from them.

and prosocial responses less favourably than do their nonaggressive peers (Crick & Dodge, 1994; Fontaine et al., 2010). In part, this is because aggressive children feel more confident of their ability to perform acts of physical and verbal aggression (Barchia & Bussey, 2011), and they expect their aggressive behaviour to result in positive outcomes (e.g., getting their way) as well as to reduce negative treatment by others (Dodge et al., 1986; Perry, Perry, & Rasmussen, 1986).

Given this evidence, it is not surprising that aggressive children are predisposed to aggressive behavioural choices (Calvete & Orue, 2012; Dodge, Lansford, & Dishion, 2006). This aggressive behaviour, in turn, appears to increase children's subsequent tendency to positively evaluate aggressive interpersonal behaviours, further increasing the level of future antisocial conduct (Fontaine et al., 2008).

It is important to note, however, that although all these aspects of functioning contribute to the prediction of children's aggression, not all aggressive children exhibit the same biases in social cognition. Children who are prone to emotionally driven, hostile aggression—labelled **reactive aggression**—are particularly likely to perceive others' motives as hostile (Crick & Dodge, 1996), to initially generate aggressive responses to provocation, and to evaluate their responses as morally acceptable (Arsenio, Adams, & Gold, 2009; Dodge et al., 1997). In contrast, children who are prone to **proactive aggression**—which, like instrumental aggression, is aimed at fulfilling a need or desire—tend to anticipate more positive social consequences for aggression (Arsenio et al., 2009; Crick & Dodge, 1996; Dodge et al., 1997; Sijtsema et al., 2009).

Family Influences on Aggression and Antisocial Behaviour

Children who experience harsh or low-quality parenting are at greater risk of becoming aggressive or antisocial than are other children (Dodge, Lansford, & Dishion, 2006; Scaramella et al., 2002). For example, children from chaotic homes—characterized by a lack of order and structure, few predictable routines, and noise—tend to be relatively high in disruptive behaviour, and this relation appears not to be due to genetics (Jaffee et al., 2012). Although it is unclear to what degree poor parenting and chaotic homes, in and of themselves, may account for children's antisocial behaviour, it is clear that they comprise several factors that can promote such behaviour.

Parental punitiveness Many children whose parents often use harsh but non-abusive physical punishment are prone to problem behaviours in the early years, aggression in childhood, and criminality in adolescence and adulthood (Burnette et al., 2012; Gershoff, 2002; Gershoff, Grogan-Kaylor et al., 2010; Gershoff et al., 2012; Olson, Lopez-Duran et al., 2011). This is especially true when the parents are cold and punitive in general (Deater-Deckard & Dodge, 1997), when the child does not have an early secure attachment (Kochanska et al., 2009; Kochanska & Kim, 2012), and when the child has a difficult temperament and is chronically angry and unregulated (Kochanska & Kim, 2012; Mulvaney & Mebert, 2007; Xu, Farver, & Zhang, 2009; Yaman et al., 2010).

Although some researchers have argued that the relation between physical punishment and children's antisocial behaviour varies across racial, ethnic, and cultural groups (Deater-Deckard & Dodge, 1997), longitudinal studies with large samples have not found this to be true. One study of more than 13,000 American families found that although African American parents did spank their 5-year-olds more than did White, Latino, or Asian American families, spanking predicted increases in children's aggression over time across all four race and ethnic groups (Gershoff et al., 2012). In an international study, both spanking and

reactive aggression emotionally driven, antagonistic aggression sparked by one's perception that other people's motives are hostile

proactive aggression unemotional aggression aimed at fulfilling a need or desire yelling were associated with higher levels of aggression in children in six countries — China, India, Kenya, Italy, the Philippines, and Thailand — although this relation was weaker if children viewed such parenting as normal (Gershoff, Grogan-Kaylor et al., 2010).

Harsh or abusive punishment is also consistently associated with the development of antisocial tendencies (Deater-Deckard et al., 1995; Luntz & Widom, 1994; Weiss et al., 1992). Very harsh physical discipline appears to lead to the kinds of social cognition that are associated with aggression, such as assuming that others have hostile intentions, generating aggressive solutions to interpersonal problems, and expecting aggressive behaviour to result in positive outcomes (Alink et al., 2012; Dodge et al., 1995).

In addition, parents who use abusive punishment provide salient models of aggressive behaviour for their children to imitate (Dogan et al., 2007). Ironically, children who are subjected to such punishment are likely to be anxious or angry and therefore unlikely to attend to their parents' instructions or demands or to be motivated to behave as their parents wish (Hoffman, 1983).

PHOTOFUSION/GETTY IMAGES

There is a reciprocal relation between children's behaviour and their parents' punitive discipline. That is, children who are high in antisocial behaviour or low in self-regulation tend to elicit harsher parenting. The harsher parenting in turn elicits more problematic behaviour from the child, leading to a coercive cycle.

There is probably a reciprocal relation between children's behaviour and their parents' punitive discipline (Arim et al., 2011; Eisenberg, Fabes et al., 1999). That is, children who are high in antisocial behaviour, who exhibit psychopathic traits (e.g., are callous, unemotional, manipulative, or remorseless), or who are low in self-regulation tend to elicit harsh parenting (Lansford et al., 2009; Salihovic et al., 2012); in turn, harsh parenting increases the children's problem behaviour (Sheehan & Watson, 2008). However, some recent research suggests that harsh physical punishment has a stronger effect on children's behaviour problems than vice versa (Lansford et al., 2011).

Ineffective discipline is often evident in the pattern of troubled family interaction described by G. R. Patterson (1982, 1995; Snyder et al., 2005), discussed in Chapter 1. In this pattern, the aggression of children who are out of control may be unintentionally reinforced by parents who, once their efforts to coerce compliance have failed, give in to their children's fits of temper and demands (Snyder, Reid, & Patterson, 2003). This cycle of parents and children behaving harshly with one another is especially probable in the case of out-of-control boys, who are much more likely than other boys to react negatively to their mother's attempts to discipline them (Patterson, Reid, & Dishion, 1992). Whether maternal coercion elicits the same pattern of response from girls as from boys is not yet known because most of the relevant research has been done with boys, but there is some reason to believe that it does not (McFadyen-Ketchum et al., 1996).

The relation between punitive parenting and children's aggression can, of course, have a genetic component, as was discussed in Chapter 3. Parents whose genes predispose them to aggressive or punitive parenting will pass those genes to their children; thus, punitive parenting can be linked to antisocial and aggressive behaviour in children both directly through genes and indirectly through a conflictual and punitive home environment (Davies, Sturge-Apple et al., 2012; Dogan et al., 2007; Thornberry et al., 2003). Recall that this indirect effect of a parent's genes on a child's behaviour is called a *passive gene–environment correlation* (see Chapter 8 and Chapter 10). Both factors appear to be at play; twin studies indicate that the relation between punitive parenting and children's antisocial

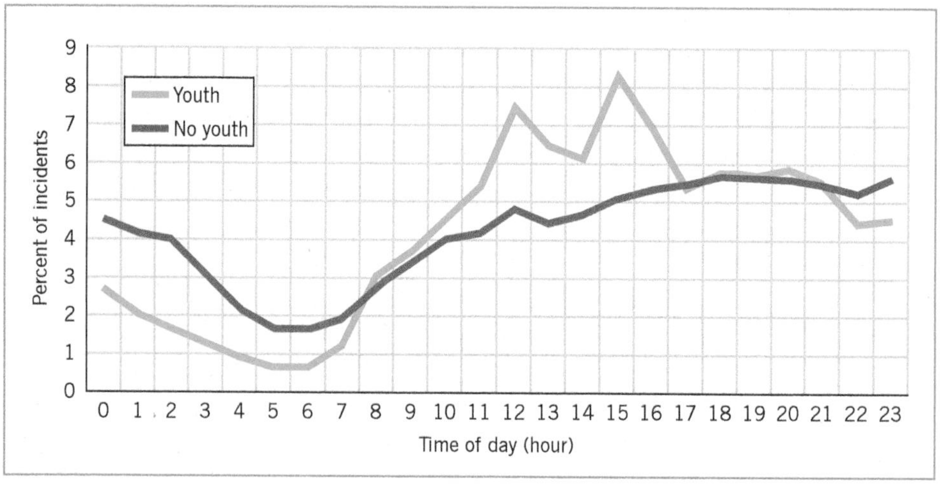

FIGURE 14.8 Crimes by time of day (weekday) Youth violent crimes occur most frequently during the noon hour and the after-school hours. Adult violent crimes do not vary dramatically by time of day. (Data from Statistics Canada, 2014)

behaviour is not entirely due to hereditary factors (Boutwell et al., 2011). Indeed, amongst monozygotic twins, the twin who receives harsher parenting and less parental warmth also develops higher levels of aggression than the co-twin (Waller et al., 2018).

Poor parental monitoring Another factor that can increase children's antisocial behaviour is parents' monitoring of where their children are, whom they are with, and what they are doing. One reason parental monitoring may be important is that it reduces the likelihood that older children and adolescents will associate with deviant, antisocial peers (Dodge et al., 2008; Patterson, Capaldi, & Bank, 1991). It also makes it more likely that parents will know whether their children are engaging in antisocial behaviour. This notion is supported by data from Statistics Canada, which finds that on weekdays, youth violent crimes peak from the noon hour to right after school (see Figure 14.8; Allen & Superle, 2016)—the potentially unsupervised hours between the end of school and when parents get home from work. Once adolescents begin engaging in aggressive and antisocial behaviours, they become even harder to monitor; parents of antisocial or aggressive youth find that monitoring can lead to such high conflict with their children that they are forced to back off (Laird et al., 2003).

Parental conflict Children who are frequently exposed to verbal and physical violence between their parents tend to be more antisocial and aggressive than other children (Cummings & Davies, 2002; Feldman, Masalha, & Derdikman-Eiron, 2010; Keller et al., 2008; Van Ryzin & Dishion, 2012). This relation holds true even when genetic factors that might have caused it are taken into account (Jaffee et al., 2002). One obvious reason is that embattled parents model aggressive behaviour for their children. Another is that children whose mothers are physically abused tend to believe that violence is an acceptable, even natural, part of family interactions (Graham-Bermann & Brescoll, 2000).

Children are more likely to develop aggressive and antisocial behaviour if they are exposed to marital conflict, especially violence. Parents who are in unhappy marriages tend to be withdrawn from and not supportive of their children, which appears to contribute to their children's problems with adjustment.

EJWHITE/GETTY IMAGES

Compared with spouses who get along well with each other, embattled spouses also tend to be less skilled and responsive, as well as more hostile and controlling, in their parenting (Buehler et al., 1997; Davies, Sturge-Apple, 2012; Emery, 1989; Gonzales et al., 2000), which, in turn, can increase their children's aggressive tendencies (Li, Putallaz, & Su, 2011). This pattern—in which marital hostility predicts hostile parenting, which, in turn, predicts children's aggression—has also been found in families with an adopted child, so these relations cannot be due solely to genes shared by parents and children (Stover et al., 2012).

Socioeconomic status and children's antisocial behaviour Children from low-income families tend to be more antisocial and aggressive than children from more prosperous homes (Goodnight et al., 2012; Keiley et al., 2000; NICHD Early Child Care Research Network, 2004; Stouthamer-Loeber et al., 2002). A large-scale Canadian study demonstrated that this pattern was particularly true for boys—that is, being male, being from an economically disadvantaged home, and having a mother with a low level of education predicted high levels of aggression for boys between 2 and 11 years of age (Côté et al., 2006). This pattern is further highlighted by the finding that when families escaped from poverty, 4- to 7-year-old children tended to become less aggressive and antisocial, whereas families' remaining in poverty or moving into poverty for the long term was associated with an increase in children's antisocial behaviour (Macmillan, McMorris, & Kruttschnitt, 2004). Many factors might account for such differences in trajectories.

One major factor is the greater number of stressors experienced by children in poor families, including stress in the family (e.g., due to illness, domestic violence, divorce, or legal problems) and neighbourhood violence (Vanfossen et al., 2010). In addition, as discussed in Chapter 12, low SES tends to be associated with living in a single-parent family or being an unplanned child of a teenage parent, and stressors of these sorts are linked to increased aggression and antisocial behaviour (Dodge, Pettit, & Bates, 1994; Linares et al., 2001; Tolan, Gorman-Smith, & Henry, 2003; Trentacosta et al., 2008). Also, because of the many stressors they face, impoverished parents are more likely than other parents to be rejecting and low in warmth; to use erratic, threatening, and harsh discipline; and to be lax in supervising their children (Conger et al., 1994; Dodge et al., 1994; Odgers et al., 2012).

Children in low-income families tend to live in low-income neighbourhoods that tend to have more violence and crime and to attend low-income schools, which are under-resourced and rate high in violence (Gershoff & Benner, 2014). Such neighbourhoods also lack appropriate mentors, job opportunities, and constructive activities (e.g., clubs and sports) that could engage children and youth and divert them from potential antisocial behaviour.

Peer Influences on Aggression and Antisocial Behaviour

As discussed in Chapter 13, aggressive children tend to socialize with other aggressive children and often become more delinquent over time if they have close friends who are aggressive. Moreover, the expression of a genetic tendency toward aggression is stronger for individuals who have aggressive friends (Brendgen et al., 2008).

Members of the larger peer group with whom older children and adolescents socialize may influence aggression even more than their close friends do (Coie & Dodge, 1998). In one study, boys exposed to peers involved in overt antisocial behaviours, such as violence and the use of a weapon, were more than 3 times as likely as other boys to engage in such acts themselves (Keenan et al., 1995). Associating with delinquent peers tends to increase delinquency because these peers model and reinforce antisocial behaviour in the peer group. At the same time, participating in delinquent activities brings adolescents into contact with more delinquent peers (Dishion, Ha, & Véronneau, 2012; Dishion, Véronneau, & Myers, 2010).

Although research findings vary somewhat, it appears that children's susceptibility to peer pressure to become involved in antisocial behaviour increases in the elementary school years peaks at about 8th or 9th grade, then declines thereafter (Berndt, 1979; Brown, Clasen, & Eicher, 1986; Steinberg & Silverberg, 1986). Although not all adolescents are susceptible to negative peer influence (Allen, Porter, & McFarland, 2006), even popular youth in early adolescence tend to increase participation in minor levels of drug use and delinquency if these behaviours are approved by peers (Allen et al., 2005).

Peer approval of relational aggression increases in middle school, and students in peer groups that are supportive of relational aggression become increasingly aggressive (Werner & Hill, 2010). However, there are exceptions to this overall pattern that appear to be related to cultural factors. For example, Mexican American immigrant youth who are less acculturated, and therefore more tied to traditional values, appear to be less susceptible to peer pressure toward antisocial behaviour than are Mexican American children who are more acculturated. Thus, it may be that peers play less of a role in promoting antisocial behaviour for adolescents who are embedded in a traditional culture oriented toward adults' expectations (e.g., deference and courtesy toward adults and adherence to adult values) (Wall, Power, & Arbona, 1993).

Biology and Socialization: Their Joint Influence on Children's Antisocial Behaviour

Recent genetically informed research illustrates that often it is a combination of genetic and environmental factors that predict children's antisocial, aggressive behaviour and that some children are more sensitive to the quality of parenting than are others. As noted in our previous discussions of differential susceptibility (see Chapter 10), children with certain gene variants related to serotonin or dopamine, which affect neurotransmission, appear to be more responsive to their environment than are children with different variants. For example, under adverse conditions (e.g., chronic stress, poor parenting, socioeconomic deprivation), children with particular variants of the serotonin transporter gene (SLC6A4), the dopamine receptor gene (DRD4), or the MAOA gene (which controls the enzyme that metabolizes serotonin and dopamine) tend to be more aggressive than children with different variants of these genes (Caspi et al., 2002; Cecil et al., 2018; Conway et al., 2012). By comparison, those same children tend to be less aggressive when they are in a supportive, resource-rich environment (Simons et al., 2011; Simons et al., 2012).

In other cases, such gene variants are related to higher risk for aggression in adverse situations like maltreatment and divorce but are not related to aggression in the absence of the adverse conditions (Cicchetti, Rogosch, & Thibodeau, 2012; Nederhof et al., 2012). Regardless of the exact nature of the gene–environment interaction, it seems clear that the degree of aggression is affected by a combination of heredity and the environment. (See Chapter 3 for further discussion of gene–environment interactions related to aggression.)

Interventions for Aggressive and Antisocial Children

Children with aggressive or antisocial problem behaviours can be successfully treated with individual psychotherapy or with a combination of psychotherapy and drug therapy (Gurnani, Ivanov, & Newcorn, 2016; Sukhodolsky et al., 2016). It is also often useful and even necessary to involve parents; interventions that teach parents how to better manage their own behaviour when interacting with their children can help reduce children's aggression and antisocial behaviour (Sukhodolsky et al., 2016).

BOX 14.4 APPLICATIONS Positive Youth Development and Service Learning

Communities and governments have long sought ways to reduce youth problem behaviours and increase positive behaviours. Beginning in the late 1800s, organizations such as Scouts Canada were established to promote leadership, citizenship, and life skills amongst youth. While such organizations continue to serve millions of young people throughout the world, a new generation of services has developed under the mantle of positive youth development.

Interventions that take a **positive youth development** approach focus attention on youths' strengths and assets, rather than on their weaknesses and deficits, and work to develop and nurture those strengths and assets (Lerner et al., 2005). The positive youth development approach emphasizes what are known as the Five Cs (Eccles & Gootman, 2002; Lerner et al., 2005):

- Competence (skill development in social, academic, cognitive, and vocational domains)
- Confidence (self-efficacy and self-worth)
- Connection (positive bonds with adults and peers in the community)
- Character (integrity and morality)
- Caring and compassion (sympathy and empathy for others)

The positive youth development approach recognizes that youth are developing within social and cultural contexts that both influence and are influenced by the youth themselves and that when youth contribute to their communities, they also benefit (Sanders & Munford, 2014). A panel convened by the National Academy of Sciences concluded that the most successful positive youth development programs are those that ensure the participants' physical and psychological safety, involve a clear structure and adult supervision, endorse positive social norms, mentor participants in skills to develop self-efficacy, and provide opportunities to belong (Eccles & Gootman, 2002). A recent meta-analysis found that positive youth development programs lead to improvements in psychological adjustment and academic outcomes (Ciocanel et al., 2017).

Service learning is a strategy for promoting positive youth development that integrates school-based instruction with community involvement in order to promote youths' civic responsibility and enhance their learning (Celio, Durlak, & Dymnicki, 2011). Service-learning programs promote positive behaviours by giving students opportunities to design and develop service projects, engage with their communities, and reflect on the benefits of their experiences, both for themselves and for the community (Chung & McBride, 2015). Participation in these activities can increase students' empathy for the needs of others, awareness of larger social issues, ability to participate in a cooperative activity, and capacity for making responsible decisions (Chung & McBride, 2015).

Dozens of research studies have examined whether service learning succeeds in promoting positive youth development. A review of 62 such studies concluded that service-learning programs at the elementary school through university levels had positive effects on youths' feelings of self-esteem and self-efficacy, attitudes toward school, civic engagement, social skills, and academic achievement (Celio et al., 2011). Students who participate in service learning also have higher grade point averages, fewer behaviour problems, and greater civic knowledge than students who do not participate in service learning (Schmidt, Shumow, & Kackar, 2007).

There is some concern that requiring youth to engage in service activities could undermine their interest, enjoyment, and intrinsic motivation to participate in volunteer work, thus counteracting any benefit that service learning may have to participants. However, when examined by researchers, no differences have been found between voluntary and mandatory service; both have positive benefits for youth (Schmidt et al., 2007). In September 1999, the Government of Ontario implemented the requirement that all high school students complete 40 hours of community involvement to graduate. A comparison of students who had to complete this requirement versus those who graduated before the requirement was enacted found that mandating community service did not have a negative influence on students' interest in and enjoyment of community engagement (Henderson et al., 2007). Furthermore, proponents of service learning argue that it can initiate habits of civic engagement and public service that will persist throughout life. The results summarized above appear to support this conclusion.

In addition to Ontario, other provinces also require high school students to engage in community service in order to graduate. For example, students in Newfoundland and Labrador must complete 30 hours of volunteering and students in the Northwest Territories must complete 25 hours. Other provinces take different approaches either by counting paid work as well as volunteer hours (e.g., British Columbia) or by offering courses where students earn credits for community service (e.g., Manitoba and Nova Scotia).

PAMELA MOORE/GETTY IMAGES

Youth who engage in service-learning projects such as cleaning up a park experience increases in self-efficacy and other positive outcomes.

There are community-based programs that aim to reduce antisocial behaviour by increasing positive behaviour through an approach called *positive youth development*. Box 14.4 presents more information about the positive youth development approach and the role played by service learning. Schools can also be settings for effective intervention with this population. For example, the Fast Track program, an intervention for children at high risk for antisocial behaviour, trained students in a special curriculum designed to promote understanding and communication of emotions, positive social behaviour, self-control, and social

positive youth development an approach to youth intervention that focuses on developing and nurturing strengths and assets rather than on correcting weaknesses and deficits

service learning a strategy for promoting positive youth development that integrates school-based instruction with community involvement in order to promote civic responsibility and enhance learning problem solving (Conduct Problems Prevention Research Group, 1999a, 1999b; Greenberg et al., 1995). Children with the most serious behaviour problems participated in an intensive intervention. The program was quite successful, with classrooms as a whole exhibiting less aggression and disruptive behaviour and a more positive atmosphere.

Numerous other programs have been used to combat bullying in schools, and many appear to reduce the incidence of bullying considerably; the more effective programs target adolescents rather than younger children (Cross et al., 2011; Salmivalli, Kärnä, & Poskiparta, 2011; Ttofi & Farrington, 2011).

REVIEW QUESTION

How does the concept of differential susceptibility explain the emergence of aggressive behaviour in some children? ■

CHAPTER SUMMARY

Moral Judgment

- Piaget delineated two age-related moral stages. In the first stage, heteronomous morality, young children tend to believe that rules are unchangeable and tend to weigh consequences more than intentions in evaluating the morality of actions. In the autonomous stage, children realize that rules are social products that can be changed, and they consider motives and intentions when evaluating behaviour. Several aspects of Piaget's theory have not held up well to scrutiny, but his theory provided the foundation for subsequent work on moral reasoning.
- Kohlberg outlined three levels of moral judgment—namely, preconventional, conventional, and postconventional—each originally containing two stages (though Stage 6 was eventually dropped from Kohlberg's scoring procedure). Kohlberg hypothesized that his sequence of stages reflects age-related, discontinuous (qualitative) changes in moral reasoning that are universal. According to Kohlberg, these changes stem from cognitive advances, particularly in perspective taking. Although there is support for the idea that higher levels of moral reasoning are related to cognitive growth, it is not clear that children's moral reasoning moves through discontinuous stages of development or develops the same way in all cultures.
- Social domain theory argues that children's moral judgments are strongly influenced by their environments, particularly by parents' socialization and by interactions with peers. This theory builds on the recognition that human social knowledge can be divided into three domains. The moral domain reflects universal concepts of fairness, justice, and rights. The societal domain includes rules and conventions dictated by a particular culture, and the personal domain pertains to individuals' choices about themselves.
- The conscience involves internalized moral standards and feelings of guilt for misbehaviour; it restrains an individual from engaging in unacceptable behaviour. The conscience develops slowly over time, beginning before age 2. Children are more likely to internalize parental standards if they are securely attached and if their parents do not rely on excessive parental power in their discipline, depending on their temperament.

Prosocial Behaviour

- Prosocial behaviour is voluntary behaviour intended to benefit another, such as helping, sharing, and comforting others.
- Prosocial behaviours emerge by the second year of life and increase in frequency with age, probably due to age-related increases in children's abilities to feel sympathy and empathy for others. Differences amongst children in these abilities contribute to individual differences in children's prosocial behaviour.
- Heredity, which contributes to differences amongst children in temperament, likely affects how empathic and prosocial children are.
- A positive parent–child relationship; authoritative parenting; the use of reasoning by parents and teachers; and exposure to prosocial models, values, and activities are associated with the development of sympathy, empathy, and prosocial behaviour. Cultural values and expectations also appear to affect the degree to which children exhibit prosocial behaviour and toward whom.
- School-based intervention programs designed to promote cooperation, perspective taking, helping, and prosocial values are associated with increased prosocial tendencies in children.

Antisocial Behaviour

- Aggressive behaviour emerges as early as the first year of life and increases in frequency during the toddler years; physical aggression starts to decline in frequency in the preschool years. In elementary school, children tend to exhibit more nonphysical aggression (e.g., relational aggression) than at younger ages, and some children increasingly engage in antisocial behaviours such as stealing.
- From preschool on, boys are more physically aggressive than girls and are more likely to engage in delinquent behaviour.
- Early individual differences in aggression and conduct problems predict antisocial behaviour in later childhood, adolescence, and adulthood.
- Biological factors that contribute to differences amongst children in temperament and neurological functioning likely affect how aggressive children become. Social cognition also affects aggression: aggressive children tend to attribute hostile motives to others and to have hostile goals themselves.
- Children's aggression is promoted by a range of environmental factors, including low parental support; chaotic families; poor monitoring; abusive, coercive, or inconsistent disciplining; and stress or conflict in the home. In addition, involvement with antisocial peers likely contributes to antisocial behaviour, although it is also likely that aggressive children seek out antisocial peers. Aggression also varies somewhat across cultures, suggesting that cultural values, norms, and socialization practices may also contribute to individual differences in aggression and antisocial behaviour.
- Children who are diagnosed with an antisocial behaviour disorder such as conduct disorder or oppositional defiant disorder display relatively severe forms of problematic behaviours.
- In high-risk schools, interventions designed to promote understanding and communication of emotions, positive social behaviour, self-control, and social problem solving can reduce the likelihood that children will develop behaviour problems, including aggression.

Test Yourself

1. According to Piaget, which of the following factors is most influential in the development of children's moral reasoning?
   a. Adult influence
   b. Interactions with peers
   c. Societal norms
   d. Heredity
2. Sarah is angry and wants to break her mother's favourite vase. However, she doesn't want to get in trouble for her actions, so she decides to punch a pillow instead. According to Kohlberg's hierarchy, Sarah's behaviour is typical of which level of moral development?
   a. Preconventional
   b. Developmental
   c. Conventional
   d. Postconventional
3. Luis does not write on his desk because the rules of the classroom forbid it, and he wants to set a good example for his classmates. According to Kohlberg's hierarchy, Luis is in which stage of moral development?
   a. Universal ethical principles
   b. Punishment and obedience orientation
   c. Instrumental and exchange orientation
   d. Social system and conscience orientation
4. According to social domain theory, at approximately what age do children begin to believe that it is more important to follow moral rules than societal conventions?
   a. 12 months
   b. 6 years
   c. 12 years
   d. 3 years
5. Prosocial behaviour is best defined as
   a. behaviour based on personal benefit.
   b. voluntary behaviour intended to benefit another.
   c. actions that contribute to society as a whole.
   d. behaviour intended to win approval.
6. Children develop a conscience
   a. through identification with the same-gender parent, at about age 4 to 6.
   b. slowly over time, and this development is affected by parental disciplinary practices.
   c. in a discontinuous process.
   d. in a standard sequence, regardless of parental practices.
7. For children with a specific variant of the gene SLC6A4, low maternal responsiveness is associated with high levels of conscience in early childhood. This pattern is an example of
   a. Piaget's stages of moral development.
   b. Kohlberg's levels of moral reasoning.
   c. goodness of fit between temperament and environment.
   d. prosocial behaviour.
8. Which of the following has been shown to influence the development of conscience?
   a. Parental discipline style
   b. Genetic factors
   c. Temperament
   d. All of the above

9. Jaden is playing with a toy car. Sam comes over and takes it from her, which makes Jaden sad. Omar watches this happen and feels sad as well. Omar is displaying what kind of emotional response?
   a. Sympathy
   b. Prosocial behaviour
   c. Altruism
   d. Empathy
10. Cooperation is a form of prosocial behaviour that may be driven by both sympathy and a child's sense of ___________.
   a. shame
   b. empathy
   c. fairness
   d. justice
11. Which of the following has been shown to influence the development of prosocial tendencies?
   a. Parental discipline style
   b. Genetic factors
   c. Temperament
   d. All of the above
12. Physical aggression is normative in development and increases in frequency beginning at around ___________ of age.
   a. 5–6 years
   b. 6 months
   c. 18 months
   d. 3 years
13. Severe antisocial and aggressive behaviours, such as cruelty to animals and patterns of bullying, are examples of
   a. conduct disorder.
   b. reactive aggression.
   c. oppositional defiant disorder.
   d. negative youth development.
14. In the school cafeteria, Lynn pushes other children out of the way in order to get ahead in the line. What type of aggression is Lynn using?
   a. Reactive
   b. Proactive
   c. Antisocial
   d. Relational
15. The youth mentoring program Big Brothers Big Sisters for at-risk youth is an example of
   a. a secondary prevention program.
   b. an aggression intervention.
   c. a positive youth development program.
   d. both A and C.

LaunchPad
macmillan learning

DON'T STOP NOW! Research shows that testing yourself is a powerful learning tool. Visit LaunchPad to access the LearningCurve adaptive quizzing system, which gives you a personalized study plan to help build your mastery of the chapter material through videos, activities, and more. **Go to launchpadworks.com.**

Critical Thinking Questions

1. Recall a recent moral dilemma in your own life. What sorts of reasoning did you use when thinking about the dilemma? On what dimensions did it differ from Kohlberg's Heinz dilemma? How might these differences have affected your reasoning about this dilemma?
2. Social domain theory emphasizes the role of the environment (nurture) in how children make moral judgments. From a social domain perspective, could a child who grew up in an environment low in morality (e.g., an abusive or neglectful home) develop into a moral person? How or why could this happen, or would it be impossible?
3. How would you design a study to determine why aggressive children and adolescents have aggressive friends? How would you determine whether aggressive youth simply choose aggressive friends or whether aggressive friends tend to make youth become more aggressive?
4. Suppose you wanted to assess children's helping behaviour that was altruistic and not due to factors such as the expectation of personal gain or concern about others' approval. How would you design a study to assess altruistic helping in 5-year-olds? How would you alter the procedure if you wanted to assess altruistic helping in 16-year-olds?
5. Using the tenets of social-learning theory (see Chapter 9), outline ways in which parents might deter the development of aggression in their children.
6. In recent decades, some advocates within the criminal justice system have pushed to try youth who commit offences as adults. Given what you have learned about moral development, should youth be considered as culpable as adults for their actions?

7. Schools are increasingly being called upon to teach children how to behave morally. What are the pros and cons of schools as settings for teaching these skills? What are the pros and cons of leaving this job solely to parents?

8. Given the pattern of juvenile violent crime peaking between 3 P.M. and 4 P.M. on school days (see Figure 14.6), what could communities do to reduce juvenile violent crime during these hours?

Key Terms

aggression, p. 508
antisocial behaviour, p. 508
conduct disorder (CD), p. 512
conscience, p. 498
instrumental aggression, p. 510
moral domain (social domain theory), p. 495
oppositional defiant disorder (ODD), p. 512
personal domain (social domain theory), p. 495
positive youth development, p. 519
primary prevention, p. 508
proactive aggression, p. 514
prosocial behaviour, p. 500
reactive aggression, p. 514
secondary prevention, p. 508
service learning, p. 519
societal domain (social domain theory), p. 495
tertiary intervention, p. 509

Answers to Test Yourself

1. b, **2.** a, **3.** d, **4.** d, **5.** b, **6.** b, **7.** c, **8.** d, **9.** d, **10.** c, **11.** d, **12.** c, **13.** a, **14.** b, **15.** d

CHAPTER

15 Gender Development

LAURIE WIGHAM/GETTY IMAGES

LAURIE WIGHAM, *Birch Lake Lagoon* (watercolour, 2015)

THEMES

NATURE AND NURTURE ▪ THE ACTIVE CHILD

THE SOCIOCULTURAL CONTEXT ▪ INDIVIDUAL DIFFERENCES

Within any group of children, individual interests, personalities, and abilities will vary. Consider four hypothetical North American 12-year-olds: Casey likes playing on the school soccer team and gets bored when sitting for too long; Taylor likes to watch science fiction programs and belongs to the school computer club; Kim likes dance classes and puts a lot of thought into what to wear each day; Alex is a cheerleader at school and babysits for extra money. You might expect that Casey and Taylor are boys and that Kim and Alex are girls. This thinking would be consistent with commonly held expectations for girls and boys in North America. In some instances, these expectations might reflect general trends amongst many boys and many girls. However, as we will explore in this chapter, empirical research challenges many widely held expectations about gender. For example, Casey or Taylor might well be girls—as many girls like sports and physical activity, as well as science fiction and computers. At the same time, Kim or Alex could be boys—as some boys enjoy dancing and dressing up, as well as belong to cheerleading squads and babysit.

The notion that girls and boys are fundamentally different in their dispositions and behaviour remains popular. The phrase "the opposite sexes" is commonly used to refer to girls and boys (and women and men). As discussed in the chapter, only a few cognitive abilities and social behaviours actually show consistent gender differences, and most of those average differences tend to be fairly small (see Table 15.1 on page 529). Even when researchers find an average gender difference in a behaviour, there is substantial overlap between the genders when individuals are considered.

For instance, take the temperamental trait of activity level (see Chapter 10). On average, boys exhibit higher activity levels than girls. However, many boys are lower in activity level than the average girl, and many girls are higher in activity level than the average boy. Thus, to understand gender development, it is important to keep in mind three points. First, girls and boys generally are not opposites; similarities are more common than differences (Hyde, 2005). Second, not all girls are alike, and not all boys are alike. There is considerable variability within each gender in abilities and behaviour. Finally, as we will explain, gender is more than simply the dichotomy of being raised as a girl or a boy (Hyde et al., 2019). At birth, children are typically labelled by doctors and parents as female or male based on their external genitalia. However, some children do not identify with the gender assigned to them at birth, or they may consider their gender identity as fluid (see Box 15.1 on page 527).

Why do many children have different gender-related preferences? Developmental psychologists generally acknowledge the combined influences of physiological, psychological, and cultural processes on gender development (Leaper, 2015a), but they differ amongst themselves in how much they stress particular factors in their explanations for observed gender differences. Some researchers argue that certain differences in females' and males' behaviour reflect underlying physiological differences that

Although this boy and girl are siblings growing up in the same household, some differences in their behaviour, attitudes, and interests are apparent. In this chapter, we compare girls' and boys' development and consider different theoretical perspectives on the development of gender differences.

JOHN GERLACH

emerged over the course of human evolution (Bjorklund & Pellegrini, 2002; Geary, 2010). In their view, average gender differences in some behaviours are partly attributable to sex-linked influences on brain structures and hormonal activity. By contrast, other psychologists place more emphasis on social and cognitive influences (Bigler & Liben, 2007; Bussey & Bandura, 1999; Martin, Ruble, & Szkrybalo, 2002; Tobin et al., 2010). They focus on the social influences of family, peers, teachers, and the culture at large, as well as on the impact of cognitive processes such as gender-related beliefs and gender identity. In general, developmental psychologists agree that gender development is a combination of *nature and nurture,* even if they might disagree on the particular factors that influence development and how they operate.

We examine two main questions in this chapter: (1) How similar or different are people based on their gender in terms of psychological variables? (2) What might account for any differences? We consider the physiological, cognitive-motivational, and cultural influences that may contribute to gender development. Next, we outline the major milestones in children's development of gender stereotypes and gender-typed behaviour. Then we compare what actually is known about the similarities and differences between girls and boys in specific areas of development, including physical development, cognitive abilities and achievement, and personality and social behaviour. But first, let's look more closely at the terms *sex* and *gender.*

Sex and Gender

Throughout our discussion, we use the terms *sex* and *gender* in distinct ways. **Sex** tends to imply innate biological origins for any differences between males and females, based on one's sex chromosomes (see Chapter 3). We usually use the term *sex* when comparing genetic females (XX) and genetic males (XY), or when referring explicitly to related physiological processes, such as the influences of sex-differentiating hormones. **Gender** refers to people's categorization of themselves or others as girls or boys (or women or men)—or possibly neither.

A variety of terms are used to distinguish amongst different gender identities. **Cisgender** refers to persons who identify with their assigned gender at birth. With few exceptions, cisgender children have been the focus of prior research on gender development. However, developmental psychologists are increasingly addressing in their research that some individuals do not identify with the gender category assigned to them at birth, a trend that we explore in Box 15.1. **Transgender** persons identify with a different gender than assigned at birth (a biological male who identifies as a girl or a biological female who identifies as a boy). **Nonbinary,** or **genderqueer,** refers to persons who do not identify exclusively with one gender category. **Gender-fluid** refers to persons who self-identify with different gender categories, depending on the context. **Bigender** refers to persons who identify with both feminine and masculine gender expressions, whereas **agender** refers to persons who do not identify with any gender category. Thus, the common notion that there are only two gender categories is being challenged through scientific evidence and people's lived experience (Hyde et al., 2019).

Although researchers are increasingly studying gender development in transgender and other non-cisgender children, there is relatively little research on these youth. Furthermore, most of the existing research with non-cisgender children has been conducted in clinical settings with an emphasis on psychological adjustment. We will address patterns of development for non-cisgender children

sex distinction between genetic females (XX) and genetic males (XY) as well as other genetic sex compositions (e.g., XO, XXY, XYY)

gender social assignment or self-categorization as "a girl" or "a boy" (or possibly both, neither, or a different category)

cisgender individuals who identify with their gender assigned at birth (or their biological sex)

transgender individuals who do not identify with the gender assigned at birth (which is typically based on their external genitalia)

nonbinary individuals who do not identify exclusively as one gender; also referred to as *genderqueer*

gender-fluid individuals who self-identify with different gender categories depending on the context

bigender individuals who identify with two genders

agender individuals who do not identify with any gender category

BOX 15.1 A CLOSER LOOK Challenges to the Gender Binary

When thinking about individuals, most people consider only two possibilities: woman or man (or girl or boy). The idea that there are only two possible categories is known as the *gender binary*. Increasingly, members of society ranging from scholars to activists have challenged this notion. Five prominent scientists — Janet Hyde, Rebecca Bigler, Daphna Joel, Charlotte Tate, and Sara van Anders — recently highlighted several problems with the gender nonbinary (Hyde et al., 2019).

First, Hyde and colleagues point out ways that scientific evidence from the field of neuroscience challenges the gender binary. They note the fallacies of thinking of sex as a *dimorphic system* — meaning that the biological system can only take one of two forms and that its effects on the brain, gender identity, or other outcomes can only take one of two forms. If sex is dimorphic, then all parts of the system must be typical of either females or males. However, neuroscience research suggests a different conclusion. Even though there are some average sex differences in brain structure, scientists do not find brain structures unique to only one sex. The human brain is a mosaic of features, some of which are more common in females and some of which are more common in males. Thus, there is no binary between having a "female brain" or a "male brain."

A second challenge comes from the field of behavioural neuroendocrinology, which studies the influence of hormones (endocrines) on brain functioning. The authors address the common belief that there are "male hormones" (such as androgens, including testosterone) and "female hormones" (such as estrogens). However, both sets of hormones are present in all humans, though there are some average sex differences in the levels of some hormones. For example, testosterone levels tend to be higher in males than females, but the average difference is small and there is overlap between females and males. Moreover, hormone levels vary depending on the situation. For example, men's testosterone levels usually decrease when engaged in nurturing parenting behaviours.

A third challenge to the gender binary is based on extensive research in the psychology of gender. As in the case of brains, behaviour is a mosaic — individuals usually exhibit a mixture of feminine-typed (i.e., more common amongst women) and masculine-typed (i.e., more common amongst men) behaviours. The authors cite one study finding that less than 1% of university students exhibited behaviours that were typical only of their self-identified gender (Hyde et al., 2019). Most people showed a mixture (e.g., a woman who plays video games *and* uses cosmetics). The reviewers also point out that meta-analyses reveal a great deal of overlap between females and males in most attitudes, abilities, and behaviours (see the section on comparisons of girls and boys later in this chapter). For instance, even though boys on average tend to prefer construction toys much more than girls, there are many girls who also like these toys and boys who do not like them.

The authors point to research with transgender and nonbinary individuals as a fourth challenge to the gender binary. Persons with transgender or nonbinary identities are found in cultures across the world, both currently and throughout history. The authors cite recent estimates that approximately 0.6% of the United States population identifies as transgender (Hyde et al., 2019). A population-based study with high school students in New Zealand found that 1.2% of students identified as transgender (Clark et al., 2014).

In their fifth challenge, Hyde and colleagues review psychology research documenting how cultural practices establish gender (or sex) as a binary category. They invoke developmental intergroup theory, also described in this chapter, to explain how environmental conditions can increase the salience of the gender binary. This process commonly occurs through cultural norms of appearance (e.g., blue for boys, pink for girls), verbal labelling (e.g., "Good morning, girls and boys"), and the use of gender categories to organize activities (e.g., gender-segregated bathrooms, toy departments, sports teams, and so on). As people notice that the world is organized in terms of this gender binary, they are more likely to stereotype others based on these categories.

Hyde and colleagues (2019) conclude that "the gender binary fundamentally misrepresents human biological and psychological states and processes" (p. 183). They propose that the emphasis on the gender binary has been an obstacle to scientific progress because it encourages a neglect of the variations within and between individuals. Furthermore, an exclusive focus on the gender binary ignores and stigmatizes individuals whose bodies or experiences do not neatly fit into the male-female dichotomy. Relatedly, the authors observe that society's attempts to force individuals to conform to the gender binary has had negative psychological consequences on transgender and nonbinary youth. At the same time, these pressures have limited cisgender youth from pursuing interests viewed as nonconforming for their gender identity.

---

when such research is available; however, in most topics related to gender development reviewed in this chapter, there is no pertinent information for children with transgender or other non-cisgender gender identities. In response to this limitation, we will periodically use the term cisgender to refer to the children being described.

Another set of terms is used to describe gender as it relates to socialization. **Gender typing** refers generally to the process of gender socialization during development. (Indeed, much of this chapter is about the gender-typing process.) **Gender-typed** refers to behaviours stereotyped for a given person's assigned gender, and **cross-gender-typed** refers to behaviours contrary to those stereotyped for a given person's assigned gender. For example, playing with dolls is gender-typed for cisgender girls and cross-gender-typed for cisgender boys. Children who are highly cross-gender-typed in relation to their assigned gender are sometimes referred to

gender typing the process of gender socialization

gender-typed behaviours stereotyped or expected for a given person's assigned gender

cross-gender-typed behaviours stereotyped or expected for the gender other than that of a given person

HILARY SWIFT/THE NEW YORK TIMES/REDUX

In recent years, developmental psychologists have begun to broaden their research to include individuals who do not identify with the gender assigned to them at birth, such as this transgender adolescent, who was born anatomically female but identifies as a transgender male.

as **gender nonconforming**. This category could include children with transgender or other non-cisgender gender identities. But the term is also used in reference to cisgender children with cross-gender-typed interests, such as a so-called tomboy—a cisgender girl who likes playing sports and dislikes playing with dolls.

Comparisons of Girls and Boys

Research has shown that only a few cognitive abilities, personality traits, and social behaviours actually show consistent gender differences—and most (but not all) of those gender differences tend to be fairly small. When evaluating group comparisons for different behaviours, it is often the case that one gender differs only *slightly* from the other: the overlap between genders is considerable, meaning that many cisgender girls and boys are similar (see Hyde, 2005). In addition, substantial variation appears within each gender: not all members of the same gender are alike. Therefore, besides knowing whether a group difference on some attribute is statistically significant—that is, unlikely to be caused by chance—it is important to consider both the *magnitude* of difference between two groups' averages and the *amount* of overlap in their distributions. This statistical index, known as **effect size**, is illustrated in Figure 15.1.

Researchers generally recognize four levels of effect sizes: *negligible* (trivial) if the two distributions overlap more than 85%; *small* but meaningful if the distributions overlap between 67% and 85% (Figure 15.1a); *medium* if the distributions overlap between 53% and 66% (Figure 15.1b); and *large* if the overlap is less than 53% (Figure 15.1c) (Cohen, 1988; Reiser & Faraggi, 1999). Moreover, some researchers refer to *very large* differences when the overlap is less than 30% (Rosenthal, 1996). Thus, sometimes even a small group difference can be statistically significant. That is, a statistically significant ($p < .05$) gender difference can have a trivial effect size!

gender nonconforming individuals who are highly cross-gender-typed in relation to their assigned gender

effect size magnitude of difference between two group's averages and the amount of overlap in their distributions

meta-analysis statistical method used to summarize average effect size and statistical significance across several research studies

Across different research studies, contradictory findings are common regarding gender differences or similarities in particular outcomes. Contradictory findings can occur because studies vary in the characteristics of their samples (e.g., participants' ages and backgrounds), the methods used (e.g., surveys, naturalistic observation, or experiments), and the situation being studied (e.g., type of play or activity, relationship amongst participants). To infer overall patterns, scientists use a statistical technique known as **meta-analysis** to summarize the average effect-size and statistical significance across studies (see Chapter 1). When available, in this section we use meta-analyses to summarize research on gender differences and similarities. Table 15.1 compiles average gender differences and effect sizes for specific behaviours. For some gender comparisons, the effect sizes are large (e.g., physical strength, toy preferences); but for most gender comparisons, the effect sizes are small or medium, and many are trivial or close to zero (e.g., math achievement, talkativeness).

Because statistically significant gender differences in cognitive abilities and social behaviours are often in the small range of effect sizes, Janet Hyde (2005)

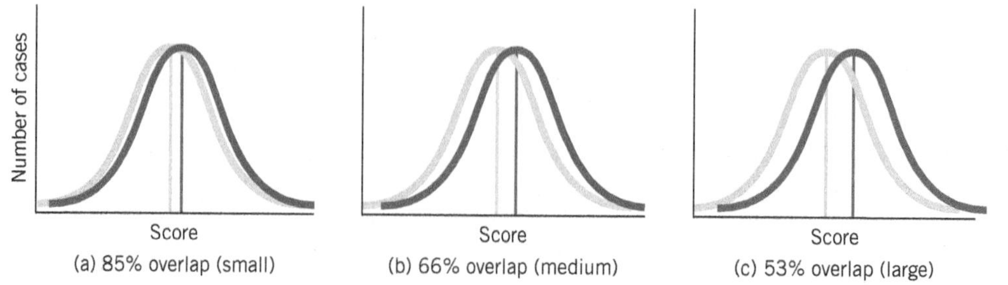

FIGURE 15.1 Effect sizes in three typical distributions of scores The effect sizes shown in graphs (a), (b), and (c) depict the overlap between males and females on three hypothetical dimensions and are typical of most gender differences. The distribution shown in yellow on each graph represents one gender, and the distribution shown in red represents the other gender. On many attributes, differences in average performance are statistically significant but very small, and the overlap between the scores for cisgender girls and boys is considerable. Note also the considerable variation on each graph within each gender, as revealed by the bell-shaped curves.

has advocated for "the gender similarities hypothesis." She argued that, when comparing girls and boys, it is important to appreciate that similarities far outweigh differences on most attributes. Later in the chapter, we review many of the topic areas addressed in Table 15.1. When discussing these research findings, we will note whether the effect size of any average gender difference in behaviour or cognition is trivial, small, medium, or large. Keep in mind, however, that even when there is a large average difference on any particular measure, many cisgender girls and boys are similar to one another. Also, some members of the group with the lower average exceed some members of the group with the higher average (see Figure 15.1). For example, there is a very large average gender difference in adult height: men are generally taller than women. At the same time, many women and men are the same height, and some women are taller than the average man.

TABLE 15.1 Summary of Average Gender Differences and Effect Sizes for Gender-Typed Cognitions and Behaviours

Statistically significant differences between two groups on any measure can range from trivial to very large. Guidelines for interpreting the effect size (magnitude of average difference) between two groups are based on the amount of overlap between the two groups' distributions of scores (see Figure 15.1). When the overlap is greater than 85%, the difference is considered *trivial*. More meaningful differences are considered *small* if the overlap is between 67% and 85%, *medium* between 53% and 66%, and *large* if less than 53% (Cohen, 1988). In this table, an overlap less than 30% indicates a *very large* difference.

Measure	Age Range	Average Finding*	Effect Size	Source
Motor Abilities				
Physical strength	Childhood	B > G	Medium	Thomas & French, 1985
	Adolescence	B > G	Very large	Thomas & French, 1985
Running speed	Childhood	B > G	Medium	Thomas & French, 1985
	Adolescence	B > G	Very large	Thomas & French, 1985
Achievement and Test Performance				
Overall school grades	Childhood and adolescence	G > B	Small	Voyer & Voyer, 2014
Overall verbal ability†	Childhood	G ≥ B	Trivial	Hyde & Linn, 1988
Reading achievement†	Childhood	G > B	Small	Nowell & Hedges, 1998; Reilly, 2012
Writing achievement†	Childhood	G > B	Medium	Nowell & Hedges, 1998
Spatial ability (mental rotation and spatial perception)	Childhood and adolescence	B > G	Small	Voyer, Voyer, & Bryden, 1995
Math achievement†	Childhood	B = G	None	Lindberg et al., 2010
		B > G	Trivial	Reilly, Neumann, & Andrews, 2015
	Adolescence	B > G	Small	Lindberg et al., 2010
		B > G	Trivial	Reilly et al., 2015
Life sciences achievement†	Adolescence	B = G	None	Halpern et al., 2007; Lindberg et al., 2010; Reilly et al., 2015
Physical sciences achievement†	Adolescence	B > G	Small	Halpern et al., 2007; Lindberg et al., 2010; Reilly et al., 2015
Gender Stereotyping	Childhood	B > G	Small	Signorella, Bigler, & Liben, 1997
Gender-Typed Play				
Preference for feminine-stereotyped toys	Childhood	G > B	Large	Todd et al., 2017
Preference for masculine-stereotyped toys	Childhood	B > G	Large	Todd et al., 2017
Rough-and-tumble play	Childhood	B > G	Large††	DiPietro, 1981
Ability Beliefs				
Athletic self-concept	Childhood and adolescence	B > G	Small	Wilgenbusch & Merrell, 1999
Verbal self-concept	Childhood and adolescence	G > B	Small	Wilgenbusch & Merrell, 1999
Math self-concept	Childhood and adolescence	B > G	Small	Wilgenbusch & Merrell, 1999; C. Huang, 2013

(continued on next page)

TABLE 15.1 Summary of Average Gender Differences and Effect Sizes for Gender-Typed Cognitions and Behaviours (continued)

Measure	Age Range	Average Finding*	Effect Size	Source
Science self-concept	Childhood and adolescence	B > G	Trivial to small	Weinburgh, 1995; Sikora & Pokropek, 2012
Computing self-concept	Childhood	B = G	None	Whitley, 1997
	Adolescence	B > G	Medium	Whitley, 1997
Personality Traits				
Activity level	Infancy	B > G	Small	Eaton & Enns, 1986
	Childhood	B > G	Medium	Eaton & Enns, 1986
Self-control	Childhood	G > B	Small to large	Else-Quest et al., 2006
Risk taking	Childhood	B > G	Small	Byrnes, Miller, & Schafer, 1999
Interpersonal Goals				
Dominance and control goals	Childhood and adolescence	B > G	Small††	Rose & Rudolph, 2006
Intimacy and support goals	Childhood and adolescence	G > B	Medium††	Rose & Rudolph, 2006
Communication with Peers				
Talkativeness	Childhood and adolescence	G = B	None	Leaper & Smith, 2004
Directive speech	Childhood and adolescence	B > G	Small	Leaper & Smith, 2004
Collaborative speech	Childhood and adolescence	G > B	Small	Leaper & Smith, 2004
Self-disclosure	Childhood	G > B	Small††	Rose & Rudolph, 2006
	Adolescence	G > B	Medium††	Rose & Rudolph, 2006
Aggression				
Direct physical aggression	Childhood and adolescence	B > G	Medium to large	Archer, 2004; Card et al., 2008
Direct verbal aggression	Childhood and adolescence	B > G	Small	Archer, 2004; Card et al., 2008
Indirect aggression	Childhood and adolescence	G ≥ B	Trivial	Card et al., 2008

*B indicates cisgender boys; G indicates cisgender girls.
†Achievement based on performance on standardized tests.
††Effect size *not* based on a meta-analysis but refers either to magnitude of difference seen in a single study or trend from a few studies summarized in the source.

REVIEW QUESTIONS

How do concepts like gender nonconformity and nonbinary gender identity challenge assumptions about child development that you have learned about up to this point in the course? How could these concepts change your thinking about the study of child development? ■

Theoretical Approaches to Gender Development

Researchers variously point to the influences of biological, cognitive-motivational, and cultural factors on gender development. First, biological differences between females and males—including the influence of sex hormones and brain structure differences—may partly account for average gender differences in some behaviours. Second, cognition and motivation—learning gender-typed roles through observation and practice—can shape children's gender development. As highlighted in cognitive-motivational explanations, boys and girls are systematically provided different role models, opportunities, and incentives for gender-typed behaviour by parents, teachers, peers, and the media. Finally, cultural factors, including the relative status of women and men in society, may shape children's gender development.

As you will see in this section, there is empirical evidence for the role of each type of influence in certain behaviours. Indeed, it is likely that most aspects of gender development result from the complex interaction of all three sets of factors.

Biological Influences

Some researchers interested in biological influences on development emphasize possible ways that gender differences in behaviour may be based partly on sex-related genetic predispositions that emerged during the course of human evolution. Other biologically oriented researchers focus more directly on identifying hormonal factors and differences in brain functioning as possible influences on gender differences in behavioural development.

Before proceeding to review some biological approaches, we want to acknowledge that trying to distinguish between biological and non-biological influences on development is potentially misleading. Notably, all behaviour and thinking are biologically based because they depend on the functioning of your brain and other organs, and all experiences lead to changes in the brain's organization (e.g., the connection of new synapses to create new memories). Nonetheless, when we refer to biological or physiological influences in this discussion, it usually refers to ways that sex-related *variations* in the physical development of the brain and the rest of the body may contribute to gender development.

Neuroscience Approaches

Researchers who take a neuroscience approach focus on testing whether and how genes, hormones, and brain functioning relate to variations in gender development (Berenbaum, 2018; Hines, 2013). Some neuroscience researchers also frame their work in terms of an evolutionary psychology perspective (Geary, 2004, 2010).

Genes As explained in the previous section, biological sex is determined by whether a person has XX (genetically female) or XY (genetically male) chromosome pairs. (There are rare conditions when a person may have a missing or an extra sex chromosome; see Box 3.1.) Some psychologists argue that females and males have genetic dispositions toward different behaviours, such as men being aggressive and women being nurturing, because they helped women and men successfully mate and protect their offspring during evolution (Benenson, 2014; Buss, 2014; Geary, 2010; Kenrick, Trost, & Sundie, 2004; see Chapter 9 for more on evolutionary theories of development). Although no research with humans has provided evidence for direct genetic influences on gender-typed behaviour, research with rodents indicates some relevant effects (Hines, 2013). For instance, studies with mice indicate links between genes on the Y chromosome and later levels of some aspects of aggressive and parenting behaviours (Hines, 2013). However, to reiterate, there are no known studies documenting direct links between genes and gender-typed behaviour in humans. As described next, there is indirect evidence of possible sex-linked genetic effects mediated by the production of hormones.

Hormones and brain functioning In the study of gender development, much attention has been paid to the possible effects of **androgens**, a class of steroid hormones that includes testosterone. Androgens are produced in the bodies of genetic females and males. As discussed in Chapter 2, around the end of the first trimester of prenatal development, the testes of genetic males increase production of particular hormones, including androgens, that lead to the formation of male genitalia in genetic males; in the absence of high levels of these hormones, female genitalia are formed in genetic females. As we will discuss later in this chapter, variations in exposure or reaction to particular hormones during the prenatal period of genetic females and males can influence the development of their sexual anatomy.

androgens class of steroid hormones that normally occur at slightly higher levels in males than in females and that affect physical development and functioning from the prenatal period onward

ASIA IMAGES GROUP/GETTY IMAGES

JOHNER/GETTY IMAGES

Amongst the most consistent average differences seen across cultures are cisgender girls' and boys' preferences for gender-typed play, as well as higher average incidences of physical aggression amongst cisgender boys than girls. However, there is variation within each gender in these trends. Also, transgender children generally show patterns of play and social behaviour that is more gender-typed for their self-identified gender than their assigned gender.

Androgens and other hormones can also have *organizing* or *activating* influences on the nervous system. **Organizing influences** occur when certain sex-linked hormones affect brain differentiation and organization during prenatal development or at puberty. For example, sex-related differences in prenatal androgens may influence the organization and functioning of the nervous system; in turn, this may be related to later average gender differences in certain play preferences (see Hines, 2013). **Activating influences** occur when fluctuations in sex-linked hormone levels influence the contemporaneous activation of certain brain and behavioural responses (Hines, 2013). For instance, the body increases androgen production in response to perceived threats, with possible implications for gender differences in aggression. These influences are discussed later in the chapter.

Brain structure and functioning Adult male and female brains show some small average differences in physical structure (Hines, 2004, 2013). However, these differences do not appear to result in any clear advantage to cognitive performance (Halpern, 2012). As noted in Box 15.1, there is a great deal of overlap between female and male brains, and no brain structures are unique to one sex (Hyde et al., 2019). Furthermore, an important limitation of research documenting sex differences in brain structure is that it is mostly based on brain-imaging studies performed on adults. Given the continual interaction of genes and experience during brain development, it is unclear to what extent any average sex differences in adult brain structure or functioning are due to genetic or environmental influences. It is also unclear to what extent these small average differences in brain structure determine any average gender differences in ability and behaviour (Halpern, 2012).

Cognitive and Motivational Influences

Cognitive theories of gender development emphasize the ways that children learn gender-typed attitudes and behaviours through observation, inference, and practice. According to these explanations, children form expectations about gender that guide their behaviour. Cognitive theories stress children's active **self-socialization:** individuals use their beliefs, expectations, and preferences to guide how they perceive the world and the actions they choose (Tobin et al., 2010). Self-socialization occurs in gender development when children seek to behave in accord with their gender identity as a girl or a boy—or possibly as transgender, gender fluid, or agender. However, cognitive theories also emphasize the role of the environment—the different role models, opportunities, and incentives that girls and boys might experience.

We next discuss four pertinent cognitive theories of gender development: cognitive developmental theory, gender schema theory, social identity theory, and social cognitive theory. As you will see, these theories complement one another in many respects (see Leaper, 2011). Some researchers have proposed theoretical models that weave together some of these approaches (for some examples, see the discussion of Integrative Theoretical Approaches later in this section).

organizing influences potential result of certain sex-linked hormones affecting brain differentiation and organization during prenatal development or at puberty

activating influences potential result of certain fluctuations in sex-linked hormone levels affecting the contemporaneous activation of the nervous system and corresponding behavioural responses

self-socialization active process during development whereby children's cognitions lead them to perceive the world and to act in accord with their expectations and beliefs

Cognitive Developmental Theory

Lawrence Kohlberg's (1966) cognitive developmental theory of gender-role development reflects a Piagetian framework (reviewed in Chapter 4). Kohlberg proposed that children actively construct knowledge about gender in the same ways that Piaget theorized children construct knowledge about the physical world. There are two distinctive contributions of Kohlberg's theory. First, he posited that children actively seek to understand the meaning of gender through observing and interacting with the world around them. (As described later, this feature is shared by other cognitive theories, including gender schema theory and social cognitive theory.) Second, Kohlberg proposed cognitive developmental changes in children's understanding of gender during early childhood.

gender identity self-identifying as a boy or a girl (or possibly as both or possibly neither)

gender stability awareness that gender remains the same over time

gender constancy realization that gender is invariant despite superficial changes in a person's appearance or behaviour

Kohlberg maintained that children's understanding of gender involves a three-stage process that occurs between approximately 2 and 6 years of age. First, by around 30 months of age, young children acquire a **gender identity**, categorizing themselves usually as either a girl or a boy (Fagot & Leinbach, 1989). However, they do not yet realize that gender is permanent. For example, young children may believe that a girl could grow up to be a father (Slaby & Frey, 1975). The second stage, which begins at about 3 or 4 years of age, is **gender stability**, wherein children come to realize that gender remains the same over time ("I'm a girl, and I'll always be a girl"). However, they are still not clear that gender is independent of superficial appearance and thus believe that a boy who has put on a dress and now looks like a girl has indeed become a girl.

The basic understanding of gender is completed in the third stage, around 6 years of age, when children achieve **gender constancy**, the understanding that gender is invariant across situations ("I'm a girl, and nothing I do will change that"). Kohlberg noted that this is the same age at which children begin to succeed on Piagetian conservation problems (see Chapter 4), and he argued that both achievements reflect the same underlying thinking processes. Kohlberg maintained that children's understanding that gender remains constant even when superficial changes occur is similar to their understanding that the amount of a substance is conserved even when its appearance is altered. For example, a ball of clay maintains the same volume after it has been mashed flat; in a similar manner, a girl remains the same gender after she gets her hair cut short and starts wearing baseball shirts. According to Kohlberg, once gender constancy is attained, children begin to seek out and attend to same-gender models to learn how to behave ("Since I'm a girl, I should like to do girl things, so I need to find out what those are").

The Boy Who Was a Girl

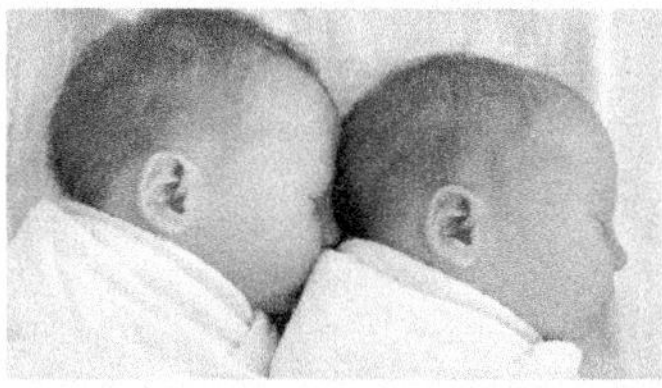

VIDEO MATERIAL IS PROVIDED BY BBC MOTIONGALLERY AND CBS NEWS ARCHIVES AND PRODUCED BY PRINCETON ACADEMIC RESOURCES. [DR. MONEY AND THE BOY WITH NO PENIS, HORIZON, BBC

Subsequent research has supported the idea that children's understanding of gender develops in the sequence Kohlberg hypothesized and that the attainment of gender constancy occurs at more or less the same age as success on conservation problems. Some studies also indicate that acquiring gender constancy might increase the likelihood of some gender-typed behaviours (Martin et al., 2002; Halim & Ruble, 2010). That is, once most children consolidate their understanding of gender, they tend to use their gender concepts to interpret the world. Gender schema theory, reviewed next, also addresses ways whereby attaining a concept of gender can affect children's gender development.

Kohlberg did not consider the possibility of children with transgender or nonbinary gender identities. Recent research studying 5-year-olds found that the gender identities of transgender children were equally as strong as those of

ROBERT DALY/GETTY IMAGES

As predicted by cognitive theories, children learn a great deal about gender roles by observing other people. Television, movies, and video games provide many examples of gender stereotypes for both sexes.

cisgender children—transgender girls were similar to cisgender girls in their gender identities, while transgender boys were similar to cisgender boys (Olson & Gülgöz, 2018). This research challenges the belief that transgender children are confused in their gender identity. With regard to gender constancy, it was observed that transgender children were more likely than cisgender children to express the view that a person's gender could sometimes change (Olson & Gülgöz, 2018). This is not surprising given transgender children's own experience with gender identity. Interestingly, the cisgender siblings of the transgender children in this study were also more likely to believe a person's gender could sometimes change—perhaps due to their own experience observing their transgender sibling.

Gender Schema Theory

Gender schema theory is an alternative to Kohlberg's explanation of children's gender development (e.g., Liben & Signorella, 1980; Martin & Halverson, 1981). In contrast to Kohlberg's view that gender-typed interests emerge after gender constancy is achieved, gender schema theory holds that the motivation to enact gender-typed behaviour begins as soon as children can label other people's and their own gender—in other words, usually by about 3 years of age (see Martin et al., 2002), which is younger than when gender constancy is attained.

According to gender schema theory, children's understanding of gender develops through their construction of **gender schemas**, which are mental representations that incorporate everything the child knows about gender. Gender schemas include memories of one's own experiences with males and females, gender stereotypes transmitted directly by adults and peers ("boys don't cry," "girls play with dolls"), and messages conveyed indirectly through the media. Children use an *ingroup/outgroup* gender schema to classify other people as being either "the same as me" or not. The motivation for cognitive consistency leads them to prefer, pay attention to, and remember more about others of their own gender. As a consequence, an *own-gender schema* is formed, consisting of detailed knowledge about how to do things that are consistent with one's own gender. Simply learning that an unfamiliar object is "for my gender" makes children like it more. Figure 15.2 illustrates how this process leads children to acquire greater knowledge and expertise with gender-consistent entities.

In one illustrative study that tested the impact of gender schemas on children's information processing, researchers presented 4- to 9-year-olds with three boxes (Bradbard et al., 1986). Each box contained objects unfamiliar to the children, and each box was separately labelled as "boys," "girls," or "boys and girls/girls and boys." The children spent more time exploring objects in boxes labelled for their own gender (or for both genders) than objects in the box labelled only for the other gender. One week later, not surprisingly, they remembered more details about the objects they had explored than about the ones with which they had spent less time. Another observational study conducted in a preschool classroom demonstrated the influence of same-gender peers in determinations of gender-appropriate behaviour. Boys approached toys that were being played with primarily by boys and shunned those that seemed popular mainly with girls (Shell & Eisenberg, 1990).

gender schemas organized mental representations (concepts, beliefs, memories) about gender, including gender stereotypes

Gender schemas are also responsible for *biased* processing and remembering of information about gender. Consistent with the research described previously,

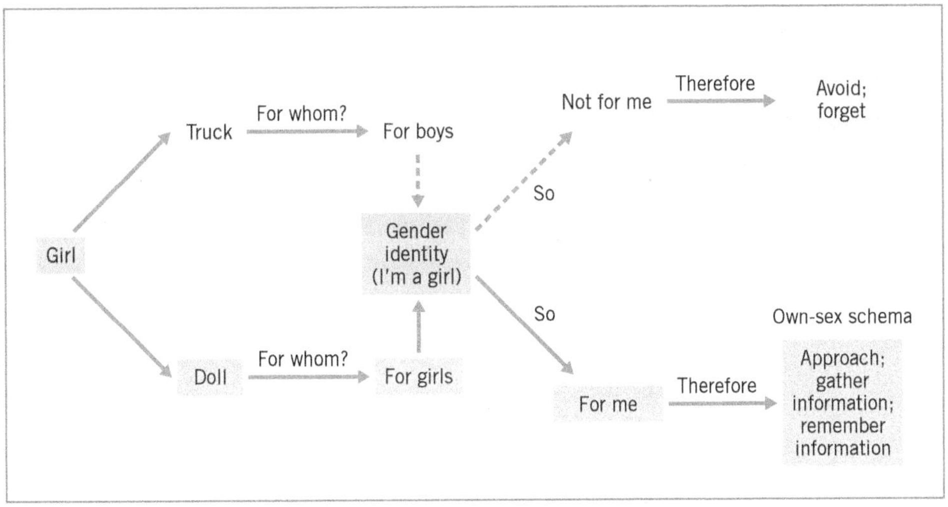

FIGURE 15.2 Gender schema theory According to gender schema theory, children classify new objects and activities as "for boys" or "for girls." They tend to investigate objects and activities that are relevant to their gender and to ignore those that are associated with the other gender.

studies show that children tend to remember more about what they observe from same-gender role models than from different-gender ones (see Blakemore, Berenbaum, & Liben, 2009; Martin et al., 2002). They are also more likely to accurately encode and remember information about story characters that behave in gender-consistent ways and to forget or distort information that is gender-inconsistent (Blakemore et al., 2009; Liben & Signorella, 1993; Martin et al., 2002). For example, in one study children were shown a series of pictures that included a combination of gender-typed images (e.g., a girl baking cookies) and cross-gender-typed images (e.g., a girl sawing wood) (Martin & Halverson, 1983). When they were later asked to recall the pictures, they showed a greater tendency to mistakenly recall cross-gender-typed images as gender-typed (e.g., remembering a picture of a girl sawing wood as a boy sawing wood) than the reverse (e.g., remembering a picture of a girl baking cookies as a boy baking cookies). This tendency to retain information that is schema-consistent and to ignore or distort schema-inconsistent information helps to perpetuate gender stereotypes that have little or no basis in reality. Furthermore, this process can perpetuate thinking about gender as a dichotomous category.

Liben and Bigler (2002) proposed that children use two kinds of filters when processing information about the world. One is a **gender schema filter** ("Is this information relevant for my gender?") and the other is an **interest filter** ("Is this information interesting?"). When encountering a new toy, for example, children might decide that it is something for girls or for boys and thus explore or ignore the toy on the basis of their gender schema filter (as depicted in Figure 15.2). However, Liben and Bigler noted that children sometimes find a new toy attractive without initially evaluating its appropriateness for their gender. In these instances, they use their interest filter to evaluate information. In turn, children sometimes use their interest filter to modify their gender schemas ("If I like this toy, it must be something that is okay for my gender"). Liben and Bigler's modification to gender schema theory helps to account for findings indicating that children are often inconsistent in their gender-typed interests (Liben & Bigler, 2002; Tobin et al., 2010). (For example, they are often more traditional in some areas than others.) It also allows for the fact that some children actively pursue certain cross-gender-typed activities simply because they enjoy them.

gender schema filter initial evaluation of information as relevant for one's own gender

interest filter initial evaluation of information as being personally interesting

Recent research finds that some (but not all) children have intense interests in particular toys, objects, or activities in early childhood. For some children,

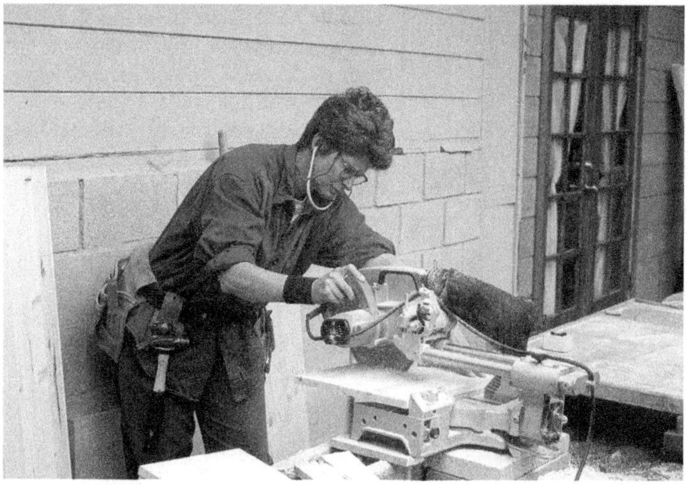

BONNIE KAMIN/PHOTOEDIT

Children's stereotyped beliefs about gender can be changed through cognitive intervention programs. Many children who learned that a person's interests and abilities were important for the kind of job the person could have showed significant reductions in gender stereotyping.

these intense interests are gender-typed, such as when a girl displays a strong interest in wearing frilly dresses and princesses or a boy demonstrates intense interest in dinosaurs or mechanical toys (DeLoache, Simcock, & Macari, 2007; Halim et al., 2014; Johnson et al., 2004). In these cases, their interests are compatible with gender-stereotyped expectations. However, some other children have intense interests in cross-gender-typed toys and activities (VanderLaan et al., 2015), such as a boy with strong interest in dress-up play or a girl with a strong preference for physical play. In these cases, the interest filter may override the gender schema filter (Leaper, 2018). That is, these children may decide to engage in the toy or activity even though they recognize it conflicts with social expectations for their assigned gender. Moreover, if the discrepancy between gender-role pressures and strong personal interests is too great, some of these children may come to identify with a more compatible gender category (see Leaper, 2018).

Although gender schemas are resistant to change, they can be modified in many children through explicit instruction and encouragement. Such an approach was demonstrated by Bigler and Liben, who created a cognitive intervention program in which elementary school children learned that a person's interests and abilities (but not gender) are important for the kind of job that the person could have (Bigler & Liben, 1990; Liben & Bigler, 1987). (The children were encouraged to see, for instance, that if Mary was strong and liked to build things, a good job for her would be to work as a carpenter.) Children who participated in this week-long program showed decreased gender stereotyping and also had better memory for gender-inconsistent stimuli (such as a picture of a girl holding a hammer). However, a limitation of interventions aimed at reducing gender stereotyping is that their impact typically fades once the intervention ends (Bigler, 1999). That is, children gradually revert back to their old gender stereotypes. Given the pervasiveness of gender stereotyping in children's everyday lives, cognitive interventions need to be sustained to have a longer-lasting effect.

Social Cognitive Theory

Kay Bussey and Albert Bandura (1999, 2004) proposed a theory of gender development based on Bandura's (1986, 1997) social cognitive theory (see pages 322–323). The theory depicts a *triadic model of reciprocal causation* amongst personal factors, environmental factors, and behaviour patterns. Personal factors include cognitive, motivational, and biological processes. Although the theory acknowledges the potential influence of biological factors, it primarily addresses cognition and motivation. Amongst its key features are sociocognitive modes of learning and self-regulatory processes.

According to social cognitive theory, learning occurs through *tuition, enactive experience,* and *observation.* **Tuition** refers to direct teaching during gender socialization, such as a father showing his son how to throw a baseball, or a mother teaching her daughter how to change a baby's diaper. **Enactive experience** occurs when children learn to guide their behaviour by taking into account the reactions their past behaviour has evoked in others. For instance, girls and boys usually receive positive reactions for behaviours that are gender-stereotypical and negative reactions for behaviours that are counter-stereotypical (Bussey & Bandura, 1999;

tuition learning through direct teaching

enactive experience learning to take into account the reactions one's past behaviour has evoked in others

Harris, 1995; Witt, 2000); they tend to use this feedback to regulate their behaviour in relevant situations. Finally, **observational learning**—the most common form of learning—occurs through seeing and encoding the consequences other people experience as a result of children's own actions. Thus, children learn a great deal about gender simply through observing the behaviour of their parents, siblings, teachers, and peers. They also learn about gender roles through media such as television, films, the Internet, and video games (see Box 15.2).

observational learning learning through watching other people and the consequences others experience as a result of their actions

Observational learning of gender-role information involves four key processes: attention, memory, production, and motivation. To learn new information, it must,

BOX 15.2 APPLICATIONS Where Are Spongesally Squarepants and Curious Jane?

Differences in the gender representation of TV, movie, and video game characters have been well documented, are very large, and have changed surprisingly little over the past four decades (Geena Davis Institute on Gender in Media, 2019; Leaper et al., 2002; Scharrer, 2013; Signorielli, 2012). Fictional characters in TV, movies, and other electronic media are commonly depicted in gender-stereotypical ways in terms of behaviour, roles, and appearance (Kirsch & Murnen, 2015; Signorielli, 2012; Walsh & Leaper, in press). For example, male characters are disproportionally portrayed as heroes, powerful, aggressive, and active; in contrast, female characters are more often shown as victims needing saving, nurturing, and concerned with romance and their appearance (Kirsch & Murnen, 2015; Signorielli, 2012; Walsh & Leaper, in press). Also, one content analysis found that boys in children's TV programs were commonly depicted as objectifying girls for their appearance, whereas girls were shown to be self-objectifying and "ego-stroking" of boys (Kirsch & Murnen, 2015).

Another striking trend is that male characters are typically overrepresented in television programs aimed at children, teens, and adults (Geena Davis Institute on Gender in Media, 2019). For example, according to one analysis of TV and movie characters, the prevalence of female characters was 28% in family films, 39% in prime-time television programs, and 31% in children's shows (Smith et al., 2013a; also see Leaper et al., 2002; Walsh & Leaper, in press, for similar results).

Portrayals of sexual minority, transgender, nonbinary, or gender-fluid characters remain rare in television or other mass media aimed at children (Kelso, 2015). However, in recent years, there have been a few exceptions, including the cartoons *Adventure Time* and *Steven Universe* (Jane, 2015). Although television may provide limited representations of gender-nonconforming youth, the Internet offers a wide variety of sites that are supportive of LGBTQ youth as they explore their identities (Craig et al., 2015; Drabbie, Keatley, & Marcelle, 2006). However, all forms of media (including television, movies, and the Internet) also provide misleading and negative messages (Drabbie et al., 2006).

From the perspectives of cognitive-motivational theories, the fact that children have so much exposure to highly stereotyped gender models matters a great deal. For example, children who watch a lot of televised and online programs have more highly stereotypic beliefs about males and females and prefer gender-typed activities to a greater extent than do children who are less avid viewers (Oppliger, 2007). Furthermore, several experimental studies have established a causal relation between TV viewing and gender stereotyping (Oppliger, 2007). For instance, when children are randomly assigned to watch shows with either gender-stereotyped or neutral content, they are more likely to endorse gender stereotypes themselves after watching the gender-stereotyped programs.

Children are, of course, exposed to media other than television, but similar gender disparities have been documented in those areas as well. For example, children's books still contain far more male than female characters, and characters of both sexes are often portrayed in gender-stereotypic ways. Males tend to be depicted as active and effective in the world at large, whereas females are frequently passive and prone to problems that require the help of males to solve (DeWitt, Cready, & Seward, 2013; Diekman & Murnen, 2004; Gooden & Gooden, 2001; Hamilton et al., 2006). Thus, although it is now possible to find more counter-stereotypical role models in children's media, most female and male characters continue to be gender-stereotyped.

Computer and online games are beginning to displace television as the primary source of children's media entertainment. Unfortunately, like television programming, many computer games portray gender in highly stereotyped ways (Downs & Smith, 2010; Scharrer, 2013). Most characters are male, and they commonly engage in highly aggressive acts; and when female characters are present, they are commonly portrayed in highly sexualized ways (e.g., Lara Croft in *Tomb Raider*).

ANDREYPOPOV/GETTY IMAGES

Computer and online games are beginning to displace television as the primary source of children's media entertainment. Unfortunately, like television programming, many computer games portray the sexes in highly stereotyped ways.

of course, be *attended* to (noticed) and then stored in *memory*. As we have noted, children often notice information that is consistent with their existing gender stereotypes. (This is the main premise of gender schema theory.) Next, children need to practice the behaviour (i.e., *production*) they have observed (assuming that the behaviour is within their capabilities). For example, cisgender girls and boys tend to practice different behaviours in play and recreation (Todd et al., 2017; Weisgram & Dinella, 2018). Finally, children's *motivation* to repeat a gender-typed behaviour will depend on the incentives or disincentives they experience relative to the behaviour. These sanctions can be experienced either directly (as when a parent praises a daughter for helping to prepare dinner) or indirectly (as when a boy observes another boy getting teased for playing with a doll). Over time, external sanctions are usually internalized as personal standards and become self-sanctions that motivate and regulate behaviour.

According to social cognitive theory, gender development becomes a process of self-regulations (or self-socialization), whereby children monitor their behaviour and evaluate how well it matches personal standards. After making this evaluation, children may feel pride or shame, depending on whether they meet their standards. When individuals experience positive self-reactions for their behaviour, they gain the sense of personal agency referred to as *self-efficacy*. Self-efficacy can develop gradually through practice (as when a son regularly plays catch with his father), through social modelling (as when a girl observes a female friend do well in math and thinks that maybe she could do well herself), and by social persuasion (as when a coach gives a pep talk to push the boys' performances on the soccer field). Researchers consistently find a strong relation between feelings of self-efficacy and motivation. For example, self-efficacy in math predicts the likelihood of girls as well as boys to take advanced math courses (Stevens et al., 2007).

Social Identity Theory

Henri Tajfel and John Turner's (1979) social identity theory addresses the influence of group membership on people's self-concepts and behaviour with others. Developmental psychologists have applied the theory to understand how group processes contribute to children's socialization and to highlight the importance of gender as a social identity in children's development (e.g., Bigler & Liben, 2007; Harris, 1995; Leaper, 2000; Nesdale, 2007; Powlishta, 1995). Indeed, gender may be the *most* central social identity in most children's lives because it is used to organize social life in every culture (Bem, 1993). Children's commitment to gender as a social identity is most readily apparent through their primary affiliation with same-gender peers (Leaper, 1994; Maccoby, 1998).

Two influential processes that occur when a person commits to an ingroup are *ingroup bias* and *ingroup assimilation*. **Ingroup bias** refers to the tendency to evaluate individuals and characteristics associated with the ingroup more positively than or as superior to those associated with the outgroup. For example, Kimberly Powlishta (1995) observed that children showed same-gender favouritism when rating peers on likeability and favourable traits. Ingroup bias is related to the process of **ingroup assimilation**, whereby individuals are socialized to conform to the group's norms. That is, peers expect ingroup members to demonstrate the characteristics that define the ingroup. Children anticipate ingroup approval for preferring same-gender peers and same-gender-typed activities, as well as for avoiding other-gender peers and cross-gender-typed activities (Banerjee & Lintern, 2000; Martin et al., 1999). As a result, children tend to become more gender-typed in their preferences as they assimilate into their same-gender peer groups (Martin & Fabes, 2001).

ingroup bias tendency to evaluate individuals and characteristics of the ingroup more positively than or as superior to those of the outgroup

ingroup assimilation process whereby individuals are socialized to conform to the group's norms, demonstrating the characteristics that define the ingroup

intersectionality the interconnection of social identities such as gender, race, ethnicity, sexual orientation, and class, especially in relation to overlapping experiences of discrimination and disadvantage

A corollary of social identity theory is that the characteristics associated with a high-status group are typically valued more than are those of a low-status group. In male-dominated societies, masculine-stereotyped attributes such as assertiveness and competition tend to be valued more highly than feminine-stereotyped attributes such as affiliation and nurturance (Feinman, 1981; Wood & Eagly, 2002). Related to this pattern is the tendency of cross-gender-typed behaviour to be more common amongst girls than amongst boys. Indeed, masculine-stereotyped behaviour in a girl can sometimes enhance her status, whereas feminine-stereotyped behaviour in a boy typically tarnishes his status (see Feinman, 1981; Leaper, 1994).

Social identity theory helps to explain why gender-typing pressures tend to be more rigid for boys than for girls (Leaper, 2000). Members of high-status groups, for example, are usually more invested in maintaining group boundaries than are members of low-status groups. In most societies, males are accorded greater status and power than are females (Wood & Eagly, 2012). Consistent with social identity theory, boys are more likely than girls to initiate and maintain role and group boundaries (Fagot, 1977; Sroufe et al., 1993). Boys are also more likely to endorse gender stereotypes (Rowley et al., 2007) and to hold sexist attitudes (Brown & Bigler, 2004).

Of course, gender is not the only social identity that shapes people's lives. As discussed in Chapter 11, many people identify with social groups based on race/ethnicity, religion, sexual orientation, social class, club membership, and so forth. Moreover, developmental psychologists are increasingly trying to understand how the intersection of multiple identities affects a person's experiences. This phenomenon is known as **intersectionality** (Cole, 2009; Mays & Ghavami, 2018). For instance, the expectations for a girl or a boy in a suburban upper-middle-class family may differ somewhat from the expectations in a poor or working-class family in an inner city. In the latter context, there may be more housework and childcare responsibilities assigned to girls in the home than would be seen in wealthier communities (Bornstein et al., 2016; Hilton & Haldeman, 1991). Also, in the poor inner-city environment, establishing one's physical and emotional toughness may be more fundamental to boys' gender identity than it would be in the suburbs; correspondingly, concerns with toughness may undermine boys' academic motivation more often in these communities than in higher-income suburbs (Anderson, 1999; Farkas & Leaper, 2016). Furthermore, as highlighted by the intersectionality approach, individuals can experience biases from multiple group identities (e.g., gender, ethnicity/race, sexual orientation, class, religion, and so on). When youth experience harassment and discrimination based on multiple group identities, it generally compounds the negative effects on their adjustment (Bucchianeri et al., 2014).

Integrative Theoretical Approaches

Most behaviours reflect the influences of physiological, cognitive, motivational, situational, and cultural processes over time. Hence, psychology theories tend to focus on one or a few of these processes. But there is room for increased synthesis across theories that are similar or complementary in their explanations (see Leaper, 2011). Two recent efforts in the developmental psychology of gender illustrate this theoretical synthesis: developmental intergroup theory and the gender self-socialization model.

Rebecca Bigler and Lynn Liben's *developmental intergroup theory (DIT)* integrates ideas from cognitive-developmental theory, gender schema theory, and social identity theory (Bigler & Liben, 2006, 2007). DIT, which was discussed in Box 15.1, highlights three key processes that contribute to the development of stereotyping and prejudice based on a person's gender (or other social identities): establishing the psychological salience of gender, categorizing individuals based on their gender, and developing stereotypes and prejudices based on this categorization.

Bigler and Liben reviewed ways in which the *psychological salience of gender* is commonly established in people's everyday lives. (Salience refers to how readily we notice something.) One way to increase the salience of gender is to make it a perceptually distinctive attribute about persons. Familiar examples include the uses of gender-differentiated colours (pink versus blue), as well as hair and clothing styles. Another common practice is to use gender labels to categorize events in our daily lives. For example, in the English language, we are typically compelled to refer to others based on their gender through the use of gendered nouns ("girl," "boy") and pronouns ("he," "she"). In other languages, such as Spanish and French, the nouns are also gendered as feminine or masculine (e.g., "ami" or "amie").

Also, many activities in children's lives are organized by gender; these range from gender-designated bathrooms to gender-segregated sports teams to single-gender schools (Leaper, 2015a). To mitigate the psychological salience of gender, some psychologists argue for changes such as dressing children in gender-neutral clothing, using gender-neutral language, and avoiding practices that unnecessarily organize children's activities based on gender (Bigler & Leaper, 2015; Bigler & Liben, 2006, 2007; Leaper, 2000).

Once the psychological salience of gender is established, the stage is set for stereotyping and prejudice. Bigler and Liben incorporate several cognitive processes previously addressed in cognitive developmental theory and social identity theory to explain how this occurs. For example, as articulated in social identity theory, this includes ingroup bias when people tend to favour characteristics associated with their own gender group (e.g., Powlishta, 1995). Another is known as *essentialism,* introduced in Chapter 7, which refers to the tendency to believe that members of a category (such as a gender group) share important qualities that make them distinct from other categories (or groups). Thus, children may view girls and boys as having inherently different traits and abilities.

Another integrative theoretical model recently introduced is David Perry and his colleagues' *gender self-socialization model (GSSM),* which bridges gender schema theory, social cognitive theory, social identity, and other theoretical approaches (Tobin et al., 2010). As with cognitive theories in general, the GSSM emphasizes how much of gender development is a process of self-socialization (Tobin et al., 2010). That is, children seek to discover their identities in relation to their understandings of the world around them. In turn, they often adapt their behaviour to match these understandings, as when they try to conform to expected norms for their gender.

In addition to incorporating ideas from gender schema theory and social identity theory, the GSSM builds on balanced identity theory from social psychology (Greenwald et al., 2002). The latter theory is based on the premise that individuals seek to attain cognitive consistency across their group identities (e.g., "I am a girl"), personal-social attributes (e.g., "I like playing dolls"), and group-attribute beliefs (e.g., "Girls play with dolls"). This model is depicted in Figure 15.3.

In their GSSM, Perry and his colleagues proposed three hypothesized ways that this balance tends to occur during gender development. First, the *stereotype emulation hypothesis* proposes that the more children identify with their gender ingroup, the more motivated they will be to adhere to the stereotypes for their gender ingroup. For example, if belonging to his same-gender peer group is important for a boy, then he might be especially prone to engage in the kinds of activities and behavioural styles expected amongst his peers. Second, the *stereotype construction hypothesis* specifies that children are apt to form generalized beliefs or stereotypes about their gender ingroup based on their own personal-social attributes. For instance, a child who likes dress-up play and identifies as a girl may assume playing dress-up is something that other girls like. Finally, the *identity construction hypothesis* states that children are more likely to identify with their gender ingroup when their own personal-social attributes match their stereotyped beliefs about their gender ingroup. For example, a boy may form a stronger gender identity if he likes playing sports and he also stereotypes sports as something for boys. This may strengthen a facet of gender identity known as *felt gender typicality*, or a sense of belonging to one's gender ingroup.

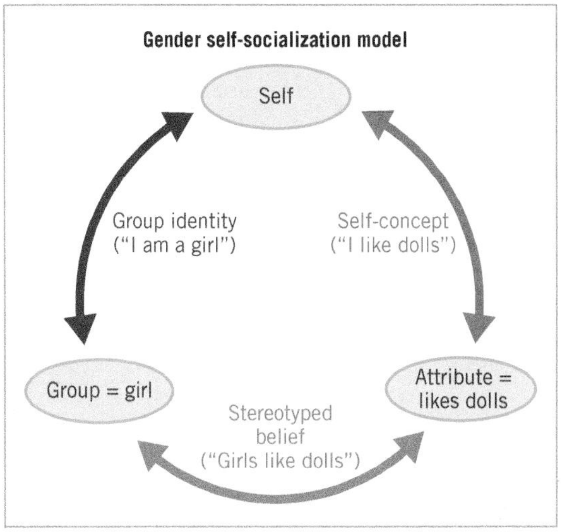

FIGURE 15.3 Depiction of the Gender Self-Socialization Model (GSSM) The GSSM is based on the premise that children seek consistency across their group identities (e.g., "I am a girl"), self-concepts ("I like playing with dolls"), and group stereotypes ("Girls like dolls"). (Information from Tobin et al., 2010)

The GSSM may help us understand why some children do not identify with their assigned gender at birth (Leaper, 2018), as in the cases noted earlier of children who have strong cross-gender-typed interests at an early age. When rejected for their gender-nonconforming interests, perhaps some of these children find they do not belong in the gender group in which they were assigned. By extension, the GSSM implies that reducing cultural gender stereotypes about personal-social attributes will mean that children will not need to associate particular activities or subjects with a particular gender.

Both DIT and GSSM are excellent illustrations of how different theories can be combined to provide a fuller picture of processes underlying children's gender development. Both theories have already generated new research that is further expanding our understanding.

Cultural Influences

The theoretical approaches we have discussed so far emphasize biological and cognitive-motivational processes involved in gender development. Complementing these approaches are theories that address the larger cultural and social-structural factors that can shape gender development (Best & Bush, 2016). More specifically, it is necessary to consider how gender inequalities in a society shape gender development (Leaper, 2000).

Bioecological Model

As described in Chapter 9, Urie Bronfenbrenner's bioecological model of human development differentiates amongst interconnected systems within the child (biological and cognitive processes) and in the child's environment (see Figure 9.3 on page 334). The environmental systems range from the microsystem (the immediate environment) to the macrosystem (the culture) and chronosystem (changes in the environment over the course of the child's development) (Bronfenbrenner, 1979; Bronfenbrenner & Morris, 1998).

A fundamental feature of the macrosystem is its **opportunity structure**, that is, the economic and social resources it offers and people's understanding of those resources (Bussey & Bandura, 1999; Leaper, 2000; Ogbu, 1981; Wood & Eagly, 2002). Opportunities for members of a cultural community can vary depending on gender, income, and other factors, and they are reflected by the dominant adult roles within that community. According to the bioecological approach, child

opportunity structure the economic and social resources offered by the macrosystem in the bioecological model, and people's understanding of those resources socialization practices in the family, peer group, classroom, and other facets of the child's microsystem serve to prepare children for these adult roles. Thus, traditional gender-typing practices perpetuate as well as reflect the existing opportunity structures for women and men in a particular community at a particular time in history (Leaper, 2000; Whiting & Edwards, 1988; Wood & Eagly, 2002).

Campbell Leaper and his colleagues have highlighted how play activities provide young children with opportunities to practice particular social behaviours and cognitive abilities (Leaper, 1994, 2000; Leaper & Bigler, 2018). For example, domestic pretend play ("playing house") provides children with contexts for practicing socioemotional skills, and playing with construction toys can help develop children's spatial skills (Leaper & Bigler, 2018). When particular play activities are differentially encouraged in one gender more than another, however, there are corresponding differences in opportunity. In turn, this may lead to later differences in preferences, attitudes, and skills that influence the kinds of occupations they pursue or their functioning in close relationships (Leaper & Bigler, 2018).

To the extent that family and occupational roles tend to be divided on the basis of gender, different behaviours are expected of women and men, as well as of girls and boys. In many countries, women have been traditionally underrepresented in politics, business, science, technology, and various other fields—a trend that continues in many societies today. In turn, girls are not expected to develop interests and skills that lead toward professions in those fields, which simply perpetuates girls' exclusion from them.

To the extent that children's development is largely an adaptation to their existing opportunities, changes in children's macrosystems and microsystems can lead to greater gender equality (see Leaper, 2000). For example, increased academic and professional opportunities for girls have led to a dramatic narrowing of the gender gap in math and science within the past few decades (Halpern, 2012; Halpern et al., 2007). In summary, the bioecological model highlights how institutionalized roles impose both opportunities and constraints on people's behaviour and beliefs in the home, schools, the labour force, and political institutions.

REVIEW QUESTION

How do the various theories described in this section fit with your own concept of gender and your personal development? ■

Milestones in Gender Development

Developmental psychologists have identified general patterns that tend to occur over the course of children's gender development. As reviewed in this section, gender-related changes are evident in children's physical, cognitive, and social development. Recall that these changes begin during prenatal development, when sexual differentiation occurs.

Infancy and Toddlerhood

During their first year, infants' perceptual abilities allow them to identify females and males. As we saw in Chapter 5, much research indicates that infants can detect complex regularities in perceptual information. Clothing, hairstyle, height, body shape, motion patterns, vocal pitch, and activities all tend to vary with gender, and these differences provide infants with gender cues.

For example, habituation studies of infant perception and categorization indicate that by about 6 to 9 months of age, infants can distinguish males from females, usually on the basis of hairstyle (Intons-Peterson, 1988). Infants can also distinguish between male and female voices and make intermodal matches on the basis of gender (Blakemore et al., 2009; Martin et al., 2002). For instance, they expect a female voice to go with a female face rather than with a male face. Although we cannot conclude that infants understand anything about what it *means* to be female or male, it does appear that older infants recognize the physical difference between females and males by using multiple perceptual cues.

Shortly after entering toddlerhood, most children begin exhibiting distinct patterns of gender development. By the latter half of their second year, children have begun to form gender-related expectations about the kinds of objects and activities typically associated with males and females. For example, research by Diane Poulin-Dubois, Lisa Serbin, and their colleagues at Concordia University in Montreal showed that 18-month-olds looked longer at a doll than at a toy car after viewing a series of female faces, and looked longer at a toy car than at a doll after habituating to male faces (Serbin et al., 2001). Another study with Canadian 24-month-olds found that counter-stereotypical matches of gender and action (e.g., a man putting on lipstick) led to longer looking times; it appeared that the children were surprised by the action's gender inconsistency (Poulin-Dubois et al., 2002). These studies suggest that, at young ages, children are learning to form gender-stereotypical associations.

Gender Development in Early Childhood

IMAGESBAZAAR/GETTY IMAGES

The clearest evidence that children have acquired the concept of gender occurs around 2½ years of age, when they begin to label other people's genders. For example, researchers might assess this ability by asking children to put pictures of children into "boys" and "girls" piles. Toddlers can also make simple gender matches, such as choosing a toy train over a doll when asked to point to the "boy's toy" (Campbell, Shirley, & Caygill, 2002). Children typically begin to show understanding of their own gender identity within a few months after labelling other people's gender. By age 2½ to 3 years, most children use gender terms such as "boy" and "girl" in their speech to refer to themselves and other children (Fenson et al., 1994).

Gender self-labelling is usually consistent with children's gender assignment at birth (based on their external genitals). However, as previously noted, some children do not identify with their assigned gender as they advance into the preschool years and older; instead, these children may identify with a different gender category (transgender), with more than one gender category (gender fluid), or with neither gender category (agender). These children usually have behavioural preferences that would be cross-gender-typed for their assigned gender at birth (see Box 15.1).

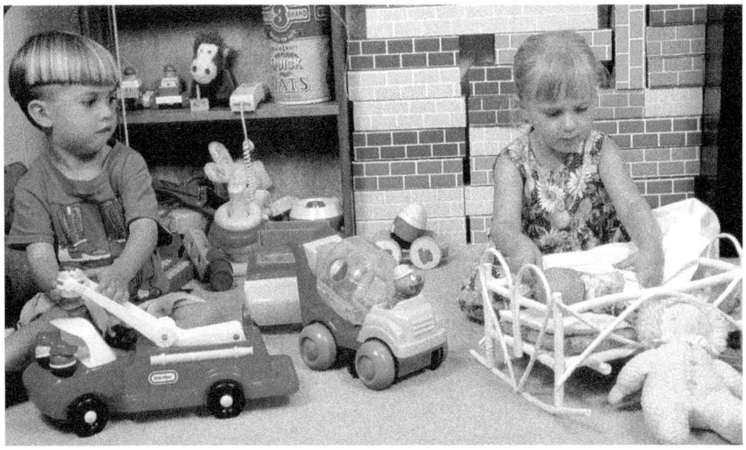

In Canada, children's play becomes differentiated by gender during the preschool period; most girls prefer to play with soft toys and to spend time in the "housekeeping" area, and most boys prefer to play with blocks and transportation toys.

MICHELLE D. BRIDWELL/PHOTOEDIT

Preschool Years

During the preschool years (approximately ages 3 to 5), children quickly learn gender stereotypes—the activities, traits, and roles associated with each gender. By about 3 years of age, most children begin to attribute

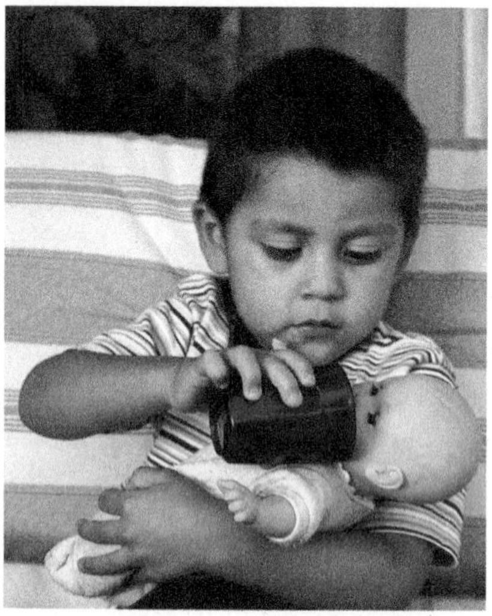

MYRLEEN PEARSON/PHOTOEDIT

During preschool, children begin to avoid peers who violate gender-role norms, and by age 5 to 7 years, they will actively tease peers who cross gender-role boundaries. This is especially true for boys: the one in this photo is likely to experience peer rejection if he continues to play with dolls and other toys strongly stereotyped as appropriate for girls.

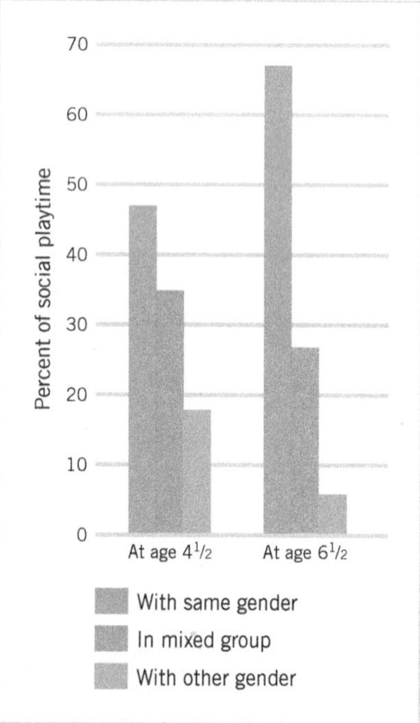

FIGURE 15.4 Gender segregation in play This graph reflects the increase in social playtime between preschool and 1st grade that children spent with playmates of their own gender and the decrease in playtime with playmates of the other gender. (Data from Maccoby, 1998)

certain toys and play activities to each gender. By about 5 years of age, they usually stereotype affiliative characteristics (e.g., nurturance, warmth) to females and assertive characteristics (e.g., directness, aggression) to males (Best & Thomas, 2004; Biernat, 1991; Liben & Bigler, 2002; Serbin, Powlishta, & Gulko, 1993). During this period, children usually lack *gender constancy:* they do not understand that gender remains stable across time and is consistent across situations. For example, a preschooler might think that a girl becomes a boy if she cuts her hair, or that a boy becomes a girl if he wears a dress. Indeed, as explained earlier in this chapter, most young children rigidly endorse gender stereotypes until they develop more cognitive flexibility during middle childhood.

Gender-Typed Behaviour

Many children begin to demonstrate preferences for some gender-typed toys by about 2 years of age. These preferences become stronger for most children during the preschool years (Cherney & London, 2006; Todd et al., 2017; Weisgram & Dinella, 2018). Indeed, during childhood, one of the largest average gender differences is in toy and play preferences, as described earlier.

Although studies find large average gender differences in play preferences, there is still some variability. First, variation exists within each gender in how strongly individual children favour gender-typed over cross-gender-typed play. That is, some cisgender children are very rigid in their preferences for gender-typed toys and play activities, whereas others are more flexible (Blakemore et al., 2009; DeLoache et al., 2007). Second, some children strongly prefer cross-gender-typed play and dislike gender-typed play. This latter group includes genetic females with congenital adrenal hyperplasia (CAH), who were exposed to unusually high levels of prenatal androgens, or genetic males with androgen insensitivity syndrome (AIS), who are unable to respond to androgen during prenatal differentiation (Berenbaum, 2018; Hines, 2013; described later in this chapter). Transgender children who identify with a gender different from the one assigned to them at birth usually prefer the play activities typically associated with their self-identified gender (Boskey, 2014; Olson & Gülgöz, 2018).

The preschool period is also when **gender segregation** emerges. Most children begin to prefer playing with same-gender peers and to avoid other-gender peers (Leaper, 1994, 2018; Maccoby, 1998). Gender segregation increases steadily between about 3 and 6 years of age, then it remains stable throughout childhood (Figure 15.4). Preference for same-gender peers is commonly seen across different cultures (Maccoby, 1998; Munroe & Romney, 2006; Whiting & Edwards, 1988).

Gender-segregated peer groups are a laboratory for cisgender children to learn what it means to be a girl or a boy. Peers are both role models and enforcers of gender-typed behaviour. Martin and Fabes (2001) identified what they termed a "social dosage effect" of belonging to same-gender peer groups during early childhood. The amount of time that preschool or kindergarten children spent with same-gender peers predicted subsequent changes in gender-typed behaviour over 6 months. For example, boys who spent more time playing with same-gender peers showed increases over time in aggression, rough-and-tumble play, activity level, and gender-typed play. Girls who spent more time playing with same-gender peers showed increases in gender-typed play and decreases in aggression and activity level.

The reasons for children's same-gender peer preferences seem to involve a combination of temperamental, cognitive, and social forces (Leaper, 2015a, 2018; Maccoby, 1998; Martin & Ruble, 2010). Their relative influences change over time. At first, some children may prefer same-gender peers partly because they have more compatible behavioural styles and interests. For instance, girls may avoid boys because boys tend to be rough and unresponsive to girls' attempts to influence them, whereas boys may prefer the company of other boys because they share similar activity levels. Around the time that children begin to exhibit a same-gender peer preference, they are also establishing a gender identity; thus, they may be drawn to peers who belong to the same ingroup.

gender segregation children's tendency to associate with same-gender peers and to avoid other-gender peers

As children become older, peer pressures may additionally motivate them to favour same-gender peers. Thus, behavioural compatibility may become a less important factor with age. For instance, physically active girls might frequently play with boys during early childhood; however, as these girls become older, they tend to affiliate more with girls—even though their activity preferences may be more compatible with some boys (Pellegrini et al., 2007). Therefore, ingroup identity and conformity pressures may supersede behavioural compatibility as reasons for gender segregation as children become older.

For some children, assimilating into same-gender peer groups may be a challenge. As explained earlier, some children demonstrate intense cross-gender-typed interests. For example, some female children may strongly prefer physical activities and rough play while some male children may strongly prefer dress-up and doll play. Many cisgender children reject peers who do not adhere to social norms in their peer group. Similarly, many parents and other adults are disapproving of gender-nonconforming behaviours in children. As a consequence, some children with strong gender-nonconforming interests may face a conflict between social pressures and their interests. This conflict puts these children at risk for depression, anxiety, and other adjustment difficulties (Connolly et al., 2016; Olson et al., 2016). Also, they may not feel like they belong with their gender ingroup, and perhaps this contributes to some of them adopting a different gender identity (see Leaper, 2018).

Middle Childhood

By about 6 years of age, cisgender children have usually attained *gender constancy,* and their ideas about gender are more consolidated. Most children continue to be highly gender-stereotyped in their views. However, because they understand that gender is not necessarily tied to a person's physical appearance, children at this age period often show a bit more flexibility in their gender stereotypes and attitudes than they did in their younger years (Katz & Ksansnak, 1994; Liben & Bigler, 2002; Serbin et al., 1993). For example, they may recognize that some boys don't like playing hockey and that some girls don't wear dresses. One recent study found that transgender children between 6 and 8 years old were less likely to endorse gender stereotypes than their cisgender peers and that the cisgender siblings of the transgender children were less likely to endorse gender stereotypes (Olson & Enright, 2018).

At approximately 9 or 10 years of age, children start to show an even clearer understanding that gender is a social category. They typically recognize that gender roles are social conventions as opposed to biological imperatives (Carter & Patterson, 1982; Conry-Murray, 2015; Killen, 2007; Stoddart & Turiel, 1985). As children come to appreciate the social basis of gender roles, they may recognize that some girls and boys may not want to do things that are typical for their gender. Even though children may understand the notion of individual variations in gender typing, they are typically aware that violating gender role norms would have social costs (Tobin et al., 2010).

assertion tendency to take action on behalf of the self through competitive, independent, or aggressive behaviours

affiliation tendency to affirm connection with others through being emotionally open, empathetic, or supportive

collaboration coordination of assertion and affiliation in behaviour, such as making initiatives for joint activity

Another development in some children's thinking in the middle childhood years is an awareness of when gender discrimination occurs, as well as the realization that it is unfair (Brown & Bigler, 2005; Killen, 2007). Killen and Stangor (2001) demonstrated this when they told children stories about a child who was excluded from a group because of the child's gender. Examples included a boy who was kept out of a ballet club and a girl who was kept out of a baseball-cards club. The researchers observed that 8- and 10-year-olds usually judged it unfair for a child to be excluded from a group solely because of gender. Yet despite their capacity to see this as wrong, children commonly exclude other children from activities based on their gender (Killen, 2007; Maccoby, 1998).

Brown and Bigler (2005) identified various factors that affect whether children recognize gender discrimination. First amongst them are cognitive prerequisites, such as an understanding of cultural stereotypes, the ability to make social comparisons, and a moral understanding of fairness and equity. These abilities are typically reached by middle childhood. People's awareness of sexism can also be influenced by individual factors such as their own self-concepts or beliefs. For instance, girls with gender-egalitarian beliefs were more likely to recognize sexism (Brown & Bigler, 2004; Leaper & Brown, 2008). Finally, the situation can affect children's likelihood of noticing discrimination. For instance, some children are more likely to notice discrimination directed toward someone else than toward themselves. Also, they are more apt to recognize gender discrimination from someone already known to be prejudiced (Brown & Bigler, 2005).

Gender-Typed Behaviour

As previously noted, most cisgender girls and boys spend time primarily in same-gender peer groups throughout childhood. On average, boys' and girls' peer groups establish somewhat different norms for behaviour (Rose & Rudolph, 2006). For this reason, some researchers have suggested that girls and boys usually construct their own "culture" during childhood (Maccoby, 1998; Maltz & Borker, 1982; Thorne & Luria, 1986). The gender-role norms seen in the social interactions of many cisgender girls and boys tend to reflect differences in the balance of assertion and affiliation (see Figure 15.5 for one model of communication styles, which plots four statement categories along these two dimensions). **Assertion** refers to one's attempts to exert influence over the environment (e.g., directive statements), whereas **affiliation** refers to making connections with others (e.g., expressing support). However, the goals of assertion and affiliation are not mutually exclusive: they are often blended together in a style known as **collaboration** (Leaper, 1991; Leaper, Tenenbaum, & Shaffer, 1999).

For example, a proposal for joint action ("Let's play a game together") or a statement that builds positively on another's idea are each simultaneously affiliative (connecting to the other) and self-assertive (influencing the situation). Thus, girls were more likely than boys to use collaborative communication that affirms both the self and the other (e.g., proposals for joint activity), whereas boys were more likely than girls to use power-assertive communication that primarily affirms the self (e.g., giving commands).

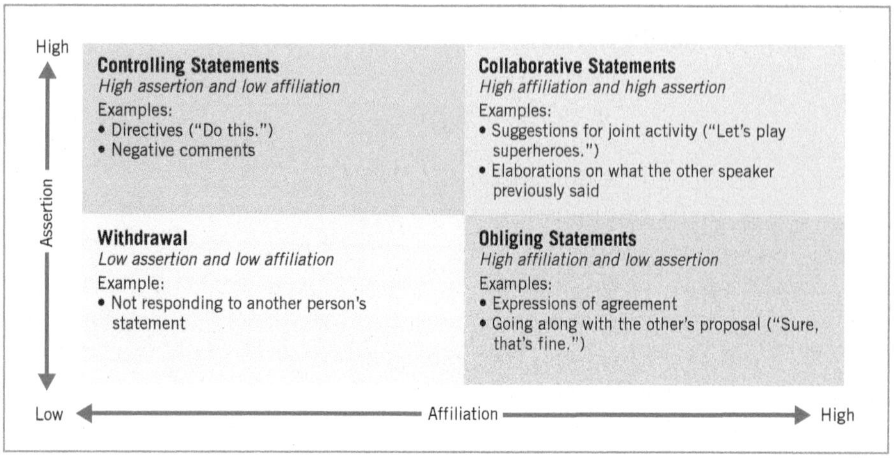

FIGURE 15.5 **Communication strategies** The figure illustrates a two-dimensional model of social interaction and communication. Assertion ranges from high to low along the vertical axis, and affiliation ranges from high to low along the horizontal axis. Collaborative acts are high in both affiliation and assertion. Controlling acts are high in assertion and low in affiliation. Obliging acts are high in affiliation and low in assertion. Withdrawing acts are low in both affiliation and assertion.

Average gender differences in girls' and boys' peer cultures reflect the organization of gender in the larger society (Leaper, 2000). The traditional masculine role in most societies stresses self-assertion and downplays interpersonal affiliation. In line with this tendency, researchers observed that boys' peer groups were more likely than girls' peer groups to maintain norms emphasizing dominance, self-reliance, competition, and hiding vulnerability. In contrast, the traditional feminine role stresses affiliation. Accordingly, in studies, girls' peer groups were more likely than boys' peer groups to reinforce norms that value interpersonal sensitivity, supportiveness, and affection (Bassen & Lamb, 2006; Best & Williams, 1993; Rose & Rudolph, 2006). However, valuing affiliation is not necessarily incompatible with self-assertion. Hence, collaborative styles of social interaction have been somewhat more common amongst girls than amongst boys (Leaper, 1991; Leaper & Smith, 2004; Leaper et al., 1999).

FUSE/THINKSTOCK

During the elementary school years, boys' and girls' groups rarely mix. Children themselves enforce gender segregation; this tendency does not seem to be due to adult influences.

As with most average gender differences, there is also considerable overlap between girls and boys in collaboration and other styles of social behaviour. For example, some boys are very collaborative while some girls are very directive. As we have noted, when children violate gender-role norms, their peers often react negatively (e.g., Fagot, 1977; Harris, 1995; Thorne & Luria, 1986), including mercilessly teasing someone who has crossed gender "borders."

Although most cisgender children typically favour same-gender peers, in certain contexts friendly mixed-gender contacts regularly occur (Sroufe et al., 1993; Strough & Covatto, 2002; Thorne, 1993; Thorne & Luria, 1986). At home and in the neighbourhood, the choice of play companions is frequently limited. As a result, girls and boys often play cooperatively with one another. In more public settings, the implicit convention is that girls and boys can be friendly if they can attribute the reason for their cross-gender contact to an external cause. For example, this might occur when a teacher assigns them to work together on a class project or when they are waiting in line together at the cafeteria. However, beyond such exceptions, the risk of peer rejection is high when children violate the social convention to avoid cross-gender contact (Sroufe et al., 1993).

Overall, gender typing during childhood tends to be more rigid amongst boys than amongst girls (Leaper, 1994; Levant, 2005). As noted earlier, amongst cisgender children, boys are more likely to endorse gender stereotypes than are girls, whereas girls are more likely than boys to endorse gender-egalitarian attitudes (Brown & Bigler, 2004). In addition, girls are less gender-typed in their behaviour. For instance, girls are more likely than boys to play with cross-gender-typed toys. Also, girls frequently pursue play activities traditionally associated with boys, such as soccer and basketball. In contrast, it is relatively rare to see cisgender boys engage in activities traditionally associated with girls, such as playing house. Furthermore, girls tend to be more flexible in coordinating interpersonal goals. For instance, as explained earlier, girls commonly coordinate both affiliative and assertive goals in their social interactions (Leaper, 1991; Leaper & Smith, 2004).

Gender segregation persists through childhood. Cross-gender teasing is used to maintain gender boundaries.

INGRAM PUBLISHING/SUPERSTOCK

gender-role intensification heightened concerns with adhering to traditional gender roles that may occur during adolescence

ambivalent sexism model of sexism that includes two components, hostile sexism (endorsement of men's dominance with negative views of women seeking equality) and benevolent sexism (the belief that men need to protect women, and that women and men have complementary traits)

gender-role flexibility recognition of gender roles as social conventions and adoption of more flexible attitudes and interests

Adolescence

According to some developmental psychologists, adolescence is a period when gender roles might become more rigid (*gender-role intensification*) or more relaxed (*gender-role flexibility*), depending on individual and contextual factors. As explained in Chapter 11, adolescence is a time when many youth are exploring their personal identities, including their values and beliefs regarding gender roles (e.g., Cooper & Grotevant, 1987). Many girls and boys internalize traditional gender roles in their personal values. As a consequence, concerns with adhering to gender-role expectations may increase (Galambos, Almeida, & Petersen, 1990; Hill & Lynch, 1983). This **gender-role intensification** commonly occurs in the context of heterosexual dating when adolescents usually adhere to traditional heterosexual scripts. For example, it remains common for both boys and girls to expect that boys will initiate and pay for dates (see Robnett & Leaper, 2013).

According to psychologists Peter Glick and Susan Fiske (2001), traditional heterosexual dating scripts stem from ambivalent sexism. **Ambivalent sexism** refers to complementary effects of *hostile sexism* (whereby men are dominant and women who seek equality are disparaged) and *benevolent sexism* (whereby men are supposed to protect women in the context of heterosexual relationships). Although benevolent sexism may seem innocent, Glick and Fiske point out that it helps to perpetuate gender differences in status and power when women are expected to rely on their male partners for financial support and safety. Both hostile and benevolent forms of sexism tend to occur together. Thus, during adolescence, rates of sexual harassment (manifestations of hostile sexism) rise during the same period that heterosexual dating is also increasing (Leaper & Robnett, 2018). Furthermore, these patterns may set the stage for observations that adults' endorsement of benevolent and hostile sexism can lead to lowered relationship satisfaction between women and men in heterosexual relationships over time (Hammond & Overall, 2017).

Gender-role intensification is also related to increases in gender discrimination during the course of adolescence (American Association of University Women [AAUW], 2011; Leaper & Brown, 2008). A national survey conducted in the United States found that most adolescent girls and boys experienced sexual harassment, and the rates increased with age—especially for girls (AAUW, 2011). A study of grade 7 and 8 students in Ontario found that 35% to 45% of students reported at least one incidence of sexual harassment during the school year (Schnoll et al., 2015). Also, instances of sexual harassment and bullying are more likely directed toward gender-nonconforming children (e.g., boys who are not athletic, girls who are not viewed as pretty or feminine), as well as LGBTQ individuals (AAUW, 2011; Martin-Storey, 2016; Mitchell, Ybarra, & Korchmaros, 2014).

Alternatively, some adolescents may reject traditional gender roles as social conventions. This inclination may lead to **gender-role flexibility**, whereby these youths pursue a flexible range of attitudes and interests (Carter & Patterson, 1982; Katz & Ksansnak, 1994). As in childhood, greater gender-role flexibility during adolescence is more likely amongst girls than amongst boys. For instance, many girls and young women in Canada and other countries participate in sports and pursue careers in business (traditionally male-dominated domains), whereas relatively few boys and young men show similar levels of interest in childcare or homemaking (traditionally female-dominated domains). For girls and boys, gender-role flexibility will partly depend on the breadth of opportunities they experience in society for their gender ingroup (Wood & Eagly, 2012). Social support (and the absence of rejection) for gender-role flexibility from peers, family, teachers, and others is also important for gender-nonconforming youth (Olson et al., 2016).

When LGBTQ adolescents encounter strong heteronormative (and cisgender) expectations in their community, they may face stigmatization and corresponding challenges in embracing their sexual identities (Toomey et al., 2010). However, in many schools in Canada, there are Straight–LGBTQ alliances that foster acceptance and support for sexual-minority and other gender-nonconforming youth (e.g., Saewyc et al., 2019).

Parents, peers, and teachers are much more tolerant of girls who engage in masculine-stereotyped activities than they are of boys who engage in feminine-stereotyped activities.

Gender-Typed Behaviour

During early adolescence, peer contacts for most youth remain primarily with members of the same gender. However, in many cultural communities, mixed-gender interactions and friendships become more common during adolescence (see Figure 15.6) (Poulin & Pedersen, 2007). These interactions can open the way to romantic relationships amongst heterosexual youth. In some cultural settings, however, there are strict rules regarding mixed-gender contacts, especially as youth enter adolescence. For example, in Orthodox Jewish, Islamic, and Amish societies, girls and boys are separated outside the home, and any mixed-gender contact must be supervised by family.

Adolescence is also a period of increased intimacy in same-gender friendships. For many girls and boys, increased emotional closeness is often attained through sharing personal feelings and thoughts, although there appears to be more variability amongst boys in the ways they experience and express closeness in friendships (Camarena, Sarigiani, & Petersen, 1990). While some boys attain intimacy through shared disclosures with same-gender friends, other boys tend to avoid self-disclosure with same-gender friends because they wish to appear strong. Instead, they usually attain a feeling of emotional closeness with friends through shared activities, such as playing sports. At the same time, many boys who avoid expressing feelings with male friends may seek emotional support with their female friends or girlfriends (Youniss & Smollar, 1985).

Self-disclosure and supportive listening are generally associated with relationship satisfaction and emotional adjustment (Rubin, Bukowski, & Parker, 2006; see Chapter 13). However, it is possible to have too much of a good thing. This occurs when friends dwell too long on upsetting events by talking to one another about them over and over. As discussed in Chapter 10, this process of *co-rumination* is more common amongst girls than amongst boys (Rose, Carlson, & Waller, 2007). To be clear, self-disclosure is generally positive for emotional adjustment, but it can be a problem when friends persistently focus on upset feelings without exploring proactive ways to cope with the distress.

FIGURE 15.6 Friends by gender and grade The data shown in this figure demonstrate that younger children tend to be friends with children who are the same gender as they are. As children move into adolescence, the number of cross-gender friends tends to increase for both boys and girls. (Data from Poulin & Pedersen, 2007)

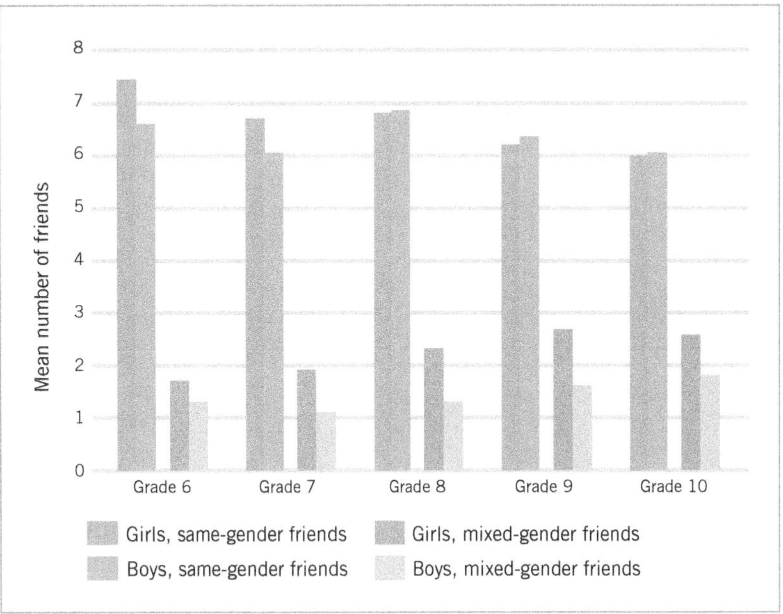

REVIEW QUESTION

What role does gender stereotyping play at the various stages of child development? ■

Patterns of Gender Development

In the following sections, we consider patterns of gender development in four areas that receive particular attention in the study of gender development: physical growth, cognitive abilities and academic achievement, interpersonal goals and communication, and aggression.

Physical Growth: Prenatal Development Through Adolescence

Sex differences in physical development appear early in prenatal development. The most dramatic of these, of course, is the emergence of male or female internal and external genitalia. Thereafter, the differences that occur between males and females are relatively subtle prior to the onset of puberty.

Prenatal Development

As noted in our earlier discussions, a key prenatal factor in sexual development is the presence or absence of androgens. Research suggests that prenatal exposure to androgens may influence the organization of the nervous system, and these effects may be partly related to some average gender differences in behaviour seen at later ages (Berenbaum, 2018; Hines, 2013).

During prenatal development, a gene on the Y chromosome of genetic males normally triggers the increased production of androgen hormones around 6 to 8 weeks after conception. This leads to a series of processes leading to the formation of male internal reproductive structures and male external genitalia. Rarely occurring recessive genes may result in a person of one genetic sex who develops the sexual structures associated with the other genetic sex or undergoes only partial development of sexual structures associated with their genetic sex. These are known as **intersex conditions** (Preves, 2003). Two intersex conditions, *congenital adrenal hyperplasia* and *androgen insensitivity syndrome,* have been of particular interest to gender development researchers.

Congenital adrenal hyperplasia (CAH) is associated with a recessive gene that leads to the production of high levels of androgen hormones during prenatal development. Although CAH can occur in genetic females and males, it primarily affects the development of genetic females. These high levels of androgens can lead to the formation of male (or partly masculinized) external genitalia in females, such as a clitoris that is enlarged and may resemble a penis, although the internal reproductive structures are usually female. Researchers studying the possible influence of androgens on later gender development have found that girls with CAH were more likely than girls without CAH to choose physically active forms of play, such as rough-and-tumble play, and to avoid sedentary forms of play, such as playing with dolls (Berenbaum, 2018; Hines, 2013; Nordenström et al., 2002). However, CAH does not have a strong impact on gender identity, as most females with CAH self-identify as girls (Hines, 2013). Research indicates that these behavioural tendencies do not appear to be caused by parents' treating these girls differently because of their masculinized genitalia (Hines, 2013).

intersex condition rare conditions in which an individual of one genetic sex can develop genitalia associated with the other genetic sex, both genetic sexes, or undergo only partial development of genitalia associated with their genetic sex

congenital adrenal hyperplasia (CAH) condition during prenatal development in which the adrenal glands produce high levels of androgens; sometimes associated with masculinization of external genitalia in genetic females and sometimes associated with higher rates of masculine-stereotyped play in genetic females

In cases of **androgen insensitivity syndrome (AIS)**, a recessive gene causes androgen receptors to malfunction in genetic males. Although increased androgen production may occur during prenatal development, the hormones do not trigger the typical physical changes in sexual differentiation. In these cases, genetic males may be born with female external genitalia (but not with female internal reproductive structures). Boys with AIS commonly self-identify as girls (and later as women). In addition, they typically show preferences for stereotypically feminine interests (Hines, 2013).

Cases of children with CAH and AIS offer evidence to support the premise that prenatal androgens may *partly* contribute to boys' and girls' gender identities and to gender-typed play preferences. In addition, this kind of evidence is sometimes used to support evolutionary accounts of gender development (Alexander, 2003). However, it is important to reiterate that there are normal variations within each genetic sex in their exposure to prenatal androgens, as well as in their later preferences for different kinds of activities and interests. Hence, there are multiple influences on children's gender development.

androgen insensitivity syndrome (AIS) condition during prenatal development in which androgen receptors malfunction in genetic males, impeding the formation of male external genitalia; in these cases, the child may be born with female external genitalia

puberty developmental period marked by the ability to reproduce and other dramatic bodily changes

menarche onset of menstruation

spermarche onset of capacity for ejaculation

Puberty

BRONEK KAMINSKI/GETTY IMAGES

Childhood and Adolescence

At birth, males, on average, weigh only about half a pound more than females do. Also, during infancy and into childhood, girls and boys grow at roughly the same rate and are essentially equal in height and weight (see Chapter 3). But during childhood, boys become notably stronger, on average, compared to girls. During adolescence, a series of dramatic bodily transformations is associated with **puberty**, the developmental period marked by the ability to reproduce—that is, the ability of males to inseminate, and the ability of females to menstruate, gestate, and lactate (Gaddis & Brooks-Gunn, 1985; Jorgensen, Keiding, & Skakkebaek, 1991). In females, puberty typically begins with enlargement of the breasts and the general growth spurt in height and weight, followed by the appearance of pubic hair and then **menarche** (the onset of menstruation). Menarche is triggered in part by the increase in body fat that typically occurs in adolescence. In males, puberty generally starts with the growth of the testes, followed by the appearance of pubic hair, the general growth spurt, growth of the penis, and **spermarche** (the capacity for ejaculation).

For both females and males, there is considerable variability in physical maturation due to both genetic and environmental factors. Genes affect growth and sexual maturation in large part by influencing the production of hormones, especially growth hormone (secreted by the pituitary gland) and thyroxin (released by the thyroid gland). The influence of environmental factors is particularly evident in the changes in physical development that have occurred over generations (see Chapter 3). In many industrialized countries, females begin menstruating several years earlier than their ancestors did 200 years ago. This change is thought to reflect improvement in nutrition over the generations.

With the changes in body composition that occur in early adolescence, particularly the substantial increase in muscle mass in boys, the gender gap in physical and motor skills greatly increases. After puberty, average gender differences are very large in strength, speed, and size: few adolescent females can run as fast or throw a ball as far as most males can (Malina & Bouchard, 1991; Thomas & French, 1985). These are amongst the largest average differences in abilities seen between females and males (see Table 15.1). Physical differences in strength, speed, and size, as well as women's childbearing capacity, may be amongst the most significant sex differences that shape the organization of gender relations

JUSTIN PUMFREY/GETTY IMAGES

In early puberty, females are typically taller than males because of females' earlier physical maturation. By the end of adolescence, males catch up and surpass females in average height and weight.

body image an individual's perception of, and feelings about, her or his own body

adrenarche period prior to the emergence of visible signs of puberty during which the adrenal glands mature, providing a major source of sex steroid hormones; correlates with the onset of sexual attraction

in a society. Psychologists Wendy Wood and Alice Eagly (2002) argued that greater gender inequalities have occurred in societies when economic subsistence favoured physical strength and disadvantaged nursing and childcare. In industrial-technological societies, physical strength is no longer an advantage for most jobs and resources such as birth control, family leave, and childcare make it possible for women (and men) to maintain engagement in the workforce.

The physical changes that males and females experience during puberty are accompanied by psychological and behavioural changes. For example, in some cultures, the increase in body fat that adolescent females undergo may be related to gender differences in **body image**—how an individual perceives and feels about his or her physical appearance. On average, girls tend to have more negative attitudes toward their bodies than boys do, and teenage girls typically want to lose several pounds regardless of how much they actually weigh (Tyrka, Graber, & Brooks-Gunn, 2000). A survey of more than 1500 Canadian preadolescents found that roughly half of both the girls and boys were dissatisfied with their bodies, but that the type of dissatisfaction varied across genders: Girls were mostly concerned about losing weight; boys, with being more muscular (Dion et al., 2016). Dissatisfaction with body image has long been associated with a host of difficulties, ranging from low self-esteem and depression to eating disorders. Surveys across different cultures indicate similar patterns of body image and eating disorders (Levine & Smolak, 2010).

Another change that accompanies physical maturation is the onset of sexual attraction, which usually begins before the physical process of puberty is complete. According to the recollections of a sample of adults in the United States, sexual attraction is first experienced at about 10 years of age—regardless of whether the attraction was for individuals of the other sex or the same sex (McClintock & Herdt, 1996). The onset of sexual attraction correlates with the maturation of the adrenal glands, which are the major source of sex steroids other than the testes and ovaries. This stage has been termed **adrenarche**, although the child's body does not yet show any outside signs of maturation. (Sexual identity and romantic relationships are reviewed in Chapters 11 and 13.)

Cognitive Abilities and Academic Achievement

The following sections summarize the evidence comparing cisgender boys' and girls' cognitive abilities and academic achievement. When average gender-differences in cognitive ability or performance have been observed, the effect sizes have usually been small (Halpern, 2012; Halpern et al., 2007; see Table 15.1). Somewhat greater differences appear when it comes to motivation for particular subjects. After summarizing these comparisons, we consider biological, cognitive-motivational, and cultural influences that might account for these findings. The relation between gender and academic achievement during childhood and adolescence has important implications for adult gender roles and equality. To the extent that cisgender girls and boys develop different cognitive abilities, academic interests, and achievement, gender differences in their future occupations and income may follow. Thus, reducing gender differences in academic motivation and achievement are critical steps toward increasing gender equality in society (Dasgupta & Stout, 2014).

To our knowledge, no research has examined the extent that children's academic interests might differ on average between cisgender children and transgender or gender-nonbinary children. However, because of the discrimination and bullying that gender-nonconforming youth often encounter in school, many transgender and nonbinary children suffer academically (Day, Perez-Brumer, & Russell, 2018).

General Intelligence and Overall Academic Achievement

Despite widespread belief to the contrary, boys and girls are equivalent in most aspects of intelligence and cognitive functioning. The average IQ scores of girls and boys are virtually identical (Halpern, 2012). However, proportionally more boys than girls have scored at both the lowest and the highest extremes. That is, somewhat more boys than girls have been diagnosed with intellectual disabilities or are classified as intellectually gifted (Halpern, 2012).

Although girls and boys are similar in general intelligence, some average differences in academic achievement were seen from elementary school through university. Recent statistics indicate that girls tend to show higher levels of school adjustment and achievement than do boys across a number of different countries (Child Trends Data Bank, 2015; Snyder & Dillow, 2010; Lam, Jimerson et al., 2012; Voyer & Voyer, 2014). In one meta-analysis carried out by researchers at the University of New Brunswick, data showed a small average difference indicating that girls tended to attain higher overall school grades than did boys (Voyer & Voyer, 2014). Also, the high school dropout rate in Canada tends to be higher for boys than for girls: in 2016, 8% of 25- to 34-year-old men had not completed high school compared to 5% of women of the same age (Uppal, 2017). Furthermore, in 2016, 57% of Canadian university graduates were women (Statistics Canada, 2018). The magnitude of gender difference in academic achievement varies somewhat across different cultural and ethnic groups and socioeconomic levels.

Verbal Skills

Compared with boys, girls have tended to be slightly advanced in early language development, including fluency and clarity of articulation and vocabulary development (Gleason & Ely, 2002). On standardized tests of children's overall verbal ability, there has been a negligible average gender difference favouring girls (Hyde & Linn, 1988). Larger average differences were seen when specific verbal skills were examined. Girls tended to achieve higher average performance in reading and writing from elementary school to high school; the effect sizes of the average differences were small for reading and medium for writing (Hedges & Nowell, 1995; Nowell & Hedges, 1998; Reilly, 2012; Voyer & Voyer, 2014; see Table 15.1). Boys were more likely to suffer speech-related difficulties, such as poor articulation and stuttering, as well as more reading-related problems such as dyslexia (Halpern, 2012).

Spatial Skills

On average, boys have tended to perform somewhat better than girls in some aspects of visual-spatial processing (see Table 15.1). This difference has typically emerged between 3 and 4 years of age and became more substantial during adolescence and adulthood (Halpern, 2012). Gender differences are most pronounced on tasks that involve mental rotation of a complex geometric figure in order to decide whether it matches another figure presented in a different orientation; on average, boys have tended to perform somewhat better than girls in that area. However, other spatial tasks—such as finding a hidden figure embedded within a larger image—have shown much smaller gender differences. Thus, the conclusion that more boys than girls have superior spatial ability depends on the particular type of spatial ability.

STEM-Related Skills

Policymakers, educators, and researchers have been concerned with gender disparities in many science, technology, engineering, and mathematics (STEM) fields (Halpern, 2012; National Science Foundation, 2017). These are amongst the fastest-growing and highest-paying occupations, and therefore women's underrepresentation in many of these fields contributes to overall gender inequities in pay and status in society (Cheryan et al., 2017). Moreover, because these fields are considered important for progress and innovation, societies should foster the talents of all interested persons starting at a young age (Cheryan et al., 2017).

Until recent decades in Canada and many other countries, boys tended to perform somewhat better on standardized tests of mathematical ability than did girls. As we have noted, however, the gender gap in mathematics achievement has closed dramatically as a result of efforts made by schools and parents to improve girls' performance. According to the most recent studies, no average gender differences in standardized test performance or basic numerical skills were seen in the elementary or middle school levels (Hutchison, Lyons, Ansari, 2019; Lindberg et al., 2010), and only a small average difference (favouring boys) was indicated at the high school level (Halpern et al., 2007; Lindberg et al., 2010; see Table 15.1). However, cross-national comparisons revealed some countries in which girls exceeded boys in average mathematics performance (Else-Quest, Hyde, & Linn, 2010).

Girls and women are also underrepresented in the engineering, computer science, and other technological fields. In Canada as of 2016, for example, 23% of postsecondary degrees and diplomas in engineering, 13.5% of postsecondary degrees and diplomas in engineering technology and related fields, and 24% of postsecondary degrees and diplomas in computer and information sciences were held by women between the ages of 25 and 34 years (Statistics Canada, 2017). Following the attention paid to the gender gap in math achievement a few decades ago, educators and researchers are increasingly addressing the gender gap in the physical sciences and engineering and technology (see Cheryan et al., 2017), and progress has been made in some of these areas—for example, 46% of degrees and diplomas in math and statistics and 39% of degrees and diplomas in the physical sciences were held by women aged 25 to 34 years, as of 2016.

Encouragement of girls' interest in STEM-related fields on the part of parents and schools has led to the dramatic closing of the achievement gap in these areas.

FSTOP123/GETTY IMAGES

In contrast to engineering and computer sciences, girls and women are attaining gender equity in the biological and health sciences. At the high school level, there is no average gender difference in achievement. At the postsecondary level as of 2016, 63% of postsecondary degrees and diplomas in biological and biomedical sciences went to women between 25 and 34 years.

Explanations for Gender Differences in Cognitive Abilities and Achievement

Researchers have variously pointed to physiological, cognitive-motivational, and cultural factors in relation to gender-related variations in cognitive abilities and achievement. We now examine each possible area of influence.

Brain and hormonal influences Some researchers have proposed that sex differences in brain structure and function may underlie some differences in how male and female brains process different types of information. However, because the research supporting this interpretation has largely been based on studies of adults, it is impossible to determine whether any differences in brain structure and function seen in adults are due to genetic or environmental influences. Also, a slight biological tendency can get exaggerated through differential experience (Halpern, 2012). For example, boys may initially have a slight average advantage over girls in some types of spatial processing. Yet, when boys spend more time playing video games and sports than girls do, they practice their spatial skills more (Moreau et al., 2012; Spence & Feng, 2010). As a consequence, the magnitude of the gender difference in spatial ability may widen. However, several studies indicate that spatial skills can be substantially improved in girls as well as boys through training (Uttal et al., 2013).

Stronger evidence for possible physiological influences is suggested by research showing that some sex differences in brain structure may be *partly* due to the influence of sex-related hormones on the developing fetal brain (Berenbaum, 2018; Hines, 2013). For instance, androgens may affect parts of the brain associated with spatial skills (Grön et al., 2000; Hines, 2013). Because males are exposed to higher levels of androgens than are females during typical prenatal development, this difference may lead to greater specialization in parts of the brain related to spatial ability, which contributes to more proficiency in spatial ability later in life. Support for this hypothesis comes from studies that have linked very high levels of prenatal androgens in girls with above-average spatial ability (Grimshaw, Sitarenios, & Finegan, 1995; Hines et al., 2003; Mueller et al., 2008). Conversely, it has been found that males with androgen insensitivity syndrome tend to score lower than average in spatial ability (Imperato-McGinley et al., 1991/2007). Keep in mind there is considerable variability within each gender group in their spatial abilities.

Cognitive and motivational influences The process of self-socialization emphasized in cognitive motivational theories plays a role in children's academic achievement. According to Eccles's *expectancy-value model of achievement* (Eccles & Wigfield, 2002), children are most motivated to achieve in areas in which they expect to succeed (i.e., self-efficacy or ability belief in a subject) and that they value (i.e., intrinsic interest and perceived importance of a subject). Gender stereotypes can shape the kinds of subjects that girls and boys tend to value (see Table 15.1). For instance, many children internalize gender stereotypes that science, technology, and math are for boys and that reading, writing, and the arts are for girls (Kessels, 2015; Papastergiou, 2008; Plante, Théorêt, & Favreau, 2009). However, some evidence suggests that these stereotypes are possibly becoming less common (Plante et al., 2009), perhaps due to the efforts of many educators, policymakers, and parents over the years.

To the extent that gender stereotyping about academic subjects does persist, perhaps it is not surprising, then, that average gender differences in interest and ability beliefs exist in these academic areas (Eccles & Wigfield, 2002; Else-Quest, Hyde, & Linn, 2010; Simpkins, Fredricks, & Eccles, 2015; Wilgenbusch & Merrell, 1999) and that these self-concepts predict academic achievement and occupational aspirations (Guo et al., 2015; Halpern, 2012; Watt, 2010; Wigfield,

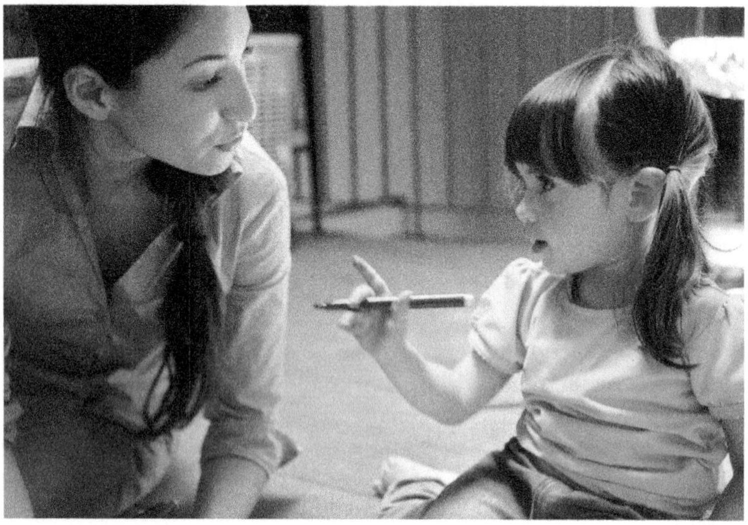

Some studies find that mothers are more talkative with daughters than with sons. Studies also find that, on average, girls acquire language at a faster rate than do boys. Does mothers' greater talkativeness with girls contribute to girls' faster language acquisition? Or does girls' faster language acquisition influence mothers' talkativeness with them?

Cambria, & Eccles, 2012). As discussed next, social and cultural factors also influence the development of gender-related variations in academic self-concepts and achievement. That is, the role models, opportunities, and incentives that children experience in their environments affect their motivation and achievement.

Parental influences As noted in Chapter 6, parents' talking to their children is a strong predictor of children's language learning. A meta-analysis of studies conducted with mostly Western middle-class families found that mothers tended to have average higher rates of verbal interaction with daughters than with sons (Leaper, Anderson, & Sanders, 1998). Thus, one possibility is that young girls learn language at a slightly faster rate than do boys partly because mothers may spend more time talking with daughters than with sons. Alternatively, because many girls tend to acquire language earlier than some boys, perhaps girls are more likely to elicit talk from their mothers (Leaper & Smith, 2004). Finally, both patterns may tend to occur—a possible bidirectional influence whereby both mothers and daughters tend to be talkative and reinforce this behaviour in one another.

Parents' gender stereotyping is also related to children's academic achievement. Many parents accept the prevailing stereotypes about boys' and girls' relative interests and aptitudes regarding various academic subjects (Eccles, 2015; Eccles et al., 2000; Leaper, 2015a), and these gender-typed expectations can affect children's achievement motivation (Eccles, 2015; Eccles et al., 2000). Observational research suggests that some parents may communicate gender-stereotyped expectations to their children through differential encouragement (Bhanot & Jovanovic, 2005; Crowley et al., 2001; Tenenbaum & Leaper, 2003). You might think that parents' beliefs about their children's academic potential would be based primarily on their children's own self-concepts and achievement, but researchers have found that parents often hold gender-typed beliefs before any average gender differences in academic interest or performance occur. In fact, longitudinal research suggests that parents' expectations can sometimes have a stronger impact on children's later achievement than the children's earlier performance in particular subject areas (Bleeker & Jacobs, 2004).

Some teachers hold gender-stereotyped expectations about girls' and boys' abilities that may affect their interactions with students.

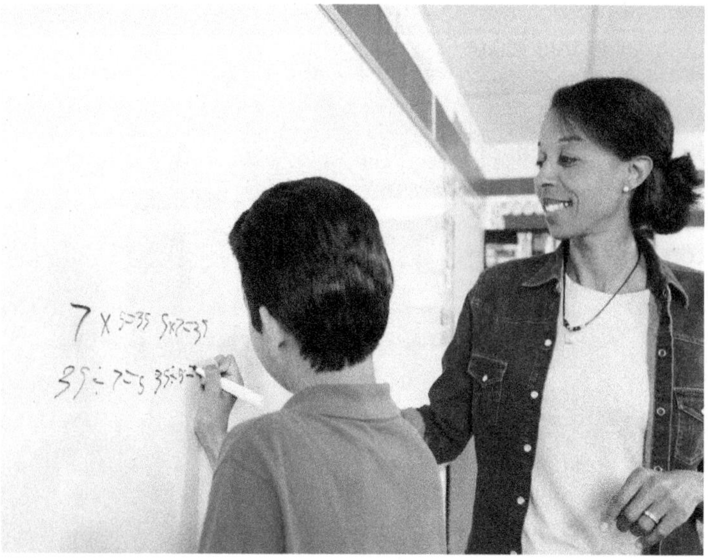

Teacher influences Teachers can influence gender differences in children's academic motivation and achievement. Some teachers may hold gender-stereotyped beliefs about girls' and boys' abilities. When this occurs, they may expect higher school achievement in girls than in boys (Jones & Myhill, 2004), or they may stereotype boys as being better at math and science (Cimpian et al., 2016; Riegle-Crumb & Humphries, 2012; Tiedemann, 2000). When teachers hold gender-typed expectations, they may differentially assess, encourage, and pay attention to students according to their gender. In this manner, teachers can lay the groundwork for self-fulfilling prophecies that affect children's later academic achievement (see Cimpian et al., 2016; Halpern,

2012; Halpern et al., 2007). However, many educators have become more aware of gender bias over the years, as in the case of proactive efforts to promote girls' participation in math, science, and technology programs (e.g., Fredricks et al., 2018; Stake & Mares, 2005).

Peer influences As described earlier in this chapter, children are usually concerned with gaining acceptance from their peers, and their interests often are shaped by the activities and values they associate with their classmates and friends. Consequently, peers can shape children's academic achievement (Wentzel, 2009). This influence begins with the kinds of play activities children practice with their peers. Many activities commonly favoured amongst boys—including construction play, sports, and video games—provide them with opportunities to develop their spatial abilities as well as math- and science-related skills. In contrast, the types of play more common amongst girls—such as domestic role-play—are talk-oriented and build verbal skills (Leaper, 2015a; Leaper & Bigler, 2018).

Girls and boys may be more likely to strive in particular school subjects when they are viewed as compatible with peer norms (Robnett & Leaper, 2013). In some schools, girls may experience negative comments if they express interest in subjects such as science or computers; and boys may experience teasing if they show interest in reading or doing well in school (Dasgupta & Stout, 2014; Leaper & Brown, 2014; Schwartz, Kelly, & Duong, 2013). Thus, peer norms regarding particular academic subjects may be related to how likely girls or boys are apt to value those subjects (Leaper, 2015b; Leaper & Brown, 2014; Schwartz et al., 2013).

Traditional masculinity norms emphasizing dominance and self-reliance may undermine some boys' academic achievement in Western industrialized countries (Farkas & Leaper, 2016; Levant, 2005; Steinmayr & Spinath, 2008; Van Houtte, 2004). That is, some boys may not consider it masculine to do well in certain subjects, such as reading and writing, or possibly in school overall (Kessels & Steinmayr, 2013; Leaper, Farkas, & Starr, 2018; Martinot, Bagès, & Désert, 2012; Santos et al., 2013; Van de Gaer et al., 2006; Van Houtte, 2004). At the same time, some U.S. research suggests that gender-role flexibility may be related to stronger interest in nontraditional majors amongst male undergraduates (Jome & Tokar, 1998; Leaper & Van, 2008).

Cultural influences The bioecological model maintains that socialization practices prepare children for their adult roles in society. If women and men tend to hold different occupations, then different abilities and preferences are apt to be encouraged in girls and boys. Therefore, where there are cultural variations in girls' and boys' academic achievement, there should be corresponding differences in socialization.

A meta-analysis conducted by Else-Quest, Hyde, and Linn (2010) pointed to cultural influences on gender-related variations in mathematics achievement. To assess possible cultural influences, the researchers considered the representation of women in higher education in the given country. They found that average gender differences in several math-related outcomes were less likely in nations with higher percentages of women in higher levels of education. This was seen for adolescents' test performance, self-confidence, and intrinsic motivation regarding math.

Peer norms can have a strong impact on girls' and boys' achievement motivation. For example, research indicates that girls are more likely to maintain their interest in science and computers when their friends support achievement in these subjects.

NANDANA DE SILVA/ALAMY

Educating Girls of the World

COURTESY OF UNICEF

One might expect the gender gap in fields such as physics, computer science, and engineering to be smaller in countries with greater gender equality. However, a recent cross-national analysis indicated the opposite (Stoet & Geary, 2018). Although the researcher noted girls performing similarly or even better than boys in most countries, there was a gender gap favouring men in attaining STEM degrees. The authors noted that the countries that were less gender-egalitarian also tended to have poorer economic conditions; additional analyses suggested that women in these countries tended to pursue STEM occupations for their economic value. In contrast, women in more egalitarian (and wealthier) countries may find they have more career options for attaining an adequate income. Furthermore, as others have argued, when women have career alternatives, they may be more likely to leave STEM majors when they experience gender bias (Cheryan et al., 2017; Leaper & Starr, 2019).

Other cultural factors have also been found to predict gender-related variations in academic achievement within Western industrialized societies. Average gender differences in overall academic success and verbal achievement tend to be less common amongst children from higher-income neighbourhoods, amongst children of highly educated parents, and amongst children of egalitarian parents (Burkam, Lee, & Smerdon, 1997; Croft et al., 2014; Ferry, Fouad, & Smith, 2000; Melby et al., 2008; Updegraff, McHale, & Crouter, 1996). Furthermore, the local community in which children are raised may have an impact. In one study, a comparison of different communities in the United States found the gender gap in physics achievement (usually favouring boys) was smaller in high schools in which more women were employed in science and technology occupations within the community (Riegle-Crumb & Moore, 2014).

Interpersonal Goals and Communication

Although average differences between cisgender (and mostly heterosexual) women's and men's speech have been documented, the magnitude of the differences has usually been in the small-to-medium range (Leaper & Ayres, 2007). The average gender differences in communication and interpersonal goals during childhood and adolescence have likewise been found to be modest (see Table 15.1).

In terms of interpersonal goals during childhood and adolescence, researchers have found average gender differences that are consistent with traditional gender roles amongst cisgender youth (Rose & Rudolph, 2006). More boys than girls tended to emphasize dominance and power as goals in their social relationships. In contrast, more girls than boys tended to favour intimacy and support as goals in their relationships. The effect sizes for these differences, however, were small to medium.

Researchers have also observed some average gender differences amongst cisgender children's communication styles with peers. Contrary to the stereotypes of talkative girls and taciturn boys, studies generally do not find average differences in talkativeness after early childhood (Leaper & Smith, 2004). However, with regard to self-disclosures about personal thoughts and feelings, there has been a small-to-medium gender difference, with higher average rates amongst girls than boys (Rose & Rudolph, 2006). Girls also tend to be somewhat more likely than boys to use collaborative statements, which reflect high affiliation and high assertion. Examples include suggestions for joint activity ("Let's play superheroes") or elaborations on what the other speaker previously said. In contrast, boys tend to be more likely than girls to use controlling statements (e.g., "Do this"), which reflect high assertion and low affiliation.

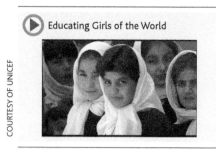

As with most average differences, there is considerable overlap between cisgender girls and boys in communication style. Although some children act in gender-stereotypical ways, many girls use controlling speech and many boys use high levels of collaborative speech. Indeed, as we have seen throughout this chapter, girls and boys are quite similar to one another in a wide variety of behaviours. As with many social behaviours, some children are more gender-typed than others. Future research could examine the interpersonal goals and communication styles of children and adolescents with transgender or gender-fluid identities, as well as cisgender youth with more gender-egalitarian attitudes. Because transgender children preferred play activities that were consistent more with their self-identified gender (Olson & Gülgöz, 2018), one might expect a similar pattern would be seen in their interpersonal goals and communication styles.

Explanations for Gender Differences in Interpersonal Goals and Communication

Researchers have identified a variety of cognitive-motivational, social-interactional, and cultural factors that are related to the likelihood of average gender differences in interpersonal goals and communication.

Cognitive and motivational influences Average gender differences in interpersonal goals and communication style are related. To the extent that some cisgender girls and boys differ in their primary goals for social relationships, they are apt to use different language styles to attain those goals (Crosby, Fireman, & Clopton, 2011; Miller, Danaher, & Forbes, 1986; Strough & Berg, 2000). For example, if a boy is especially interested in establishing dominance, using directive statements may help him attain that goal; and if a girl wants to establish intimacy, then talking about personal feelings or elaborating on the other person's thoughts would help realize that goal. Individual differences in interpersonal goals within any gender group may partly account for corresponding variations in whether particular children exhibit highly gender-typed behaviours.

Parental influences Many children observe their parents modelling gender-typed communication patterns. One meta-analysis summarized trends across studies (most of which were conducted with Western middle-class families with heterosexual parents) comparing mothers' and fathers' speech to their children (Leaper et al., 1998). The results indicated small average effect sizes: first, mothers were more likely than fathers to use affiliative speech; in contrast, fathers were more likely than mothers to use controlling (high in assertion and low in affiliation) speech. Additional research is needed to explore variations in parents' gender-typed communication depending on their gender attitudes, sexual orientation, and cultural background. Moreover, a larger question to address in longitudinal research is whether and how parental modelling shapes the kinds of communication strategies their children will favour as they get older.

Peer influences The social norms and activities traditionally practiced within children's gender-segregated peer groups foster different interpersonal goals in cisgender girls and boys. For example, in their peer interactions, many girls commonly engage in domestic scenarios ("playing house") that are structured around collaborative and affectionate interchanges. Boys' play is more likely to involve competitive contexts ("playing war" or sports) that are structured around dominance and power. The impact of same-gender peer norms was implicated in Leaper and Smith's (2004) meta-analysis, which found that gender differences in communication were more likely to be detected in studies of same-gender interactions than in mixed-gender interactions.

Cultural influences Cross-cultural comparisons generally find a similar pattern of average gender difference in social behaviour. That is, affiliative social behaviour tends to be more common amongst girls and women than amongst boys and men, whereas directive social behaviour tends to be more common amongst boys and men than amongst girls and women (Best, 2010). However, there are cultural variations in the degree to which these behaviours might be seen. For instance, in many Asian cultures, such as Japan, it is generally considered important for boys as well as girls to show high levels of affiliation in social interaction. Yet, within these cultures, boys and men tend to be more direct in their speech than do girls and women (Smith, 1992). Also, there are cultural variations within diverse nations, such as the United States. For example, some researchers have observed highly direct social interactions amongst African American girls from working-class and low-income neighbourhoods in contrast to European American girls from middle-class communities (Kyratzis, 2004).

Aggressive Behaviour

The conventional wisdom is that boys are more aggressive than girls. In support of this expectation, research studies indicate a reliable average gender difference in aggression. But the magnitude of the gender difference is not as great as many people expect. Also, this difference depends partly on the type of aggression being considered (see Table 15.1).

As noted in Chapter 13, researchers distinguish between direct and indirect forms of aggression (Archer & Coyne, 2005; Björkqvist, Österman, & Kaukiainen, 1992). *Direct aggression* involves overt physical or verbal acts openly intended to cause harm, whereas *indirect aggression* (also known as relational or social aggression) involves attempts to damage a person's social standing or group acceptance through covert means such as negative gossip and social exclusion.

Indirect aggression includes behaviours such as criticizing and spreading rumors about a peer or excluding a peer from the friendship group. Contrary to the "mean girl" stereotype in popular media, average rates of indirect aggression appear similar for girls and boys. However, boys use higher average rates of direct physical and verbal aggression. Therefore, when acting aggressively, girls may tend to use *proportionally* more indirect than direct aggression than boys do.

SPENCER GRANT/PHOTOEDIT

Average gender differences in the incidence of physical aggression emerge gradually during the preschool years (Hay, 2007). In two comprehensive meta-analyses of studies comparing boys' and girls' aggressive behaviour, both physical and verbal forms of direct aggression occurred more often amongst boys than amongst girls (Archer, 2004; Card et al., 2008). The average difference was small during childhood and medium to large during adolescence. Although direct aggression generally declined for both boys and girls with age, the drop was more pronounced for girls than for boys (Archer, 2004).

There appears to be no average gender difference during childhood in the use of indirect aggression. In a meta-analysis of studies testing for such gender differences (Card et al., 2008), only a negligible effect size during adolescence was indicated, with girls slightly more likely than boys to use indirect aggression. The trivial effect size may seem surprising given the popular notion of "mean girls" who use indirect strategies such as negative gossip and social exclusion. However, because direct aggression is less likely amongst girls than boys, girls tend to use proportionally more indirect than direct aggression than boys, on average. Thus, when most girls do express aggression, they may be more apt to use indirect rather than direct physical or verbal aggression (Leaper, 2013). Many boys may use a similar amount of indirect aggression as girls and additionally use more direct aggression.

Average gender differences in aggression have been found primarily in research on same-gender interactions. Research conducted with mostly European American children suggests that different rules may apply when some girls and boys have conflicts with one another. Beginning in early childhood, boys are more likely than girls to ignore the other gender's attempts to exert influence (Maccoby, 1998). Thus, when they are more assertive and less affiliative, boys may be more apt to get their way in unsupervised mixed-gender groups.

Studies in the United States comparing children's behaviour in same-gender versus cross-gender conflicts revealed another interesting pattern. In same-gender conflicts, boys were more likely to use power-assertive strategies (e.g., threats, demands) and girls were more likely to use conflict-mitigation strategies (e.g., compromise, change the topic). Yet in cross-gender conflicts, girls' use of power-assertive strategies increased, while boys' use of conflict-mitigation strategies did not change (Miller et al., 1986; Sims, Hutchins, & Taylor, 1998). These studies suggest that cisgender girls often may find it necessary to play by the boys' rules to gain influence in mixed-gender settings.

Explanations for Gender Differences in Aggression

Possible explanations for gender differences in aggression range from the effects of physiological factors to the socializing influences of family, peers, the media, and the culture at large. Each factor likely has a contributing role.

Brain and hormonal influences It is well known that, on average, males have higher baseline levels of testosterone than do females. Many people assume that this accounts for gender differences in aggression. Contrary to this popular belief, there does *not* appear to be a direct association between aggression and baseline testosterone levels (Archer, Graham-Kevan, & Davies, 2005). However, there is an indirect one: the body increases its production of testosterone in response to perceived threats and challenges, and this increase can lead to more aggressive behaviour (Archer, 2006). Furthermore, people who are impulsive and less inhibited are more likely to perceive the behaviour of others as threatening. Thus, because boys, on average, have more difficulty regulating emotional arousal (Else-Quest et al., 2006), they may be more prone to engage in direct aggression (Hay, 2007). Conversely, greater average emotion regulation amongst girls (compared to boys) may contribute to higher rates of prosocial behaviour and lower rates of direct aggressive behaviour.

Cognitive and motivational influences Average gender differences in empathy and prosocial behaviour may be related to differences in boys' and girls' rates of aggression (Knight, Fabes, & Higgins, 1996; Lemerise & Arsenio, 2000; Levant, 2005; Mayberry & Espelage, 2007). On average, girls are somewhat more likely than boys to report feelings of empathy and sympathy in response to people's distress (Eisenberg & Fabes, 1998), and they also tend to display more concern in their behavioural reactions (e.g., looks of concern and attempts to help). Direct aggression may be more likely amongst children who are less empathetic and have fewer prosocial skills. In support of this explanation, one study found average gender differences, with boys demonstrating higher rates of direct aggression and lower rates of empathy than girls, but both aggressive girls and aggressive boys were rated lower on empathy than were nonaggressive girls and boys (Mayberry & Espelage, 2007).

The gender-typed social norms and goals regarding assertion and affiliation may further contribute to the average gender difference in conflict and aggression (Chang, 2004; Miller et al., 1986; Rose & Rudolph, 2006; see Table 15.1). More boys than girls tend to favour assertive over affiliative goals (e.g., being dominant), whereas more girls than boys tend to endorse affiliative goals or a combination of affiliative and assertive goals (e.g., maintaining intimacy). When some boys focus on dominance goals, they may be more likely to appraise conflicts as competitions that require the use of direct aggression. In addition, some boys may initiate direct aggression as a way to enhance their status.

In contrast, by emphasizing intimacy and nurturance goals, many girls may be more likely to view relationship conflicts as threats to interpersonal harmony that need to be resolved through compromise (Miller et al., 1986). The normative social pressures amongst many girls to act "nice" may also lead them to avoid direct confrontation. However, when girls who adhere to these norms are unable to resolve a conflict, they may try to hurt one another through indirect strategies such as criticizing or excluding the offender or sharing secret information about the offender with other girls (Murray-Close, Ostrov, & Crick, 2007; Underwood, 2003).

Parental and other adult influences In general, most parents and other adults disapprove of physical aggression in both boys and girls. After the preschool years, however, adults tend to be more tolerant of aggression in boys and often adopt a "boys will be boys" attitude toward it (Martin & Ross, 2005). In a classic experiment demonstrating this effect, researchers asked people to watch a short film of two children engaged in rough-and-tumble play in the snow and to rate the level of the play's aggressiveness (Condry & Ross, 1985). The children were dressed in gender-neutral snowsuits and filmed at a distance that made their gender undeterminable. Some viewers were told that both children were boys; others were told that the children were both girls; still others were told that the children were a boy and girl. Viewers who thought that both children were boys rated their play as much less aggressive than did viewers who thought that both children were girls. A subsequent Canadian study showed that this "boys will be boys" bias may vary somewhat with observer gender: male early childhood educators were less concerned about boys' physical aggression than were female early childhood educators (Bosacki et al., 2015).

Children also appear aware of this "boys will be boys" bias. They believe that physical aggression is more acceptable, and less likely to be punished, when enacted by boys than when enacted by girls (Giles & Heyman, 2005; Perry, Perry, & Weiss, 1989). Thus, girls' average reliance on primarily indirect strategies of aggression—that are covert and easily denied if detected—may reflect their recognition that displays of physical aggression on their part will attract adult attention and punishment.

Parenting style may also factor into children's manifestations of aggression. Harsh, inconsistent parenting and poor monitoring increase the likelihood of physical aggression in childhood (Leve, Pears, & Fisher, 2002; Vitaro et al., 2006). Children who experience such parenting may learn to mistrust others and make hostile attributions about other people's intentions (Crick & Dodge, 1996). The association between harsh parenting and later physical aggression is stronger for boys than for girls. Also, as noted in Chapter 14, poor parental monitoring increases children's susceptibility to negative peer influences and is correlated with higher rates of aggression and delinquency (Jacobson & Crockett, 2000). Thus, the fact that parents monitor daughters more closely than sons may contribute to gender differences in aggression.

Peer influences Gender differences in aggression are consistent with the gender-typed social norms of girls' and boys' same-gender peer groups. For example, a study conducted in China of 82 junior high school classrooms (with 50–60 students each) found that average gender differences in rates of aggression varied across classrooms, depending on whether there were gender differences in classroom norms for accepting aggression (Chang, 2004). However, it is worth noting that children who are high in aggression *and* low in prosocial behaviour are typically rejected in both male and female peer groups (Hawley, Little, & Card, 2008). These children tend to seek out marginal peer groups of other similarly rejected peers; these contacts strengthen the likelihood of physical aggression over time (Werner & Crick, 2004).

Another peer influence on aggression may be boys' regular participation in aggressive contact sports, which sanction the use of physical force and may contribute to higher rates of direct aggression amongst boys (Kidd, 2013; Messner, 2002). Support for this proposal is the finding that participation in aggressive sports, such as football, in high school is correlated with a higher likelihood of sexual aggression in university (Forbes et al., 2006). As explained in Box 15.3, aggressive behaviours may also involve sexual harassment.

Media influences A common question raised by parents and researchers is whether frequently watching violent TV shows and movies or playing violent video games has a negative impact on children. As you might expect, boys are more likely than girls to devote time to these activities (Cherney & London, 2006). One possible inference is that consuming more violent media may contribute to average gender differences in physical aggression.

Our discussion of media violence in Chapter 9 makes clear that viewing aggression in movies, TV programming, and video games is associated with children's aggressive behaviour and that this holds true for girls as well as boys. As also noted in that chapter, the degree and nature of this relationship remains a topic of debate.

Whereas boys are more likely than girls to favour TV shows and movies with violent content, one study found that adolescent girls were more likely than boys to prefer shows depicting indirect aggression (Coyne & Archer, 2005). Furthermore, an experimental study demonstrated that observing indirect aggression on TV increased the subsequent likelihood of indirect aggressive behaviour but had no impact on direct aggression (Coyne, Archer, & Eslea, 2004).

Other cultural influences Although gender differences in aggression have been observed in all cultures, cultural norms also play an important role in determining the levels of aggression that are observed in boys and girls. Douglas Fry (1988) studied rural communities in the mountains of Mexico and found that the levels of childhood aggression that were considered normal varied widely from one area to another. Boys in each community showed more aggression than girls did. However, girls in the high-aggression communities were more aggressive than boys in the low-aggression communities.

The community context must also be considered in relation to the emergence of differential rates of aggression. More than 60% of children (under 18 years) in the United States are

Boys are more likely to witness violent events, and these experiences may contribute to higher average rates of aggression for boys compared with girls.

JOAN BARNETT LEE/MODESTO BEE/MCT/NEWSCOM

BOX 15.3 APPLICATIONS Sexual Harassment and Dating Violence

Sexual harassment commonly affects children and adolescents, and it can involve direct (physical or verbal) or indirect (relational) aggression. Physical sexual harassment involves inappropriate touching or forced sexual activity. Verbal sexual harassment involves unwanted, demeaning, or homophobic sexual comments, whether spoken directly to the target or indirectly, behind her or his back. Also, verbal harassment commonly spreads via electronic media (Ybarra & Mitchell, 2007).

Surveys in the United States and Canada indicate that the vast majority of youth of all genders have experienced sexual harassment during adolescence (AAUW, 2011; Leaper & Brown, 2008; McMaster et al., 2002; Mitchell et al., 2014). Most teen sexual harassment occurs in school hallways and classrooms, and the perpetrators are more likely to be peers rather than teachers or other adults. In a large-scale study of Canadian students, 41% of girls and 30% of boys in grade 10 reported having experienced sexual harassment at least once during the prior two months (Craig, Lambe, & McIver, 2016).

A more recent online survey of adolescent Internet users in the United States (Mitchell et al., 2014) examined rates of reported sexual harassment separately for youth based on their gender and self-identified sexual orientation. Across ages (13 to 18 years), the percent reporting sexual harassment was 43% for heterosexual girls, 72% for lesbian girls, 66% for bisexual girls, 23% for heterosexual boys, 82% for transgender youth, 66% for gay boys, and 50% for bisexual boys. The findings from Mitchell and colleagues' survey are consistent with other reports, including data from Canadian adolescents, that rates of sexual harassment may be higher for sexual-minority (lesbian, gay, bisexual), transgender, and other gender-nonconforming youths (AAUW, 2011; Williams et al., 2005).

When the adolescents in a U.S. national survey were asked to indicate whether and how sexual harassment affected them, girls were more likely than boys to report negative effects (AAUW, 2011; also found in Mitchell et al., 2014). The most common responses to sexual harassment in this survey included not wanting to go to school (37% of girls, 25% of boys) and finding it difficult to study (34% of girls, 24% of boys). Boys were more likely than girls to report that experiences with sexual harassment had no effect on them (17% of boys, 10% of girls).

Amongst cisgender heterosexual youth, girls appear to have more negative reactions to sexual harassment on average than do boys—perhaps partly because girls are somewhat more likely than boys to experience repeated sexual harassment (AAUW, 2011). Also, because of traditional masculine socialization, boys may be more reluctant to admit vulnerability (Farkas & Leaper, 2016). For any individual, repeated experiences with sexual harassment can have long-term negative consequences on self-esteem and adjustment (Bucchianeri et al., 2014; Leaper & Brown, 2008; Olson et al., 2016).

Sexual harassment and violence also occur in dating relationships. Physical aggression occurs in an estimated one-fourth of adolescent heterosexual dating relationships in the United States (Hickman, Jaycox, & Aronoff, 2004; O'Leary et al., 2008), with boys the more likely perpetrators (Swahn et al., 2008; Wolitzky-Taylor et al., 2008). A recent study in British Columbia suggests that physical aggression in adolescent dating relationships has declined slightly over the past 10 years, perhaps due to programming that emphasizes healthy relationships (Shaffer et al., 2018).

In a recent nationwide survey of 9th- to 12th-grade students in the United States (Kann et al., 2016), the reported incidence of having been forced to have unwanted sexual intercourse was 18% for gay, lesbian, and bisexual respondents compared to 5% for heterosexual respondents. In addition, 18% of gay, lesbian, and bisexual students reported being victims of dating violence in the past year compared with 8% of heterosexual students (Kann et al., 2016).

The surveys described above were primarily conducted in the United States but generally align with Canadian data. Other studies indicate that sexual harassment and sexual violence are also problems for teens in many parts of the world (see Leaper & Robnett, 2018). A cross-national comparison indicated that rates of sexual violence against women were higher in countries with greater societal gender inequality (Yodanis, 2004).

estimated to have experienced or witnessed violence in their community within the past year (Child Trends Data Bank, 2016; Finkelhor et al., 2009). Moreover, these experiences are more common for children living in low-income, inner-city environments than those in wealthier suburbs. When children are exposed to violence in their homes and communities, boys and girls both experience an increased risk of emotional and behavioural problems and show an increase in aggressive behaviours. However, boys are more likely than girls to be exposed to the highest levels of violence, and the average impact of exposure is also greater for boys than for girls (Guerra, Huesmann, & Spindler, 2003).

REVIEW QUESTION

How do social cultural norms influence the various patterns of gender development discussed in this section? ■

CHAPTER SUMMARY

Sex and Gender

- *Sex* describes distinctions between genetic females (XX) and genetic males (XY), as well as other genetic sex compositions; *gender* indicates social assignment or self-categorization as female or male (or neither).
- A variety of terms are used to distinguish between different gender identities, including cisgender, transgender, nonbinary (genderqueer), gender-fluid, bigender, and agender. Terms are also used to describe how gender is socialized: gender typing refers to the process of gender socialization during development, and terms such as cross-gender-typed and gender nonconforming describe behaviours contrary to those stereotyped for a given person's assigned gender.
- Research has shown gender differences in some areas, including cognitive abilities, personality traits, and social behaviours, but these differences tend to be small and there is often considerable overlap between genders. Hyde's *gender similarities hypothesis* argues that similarities between genders far outweigh differences on most attributes.

Theoretical Approaches to Gender Development

- Biosocial theory focuses on the impact of evolved *physical* differences between females (childbearing and nursing capacities) and males (greater strength, speed, and size) in relation to the social ecology.
- Other biological researchers take a neuroscience approach to gender development by focusing on sex differences in brain organization and the influences of sex hormones (such as androgens) both before birth and after.
- Another approach, which addresses cognitive and motivational influences on gender development, includes cognitive developmental theory, gender schema theory, social cognitive theory, and social identity theory. All emphasize children's active participation in learning gender roles and adopting the preferences and behaviours considered appropriate for their gender, thereby highlighting how gender development is largely a process of self-socialization.
- According to cognitive developmental theory, once children realize that their gender is consistent across situations (gender constancy), they pay close attention to same-gender models to learn how to behave.
- Gender schema theory maintains that children construct mental representations of gender based on their own experience and the gender-related ideas they are exposed to. Children begin to acquire same-gender interests and values as soon as they can identify their own gender. Subsequently, children pay greater attention to, and learn more about, those things that they regard as relevant for their own gender.
- Social cognitive theory addresses many processes involved in learning gender-typed values and behaviours, including observing others' behaviour and determining the consequences of particular behaviours in relation to one's own or other people's gender. Children internalize gender-typed norms, standards that they use to monitor their own behaviour.
- Social identity theory also stresses the importance of adopting a gender identity and proposes that children tend to form an ingroup bias favouring attributes associated with their own gender and also to enforce conformity to gender-role norms.
- Two recent theoretical approaches have attempted to integrate aspects of physiological, cognitive, motivational, situation, and cultural influences on gender development. Developmental intergroup theory (DIT) describes how diverse processes contribute to the development of stereotyping and prejudice based on a person's gender. The gender self-socialization model (GSSM) emphasizes the degree to which children's efforts to form an identity and understand the world around them contributes to their gender development.
- The bioecological model characterizes children's development as embedded in nested systems ranging from the microsystem (immediate environment) to the macrosystem (society). A key feature of the macrosystem is its opportunity structure and the corresponding roles available to women and men that shape the ways in which girls and boys are socialized.

Milestones in Gender Development

- Between 6 and 8 weeks of prenatal development, sexual differentiation begins. External and internal genitalia are normally completed by the end of the first trimester.
- During their first year, infants learn to distinguish male from female faces. Between ages 2 and 3, children learn to identify their own gender, start to acquire stereotypes about males and females, and begin to prefer gender-typed toys and play activities.
- During preschool, children begin to gravitate toward same-gender peers, and a strong tendency for children to self-segregate by gender persists until adolescence. Preschool children also stereotype certain traits and activities for each gender. Preferences for gender-typed play become stronger from early to middle childhood.
- At about 6 years of age, children develop gender constancy. In addition, during middle childhood, they come to understand that gender roles are social conventions. They also may understand that gender discrimination is unfair and notice when it occurs. Average gender differences in social behaviour begin to emerge, with boys more likely than girls to stress assertion over affiliation, and girls more apt to emphasize affiliation or a combination of affiliation and assertion.

- During adolescence, gender roles sometimes become more flexible (due to increased cognitive flexibility) or more rigid (due to concerns with heterosexual roles and adoption of conventional gender attitudes).

Patterns of Gender Development

- Boys and girls are quite similar in physical development until puberty, which begins earlier for girls than for boys. Amongst the largest average gender differences are physical strength, speed, and size after puberty, and a moderate difference exists in physical activity level.
- Girls and boys score similarly on tests of general intelligence. Slight-to-small average gender differences have been reported in specific cognitive abilities: boys show higher proficiency with certain types of spatial reasoning and mathematic ability, and girls show a small advantage in verbal ability. In academic achievement, girls have tended to do better than boys in reading and writing, whereas boys have tended to do better than girls in the physical sciences. Girls also tend to do better in overall school performance.
- Biological, cognitive-motivational, and cultural factors may contribute to gender-related variations in academic achievement. Researchers find academic achievement in particular domains is related to the expectations of parents, peers, and teachers. The gender gap in U.S. achievement in STEM fields has dramatically closed in recent decades, and such differences are less likely in societies characterized by greater overall gender equality.
- Average gender differences in communication and interpersonal goals during childhood and adolescence have been found to be modest. More boys than girls tended to emphasize dominance and power as goals in their social relationships, and more girls than boys tended to favour intimacy and support as goals in their relationships.
- Direct (physical and verbal) aggression is associated with an average gender difference of moderate effect size, with higher rates amongst boys than amongst girls. No meaningful average gender difference appears in indirect aggression (such as social exclusion or negative gossip). However, indirect aggression constitutes a larger proportion of all aggressive behaviours amongst girls than amongst boys. Lower average levels of self-regulation may be partly related to the higher incidence of direct aggression amongst boys. Some cultural variations in the magnitude of gender difference in direct aggression are related to the degree that behaviours such as sexual harassment are tolerated in a particular culture.

Test Yourself

1. The gender similarities hypothesis emphasizes that in areas of cognitive behaviours and social abilities
   a. all measurable differences between the sexes are trivial.
   b. boys and girls develop on parallel but unequal tracks.
   c. similarities between boys and girls far outweigh differences.
   d. differences between boys and girls outweigh similarities.

2. Rose is a 9-year-old girl. She strongly prefers wearing T-shirts and jeans to dresses and other "girly" clothes. She loves sports and hates playing with dolls. Rose's preferences are an example of ____________.
   a. gender-role intensification
   b. cross-gender-typed behaviour
   c. cisgender modelling
   d. gender segregation

3. Gender typing refers to
   a. the identification of an individual based on sex chromosomes.
   b. an individual's personal identification as male, female, or neither.
   c. the process of gender socialization that occurs during development.
   d. the genetic forces that determine an individual's sex during prenatal development.

4. The use of gendered nouns and pronouns, the association of certain hairstyles with specific genders, and the gender differentiation of specific colours are all examples of which of the following?
   a. The psychological salience of gender
   b. Gender identity
   c. Organizational influences
   d. Gender-role intensification

5. Finnegan, a 5-year-old boy, is given a choice between playing with a toy truck or a ballerina doll. He chooses the truck because he has learned that boys play with trucks and girls play with dolls. This episode illustrates the child's ____________.
   a. interest filter
   b. intersectionality
   c. gender schema filter
   d. gender segregation

6. Exposure to high levels of prenatal androgens in genetic females may influence the development of their nervous system in such a way that results in certain cross-gender-typed behaviours. This example demonstrates the effect of ____________.
   a. activating influences
   b. cisgender disposition
   c. organizing influences
   d. self-socialization

7. Which of the following statements is most representative of Kohlberg's conception of the gender constancy stage?
   a. "Girls can have babies, boys cannot."
   b. "I am a boy today, but could be a girl tomorrow."
   c. "Even if I cut my hair and dress like a boy, I am a girl."
   d. "I will always be a girl."
8. The complex web of influences—including gender, sexual orientation, race, social class, and other group affiliations—that shape an individual's social identity and experiences is known as ____________.
   a. gender schema
   b. in-group assimilation
   c. intersectionality
   d. collaboration
9. Alex is a 6-year-old boy. His father disapproves when Alex plays with his sister's dolls but happily engages with him when Alex plays with trucks. This scenario is an example of the influence of ____________ in shaping Alex's gender identity.
   a. observational learning
   b. collaboration
   c. enactive experience
   d. intersectionality
10. Gender segregation refers to
    a. the tendency of young children to associate with same-gender peers and avoid other-gender peers.
    b. the difference between the sexes in cognitive and behavioural tendencies.
    c. the tendency for an individual to engage in gender-typed behaviours.
    d. the tendency of an individual to retain information that is gender schema-consistent.
11. An individual who is high in both assertion and affiliation is likely to display which of the following communication styles?
    a. Collaboration
    b. Withdrawal
    c. Obliging statements
    d. Controlling statements
12. The tendency of adolescents to integrate elements of traditional gender roles into their personal values, which can lead to increased gender discrimination, is known as ____________.
    a. gender-role flexibility
    b. gender-role intensification
    c. assimilation
    d. collaboration
13. Some people believe that men are supposed to protect women. They may also believe that men and women possess complementary traits, such as men are leaders and protectors and women are submissive and nurturing. These attitudes reflect ____________.
    a. gender constancy
    b. the interest filter
    c. benevolent sexism
    d. hostile sexism
14. Children tend to be motivated to achieve in those areas that they find personally valuable and in which they expect to succeed. This tendency is described by which of the following models?
    a. Gender self-socialization model
    b. Developmental intergroup model
    c. Expectancy-value model of achievement
    d. Affiliation-assertion model
15. Small but consistent gender differences have been found in all of the following domains except ____________.
    a. self-concept
    b. general intelligence
    c. communication skills
    d. mental spatial rotation tasks

LaunchPad
macmillan learning

DON'T STOP NOW! Research shows that testing yourself is a powerful learning tool. Visit LaunchPad to access the LearningCurve adaptive quizzing system, which gives you a personalized study plan to help build your mastery of the chapter material through videos, activities, and more. **Go to launchpadworks.com.**

Critical Thinking Questions

1. The four children described at the start of the chapter were portrayed to highlight variations in gender-typed behaviour and interests both between gender and within genders. How would the different theories outlined in this chapter attempt to explain these differences and similarities? How would different theories account for other children who have more flexible gender-typed behaviours and interests?
2. Think about how females and males were portrayed in shows, movies, and video games as you were growing up. How might these depictions have affected your gender development?

3. Imagine that you wanted to raise your own children to be as minimally gender-typed as possible. Which of the theoretical perspectives outlined in the chapter would you rely on most? Do you think you would be more likely to achieve your goal with a daughter or a son?
4. Historically, men have held dominant status in society, but over the course of the last several decades, women have significantly increased their status and power in Canada and in many other countries. Women now occupy top ranks in many occupations, and it is no longer uncommon to see men engaged in childcare and housework. How do you think this trend toward gender equality amongst adults will affect the kinds of play activities and behaviours in which girls and boys engage in the future?
5. Research on gender development has tended to focus on cisgender children. How might the inclusion of a wider range of gender identities affect our understanding of gender differences and gender development in the future?

Key Terms

activating influences, p. 532
adrenarche, p. 552
affiliation, p. 546
agender, p. 526
ambivalent sexism, p. 548
androgen insensitivity syndrome (AIS), p. 551
androgens, p. 531
assertion, p. 546
bigender, p. 526
body image, p. 552
cisgender, p. 526
collaboration, p. 546
congenital adrenal hyperplasia (CAH), p. 550
cross-gender-typed, p. 527
effect size, p. 528
enactive experience, p. 536
gender, p. 526
gender constancy, p. 533
gender-fluid, p. 526
gender identity, p. 533
gender nonconforming, p. 528
gender schema filter, p. 535
gender schemas, p. 534
gender segregation, p. 544
gender stability, p. 533
gender-typed, p. 527
gender typing, p. 527
gender-role flexibility, p. 548
gender-role intensification, p. 548
ingroup assimilation, p. 538
ingroup bias, p. 538
interest filter, p. 535
intersectionality, p. 539
intersex condition, p. 550
menarche, p. 551
meta-analysis, p. 528
nonbinary (genderqueer), p. 526
observational learning, p. 537
opportunity structure, p. 541
organizing influences, p. 532
puberty, p. 551
self-socialization, p. 532
sex, p. 526
spermarche, p. 551
transgender, p. 526
tuition, p. 536

Answers to Test Yourself

1. c, **2.** b, **3.** c, **4.** a, **5.** c, **6.** c, **7.** c, **8.** c, **9.** c, **10.** a, **11.** a, **12.** b, **13.** c, **14.** c, **15.** b

CHAPTER

Conclusions

16

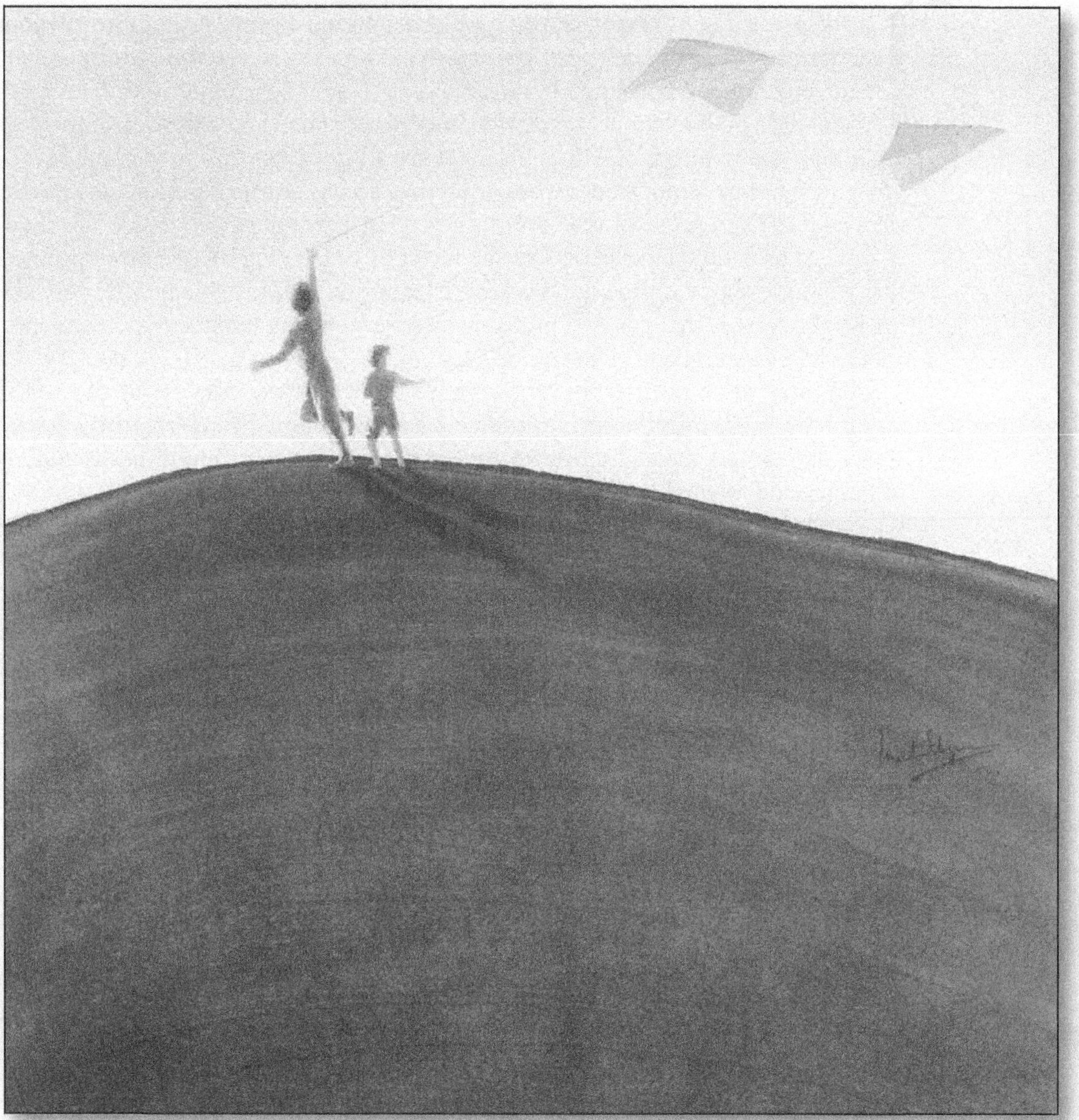

LINCOLN SELIGMAN/PRIVATE COLLECTION/BRIDGEMAN IMAGES

LINCOLN SELIGMAN, *Kite Flying* (watercolour on paper, 2000)

THEMES

NATURE AND NURTURE ■ THE ACTIVE CHILD ■ CONTINUITY/DISCONTINUITY ■ MECHANISMS OF CHANGE
THE SOCIOCULTURAL CONTEXT ■ INDIVIDUAL DIFFERENCES ■ RESEARCH AND CHILDREN'S WELFARE

In the preceding 15 chapters, you have encountered a great deal of information about how children develop. You learned about the development of perception, attachment, conceptual understanding, language, intelligence, emotional regulation, peer relations, aggression, morality, gender, and a host of other vital human characteristics. Although these are all important parts of child development, the sheer amount of information may seem daunting: getting lost in the trees and losing a sense of the forest is a real risk. We therefore devote this final chapter to providing an overview of the forest by organizing many of the specifics that you have learned into an integrative framework. A likely side benefit of reading this chapter is that you will probably discover that you understand much more about child development than you realized.

The integrative framework that organizes this chapter consists of the seven themes that were introduced in Chapter 1 and highlighted throughout the book. As we have noted, most child-development research is ultimately aimed at understanding fundamental issues related to these themes. This is true regardless of the type of development that the research addresses and regardless of whether the research focuses on fetuses, infants, toddlers, preschoolers, school-age children, or adolescents. Beneath the myriad details, the seven themes emerge again and again.

Theme 1: Nature and Nurture: All Interactions, All the Time

When people think about a child's nature, they typically focus on the biological characteristics with which the child enters the world. When they think of the child's nurture, they focus on the child-rearing experiences provided by parents, caregivers, and other adults. Within this view, nurture is like a sculptor, shaping the raw material provided by the child's nature into ever closer approximations of its final form.

Although this metaphor is appealing, the reality is much more complex. Unlike the sculptor's passive media of marble and clay, children are active participants in their own development. They seek out experiences based on their inclinations and interests. They also influence other people's behaviour toward them: from birth onward, their nature influences the nurture they receive. In addition, rather than nature doing its work before birth and nurture doing its work after, nurture influences development even before birth, and nature is just as influential in adolescence and adulthood as earlier. In this section, we review how nature and nurture interact to produce development.

Nature and Nurture Begin Interacting Before Birth

When prenatal development proceeds normally, it is easy to think of it as a simple unfolding of innate potential, one in which the environment matters little. When things go wrong, however, the interaction of nature and nurture is all too apparent. Consider the effects of teratogens. Prenatal exposure to these potentially harmful substances—which include toxins in the general environment, such as mercury, radiation, lead, insects (e.g., mosquitoes carrying the Zika virus), and air pollution, as well as toxins that depend on parental behaviour (e.g., cigarettes, alcohol, and illegal drugs)—can cause a wide variety of physical and cognitive impairments. Nevertheless, whether and how much a given baby will actually be affected depends on innumerable interactions amongst the genetics of the mother, the genetics of the fetus, and a host of environmental factors such as the particular teratogen and the timing and amount of exposure.

The interaction of nature and nurture during the prenatal period is also evident in fetal learning. The experience of hearing the mother's voice while in the womb leads a newborn to prefer her voice to that of other women. The influence of prenatal experience can be long-lasting; for example, prenatal exposure to garlic-flavoured food influences liking of such flavours amongst 8- and 9-year-olds. Thus, preferences that are often thought of as being determined purely by nature reflect nurture as well.

Infants' Nature Elicits Nurture

Nature equips babies with a host of qualities that elicit appropriate nurture from parents and other caregivers. One big factor in babies' favour is that they are cute; most people enjoy watching and interacting with them. By looking and smiling at other people, babies motivate others to feel warmly toward them and to care for them. Their emotional expressions—cries, coos, and smiles—guide caregivers' efforts to figure out what to do to make them happy and comfortable. In addition, their attentiveness to sights and sounds that they find interesting encourages others to talk to them and to provide the stimulation necessary for learning. One simple example of this interactive relationship is the fact that parents everywhere sing to their infants; infants throughout the world find singing soothing, bounce in response to rhythm, and respond positively to melodies.

Timing Matters

The effects of an experience on development depend on the state of the organism at the time of the experience. Timing of exposure to teratogens greatly influences their effects on prenatal development. For example, if a pregnant woman comes down with rubella early in pregnancy, when the developing visual and auditory systems are at a particularly sensitive point, her baby may be born deaf or blind; if she comes down with rubella late in pregnancy, the risk that damage will occur is considerably lower.

Timing also influences many aspects of development in the months and years following birth. The development of perceptual capabilities presents numerous illustrations of the importance of appropriate experience at the appropriate time. The general rule in such cases is "use it or lose it": for normal development to occur, children must encounter the relevant experiences during a certain window of time.

Auditory development provides a good example. Until 8 months of age, infants can discriminate between phonemes regardless of whether they occur in the language the infants hear daily. By age

Infants' expressions of contentment and happiness when engaging in certain activities motivate their parents and other adults to engage in the activities with them.

ALLEN DONIKOWSKI/GETTY IMAGES

12 months, however, infants lose the ability to hear the difference between similar sounds that they do not ordinarily encounter or that are not meaningfully different in their native language.

Similar sensitive periods occur in grammatical development. Children from East Asia who move to the United States and begin to learn English as a second language before age 7 acquire grammatical competence in English that eventually matches that of native-born American children. Those who arrive between ages 7 and 11 learn almost as well. However, individuals who arrive at later ages rarely master English grammar, even after many years of hearing and speaking the language of their adopted land. Deaf children's learning of sign language shows a similar pattern: early exposure results in more complete grammatical mastery.

The importance of normal early experience is also evident in social, emotional, and intellectual development. Infants and toddlers who do not have an emotional connection with any caregiver, such as the children who spent their first years in the infamous orphanages of Romania in the 1980s or in concentration camps during World War II, often continue to interact atypically with other people long after being placed in loving homes. Those who spent their first 2 years or more in the Romanian orphanages also had unusually high rates of low IQ for many years after they were adopted into the loving families. Thus, in many aspects of the development of perception, language, intelligence, emotions, and social behaviour, the timing of experience is crucial.

Differences in running speeds are partially attributable to genetic differences that are present at birth, but nature takes time to reveal itself. Who could have looked at these children when they were newborns and predicted who would be the best runners?

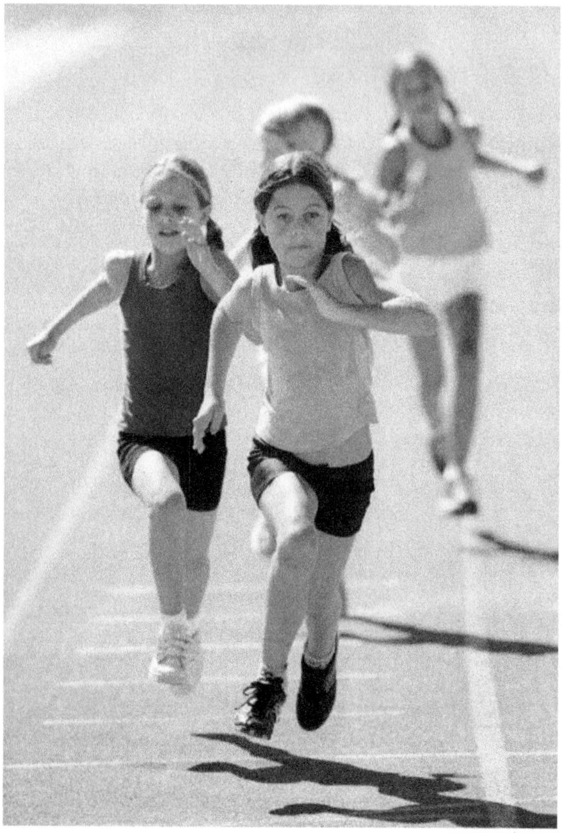

POLKA DOT IMAGES/GETTY IMAGES

Nature Does Not Reveal Itself All at Once

Many genetically influenced properties do not become evident until middle childhood, adolescence, or adulthood. One obvious example is the physical changes that occur at puberty. A less obvious example involves nearsightedness. Many children are born with genes that predispose them to become nearsighted, but most do not become so until late childhood or early adolescence. A third example involves the steep rise during adolescence in the incidence of depression. Depression has a genetic component, but the increased rate of depression in adolescence, especially in girls, is also attributable to the many challenges of dealing with the world of adolescence, such as encountering cruel comments on social media.

The development of schizophrenia follows a similar path. Schizophrenia is highly influenced by genes inherited at conception, but most people who become schizophrenic do not do so until late adolescence or early adulthood. As with other aspects of development, the emergence of schizophrenia reflects a complex interplay between nature and nurture. Children with a schizophrenic biological parent who are raised by nonschizophrenic parents are more likely to become schizophrenic themselves than are the biological children of the nonschizophrenic parents. Children who are raised in troubled homes are also more likely than others to become schizophrenic. However, the only children with a substantial likelihood of becoming schizophrenic are those who grow up in a troubled family *and* have a biological parent who is schizophrenic. As in other contexts, the interaction between the children's nature and the nurture they receive is crucial.

Perhaps the most surprising and compelling evidence for the interaction of nature and nurture comes from the emerging field of epigenetics. Although people often think of the genotype as being "fixed" at birth, experience can enhance or silence gene expression. Early stressful environments, such as those imposed by poverty, seem to especially influence later gene expression. Thus, adults who grew up in low-income families exhibit different patterns of gene expression decades later than do adults who grew up in high-income homes, regardless of their incomes as adults. Even more remarkably, some of these effects of the early environment on the genome are passed down to the next generation, perhaps through the mechanism of early adversity influencing methylation of sperm cells. Thus, not only does nature not reveal itself all at once, but nature itself changes as a result of nurture.

Everything Influences Everything

One common reaction to learning about the complex interactions between nature and nurture is "It sounds like everything influences everything else." Although it sounds glib, this conclusion is basically accurate. Consider some of the factors that influence children's and adolescents' self-esteem. Genes matter; the closer the biological relation between two children or adolescents, the more similar their degree of self-esteem is likely to be. A large part of the reason for this genetic influence on self-esteem is that genes influence a wide range of *other* characteristics that themselves influence self-esteem. For example, genes strongly affect attractiveness, athletic talent, and academic success, all of which contribute to self-esteem.

Factors other than genes also play large roles in the development of self-esteem. Support from one's family and peers contribute in positive ways; poverty and unpopularity contribute in negative ways. Unrelated adults also can have positive or negative influences on self-esteem. For example, having a supportive teacher can promote a child's self-esteem, and having a hostile or demeaning teacher can reduce it. Values of the broader society are also influential. East Asian societies tend to emphasize the importance of self-criticism, and children and adolescents in those societies report lower levels of self-esteem than do peers in Western societies.

Complex interactions are not limited to the development of self-esteem or to social development; they are characteristic of development in all areas. For example, in the development of intelligence, the influence of genetics seems to be greater than that of shared environment for children from middle- and upper-income backgrounds, but the opposite seems to be true for children from impoverished backgrounds. Similarly, parental involvement in school is more closely related to academic achievement in low-income families than in more affluent families. Thus, children's nature—their genes, personal characteristics, and behavioural tendencies—interact with the nurture they receive from parents, teachers, peers, the broader society, and the physical environment to shape their self-esteem, intellect, and other qualities.

Theme 2: Children Play Active Roles in Their Own Development

Physical activity begins even before the fetus leaves the womb; the kicking that thrills prospective parents is perhaps the most obvious example. Less obviously, fetuses are also mentally active. While still in the womb, they can learn enough about the sounds in a story their mother repeatedly reads aloud that, as newborns, they react differently to that story than to ones their mother did not read aloud. Moreover, from their first minutes outside the womb, infants selectively focus on

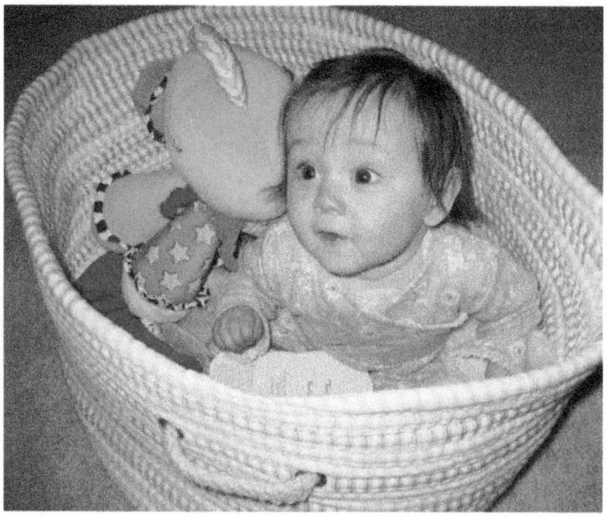

COURTESY OF ROBERT SIEGLER

As this infant's eager gaze suggests, children's choices of where to look are amongst the ways in which they shape their own development.

objects and events that interest them rather than passively gazing at whatever appears before their eyes.

Infants' and older children's actions also produce reactions in other people, which further shape the children's development. In this section, we examine four ways in which children contribute to their own development: through physically interacting with the environment, interpreting their experience, regulating their behaviour, and eliciting reactions from other people.

Self-Initiated Activity

Even in the womb, typical development depends on the activity of the fetus. Fetuses make breathing movements that strengthen their lungs, and they swallow amniotic fluid that prepares their digestive system to function properly after birth. They also "work out" various muscles by tugging on their umbilical cord, sucking their thumb, kicking, and turning somersaults.

From the day they are born, infants display looking preferences that guide their attention to the most informative aspects of the environment that their processing abilities can handle. They like looking at objects rather than at blank fields. They like looking at moving objects rather than at stationary ones and at the edges of objects rather than at their interiors. And they particularly like looking at faces, especially their mother's.

Infants' ability to interact with the environment expands greatly during the first year. At about 3 months, most infants become able to fairly smoothly follow moving objects with their eyes, which improves their ability to learn about the actions occurring around them. At 6 or 7 months, many become able to crawl on their bellies and, soon after, on their hands and knees; as a result, they no longer have to wait for the world to come to them. By 8 or 9 months, most can hold up their heads, which allows them to reach accurately for objects even when they are not being supported. And by 13 or 14 months, most begin to walk independently, which opens new frontiers for exploration.

As development proceeds, children's self-initiated activity extends to additional domains such as language. Toddlers delight in telling their parents the names of objects—for no reason beyond the joy of doing so. They practice talking in their cribs, even when nobody else is present to hear them. They and older children, both deaf and hearing, invent gestures and words to represent objects and events. As their language proficiency develops, children become skilled at initiating conversations that bring them information, allow them to express their feelings and desires, and help them regulate their emotions.

The effects of self-initiated activities are also seen at older ages in other areas, such as self-socialization and antisocial behaviour. Throughout the world, boys and girls choose to play predominantly with members of their own gender, especially between the ages of 6 and 10 years. The play patterns reflect the children's own choices. Gender segregation is rarely imposed by adults; rather, it arises from differences in the kinds of play that boys and girls tend to prefer. Beginning in the school years, these preferences tend to be reinforced by unkind comments and ridicule from peers when a child crosses the "gender border."

Children's choices of activities shape their development. This child's interest in print led him to learn to read and write at age 3; the fact that he is one of the authors' children also probably had something to do with his early interest in these skills. (He also is now the father of the baby in the preceding photo.)

COURTESY OF ROBERT SIEGLER

In later childhood and adolescence, children's choices of friends and peer groups become important influences on their own behaviour, in that children tend to increasingly act like their friends and others in their social group in both positive and negative ways. Thus, from the prenatal period through adolescence, children's self-initiated activities contribute to their development.

Active Interpretation of Experience

Children also contribute to their development by trying to understand the world around them. Even in the first year, infants gain a sense of what is possible in the physical world. Thus, they look longer at an "impossible" event—such as when one solid object appears to move through the space occupied by another object, or when an object seems to be suspended in midair without support—than they do at an event that is similar but physically possible. Toddlers' and preschoolers' continuous "why" questions, and school-age children's searching for the explanations of magic tricks, provide other compelling examples of children's eagerness to understand the world.

This desire to understand also motivates young children to construct informal theories concerning inanimate objects, living things, and people. These theories allow children to go beyond the data provided by their senses to infer underlying causes. For example, preschoolers reason that there must be something inside animals that causes them to grow, breathe, have babies, get sick, and so on, even though they do not know what that something is. They also reason that inanimate objects must have different material inside them than living things do.

Children's and adolescents' interpretations of their experiences extend to inferences about themselves as well as about the external world. When some children fail to solve a problem, for example, they feel sad and question their ability. Other children who fail on the same task take the failure as a challenge and an opportunity to learn. Similarly, in ambiguous social situations, aggressive children tend to attribute hostile intent to others even when the others' motives are unclear; this interpretation sometimes leads aggressive children to lash out before the other person can hurt them. Thus, subjective interpretations of experiences, as well as objective reality, shape development.

Self-Regulation

Another way in which children contribute to their own development is by regulating their behaviour. Consider how they regulate their emotions. In the first months after they are born, infants rely almost entirely on parents and other caregivers to help them cope with fright and frustration. By age 6 months, they learn to cope with some upsetting situations by rubbing their bodies to soothe themselves. During the toddler and preschool periods, children become increasingly adept at using physical strategies, such as looking away, when faced with stressors or temptation. During elementary school, they increasingly use cognitive strategies, such as reminding themselves that an unpleasant experience will soon be over, to cope with negative situations. Across a wide range of ages, children who successfully regulate their emotions tend to be more popular and more socially competent than those who are less skilled at emotional regulation.

These early self-regulation skills are related to long-term developmental outcomes. For example, boys who exhibit strong self-regulation abilities in the preschool and early elementary school periods are less likely as adults to use cocaine and other drugs. Children's early self-control also has been found to be a strong predictor of their later grades in school and of occupational and economic success in adulthood.

Over the course of childhood and adolescence, children increasingly regulate their development through their choice of activities. Whether young children go to sports events, movies, libraries, or religious services depends mainly on whether their parents take them there. Whether adolescents engage in the same activities depends mainly on their own preferences. Selecting moral values, choosing a romantic partner, pursuing an occupation, and deciding whether to have children are just a few of the major decisions that adolescents and young adults face. The wisdom of their choices strongly influences their subsequent lives.

Eliciting Reactions from Other People

Because children of all ages differ from one another in behaviour and appearance, they evoke different reactions from other people. For example, babies with easy temperaments elicit more positive reactions from their parents than do cranky or fussy babies. Similarly, attractive babies elicit more affectionate and playful mothering than do less attractive ones. And in trying times, attractive children are less likely to suffer parental rejection and punishment than are less attractive ones. Other adults also are influenced by children's actions. For example, when children encounter difficulty learning particular material, teachers act in more encouraging ways if the child has generally been well behaved than if the child has been badly behaved in the past.

The effects that children's initial inclinations have on their parents' behaviour toward them multiply over time. Most parents of children who are disobedient, angry, and challenging try to be supportive but firm with them. However, if the negative behaviour and defiance continue, many parents become hostile and punitive. Other parents, faced with belligerence and aggression, back down from confrontations and increasingly give in to their children's demands. Once such negative cycles are established, they are difficult to stop. If teenagers act disruptively, and parents respond with hostility, problems generally worsen over the course of adolescence.

It is all too easy for relations between parents and children to spiral downward, with disobedience and anger from children eliciting anger and hostility from parents, which then elicits more disobedience and anger from children, and so on.

STEVE DEBENPORT/GETTY IMAGES

Children's characteristics and behaviour influence not just their parents' and teachers' reactions but also those of their peers. At all ages, children who are cooperative, friendly, sociable, and sensitive to others tend to be popular with their peers, whereas those who are aggressive or disruptive tend to be disliked and rejected. In some cases, peers' reactions to one another's behaviour change with age; for example, kindergartners tend to neither like nor dislike withdrawn peers, but older elementary and middle school students tend to dislike such children. Peer reactions to children's behaviour often have long-term consequences; children who were rejected by peers when younger are more likely than children who were popular to have difficulty later in school and to engage in criminal activity. In many ways, then, children influence their own development not only by initiating actions, interpreting their experiences, and regulating their emotions, but also by eliciting reactions from other people that then shape their subsequent behaviour.

Theme 3: Development Is Both Continuous and Discontinuous

Long before there was a scientific discipline of child development, philosophers and others interested in human nature argued about whether development is continuous or discontinuous. Current disputes between those who believe that development is continuous, such as social-learning theorists, and those who believe it is discontinuous, such as stage theorists, thus have a long history. Both positions have endured so long for good reason: each captures important truths about development, yet neither captures the whole truth. Two particularly important issues in this long-standing debate involve continuity/discontinuity of individual differences and continuity/discontinuity of the standard course of development with age.

Continuity/Discontinuity of Individual Differences

One sense of continuity/discontinuity involves stability of individual differences over time. The basic question is whether children who initially are higher or lower than most peers in some quality continue to be higher or lower in that quality years later. It turns out that many individual differences in psychological properties are moderately stable over the course of development, but the stability is always far from 100%.

Consider the development of intelligence. Some stability is present from infancy onward. For instance, the faster that infants habituate to repeated presentation of the same display, the higher their IQ scores tend to be 10 or more years later. Infants' patterns of electrical brain activity also are related to their speed of processing and attention regulation more than 10 years later. The amount of stability increases with age. IQ scores show some stability from age 3 to age 13, considerable stability from age 5 to age 15, and substantial stability from age 8 to age 18.

Even in later childhood, however, IQ scores vary from occasion to occasion. For example, when the same children take IQ tests at ages 8 and 17, the two scores differ on average by 9 points. Part of this variability reflects random fluctuations in how sharp the person is on the day of testing and in the person's knowledge about the particular questions on each test. Another part of the variability reflects the fact that even if two children start out with equal intelligence, one may show greater intellectual growth over time.

Individual differences in social and personality characteristics also show some continuity over time. Shy toddlers tend to grow into shy children, fearful toddlers into fearful children, aggressive children into aggressive adolescents, generous children into generous adults, and so on. The continuity also carries over into situations quite different from any that the children faced at the earlier time; for example, secure attachments in infancy predict positive romantic relationships in adolescence.

Although there is some continuity of individual differences in social, emotional, and personality development, the degree of continuity is generally lower than in intellectual development. For example, whereas children who are high in reading and math achievement in 5th grade generally remain so in 7th grade, children who are popular in 5th grade may or may not be popular in 7th grade. In addition, aspects of temperament such as fearfulness and shyness often change considerably over the course of early and middle childhood.

Regardless of whether the focus is on intellectual, social, or emotional development, the stability of individual differences is influenced by the stability of the environment. For instance, an infant's attachment to his or her mother correlates positively with the infant's long-term security, but the correlation is higher if the home environment is consistent than if serious disruptions occur. Similarly, IQ scores are more stable if the home environment remains stable. Thus, continuities in individual differences reflect continuities in children's environments as well as in their genes.

Continuity/Discontinuity of Overall Development: The Question of Stages

Many of the most prominent theories of development divide childhood and adolescence into a small number of discrete stages. Piaget's theory of cognitive development, Freud's theory of psychosexual development, Erikson's theory of psychosocial development, and Kohlberg's theory of moral development all describe development in this way. The enduring popularity of these stage approaches is easy to understand: they simplify the enormously complicated process of development by dividing it into a few distinct periods; they point to important characteristics of behaviour during each period; and they impart an overall sense of coherence to the developmental process.

Although stage theories differ in their particulars, they share four key assumptions: (1) development progresses through a series of qualitatively distinct stages; (2) when children are in a given stage, a fairly broad range of their thinking and behaviour exhibits the features characteristic of that stage; (3) the stages occur in the same order for all children; and (4) transitions between stages occur quickly.

Development turns out to be considerably less tidy than stage approaches imply, however. For example, children who exhibit preoperational reasoning on some tasks often exhibit concrete operational reasoning on others; children who reason in a preconventional way about some moral dilemmas often reason in a conventional way about others; and so on. Rarely is a sudden change evident across a broad range of tasks.

In addition, developmental processes often show a great deal of continuity. Throughout childhood and adolescence, there are gradual, continuous increases in the ability to regulate emotions, make friends, take other people's perspectives, remember events, solve problems, and engage in many other activities.

This does not mean that there are no sudden jumps. When we consider specific tasks and processes, rather than broad domains, we see many discontinuities. Typically, 3-month-olds move from having almost no binocular depth perception to having adultlike levels within 1 or 2 weeks. Fear of strangers is rare at 4 months but very common by 8 months. Many toddlers move in a single day from being unable to walk without support to walking unsupported for a number of steps. After acquiring about one word per week between ages 12 and 18 months, many toddlers undergo a vocabulary explosion, in which the number of words they know and use expands rapidly for years thereafter. Thus, although broad domains, such as intelligence and personality, rarely show discontinuous changes, specific aspects of development fairly often do.

Whether development appears to be continuous or discontinuous often depends on whether the focus is on behaviour or on underlying processes. Behaviours that emerge or disappear quite suddenly may reflect continuous underlying processes. Recall the case of infants' stepping reflex. For the first 2 months after birth, if infants are supported in an upright position with their feet touching the ground, they will first lift one leg and then the other in a pattern similar to walking. At around age 2 months, this reflex suddenly disappears. Underlying the abrupt change in behaviour, however, are gradual changes in two dimensions—the infant's weight and leg strength. As babies grow, their gain in weight temporarily outstrips their gain in leg strength, and they become unable to lift their legs without help. When babies who have stopped exhibiting the stepping reflex are supported in a tank of water, making it easier for them to lift their legs, the stepping reflex reappears.

Whether development appears continuous or discontinuous also depends on the timescale being considered. Recall that when a child's height was measured every 6 months from birth to 18 years, the growth looked continuous (see Figure 1.3, page 16). When height was measured daily, however, development looked discontinuous, with occasional "growth days" sprinkled amongst numerous days without growth.

One useful framework for thinking about developmental continuities and discontinuities is to envision development as a road trip across Canada, from St. John's to Victoria. In one sense, the drive is a continuous progression westward along the Trans-Canada Highway (with a few ferry rides along the way!). In another sense, the drive starts in the East and then proceeds (in an invariant order, without the possibility of skipping a region) through the Atlantic provinces, central Canada, the Prairies, and the Rocky Mountains before reaching its end point in British Columbia. The East includes the Atlantic provinces, and they tend to be hilly, cloudy, and green; central Canada is made up of lowlands, lakes, and rivers; the Prairies tend to be flatter, drier, and sunnier; and the West has extensive mountainous areas where heavy snow falls. The differences between regions in climate, colour, and topography are large and real, but the boundaries between them are arbitrary. For example, is Quebec the westernmost Atlantic province (given its extensive Atlantic coast) or the eastern part of Central Canada?

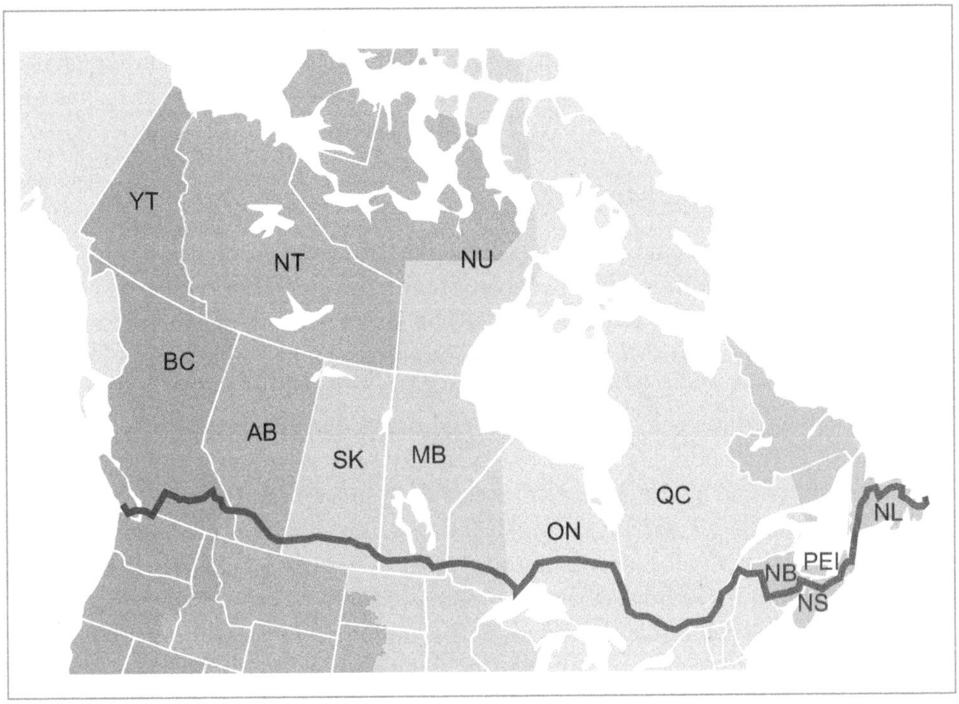

A trip along the Trans-Canada Highway (and on a few ferries) from St. John's to Victoria takes a driver through six time zones in which the main features of the land change dramatically. The changes in topography, like those in development, however, are not discontinuous. Adjacent areas tend to be highly similar, and classification of a border area as being in one zone or another is often quite arbitrary. In all of these ways, the journey resembles psychological development.

The continuities and discontinuities in development are a lot like those on the road trip. Consider children's conceptions of the self. At one level of analysis, the development of the self is continuous. Over the course of development, children (and adults) understand more and more about themselves. At another level of analysis, milestones characterize each period of development. During infancy, children come to distinguish between themselves and other people, but they rarely if ever see themselves from another person's perspective. During the toddler period, children increasingly view themselves as others might, which allows them to feel such emotions as shame and guilt. During the preschool period, children realize that certain of their personal characteristics are permanent, and they use this knowledge to guide their behaviour. During the elementary school years, children increasingly think of themselves in terms of their competencies relative to other children's (intelligence, athletic skill, popularity, and so forth). During adolescence, they come to recognize how differently they themselves act in different situations.

Thus, any statement about when a given competency emerges is somewhat arbitrary, much like a statement about where a geographic region begins. Nonetheless, identifying the milestones helps us understand roughly where we are on the map.

Theme 4: Mechanisms of Developmental Change

As with so many other issues, contemporary thinking about developmental change owes a large debt to the ideas of Jean Piaget. Within Piaget's theory, change occurs through the interaction of assimilation and accommodation. Through assimilation, children interpret new experiences in terms of their existing mental structures; through accommodation, they revise their existing mental structures in accordance with the new experiences. Thus, when we hear a truly unfamiliar type of music (for most of us, Javanese 12-tone music would fit this description), we assimilate the sounds to more familiar musical patterns to the extent we can. At the same time, our understanding accommodates to the experience so that when we next encounter the unfamiliar music, it will be a little easier to grasp and will feel a little less strange.

A great deal has been learned about developmental mechanisms since Piaget formulated his theory. Some of the advances have come in understanding change at the biological level, others in understanding it at the behavioural level, and still others in understanding it at the level of cognitive processes.

Biological Change Mechanisms

Biological change mechanisms come into play from the moment a sperm unites with an egg. The sperm and egg each contain half of the DNA that will constitute the child's genotype throughout life. The genotype contains instructions that specify the rough outline of development, but all particulars are filled in by subsequent interactions between the genotype and the environment.

The way in which the brain forms after conception illustrates the complexity of change at the biological level. The first key process in brain development is *neurogenesis,* which by the 3rd or 4th week after conception is producing roughly 10,000 brain cells *per minute.* About 100 days later, the brain contains almost all the neurons it ever will have. As neurons form, a process of *cell migration* causes many of them to travel from where they were produced to their long-term location.

Once neurons reach their destination, they undergo a process of *differentiation,* in which dendrites and axons grow out from the original cell body. Later in the prenatal period, the process of *myelination* adds an insulating sheath over certain axons, which speeds up the rate of transmission of electrical signals along them. Myelination continues through childhood and into adolescence.

Yet another process, *synaptogenesis,* involves formation of synapses between the ends of axons and the beginnings of dendrites that allow neurotransmitters to transmit signals from neuron to neuron. The number of synapses increases rapidly from the prenatal period to early or middle childhood (depending on the particular brain area). By the end of this period of explosive growth, the number of synapses in a given area far exceeds the number in the brains of adults. A process of *pruning* then reduces the number of synapses. The greatest pruning occurs at different times in different brain areas; in some areas, notably the prefrontal cortex, the pruning process occurs throughout adolescence and beyond. Those synapses that are frequently used are maintained; those that are not are eliminated (reflecting "use it or lose it" at the biological level). The pruning of unused synapses increases the efficiency of information processing.

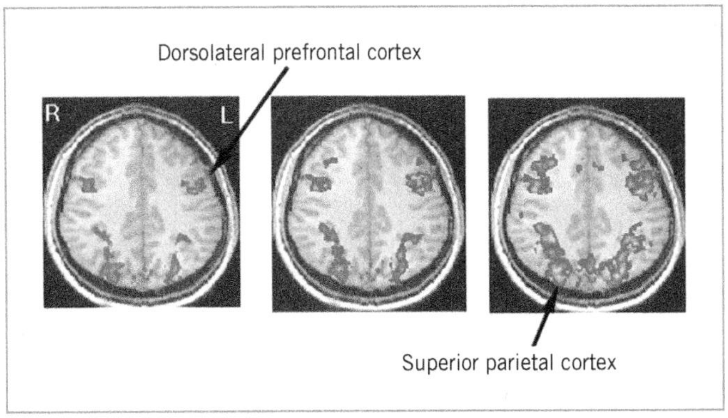

The scans show the group average pattern of brain activation for each of three increasingly difficult items (from left to right) on a problem-solving task that requires both executive functioning and spatial processing. As shown, with increasing problem difficulty, the amount of neural activity increases in the prefrontal cortex (toward the front of the brain, often involved in executive functioning) and in the superior parietal cortex (toward the back of the brain, often involved in spatial processing).

The brain includes a number of areas that are specialized for specific functions. This specialization makes possible rapid and universal development of these functions and thus enhances learning of the relevant type of information. Some of the functions are closely linked to sensory and motor systems. The visual cortex is particularly active in processing sights; the auditory cortex is particularly active in processing sounds; the motor cortex is particularly active in making movements; and so on.

Other brain areas are specialized for functions that are not specific to any one sensory or motor system. The limbic system, located in the lower part of the brain, is particularly prominent in producing emotions. The prefrontal cortex is particularly involved in executive functioning. Some areas in the parietal lobe are particularly active in processing space, time, and number. All of these areas are involved in numerous other types of processing, and all types of processing involve numerous brain areas, but each of the areas is especially active in processing the type of information associated with it. Thus, biological mechanisms underlie both specific and broad changes.

Behavioural Change Mechanisms

Behavioural change mechanisms describe responses to environmental contingencies that contribute to development. These learning mechanisms shape behaviour from the prenatal period onward.

Habituation, Conditioning, Statistical Learning, and Rational Learning

The capacity to habituate to familiar stimuli begins before fetuses leave the womb. By 30 weeks after conception (8 to 10 weeks before the typical time of birth), the central nervous system is sufficiently developed for habituation to occur, as reflected in a fetus's heart rate initially slowing down (a sign of interest) when a bell is rung next to the mother's belly and then the heart rate returning toward the typical rate as the bell is rung repeatedly. Habituation continues after birth as well, and it is seen in changes in looking patterns as well as in heart-rate patterns. For example, when a picture of a face is shown repeatedly, infants reduce the time they spend looking at it, but they show renewed interest when a different face appears. Habituation motivates babies to seek new stimulation when they have already learned from an experience and thus helps them learn more.

From their first days in the outside world, infants also can learn through classical conditioning. If an initially neutral stimulus is repeatedly presented just before an unconditioned stimulus, it comes to elicit a similar response to that elicited by the unconditioned stimulus. For example, when a tone is presented simultaneously with a puff of air to a newborn's eye, the infant learns to blink when the tone is sounded, even without the air puff.

Like older children, infants also learn through instrumental conditioning; behaviours that are rewarded become more frequent, and behaviours that do not lead to rewards become less frequent. Even young infants appear highly motivated to learn in this way: 2-month-olds express joy and interest when they see a behaviour produce a desired outcome, and they cry and express anger when a learned response no longer produces the desired results. Infants in their first year generalize their instrumental learning to somewhat novel situations, as well as learning about the specific earlier situation. Thus, after learning to kick in order to make a particular mobile jiggle, 6-month-olds (though not 3-month-olds) generalize the kicking to other mobiles. As this example illustrates, instrumental learning is narrower early in infancy than it will be later.

Yet another mechanism that allows infants to acquire information rapidly is statistical learning. From birth onward, infants quickly learn the likelihood that one sight or sound will follow another. Because many events, including the sounds within words and certain daily routines, occur in predictable orders, statistical learning helps infants anticipate other people's actions and generate similar sequences of behaviour themselves.

Closely related to statistical learning is rational learning, which involves integrating the learner's prior beliefs and biases with what actually occurs in the environment. When, for example, infants observe an adult pulling balls of two different colours out of a transparent box, seemingly at random, and the ratio of the colours of those balls deviates greatly from that of the total set of balls in the box, the infants' looking times suggest that they are surprised. Together with habituation, classical conditioning, generalization, and instrumental and statistical learning, such rational learning allows infants to acquire knowledge of the world from the first days following birth.

Social Learning

Children (and adults) learn a great deal from observing and interacting with other people. This social learning pervades our lives to such an extent that it is difficult to think of it as a specific learning capability. However, when we compare humans with other animals—even close relatives such as chimpanzees and other apes—the centrality of social learning in people's lives becomes apparent. Humans are far more skillful than any other animal in learning what others are trying to teach us; we also are far more inclined to teach others what we know. Amongst the crucial contributors to this social learning are imitation, social referencing, language, and guided participation.

The first discernible form of social learning is imitation. At first, the imitation is limited to behaviours that infants sometimes spontaneously produce on their own, such as sticking out the tongue, and even that is inconsistent. However, by the second half of the first year, infants imitate novel behaviours that they never make spontaneously. By 15 months, toddlers not only learn novel behaviours but can also remember and continue to produce them for at least a week. This imitation is not just "monkey see, monkey do." When children of this age see a model unsuccessfully try to do something, they imitate what the model was trying to do rather than what the model actually did and use alternative means to reach what they see as the intended goal.

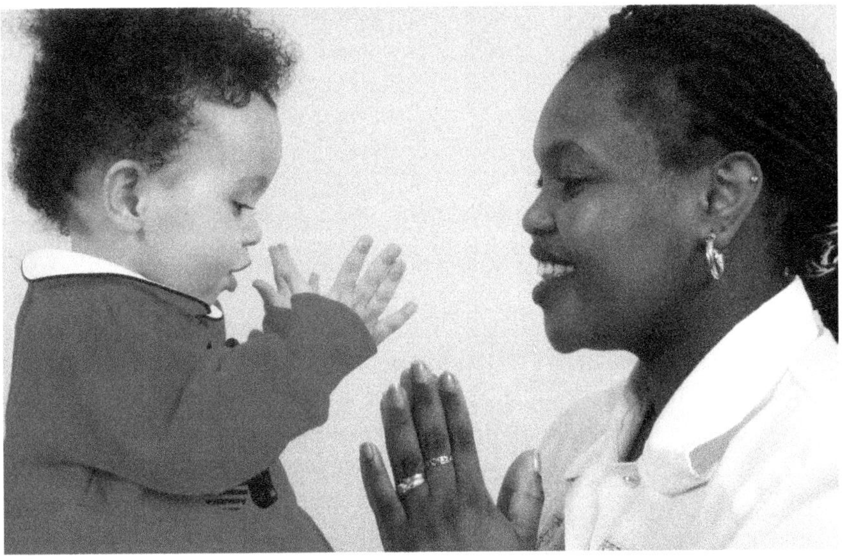

HAMPTON PICTURE LIBRARY/ALAMY STOCK PHOTO

Imitation starts in infancy.

Social learning influences socioemotional development as well as knowledge acquisition. When an unfamiliar person enters the room, 12-month-olds look to their mother for guidance. If the mother's face or voice shows fear, the baby tends to stay close to her; if the mother smiles, the baby is more likely to approach the stranger. Similarly, in the laboratory, a baby of this age will often cross the visual cliff—in which a transparent plexiglass floor is placed over what looks like a steep drop off—but only if the mother smiles; they rarely will cross if she looks worried.

Social learning also shapes children's standards and values. From the second year of life, toddlers internalize their parents' values and standards and use them to guide and evaluate their own conduct. Later in development, peers, teachers, and other adults also influence children's standards and values through the process of social learning. Peers, in particular, play a steadily increasing role over the course of childhood and adolescence.

Imitation is not the only mechanism of social learning. Another is social scaffolding. In this change mechanism, a more knowledgeable person may provide the learner with an overview of a given task, demonstrate how to do the most difficult parts, provide help with the most difficult parts, and offer suggestions to the learner on how to proceed. Such scaffolding allows a beginner to do more than he or she could do without help. Then, as the learner masters the basics of the task, the more expert person transfers more and more responsibility to the learner until the learner is doing the entire task. Thus, children and other people collaborate to produce social learning.

Using tools to build and repair things is a common context for social scaffolding, in which the more experienced person helps the younger and less experienced person to operate at a higher level than would otherwise be possible.

PLUSH STUDIOS/BILL REITZEL/THINKSTOCK

Cognitive Change Mechanisms

Many of the most compelling analyses of developmental change are at the level of cognitive processes. Both general and specific information-processing mechanisms play important roles.

General Information-Processing Mechanisms

Four types of information-processing mechanisms are especially general and pervasive: basic processes, strategies, metacognition, and content knowledge.

Basic processes are the simplest, most broadly applicable, and earliest-developing general information-processing mechanisms. They overlap considerably with behavioural learning processes and include associating

TOPFOTO/THE IMAGE WORKS

Exceptional content knowledge can outweigh all of adults' usual intellectual advantages over children. On the day this photograph was taken, this 8-year-old boy became the youngest person ever to defeat a chess grandmaster (the ranking awarded to the greatest chess players in the world).

events with each other, recognizing objects as familiar, recalling facts and procedures, encoding key features of events, and generalizing from one instance to another. Changes with age occur in the speed and efficiency of these basic processes, but all of the basic processes are present from early infancy onward. These basic processes provide a foundation that allows infants to learn about the world from their very first days.

Strategies also contribute to many types of development. Toddlers, for example, form strategies for achieving goals such as obtaining a toy that is out of reach or descending a steep ramp; preschoolers form strategies for counting and solving arithmetic problems; school-age children form strategies for playing games and getting along with others; and so on. Often, children acquire multiple strategies for solving a single kind of problem—for example, strategies for approaching unfamiliar children on a playground or for solving arithmetic problems. Knowing multiple strategies allows children to adapt to the demands of different problems and situations.

Metacognition is a third type of cognitive process that contributes to development in large ways. For instance, increasing use of memory strategies stems in large part from children's increasing realization that they are unlikely to remember large amounts of material verbatim without such strategies. Amongst the most important applications of metacognition is adaptive choice amongst alternative strategies, such as whether to reread to understand text, whether to count or state a retrieved answer to solve an arithmetic problem, and whether to write an outline before beginning an essay. The cognitive control involved in executive functioning—for example, inhibiting tempting but counterproductive actions, being cognitively flexible, and considering other people's perspectives—is another crucial type of metacognition.

Content knowledge is a fourth pervasive contributor to cognitive change. The more children know about any topic—whether it be chess, soccer, dinosaurs, or language—the better able they are to learn and remember new information about it. Knowledge also facilitates learning of unfamiliar content by allowing children to draw analogies between the new content and previously acquired information.

Domain-Specific Learning Mechanisms

Infants acquire some complex competencies surprisingly rapidly, including basic perception, understanding of the physical world, language comprehension and production, interpretation of emotions, and attachment to caregivers. What seems to unite the varied capabilities that children acquire especially rapidly is their importance for further learning and survival.

A number of theorists have posited that the nearly universal, rapid learning in these domains is produced by domain-specific learning mechanisms that operate on everyday experience to produce accurate conclusions about the world. For example, even infants in their first year seem to expect stationary objects to be more strongly affected by collisions with bigger moving objects than with smaller moving objects. Similarly, toddlers' word learning seems to be aided by the whole-object assumption (the idea that words used to label objects refer to the whole object rather than to a part of it) and the mutual exclusivity assumption (the idea that each object has a single name). These assumptions are usually correct for the words that toddlers hear, thus helping them learn what the words mean.

Children's informal theories about the main types of entities in the world—inanimate objects, people, and other living things—also facilitate their learning about them. The value of learning rapidly about the properties of people, other living things, and inanimate objects is clear; saying "More juice" to another person, for example, is considerably more likely to yield the desired outcome than is saying the same words to a dog, no matter how intelligent the dog is. Crucial in children's informal theories, as in scientists' formal ones, are causal relations that explain a large number of observations in terms of a few basic unobservable processes.

Possessing basic understanding of key concepts—such as inertia and solidity for inanimate objects; goal-directed movement and growth for living things; and intentions, beliefs, and desires for people—helps children act appropriately in new situations. For example, a preschooler who meets an unfamiliar peer assumes that the other child will have intentions, beliefs, and desires—an assumption that helps the preschooler understand the other child's actions and react appropriately to them. These assumptions about other people's minds aid the social understanding of children in all societies. Thus, both general and domain-specific cognitive learning mechanisms help children understand the world around them.

Change Mechanisms Work Together

Although it is often easiest to discuss different change mechanisms separately, it is crucial to remember that biological, cognitive, and behavioural mechanisms all reflect interactions between the person and the environment and that all types of mechanisms work together to produce change. For instance, consider effortful attention. The development of this capability reflects a combination of biological and environmental factors. On the biological side, genes influence the production of neurotransmitters that affect children's ability to focus and ignore distractions. Effortful attention also relies on the development of connections between two parts of the brain—the anterior cingulate, which is active in attention to goals, and the limbic area, which is active in emotional reactions. On the environmental side, the development of effortful attention is influenced by the quality of parenting a child receives—though this is true primarily for children with a particular genotype. For children with one form of a relevant gene, quality of parenting substantially influences the development of effortful attention, whereas for children with another form of the gene, quality of parenting has little effect on its development.

Specific experiences can also be influential; for example, playing specially designed computer games increases the activity of the anterior cingulate and thus may aid the ability to sustain attention on both experimental tasks and intelligence tests. In short, varied types of mechanisms work together to produce development of even a single capability.

Theme 5: The Sociocultural Context Shapes Development

Children develop within a personal context of other people: families, friends, neighbours, teachers, and classmates. They also develop within an impersonal context of historical, economic, technological, and political forces, as well as societal beliefs, attitudes, and values. The impersonal context is important in shaping development, just as the personal one is. There is little reason to think that parents in economically advanced societies in the twenty-first century love their children more than parents of the past did. Yet children today die less often, get sick less often, eat a more nutritious diet, and receive more formal education than did children from even the wealthiest families of 100 or 200 years ago. Thus, when and where children grow up profoundly influences their lives.

Growing Up in Societies with Different Practices and Values

Values and practices that people within a society take for granted as "natural" often vary substantially amongst societies. These variations influence the rate and form of development. Throughout the book, you have encountered examples of this in every aspect of development, including in domains that are commonly thought of as being governed entirely by maturation. For example, people often assume that the timing of walking and other motor skills in infancy is determined solely by biology, but babies who grow up in African tribes that strongly encourage infants' motor development tend to walk and reach other motor milestones earlier than do infants in Canada and the United States. Similarly, infants in societies where babies sleep with their mothers for several years exhibit less fear at bedtime than do children in Canada and the United States, where babies rarely sleep in the same bed or even the same room as their mothers past the first 6 months of their lives.

Emotional reactions provide another example of how cultural practices and values influence behaviour, even when we might not expect them to do so. Infants in all societies that have been studied show the same attachment patterns, but the frequency of occurrence of each pattern varies with the values of the society. Relative to babies in Canada and the United States, for instance, Japanese and Korean babies who are placed in the Strange Situation more often become very upset, showing the insecure/resistant attachment pattern (see Chapter 11). These differences in attachment patterns appear to be due to differing cultural values and practices. Japanese and Korean mothers traditionally encourage dependence in children and rarely leave their babies alone, which may lead the babies to become especially upset when they are left alone in the Strange Situation. In contrast, Canadian and U.S. parents emphasize independence to a greater degree and more often leave babies alone in a room or with other people.

Cultural influences such as these continue well beyond infancy. Japanese culture, for instance, places a higher value on hiding negative emotions, especially anger, than does American culture, and Japanese mothers discourage their children from expressing negative emotions. Quite likely because of these cultural influences, Japanese preschoolers and school-age children less often express anger and other negative emotions than do U.S. peers. Similarly, child rearing in rural Mexican villages emphasizes cooperation and caring about others, and children raised in these villages are more likely to share their possessions than are children from Mexican cities.

The culture of Mexican villages successfully encourages cooperation and helping amongst children and others.

YURI CORTEZ/GETTY IMAGES

Culture influences not only parents' actions but also children's interpretations of those actions. For example, harsh parenting is associated with more aggressive behaviour at school for children from European-Canadian families, but it is associated with less aggressive behaviour in children from South-Asian Canadian families (C. Ho et al., 2008). The differing effectiveness of the disciplinary approaches may reflect children's interpretations of their parents' behaviour. If children believe that scolding and inducing shame and guilt are in their best interest, those behaviours can be effective. However, if children see such disciplinary approaches as reflecting negative parental feelings toward them, the discipline tends to be ineffective or harmful.

Sociocultural differences exert a similar influence on cognitive development. They help determine which skills and knowledge children acquire—for instance, whether children learn to operate abacuses, iPads, or both. They also influence how well children learn skills that everyone acquires to some degree; for example, Australian aboriginal children, whose adult lives will depend on their ability to trek through the desert to distant oases, develop spatial skills superior to those of urban Australian children. Finally, cultural values influence the educational system, which in turn influences what and how deeply children learn. For instance, students in community-of-learners classrooms learn about fewer scientific topics than do children in traditional classrooms, but they learn about them in greater depth.

Growing Up in Different Times and Places

When and where children grow up profoundly influences their development. As noted earlier, in modern societies, children's lives are greatly improved over what they were in the past, in terms of health, nutrition, shelter, and other material factors. Modern life also enhances some types of opportunities for learning; for example, watching the children's television program *Sesame Street* appears to have enhanced children's learning in countries around the world. Not all of the changes in modern societies have promoted children's well-being, however. For example, in North America and Europe, far more children grow up with divorced parents than in the past, and these children are at risk for many problems. On average, they are more prone to sadness and depression, have lower self-esteem, do less well in school, and are less socially competent than peers who live in intact families. Although most children from divorced families do not have serious problems, a minority do: engaging in delinquent activities, dropping out of school, and having children out of wedlock all are more common amongst children whose parents are divorced.

Other historical changes result in children's lives being different but not necessarily better or worse. The great expansion of childcare outside the home is one such case. In Canada, about 60% of children under 5 currently receive childcare outside their homes—a figure that has grown significantly since the 1960s. As this change was occurring, many people feared that such care would weaken attachment between babies and mothers. Others expressed hopes that such care would greatly stimulate cognitive development, especially of children from impoverished backgrounds, because of the greater opportunities for interaction with other children and adults. In fact, the data indicate that neither the fears nor the hopes were justified. In almost all respects, children who receive care outside the home tend to develop similarly, both emotionally and cognitively, to those who do not.

More generally, the same cultural or technological change can bring either positive or negative effects, depending on who the child is and how the innovation is used. For instance, the Internet can be used to communicate with friends, which tends to strengthen friendships, but it can also be used for cyberbullying. Playing certain electronic games stimulates development of attention, but very high frequency of playing such games can harm the quality of friendships. Similarly, moderate amounts of digital screen time do not appear to affect adolescents' mental health, but high amounts are associated with greater risk of adolescents' developing mental health problems. Thus, in terms of health, comfort, intellectual stimulation, and material well-being, children growing up today in modern societies are, on the whole, better off than those who grew up in the past, but in other ways, the picture is more mixed.

Growing Up in Different Circumstances Within a Society

Even amongst children growing up at the same time in the same society, differences in economic circumstances, family relationships, and peer groups lead to large differences in children's lives.

Economic Influences

In every society, the economic circumstances of a child's family considerably influence the child's life. However, the degree of economic inequality within each society influences how large a difference the economic circumstances make. In societies with large income inequalities, such as the United States, poor children's academic achievement is far lower than that of children from wealthier families. In societies with smaller inequalities, such as Canada, Japan, and Sweden, children from affluent families also do better academically than children from poorer families, but the differences are smaller.

It is not just academic achievement that is influenced by economic circumstances; all aspects of development are. Infants from impoverished families more often are insecurely attached to their mothers. Children and adolescents from impoverished families more often are rejected as friends and more often report being lonely. Illegal substance use, crime, and depression also are more common amongst poor adolescents than amongst peers from wealthier backgrounds.

These negative outcomes are unsurprising, given the many disadvantages that children from impoverished families face. Relative to children who grow up in more affluent environments, poor children more often live in dangerous neighbourhoods; grow up in homes with one or no biological parents; attend inferior childcare centres and schools; less often are read to and spoken to by their parents; and have fewer books, magazines, and other intellectually stimulating material in their homes. The cumulative burden of these disadvantages, rather than any one of them, poses the greatest obstacle to successful development.

The Great Depression of the 1930s greatly increased the number of children in the United States, Canada, and other countries growing up in extreme poverty. How might the extreme poverty and instability faced by these children have affected their development, compared to that of their more affluent peers?

Influences of Family and Peers

Families and peer groups vary considerably in ways other than income, and many of these differences also have a substantial influence on development. In some families, regardless of income, parents are sensitive to babies' needs and form close attachments with them; in others, this does not occur. In some families, again regardless of income, parents read to their children each night, thus helping the children learn to read; in others, this practice does not occur.

The influence of friends, other peers, teachers, and other adults varies in as many ways as that of families. Friends, for example, can provide companionship and feedback, contribute to self-esteem, and serve as a buffer against stress; during adolescence, they can be particularly important sources of sympathy and support. On the other hand, friends can also have negative influences, drawing children and adolescents into reckless and aggressive behaviour, including crime, drinking, and drug use.

Thus, personal relationships, like economic circumstances, culture, and technology, influence development, but the effects of these influences vary with the particulars.

Theme 6: Individual Differences

Children differ on a huge number of dimensions—demographic characteristics (gender, race, ethnicity, socioeconomic status), psychological characteristics (intellect, personality, artistic ability), experiences (where they grow up; whether their parents are divorced; whether they participate in plays, bands, or organized sports), and so on. How can we tell which individual differences are the crucial ones for understanding children and predicting their futures?

As illustrated in Figure 16.1, three variables—breadth of related characteristics, stability over time, and predictive value—are crucial in determining the importance of any dimension of individual differences. First, as shown by the red arrows in Figure 16.1, children's status on the most important dimensions is associated with their status at that time on other important dimensions. Thus, one reason intelligence is considered a central individual difference is that the higher a child's IQ at a given age, the higher the child's grades, achievement test scores, and general knowledge tend to be at the same time. A second key characteristic is stability over time (the blue arrows in Figure 16.1). A dimension of individual differences is of greater interest if the higher or lower that children score on it early in development, the higher or lower they are likely to score on it later. Thus, another reason for interest in IQ is that children with high (or low) IQs usually grow into adults with high (or low) IQs. A third characteristic of major dimensions of individual differences is that a child's status on a dimension predicts outcomes on other important characteristics in the future (the green arrows in Figure 16.1). Thus, a third reason for interest in IQ scores is that a person's IQ during middle childhood and adolescence predicts that person's later earnings, occupational status, and years of education.

This analysis makes clear why demographic variables such as gender, race, ethnicity, and SES are studied so often. Consider gender, for example. Gender differences are related to a wide variety of other differences. On average, cisgender boys tend to be larger, stronger, more physically active, and more physically aggressive; to play in larger groups; to be better at some forms of spatial thinking; and more often to have ADHD and math or reading disabilities. On average, cisgender girls tend to be more verbal, quicker to perceive emotions, better at

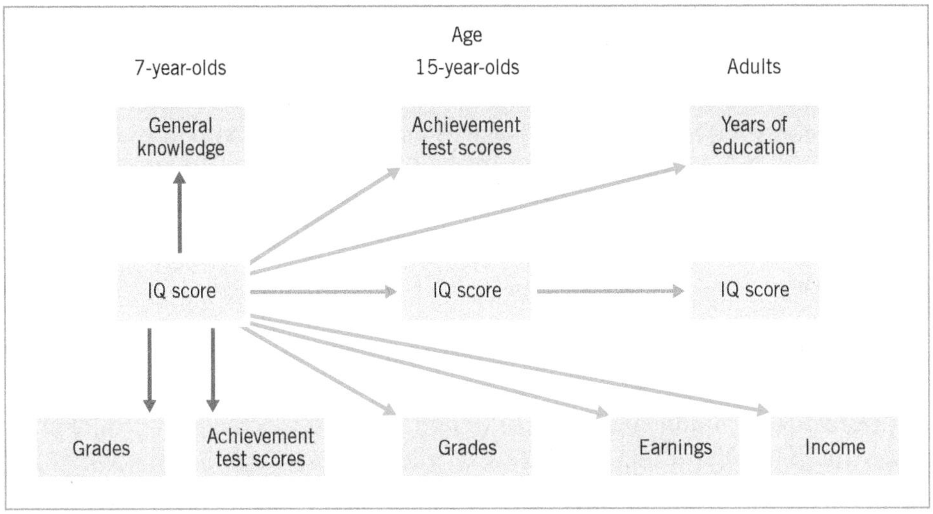

FIGURE 16.1 Intelligence and individual differences Intelligence is considered a crucial dimension of individual differences because IQ scores (1) correlate with other conceptually related dimensions such as general knowledge and grades at any one age (red arrows extending from IQ to other outcomes at age 7); (2) show considerable continuity over age (blue arrows); and (3) predict future outcomes, such as years of education and income in adulthood (green arrows connecting IQ score at age 7 to other later outcomes).

writing, and more likely to express sympathy and empathy for people in distress. Gender identity as male or female also is generally stable over time. Finally, being male or female predicts future individual differences. If a newborn is female, it is likely that, compared with males, she will be more self-revealing with friends, more vulnerable to depression, more inclined to prosocial behaviour, and more disposed to using indirect aggression. However, keep in mind a few points.

First, the correlation between a person's gender and future individual differences reflects complex interactions amongst social and biological influences. Neither biological nor social factors in isolation cause these characteristics—they both do. For example, one reason that a person's gender may predict their later behaviour is because girls and boys tend to be treated differently. Second, there is much variability within each gender. For example, not all boys are physically active and not all girls are good at perceiving emotions. Finally, there is much overlap between females and males in each of these behaviours, as can be seen in Table 15.1. For example, many girls and boys are good at spatial skills or verbal skills, and many girls and boys score poorly in these domains.

We next consider the extent to which several other variables show these three key features of individual differences.

Breadth of Individual Differences at a Given Time

Individual differences are not randomly distributed. Children who are high on one dimension also tend to be high on other, conceptually related dimensions. Thus, children who do well on one measure of intellect—language, memory, conceptual understanding, problem solving, reading, or mathematics—tend to do well on others. Similarly, children who do well on one measure of social or emotional functioning—relations with parents, relations with peers, relations with teachers, self-esteem, prosocial behaviour, and lack of aggression and lying—also tend to do well on others. Sometimes, as with the relation between intelligence and school achievement, the connections are very strong. More often, the relations are moderate. Thus, although children who get along well with their parents also tend to get along well with peers, there are many exceptions.

Beyond intelligence and gender, two other crucial dimensions of individual differences are attachment and self-esteem. Compared with their insecurely attached peers, a toddler who is securely attached to his or her mother tends to be more enthusiastic and positive about solving problems with her, to comply more often with her directives, and to obey her requests even when she isn't present. Such children also tend to get along better with other toddlers and to be more sociable and more socially competent. Similarly, children and adolescents who are high in self-esteem also tend to be strong on many other dimensions of social and emotional functioning. They tend to be generally hopeful and popular, to have many friends, and to have good academic and self-regulation skills. In contrast, those with low self-esteem tend to feel hopeless and to be prone to problems such as depression, aggression, and social withdrawal.

Stability Over Time

Many individual differences show moderate stability over time. For instance, people who have easy temperaments during infancy tend to continue to have easy temperaments in middle and later childhood. Similarly, elementary school children with ADHD, reading disabilities, or mathematics disabilities usually have lifelong difficulties in those areas.

The reasons for such stability of psychological characteristics are to be found in the stability of both genes and environment. A child's genotype remains identical over the course of development (though particular genes switch on and off at different times). Most children's environments remain fairly stable as well. Families that are middle class when a child is born tend to remain middle class; families that value education when the child is born usually continue to value education; parents who are sensitive and supportive generally remain that way; and so on. Major changes, such as divorce and job loss, do occur, and they affect children's happiness, self-esteem, and other characteristics. Nonetheless, the stability of children's environments, like the stability of their genes, contributes to the stability of their psychological functioning over time.

Predicting Future Individual Differences on Other Dimensions

Individual differences on some dimensions are related not only to future status on that dimension but also to future status on other dimensions. For instance, children who are securely attached as infants tend as toddlers and preschoolers to have more social ties to their peers than do children who were insecurely attached as infants. When they reach school age, these securely attached children tend to understand other children's emotions relatively well and to be relatively skilled in resolving conflicts. When they reach adolescence and adulthood, they tend to form close attachments with romantic partners. All of these outcomes are consistent with the view that secure early attachment provides a working model that influences subsequent relationships with other people.

As with stability over time of a single dimension, the relative stability of most children's environments contributes to these long-term continuities of psychological functioning. If children's environments change in important ways, the typical continuities may be disrupted. Thus, stressful events such as divorce reduce the likelihood that children who were securely attached during infancy will continue to show the positive relations with peers usually associated with secure attachment.

Determinants of Individual Differences

Individual differences, like all other aspects of development, are ultimately attributable to the interaction of children's genes and the environments they encounter.

Genetics

For a number of important characteristics—including IQ, prosocial behaviour, and empathy—about 50% of the differences amongst individuals in a given population are attributable to differences in genetic inheritance. The degree of genetic influence on individual differences tends to increase over the course of development. For example, correlations between the IQs of adopted children and their biological parents steadily increase over the course of childhood and adolescence, even if the children never meet or have any contact with their biological parents. One reason is that many genes related to intellectual functioning do not exercise their effects until late childhood or adolescence. Another reason is that over the course of development, children become increasingly free to choose environments that are in accord with their genetic predispositions.

Genetic similarities sometimes produce a striking physical resemblance between parent and child. We can only wonder whether this baby, as she develops, will come to resemble her father in other ways as well.

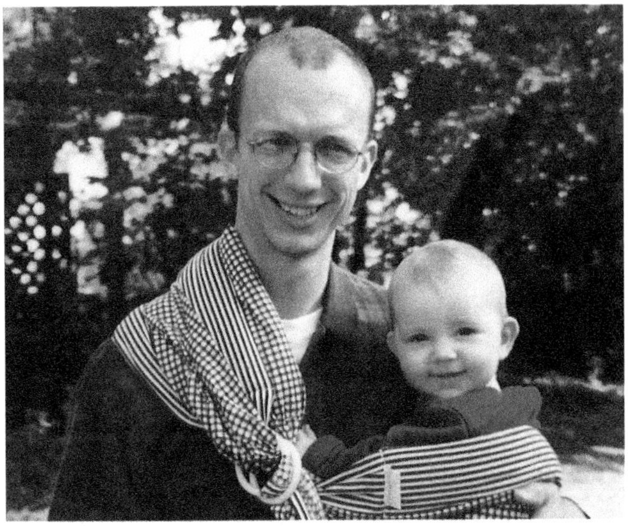

COURTESY OF BETHANY RITTLE-JOHNSON

Experience

Individual differences reflect children's experiences as well as their genes. Consider just one major environmental influence: the parents who raise the children. The more that parents address speech to their toddlers, the more rapidly the toddlers recognize familiar words and learn new ones. The more that parents aim their scaffolding at, but not beyond, the upper end of their children's capabilities, the greater the improvement in their children's problem solving. The more stimulating and responsive the home intellectual environment, the higher children's IQ tends to be.

Parents exert at least as large an influence on their children's social and emotional development as on their intellectual development. For example, the likelihood that children will adopt their parents' standards and values appears to be influenced by the type of discipline their parents use with them. Similarly, parents influence their children's willingness to share, especially if they discuss the reasons for sharing with their children and have good relationships with them.

The effects of different types of parenting, like the effects of children's other experiences, depends on the child. One example of this involves the development of conscience. For fearful children, the key factor determining whether the child internalizes the parents' moral values is gentle discipline. Fearful children may become so anxious in the face of rigorous discipline that they cannot focus on the moral values that the parents are trying to instill. For fearless children, on the other hand, the key factor is a positive relationship with one's parents. Such fearless children often do not respond to gentle discipline; they tend to internalize their parents' values only if they feel close to them. As an old adage states, "It's a wise parent who knows his child."

Theme 7: Child-Development Research Can Improve Children's Lives

One of the few goals shared by virtually everyone is for children to be as happy and healthy as possible. Understanding how children develop can contribute to this goal. Theories of development provide general principles for interpreting children's behaviour and for analyzing their problems. Many empirical studies yield specific lessons regarding how to promote children's physical well-being, positive relationships with other people, and learning. In this section, we review practical implications of child-development research for raising children, educating them, and helping them overcome problems.

Implications for Parenting

Several principles of good parenting are so obvious that noting them might seem unnecessary. However, the number of children who are disadvantaged each year by poor parenting makes it clear that these principles cannot be stated too often.

Pick a Good Partner

The first principle of good parenting comes into play before parenthood even begins: pick a good partner. Given the importance of the environment, if you think you might want to have children, pick a partner whose intellectual and emotional characteristics seem likely to lead to their becoming a good mother or father. In terms of your child's development, no decision is more important than your choice of partner.

Ensure a Healthy Pregnancy

An expectant mother should maintain a healthy diet, have regular checkups, and keep stress levels as low as possible to increase the likelihood of a successful pregnancy. Equally important is avoiding teratogens such as tobacco, alcohol, and harmful drugs.

Know Which Decisions Are Likely to Have a Long-Term Impact

In addition to the joy they feel when their baby is born, new parents face a daunting number of decisions. Fortunately, babies are quite resilient. In the context of a loving and supportive home, a wide range of choices work out about equally well. Some decisions that seem minor, however, can have important effects. One such decision involves the baby's sleeping position: having a baby sleep on his or her back, rather than on his or her stomach, reduces the possibility of SIDS. Another decision with important long-term impact is vaccinating children against German measles and other diseases that are common in childhood or can negatively affect children's development; this is important not only for the health of one's own child but also for the health of other children in the community.

In other cases, the lesson of child-development research is that early problems are often transitory, so there is no reason to worry about them. Colic, which affects about 10% of babies, is one such problem. A colicky baby's frequent, high-pitched, grating, sick-sounding cries are difficult for parents to bear, but they have no long-term implications for the baby's development. In the short run, the best approach is to soothe the baby to the extent possible and not feel at fault if the effort fails. In the longer run, the best path for parents is to relax, seek social support, and obtain help to allow some time off from caregiving—and to remember that colic usually ends by the time babies are 3 months old.

Form a Secure Attachment

Most parents have no difficulty forming a secure attachment with their baby, but some parents and babies do not form such bonds. One reason is genetics: variant forms of certain genes can influence the likelihood of a child's forming a secure parental attachment in at least some circumstances. Of course, no one can control the genes that babies inherit, but parents and other caretakers can maximize the likelihood of a baby's becoming securely attached by maintaining a positive approach in their caregiving and by being responsive to the baby's needs. This is easier said than done, of course, and other dimensions of a baby's temperament, as well as the parents' attitude and responsiveness, influence the quality of attachment. However, even when babies are initially irritable and difficult, programs that teach parents how to be responsive and positive with them can lead to more secure attachments.

Provide a Stimulating Environment

The home environment has a great deal to do with children's learning. One good example involves reading acquisition. Reading to young children positively influences their later reading achievement. One reason is that such activities promote phonological awareness (the ability to identify the component sounds within words). Nursery rhymes seem to be particularly effective in this regard; children who repeatedly hear *Green Eggs and Ham,* for instance, generally learn to appreciate the similarities and differences in *Sam, ham, am,* and related words. Phonological awareness helps children learn to sound out words, which, in turn, helps them learn to retrieve the words' identities quickly and effortlessly. Successful early reading leads children to read more, which helps them improve their reading further over

ASIA IMAGES GROUP PTE LTD/ALAMY

Family activities, such as looking at photo albums and reminiscing about the people and settings they depict, provide both stimulation and warm, positive feelings for many children.

the course of schooling. More generally, the more stimulating the intellectual environment, the more eager children are to learn.

Implications for Education

Theories and research on child development hold a number of further lessons for how to educate children most effectively. Consider the instructional implications of several major theories of cognitive development.

Piaget's theory emphasizes the importance of the child's active involvement, both mental and physical, in the learning process. This active involvement is especially important in helping children master counterintuitive ideas. For example, the physical experience of walking around a pivot while holding a long metal rod at points close to and far from the pivot allowed children to overcome a widely held misconception that previous paper-and-pencil physics lessons had failed to correct—the misconception that all parts of an object must move at the same speed.

Information-processing theories suggest that analyzing the types of information available to children in everyday activities can improve learning. One such analysis indicated that the simple board game Snakes and Ladders provides visual, auditory, kinesthetic, and temporal information that can help children learn the sizes of numbers. Consistent with this analysis, having children from low-income families play a game based on Snakes and Ladders improved the children's understanding of the sizes of numbers, as well as their counting, recognition of numbers, and arithmetic learning.

Sociocultural theories emphasize the need to turn classrooms into communities of learners, in which children cooperate with one another in their pursuit of knowledge. Rather than following the traditional model of instruction in which teachers lecture and children take notes, community-of-learners classrooms follow an approach in which teachers provide the minimum guidance needed for children to learn and gradually decrease their directive role as children's competence increases. Such programs also encourage children to make use of the resources of the broader community—children and teachers at other schools, outside experts, reference books, websites, and so on. The approach can be effective not only in building intellectual skills but also in promoting desirable values, such as personal responsibility and mutual respect.

Implications for Helping Children at Risk

Several principles that have emerged from empirical research offer valuable guidance for helping children at risk for serious developmental problems.

The Importance of Timing

Providing interventions at the optimal time is crucial in a variety of developmental contexts. One important example involves efforts to help children at risk for learning difficulties. All theories of cognitive development indicate that such difficulties should be addressed early, before children lose confidence in their ability to learn and before they become resentful toward schools and teachers. This realization, together with research documenting that many children from impoverished backgrounds have difficulty in school, laid the groundwork for various early intervention and prevention programs. Evaluations of the programs' effects indicate that these programs increase children's IQs and achievement test scores by the end of the programs and briefly thereafter. Subsequently, the positive effects on IQ and academic achievement usually fade, but other positive effects continue. At-risk children who participate in such programs are less likely to ever be held back in school or assigned to special-education classes than are those who do not participate, and they are more likely to graduate from high school and go to university. These are important gains.

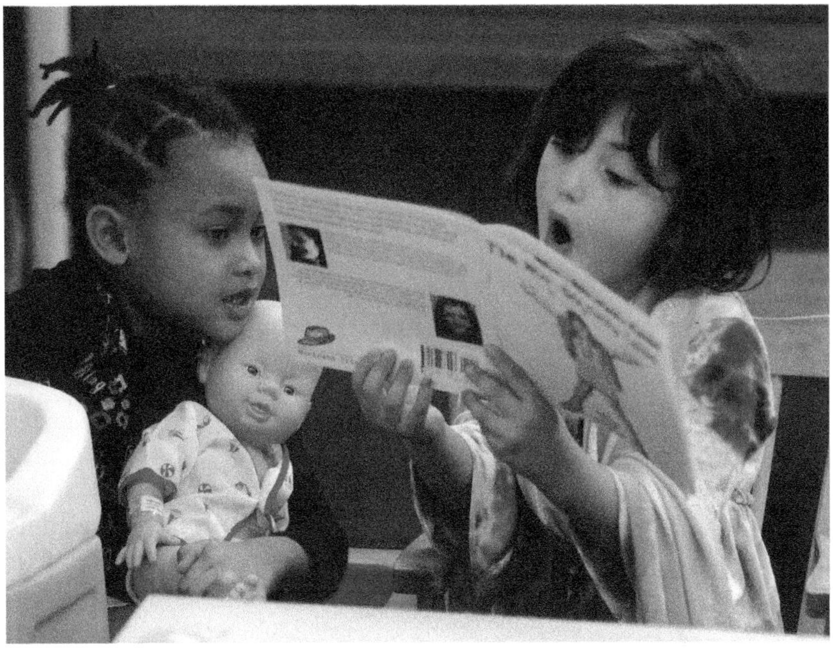
COLIN MCCONNELL/GETTY IMAGES

Experiences such as this one in classrooms with early intervention programs lead to a variety of lasting benefits.

Even greater positive effects of early educational programs are possible, as illustrated by the Better Beginnings, Better Futures (BBBF) project and the Carolina Abecedarian Project. BBBF offered a variety of child-, parent-, and family- and community-focused programming to families with children between the ages of 4 and 8 years living in four Ontario communities considered "at risk." Similarly, the Carolina Abecedarian Project was designed to show what could be achieved through an optimally staffed, highly funded, and carefully designed program that started during infancy and lasted through age 5. The Abecedarian Project produced large gains in both academic achievement and social skills that continued throughout childhood and adolescence. Its results demonstrate that it is possible for intensive programs that start early to have substantial, lasting benefits on poor children's academic achievement.

Early detection of child maltreatment and rapid intervention to end it are also crucial. Neglect, physical abuse, and sexual abuse are the three most common forms of child maltreatment. Parents who are stressed economically, have few friends, use alcohol and illegal drugs, or are being abused by their partner are the most likely to mistreat their children.

Knowing the characteristics of abused and neglected children can help teachers and others who come into contact with children recognize potential problems early and alert social service agencies so that they can investigate and remedy the problems. Children who are maltreated tend to have difficult temperaments, to have few friends, to be in poor physical and mental health, to do poorly in school, and to show atypical aggression or passivity. Adolescents who are maltreated may be depressed or hyperactive, use drugs or alcohol, and have sexual problems such as promiscuity or atypical fearfulness. Early recognition of such signs of abuse can literally save children's lives.

Biology and Environment Work Together

Another principle with important practical implications is that biology and environment work together to produce all behaviour. This principle has proved important in designing treatments for ADHD. Although stimulant drugs such as

Ritalin are the best-known treatment for this problem, research has shown that when medications are used alone, their benefits usually end as soon as children stop taking them. Longer-lasting benefits require behavioural therapy as well as medication. One effective treatment is to teach children cognitive strategies for screening out distractions. The medications calm children with ADHD sufficiently that they can benefit from the therapy; the therapy helps them learn effective ways for coping with their problems and for interacting with other people.

Every Problem Has Many Causes

An additional principle that has proved useful for helping children is that trying to identify *the* cause of any particular problem is futile; problems almost always have multiple causes. The greater the number of risks, the more likely a child is to have low IQ, poor socioemotional skills, and psychiatric disorders. Accordingly, providing effective treatment often requires addressing many particular difficulties. This principle has provided useful guidance for intervening with children who are rejected by other children. Helping these children gain better social skills requires increasing their understanding of other people. It also requires helping them learn new strategies, such as how to enter an ongoing group interaction unobtrusively and how to resolve conflicts without resorting to aggression. It also requires helping them learn from their own experience—for example, by monitoring the success of the different strategies they try and, when necessary, analyzing what went wrong. Together, these approaches can help rejected children make friends and become better accepted.

Improving Social Policy

Even if you do not have children of your own and do not interact with children in your own work, your actions as a citizen can influence the lives of the children in your community. Votes in elections and referenda, opinions expressed in informal discussions, and participation in advocacy organizations all can make a difference. Knowledge of child-development research can inform your perspectives on many issues relevant to children.

The conclusions that you reach will, and should, reflect your values as well as the evidence. For example, reductions in class size in kindergarten through 3rd-grade classrooms have had variable effects on student achievement. A large-scale, well-implemented study in Tennessee indicated positive effects on student achievement (Krueger, 1999), whereas a large-scale, well-implemented study in California did not show any effect on achievement (Stecher, McCaffrey, & Bugliari, 2003). Teachers and parents appeared to be pleased with the class-size reductions in both cases and believed that the smaller classes helped their children.

Are these outcomes worth the many billions of dollars that hiring the number of teachers needed to implement such a reform throughout a large country would cost? Research cannot answer this question because the answer depends on values as well as data. How expensive is too expensive? Nonetheless, as the example illustrates, knowing the scientific evidence can help us, as citizens, make better-informed decisions.

Parental Leave

Should society require employers to grant paid parental leave in the months after a baby is born, and if so, for how long? Canada is amongst the many countries in the world that have a national parental leave policy, but the duration of leave varies significantly across these countries, and there are some countries, including the United States, with no such policy in place. Long hours of lower quality childcare before an infant is 9 months old can have negative effects on early social development; therefore, we could say that society should make it easier for parents to take leave for that period of time. However, other considerations, such as economic costs, are also important: Should governments require all employers to provide paid leave, or should small or very small businesses be exempted from the requirement? For how long should paid leave be required? Should the amount of paid leave be equal to the employee's usual salary or a reduced amount? Should the length of paid leave be identical for both parents, longer for the primary caretaker, or only provided for the primary caretaker? As noted earlier, scientific evidence can never answer such questions, which inevitably reflect values and priorities.

Childcare

Should the general society subsidize childcare payments for parents of young children? One argument against such a policy has been the claim that children develop more successfully if they stay at home with one of their parents or another relative than if they attend day care. This argument has turned out to be incorrect, however. Children who attend good-quality day care develop similarly to children who receive care at home from their parents.

Eyewitness Testimony

Understanding child development is also vital for deciding whether children should be allowed to testify in court cases and for obtaining the most accurate testimony possible from them. Each year, tens of thousands of children in Canada testify in legal cases, either about crimes they experienced or witnessed. Often, the child and the accused are the only ones who witnessed the events. Research indicates that, in general, the accuracy of testimony increases with age; 8-year-olds recall more than do 6-year-olds, and 6-year-olds recall more than do 4-year-olds. However, when children are shielded from misleading and repeated questioning, even 4- and 5-year-olds usually provide accurate testimony about the types of

BLUE JEAN IMAGES/ALAMY

Children are naturally curious about the world; encouraging this curiosity and channeling it in fruitful directions are amongst the most vital goals facing both parents and society.

issues that are central in court cases. Given the high stakes in such cases, using the lessons of research to elicit the most accurate possible testimony from children is essential for just verdicts.

Child-development research holds lessons for numerous other social problems as well. Research on the causes of aggression has led to programs such as Fast Track, which are designed to teach aggressive children to manage their anger and avoid violence. Research on the development of helping and sharing behaviour has led to programs such as Roots of Empathy, designed to promote children's prosocial behaviours and decrease their aggressive behaviours. Research on the effects of poverty has provided the basis for the Better Beginnings, Better Futures project, the Carolina Abecedarian Project, and other early education efforts. There is no end of social problems; understanding child development can help address the ones that affect children's futures.

Test Yourself

1. Which of the following statements accurately describes the interaction of nature and nurture?
   a. Nature does its work before birth, and nurture takes over only after birth.
   b. Nature's influence continues through infancy before giving way to the influence of nurture.
   c. Nature and nurture begin interacting on the fetus in the womb, and both continue to shape the individual's development throughout life.
   d. The role that both nature and nurture play in development is often overstated.
2. Which of the following is an example of the crucial role that timing plays in the potential impact of a teratogen?
   a. The diet of a pregnant mother will influence taste preferences that the fetus will exhibit after birth.
   b. By age 12 months, infants lose the ability to hear the difference between similar sounds that they do not encounter on a regular basis.
   c. A virus will cause damage to the development of a fetus if contracted by the pregnant mother at specific sensitive times during pregnancy.
   d. It is more difficult for children older than 11 or 12 years of age to gain competence in a new language than it is for younger children.
3. The emerging field of epigenetics has helped to explain the ways in which a child's environment can influence gene expression. Which of the following is an example of this interaction?
   a. Children with certain types of brain damage will perform on par with other children on IQ tests up to a certain age but will fall behind after that point.
   b. It is more difficult for children older than 11 or 12 years of age to gain competence in a new language than it is for younger children.
   c. A child who loses capability in one sense, such as sight, will often compensate with enhanced ability in another sense.
   d. The amount of stress that a mother experiences during her child's infancy can affect that child's ability to regulate reaction to stress later in life.
4. Looking preferences, self-initiated activities, self-socialization, and even the manner in which infants react to their parents are all examples of
   a. the active role children play in their development.
   b. the greater influence that nurture plays compared with nature in child development.
   c. the ways in which development is discontinuous.
   d. the ways in which the sociocultural context shapes development.
5. Which of the following is an example of the theme of the active child?
   a. The stability of IQ scores on average tends to increase with age.
   b. Stressful maternal experiences, such as a periodic shortage of food at certain points during pregnancy, will influence the future physical development of the child.
   c. Children who exhibit preoperational reasoning in some contexts may also exhibit concrete operational reasoning in others.
   d. Children who are better able to regulate their emotions tend to be more socially competent and, therefore, elicit more positive reactions from other people than those who are less skilled at emotion regulation.

6. Piaget's theory of cognitive development, Freud's theory of psychosexual development, and Erikson's theory of psychosocial development are all examples of
   a. social learning theory.
   b. the stage approach to development.
   c. theories based on an empiricist perspective of development.
   d. theories based on the nativist approach to child development.
7. An infant's attachment to his or her mother will more reliably predict that child's long-term security if there are no significant disruptions in the home environment. This example illustrates
   a. the degree to which genetic influence on individual differences tends to decrease over time.
   b. how continuity in individual differences is influenced by continuity in the environment.
   c. the manner in which sociocultural differences exert influence on cognitive development.
   d. the role of domain-specific learning mechanisms in child development.
8. Which of the following statements accurately expresses a key understanding regarding the continuity and discontinuity of development?
   a. Child psychologists today generally believe that, for the vast majority of traits, development occurs in a discontinuous manner.
   b. Very few individual differences in psychological properties show stability over time.
   c. Contrary to the theories by early behavioural psychologists like Piaget and Erikson, developmental processes rarely show a great deal of continuity.
   d. The apparent continuity or discontinuity of a given developmental trait depends on the timescale on which it is considered.
9. Before writing an essay, a child first considers what readers already know about the topic. Which of the four general information-processing mechanisms is illustrated by this example?
   a. Strategy formation
   b. Basic processes
   c. Metacognition
   d. Content knowledge
10. Which of the following statements is *not* true of the development of a child's cognitive abilities?
   a. A child's content knowledge in a given area can outweigh an adult's general intellectual ability.
   b. Statistical learning emerges in middle childhood, after the child has begun to understand basic mathematical properties.
   c. Understanding basic causal relationships allows children to infer explanations for a wide variety of observations.
   d. Knowing multiple strategies for achieving goals helps children adapt to different problems and situations they will face.
11. Babies who grow up in African tribes that strongly encourage infants' motor development tend to walk and reach other motor milestones earlier than do infants in Canada. This is an example of the effect of ____________ on development.
   a. change mechanisms
   b. historical change
   c. discontinuity
   d. the sociocultural context
12. Which of the following is *not* a reason why demographic variables such as gender, race, ethnicity, and socioeconomic status are particularly useful to child-development researchers?
   a. Each of these variables relates directly to a wide variety of other individual differences.
   b. These variables tend to remain stable over time.
   c. These variables have been shown to reliably predict some future outcomes.
   d. These variables tend to be unaffected by environmental factors.
13. Which of the following is an important contribution that Piaget's theory has made to children's education?
   a. Piaget helped to delineate the interactions between a child's genes and his or her environment.
   b. Piaget's theory emphasizes the importance of the child's active involvement in the learning process.
   c. Piaget brought attention to the role that cultural influences play in a child's learning.
   d. Piaget explained cognitive development as a continuous process rather than as a series of stages.
14. Habituation is a learning process in which a child becomes familiar with a repeated stimulus. This process can motivate the child to seek out new stimulation. Besides illustrating the role of behavioural mechanisms in a child's development, this example also demonstrates which other theme of child development?
   a. The sociocultural context of an individual's development
   b. The role of the active child
   c. The discontinuity of change over time
   d. The influence of nature over nurture
15. Consider the statement "Individual differences are not randomly distributed." What is meant by this observation?
   a. A child's performance in one area of development will predict the child's achievement in another, related area.
   b. A child's genotype will always exert a stronger influence on the child's outcomes than will any environmental factors.
   c. Each individual child is different from all other children.
   d. A child's performance on one measure of intelligence will not predict the child's performance in another.

LaunchPad
macmillan learning

DON'T STOP NOW! Research shows that testing yourself is a powerful learning tool. Visit LaunchPad to access the LearningCurve adaptive quizzing system, which gives you a personalized study plan to help build your mastery of the chapter material through videos, activities, and more. **Go to launchpadworks.com.**

Critical Thinking Questions

1. What qualities of children influence the way that other people act toward them, and how do these actions influence their development?
2. Individual differences show some stability over time. How do genes and environment contribute to this stability?
3. How would growing up in one modern society rather than another—for example, Canada rather than Japan—be expected to influence a child's development?
4. How have the changes that have taken place in Canada over the past century influenced children's development? Has the overall effect of the changes on children been predominantly beneficial or predominantly harmful?
5. What findings that you read about in this book surprised you the most? Were there any findings or conclusions that you just don't believe?
6. What practical lessons have you learned from this course that will influence how you might raise your children if you have them?

Answers to Test Yourself

1. c, **2.** c, **3.** d, **4.** a, **5.** d, **6.** b, **7.** b, **8.** d, **9.** c, **10.** b, **11.** d, **12.** d, **13.** b, **14.** b, **15.** a

Glossary

accommodation the process by which people adapt current knowledge structures in response to new experiences.

acculturation the process of adjusting to a new culture while retaining some aspects of one's culture of origin.

achievement motivation refers to whether children are motivated by mastery or by others' views of their success.

activating influences potential result of certain fluctuations in sex-linked hormone levels affecting the contemporaneous activation of the nervous system and corresponding behavioural responses.

active learning learning by engaging with the world, rather than passively observing objects and events.

adrenarche period prior to the emergence of visible signs of puberty during which the adrenal glands mature, providing a major source of sex steroid hormones; correlates with the onset of sexual attraction.

adverse childhood experiences (ACEs) traumatic childhood experiences, such as abuse, neglect, violence exposure, or death of a parent, that are linked to mental and physical health problems later in life.

affiliation tendency to affirm connection with others through being emotionally open, empathetic, or supportive.

affordances the possibilities for action offered, or afforded, by objects and situations.

agender individuals who do not identify with any gender category.

aggression behaviour aimed at physically or emotionally harming or injuring others.

aggressive-rejected (peer status) children who are viewed by their peers as especially prone to physical aggression, disruptive behaviour, delinquency, and negative behaviour such as hostility and threatening others.

alleles two or more different forms of a gene.

ambivalent sexism model of sexism that includes two components, hostile sexism (endorsement of men's dominance with negative views of women seeking equality) and benevolent sexism (the belief that men need to protect women, and that women and men have complementary traits).

amniotic sac a transparent, fluid-filled membrane that surrounds and protects the fetus.

amygdala an area of the brain that is involved in emotional reactions.

anal stage the second stage in Freud's theory, lasting from the second year through the third year, in which the primary source of pleasure comes from defecation.

androgen insensitivity syndrome (AIS) condition during prenatal development in which androgen receptors malfunction in genetic males, impeding the formation of male external genitalia; in these cases, the child may be born with female external genitalia.

androgens class of steroid hormones that normally occur at slightly higher levels in males than in females and that affect physical development and functioning from the prenatal period onward.

A-not-B error the tendency to reach for a hidden object where it was last found rather than in the new location where it was last hidden.

antisocial behaviour disruptive, hostile, or aggressive behaviour that violates social norms or rules and that harms or takes advantage of others.

anxiety disorders a set of mental disorders that involve the inability to regulate fear and worry.

Apgar score method for evaluating the health of the newborn immediately following birth based on skin tone, pulse rate, facial response, arm and leg activity, and breathing.

apoptosis genetically programmed cell death.

arborization formation of new dendritic trees and branches.

assertion tendency to take action on behalf of the self through competitive, independent, or aggressive behaviours.

assimilation the process by which people translate incoming information into a form that fits concepts they already understand.

association areas parts of the brain that lie between the major sensory and motor areas and that process and integrate input from those areas.

attachment an emotional bond with a specific person that is enduring across space and time.

attachment theory theory based on John Bowlby's work that posits that children are biologically predisposed to develop attachments to caregivers as a means of increasing the chances of their own survival.

attention-deficit hyperactivity disorder (ADHD) a syndrome that involves difficulty in sustaining attention.

auditory localization perception of the location in space of a sound source.

authoritarian parenting a parenting style that is high in demandingness and low in responsiveness. Authoritarian parents are nonresponsive to their children's needs and tend to enforce their demands through the exercise of parental power and the use of threats and punishment. They are oriented toward obedience and authority and expect their children to comply with their demands without question or explanation.

authoritative parenting a parenting style that is high in demandingness and supportiveness. Authoritative parents set clear standards and limits for their children and are firm about enforcing them; at the same time, they allow their children considerable autonomy within those limits, are attentive and responsive to their children's concerns and needs, and respect and consider their children's perspective.

axons neural fibres that conduct electrical signals away from the cell body to connections with other neurons.

babbling repetitive consonant–vowel sequences ("bababa …") or hand movements (for learners of sign languages).

basic level the middle level, and often the first level learned, within a category hierarchy, such as "dog" in the animal/dog/poodle example.

basic processes the simplest and most frequently used mental activities.

behaviour genetics the science concerned with how variation in behaviour and development results from the combination of genetic and environmental factors.

behaviour modification a form of therapy based on principles of operant conditioning in which reinforcement contingencies are changed to encourage more adaptive behaviour.

Better Beginnings, Better Futures (BBBF) Ontario-based prevention project designed for young children who have multiple risks for poorer child development.

bidirectionality of parent–child interactions the idea that parents and their children are mutually affected by one another's characteristics and behaviours.

bigender individuals who identify with two genders.

bilingualism fluency in two languages.

binocular disparity the difference between the retinal image of an object in each eye that results in two slightly different signals being sent to the brain.

body image an individual's perception of, and feelings about, her or his own body.

Carolina Abecedarian Project comprehensive and successful enrichment program in the United States for children from low-income families.

carrier genetic testing genetic testing used to determine whether prospective parents are carriers of specific disorders.

categorical perception the perception of phonemes as belonging to discrete categories.

category hierarchy a category that is organized by set–subset relations, such as animal/dog/poodle.

cell body a component of the neuron that contains the basic biological material that keeps the neuron functioning.

centration the tendency to focus on a single, perceptually striking feature of an object or event.

cephalocaudal development the pattern of growth in which areas near the head develop earlier than areas farther from the head.

cerebral cortex the "grey matter" of the brain, consisting of four distinct lobes.

cerebral hemispheres the two halves of the cortex.

cerebral lateralization the specialization of the hemispheres of the brain for different modes of processing.

child maltreatment action or failure to act on the part of a parent or caretaker that results in physical or emotional harm to a child or a risk of serious harm.

chromosomes molecules of DNA that transmit genetic information; chromosomes are made up of DNA.

chronosystem historical changes that influence the other systems.

cisgender individuals who identify with their gender assigned at birth (or their biological sex).

classical conditioning a form of learning that consists of associating an initially neutral stimulus with a stimulus that always evokes a particular reflexive response.

clinical interview a procedure in which questions are adjusted in accord with the answers the interviewee provides.

cognitive development the development of thinking and reasoning.

colic excessive, inconsolable crying by a young infant for no apparent reason.

collaboration coordination of assertion and affiliation in behaviour, such as making initiatives for joint activity.

collective monologue conversation between children that involves a series of non sequiturs.

comprehension monitoring process of keeping track of one's understanding of a verbal description or text.

computer simulation a type of mathematical model that expresses ideas about mental processes in precise ways.

conception the union of an egg from the mother and a sperm from the father.

concepts general ideas or understandings that can be used to group together objects, events, qualities, or abstractions that are similar in some way.

concrete operational stage the period (7 to 12 years) within Piaget's theory in which children become able to reason logically about concrete objects and events.

conditioned response (CR) the originally reflexive response that comes to be elicited by the conditioned stimulus.

conditioned stimulus (CS) the neutral stimulus that is repeatedly paired with the unconditioned stimulus.

conduct disorder (CD) a disorder that involves severe antisocial and aggressive behaviours that inflict pain on others or involve destruction of property or denial of the rights of others.

cone cells light-sensitive neurons that are highly concentrated in the fovea (the central region of the retina).

congenital adrenal hyperplasia (CAH) condition during prenatal development in which the adrenal glands produce high levels of androgens; sometimes associated with masculinization of external genitalia in genetic females and sometimes associated with higher rates of masculine-stereotyped play in genetic females.

connectionism a computational modelling approach that emphasizes the simultaneous activity of numerous interconnected processing units.

conscience an internal regulatory mechanism that increases an individual's ability to conform to standards of conduct accepted in their culture.

conservation concept the idea that merely changing the appearance of objects does not necessarily change the objects' other key properties.

constructivism the theory that infants build increasingly advanced understanding by combining rudimentary innate knowledge with subsequent experiences.

continuous development the idea that changes with age occur gradually, in small increments, like that of a pine tree growing taller and taller.

contrast sensitivity the ability to detect differences in light and dark areas in a visual pattern.

control group the group of participants in an experimental design who are not presented the experience of interest but in other ways are treated similarly.

controversial (peer status) children or adolescents who are liked by quite a few peers and are disliked by quite a few others.

core-knowledge theories approaches that view children as having some innate knowledge in domains of special evolutionary importance and domain-specific learning mechanisms for rapidly and effortlessly acquiring additional information in those domains.

co-regulation the process by which a caregiver provides the needed comfort or distraction to help a child reduce his or her distress.

corpus callosum a dense tract of nerve fibres that enable the two hemispheres of the brain to communicate.

correlation the association between two variables.

correlational designs studies intended to indicate how two variables are related to each other.

co-rumination extensively discussing and self-disclosing emotional problems with another person.

cross-gender-typed behaviours stereotyped or expected for the gender other than that of a given person.

crossing over the process by which sections of DNA switch from one chromosome to the other; crossing over promotes variability among individuals.

cross-sectional design a research method in which participants of different ages are compared on a given behaviour or characteristic over a short period.

cross-situational word learning determining word meanings by tracking the correlations between labels and meanings across scenes and contexts.

crystallized intelligence factual knowledge about the world.

cultural tools the innumerable products of human ingenuity that enhance thinking.

cumulative risk the accumulation of disadvantages over years of development.

cyberbullying repeated and intentional harassment or mistreatment of an individual via digital devices such as cell phones, computers, and tablets.

deferred imitation the repetition of other people's behaviour a substantial time after it originally occurred.

dendrites neural fibres that receive input from other cells and conduct it toward the cell body in the form of electrical impulses.

dependent variable a behaviour that is measured to determine whether it is affected by exposure to the independent variable.

depression a mental disorder that involves a sad or irritable mood along with physical and cognitive changes that interfere with daily life.

developmental resilience successful development in spite of multiple and seemingly overwhelming developmental hazards.

differential susceptibility a circumstance in which the same temperament characteristic that puts some children at high risk for negative outcomes when exposed to a harsh home environment also causes them to blossom when their home environment is positive.

direction-of-causation problem the concept that a correlation between two variables does not indicate which, if either, variable is the cause of the other.

discipline the set of strategies and behaviours parents use to teach children how to behave appropriately.

discontinuous development the idea that changes with age include occasional large shifts, like the transition from caterpillar to cocoon to butterfly.

discrete emotions theory a theory in which emotions are viewed as innate, and each emotion has a specific and distinctive set of bodily and facial reactions.

dishabituation the introduction of a new stimulus rekindles interest following habituation to a repeated stimulus.

disorganized/disoriented attachment a type of insecure attachment in which infants or young children have no consistent way of coping with the stress of the Strange Situation. Their behaviour is confused or even contradictory, and they often appear dazed or disoriented.

display rules a social group's informal norms about when, where, and how much one should show emotions and when and where displays of emotion should be suppressed or masked by displays of other emotions.

distributional properties of speech in any language, certain sounds are more likely to occur together than are others.

DNA (deoxyribonucleic acid) molecules that carry all the biochemical instructions involved in the formation and functioning of an organism.

domain specific information about a particular content area.

dominant allele the allele that, if present, gets expressed.

dose–response relation a relation in which the effect of exposure to an element increases with the extent of exposure (prenatally, the more exposure a fetus has to a potential teratogen, the more severe its effect is likely to be).

dual representation treating a symbolic artefact both as a real object and as a symbol for something other than itself.

dynamic-systems theories a class of theories that focus on how change occurs over time in complex systems.

dyslexia inability to read and spell well despite having normal intelligence.

effect size magnitude of difference between two group's averages and the amount of overlap in their distributions.

ego in psychoanalytic theory, the second personality structure to develop. It is the rational, logical, problem-solving component of personality.

egocentric spatial representations coding of spatial locations relative to one's own body, without regard to the surroundings.

egocentrism the tendency to perceive the world solely from one's own point of view.

embryo the developing organism from the 3rd to 8th week of prenatal development.

embryonic stem cells embryonic cells, which can develop into any type of body cell.

emotion coaching the use of discussion and other forms of instruction to teach children how to cope with and properly express emotions.

emotion regulation a set of both conscious and unconscious processes used to both monitor and modulate emotional experiences and expressions.

emotion socialization the process through which children acquire the values, standards, skills, knowledge, and behaviours that are regarded as appropriate for their present and future roles in their particular culture.

emotional intelligence the ability to cognitively process information about emotions and to use that information to guide both thought and behaviour.

emotions neural and physiological responses to the environment, subjective feelings, cognitions related to those feelings, and the desire to take action.

enactive experience learning to take into account the reactions one's past behaviour has evoked in others.

encoding the process of representing in memory information that draws attention or is considered important.

endophenotypes intermediate phenotypes, including the brain and nervous systems, that do not involve overt behaviour.

entity theory a theory that a person's level of intelligence is fixed and unchangeable.

entity/helpless orientation a tendency to attribute success and failure to enduring aspects of the self and to give up in the face of failure.

environment every aspect of individuals and their surroundings other than genes.

epigenesis the emergence of new structures and functions in the course of development.

epigenetics the study of stable changes in gene expression that are mediated by the environment.

equifinality the concept that various causes can lead to the same mental disorder.

equilibration the process by which children (or other people) balance assimilation and accommodation to create stable understanding.

erogenous zones in Freud's theory, areas of the body that become erotically sensitive in successive stages of development.

essentialism the view that living things have an essence inside them that makes them what they are.

ethnic and racial identity the beliefs and attitudes an individual has about the ethnic or racial groups to which they belong.

ethology the study of the evolutionary bases of behaviour.

exosystem environmental settings that a child does not directly experience but that can affect the child indirectly.

experience-dependent plasticity the process through which neural connections are created and reorganized throughout life as a function of an individual's experiences.

experience-expectant plasticity the process through which the normal wiring of the brain occurs in part as a result of species-typical experiences.

experimental control the ability of researchers to determine the specific experiences of participants during the course of an experiment.

experimental designs a group of approaches that allow inferences about causes and effects to be drawn.

experimental group the group of participants in an experimental design who are presented the experience of interest.

external validity the degree to which results can be generalized beyond the particulars of the research.

false-belief problems tasks that test a child's understanding that other people will act in accord with their own beliefs even when the child knows that those beliefs are incorrect.

family a group that involves at least one adult who is related to the child by birth, marriage, adoption, or foster status and who is responsible for providing basic necessities as well as love, support, safety, stability, and opportunities for learning.

family dynamics the way in which family members interact through various relationships: mother with each child, father with each child, mother with father, and siblings with one another.

family structure the number of and relationships amongst the people living in a household.

fetal alcohol spectrum disorder (FASD) the harmful effects of maternal alcohol consumption on a developing fetus. Fetal alcohol syndrome (FAS) involves a range of effects, including facial deformities, intellectual disabilities, attention problems, hyperactivity, and other defects. Fetal alcohol effects (FAE) is a term used for individuals who show some, but not all, of the standard effects of FAS.

fetus the developing organism from the 9th week to birth.

fluid intelligence ability to think on the spot to solve novel problems.

Flynn effect consistent rise in average IQ scores that has occurred over the past 80 years in many countries.

formal operational stage the period (12 years and beyond) within Piaget's theory in which people become able to think about abstractions and hypothetical situations.

fraternal (dizygotic) twins twins that result when two eggs happen to be released into the fallopian tube at the same time and are fertilized by two different sperm; fraternal twins have only half their genes in common.

friend a person with whom an individual has an intimate, reciprocated, positive relationship.

frontal lobe major area of the cortex that is associated with working memory and cognitive control.

functionalist perspective a theory which argues that the basic function of emotions is to promote action toward achieving a goal. In this view, emotions are not discrete from one another and vary somewhat based on the social environment.

***g* (general intelligence)** cognitive processes that influence the ability to think and learn on all intellectual tasks.

gametes (germ cells) reproductive cells—egg and sperm—that contain only half the genetic material of all the other cells in the body.

gender social assignment or self-categorization as "a girl" or "a boy" (or possibly both, neither, or a different category).

gender constancy realization that gender is invariant despite superficial changes in a person's appearance or behaviour.

gender-fluid individuals who self-identify with different gender categories depending on the context.

gender identity self-identifying as a boy or a girl (or possibly as both or possibly neither).

gender nonconforming individuals who are highly cross-gender-typed in relation to their assigned gender.

gender-role flexibility recognition of gender roles as social conventions and adoption of more flexible attitudes and interests.

gender-role intensification heightened concerns with adhering to traditional gender roles that may occur during adolescence.

gender schema filter initial evaluation of information as relevant for one's own gender.

gender schemas organized mental representations (concepts, beliefs, memories) about gender, including gender stereotypes.

gender segregation children's tendency to associate with same-gender peers and to avoid other-gender peers.

gender stability awareness that gender remains the same over time.

gender-typed behaviours stereotyped or expected for a given person's assigned gender.

gender typing the process of gender socialization.

generative a system in which a finite set of words can be combined to generate an infinite number of sentences.

genes sections of chromosomes that are the basic unit of heredity in all living things.

genital stage the final stage in Freud's theory, beginning in adolescence, in which sexual maturation is complete.

genome each person's complete set of hereditary information; the complete set of DNA of any organism, including all of its genes.

genotype the genetic material an individual inherits.

gesture–speech mismatches phenomenon in which hand movements and verbal statements convey different ideas.

glial cells cells in the brain that provide a variety of critical supportive functions.

goodness of fit the degree to which an individual's temperament is compatible with the demands and expectations of his or her social environment.

guided participation a process in which more knowledgeable individuals organize activities in ways that allow less knowledgeable people to learn.

habituation a simple form of learning that involves a decrease in response to repeated or continued stimulation.

heritability a statistical estimate of the proportion of the measured variance on a trait among individuals in a given population that is attributable to genetic differences among those individuals.

heritable refers to characteristics or traits that are genetically transmitted.

heterozygous having two different alleles for a trait.

homozygous having two of the same allele for a trait.

hostile attributional bias in Dodge's theory, the tendency to assume that other people's ambiguous actions stem from hostile intent.

hypotheses testable predictions of the presence or absence of phenomena or relations.

id in psychoanalytic theory, the earliest and most primitive personality structure. It is unconscious and operates with the goal of seeking pleasure.

identical (monozygotic) twins twins that result from the splitting in half of the zygote, resulting in each of the two resulting zygotes having exactly the same set of genes.

identity a description of the self that is often externally imposed, such as through membership in a group.

identity achievement an integration of various aspects of the self into a coherent whole that is stable over time and across events.

identity diffusion period in which the individual does not have firm commitments regarding the issues in question and is not making progress toward developing them.

identity foreclosure period in which the individual has not engaged in any identity experimentation and has established a vocational or ideological identity based on the choices or values of others.

imaginary audience the belief, stemming from adolescent egocentrism, that everyone else is focused on the adolescent's appearance and behaviour.

imprinting a form of learning in which the newborns of some species become attached to and follow adult members of the species.

incremental theory a theory that a person's intelligence can grow as a function of experience.

incremental/mastery orientation a general tendency to attribute success and failure to the amount of effort expended and to persist in the face of failure.

independent variable the experience that participants in the experimental group receive and that those in the control group do not receive.

infant-directed speech (IDS) the distinctive mode of speech used when speaking to infants and toddlers.

infant mortality death during the first year after birth.

information-processing theories a class of theories that focus on the structure of the cognitive system and the mental activities used to deploy attention and memory to solve problems.

ingroup assimilation process whereby individuals are socialized to conform to the group's norms, demonstrating the characteristics that define the ingroup.

ingroup bias tendency to evaluate individuals and characteristics of the ingroup more positively than or as superior to those of the outgroup.

insecure/avoidant attachment a type of insecure attachment in which infants or young children seem somewhat indifferent toward their caregiver and may even avoid the caregiver. If the infant gets upset when left alone, he or she is as easily comforted by a stranger as by a parent.

insecure/resistant attachment a type of insecure attachment in which infants or young children are clingy and stay close to their caregiver rather than exploring their environment. In the Strange Situation, insecure/resistant infants tend to become very upset when the caregiver leaves them alone in the room. When their caregiver returns, they are not easily comforted and both seek comfort and resist efforts by the caregiver to comfort them.

instrumental aggression aggression motivated by the desire to obtain a concrete goal.

instrumental (operant) conditioning learning the relation between one's own behaviour and the consequences that result from it.

interest filter initial evaluation of information as being personally interesting.

intermittent reinforcement inconsistent response to a behaviour; for example, sometimes punishing unacceptable behaviours, and other times ignoring it.

intermodal perception the combining of information from two or more sensory systems.

internal validity the degree to which effects observed within experiments can be attributed to the factor that the researcher is testing.

internal working model of attachment the child's mental representation of the self, of attachment figure(s), and of relationships in general that is constructed as a result of experiences with caregivers. The working model guides children's interactions with caregivers and other people in infancy and at older ages.

internalization the process by which children learn and accept the reasons for desired behaviour.

interrater reliability the amount of agreement in the observations of different raters who witness the same behaviour.

intersectionality the interconnection of social identities such as gender, race, ethnicity, sexual orientation, and class, especially in relation to overlapping experiences of discrimination and disadvantage.

intersex condition rare conditions in which an individual of one genetic sex can develop genitalia associated with the other genetic sex, both genetic sexes, or undergo only partial development of genitalia associated with their genetic sex.

intersubjectivity the mutual understanding that people share during communication.

IQ (intelligence quotient) a quantitative measure of a child's intelligence relative to that of other children of the same age.

joint attention a process in which social partners intentionally focus on a common referent in the external environment.

language comprehension understanding what others say (or sign or write).

language production the process of speaking (or signing or writing).

latency period the fourth stage in Freud's theory, lasting from age 6 to age 12, in which sexual energy gets channelled into socially acceptable activities.

longitudinal design a method of study in which the same participants are studied twice or more over a substantial length of time.

long-term memory information retained on an enduring basis.

low birth weight (LBW) a birth weight of less than 2500 grams.

macrosystem the larger cultural and social context within which the other systems are embedded.

mathematical equality concept that the values on each side of the equal sign must be equivalent.

meiosis cell division that produces gametes.

menarche onset of menstruation.

mental disorder a state of having problems with emotional reactions to the environment and with social relationships in ways that affect daily life.

mental health children's sense of well-being both internally, such as in their emotions and stress levels, and externally, such as in their relationships with family members and peers.

mesosystem the interconnections among immediate, or microsystem, settings.

meta-analysis a statistical method for combining the results from independent studies to reach conclusions based on all of them; used to summarize average effect size and statistical significance across several research studies.

methylation a biochemical process that influences behaviour by suppressing gene activity and expression.

microgenetic design a method of study in which the same participants are studied repeatedly over a short period.

microsystem the immediate environment that an individual child personally experiences and participates in.

mitosis cell division that results in two identical cells.

monocular depth (pictorial) cues the perceptual cues of depth (such as relative size and interposition) that can be perceived by one eye alone.

moral domain an area of social knowledge based on concepts of right and wrong, fairness, justice, and individual rights; these concepts apply across contexts and supersede rules or authority.

moratorium period in which the individual is exploring various occupational and ideological choices and has not yet made a clear commitment to them.

morphemes the smallest units of meaning in a language.

multifinality the concept that certain risk factors do not always lead to a mental disorder.

multiple intelligences theory Gardner's theory of intellect, based on the view that people possess at least eight types of intelligence.

mutation a change in a section of DNA.

myelin sheath a fatty sheath that forms around certain axons in the body and increases the speed and efficiency of information transmission.

myelination the formation of myelin (a fatty sheath) around the axons of neurons that speeds and increases information-processing abilities.

naïve psychology a commonsense level of understanding of other people and oneself.

narratives story-like structured descriptions of past events.

nativism the theory that infants have substantial innate knowledge of evolutionarily important domains.

naturalistic observation examination of ongoing behaviour in an environment not controlled by the researcher.

nature our biological endowment; the genes we receive from our parents.

neglected (peer status) children or adolescents who are infrequently mentioned as either liked or disliked; they simply are not noticed much by peers.

neural tube a groove formed in the top layer of differentiated cells in the embryo that eventually becomes the brain and spinal cord.

neurogenesis the proliferation of neurons through cell division.

neurons cells that are specialized for sending and receiving messages between the brain and all parts of the body, as well as within the brain itself.

neurotransmitters chemicals involved in communication among brain cells.

newborn screening tests used to screen newborn infants for a range of genetic and non-genetic disorders.

nonbinary individuals who do not identify exclusively as one gender; also referred to as *genderqueer*.

non-REM sleep a quiet or deep sleep state characterized by the absence of motor activity or eye movements and more regular, slow brain waves, breathing, and heart rate.

normal distribution pattern of data in which scores fall symmetrically around a mean value, with most scores falling close to the mean and fewer and fewer scores farther from it.

numerical equality the realization that all sets of *N* objects have something in common.

numerical magnitude representations mental models of the sizes of numbers, ordered along a less-to-more dimension.

nurture the environments, both physical and social, that influence our development.

object permanence the knowledge that objects continue to exist even when they are out of view.

object segregation the identification of separate objects in a visual array.

object substitution a form of pretense in which an object is used as something other than itself, for example, using a broom to represent a horse.

observational learning learning through watching other people and the consequences others experience as a result of their actions.

occipital lobe major area of the cortex that is primarily involved in processing visual information.

opportunity structure the economic and social resources offered by the macrosystem in the bioecological model, and people's understanding of those resources.

oppositional defiant disorder (ODD) a disorder characterized by age-inappropriate and persistent displays of angry, defiant, and irritable behaviours.

optical expansion a depth cue in which an object occludes increasingly more of the background, indicating that the object is approaching.

oral stage the first stage in Freud's theory, occurring in the first year, in which the primary source of satisfaction and pleasure is oral activity.

organizing influences potential result of certain sex-linked hormones affecting brain differentiation and organization during prenatal development or at puberty.

overextension an overly broad interpretation of the meaning of a word.

overlapping waves theory an information-processing approach that emphasizes the variability of children's thinking.

overregularization speech errors in which children treat irregular forms of words as if they were regular.

parental-investment theory a theory that stresses the evolutionary basis of many aspects of parental behaviour that benefit their offspring.

parental sensitivity caregiving behaviour that involves the expression of warmth and contingent responsiveness to children, such as when they require assistance or are in distress.

parenting style parenting behaviours and attitudes that set the emotional climate in regard to parent–child interactions, such as parental responsiveness and demandingness.

parietal lobe major area of the cortex that is associated with spatial processing and sensory information integration.

peers people of approximately the same age and status who are unrelated to one another.

perception the process of organizing and interpreting sensory information.

perceptual categorization the grouping together of objects that have similar appearances.

perceptual constancy the perception of objects as being of constant size, shape, colour, and so on, in spite of physical differences in the retinal image of the object.

perceptual narrowing developmental changes in which experience fine-tunes the perceptual system.

permissive parenting a parenting style that is high in responsiveness but low in demandingness. Permissive parents are responsive to their children's needs and do not require their children to regulate themselves or act in appropriate or mature ways.

personal domain an area of social knowledge that pertains to actions in which individual preferences are the main consideration; there are no right or wrong choices.

personal fable a form of adolescent egocentrism that involves beliefs in the uniqueness of one's own feelings and thoughts.

phallic stage the third stage in Freud's theory, lasting from age 3 to age 6, in which sexual pleasure is focused on the genitalia.

phenotype the observable expression of the genotype, including both body characteristics and behaviour.

phenylketonuria (PKU) a disorder related to a defective recessive gene on chromosome 12 that prevents metabolism of the amino acid phenylalanine.

phonemes the smallest units of meaningful sound.

phonemic awareness ability to identify component sounds within words.

phonological recoding skills ability to translate letters into sounds and to blend sounds into words; informally called *sounding out.*

phylogenetic continuity the idea that because of our common evolutionary history, humans share many characteristics, behaviours, and developmental processes with non-human animals, especially mammals.

Piaget's theory the theory of Swiss psychologist Jean Piaget, which posits that cognitive development involves a sequence of four stages—the sensorimotor, preoperational, concrete operational, and formal operational stages—that are constructed through the processes of assimilation, accommodation, and equilibration.

placenta a support organ for the fetus; it keeps the circulatory systems of the fetus and mother separate, but a semipermeable membrane permits the exchange of some materials between them (oxygen and nutrients from mother to fetus, and carbon dioxide and waste products from fetus to mother).

plasticity the capacity of the brain to be affected by experience.

play voluntary activities, particularly those of children, with no specific motivation beyond their inherent enjoyment.

polygenic inheritance inheritance pattern in which traits are governed by more than one gene.

polyvictimization the co-occurrence of multiple forms of maltreatment.

popular (peer status) children or adolescents who are viewed positively (liked) by many peers and are viewed negatively (disliked) by few peers.

positive reinforcement a reward that reliably follows a behaviour and increases the likelihood that the behaviour will be repeated.

positive youth development an approach to youth intervention that focuses on developing and nurturing strengths and assets rather than on correcting weaknesses and deficits.

pragmatic cues aspects of the social context used for word learning.

pragmatics knowledge about how language is used.

preferential-looking technique a method for studying visual attention in infants that involves showing infants two images simultaneously to see if the infants prefer one over the other (indexed by longer looking).

premature any child born at 37 weeks after conception or earlier (as opposed to the normal term of 38 weeks).

prenatal testing genetic testing used to assess the fetus's risk for genetic disorders.

preoperational stage the period (2 to 7 years) within Piaget's theory in which children become able to represent their experiences in language, mental imagery, and symbolic thought.

pre-reaching movements clumsy swiping movements by young infants toward objects they see.

pretend play make-believe activities in which children create new symbolic relations, acting as if they were in a situation different from their actual one.

primary mental abilities seven abilities proposed by Thurstone as crucial to intelligence.

primary prevention a program targeting all individuals in a particular setting (e.g., a school) in order to prevent the occurrence of a problematic behaviour or condition.

private speech the second phase of Vygotsky's internalization-of-thought process, in which children develop self-regulation and problem-solving abilities by telling themselves aloud what to do, much as their parents did in the first stage.

proactive aggression unemotional aggression aimed at fulfilling a need or desire.

problem solving the process of attaining a goal by using a strategy to overcome an obstacle.

prosocial behaviour voluntary behaviour intended to benefit another, such as helping, sharing with, and comforting others.

prosody the characteristic rhythm and intonational patterns with which a language is spoken.

puberty developmental period marked by the ability to reproduce and other dramatic bodily changes.

punishment a negative stimulus that follows a behaviour to reduce the likelihood that the behaviour will occur again.

questionnaire a method that allows researchers to gather information from a large number of participants simultaneously by presenting them a uniform set of printed questions.

random assignment a procedure in which each participant has an equal chance of being assigned to each group within an experiment.

rapid eye movement (REM) sleep an active sleep state characterized by quick, jerky eye movements under closed lids and associated with dreaming in adults.

rational learning the ability to use prior experiences to predict what will occur in the future.

reactive aggression emotionally driven, antagonistic aggression sparked by one's perception that other people's motives are hostile.

recessive allele the allele that is not expressed if a dominant allele is present.

reciprocal determinism child–environment influences operate in both directions; children are both affected by and influence aspects of their environment.

reflexes fixed patterns of action that occur in response to particular stimulation.

regulator genes genes that control the activity of other genes.

rehearsal the process of repeating information multiple times to aid memory of it.

rejected (peer status) children or adolescents who are liked by few peers and disliked by many peers.

relational aggression a kind of aggression that involves excluding others from the social group and attempting to do harm to other people's relationships; it includes spreading rumors about peers, withholding friendship to inflict harm, and ignoring peers when angry or frustrated or trying to get one's own way.

reliability the degree to which independent measurements of a given behaviour are consistent.

role taking being aware of the perspective of another person.

rumination the act of focusing on one's own negative emotions and negative self-appraisals and on their causes and consequences, without engaging in efforts to improve one's situation.

scale error the attempt by a young child to perform an action on a miniature object that is impossible due to the large discrepancy in the relative sizes of the child and the object.

scientific method an approach to testing beliefs that involves choosing a question, formulating a hypothesis, testing the hypothesis, and drawing a conclusion.

script typical sequence of actions used to organize and interpret repeated events, such as eating at restaurants, going to doctors' appointments, and writing reports.

secondary prevention a program designed to help individuals at risk for developing a problem or condition, with the goal of preventing the problem or condition.

secular trends marked changes in physical development that have occurred over generations.

secure attachment a pattern of attachment in which infants or young children have a positive and trusting relationship with their attachment figure. In the Strange Situation, a securely attached infant may be upset when the caregiver leaves but may be happy to see the caregiver return, recovering quickly from any distress. When children are securely attached, they can use caregivers as a secure base for exploration.

secure base refers to the idea that the presence of a trusted caregiver provides an infant or toddler with a sense of security that makes it possible for the child to explore the environment.

selective attention the process of intentionally focusing on the information that is most relevant to the current goal.

self-comforting behaviours repetitive actions that regulate arousal by providing a mildly positive physical sensation.

self-concept a conceptual system made up of one's thoughts and attitudes about oneself.

self-conscious emotions emotions such as guilt, shame, embarrassment, and pride that relate to our sense of self and our consciousness of others' reactions to us.

self-discipline ability to inhibit actions, follow rules, and avoid impulsive reactions.

self-distraction looking away from an upsetting stimulus in order to regulate one's level of arousal.

self-esteem an individual's overall subjective evaluation of his or her worth and the feelings he or she has about that evaluation.

self-locomotion the ability to move oneself around in the environment.

self-socialization active process during development whereby children's cognitions lead them to perceive the world and to act in accord with their expectations and beliefs, through their activity preferences, friendship choices, and so on.

sensation the processing of basic information from the external world via receptors in the sense organs (eyes, ears, skin, etc.) and brain.

sensitive period the period of time during which a developing organism is most sensitive to the effects of external factors.

sensorimotor stage the period (birth to 2 years) within Piaget's theory in which intelligence is expressed through sensory and motor abilities.

separation anxiety feelings of distress that children, especially infants and toddlers, experience when they are separated, or expect to be separated, from individuals to whom they are emotionally attached.

service learning a strategy for promoting positive youth development that integrates school-based instruction with community involvement in order to promote civic responsibility and enhance learning.

sex distinction between genetic females (XX) and genetic males (XY) as well as other genetic sex compositions (e.g., XO, XXY, XYY).

sex chromosomes the chromosomes (X and Y) that determine an individual's designated sex at birth.

sexual identity one's sense of oneself as a sexual being.

sexual-minority youth young people who experience same-sex attractions.

sexual orientation a person's preference in regard to males or females as objects of erotic feelings.

simple view of reading perspective that comprehension depends solely on decoding skill and comprehension of oral language.

situation model cognitive processes used to represent a situation or sequence of events.

small for gestational age babies who weigh substantially less than is normal for whatever their gestational age.

smooth pursuit eye movements visual behaviour in which the viewer's gaze shifts at the same rate and angle as a moving object.

social comparison the process of comparing aspects of one's own psychological, behavioural, or physical functioning to that of others in order to evaluate oneself.

social competence the ability to achieve personal goals in social interactions while simultaneously maintaining positive relationships with others.

social referencing the use of a parent's or another adult's facial expression or vocal cues to decide how to deal with novel, ambiguous, or possibly threatening situations.

social scaffolding a process in which more competent people provide a temporary framework that supports children's thinking at a higher level than children could manage on their own.

social smiles smiles that are directed at people; they first emerge around the third month of life.

socialization the process through which children acquire the values, standards, skills, knowledge, and behaviours that are regarded as appropriate for their present and future roles in their particular culture.

societal domain an area of social knowledge that encompasses concepts regarding the rules and conventions through which societies maintain order.

sociocultural context the physical, social, cultural, economic, and historical circumstances that make up any child's environment.

sociocultural theories approaches that emphasize that other people and the surrounding culture contribute greatly to children's development.

sociodramatic play activities in which children enact miniature dramas with other children or adults, such as "mother comforting baby."

socioeconomic status (SES) a measure of social class based on income and education.

sociometric status a measurement that reflects the degree to which children are liked or disliked by their peers as a group.

spermarche onset of capacity for ejaculation.

spines formations on the dendrites of neurons that increase the dendrites' capacity to form connections with other neurons.

stage theories approaches proposing that development involves a series of large, discontinuous, age-related phases.

standard deviation (SD) measure of the variability of scores in a distribution; in a normal distribution, 68% of scores fall within 1 SD of the mean, and 95% of scores fall within 2 SDs of the mean.

state level of arousal and engagement in the environment, ranging from deep sleep to intense activity.

stepping reflex a neonatal reflex in which an infant lifts first one leg and then the other in a coordinated pattern like walking.

stereopsis the process by which the visual cortex combines the differing neural signals caused by binocular disparity, resulting in the perception of depth.

Strange Situation a procedure developed by Mary Ainsworth to assess infants' attachment to their primary caregiver.

strategy–choice process procedure for selecting among alternative ways to solve a problem.

stress a physiological reaction to some change or threat in the environment.

structured interview a research procedure in which all participants are asked to answer the same questions.

structured observation a method that involves presenting an identical situation to each participant and recording the participant's behaviour.

subordinate level the most specific level within a category hierarchy, such as "poodle" in the animal/dog/poodle example.

sudden infant death syndrome (SIDS) the sudden, unexpected death of an infant less than 1 year of age that has no identifiable cause.

superego in psychoanalytic theory, the third personality structure, consisting of internalized moral standards.

superordinate level the general level within a category hierarchy, such as "animal" in the animal/dog/poodle example.

swaddling a soothing technique, used in many cultures, that involves wrapping a baby tightly in cloths or a blanket.

symbolic representation the use of one object to stand for another.

symbols systems for representing our thoughts, feelings, and knowledge, and for communicating them to other people.

synapses microscopic junctions between the axon terminal of one neuron and the dendritic branches or cell body of another.

synaptic pruning the normal developmental process through which synapses that are rarely activated are eliminated.

synaptogenesis the process by which neurons form synapses with other neurons, resulting in trillions of connections.

syntactic bootstrapping the strategy of using grammatical structure to infer the meaning of a new word.

syntax rules specifying how words from different categories (nouns, verbs, adjectives, etc.) can be combined.

task analysis the research technique of specifying the goals, obstacles to their realization, and potential solution strategies involved in problem solving.

telegraphic speech short utterances that leave out non-essential words.

temperament individual differences in emotion, activity level, and attention that are exhibited across contexts and that are present from infancy and thus thought to be genetically based.

temporal lobe major area of the cortex that is associated with speech and language, music, and emotional information.

teratogen an external agent that can cause damage or death during prenatal development.

tertiary intervention a program designed to help individuals who already exhibit a problem or condition.

test–retest reliability the degree of similarity of a participant's performance on two or more occasions.

theory of mind an organized understanding of how mental processes such as intentions, desires, beliefs, perceptions, and emotions influence behaviour.

theory of mind module (TOMM) a hypothesized brain mechanism devoted to understanding other human beings.

theory of successful intelligence Sternberg's theory of intellect, based on the view that intelligence is the ability to achieve success in life.

third-variable problem the concept that a correlation between two variables may stem from both being influenced by some third variable.

three-stratum theory of intelligence Carroll's model that places *g* at the top of the intelligence hierarchy, eight moderately general abilities in the middle, and many specific processes at the bottom.

toxic stress the experience of overwhelming levels of stress without support from adults to help mitigate the effects of that stress.

transgender individuals who do not identify with the gender assigned at birth (which is typically based on their external genitalia).

tuition learning through direct teaching.

umbilical cord a tube containing the blood vessels connecting the fetus and placenta.

unconditioned response (UCR) a reflexive response that is elicited by the unconditioned stimulus.

unconditioned stimulus (UCS) a stimulus that evokes a reflexive response.

underextension an overly narrow interpretation of the meaning of a word.

uninvolved parenting a parenting style that is low in both demandingness and responsiveness to their children; in other words, this style describes parents who are generally disengaged.

Universal Grammar a proposed set of highly abstract structures that are common to all languages.

validity the degree to which a test measures what it is intended to measure.

variables attributes that vary across individuals and situations, such as age, sex, and popularity.

vicarious reinforcement observing someone else receive a reward or punishment.

violation-of-expectancy a procedure used to study infant cognition in which infants are shown an event that should evoke surprise or interest if it goes against something the infant knows.

visual acuity the sharpness and clarity of vision.

visually based retrieval proceeding directly from the visual form of a word to its meaning.

voice onset time (VOT) the length of time between when air passes through the lips and when the vocal cords start vibrating.

Wechsler Intelligence Scale for Children (WISC) widely used test designed to measure the intelligence of children 6 years and older.

withdrawn-rejected (peer status) rejected children who are socially withdrawn, wary, and often timid.

word segmentation discovering where words begin and end in fluent speech.

working memory memory system that involves actively attending to, maintaining, and processing information.

zygote a fertilized egg cell.

References

AAP Council on Communications and Media. (2016). Media and young minds. *Pediatrics, 138*(5), e20162591.

Abar, C. C., Jackson, K. M., & Wood, M. (2014). Reciprocal relations between perceived parental knowledge and adolescent substance use and delinquency: The moderating role of parent–teen relationship quality. *Developmental Psychology, 50,* 2176–2187. doi:10.1037/a0037463

Abbas, R., & Mesch, G. (2018). Do rich teens get richer? Facebook use and the link between offline and online social capital among Palestinian youth in Israel. *Information, Communication, & Society, 21,* 63–79. doi:10.1080/1369118X.2016.1261168

Abela, J. R., Hankin, B. L., Sheshko, D. M., Fishman, M. B., & Stolow, D. (2012). Multi-wave prospective examination of the stress-reactivity extension of response styles theory of depression in high-risk children and early adolescents. *Journal of Abnormal Child Psychology, 40,* 277–287. doi:10.1007/s10802-011-9563-x

Aboud, F. E., & Mendelson, M. J. (1996). Determinants of friendship selection and quality: Developmental perspectives. In W. M. Bukowski, A. F. Newcomb, & W. W. Hartup (Eds.), *The company they keep: Friendship in childhood and adolescence* (pp. 87–112). New York: Cambridge University Press.

Aboud, F. E., & Sankar, J. (2007). Friendship and identity in a language-integrated school. *International Journal of Behavioral Development, 31*(5), 445–453.

Abramovitch, R., Corter, C., & Lando, B. (1979). Sibling interaction in the home. *Child Development, 50,* 997–1003. doi:10.2307/1129325

Acredolo, C., & Schmid, J. (1981). The understanding of relative speeds, distances, and durations of movement. *Developmental Psychology, 17,* 490–493. doi:10.1037/0012-1649.17.4.490

Acredolo, L. P., & Goodwyn, S. W. (1990). Sign language in babies: The significance of symbolic gesturing for understanding language development. In R. Vasta (Ed.), *Annals of child development* (Vol. 7, pp. 1–42). London: Jessica Kingsley.

Adams, R. E., Santo, J. B., & Bukowski, W. M. (2011). The presence of a best friend buffers the effects of negative experiences. *Developmental Psychology, 47,* 1786–1791. doi:10.1037/a0025401

Adibpour, P., Dubois, J., & Dehaene-Lambertz, G. (2018). Right but not left hemispheric discrimination of faces in infancy. *Nature Human Behaviour, 2*(1), 67.

Adler, S. A., Haith, M. M., Arehart, D. M., & Lanthier, E. C. (2008). Infants' visual expectations and the processing of time. *Journal of Cognition and Development, 9,* 1–25.

Adolph, K. E., & Berger, S. E. (2015). Physical and motor development. In M. H. Bornstein & M. E. Lamb (Eds.), *Developmental Science: An advanced textbook* (7th ed., pp. 261–333). New York: Psychology Press/Taylor & Francis.

Adolph, K. E., & Hoch, J. E. (2019). Motor development: Embodied, embedded, enculturated, and enabling. *Annual Review of Psychology, 70,* 141–164. doi:10.1146/annurev-psych-010418-102836

Adolph, K. E., & Robinson, S. R. (2013). The road to walking: What learning to walk tells us about development. In P. D. Zelazo (Ed.), *Oxford handbook of developmental psychology: Vol. 1. Body and mind* (pp. 403–446). New York: Oxford University Press.

Adolph, K. E., & Robinson, S. R. (2015). Motor development. In R. M. Lerner (Series Eds.) & L. Liben & U. Muller (Vol. Eds.), *Handbook of child psychology and developmental science: Vol. 2: Cognitive processes* (7th ed., pp. 114–157). Hoboken, NJ: Wiley. doi:10.1002/9781118963418.childpsy204

Adolph, K. E., Cole, W. G., Komati, M., Garciaguirre, J. S., Badaly, D., Lingeman, J. M., . . . Sotsky, R. B. (2012). How do you learn to walk? Thousands of steps and dozens of falls per day. *Psychological Science, 23,* 1387–1394. doi:10.1177/0956797612446346

Adolph, K. E., Karasik, L. B., & Tamis-LeMonda, C. S. (2010). Motor skills. In M. H. Bornstein (Ed.), *Handbook of Cultural Developmental Science* (pp. 61–88). New York: Taylor & Francis.

Adolph, K. E., Vereijken, B., & Denny, M. A. (1998). Learning to crawl. *Child Development, 69,* 1299–1312.

Afifi, T. D., Afifi, W. A., & Coho, A. (2009). Adolescents' physiological reactions to their parents' negative disclosures about the other parent in divorced and nondivorced families. *Journal of Divorce and Remarriage, 50,* 517–540. doi:10.1080/10502550902970496

Afifi, T. D., & McManus, T. (2010). Divorce disclosures and adolescents' physical and mental health and parental relationship quality. *Journal of Divorce and Remarriage, 51,* 83–107. doi:10.1080/10502550903455141

Agrillo, C., Piffer, L., & Bisazza, A. (2011). Number versus continuous quantity in numerosity judgments by fish. *Cognition, 119*(2), 281–287. doi:10.1016/j.cognition.2010.10.022

Aguilar, B., Sroufe, L. A., Egeland, B., & Carlson, E. (2000). Distinguishing the early-onset/persistent and adolescence-onset antisocial behavior types: From birth to 16 years. *Development and Psychopathology, 12,* 109–132.

Agyei, S. B., van der Weel, F. R., & van der Meer, A. L. (2016). Development of visual motion perception for prospective control: Brain and behavioral studies in infants. *Frontiers in Psychology, 7*(100). doi:10.3389/fpsyg.2016.00100

Ainsworth, M. D. (1967). *Infancy in Uganda: Infant care and the growth of love.* Baltimore, MD: Johns Hopkins Press.

Ainsworth, M. D. S. (1973). The development of infant-mother attachment. In B. M. Caldwell & H. N. Ricciuti (Eds.), *Review of child development research* (Vol. 3, pp. 1–94). Chicago: University of Chicago Press.

Ainsworth, M. D. S., Blehar, M. C., Waters, E., & Wall, S. (1978). *Patterns of attachment: A psychological study of the strange situation.* Hillsdale, NJ: Erlbaum.

Akbari, E., & McCuaig, K. (2017). *Early Childhood Education Report 2017.* University of Toronto Ontario Institute for Studies in Education. Retrieved from http://ecereport.ca/media/uploads/2017-report-pdfs/ece-report2017-en-feb6.pdf

Akhtar, N., & Gernsbacher, M. A. (2008). On privileging the role of gaze in infant social cognition. *Child Development Perspectives, 2,* 59–65. doi:10.1111/j.1750-8606.2008.00044.x

Aknin, L. B., Broesch, T., Hamlin, J. K., & Van de Vondervoort, J. W. (2015). Prosocial behavior leads to happiness in a small-scale rural society. *Journal of Experimental Psychology: General, 144*(4), 788–795. http://dx.doi.org/10.1037/xge0000082

Aknin, L. B., Hamlin, J. K., & Dunn, E. W. (2012). Giving leads to happiness in young children. *PLoS ONE, 7,* e39211. doi:10.1371/journal.pone.0039211

Aksan, N., & Kochanska, G. (2005). Conscience in childhood: Old questions, new answers. *Developmental Psychology, 41,* 506–516. doi:10.1037/0012-1649.41.3.506

Aksan, N., Kochanska, G., & Ortmann, M. R. (2006). Mutually responsive orientation between parents and their young children: Toward methodological advances in the science of relationships. *Developmental Psychology, 42,* 833–848. doi:10.1037/0012-1649.42.5.833

Albareda-Castellot, B., Pons, F., & Sebastián-Gallés, N. (2011). The acquisition of phonetic categories in bilingual infants: New data from an anticipatory eye movement paradigm. *Developmental Science, 14,* 395–401.

Albert, R. R., Schwade, J. A., & Goldstein, M. H. (2018). The social functions of babbling: Acoustic and contextual characteristics that facilitate maternal responsiveness. *Developmental Science, 21*(5), e12641.

Alberts, A., Elkind, D., & Ginsberg, S. (2007). The personal fable and risk-taking in early adolescence. *Journal of Youth and Adolescence, 36,* 71–76. doi:10.1007/s10964-006-9144-4

Alexander, G. M. (2003). An evolutionary perspective of sex-typed toy preferences: Pink, blue, and the brain. *Archives of Sexual Behavior, 32,* 7–14. doi:10.1023/A:1021833110722

Alexander, K. L., Entwisle, D. R., & Olson, L. S. (2007). Lasting consequences of the summer learning gap. *American Sociological Review, 72,* 167–180.

Ali, J. B., Spence, C., & Bremner, A. J. (2015). Human infants' ability to perceive touch in external space develops postnatally. *Current Biology, 25*(20), R978–R979.

Alibali, M. W., Spencer, R. C., Knox, L., & Kita, S. (2011). Spontaneous gestures influence strategy choices in problem solving. *Psychological Science, 22,* 1138–1144. doi:10.1177/0956797611417722

Alink, L. R. A., Cicchetti, D., Kim, J., & Rogosch, F. A. (2012). Longitudinal associations among child maltreatment, social functioning, and cortisol regulation. *Developmental Psychology, 48,* 224–236. doi:10.1037/a0024892

Alink, L. R. A., Mesman, J., Van Zeijl, J., Stolk, M. N., Juffer, F., Koot, H. M., . . . van IJzendoorn, M. H. (2006). The early childhood aggression curve: Development of physical aggression in 10- to 50-month-old children. *Child Development, 77,* 954–966. doi:10.1111/j.1467-8624.2006.00912.x

Allen, J. P., Chango, J., Szwedo, D., Schad, M., & Marston, E. (2012). Predictors of susceptibility to peer influence regarding substance use in adolescence. *Child Development, 83,* 337–350. doi:10.1111/j.1467-8624.2011.01682.x

Allen, J. P., Porter, M. R., & McFarland, F. C. (2006). Leaders and followers in adolescent close friendships: Susceptibility to peer influence as a predictor of risky behavior, friendship instability, and depression. *Development and Psychopathology, 18,* 155–172. doi:10.1017/S0954579406060093

Allen, J. P., Porter, M. R., McFarland, F. C., Marsh, P., & McElhaney, K. B. (2005). The two faces of adolescents' success with peers: Adolescent popularity, social adaptation, and deviant behavior. *Child Development, 76,* 747–760. doi:10.1111/j.1467-8624.2005.00875.x

Allen, M. K., & Superle, T. (2016). Youth crime in Canada, 2014. Statistics Canada Catalogue no. 85-002-X ISSN 1209-6393.

Altenhofen, S., Sutherland, K., & Biringen, Z. (2010). Families experiencing divorce: Age at onset of overnight stays, conflict, and emotional availability as predictors of child attachment. *Journal of Divorce & Remarriage, 51*(3), 141–156. doi:10.1080/10502551003597782

Altermatt, E. R., & Pomerantz, E. M. (2003). The development of competence-related and motivational beliefs: An investigation of similarity and influence among friends. *Journal of Educational Psychology, 95,* 111–123. doi:10.1037/0022-0663.95.1.111

Altschul, I., Lee, S. J., & Gershoff, E. T. (2016). Hugs, not hits: Maternal warmth, not spanking, predicts positive child behaviors in the first five years of life. *Journal of Marriage and Family, 78,* 695–714. doi:10.1111/jomf.12306

Amano, S., Shrestha, B. P., Chaube, S. S., Higuchi, M., Manandhar, D. S., Osrin, D., . . . Saville, N. (2014). Effectiveness of female community health volunteers in the detection and management of low-birth-weight in Nepal. *Rural and Remote Health, 14*(1), 2508.

Amaral, D. G., Schumann, C. M., & Nordahl, C. W. (2008). Neuroanatomy of autism. *Trends in Neurosciences, 31,* 137–145. doi:10.1016/j.tins.2007.12.005

Amato, P. R. (2010). Research on divorce: Continuing trends and new developments. *Journal of Marriage and Family, 72,* 650–666. doi:10.1111/j.1741-3737.2010.00723.x

Amato, P. R., Loomis, L. S., & Booth, A. (1995). Parental divorce, marital conflict, and offspring well-being during early adulthood. *Social Forces, 73,* 895–915. doi:10.1093/sf/73.3.895

American Academy of Pediatrics. (2016). *Early brain and child development: Building brains, forging futures.* Retrieved from https://www.aap.org/en-us/advocacy-and-policy/aap-health-initiatives/EBCD/Pages/default.aspx

American Association of University Women (AAUW). (2011). *Crossing the line: Sexual harassment at school.* Washington, DC: Author.

American Psychiatric Association. (2013). *Diagnostic and statistical manual of mental disorders* (5th ed.). Arlington, VA: American Psychiatric Publishing.

Anda, R. F., Felitti, V. J., Walker, J., Whitfield, C. L., Bremner, J. D., Perry, B. D., . . . Giles, W. H. (2006). The enduring effects of abuse and related adverse experiences in childhood: A convergence of evidence from neurobiology and epidemiology. *European Archives of Psychiatry and Clinical Neurosciences, 56,* 174–186. doi:10.1007/s00406-005-0624-4

Anderson, C. A., & Bushman, B. J. (2001). Effects of violent video games on aggressive behavior, aggressive cognition, aggressive affect, physiological arousal, and prosocial behavior: A meta-analytic review of the scientific literature. *Psychological Science, 12,* 353–359. doi:10.1111/1467-9280.00366

Anderson, E. (1999). *Code of the street: Decency, violence, and the moral life of the inner city.* New York: W. W. Norton.

Anderson, M., & Jiang, J. (2018). Teens' social media habits and experiences. *Pew Research Center: Internet & Technology,* November 28, 2018.

Anderson, M., & Silver, L. (2019). 7 key findings about mobile phone and social media use in emerging economies. *Pew Research Center,* March 7, 2019.

Anderson, R. C., Wilson, P. T., & Fielding, L. G. (1988). Growth in reading and how children spend their time outside of school. *Reading Research Quarterly, 23,* 285–303.

Anderson, S. F., Salk, R. H., & Hyde, J. S. (2015). Stress in romantic relationships and adolescent depressive symptoms: Influence of parental support. *Journal of Family Psychology, 29,* 339–348. doi:10.1037/fam0000089

Angeleri, R., & Airenti, G. (2014). The development of joke and irony understanding: A study with 3- to 6-year-old children. *Canadian Journal of Experimental Psychology, 68,* 133–146. https://doi.org/10.1037/cep0000011.supp

Anglin, J. M. (1993). Vocabulary development: A morphological analysis. *Monographs of the Society for Research in Child Development, 58*(10, Serial No. 238).

Angulo-Barroso, R. M., Peciña, S., Lin, X., Li, M., Sturza, J., Shao, J., & Lozoff, B. (2017). Implicit learning and emotional responses in nine-month-old infants. *Cognition and Emotion, 31,* 1031–1040.

Angus Reid Institute. (2016). Extra-terrestrials and other strange things: Four-in-five Canadians believe. Retrieved from http://angusreid.org/extra-terrestrials-stranger-things/

Ansari, D. (2008). Effects of development and enculturation on number representation in the brain. *Nature Reviews Neuroscience, 9,* 278–291. doi:10.1038/nrn2334

Antovich, D. M., & Graf Estes, K. (2018). Learning across languages: Bilingual experience supports dual language statistical word segmentation. *Developmental Science, 21*(2), e12548.

Anzman-Frasca, S., Ventura, A. K., Ehrenberg, S., & Myers, K. P. (2018). Promoting healthy food preferences from the start: A narrative review of food preference learning from the prenatal period through early childhood. *Obesity Reviews, 19*(4), 576–604.

Anzures, G., Wheeler, A., Quinn, P. C., Pascalis, O., Slater, A. M., Heron-Delaney, M., . . . Lee, K. (2012). Brief daily exposures to Asian females reverses perceptual narrowing for Asian faces in Caucasian infants. *Journal of Experimental Child Psychology, 112*(4), 484–495.

Appelhans, B. M., Fitzpatrick, S. L., Li, H., Cail, V., Waring, M. E., Schneider, K. L., . . . Pagoto, S. L. (2014). The home environment and childhood obesity in low-income households: Indirect effects via sleep duration and screen time. *BMC Public Health, 14*(1160). doi:10.1186/1471-2458-14-1160

Aptekar, L., & Ciano-Federoff, L. M. (1999). Street children in Nairobi: Gender differences in mental health. In M. Raffaelli & R. W. Larson (Eds.), *New Directions for Child and Adolescent Development: No. 85. Homeless and working youth around the world: Exploring developmental issues* (Vol. 1999, pp. 35–46). San Francisco: Jossey-Bass.

Aptekar, L., & Stoecklin, D. (2014) *Street children and homeless youth: A cross-cultural perspective.* doi:10.1007/978-94-007-7356-1_2

Apthorp, H., Randel, B., Cherasaro, T., Clark, T., McKeown, M., & Beck, I. (2012). Effects of a supplemental vocabulary program on word knowledge and passage comprehension. *Journal of Research on Educational Effectiveness, 5*(2), 160–188. doi:10.1080/19345747.2012.660240

Archer, J. (2004). Sex differences in aggression in real-world settings: A meta-analytic review. *Review of General Psychology, 8,* 291–322. doi:10.1037/1089-2680.8.4.291

Archer, J. (2006). Testosterone and human aggression: An evaluation of the challenge hypothesis. *Neuroscience and Biobehavioral Reviews, 30,* 319–345. doi:10.1016/j.neubiorev.2004.12.007

Archer, J. (2013). Can evolutionary principles explain patterns of family violence? *Psychological Bulletin, 139*(2), 403–440.

Archer, J., & Coyne, S. M. (2005). An integrated review of indirect, relational, and social aggression. *Personality and Social Psychology Review, 9,* 212–230. doi:10.1207/s15327957pspr0903_2

Archer, J., Graham-Kevan, N., & Davies, M. (2005). Testosterone and aggression: A reanalysis of Book, Starzyk, and Quinsey's (2001) study. *Aggression and Violent Behavior, 10,* 241–261. doi:10.1016/j.avb.2004.01.001

Arck, P. C., Rücke, M., Rose, M., Szekeres-Bartho, J., Douglas, A. J., Pritsch, M., . . . Nakamura, K. (2008). Early risk factors for miscarriage: A prospective cohort study in pregnant women. *Reproductive Biomedicine Online, 17*(1), 101–113.

Ardizzi, M., Martini, F., Umiltà, M. A., Evangelista, V., Ravera, R., & Gallese, V. (2015). Impact of childhood maltreatment on the recognition of facial expressions of emotions. *PloS ONE, 10*(10), e0141732. doi:10.1371/journal.pone.0141732

Arim, R. G., Dahinten, V. S., Marshall, S. K., & Shapka, J. D. (2011). An examination of the reciprocal relationships between adolescents' aggressive behaviors and their perceptions of parental nurturance. *Journal of Youth and Adolescence, 40,* 207–220. doi:10.1007/s10964-009-9493-x

Aristotle. (1954). *The Nicomachean ethics* (D. Ross, Trans.). London: Oxford University Press.

Armenta, B. E., Knight, G. P., Carlo, G., & Jacobson, R. P. (2011). The relation between ethnic group attachment and prosocial tendencies: The mediating role of cultural values. *European Journal of Social Psychology, 41,* 107–115.

Arndorfer, C., & Stormshak, E. (2008). Same-sex versus other-sex best friendship in early adolescence: Longitudinal predictors of antisocial behavior throughout adolescence. *Journal of Youth and Adolescence, 37,* 1059–1070. doi:10.1007/s10964-008-9311-x

Arsenio, W. F., Adams, E., & Gold, J. (2009). Social information processing, moral reasoning, and emotion attributions: Relations with adolescents' reactive and proactive aggression. *Child Development, 80,* 1739–1755. doi:10.1111/j.1467-8624.2009.01365.x

Arterberry, M. E., & Kellman, P. J. (2016). *Development of perception in infancy: The cradle of knowledge revisited.* Oxford: Oxford University Press.

Asendorpf, J. B. (1990). Development of inhibition during childhood: Evidence for situational specificity and a two-factor model. *Developmental Psychology, 26,* 721–730. doi:10.1037/0012-1649.26.5.721

Ashcraft, M. H., & Ridley, K. S. (2005). Math anxiety and its cognitive consequences. In J. I. D. Campbell (Ed.), *Handbook of mathematical cognition* (pp. 315–327). New York: Psychology Press.

Asher, S. R., & Dodge, K. A. (1986). Identifying children who are rejected by their peers. *Developmental Psychology, 22,* 444–449. doi:10.1037/0012-1649.22.4.444

Assini-Meytin, L. C., & Green, K. M. (2015). Long-term consequences of adolescent parenthood among African American urban youth: A propensity matching approach. *Journal of Adolescent Health, 56,* 529–535. doi:10.1016/j.jadohealth.2015.01.005

Association for the Accreditation of Early Learning and Care Services, Alberta Human Services (2013). Alberta Child Care Accreditation Standards. Alberta Government. Retrieved from http://www.humanservices.alberta.ca/documents/accreditation-standards.pdf

Atran, S. (1990). *Cognitive foundations of natural history: Towards an anthropology of science.* Cambridge: Cambridge University Press.

Atran, S. (2002). Modular and cultural factors in biological understanding: An experimental approach to the cognitive basis of science. In P. Carruthers, S. P. Stich, & M. Siegal (Eds.), *The cognitive basis of science* (pp. 41–72). New York: Cambridge University Press.

Attili, G., Vermigli, P., & Schneider, B. H. (1997). Peer acceptance and friendship patterns among Italian schoolchildren within a cross-cultural perspective. *International Journal of Behavioral Development, 21,* 277–288. doi:10.1080/016502597384866

Auerbach, R. P., Bigda-Peyton, J. S., Eberhart, N. K., Webb, C. A., & Ho, M.-H. R. (2011). Conceptualizing the prospective relationship between social support, stress, and depressive symptoms among adolescents. *Journal of Abnormal Child Psychology, 39,* 475–487.

Austad, S. N. (2015). The human prenatal sex ratio: A major surprise. *Proceedings of the National Academy of Sciences, 112*(16), 4839–4840.

Austin, G., Groppe, K., & Elsner, B. (2014). The reciprocal relationship between executive function and theory of mind in middle childhood: A 1-year longitudinal perspective. *Frontiers in Psychology, 5,* 655. doi:10.3389/fpsyg.2014.00655

Avenevoli, S., Swendsen, J., He, J., Burstein, M., & Merikangas, K. R. (2015). Major depression in the National Comorbidity Survey—Adolescent Supplement: Prevalence, correlates, and treatment. *Journal of the American Academy of Child and Adolescent Psychiatry, 54,* 37–44.e2.

Ayduk, O., Mendoza-Denton, R., Mischel, W., Downey, G., Peake, P. K., & Rodriguez, M. (2000). Regulating the interpersonal self: Strategic self-regulation for coping with rejection sensitivity. *Journal of Personality and Social Psychology, 79,* 776–792.

Azmitia, M., & Montgomery, R. (1993). Friendship, transactive dialogues, and the development of scientific reasoning. *Social Development, 2,* 202–221. doi:10.1111/j.1467-9507.1993.tb00014.x

Backscheider, A. G., Shatz, M., & Gelman, S. A. (1993). Preschoolers' ability to distinguish living kinds as a function of regrowth. *Child Development, 64,* 1242–1257. doi:10.1111/j.1467-8624.1993.tb04198.x

Badr, L. K., Abdallah, B., & Kahale, L. (2015). A meta-analysis of preterm infant massage: An ancient practice with contemporary applications. *MCN: The American Journal of Maternal/Child Nursing, 40*(6), 344–358.

Bagwell, C. L., & Bukowski, W. M. (2018). Friendship in childhood and adolescence: Features, effects, and processes. In W. M. Bukowski, B. Laursen, & K. H. Rubin (Eds.), *Handbook of peer interactions, relationships, and groups* (2nd ed., pp. 371–390). New York: Guilford.

Bagwell, C. L., Newcomb, A. F., & Bukowski, W. M. (1998). Preadolescent friendship and peer rejection as predictors of adult adjustment. *Child Development, 69,* 140–153. doi:10.1111/j.1467-8624.1998.tb06139.x

Baham, M. E., Weimer, A. A., Braver, S. L., & Fabricius, W. V. (2008). Sibling relationships in blended families. In J. Pryor (Ed.), *The international handbook of stepfamilies: Policy and practice in legal, research, and clinical environments* (pp. 175–207). Hoboken, NJ: Wiley.

Bahrick, H. P., & Phelps, E. (1987). Retention of Spanish vocabulary over 8 years. *Journal of Experimental Psychology: Learning, Memory, and Cognition, 13*(2), 344. doi:10.1037/0278-7393.13.2.344

Bail, A., Morini, G., & Newman, R. S. (2015). Look at the gato! Code-switching in speech to toddlers. *Journal of Child Language, 42*(05), 1073–1101.

Bailey, D. H., Nguyen, T. Jenkins, J. M., Domina, T., Clements, D. H., & Sarama, J. S. (2016). Fadeout in an early mathematics intervention: Constraining content of preexisting differences? *Developmental Psychology, 52*(9), 1457–1469. doi:10.1037/dev0000188

Bailey, D. H., Zhou, X., Zhang, Y., Cui, J., Fuchs, L. S., Jordan, N. C., . . . Siegler, R. S. (2015). Development of fraction concepts and procedures in U.S. and Chinese children. *Journal of Experimental Child Psychology, 129,* 68–83. doi:10.1016/j.jecp.2014.08.006

Bailey, Z. D., Krieger, N., Agénor, M., Graves, J., Linos, N., & Bassett, M. T. (2017). Structural racism and health inequities in the USA: Evidence and interventions. *Lancet, 389*(10077), 1453–1463.

Baillargeon, R. (1987a). Object permanence in 3½- and 4½-month-old infants. *Developmental Psychology, 23,* 655–664.

Baillargeon, R. (1987b). Young infants' reasoning about the physical and spatial properties of a hidden object. *Cognitive Development, 2,* 179–200. doi:10.1016/S0885-2014(87)90043-8

Baillargeon, R. (1993). The object concept revisited: New directions in the investigation of infants' physical knowledge. In C. E. Granrud (Ed.), *Visual perception and cognition in infancy* (Vol. 23, pp. 265–315). Hillsdale, NJ: Erlbaum.

Baillargeon, R. (1998). Infants' understanding of the physical world. In M. Sabourin, F. Craik, & M. Robert (Eds.), *Advances in psychological science: Vol. 2. Biological and cognitive aspects* (pp. 503–529). Hove, England: Psychology Press.

Baillargeon, R. (2004). Infants' physical world. *Current Directions in Psychological Science, 13*(3), 89–94. doi:10.1111/j.0963-7214.2004.00281.x

Baillargeon, R., Needham, A., & DeVos, J. (1992). The development of young infants' intuitions about support. *Early Development and Parenting, 1,* 69–78. doi:10.1002/edp.2430010203

Baillargeon, R., Spelke, E. S., & Wasserman, S. (1985). Object permanence in five-month-old infants. *Cognition, 20,* 191–208. doi:10.1016/0010-0277(85)90008-3

Baines, E., & Blatchford, P. (2011). Children's games and playground activities in school and their role in development. In A. D. Pellegrini (Ed.) & P. E. Nathan (Series Ed.), *The Oxford Handbook of the Development of Play* (1st ed., pp. 260–283). New York: Oxford University Press.

Baio, J., Wiggins, L., Christensen, D. L., Maenner, M. J., Daniels, J., Warren, Z., . . . Dowling, N. F. (2018). Prevalence of autism spectrum disorder among children aged 8 years—Autism and Developmental Disabilities Monitoring Network, 11 sites, United States, 2014. *MMWR Surveillance Summary, 67*(No. SS-6), 1–23. http://dx.doi.org/10.15585/mmwr.ss6706a1

Baker, J. K., Fenning, R. M., & Crnic, K. A. (2011). Emotion socialization by mothers and fathers: Coherence among behaviors and associations with parent attitudes and children's social competence. *Social Development, 20,* 412–430. doi:10.1111/j.1467-9507.2010.00585.x

Baker, S. T., Friedman, O., & Leslie, A. M. (2010). The opposites task: Using general rules to test cognitive flexibility in preschoolers. *Journal of Cognition and Development, 11,* 240–254. doi:10.1080/15248371003699944

Bakermans-Kranenburg, M. J., Dobrova-Krol, N., & van IJzendoorn, M. (2012). Impact of institutional care on attachment disorganization and insecurity of Ukrainian preschoolers: Protective effect of the long variant of the serotonin transporter gene (5HTT). *International Journal of Behavioral Development, 36,* 11–18. doi:10.1177/0165025411406858

Bakermans-Kranenburg, M. J., & van IJzendoorn, M. H. (2016). Attachment, parenting, & genetics. In J. Cassidy & P. R. Shaver (Eds.), *Handbook of attachment: Theory, research, and clinical applications,* 3rd ed. (pp. 155–179). New York: Guilford.

Bakermans-Kranenburg, M. J., & van IJzendoorn, M. H. (2007). Research review: Genetic vulnerability or differential susceptibility in child development: The case of attachment. *Journal of Child Psychology and Psychiatry, 48,* 1160–1173. doi:10.1111/j.1469-7610.2007.01801.x

Bakermans-Kranenburg, M. J., & van IJzendoorn, M. H. (2011). Differential susceptibility to rearing environment depending on dopamine-related genes: New evidence and a meta-analysis. *Development and Psychopathology, 23,* 39–52. doi:10.1017/S0954579410000635

Bakermans-Kranenburg, M. J., van IJzendoorn, M. H., & Juffer, F. (2003). Less is more: Meta-analyses of sensitivity and attachment interventions in early childhood. *Psychological Bulletin, 129,* 195–215. doi:10.1037/0033-2909.129.2.195

Baldwin, D. A. (1991). Infants' contribution to the achievement of joint reference. *Child Development, 62,* 874–890. doi:10.1111/j.1467-8624.1991.tb01577.x

Baldwin, D. A. (1993). Early referential understanding: Infants' ability to recognize referential acts for what they are. *Developmental Psychology, 29,* 832–843. doi:10.1037/0012-1649.29.5.832

Balsam, K. E., Molina, Y., Blayney, J. A., Dillworth, T., Zimmerman, L., & Kaysen, D. (2015). Racial /ethnic differences in identity and mental health outcomes among young sexual minority women. *Cultural Diversity and Ethnic Minority Psychology, 21,* 380–390. doi:10.1037/a0038680

Bámaca, M. Y., Umaña-Taylor, A. J., Shin, N., & Alfaro, E. C. (2005). Latino adolescents' perception of parenting behaviors and self-esteem: Examining the role of neighborhood risk. *Family Relations, 54,* 621–632. doi:10.1111/j.1741-3729.2005.00346.x

Bandura, A. (1965). Influence of models' reinforcement contingencies on the acquisition of imitative responses. *Journal of Personality and Social Psychology, 1,* 589–595. doi:10.1037/h0022070

Bandura, A. (1977). *Social learning theory.* Englewood Cliffs, NJ: Prentice Hall.

Bandura, A. (1986). *Social foundations of thought and action: A social cognitive theory.* Englewood Cliffs, NJ: Prentice Hall.

Bandura, A. (1997). *Self-efficacy: The exercise of control.* New York: W. H. Freeman/Times Books/Henry Holt & Co.

Bandura, A., Ross, D., & Ross, S. A. (1963). Imitation of film-mediated aggressive models. *Journal of Abnormal and Social Psychology, 66,* 3–11. doi:10.1037/h0048687

Banerjee, M. (1997). Hidden emotions: Preschoolers' knowledge of appearance-reality and emotion display rules. *Social Cognition, 15,* 107–132. doi:10.1521 /soco.1997.15.2.107

Banerjee, R., & Lintern, V. (2000). Boys will be boys: The effect of social evaluation concerns on gender-typing. *Social Development, 9,* 397–408.

Banks, M. S., Aslin, R. N., & Letson, R. D. (1975). Sensitive period for the development of human binocular vision. *Science, 190*(4215), 675–677.

Banks, M. S., & Dannemiller, J. L. (1987). Infant visual psychophysics. In P. Salapatek & L. B. Cohen (Eds.), *Handbook of infant perception* (Vol. 1, pp. 115–184). Orlando, FL: Academic Press.

Barchia, K., & Bussey, K. (2011). Individual and collective social cognitive influences on peer aggression: Exploring the contribution of aggression efficacy, moral disengagement, and collective efficacy. *Aggressive Behavior, 37,* 107–120. doi:10.1002/ab.20375

Bar-Haim, Y., Ziv, T., Lamy, D., & Hodes, R. M. (2006). Nature and nurture in own-race face processing. *Psychological Science, 17,* 159–163. doi:10.1111/j.1467-9280.2006.01679.x

Barnes, J. C., Beaver, K. M., & Miller, J. M. (2010). Estimating the effect of gang membership on nonviolent and violent delinquency: A counterfactual analysis. *Aggressive Behavior, 36,* 437–451. doi:10.1002/ab.20359

Baron-Cohen, S. (1991). The development of a theory of mind in autism: Deviance and delay? *Psychiatric Clinics of North America, 14,* 33–51.

Baron-Cohen, S. (1993). From attention-goal psychology to belief-desire psychology: The development of a theory of mind, and its dysfunction. In S. Baron-Cohen, H. Tager-Flusberg, & D. J. Cohen (Eds.), *Understanding other minds: Perspectives from autism* (pp. 59–82). Oxford: Oxford University Press.

Baron-Cohen, S. (1995). *Mindblindness: An essay on autism and theory of mind.* Cambridge, MA: MIT Press.

Barr, R. G., Barr, M., Rajabali, F., Humphreys, C., Pike, I., Brant, R., . . . Singhal, A. (2018). Eight-year outcome of implementation of abusive head trauma prevention. *Child Abuse & Neglect, 84,* 106–114.

Barr, R. G., Rajabali, F., Aragon, M., Colbourne, M., & Brant, R. (2015). Education about crying in normal infants is associated with a reduction in pediatric emergency room visits for crying complaints. *Journal of Developmental & Behavioral Pediatrics, 36*(4), 252–257.

Barrett, K. C., Zahn-Waxler, C., & Cole, P. M. (1993). Avoiders vs. amenders: Implications for the investigation of guilt and shame during toddlerhood? *Cognition and Emotion, 7,* 481–505.

Barrouillet, P., & Camos, V. (2015). *Working memory: Loss and reconstruction.* New York: Psychology Press.

Barry, R. A., & Kochanska, G. (2010). A longitudinal investigation of the affective environment in families with young children: From infancy to early school age. *Emotion, 10,* 237–249.

Bartrip, J., Morton, J., & de Schonen, S. (2001). Responses to mother's face in 3-week to 5-month-old infants. *British Journal of Developmental Psychology, 19,* 219–232. doi:10.1348/026151001166047

Bartsch, K., & Wellman, H. M. (1995). *Children talk about the mind.* New York: Oxford University Press.

Bassen, C. R., & Lamb, M. E. (2006). Gender differences in adolescents' self-concepts of assertion and affiliation. *European Journal of Developmental Psychology, 3,* 71–94.

Bastaits, K., & Mortelmans, D. (2016). Parenting as mediator between post-divorce family structure and children's well-being. *Journal of Child and Family Studies, 25,* 2178–2188. doi:10.1007/s10826-016-0395-8

Bates, J. E., Schermerhorn, A. C., & Petersen, I. T. (2012). Temperament and parenting in developmental perspective. In M. R. Zentner & R. L. Shiner (Eds.), *Handbook of temperament* (pp. 425–441). New York: Guilford Press.

Baudry, C., Tarbulsy, G. M., Atkinson, L., Pearson, J., & St-Pierre, A. (2017). Intervention with adolescent mother–child dyads and cognitive development in early childhood: A meta-analysis. *Prevention Science, 18,* 116–130. doi:10.1007/s11121-016-0731-7

Bauer, P. J. (1995). Recalling past events: From infancy to early childhood. In R. Vasta (Ed.), *Annals of child development* (Vol. 11, pp. 25–71). London: Jessica Kingsley.

Bauer, P. J. (2007). *Remembering the times of our lives: Memory in infancy and beyond.* Mahwah, NJ: Erlbaum.

Baumeister, R. F. (2005). Self-concept, self-esteem, and identity. In V. Derlega, B. Winstead, & W. Jones (Eds.), *Personality: Contemporary Theory and Research* (3rd ed., pp. 246–280). San Francisco: Wadsworth.

Baumgartner, H. A., & Oakes, L. M. (2013). Investigating the relation between infants' manual activity with objects and their perception of dynamic events. *Infancy, 18*(6), 983–1006. doi:10.1111 /infa.12009

Bauminger, N., Finzi-Dottan, R., Chason, S., & Har-Even, D. (2008). Intimacy in adolescent friendship: The roles of attachment, coherence, and self-disclosure. *Journal of Social and Personal Relationships, 25,* 409–428. doi:10.1177/0265407508090866

Baumrind, D. (1973). The development of instrumental competence through socialization. In A. D. Pick (Ed.), *Minnesota Symposia on Child Psychology* (Vol. 7, pp. 3–46). Minneapolis: University of Minnesota Press.

Baumrind, D. (1991a). The influence of parenting style on adolescent competence and substance use. *Journal of Early Adolescence, 11,* 56–95. doi:10.1177/0272431691111004

Baumrind, D. (1991b). Parenting styles and adolescent development. In R. M. Lerner, A. C. Petersen, & J. Brooks-Gunn (Eds.), *Encyclopedia of adolescence* (pp. 746–758). New York: Garland.

Beach, S. R. H., Lei, M. K., Brody, G. H., Simons, R. L., Cutrona, C., & Philibert, R. A. (2012). Genetic moderation of contextual effects on negative arousal and parenting in African-American parents. *Journal of Family Psychology, 26,* 46–55. doi:10.1037/a0026236

Beardsall, L., & Dunn, J. (1992). Adversities in childhood: Siblings' experiences, and their relations to self-esteem. *Journal of Child Psychology and Psychiatry, 33,* 349–359.

Beckett, C., Maughan, B., Rutter, M., Castle, J., Colvert, E., Groothues, C., . . . Sonuga-Barke, E. J. (2006). Do the effects of early severe deprivation on cognition persist into early adolescence? Findings from the English and Romanian adoptees study. *Child Development, 77,* 696–711. doi:10.1111/j.1467-8624.2006.00898.x

Begus, K., Gliga, T., & Southgate, V. (2014). Infants learn what they want to learn: Responding to infant pointing leads to superior learning. *PLoS ONE, 9*(10), e108817.

Behl-Chadha, G. (1996). Basic-level and superordinate-like categorical representations in early infancy. *Cognition, 60,* 105–141.

Behne, T., Liszkowski, U., Carpenter, M., & Tomasello, M. (2012). Twelve-month-olds' comprehension and production of pointing. *British Journal of Developmental Psychology, 30,* 359–375. doi:10.1111/j.2044-835X.2011.02043.x

Behnke, A. O., Plunkett, S. W., Sands, T., & Bámaca-Colbert, M. Y. (2011). The relationship between Latino adolescents' perceptions of discrimination, neighborhood risk, and parenting on self-esteem and depressive symptoms. *Journal of Cross-Cultural Psychology, 42,* 1179–1197. doi:10.1177/0022022110383424

Behnke, M., Smith, V. C., Levy, S., Ammerman, S. D., Gonzalez, P. K., Ryan, S. A., . . . Cummings, J. J. (2013). Prenatal substance abuse: Short- and long-term effects on the exposed fetus. *Pediatrics, 131*(3), e1009–e1024.

Beilock, S. L., Gunderson, E. A., Ramirez, G., & Levine, S. C. (2010). Female teachers' math anxiety affects girls' math achievement. *Proceedings of the National Academy of Sciences of the United States of America, 107,* 1860–1863.

Beilock, S. L., & Willingham, D. T. (2014, Summer). Math anxiety: Can teachers help students reduce it? American Educator. Retrieved from http://www.aft.org /sites/default/files/-periodicals/beilock.pdf

Bell, M. L., & Ebisu, K. (2012). Environmental inequality in exposures to airborne particulate matter components in the United States. *Environmental Health Perspectives, 120*(12), 1699. doi:10.1289/ehp.1205201

Bell, S. M., & Ainsworth, M. D. S. (1972). Infant crying and maternal responsiveness. *Child Development, 43*(4), 1171–1190.

Belsky, J. (1986). Infant day care: A cause for concern? *Zero to Three, 7*(1), 1–7.

Belsky, J., Bakermans-Kranenburg, M. J., & van IJzendoorn, M. H. (2007). For better and for worse: Differential susceptibility to environmental influences. *Current Directions in Psychological Science, 16,* 300–304. doi:10.1111/j.1467-8721.2007.00525.x

Belsky, J., Newman, D. A., Widaman, K. F., Rodkin, P., Pluess, M., Fraley, R. C., . . . Roisman, G. I. (2015). Differential susceptibility to effects of maternal sensitivity? A study of candidate plasticity genes. *Development and Psychopathology, 27,* 725–746. doi:10.1017/S0954579414000844

Belsky, J., & Pluess, M. (2009). Beyond diathesis stress: Differential susceptibility to environmental influences. *Psychological Bulletin, 135,* 885–908. doi:10.1037/a0017376

Belsky, J., Schlomer, G. L., & Ellis, B. J. (2012). Beyond cumulative risk: Distinguishing harshness and unpredictability as determinants of parenting and early life history strategy. *Developmental Psychology, 48,* 662–673. doi:10.1037/a0024454

Bem, S. L. (1993). *The lenses of gender: Transforming the debate on sexual inequality.* New Haven, CT: Yale University Press.

Benenson, J. (2014). *Warriors and worriers: The survival of the sexes.* New York: Oxford University Press.

Benenson, J. F., & Christakos, A. (2003). The greater fragility of females' versus males' closest same-sex friendships. *Child Development, 74,* 1123–1129. doi:10.1111/1467-8624.00596

Benitez, V. L., & Saffran, J. R. (2018). Predictable events enhance word learning in toddlers. *Current Biology, 28*(17), 2787–2793.

Benitez, V. L., & Smith, L. B. (2012). Predictable locations aid early object name learning. *Cognition, 125*(3), 339–352.

Benner, A. D., & Kim, S. Y. (2010). Understanding Chinese American adolescents' developmental outcomes: Insights from the family stress model. *Journal of Research on Adolescence, 20,* 1–12. doi:10.1111/j.1532-7795.2009.00629.x

Benson, J. E., Sabbagh, M. A., Carlson, S. M., & Zelazo, P. D. (2013). Individual differences in executive functioning predict preschoolers' improvement from theory-of-mind training. *Developmental Psychology, 49*(9), 1615–1627. doi:10.1037/a0031056

Beran, T., Mishna, F., McInroy, L. B., & Shariff, S. (2015). Children's experiences of cyberbullying: A Canadian national study. *Children & Schools, 37*(4), 207–214.

Bérard, A., & Sheehy, O. (2014). The Quebec pregnancy cohort–prevalence of medication use during gestation and pregnancy outcomes. *PloS One, 9*(4), e93870.

Berenbaum, S. A. (2018). Beyond pink and blue: The complexity of early androgen effects on gender development. *Child Development Perspectives, 12*(1), 58–64. http://dx.doi.org/10.1111/cdep.12261

Berg, C. A., Strough, J., Calderone, K., Meegan, S. P., & Sansone, C. (1997). Planning to prevent everyday problems from occurring. In S. L. Friedman & E. K. Scholnick (Eds.), *The developmental psychology of planning: Why, how, and when do we plan?* (pp. 209–236). Mahwah, NJ: Erlbaum.

Berg, N. E., & Mussen, P. (1975). The origins and development of concepts of justice. *Journal of Social Issues, 31,* 183–201. doi:10.1111/j.1540-4560.1975.tb01003.x

Bergelson, E., & Swingley, D. (2012). At 6–9 months, human infants know the meanings of many common nouns. *Proceedings of the National Academy of Sciences of the United States of America, 109,* 3253–3258. doi:10.1073/pnas.1113380109

Berger, A. (2011). *Self-regulation: Brain, cognition, and development.* Washington, DC: American Psychological Association.

Berger, L., Brooks-Gunn, J., Paxson, C., & Waldfogel, J. (2008). First-year maternal employment and child outcomes: Differences across racial and ethnic groups. *Children and Youth Services Review, 30,* 365–387. doi:10.1016/j.childyouth.2007.10.010

Berkel, C., Murry, V. M., Hurt, T. R., Chen, Y.-f., Brody, G. H., Simons, R. L., . . . Gibbons, F. X. (2009). It takes a village: Protecting rural African American youth in the context of racism. *Journal of Youth and Adolescence, 38,* 175–188. doi:10.1007/s10964-008-9346-z

Berko, J. (1958). The child's learning of English morphology. *Word, 14,* 150–177.

Berkowitz, T., Schaeffer, M. W., Maloney, E. A., Peterson, L., Gregor, C., Levine, S. C., & Beilock, S. L. (2015). Math at home adds up to achievement in school. *Science, 350*(6257), 196–198. doi:10.1126/science.aac7427

Berlin, L. J., Ispa, J. M., Fine, M. A., Malone, P. S., Brooks-Gunn, J., Brady-Smith, C., . . . Bai, Y. (2009). Correlates and consequences of spanking and verbal punishment for low-income White, African American, and Mexican American toddlers. *Child Development, 80,* 1403–1420. doi:10.1111/j.1467-8624.2009.01341.x

Berman, J. M. J., Chambers, C. G., & Graham, S. A. (2010). Preschoolers' appreciation of speaker vocal affect as a cue to referential intent. *Journal of Experimental Child Psychology, 107,* 87–99. doi:10.1016/j.jecp.2010.04.012

Bernard, K., & Dozier, M. (2010). Examining infants' cortisol responses to laboratory tasks among children varying in attachment disorganization: Stress reactivity or return to baseline? *Developmental Psychology, 46,* 1771–1778. doi:10.1037/a0020660

Bernard, K., Dozier, M., Bick, J., Lewis-Morrarty, E., Lindhiem, O., & Carlson, E. (2012). Enhancing attachment organization among maltreated children: Results of a randomized clinical trial. *Child Development, 83,* 623–636. doi:10.1111/j.1467-8624.2011.01712.x

Berndt, T. J. (1979). Developmental changes in conformity to peers and parents. *Developmental Psychology, 15,* 608–616. doi:10.1037/0012-1649.15.6.608

Berndt, T. J., Hawkins, J. A., & Jiao, Z. (1999). Influences of friends and friendships on adjustment to junior high school. *Merrill-Palmer Quarterly, 45,* 13–41.

Berninger, V. W., & Richards, T. L. (2002b). Building a writing brain neurologically. In V. W. Berninger & T. L. Richards (Eds.), *Brain literacy for educators and psychologists* (pp. 247–271). San Diego, CA: Academic Press.

Berteletti, I., Lucangeli, D., Piazza, M., Dehaene, S., & Zorzi, M. (2010). Numerical estimation in preschoolers. *Developmental Psychology, 46,* 545–551. doi:10.1037/a0017887

Bertenthal, B. I. (1993). Infants' perception of biomechanical motions: Intrinsic image and knowledge-based constraints. In C. Granrud (Ed.), *Visual perception and cognition in infancy* (pp. 175–214). Hillsdale, NJ: Erlbaum.

Bertenthal, B. I., Campos, J. J., & Kermoian, R. (1994). An epigenetic perspective on the development of self-produced locomotion and its consequences. *Current Directions in Psychological Science, 3,* 140–145. doi:10.2307/20182292

Bertenthal, B. I., & Clifton, R. K. (1998). Perception and action. In W. Damon (Series Ed.) & D. Kuhn & R. S. Siegler (Vol. Eds.), *Handbook of child psychology: Vol. 2. Cognition, perception, and language* (5th ed., pp. 51–102). New York: Wiley.

Best, D. L. (2010). Gender. In M. H. Bornstein (Ed.), *Handbook of cultural developmental science* (pp. 209–222). New York: Psychology Press.

Best, D. L., & Bush, C. D. (2016). Gender roles in childhood and adolescence. In U. P. Gielen & J. L. Roopnarine (Eds.), *Childhood and adolescence: Cross-cultural perspectives and applications* (pp. 209–239). Santa Barbara, CA: Praeger.

Best, D. L., & Thomas, J. J. (2004). Cultural diversity and cross-cultural perspectives. In A. H. Eagly, A. E. Beall, & R. J. Sternberg (Eds.), *The psychology of gender* (2nd ed., pp. 296–327). New York: Guilford Press.

Best, D. L., & Williams, J. E. (1993). A cross-cultural viewpoint. In A. E. Beall & R. J. Sternberg (Eds.), *The psychology of gender* (pp. 215–248). New York: Guilford Press.

Best, J. R., & Miller, P. H. (2010). A developmental perspective on executive function. *Child Development, 81*(6), 1641–1660. doi:10.1111/j.1467-8624.2010.01499.x

Beyers, W., & Goossens, L. (2008). Dynamics of perceived parenting and identity formation in late adolescence. *Journal of Adolescence, 31,* 165–184. doi:10.1016/j.adolescence.2007.04.003

Bezdjian, S., Raine, A., Baker, L. A., & Lynam, D. R. (2011). Psychopathic personality in children: Genetic and environmental contributions. *Psychological Medicine, 41,* 589–600. doi:10.1017/S0033291710000966

Bhanot, R., & Jovanovic, J. (2005). Do parents' academic gender stereotypes influence whether they intrude on their children's homework? *Sex Roles, 52,* 597–607. doi:10.1007/s11199-005-3728-4

Bialystok, E. (2000). Symbolic representation across domains in preschool children. *Journal of Experimental Child Psychology, 76,* 173–189.

Bialystok, E. (2009). Bilingualism: The good, the bad, and the indifferent. *Bilingualism: Language and Cognition, 12*(1), 3–11.

Bialystok, E., & Craik, F. I. M. (2010). Cognitive and linguistic processing in the bilingual mind. *Current Directions in Psychological Science, 19,* 19–23. doi:10.1177/0963721409358571

Bibok, M. B., Carpendale, J. I., & Müller, U. (2009). Parental scaffolding and the development of executive function. *New Directions for Child and Adolescent Development, 2009*(123), 17–34. doi:10.1002/cd.233

Bick, J., Dozier, M., & Perkins, E. (2012). Convergence between attachment classifications and natural reunion behavior among children and parents in a child care setting. *Attachment & Human Development, 14,* 1–10. doi:10.1080/14616734.2012.636645

Bick, J., Zhu, T., Stamoulis, C., Fox, N. A., Zeanah, C. H., & Nelson, C. A. (2015). Effect on early institutionalization and foster care on long-term white matter development: A randomized clinical trial. *JAMA Pediatrics, 169,* 211–219. doi:10.1001/jamapediatrics.2014.3212

Biehle, S. N., & Mickelson, K. D. (2012). First-time parents' expectations about the division of childcare and play. *Journal of Family Psychology, 26,* 36–45. doi:10.1037/a0026608

Bierman, K. L., Coie, J. D., Dodge, K. A., Greenberg, M. T., Lochman, J. E., McMahon, R. J., . . . Conduct Problems Prevention Research Group. (2010). The effects of a multiyear universal social–emotional learning program: The role of student and school characteristics. *Journal of Consulting and Clinical Psychology, 78,* 156–168. doi:10.1037/a0018607

Biernat, M. (1991). Gender stereotypes and the relationship between masculinity and femininity: A developmental analysis. *Journal of Personality and Social Psychology, 61,* 351–365. doi:10.1037/0022-3514.61.3.351

Biesele, M. (1997). An ideal of unassisted birth. In R. E. Davis-Floyd & C. F. Sargent (Eds.), *Childbirth and Authoritative Knowledge: Cross-Cultural Perspectives.* Oakland: University of California Press.

Bigelow, A. E. (1996). Blind and sighted children's spatial knowledge of their home environments. *International Journal of Behavioral Development, 19*(4), 797–816.

Bigelow, A. E., MacLean, K., Proctor, J., Myatt, T., Gillis, R., & Power, M. (2010). Maternal sensitivity throughout infancy: Continuity and relation to attachment security. *Infant Behavior and Development, 33*(1), 50–60.

Bigler, R. S. (1999). Psychological interventions designed to counter sexism in children: Empirical limitations and theoretical foundations. In J. W. B. Swann, J. H. Langlois, & L. A. Gilbert (Eds.), *Sexism and stereotypes in modern society: The gender science of Janet Taylor Spence* (pp. 129–151). Washington, DC: American Psychological Association.

Bigler, R. S., & Leaper, C. (2015). Gendered language: Psychological principles, evolving practices, and inclusive policies. *Policy Insights from the Behavioral and Brain Sciences, 2*(1), 187–194. https://doi.org/10.1177/2372732215600452

Bigler, R. S., & Liben, L. S. (1990). The role of attitudes and interventions in gender-schematic processing. *Child Development, 61,* 1440–1452.

Bigler, R. S., & Liben, L. S. (2006). A developmental intergroup theory of social stereotypes and prejudice. In R. V. Kail (Ed.), *Advances in child development and behavior* (Vol. 34, pp. 39–89). San Diego, CA: Elsevier Academic Press.

Bigler, R. S., & Liben, L. S. (2007). Developmental intergroup theory: Explaining and reducing children's social stereotyping and prejudice. *Current Directions in Psychological Science, 16*(3), 162–166. http://dx.doi.org/10.1111/j.1467-8721.2007.00496.x

Bird, A., Reese, E., & Tripp, G. (2006). Parent–child talk about past emotional events: Associations with child temperament and goodness-of-fit. *Journal of Cognition and Development, 7,* 189–210.

Birulés, J., Bosch, L., Brieke, R., Pons, F., & Lewkowicz, D. J. (2018). Inside bilingualism: Language background modulates selective attention to a talker's mouth. *Developmental Science,* e12755–e12755.

Bishop, D. V. (2015). The interface between genetics and psychology: Lessons from developmental dyslexia. *Proceedings of the Royal Society B: Biological Sciences, 282*(1806). https://doi.org/10.1098/rspb.2014.3139

Bjorklund, D. F. (1997). The role of immaturity in human development. *Psychological Bulletin, 122,* 153–169.

Bjorklund, D. F., & Pellegrini, A. D. (2002). *The origins of human nature: Evolutionary developmental psychology.* Washington, DC: American Psychological Association.

Björkqvist, K., Österman, K., & Kaukiainen, A. (1992). The development of direct and indirect aggressive strategies in males and females. In K. Björkqvist & P. Niemelä (Eds.), *Of mice and women: Aspects of female aggression* (pp. 51–64). San Diego, CA: Academic Press.

Blackstock, C. (2003). First Nations child and family services: Restoring peace and harmony in First Nations communities. *Child Welfare: Connecting Research Policy and Practice,* 331–342.

Blackwell, L. S., Trzesniewski, K. H., & Dweck, C. S. (2007). Implicit theories of intelligence predict achievement across an adolescent transition: A longitudinal study and an intervention. *Child Development, 78,* 246–263. doi:10.1111/j.1467-8624.2007.00995.x

Blair, C. (2016). Developmental science and executive function. *Current Directions in Psychological Science, 25*(1), 3–7. doi:10.1177/0963721415622634

Blair, C., & Raver, C. C. (2015). School readiness and self-regulation: A developmental psychobiological approach. *Annual Review of Psychology, 66,* 711. doi:10.1146/annurev-psych-010814-015221

Blair, J. R. (2016). The neurobiology of disruptive behavior disorder. *American Journal of Psychiatry, 173*(11), 1073–1074. doi:10.1176/appi.ajp.2016.16080971

Blake, J., & de Boysson-Bardies, B. (1992). Patterns in babbling: A cross-linguistic study. *Journal of Child Language, 19*(01), 51–74.

Blake, P. R., Corbit, J., Callaghan, T. C., & Warneken, F. (2016). Give as I give: Adult influence on children's giving in two cultures. *Journal of Experimental Child Psychology, 152,* 149–160. doi:10.1016/j.jecp.2016.07.010

Blake, P. R., McAuliffe, K., Corbit, J., Callaghan, T. C., Barry, O., Bowie, A., . . . Warneken, F. (2015). The ontogeny of fairness in seven societies. *Nature, 528,* 258–261. doi:10.1038/nature15703

Blakemore, J. E. O., Berenbaum, S. A., & Liben, L. S. (2009). *Gender development.* New York: Taylor & Francis.

Blakemore, S. J., & Mills, K. L. (2014). Is adolescence a sensitive period for sociocultural processing? *Annual Review of Psychology, 65,* 187–207.

Blandon, A. Y., Calkins, S. D., Keane, S. P., & O'Brien, M. (2008). Individual differences in trajectories of emotion regulation processes: The effects of maternal depressive symptomatology and children's physiological regulation. *Developmental Psychology, 44,* 1110–1123. doi:10.1037/0012-1649.44.4.1110

Bleeker, M. M., & Jacobs, J. E. (2004). Achievement in math and science: Do mothers' beliefs matter 12 years later? *Journal of Educational Psychology, 96,* 97–109. doi:10.1037/0022-0663.96.1.97

Bleidorn, W., Arslan, R. C., Denissen, J. A., Rentfrow, P. J., Gebauer, J. E., Potter, J., & Gosling, S. D. (2016). Age and gender differences in self-esteem: A cross-cultural window. *Journal of Personality and Social Psychology, 111,* 396–410. doi:10.1037/pspp0000078

Blesa, M., Sullivan, G., Anblagan, D., Telford, E. J., Quigley, A. J., Sparrow, S. A., . . . Boardman, J. P. (2019). Early breast milk exposure modifies brain connectivity in preterm infants. *NeuroImage, 184,* 431–439.

Bloom, L. (1973). *One word at a time: The use of single word utterances before syntax.* The Hague, Netherlands: Mouton.

Bloom, L. (1998). Language acquisition in its developmental context. In W. Damon (Series Ed.) & D. Kuhn & R. S. Siegler (Vol. Eds.), *Handbook of child psychology: Vol. 2. Cognition, perception, and language* (5th ed., pp. 309–370). Hoboken, NJ: Wiley.

Bloom, P. (2000). *How children learn the meanings of words.* Cambridge, MA: MIT Press.

Blumberg, F. C., Deater-Deckard, K., Calvert, S. L., Flynn, R. M., Green, C. S., Arnold, D. & Brooks P. J. (2019). Digital games as a context for children's cognitive development: Research recommendations and considerations. *Social Policy Report, 32*(1), 1–33. doi:10.1002/sop2.3

Blumberg, F. C., & Randall, J. D. (2013). What do children and adolescents say they do during video game play? *Journal of Applied Developmental Psychology, 34*(2), 82–88. doi:10.1016/j.appdev.2012.11.004

Blumberg, M. S. (2015). Developing sensorimotor systems in our sleep. *Current Directions in Psychological Science, 24*(1), 32–37.

Bode, L., Kuhn, L., Kim, H. Y., Hsiao, L., Nissan, C., Sinkala, M., . . . Aldrovandi, G. M. (2012). Human milk oligosaccharide concentration and risk of postnatal transmission of HIV through breastfeeding. *American Journal of Clinical Nutrition, 96,* 831–839. doi:10.3945/ajcn.112.039503

Boden, J. M., Fergusson, D. M., & Horwood, L. J. (2008). Does adolescent self-esteem predict later life outcomes? A test of the causal role of self-esteem. *Development and Psychopathology, 20,* 319–339. doi:10.1017/S0954579408000151

Boeke, J. D., Church, G., Hessel, A., Kelley, N. J., Arkin, A., Cai, Y., . . . Isaacs, F. J. (2016). The Genome Project-Write. *Science, 353*(6295), 126–127.

Bohlin, G., Hagekull, B., & Rydell, A.-M. (2000). Attachment and social functioning: A longitudinal study from infancy to middle childhood. *Social Development, 9,* 24–39. doi:10.1111/1467-9507.00109

Bohnert, N., Milan, A., & Lathe, H. (2014). Living arrangements of children in Canada: A century of change. Ottowa: Minister of Industry.

Boivin, M., & Hertzman, C. (Eds.). (2012). Early childhood development: Adverse experiences and developmental health. Royal Society of Canada—Canadian Academy of Health Sciences Expert Panel (with Ronald Barr, Thomas Boyce, Alison Fleming, Harriet MacMillan, Candice Odgers, Marla Sokolowski, & Nico Trocmé). Ottawa, ON, Canada: Royal Society of Canada. Retrieved from https://rsc-src.ca/sites/default/files/pdf/ECD%20Report_0.pdf

Bokhorst, C. L., Bakermans-Kranenburg, M. J., Pasco Fearon, R. M., van IJzendoorn, M. H., Fonagy, P., & Schuengel, C. (2003). The importance of shared environment in mother–infant attachment security: A behavioral genetic study. *Child Development, 74,* 1769–1782. doi:10.1046/j.1467-8624.2003.00637.x

Bokhorst, C. L., Sumter, S. R., & Westenberg, P. M. (2010). Social support from parents, friends, classmates, and teachers in children and adolescents aged 9 to 18 years: Who is perceived as most supportive? *Social Development, 19,* 417–426. doi:10.1111/j.1467-9507.2009.00540.x

Bolger, K. E., & Scarr, S. (1995). Not so far from home: How family characteristics predict child care quality. *Early Development and Parenting, 4,* 103–112. doi:10.1002/edp.2430040303

Bolkan, C., Sano, Y., De Costa, J., Acock, A. C., & Day, R. D. (2010). Early adolescents' perceptions of mothers' and fathers' parenting styles and problem behavior. *Marriage and Family Review, 46,* 563–579. doi:10.1080/01494929.2010.543040

Bona, K., Blonquist, T. M., Neuberg, D. S., Silverman, L. B., & Wolfe, J. (2016). Impact of socioeconomic status on timing of relapse and overall survival for children treated on Dana-Farber Cancer Institute ALL consortium protocols (2000–2010). *Pediatric Blood & Cancer, 63,* 1012–1018. doi:10.1002/pbc.25928

Bonica, C., Arnold, D. H., Fisher, P. H., Zeljo, A., & Yershova, K. (2003). Relational aggression, relational victimization, and language development in preschoolers. *Social Development, 12,* 551–562. doi:10.1111/1467-9507.00248

Bonner, J. T. (1988). *The evolution of culture in animals.* Princeton, NJ: Princeton University Press.

Booth-LaForce, C., & Groh, A. M. (2018). Parent-child attachment and peer relations. In W. M. Bukowski, B. Laursen, & K. H. Rubin (Eds.), *Handbook of peer interactions, relationships, and groups* (2nd ed., pp. 349–370). New York: Guilford.

Booth-Laforce, C., Oh, W., Kennedy, A. E., Rubin, K. H., Rose-Krasnor, L., & Laursen, B. (2012). Parent and peer links to trajectories of anxious withdrawal from grades 5 to 8. *Journal of Clinical Child and Adolescent Psychology, 41,* 138–149. doi:10.1080/15374416.2012.651995

Booth-LaForce, C., & Oxford, M. L. (2008). Trajectories of social withdrawal from grades 1 to 6: Prediction from early parenting, attachment, and temperament. *Developmental Psychology, 44,* 1298–1313. doi:10.1037/a0012954

Borelli, J. L., Crowley, M. J., David, D. H., Sbarra, D. A., Anderson, G. M., & Mayes, L. C. (2010). Attachment and emotion in school-aged children. *Emotion, 10,* 475–485. doi:10.1037/a0018490

Borge, A. I. H., Rutter, M., Côté, S., & Tremblay, R. E. (2004). Early childcare and physical aggression: Differentiating social selection and social causation. *Journal of Child Psychology and Psychiatry, 45,* 367–376. doi:10.1111/j.1469-7610.2004.00227.x

Bornstein, M. H. (2007). On the significance of social relationships in the development of children's earliest symbolic play: An ecological perspective. In A. Göncü & S. Gaskins (Eds.), *Play and development: Evolutionary, sociocultural, and functional perspectives* (pp. 101–129). New York: Erlbaum.

Bornstein, M. H., Hahn, C. S., & Suwalsky, J. T. (2013). Physically developed and exploratory young infants contribute to their own long-term academic achievement. *Psychological Science, 24*(10), 1906–1917.

Bornstein, M. H., Hahn, C. S., & Wolke, D. (2013). Systems and cascades in cognitive development and academic achievement. *Child Development, 84*(1), 154–162.

Bornstein, M. H., & Putnick, D. L. (2012). Cognitive and socioemotional caregiving in developing countries. *Child Development, 83,* 46–61. doi:10.1111/j.1467-8624.2011.01673.x

Bornstein, M. H., Putnick, D. L., Bradley, R. H., Deater-Deckard, K., & Lansford, J. E. (2016). Gender in low- and middle-income countries: I. Introduction. *Monographs of the Society for Research in Child Development, 81*(1), 1–144.

Bornstein, M. H., Putnick, D. L., Gartstein, M. A., Hahn, C., Auestad, N., & O'Connor, D. L. (2015). Infant temperament: Stability by age, gender, birth order, term status, and socioeconomic status. *Child Development, 86,* 844–863. doi:10.1111/cdev.12367

Borstelmann, L. J. (1983). Children before psychology: Ideas about children from antiquity to the late 1800s. In P. H. Mussen (Series Ed.) & W. Kessen (Vol. Ed.), *Handbook of child psychology: Vol. 1. History, theory, and methods* (4th ed., pp. 1–40). New York: Wiley.

Bortfeld, H., Fava, E., & Boas, D. A. (2009). Identifying cortical lateralization of speech processing in infants using near-infrared spectroscopy. *Developmental Neuropsychology, 34,* 52–65. doi:10.1080/87565640802564481

Bortfeld, H., Morgan, J. L., Golinkoff, R. M., & Rathbun, K. (2005). Mommy and me: Familiar names help launch babies into speech-stream segmentation. *Psychological Science, 16,* 298–304. doi:10.1111/j.0956-7976.2005.01531.x

Bos, H. M. W., Knox, J. R, van Rijn-van Gelderen, L., & Gatrell, N. K. (2016). Same-sex and different-sex parent households and child health outcomes: Findings from the National Survey of Children's Health. *Journal of Developmental and Behavioral Pediatrics, 37,* 179–187. doi:10.1097/DBP.0000000000000288

Bos, H. M. W., Kuyper, L., & Gartrell, N. K. (2018). A population-based comparison of female and male same-sex parent and different-sex parent households. *Family Process, 57,* 148–164. doi:10.1111/famp.12278

Bosacki, S., Woods, H., & Coplan, R. (2015). Canadian female and male early childhood educators' perceptions of child aggression and rough-and-tumble play. *Early Child Development and Care, 185*(7), 1134–1147.

Boskey, E. R. (2014). Understanding transgender identity development in childhood and adolescence. *American Journal of Sexuality Education, 9,* 445–463.

Bosma, H. A., & Kunnen, E. S. (2001). Determinants and mechanisms in ego identity development: A review and synthesis. *Developmental Review, 21,* 39–66. doi:10.1006/drev.2000.0514

Botto, S. V., & Rochat, P. (2018). Sensitivity to the evaluation of others emerges by 24 months. *Developmental Psychology, 54*(9), 1723–1734. doi:10.1037/dev0000548

Bouchard, T. J., Jr., Lykken, D. T., McGue, M., Segal, N. L., & Tellegen, A. (1990, October 12). Sources of human psychological differences: The Minnesota Study of Twins Reared Apart. *Science, 250,* 223–228.

Boucher, O., Jacobson, S. W., Plusquellec, P., Dewailly, É., Ayotte, P., Forget-Dubois, N., . . . Muckle, G. (2012). Prenatal methylmercury, postnatal lead exposure, and evidence of attention deficit/hyperactivity disorder among Inuit children in Arctic Québec. *Environmental Health Perspectives, 120*(10), 1456.

Boucher, O., Muckle, G., Jacobson, J. L., Carter, R. C., Kaplan-Estrin, M., Ayotte, P., Dewailly, É., & Jacobson, S. W. (2014). Domain-specific effects of prenatal exposure to PCBs, mercury, and lead on infant cognition: Results from the Environmental Contaminants and Child Development Study in Nunavik. *Environmental Health Perspectives, 122,* 310–316. http://dx.doi.org/10.1289/ehp.1206323

Boulet, V., & Badets, N. (2017). Early motherhood among off-reserve First Nations, Métis and Inuit women. *Statistics Canada Catalogue, 75-006-X,* ISSN 2291-0840.

Boutwell, B. B., Franklin, C. A., Barnes, J. C., & Beaver, K. M. (2011). Physical punishment and childhood aggression: The role of gender and gene–environment interplay. *Aggressive Behavior, 37,* 559–568. doi:10.1002/ab.20409

Boutwell, B. B., Young, J. T., & Meldrum, R. C. (2018). On the positive relationship between breastfeeding & intelligence. *Developmental Psychology, 54*(8), 1426.

Bouwer, R., Koster, M., & van den Bergh, H. (2018). Effects of a strategy-focused instructional program on the writing quality of upper elementary students in the Netherlands. *Journal of Educational Psychology, 110*(1), 58–71. doi:10.1037/edu0000206

Bowker, J. C., & Raja, R. (2011). Social withdrawal subtypes during early adolescence in India. *Journal of Abnormal Child Psychology, 39,* 201–212. doi:10.1007/s10802-010-9461-7

Bowlby, J. (1953). *Child care and the growth of love* (M. Fry, Ed.). London: Penguin Books.

Bowlby, J. (1969). *Attachment and loss: Vol. 1. Attachment.* New York: Basic Books.

Bowlby, J. (1973). *Attachment and loss: Vol. 2. Separation: Anxiety and anger.* New York: Basic Books.

Bowlby, J. (1980). *Attachment and loss: Vol. 3. Loss.* New York: Basic Books.

Boxer, P., Groves, C. L., & Docherty, M. (2015). Video games do indeed influence children and adolescents' aggression, prosocial behavior, and academic performance: A clearer reading of Ferguson (2015). *Perspectives on Psychological Science, 10*(5), 671–673.

Boyce, W. T., & Ellis, B. J. (2005). Biological sensitivity to context: I. An evolutionary-developmental theory of the origins and functions of stress reactivity. *Development and Psychopathology, 17,* 271–301. doi:10.1017/S0954579405050145

Boys and Girls Club, Big Brothers Big Sisters of Edmonton and Area [BGCBIGS]. (2014). How do parents feel about their children's potential? New Survey Release from BBBS Canada. Retrieved from https://bgcbigs.ca/how-do-parents-feel-about-their-childrens-potential-new-survey-release-from-bbbs-canada/

Bradbard, M. R., Martin, C. L., Endsley, R. C., & Halverson, C. F. (1986). Influence of sex stereotypes on children's exploration and memory: A competence versus performance distinction. *Developmental Psychology, 22,* 481–486. doi:10.1037/0012-1649.22.4.481

Bradley, R. H., & Caldwell, B. M. (1979). Home observation for measurement of the environment: A revision of the preschool scale. *American Journal of Mental Deficiency, 84,* 235–244.

Bradley, R. H., & Caldwell, B. M. (1984). 174 children: A study of the relationship between home environment and cognitive development during the first 5 years. In A. W. Gottfried (Ed.), *Home environment and early cognitive development* (pp. 5–56). New York: Academic Press.

Bradley, R. H., Caldwell, B. M., Rock, S. L., Ramey, C. T., Barnard, K. E., Gray, C., . . . Johnson, D. L. (1989). Home environment and cognitive development in the first 3 years of life: A collaborative study involving six sites and three ethnic groups in North America. *Developmental Psychology, 25*(2), 217–235.

Bradley, R. H., Convyn, R. F., Burchinal, M., McAdoo, H. P., & García Coll, C. (2001). The home environments of children in the United States: Part II. Relations with behavioral development through age thirteen. *Child Development, 72,* 1868–1886.

Bradley, R. H., Whiteside, L., Mundrom, D. J., Casey, P. H., Kelleher, K. J., & Pope, S. K. (1994). Contribution of early intervention and early caregiving experiences to resilience in low-birthweight, premature children living in poverty. *Journal of Clinical Child Psychology, 23,* 425–434.

Bradshaw, C. P., Waasdorp, T. E., & Leaf, P. J. (2012). Effects of school-wide positive behavioral interventions and supports on child behavior problems. *Pediatrics, 130,* e1136–e1145. doi:10.1542/peds.2012-0243

Braine, M. D. S. (1976). [Review of the book *The acquisition of phonology,* by N. V. Smith]. *Language, 52,* 489–498.

Bramlett, M. D., & Mosher, W. D. (2002). *Vital and health statistics: Series 22. Cohabitation, marriage, divorce, and remarriage in the United States.* Hyattsville, MD: National Center for Health Statistics.

Brannon, E. M., Lutz, D., & Cordes, S. (2006). The development of area discrimination and its implications for number representation in infancy. *Developmental Science, 9,* F59–F64. doi:10.1111/j.1467-7687.2006.00530.x

Brannon, E. M., Suanda, S., & Libertus, K. (2007). Temporal discrimination increases in precision over development and parallels the development of numerosity discrimination. *Developmental Science, 10,* 770–777. doi:10.1111/j.1467-7687.2007.00635.x

Braungart-Rieker, J. M., Hill-Soderlund, A. L., & Karrass, J. (2010). Fear and anger reactivity trajectories from 4 to 16 months: The roles of temperament, regulation, and maternal sensitivity. *Developmental Psychology, 46,* 791–804. doi:10.1037/a0019673

Braveman, P., Heck, K., Egerter, S., Dominguez, T. P., Rinki, C., Marchi, K. S., & Curtis, M. (2017). Worry about racial discrimination: A missing piece of the puzzle of Black–White disparities in preterm birth? *PloS One, 12*(10), e0186151.

Braver, S. L., Ellman, I. M., & Fabricius, W. V. (2003). Relocation of children after divorce and children's best interests: New evidence and legal considerations. *Journal of Family Psychology, 17,* 206–219. doi:10.1037/0893-3200.17.2.206

Bray, J. H., Adams, G. J., Getz, J. G., & McQueen, A. (2003). Individuation, peers, and adolescent alcohol use: A latent growth analysis. *Journal of Consulting and Clinical Psychology, 71,* 553–564. doi:10.1037/0022-006X.71.3.553

Bray, J. H., & Berger, S. H. (1993). Developmental issues in StepFamilies Research Project: Family relationships and parent–child interactions. *Journal of Family Psychology, 7,* 76–90. doi:10.1037/0893-3200.7.1.76

Breazeal (Ferrell), C. (1998). Early experiments using motivations to regulate human-robot interaction. In *Proceedings of 1998 AAAI Fall Symposium: Emotional and Intelligent, The Tangled Knot of Cognition,* Orlando, FL, 31–36.

Bremner, J. G. (1978). Spatial errors made by infants: Inadequate spatial cues or evidence of egocentrism? *British Journal of Psychology, 69,* 77–84. doi:10.1111/j.2044-8295.1978.tb01634.x

Brendgen, M., Boivin, M., Dionne, G., Barker, E. D., Vitaro, F., Girard, A., . . . Pérusse, D. (2011). Gene–environment processes linking aggression, peer victimization, and the teacher–child relationship. *Child Development, 82,* 2021–2036. doi:10.1111/j.1467-8624.2011.01644.x

Brendgen, M., Boivin, M., Vitaro, F., Bukowski, W. M., Dionne, G., Tremblay, R. E., & Pérusse, D. (2008). Linkages between children's and their friends' social and physical aggression: Evidence for a gene–environment interaction? *Child Development, 79,* 13–29. doi:10.1111/j.1467-8624.2007.01108.x

Brendgen, M., Vitaro, F., Bukowski, W. M., Doyle, A. B., & Markiewicz, D. (2001). Developmental profiles of peer social preference over the course of elementary school: Associations with trajectories of externalizing and internalizing behavior. *Developmental Psychology, 37,* 308–320.

Brentari, D., & Goldin-Meadow, S. (2017). Language emergence. *Annual Review of Linguistics, 3,* 363–388.

Bretherton, I., & Munholland, K. A. (2016). The internal working model construct in light of contemporary neuroimaging research. In J. Cassidy & P. R. Shaver (Eds.), *Handbook of attachment: Theory, research, and clinical applications, 3rd ed.* (pp. 63–88). New York: Guilford.

Briars, D. J., & Siegler, R. S. (1984). A featural analysis of preschoolers' counting knowledge. *Developmental Psychology, 20*(4), 607–618. doi:10.1037/0012-1649.20.4.607

Bridges, L. J., & Grolnick, W. S. (1995). The development of emotional self-regulation in infancy and early childhood. In N. Eisenberg (Ed.), *Review of personality and social psychology: Vol. 15. Social development* (pp. 185–211). Thousand Oaks, CA: Sage.

Bright, F. M., Vink, R., & Byard, R. W. (2018). Neuropathological developments in sudden infant death syndrome. *Pediatric and Developmental Pathology.* doi:10.1177/1093526618776439

Bril, B., & Sabatier, C. (1986). The cultural context of motor development: Postural manipulations in the daily life of Bambara babies (Mali). *International Journal of Behavioral Development, 9,* 439–453.

Bringewatt, E. H., & Gershoff, E. T. (2010). Falling through the cracks: Gaps and barriers in the mental health system for America's disadvantaged children. *Children and Youth Services Review, 32,* 1291–1299. doi:10.1016/j.childyouth.2010.04.021

Broadbent, H. J., Farran, E. K., & Tolmie, A. (2014). Egocentric and allocentric navigation strategies in Williams syndrome and typical development. *Developmental Science, 17*(6), 920–934. doi:10.1111/desc.12176

Broberg, A. G., Wessels, H., Lamb, M. E., & Hwang, C. P. (1997). Effects of day care on the development of cognitive abilities in 8-year-olds: A longitudinal study. *Developmental Psychology, 33*(1), 62.

Brody, N. (1992). *Intelligence* (2nd ed.). San Diego, CA: Academic Press.

Broesch, T., Rochat, P., Olah, K., Broesch, J., & Henrich, J. (2016). Similarities and differences in maternal responsiveness in three societies: Evidence from Fiji, Kenya, and the United States. *Child Development, 87*(3), 700–711.

Broesch, T. L., Callaghan, T., Henrich, J., Murphy, C., & Rochat, P. (2010). Cultural variations in children's mirror self-recognition. *Journal of Cross-Cultural Psychology, 42,* 1018–1029. doi:10.1177/0022022110381114

Brogly, S. B., Turner, S., Lajkosz, K., Davies, G., Newman, A., Johnson, A., & Dow, K. (2017). Infants born to opioid-dependent women in Ontario, 2002–2014. *Journal of Obstetrics and Gynaecology Canada, 39*(3), 157–165.

Bronfenbrenner, U. (1979). *The ecology of human development: Experiments by nature and design.* Cambridge, MA: Harvard University Press.

Bronfenbrenner, U. (1993). The ecology of cognitive development: Research models and fugitive findings. In R. H. Wozniak & K. W. Fischer (Eds.), *Development in context: Acting and thinking in specific environments* (pp. 3–44). Hillsdale, NJ: Erlbaum.

Bronfenbrenner, U., & Morris, P. A. (1998). The ecology of developmental processes. In W. Damon (Series Ed.) & R. M. Lerner (Vol. Ed.), *Handbook of child psychology: Vol. 1. Theoretical models of human development* (5th ed., pp. 993–1028). New York: Wiley.

Brooker, I., & Poulin-Dubois, D. (2013). Is a bird an apple? The effect of speaker labeling accuracy on infants' word learning, imitation, and helping behaviors. *Infancy, 18*(s1), E46–E68. doi:10.1111/infa.12027

Brooks, R., & Meltzoff, A. N. (2008). Infant gaze following and pointing predict accelerated vocabulary growth through two years of age: A longitudinal, growth curve modeling study. *Journal of Child Language, 35,* 207–220. doi:10.1017/S030500090700829X

Brooks-Gunn, J., Han, W.-J., & Waldfogel, J. (2010). First-year maternal employment and child development in the first 7 years: III. What distinguishes women who work full-time, part-time, or not at all in the 1st year? *Monographs of the Society for Research in Child Development, 75*(2, Serial No. 296), 35–49.

Brophy-Herb, H. E., Schiffman, R. F., Bocknek, E. L., Dupuis, S. B., Fitzgerald, H. E., Horodynski, M., . . . Hillaker, B. (2011). Toddlers' social-emotional competence in the contexts of maternal emotion socialization and contingent responsiveness in a low-income sample. *Social Development, 20,* 73–92.

Brown, A. L. (1997). Transforming schools into communities of thinking and learning about serious matters. *American Psychologist, 52,* 399–413. doi:10.1037/0003-066X.52.4.399

Brown, B. B., Clasen, D. R., & Eicher, S. A. (1986). Perceptions of peer pressure, peer conformity dispositions, and self-reported behavior among adolescents. *Developmental Psychology, 22,* 521–530. doi:10.1037/0012-1649.22.4.521

Brown, C. S., & Bigler, R. S. (2004). Children's perceptions of gender discrimination. *Developmental Psychology, 40,* 714–726. doi:10.1037/0012-1649.40.5.714

Brown, C. S., & Bigler, R. S. (2005). Children's perceptions of discrimination: A developmental model. *Child Development, 76,* 533–553. doi:10.1111/j.1467-8624.2005.00862.x

Brown, G. L., Mangelsdorf, S. C., & Neff, C. (2012). Father involvement, paternal sensitivity, and father–child attachment security in the first 3 years. *Journal of Family Psychology, 26,* 421–430. doi:10.1037/a0027836

Brown, J. R., & Dunn, J. (1996). Continuities in emotion understanding from three to six years. *Child Development, 67,* 789–802.

Brown, R. (1973). *A first language: The early stages.* Cambridge, MA: Harvard University Press.

Brown, R., & Hanlon, C. (1970). Derivational complexity and order of acquisition in child speech.

In J. R. Hayes (Ed.), *Cognition and the development of language* (Vol. 8, pp. 11–53). New York: Wiley.

Brown, R. W. (1957). Linguistic determinism and the part of speech. *Journal of Abnormal Psychology and Social Psychology, 55,* 1–5.

Brown, S. L., Manning, W. D., & Stykes, J. B. (2015). Family structure and child well-being: Integrating family complexity. *Family Relations, 77,* 177–190. doi:10.1111/jomf.12145

Brownell, C. A., Ramani, G. B., & Zerwas, S. (2006). Becoming a social partner with peers: Cooperation and social understanding in one- and two-year-olds. *Child Development, 77,* 803–821. doi:10.1111/j.1467-8624.2006.t01-1-.x-i1

Brownell, C. A., Svetlova, M., & Nichols, S. (2009). To share or not to share: When do toddlers respond to another's needs? *Infancy, 14,* 117–130. doi:10.1080/15250000802569868

Brownell, C. A., Zerwas, S., & Ramani, G. B. (2007). "So big": The development of body self-awareness in toddlers. *Child Development, 78,* 1426–1440. doi:10.1111/j.1467-8624.2007.01075.x

Bruck, M., Ceci, S. J., & Principe, G. F. (2006). The child and the law. In W. Damon & R. M. Lerner (Series Eds.) & K. A. Renninger & I. E. Sigel (Vol. Eds.), *Handbook of child psychology: Vol. 4. Child psychology in practice* (6th ed., pp. 776–816). Hoboken, NJ: Wiley.

Brumariu, L. E., & Kerns, K. A. (2010). Parent–child attachment and internalizing symptoms in childhood and adolescence: A review of empirical findings and future directions. *Development and Psychopathology, 22,* 177–203. doi:10.1017/S0954579409990344

Brummelman, E., Crocker, J., & Bushman, B. J. (2016). The praise paradox: When and why praise backfires in children with low self-esteem. *Child Development Perspectives, 10,* 111–115. doi:10.1111/cdep.12171

Brummelman, E., Thomaes, S., de Castro, B. O., Overbeek, G., & Bushman, B. J. (2014). "That's not just beautiful—That's incredibly beautiful!" The adverse impact of inflated praise on children with low self-esteem. *Psychological Science, 25,* 728–735. doi:0956797613514251

Brummelte, S., & Galea, L. A. (2016). Postpartum depression: Etiology, treatment and consequences for maternal care. *Hormones and Behavior, 77,* 153–166.

Bruner, J. S. (1977). Early social interaction and language acquisition. In H. R. Schaffer (Ed.), *Studies in mother–infant interaction* (pp. 271–289). London: Academic Press.

Bryant, J. B., & Polkosky, M. (2001, April). *Parents responses to pre-schoolers' lexical innovations.* Paper presented at the Biennial Meeting of the Society for Research in Child Development, Minneapolis, MN.

Bucchianeri, M. M., Eisenberg, M. E., Wall, M. M., Piran, N., & Neumark-Sztainer, D. (2014). Multiple types of harassment: Associations with emotional well-being and unhealthy behaviors in adolescents. *Journal of Adolescent Health, 54*(6), 724–729. https://doi.org/10.1016/j.jadohealth.2013.10.205

Buchanan, C. M., Maccoby, E. E., & Dornbusch, S. M. (1991). Caught between parents: Adolescents' experience in divorced homes. *Child Development, 62,* 1008–1029. doi:10.1111/j.1467-8624.1991.tb01586.x

Buckner, J. C., Bassuk, E. L., Weinreb, L. F., & Brooks, M. G. (1999). Homelessness and its relation to the mental health and behavior of low-income school-age children. *Developmental Psychology, 35,* 246–257. doi:10.1037/0012-1649.35.1.246

Buehler, C., Anthony, C., Krishnakumar, A., Stone, G., Gerard, J., & Pemberton, S. (1997). Interparental conflict and youth problem behaviors: A meta-analysis. *Journal of Child and Family Studies, 6,* 233–247. doi:10.1023/A:1025006909538

Buehler, C., Lange, G., & Franck, K. L. (2007). Adolescents' cognitive and emotional responses to marital hostility. *Child Development, 78,* 775–789. doi:10.1111/j.1467-8624.2007.01032.x

Buist, K. L., Paalman, C. H., Branje, S. J., Deković, M., Reitz, E., Verhoeven, M., . . . Hale, W. W., III (2014). Longitudinal effects of sibling relationship quality on adolescent problem behavior: A cross-ethnic comparison. *Cultural Diversity and Ethnic Minority Psychology, 20*(2), 266. doi:10.1037/a0033675

Bukowski, W. M., Cillessen, A. H. N., & Velasquez, A. M. (2012). Peer ratings. In B. Laursen, T. D. Little, & N. A. Card (Eds.), *Handbook of developmental research methods* (pp. 211–230). New York: Guilford Press.

Bukowski, W. M., Gauze, C., Hoza, B., & Newcomb, A. F. (1993). Differences and consistency between same-sex and other-sex peer relationships during early adolescence. *Developmental Psychology, 29,* 255–263. doi:10.1037/0012-1649.29.2.255

Bukowski, W. M., Laursen, B., & Hoza, B. (2010). The snowball effect: Friendship moderates escalations in depressed affect among avoidant and excluded children. *Development and Psychopathology, 22,* 749–757. doi:10.1017/S095457941000043X

Bukowski, W. M., Newcomb, A. F., & Hartup, W. W. (1996). Friendship and its significance in childhood and adolescence: Introduction and comment. In W. M. Bukowski, A. F. Newcomb, & W. W. Hartup (Eds.), *The company they keep: Friendship in childhood and adolescence* (pp. 1–15). Cambridge: Cambridge University Press.

Bulf, H., Johnson, S. P., & Valenza, E. (2011). Visual statistical learning in the newborn infant. *Cognition, 121,* 127–132. doi:10.1016/j.cognition.2011.06.010

Bullens, J., Iglói, K., Berthoz, A., Postma, A., & Rondi-Reig, L. (2010). Developmental time course of the acquisition of sequential egocentric and allocentric navigation strategies. *Journal of Experimental Child Psychology, 107*(3), 337–350. doi:10.1016/j.jecp.2010.05.010

Burchinal, M. R., Campbell, F. A., Brayant, D. M., Wasik, B. H., & Ramey, C. T. (1997). Early intervention and mediating processes in cognitive performance of children of low-income African American families. *Child Development, 68,* 935–954.

Burchinal, M. R., & Clarke-Stewart, K. A. (2007). Maternal employment and child cognitive outcomes: The importance of analytic approach. *Developmental Psychology, 43,* 1140–1155. doi:10.1037/0012-1649.43.5.1140

Bureau, J. F., Martin, J., Yurkowski, K., Schmiedel, S., Quan, J., Moss, E., . . . Pallanca, D. (2017). Correlates of child–father and child–mother attachment in the preschool years. *Attachment & Human Development, 19*(2), 130–150.

Burgess, K. B., Marshall, P. J., Rubin, K. H., & Fox, N. A. (2003). Infant attachment and temperament as predictors of subsequent externalizing problems and cardiac physiology. *Journal of Child Psychology and Psychiatry, 44,* 819–831. doi:10.1111/1469-7610.00167

Burkam, D. T., Lee, V. E., & Smerdon, B. A. (1997). Gender and science learning early in high school: Subject matter and laboratory experiences. *American Educational Research Journal, 34,* 297–331. doi:10.3102/00028312034002297

Burnette, M. L., Oshri, A., Lax, R., Richards, D., & Ragbeer, S. N. (2012). Pathways from harsh parenting to adolescent antisocial behavior: A multidomain test of gender moderation. *Development and Psychopathology, 24,* 857–870. doi:10.1017/S0954579412000417

Burnham, D., & Dodd, B. (2004). Auditory–visual speech integration by prelinguistic infants: Perception of an emergent consonant in the McGurk effect. *Developmental Psychobiology, 45*(4), 204–220.

Burt, S. A., Barnes, A. R., McGue, M., & Iacono, W. G. (2008). Parental divorce and adolescent delinquency: Ruling out the impact of common genes. *Developmental Psychology, 44,* 1668–1677. doi:10.1037/a0013477

Burt, S. A., Donnellan, M. B., Iacono, W., & McGue, M. (2011). Age-of-onset or behavioral sub-types? A prospective comparison of two approaches to characterizing the heterogeneity within antisocial behavior. *Journal of Abnormal Child Psychology, 39,* 633–644. doi:10.1007/s10802-011-9491-9

Burton, L. M., Bonilla-Silva, E., Ray, V., Buckelew, R., & Freeman, E. H. (2010). Critical race theories, colorism, and the decade's research on families of color. *Journal of Marriage and Family, 72,* 440–459. doi:10.1111/j.1741-3737.2010.00712.x

Bushnell, E. W., McKenzie, B. E., Lawrence, D. A., & Connell, S. (1995). The spatial coding strategies of one-year-old infants in a locomotor search task. *Child Development, 66,* 937–958.

Bushnell, I. W. R., Sai, F., & Mullin, J. T. (2011). Neonatal recognition of the mother's face. *British Journal of Developmental Psychology, 7,* 3–15. doi:10.1111/j.2044-835X.1989.tb00784.x

Buss, A. T., & Spencer, J. P. (2014). The emergent executive: A dynamic field theory of the development of executive function. *Monographs of the Society for Research in Child Development, 79*(2), vii–103. doi:10.1002/mono.12096

Buss, D. M. (2014). *Evolutionary psychology: The new science of the mind* (5th ed.). New York: Psychology Press.

Buss, K. A., & Kiel, E. J. (2011). Do maternal protective behaviors alleviate toddlers' fearful distress? *International Journal of Behavioral Development, 35,* 136–143. doi:10.1177/0165025410375922

Bussey, K., & Bandura, A. (1999). Social cognitive theory of gender development and differentiation. *Psychological Review, 106,* 676–713.

Bussey, K., & Bandura, A. (2004). Social cognitive theory of gender development and functioning. In A. H. Eagly, A. E. Beall, & R. J. Sternberg (Eds.), *The Psychology of Gender* (2nd ed., pp. 92–119). New York: Guilford Press.

Byers-Heinlein, K. (2013). Parental language mixing: Its measurement and the relation of mixed input to young bilingual children's vocabulary size. *Bilingualism: Language and Cognition, 16*(01), 32–48.

Byers-Heinlein, K. (2017). Bilingualism affects 9-month-old infants' expectations about how words refer to kinds. *Developmental Science, 20*(1), e12486.

Byers-Heinlein, K., Burns, T. C., & Werker, J. F. (2010). The roots of bilingualism in newborns. *Psychological Science, 21,* 343–348. doi:10.1177/0956797609360758

Byers-Heinlein, K., Morin-Lessard, E., & Lew-Williams, C. (2017). Bilingual infants control their languages as they listen. *Proceedings of the National Academy of Sciences, 114*(34), 9032–9037.

Byers-Heinlein, K., & Werker, J. F. (2009). Monolingual, bilingual, trilingual: Infants' language experience influences the development of a word-learning heuristic. *Developmental Science, 12,* 815–823. doi:10.1111/j.1467-7687.2009.00902.x

Byrd-Bredbenner, C., Martin-Biggers, J., Povis, G. A., Worobey, J., Hongu, N., & Quick, V. (2018). Promoting healthy home environments and lifestyles in families with preschool children: HomeStyles, a randomized controlled trial. *Contemporary Clinical Trials, 64,* 139–151.

Byrnes, J. P., Miller, D. C., & Schafer, W. D. (1999). Gender differences in risk taking: A meta-analysis. *Psychological Bulletin, 125,* 367–383. doi:10.1037/0033-2909.125.3.367

Cahan, S., & Cohen, N. (1989). Age versus schooling effects on intelligence development. *Child Development, 60,* 1239–1249.

Cai, H., Brown, J. D., Deng, C., & Oakes, M. A. (2007). Self-esteem and culture: Differences in cognitive self-evaluations or affective self-regard? *Asian Journal of Social Psychology, 10,* 162–170. doi:10.1111/j.1467-839X.2007.00222.x

Cain, K. M., & Dweck, C. S. (1995). The relation between motivational patterns and achievement cognitions through the elementary school years. *Merrill-Palmer Quarterly, 41,* 25–52. doi:10.2307/23087453

Calati, R., Pedrini, L., Alighieri, S., Alvarez, M. I., Desideri, L., Durante, D., . . . Pericoli, V. (2011). Is cognitive behavioural therapy an effective complement to antidepressants in adolescents? A meta-analysis. *Acta Neuropsychiatrica, 23,* 263–271.

Caldwell, M. S., Rudolph, K. D., Troop-Gordon, W., & Kim, D.-Y. (2004). Reciprocal influences among relational self-views, social disengagement, and peer stress during early adolescence. *Child Development, 75,* 1140–1154. doi:10.1111/j.1467-8624.2004.00730.x

Calkins, S. D., & Williford, A. P. (2009). Taming the terrible twos: Self-regulation and school readiness. In O. A. Barbarin & B. H. Wasik (Eds.), *Handbook of child development and early education: Research to practice* (pp. 172–198). New York: Guilford.

Callaghan, T., Moll, H., Rakoczy, H., Warneken, F., Liszkowski, U., Behne, T., & Tomasello, M. (2011). Early social cognition in three cultural contexts. *Monographs of the Society for Research in Child Development, 76*(2, Serial No. 299), vii–142. doi:10.1111/j.1540-5834.2011.00603.x

Callaghan, T., Moll, H., Rakoczy, H., Warneken, F., Liszkowski, U., Behne, T., & Tomasello, M. (2011). Early social cognition in three cultural contexts. *Monographs of the Society for Research in Child Development, 76*(2, Serial No. 299), vii–142. doi:10.1111/j.1540-5834.2011.00603.x

Callaghan, T., Rochat, P., Lillard, A., Claux, M. L., Odden, H., Itakura, S., . . . Singh, S. (2005). Synchrony in the onset of mental-state reasoning: Evidence from five cultures. *Psychological Science, 16,* 378–384. doi:10.1111/j.0956-7976.2005.01544.x

Callaghan, T. C. (1999). Early understanding and production of graphic symbols. *Child Development, 70,* 1314–1324. doi:10.1111/1467-8624.00096

Callaghan, T. C., Rochat, P., & Corbit, J. (2012). Young children's knowledge of the representational function of pictorial symbols: Development across the preschool years in three cultures. *Journal of Cognition and Development, 13*(3), 320–353.

Callanan, M. A. (1990). Parents' descriptions of objects: Potential data for children's inferences about category principles. *Cognitive Development, 5,* 101–122. doi:10.1016/0885-2014(90)90015-L

Callanan, M. A., & Sabbagh, M. A. (2004). Multiple labels for objects in conversations with young children: Parents' language and children's developing expectations about word meanings. *Developmental Psychology, 40,* 746–762.

Calvete, E., & Orue, I. (2012). Social information processing as a mediator between cognitive schemas and aggressive behavior in adolescents. *Journal of Abnormal Child Psychology, 40,* 105–117. doi:10.1007/s10802-011-9546-y

Camarena, P. M., Sarigiani, P. A., & Petersen, A. C. (1990). Gender-specific pathways to intimacy in early adolescence. *Journal of Youth and Adolescence, 19,* 19–32. doi:10.1007/BF01539442

Campbell, A., Shirley, L., & Caygill, L. (2002). Sex-typed preferences in three domains: Do two-year-olds need cognitive variables? *British Journal of Psychology, 93,* 203–217. doi:10.1348/000712602162544

Campbell, F. A., Pungello, E. P., Burchinal, M., Kainz, K., Pan, Y., Wasik, B. H., . . . Ramey, C. T. (2012). Adult outcomes as a function of an early childhood educational program: An Abecedarian Project follow-up. *Developmental Psychology, 48,* 1033–1043.

Campbell, F. A., Pungello, E. P., Miller-Johnson, S., Burchinal, M., & Ramey, C. T. (2001). The development of cognitive and academic abilities: Growth curves from an early childhood educational experiment. *Developmental Psychology, 37,* 231–242.

Campbell, S. B., Spieker, S., Vandergrift, N., Belsky, J., Burchinal, M., & NICHD Early Child Care Research Network. (2010). Predictors and sequelae of trajectories of physical aggression in school-age boys and girls. *Development and Psychopathology, 22,* 133–150.

Campos, J. J., Anderson, D. I., Barbu-Roth, M. A., Hubbard, E. M., Hertenstein, M. J., & Witherington, D. (2000). Travel broadens the mind. *Infancy, 1,* 149–219.

Campos, J. J., Frankel, C. B., & Camras, L. (2004). On the nature of emotion regulation. *Child Development, 75,* 377–394. doi:10.1111/j.1467-8624.2004.00681.x

Campos, J. J., Kermoian, R., & Zumbahlen, M. R. (1992). Socioemotional transformations in the family system following infant crawling onset. In N. Eisenberg & R. A. Fabes (Eds.), *New Directions for Child and Adolescent Development: No. 55. Emotion and its regulation in early development* (pp. 25–40). San Francisco: Jossey-Bass.

Campos, J. J., Mumme, D. L., Kermoian, R., & Campos, R. G. (1994). A functionalist perspective on the nature of emotion. *Monographs of the Society for Research in Child Development, 59*(2–3, Serial No. 240), 284–303.

Campos, J. J., Witherington, D., Anderson, D. I., Frankel, C. I., Uchiyama, I., & Barbu-Roth, M. (2008). Rediscovering development in infancy. *Child Development, 79,* 1625–1632. doi:10.1111/j.1467-8624.2008.01212.x

Camras, L. A., Malatesta, C., & Izard, C. E. (1991). The development of facial expressions in infancy. In R. S. Feldman & B. Rimé (Eds.), *Fundamentals of nonverbal behavior* (pp. 73–105). New York: Cambridge University Press.

Canadian Department of Justice. (2017). Child custody and access. Retrieved from https://www.justice.gc.ca/eng/rp-pr/jr/jf-pf/2017/docs/nov02.pdf

Canadian Institute for Health Information. (n.d.). Health Indicators Interactive Tool. Retrieved from https://yourhealthsystem.cihi.ca/epub/

Canadian Institute for Health Information. (2016). Child and Youth Mental Health in Canada. Infographic. Retrieved from https://www.cihi.ca/sites/default/files/infographic_youthandmentalhealth2016-en.pdf

Canadian Paediatric Society. (2016). *Endorsement of Joint Statement on Physical Punishment of Children and Youth.* Retrieved from https://www.cps.ca/en/documents/authors-auteurs/child-and-youth-maltreatment-section

Canadian Pediatric Society. (2017). Screen time and young children: Promoting health and development in a digital world. *Pediatrics and Child Health, 22,* 461–468.

Canadian Pediatric Society. (2019). Digital media: Promoting healthy screen use in school-aged children and adolescents. Retrieved from https://www.cps.ca/en/documents/position/digital-media

Canadian Psychological Association. (2004). *Policy and position statements: Physical punishment of children and youth.* Retrieved from https://cpa.ca/aboutcpa/policystatements/#physical

Canli, T., Omura, K., Haas, B. W., Fallgatter, A., Constable, R. T., & Lesch, K. P. (2005). Beyond affect: A role for genetic variation of the serotonin transporter in neural activation during a cognitive attention task. *Proceedings of the National Academy of Sciences of the United States of America, 102,* 12224–12229. doi:10.1073/pnas.0503880102

Cannon, E. N., & Woodward, A. L. (2012). Infants generate goal-based action predictions. *Developmental Science, 15,* 292–298. doi:10.1111/j.1467-7687.2011.01127.x

Canobi, K. H., Reeve, R. A., & Pattison, P. E. (2002). Young children's understanding of addition concepts. *Educational Psychology, 22,* 513–532.

Cantin, R. H., Gnaedinger, E. K., Gallaway, K. C., Hesson-McInnis, M. S., & Hund, A. M. (2016). Executive functioning predicts reading, mathematics, and theory of mind during the elementary years. *Journal of Experimental Child Psychology, 146,* 66–78. doi:10.1016/j.jecp.2016.01.014

Caputi, M., Lecce, S., Pagnin, A., & Banerjee, R. (2012). Longitudinal effects of theory of mind on later peer relations: The role of prosocial behavior. *Developmental Psychology, 48,* 257–270. doi:10.1037/a0025402

Cárcamo, R. A., Vermeer, H. J., van der Veer, R., & van IJzendoorn, M. H. (2016). Early full-time day care, mother–child attachment, and quality of the home environment in Chile: Preliminary findings. *Early Education and Development, 27,* 457–477. doi:10.1080/10409289.2016.1091971

Card, N. A., Stucky, B. D., Sawalani, G. M., & Little, T. D. (2008). Direct and indirect aggression during childhood and adolescence: A meta-analytic review of gender differences, intercorrelations, and relations to maladjustment. *Child Development, 79,* 1185–1229. doi:10.1111/j.1467-8624.2008.01184.x

Cardno, A. G., & Gottesman, I. I. (2000). Twin studies of schizophrenia: From bow-and-arrow concordances to Star Wars Mx and functional genomics. *American Journal of Medical Genetics, 97,* 12–17.

Carey, S. (1985). *Conceptual change in childhood.* Cambridge, MA: MIT Press.

Carey, S. (1999). Sources of conceptual change. In E. K. Scholnick, K. Nelson, S. A. Gelman, & P. H. Miller (Eds.), *Conceptual development: Piaget's legacy* (pp. 293–326). Mahwah, NJ: Erlbaum.

Carlo, G., Mestre, M. V., Samper, P., Tur, A., & Armenta, B. E. (2010). Feelings or cognitions? Moral cognitions and emotions as longitudinal predictors of prosocial and aggressive behaviors. *Personality and Individual Differences, 48,* 872–877. doi:10.1016/j.paid.2010.02.010

Carlson, E. A., Sroufe, L. A., & Egeland, B. (2004). The construction of experience: A longitudinal study of representation and behavior. *Child Development, 75,* 66–83. doi:10.1111/j.1467-8624.2004.00654.x

Carlson, S., Hyvärinen, L., & Raninen, A. (1986). Persistent behavioural blindness after early visual deprivation and active visual rehabilitation: A case report. *British Journal of Ophthalmology, 70,* 607–611. doi:10.1136/bjo.70.8.607

Carlson, S. M., Gum, J., Davis, A., & Malloy, A. (2003, June). *Predictors of imaginary companion in early childhood.* Poster session presented at the annual meeting of the Jean Piaget Society, Chicago, IL.

Carlson, S. M., Mandell, D. J., & Williams, L. (2004). Executive function and theory of mind: Stability and prediction from ages 2 to 3. *Developmental Psychology, 40,* 1105–1122. doi:10.1037/0012-1649.40.6.1105

Carlson, S. M., Moses, L. J., & Hix, H. R. (1998). The role of inhibitory processes in young children's difficulties with deception and false belief. *Child Development, 69*(3), 672–691. doi:10.1111/j.1467-8624.1998.tb06236.x

Carlson, S. M., Taylor, M., & Levin, G. R. (1998). The influence of culture on pretend play: The case of Mennonite children. *Merrill Palmer Quarterly, 44,* 538–565.

Carpendale, J. I. (2000). Kohlberg and Piaget on stages and moral reasoning. *Developmental Review, 20*(2), 181–205.

Carpenter, M., Nagell, K., & Tomasello, M. (1998). Social cognition, joint attention, and communicative competence from 9 to 15 months of age. *Monographs of the Society for Research in Child Development, 63*(4, Serial No. 255).

Carra, C., Lavelli, M., & Keller, H. (2014). Differences in practices of body stimulation during the first 3 months: Ethnotheories and behaviors of Italian mothers and West African immigrant mothers. *Infant Behavior & Development, 37,* 5–15.

Carroll, J. B. (1993). *Human cognitive abilities: A survey of factor-analytic studies.* New York: Cambridge University Press.

Carroll, J. B. (2005). The three-stratum theory of cognitive abilities. In D. P. Flanagan & P. L. Harrison (Eds.), *Contemporary intellectual assessment: Theories, tests, and issues* (2nd ed., pp. 69–76). New York: Guilford Press.

Carson, G., Cox, L. V., Crane, J., Croteau, P., Graves, L., Kluka, S., . . . Poole, N. (2017). No. 245-Alcohol use and pregnancy consensus clinical guidelines. *Journal of Obstetrics and Gynaecology Canada, 39*(9), e220–e254.

Carter, D. B., & Patterson, C. J. (1982). Sex roles as social conventions: The development of children's conceptions of sex-role stereotypes. *Developmental Psychology, 18,* 812–824. doi:10.1037/0012-1649.18.6.812

Carver, L. J., & Vaccaro, B. G. (2007). 12-month-old infants allocate increased neural resources to stimuli associated with negative adult emotion. *Developmental Psychology, 43,* 54–69. doi:10.1037/0012-1649.43.1.54

Casasola, M. (2008). The development of infants' spatial categories. *Current Directions in Psychological Science, 17,* 21–25. doi:10.1111/j.1467-8721.2008.00541.x

Case, R. (1998). The development of conceptual structures. In W. Damon (Series Ed.) & D. Kuhn & R. S. Siegler (Vol. Eds.), *Handbook of child psychology: Vol. 2. Cognition, perception, and language* (5th ed., pp. 745–800). New York: Wiley.

Case, R., Griffin, S., & Kelly, W. M. (1999). Socioeconomic gradients in mathematical ability and their responsiveness to intervention during early childhood. In D. P. Keating & C. Hertzman (Eds.), *Developmental health and the wealth of nations: Social, biological, and educational dynamics* (pp. 125–149). New York: Guilford Press.

Casey, B. J., Somerville, L. H., Gotlib, I. H., Ayduk, O., Franklin, N. T., Askren, M. K., . . . Shoda, Y. (2011). Behavioral and neural correlates of delay of gratification 40 years later. *Proceedings of the National Academy of Sciences of the United States of America, 108,* 14998–15003. doi:10.1073/pnas.1108561108

Casey, B. J., Tottenham, N., Liston, C., & Durston, S. (2005). Imaging the developing brain: What have we learned about cognitive development? *Trends in Cognitive Sciences, 9,* 104–110.

Cashon, C. H., Ha, O. R., Graf Estes, K., Saffran, J. R., & Mervis, C. B. (2016). Infants with Williams syndrome detect statistical regularities in continuous speech. *Cognition, 154,* 165–168.

Casiglia, A. C., Lo Coco, A., & Zappulla, C. (1998). Aspects of social reputation and peer relationships in Italian children: A cross-cultural perspective. *Developmental Psychology, 34,* 723–730. doi:10.1037/0012-1649.34.4.723

Caspi, A., Henry, B., McGee, R. O., Moffitt, T. E., & Silva, P. A. (1995). Temperamental origins of child and adolescent behavior problems: From age three to age fifteen. *Child Development, 66,* 55–68.

Caspi, A., McClay, J., Moffitt, T. E., Mill, J., Martin, J., Craig, I. W., . . . Poulton, R. (2002, August 2). Role of genotype in the cycle of violence in maltreated children. *Science, 297,* 851–854.

Caspi, A., & Silva, P. A. (1995). Temperamental qualities at age three predict personality traits in young adulthood: Longitudinal evidence from a birth cohort. *Child Development, 66,* 486–498.

Cassidy, J. (1994). Emotion regulation: Influences of attachment relationships. *Monographs of the Society for Research in Child Development, 59*(2–3, Serial No. 240), 228–249.

Cassidy, J. (2016). The nature of the child's ties. In J. Cassidy & P. R. Shaver (Eds.), *Handbook of attachment: Theory, research, and clinical applications, 3rd ed.* (pp. 3–24). New York: Guilford

Cassidy, J., Ziv, Y., Mehta, T. G., & Feeney, B. C. (2003). Feedback seeking in children and adolescents: Associations with self-perceptions, attachment representations, and depression. *Child Development, 74,* 612–628. doi:10.1111/1467-8624.7402019

Castillo, R., Salguero, J. M., Fernández-Berrocal, P., & Balluerka, N. (2013). Effects of an emotional intelligence intervention on aggression and empathy among adolescents. *Journal of Adolescence, 36,* 883–892. doi:10.1016/j.adolescence.2013.07.001

Castles, A., Rastle, K., & Nation, K. (2018). Ending the reading wars: Reading acquisition from novice to expert. *Psychological Science in the Public Interest, 19*(1), 5–51. doi:10.1177/1529100618772271

Castro, D. C., Páez, M. M., Dickinson, D. K., & Frede, E. (2011). Promoting language and literacy in young dual language learners: Research, practice, and policy. *Child Development Perspectives, 5,* 15–21. doi:10.1111/j.1750-8606.2010.00142.x

Castro, V. L., Cooke, A. N., Halberstadt, A. G., & Garrett-Peters, P. (2018). Bidirectional linkages between emotion recognition and problem behaviors in elementary school children. *Journal of Nonverbal Behavior, 42,* 155–178. doi:10.1007/s10919-017-0269-9

Cavanagh, S. E., & Huston, A. C. (2006). Family instability and children's early behavior problems. *Social Forces, 85,* 551–585. doi:10.1353/sof.2006.0120

Cecchini, M., Baroni, E., Di Vito, C., & Lai, C. (2011). Smiling in newborns during communicative wake and active sleep. *Infant Behavior and Development, 34,* 417–423. doi:10.1016/j.infbeh.2011.04.001

Ceci, S. J. (1996). *On intelligence: A bioecological treatise on intellectual development.* Cambridge, MA: Harvard University Press.

Ceci, S. J., & Bruck, M. (1998). Children's testimony: Applied and basic issues. In W. Damon (Series Ed.) & I. E. Sigel & K. A. Renninger (Vol. Eds.), *Handbook of child psychology: Vol. 4. Child psychology in practice* (5th ed., pp. 713–774). New York: Wiley.

Cecil, C. A., Walton, E., Pingault, J. B., Provençal, N., Pappa, I., Vitaro, F., . . . Viding, E. (2018). DRD4 methylation as a potential biomarker for physical aggression: An epigenome-wide, cross-tissue investigation. *American Journal of Medical Genetics Part B: Neuropsychiatric Genetics, 177*(8), 746–764.

Celio, C. I., Durlak, J., & Dymnicki, A. (2011). A meta-analysis of the impact of service-learning on students. *Journal of Experiential Education, 34,* 164–181. doi:10.5193/JEE34.2.164

Cénat, J. M., Blais, M., Hébert, M., Lavoie, F., & Guerrier, M. (2015). Correlates of bullying in Quebec high school students: The vulnerability of sexual-minority youth. *Journal of Affective Disorders, 183,* 315–321.

Centers for Disease Control and Prevention. (2017a). Data and statistics on Down syndrome. Retrieved from https://www.cdc.gov/ncbddd/birthdefects/downsyndrome/data.html

Centers for Disease Control and Prevention. (2017b). High School YRBS: 2017 Results. Retrieved from https://nccd.cdc.gov/Youthonline/App/

Centers for Disease Control and Prevention. (2018). Breastfeeding among U.S. children born 2009–2015, CDC National Immunization Survey. Retrieved from https://www.cdc.gov/breastfeeding/data/nis_data/results.html

Centers for Disease Control and Prevention. (2019). Child abuse & neglect: Risk and protective factors. Retrieved from https://www.cdc.gov/violenceprevention/childabuseandneglect/riskprotectivefactors.html

Central Intelligence Agency (CIA). (2018). *The World Factbook.* Retrieved from https://www.cia.gov/library/publications/the-world-factbook/rankorder/2091rank.html

Ceyhan-Birsoy, O., Murry, J. B., Machini, K., Lebo, M. S., Timothy, W. Y., Fayer, S., . . . Holm, I. A. (2019). Interpretation of genomic sequencing results in healthy and ill newborns: Results from the BabySeq Project. *The American Journal of Human Genetics, 104*(1), 76–93.

Chabris, C. F., Lee, J. J., Cesarini, D., Benjamin, D. J., & Laibson, D. I. (2015). The fourth law of behavior genetics. *Current Directions in Psychological Science, 24*(4), 304–312. doi:10.1177/0963721415580430

Chall, J. (1979). The great debate: Ten years later, with a modest proposal for reading stages. In L. B. Resnick & P. A. Weaver (Eds.), *Theory and practice of early reading* (Vol. 1, pp. 29–55). Hillsdale, NJ: Erlbaum.

Chall, J. S. (1983). *Stages of reading development.* New York: McGraw-Hill.

Chalmers, D., & Lawrence, J. A. (1993). Investigating the effects of planning aids on adults' and adolescents' organisation of a complex task. *International Journal of Behavioral Development, 16,* 191–214.

Chambers, C. G., Graham, S. A., & Turner, J. N. (2008). When hearsay trumps evidence: How generic language guides preschoolers' inferences about unfamiliar things. *Language and Cognitive Processes, 23*(5), 749–766.

Chan, A., & Poulin, F. (2007). Monthly changes in the composition of friendship networks in early adolescence. *Merrill-Palmer Quarterly, 53,* 578–602.

Chan, K., Penner, K., Mah, J. W., & Johnston, C. (2010). Assessing parenting behaviors in Euro-Canadian and East Asian immigrant mothers: Limitations to observations of responsiveness. *Child & Family Behavior Therapy, 32*(2), 85–102.

Chang, L. (2004). The role of classroom norms in contextualizing the relations of children's social behaviors to peer acceptance. *Developmental Psychology, 40*(5), 691–702.

Chang, L., Lansford, J. E., Schwartz, D., & Farver, J. M. (2004). Marital quality, maternal depressed affect, harsh parenting, and child externalising in Hong Kong Chinese families. *International Journal of Behavioral Development, 28,* 311–318. doi:10.1080/01650250344000523

Chang, Z., Lichtenstein, P., Asherson, P. J., & Larsson, H. (2013). Developmental twin study of attention problems: High heritabilities throughout development. *Journal of the American Medical Association Psychiatry, 70*(3), 311–318.

Chao, R. K. (1994). Beyond parental control and authoritarian parenting style: Understanding Chinese parenting through the cultural notion of training. *Child Development, 65,* 1111–1119. doi:10.1111/j.1467-8624.1994.tb00806.x

Chaplin, T. M., & Aldao, A. (2013). Gender differences in emotion expression in children: A meta-analytic review. *Psychological Bulletin, 139*(4), 735–765. doi:10.1037/a0030737

Chayer, M.-H., & Bouffard, T. (2010). Relations between impostor feelings and upward and downward identification and contrast among 10- to 12-year-old students. *European Journal of Psychology of Education, 25,* 125–140. doi:10.1007/s10212-009-0004-y

Cheah, C., & Rubin, K. (2004). European American and Mainland Chinese mothers' responses to aggression and social withdrawal in preschoolers. *International Journal of Behavioral Development, 28,* 83–94.

Cheah, C. S. L., Leung, C. Y. Y., Tahseen, M., & Schultz, D. (2009). Authoritative parenting among immigrant Chinese mothers of preschoolers. *Journal of Family Psychology, 23,* 311–320. 10.1037/a0015076

Chen, A., Oster, E., & Williams, W. (2016). Why is infant mortality higher in the United States than in Europe? *American Economic Journal: Economic Policy,* 8(2), 89–124.

Chen, E., & Miller, G. E. (2012). "Shift-and-persist" strategies: Why being low in socioeconomic status isn't always bad for health. *Perspectives on Psychological Science, 7,* 135–158. doi:10.1177/1745691612436694

Chen, X., Cen, G., Li, D., & He, Y. (2005). Social functioning and adjustment in Chinese children: The imprint of historical time. *Child Development, 76,* 182–195. doi:10.1111/j.1467-8624.2005.00838.x

Chen, X., Chang, L., He, Y., & Liu, H. (2005). The peer group as a context: Moderating effects on relations between maternal parenting and social and school adjustment in Chinese children. *Child Development, 76,* 417–434. doi:10.1111/j.1467-8624.2005.00854.x

Chen, X., Rubin, K. H., & Li, B. (1995). Social and school adjustment of shy and aggressive children in China. *Development and Psychopathology, 7,* 337–349. doi:10.1017/S0954579400006544

Chen, X., Rubin, K. H., Li, B.-s., & Li, D. (1999). Adolescent outcomes of social functioning in Chinese children. *International Journal of Behavioral Development, 23,* 199–223. doi:10.1080/016502599384071

Chen, X., Rubin, K. H., & Li, Z.-y. (1995). Social functioning and adjustment in Chinese children: A longitudinal study. *Developmental Psychology, 31,* 531–539. doi:10.1037/0012-1649.31.4.531

Chen, X., Rubin, K. H., & Sun, Y. (1992). Social reputation and peer relationships in Chinese and Canadian children: A cross-cultural study. *Child Development, 63,* 1336–1343. doi:10.1111/j.1467-8624.1992.tb01698.x

Chen, X., Wang, L., & Cao, R. (2011). Shyness-sensitivity and unsociability in rural Chinese children: Relations with social, school, and psychological adjustment. *Child Development, 82,* 1531–1543. doi:10.1111/j.1467-8624.2011.01616.x

Chen, X., Wang, L., & Wang, Z. (2009). Shyness-sensitivity and social, school, and psychological adjustment in rural migrant and urban children in China. *Child Development, 80,* 1499–1513. doi:10.1111/j.1467-8624.2009.01347.x

Chen, Z., Mo, L., & Honomichl, R. (2004). Having the memory of an elephant: Long-term retrieval and the use of analogues in problem solving. *Journal of Experimental Psychology: General, 133,* 415–433.

Chen, Z., & Siegler, R. (2000). Across the great divide: Bridging the gap between understanding of toddlers' and older children's thinking. *Monographs of the Society for Research in Child Development, 65*(2, Serial No. 261).

Cheour, M., Martynova, O., Näätänen, R., Erkkola, R., Sillanpää, M., Kero, P., . . . Hämäläinen, H. (2002, February 7). Speech sounds learned by sleeping newborns. *Nature, 415,* 599–600.

Cherney, I. D., & London, K. (2006). Gender-linked differences in the toys, television shows, computer games, and outdoor activities of 5- to 13-year-old children. *Sex Roles, 54,* 717–726. doi:10.1007/s11199-006-9037-8

Cheryan, S., Ziegler, S. A., Montoya, A. K., & Jiang, L. (2017). Why are some STEM fields more gender balanced than others? *Psychological Bulletin, 143*(1), 1–35. http://dx.doi.org/10.1037/bul0000052

Chi, M. T. H., & Ceci, S. J. (1987). Content knowledge: Its role, representation, and restructuring in memory development. In H. W. Reese (Ed.), *Advances in child development and behavior* (Vol. 20, pp. 91–142). San Diego, CA: Academic Press.

Chiappe, P., & Siegel, L. S. (1999). Phonological awareness and reading acquisition in English- and Punjabi-speaking Canadian children. *Journal of Educational Psychology, 91*(1), 20–28.

Child Abuse Prevention and Treatment Act of 2010. Public Law 111-320, § 5101, Note (§ 3).

Child and Family Services Reviews Information Portal. (2019). *Types of maltreatment.* Retrieved from https://training.cfsrportal.acf.hhs.gov/book/export/html/2979

Child Care Aware of America. (2018). *The U.S. and the high cost of child care.* Retrieved from https://usa.childcareaware.org/advocacy-public-policy/resources/research/costofcare/

Child Trends Data Bank. (2015). *High school dropout rates: Indicators on children and youth.* Retrieved from http://www.childtrends.org/

Child Trends Data Bank. (2016). *Children's exposure to violence: Indicators on children and youth.* Retrieved from http://www.childtrends.org/

Children's Defense Organization. (2018, September 12). *Child poverty in America, 2017: National analysis.* Retrieved from https://www.childrensdefense.org/policy/resources/fact-sheets-and-issue-briefs/

Chisholm, J. S. (1983). *Navajo infancy: An ethological study of child development.* Hawthorne, NY: Aldine.

Chisholm, K. (1998). A three-year follow-up of attachment and indiscriminate friendliness in children adopted from Romanian orphanages. *Child Development, 69*(4), 1092–1106.

Choi, K., & Kirkorian, H. L. (2016). Touch or watch to learn? Toddlers' object retrieval using contingent and noncontingent video. *Psychological Science, 27*(5), 726–736.

Choi, U. S., Sung, Y. W., Hong, S., Chung, J. Y., & Ogawa, S. (2015). Structural and functional plasticity specific to musical training with wind instruments. *Frontiers in Human Neuroscience, 9,* 597. doi:10.3389/fnhum.2015.00597

Chomsky, N. (1957). *Syntactic Structures.* The Hague, Netherlands/Paris, France: Mouton.

Chomsky, N. (1959). A review of B. F. Skinner's *Verbal Behavior. Language, 35,* 26–58.

Chomsky, N. (1988). *Language and problems of knowledge: The Managua lectures (Vol. 16).* Cambridge, MA: MIT Press.

Chouinard, M. M. (2007). Children's questions: A mechanism for cognitive development. *Monographs of the Society for Research in Child Development, 72*(1, Serial No. 286).

Chugani, H. T., Behen, M. E., Muzik, O., Juhasz, C., Nagy, F., & Chugani, D. C. (2001). Local brain functional activity following early deprivation: A study of postinstitutionalized Romanian orphans. *Neuroimage, 14,* 1290–1301. doi:10.1006/nimg.2001.0917

Chung, S., & McBride, A. M. (2015). Social and emotional learning in middle school curricula: A service learning model based on positive youth development. *Children and Youth Services Review, 53,* 192–200. doi:10.1016/j.childyouth.2015.04.008

Chung-Hall, J., & Chen, X. (2010). Aggressive and prosocial peer group functioning: Effects on children's social, school, and psychological adjustment. *Social Development, 19,* 659–680. doi:10.1111/j.1467-9507.2009.00556.x

Church, R. B. (1999). Using gesture and speech to capture transitions in learning. *Cognitive Development, 14,* 313–342.

Cianciolo, A. T., Matthew, C., Sternberg, R. J., & Wagner, R. K. (2006). Tacit knowledge, practical intelligence, and expertise. In K. A. Ericsson, N. Charness, P. J. Feltovich, & R. R. Hoffman (Eds.), *The Cambridge handbook of expertise and expert performance* (pp. 613–632). New York: Cambridge University Press.

Cicchetti, D., & Ng, R. (2014). Emotional development in maltreated children. In K. H. Lagattuta (Ed.), *Children and emotion: New insights into developmental affective sciences* (pp. 29–41). Basel, Switzerland: Karger.

Cicchetti, D., & Rogosch, F. A. (1996). Equifinality and multifinality in developmental psychopathology. *Development and Psychopathology, 8,* 597–600. doi:10.1017/S0954579400007318

Cicchetti, D., Rogosch, F. A., & Thibodeau, E. L. (2012). The effects of child maltreatment on early signs of antisocial behavior: Genetic moderation by tryptophan hydroxylase, serotonin transporter, and monoamine oxidase A genes. *Development and Psychopathology, 24,* 907–928.

Cicchetti, D., & Toth, S. L. (2006). Developmental psychopathology and preventive intervention. In W. Damon & R. M. Lerner (Series Eds.) & K. A. Renninger & I. E. Sigel (Vol. Eds.), *Handbook of child psychology: Vol. 4. Child psychology in practice* (6th ed., pp. 497–547). Hoboken, NJ: Wiley.

Cillessen, A. H. N. (2011). Toward a theory of popularity. In A. H. N. Cillessen, D. Schwartz, & L. Mayeux, *Popularity in the peer system* (pp. 273–299). New York: Guilford Press.

Cillessen, A. H. N., & Mayeux, L. (2004). From censure to reinforcement: Developmental changes in the association between aggression and social status. *Child Development, 75,* 147–163. doi:10.2307/3696572

Cimpian, A., & Scott, R. M. (2012). Children expect generic knowledge to be widely shared. *Cognition, 123,* 419–433. doi:10.1016/j.cognition.2012.02.003

Cimpian, J. R., Lubienski, S. T., Timmer, J. D., Makowski, M. B., & Miller, E. K. (2016). Have gender gaps in math closed? Achievement, teacher perceptions, and learning behaviors across two ECLS-K cohorts. AERA Open. doi:10.1177/2332858416673617

Ciocanel, O., Power, K., Eriksen, A., & Gillings, K. (2017). Effectiveness of positive youth development interventions: A meta-analysis of randomized controlled trials. *Journal of Youth and Adolescence, 46,* 483–504. doi:10.1007/s10964-016-0555-6

Cito, G., Luisi, S., Mezzesdimi, A., Cavicchioli, C., Calonaci, G., & Petraglia, F. (2005). Maternal position during non-stress test and fetal heart rate patterns. *Acta Obstetricia et Gynecologica Scandinavica, 84,* 335–338. doi:10.1111/j.0001-6349.2005.00644.x

Clark, E. V. (1993). *The lexicon in acquisition.* Cambridge: Cambridge University Press.

Clark, T. C., Lucassen, M. F., Bullen, P., Denny, S. J., Fleming, T. M., Robinson, E. M., & Rossen, F. V. (2014). The health and well-being of transgender high school students: Results from the New Zealand adolescent health survey (Youth'12). *Journal of Adolescent Health, 55*(1), 93–99.

Clarke-McLean, J. G. (1996). Social networks among incarcerated juvenile offenders. *Social Development, 5,* 203–217. doi:10.1111/j.1467-9507.1996.tb00081.x

Clearfield, M. (2006). A dynamic account of infant looking behavior in small and large number tasks. In M. A. Vanchevsky (Ed.), *Focus on cognitive psychology research* (pp. 59–83). New York: Nova Science.

Clearfield, M. W., Dineva, E., Smith, L. B., Diedrich, F. J., & Thelen, E. (2009). Cue salience and infant perseverative reaching: Tests of the dynamic field theory. *Developmental Science, 12,* 26–40. doi:10.1111/j.1467-7687.2008.00769.x

Clément, M. E., & Chamberland, C. (2014). Trends in corporal punishment and attitudes in favor of this practice: Toward a change in societal norms. *Canadian Journal of Community Mental Health, 33,* 13–17. doi:10.7870/cjcmh-2014-013

Clifton, R. K., Rochat, P., Litovsky, R. Y., & Perris, E. E. (1991). Object representation guides infants' reaching in the dark. *Journal of Experimental Psychology: Human Perception and Performance, 17,* 323–329. doi:10.1037/0096-1523.17.2.323

Clore, G. (1981). *The wit and wisdom of Benjamin Clore.* Unpublished manuscript.

Coe, C. L., & Lubach, G. R. (2008). Fetal programming: Prenatal origins of health and illness. *Current Directions in Psychological Science, 17,* 36–41. doi:10.1111/j.1467-8721.2008.00544.x

Coe, H., Chan, J., & Freeman, J. (2016). Chapter 4: Peers. In J. Freeman, M. King, & W. Pickett (Eds.), *Health Behaviour in School-Aged Children (HBSC) in Canada: Focus on Relationships.* Public Health Agency of Canada. Retrieved from http://healthycanadians.gc.ca/publications/science-research-sciences-recherches/health-behaviour-children-canada-2015-comportements-sante-jeunes/index-eng.php

Cohain, J. S., Buxbaum, R. E., & Mankuta, D. (2017). Spontaneous first trimester miscarriage rates per woman among parous women with 1 or more pregnancies of 24 weeks or more. *BMC Pregnancy and Childbirth, 17*(1), 437.

Cohen, D. J. (1980). The pathology of the self in primary childhood autism and Gilles de la Tourette syndrome. *Psychiatric Clinics of North America, 3,* 383–402.

Cohen, J. (1988). *Statistical power analysis for the behavioral sciences* (2nd ed.). Hillsdale, NJ: Erlbaum.

Cohen, J. (2018). What now for human gene editing? *Science, 362*(6419), 1090–1092.

Cohen, L. B., & Cashon, C. H. (2006). Infant cognition. In W. Damon & R. M. Lerner (Series Eds.) & D. Kuhn & R. S. Siegler (Vol. Eds.), *Handbook of child psychology: Vol. 2. Cognition, perception, and language* (6th ed., pp. 214–251). Hoboken, NJ: Wiley.

Coie, J. D., & Dodge, K. A. (1983). Continuities and changes in children's social status: A five-year longitudinal study. *Merrill-Palmer Quarterly, 29,* 261–282.

Coie, J. D., & Dodge, K. A. (1998). Aggression and antisocial behavior. In W. Damon (Series Ed.) & N. Eisenberg (Vol. Ed.), *Handbook of child psychology: Vol. 3. Social, emotional, and personality development* (5th ed., pp. 779–862). Hoboken, NJ: Wiley.

Coie, J. D., Dodge, K. A., & Kupersmidt, J. B. (1990). Peer group behavior and social status. In S. R. Asher & J. D. Coie (Eds.), *Peer rejection in childhood* (pp. 17–59). New York: Cambridge University Press.

Coker, T. R., Austin, S. B., & Schuster, M. A. (2010). The health and health care of lesbian, gay, and bisexual adolescents. *Annual Review of Public Health, 31,* 457–477. doi:10.1146/annurev.publhealth.012809.103636

Colby, A., & Kohlberg, L. (1987a). *The measurement of moral judgment* (Vol. 1). New York: Cambridge University Press.

Colby, A., & Kohlberg, L. (1987b). *The measurement of moral judgment* (Vol. 2). New York: Cambridge University Press.

Colby, A., Kohlberg, L., Gibbs, J., Lieberman, M., Fischer, K., & Saltzstein, H. D. (1983). A longitudinal study of moral judgment. *Monographs of the Society for Research in Child Development, 48*(1–2, Serial No. 200), 1–124. doi:10.2307/1165935

Cole, P. M. (1986). Children's spontaneous control of facial expression. *Child Development, 57,* 1309–1321.

Cole, P. M., & Dennis, T. A. (1998). Variations on a theme: Culture and the meaning of socialization practices and child competence. *Psychological Inquiry, 9,* 276–278.

Cole, P. M., & Jacobs, A. E. (2018). From children's expressive control to emotion regulation: Looking back, looking ahead. *European Journal of Developmental Psychology, 15*(6), 658–677. doi:10.1080/17405629.2018.1438888

Cole, P. M., & Tamang, B. L. (1998). Nepali children's ideas about emotional displays in hypothetical challenges. *Developmental Psychology, 34,* 640–646.

Cole, P. M., Tamang, B. L., & Shrestha, S. (2006). Cultural variations in the socialization of young children's anger and shame. *Child Development, 77,* 1237–1251. doi:10.1111/j.1467-8624.2006.00931.x

Cole, P. M., Tan, P. Z., Hall, S. E., Zhang, Y., Crnic, K. A., Blair, C. B., & Li, R. (2011). Developmental changes in anger expression and attention focus: Learning to wait. *Developmental Psychology, 47,* 1078–1089. doi:10.1037/a0023813

Cole, S. W. (2009). Social regulation of human gene expression. *Current Directions in Psychological Science, 18,* 132–137. doi:10.1111/j.1467-8721.2009.01623.x

Cole, W. G., Lingeman, J. M., & Adolph, K. E. (2012). Go naked: Diapers affect infant walking. *Developmental Science, 15,* 783–790. doi:10.1111/j.1467-7687.2012.01169.x

Coleman, J. R., Bryois, J., Gaspar, H. A., Jansen, P. R., Savage, J. E., Skene, N., . . . Hjerling-Leffler, J. (2019). Biological annotation of genetic loci associated with intelligence in a meta-analysis of 87,740 individuals. *Molecular Psychiatry, 24*(2), 182–197.

Coley, J. D. (2000). On the importance of comparative research: The case of folkbiology. *Child Development, 71,* 82–90.

Coley, R. L., & Lombardi, C. M. (2013). Does maternal employment following childbirth support or inhibit low-income children's long-term development? *Child Development, 84,* 178–197. doi:10.1111/j.1467-8624.2012.01840.x

Collie, R., & Hayne, H. (1999). Deferred imitation by 6- and 9-month-old infants: More evidence for declarative memory. *Developmental Psychobiology, 35,* 83–90.

Collier, L. (2018). Young victims of the opioid crisis. *Monitor on Psychology, 49,* 18–20.

Collignon, O., Dormal, G., de Heering, A., Lepore, F., Lewis, T. L., & Maurer, D. (2015). Long-lasting cross-modal cortical reorganization triggered by brief postnatal visual deprivation. *Current Biology, 25*(18), 2379–2383.

Collins, S. A., Surmala, P., Osborne, G., Greenberg, C., Bathory, L. W., Edmunds-Potvin, S., & Arbour, L. (2012). Causes and risk factors for infant mortality in Nunavut, Canada 1999–2011. *BMC Pediatrics, 12*(1), 1.

Collins, W. A., Hennighausen, K. C., Schmit, D. T., & Sroufe, L. A. (1997). Developmental precursors of romantic relationships: A longitudinal analysis. In S. Shulman & W. A. Collins (Eds.), *New directions for child and adolescent development: No. 78. Romantic relationships in adolescence: Developmental perspectives* (pp. 69–84). San Francisco: Jossey-Bass.

Collisson, B. A., Graham, S. A., Preston, J. L., Rose, M. S., McDonald, S., & Tough, S. (2016). Risk and protective factors for late talking: An epidemiologic investigation. *Journal of Pediatrics, 172,* 168–174.

Colombo, J., & Richman, W. A. (2002). Infant timekeeping: Attention and temporal estimation in 4-month-olds. *Psychological Science, 13,* 475–479.

Colombo, J., Shaddy, D. J., Richman, W. A., Maikranz, J. M., & Blaga, O. M. (2004). The developmental course of habituation in infancy and preschool outcome. *Infancy, 5,* 1–38. doi:10.1207/s15327078in0501_1

Combs-Ronto, L., Olson, S., Lunkenheimer, E., & Sameroff, A. (2009). Interactions between maternal parenting and children's early disruptive behavior: Bidirectional associations across the transition from preschool to school entry. *Journal of Abnormal Child Psychology, 37,* 1151–1163. doi:10.1007/s10802-009-9332-2

Common Sense. (2018). Social media, social life: Teens reveal their experiences. Common Sense Media: San Francisco, CA. Retrieved from https://www.commonsensemedia.org/research/social-media-social-life-2018.

Compian, L., Gowen, L. K., & Hayward, C. (2004). Peripubertal girls' romantic and platonic involvement with boys: Associations with body image and depression symptoms. *Journal of Research on Adolescence, 14,* 23–47.

Compton, D. L., Miller, A. C., Elleman, A. M., & Steacy, L. M. (2014). Have we forsaken reading theory in the name of "quick fix" interventions for children with reading disability? *Scientific Studies of Reading, 18*(1), 55–73. doi:10.1080/10888438.2013.836200

Conde-Agudelo, A., & Díaz-Rossello, J. L. (2014). Kangaroo mother care to reduce morbidity and mortality in low birthweight infants. *Cochrane Database of Systematic Reviews, 4,* Art. No.: CD002771. doi:10.1002/14651858.CD002771.pub3

Condry, J. C., & Ross, D. F. (1985). Sex and aggression: The influence of gender label on the perception of aggression in children. *Child Development, 56,* 225–233. doi:10.2307/1130189

Conduct Problems Prevention Research Group. (1999a). Initial impact of the Fast Track prevention trial for conduct problems: I. The high-risk sample. *Journal of Consulting and Clinical Psychology, 67,* 631–647. doi:10.1037/0022-006X.67.5.631

Conduct Problems Prevention Research Group. (1999b). Initial impact of the Fast Track prevention trial for conduct problems: II. Classroom effects. *Journal of Consulting and Clinical Psychology, 67,* 648–657. doi:10.1037/0022-006X.67.5.648

Conduct Problems Prevention Research Group. (2002). The implementation of the Fast Track Program: An example of a large-scale prevention science efficacy trial. *Journal of Abnormal Child Psychology, 30*(1), 1–17.

Conger, R. D., Ge, X., Elder, G. H., Jr., Lorenz, F. O., & Simons, R. L. (1994). Economic stress, coercive family process, and developmental problems of adolescents. *Child Development, 65,* 541–561. doi:10.2307/1131401

Conner, D. B., Knight, D. K., & Cross, D. R. (1997). Mothers' and fathers' scaffolding of their 2-year-olds during problem-solving and literacy interactions. *British Journal of Developmental Psychology, 15,* 323–338. doi:10.1111/j.2044-835X.1997.tb00524.x

Connolly, M. D. Zervos, M. J., Barone, C. J., Johnson, C. C., & Joseph C. L. (2016). The mental health of transgender youth: Advances in understanding. *Journal of Adolescent Health, 59*(5), 489–495. doi:10.1016/j.jadohealth.2016.06.012

Conradt, E. (2017). Using principles of behavioral epigenetics to advance research on early-life stress. *Child Development Perspectives, 11*(2), 107–112.

Conry-Murray, C. (2015). Children's judgments of inequitable distributions that conform to gender norms. *Merrill-Palmer Quarterly, 61,* 319–344.

Constantino, J. N., Kennon-McGill, S., Weichselbaum, C., Marrus, N., Haider, A., Glowinski, A. L., . . . Jones, W. (2017). Infant viewing of social scenes is under genetic control and is atypical in autism. *Nature, 547*(7663), 340.

Conway, C. C., Keenan-Miller, D., Hammen, C., Lind, P. A., Najman, J. M., & Brennan, P. A. (2012). Coaction of stress and serotonin transporter genotype in predicting aggression at the transition to adulthood. *Journal of Clinical Child and Adolescent Psychology, 41,* 53–63. doi:10.1080/15374416.2012.632351

Cooklin, A. R., Westrupp, E., Strazdins, L., Giallo, R., Martin, A., & Nicholson, J. M. (2015), Mothers' work–family conflict and enrichment: Associations with parenting quality and couple relationship. *Child, 41*(2), 266–277. doi:10.1111/cch.12137

Cooley, C. H. (1902). *Human nature and the social order.* New York: Charles Scribner's Sons.

Cooper, C. R., & Grotevant, H. D. (1987). Gender issues in the interface of family experience and adolescents' friendship and dating identity. *Journal of Youth & Adolescence, 16,* 247–264.

Cooper, R. P., & Aslin, R. N. (1994). Developmental differences in infant attention to the spectral properties of infant-directed speech. *Child Development, 65,* 1663–1677.

Cooper, S. M., & McLoyd, V. C. (2011). Racial barrier socialization and the well-being of African American adolescents: The moderating role of mother–adolescent relationship quality. *Journal of Research on Adolescence, 21,* 895–903. doi:10.1111/j.1532-7795.2011.00749.x

Coplan, R. J., Arbeau, K. A., & Armer, M. (2008). Don't fret, be supportive! Maternal characteristics linking child shyness to psychosocial and school adjustment in kindergarten. *Journal of Abnormal Child Psychology, 36*(3), 359–371. doi:10.1007/s10802-007-9183-7

Coplan, R. J., & Armer, M. (2007). A "multitude" of solitude: A closer look at social withdrawal and nonsocial play in early childhood. *Child Development Perspectives, 1,* 26–32. doi:10.1111/j.1750-8606.2007.00006.x

Corbeil, M., Trehub, S. E., & Peretz, I. (2015). Singing delays the onset of infant distress. *Infancy, 21,* 373–391.

Cordes, S., & Brannon, E. M. (2008). Quantitative competencies in infancy. *Developmental Science, 11*(6), 803–808. doi:10.1111/j.1467-7687.2008.00770.x

Corenblum, B. (2014). Relationships between racial–ethnic identity, self-esteem and in-group attitudes among First Nation children. *Journal of Youth and Adolescence, 43*(3), 387–404.

Cormier, D. C., Kennedy, K. E., & Aquilina, A. M. (2016). Test review: "Wechsler, D. (2014)," Wechsler Intelligence Scale for Children: Canadian 322 (WISC-V CDN). Toronto, Ontario: Pearson Canada Assessment. *Canadian Journal of School Psychology, 31*(4), 322–334.

Cornell, C. (2011). The real cost of raising a child. *Money Sense Magazine.* Retrieved from http://www.-money sense.ca/2011/08/10/the-real-cost-of-raising-kids/

Cornell, E. H., Heth, C. D., Kneubuhler, Y., & Sehgal, S. (1996). Serial position effects in children's route reversal errors: Implications for police search operations. *Applied Cognitive Psychology, 10,* 301–326.

Corsi, D. J., Hsu, H., Weiss, D., Fell, D. B., & Walker, M. (2019). Trends and correlates of cannabis use in pregnancy: A population-based study in Ontario, Canada from 2012 to 2017. *Canadian Journal of Public Health, 110,* 76–84.

Costa, A., Hernández, M., & Sebastián-Gallés, N. (2008). Bilingualism aids conflict resolution: Evidence from the ANT task. *Cognition, 106,* 59–86. doi:10.1016/j.cognition.2006.12.013

Costello, D. M., Swendsen, J., Rose, J. S., & Dierker, L. C. (2008). Risk and protective factors associated with trajectories of depressed mood from adolescence to early adulthood. *Journal of Consulting and Clinical Psychology, 76,* 173–183. doi:10.1037/0022-006X.76.2.173

Costello, E. J., Copeland, W., & Angold, A. (2011). Trends in psychopathology across the adolescent years: What changes when children become adolescents, and when adolescents become adults? *Journal of Child Psychology and Psychiatry, 52,* 1015–1025. doi:10.1111/j.1469-7610.2011.02446.x

Costigan, C. L., Koryzma, C. M., Hua, J. M., & Chance, L. J. (2010). Ethnic identity, achievement, and psychological adjustment: Examining risk and resilience among youth from immigrant Chinese families in Canada. *Cultural Diversity and Ethnic Minority Psychology, 16*(2), 264–273.

Côté, S. M., Borge, A. I., Geoffroy, M.-C., Rutter, M., & Tremblay, R. E. (2008). Nonmaternal care in infancy and emotional/behavioral difficulties at 4 years old: Moderation by family risk characteristics. *Developmental Psychology, 44,* 155–168. doi:10.1037/0012-1649.44.1.155

Côté, S. M., Doyle, O., Petitclerc, A., & Timmins, L. (2013). Child care in infancy and cognitive performance until middle childhood in the Millennium Cohort Study. *Child Development, 84,* 1191–1208. doi:10.1111/cdev.12049

Côté, S., Vaillancourt, T., LeBlanc, J. C., Nagin, D. S., & Tremblay, R. E. (2006). The development of physical aggression from toddlerhood to pre-adolescence: A nationwide longitudinal study of Canadian children. *Journal of Abnormal Child Psychology, 34*(1), 68–82.

Courage, M. L., Edison, S. C., & Howe, M. L. (2004). Variability in the early development of visual self-recognition. *Infant Behavior and Development, 27,* 509–532. doi:10.1016/j.infbeh.2004.06.001

Cowan, N. (2016). Working memory maturation: Can we get at the essence of cognitive growth? *Perspectives on Psychological Science, 11*(2), 239–264. doi:10.1177/1745691615621279

Cowell, J. M., Lee, K., Malcolm-Smith, S., Selcuk, B., Zhou, X., & Decety, J. (2017). The development of generosity and moral cognition across five cultures. *Developmental Science, 20,* e12403. doi:10.1111/desc.12403

Cox, J. E., Harris, S. K., Conroy, K., Engelhart, T., Vyavaharkar, A., Federico, A., & Woods, E. R. (2019). A parenting and life skills intervention for teen mothers: A randomized controlled trial. *Pediatrics, 143,* e20182303.

Coyle, T. R., Pillow, D. R., Snyder, A. C., & Kochunov, P. (2011). Processing speed mediates the development of general intelligence (g) in adolescence. *Psychological Science, 22,* 1265–1269. doi:10.1177/0956797611418243

Coyne, S. M., & Archer, J. (2005). The relationship between indirect and physical aggression on television and in real life. *Social Development, 14,* 324–338. doi:10.1111/j.1467-9507.2005.00304.x

Coyne, S. M., Archer, J., & Eslea, M. (2004). Cruel intentions on television and in real life: Can viewing indirect aggression increase viewers' subsequent indirect aggression? *Journal of Experimental Child Psychology, 88,* 234–253. doi:10.1016/j.jecp.2004.03.001

Cragg, L., & Gilmore, C. (2014). Skills underlying mathematics: The role of executive function in the development of mathematics proficiency. *Trends in Neuroscience and Education, 3*(2), 63–68. doi:10.1016/j.tine.2013.12.001

Craig, S. L., McInroy, L., McCready, L. T., & Alaggia, R. (2015). Media: A catalyst for resilience in lesbian, gay, bisexual, transgender, and queer youth. *Journal of LGBT Youth, 12*(3), 254–275. http://dx.doi.org/10.1080/19361653.2015.1040193

Craig, W., Lambe, L., & McIver, T. (2016). Chapter 15: Bullying and fighting. In J. Freeman, M. King, & W. Pickett (Eds.), *Health behaviour in school-aged children (HBSC) in Canada: Focus on relationships.* Public Health Agency of Canada. Retrieved from http://healthycanadians.gc.ca/publications/science-research-sciences-recherches/health-behaviour-children-canada-2015-comportements-sante-jeunes/index-eng.php

Craik, F. I., Bialystok, E., & Freedman, M. (2010). Delaying the onset of Alzheimer disease: Bilingualism as a form of cognitive reserve. *Neurology, 75*(19), 1726–1729.

Crean, H. F., & Johnson, D. B. (2013). Promoting Alternative Thinking Strategies (PATHS) and elementary school aged children's aggression: Results from a cluster randomized trial. *American Journal of Community Psychology, 52,* 56–72. doi:10.1007/s10464-013-9576-4

Crick, N. R., & Dodge, K. A. (1994). A review and reformulation of social information-processing mechanisms in children's social adjustment. *Psychological Bulletin, 115,* 74–101. doi:10.1037/0033-2909.115.1.74

Crick, N. R., & Dodge, K. A. (1996). Social information-processing mechanisms in reactive and proactive aggression. *Child Development, 67,* 993–1002. doi:10.2307/1131875

Crick, N. R., Casas, J. F., & Mosher, M. (1997). Relational and overt aggression in preschool. *Developmental Psychology, 33,* 579–588. doi:10.1037/0012-1649.33.4.579

Cristia, A., Dupoux, E., Gurven, M., & Stieglitz, J. (2017). Child-directed speech is infrequent in a forager-farmer population: A time allocation study. *Child Development, 90,* 759–773.

Crocetti, E. (2017). Identify formation in adolescence: The dynamic of forming and consolidating identity commitments. *Child Development Perspectives, 11,* 145–150. doi:10.1111/cdep.12226

Croft, A., Schmader, T., Block, K., & Baron, A. S. (2014). The second shift reflected in the second generation: Do parents' gender roles at home predict children's aspirations? *Psychological Science, 25,* 1418–1428.

Crosby, D. A., Dowsett, C. J., Gennetian, L. A., & Huston, A. C. (2010). A tale of two methods: Comparing regression and instrumental variables estimates of the effects of preschool child care type on the subsequent externalizing behavior of children in low-income families. *Developmental Psychology, 46,* 1030–1048. doi:10.1037/a0020384

Crosby, K. A., Fireman, G. D., & Clopton, J. R. (2011). Differences between non-aggressive, rejected children and popular children during peer collaboration. *Child & Family Behavior Therapy, 33*(1), 1–19.

Cross, D., Epstein, M., Hearn, L., Slee, P., Shaw, T., & Monks, H. (2011). National Safe Schools Framework: Policy and practice to reduce bullying in Australian schools. *International Journal of Behavioral Development, 35,* 398–404. doi:10.1177/0165025411407456

Cross, D., Shaw, T., Hadwen, K., Cardoso, P., Slee, P., Roberts, C., & Barnes, A. (2016). Longitudinal impact of the Cyber Friendly Schools program on adolescents' cyberbullying behavior. *Aggressive Behavior, 42,* 166–180. doi:10.1002/ab.21609

Crowley, K., Callanan, M. A., Tenenbaum, H. R., & Allen, E. (2001). Parents explain more often to boys than to girls during shared scientific thinking. *Psychological Science, 12,* 258–261. doi:10.1111/1467-9280.00347

Cruz, J. E., Emery, R. E., & Turkheimer, E. (2012). Peer network drinking predicts increased alcohol use from adolescence to early adulthood after controlling for genetic and shared environmental selection. *Developmental Psychology, 48,* 1390–1402. doi:10.1037/a0027515

Cummings, E. M., & Davies, P. T. (2002). Effects of marital conflict on children: Recent advances and emerging themes in process-oriented research. *Journal of Child Psychology and Psychiatry, 43,* 31–63. doi:10.1111/1469-7610.00003

Cunningham, A. J., & Stevens, L. (2011). *Helping a child be a witness in court: 101 things to know, say and do.* Centre for Children and Families in the Justice System—Centre des enfants, des familles et le système de justice.

Curry, D., Schmitt, M. J., & Waldron, S. (1996). A framework for adult numeracy standards: The mathematical skills and abilities adults need to be equipped for the future. Retrieved from http://shell04.theworld.com/std/anpn//framewk

Curtin, S., Mintz, T. H., & Christiansen, M. H. (2005). Stress changes the representational landscape: Evidence from word segmentation. *Cognition, 96,* 233–262. doi:10.1016/j.cognition.2004.08.005

Curtiss, S. (1977). *Genie: A psycholinguistic study of a modern-day "wild child."* New York: Academic Press.

Curtiss, S. (1989). The independence and task-specificity of language. In M. H. Bornstein & J. S. Bruner (Eds.), *Interaction in human development* (pp. 105–137). Hillsdale, NJ: Erlbaum.

Cushon, J. A., Vu, L. T., Janzen, B. L., & Muhajarine, N. (2011). Neighborhood poverty impacts children's physical health and well-being over time: Evidence from the Early Development Instrument. *Early Education and Development, 22*(2), 183–205.

Cyr, C., Euser, E. M., Bakermans-Kranenburg, M. J., & van Ijzendoorn, M. H. (2010). Attachment security and disorganization in maltreating and high-risk families: A series of meta-analyses. *Development & Psychopathology, 22,* 87–108.

Daly, M., & Wilson, M. I. (1996). Violence against stepchildren. *Current Directions in Psychological Science, 5,* 77–80. doi:10.1111/1467-8721.ep10772793

Damasio, A. R. (1999). *The feeling of what happens: Body and emotion in the making of consciousness.* New York: Harcourt Brace.

Damon, W., & Hart, D. (1988). *Self-understanding in childhood and adolescence.* Cambridge: Cambridge University Press.

Danese, A., & McEwen, B. S. (2012). Adverse child experiences, allostasis, allostatic load, and age-related disease. *Physiology and Behavior, 106,* 29–39. doi:10.1016/j.physbeh

Darling, N., & Steinberg, L. (1993). Parenting style as context: An integrative model. *Psychological Bulletin, 113,* 487–496. doi:10.1037/0033-2909.113.3.487

Dasgupta, N., & Stout, J. G. (2014). Girls and women in science, technology, engineering, and mathematics: STEMing the tide and broadening participation in STEM careers. *Policy Insights from the Behavioral and Brain Sciences, 1*(1), 21–29. doi:10.1177/2372732214549471

Davidov, M., & Grusec, J. E. (2006). Untangling the links of parental responsiveness to distress and warmth to child outcomes. *Child Dvelopment, 77*(1), 44–58.

Davidson, J., Dunne, R., Eccles, J. S., Engle, A., Greenberg, M., Jennings, P., . . . Roeser, R. W. (2012). Contemplative practices and mental training: Prospects for American education. *Child Development Perspectives, 6*(2), 146–153.

Davies, P. T., Cummings, E. M., & Winter, M. A. (2004). Pathways between profiles of family functioning, child security in the interparental subsystem, and child psychological problems. *Development and Psychopathology, 16,* 525–550. doi:10.1017/S0954579404004651

Davies, P. T., Sturge-Apple, M. L., Cicchetti, D., Manning, L. G., & Vonhold, S. E. (2012). Pathways and processes of risk in associations among maternal antisocial personality symptoms, interparental aggression, and preschooler's psychopathology. *Development and Psychopathology, 24,* 807–832. doi:10.1017/S0954579412000387

Davis, O. S. P., Band, G., Pirinen, M., Haworth, C. M. A., Meaburn, E. L., . . . Spencer, C. C. A. (2014). The correlation between reading and mathematics ability at age twelve has a substantial genetic component. *Nature Communications, 5,* 4204.

Dawson, G., Rogers, S., Munson, J., Smith, M., Winter, J., Greenson, J., . . . Varley, J. (2010). Randomized, controlled trial of an intervention for toddlers with autism: The Early Start Denver Model. *Pediatrics, 125,* e17–e23. doi:10.1542/peds.2009-0958

Day, J. K., Perez-Brumer, A., & Russell, S. T. (2018). Safe schools? Transgender youth's school experiences and perceptions of school climate. *Journal of Youth and Adolescence, 47*(8), 1731–1742. http://dx.doi.org/10.1007/s10964-018-0866-x

de Boysson-Bardies, B. (1999). *How language comes to children: From birth to two years* (M. B. DeBevoise, Trans.). Cambridge, MA: MIT Press. (Original work published 1996)

De Brito, S. A., Hodgins, S., McCrory, E. J. P., Mechelli, A., Wilke, M., Jones, A. P., & Viding, E. (2009). Structural neuroimaging and the antisocial brain: Main findings and methodological challenges. *Criminal Justice and Behavior, 36,* 1173–1186. doi:10.1177/0093854809342883

De Goede, I. H. A., Branje, S. J. T., & Meeus, W. H. J. (2009). Developmental changes and gender differences in adolescents' perceptions of friendships. *Journal of Adolescence, 32,* 1105–1123. doi:10.1016/j.adolescence.2009.03.002

de Guzman, M. R. T., Carlo, G., & Edwards, C. P. (2008). Prosocial behaviors in context: Examining the role of children's social companions. *International Journal of Behavioral Development, 32,* 522–530. doi:10.1177/0165025408095557

de Heering, A., & Maurer, D. (2014). Face memory deficits in patients deprived of early visual input by bilateral congenital cataracts. *Developmental Psychobiology, 56*(1), 96–108.

de Hevia, M. D., & Spelke, E. S. (2010). Number-space mapping in human infants. *Psychological Science, 21,* 653–660. doi:10.1177/0956797610366091

de Rooij, S. R., Wouters, H., Yonker, J. E., Painter, R. C., & Roseboom, T. J. (2010). Prenatal undernutrition and cognitive function in late adulthood. *Proceedings of the National Academy of Sciences of the United States of America, 107,* 16881–16886.

de Wied, M., van Boxtel, A., Matthys, W., & Meeus, W. (2012). Verbal, facial and autonomic responses to empathy-eliciting film clips by disruptive male adolescents with high versus low callous-unemotional traits. *Journal of Abnormal Child Psychology, 40,* 211–223. doi:10.1007/s10802-011-9557-8

Deák, G. O. (2015, August). When and where do infants follow gaze? *2015 Joint IEEE International Conference on Development and Learning and Epigenetic Robotics (ICDL-EpiRob),* Brown University (pp. 182–187). doi:10.1109/DEVLRN.2015.7346138

DeAnda, S., Hendrickson, K., Zesiger, P., Poulin-Dubois, D., & Friend, M. (2016). Lexical access in the second year: A cross-linguistic study of monolingual and bilingual vocabulary development. *San Diego Linguistic Papers, 6,* 14–28.

Deary, I. J. (2012). Intelligence. *Annual Review of Psychology, 63,* 453–482.

Deater-Deckard, K., & Dodge, K. A. (1997). Externalizing behavior problems and discipline revisited: Nonlinear effects and variation by culture, context, and gender. *Psychological Inquiry, 8,* 161–175. doi:10.1207/s15327965pli0803_1

Deater-Deckard, K., Dodge, K. A., Bates, J. E., & Pettit, G. S. (1995, April). *Risk factors for the development of externalizing behavior problems: Are there ethnic group differences in process?* Paper presented at the biennial meeting of the Society for Research in Child Development, Indianapolis, IN.

Deater-Deckard, K., El Mallah, S., Chang, M., Evans, M. A., & Norton, A. (2014). Student behavioral engagement during mathematics educational video game instruction with 11–14 year olds. *International Journal of Child-Computer Interaction, 2*(3), 101–108. doi:10.1016/j.ijcci.2014.08.001

Deater-Deckard, K., Pike, A., Petrill, S. A., Cutting, A. L., Hughes, C., & O'Connor, T. G. (2001). Nonshared environmental processes in social-emotional development: An observational study of identical twin differences in the preschool period. *Developmental Science, 4*(2), F1–F6. doi:10.1111/1467-7687.00157

Deb-Rinker, P., León, J. A., Gilbert, N. L., Rouleau, J., Andersen, A. M. N., Bjarnadóttir, R. I., . . . Zhang, X. (2015). Differences in perinatal and infant mortality in high-income countries: Artifacts of birth registration or evidence of true differences? *BMC Pediatrics, 15*(1), 112.

DeCasper, A. J., & Spence, M. J. (1986). Prenatal maternal speech influences newborns' perception of speech sounds. *Infant Behavior and Development, 9,* 133–150. doi:10.1016/0163-6383(86)90025-1

DeCasper, A., & Fifer, W. (1980, June 6). Of human bonding: Newborns prefer their mothers' voices. *Science, 208,* 1174–1176.

Deen, B., Richardson, H., Dilks, D. D., Takahashi, A., Keil, B., Wald, L. L., . . . Saxe, R. (2017). Organization of high-level visual cortex in human infants. *Nature Communications, 8,* 13995.

Dehaene, S., & Brannon, E. (Eds.). (2011). *Space, time and number in the brain: Searching for the foundations of mathematical thought.* San Diego, CA: Academic Press.

Dehaene-Lambertz, G. (2017). The human infant brain: A neural architecture able to learn language. *Psychonomic Bulletin & Review, 24*(1), 48–55.

Dehaene-Lambertz, G., Dehaene, S., & Hertz-Pannier, L. (2002, December 6). Functional neuroimaging of speech perception in infants. *Science, 298,* 2013–2015.

DeJesus, J. M., Shutts, K., & Kinzler, K. D. (2018). Mere social knowledge impacts children's consumption and categorization of foods. *Developmental Science, 21*(5), e12627.

Del Rey, R., Casas, J. A., & Ortega, R. (2016). Impact of the ConRed program on different cyberbullying roles. *Aggressive Behavior, 42,* 123–135. doi:10.1002/ab.21608

Delaney, C. (2000). Making babies in a Turkish village. In J. S. DeLoache & A. Gottlieb (Eds.), *A world of babies: Imagined childcare guides for seven societies* (pp. 117–144). New York: Cambridge University Press.

Dellicour, S., Aol, G., Ouma, P., Yan, N., Bigogo, G., Hamel, M. J., . . . Feikin, D. (2016). Weekly miscarriage rates in a community-based prospective cohort study in rural western Kenya. *BMJ Open, 6*(4), e011088.

DeLoache, J. S. (1987, December 11). Rapid change in the symbolic functioning of very young children. *Science, 238,* 1556–1557.

DeLoache, J. S., Chiong, C., Sherman, K., Islam, N., Vanderborght, M., Troseth, G. L., . . . O'Doherty, K. (2010). Do babies learn from baby media? *Psychological Science, 21,* 1570–1574. doi:10.1177/0956797610384145

DeLoache, J. S., & Marzolf, D. P. (1995). The use of dolls to interview young children: Issues of symbolic representation. *Journal of Experimental Child Psychology, 60,* 155–173.

DeLoache, J. S., Miller, K. F., & Rosengren, K. S. (1997). The credible shrinking room: Very young children's performance with symbolic and nonsymbolic relations. *Psychological Science, 8,* 308–313. doi:10.1111/j.1467-9280.1997.tb00443.x

DeLoache, J. S., Pierroutsakos, S. L., Uttal, D. H., Rosengren, K. S., & Gottlieb, A. (1998). Grasping the nature of pictures. *Psychological Science, 9,* 205–210. doi:10.1111/1467-9280.00039

DeLoache, J. S., Simcock, G., & Macari, S. (2007). Planes, trains, automobiles—and tea sets: Extremely intense interests in very young children. *Developmental Psychology, 43*(6), 1579–1586. http://dx.doi.org/10.1037/0012-1649.43.6.1579

DeLoache, J. S., Strauss, M. S., & Maynard, J. (1979). Picture perception in infancy. *Infant Behavior and Development, 2,* 77–89. doi:10.1016/S0163-6383(79)80010-7

DeLoache, J. S., Uttal, D. H., & Rosengren, K. S. (2004, May 14). Scale errors offer evidence for a perception-action dissociation early in life. *Science, 304,* 1027–1029.

Deluty, R. H. (1985). Cognitive mediation of aggressive, assertive, and submissive behavior in children. *International Journal of Behavioral Development, 8,* 355–369. doi:10.1177/016502548500800309

DeMarie-Dreblow, D., & Miller, P. H. (1988). The development of children's strategies for selective attention: Evidence for a transitional period. *Child Development, 59,* 1504–1513.

Denham, S. A. (1986). Social cognition, prosocial behavior, and emotion in preschoolers: Contextual validation. *Child Development, 57,* 194–201.

Denham, S. A. (1998). *Emotional development in young children.* New York: Guilford Press.

Denham, S. A. (2006). The emotional basis of learning and development in early childhood education. In B. Spodek & O. N. Saracho (Eds.), *Handbook of research on the education of young children* (2nd ed., pp. 85–103). Mahwah, NJ: Erlbaum.

Denham, S. A., & Burton, R. (1996). A social-emotional intervention for at-risk 4-year-olds. *Journal of School Psychology, 34,* 225–245. doi:10.1016/0022-4405(96)00013-1

Denham, S. A., Warren-Khot, H. K., Bassett, H. H., Wyatt, T., & Perna, A. (2012). Factor structure of self-regulation in preschoolers: Testing models of a field-based assessment for predicting early school readiness. *Journal of Experimental Child Psychology, 111,* 386–404. doi:10.1016/j.jecp.2011.10.002

Denham, S. A., Zoller, D., & Couchoud, E. A. (1994). Socialization of preschoolers' emotion understanding. *Developmental Psychology, 30,* 928–936.

DeNigris, D., & Brooks, P. J. (2018). The role of language in temporal cognition in 6- to 10-year-old children. *Journal of Cognition and Development, 19*(4), 431–455.

Denison, S., & Xu, F. (2010). Integrating physical constraints in statistical inference by 11-month-old infants. *Cognitive Science, 34,* 885–908. doi:10.1111/j.1551-6709.2010.01111.x

Denison, S., Reed, C., & Xu, F. (2013). The emergence of probabilistic reasoning in very young infants: Evidence from 4.5- and 6-month-olds. *Developmental Psychology, 49,* 243–249. doi:10.1037/a0028278

Denissen, J. J. A., van Aken, M. A. G., & Dubas, J. S. (2009). It takes two to tango: How parents' and adolescents' personalities link to the quality of their mutual relationship. *Developmental Psychology, 45,* 928–941. doi:10.1037/a0016230

Dennis, T., Bendersky, M., Ramsay, D., & Lewis, M. (2006). Reactivity and regulation in children prenatally exposed to cocaine. *Developmental Psychology, 42,* 688–697. doi:10.1037/0012-1649.42.4.688

Dennis, W., & Najarian, P. (1957). Infant development under environmental handicap. *Psychological Monographs: General and Applied, 71*(7), 1–13.

Deoni, S., Dean, D., III, Joelson, S., O'Regan, J., & Schneider, N. (2018). Early nutrition influences developmental myelination and cognition in infants and young children. *Neuroimage, 178,* 649–659.

Department of Statistics Singapore. (2016). General Household Survey 2015. Retrieved from http://www.singstat.gov.sg/publications/publications-and-papers/GHS/ghs2015content

Després, C., Beuter, A., Richer, F., Poitras, K., Veilleux, A., Ayotte, P., . . . Muckle, G. (2005). Neuromotor functions in Inuit preschool children exposed to Pb, PCBs, and Hg. *Neurotoxicology and Teratology, 27,* 245–257. doi:10.1016/j.ntt.2004.12.001

Depue, R. A., & Fu, Y. (2012). Neurobiology and neurochemistry of temperament (adults). In M. R. Zentner & R. L. Shiner (Eds.), *Handbook of temperament* (pp. 368–399). New York: Guilford Press.

DeRosier, M. E., Kupersmidt, J. B., & Patterson, C. J. (1994). Children's academic and behavioral adjustment as a function of the chronicity and proximity of peer rejection. *Child Development, 65,* 1799–1813. doi:10.1111/j.1467-8624.1994.tb00850.x

Desjarlais, M., & Willoughby, T. (2010). A longitudinal study of the relation between adolescent boys' and girls' computer use with friends and friendship quality: Support for the social compensation or the rich-get-richer hypothesis? *Computers in Human Behavior, 26,* 896–905. doi:10.1016/j.chb.2010.02.004

DeSnoo, K. (1937). The drinking child in the uterus. *Journal of Obstetric Gynecology, 105,* 88–97.

Devine, A., Fawcett, K., Szücs, D., & Dowker, A. (2012). Gender differences in mathematics anxiety and the relation to mathematics performance while controlling for test anxiety. *Behavioral and Brain Functions, 8*(33). doi:10.1186/1744-9081-8-33

DeWitt, A. L., Cready, C. M., & Seward, R. R. (2013). Parental role portrayals in twentieth century children's picture books: More egalitarian or ongoing stereotyping? *Sex Roles, 69,* 89–106.

Di Giorgio, E., Leo, I., Pascalis, O., & Simion, F. (2012). Is the face-perception system human-specific at birth? *Developmental Psychology, 48,* 1083–1090. doi:10.1037/a0026521

Di Giunta, L., Pastorelli, C., Eisenberg, N., Gerbino, M., Castellani, V., & Bombi, A. (2010). Developmental trajectories of physical aggression: Prediction of overt and covert antisocial behaviors from self- and mothers' reports. *European Child and Adolescent Psychiatry, 19,* 873–882. doi:10.1007/s00787-010-0134-4

Diamond, A. (1985). Development of the ability to use recall to guide action, as indicated by infants' performance on $A\overline{B}$. *Child Development, 56,* 868–883. doi:10.2307/1130099

Diamond, A. (2013). Executive functions. *Annual Review of Psychology, 64,* 135–168. doi:10.1146/annurev-psych-113011-143750

Diamond, A., Briand, L., Fossella, J., & Gehlbach, L. (2004). Genetic and neurochemical modulation of prefrontal cognitive functions in children. *American Journal of Psychiatry, 161,* 125–132.

Diamond, A., & Goldman-Rakic, P. S. (1989). Comparison of human infants and rhesus monkeys on Piaget's AB task: Evidence for dependence on dorsolateral prefrontal cortex. *Experimental Brain Research, 74,* 24–40. doi:10.1007/BF00248277

Diamond, A., & Lee, K. (2011, August 19). Interventions shown to aid executive function development in children 4 to 12 years old. *Science, 333,* 959–964.

Diamond, L. M. (2008). Female bisexuality from adolescence to adulthood: Results from a 10-year longitudinal study. *Developmental Psychology, 44,* 5–14. doi:10.1037/0012-1649.44.1.5

Diamond, L. M., Bonner, S. B., & Dickenson, J. (2015). The development of sexuality. In M. E. Lamb (Vol. Ed.) & R. M. Lerner (Editor-in-Chief), *Handbook of Child Psychology and Developmental Science* (7th ed.), Volume 3: Socioemotional processes (pp. 888–931). Hoboken, NJ: Wiley.

Diaz, C. J., & Fiel, J. E. (2016). The effect(s) of teen pregnancy: Reconciling theory, methods, and findings. *Demography, 53,* 85–116. doi:10.1007/s13524-015-0446-6

Díaz, R. M., & Berk, L. E. (Eds.). (2014). *Private speech: From social interaction to self-regulation.* New York: Psychology Press.

DiBiase, R., & Waddell, S. (1995). Some effects of homelessness on the psychological functioning of preschoolers. *Journal of Abnormal Child Psychology, 23,* 783–792. doi:10.1007/BF01447477

Dick, D. M., Pagan, J. L., Holliday, C., Viken, R., Pulkkinen, L., Kaprio, J., & Rose, R. J. (2007). Gender differences in friends' influences on adolescent drinking: A genetic epidemiological study. *Alcoholism: Clinical and Experimental Research, 31,* 2012–2019. doi:10.1111/j.1530-0277.2007.00523.x

Dickinson, D. K. (2011, August 19). Teachers' language practices and academic outcomes of preschool children. *Science, 333,* 964–967.

Dickinson, D. K., & Porche, M. V. (2011). Relation between language experiences in preschool classrooms and children's kindergarten and fourth-grade language and reading abilities. *Child Development, 82,* 870–886. doi:10.1111/j.1467-8624.2011.01576.x

DiCorcia, J. A., Snidman, N., Sravish, A. V., & Tronick, E. (2015). Evaluating the nature of the still-face effect in the double face-to-face still-face paradigm using different comparison groups. *Infancy, 21,* 332–352. doi:10.1111/infa.12123

Diekelmann, S., & Born, J. (2010). The memory function of sleep. *Nature Reviews Neuroscience, 11,* 114–126. doi:10.1038/nrn2762

Diekman, A. B., & Murnen, S. K. (2004). Learning to be little women and little men: The inequitable gender equality of nonsexist children's literature. *Sex Roles, 50,* 373–385. doi:10.1023/B:SERS.0000018892.26527.ea

Diener, M. (2000). Gift from the gods: A Balinese guide to early child rearing. In J. S. DeLoache & A. Gottlieb (Eds.), *A world of babies: Imagined childcare guides for seven societies* (pp. 96–116). New York: Cambridge University Press.

Diener, M. L., & Lucas, R. E. (2004). Adults' desires for children's emotions across 48 countries: Associations with individual and national characteristics. *Journal of Cross-Cultural Psychology, 35,* 525–547. doi:10.1177/0022022104268387

Dijkstra, J. K., Cillessen, A. H. N., & Borch, C. (2013). Popularity and adolescent friendship networks: Selection and influence dynamics. *Developmental Psychology, 49,* 1242–1252. doi:10.1037/a0030098

Dillon, M. R., & Spelke, E. S. (2015). Core geometry in perspective. *Developmental Science, 18*(6), 894–908.

Dimidjian, S., & Goodman, S. H. (2014). Preferences and attitudes toward approaches to depression relapse /recurrence prevention among pregnant women. *Behaviour Research and Therapy, 54,* 7–11.

Dimidjian, S., Goodman, S. H., Sherwood, N. E., Simon, G. E., Ludman, E., Gallop, R., . . . Powers, J. D. (2017). A pragmatic randomized clinical trial of behavioral activation for depressed pregnant women. *Journal of Consulting and Clinical Psychology, 85*(1), 26.

Dimond, D., Schuetze, M., Smith, R. E., Dhollander, T., Cho, I., Vinette, S., . . . Connelly, A. (2019). Reduced white matter fiber density in autism spectrum disorder. *Cerebral Cortex, 29*(4), 1778–1788. https://doi.org/10.1093/cercor/bhy348

Dinstein, I., Heeger, D. J., Lorenzi, L., Minshew, N. J., Malach, R., & Behrmann, M. (2012). Unreliable evoked responses in autism. *Neuron, 75*(6), 981–991. doi:10.1016/j.neuron.2012.07.026

Dion, J., Hains, J., Vachon, P., Plouffe, J., Laberge, L., Perron, M., . . . Leone, M. (2016). Correlates of body dissatisfaction in children. *Journal of Pediatrics, 171,* 202–207.

Dionne, G., Tremblay, R., Boivin, M., Laplante, D., & Pérusse, D. (2003). Physical aggression and expressive vocabulary in 19-month-old twins. *Developmental Psychology, 39,* 261–273. doi:10.1037/0012-1649.39.2.261

DiPietro, J. A. (1981). Rough and tumble play: A function of gender. *Developmental Psychology, 17,* 50.

DiPietro, J. A., Costigan, K. A., & Voegtline, K. M. (2015). Studies in fetal behavior: Revisited, renewed and reimagined. *Monographs for the Society of Research in Child Development, 80*(3), vii, 1–94.

DiPietro, J. A., & Voegtline, K. M. (2017). The gestational foundation of sex differences in development and vulnerability. *Neuroscience, 342,* 4–20.

DiPietro, J. A., Voegtline, K. M., Pater, H. A., & Costigan, K. A. (2018). Predicting child temperament and behavior from the fetus. *Development and Psychopathology, 30*(3), 855–870.

Dirks, J., & Gibson, E. (1977). Infants' perception of similarity between live people and their photographs. *Child Development, 48,* 124–130. doi:10.2307/1128890

Dirks, M. A., Persram, R., Recchia, H. E., & Howe, N. (2015). Sibling relationships as sources of risk and resilience in the development and maintenance of internalizing and externalizing problems during childhood and adolescence. *Clinical Psychology Review, 42,* 145–155. doi:10.1016/j.cpr.2015.07.003

Dishion, T. J. (1990). The family ecology of boys' peer relations in middle childhood. *Child Development, 61,* 874–892. doi:10.1111/j.1467-8624.1990.tb02829.x

Dishion, T. J., Andrews, D. W., & Crosby, L. (1995). Antisocial boys and their friends in early adolescence: Relationship characteristics, quality, and interactional process. *Child Development, 66,* 139–151. doi:10.1111/j.1467-8624.1995.tb00861.x

Dishion, T. J., Ha, T., & Véronneau, M.-H. (2012). An ecological analysis of the effects of deviant peer clustering on sexual promiscuity, problem behavior, and childbearing from early adolescence to adulthood: An enhancement of the life history framework. *Developmental Psychology, 48,* 703–717. doi:10.1037/a0027304

Dishion, T. J., & Tipsord, J. M. (2011). Peer contagion in child and adolescent social and emotional development. *Annual Review of Psychology, 62,* 189–214. doi:10.1146/annurev.psych.093008.100412

Dishion, T. J., Véronneau, M.-H., & Myers, M. W. (2010). Cascading peer dynamics underlying the progression from problem behavior to violence in early to late adolescence. *Development and Psychopathology, 22,* 603–619. doi:10.1017/S0954579410000313

Dix, T., & Grusec, J. E. (1983). Parental influence techniques: An attributional analysis. *Child Development, 54,* 645–652. doi:10.2307/1130051

Doan, S. N., Fuller-Rowell, T. E., & Evans, G. W. (2012). Cumulative risk and adolescent's internalizing and externalizing problems: The mediating roles of maternal responsiveness and self-regulation. *Developmental Psychology, 48,* 1529–1539. doi:10.1037/a0027815

Doan, S. N., Fuller-Rowell, T. E., & Evans, G. W. (2012). Cumulative risk and adolescent's internalizing and externalizing problems: The mediating roles of maternal responsiveness and self-regulation. *Developmental Psychology, 48,* 1529–1539. doi:10.1037/a0027815

Doan, S. N., & Wang, Q. (2010). Maternal discussions of mental states and behaviors: Relations to emotion situation knowledge in European American and immigrant Chinese children. *Child Development, 81,* 1490–1503. doi:10.1111/j.1467-8624.2010.01487.x

Dodge, K. A. (1980). Social cognition and children's aggressive behavior. *Child Development, 51,* 162–170. doi:10.2307/1129603

Dodge, K. A. (1986). A social information processing model of social competence in children. In M. Perlmutter (Ed.), *Minnesota Symposia on Child Psychology: Vol. 18. Cognitive perspectives on children's social and behavioral development* (pp. 77–125). Hillsdale, NJ: Erlbaum.

Dodge, K. A., Dishion, T. J., & Lansford, J. E. (Eds.). (2006). *Deviant peer influences in programs for youth: Problems and solutions.* New York: Guilford Press.

Dodge, K. A., Godwin, J., & Conduct Problems Prevention Research Group. (2013). Social-information-processing patterns mediate the impact of preventive intervention on adolescent antisocial behavior. *Psychological Science, 24*(4), 456–465.

Dodge, K. A., Greenberg, M. T., Malone, P. S., & Conduct Problems Prevention Research Group. (2008). Testing an idealized dynamic cascade model of the development of serious violence in adolescence. *Child Development, 79,* 1907–1927. doi:10.1111/j.1467-8624.2008.01233.x

Dodge, K. A., Lansford, J. E., Burks, V. S., Bates, J. E., Pettit, G. S., Fontaine, R., & Price, J. M. (2003). Peer rejection and social information-processing factors in the development of aggressive behavior problems in children. *Child Development, 74,* 374–393. doi:10.1111/1467-8624.7402004

Dodge, K. A., Lansford, J. E., & Dishion, T. J. (2006). The problem of deviant peer influences in intervention programs. In K. A. Dodge, T. J. Dishion, & J. E. Lansford (Eds.), *Deviant peer influences in programs for youth: Problems and solutions* (pp. 3–13). New York: Guilford Press.

Dodge, K. A., Lochman, J. E., Harnish, J. D., Bates, J. E., & Pettit, G. S. (1997). Reactive and proactive aggression in school children and psychiatrically impaired chronically assaultive youth. *Journal of Abnormal Psychology, 106,* 37–51.

Dodge, K. A., Malone, P. S., Lansford, J. E., Sorbring, E., Skinner, A. T., Tapanya, S., . . . Bacchini, D. (2015). Hostile attributional bias and aggressive behavior in global context. *Proceedings of the National Academy of Sciences, 112*(30), 9310–9315.

Dodge, K. A., Pettit, G. S., & Bates, J. E. (1994). Socialization mediators of the relation between socioeconomic status and child conduct problems. *Child Development, 65,* 649–665. doi:10.2307/1131407

Dodge, K. A., Pettit, G. S., Bates, J. E., & Valente, E. (1995). Social information-processing patterns partially mediate the effect of early physical abuse on later conduct problems. *Journal of Abnormal Psychology, 104,* 632–643. doi:10.1037/0021-843X.104.4.632

Dodge, K. A., Pettit, G. S., McClaskey, C. L., Brown, M. M., & Gottman, J. M. (1986). Social competence in children. *Monographs of the Society for Research in Child Development, 51*(2, Serial No. 213), i–85. doi:10.2307/1165906

Dogan, S. J., Conger, R. D., Kim, K. J., & Masyn, K. E. (2007). Cognitive and parenting pathways in the transmission of antisocial behavior from parents to adolescents. *Child Development, 78,* 335–349. doi:10.1111/j.1467-8624.2007.01001.x

Doherty, M. J. (2008). *Theory of mind: How children understand others' thoughts and feelings.* New York: Psychology Press. doi:10.4324/9780203929902

Dolgin, E. (2018). Scientists downsize bold plan to make human genome from scratch. *Nature, 557,* 16–17.

Dollard, J., & Miller, N. E. (1950). *Personality and psychotherapy.* New York: McGraw-Hill.

Dombroski, J., & Newman, R. S. (2014). Toddlers' ability to map the meaning of new words in multi-talker environments. *Journal of the Acoustic Society of America, 136*(5), 2807–2815.

Domitrovich, C. E., Bradshaw, C. P., Greenberg, M. T., Embry, D., Poduska, J. M., & Ialongo, N. S. (2010). Integrated models of school-based prevention: Logic and theory. *Psychology in the Schools, 47,* 71–88. doi:10.1002/pits.20452

Domitrovich, C. E., Cortes, R. C., & Greenberg, M. T. (2007). Improving young children's social and emotional competence: A randomized trial of the preschool "PATHS" curriculum. *Journal of Primary Prevention, 28,* 67–91. doi:10.1007/s10935-007-0081-0

Dontigny, L., Arsenault, M. Y., & Martel, M. J. (2018). No. 203-Rubella in Pregnancy. *Journal of Obstetrics and Gynaecology Canada, 40*(8), e615–e621.

Downs, E., & Smith, S. L. (2010). Keeping abreast of hypersexuality: A video game character content analysis. *Sex Roles, 62,* 721–733.

Doyle, A. B., Lawford, H., & Markiewicz, D. (2009). Attachment style with mother, father, best friend, and romantic partner during adolescence. *Journal of Research on Adolescence, 19,* 690–714. doi:10.1111/j.1532-7795.2009.00617.x

Dozier, M., & Bernard, K. (2017). Attachment and biobehavioral catch-up: Addressing the needs of infants and toddlers exposed to inadequate or problematic caregiving. *Current Opinion in Psychology, 15,* 111–117. doi:10.1016/j.copsyc.2017.03.003

Drabbie, L., Keatley, J. G., & Marcelle, G. (2006). Media strategies for advancing health in lesbian, gay, bisexual, and transgender communities. In M. D. Shankle (Ed.), *The handbook of lesbian, gay, bisexual, and transgender public health: A practitioner's guide to service* (pp. 335–352). Harrington Park Press/The Haworth Press: Binghamton, NY.

Drake, K., Belsky, J., & Fearon, R. P. (2014). From early attachment to engagement with learning in school: The role of self-regulation and persistence. *Developmental Psychology, 50,* 1350–1361. doi:10.1037/a0032779

Drevenstedt, G. L., Crimmins, E. M., Vasunilashorn, S., & Finch, C. E. (2008). The rise and fall of excess male infant mortality. *Proceedings of the National Academy of Sciences, 105*(13), 5016–5021.

Driscoll, A. K., Russell, S. T., & Crockett, L. J. (2008). Parenting styles and youth well-being across immigrant generations. *Journal of Family Issues, 29,* 185–209. doi:10.1177/0192513x07307843

Drummond, K. D., Bradley, S. J., Peterson-Badali, M., & Zucker, K. J. (2008). A follow-up study of girls with gender identity disorder. *Developmental Psychology, 44,* 34–45. doi:10.1037/0012-1649.44.1.34

Dubois, J., Dehaene-Lambertz, G., Kulikova, S., Poupon, C., Hüppi, P. S., & Hertz-Pannier, L. (2014). The early development of brain white matter: A review of imaging studies in fetuses, newborns and infants. *Neuroscience, 276,* 48–71.

Duckworth, A. L., Quinn, P. D., Lynam, D. R., Loeber, R., & Stouthamer-Loeber, M. (2011). Role of test motivation in intelligence testing. *Proceedings of the National Academy of Sciences, 108*(19), 7716–7720. doi:10.1073/pnas.1018601108

Duckworth, A. L., Quinn, P. D., & Tsukayama, E. (2012). What *No Child Left Behind* leaves behind: The roles of IQ and self-control in predicting standardized achievement test scores and report card grades. *Journal of Educational Psychology, 104,* 439–451. doi:10.1037/a0026280

Duff, C. K., & Flattery, J. J. (2014). Developing mirror self-awareness in students with autism spectrum disorder. *Journal of Autism and Developmental Disorders, 44,* 1027–1038. doi:10.1007/s10803-013-1954

Duncan, G. J., & Murnane, R. J. (2011). *Whither opportunity? Rising inequality, schools, and children's life chances.* New York: Russell Sage Foundation.

Duncan, G. J., Dowsett, C. J., Claessens, A., Magnuson, K., Huston, A. C., Klebanov, P., . . . Japel, C. (2007). School readiness and later achievement. *Developmental Psychology, 43,* 1428–1446. doi:10.1037/0012-1649.43.6.1428

Duncan, G. J., & Murnane, R. J. (2014). *Restoring opportunity: The crisis of inequality and the challenge for American education.* Retrieved from http://escholarship.org/uc/item/2v8169pn

Dunfield, K., Kuhlmeier, V. A., O'Connell, L., & Kelley, E. (2011). Examining the diversity of prosocial behavior: Helping, sharing, and comforting in infancy. *Infancy, 16,* 227–247. doi:10.1111/j.1532-7078.2010.00041.x

Dunfield, K. A., & Kuhlmeier, V. A. (2013). Classifying prosocial behavior: Children's responses to instrumental need, emotional distress, and material desire. *Child Development, 84,* 1766–1776. doi:10.1111/cdev.12075

Dunifon, R., Kalil, A., Crosby, D. A., & Su, J. H. (2013). Mothers' night work and children's behavior problems. *Developmental Psychology, 49,* 1874–1885. doi:10.1037/a0031241

Dunn, J. (2004). *Children's friendships: The beginnings of intimacy.* Malden, MA: Blackwell.

Dunn, J. (2014). Moral development in early childhood and social interaction in the family. In M. Killen & J. G. Smetana (Eds.), *Handbook of moral development* (2nd ed., pp. 135–159). New York: Psychology Press.

Dunn, J., & Brown, J. (1994). Affect expression in the family, children's understanding of emotions, and their interactions with others. *Merrill-Palmer Quarterly, 40,* 120–137.

Dunn, J., Brown, J., & Beardsall, L. (1991). Family talk about feeling states and children's later understanding of others' emotions. *Developmental Psychology, 27,* 448–455.

Dunn, J., Brown, J., Slomkowski, C., Tesla, C., & Youngblade, L. (1991). Young children's understanding of other people's feelings and beliefs: Individual differences and their antecedents. *Child Development, 62,* 1352–1366.

Duong, M. T., Schwartz, D., Chang, L., Kelly, B. M., & Tom, S. R. (2009). Associations between maternal physical discipline and peer victimization among Hong Kong Chinese children: The moderating role of child aggression. *Journal of Abnormal Child Psychology, 37,* 957–966. doi:10.1007/s10802-009-9322-4

Durbin, C. E. (2010). Validity of young children's self-reports of their emotion in response to structured laboratory tasks. *Emotion, 10,* 519–535. doi:10.1037/a0019008

Durbin, C. E., Hayden, E. P., Klein, D. N., & Olino, T. M. (2007). *Emotion, 7,* 388–399.

Durrant, J., Trocmé, N., Fallon, B., Milne, C., Black, T., & Knoke, D. (2006). *Punitive violence against children in Canada* (CECW Information Sheet #41E). Retrieved from University of Toronto, Faculty of Social Work website: http://cwrp.ca/publications/497

Duschinsky, R. (2015). The emergence of the disorganized/disoriented (D) attachment classification, 1979–1982. *History of Psychology, 18,* 32–46. doi:10/1037/a0038524

Dweck, C. S. (1999). *Self-theories: Their role in motivation, personality, and development.* Philadelphia: Psychology Press.

Dweck, C. S. (2006). *Mindset: The new psychology of success.* New York: Random House.

Dweck, C. S. (2012). Mindsets and human nature: Promoting change in the Middle East, the schoolyard, the racial divide, and willpower. *American Psychologist, 67*(8), 614–622. doi:10.1037/a0029783

Dweck, C. S., & Leggett, E. L. (1988). A social-cognitive approach to motivation and personality. *Psychological Review, 95,* 256–273.

Dwyer, K. M., Fredstrom, B. K., Rubin, K. H., Booth-LaForce, C., Rose-Krasnor, L., & Burgess, K. B. (2010). Attachment, social information processing, and friendship quality of early adolescent girls and boys. *Journal of Social and Personal Relationships, 27,* 91–116. doi:10.1177/0265407509346420

Eaton, W. O., & Enns, L. R. (1986). Sex differences in human motor activity level. *Psychological Bulletin, 100,* 19–28. doi:10.1037/0033-2909.100.1.19

Eccles, J. S. (2015). Gender socialization of STEM interests in the family. *International Journal of Gender, Science, & Technology, 7,* 116–132.

Eccles, J. S., Freedman-Doan, C., Frome, P., Jacobs, J., & Yoon, K. S. (2000). Gender-role socialization in the family: A longitudinal approach. In T. Eckes & H. M. Trautner (Eds.), *The developmental social psychology of gender* (pp. 333–360). Mahwah, NJ: Erlbaum.

Eccles, J. S., & Gootman, J. (Eds.). (2002). *Community programs to promote youth development.* Washington, DC: National Academy Press.

Eccles, J. S., & Wigfield, A. (2002). Motivational beliefs, values, and goals. *Annual Review of Psychology, 53,* 109–132. doi:10.1146/annurev.psych.53.100901.135153

Eccles, J. S., Wigfield, A., Flanagan, C. A., Miller, C., Reuman, D. A., & Yee, D. (1989). Self-concepts, domain values, and self-esteem: Relations and changes at early adolescence. *Journal of Personality, 57,* 283–310. doi:10.1111/j.1467-6494.1989.tb00484.x

Eder, D. (1985). The cycle of popularity: Interpersonal relations among female adolescents. *Sociology of Education, 58,* 154–165. doi:10.2307/2112416

Edgin, J. O., Tooley, U., Demara, B., Nyhuis, C., Anand, P., & Spanò, G. (2015). Sleep disturbance and expressive language development in preschool-age children with Down syndrome. *Child Development, 86*(6), 1984–1998. doi:10.1111/cdev.12443

Ehri, L. C. (2014). Orthographic mapping in the acquisition of sight word reading, spelling memory, and vocabulary learning. *Scientific Studies of Reading, 18*(1), 5–21. doi:10.1080/10888438.2013.819356

Eiden, R. D., Colder, C., Edwards, E. P., & Leonard, K. E. (2009). A longitudinal study of social competence among children of alcoholic and non-alcoholic parents: Role of parental psychopathology, parental warmth, and self-regulation. *Psychology of Addictive Behaviors, 23,* 36–46.

Eigsti, I. M., Zayas, V., Mischel, W., Shoda, Y., Ayduk, O., Dadlani, M. B., . . . Casey, B. J. (2006). Predicting cognitive control from preschool to late adolescence and young adulthood. *Psychological Science, 17,* 478–484. doi:10.1111/j.1467-9280.2006.01732.x

Eimas, P. D., Siqueland, E. R., Jusczyk, P., & Vigorito, J. (1971, January 22). Speech perception in infants. *Science, 171,* 303–306.

Eisenberg, N. (2000). Emotion, regulation, and moral development. *Annual Review of Psychology, 51,* 665–697. doi:10.1146/annurev.psych.51.1.665

Eisenberg, N., Chang, L., Ma, Y., & Huang, X. (2009). Relations of parenting style to Chinese children's effortful control, ego resilience, and maladjustment. *Development and Psychopathology, 21,* 455–477. doi:10.1017/S095457940900025X

Eisenberg, N., Cumberland, A., & Spinrad, T. L. (1998). Parental socialization of emotion. *Psychological Inquiry, 9,* 241–273.

Eisenberg, N., & Fabes, R. A. (1998). Prosocial development. In W. Damon (Series Ed.) & N. Eisenberg (Vol. Ed.), *Handbook of child psychology: Vol. 3. Social, emotional, and personality development* (5th ed., pp. 701–778). New York: Wiley.

Eisenberg, N., Fabes, R. A., Shepard, S. A., Guthrie, I. K., Murphy, B. C., & Reiser, M. (1999). Parental reactions to children's negative emotions: Longitudinal relations to quality of children's social functioning. *Child Development, 70,* 513–534.

Eisenberg, N., Fabes, R. A., & Spinrad, T. L. (2006). Prosocial development. In N. Eisenberg, W. Damon, & R. M. Lerner (Eds.), *Handbook of child psychology: Social, emotional, and personality development* (pp. 646–718). Hoboken, NJ: Wiley.

Eisenberg, N., Michalik, N., Spinrad, T. L., Hofer, C., Kupfer, A., Valiente, C., . . . Reiser, M. (2007). The relations of effortful control and impulsivity to children's sympathy: A longitudinal study. *Cognitive Development, 22,* 544–567. doi:10.1016/j.cogdev.2007.08.003

Eisenberg, N., Sallquist, J., French, D. C., Purwono, U., Suryanti, T. A., & Pidada, S. (2009). The relations of majority-minority group status and having an other-religion friend to Indonesian youths' socioemotional functioning. *Developmental Psychology, 45,* 248–259. doi:10.1037/a0014028

Eisenberg, N., Shell, R., Pasternack, J., Lennon, R., Beller, R., & Mathy, R. M. (1987). Prosocial development in middle childhood: A longitudinal study. *Developmental Psychology, 23*(5), 712–718. http://dx.doi.org/10.1037/0012-1649.23.5.712

Eisenberg, N., Spinrad, T. L., & Knafo-Noam, A. (2015). Prosocial development. In M. E. Lamb (Ed.) & R. M. Lerner (Series Ed.), *Handbook of child psychology and developmental science: Vol. 3* (7th ed., pp. 610–656). Hoboken, NJ: Wiley.

Eisenberg, N., Valiente, C., Spinrad, T. L., Cumberland, A., Liew, J., Reiser, M., . . . Losoya, S. H. (2009). Longitudinal relations of children's effortful control, impulsivity, and negative emotionality to their externalizing, internalizing, and co-occurring behavior problems. *Developmental Psychology, 45,* 988–1008. doi:10.1037/a0016213

Eisenberg, N., Zhou, Q., Spinrad, T. L., Valiente, C., Fabes, R. A., & Liew, J. (2005). Relations among positive parenting, children's effortful control, and externalizing problems: A three-wave longitudinal study. *Child Development, 76,* 1055–1071. doi:10.1111/j.1467-8624.2005.00897.x

Eisenberg-Berg, N., & Geisheker, E. (1979). Content of preachings and power of the model/preacher: The effect on children's generosity. *Developmental Psychology, 15,* 168–175.

Eisner, M. P., & Malti, T. (2015). Aggressive and violent behavior. In M. E. Lamb (Ed.) & R. M. Lerner (Series Ed.), *Handbook of child psychology and developmental science: Vol. 3* (7th ed., pp. 794–841). Hoboken, NJ: Wiley.

Ekas, N. V., Lickenbrock, D. M., & Braungart-Rieker, J. (2013). Developmental trajectories of emotion regulation across infancy: Do age and the social partner influence temporal patterns? *Infancy, 18,* 729–754. doi:10.1111/infa.12003

Ekman, P., & Cordaro, D. (2011). What is meant by calling emotions basic. *Emotion Review, 3,* 364–370. doi:10.1177/1754073911410740

Elam, K. K., Sandler, I., Wolchik, S., & Tein, J. (2016). Non-residential father–child involvement, interparental conflict and mental health of children following divorce: A person-focused approach. *Journal of Youth and Adolescence, 45,* 581–593. doi:10.1007/s10964-015-0399-5

Elicker, J., Englund, M., & Sroufe, L. A. (1992). Predicting peer competence and peer relationships in childhood from early parent–child relationships. In R. D. Parke & G. W. Ladd (Eds.), *Family-peer relationships: Modes of linkage* (pp. 77–106). Hillsdale, NJ: Erlbaum.

Elkind, D. (1967). Egocentrism in adolescence. *Child Development, 38,* 1025–1034.

Elledge, L. C., Williford, A., Boulton, A. J., DePaolis, K. J., Little, T. D., & Salmivalli, C. (2013). Individual and contextual predictors of cyberbullying: The influence of children's provictim attitudes and teachers' ability to intervene. *Journal of Youth and Adolescence, 42,* 698–710. doi:10.1007/s10964-013-9920-x

Elliott, C., & Scime, N.V. (2019). Nutrient profiling and child-targeted supermarket foods: Assessing a "Made in Canada" policy approach. *International Journal of Environmental Research and Public Health, 16,* 639. doi:10.3390/ijerph16040639

Ellis, B. J., Bates, J. E., Dodge, K. A., Fergusson, D. M., Horwood, L. J., Pettit, G. S., & Woodward, L. (2003). Does father absence place daughters at special risk for early sexual activity and teenage pregnancy? *Child Development, 74,* 801–821. doi:10.1111/1467-8624.00569

Ellis, C. T., & Turk-Browne, N. B. (2018). Infant fMRI: A model system for cognitive neuroscience. *Trends in Cognitive Sciences, 22,* 375–387.

Else-Quest, N. M., Hyde, J. S., & Linn, M. C. (2010). Cross-national patterns of gender differences in mathematics: A meta-analysis. *Psychological Bulletin, 136,* 103–127. doi:10.1037/a0018053

Else-Quest, N. M., Hyde, J. S., Goldsmith, H. H., & Van Hulle, C. A. (2006). Gender differences in temperament: A meta-analysis. *Psychological Bulletin, 132,* 33–72. doi:10.1037/0033-2909.132.1.33

Emery, R. E. (1989). Family violence. *American Psychologist, 44,* 321–328. doi:10.1037/0003-066X.44.2.321

Engle, J. M., & McElwain, N. L. (2011). Parental reactions to toddlers' negative emotions and child negative emotionality as correlates of problem behavior at the age of three. *Social Development, 20,* 251–271.

Engle, J. M., McElwain, N. L., & Lasky, N. (2011). Presence and quality of kindergarten children's friendships: Concurrent and longitudinal associations with child adjustment in the early school years. *Infant and Child Development, 20,* 365–386. doi:10.1002/icd.706

Englund, M. M., Kuo, S. I.-C., Puig, J., & Collins, W. A. (2011). Early roots of adult competence: The significance of close relationships from infancy to early adulthood. *International Journal of Behavioral Development, 35,* 490–496. doi:10.1177/0165025411422994

Ensor, R., & Hughes, C. (2008). Content or connectedness? Mother–child talk and early social understanding. *Child Development, 79,* 201–216.

Entertainment Software Rating Board. (n.d.). Frequently asked questions. Retrieved from http://www.esrb.org/ratings/faq.aspx#20

Eppig, C., Fincher, C. L., & Thornhill, R. (2010). Parasite prevalence and the worldwide distribution of cognitive ability. *Proceedings of the Royal Society B: Biological Sciences, 277,* 3801–3808. doi:10.1098/rspb.2010.0973

Erel, O., Margolin, G., & John, R. S. (1998). Observed sibling interaction: Links with the marital and the mother–child relationship. *Developmental Psychology, 34,* 288–298. doi:10.1037/0012-1649.34.2.288

Erel, O., Oberman, Y., & Yirmiya, N. (2000). Maternal versus nonmaternal care and seven domains of children's development. *Psychological Bulletin, 126,* 727–747. doi:10.1037/0033-2909.126.5.727

Erickson, M. F., Sroufe, L. A., & Egeland, B. (1985). The relationship between quality of attachment and behavior problems in preschool in a high-risk sample. *Monographs of the Society for Research in Child Development, 50*(1–2, Serial No. 209), 147–166. doi:10.2307/3333831

Erikson, E. H. (1950). *Childhood and society.* New York: Norton.

Erikson, E. H. (1968). *Identity: Youth and crisis.* New York: Norton.

Eron, L. D., Huesmann, L. R., Dubow, E., Romanoff, R., & Yarmel, P. W. (1987). Aggression and its correlates over 22 years. In D. H. Crowell, I. M. Evans, & C. R. O'Donnell (Eds.), *Childhood aggression and violence: Sources of influence, prevention, and control* (pp. 249–262). New York: Plenum.

Espy, K. A., Sheffield, T. D., Wiebe, S. A., Clark, C. A. C., & Moehr, M. J. (2011). Executive control and dimensions of problem behaviors in preschool children. *Journal of Child Psychology and Psychiatry, 52,* 33–46. doi:10.1111/j.1469-7610.2010.02265.x

Essex, M. J., Boyce, T. W., Hertzman, C., Lam, L. L., Armstrong, J. M., Neumann, S. M. A., & Kobor, M. S. (2013). Epigenetic vestiges of early developmental adversity: Childhood stress exposure and DNA methylation in adolescence. *Child Development, 84,* 58–75. doi:10.1111/j.1467-8624.2011.01641.x

Evans, A. B., Banerjee, M., Meyer, R., Aldana, A., Foust, M., & Rowley, S. (2012). Racial socialization as a mechanism for positive development among African American youth. *Child Development Perspectives, 6,* 251–257. doi:10.1111/j.1750-8606.2011.00226.x

Evans, A. D., Xu, F., & Lee, K. (2011). When all signs point to you: Lies told in the face of evidence. *Developmental Psychology, 47,* 39–49.

Evans, E. M. (2008). Conceptual change and evolutionary biology: A developmental analysis. In S. Vosniadou (Ed.), *International handbook of research on conceptual change* (pp. 263–294). New York: Routledge.

Evans, E. M., Legare, C., & Rosengren, K. (2011). Engaging multiple epistemologies: Implications for science education. In R. Taylor & M. Ferrari (Eds.), *Epistemology and science education: Understanding the evolution vs. intelligent design controversy* (pp. 111–139). New York: Routledge.

Evans, G. W., & Cassells, R. C. (2014). Childhood poverty, cumulative risk exposure, and mental health in emerging adults. *Clinical Psychological Science, 2*(3), 287–296. doi:10.1177/2167702613501496

Evans, G. W., Li, D., & Whipple, S. S. (2013). Cumulative risk and child development. *Psychological Bulletin, 139*(6), 1342–1396. doi:10.1037/a0031808

Evans, M. A., Shaw, D., & Bell, M. (2000). Home literacy activities and their influence on early literacy skills. *Canadian Journal of Experimental Psychology, 2,* 65–75.

Ezkurdia, I., Juan, D., Rodriguez, J. M., Frankish, A., Diekhans, M., Harrow, J., . . . Tress, M. L. (2014). Multiple evidence strands suggest that there may be as few as 19,000 human protein-coding genes. *Human Molecular Genetics, 23*(22), 5866–5878.

Fabes, R. A., & Eisenberg, N. (1992). Young children's coping with interpersonal anger. *Child Development, 63,* 116–128. doi:10.1111/j.1467-8624.1992.tb03600.x

Fabricius, W. V., & Braver, S. L. (2006). Relocation, parent conflict, and domestic violence: Independent risk factors for children of divorce. *Journal of Child Custody, 3,* 7–27. doi:10.1300/j190v03n03_02

Fagg, J. H., Curtis, S. E., Cummins, S., Stansfeld, S. A., & Quesnel-Vallée, A. (2013). Neighbourhood deprivation and adolescent self-esteem: Exploration of the "socio-economic equalisation in youth" hypothesis in Britain and Canada. *Social Science & Medicine, 91,* 168–177.

Fagot, B. I. (1977). Consequences of moderate cross-gender behavior in preschool children. *Child Development, 48,* 902–907. doi:10.2307/1128339

Fagot, B. I., & Leinbach, M. D. (1989). The young child's gender schema: Environmental input, internal organization. *Child Development, 60,* 663–672. doi:10.2307/1130731

Fallang, B., Saugstad, O. D., Grogaard, J., & Hadders-Algra, M. (2003). Kinematic quality of reaching movements in preterm infants. *Pediatric Research, 53,* 836–842. doi:10.1203/01.PDR.0000058925.94994.BC

Fallon, B., Van Wert, M., Trocmé, N., MacLaurin, B., Sinha, V., Lefebvre, R., . . . Goel, S. (2015). *Ontario incidence study of reported child abuse and neglect—2013 (OIS-2013).* Toronto: Child Welfare Research Portal. Retrieved from http://cwrp.ca/sites/default/files/publications/en/ois-2013_final.pdf

Fan, S. P., Liberman, Z., Keysar, B., & Kinzler, K. D. (2015). The exposure advantage: Early exposure to a multilingual environment promotes effective communication. *Psychological Science, 26*(7), 1090–1097.

Fanger, S. M., Frankel, L. A., & Hazen, N. (2012). Peer exclusion in preschool children's play: Naturalistic observations in a playground setting. *Merrill-Palmer Quarterly, 58,* 224–254. doi:10.1353/mpq.2012.0007

Fantz, R. L. (1961, May). The origin of form perception. *Scientific American, 204*(5), 66–72.

Farkas, T., & Leaper, C. (2016). The psychology of boys. In Y. J. Wong, & S. R. Wester. (Eds.), *APA handbook of men and masculinities* (pp. 357–387). Washington, DC: American Psychological Association.

Farr, R. H. (2017). Does parental sexual orientation matter? A longitudinal follow-up of adoptive families with school-age children. *Developmental Psychology, 53,* 252–264. doi:10.1037/dev0000228

Farr, R. H., Bruun, S. T., Doss, K. M., & Patterson, C. J. (2018). Children's gender-typed behavior from early to middle childhood in adoptive families with lesbian, gay, and heterosexual parents. *Sex Roles, 78,* 528–541. doi:10.1007/s11199-017-0812-5

Farr, R. H., Forssell, S. L., & Patterson, C. J. (2010). Parenting and child development in adoptive families: Does parental sexual orientation matter? *Applied Developmental Science, 14,* 164–178. doi:10.1080/10888691.2010.500958

Farr, R. H., & Patterson, C. J. (2013). Coparenting among lesbian, gay, and heterosexual couples: Associations with adopted children's outcomes. *Child Development, 84,* 1226–1240. doi:10.1111/cdev.12046

Farrant, B. M., Devine, T. A. J., Maybery, M. T., & Fletcher, J. (2012). Empathy, perspective taking and prosocial behaviour: The importance of parenting practices. *Infant and Child Development, 21,* 175–188. doi:10.1002/icd.740

Fausey, C. M., Jayaraman, S., & Smith, L. B. (2016). From faces to hands: Changing visual input in the first two years. *Cognition, 152,* 101–107.

Fazio, L. K., DeWolf, M., & Siegler, R. S. (2016). Strategy use and strategy choice in fraction magnitude comparison. *Journal of Experimental Psychology: Learning, Memory, and Cognition, 42,* 1–16. doi:10.1037/xlm0000153

Fearon, R. P., Bakermans-Kranenburg, M. J., van IJzendoorn, M. H., Lapsley, A.-M., & Roisman, G. I. (2010). The significance of insecure attachment and disorganization in the development of children's externalizing behavior: A meta-analytic study. *Child Development, 81,* 435–456. doi:10.1111/j.1467-8624.2009.01405.x

Feddes, A. R., Noack, P., & Rutland, A. (2009). Direct and extended friendship effects on minority and majority children's interethnic attitudes: A longitudinal study. *Child Development, 80,* 377–390. doi:10.1111/j.1467-8624.2009.01266.x

Federal Bureau of Investigation. (2018). Hate crime statistics, 2017. Retrieved from https://ucr.fbi.gov/hate-crime/2017/topic-pages/victims.pdf

Fedewa, A. L., Black, W. W., & Ahn, S. (2015). Children and adolescents with same-gender parents: A meta-analytic approach in assessing outcomes. *Journal of GLBT Family Studies, 11,* 1–34. doi:10.1080/1550428X.2013.869486

Feigenson, L. (2016). Surprise enhances early learning. In D. Barner & A. S. Baron (Eds.), *Core knowledge and conceptual change* (pp. 89–102). New York: Oxford University Press.

Feigenson, L., Carey, S., & Hauser, M. (2002). The representations underlying infants' choice of more: Object files versus analog magnitudes. *Psychological Science, 13*(2), 150–156.

Feigenson, L., Dehaene, S., & Spelke, E. (2004). Core systems of number. *Trends in cognitive sciences, 8*(7), 307–314. doi:10.1016/j.tics.2004.05.002

Feinman, S. (1981). Why is cross-sex-role behavior more approved for girls than boys? A status characteristics approach. *Sex Roles: A Journal of Research, 7*(3), 289–300. http://dx.doi.org/10.1007/BF00287543

Feitelson, D., & Goldstein, Z. (1986). Patterns of book ownership and reading to young children in Israeli school-oriented and nonschool-oriented families. *The Reading Teacher, 39,* 924–930.

Feldman, R. (2012). Oxytocin and social affiliation in humans. *Hormones and Behavior, 61,* 380–391. doi:10.1016/j.yhbeh.2012.01.008

Feldman, R., & Masalha, S. (2010). Parent–child and triadic antecedents of children's social competence: Cultural specificity, shared process. *Developmental Psychology, 46,* 455–467. doi:10.1037/a0017415

Feldman, R., Masalha, S., & Derdikman-Eiron, R. (2010). Conflict resolution in the parent–child, marital, and peer contexts and children's aggression in the peer group: A process-oriented cultural perspective. *Developmental Psychology, 46,* 310–325. doi:10.1037/a0018286

Felson, J. (2014). What can we learn from twin studies? A comprehensive evaluation of the equal environments assumption. *Social Science Research, 43,* 184–199.

Fenson, L., Dale, P. S., Reznick, J. S., Bates, E., Thal, D. J., & Pethick, S. J. (1994). Variability in early communicative development. *Monographs of the Society for Research in Child Development, 59*(5, Serial No. 242), 1–173.

Ferguson, B., Graf, E., & Waxman, S. R. (2018). When veps cry: Two-year-olds efficiently learn novel words from linguistic contexts alone. *Language Learning and Development, 14*(1), 1–12.

Ferguson, C. J. (2015). Do angry birds make for angry children? A meta-analysis of video game influences on children's and adolescents' aggression, mental health, prosocial behavior, and academic performance. *Perspectives on Psychological Science, 10*(5), 646–666. doi:10.1177/1745691615592234

Fergusson, E., Maughan, B., & Golding, J. (2008). Which children receive grandparental care and what effect does it have? *Journal of Child Psychology and Psychiatry, 49,* 161–169. doi:10.1111/j.1469-7610.2007.01840.x

Ferjan Ramírez, N., Lytle, S. R., Fish, M., & Kuhl, P. K. (2018). Parent coaching at 6 and 10 months improves language outcomes at 14 months: A randomized controlled trial. *Developmental Science, 22*(3), e12762.

Fernald, A. (1993). Approval and disapproval: Infant responsiveness to vocal affect in familiar and unfamiliar languages. *Child Development, 64,* 657–674.

Fernald, A., & Marchman, V. A. (2012). Individual differences in lexical processing at 18 months predict vocabulary growth in typically developing and late-talking toddlers. *Child Development, 83,* 203–222. doi:10.1111/j.1467-8624.2011.01692.x

Fernald, A., Perfors, A., & Marchman, V. A. (2006). Picking up speed in understanding: Speech processing efficiency and vocabulary growth across the 2nd year. *Developmental Psychology, 42,* 98–116. doi:10.1037/0012-1649.42.1.98

Fernald, A., Taeschner, T., Dunn, J., Papousek, M., de Boysson-Bardies, B., & Fukui, I. (1989). A cross-language study of prosodic modifications in mothers' and fathers' speech to preverbal infants. *Journal of Child Language, 16,* 477–501.

Ferrao, V. (2010). Women in Canada: A gender-based statistical report. Paid work. Ministry of Industry. Retrieved from http://www.statcan.gc.ca/pub/89-503-x/2010001/article/11387-eng.pdf

Ferrari, M., & Chi, M. T. H. (1998). The nature of naïve explanations of natural selection. *International Journal of Science Education, 20*(10), 1231–1256. doi:10.1080/0950069980201005

Ferrari, P. F., Vanderwert, R. E., Paukner, A., Bower, S., Suomi, S. J., & Fox, N. A. (2012). Distinct EEG amplitude suppression to facial gestures as evidence for a mirror mechanism in newborn monkeys. *Journal of Cognitive Neuroscience, 24*(5), 1165–1172.

Ferry, T. R., Fouad, N. A., & Smith, P. L. (2000). The role of family context in a social cognitive model for career-related choice behavior: A math and science perspective. *Journal of Vocational Behavior, 57,* 348–364. doi:10.1006/jvbe.1999.1743

Field, D. (1987). A review of preschool conservation training: An analysis of analyses. *Developmental Review, 7,* 210–251. doi:10.1016/0273-2297(87)90013-X

Field, T. (2017). Newborn massage therapy. *International Journal of Pediatrics and Neonatal Health, 1*(1), 54–64.

Fifer, W. P., Byrd, D. L., Kaku, M., Eigsti, I.-M., Isler, J. R., Grose-Fifer, J., . . . Balsam, P. D. (2010). Newborn infants learn during sleep. *Proceedings of the National Academy of Sciences of the United States of America, 107,* 10320–10323. doi:10.1073/pnas.1005061107

Filippi, C. A., Cannon, E. N., Fox, N. A., Thorpe, S. G., Ferrari, P. F., & Woodward, A. L. (2016). Motor system activation predicts goal imitation in 7-month-old infants. *Psychological Science, 27*(5), 675–684.

Findlay, L. C., & Kohen, D. E. (2012). Leave practices of parents after the birth or adoption of young children. *Canadian Social Trends, Statistics Canada, Cat. No. 11-008X.* Retrieved from https://www150.statcan.gc.ca/n1/en/pub/11-008-x/2012002/article/11697-eng.pdf?st=akS6srDN

Fingher, N., Dinstein, I., Ben-Shachar, M., Haar, S., Dale, A. M., Eyler, L., . . . Courchesne, E. (2017). Toddlers later diagnosed with autism exhibit multiple structural abnormalities in temporal corpus callosum fibers. *Cortex, 97,* 291–305.

Finkelhor, D., Turner, H., Ormrod, R., Hamby, S., and Kracke, K. (2009). *Children's Exposure to Violence: A Comprehensive National Survey. Bulletin.* Washington, DC: U.S. Department of Justice, Office of Justice Programs, Office of Juvenile Justice and Delinquency Prevention. Retrieved from https://www.ncjrs.gov/pdffiles1/ojjdp/227744.pdf

Finnie, V., & Russell, A. (1988). Preschool children's social status and their mothers' behavior and knowledge in the supervisory role. *Developmental Psychology, 24,* 789–801. doi:10.1037/0012-1649.24.6.789

Fischer, K. W., & Bidell, T. R. (2006). Dynamic development of action and thought. In W. Damon & R. M. Lerner (Series Eds.) & R. M. Lerner (Vol. Ed.), *Handbook of child psychology: Vol. 1. Theoretical models of human development* (6th ed., pp. 313–399). Hoboken, NJ: Wiley.

Fish, J. N., Baams, L., Wojciak, A. S., & Russell, S. T. (2019). Are sexual minority youth overrepresented in foster care, child welfare, and out-of-home placement? Findings from nationally representative data. *Child Abuse & Neglect, 89,* 203–211. doi:10.1016/j.chiabu.2019.01.005

Fisher, C. (1999). From form to meaning: A role for structural alignment in the acquisition of language. *Advances in Child Development and Behavior, 27,* 1–53.

Fisher, C., Gleitman, H., & Gleitman, L. R. (1991). On the semantic content of subcategorization frames. *Cognitive Psychology, 23,* 331–392.

Fisher, P. A., Gunnar, M. R., Chamberlain, P., & Reid, J. B. (2000). Preventive intervention for maltreated preschool children: Impact on children's behavior, neuroendocrine activity, and foster parent functioning. *Journal of the American Academy of Child and Adolescent Psychiatry, 39,* 1356–1364. doi:10.1097/00004583-200011000-00009

Fitzgerald, J. (1992). Variant views about good thinking during composing: Focus on revision. In M. Pressley, K. R. Harris, & J. T. Guthrie (Eds.), *Promoting academic competence and literacy in school* (pp. 337–358). Bingley, England: Emerald Group.

Flavell, J. H. (1986). The development of children's knowledge about the appearance-reality distinction. *American Psychologist, 41,* 418–425.

Fleischer, N. L., Merialdi, M., van Donkelaar, A., Vadillo-Ortega, F., Martin, R. V., Betran, A. P., & Souza, J. P. (2015). Outdoor air pollution, preterm birth, and low birth weight: Analysis of the World Health Organization global survey on maternal and perinatal health. *Environmental Health Perspectives, 22*(4), 425–430.

Fletcher, A. C., Rollins, A., & Nickerson, P. (2004). The extension of school-based inter- and intraracial children's friendships: Influences on psychosocial well-being. *American Journal of Orthopsychiatry, 74,* 272–285. doi:10.1037/0002-9432.74.3.272

Fló, A., Brusini, P., Macagno, F., Nespor, M., Mehler, J., & Ferry, A. L. (2019). Newborns are sensitive to multiple cues for word segmentation in continuous speech. *Developmental Science,* e12802. https://doi.org/10.1111/desc.12802

Flook, L., Goldberg, S. B., Pinger, L. J., & Davidson, R. J. (2015). Promoting prosocial behavior and self-regulatory skills in preschool children through a mindfulness-based kindness curriculum. *Developmental Psychology, 51*(1), 44–51.

Flynn, J. R. (1987). Massive IQ gains in 14 nations: What IQ tests really measure. *Psychological Bulletin, 101,* 171–191.

Flynn, J. R. (2009). *What is intelligence? Beyond the Flynn effect.* Cambridge: Cambridge University Press.

Flynn, J. R., & Weiss, L. G. (2007). American IQ gains from 1931 to 2002: The WISC subtests and educational progress. *International Journal of Testing, 7,* 209–224.

Flynn, R. M., & Richert, R. A. (2018). Cognitive, not physical, engagement in video gaming influences executive functioning. *Journal of Cognition and Development, 19*(1), 1–20. doi:10.1080/15248372.2017.1419246

Fontaine, R. G., Tanha, M., Yang, C., Dodge, K. A., Bates, J. E., & Pettit, G. S. (2010). Does response evaluation and decision (RED) mediate the relation between hostile attributional style and antisocial behavior in adolescence? *Journal of Abnormal Child Psychology, 38,* 615–626. doi:10.1007/s10802-010-9397-y

Fontaine, R. G., Yang, C., Dodge, K. A., Bates, J. E., & Pettit, G. S. (2008). Testing an individual systems model of response evaluation and decision (RED) and antisocial behavior across adolescence. *Child Development, 79,* 462–475. doi:10.1111/j.1467-8624.2007.01136.x

Fontaine, R. G., Yang, C., Dodge, K. A., Pettit, G. S., & Bates, J. E. (2009). Development of response evaluation and decision (RED) and antisocial behavior in childhood and adolescence. *Developmental Psychology, 45,* 447–459. doi:10.1037/a0014142

Fontenot, K., Semega, J., & Kollar, M. (2018). Income and poverty in the United States: 2017. *Current Population Reports (P60-263).* Washington, DC: U.S. Census Bureau. Retrieved from https://www.census.gov/content/dam/Census/library/publications/2018/demo/p60-263.pdf

Foorman, B., Beyler, N., Borradaile, K., Coyne, M., Denton, C. A., Dimino, J., . . . Wissel, S. (2016). *Foundational skills to support reading for understanding in kindergarten through 3rd grade* (NCEE 2016-4008). Washington, DC: National Center for Education Evaluation and Regional Assistance (NCEE), Institute of Education Sciences, U.S. Department of Education. Retrieved from http://ies.ed.gov/ncee/wwc/PracticeGuide.aspx?sid=21

Forbes, G. B., Adams-Curtis, L. E., Pakalka, A. H., & White, K. B. (2006). Dating aggression, sexual coercion, and aggression-supporting attitudes among college men as a function of participation in aggressive high school sports. *Violence Against Women, 12,* 441–455. doi:10.1177/1077801206288126

Fortson, B. L., Klevens, J., Merrick, M. T., Gilbert, L. K., & Alexander, S. P. (2016). *Preventing child abuse and neglect: A technical package for policy, norm, and programmatic activities.* Atlanta, GA: National Center for Injury Prevention and Control, Centers for Disease Control and Prevention. Retrieved from https://www.cdc.gov/violenceprevention/pdf/CAN-Prevention-Technical-Package.pdf

Fox, N. A., & Calkins, S. D. (1993). Pathways to aggression and social withdrawal: Interactions among temperament, attachment, and regulation. In K. H. Rubin & J. B. Asendorpf (Eds.), *Social withdrawal, inhibition, and shyness in childhood* (pp. 81–100). Hillsdale, NJ: Erlbaum.

Fraley, R. C., & Spieker, S. J. (2003). Are infant attachment patterns continuously or categorically distributed? A taxometric analysis of Strange Situation Behavior. *Developmental Psychology, 39,* 387–404. doi:10.1037/0012-1649.39.3.387

Franceschini, S., Trevisan, P., Ronconi, L., Bertoni, S., Colmar, S., Double, K., . . . Gori, S. (2017). Action video games improve reading abilities and visual-to-auditory attentional shifting in English-speaking children with dyslexia. *Scientific Reports, 7*(1), 5863. doi:10.1038/s41598-017-05826-8

Franchak, J. M., Kretch, K. S., & Adolph, K. E. (2018). See and be seen: Infant–caregiver social looking during locomotor free play. *Developmental Science, 21*(4), e12626.

Franke, K., Gaser, C., Roseboom, T. J., Schwab, M., & de Rooij, S. R. (2018). Premature brain aging in humans exposed to maternal nutrient restriction during early gestation. *NeuroImage, 173,* 460–471.

Frazier, T. W., Strauss, M., Klingemier, E. W., Zetzer, E. E., Hardan, A. Y., Eng, C., & Youngstrom, E. A. (2017). A meta-analysis of gaze differences to social and nonsocial information between individuals with and without autism. *Journal of the American Academy of Child & Adolescent Psychiatry, 56*(7), 546–555.

Fréchette, S., & Romano, E. (2015). Change in corporal punishment over time in a representative sample of Canadian parents. *Journal of Family Psychology, 29*(4), 507–517.

Fredricks, J. A., Hofkens, T., Wang, M., Mortenson, E., & Scott, P. (2018). Supporting girls' and boys' engagement in math and science learning: A mixed methods study. *Journal of Research in Science Teaching, 55*(2), 271–298. http://dx.doi.org/10.1002/tea.21419

Freitag, M. K., Belsky, J., Grossmann, K., Grossmann, K. E., & Scheuerer-Englisch, H. (1996). Continuity in parent–child relationships from infancy to middle childhood and relations with friendship competence. *Child Development, 67,* 1437–1454. doi:10.2307/1131710

French, D. C., Setiono, K., & Eddy, J. M. (1999). Bootstrapping through the cultural comparison minefield: Childhood social status and friendship in the United States and Indonesia. In W. A. Collins & B. Laursen (Eds.), *Minnesota Symposia on Child Psychology: Vol. 30. Relationships as developmental contexts* (pp. 109–131). Mahwah, NJ: Erlbaum.

Freud, S. (1964a). *New introductory lectures on psychoanalysis: The standard edition* (J. Strachey, Ed. & Trans.). New York: Norton. (Original work published 1933)

Frick, P. J., & Morris, A. S. (2004). Temperament and developmental pathways to conduct problems. *Journal of Clinical Child and Adolescent Psychology, 33,* 54–68. doi:10.1207/S15374424JCCP3301_6

Friedlmeier, W., Corapci, F., & Cole, P. M. (2011). Emotion socialization in cross-cultural perspective. *Social and Personality Psychology Compass, 5,* 410–427.

Friedman, E. M., Karlamangla, A. S., Gruenewald, T., & Seeman, T. E. (2015). Early life adversity and adult biological risk profiles. *Psychosomatic Medicine, 77*(2), 176–185.

Friedman, M. S., Marshal, M. P., Guadamuz, T. E., Wei, C., Wong, C. F., Saewyc, E. M., & Stall, R. (2011). A meta-analysis of disparities in childhood sexual abuse, parental physical abuse, and peer victimization among sexual minority and sexual nonminority individuals. *American Journal of Public Health, 101,* 1481–1494. doi:10.2105/AJPH.2009.190009

Friedman, W. J. (1991). The development of children's memory for the time of past events. *Child Development, 62,* 139–155. doi:10.1111/j.1467-8624.1991.tb01520.x

Friedman, W. J. (2000). The development of children's knowledge of the times of future events. *Child Development, 71,* 913–932.

Friedman, W. J. (2003). The development of a differentiated sense of the past and the future. *Advances in Child Development and Behavior, 31,* 229–269.

Friedman, W. J. (2008). Developmental perspectives on the psychology of time. In S. Grondin (Ed.), *Psychology of time* (pp. 345–366). Bingley, England: Emerald.

Friedman, W. J., & Lyon, T. D. (2005). Development of temporal-reconstructive abilities. *Child Development, 76,* 1202–1216. doi:10.1111/j.1467-8624.2005.00845.x

Friedman-Krauss, A. H., Barnett, W. S., Garver, K. A., Hodges, K. S., Weisenfeld, G. G., & DiCrecchio, N. (2019). *The state of preschool 2018: State preschool yearbook.* National Institute for Early Education Research. Retrieved from http://nieer.org/wp-content/uploads/2019/04/YB2018_Full-ReportR2.pdf

Friedrich, M., Wilhelm, I., Born, J., & Friederici, A. D. (2015). Generalization of word meaning during infant sleep. *Nature Communications, 6,* 1–9. doi:10.1038/ncomms7004

Fry, D. P. (1988). Intercommunity differences in aggression among Zapotec children. *Child Development, 59,* 1008–1019. doi:10.2307/1130267

Frye, D., Braisby, N., Lowe, J., Maroudas, C., & Nicholls, J. (1989). Young children's understanding of counting and cardinality. *Child Development, 60,* 1158–1171.

Frye, D., Zelazo, P. D., Brooks, P. J., & Samuels, M. C. (1996). Inference and action in early causal reasoning. *Developmental Psychology, 32,* 120–131.

Fuchs, L. S., Schumacher, R. F., Long, J., Namkung, J., Hamlett, C. L., Cirino, P. T., . . . Changas, P. (2013). Improving at-risk learners' understanding of fractions. *Journal of Educational Psychology, 105,* 683–700. doi:10.1037/a0032446

Fuhrmann, D., Knoll, L. J., & Blakemore, S. J. (2015). Adolescence as a sensitive period of brain development. *Trends in Cognitive Sciences, 19*(10), 558–566.

Fujiwara, T., Ito, J., & Kawachi, I. (2013). Income inequality, parental socioeconomic status, and birth outcomes in Japan. *American Journal of Epidemiology, 177*(10), 1042–1052.

Fukuda, M., Fukuda, K., Shimizu, T., Nobunaga, M., Mamsen, L. S., & Andersen, C. Y. (2014). Climate change is associated with male:female ratios of fetal deaths and newborns infants in Japan. *Fertility and Sterility, 102*(5), 1364–1370.

Fung, H., & Chen, E. C.-H. (2001). Across time and beyond skin: Self and transgression in the everyday socialization of shame among Taiwanese preschool children. *Social Development, 10,* 419–437.

Furman, W., Simon, V. A., Shaffer, L., & Bouchey, H. A. (2002). Adolescents' working models and styles for relationships with parents, friends, and romantic partners. *Child Development, 73,* 241–255. doi:10.1111/1467-8624.00403

Furnes, B., & Samuelsson, S. (2011). Phonological awareness and rapid automatized naming predicting early development in reading and spelling: Results from a cross-linguistic longitudinal study. *Learning and Individual Differences, 21,* 85–95. doi:10.1016/j.lindif.2010.10.005

Furukawa, E., Tangney, J., & Higashibara, F. (2012). Cross-cultural continuities and discontinuities in shame, guilt, and pride: A study of children residing in Japan, Korea and the USA. *Self and Identity, 11,* 90–113.

Furuya-Kanamori, L., & Doi, S. (May 2016). Angry birds, angry children, and angry meta-analysts: A reanalysis. *Perspectives on Psychological Science, 11*(3), 408–414. doi:10.1177/1745691616635599

Gaddis, A., & Brooks-Gunn, J. (1985). The male experience of pubertal change. *Journal of Youth and Adolescence, 14,* 61–69. doi:10.1007/BF02088647

Gaetz, S., Gulliver, T., & Richter, T. (2014). *The state of homelessness in Canada: 2014.* Toronto, Canada: Homeless Hub Press.

Gaetz, S., O'Grady, B., Buccieri, K., Karabanow, J., & Marsolais, A. (Eds.). (2013). *Youth homelessness in Canada: Implications for policy and practice.* Toronto, Canada: Canadian Homelessness Research Network Press.

Gaither, S. E., Pauker, K., & Johnson, S. P. (2012). Biracial and monoracial infant own-race face perception: An eye tracking study. *Developmental Science, 15,* 775–782. doi:10.1111/j.1467-7687.2012.01170.x

Galambos, N. L., Almeida, D. M., & Petersen, A. C. (1990). Masculinity, femininity, and sex role attitudes in early adolescence: Exploring gender intensification. *Child Development, 61,* 1905–1914. doi:10.1111/j.1467-8624.1990.tb03574.x

Galambos, N., Leadbeater, B., & Barker, E. (2004). Gender differences in and risk factors for depression in adolescence: A 4-year longitudinal study. *International Journal of Behavioral Development, 28,* 16–25.

Gallese, V., Fadiga, L., Fogassi, L., & Rizzolatti, G. (1996). Action recognition in the premotor cortex. *Brain, 119,* 593–609. doi:10.1093/brain/119.2.593

Galliher, R. V., Jones, M. D., & Dahl, A. (2011). Concurrent and longitudinal effects of ethnic identity and experiences of discrimination on psychosocial adjustment of Navajo adolescents. *Developmental Psychology, 47,* 509–526. doi:10.1037/a0021061

Gal-Szabo, D. E., Spinrad, T. L., Eisenberg, N., Sulik, M. J. (2019). The relations of children's emotion knowledge to their observed social play and reticent /uninvolved behavior in preschool: Moderation by effortful control. *Social Development, 28,* 57–73. https://doi.org/10.1111/sode.12321

Gamble, W. C., Yu, J. J., & Kuehn, E. D. (2011). Adolescent sibling relationship quality and adjustment: Sibling trustworthiness and modeling, as factors directly and indirectly influencing these associations. *Social Development, 20,* 605–623. doi:10.1111/j.1467-9507.2010.00591.x

Gampe, A., Wermelinger, S., & Daum, M. M. (2019). Bilingual children adapt to the needs of their communication partners, monolinguals do not. *Child Development, 90*(1), 98–107.

Gandelman, R. (1992). *The psychobiology of behavioral development.* New York: Oxford University Press.

Ganiban, J. M., Ulbricht, J., Saudino, K. J., Reiss, D., & Neiderhiser, J. M. (2011). Understanding child-based effects on parenting: Temperament as a moderator of genetic and environmental contributions to parenting. *Developmental Psychology, 47,* 676–692.

Ganong, L., Coleman, M., & Jamison, T. (2011). Patterns of stepchild–stepparent relationship development. *Journal of Marriage and Family, 73,* 396–413. doi:10.111/j.1741-3737.2010.00814.x

Ganong, L., Coleman, M., & Russell, L. T. (2015). Children in diverse families. In M. H. Bornstein & T. Leventhal (Vol. Eds.) & R. M. Lerner (Editor in Chief), *Handbook of child psychology and developmental science, Vol. 4: Ecological settings and processes* (pp. 133–174). Hoboken, NJ: Wiley.

Ganzach, Y., Gotlibobski, C., Greenberg, D., & Pazy, A. (2013). General mental ability and pay: Nonlinear effects. *Intelligence, 41*(5), 631–637. doi:10.1016/j.intell.2013.07.015

Garber, J., & Cole, D. A. (2010). Intergenerational transmission of depression: A launch and grow model of change across adolescence. *Development and Psychopathology, 22,* 819–830. doi:10.1017 /S0954579410000489

Gardner, D., Harris, P. L., Ohmoto, M., & Hamazaki, T. (1988). Japanese children's understanding of the distinction between real and apparent emotion. *International Journal of Behavioral Development, 11,* 203–218.

Gardner, H. (1993). *Multiple intelligences: The theory in practice.* New York: Basic Books.

Gardner, H. (1999). *Intelligence reframed: Multiple intelligences for the 21st Century.* New York: Basic Books.

Gardner, R. A., & Gardner, B. T. (1969, August 15). Teaching sign language to a chimpanzee. *Science, 165,* 664–672.

Gargus, R. A., Vohr, B. R., Tyson, J. E., High, P., Higgins, R. D., Wrage, L. A., & Poole, K. (2009). Unimpaired outcomes for extremely low birth weight infants at 18 to 22 months. *Pediatrics, 124,* 112–121. doi:10.1542/peds.2008-2742

Garrett-Bakelman, F. E., Darshi, M., Green, S. J., Gur, R. C., Lin, L., Macias, B. R., . . . Piening, B. D. (2019). The NASA Twins Study: A multidimensional analysis of a year-long human spaceflight. *Science, 364*(6436), eaau8650.

Gartstein, M. A., & Rothbart, M. K. (2003). Studying infant temperament via the Revised Infant Behavior Questionnaire. *Infant Behavior and Development, 26*(1), 64–86.

Gass, K., Jenkins, J., & Dunn, J. (2007). Are sibling relationships protective? A longitudinal study. *Journal of Child Psychology and Psychiatry, 48,* 167–175. doi:10.1111/j.1469-7610.2006.01699.x

Gatzke-Kopp, L. M., Beauchaine, T. P., Shannon, K. E., Chipman, J., Fleming, A. P., Crowell, S. E., . . . Aylward, E. (2009). Neurological correlates of reward responding in adolescents with and without externalizing behavior disorders. *Journal of Abnormal Psychology, 118,* 203–213. doi:10.1037/a0014378

Gauvain, M. (2001). *The social context of cognitive development.* New York: Guilford Press.

Gaylord-Harden, N. K., Burrow, A. L., & Cunningham, J. A. (2012). A cultural-asset framework for investigating successful adaptation to stress in African American youth. *Child Development Perspectives, 6,* 264–271. doi:10.1111/j.1750-8606.2012.00236.x

Gazzaniga, M. S., Ivry, R., & Mangun, G. R. (2013). *Cognitive neuroscience: the biology of mind* (4th ed.). New York: W. W. Norton.

Ge, X., Natsuaki, M. N., & Conger, R. D. (2006). Trajectories of depressive symptoms and stressful life events among male and female adolescents in divorced and nondivorced families. *Development and Psychopathology, 18,* 253–273. doi:10.1017 /S0954579406060147

Geangu, E., Ichikawa, H., Lao, J., Kanazawa, S., Yamaguchi, M., Caldara, R., & Turati, C. (2016). Culture shapes 7-month-olds' perceptual strategies in discriminating facial expressions of emotion. *Current Biology, 26,* R1–R3.

Geary, D. C. (2004). Mathematics and learning disabilities. *Journal of Learning Disabilities, 37,* 4–15. doi :10.1177/00222194040370010201

Geary, D. C. (2005). *The origin of mind: Evolution of brain, cognition, and general intelligence.* Washington, DC: American Psychological Association.

Geary, D. C. (2006). Development of mathematical understanding. In W. Damon & R. M. Lerner (Series Eds.) & D. Kuhn & R. S. Siegler (Vol. Eds.), *Handbook of child psychology: Vol. 2. Cognition, perception, and language* (6th ed., pp. 777–810). Hoboken, NJ: Wiley.

Geary, D. C. (2009). *Male, female: The evolution of human sex differences* (2nd ed.). Washington, DC: American Psychological Association.

Geary, D. C. (2010). *Male, female: The evolution of human sex differences* (2nd ed.). Washington, DC: American Psychological Association.

Geary, D. C., Hoard, M. K., Byrd-Craven, J., Nugent, L., & Numtee, C. (2007). Cognitive mechanisms underlying achievement deficits in children with mathematical learning disability. *Child Development, 78,* 1343–1359. doi:10.1111/j.1467-8624.2007.01069.x

Geary, D. C., Hoard, M. K., Nugent, L., & Bailey, D. H. (2012). Mathematical cognition deficits in children with learning disabilities and persistent low achievement: A five-year prospective study. *Journal of Educational Psychology, 104,* 206–223. doi:10.1037 /a0025398

Geena Davis Institute on Gender in Media. (2019). *Key findings.* Retrieved from https://seejane.org /research-informs-empowers/

Gejman, P. V., Sanders, A. R., & Duan, J. (2010). The role of genetics in the etiology of schizophrenia. *Psychiatric Clinics of North America, 33*(1), 35–66. doi:10.1016/j.psc.2009.12.003

Gelman, R., & Gallistel, C. R. (1978). *The child's understanding of number.* Cambridge, MA: Harvard University Press.

Gelman, R., Meck, E., & Merkin, S. (1986). Young children's numerical competence. *Cognitive Development, 1,* 1–29.

Gelman, R., & Williams, E. M. (1998). Enabling constraints for cognitive development and learning: Domain specificity and epigenesis. In W. Damon (Series Ed.) & D. Kuhn & R. S. Siegler (Vol. Eds.), *Handbook of child psychology: Vol. 2: Cognition, perception, and language* (5th ed., pp. 575–630). Hoboken, NJ: Wiley.

Gelman, S. A. (2003). *The essential child: Origins of essentialism in everyday thought.* New York: Oxford University Press.

Gelman, S. A., Coley, J. D., Rosengren, K. S., Hartman, E., & Pappas, A. (1998). Beyond labeling: The role of maternal input in the acquisition of richly structured categories. *Monographs of the Society for Research in Child Development, 63*(1, Serial No. 253).

Gelman, S. A., & Kalish, C. W. (2006). Conceptual development. In W. Damon & R. M. Lerner (Series Eds.) & D. Kuhn & R. S. Siegler (Vol. Eds.), *Handbook of child psychology: Vol. 2. Cognition, perception, and language* (6th ed., pp. 687–733). Hoboken, NJ: Wiley.

Gelman, S. A., & Noles, N. S. (2011). Domains and naïve theories. *Wiley Interdisciplinary Reviews: Cognitive Science, 2*(5), 490–502. doi:10.1002/wcs.124

Genesee, F., Boivin, I., & Nicoladis, E. (1996). Talking with strangers: A study of bilingual children's communicative competence. *Applied Psycholinguistics, 17*(4), 427–442.

Genesee, F., & Nicoladis, E. (2007). Bilingual first language acquisition. *Handbook of Language Development,* 324–342.

Gentile, B., Grabe, S., Dolan-Pascoe, B., Twenge, J. M., & Wells, B. E. (2009). Gender differences in domain-specific self-esteem: A meta-analysis. *Review of General Psychology, 13,* 34–45. doi:10.1037/a0013689

Gentile, D. A. (2015). What is a good skeptic to do? The case for skepticism in the media violence discussion. *Perspectives on Psychological Science, 10*(5), 674–676.

Georgiades, K., Duncan, L., Wang, L., Comeau, J., & Boyle, M. H. (2019). Six-month prevalence of mental disorders and service contacts among children and youth in Ontario: Evidence from the 2014 Ontario Child Health Study. *Canadian Journal of Psychiatry, 64*(4), 246–255. https://doi.org/10.1177/0706743719830024

Gergely, G., Bekkering, H., & Kiraly, I. (2002, February 14). Developmental psychology: Rational imitation in preverbal infants. *Nature, 415,* 755.

Gerken, L., Balcomb, F. K., & Minton, J. L. (2011). Infants avoid "labouring in vain" by attending more to learnable than unlearnable linguistic patterns. *Developmental Science, 14,* 972–979. doi:10.1111/j.1467-7687.2011.01046.x

Gerken, L., Wilson, R., & Lewis, W. (2005). Infants can use distributional cues to form syntactic categories. *Journal of Child Language, 32,* 249–268. doi:10.1017/S0305000904006786

German, T. P., & Nichols, S. (2003). Children's counterfactual inferences about long and short causal chains. *Developmental Science, 6,* 514–523. doi:10.1111/1467-7687.00309

Gershoff, E. T. (2002). Corporal punishment by parents and associated child behaviors and experiences: A meta-analytic and theoretical review. *Psychological Bulletin, 128,* 539–579.

Gershoff, E. T. (2013). Spanking and child development: We know enough now to stop hitting our children. *Child Development Perspectives, 7,* 133–137. doi:10.1111/cdep.12038

Gershoff, E. T., Aber, J. L., Raver, C. C., & Lennon, M. C. (2007). Income is not enough: Incorporating material hardship into models of income associations with parent mediators and child outcomes. *Child Development, 78*(1), 70–95. doi:10.1111/j.1467-8624.2007.00986.x

Gershoff, E. T., Aber, J. L., Ware, A., & Kotler, J. (2010). Exposure to 9/11 among youth and their mothers in New York City: Enduring associations with mental health and sociopolitical attitudes. *Child Development, 81,* 1142–1160.

Gershoff, E. T., & Benner, A. D. (2014). Neighborhood and school contexts in the lives of children. In E. T. Gershoff, R. S. Mistry, & D. A. Crosby (Eds.), *Societal contexts of child development.* New York: Oxford University Press.

Gershoff, E. T., & Grogan-Kaylor, A. (2016a). Corporal punishment by parents and its consequences for children: Old controversies and new meta-analyses. *Journal of Family Psychology, 30,* 453–469. doi:10.1037/fam0000191

Gershoff, E. T., & Grogan-Kaylor, A. (2016b). Cultural normativeness, race, and spanking: Preliminary meta-analytic findings. *Family Relations, 65,* 490–501. doi:10.1111/fare.12205

Gershoff, E. T., Grogan-Kaylor, A., Lansford, J. E., Chang, L., Zelli, A., Deater-Deckard, K., & Dodge, K. A. (2010). Parent discipline practices in an international sample: Associations with child behaviors and moderation by perceived normativeness. *Child Development, 81,* 487–502. doi:10.1111/j.1467-8624.2009.01409.x

Gershoff, E. T., Lansford, J. E., Sexton, H. R., Davis-Kean, P., & Sameroff, A. J. (2012). Longitudinal links between spanking and children's externalizing behaviors in a national sample of White, Black, Hispanic, and Asian American families. *Child Development, 83,* 838–843. doi:10.1111/j.1467-8624.2011.01732.x

Gesell, A., & Thompson, H. (1938). *The psychology of early growth, including norms of infant behavior and a method of genetic analysis.* New York: Macmillan.

Gest, S. D., Graham-Bermann, S. A., & Hartup, W. W. (2001). Peer experience: Common and unique features of number of friendships, social network centrality, and sociometric status. *Social Development, 10,* 23–40. doi:10.1111/1467-9507.00146

Gfellner, B. M., & Armstrong, H. D. (2012). Ego development, ego strengths, and ethnic identity among First Nation adolescents. *Journal of Research on Adolescence, 22,* 225–234. doi:10.1111/j.1532-7795.2011.00769.x

Gianino, A., & Tronick, E. Z. (1988). The mutual regulation model: The infant's self and interactive regulation and coping and defensive capacities. In T. M. Field, P. M. McCabe, & N. Schneiderman (Eds.), *Stress and coping across development* (pp. 47–68). Hillsdale, NJ: Erlbaum.

Gibbs, J. C., Basinger, K. S., Grime, R. L., & Snarey, J. R. (2007). Moral judgment development across cultures: Revisiting Kohlberg's universality claims. *Developmental Review, 27,* 443–500. doi:10.1016/j.dr.2007.04.001te

Gibson, E. J. (1988). Exploratory behavior in the development of perceiving, acting, and the acquiring of knowledge. *Annual Review of Psychology, 39,* 1–42. doi:10.1146/annurev.ps.39.020188.000245

Gibson, E. J., Riccio, G., Schmuckler, M. A., Stoffregen, T. A., Rosenberg, D., & Taormina, J. (1987). Detection of the traversability of surfaces by crawling and walking infants. *Journal of Experimental Psychology: Human Perception and Performance, 13,* 533–544. doi:10.1037/0096-1523.13.4.533

Gibson, E. J., & Schmuckler, M. A. (1989). Going somewhere: An ecological and experimental approach to development of mobility. *Ecological Psychology, 1,* 3–25. doi:10.1207/s15326969eco0101_2

Gibson, E. J., & Walk, R. D. (1960, April). The "visual cliff." *Scientific American, 202*(4), 64–71.

Giedd, J. N., Blumenthal, J., Jeffries, N. O., Castellanos, F. X., Liu, H., Zijdenbos, A., . . . Rapoport, J. L. (1999). Brain development during childhood and adolescence: A longitudinal MRI study. *Nature Neuroscience, 2,* 861–863.

Gilbert, N. L., Auger, N., Wilkins, R., & Kramer, M. S. (2013). Neighbourhood income and neonatal, postneonatal and sudden infant death syndrome (SIDS) mortality in Canada, 1991–2005. *Canadian Journal of Public Health, 104*(3), 187–192.

Giles, J. W., & Heyman, G. D. (2005). Young children's beliefs about the relationship between gender and aggressive behavior. *Child Development, 76,* 107–121. doi:10.1111/j.1467-8624.2005.00833.x

Giletta, M., Scholte, R. H., Burk, W. J., Engels, R. C., Larsen, J. K., Prinstein, M. J., & Ciairano, S. (2011). Similarity in depressive symptoms in adolescents' friendship dyads: Selection or socialization? *Developmental Psychology, 47,* 1804–1814. doi:10.1037/a0023872

Gilligan, C. (1982). *In a different voice: Psychological theory and women's development.* Cambridge, MA: Harvard University Press.

Gilligan, C., & Attanucci, J. (1988). Two moral orientations: Gender differences and similarities. *Merrill-Palmer Quarterly, 34,* 223–237. doi:10.2307/23086381

Gilmore, J. H., Knickmeyer, R. C., & Gao, W. (2018). Imaging structural and functional brain development in early childhood. *Nature Reviews Neuroscience, 19*(3), 123.

Gitterman, B. A., Flanagan, P. J., Cotton, W. H., Dilley, K. J., Duffee, J. H., Green, A. E., . . . Nelson, J. L. (2016). Poverty and child health in the United States. *Pediatrics, 137*(4), e20160339. doi:10.1542/peds.2016-0339

Gladwell, M. (2008). *Outliers: The story of success.* New York: Little, Brown.

Glass, B. D., Maddox, W. T., & Love, B. C. (2013). Real-time strategy game training: Emergence of a cognitive flexibility trait. *PLoS ONE, 8*(8), Article e70350. Retrieved from http://journals.plos.org/plosone/article?id=10.1371/journal.pone.0070350

Gleason, J. B., & Ely, R. (2002). Gender differences in language development. In A. V. McGillicuddy-De Lisi & R. De Lisi (Eds.), *Biology, society, and behavior: The development of sex differences in cognition* (Vol. 21, pp. 127–154). Westport, CT: Ablex.

Glick, G. C., & Rose, A. J. (2011). Prospective associations between friendship adjustment and social strategies: Friendship as a context for building social skills. *Developmental Psychology, 47,* 1117–1132.

Glick, P., & Fiske, S. T. (2001). An ambivalent alliance: Hostile and benevolent sexism as complementary justifications for gender inequality. *American Psychologist, 56*(2), 109–118.

Global Initiative to End All Corporal Punishment of Children. (2019). *Global progress.* Retrieved from https://endcorporalpunishment.org/countdown/

Glocker, M. L., Langleben, D. D., Ruparel, K., Loughead, J. W., Valdez, J. N., Griffin, M. D., . . . Gur, R. C. (2009). Baby schema modulates the brain reward system in nulliparous women. *Proceedings of the National Academy of Sciences, 106*(22), 9115–9119.

Glover, V., O'Donnell, K. J., O'Connor, T. G., & Fisher, J. (2018). Prenatal maternal stress, fetal programming, and mechanisms underlying later psychopathology—A global perspective. *Development and Psychopathology, 30*(3), 843–854.

Godlee, F., Smith, J., & Marcovitch, H. (2011). Wakefield's article linking MMR vaccine and autism was fraudulent. *BMJ, 342.* doi:10.1136/bmj.c7452

Gogtay, N., Giedd, J. N., Lusk, L., Hyashi, K. M., Greenstein, D., Vaituzis, A.C., . . . Thompson, P. M. (2004). Dynamic mapping of human cortical development during childhood through early adulthood. *PNAS, 101*(21), 8174–8179.

Goldin-Meadow, S., Cook, S. W., & Mitchell, Z. A. (2009). Gesturing gives children new ideas about math. *Psychological Science, 20,* 267–272.

Goldsmith, H. H., Pollak, S. D., & Davidson, R. J. (2008). Developmental neuroscience perspectives on emotion regulation. *Child Development Perspectives, 2,* 132–140.

Goldstein, M. H., King, A. P., & West, M. J. (2003). Social interaction shapes babbling: Testing parallels between birdsong and speech. *Proceedings of the National Academy of Sciences of the United States of America, 100,* 8030–8035. doi:10.1073/pnas.1332441100

Goldstein, M. H., & Schwade, J. A. (2008). Social feedback to infants' babbling facilitates rapid phonological learning. *Psychological Science, 19,* 515–523. doi:10.1111/j.1467-9280.2008.02117.x

Goldstein, M. H., Schwade, J., Briesch, J., & Syal, S. (2010). Learning while babbling: Prelinguistic object-directed vocalizations indicate a readiness to learn. *Infancy, 15,* 362–391. doi:10.1111/j.1532-7078.2009.00020.x

Goldstein, T. R., & Winner, E. (2011). Enhancing empathy and theory of mind. *Journal of Cognition and Development, 13,* 19–37. doi:10.1080/15248372.2011.573514

Golish, T. D. (2003). Stepfamily communication strengths. *Human Communication Research, 29,* 41–80. doi:10.1111/j.1468-2958.2003.tb00831.x

Gómez, R. L. (2002). Variability and detection of invariant structure. *Psychological Science, 13,* 431–436.

Gómez, R. L., Bootzin, R. R., & Nadel, L. (2006). Naps promote abstraction in language-learning infants. *Psychological Science, 17,* 670–674. doi:10.1111/j.1467-9280.2006.01764.x

Gómez, R. L., & Edgin, J. O. (2015). Sleep as a window into early neural development: Shifts in sleep-dependent learning effects across early childhood. *Child Development Perspectives, 9*(3), 183–189. doi:10.1111/cdep.12130

Gonzales, N. A., Pitts, S. C., Hill, N. E., & Roosa, M. W. (2000). A mediational model of the impact of interparental conflict on child adjustment in a multiethnic, low-income sample. *Journal of Family Psychology, 14,* 365–379. doi:10.1037/0893-3200.14.3.365

Good, T. L., & Brophy, J. E. (1996). *Looking in classrooms* (7th ed.). New York: Longman.

Gooden, A. M., & Gooden, M. A. (2001). Gender representation in notable children's picture books: 1995–1999. *Sex Roles, 45,* 89–101. doi:10.1023/A:1013064418674

Goodman, A., Gregg, P., & Washbrook, E. (2011). Children's educational attainment and the aspirations, attitudes and behaviours of parents and children through childhood. *Longitudinal and Life Course Studies, 2*(1), 1–18. doi:10.14301/llcs.v2i1.147

Goodnight, J. A., Lahey, B. B., Van Hulle, C. A., Rodgers, J. L., Rathouz, P. J., Waldman, I. D., & D'Onofrio, B. M. (2012). A quasi-experimental analysis of the influence of neighborhood disadvantage on child and adolescent conduct problems. *Journal of Abnormal Psychology, 121,* 95–108. doi:10.1037/a0025078

Gooren, E. M. J. C., van Lier, P. A. C., Stegge, H., Terwogt, M. M., & Koot, H. M. (2011). The development of conduct problems and depressive symptoms in early elementary school children: The role of peer rejection. *Journal of Clinical Child and Adolescent Psychology, 40,* 245–253. doi:10.1080/15374416.2011.546045

Gopnik, A., & Astington, J. W. (1988). Children's understanding of representational change and its relation to the understanding of false belief and the appearance-reality distinction. *Child Development, 59,* 26–37.

Gopnik, A., & Slaughter, V. (1991). Young children's understanding of changes in their mental states. *Child Development, 62,* 98–110. doi:10.1111/j.1467-8624.1991.tb01517.x

Gopnik, A., & Wellman, H. M. (2012). Reconstructing constructivism: Causal models, Bayesian learning mechanisms, and the theory theory. *Psychological Bulletin, 138*(6), 1085–1108. doi:10.1037/a0028044

Gordon, K., Murin, M., Baykaner, O., Roughan, L., Livermore-Hardy, V., Skuse, D., & Mandy, W. (2015). A randomised controlled trial of PEGASUS, a psychoeducational programme for young people with high-functioning autism spectrum disorder. *Journal of Child Psychology and Psychiatry, 56,* 468–476. doi:10.1111/jcpp.12304

Gordon, M. (2009). *Roots of empathy: Changing the world child by child.* Workman Publishing.

Gosselin, J., & David, H. (2007). Risk and resilience factors linked with the psychosocial adjustment of adolescents, stepparents and biological parents. *Journal of Divorce and Remarriage, 48,* 29–53. doi:10.1300/j087v48n01_02

Gottesman, I. I. (with Wolfgram, D. L.). (1991). *Schizophrenia genesis: The origins of madness.* New York: Freeman.

Gottfredson, L. S. (1997). Why g matters: The complexity of everyday life. *Intelligence, 24,* 79–132.

Gottfredson, L. S. (2011). Intelligence and social inequality: Why the biological link? In T. Chamorro-Premuzic, S. von Stumm, & A. Furnham (Eds.), *Handbook of individual differences* (pp. 538–575). Chichester, West Sussex, England: Wiley-Blackwell.

Gottlieb, A. (2004). *The afterlife is where we come from: The culture of infancy in West Africa.* Chicago: University of Chicago Press.

Gottman, J. M., Katz, L. F., & Hooven, C. (1997). *Meta-emotion: How families communicate emotionally.* Mahwah, NJ: Erlbaum.

Gould, E., & Cooke, T. (2015, October). High-quality child care is out of reach for working families (Issue Brief No. 404). Washington, DC: Economic Policy Institute. Retrieved from Economic Policy Institute website: http://www.epi.org/publication/child-care-affordability/

Gradisar, M., Jackson, K., Spurrier, N. J., Gibson, J., Whitham, J., Williams, A. S., . . . Kennaway, D. J. (2016). Behavioral interventions for infant sleep problems: A randomized controlled trial. *Pediatrics,* e20151486.

Grady, C. L., Mondloch, C. J., Lewis, T. L., & Maurer, D. (2014). Early visual deprivation from congenital cataracts disrupts activity and functional connectivity in the face network. *Neuropsychologia, 57*(May), 122–139. doi:10.1016/j.neuropsychologia.2014.03.005

Graf Estes, K., & Hay, J. F. (2015). Flexibility in bilingual infants' word learning. *Child Development, 86*(5), 1371–1385.

Graham, S. [Sandra], & Hudley, C. (1994). Attributions of aggressive and nonaggressive African-American male early adolescents: A study of construct accessibility. *Developmental Psychology, 30,* 365–373. doi:10.1037/0012-1649.30.3.365

Graham, S., McKeown, D., Kiuhara, S., & Harris, K. R. (2012). A meta-analysis of writing instruction for students in the elementary grades. *Journal of Educational Psychology, 104*(4), 879. doi:10.1037/a0029185

Graham, S. A., & Diesendruck, G. (2010). Fifteen-month-old infants attend to shape over other perceptual properties in an induction task. *Cognitive Development, 25*(2), 111–123.

Graham, S. A., & Fisher, S. E. (2015). Understanding language from a genomic perspective. *Annual Review of Genetics, 49,* 131–160. doi:10.1146/annurev-genet-120213-092236

Graham, S. A., Nayer, S. L., & Gelman, S. A. (2011). Two year olds use the generic/nongeneric distinction to guide their inferences about novel kinds. *Child Development, 82*(2), 493–507.

Graham, S. A., & Poulin-Dubois, D. (1999). Infants' reliance on shape to generalize novel labels to animate and inanimate objects. *Journal of Child Language, 26,* 295–320.

Graham-Bermann, S. A., & Brescoll, V. (2000). Gender, power, and violence: Assessing the family stereotypes of the children of batterers. *Journal of Family Psychology, 14,* 600–612. doi:10.1037/0893-3200.14.4.600

Granier-Deferre, C., Ribeiro, A., Jacquet, A. Y., & Bassereau, S. (2011). Near-term fetuses process temporal features of speech. *Developmental Science, 14,* 336–352.

Granot, D., & Mayseless, O. (2001). Attachment security and adjustment to school in middle childhood. *International Journal of Behavioral Development, 25,* 530–541. doi:10.1080/01650250042000366

Granqvist, P., Sroufe, A. L., Dozier, M., Hesse, E., Steele, M., . . . Duschinsky, R. (2017). Disorganized attachment in infancy: A review of the phenomenon and its implications for clinicians and policy-makers. *Attachment & Human Development, 19,* 534–558. doi:10.1080/14616734.2017.1354040

Gray-Little, B., & Hafdahl, A. R. (2000). Factors influencing racial comparisons of self-esteem: A quantitative review. *Psychological Bulletin, 126,* 26–54. doi:10.1037/0033-2909.126.1.26

Greenberg, M. T., Kusché, C. A., Cook, E. T., & Quamma, J. P. (1995). Promoting emotional competence in school-aged children: The effects of the PATHS curriculum. *Development and Psychopathology, 7,* 117–136. doi:10.1017/S0954579400006374

Greenfield, P. M. (2004). Inadvertent exposure to pornography on the Internet: Implications of peer-to-peer file-sharing networks for child development and families. *Journal of Applied Developmental Psychology, 25,* 741–750. doi:10.1016/j.appdev.2004.09.009

Greenfield, P. M., Suzuki, L. K., & Rothstein-Fisch, C. (2006). Cultural pathways through human development. In W. Damon & R. M. Lerner (Series Eds.) & K. A. Renninger & I. E. Sigel (Vol. Eds.), *Handbook of child psychology: Vol. 4: Child psychology in practice* (6th ed., pp. 655–699). Hoboken, NJ: Wiley.

Greenough, W. T., Black, J. E., & Wallace, C. S. (1987). Experience and brain development. *Child Development, 58,* 539–559.

Greenwald, A. G., Banaji, M. R., Rudman, L. A., Farnham, S. D., Nosek, B. A., & Mellott, D. S. (2002). A unified theory of implicit attitudes, stereotypes, self-esteem, and self-concept. *Psychological Review, 109*(1), 3–25. http://dx.doi.org/10.1037/0033-295X.109.1.3

Gregory, A. M., Light-Häusermann, J. H., Rijsdijk, F., & Eley, T. C. (2009). Behavioral genetic analyses of prosocial behavior in adolescents. *Developmental Science, 12,* 165–174. doi:10.1111/j.1467-7687.2008.00739.x

Gregory, T. R. (2009). Understanding natural selection: Essential concepts and common misconceptions. *Evolution: Education & Outreach, 2,* 156–175. doi:10.1007/s12052-009-0128-1

Grieco-Calub, T. M., Saffran, J. R., & Litovsky, R. Y. (2009). Spoken word recognition in toddlers who use cochlear implants. *Journal of Speech, Language, and Hearing Research, 52,* 1390–1400. doi:10.1044/1092-4388(2009/08-0154)

Grimshaw, G. M., Sitarenios, G., & Finegan, J.-A. K. (1995). Mental rotation at 7 years: Relations with prenatal testosterone levels and spatial play experiences. *Brain and Cognition, 29,* 85–100. doi:10.1006/brcg.1995.1269

Groh, A. M., Fearon, R. P., Bakermans-Kranenburg, M. J., van IJzendoorn, M. H., Steele, R. D., & Roisman, G. I. (2014). The significance of attachment security for children's social competence with peers: A meta-analytic study. *Attachment & Human Development, 16,* 103–136.

Groh, A. M., Roisman, G. I., van IJzendoorn, M. H., Bakermans-Kranenburg, M. J., & Fearon, R. P. (2012). The significance of insecure and disorganized attachment for children's internalizing symptoms: A meta-analytic study. *Child Development, 83,* 591–610. doi:10.1111/j.1467-8624.2011.01711.x

Grön, G., Wunderlich, A. P., Spitzer, M., Tomczak, R., & Riepe, M. W. (2000). Brain activation during human navigation: Gender-different neural networks as substrate of performance. *Nature Neuroscience, 3,* 404–408.

Gross, D., & Harris, P. L. (1988). False beliefs about emotion: Children's understanding of misleading emotional displays. *International Journal of Behavioral Development, 11*(4), 475–488.

Grossmann, T. (2010). The development of emotion perception in face and voice during infancy. *Restorative Neurology and Neuroscience, 28,* 219–236. doi:10.3233/RNN-2010-0499

Grueneich, R. (1982). Issues in the developmental study of how children use intention and consequence information to make moral evaluations. *Child Development, 53,* 29–43. doi:10.2307/1129636

Grünebaum, A., McCullough, L. B., Arabin, B., Brent, R. L., Levene, M. I., & Chervenak, F. A. (2016). Neonatal mortality of planned home birth in the United States in relation to professional certification of birth attendants. *PLoS ONE, 11*(5), e0155721. doi:10.1371/journal.pone.0155721

Grusec, J. E., & Goodnow, J. J. (1994). Impact of parental discipline methods on the child's internalization of values: A reconceptualization of current points of view. *Developmental Psychology, 30,* 4–19. doi:10.1037/0012-1649.30.1.4

Grusec, J. E., Goodnow, J. J., & Cohen, L. (1996). Household work and the development of concern for others. *Developmental Psychology, 32,* 999–1007.

Grych, J. H., Harold, G. T., & Miles, C. J. (2003). A prospective investigation of appraisals as mediators of the link between interparental conflict and child adjustment. *Child Development, 74,* 1176–1193. doi:10.1111/1467-8624.00600

Grych, J. H., Raynor, S. R., & Fosco, G. M. (2004). Family processes that shape the impact of interparental conflict on adolescents. *Development and Psychopathology, 16,* 649–665. doi:10.1017/S0954579404004717

Guerra, N. G., Huesmann, L. R., & Spindler, A. (2003). Community violence exposure, social cognition, and aggression among urban elementary school children. *Child Development, 74,* 1561–1576. doi:10.1111/1467-8624.00623

Gullone, E. (2000). The development of normal fear: A century of research. *Clinical Psychology Review, 20,* 429–451. doi:10.1016/S0272-7358(99)00034-3

Gummerum, M., & Keller, M. (2008). Affection, virtue, pleasure, and profit: Developing an understanding of friendship closeness and intimacy in western and Asian societies. *International Journal of Behavioral Development, 32,* 218–231. doi:10.1177/0165025408089271

Gunderson, E. A., Gripshover, S. J., Romero, C., Dweck, C. S., Goldin-Meadow, S., & Levine, S. C. (2013). Parent praise to 1- to 3-year-olds predicts children's motivational frameworks 5 years later. *Child Development, 84*(5), 1526–1541.

Gunderson, E. A., Sorhagen, N. S., Gripshover, S. J., Dweck, C. S., Goldin-Meadow, S., & Levine, S. C. (2018). Parent praise to toddlers predicts fourth grade academic achievement via children's incremental mindsets. *Developmental Psychology, 54*(3), 397–409.

Guo, J., Marsh, H. W., Morin, A. J. S., Parker, P. D., & Kaur, G. (2015). Directionality of the associations of high school expectancy-value, aspirations, and attainment: A longitudinal study. *American Educational Research Journal, 52*(2), 371–402. doi:10.3102/0002831214565786

Gurnani, T., Ivanov, I., & Newcorn, J. H. (2016). Pharmacotherapy of aggression in child and adolescent psychiatric disorders. *Journal of Child and Adolescent Psychopharmacology, 26,* 65–73. doi:10.1089/cap.2015.0167

Guthrie, J. T., Wigfield, A., Metsala, J. L., & Cox, K. E. (1999). Motivational and cognitive predictors of text comprehension and reading amount. *Scientific Studies of Reading, 3,* 231–256. doi:10.1207/s1532799xssr0303_3

Gutman, L. M., Sameroff, A. J., & Cole, R. (2003). Academic growth curve trajectories from 1st grade to 12th grade: Effects of multiple social risk factors and preschool child factors. *Developmental Psychology, 39,* 777–790.

Gweon, H., & Schulz, L. (2011). 16-month-olds rationally infer causes of failed actions. *Science, 332*(6037), 1524.

Gwiazda, J., Grice, K., Held, R., McLellan, J., & Thorn, F. (2000). Astigmatism and the development of myopia in children. *Vision Research, 40,* 1019–1026.

Hagerman, M. A. (2017). White racial socialization: Progressive fathers on raising "antiracist" children. *Journal of Marriage and Family, 79,* 60–74. doi:10.1111/jomf.12325

Haith, M. M., Bergman, T., & Moore, M. J. (1977, November). Eye contact and face scanning in early infancy. *Science, 198,* 853–855.

Haith, M. M., Wentworth, N., & Canfield, R. L. (1993). The formation of expectations in early infancy. In C. Rovee-Collier & L. P. Lipsitt (Eds.), *Advances in infancy research* (Vol. 8, pp. 251–297). Norwood, NJ: Ablex.

Hakvoort, E. M., Bos, H. M. W., van Balen, F., & Hermanns, J. M. A. (2011). Postdivorce relationships in families and children's psychosocial adjustment. *Journal of Divorce and Remarriage, 52,* 125–146. doi:10.1080/10502556.2011.546243

Halberda, J., & Feigenson, L. (2008). Developmental change in the acuity of the "Number Sense": The approximate number system in 3-, 4-, 5-, and 6-year-olds and adults. *Developmental Psychology, 44*(5), 1457–1465. doi:10.1037/a0012682

Halberstadt, A. G., & Eaton, K. L. (2003). A meta-analysis of family expressiveness and children's emotion expressiveness and understanding. *Marriage & Family Review, 34*(1–2), 35–62. doi:10.1300/J002v34n01_03

Halim, M. L., & Ruble, D. (2010). Gender identity and stereotyping in early and middle childhood. In J. C. Chrisler, & D. R. McCreary (Eds.), *Handbook of gender research in psychology, Vol 1: Gender research in general and experimental psychology* (pp. 495–525). New York: Springer. http://dx.doi.org/10.1007/978-1-4419-1465-1_24

Halim, M. L., Ruble, D. N., Tamis-LeMonda, C., Zosuls, K. M., Lurye, L. E., & Greulich, F. K. (2014). Pink frilly dresses and the avoidance of all things "girly": Children's appearance rigidity and cognitive theories of gender development. *Developmental Psychology, 50*(4), 1091–1101. http://dx.doi.org/10.1037/a0034906

Hallers-Haalboom, E. T., Mesman, J., Groeneveld, M. G., Endendijk, J. J., van Berkel, S. R., van der Pol, L. D., & Bakermans-Kranenburg, M. J. (2014). Mothers, fathers, sons and daughters: Parental sensitivity in families with two children. *Journal of Family Psychology, 28*(2), 138. doi:10.1037/a0036004

Halligan, S. L., & Philips, K. J. (2010). Are you thinking what I'm thinking? Peer group similarities in adolescent hostile attribution tendencies. *Developmental Psychology, 46,* 1385–1388. doi:10.1037/a0020383

Halpern, D. F. (2012). *Sex differences in cognitive abilities* (4th ed.). New York: Psychology Press.

Halpern, D. F., Benbow, C. P., Geary, D. C., Gur, R. C., Hyde, J. S., & Gernsbacher, M. A. (2007). The science of sex differences in science and mathematics. *Psychological Science in the Public Interest, 8,* 1–51. doi:10.1111/j.1529-1006.2007.00032.x

Haltigan, J. D., & Vaillancourt, T. (2014). Joint trajectories of bullying and peer victimization across elementary and middle school and associations with symptoms of psychopathology. *Developmental Psychology, 50,* 2426–2436. doi:10.1037/a0038030

Hamamura, T., Heine, S. J., & Paulhus, D. L. (2008). Cultural differences in response styles: The role of dialectical thinking. *Personality and Individual Differences, 44,* 932–942. doi:10.1016/j.paid.2007.10.034

Hamilton, M. C., Anderson, D., Broaddus, M., & Young, K. (2006). Gender stereotyping and under-representation of female characters in 200 popular children's picture books: A twenty-first century update. *Sex Roles, 55,* 757–765.

Hamlin, J. K. (2013). Moral judgment and action in preverbal infants and toddlers: Evidence for an innate moral core. *Current Directions in Psychological Science, 22,* 186–193. doi:10.1177/0963721412470687

Hamlin, J. K., Wynn, K., & Bloom, P. (2007, September 24). Social evaluation by preverbal infants. *Nature, 450,* 557–559. doi:10.1038/nature06288

Hammond, M. D., & Overall, N. C. (2017). Dynamics within intimate relationships and the causes, consequences, and functions of sexist attitudes. *Current Directions in Psychological Science, 26*(2), 120–125. http://dx.doi.org/10.1177/0963721416686213

Han, J. Y., Kwon, H. J., Ha, M., Paik, K. C., Lim, M. H., Lee, S. G., . . . Kim, E. J. (2015). The effects of prenatal exposure to alcohol and environmental tobacco smoke on risk for ADHD: A large population-based study. *Psychiatry Research, 225*(1), 164–168.

Han, W.-J., Miller, D. P., & Waldfogel, J. (2010). Parental work schedules and adolescent risky behaviors. *Developmental Psychology, 46,* 1245–1267. doi:10.1037/a0020178

Hanania, R., & Smith, L. B. (2010). Selective attention and attention switching: Towards a unified developmental approach. *Developmental Science, 13*(4), 622–635. doi:10.1111/j.1467-7687.2009.00921.x

Hankin, B. L., & Abramson, L. Y. (1999). Development of gender differences in depression: Description and possible explanations. *Annals of Medicine, 31,* 372–379.

Hankin, B. L., Abramson, L. Y., Moffitt, T. E., Silva, P. A., McGee, R., & Angell, K. E. (1998). Development of depression from preadolescence to young adulthood: Emerging gender differences in a 10-year longitudinal study. *Journal of Abnormal Psychology, 107,* 128–140. doi:10.1037/0021-843X.107.1.128

Hankin, B. L., Stone, L., & Wright, P. A. (2010). Corumination, interpersonal stress generation, and internalizing symptoms: Accumulating effects and transactional influences in a multiwave study of adolescents. *Development and Psychopathology, 22,* 217–235. doi:10.1017/S0954579409990368

Hankin, B. L., Young, J. F., Abela, J. Z., Smolen, A., Jenness, J. L., Gulley, L. D., . . . Oppenheimer, C. W. (2015). Depression from childhood into late adolescence: Influence of gender, development, genetic susceptibility, and peer stress. *Journal of Abnormal Psychology, 124*(4), 803–816. doi:10.1037/abn0000089

Hanks, A. S., Just, D. R., & Brumberg, A. (2016). Marketing vegetables in elementary school cafeterias to increase uptake. *Pediatrics, 138*(2), e20151720.

Hannon, E. E., & Trehub, S. E. (2005a). Metrical categories in infancy and adulthood. *Psychological Science, 16,* 48–55. doi:10.1111/j.0956-7976.2005.00779.x

Hannon, E. E., & Trehub, S. E. (2005b). Tuning in to musical rhythms: Infants learn more readily than adults. *Proceedings of the National Academy of Sciences of the United States of America, 102,* 12639–12643. doi:10.1073/pnas.0504254102

Hannon, E. E., Nave-Blodgett, J. E., & Nave, K. M. (2018). The developmental origins of the perception and production of musical rhythm. *Child Development Perspectives, 12*(3), 194–198.

Hanson, J. L., Hair, N., Shen, D. G., Shi, F., Gilmore, J. H., Wolfe, B. L., & Pollak, S. D. (2013). Family poverty affects the rate of human infant brain growth. *PLoS ONE, 8*(12), e80954.

Harkness, S., & Super, C. M. (1995). Culture and parenting. In M. H. Bornstein (Ed.), *Handbook of Parenting* (Vol. 2, pp. 211–234). Mahwah, NJ: Erlbaum.

Harlow, H. F. (1958). The nature of love. *American Psychologist, 13,* 673–685. doi:10.1037/h0047884

Harmon-Jones, E., & Harmon-Jones, C. (2016). Anger. In L. F. Barrett, M. Lewis, & J. M. Haviland-Jones (Eds.), *Handbook of emotions* (4th ed., pp. 774–791). New York: Guilford.

Harris, F. R., Wolf, M. M., & Baer, D. M. (1967). Social reinforcement effects on child behavior. In W. W. Hartup & N. L. Smothergill (Eds.), *The young child: Reviews of research* (pp. 13–26). Washington, DC: National Association for the Education of Young Children.

Harris, J. R. (1995). Where is the child's environment? A group socialization theory of development. *Psychological Review, 102,* 458–489. doi:10.1037/0033-295X.102.3.458

Harris, P. L. (2000). *The work of the imagination.* Oxford: Blackwell.

Harris, P. L. (2006). Social cognition. In W. Damon & R. M. Lerner (Series Eds.) & D. Kuhn & R. S. Siegler (Vol. Eds.), *Handbook of child psychology: Vol. 2. Cognition, perception, and language* (6th ed., pp. 811–858). Hoboken, NJ: Wiley.

Harris, P. L., & Giménez, M. (2005). Children's acceptance of conflicting testimony: The case of death. *Journal of Cognition and Culture, 5*(1), 143–164. doi:10.1163/1568537054068606

Harris, P. L., Koenig, M. A., Corriveau, K. H., & Jaswal, V. K. (2018). Cognitive foundations of learning from testimony. *Annual Review of Psychology, 69,* 251–273.

Harrist, A. W., Swindle, T. M., Hubbs Tait, L., Topham, G. L., Shriver, L. H., & Page, M. C. (2016). The social and emotional lives of overweight, obese, and severely obese children. *Child Development, 87*(5), 1564–1580. doi:10.1111/cdev.12548

Harrist, A. W., Zaia, A. F., Bates, J. E., Dodge, K. A., & Pettit, G. S. (1997). Subtypes of social withdrawal in early childhood: Sociometric status and social-cognitive differences across four years. *Child Development, 68,* 278–294. doi:10.2307/1131850

Harstad, E. B., Weaver, A. L., Katusic, S. K., Colligan, R. C., Kumar, S., Chan, E., . . . Barbaresi, W. J. (2014). ADHD, stimulant treatment, and growth: A longitudinal study. *Pediatrics, 134*(4), e935–e944.

Hart, B., & Risley, T. R. (1995). *Meaningful differences in the everyday experience of young American children.* Baltimore, MD: Brookes.

Hart, B., & Risley, T. R. (2003, Spring). The early catastrophe: The 30 million word gap by age 3. *American Educator, 27*(1), 4–9.

Hart, C. H., Ladd, G. W., & Burleson, B. R. (1990). Children's expectations of the outcomes of social strategies: Relations with sociometric status and maternal disciplinary styles. *Child Development, 61,* 127–137. doi:10.1111/j.1467-8624.1990.tb02766.x

Hart, D., Donnelly, T. M., Youniss, J., & Atkins, R. (2007). High school community service as a predictor of adult voting and volunteering. *American Educational Research Journal, 44,* 197–219. doi:10.3102/0002831206298173

Hart, D., & Fegley, S. (1995). Prosocial behavior and caring in adolescence: Relations to self-understanding and social judgment. *Child Development, 66,* 1346–1359. doi:10.1111/j.1467-8624.1995.tb00939.x

Harter, S. (1999). *The construction of the self: A developmental perspective.* New York: Guilford Press.

Harter, S. (2006). The self. In W. Damon & R. M. Lerner (Series Eds.) & N. Eisenberg (Vol. Ed.), *Handbook of child psychology: Vol. 3. Social, emotional, and personality development* (6th ed., pp. 505–570). Hoboken, NJ: Wiley.

Harter, S. (2012). *The construction of the self: Developmental and sociocultural foundations* (2nd ed.). New York: Guilford Press.

Hartman, L. R., Magalhães, L., & Mandich, A. (2011). What does parental divorce or marital separation mean for adolescents? A scoping review of North American literature. *Journal of Divorce and Remarriage, 52,* 490–518. doi:10.1080/10502556.2011.609432

Hartshorne, J. K., Tenenbaum, J. B., & Pinker, S. (2018). A critical period for second language acquisition: Evidence from 2/3 million English speakers. *Cognition, 177,* 263–277.

Hartup, W. W. (1974). Aggression in childhood: Developmental perspectives. *American Psychologist, 29,* 336–341. doi:10.1037/h0037622

Hartup, W. W. (1983). Peer relations. In P. H. Mussen (Series Ed.) & E. M. Hetherington (Vol. Ed.), *Handbook of child psychology: Vol. 4. Socialization, personality, and social development* (4th ed., pp. 103–196). New York: Wiley.

Hartup, W. W. (1996). The company they keep: Friendships and their developmental significance. *Child Development, 67,* 1–13. doi:10.1111/j.1467-8624.1996.tb01714.x

Haselager, G. J. T., Hartup, W. W., van Lieshout, C. F. M., & Riksen-Walraven, J. M. A. (1998). Similarities between friends and nonfriends in middle childhood. *Child Development, 69,* 1198–1208. doi:10.1111/j.1467-8624.1998.tb06167.x

Hastings, P. D., & De, I. (2008). Parasympathetic regulation and parental socialization of emotion: Biopsychosocial processes of adjustment in preschoolers. *Social Development, 17,* 211–238.

Hastings, P. D., McShane, K. E., Parker, R., & Ladha, F. (2007). Ready to make nice: Parental socialization of young sons' and daughters' prosocial behaviors with peers. *Journal of Genetic Psychology, 168,* 177–200. doi:10.3200/GNTP.168.2.177-200

Hastings, P. D., Miller, J. G., Kahle, S., & Zahn-Waxler, C. (2014). The neurobiological bases of empathic concern for others. In M. Killen & J. G. Smetana (Eds.), *Handbook of moral development* (2nd ed., pp. 411–434). New York: Psychology Press.

Hastings, P. D., Miller, J. G., & Troxel, N. R. (2015). Making good: The socialization of children's prosocial development. In J. E. Grusec & P. D. Hastings (Eds.), *Handbook of socialization: Theory and research* (pp. 637–685). New York: Guilford.

Hastings, P. D., Zahn-Waxler, C., & McShane, K. E. (2005). We are, by nature, moral creatures: Biological bases of concern for others. In M. Killen & J. Smetana (Eds.), *Handbook of moral development* (pp. 483–516). Hillsdale, NJ: Erlbaum.

Hastings, P. D., Zahn-Waxler, C., Robinson, J., Usher, B., & Bridges, D. (2000). The development of concern for others in children with behavior problems. *Developmental Psychology, 36,* 531–546. doi:10.1037/0012-1649.36.5.531

Hatano, G., Siegler, R. S., Richards, D. D., Inagaki, K., Stavy, R., & Wax, N. (1993). The development of biological knowledge: A multi-national study. *Cognitive Development, 8,* 47–62. doi:10.1016/0885-2014(93)90004-O

Hatzichristou, C., & Hopf, D. (1996). A multiperspective comparison of peer sociometric status groups in childhood and adolescence. *Child Development, 67,* 1085–1102. doi:10.2307/1131881

Hawkins, D. L., Pepler, D. J., & Craig, W. M. (2001). Naturalistic observations of peer interventions in bullying. *Social Development, 10,* 512–527. doi:10.1111/1467-9507.00178

Hawley, P. H., Little, T. D., & Card, N. A. (2008). The myth of the alpha male: A new look at dominance-related beliefs and behaviors among adolescent males and females. *International Journal of Behavioral Development, 32,* 76–88. doi:10.1177/0165025407084054

Haworth, C. M. A., Wright, M. J., Luciano, M., Martin, N. G., de Geus, E. J. C., van Beijsterveldt, C. E. M., . . . Plomin, R. (2010). The heritability of general cognitive ability increases linearly from childhood to young adulthood. *Molecular Psychiatry, 15,* 1112–1120. doi:10.1038/mp.2009.55

Hay, D. F. (2007). The gradual emergence of sex differences in aggression: Alternative hypotheses. *Psychological Medicine, 37,* 1527–1537. doi:10.1017/S0033291707000165

Hay, D. F., Caplan, M., & Nash, A. (2018). The beginnings of peer relations. In W. M. Bukowski, B. Laursen, & K. H. Rubin (Eds.), *Handbook of peer interactions, relationships, and groups* (2nd ed., pp. 200–221). New York: Guilford.

Hay, D. F., Hurst, S.-L., Waters, C. S., & Chadwick, A. (2011). Infants' use of force to defend toys: The origins of instrumental aggression. *Infancy, 16,* 471–489. doi:10.1111/j.1532-7078.2011.00069.x

Hay, D. F., Mundy, L., Roberts, S., Carta, R., Waters, C. S., Perra, O., . . . van Goozen, S. (2011). Known risk factors for violence predict 12-month-old infants' aggressiveness with peers. *Psychological Science, 22,* 1205–1211. doi:10.1177/0956797611419303

Haynes, R. L., Frelinger, A. L., Giles, E. K., Goldstein, R. D., Tran, H., Kozakewich, H. P., . . . Paterson, D. S. (2017). High serum serotonin in sudden infant death syndrome. *Proceedings of the National Academy of Sciences, 114*(29), 7695–7700.

Hazel, N. A., Oppenheimer, C. W., Technow, J. R., Young, J. F., & Hankin, B. L. (2014). Parent relationship quality buffers against the effect of peer stressors on depressive symptoms from middle childhood to adolescence. *Developmental Psychology, 50,* 2115–2123. doi:10.1037/a0037192

He, H., Xiao, L., Torrie, J. E., Auger, N., McHugh, N. G. L., Zoungrana, H., & Luo, Z. C. (2017). Disparities in infant hospitalizations in Indigenous and non-Indigenous populations in Quebec, Canada. *Canadian Medical Association Journal, 189*(21), E739–E746.

He, M., Walle, E. A., & Campos, J. J. (2015). A cross-national investigation of the relationship between infant walking and language development. *Infancy, 20*(3), 283–305.

Health Canada. (2019). Health Canada's healthy eating strategy. Retrieved from https://www.canada.ca/en/services/health/campaigns/vision-healthy-canada/healthy-eating.html#a4

Health Canada. (1998, October). Aboriginal Head Start Initiative for Urban and Northern Communities. Ottawa: Health Canada. Government of Canada. Retrieved from http://www.hc-sc.gc.ca/ahc-asc/media/nr-cp/1998/1998_71bk2_e.html

Heathcock, J. C., Lobo, M., & Galloway, J. C. (2008). Movement training advances the emergence of reaching in infants born at less than 33 weeks of gestational age: A randomized clinical trial. *Physical Therapy, 88,* 310–322. doi:10.2522/ptj.20070145

Heatherington, L., & Lavner, J. A. (2008). Coming to terms with coming out: Review and recommendations for family systems-focused research. *Journal of Family Psychology, 22,* 329–343. doi:10.1037/0893-3200.22.3.329

Heaven, P., & Ciarrochi, J. (2008). Parental styles, gender and the development of hope and self-esteem. *European Journal of Personality, 22,* 707–724. doi:10.1002/per.699

Hebb, D. O. (1949). *The organization of behavior: A neuropsychological theory.* New York: Wiley.

Heckman, J. J. (2011, Spring). The economics of inequality. *American Educator,* 31–35, 47.

Hedges, L. V., & Nowell, A. (1995, July 7). Sex differences in mental test scores, variability, and numbers of high-scoring individuals. *Science, 269,* 41–45.

Heffer, T., Good, M., Daly, O., MacDonell, E., & Willoughby, T. (2019). The longitudinal association between social-media use and depressive symptoms among adolescents and young adults: An empirical reply to Twenge et al. (2018). *Clinical Psychological Science, 7*(3), 462–470. doi:2167702618812727

Heine, S. J., Lehman, D. R., Markus, H. R., & Kitayama, S. (1999). Is there a universal need for positive self-regard? *Psychological Review, 106,* 766–794.

Held, R., Birch, E., & Gwiazda, J. (1980). Stereoacuity of human infants. *Proceedings of the National Academy of Sciences of the United States of America, 77,* 5572–5574.

Held, R., Ostrovsky, Y., de Gelder, B., Gandhi, T., Ganesh, S., Mathur, U., & Sinha, P. (2011). The newly sighted fail to match seen with felt. *Nature Neuroscience, 14*(5), 551–553.

Henderson, A., Brown, S. D., Pancer, S. M., & Ellis-Hale, K. (2007). Mandated community service in high school and subsequent civic engagement: The case of the "double cohort" in Ontario, Canada. *Journal of Youth and Adolescence, 36*(7), 849–860.

Henry, C. S., Sager, D. W., & Plunkett, S. W. (1996). Adolescents' perceptions of family system characteristics, parent–adolescent dyadic behaviors, adolescent qualities, and adolescent empathy. *Family Relations, 45,* 283–292. doi:10.2307/585500

Hepper, P. G., Wells, D. L., & Lynch, C. (2005). Prenatal thumb sucking is related to postnatal handedness. *Neuropsychologia, 43*(3), 313–315.

Herman, M. (2004). Forced to choose: Some determinants of racial identification in multiracial adolescents. *Child Development, 75,* 730–748. doi:10.1111/j.1467-8624.2004.00703.x

Herold, K., & Akhtar, N. (2014). Two-year-olds' understanding of self-symbols. *British Journal of Developmental Psychology, 32*(3), 262–275.

Heron-Delaney, M., Anzures, G., Herbert, J. S., Quinn, P. C., Slater, A. M., Tanaka, J. W., . . . Pascalis, O. (2011). Perceptual training prevents the emergence of the other race effect during infancy. *PLoS ONE, 6*(5), e19858.

Herrera, M. O., Mathiesen, M. E., Merino, J. M., & Recart, I. (2005). Learning contexts for young children in Chile: Process quality assessment in preschool centres. *International Journal of Early Years Education, 13*(1), 13–27.

Herrmann, E., Call, J., Hernàndez-Lloreda, M. V., Hare, B., & Tomasello, M. (2007, September 7). Humans have evolved specialized skills of social cognition: The cultural intelligence hypothesis. *Science, 317,* 1360–1366.

Hertenstein, M. J., & Campos, J. J. (2004). The retention effects of an adult's emotional displays on infant behavior. *Child Development, 75,* 595–613. doi:10.1111/j.1467-8624.2004.00695.x

Hespos, S. J., Ferry, A. L., Anderson, E. M., Hollenbeck, E. N., & Rips, L. J. (2016). Five-month-old infants have general knowledge of how nonsolid substances behave and interact. *Psychological Science, 27*(2), 244–256.

Hespos, S. J., & Spelke, E. S. (2004, July 22). Conceptual precursors to language. *Nature, 430,* 453–456. doi:10.1038/nature02634

Hespos, S. J., & vanMarle, K. (2012). Physics for infants: Characterizing the origins of knowledge about objects, substances, and number. *Wiley Interdisciplinary Reviews: Cognitive Science, 3*(1), 19–27. doi:10.1002/wcs.157

Hesse, E., & Main, M. (2006). Frightened, threatening, and dissociative parental behavior in low-risk samples: Description, discussion, and interpretations. *Development and Psychopathology, 18,* 309–343.

Hetherington, E. M. (1999). Social capital and the development of youth from nondivorced, divorced and remarried families. In W. A. Collins & B. Laursen (Eds.), *Minnesota Symposia on Child Psychology: Vol. 30. Relationships as developmental contexts* (pp. 177–209). Mahwah, NJ: Erlbaum.

Hetherington, E. M., Bridges, M., & Insabella, G. M. (1998). What matters? What does not? Five perspectives on the association between marital transitions and children's adjustment. *American Psychologist, 53,* 167–184. doi:10.1037/0003-066X.53.2.167

Hetherington, E. M., Henderson, S. H., Reiss, D. (with Anderson, E. R., Bridges, M., Chan, R. W., Insabella, G. M., Jodl, K. M., Kim, J. E., Mitchell, A. S., O'Connor, T. G., Skaggs, M. J., & Taylor, L. C.). (1999). Adolescent siblings in stepfamilies: Family functioning and adolescent adjustment, with commentary by James H. Bray. *Monographs of the Society for Research in Child Development, 64*(4, Serial No. 259), i–209.

Hickling, A. K., & Gelman, S. A. (1995). How does your garden grow? Early conceptualization of seeds and their place in the plant growth cycle. *Child Development, 66,* 856–876. doi:10.1111/j.1467-8624.1995.tb00910.x

Hickman, L. J., Jaycox, L. H., & Aronoff, J. (2004). Dating violence among adolescents: Prevalence, gender distribution, and prevention program effectiveness. *Trauma, Violence, and Abuse, 5,* 123–142. doi:10.1177/1524838003262332

Higgins, E. T. (1991). Development of self-regulatory and self-evaluative processes: Costs, benefits, and tradeoffs. In M. R. Gunnar & L. A. Sroufe (Eds.), *Self processes and development* (pp. 125–165). Hillsdale, NJ: Erlbaum.

High, P. C., Klass, P., Donoghue, E., Glassy, D., DelConte, B., Earls, M., . . . Schulte, E. E. (2014). Literacy promotion: An essential component of primary care pediatric practice. *Pediatrics, 134*(2), 404–409.

Hill, J., Emery, R. E., Harden, K. P., Mendle, J., & Turkheimer, E. (2008). Alcohol use in adolescent twins and affiliation with substance using peers. *Journal of Abnormal Child Psychology, 36,* 81–94. doi:10.1007/s10802-007-9161-0

Hill, J. P., & Lynch, M. E. (1983). The intensification of gender-related role expectations during early adolescence. In J. Brooks-Gunn & A. C. Petersen (Eds.), *Girls at puberty: Biological and psychosocial perspectives* (pp. 201–228). New York: Springer.

Hilt, L. M., & Nolen-Hoeksema, S. (2009). The emergence of gender differences in depression in adolescence. In S. Nolen-Hoeksema & L. M. Hilt (Eds.), *Handbook of depression in adolescents* (pp. 111–135). New York: Routledge/Taylor & Francis Group.

Hilt, L. M., & Pollak, S. D. (2012). Getting out of rumination: Comparison of three brief interventions in a sample of youth. *Journal of Abnormal Child Psychology, 40*(7), 1157–1165.

Hilton, J. M., & Haldeman, V. A. (1991). Gender differences in the performance of household tasks by adults and children in single-parent and two-parent, two-earner families. *Journal of Family Issues, 12*(1), 114–130.

Hindman, A. H., Wasik, B. A., & Snell, E. K. (2016). Closing the 30 million word gap: Next steps in designing research to inform practice. *Child Development Perspectives, 10*(2), 134–139.

Hinduja, S., & Patchin, J. W. (2019). *2016 Cyberbullying Data.* Cyberbullying Research Center. Retrieved from https://cyberbullying.org/2016-cyberbullying-data

Hineline, P. N., & Rosales-Ruiz, J. (2012). Behavior in relation to aversive events: Punishment and negative reinforcement. In G. J. Madden, W. V. Dube, T. Hackenberg, G. Hanley, & K. A. Lattal (Eds.), *APA Handbook of Operant Behavior* (pp. 483–512). Washington, DC: American Psychological Association.

Hines, M. (2004). *Brain gender.* Oxford: Oxford University Press.

Hines, M. (2013). Sex and sex differences. In P. D. Zelazo (Ed.), *Oxford handbook of developmental psychology* (Vol. 1, pp. 164–201). New York: Oxford University Press.

Hines, M., Fane, B. A., Pasterski, V. L., Mathews, G. A., Conway, G. S., & Brook, C. (2003). Spatial abilities following prenatal androgen abnormality: Targeting and mental rotations performance in individuals with congenital adrenal hyperplasia. *Psychoneuroendocrinology, 28,* 1010–1026. doi:10.1016/S0306-4530(02)00121-X

Hinshaw, S. P. (2015). Developmental psychopathology, ontogenic process models, gene–environment interplay, and brain development: An emerging synthesis. *Journal of Abnormal Psychology, 124*(4), 771–775. doi:10.1037/abn0000110

Hinshaw, S. P. (2018). Attention deficit hyperactivity disorder (ADHD): Controversy, developmental mechanisms, and multiple levels of analysis. *Annual Review of Clinical Psychology, 14,* 291–316.

Hinshaw, S. P., & Arnold, L. E. (2015). Attention-deficit hyperactivity disorder, multimodal treatment, and longitudinal outcome: Evidence, paradox, and challenge. *Wiley Interdisciplinary Reviews: Cognitive Science, 6*(1), 39–52.

Hinshaw, S. P., & Lee, S. S. (2003). Conduct and oppositional defiant disorders. In E. J. Mash & R. A. Barkley (Eds.), *Child psychopathology* (2nd ed., pp. 144–198). New York: Guilford Press.

Hirsh-Pasek, K., Adamson, L. B., Bakeman, R., Owen, M. T., Golinkoff, R. M., Pace, A., . . Suma, K. (2015). The contribution of early communication quality to low-income children's language success. *Psychological Science, 26*(7), 1071–1083.

Hirsh-Pasek, K., & Golinkoff, R. M. (1996). The preferential looking paradigm reveals emerging language comprehension. In D. McDaniel, C. McKee, & H. Cairns (Eds.), *Methods for Assessing Children's Syntax* (pp. 105–124). Cambridge, MA: MIT Press.

Hirsh-Pasek, K., Golinkoff, R. M., Berk, L. E., & Singer, D. G. (2009). *A mandate for playful learning in preschool: Presenting the evidence.* New York: Oxford University Press.

Hirsh-Pasek, K., Zosh, J. M., Golinkoff, R. M., Gray, J. H., Robb, M. B., & Kaufman, J. (2015). Putting education in "educational" apps: Lessons from the science of learning. *Psychological Science in the Public Interest, 16*(1), 3–34.

Ho, D. Y. F. (1986). Chinese patterns of socialization: A critical review. In M. H. Bond (Ed.), *The psychology of the Chinese people* (pp. 1–37). New York: Oxford University Press.

Hobson, J. A., Harris, R., Garcia-Perez, R., & Hobson, R. P. (2009). Anticipatory concern: A study in autism. *Developmental Science, 12,* 249–263. doi:10.1111/j.1467-7687.2008.00762.x

Hochberg, J., & Brooks, V. (1962). Pictorial recognition as an unlearned ability: A study of one child's performance. *American Journal of Psychology, 75,* 624–628. doi:10.2307/1420286

Hoehl, S., Hellmer, K., Johansson, M., & Gredebäck, G. (2017). Itsy bitsy spider . . . : Infants react with increased arousal to spiders and snakes. *Frontiers in Psychology, 8,* 1710. doi:10.3389/fpsyg.2017.01710

Hoeve, M., Dubas, J. S., Gerris, J. R. M., van der Laan, P. H., & Smeenk, W. (2011). Maternal and paternal parenting styles: Unique and combined links to adolescent and early adult delinquency. *Journal of Adolescence, 34,* 813–827. doi:10.1016/j.adolescence.2011.02.004

Hoeve, M., Stams, G. J. J. M., Put, C. E., Dubas, J. S., Laan, P. H., & Gerris, J. R. M. (2012). A meta-analysis of attachment to parents and delinquency. *Journal of Abnormal Child Psychology, 40,* 771–785. doi:10.1007/s10802-011-9608-1

Hoff, K. E., Reese-Weber, M., Schneider, W. J., & Stagg, J. W. (2009). The association between high status positions and aggressive behavior in early adolescence. *Journal of School Psychology, 47,* 395–426. doi:10.1016/j.jsp.2009.07.003

Hoffman, M. L. (1976). Empathy, role-taking, guilt and development of altruistic motives. In T. Lickona (Ed.), *Moral development and behavior: Theory, research, and social issues.* New York: Holt, Rinehart, & Winston.

Hoffman, M. L. (1982). Development of prosocial motivation: Empathy and guilt. In N. Eisenberg (Ed.), *The development of prosocial behavior* (pp. 281–313). New York: Academic Press.

Hoffman, M. L. (1983). Affective and cognitive processes in moral internalization. In E. T. Higgins, D. N. Ruble, & W. W. Hartup (Eds.), *Social cognition and social development: A sociocultural perspective* (pp. 236–274). Cambridge: Cambridge University Press.

Hoffman, M. L. (2000). *Empathy and moral development: Implications for caring and justice.* Cambridge: Cambridge University Press.

Hofmann, S. G., Asnaani, A., Vonk, I. J. J., Sawyer, A. T., & Fang, A. (2012). The efficacy of cognitive behavioral therapy: A review of meta-analyses. *Cognitive Therapy and Research, 36,* 427–440. doi:10.1007/s10608-013-9595-3

Honein, M. A., Dawson, A. L., Petersen, E. E., Jones, A. M., Lee, E. H., Yazdy, M. M., . . . Ellington, S. R. (2017). Birth defects among fetuses and infants of U.S. women with evidence of possible Zika virus infection during pregnancy. *Journal of the American Medical Association, 317*(1), 59–68.

Hong, H.-Y., & Lin-Siegler, X. (2012). How learning about scientists' struggles influences students' interest and learning in physics. *Journal of Educational Psychology, 104*(2), 469–484. doi:10.1037/a0026224

Hong, J. S., Tillman, R., & Luby, J. L. (2015). Disruptive behavior in preschool children: Normal misbehavior from markers of current and later childhood conduct disorder. *Journal of Pediatrics, 166,* 723–730. doi:10.1016/j.jpeds.2014.11.041

Horn, J. L., & McArdle, J. J. (2007). Understanding human intelligence since Spearman. In R. Cudeck & R. C. MacCallum (Eds.), *Factor analysis at 100: Historical developments and future directions* (pp. 205–247). Mahwah, NJ: Erlbaum.

Houltberg, B. J., Morris, A. S., Cui, L., Henry, C. S., & Criss, M. M. (2014). The role of youth anger in explaining links between parenting and early adolescent prosocial and antisocial behavior. *Journal of Early Adolescence.* doi:10.1177/0272431614562834.

Houston, D. M., & Miyamoto, R. T. (2010). Effects of early auditory experience on word learning and speech perception in deaf children with cochlear implants: Implications for sensitive periods of language development. *Otology and Neurotology, 31,* 1248–1253.

Howe, M. L., & Courage, M. L. (1997). The emergence and early development of autobiographical memory. *Psychological Review, 104,* 499–523.

Howe, N., Aquan-Assee, J., & Bukowski, W. M. (2001). Predicting sibling relations over time: Synchrony between maternal management styles and sibling relationship quality. *Merrill-Palmer Quarterly, 47,* 121–141.

Howe, N., & Leach, J. (2018). Children's play and peer relations. In W. M. Bukowski, B. Laursen, & K. H. Rubin (Eds.), *Handbook of peer interactions, relationships, and groups* (2nd ed., pp. 222–242). New York: Guilford.

Howell, E. A. (2018). Reducing disparities in severe maternal morbidity and mortality. *Clinical Obstetrics and Gynecology, 61*(2), 387–399.

Howes, D. (2012). Hiccups: A new explanation for the mysterious reflex. *Bioessays, 34,* 451–453. doi:10.1002/bies.201100194

Hoynes, H., Schanzenbach, D. W., & Almond, D. (2016). Long-run impacts of childhood access to the safety net. *American Economic Review, 106*(4), 903–934.

Hruschka, D. J., Medin, D. L., Rogoff, B., & Henrich, J. (2018). Pressing questions in the study of psychological and behavioral diversity. *Proceedings of the National Academy of Sciences, 115*(45), 11366–11368.

Huang, C. (2013). Gender differences in academic self-efficacy: A meta-analysis. *European Journal of Psychology of Education, 28*(1), 1–35. http://dx.doi.org/10.1007/s10212-011-0097-y

Huang, F. L., & Cornell, D. G. (2015). The impact of definition and question order on the prevalence of bullying victimization using student self-reports. *Psychological Assessment, 27,* 1484–1493. doi:10.1037/pas0000149

Hubbard, F. O. A., & van IJzendoorn, M. H. (1991). Maternal unresponsiveness and infant crying across the first 9 months: A naturalistic longitudinal study. *Infant Behavior and Development, 14,* 299–312. doi:10.1016/0163-6383(91)90024-M

Hubel, D. H., & Wiesel, T. N. (1962). Receptive fields, binocular interaction and functional architecture in the cat's visual cortex. *The Journal of Physiology, 160*(1), 106–154.

Hubel, D. H., & Wiesel, T. N. (1970). The period of susceptibility to the physiological effects of unilateral eye closure in kittens. *The Journal of Physiology, 206*(2), 419.

Huber, A., McMahon, C. A., & Sweller, N. (2015). Efficacy of the 20-week Circle of Security intervention: Changes in caregiver reflective functioning, representations, and child attachment in an Australian clinical sample. *Infant Mental Health Journal, 36,* 556–574. doi:10.1002/imhj.21540

Hudson, J. A., Sosa, B., & Shapiro, L. R. (1997). Scripts and plans: The development of preschool children's event knowledge and event planning. In S. L. Friedman & E. K. Scholnick (Eds.), *The developmental psychology of planning: Why, how, and when do we plan?* (pp. 77–102). Mahwah, NJ: Erlbaum.

Hughes, C., & Dunn, J. (1998). Understanding mind and emotion: Longitudinal associations with mental-state talk between young friends. *Developmental Psychology, 34,* 1026–1037. doi:10.1037/0012-1649.34.5.1026

Hughes, D., Way, N., & Rivas-Drake, D. (2011). Stability and change in private and public ethnic regard among African American, Puerto Rican, Dominican, and Chinese American early adolescents. *Journal of Research on Adolescence, 21,* 861–870. doi:10.1111/j.1532-7795.2011.00744.x

Huguet, G., Benabou, M., & Bourgeron, T. (2016). The genetics of autism spectrum disorders. In P. Sassone-Corsi & Y. Christen (Eds.), *A time for metabolism and hormones* (pp. 101–129). Heidelberg, Germany; New York, NY; Dordrecht, Netherlands; London: Springer International Publishing.

Huizink, A. C. (2008). Prenatal stress exposure and temperament: A review. *International Journal of Developmental Science, 2,* 77–99. doi:10.3233/DEV-2008-21206

Huizink, A. C. (2012). Prenatal factors in temperament: The role of prenatal stress and substance use exposure. In M. R. Zentner & R. L. Shiner (Eds.), *Handbook of temperament* (pp. 297–314). New York: Guilford Press.

Hulslander, J., Olson, R. K., Willcutt, E. G., Wadsworth, S. J. (2011). Longitudinal stability of reading-related skills and their prediction of reading development. *Scientific Studies of Reading, 14,* 111–136. doi:10.1080/10888431003604058205632 41

Human Rights Campaign. (2012). *Growing up LGBT in America: At home, at school, and in the community.* Washington, DC: Author. Retrieved from http://www.hrc.org/files/assets/resources/Growing-Up-LGBT-in-America_Report.pdf

Human Rights Campaign. (2018). *HRC 2018 LGBTQ youth report.* Washington, DC: Author. Retrieved from https://www.hrc.org/resources/2018-lgbtq-youth-report

Humphreys, L. G. (1989). Intelligence: Three kinds of instability and their consequences for policy. In R. L. Linn (Ed.), *Intelligence* (pp. 193–216). Urbana: University of Illinois Press.

Hunt, J. M. (1961). *Intelligence and experience.* New York: Ronald Press.

Hurtado, N., Marchman, V. A., & Fernald, A. (2008). Does input influence uptake? Links between maternal talk, processing speed and vocabulary size in Spanish-learning children. *Developmental Science, 11,* F31–F39. doi:10.1111/j.1467-7687.2008.00768.x

Hutchinson, E. A., De Luca, C. R., Doyle, L. W., Roberts, G., Anderson, P. J., & Victorian Infant Collaborative Study Group. (2013). School-age outcomes of extremely preterm or extremely low birth weight children. *Pediatrics, 131*(4), e1053–e1061.

Hutchison, J. E., Lyons, I. M., & Ansari, D. (2019). More similar than different: Gender differences in children's basic numerical skills are the exception not the rule. *Child Development, 90*(1), e66–e79.

Huttenlocher, J., Levine, S., & Vevea, J. (1998). Environmental input and cognitive growth: A study using time-period comparisons. *Child Development, 69,* 1012–1029.

Hutton, E. K., Cappelletti, A., Reitsma, A. H., Simioni, J., Horne, J., McGregor, C., & Ahmed, R. J. (2015, December 22). Outcomes associated with planned place of birth among women with low-risk pregnancies. *Canadian Medical Association Journal,* cmaj-150564. doi:10.1503/cmaj.150564

Hviid, A., Hansen, J. V., Frisch, M., & Melbye, M. (2019). Measles, mumps, rubella vaccination and autism: A nationwide cohort study. *Annals of Internal Medicine, 170,* 513–520.

Hwang, J. M., Cheong, P. H., & Feeley, T. H. (2009). Being young and feeling blue in Taiwan: Examining adolescent depressive mood and online and offline activities. *New Media and Society, 11,* 1101–1121. doi:10.1177/1461444809341699

Hyde, J. S. (2005). The gender similarities hypothesis. *American Psychologist, 60,* 581–592. doi:10.1037/0003-066X.60.6.581

Hyde, J. S., Bigler, R. S., Joel, D., Tate, C. C., & van Anders, S. M. (2019). The future of sex and gender in psychology: Five challenges to the gender binary. *American Psychologist, 74*(2), 171–193. http://dx.doi.org/10.1037/amp0000307

Hyde, J. S., & Linn, M. C. (1988). Gender differences in verbal ability: A meta-analysis. *Psychological Bulletin, 104,* 53–69. doi:10.1037/0033-2909.104.1.53

Hymel, S., Bowker, A., & Woody, E. (1993). Aggressive versus withdrawn unpopular children: Variations in peer and self-perceptions in multiple domains. *Child Development, 64,* 879–896. doi:10.1111/j.1467-8624.1993.tb02949.x

Imperato-McGinley, J., Pichardo, M., Gautier, T., Voyer, D., & Bryden, M. P. (2007). Cognitive abilities in androgen-insensitive subjects: Comparison with control males and females from the same kindred. In G. Einstein (Ed.), *Sex and the brain* (pp. 555–560). Cambridge, MA: MIT Press. (Reprinted from *Clinical Endocrinology, 34,* pp. 341–347, 1991)

Inagaki, K., & Hatano, G. (1993). Young children's understanding of the mind-body distinction. *Child Development, 64,* 1534–1549.

Inagaki, K., & Hatano, G. (1996). Young children's recognition of commonalities between animals and plants. *Child Development, 67,* 2823–2840. doi:10.1111/j.1467-8624.1996.tb01890.x

Inagaki, K., & Hatano, G. (2002). *Young children's naive thinking about the biological world.* New York: Psychology Press.

Inagaki, K., & Hatano, G. (2008). Conceptual change in naïve biology. In S. Vosniadou (Ed.), *International handbook of research on conceptual change* (pp. 240–262). New York: Routledge/Taylor & Francis.

Inam, A., Tariq, P. N., & Zaman, S. (2015). Cultural adaptation of preschool PATHS (Promoting Alternative Thinking Strategies) curriculum for Pakistani children. *International Journal of Psychology, 50,* 232–239. doi:10.1002/ijop.12090

Inhelder, B., & Piaget, J. (1958). *The growth of logical thinking from childhood to adolescence: An essay on the construction of formal operational structures.* New York: Basic Books.

Inlow, J. K., & Restifo, L. L. (2004). Molecular and comparative genetics of mental retardation. *Genetics, 166,* 835–881.

Intons-Peterson, M. J. (1988). *Children's concepts of gender.* Norwood, NJ: Ablex.

Isabella, R. A. (1993). Origins of attachment: Maternal interactive behavior across the first year. *Child Development, 64,* 605–621. doi:10.1111/j.1467-8624.1993.tb02931.x

It Gets Better Project. (n.d.). What is the It Gets Better Project? Los Angeles. Retrieved from http://www.itgetsbetter.org/about

Iverson, J. M., & Goldin-Meadow, S. (1998, November 26). Why people gesture when they speak. *Nature, 396,* 228.

Iyer, R. V., Kochenderfer-Ladd, B., Eisenberg, N., & Thompson, M. (2010). Peer victimization and effortful control: Relations to school engagement and academic achievement. *Merrill-Palmer Quarterly, 56,* 361–387.

Izard, C. E. (2010). The many meanings/aspects of emotion: Definitions, functions, activation, and regulation. *Emotion Review, 2,* 363–370.

Izard, C. E., & Dougherty, L. (1980). *A system for identifying affect expressions by holistic judgments (AFFEX).* Newark, DE: University of Delaware, Instructional Resources Center.

Izard, C. E., King, K. A., Trentacosta, C. J., Morgan, J. K., Laurenceau, J. P., Krauthamer-Ewing, E. S., & Finlon, K. J. (2008). Accelerating the development of emotion competence in Head Start children: Effects on adaptive and maladaptive behavior. *Development and Psychopathology, 20,* 369–397. doi:10.1017/S0954579408000175

Izard, C. E., Woodburn, E. M., & Finlon, K. J. (2010). Extending emotion science to the study of discrete emotions in infants. *Emotion Review, 2,* 134–136. doi:10.1177/1754073909355003

Izard, V., Sann, C., Spelke, E. S., & Streri, A. (2009). Newborn infants perceive abstract numbers. *Proceedings of the National Academy of Sciences of the United States of America, 106,* 10382–10385. doi:10.1073/pnas.0812142106

Jack, R. E., Garrod, O. G., Yu, H., Caldara, R., & Schyns, P. G. (2012). Facial expressions of emotion are not culturally universal. *Proceedings of the National Academy of Sciences, 109*(19), 7241–7244.

Jacobson, K. C., & Crockett, L. J. (2000). Parental monitoring and adolescent adjustment: An ecological perspective. *Journal of Research on Adolescence, 10,* 65–97. doi:10.1207/SJRA1001_4

Jaffee, S., & Hyde, J. S. (2000). Gender differences in moral orientation: A meta-analysis. *Psychological Bulletin, 126,* 703–726. doi:10.1037/0033-2909.126.5.703

Jaffee, S. R., & Christian, C. W. (2014). The biological embedding of child abuse and neglect: Implications for policy and practice. *Social Policy Report, 28,* 3–19.

Jaffee, S. R., Hanscombe, K. B., Haworth, C. M. A., Davis, O. S. P., & Plomin, R. (2012). Chaotic homes and children's disruptive behavior: A longitudinal cross-lagged twin study. *Psychological Science, 23,* 643–650. doi:10.1177/0956797611431693

Jaffee, S. R., Moffitt, T. E., Caspi, A., Taylor, A., & Arseneault, L. (2002). Influence of adult domestic violence on children's internalizing and externalizing problems: An environmentally informative twin study. *Journal of the American Academy of Child and Adolescent Psychiatry, 41,* 1095–1103. doi:10.1097/00004583-200209000-00010

Jahromi, L. B., Putnam, S. P., & Stifter, C. A. (2004). Maternal regulation of infant reactivity from 2 to 6 months. *Developmental Psychology, 40,* 477–487. doi:10.1037/0012-1649.40.4.477

Jain, A., Marshall, J., Buikema, A., Bancroft, T., Kelly, J. P., & Newschaffer, C. G. (2015). Autism occurrence by MMR vaccine status among U.S. children with older siblings with and without autism. *Journal of the American Medical Association, 313,* 1534–1540.

Jane, E. A. (2015). "Gunter's a woman?!"—Doing and undoing gender in cartoon network's adventure time. *Journal of Children and Media, 9*(2), 231–247. http://dx.doi.org/10.1080/17482798.2015.1024002

Janssens, J. M. A. M., & Deković, M. (1997). Child rearing, prosocial moral reasoning, and prosocial behaviour. *International Journal of Behavioral Development, 20,* 509–527. doi:10.1080/016502597385252

Janus, M., & Duku, E. (2007). The school entry gap: Socioeconomic, family, and health factors associated with children's school readiness to learn. *Early Education and Development, 18*(3), 375–403.

Janus, M., & Reid-Westoby, C. (2016). Monitoring the development of all children: The Early Development Instrument. In T. Moreno (Ed.), *Early childhood matters* (pp. 40–45). The Hague, Netherlands: Bernard van Leer Foundation.

Jaser, S. S., Champion, J. E., Reeslund, K. L., Keller, G., Merchant, M. J., Benson, M., & Compas, B. E. (2007). Cross-situational coping with peer and family stressors in adolescent offspring of depressed parents. *Journal of Adolescence, 30,* 917–932.

Jayaraman, S., Fausey, C. M., & Smith, L. B. (2015). The faces in infant-perspective scenes change over the first year of life. *PLoS ONE, 10*(5), e0123780. doi:10.1371/journal.pone.0123780

Jenkins, J. (1992). Sibling relationships in disharmonious homes: Potential difficulties and protective effects. In F. Boer & J. Dunn (Eds.), *Children's sibling relationships: Developmental and clinical issues* (pp. 125–138). Hillsdale, NJ: Erlbaum.

Jenkins, J. M., & Astington, J. W. (1996). Cognitive factors and family structure associated with theory of mind development in young children. *Developmental Psychology, 32,* 70–78.

Jennings, P. A., & Greenberg, M. T. (2009). The prosocial classroom: Teacher social and emotional competence in relation to student and classroom outcomes. *Review of Educational Research, 79,* 491–525. doi:10.3102/0034654308325693

Jensen, A. R. (1973). *Educability and group differences.* New York: Harper & Row.

Jensen, T. M., Shafer, K., & Holmes, E. K. (2017). Transitioning to stepfamily life: The influence of closeness with biological parents and stepparents on children's stress. *Child & Family Social Work, 22,* 275–286. doi:10.1111/cfs.12237

Jiang, J. (2018). How teens and parents navigate screen time and device distractions. Pew Research Center for Internet and Technology. Retrieved from http://www.pewinternet.org/2018/08/22/how-teens-and-parents-navigate-screen-time-and-device-distractions

Jiang, M. J., & Rosengren, K. S. (2018). Action errors: A window into the early development of perception–action system. *Advances in Child Development and Behavior, 55,* 145–171.

Jiang, M. J., & Rosengren, K. S. (2018). Action errors: A window into the early development of perception–action system. *Advances in Child Development and Behavior, 55,* 145–171.

Jiang, N., Lee, L., Zelikoff, J. T., & Weitzman, M. (2018). E-cigarettes: Effects on the fetus. *Pediatrics in Review, 39,* 156–158.

Jirout, J. J., & Newcombe, N. S. (2015). Building blocks for developing spatial skills: Evidence from a large, representative U.S. sample. *Psychological Science, 26*(3), 302–310. doi:10.1177/0956797614563338

Johnson, D. E., & Gunnar, M. R. (2011). IV. Growth failure in institutionalized children. *Monographs of the Society for Research in Child Development, 76*(4, Serial No. 301), 92–126. doi:10.1111/j.1540-5834.2011.00629.x

Johnson, E. K., & Jusczyk, P. W. (2001). Word segmentation by 8-month-olds: When speech cues count more than statistics. *Journal of Memory and Language, 44,* 548–567. doi:10.1006/jmla.2000.2755

Johnson, J. L., McWilliams, K., Goodman, G. S., Shelley, A. E., & Piper, B. (2016). Basic principles of interviewing the child eyewitness. In *Forensic interviews regarding child sexual abuse* (pp. 179–195). Springer International Publishing.

Johnson, J. S., & Newport, E. L. (1989). Critical period effects in second language learning: The influence of maturational state on the acquisition of English as a second language. *Cognitive Psychology, 21,* 60–99.

Johnson, K. E., Alexander, J. M., Spencer, S., Leibham, M. E., & Neitzel, C. (2004). Factors associated with the early emergence of intense interests within conceptual domains. *Cognitive Development, 19*(3), 325–343. http://dx.doi.org/10.1016/j.cogdev.2004.03.001

Johnson, K. E., & Mervis, C. B. (1994). Microgenetic analysis of first steps in children's acquisition of expertise on shorebirds. *Developmental Psychology, 30,* 418–435.

Johnson, M. H. (2011). Interactive specialization: A domain-general framework for human functional brain development? *Developmental Cognitive Neuroscience, 1*(1), 7–21. doi:10.1016/j.dcn.2010.07.003

Johnson, S., & Marlow, N. (2011). Preterm birth and childhood psychiatric disorders. *Pediatric Research, 69,* 11R–18R.

Johnson, S. C., & Chen, F. S. (2011). Socioemotional information processing in human infants: From genes to subjective construals. *Emotion Review, 3,* 169–178. doi:10.1177/1754073910387945

Johnson, S. C., Dweck, C. S., & Chen, F. S. (2007). Evidence for infants' internal working models of attachment. *Psychological Science, 18,* 501–502. doi:10.1111/j.1467-9280.2007.01929.x

Johnson, S. C., & Solomon, G. E. A. (1997). Why dogs have puppies and cats have kittens: The role of birth in young children's understanding of biological origins. *Child Development, 68,* 404–419. doi:10.1111/j.1467-8624.1997.tb01948.x

Johnson, S. P. (Ed.). (2010). *Neoconstructivism: The new science of cognitive development.* New York: Oxford University Press.

Johnson, S. P., Amso, D., & Slemmer, J. A. (2003). Development of object concepts in infancy: Evidence for early learning in an eye-tracking paradigm. *Proceedings of the National Academy of Sciences of the United States of America, 100,* 10568–10573. doi:10.1073/pnas.1630655100

Johnson, S. P., & Aslin, R. N. (1995). Perception of object unity in 2-month-old infants. *Developmental Psychology, 31,* 739–745. doi:10.1037/0012-1649.31.5.739

Johnson, W., McGue, M., & Iacono, W. G. (2006). Genetic and environmental influences on academic achievement trajectories during adolescence. *Developmental Psychology, 42,* 514–532. doi:10.1037/0012-1649.42.3.514

Jome, L. M., & Tokar, D. M. (1998). Dimensions of masculinity and major choice traditionality. *Journal of Vocational Behavior, 52,* 120–134. doi:10.1006/jvbe.1996.1571

Jones, C. R., Simonoff, E., Baird, G., Pickles, A., Marsden, A. J., Tregay, J., . . . Charman, T. (2018). The association between theory of mind, executive function, and the symptoms of autism spectrum disorder. *Autism Research, 11*(1), 95–109.

Jones, S., & Myhill, D. (2004). "Troublesome boys" and "compliant girls": Gender identity and perceptions of achievement and underachievement. *British Journal of Sociology of Education, 25,* 547–561. doi:10.2307/4128701

Jonson-Reid, M., Kohl, P. L., & Drake, B. (2012). Child and adult outcomes of chronic child maltreatment. *Pediatrics, 129*(5), 839–845.

Jordan, N. C. (2007). Do words count? Connections between mathematics and reading difficulties. In D. B. Berch & M. M. M. Mazzocco (Eds.), *Why is math so hard for some children? The nature and origins of mathematical learning difficulties and disabilities* (pp. 107–120). Baltimore, MD: Paul H. Brookes.

Jordan, N. C., Hansen, N., Fuchs, L. S., Siegler, R. S., Gersten, R., & Micklos, D. (2013). Developmental predictors of fraction concepts and procedures. *Journal of Experimental Child Psychology, 116,* 45–58. doi:10.1016/j.jecp.2013.02.001

Jorgensen, M., Keiding, N., & Skakkebaek, N. E. (1991). Estimation of spermarche from longitudinal spermaturia data. *Biometrics, 47,* 177–193. doi:10.2307/2532505

Joshi, M. S., & MacLean, M. (1994). Indian and English children's understanding of the distinction between real and apparent emotion. *Child Development, 65,* 1372–1384.

Jowkar-Baniani, G., & Schmuckler, M. A. (2011). Picture perception in infants: Generalization from two-dimensional to three-dimensional displays. *Infancy, 16*(2), 211–226.

Juel, C. (1988). Learning to read and write: A longitudinal study of 54 children from first through fourth grades. *Journal of Educational Psychology, 80,* 437–447. doi:10.1037/0022-0663.80.4.437

Jung, R. E., & Haier, R. J. (2007). The Parieto-Frontal Integration Theory (P-FIT) of intelligence: Converging neuroimaging evidence. *Behavioral and Brain Sciences, 30,* 135–154. doi:10.1017/S0140525X07001185

Jusczyk, P. W., & Aslin, R. N. (1995). Infants' detection of the sound patterns of words in fluent speech. *Cognitive Psychology, 29,* 1–23. doi:10.1006/cogp.1995.1010

Justice, L. M., Petscher, Y., Schatschneider, C., & Mashburn, A. (2011). Peer effects in preschool classrooms: Is children's language growth associated with their classmates' skills? *Child Development, 82,* 1768–1777. doi:10.1111/j.1467-8624.2011.01665.x

Kabali, H. K., Irigoyen, M. M., Nunez-Davis, R., Budacki, J. G., Mohanty, S. H., Leister, K. P., & Bonner, R. L. (2015). Exposure and use of mobile media devices by young children. *Pediatrics, 136,* 1–7.

Kagan, J. (1976). Emergent themes in human development. *American Scientist, 64,* 186–196.

Kagan, J. (2000). *Three seductive ideas* (Revised ed.). Harvard University Press: Cambridge, MA.

Kagan, J. (2008). In defense of qualitative changes in development. *Child Development, 79,* 1606–1624. doi:10.1111/j.1467-8624.2008.01211.x

Kagan, J., & Fox, N. A. (2006). Biology, culture, and temperamental biases. In W. Damon & R. M. Lerner (Series Eds.) & N. Eisenberg (Vol. Ed.), *Handbook of child psychology: Vol. 3. Social, emotional, and personality development* (6th ed., pp. 167–225). Hoboken, NJ: Wiley.

Kahen, V., Katz, L. F., & Gottman, J. M. (1994). Linkages between parent–child interaction and conversations of friends. *Social Development, 3,* 238–254. doi:10.1111/j.1467-9507.1994.tb00043.x

Kail, R. (1991). Developmental change in speed of processing during childhood and adolescence. *Psychological Bulletin, 109,* 490–501.

Kail, R. V. (1984). *The development of memory in children* (2nd ed.). New York: Freeman.

Kail, R. V., Lervåg, A., Hulme, C. (2016). Longitudinal evidence linking processing speed to the development of reasoning. *Developmental Science, 19*(6), 1067–1074. doi:10.1111/desc.12352

Kaler, S. R., & Kopp, C. B. (1990). Compliance and comprehension in very young toddlers. *Child Development, 61,* 1997–2003.

Kalish, C. (1997). Preschoolers' understanding of mental and bodily reactions to contamination: What you don't know can hurt you, but cannot sadden you. *Developmental Psychology, 33,* 79–91.

Kam, C., Wong, L. W., & Fung, K. M. (2011). Promoting social-emotional learning in Chinese schools: A feasibility study of PATHS implementation in Hong Kong. *The International Journal of Emotional Education, 3,* 30–47.

Kam, C.-M., Greenberg, M. T., Bierman, K. L., Coie, J. D., Dodge, K. A., Foster, M. E., . . . Pinderhughes, E. E. (2011). Maternal depressive symptoms and child social preference during the early school years: Mediation by maternal warmth and child emotion regulation. *Journal of Abnormal Child Psychology, 39,* 365–377. doi:10.1007/s10802-010-9468-0

Kaminski, J., Call, J., & Fischer, J. (2004, June 11). Word learning in a domestic dog: Evidence for "fast mapping." *Science, 304,* 1682–1683.

Kanazawa, S. (2015). Breastfeeding is positively associated with child intelligence even net of parental IQ. *Developmental Psychology, 51*(12), 1683–1689.

Kang, C. Y., Duncan, G. J., Clements, D. H., Sarama, J., & Bailey, D. H. (2019). The roles of transfer of learning and forgetting in the persistence and fadeout of early childhood mathematics interventions. *Journal of Educational Psychology, 111*(4), 590–603. doi:10.1037/edu0000297

Kann, L., Olsen, E. O., McManus, T., Harris, W. A., Shanklin, S. L., Flint, K. H., . . . Zaza, S. (2016, August 12). Sexual identity, sex of sexual contacts, and health-related behaviors among students in grades 9–12—United States and selected sites, 2015. *Surveillance Summaries, 65*(9), 1–202.

Kaplan, H., & Dove, H. (1987). Infant development among the Ache of eastern Paraguay. *Developmental Psychology, 23,* 190–198. doi:10.1037/0012-1649.23.2.190

Karasewich, T. A., Kuhlmeier, V. A., Beier, J. S., & Dunfield, K. A. (2019). Getting help for others: An examination of indirect helping in young children. *Developmental Psychology, 55*(3), 606.

Karasik, L. B., Tamis-LeMonda, C. S., Adolph, K. E., & Bornstein, M. H. (2015). Places and postures: A cross-cultural comparison of sitting in 5-month-olds. *Journal of Cross-Cultural Psychology, 46,* 1023–1038.

Karavasilis Karos, L., Howe, N., & Aquan-Assee, J. (2008). Reciprocal and complementary sibling interactions, relationship quality and socio-emotional problem solving. *Infant and Child Development, 6*(16), 577–596.

Karmiloff-Smith, A., Broadbent, H., Farran, E. K., Longhi, E., D'Souza, D., Metcalfe, K., . . . Sansbury, F. (2012). Social cognition in Williams syndrome: Genotype/phenotype insights from partial deletion patients. *Frontiers in Psychology, 3,* 168. doi:10.3389/fpsyg.2012.00168

Karriker-Jaffe, K. J., Foshee, V. A., Ennett, S. T., & Suchindran, C. (2008). The development of aggression during adolescence: Sex differences in trajectories of physical and social aggression among youth in rural areas. *Journal of Abnormal Child Psychology, 36,* 1227–1236. doi:10.1007/s10802-008-9245-5

Kärtner, J., Keller, H., & Chaudhary, N. (2010). Cognitive and social influences on early prosocial behavior in two sociocultural contexts. *Developmental Psychology, 46,* 905–914. doi:10.1037/a0019718

Katz, C., Barnetz, Z., & Hershkowitz, I. (2014). The effect of drawing on children's experiences of investigations following alleged child abuse. *Child Abuse & Neglect, 38*(5), 858–867.

Katz, L. F., Hunter, E., & Klowden, A. (2008). Intimate partner violence and children's reaction to peer provocation: The moderating role of emotion coaching. *Journal of Family Psychology, 22,* 614–621. doi:10.1037/a0012793

Katz, L. F., Maliken, A. C., & Stettler, N. M. (2012). Parental meta-emotion philosophy: A review of research and theoretical framework. *Child Development Perspectives, 6,* 417–422. doi:10.1111/j.1750-8606.2012.00244.x

Katz, P. A., & Ksansnak, K. R. (1994). Developmental aspects of gender role flexibility and traditionality in middle childhood and adolescence. *Developmental Psychology, 30,* 272–282. doi:10.1037/0012-1649.30.2.272

Katz, S. J., Conway, C. C., Hammen, C. L., Brennan, P. A., & Najman, J. M. (2011). Childhood social withdrawal, interpersonal impairment, and young adult depression: A mediational model. *Journal of Abnormal Child Psychology, 39,* 1227–1238. doi:10.1007/s10802-011-9537-z

Kaufman, T., Kretschmer, T., Huitsing, G., & Veenstra, R. (2019). Caught in a vicious cycle? Explaining bidirectional spillover between parent–child relationships and peer victimization. *Development and Psychopathology,* 1–10. Advance online publication. doi:10.1017/S0954579418001360

Kavanaugh, R. D., & Engel, S. (1998). The development of pretense and narrative in early childhood. In O. N. Saracho & B. Spodek (Eds.), *Multiple perspectives on play in early childhood education* (pp. 80–99). Albany: State University of New York Press.

Kawabata, Y., & Crick, N. R. (2008). The role of cross-racial/ethnic friendships in social adjustment. *Developmental Psychology, 44,* 1177–1183. doi:10.1037/0012-1649.44.4.1177

Kawabata, Y., & Crick, N. R. (2011). The significance of cross-racial/ethnic friendships: Associations with peer victimization, peer support, sociometric status, and classroom diversity. *Developmental Psychology, 47,* 1763–1775. doi:10.1037/a0025399

Kawabata, Y., Crick, N. R., & Hamaguchi, Y. (2010). Forms of aggression, social-psychological adjustment, and peer victimization in a Japanese sample: The moderating role of positive and negative friendship quality. *Journal of Abnormal Child Psychology, 38,* 471–484. doi:10.1007/s10802-010-9386-1

Kaye, K. L., & Bower, T. G. R. (1994). Learning and intermodal transfer of information in newborns. *Psychological Science, 5,* 286–288. doi:10.1111/j.1467-9280.1994.tb00627.x

Kearins, J. M. (1981). Visual spatial memory in Australian Aboriginal children of desert regions. *Cognitive Psychology, 13,* 434–460.

Kearney, M. S., & Levine, P. B. (2015). *Early childhood education by MOOC: Lessons from Sesame Street* (Report No. w21229). Cambridge, Massachusetts: National Bureau of Economic Research. doi:10.3386/w21229

Keates, J., Graham, S. A., & Ganea, P. A. (2014). Infants transfer nonobvious properties from pictures to real-world objects. *Journal of Experimental Child Psychology, 125,* 35–47.

Keen, R. E., & Berthier, N. E. (2004). Continuities and discontinuities in infants' representation of objects and events. In V. K. Robert (Ed.), *Advances in child development and behavior* (Vol. 32, pp. 243–279). San Diego, CA: Elsevier.

Keenan, K., Loeber, R., Zhang, Q., Stouthamer-Loeber, M., & van Kammen, W. B. (1995). The influence of deviant peers on the development of boys' disruptive and delinquent behavior: A temporal analysis. *Development and Psychopathology, 7,* 715–726. doi:10.1017/S0954579400006805

Keenan, K., Wroblewski, K., Hipwell, A., Loeber, R., & Stouthamer-Loeber, M. (2010). Age of onset, symptom threshold, and expansion of the nosology of conduct disorder for girls. *Journal of Abnormal Psychology, 119,* 689–698. doi:10.1037/a0019346

Keil, F. C. (1979). *Semantic and conceptual development: An ontological perspective.* Cambridge, MA: Harvard University Press.

Keil, F. C. (1992). The origins of an autonomous biology. In M. R. Gunnar & M. Maratsos (Eds.), *Minnesota Symposia on Child Psychology: Vol. 25. Modularity and constraints in language and cognition* (pp. 103–137). Hillsdale, NJ: Erlbaum.

Keiley, M. K., Bates, J. E., Dodge, K. A., & Pettit, G. S. (2000). A cross-domain growth analysis: Externalizing and internalizing behaviors during 8 years of childhood. *Journal of Abnormal Child Psychology, 28,* 161–179. doi:10.1023/A:1005122814723

Kelemen, D., & DiYanni, C. (2005). Intuitions about origins: Purpose and intelligent design in children's reasoning about nature. *Journal of Cognition and Development, 6,* 3–31. doi:10.1207/s15327647jcd0601_2

Kelemen, D., Emmons, N. A., Schillaci, R. S., & Ganea, P. A. (2014). Young children can be taught basic natural selection using a picture-storybook intervention. *Psychological Science, 25*(4), 893–902. doi:10.1177/0956797613516009

Kell, H. J., Lubinski, D., & Benbow, C. P. (2013). Who rises to the top? Early indicators. *Psychological Science, 24*(5), 648–659. doi:10.1177/0956797612457784

Keller, P. S., Cummings, E. M., Davies, P. T., & Mitchell, P. M. (2008). Longitudinal relations between parental drinking problems, family functioning, and child adjustment. *Development and Psychopathology, 20,* 195–212. doi:10.1017/S0954579408000096

Kellman, P. J., & Spelke, E. S. (1983). Perception of partly occluded objects in infancy. *Cognitive Psychology, 15,* 483–524. doi:10.1016/0010-0285(83)90017-8

Kelly, D. J., Liu, S., Ge, L., Quinn, P. C., Slater, A. M., Lee, K., . . . Pascalis, O. (2007). Cross-race preferences for same-race faces extend beyond the African versus Caucasian contrast in 3-month-old infants. *Infancy, 11,* 87–95.

Kelly, D. J., Liu, S., Lee, K., Quinn, P. C., Pascalis, O., Slater, A. M., & Ge, L. (2009). Development of the other-race effect during infancy: Evidence toward universality? *Journal of Experimental Child Psychology, 104,* 105–114. doi:10.1016/j.jecp.2009.01.006

Kelly, D. J., Quinn, P. C., Slater, A. M., Lee, K., Ge, L., & Pascalis, O. (2007). The other-race effect develops during infancy: Evidence of perceptual narrowing. *Psychological Science, 18,* 1084–1089. doi:10.1111/j.1467-9280.2007.02029.x

Kelly, D. J., Quinn, P. C., Slater, A. M., Lee, K., Gibson, A., Smith, M., . . . Pascalis, O. (2005). Three-month-olds, but not newborns, prefer own-race faces. *Developmental Science, 8,* F31–F36. doi:10.1111/j.1467-7687.2005.0434a.x

Kelly, M. B. (2012). Divorce cases in civil court, 2010/2011. *Statistics Canada Catalogue, 85-002-X,* ISSN 1209-6393.

Kelly, Y., Zilanawala, A., Sacker, A., Hiatt, R., & Viner, R. (2017). Early puberty in 11-year-old girls: Millennium Cohort Study findings. *Archives of Disease in Childhood, 102*(3), 232–237.

Kelso, T. (2015). Still trapped in the U.S. media's closet: Representations of gender-variant pre-adolescent children. *Journal of Homosexuality, 62,* 1058–1079. doi:10.1080/00918369.2015.1021634

Kempermann, G., Gage, F. H., Aigner, L., Song, H., Curtis, M. A., Thuret, S., . . . Gould, E. (2018). Human adult neurogenesis: Evidence and remaining questions. *Cell Stem Cell, 23,* 25–30.

Kenrick, D. T., Trost, M. R., & Sundie, J. M. (2004). Sex roles as adaptations: An evolutionary perspective on gender differences and similarities. In A. H. Eagly, A. E. Beall, & R. J. Sternberg (Eds.), *The psychology of gender* (2nd ed., pp. 65–91). New York: Guilford Press.

Kerns, K. A., Abraham, M. M., Schlegelmilch, A., & Morgan, T. A. (2007). Mother–child attachment in later middle childhood: Assessment approaches and associations with mood and emotion regulation. *Attachment and Human Development, 9,* 33–53. doi:10.1080/14616730601151441

Kerr, M., Stattin, H., & Özdemir, M. (2012). Perceived parenting style and adolescent adjustment: Revisiting directions of effects and the role of parental knowledge. *Developmental Psychology, 48,* 1540–1553. doi:10.1037/a0027720

Kessels, U. (2015). Bridging the gap by enhancing the fit: How stereotypes about STEM clash with stereotypes about girls. *International Journal of Gender, Science, & Technology, 7,* 280–296.

Kessels, U., & Steinmayr, R. (2013). Macho-man in school: Toward the role of gender role self-concepts and help seeking in school performance. *Learning and Individual Differences, 23,* 234–240.

Kessen, W. (1965). *The child.* New York: Wiley.

Kestenbaum, R., Farber, E. A., & Sroufe, L. A. (1989). Individual differences in empathy among preschoolers: Relation to attachment history. In N. Eisenberg (Ed.), *New Directions for Child and Adolescent Development: No. 44. Empathy and related emotional responses* (pp. 51–64). San Francisco: Jossey-Bass.

Kety, S. S., Wender, P. H., Jacobsen, B., Ingraham, L. J., Jansson, L., Faber, B., & Kinney, D. K. (1994). Mental illness in the biological and adoptive relatives of schizophrenic adoptees: Replication of the Copenhagen Study in the rest of Denmark. *Archives of General Psychiatry, 51,* 442–455.

Keys, T. D., Farkas, G., Burchinal, M. R., Duncan, G. J., Vandell, D. L., Li, W., . . . Howes, C. (2013). Preschool center quality and school readiness: Quality effects and variation by demographic and child characteristics. *Child Development, 84,* 1171–1190. doi:10.1111/cdev.12048

Khaleque, A., & Rohner, R. P. (2012). Pancultural associations between perceived parental acceptance and psychological adjustment of children and adults: A meta-analytic review of worldwide research. *Journal of Cross-Cultural Psychology, 43*(5), 784–800. doi:10.1177/0022022111406120

Khan, S., Gagné, M., Yang, L., & Shapka, J. (2016). Exploring the relationship between adolescents' self-concept and their offline and online social worlds. *Computers in Human Behavior, 55,* 940–945. doi:10.1016/j.chb.2015.09.046

Khu, M., Chambers, C., & Graham, S. A. (2018). When you're happy and I know it: Four-year-olds' emotional perspective taking during online language comprehension. *Child Development, 89*(6), 2264–2281.

Khundrakpam, B. S., Lewis, J. D., Kostopoulos, P., Carbonell, F., & Evans, A. C. (2017). Cortical thickness abnormalities in autism spectrum disorders through late childhood, adolescence, and adulthood: A large-scale MRI study. *Cerebral Cortex, 27*(3), 1721–1731.

Kiang, L., Yip, T., & Fuligni, A. J. (2008). Multiple social identities and adjustment in young adults from ethnically diverse backgrounds. *Journal of Research on Adolescence, 18,* 643–670. doi:10.1111/j.1532-7795.2008.00575.x

Kibbe, M. (2015). Varieties of visual working memory representation in infancy and beyond. *Current Directions in Psychological Science, 24*(6), 433–439.

Kidd, B. (2013). Sports and masculinity. *Sport in Society, 16,* 553–564.

Kidd, C., Piantadosi, S. T., & Aslin, R. N. (2012). The Goldilocks effect: Human infants allocate attention to visual sequences that are neither too simple nor too complex. *PLoS ONE, 7*(5), e36399. doi:10.1371/journal.pone.0036399

Kidd, C., Piantadosi, S. T., & Aslin, R. N. (2014). The Goldilocks effect in infant auditory attention. *Child Development, 85*(5), 1795–1804

Kiesner, J., Poulin, F., & Dishion, T. J. (2010). Adolescent substance use with friends: Moderating and mediating effects of parental monitoring and peer activity contexts. *Merrill Palmer Quarterly, 56,* 529–556.

Kiff, C. J., Lengua, L. J., & Zalewski, M. (2011). Nature and nurturing: Parenting in the context of child temperament. *Clinical Child and Family Psychology Review, 14,* 251–301. doi:10.1007/s10567-011-0093-4

Killen, M. (2007). Children's social and moral reasoning about exclusion. *Current Directions in Psychological Science, 16,* 32–36. doi:10.1111/j.1467-8721.2007.00470.x

Killen, M., & Smetana, J. G. (2015). Origins and development of morality. In M. E. Lamb (Ed.) & R. M. Lerner (Series Ed.), *Handbook of child psychology and developmental science, Vol. 3* (7th ed., pp. 701–749). Hoboken, NJ: Wiley.

Killen, M., & Stangor, C. (2001). Children's social reasoning about inclusion and exclusion in gender and race peer group contexts. *Child Development, 72,* 174–186. doi:10.2307/1132478

Kim, C. R., Counotte, M., Bernstein, K., Deal, C., Mayaud, P., Low, N., & Broutet, N. (2018). Investigating the sexual transmission of Zika virus. *Lancet Global Health, 6*(1), e24–e25.

Kim, E. Y., & Song, H. J. (2015). Six-month-olds actively predict others' goal-directed actions. *Cognitive Development, 33,* 1–13.

Kim, I. K., & Spelke, E. S. (1992). Infants' sensitivity to effects of gravity on visible object motion. *Journal of Experimental Psychology: Human Perception and Performance, 18,* 385–393. doi:10.1037/0096-1523.18.2.385

Kim, J.-Y., McHale, S. M., Wayne Osgood, D., & Crouter, A. C. (2006). Longitudinal course and family correlates of sibling relationships from childhood through adolescence. *Child Development, 77,* 1746–1761. doi:10.1111/j.1467-8624.2006.00971.x

Kim, K. H., Relkin, N. R., Lee, K. M., & Hirsch, J. (1997, July 10). Distinct cortical areas associated with native and second languages. *Nature, 388,* 171–174.

Kim, P., Evans, G. W., Angstadt, M., Ho, S. S., Sripada, C. S., Swain, J. E., . . . Phan, K. L. (2013). Effects of childhood poverty and chronic stress on emotion regulatory brain function in adulthood. *The Proceedings of the National Academy of Sciences, 110,* 18442–18447.

Kingery, J. N., Erdley, C. A., & Marshall, K. C. (2011). Peer acceptance and friendship as predictors of early adolescents' adjustment across the middle school transition. *Merrill-Palmer Quarterly, 57,* 215–243.

Kinzler, K. D., Dupoux, E., & Spelke, E. S. (2007). The native language of social cognition. *Proceedings of the National Academy of Sciences of the United States of America, 104,* 12577–12580. doi:10.1073/pnas.0705345104

Kirkham, N. Z., Slemmer, J. A., & Johnson, S. P. (2002). Visual statistical learning in infancy: Evidence for a domain general learning mechanism. *Cognition, 83,* B35–B42. doi:10.1016/S0010-0277(02)00004-5

Kirsch, A. C., & Murnen, S. K. (2015). "Hot" girls and "cool dudes": Examining the prevalence of the heterosexual script in American children's television media. *Psychology of Popular Media Culture, 4*(1), 18–30. http://dx.doi.org/10.1037/ppm0000017

Kisilevsky, B. S., Hains, S. M., Lee, K., Xie, X., Huang, H., Ye, H. H., . . . Wang, Z. (2003). Effects of experience on fetal voice recognition. *Psychological Science, 14,* 220–224.

Klahr, D. (1978). Goal formation, planning, and learning by pre-school problem solvers or: "My socks are in the dryer." In R. Siegler (Ed.), *Children's thinking: What develops?* (pp. 181–212). Hillsdale, NJ: Erlbaum.

Klein, D. N., Kujawa, A. J., Black, S. R., & Pennock, A. T. (2013). Depressive disorders. In T. P. Beauchaine & S. P. Hinshaw (Eds.), *Child and adolescent psychopathology* (2nd ed., pp. 543–575). New York: Wiley.

Klimes-Dougan, B., & Kopp, C. B. (1999). Children's conflict tactics with mothers: A longitudinal investigation of the toddler and preschool years. *Merrill-Palmer Quarterly, 45,* 226–241.

Klin, A., Jones, W., Schultz, R., & Volkmar, F. (2004). The enactive mind, or from actions to cognition: Lessons from autism. In U. Frith & E. L. Hill (Eds.), *Autism, mind, and brain* (pp. 127–160). Oxford: Oxford University Press.

Kline, M. A., Shamsudheen, R., & Broesch, T. (2018). Variation is the universal: Making cultural evolution work in developmental psychology. *Philosophical Transactions of the Royal Society B: Biological Sciences, 373*(1743). https://dx.doi.org/10.1098/rstb.2017.0059

Knafo, A., & Israel, S. (2010). Genetic and environmental influences on prosocial behavior. In M. Mikulincer & P. R. Shaver (Eds.), *Prosocial motives, emotions, and behavior: The better angels of our nature* (pp. 149–167). Washington, DC: American Psychological Association.

Knafo, A., & Plomin, R. (2006a). Parental discipline and affection and children's prosocial behavior: Genetic and environmental links. *Journal of Personality and Social Psychology, 90,* 147–164. doi:10.1037/0022-3514.90.1.147

Knafo, A., & Plomin, R. (2006b). Prosocial behavior from early to middle childhood: Genetic and environmental influences on stability and change. *Developmental Psychology, 42,* 771–786. doi:10.1037/0012-1649.42.5.771

Knafo, A., Zahn-Waxler, C., Van Hulle, C., Robinson, J. L., & Rhee, S. H. (2008). The developmental origins of a disposition toward empathy: Genetic and environmental contributions. *Emotion, 8,* 737–752. doi:10.1037/a0014179

Knecht, A. B., Burk, W. J., Weesie, J., & Steglich, C. (2011). Friendship and alcohol use in early adolescence: A multilevel social network approach. *Journal of Research on Adolescence, 21,* 475–487. doi:10.1111/j.1532-7795.2010.00685.x

Knecht, A., Snijders, T. A. B., Baerveldt, C., Steglich, C. E. G., & Raub, W. (2010). Friendship and delinquency: Selection and influence processes in early adolescence. *Social Development, 19,* 494–514. doi:10.1111/j.1467-9507.2009.00564.x

Knight, G. P., Cota, M. K., & Bernal, M. E. (1993). The socialization of cooperative, competitive, and individualistic preferences among Mexican American children: The mediating role of ethnic identity. *Hispanic Journal of Behavioral Sciences, 15,* 291–309. doi:10.1177/07399863930153001

Knight, G. P., Fabes, R. A., & Higgins, D. A. (1996). Concerns about drawing causal inferences from meta-analyses: An example in the study of gender differences in aggression. *Psychological Bulletin, 119,* 410–421. doi:10.1037/0033-2909.119.3.410

Knudsen, E. I., Heckman, J. J., Cameron, J. L., & Shonkoff, J. P. (2006). Economic, neurobiological, and behavioral perspectives on building America's future workforce. *Proceedings of the National Academy of Sciences of the United States of America, 103,* 10155–10162. doi:10.1073/pnas.0600888103

Kobasigawa, A., Ransom, C. C., & Holland, C. J. (1980). Children's knowledge about skimming. *Alberta Journal of Educational Research, 26,* 169–182.

Kobiella, A., Grossmann, T., Reid, V. M., & Striano, T. (2008). The discrimination of angry and fearful facial expressions in 7-month-old infants: An event-related potential study. *Cognition and Emotion, 22,* 134–146.

Kochanska, G. (1993). Toward a synthesis of parental socialization and child temperament in early development of conscience. *Child Development, 64,* 325–347. doi:10.2307/1131254

Kochanska, G. (1997). Mutually responsive orientation between mothers and their young children: Implications for early socialization. *Child Development, 68,* 94–112. doi:10.2307/1131928

Kochanska, G. (2001). Emotional development in children with different attachment histories: The first three years. *Child Development, 72,* 474–490.

Kochanska, G. (2002). Committed compliance, moral self, and internalization: A mediational model. *Developmental Psychology, 38,* 339–351. doi:10.1037/0012-1649.38.3.339

Kochanska, G., & Aksan, N. (2006). Children's conscience and self-regulation. *Journal of Personality, 74,* 1587–1618. doi:10.1111/j.1467-6494.2006.00421.x

Kochanska, G., Aksan, N., & Joy, M. E. (2007). Children's fearfulness as a moderator of parenting in early socialization: Two longitudinal studies. *Developmental Psychology, 43,* 222–237. doi:10.1037/0012-1649.43.1.222

Kochanska, G., Barry, R. A., Aksan, N., & Boldt, L. J. (2008). A developmental model of maternal and child contributions to disruptive conduct: The first six years. *Journal of Child Psychology and Psychiatry, 49,* 1220–1227. doi:10.1111/j.1469-7610.2008.01932.x

Kochanska, G., Barry, R. A., Stellern, S. A., & O'Bleness, J. J. (2009). Early attachment organization moderates the parent–child mutually coercive pathway to children's antisocial conduct. *Child Development, 80,* 1288–1300. doi:10.1111/j.1467-8624.2009.01332.x

Kochanska, G., Coy, K. C., & Murray, K. T. (2001). The development of self-regulation in the first four years of life. *Child Development, 72,* 1091–1111.

Kochanska, G., Forman, D. R., Aksan, N., & Dunbar, S. B. (2005). Pathways to conscience: Early mother–child mutually responsive orientation and children's moral emotion, conduct, and cognition. *Journal of Child Psychology and Psychiatry, 46,* 19–34. doi:10.1111/j.1469-7610.2004.00348.x

Kochanska, G., Gross, J. N., Lin, M. H., & Nichols, K. E. (2002). Guilt in young children: Development, determinants, and relations with a broader system of standards. *Child Development, 73,* 461–482. doi:10.1111/1467-8624.00418

Kochanska, G., Gross, J. N., Lin, M. H., & Nichols, K. E. (2002). Guilt in young children: Development, determinants, and relations with a broader system of standards. *Child Development, 73,* 461–482. doi:10.1111/1467-8624.00418

Kochanska, G., & Kim, S. (2012). Toward a new understanding of legacy of early attachments for future antisocial trajectories: Evidence from two longitudinal studies. *Development and Psychopathology, 24,* 783–806. doi:10.1017/S0954579412000375

Kochanska, G., & Kim, S. (2013). Early attachment organization with both parents and future behavior problems: From infancy to middle childhood. *Child Development, 84,* 283–296. doi:10.1111/j.1467-8624.2012.01852.x

Kochanska, G., Kim, S., Barry, R. A., & Philibert, R. A. (2011). Children's genotypes interact with maternal responsive care in predicting children's competence: Diathesis–stress or differential susceptibility? *Development and Psychopathology, 23,* 605–616. doi:10.1017/S0954579411000071

Kochanska, G., Koenig, J. L., Barry, R. A., Kim, S., & Yoon, J. E. (2010). Children's conscience during toddler and preschool years, moral self, and a competent, adaptive developmental trajectory. *Developmental Psychology, 46,* 1320–1332. doi:10.1037/a0020381

Kochanska, G., Philibert, R. A., & Barry, R. A. (2009). Interplay of genes and early mother–child relationship in the development of self-regulation from toddler to preschool age. *Journal of Child Psychology and Psychiatry, 50,* 1331–1338. doi:10.1111/j.1469-7610.2008.02050.x

Kochel, K. P., Ladd, G. W., & Rudolph, K. D. (2012). Longitudinal associations among youth depressive symptoms, peer victimization, and low peer acceptance: An interpersonal process perspective. *Child Development, 83,* 637–650.

Kohlberg, L. (1966). A cognitive-developmental analysis of children's sex-role concepts and attitudes. In E. E. Maccoby (Ed.), *The development of sex differences* (Vol. 5, pp. 82–173). Palo Alto, CA: Stanford University Press.

Kohlberg, L. (1976). Moral stages and moralization: The cognitive–developmental approach. In T. Lickona (Ed.), *Moral development and behavior: Theory, research, and social issues* (pp. 31–53). New York: Holt, Rinehart and Winston.

Kolata, G. (2019) These patients had sickle-cell disease. Experimental therapies might have cured them. *The New York Times,* January 27, 2019.

Kolbert, E. (2018, April). There's no scientific basis for race—It's a made-up label. *National Geographic.* Retrieved from https://www.nationalgeographic.com/magazine/2018/04/race-genetics-science-africa/

Kong, A., Thorleifsson, G., Frigge, M. L., Vilhjalmsson, B. J., Young, A. I., Thorgeirsson, T. E., . . . Gudbjartsson, D. F. (2018). The nature of nurture: Effects of parental genotypes. *Science, 359*(6374), 424–428.

Kopp, C. B. (1989). Regulation of distress and negative emotions: A developmental view. *Developmental Psychology, 25,* 343–354. doi:10.1037/0012-1649.25.3.343

Kopp, C. B. (1992). Emotional distress and control in young children. In R. A. Fabes & N. Eisenberg (Eds.), *New Directions for Child and Adolescent Development: No. 55. Emotion and its regulation in early development* (Vol. 1992, pp. 41–56). San Francisco: Jossey-Bass.

Kopp, C. B. (2001). Self-regulation in childhood. In N. J. Smelser & P. B. Baltes (Eds.), *International encyclopedia of the social and behavioral sciences* (pp. 13862–13866). London: Elsevier.

Korenman, S., Miller, J. E., & Sjaastad, J. E. (1995). Long-term poverty and child development in the United States: Results from the NLSY [Special Issue on Child Poverty, Public Practices, and Welfare Reform]. *Children and Youth Services Review, 17,* 127–155.

Kosenko, K. A., Bond, B. J., & Hurley, R. J. (2018). An exploration into the uses and gratifications of media for transgender individuals. *Psychology of Popular Media Culture, 7*(3), 274–288. http://dx.doi.org/10.1037/ppm0000135

Kouros, C. D., Cummings, E. M., & Davies, P. T. (2010). Early trajectories of interparental conflict and externalizing problems as predictors of social competence in preadolescence. *Development and Psychopathology, 22,* 527–537.

Koutamanis, M., Vossen, H. G. M., Peter, J., & Valkenberg, P. M. (2013). Practice makes perfect: The longitudinal effect of adolescents' instant messaging on their ability to initiate offline friendships. *Computers in Human Behavior, 29,* 2265–2272. doi:10.1016/j.chb. 2013.04.033

Koutsandréou, F., Wegner, M., Niemann, C., & Budde, H. (2016). Effects of motor versus cardiovascular exercise training on children's working memory. *Medicine & Science in Sports & Exercise, 48*(6), 1144–1152. doi:10.1249/MSS.0000000000000869

Kovács, Á. M., & Mehler, J. (2009a). Cognitive gains in 7-month-old bilingual infants. *Proceedings of the National Academy of Sciences of the United States of America, 106,* 6556–6560. doi:10.1073/pnas.0811323106

Kovács, Á. M., & Mehler, J. (2009b, July 31). Flexible learning of multiple speech structures in bilingual infants. *Science, 325,* 611–612.

Kovas, Y., & Plomin, R. (2007). Learning abilities and disabilities: Generalist genes, specialist environments. *Current Directions in Psychological Science, 16,* 284–288. doi:10.1111/j.1467-8721.2007.00521.x

Kowal, A. K., Krull, J. L., & Kramer, L. (2004). How the differential treatment of siblings is linked with parent–child relationship quality. *Journal of Family Psychology, 18,* 658–665. doi:10.1037/0893-3200.18.4.658

Kowalski, R. M., Giumetti, G. W., Schroeder, A. N., & Lattanner, M. R. (2014). Bullying in the digital age: A critical review and meta-analysis of cyberbullying research among youth. *Psychological Bulletin, 140,* 1073–1137. doi:10.1037/a0035618

Kraak, V. I., & Story, M. (2015). Influence of food companies' brand mascots and entertainment companies' cartoon media characters on children's diet and health: A systematic review and research needs. *Obesity Reviews, 16*(2), 107–126.

Krapohl, E., & Plomin, R. (2016). Genetic link between family socioeconomic status and children's educational achievement estimated from genome-wide SNPs. *Molecular Psychiatry, 21*(3), 437–443.

Krascum, R. M., & Andrews, S. (1998). The effects of theories on children's acquisition of family-resemblance categories. *Child Development, 69,* 333–346. doi:10.1111/j.1467-8624.1998.tb06192.x

Kraus, N., & Chandrasekaran, B. (2010). Music training for the development of auditory skills. *Nature Reviews Neuroscience, 11*(8), 599–605.

Kreppner, J. M., Rutter, M., Beckett, C., Castle, J., Colvert, E., Groothues, C., . . . Sonuga-Barke, E. J. (2007). Normality and impairment following profound early institutional deprivation: A longitudinal follow-up into early adolescence. *Developmental Psychology, 43,* 931–946. doi:10.1037/0012-1649.43.4.93

Krevans, J., & Gibbs, J. C. (1996). Parents' use of inductive discipline: Relations to children's empathy and prosocial behavior. *Child Development, 67,* 3263–3277. doi:10.1111/j.1467-8624.1996.tb01913.x

Kroger, J., Martinussen, M., & Marcia, J. E. (2010). Identity status change during adolescence and young adulthood: A meta-analysis. *Journal of Adolescence, 33,* 683–698. doi:10.1016/j.adolescence.2009.11.002

Kromm, H., Färber, M., & Holodynski, M. (2015). Felt or false smiles? Volitional regulation of emotional expression in 4-, 6-, and 8-year-old children. *Child Development, 86,* 579–597. doi:10.1111/cdev.12315

Krueger, A. B. (1999). Experimental estimates of educational production functions. *Quarterly Journal of Economics, 114,* 497–532.

Kruger, A. C., & Konner, M. (2010). Who responds to crying? Maternal care and allocare among the !Kung. *Human Nature, 21,* 309–329. doi:10.1007/s12110-010-9095-z

Kudo, N., Nonaka, Y., Mizuno, N., Mizuno, K., & Okanoya, K. (2011). On-line statistical segmentation of a non-speech auditory stream in neonates as demonstrated by event-related brain potentials. *Developmental Science, 14,* 1100–1106. doi:10.1111/j.1467-7687. 2011.01056.x

Kuhl, P. K., Andruski, J. E., Chistovich, I. A., Chistovich, L. A., Kozhevnikova, E. V., Ryskina, V. L., . . . Lacerda, F. (1997, August 1). Cross-language analysis of phonetic units in language addressed to infants. *Science, 277,* 684–686.

Kuhl, P. K., Tsao, F.-M., & Liu, H.-M. (2003). Foreign-language experience in infancy: Effects of short-term exposure and social interaction on phonetic learning. *Proceedings of the National Academy of Sciences of the United States of America, 100,* 9096–9101. doi:10.1073/pnas.1532872100

Kuhl, P. K., Williams, K. A., Lacerda, F., Stevens, K. N., & Lindblom, B. (1992, January 31). Linguistic experience alters phonetic perception in infants by 6 months of age. *Science, 255,* 606–608.

Kuhn, D., & Franklin, S. (2006). The second decade: What develops (and how). In W. Damon & R. M. Lerner (Series Eds.) & D. Kuhn & R. Siegler (Vol. Eds.), *Handbook of child psychology: Vol. 2. Cognition, perception, and language* (6th ed., pp. 953–993). Hoboken, NJ: Wiley.

Kurdziel, L., Duclos, K., & Spencer, R. M. (2013). Sleep spindles in midday naps enhance learning in preschool children. *Proceedings of the National Academy of Sciences, 110*(43), 17267–17272. doi:10.1073/pnas.1306418110

Kuryluk, A., Cohen, R., & Audley-Piotrowski, S. (2011). The role of respect in the relation of aggression to popularity. *Social Development, 20,* 703–717. doi:10.1111/j.1467-9507.2011.00613.x

Kushnerenko, E., Teinonen, T., Volein, A., & Csibra, G. (2008). Electrophysiological evidence of illusory audiovisual speech percept in human infants. *Proceedings of the National Academy of Sciences, 105*(32), 11442–11445.

Kutnick, P. (1986). The relationship of moral judgment and moral action: Kohlberg's theory, criticism and revision. In S. Modgil & C. Modgil (Eds.), *Lawrence Kohlberg: Consensus and controversy* (pp. 125–148). Philadelphia: Falmer Press.

Kyratzis, A. (2004). Talk and interaction among children and the co-construction of peer groups and peer culture. *Annual Review of Anthropology, 33,* 625–649.

LaBounty, J., Wellman, H. M., Olson, S., Lagattuta, K., & Liu, D. (2008). Mothers' and fathers' use of internal state talk with their young children. *Social Development, 17,* 757–775.

Lacourse, E., Boivin, M., Brendgen, M., Petitclerc, A., Girard, A., Vitaro, F., . . . Tremblay, R. E. (2014). A longitudinal twin study of physical aggression during early childhood: Evidence for a developmentally dynamic genome. *Psychological Medicine, 44*(12), 2617–2627.

Ladd, G. W. (1992). Themes and theories: Perspectives on processes in family-peer relationships. In R. D. Parke & G. W. Ladd (Eds.), *Family-peer relationships: Modes of linkage* (pp. 1–34). Hillsdale, NJ: Erlbaum.

Ladd, G. W., & Coleman, C. C. (1997). Children's classroom peer relationships and early school attitudes: Concurrent and longitudinal associations. *Early Education and Development, 8,* 51–66. doi:10.1207/s15566935eed0801_5

Ladd, G. W., & Hart, C. H. (1992). Creating informal play opportunities: Are parents' and preschoolers' initiations related to children's competence with peers? *Developmental Psychology, 28,* 1179–1187. doi:10.1037/0012-1649.28.6.1179

Ladd, G. W., Herald-Brown, S. L., & Reiser, M. (2008). Does chronic classroom peer rejection predict the development of children's classroom participation during the grade school years? *Child Development, 79,* 1001–1015. doi:10.1111/j.1467-8624.2008.01172.x

Ladd, G. W., Kochenderfer, B. J., & Coleman, C. C. (1996). Friendship quality as a predictor of young children's early school adjustment. *Child Development, 67,* 1103–1118. doi:10.1111/j.1467-8624.1996.tb01785.x

Lagacé-Séguin, D. G., & Gionet, A. (2009). Parental meta-emotion and temperament predict coping skills in early adolescence. *International Journal of Adolescence and Youth, 14,* 367–382.

Lagattuta, K. H., Nucci, L., & Bosacki, S. L. (2010). Bridging theory of mind and the personal domain: Children's reasoning about resistance to parental control. *Child Development, 81,* 616–635. doi:10.1111/j.1467-8624.2009.01419.x

Lagattuta, K. H., & Thompson, R. A. (2007). The development of self-conscious emotions: Cognitive processes and social influences. In J. L. Tracy, R. W. Robins, & J. P. Tangney (Eds.), *The self-conscious emotions: Theory and research* (pp. 91–113). New York: Guilford Press.

Laghi, F., Schneider, B. H., Vitoroulis, R. J., Coplan, R. J., & Baiocco, R. (2013). Knowing when not to use the internet: Shyness and adolescents' on-line and off-line interactions with friends. *Computers in Human Behavior, 29,* 51–57. doi:10.1016/j.chb.2012.07.015

Lahey, B. B., Schwab-Stone, M., Goodman, S. H., Waldman, I. D., Canino, G., Rathouz, P. J., . . . Jensen, P. S. (2000). Age and gender differences in oppositional behavior and conduct problems: A cross-sectional household study of middle childhood and adolescence. *Journal of Abnormal Psychology, 109,* 488–503. doi:10.1037/0021-843X.109.3.488

Laible, D., Eye, J., & Carlo, G. (2008). Dimensions of conscience in mid-adolescence: Links with social behavior, parenting, and temperament. *Journal of Youth and Adolescence, 37,* 875–887. doi:10.1007/s10964-008-9277-8

Laird, R. D., Pettit, G. S., Bates, J. E., & Dodge, K. A. (2003). Parents' monitoring-relevant knowledge and adolescents' delinquent behavior: Evidence of correlated developmental changes and reciprocal influences. *Child Development, 74,* 752–768. doi:10.1111/1467-8624.00566

Laird, R. D., Pettit, G. S., Mize, J., Brown, E. G., & Lindsey, E. (1994). Mother–child conversations about peers: Contributions to competence. *Family Relations, 43,* 425–432. doi:10.2307/585374

Lam, C. B., McHale, S. M., & Crouter, A. C. (2014). Time with peers from middle childhood to late adolescence: Developmental course and adjustment correlates. *Child Development, 85,* 1677–1693. doi:10.1111/cdev.12235

Lam, E. T., Hastie, A., Lin, C., Ehrlich, D., Das, S. K., Austin, M. D., . . . Kwok, P. Y. (2012). Genome mapping on nanochannel arrays for structural variation analysis and sequence assembly. *Nature Biotechnology, 30*(8), 771–776. doi:10.1038/nbt.2303

Lam, S. F., Jimerson, S., Kikas, E., Cefai, C., Veiga, F. H., Nelson, B., . . . Farrell, P. (2012). Do girls and boys perceive themselves as equally engaged in school? The results of an international study from 12 countries. *Journal of School Psychology, 50*(1), 77–94.

Lamb, M. E. (1998). Nonparental child care: Context, quality, correlates, and consequences. In W. Damon (Series Ed.) & I. E. Sigel & K. A. Renninger (Vol. Eds.), *Handbook of child psychology: Vol. 4. Child psychology in practice* (5th ed., pp. 135–210). New York: Wiley.

Lamborn, S. D., Mounts, N. S., Steinberg, L., & Dornbusch, S. M. (1991). Patterns of competence and adjustment among adolescents from authoritative, authoritarian, indulgent, and neglectful families. *Child Development, 62,* 1049–1065. doi:10.1111/j.1467-8624.1991.tb01588.x

Landau, B., Smith, L. B., & Jones, S. S. (1988). The importance of shape in early lexical learning. *Cognitive Development, 3,* 299–321. doi:10.1016/0885-2014(88)90014-7

Lane, D. M., & Chang, Y. A. (2018). Chess knowledge predicts chess memory even after controlling for chess experience: Evidence for the role of high-level processes. *Memory & Cognition, 46*(3), 337–348. doi:10.3758/s13421-017-0768-2

Lange, S., Probst, C., Quere, M., Rehm, J., & Popova, S. (2015). Alcohol use, smoking and their co-occurrence during pregnancy among Canadian women, 2003 to 2011/12. *Addictive Behaviors, 50,* 102–109.

Lange, S., Probst, C., Rehm, J., & Popova, S. (2017). Prevalence of binge drinking during pregnancy by country and World Health Organization region: Systematic review and meta-analysis. *Reproductive Toxicology, 73,* 214–221.

Langley, K., Heron, J., Smith, G. D., & Thapar, A. (2012). Maternal and paternal smoking during pregnancy and risk of ADHD symptoms in offspring: Testing for intrauterine effects. *American Journal of Epidemiology, 176*(3), 261–268.

Langlois, J. H., Kalakanis, L., Rubenstein, A. J., Larson, A., Hallam, M., & Smoot, M. (2000). Maxims or myths of beauty? A meta-analytic and theoretical review. *Psychological Bulletin, 126,* 390–423. doi:10.1037//0033-2909.126.3.390

Langlois, J. H., Ritter, J. M., Roggman, L. A., & Vaughn, L. S. (1991). Facial diversity and infant preferences for attractive faces. *Developmental Psychology, 27,* 79–84. doi:10.1037/0012-1649.27.1.79

Langlois, J. H., Roggman, L. A., Casey, R. J., Ritter, J. M., Rieser-Danner, L. A., & Jenkins, V. Y. (1987). Infant preferences for attractive faces: Rudiments of a stereotype? *Developmental Psychology, 23,* 363–369. doi:10.1037/0012-1649.23.3.363

Langlois, J. H., Roggman, L. A., & Rieser-Danner, L. A. (1990). Infants' differential social responses to attractive and unattractive faces. *Developmental Psychology, 26,* 153–159. doi:10.1037/0012-1649.26.1.153

Lansford, J., Putallaz, M., Grimes, C., Schiro-Osman, K., Kupersmidt, J., & Coie, J. (2006). Perceptions of friendship quality and observed behaviors with friends: How do sociometrically rejected, average, and popular girls differ? *Merrill-Palmer Quarterly, 52*(4), 694–720.

Lansford, J. E., Criss, M. M., Dodge, K. A., Shaw, D. S., Pettit, G. S., & Bates, J. E. (2009). Trajectories of physical discipline: Early childhood antecedents and developmental outcomes. *Child Development, 80,* 1385–1402. doi:10.1111/j.1467-8624.2009.01340.x

Lansford, J. E., Criss, M. M., Laird, R. D., Shaw, D. S., Pettit, G. S., Bates, J. E., & Dodge, K. A. (2011). Reciprocal relations between parents' physical discipline and children's externalizing behavior during middle childhood and adolescence. *Development and Psychopathology, 23,* 225–238. doi:10.1017/S0954579410000751

Lansford, J. E., Godwin, J., Al-Hassan, S. M., Bacchini, D., Bornstein, M. H., Chang, L., . . . Zelli, A. (2018). Longitudinal associations between parenting and youth adjustment in twelve cultural groups: Cultural normativeness of parenting as a moderator. *Developmental Psychology, 54,* 362–377. https://doi.org/10.1037/dev0000416

Lansford, J. E., Malone, P. S., Dodge, K. A., Pettit, G. S., & Bates, J. E. (2010). Developmental cascades of peer rejection, social information processing biases, and aggression during middle childhood. *Development and Psychopathology, 22,* 593–602. doi:10.1017/S0954579410000301

Lansford, J. E., Skinner, A. T., Sorbring, E., Giunta, L. D., Deater-Deckard, K., Dodge, K. A., . . . Chang, L. (2012), Boys' and girls' relational and physical aggression in nine countries. *Aggressive Behavior, 38,* 298–308. doi:10.1002/ab.21433

Lapsley, D. K. (2006). Moral stage theory. In J. S. Melanie Killen (Ed.), *Handbook of moral development* (pp. 37–66). Mahwah, NJ: Erlbaum.

Larsen, J. K., Hermans, R. C., Sleddens, E. F., Engels, R. C., Fisher, J. O., & Kremers, S. P. (2015). How parental dietary behavior and food parenting practices affect children's dietary behavior. Interacting sources of influence? *Appetite, 89,* 246–257.

Larson, K., Russ, S. A., Nelson, B. B., Olson, L. M., & Halfon, N. (2015). Cognitive ability at kindergarten entry and socioeconomic status. *Pediatrics, 135,* e440–e448. doi:10.1542/peds.2014-0434

Larsson, H., Chang, Z., D'Onofrio, B. M., & Lichtenstein, P. (2014). The heritability of clinically diagnosed attention deficit hyperactivity disorder across the lifespan. *Psychological Medicine, 44*(10), 2223–2229.

Laski, E. V., & Siegler, R. S. (2014). Learning from number board games: You learn what you encode. *Developmental Psychology, 50,* 853–864. doi:10.1037/a0034321

Laski, E. V., & Yu, Q. (2014). Number line estimation and mental addition: Examining the potential roles of language and education. *Journal of Experimental Child Psychology, 117,* 29–44. doi:10.1016/j.jecp.2013.08.007

Laughlin, J. (2014). *A child's day: Living arrangements, nativity, and family transitions: 2011* (Current Population Reports, P70–139). Retrieved from U.S. Census Bureau website: https://www.census.gov/content/dam/Census/library/publications/2014/demo/p70-139.pdf

Laughlin, L. (2013). *Who's minding the kids? Child care arrangements: Spring 2011* (Current Population Reports, P70-135). Washington, DC: U.S. Census Bureau. Retrieved from U.S. Census Bureau website: http://www.census.gov/content/dam/Census/library/publications/2013/demo/p70-135.pdf

Laurence, S., & Mondloch, C. J. (2016). That's my teacher! Children's ability to recognize personally familiar and unfamiliar faces improves with age. *Journal of Experimental Child Psychology, 143,* 123–138.

Laurin, J. C., Joussemet, M., Tremblay, R. E., & Boivin, M. (2015). Early forms of controlling parenting and the development of childhood anxiety. *Journal of Child and Family Studies, 24*(11), 3279–3292.

Laursen, B., Bukowski, W. M., Aunola, K., & Nurmi, J.-E. (2007). Friendship moderates prospective associations between social isolation and adjustment problems in young children. *Child Development, 78,* 1395–1404. doi:10.1111/j.1467-8624.2007.01072.x

Laursen, B., Finkelstein, B. D., & Betts, N. T. (2001). A developmental meta-analysis of peer conflict resolution. *Developmental Review, 21,* 423–449. doi:10.1006/drev.2000.0531

Lavelli, M., & Fogel, A. (2005). Developmental changes in the relationship between the infant's attention and emotion during early face-to-face communication: The 2-month transition. *Developmental Psychology, 41,* 265–280.

Lavelli, M., & Fogel, A. (2013). Interdyad differences in early mother–infant face-to-face communication: Real-time dynamics and developmental pathways. *Developmental Psychology, 49*(12), 2257–2271. http://dx.doi.org/10.1037/a0032268

Lavigne, J. V., Bryant, F. B., Hopkins, J., & Gouze, K. R. (2019). Age 4 predictors of oppositional defiant disorder in early grammar school. *Journal of Clinical Child & Adolescent Psychology, 48,* 93–107. doi:10.1080/15374416.2017.1280806

Lawford, H., Pratt, M. W., Hunsberger, B., & Pancer, S. M. (2005). Adolescent generativity: A longitudinal study of two possible contexts for learning concern for future generations. *Journal of Research on Adolescence, 15,* 261–273. doi:10.1111/j.1532-7795.2005.00096.x

Layton, T. J., Barnett, M. L., Hicks, T. R., & Jena, A. B. (2018). Attention deficit–hyperactivity disorder and month of school enrollment. *New England Journal of Medicine, 379*(22), 2122–2130.

Lazar, I., Darlington, R., Murray, H., Royce, J., & Snipper, A. (1982). Lasting effects of early education: A report from the Consortium for Longitudinal Studies. *Monographs of the Society for Research in Child Development, 47*(2/3, Serial No. 195).

Lazenby, D. C., Sideridis, G. D., Huntington, N., Prante, M., Dale, P. S., Curtin, S., . . . Akshoomoff, N. (2016). Language differences at 12 months in infants who develop autism spectrum disorder. *Journal of Autism and Developmental Disorders, 46*(3), 899–909.

Le Corre, M., & Carey, S. (2007). One, two, three, four, nothing more: An investigation of the conceptual sources of the verbal counting principles. *Cognition, 105,* 395–438. doi:10.1016/j.cognition.2006.10.005

Le Corre, M., Van de Walle, G., Brannon, E. M., & Carey, S. (2006). Re-visiting the competence/performance debate in the acquisition of the counting principles. *Cognitive Psychology, 52*(2), 130–169. doi:10.1016/j.cogpsych.2005.07

Le Grand, R., Mondloch, C. J., Maurer, D., & Brent, H. P. (2001, April 19). Early visual experience and face processing. *Nature, 410,* 890. doi:10.1038/35073749

Le Grand, R., Mondloch, C. J., Maurer, D., & Brent, H. P. (2003). Expert face processing requires visual input to the right hemisphere during infancy. *Nature Neuroscience, 6,* 1108–1112. doi:10.1038/nn1121

Le Mare, L., & Audet, K. (2006). A longitudinal study of the physical growth and health of post-institutionalized Romanian adoptees. *Paediatrics & Child Health, 11*(2), 85–91.

Le, H.-N. (2000). Never leave your little one alone: Raising an Ifaluk child. In J. S. DeLoache & A. Gottlieb (Eds.), *A world of babies: Imagined childcare guides for seven societies* (pp. 199–220). New York: Cambridge University Press.

Leadbeater, B. J., & Hoglund, W. L. G. (2009). The effects of peer victimization and physical aggression on changes in internalizing from first to third grade. *Child Development, 80,* 843–859. doi:10.1111/j.1467-8624.2009.01301.x

Leaper, C. (1991). Influence and involvement in children's discourse: Age, gender, and partner effects. *Child Development, 62,* 797–811.

Leaper, C. (1994). Exploring the consequences of gender segregation on social relationships: Social relationships in childhood, adolescence and adulthood. In C. Leaper (Ed.), *New Directions for Child and Adolescent Development: No. 65. Childhood gender segregation: Causes and consequences* (pp. 67–86). San Francisco: Jossey-Bass.

Leaper, C. (2000). The social construction and socialization of gender during development. In P. H. Miller, & E. Kofsky Scholnick (Eds.), *Toward a feminist developmental psychology* (pp. 127–152). Taylor & Frances/Routledge: Florence, KY.

Leaper, C. (2011). More similarities than differences in contemporary theories of social development? A plea for theory bridging. In J. B. Benson (Ed.), *Advances in child development and behavior: Vol. 40* (pp. 337–378). San Diego, CA: Elsevier Academic Press. http://dx.doi.org/10.1016/B978-0-12-386491-8.00009-8

Leaper, C. (2013). Gender development during childhood. In P. D. Zelazo (Ed.), *Oxford handbook of developmental psychology: Vol. 2. Self and other* (pp. 326–376). New York: Oxford University Press.

Leaper, C. (2015a). Gender and social-cognitive development. In R. M. Lerner (Series Ed.), L. S. Liben & U. Muller (Vol. Eds.), *Handbook of child psychology and developmental science* (7th ed.), *Vol. 2: Cognitive processes* (pp. 806–853). Hoboken, NJ: Wiley.

Leaper, C. (2015b). Do I belong? Gender, peer groups, and STEM achievement. *International Journal of Gender, Science, & Technology, 7,* 166–179.

Leaper, C. (2018). Gender, dispositions, peer relations, and identity: Toward an integrative developmental model. In N. K. Dess, J. Marecek, & L. C. Bell (Eds.), *Gender, sex, and sexualities: Psychological perspectives* (pp. 219–245). New York: Oxford University Press.

Leaper, C., Anderson, K. J., & Sanders, P. (1998). Moderators of gender effects on parents' talk to their children: A meta-analysis. *Developmental Psychology, 34,* 3–27. doi:10.1037/0012-1649.34.1.3

Leaper, C., & Ayres, M. M. (2007). A meta-analytic review of gender variations in adults' language use: Talkativeness, affiliative speech, and assertive speech. *Personality and Social Psychology Review, 11,* 328–363. doi:10.1177/1088868307302221

Leaper, C., & Bigler, R. S. (2018). Societal causes and consequences of gender typing of children's toys. In E. S. Weisgram & L. M. Dinella (Eds.), *Gender typing of children's toys: How early play experiences impact development* (pp. 287–308). Washington, DC: American Psychological Association. http://dx.doi.org/10.1037/0000077-013

Leaper, C., Breed, L., Hoffman, L., & Perlman, C. A. (2002). Variations in the gender-stereotyped content of children's television cartoons across genres. *Journal of Applied Social Psychology, 32,* 1653–1662. doi:10.1111/j.1559-1816.2002.tb02767.x

Leaper, C., & Brown, C. S. (2008). Perceived experiences with sexism among adolescent girls. *Child Development, 79,* 685–704. doi:10.1111/j.1467-8624.2008.01151.x

Leaper, C., & Brown, C. S. (2014). Sexism in schools. In L. S. Liben & R. S. Bigler (Eds.), *Advances in child development and behavior, Vol. 47: The role of gender in educational contexts and outcomes* (pp. 189–223). San Diego, CA: Elsevier Academic Press. http://dx.doi.org/10.1016/bs.acdb.2014.04.001

Leaper, C., Farkas, T., & Starr, C. R. (2018, October 1). Traditional masculinity, help avoidance, and intrinsic interest in relation to high school students' English and math performance. *Psychology of Men & Masculinities, 20*(4), 603–611. http://dx.doi.org/10.1037/men0000188

Leaper, C., & Robnett, R. D. (2018). Sexism. In R. J. R. Levesque (Ed.), *Encyclopedia of adolescence* (2nd ed., pp. 3502–3511). New York: Springer. https://doi.org/10.1007/978-3-319-33228-4_226

Leaper, C., & Smith, T. E. (2004). A meta-analytic review of gender variations in children's language use: Talkativeness, affiliative speech, and assertive speech. *Developmental Psychology, 40,* 993–1027. doi:10.1037/0012-1649.40.6.993

Leaper, C., & Starr, C. R. (2019). Helping or hindering undergraduate women's STEM motivation: Experiences with STEM support, STEM-related gender bias, and sexual harassment. *Psychology of Women Quarterly, 43*(2), 165–183. https://doi.org/10.1177/0361684318806302

Leaper, C., Tenenbaum, H. R., & Shaffer, T. G. (1999). Communication patterns of African American girls and boys from low-income, urban backgrounds. *Child Development, 70,* 1489–1503. doi:10.1111/1467-8624.00108

Leaper, C., & Van, S. R. (2008). Masculinity ideology, covert sexism, and perceived gender typicality in relation to young men's academic motivation and choices in college. *Psychology of Men & Masculinities, 9,* 139–153. doi:10.1037/1524-9220.9.3.139

Lebel, C., Walton, M., Letourneau, N., Giesbrecht, G. F., Kaplan, B. J., & Dewey, D. (2016). Prepartum and postpartum maternal depressive symptoms are related to children's brain structure in preschool. *Biological Psychiatry, 80*(11), 859–868.

Lecanuet, J.-P., & Jacquet, A.-Y. (2002). Fetal responsiveness to maternal passive swinging in low heart rate variability state: Effects of stimulation direction and duration. *Developmental Psychobiology, 40,* 57–67. doi:10.1002/dev.10013

Lee, B. K., & McGrath, J. J. (2015). Advancing parental age and autism: Multifactorial pathways. *Trends in Molecular Medicine, 21*(2), 118–125.

Lee, C. C., Jhang, Y., Chen, L. M., Relyea, G., & Oller, D. K. (2016). Subtlety of ambient-language effects in babbling: A study of English- and Chinese-learning infants at 8, 10, and 12 months. *Language Learning and Development.* doi:10.1080/15475441.2016.1180983

Lee, D., & McLanahan, S. (2015). Family structure transitions and child development: Instability, selection, and population heterogeneity. *American Sociological Review, 80,* 738–763. doi:10.1177/0003122415592129

Lee, E. H., Zhou, Q., Eisenberg, N., & Wang, Y. (2013). Bidirectional relations between temperament and parenting styles in Chinese children. *International Journal of Behavioral Development, 37,* 57–67. doi:10.1177/0165025412460795

Lee, G. Y., & Kisilevsky, B. S. (2014). Fetuses respond to father's voice but prefer mother's voice after birth. *Developmental Psychobiology, 56*(1), 1–11.

Lee, K. (2013). Little liars: Development of verbal deception in children. *Child Development Perspectives, 7*(2), 91–96. doi:10.1111/cdep.12023

Lee, K., & Lee, J. (2012). Self-esteem and delinquency in South Korean adolescents: Latent growth modeling. *School Psychology International, 33,* 54–68. doi:10.1177/0143034311409856

Lee, K., Cameron, C. A., Xu, F., Fu, G., & Board, J. (1997). Chinese and Canadian children's evaluations of lying and truth telling: Similarities and differences in the context of pro and antisocial behaviors. *Child Development, 68*(5), 924–934.

Lee, L., Howes, C., & Chamberlain, B. (2007). Ethnic heterogeneity of social networks and cross-ethnic friendships of elementary school boys and girls. *Merrill-Palmer Quarterly, 53,* 325–346.

Lee, S., & Edmonston, B. (2013). Canada's immigrant families: Growth, diversity and challenges. *Population Change and Lifecourse Strategic Knowledge Cluster Discussion Paper Series, 1*(1). Article 4.

Lee, S. J., Altschul, I., & Gershoff, E. T. (2013). Does warmth moderate longitudinal associations between maternal spanking and child aggression in early childhood? *Developmental Psychology, 49,* 2017–2028. doi:10.1037/a0031630

Lee, S. J., Grogan-Kaylor, A., & Berger, L. M. (2014). Parental spanking of 1-year-old children and subsequent protective services involvement. *Child Abuse & Neglect, 38,* 875–883. doi:10.1016/j.chiabu.2014.01.018

Leerkes, E. M., Parade, S. H., & Gudmundson, J. A. (2011). Mothers' emotional reactions to crying pose risk for subsequent attachment insecurity. *Journal of Family Psychology, 25,* 635–643. doi:10.1037/a0023654

LeFevre, J.-A., Bisanz, J., Daley, K. E., Buffone, L., Greenham, S. L., & Sadesky, G. S. (1996). Multiple routes to solution of single-digit multiplication problems. *Journal of Experimental Psychology: General, 125,* 284–306.

Legare, C. H., & Gelman, S. A. (2008). Bewitchment, biology, or both: The co-existence of natural and supernatural explanatory frameworks across development. *Cognitive Science, 32*(4), 607–642. doi:10.1080/03640210802066766

Legare, C. H., & Gelman, S. A. (2014). Examining explanatory biases in young children's biological reasoning. *Journal of Cognition and Development, 15*(2), 287–303. doi:10.1080/15248372.2012.749480

Leigh, J., Dettman, S., Dowell, R., & Briggs, R. (2013). Communication development in children who receive a cochlear implant by 12 months of age. *Otology & Neurotology, 34*(3), 443–450.

Lemaire, P., & Brun, F. (2016). Age-related differences in children's strategy repetition: A study in arithmetic. *Journal of Experimental Child Psychology, 150,* 227–240. doi:10.1016/j.jecp.2016.05.014

Lemerise, E. A., & Arsenio, W. F. (2000). An integrated model of emotion processes and cognition in social information processing. *Child Development, 71,* 107–118. doi:10.1111/1467-8624.00124

Lemerise, E. A., & Dodge, K. A. (2008). The development of anger and hostile interactions. In M. Lewis, J. M. Haviland-Jones, & L. F. Barrett (Eds.), Handbook of emotions (3rd ed., pp. 730–741). New York: Guilford.

Lemery-Chalfant, K., Kao, K., Swann, G., & Goldsmith, H. H. (2013). Childhood temperament: Passive gene–environment correlation, gene–environment interaction, and the hidden importance of the family environment. *Development and Psychopathology, 25*(1), 51–63. doi:10.1017/S0954579412000892

Lengua, L. J., Bush, N. R., Long, A. C., Kovacs, E. A., & Trancik, A. M. (2008). Effortful control as a moderator of the relation between contextual risk factors and growth in adjustment problems. *Development and Psychopathology, 20,* 509–528.

Lenhart, A. (2015). *How teens hang out and stay in touch with their closest friends.* Pew Research Center. Retrieved from http://www.pewinternet.org/2015/08/06/chapter-2-how-teens-hang-out-and-stay-in-touch-with-their-closest-friends/

Lenhart, A., Smith, A., & Anderson, M. (2015). *Teens, technology and romantic relationships.* Pew Research Center. Retrieved from http://www.pewinternet.org/files/2015/10/PI_2015-10-01_teens-technology-romance_FINAL.pdf

Leonard, J. A., Lee, Y., & Schulz, L. E. (2017). Infants make more attempts to achieve a goal when they see adults persist. *Science, 357*(6357), 1290–1294.

Leppänen, J. M., & Nelson, C. A. (2012). Early development of fear processing. *Current Directions in Psychological Science, 21*(3), 200–204. https://doi.org/10.1177/0963721411435841

Lereya, S. T., Copeland, W. E., Zammit, S., & Wolke, D. (2015). Bully/victims: A longitudinal, population-based cohort study of their mental health. *European Child & Adolescent Psychiatry, 24,* 1461–1471. doi:10.1007/s00787-015-0705-5

Lerner, R. M., Lerner, J. V., Almerigi, J. B., Theokas, C., Phelps, E., Gestsdottir, T., . . . von Eye, A. (2005). Positive youth development, participation in community youth development programs, and community contributions of fifth-grade adolescents: Findings from the first wave of the 4-H study of positive youth development. *The Journal of Early Adolescence, 25,* 17–71. doi:10.1177/0272431604272461

Lervåg, A., Hulme, C., & Melby-Lervåg, M. (2018). Unpicking the developmental relationship between oral language skills and reading comprehension: It's simple, but complex. *Child Development, 89*(5), 1821–1838. doi:10.1111/cdev.12861

Leslie, A. M. (1986). Getting development off the ground: Modularity and the infant's perception of causality. In P. van Geert (Ed.), *Theory building in developmental psychology* (pp. 406–437). New York: Elsevier.

Leslie, A. M. (2000). How to acquire a representational theory of mind. In D. Sperber (Ed.), *Metarepresentations: A multidisciplinary perspective* (pp. 197–223). Oxford: Oxford University Press.

Leslie, A. M., Friedman, O., & German, T. P. (2004). Core mechanisms in 'theory of mind.' *Trends in Cognitive Sciences, 8*(12), 528–533. doi:10.1016/j.tics.2004.10.001

Lester, B. M., Conradt, E., & Marsit, C. (2016). Introduction to the special section on epigenetics. *Child Development, 87*(1), 29–37.

Letourneau, N., Tryphonopoulos, P., Giesbrecht, G., Dennis, C., Bhogal, S., & Watson, B. (2015). Narrative and meta-analytic review of interventions aiming to improve maternal-child attachment security. *Infant Mental Health Journal, 36,* 366–387. doi:10.1002/imhj.21525

Leung, F. K. S., Park, K., Shimizu, Y., & Xu, B. (2015). Mathematics education in East Asia. In S. J. Cho (Ed.), *The proceedings of the 12th International Congress on Mathematical Education* (pp. 123–143). New York: Springer. doi:10.1007/978-3-319-12688-3_11

Levant, R. F. (2005). The crises of boyhood. In G. E. Good & G. R. Brooks (Eds.), *The new handbook of psychotherapy and counseling with men: A comprehensive guide to settings, problems, and treatment approaches* (Rev. and abridged ed., pp. 161–171). San Francisco: Jossey-Bass.

Leve, L. D., Pears, K. C., & Fisher, P. A. (2002). Competence in early development. In J. B. Reid, G. R. Patterson, & J. Snyder (Eds.), *Antisocial behavior in children and adolescents: A developmental analysis and model for intervention* (pp. 45–64). Washington, DC: American Psychological Association.

Levin, I. (1982). The nature and development of time concepts in children: The effects of interfering cues. In W. J. Friedman (Ed.), *Developmental psychology of time* (pp. 47–85). New York: Academic Press.

Levin, I., & Aram, D. (2013). Promoting early literacy via practicing invented spelling: A comparison of different mediation routines. *Reading Research Quarterly, 48,* 221–236. doi:10.1002/rrq.48

Levin, I., & Korat, O. (1993). Sensitivity to phonological, morphological, and semantic cues in early reading and writing in Hebrew. *Merrill-Palmer Quarterly, 39,* 213–232.

Levin, I., Siegler, R. S., & Druyan, S. (1990). Misconceptions about motion: Development and training effects. *Child Development, 61,* 1544–1557. doi:10.1111/j.1467-8624.1990.tb02882.x

Levine, M. P., & Smolak, L. (2010). Cultural influences on body image and the eating disorders. In W. S. Agras (Ed.), *The Oxford handbook of eating disorders* (pp. 223–246). New York: Oxford University Press.

LeVine, R. A. (1988). Human parental care: Universal goals, cultural strategies, individual behavior. In R. A. LeVine, P. M. Miller, & M. M. West (Eds.), *New Directions for Child and Adolescent Development: No. 40. Parental behavior in diverse societies* (pp. 3–12). San Francisco: Jossey-Bass.

Levine, S. C., Ratliff, K. R., Huttenlocher, J., & Cannon, J. (2012). Early puzzle play: A predictor of preschoolers' spatial transformation skill. *Developmental Psychology, 48,* 530–542. doi:10.1037/a0025913

Lew, A. R. (2011). Looking beyond the boundaries: Time to put landmarks back on the cognitive map? *Psychological Bulletin, 137,* 484–507. doi:10.1037/a0022315

Lewin, H. A., Robinson, G. E., Kress, W. J., Baker, W. J., Coddington, J., Crandall, K. A., . . . Goldstein, M. M. (2018). Earth BioGenome Project: Sequencing life for the future of life. *Proceedings of the National Academy of Sciences, 115*(17), 4325–4333.

Lewis, E. E., Dozier, M., Ackerman, J., & Sepulveda-Kozakowski, S. (2007). The effect of placement instability on adopted children's inhibitory control abilities and oppositional behavior. *Developmental Psychology, 43,* 1415–1427. doi:10.1037/0012-1649.43.6.1415

Lewis, M. (1995). Embarrassment: The emotion of self-exposure and evaluation. In J. P. Tangney & K. W. Fischer (Eds.), *Self-conscious emotions: The psychology of shame, guilt, embarrassment, and pride* (pp. 198–218). New York: Guilford Press.

Lewis, M. (1998). Emotional competence and development. In D. Pushkar, W. M. Bukowski, A. E. Schwartzman, D. M. Stack, & D. R. White (Eds.), *Improving competence across the lifespan: Building interventions based on theory and research* (pp. 27–36). New York: Plenum Press.

Lewis, M. (2016). Self-conscious emotions: Embarrassment, pride, shame, guilt and hubris. In L. F. Barrett, M. Lewis, & J. M. Haviland-Jones (Eds.), *Handbook of emotions* (4th ed., pp. 792–814). New York: Guilford.

Lewis, M., Alessandri, S. M., & Sullivan, M. W. (1990). Violation of expectancy, loss of control, and anger expressions in young infants. *Developmental Psychology, 26,* 745–751.

Lewis, M., & Brooks-Gunn, J. (1979). *Social cognition and the acquisition of self.* New York: Plenum Press.

Lewkowicz, D. J. (2004). Perception of serial order in infants. *Developmental Science, 7,* 175–184.

Lewkowicz, D. J., & Ghazanfar, A. A. (2006). The decline of cross-species intersensory perception in human infants. *Proceedings of the National Academy of Sciences of the United States of America, 103,* 6771–6774. doi:10.1073/pnas.0602027103

Lewkowicz, D. J., & Hansen-Tift, A. M. (2012). Infants deploy selective attention to the mouth of a talking face when learning speech. *Proceedings of the National Academy of Sciences, 109*(5), 1431–1436.

Lewkowicz, D. J., & Minar, N. J. (2014). Infants are not sensitive to synesthetic cross-modality correspondences: A comment on Walker et al. (2010). *Psychological Science, 25*(3), 832–834.

Lew-Williams, C., & Fernald, A. (2007). Young children learning Spanish make rapid use of grammatical gender in spoken word recognition. *Psychological Science, 18,* 193–198. doi:10.1111/j.1467-9280.2007.01871.x

Li, R., Montpetit, A., Rousseau, M., Wu, S. Y. M., Greenwood, C. M., Spector, T. D., . . . Richards, J. B. (2014). Somatic point mutations occurring early in development: A monozygotic twin study. *Journal of Medical Genetics, 51,* 28–43. doi:10.1136/jmedgenet-2013-101712

Li, Y., Putallaz, M., & Su, Y. (2011). Interparental conflict styles and parenting behaviors: Associations with overt and relational aggression among Chinese children. *Merrill-Palmer Quarterly, 57,* 402–428.

Liben, L. S., & Bigler, R. S. (1987). Children's gender schemata. In L. S. Liben & M. L. Signorella (Eds.), *New Directions for Child and Adolescent Development: No. 38. Children's gender schemata* (Vol. 1987, pp. 89–105). San Francisco: Jossey-Bass.

Liben, L. S., & Bigler, R. S. (2002). The developmental course of gender differentiation: Conceptualizing, measuring, and evaluating constructs and pathways. *Monographs of the Society for Research in Child Development, 67*(2, Serial No. 269), i–183. doi:10.2307/3181530

Liben, L. S., & Myers, L. J. (2007). Developmental changes in children's understanding of maps: What, when, and how. In J. M. Plumert & J. P. Spence (Eds.), *The emerging spatial mind* (pp. 193–218). Oxford: Oxford University Press.

Liben, L. S., & Signorella, M. L. (1980). Gender-related schemata and constructive memory in children. *Child Development, 51,* 11–18.

Liben, L. S., & Signorella, M. L. (1993). Gender-schematic processing in children: The role of initial interpretations of stimuli. *Developmental Psychology, 29,* 141–149. doi:10.1037/0012-1649.29.1.141

Liberman, Z., Woodward, A. L., Keysar, B., & Kinzler, K. D. (2017). Exposure to multiple languages enhances communication skills in infancy. *Developmental Science, 20*(1), e12420.

Liberman, Z., Woodward, A. L., Sullivan, K., & Kinzler, K. (2016). Early emerging system for reasoning about the social nature of food. *Proceedings of the National Academy of Sciences, 113*(34). doi:10.1073/pnas.1605456113

Libertus, K., Joh, A. S., & Needham, A. W. (2015). Motor training at 3 months affects object exploration 12 months later. *Developmental Science, 19*(6), 1058–1066. doi:10.1111/desc.12370

Libertus, K., & Needham, A. (2010). Teach to reach: The effects of active vs. passive reaching experiences on action and perception. *Vision Research, 50,* 2750–2757. doi:10.1016/j.visres.2010.09.001

Libertus, M. E., & Brannon, E. M. (2010). Stable individual differences in number discriminations in infancy. *Developmental Science, 13*(6), 900–906. doi:10.1111/j.1467-7687.2009.00948.x

Lickona, T. (1976). Research on Piaget's theory of moral development. In T. Lickona (Ed.), *Moral development and behavior: Theory, research, and social issues* (pp. 219–240). New York: Holt, Rinehart and Winston.

Liew, J., Eisenberg, N., Spinrad, T. L., Eggum, N. D., Haugen, R. G., Kupfer, A., . . . Baham, M. E. (2011). Physiological regulation and fearfulness as predictors of young children's empathy-related reactions. *Social Development, 20,* 111–134. doi:10.1111/j.1467-9507.2010.00575.x

Lillard, A. (2007). Guided participation: How mothers structure and children understand pretend play. In A. Göncü & S. Gaskins (Eds.), *Play and development: Evolutionary, sociocultural, and functional perspectives* (pp. 131–154). Mahwah, NJ: Erlbaum.

Lillard, A. S. (2015). The development of play. In R. M. Lerner (Series Ed.), L. S. Liben & U. Müeller (Vol. Eds.), *Handbook of child psychology and developmental science, Volume 2, Cognitive processes,* 7th ed. (pp. 425–468). New York: Wiley.

Lillard, A. S. (2017). Why do the children (pretend) play? *Trends in Cognitive Sciences, 21*(11), 826–834. doi:10.1016/j.tics.2017.08.001

Lillard, A. S., & Flavell, J. H. (1992). Children's understanding of different mental states. *Developmental Psychology, 28,* 626–634.

Lillard, A. S., Lerner, M. D., Hopkins, E. J., Dore, R. A., Smith, E. D., & Palmquist, C. M. (2013). The impact of pretend play on children's development: A review of the evidence. *Psychological Bulletin, 139,* 1–34. doi:10.1037/a0029321

Lin, Y.-W., & Bratton, S. C. (2015). A meta-analytic review of child-centered play therapy approaches. *Journal of Counseling & Development, 93,* 45–58. doi:10.1002/j.1556-6676.2015.00180.x

Linares, L. O., Heeren, T., Bronfman, E., Zuckerman, B., Augustyn, M., & Tronick, E. (2001). A mediational model for the impact of exposure to community violence on early child behavior problems. *Child Development, 72,* 639–652. doi:10.1111/1467-8624.00302

Lindberg, M. (1991). A taxonomy of suggestibility and eyewitness memory: Age, memory process, and focus of analysis. In J. Doris (Ed.), *The suggestibility of children's recollection: Implications for eyewitness memory* (pp. 47–55). Washington, DC: American Psychological Association.

Lindberg, S. M., Hyde, J. S., Petersen, J. L., & Linn, M. C. (2010). New trends in gender and mathematics performance: A meta-analysis. *Psychological Bulletin, 136,* 1123–1135.

Lindquist, K. A., Siegel, E. H., Quigley, K. S., & Barrett, L. F. (2013). The hundred-year emotion war: Are emotions natural kinds or psychological constructions? Comment on Lench, Flores, and Bench (2011). *Psychological Bulletin, 139,* 255–263. doi:10.1037/a0029038

Lindsey, E. W., & Colwell, M. (2013). Pretend and physical play: Links to preschoolers' affective social competence. *Merrill-Palmer Quarterly, 59,* 330–360. doi:10.1353/mpq.2013.0015

Lingwood, J., Blades, M., Farran, E. K., Courbois, Y., & Matthews, D. (2018). Using virtual environments to investigate wayfinding in 8- to 12-year-olds and adults. *Journal of Experimental Child Psychology, 166,* 178–189. doi:10.1016/j.jecp.2017.08.012

Lins-Dyer, M. T., & Nucci, L. (2007). The impact of social class and social cognitive domain on northeastern Brazilian mothers' and daughters' conceptions of parental control. *International Journal of Behavioral Development, 31,* 105–114. doi:10.1177/0165025407073577

Lin-Siegler, X., Ahn, J. N., Chen, C., Fang, F.-F. A., & Luna-Lucero, M. (2016). Even Einstein struggled: Effects of learning about great scientists' struggles on high school students' motivation to learn science. *Journal of Educational Psychology, 108*(3), 314–328. doi:10.1037.edu0000092

Lipman, E. L., Georgiades, K., & Boyle, M. H. (2011). Young adult outcomes of children born to teen mothers: Effects of being born during their teen or later years. *Journal of the American Academy of Child and Adolescent Psychiatry, 50,* 232–241.e4. doi:10.1016/j.jaac.2010.12.007

Lipton, J. S., & Spelke, E. S. (2003). Origins of number sense large-number discrimination in human infants. *Psychological Science, 14,* 396–401.

Lister-Landman, K. M., Domoff, S. E., & Dubow, E. F. (2015, October 5). The role of compulsive texting in adolescents' academic functioning. *Psychology of Popular Media Culture.* Advance online publication. doi:10.1037/ppm0000100

Litwack, S. D., Wargo Aikins, J., & Cillessen, A. H. N. (2012). The distinct roles of sociometric and perceived popularity in friendship: Implications for adolescent depressive affect and self-esteem. *Journal of Early Adolescence, 32,* 226–251. doi:10.1177/0272431610387142

Liu, C. H., Giallo, R., Doan, S. N., Seidman, L. J., & Tronick, E. (2016). Racial and ethnic differences in prenatal life stress and postpartum depression symptoms. *Archives of Psychiatric Nursing, 30,* 7–12.

Liu, S., Xiao, N. G., Quinn, P. C., Zhu, D., Ge, L., . . . Lee, K. (2015). Asian infants show preference for own-race but not other-race female faces: The role of infant caregiving arrangements. *Frontiers in Psychology, 6,* 593.

Lobo, M. A., Galloway, J. C., & Savelsbergh, G. J. (2004). General and task-related experiences affect early object interaction. *Child Development, 75,* 1268–1281. doi:10.1111/j.1467-8624.2004.00738.x

Loeber, R. (1982). The stability of antisocial and delinquent child behavior: A review. *Child Development, 53,* 1431–1446. doi:10.2307/1130070

Loeber, R., & Burke, J. D. (2011). Developmental pathways in juvenile externalizing and internalizing problems. *Journal of Research on Adolescence, 21,* 34–46. doi:10.1111/j.1532-7795.2010.00713.x

Lomas, J., Stough, C., Hansen, K., & Downey, L. A. (2012). Emotional intelligence, victimization, and bullying in adolescents. *Journal of Adolescence, 35,* 207–211. doi:10.1016/j.adolescence.2011.03.002

Longacre, M. R., Drake, K. M., Titus, L. J., Cleveland, L. P., Langeloh, G., Hendricks, K., & Dalton, M. A. (2016). A toy story: Association between young children's knowledge of fast food toy premiums and their fast food consumption. *Appetite, 96,* 473–480.

Lonigan, C. J. (2015). Early literacy. In R. M. Lerner (Ed.-in-Chief), L. S. Liben & U. M. Müller (Vol. Eds.), *Handbook of child psychology and developmental science: Vol. 2.* Cognitive processes (7th ed., pp. 763–805). Hoboken, NJ: Wiley.

Loomis, J. M., Klatzky, R. L., Golledge, R. G., Cicinelli, J. G., Pellegrino, J. W., & Fry, P. A. (1993). Nonvisual navigation by blind and sighted: Assessment of path integration ability. *Journal of Experimental Psychology: General, 122,* 73–91.

Lopez-Duran, N. L., Kuhlman, K. R., George, C., & Kovacs, M. (2013). Facial emotion expression recognition by children at familial risk for depression: High-risk boys are oversensitive to sadness. *Journal of Child Psychology and Psychiatry, 54,* 565–574. doi:10.1111/jcpp.12005

Lorenz, K. (1935). Der Kumpan in der Umwelt des Vogels. Der Artgenosse als auslosendes Moment sozialer Verhaltungsweisen [The companion in the bird's world. The fellow-member of the species as releasing factor of social behavior]. *Journal für Ornithologie, Beiblatt (Leipzig), 83,* 137–213.

Lorenz, K. (1952). *King Solomon's ring: New light on animal ways.* New York: Crowell.

Lorenz, K. (1971). *Studies in Animal and Human Behavior.* Cambridge, MA: Harvard University Press.

Lortie-Forgues, H., Tian, J., & Siegler, R. S. (2015). Why is learning fraction and decimal arithmetic so difficult? *Developmental Review, 38,* 201–221, doi:10.1016/j.dr.2015.07.008

Lourenco, S. F., & Longo, M. R. (2010). General magnitude representation in human infants. *Psychological Science, 21,* 873–881. doi:10.1177/0956797610370158

Love, J. M., Chazan-Cohen, R., & Raikes, H. (2007). Forty years of research knowledge and use: From Head Start to Early Head Start and beyond. In J. L. Aber, S. J. Bishop-Josef, S. M. Jones, K. T. McLearn, & D. A. Phillips (Eds.), *Child development and social policy: Knowledge for action* (pp. 79–95). Washington, DC: American Psychological Association.

Love, J. M., Harrison, L., Sagi-Schwartz, A., van IJzendoorn, M. H., Ross, C., Ungerer, J. A., . . . Chazan-Cohen, R. (2003). Child care quality matters: How conclusions may vary with context. *Child Development, 74,* 1021–1033. doi:10.1111/1467-8624.00584

Lubinski, D., Benbow, C. P., & Kell, H. J. (2014). Life paths and accomplishments of mathematically precocious males and females four decades later. *Psychological Science, 25*(12), 2217–2232. doi:10.1177/0956797614551371

Lubinski, D., & Humphreys, L. G. (1997). Incorporating general intelligence into epidemiology and the social sciences. *Intelligence, 24,* 159–201.

Lubinski, D., Webb, R. M., Morelock, M. J., & Benbow, C. P. (2001). Top 1 in 10,000: A 10-year follow-up of the profoundly gifted. *Journal of Applied Psychology, 86,* 718–729.

Lucassen, N., Tharner, A., van IJzendoorn, M. H., Bakermans-Kranenburg, M. J., Volling, B. L., Verhulst, F. C., . . . Tiemeier, H. (2011). The association between paternal sensitivity and infant-father attachment security: A meta-analysis of three decades of research. *Journal of Family Psychology, 25,* 986–992. doi:10.1037/a0025855

Luebbe, A. M., Kiel, E. J., & Buss, K. A. (2011). Toddlers' context-varying emotions, maternal responses to emotions, and internalizing behaviors. *Emotion, 11,* 697–703.

Luengo Kanacri, B. P., Pastorelli, C., Eisenberg, N., Zuffianò, A., & Caprara, G. V. (2013). The development of prosociality from adolescence to early adulthood: The role of effortful control. *Journal of Personality, 81,* 302–312. doi:10.1111/jopy.12001

Luijk, M. P. C. M., Saridjan, N., Tharner, A., van IJzendoorn, M. H., Bakermans-Kranenburg, M. J., Jaddoe, V. W. V., . . . Tiemeier, H. (2010). Attachment, depression, and cortisol: Deviant patterns in insecure-resistant and disorganized infants. *Developmental Psychobiology, 52,* 441–452. doi:10.1002/dev.20446

Lumeng, J. C., Taveras, E. M., Birch, L., & Yanovski, S. Z. (2015). Prevention of obesity in infancy and early childhood: A National Institutes of Health workshop. *Journal of the American Medical Association Pediatrics, 169*(5), 484–490.

Luna, B., Garver, K. E., Urban, T. A., Lazar, N. A., & Sweeney, J. A. (2004). Maturation of cognitive processes from late childhood to adulthood. *Child Development, 75,* 1357–1372. doi:10.1111/j.1467-8624.2004.00745.x

Luntz, B. K., & Widom, C. S. (1994). Antisocial personality disorder in abused and neglected children grown up. *American Journal of Psychiatry, 151,* 670–674.

Luo, Z. C., Wilkins, R., Heaman, M., Smylie, J., Martens, P. J., McHugh, N. G., . . . Fraser, W. D. (2012). Birth outcomes and infant mortality among First Nations Inuit, and non-Indigenous women by northern versus southern residence, Quebec. *Journal of Epidemiology and Community Health, 66*(4), 328–333.

Lusskin, S. I., Khan, S. J., Ernst, C., Habib, S., Fersh, M. E., & Albertini, E. S. (2018). Pharmacotherapy for perinatal depression. *Clinical Obstetrics and Gynecology, 61*(3), 544–561.

Luthar, S. S., Barkin, S. H., & Crossman, E. J. (2013). "I can, therefore I must": Fragility in the upper-middle classes [Monograph]. *Development and Psychopathology, 25*(4, Pt. 2), 1529–1549. doi:10.1017/S0954579413000758

Luyckx, K., Soenens, B., & Goossens, L. (2006). The personality-identity interplay in emerging adult women: Convergent findings from complementary analyses. *European Journal of Personality, 20,* 195–215.

Luyckx, K., Soenens, B., Vansteenkiste, M., Goossens, L., & Berzonsky, M. D. (2007). Parental psychological control and dimensions of identity formation in emerging adulthood. *Journal of Family Psychology, 21,* 546–550. doi:10.1037/0893-3200.21.3.546

Lynn, R. (2009). What has caused the Flynn effect? Secular increases in the Development Quotients of infants. *Intelligence, 37,* 16–24.

Lyons, I. M., & Ansari, D. (2015). Chapter three: Foundations of children's numerical and mathematical skills: The roles of symbolic and nonsymbolic representations of numerical magnitude. *Advances in Child Development and Behavior, 48,* 93–116. doi:10.1016/bs.acdb.2014.11.003

Lyons, I. M., & Beilock, S. L. (2012). When math hurts: Math anxiety predicts pain network activation in anticipation of doing math. *PLoS ONE, 7,* e48076. doi:10.1371/journal.pone.0048076

Lytle, S. R., Garcia-Sierra, A., & Kuhl, P. K. (2018). Two are better than one: Infant language learning from video improves in the presence of peers. *Proceedings of the National Academy of Sciences, 115*(40), 9859–9866.

Ma, W., Golinkoff, R. M., Houston, D. M., & Hirsh-Pasek, K. (2011). Word learning in infant- and adult-directed speech. *Language Learning and Development, 7,* 185–201. doi:10.1080/15475441.2011.579839

Mabbott, D. J., & Bisanz, J. (2003). Developmental change and individual differences in children's multiplication. *Child Development, 74,* 1091–1107.

MacBrayer, E. K., Milich, R., & Hundley, M. (2003). Attributional biases in aggressive children and their mothers. *Journal of Abnormal Psychology, 112,* 698–708. doi:10.1037/0021-843X.112.4.598

Macchi Cassia, V., Kuefner, D., Westerlund, A., & Nelson, C. A. (2006). A behavioural and ERP investigation of 3-month-olds' face preferences. *Neuropsychologia, 44,* 2113–2125. doi:10.1016/j.neuropsychologia.2005.11.014

Macchi Cassia, V., Turati, C., & Simion, F. (2004). Can a nonspecific bias toward top-heavy patterns explain newborns' face preference? *Psychological Science, 15,* 379–383. doi:10.1111/j.0956-7976.2004.00688.x

Maccoby, E. E. (1998). *The two sexes: Growing up apart, coming together.* Cambridge, MA: Harvard University Press.

Maccoby, E. E. (2000). Perspectives on gender development. *International Journal of Behavioral Development, 24,* 398–406. doi:10.1080/016502500750037946

Maccoby, E. E. (2015). Historical overview of socialization research and theory. In J. E. Grusec & P. D. Hastings (Eds.), *Handbook of socialization: Theory and research* (pp. 3–32). New York: Guilford.

Maccoby, E. E., & Martin, J. A. (1983). Socialization in the context of the family: Parent–child interaction. In P. H. Mussen (Series Ed.) & E. M. Hetherington (Vol. Ed.), *Handbook of child psychology: Vol. 4. Socialization, personality, and social development* (4th ed., pp. 1–101). New York: Wiley.

Macdonald, D., & Friendly, M. (2014, November). The parent trap: Child care fees in Canada's big cities. Canadian Centre for Policy Alternatives. Retrieved from www.policyalternatives.ca/parent-trap

Macdonald, D., & Wilson, D. (2016). Shameful neglect: Indigenous child poverty in Canada. Canadian Centre for Policy Alternatives. Retrieved from https://www.policyalternatives.ca/publications/reports/shameful-neglect

MacDonald, G. W., & Cornwall, A. (1995). The relationship between phonological awareness and reading and spelling achievement eleven years later. *Journal of Learning Disabilities, 28,* 523–527.

MacDonald, K., & MacDonald, T. M. (2010). The peptide that binds: A systematic review of oxytocin and its prosocial effects in humans. *Harvard Review of Psychiatry, 18,* 1–21. doi:10.3109/10673220903523615

MacEvoy, J. P., & Asher, S. R. (2012). When friends disappoint: Boys' and girls' responses to transgressions of friendship expectations. *Child Development, 83,* 104–119. doi:10.1111/j.1467-8624.2011.01685.x

Mackey, A. P., Finn, A. S., Leonard, J. A., Jacoby-Senghor, D. S., West, M. R., Gabrieli, C. F., & Gabrieli, J. D. (2015). Neuroanatomical correlates of the income-achievement gap. *Psychological Science, 26*(6), 925–933.

Maclean, M., Bryant, P., & Bradley, L. (1987). Rhymes, nursery rhymes, and reading in early childhood. *Merrill-Palmer Quarterly, 33,* 255–281.

Macmillan, R., McMorris, B. J., & Kruttschnitt, C. (2004). Linked lives: Stability and change in maternal circumstances and trajectories of antisocial behavior in children. *Child Development, 75,* 205–220. doi:10.1111/j.1467-8624.2004.00664.x

Madigan, S., Browne, D., Racine, N., Mori, C., & Tough, S. (2019). Association between screen time and children's performance on a developmental screening Test. *Journal of the American Medical Association Pediatrics, 173*(3), 244–250.

Madigan, S., Brumariu, L. E., Villani, V., Atkinson, L., & Lyons-Ruth, K. (2016). Representational and questionnaire measures of attachment: A meta-analysis of relations to child internalizing and externalizing problems. *Psychological Bulletin, 142,* 367–399. doi:10.1037/bul0000029

Madigan, S., Moran, G., & Pederson, D. R. (2006). Unresolved states of mind, disorganized attachment relationships, and disrupted interactions of adolescent mothers and their infants. *Developmental Psychology, 42,* 293–304. doi:10.1037/0012-1649.42.2.293

Madole, K. L., & Oakes, L. M. (1999). Making sense of infant categorization: Stable processes and changing representations. *Developmental Review, 19,* 263–296. doi:10.1006/drev.1998.0481

Mage, D. T., & Donner, E. M. (2014). Is excess male infant mortality from sudden infant death syndrome and other respiratory diseases X-linked? *Acta Paediatrica, 103,* 188–193.

Maguire, M. C., & Dunn, J. (1997). Friendships in early childhood, and social understanding. *International Journal of Behavioral Development, 21,* 669–686. doi:10.1080/016502597384613

Maher, C., Olds, T. S., Eisenmann, J. C., & Dollman, J. (2012). Screen time is more strongly associated than physical activity with overweight and obesity in 9- to 16-year-old Australians. *Acta Pædiatrica, 101*(11), 1170–1174.

Mahy, C. E., Moses, L. J., & Pfeifer, J. H. (2014). How and where: Theory-of-mind in the brain. *Developmental Cognitive Neuroscience, 9,* 68–81. doi:10.1016/j.dcn.2014.01.002

Main, M., & Solomon, J. (1990). Procedures for identifying infants as disorganized/disoriented during the Ainsworth Strange Situation. In M. T. Greenberg, D. Cicchetti, & E. M. Cummings (Eds.), *Attachment in the preschool years: Theory, research, and intervention* (pp. 121–160). Chicago: University of Chicago Press.

Maitre, N. L., Key, A. P., Chorna, O. D., Slaughter, J. C., Matusz, P. J., Wallace, M. T., & Murray, M. M. (2017). The dual nature of early-life experience on somatosensory processing in the human infant brain. *Current Biology, 27*(7), 1048–1054.

Makel, M. C., Kell, H. J., Lubinski, D., Putallaz, M., & Benbow, C. P. (2016). When lightning strikes twice: Profoundly gifted, profoundly accomplished. *Psychological Science, 27*(7), 1004–1018. doi:10.1177/0956797616644735

Malina, R. M., & Bouchard, C. (1991). *Growth, maturation, and physical activity.* Champaign, IL: Human Kinetics.

Maloney, E. A., Ramirez, G., Gunderson, E. A., Levine, S. C., & Beilock, S. L. (2015). Intergenerational effects of parents' math anxiety on children's math achievement and anxiety. *Psychological Science, 26*(9), 1480–1488. doi:10.1177/0956797615592630

Maltz, D. N., & Borker, R. (1982). A cultural approach to male-female miscommunication. In J. J. Gumperz (Ed.), *Language and social identity* (pp. 196–216). Cambridge: Cambridge University Press.

Malvaso, C., Delfabbro, P., Proeve, M., & Nobes, G. (2015). Predictors of child injury in biological and stepfamilies. *Journal of Child & Adolescent Trauma, 8*(3), 149–159. doi:10.1111/j.1467-8624.2009.01360.x

Mandel, D. R., Jusczyk, P. W., & Pisoni, D. B. (1995). Infants' recognition of the sound patterns of their own names. *Psychological Science, 6,* 314–317. doi:10.1111/j.1467-9280.1995.tb00517.x

Mandler, J. M., & McDonough, L. (1998). Studies in inductive inference in infancy. *Cognitive Psychology, 37,* 60–96. doi:10.1006/cogp.1998.0691

Manicklal, S., Emery, V. C., Lazzarotto, T., Boppana, S. B., & Gupta, R. K. (2013). The "silent" global burden of congenital cytomegalovirus. *Clinical Microbiology Reviews, 26*(1), 86–102.

Männikkö, R., Wong, L., Tester, D. J., Thor, M. G., Sud, R., Kullmann, D. M., . . . Evans, M. J. (2018). Dysfunction of NaV1.4, a skeletal muscle voltage-gated sodium channel, in sudden infant death syndrome: A case-control study. *Lancet, 391*(10129), 1483–1492.

Marceau, K., Horwitz, B. N., Narusyte, J., Ganiban, J. M., Spotts, E. L., Reiss, D., & Neiderhiser, J. M. (2013). Gene–environment correlation underlying the association between parental negativity and adolescent externalizing problems. *Child Development, 84,* 2031–2046. doi:10.1111/cdev.12094

Marcia, J. E. (1980). Identity in adolescence. In J. Adelson (Ed.), *Handbook of adolescent psychology* (pp. 159–187). New York: Wiley.

Marcus, G. F., Vijayan, S., Bandi Rao, S., & Vishton, P. M. (1999, January 1). Rule learning by seven-month-old infants. *Science, 283,* 77–80.

Mares, M. L., & Pan, Z. (2013). Effects of Sesame Street: A meta-analysis of children's learning in 15 countries. *Journal of Applied Developmental Psychology, 34*(3), 140–151.

Margett, T. E., & Witherington, D. C. (2011). The nature of preschoolers' concept of living and artificial objects. *Child Development, 82,* 2067–2082. doi:10.1111/j.1467-8624.2011.01661.x

Margoni, F., & Surian, L. (2018). Infants' evaluation of prosocial and antisocial agents: A meta-analysis. *Developmental Psychology, 54*(8), 1445. doi:10.1037/dev0000538

Marin, M. M., Rapisardi, G., & Tani, F. (2015). Two-day-old newborn infants recognise their mother by her axillary odour. *Acta Paediatrica, 104*(3), 237–240.

Markman, E. M. (1989). *Categorization and naming in children: Problems of induction.* Cambridge, MA: MIT Press.

Markman, E. M., & Wachtel, G. F. (1988). Children's use of mutual exclusivity to constrain the meanings of words. *Cognitive Psychology, 20,* 121–157.

Marks, A. K., Patton, F., & García Coll, C. (2011). Being bicultural: A mixed-methods study of adolescents' implicitly and explicitly measured multiethnic identities. *Developmental Psychology, 47,* 270–288. doi:10.1037/a0020730

Markson, L., & Bloom, P. (1997, February 27). Evidence against a dedicated system for word learning in children. *Nature, 385,* 813–815. doi:10.1038/385813a0

Marlier, L., & Schaal, B. (2005). Human newborns prefer human milk: Conspecific milk odor is attractive without postnatal exposure. *Child Development, 76,* 155–168. doi:10.1111/j.1467-8624.2005.00836.x

Marshall, K. (2010). Employer top-ups. *Statistics Canada Catalogue 75-001-X.*

Marshall, P. J., & Meltzoff, A. N. (2014). Neural mirroring mechanisms and imitation in human infants. *Philosophical Transactions of the Royal Society of B: Biological Sciences, 369*(1644). doi:10.1098/rstb.2013.0620

Martin, C. L., & Fabes, R. A. (2001). The stability and consequences of young children's same-sex peer interactions. *Developmental Psychology, 37,* 431–446. doi:10.1037/0012-1649.37.3.431

Martin, C. L., Fabes, R. A., Evans, S. M., & Wyman, H. (1999). Social cognition on the playground: Children's beliefs about playing with girls versus boys and their relations to sex segregated play. *Journal of Social and Personal Relationships, 16,* 751–771. doi:10.1177/0265407599166005

Martin, C. L., & Halverson, C. F., Jr. (1981). A schematic processing model of sex typing and stereotyping in children. *Child Development, 52,* 1119–1134. doi:10.2307/1129498

Martin, C. L., & Halverson, C. F., Jr. (1983). The effects of sex-typing schemas on young children's memory. *Child Development, 54,* 563–574. doi:10.2307/1130043

Martin, C. L., Kornienko, O., Schaefer, D. R., Hanish, L. D., Fabes, R. A., & Goble, P. (2013). The role of sex of peers and gender-typed activities in young children's peer affiliative networks: A longitudinal analysis of selection and influence. *Child Development, 84,* 921–937. doi:10.1111/cdev.12032

Martin, C. L., & Ruble, D. N. (2010). Patterns of gender development. *Annual Review of Psychology, 61,* 353–381. http://dx.doi.org/10.1146/annurev.psych.093008.100511

Martin, C. L., Ruble, D. N., & Szkrybalo, J. (2002). Cognitive theories of early gender development. *Psychological Bulletin, 128,* 903–933.

Martin, J., & Ross, H. (2005). Sibling aggression: Sex differences and parents' reactions. *International Journal of Behavioral Development, 29,* 129–138. doi:10.1080/01650250444000469

Martin, J. A., Hamilton, B. E., & Osterman, M. J. (2018). Births in the USA, 2017. *National Center for Health Statistics Data Brief, no. 318.* Hyattsville, MD: National Center for Health Statistics.

Martin, J. A., Hamilton, B. E., Osterman, M. J., Driscoll, A. K., & Drake, P. (2018). Births: Final data for 2016. *National Vital Statistics Reports, 67*(8), 1–49.

Martin, N. G., Maza, L., McGrath, S. J., & Phelps, A. E. (2014). An examination of referential and affect specificity with five emotions in infancy. *Infant Behavior and Development, 37,* 286–297. doi:10.1016/j.infbeh.2014.04.009

Martini, F., & Sénéchal, M. (2012). Learning literacy skills at home: Parent teaching, expectations and child interest. *Canadian Journal of Behavioural Sciences, 44,* 210–221. doi:10.1037/a0026758

Martinot, D., Bagès, C., & Désert, M. (2012). French children's awareness of gender stereotypes about mathematics and reading: When girls improve their reputation in math. *Sex Roles, 66,* 210–219. doi:10.1007/s11199-011-0032-3

Martin-Storey, A. (2016). Gender, sexuality, and gender nonconformity: Understanding variation in functioning. *Child Development Perspectives, 10*(40), 257–262. doi:10.1111/cdep.12194

Martin-Storey, A., & Crosnoe, R. (2012). Sexual minority status, peer harassment, and adolescent depression. *Journal of Adolescence, 35,* 1001–1011. doi:10.1016/j.adolescence.2012.02.006

Martos, A. J., Nezhad, S., & Meyer, I. H. (2015). Variations in sexual identity milestones among lesbians, gay men, and bisexuals. *Sexuality Research & Social Policy: A Journal of the NSRC, 12,* 24–33. doi:10.1007/s13178-014-0167-4

Marufu, T. C., Ahankari, A., Coleman, T., & Lewis, S. (2015). Maternal smoking and the risk of still birth: Systematic review and meta-analysis. *BMC Public Health, 15,* 239. doi:10.1186/s12889-015-1552-5

Masataka, N. (1992). Motherese in a signed language. *Infant Behavior and Development, 15,* 453–460. doi:10.1016/0163-6383(92)80013-K

Masataka, N. (1999). Preference for infant-directed singing in 2-day-old hearing infants of deaf parents. *Developmental Psychology, 35,* 1001–1005. doi:10.1037/0012-1649.35.4.1001

Masataka, N. (2006). Preference for consonance over dissonance by hearing newborns of deaf parents and of hearing parents. *Developmental Science, 9,* 46–50. doi:10.1111/j.1467-7687.2005.00462.x

Mascolo, M. F., Fischer, K. W., & Li, J. (2003). Dynamic development of component systems of emotions: Pride, shame, and guilt in China and the United States. In R. J. Davidson, K. R. Scherer, & H. H. Goldsmith (Eds.), *Handbook of affective sciences* (pp. 375–408). Oxford: Oxford University Press.

Mason, M. G., & Gibbs, J. C. (1993). Social perspective taking and moral judgment among college students. *Journal of Adolescent Research, 8,* 109–123. doi:10.1177/074355489381008

Mason, S. M., Schnitzer, P. G., Danilack, V. A., Elston, B., & Savitz, D. A. (2018). Risk factors for maltreatment-related infant hospitalizations in New York City, 1995–2004. *Annals of Epidemiology, 28,* 590–596.

Masten, A. S. (2007). Resilience in developing systems: Progress and promise as the fourth wave rises. *Development and Psychopathology, 19,* 921–930. doi:10.1017/S0954579407000442

Masten, A. S. (2014). Global perspectives on resilience in children and youth. *Child Development, 85*(1), 6–20. doi:10.1111/cdev.12205

Masten, A. S., Best, K. M., & Garmezy, N. (1990). Resilience and development: Contributions from the study of children who overcome adversity. *Development and Psychopathology, 2,* 425–444. doi:10.1017/S0954579400005812

Masten, A. S., & Cicchetti, D. (2010). Developmental cascades. *Development and Psychopathology, 22,* 491–495. doi:10.1017/S0954579410000222

Masten, A. S., Cutuli, J. J., Herbers, J. E., Hinz, E., Obradović, J., & Wenzel, A. J. (2014). Academic risk and resilience in the context of homelessness. *Child Development Perspectives, 8,* 201–206. doi:10.1111/cdep.12088

Matsumoto, D. R. (1996). *Unmasking Japan: Myths and realities about the emotions of the Japanese.* Stanford, CA: Stanford University Press.

Matuz, T., Govindan, R. B., Preissl, H., Siegel, E. R., Muenssinger, J., Murphy, P., . . . Eswaran, H. (2012). Habituation of visual evoked responses in neonates and fetuses: A MEG study. *Developmental Cognitive Neuroscience, 2*(3), 303–316.

Maughan, B., Collishaw, S., & Stringaris, A. (2013). Depression in childhood and adolescence. *Journal of the Canadian Academy of Child and Adolescent Psychiatry, 22*(1), 35–40.

Maurer, D., Le Grand, R., & Mondloch, C. J. (2002). The many faces of configural processing. *Trends in Cognitive Sciences, 6*(6), 255–260.

Maurer, D., & Maurer, C. (1988). *The world of the newborn.* New York: Basic Books.

Maurer, D., & Salapatek, P. (1976). Developmental changes in the scanning of faces by young infants. *Child Development, 47,* 523–527. doi:10.2307/1128813

Maya-Vetencourt, J. F., & Origlia, N. (2012). Visual cortex plasticity: A complex interplay of genetic and environmental influences. *Neural Plasticity, 2012.* doi:10.1155/2012/631965

Mayberry, M. L., & Espelage, D. L. (2007). Associations among empathy, social competence, & reactive/proactive aggression subtypes. *Journal of Youth and Adolescence, 36,* 787–798. doi:10.1007/s10964-006-9113-y

Mayberry, R. I., Davenport, T., Roth, A., & Halgren, E. (2018). Neurolinguistic processing when the brain matures without language. *Cortex, 99,* 390–403. doi.org/10.1016/j.cortex.2017.12.011

Mayberry, R. I., & Kluender, R. (2018). Rethinking the critical period for language: New insights into an old question from American Sign Language. *Bilingualism: Language and Cognition, 21*(5), 886–905.

Mayberry, R. I., Lock, E., & Kazmi, H. (2002). Development: Linguistic ability and early language exposure. *Nature, 417*(6884), 38.

Mayer, J. D., Roberts, R. D., & Barsade, S. G. (2008). Human abilities: Emotional intelligence. *Annual Review of Psychology, 59,* 507–537. doi:10.1146/annurev.psych.59.103006.093646

Mayeux, L., & Cillessen, A. H. N. (2008). It's not just being popular, it's knowing it, too: The role of self-perceptions of status in the associations between peer status and aggression. *Social Development, 17,* 871–888. doi:10.1111/j.1467-9507.2008.00474.x

Mayor, J., & Plunkett, K. (2014). Shared understanding and idiosyncratic expression in early vocabularies. *Developmental Science, 17*(3), 412–423.

Mays, V. M., & Ghavami, N. (2018). History, aspirations, and transformations of intersectionality: Focusing on gender. In C. B. Travis, J. W. White, A. Rutherford, W. S. Williams, S. L. Cook, & K. F. Wyche (Eds.), *APA handbooks in psychology series. APA handbook of the psychology of women: History, theory, and battlegrounds* (pp. 541–566). Washington, DC: American Psychological Association. doi:10.1037/0000059-028

Mbachu, I. I., Ezeama, C., Osuagwu, K., Umeononihu, O. S., Obiannika, C., & Ezeama, N. (2017). A cross-sectional study of maternal near miss and mortality at a rural tertiary centre in southern Nigeria. *BMC Pregnancy and Childbirth, 17*(1), 251.

McAdams, D. P., & Olson, B. D. (2010). Personality development: Continuity and change over the life course. *Annual Review of Psychology, 61,* 517–542. doi:10.1146/annurev.psych.093008.100507

McBride-Chang, C. (2004). *Children's literacy development.* New York: Oxford University Press.

McCabe, A., & Peterson, C. (1991). Getting the story: A longitudinal study of parental styles in eliciting narratives and developing narrative skill. In A. McCabe & C. Peterson (Eds.), *Developing narrative structure* (pp. 217–253). Hillsdale, NJ: Erlbaum.

McCabe, A., Tamis-LeMonda, C. S., Bornstein, M. H., Cates, C. B., Golinkoff, R., Guerra, A. W., . . . Mendelsohn, A. (2013). Multilingual children. *Social Policy Report, 27*(4), 1–21.

McCall, R. B., van IJzendoorn, M. H., Juffer, F., Groark, C. J., & Groza, V. K. (2011). Children without permanent parents: Research, practice, and policy. *Monographs of the Society for Research in Child Development, 76*(4, Serial No. 301), 1–318.

McCarthy, A., & Lee, K. (2009). Children's knowledge of deceptive gaze cues and its relation to their actual lying behavior. *Journal of Experimental Child Psychology, 103,* 117–134. doi:10.1016/j.jecp.2008.06.005

McClelland, J. L., McNaughton, B. L., & O'Reilly, R. C. (1995). Why there are complementary learning systems in the hippocampus and neocortex: Insights from the successes and failures of connectionist models of learning and memory. *Psychological Review, 102*(3), 419–457. doi:10.1037/0033-295X.102.3.419

McClintock, M. K., & Herdt, G. (1996). Rethinking puberty: The development of sexual attraction. *Current Directions in Psychological Science, 5,* 178–183. doi:10.1111/1467-8721.ep11512422

McCloskey, M. (2007). Quantitative literacy and developmental dyscalculias. In D. B. Berch & M. M. M. Mazzocco (Eds.), *Why is math so hard for some children? The nature and origins of mathematical learning difficulties and disabilities* (pp. 415–429). Baltimore, MD: Paul H. Brookes.

McCoy, D. C., & Raver, C. C. (2011). Caregiver emotional expressiveness, child emotion regulation, and child behavior problems among Head Start families. *Social Development, 20,* 741–761.

McCrink, K., & Wynn, K. (2004). Large-number addition and subtraction by 9-month-old infants. *Psychological Science, 15*(11), 776–781. doi:10.1111/j.0956-7976.2004.00755.x

McCrory, E. J., De Brito, S. A., Kelly, P. A., Bird, G., Sebastian, C. L., Mechelli, A., . . . Viding, E. (2013). Amygdala activation in maltreated children during pre-attentive emotional processing. *British Journal of Psychiatry, 202,* 269–276.

McCrory, E. J., & Viding, E. (2015). The theory of latent vulnerability: Reconceptualizing the link between childhood maltreatment and psychiatric disorder. *Development and Psychopathology, 27*(2), 493–505.

McCutchen, D. (2011). From novice to expert: Implications of language skills and writing-relevant knowledge for memory during the development of writing skill. *Journal of Writing Research, 3*(1), 51–68. doi:10.17239/jowr-2011.03.01.3

McDaniel, M. A. (2005). Big-brained people are smarter: A meta-analysis of the relationship between in vivo brain volume and intelligence. *Intelligence, 33,* 337–346. doi:10.1016/j.intell.2004.11.005

McDonald, K. L., Malti, T., Killen, M., & Rubin, K. H. (2014). Best friends' discussions of social dilemmas. *Journal of Youth and Adolescence, 43,* 233–244. doi:10.1007/s10964-013-9961-1

McDonald, K. L., Putallaz, M., Grimes, C. L., Kupersmidt, J. B., & Coie, J. D. (2007). Girl talk: Gossip, friendship, and sociometric status. *Merrill-Palmer Quarterly, 53,* 381–411.

McDonald, S. W., Madigan, S., Racine, N., Benzies, K., Tomfohr, L., & Tough, S. (2019). Maternal adverse childhood experiences, mental health, and child behaviour at age 3: The all our families community cohort study. *Preventive Medicine, 118,* 286–294.

McDougall, P., & Hymel, S. (2007). Same-gender versus cross-gender friendship conceptions: Similar or different? *Merrill-Palmer Quarterly, 53,* 347–380.

McDowell, D. J., & Parke, R. D. (2009). Parental correlates of children's peer relations: An empirical test of a tripartite model. *Developmental Psychology, 45,* 224–235. doi:10.1037/a0014305

McElwain, N. L., Booth-LaForce, C., & Wu, X. (2011). Infant–mother attachment and children's friendship quality: Maternal mental-state talk as an intervening mechanism. *Developmental Psychology, 47,* 1295–1311. doi:10.1037/a0024094

McFadyen-Ketchum, S. A., Bates, J. E., Dodge, K. A., & Pettit, G. S. (1996). Patterns of change in early childhood aggressive-disruptive behavior: Gender differences in predictions from early coercive and affectionate mother–child interactions. *Child Development, 67,* 2417–2433. doi:10.2307/1131631

McGill, R. K., Way, N., & Hughes, D. (2012). Intra- and interracial best friendships during middle school: Links to social and emotional well-being. *Journal of Research on Adolescence, 22,* 722–738. doi:10.1111/j.1532-7795.2012.00826.x

McGowan, P. O., Sasaki, A., D'Alessio, A. C., Dymov, S., Labonté, B., Szyf, M., . . . Meaney, M. J. (2009). Epigenetic regulation of the glucocorticoid receptor in human brain associates with childhood abuse. *Nature Neuroscience, 12,* 342–348. doi:10.1038/nn.2270

McGraw, M. B. (1943). *The neuromuscular maturation of the human infant.* New York: Columbia University Press.

McGue, M., Bouchard, T. J., Jr., Iacono, W. G., & Lykken, D. T. (1993). Behavioral genetics of cognitive ability: A life-span perspective. In R. Plomin & G. E. McClearn (Eds.), *Nature, nurture and psychology* (pp. 59–76). Washington, DC: American Psychological Association.

McGuire, S., McHale, S. M., & Updegraff, K. (1996). Children's perceptions of the sibling relationship in middle childhood: Connections within and between family relationships. *Personal Relationships, 3,* 229–239. doi:10.1111/j.1475-6811.1996.tb00114.x

McGurk, H., & MacDonald, J. (1976, December 23–30). Hearing lips and seeing voices. *Nature, 264,* 746–748.

McHale, S. M., Bissell, J., & Kim, J.-Y. (2009). Sibling relationship, family, and genetic factors in sibling similarity in sexual risk. *Journal of Family Psychology, 23,* 562–572. doi:10.1037/a0014982

McHale, S. M., Updegraff, K. A., Shanahan, L., Crouter, A. C., & Killoren, S. E. (2005). Siblings' differential treatment in Mexican American families. *Journal of Marriage and Family, 67,* 1259–1274. doi:10.1111/j.1741-3737.2005.00215.x

McIntosh, K. (2014). Positive Behavioral Interventions and Supports—Soutien au comportement positif (PBIS-SCP) in Canada: Deep history, promising future. *Canadian Journal of School Psychology, 29,* 155–160.

McKenna, K. Y. A., & Bargh, J. (1998). Coming out in the age of the internet: Identity "demarginalization" through virtual group participation. *Journal of Personality and Social Psychology, 75,* 681–694. doi:10.1037/0022-3514.75.3.681

McMahon, A. W., Iskander, J. K., Haber, P., Braun, M. M., & Ball, R. (2008). Inactivated influenza vaccine (IIV) in children <2 years of age: Examination of selected adverse events reported to the Vaccine Adverse Event Reporting System (VAERS) after thimerosal-free or thimerosal-containing vaccine. *Vaccine, 26,* 427–429. doi:10.1016/j.vaccine.2007.10.071

McMaster, L. E., Connolly, J., Pepler, D., & Craig, W. M. (2002). Peer to peer sexual harassment in early adolescence: A developmental perspective. *Development and Psychopathology, 14,* 91–105.

McMillan, B., & Saffran, J. R. (2016). Learning in complex environments: The effects of background speech on early word learning. *Child Development, 87*(6), 1841–1855. doi:10.1111/cdev.12559

McMurray, B. (2007, August 3). Defusing the childhood vocabulary explosion. *Science, 317,* 631.

McMurray, B., Horst, J. S., & Samuelson, L. K. (2012). Word learning emerges from the interaction of online referent selection and slow associative learning. *Psychological Review, 119*(4), 831–877. doi:10.1037/a0029872

McNeil, N. M., Fyfe, E. R., Petersen, L. A., Dunwiddie, A. E., & Brletic-Shipley, H. (2011). Benefits of practicing 4 = 2 + 2: Nontraditional problem formats facilitate children's understanding of mathematical equivalence. *Child Development, 82,* 1620–1633.

Meaney, M. J. (2001). Maternal care, gene expression, and the transmission of individual differences in stress reactivity across generations. *Annual Review of Neuroscience, 24,* 1161–1192. doi:10.1146/annurev.neuro.24.1.1161

Meaney, M. J. (2010). Epigenetics and the biological definition of gene × environment interactions. *Child Development, 81,* 41–79.

Meeus, W. (2011). The study of adolescent identity formation 2000–2010: A review of longitudinal research. *Journal of Research on Adolescence, 21,* 75–94. doi:10.1111/j.1532-7795.2010.00716.x

Meeus, W., Van De Schoot, R., Keijsers, L., Schwartz, S. J., & Branje, S. (2010). On the progression and stability of adolescent identity formation: A five-wave longitudinal study in early-to-middle and middle-to-late adolescence. *Child Development, 81,* 1565–1581. doi:10.1111/j.1467-8624.2010.01492.x

Mehler, J., Jusczyk, P., Lambertz, G., Halsted, N., Bertoncini, J., & Amiel-Tison, C. (1988). A precursor of language acquisition in young infants. *Cognition, 29,* 143–178.

Melby, J. N., Conger, R. D., Fang, S., Wickrama, K. A. S., & Conger, K. J. (2008). Adolescent family experiences and educational attainment during early adulthood. *Developmental Psychology, 44,* 1519–1536.

Meltzoff, A. N. (1988). Infant imitation and memory: Nine-month-olds in immediate and deferred tests. *Child Development, 59,* 217–225.

Meltzoff, A. N. (1990). Towards a developmental cognitive science. The implications of cross-modal matching and imitation for the development of representation and memory in infancy. *Annals of the New York Academy of Sciences, 608,* 1–31.

Meltzoff, A. N. (1995). Understanding the intentions of others: Re-enactment of intended acts by 18-month-old children. *Developmental Psychology, 31,* 838–850. doi:10.1037/0012-1649.31.5.838

Meltzoff, A. N., & Borton, R. W. (1979, November 22). Intermodal matching by human neonates. *Nature, 282,* 403–404.

Meltzoff, A. N., & Brooks, R. (2008). Self-experience as a mechanism for learning about others: A training study in social cognition. *Developmental Psychology, 44*(5), 1257. doi:10.1017/S030500090700829X

Meltzoff, A. N., & Marshall, P. J. (2018). Human infant imitation as a social survival circuit. *Current Opinion in Behavioral Sciences, 24,* 130–136.

Meltzoff, A. N., & Moore, M. K. (1977, October 7). Imitation of facial and manual gestures by human neonates. *Science, 198,* 75–78.

Meltzoff, A. N., & Moore, M. K. (1983). Newborn infants imitate adult facial gestures. *Child Development, 54,* 702–709.

Meltzoff, A. N., Murray, L., Simpson, E., Heimann, M., Nagy, E., Nadel, J., . . . Ferrari, P. F. (2018). Re-examination of Oostenbroek et al. (2016): Evidence for neonatal imitation of tongue protrusion. *Developmental Science, 21*(4), e12609. https://doi.org/10.1111/desc.12609

Meltzoff, A. N., Murray, L., Simpson, E., Heimann, M., Nagy, E., Nadel, J., . . . Subiaul, F. (2019). Eliciting imitation in early infancy. *Developmental Science, 22,* e12738. https://doi.org/10.1111/desc.12738

Meltzoff, A. N., Ramírez, R. R., Saby, J. N., Larson, E., Taulu, S., & Marshall, P. J. (2018). Infant brain responses to felt and observed touch of hands and feet: An MEG study. *Developmental Science, 21,* e12651.

Mennella, J. A., Jagnow, C. P., & Beauchamp, G. K. (2001). Prenatal and postnatal flavor learning by human infants. *Pediatrics, 107*(6), e88. doi:10.1542/peds.107.6.e88

Menon, M., Tobin, D. D., Corby, B. C., Menon, M., Hodges, E. V., & Perry, D. G. (2007). The developmental costs of high self-esteem for antisocial children. *Child Development, 78,* 1627–1639.

Merz, E. C., Maskus, E. A., Melvin, S. A., He, X., & Noble, K. G. (2019). Socioeconomic disparities in language input are associated with children's language-related brain structure and reading skills. *Child Development.* https://doi.org/10.1111/cdev.13239

Mesman, J., Stoel, R., Bakermans-Kranenburg, M. J., van IJzendoorn, M. H., Juffer, F., Koot, H. M., & Alink, L. R. (2009). Predicting growth curves of early childhood externalizing problems: Differential susceptibility of children with difficult temperament. *Journal of Abnormal Child Psychology, 37,* 625–636. doi:10.1007/s10802-009-9298-0

Mesman, J., van IJzendoorn, M. H., & Sagi-Schwartz, A. (2016). Cross-cultural patterns of attachment: Universal and contextual dimensions. In J. Cassidy & P. R. Shaver (Eds.), *Handbook of attachment: Theory, research, and clinical applications, 3rd ed.* (pp. 790–815). New York: Guilford.

Mesquita, B., & Frijda, N. H. (1992). Cultural variations in emotions: A review. *Psychological Bulletin, 112,* 179–204.

Messner, M. (2002). *Taking the field: Women, men, and sports.* Minneapolis, MN: University of Minnesota Press.

Meter, D. J., & Card, N. A. (2016). Stability of children's and adolescents' friendships: A meta-analytic review. *Merrill-Palmer Quarterly, 62*(3), 252–284. doi:10.13110/merrpalmquar1982.62.3.0252

Metz, E., & Youniss, J. (2003). A demonstration that school-based required service does not deter—but heightens—volunteerism. *Political Science and Politics, 36,* 281–286. doi:10.1017/S1049096503002221

Meunier, J. C., Boyle, M., O'Connor, T. G., & Jenkins, J. M. (2013). Multilevel mediation: Cumulative contextual risk, maternal differential treatment, and children's behavior within families. *Child Development, 84,* 1594–1615. doi:10.1111/cdev.12066

MHASEF Research Team. (2015). *The mental health of children and youth in Ontario: A baseline scorecard.* Toronto, ON: Institute for Clinical Evaluative Sciences.

Michalik, N. M., Eisenberg, N., Spinrad, T. L., Ladd, B., Thompson, M., & Valiente, C. (2007). Longitudinal relations among parental emotional expressivity and sympathy and prosocial behavior in adolescence. *Social Development, 16,* 286–309. doi:10.1111/j.1467-9507.2007.00385.x

Michalson, L., & Lewis, M. (1985). What do children know about emotions and when do they know it? In M. Lewis & L. A. Rosenblum (Series Eds.) & M. Lewis & C. Saarni (Vol. Eds.), *Genesis of behavior: Vol. 5. The socialization of emotions* (pp. 117–139). New York: Plenum Press.

Miell, D., & MacDonald, R. (2000). Children's creative collaborations: The importance of friendship when working together on a musical composition. *Social Development, 9,* 348–369. doi:10.1111/1467-9507.00130

Mikami, A. Y., Szwedo, D. E., Allen, J. P., Evans, M. A., & Hare, A. L. (2010). Adolescent peer relationships and behavior problems predict young adults' communication on social networking websites. *Developmental Psychology, 46,* 46–56. doi:10.1037/a0017420

Miklikowska, M., Duriez, B., & Soenens, B. (2011). Family roots of empathy-related characteristics: The role of perceived maternal and paternal need support in adolescence. *Developmental Psychology, 47,* 1342–1352. doi:10.1037/a0024726

Milewski, A. E. (1976). Infants' discrimination of internal and external pattern elements. *Journal of Experimental Child Psychology, 22,* 229–246. doi:10.1016/0022-0965(76)90004-7

Miller, G. A., & Gildea, P. M. (1987, September). How children learn words. *Scientific American, 257*(3), 94–99.

Miller, G. E., Chen, E., & Parker, K. J. (2011). Psychological stress in childhood and susceptibility to the chronic diseases of aging: Moving toward a model of behavioral and biological mechanisms. *Psychological Bulletin, 137*(6), 959–997.

Miller, J. G., Bersoff, D. M., & Harwood, R. L. (1990). Perceptions of social responsibilities in India and in the United States: Moral imperatives or personal decisions? *Journal of Personality and Social Psychology, 58,* 33–47. doi:10.1037/0022-3514.58.1.33

Miller, J. L. (2014). Effects of familiar contingencies on infants' vocal behavior in new communicative contexts. *Developmental Psychobiology, 56*(7), 1518–1527.

Miller, K. (1984). Child as the measurer of all things: Measurement of procedures and the development of quantitative concepts. In C. Sophian (Ed.), *Origins of cognitive skills: The Eighteenth Annual Carnegie Symposium on Cognition* (pp. 193–228). Hillsdale, NJ: Erlbaum.

Miller, K. F., Smith, C. M., Zhu, J., & Zhang, H. (1995). Preschool origins of cross-national differences in mathematical competence: The role of number-naming systems. *Psychological Science, 6,* 56–60. doi:10.1111/j.1467-9280.1995.tb00305.x

Miller, P. H. (2002). *Theories of developmental psychology* (4th ed.). New York: Worth.

Miller, P. H. (2011). *Theories of developmental psychology* (5th ed.). New York: Worth.

Miller, P. H., & Coyle, T. R. (1999). Developmental change: Lessons from microgenesis. In E. K. Scholnick, K. Nelson, S. A. Gelman, & P. H. Miller (Eds.), *Conceptual development: Piaget's legacy* (pp. 209–239). Mahwah, NJ: Erlbaum.

Miller, P. M., Danaher, D. L., & Forbes, D. (1986). Sex-related strategies for coping with interpersonal conflict in children aged five and seven. *Developmental Psychology, 22,* 543–548. doi:10.1037/0012-1649.22.4.543

Miller, S. A. (2012). *Theory of mind: Beyond the preschool years.* New York: Psychology Press.

Miner, J. L., & Clarke-Stewart, K. A. (2008). Trajectories of externalizing behavior from age 2 to age 9: Relations with gender, temperament, ethnicity, parenting, and rater. *Developmental Psychology, 44,* 771–786. doi:10.1037/0012-1649.44.3.771

Mireault, G. C., Crockenberg, S. C., Sparrow, J. E., Cousineau, K., Pettinato, C., & Woodard, K. (2015). Laughing matters: Infant humor in the context of parental affect. *Journal of Experimental Child Psychology, 136,* 30–41. https://doi.org/10.1016/j.jecp.2015.03.012

Mischel, W. (2015). *The marshmallow test: Why self-control is the engine of success.* New York: Little, Brown.

Mitchell, K. J., Ybarra, M. L., & Korchmaros, J. D. (2014). Sexual harassment among adolescents of different sexual orientations and gender identities. *Child Abuse & Neglect, 38,* 280–295.

Mobin, A., Feng, C. X., & Neudorf, C. (2017). Cybervictimization among preadolescents in a community-based sample in Canada: Prevalence and predictors. *Canadian Journal of Public Health, 108*(5–6), e475–e481.

Modecki, K. L., Barber, B. L., & Vernon, L. (2013). Mapping developmental precursors of cyber-aggression: Trajectories of risk predict perpetration and victimization. *Journal of Youth and Adolescence, 42,* 651–661. doi:10.1007/s10964-012-9887-z

Modin, B., Östberg, V., & Almquist, Y. (2011). Childhood peer status and adult susceptibility to anxiety and depression: A 30-year hospital follow-up. *Journal of Abnormal Child Psychology, 39,* 187–199. doi:10.1007/s10802-010-9462-6

Moffitt, T. E. (1993a). Adolescence-limited and life-course-persistent antisocial behavior: A developmental taxonomy. *Psychological Review, 100,* 674–701. doi:10.1037/0033-295X.100.4.674

Moffitt, T. E., & Caspi, A. (2001). Childhood predictors differentiate life-course persistent and adolescence-limited antisocial pathways among males and females. *Development and Psychopathology, 13,* 355–375.

Moffitt, T. E., Caspi, A., Harrington, H., & Milne, B. J. (2002). Males on the life-course-persistent and adolescence-limited antisocial pathways: Follow-up at age 26 years. *Development and Psychopathology, 14,* 179–207.

Mollborn, S., & Dennis, J. A. (2012). Investigating the life situations and development of teenage mothers' children: Evidence from the ECLS-B. *Population Research and Policy Review, 31,* 31–66. doi:10.1007/s11113-011-9218-1

Möller, E. L., Nickolić, M., Majdandžić, M., & Bögels, S. M. (2016). Associations between maternal and paternal parenting behaviors, anxiety and its precursors in early childhood: A meta-analysis. *Clinical Psychology Review, 45,* 17–33. doi:10.1016/j.cpr.2016.03.002

Monahan, K. C., Steinberg, L., Cauffman, E., & Mulvey, E. P. (2009). Trajectories of antisocial behavior and psychosocial maturity from adolescence to young adulthood. *Developmental Psychology, 45,* 1654–1668. doi:10.1037/a0015862

Monnery-Patris, S., Wagner, S., Rigal, N., Schwartz, C., Chabanet, C., Issanchou, S., & Nicklaus, S. (2015). Smell differential reactivity, but not taste differential reactivity, is related to food neophobia in toddlers. *Appetite, 95,* 303–309.

Montag, J. L., Jones, M. N., & Smith, L. B. (2015). The words children hear: Picture books and the statistics for language learning. *Psychological Science, 26*(9), 1489–1496.

Montirosso, R., Peverelli, M., Frigerio, E., Crespi, M., & Borgatti, R. (2010). The development of dynamic facial expression recognition at different intensities in 4- to 18-year-olds. *Social Development, 19,* 71–92.

Moon, C., Cooper, R. P., & Fifer, W. P. (1993). Two-day-olds prefer their native language. *Infant Behavior and Development, 16,* 495–500.

Moon, C., & Fifer, W. (1990, April). *Newborns prefer a prenatal version of mother's voice.* Poster session presented at the Biannual Meeting of the International Society of Infant Studies, Montreal, Canada.

Moon, M., & Hoffman, C. D. (2008). Mothers' and fathers' differential expectancies and behaviors: Parent × child gender effects. *Journal of Genetic Psychology, 169,* 261–280. doi:10.3200/GNTP.169.3.261-280

Moore, A. M., & Ashcraft, M. H. (2013). Emotionality in mathematical problem solving. In C. Mohiyeddini, M. Eysenck, & S. Bauer (Eds.), *Handbook of psychology of emotions: Recent theoretical perspectives and novel empirical findings* (pp. 115–141). Hauppauge, NY: Nova Science Publishers.

Moore, C. F. (2003). *Silent scourge: Children, pollution, and why scientists disagree.* New York: Oxford University Press.

Moore, K. A., Manlove, J., Glei, D. A., & Morrison, D. R. (1998). Nonmarital school-age motherhood: Family, individual, and school characteristics. *Journal of Adolescent Research, 13,* 433–457. doi:10.1177/0743554898134004

Moore, K. L., & Persaud, T. V. N. (1993). *Before we are born: Essentials of embryology and birth defects* (4th ed.). Philadelphia: Saunders.

Moors, A., Phoebe C., Ellsworth, P. C., Scherer, K. R., & Frijda, N. H. (2013). Appraisal theories of emotion: State of the art and future development. *Emotion Review, 5,* 119–124. doi:10.1177/1754073912468165

Morales, J. R., & Guerra, N. G. (2006). Effects of multiple context and cumulative stress on urban children's adjustment in elementary school. *Child Development, 77,* 907–923. doi:10.1111/j.1467-8624.2006.00910.x

Moreau, D., Clerc, J., Mansy-Dannay, A., & Guerrien, A. (2012). Enhancing spatial ability through sport practice: Evidence for an effect of motor training on mental rotation performance. *Journal of Individual Differences, 33,* 83–88. doi:10.1027/1614-0001/a000075

Morelen, D., & Suveg, C. (2012). A real-time analysis of parent–child emotion discussions: The interaction is reciprocal. *Journal of Family Psychology, 26,* 998–1003. doi:10.1037/a0030148

Morelen, D., Southam-Gerow, M., & Zeman, J. (2016). Child emotion regulation and peer victimization: The moderating role of child sex. *Journal of Child and Family Studies, 25,* 1941–1953. doi:10.1007/s10826-016-0360-6

Morelli, G. A., Rogoff, B., Oppenheim, D., & Goldsmith, D. (1992). Cultural variation in infants' sleeping arrangements: Questions of independence. *Developmental Psychology, 28,* 604–613. doi:10.1037/0012-1649.28.4.604

Morgan, J., Shaw, D., & Olino, T. (2012). Differential susceptibility effects: The interaction of negative emotionality and sibling relationship quality on childhood internalizing problems and social skills. *Journal of Abnormal Child Psychology, 40,* 885–899. doi:10.1007/s10802-012-9618-7

Morgan, J. K., Izard, C. E., & Hyde, C. (2014). Emotional reactivity and regulation in Head Start children: Links to ecologically valid behaviors and internalizing problems. *Social Development, 23*(2), 250–266. doi:10.1111/sode.12049

Morin-Lessard, E., Poulin-Dubois, D., Segalowitz, N., & Byers-Heinlein, K. (2019). Selective attention to the mouth of talking faces in monolinguals and bilinguals aged 5 months to 5 years. *Developmental Psychology.* doi:10.1037/dev0000750

Morris, A. S., Silk, J. S., Steinberg, L., Myers, S. S., & Robinson, L. R. (2007). The role of the family context in the development of emotion regulation. *Social Development, 16,* 361–388. doi:10.1111/j.1467-9507.2007.00389.x

Morsunbul, U., Crocetti, E., Cok, F., & Meeus, W. (2016). Identity statuses and psychosocial functioning in Turkish youth: A person-centered approach. *Journal of Adolescence, 47,* 145–155. doi:10.1016/j.adolescence.2015.09.001

Moss, E., Dubois-Comtois, K., Cyr, C., Tarabulsy, G. M., St-Laurent, D., & Bernier, A. (2011). Efficacy of a home-visiting intervention aimed at improving maternal sensitivity, child attachment, and behavioral outcomes for maltreated children: A randomized control trial. *Development and Psychopathology, 23*(1), 195–210.

Moss, E., & St-Laurent, D. (2001). Attachment at school age and academic performance. *Developmental Psychology, 37*(6), 863.

Mounts, N. S. (2002). Parental management of adolescent peer relationships in context: The role of parenting style. *Journal of Family Psychology, 16,* 58–69. doi:10.1037/0893-3200.16.1.58

Mounts, N. S., & Steinberg, L. (1995). An ecological analysis of peer influence on adolescent grade point average and drug use. *Developmental Psychology, 31,* 915–922. doi:10.1037/0012-1649.31.6.915

Moyser, M. (2017). Women and paid work. Statistics Canada, Catalogue no. 89-503-X. Retrieved from https://www150.statcan.gc.ca/n1/en/pub/89-503-x/2015001/article/14694-eng.pdf?st=VHA35krZ

Mueller, S. C., Temple, V., Oh, E., VanRyzin, C., Williams, A., Cornwell, B., . . . Merke, D. P. (2008). Early androgen exposure modulates spatial cognition in congenital adrenal hyperplasia (CAH). *Psychoneuroendocrinology, 33,* 973–980. doi:10.1016/j.psyneuen.2008.04.005

Muenssinger, J., Matuz, T., Schleger, F., Kiefer-Schmidt, I., Goelz, R., Wacker-Gussmann, A., . . . Preissl, H. (2013). Auditory habituation in the fetus and neonate: An fMEG study. *Developmental Science, 16*(2), 287–295.

Mukherjee, H. B. (2016). *Education for fullness: A study of the educational thought and experiment of Rabindranath Tagore.* New York: Routledge.

Mullally, S. L., & Maguire, E. A. (2014). Learning to remember: The early ontogeny of episodic memory. *Developmental Cognitive Neuroscience, 9*(100), 12–29. doi:10.1016/j.dcn.2013.12.006

Mulvaney, M. K., & Mebert, C. J. (2007). Parental corporal punishment predicts behavior problems in early childhood. *Journal of Family Psychology, 21,* 389–397. doi:10.1037/0893-3200.21.3.389

Munakata, Y., & McClelland, J. L. (2003). Connectionist models of development. *Developmental Science, 6*(4), 413–429. doi:10.1111/1467-7687.00296

Munakata, Y., McClelland, J. L., Johnson, M. H., & Siegler, R. S. (1997). Rethinking infant knowledge: Toward an adaptive process account of successes and failures in object permanence tasks. *Psychological Review, 104,* 686–713. doi:10.1037/0033-295X.104.4.686

Munakata, Y., Snyder, H. R., & Chatham, C. H. (2012). Developing cognitive control: Three key transitions. *Current Directions in Psychological Science, 21,* 71–77. doi:10.1177/0963721412436807

Munroe, R. L., & Romney, A. K. (2006). Gender and age differences in same-sex aggregation and social behavior: A four-culture study. *Journal of Cross-Cultural Psychology, 37*(1), 3–19. https://doi.org/10.1177/0022022105282292

Muresan, R. (2016). One in 10 visitors of porn sites is under 10 years old. Bitdefender. Retrieved from https://hotforsecurity.bitdefender.com/blog/one-in-10-visitors-of-porn-sites-is-under-10-years-old-16675.html

Murray, M. M., Lewkowicz, D. J., Amedi, A., & Wallace, M. T. (2016). Multisensory processes: A balancing act across the lifespan. *Trends in Neurosciences.* doi:10.1016/j.tins.2016.05.003

Murray-Close, D., Ostrov, J. M., & Crick, N. R. (2007). A short-term longitudinal study of growth of relational aggression during middle childhood: Associations with gender, friendship intimacy, and internalizing problems. *Development and Psychopathology, 19,* 187–203.

Myers, L. J., LeWitt, R. B., Gallo, R. E., & Maselli, N. M. (2017). Baby FaceTime: Can toddlers learn from online video chat? *Developmental Science, 20*(4), e12430.

Myowa-Yamakoshi, M., & Takeshita, H. (2006). Do human fetuses anticipate self-oriented actions? A study by four-dimensional (4D) ultrasonography. *Infancy, 10,* 289–301.

Naigles, L. (1990). Children use syntax to learn verb meanings. *Journal of Child Language, 17,* 357–374. doi:10.1017/S0305000900013817

Nair, R. J., Roche, K. M., & White, R. M. B. (2018). Acculturation gap distress among Latino youth: Prospective links to family processes and youth depressive symptoms, alcohol use, and academic performance. *Journal of Youth and Adolescence, 47,* 105–120. doi:10.1007/s10964-017-0753-x

Nakamichi, N. (2015). Maternal behavior modifications during pretense and their long-term effects on toddlers' understanding of pretense. *Journal of Cognition and Development, 16*(4), 541–558. doi:10.1080/15248372.2014.926271

Náñez, J. (1988). Perception of impending collision in 3- to 6-week-old human infants. *Infant Behavior & Development, 11,* 447–463.

Nantel-Vivier, A., Kokko, K., Caprara, G. V., Pastorelli, C., Gerbino, M. G., Paciello, M., . . . Tremblay, R. E. (2009). Prosocial development from childhood to adolescence: A multi-informant perspective with Canadian and Italian longitudinal studies. *Journal of Child Psychology and Psychiatry, 50,* 590–598. doi:10.1111/j.1469-7610.2008.02039.x

Naoi, N., Minagawa-Kawai, Y., Kaboyashi, A., Takeuchi, K., Nakamura, K., Yamamoto, J., & Kojima, S. (2012). Cerebral responses to infant-directed speech and the effect of talker familiarity. *NeuroImage, 59,* 1735–1744.

Naterer, A., & Godina, V. (2011). Bomzhji and their subculture: An anthropolitical study of street children subculture in Makeevka, Eastern Ukraine. *Childhood, 18,* 20–38. doi:10.1177/0907568210379924

Naterer, A., & Lavrič, M. (2016). Using social indicators in assessing factors and numbers of street children in the world. *Child Indicators Research, 9,* 21–37. doi:10.1007/s12187-015-9306-6L

Nation, K. (2008). Learning to read words. *Quarterly Journal of Experimental Psychology, 61,* 1121–1133. doi:10.1080/17470210802034603

National Association for the Education of Young Children (NAEYC). (2018). *NAEYC Early Learning Program Standards.* Retrieved from https://www.naeyc.org/sites/default/files/globally-shared/downloads/PDFs/accreditation/early-learning/overview_of_the_standards.pdf

National Association for the Education of Young Children. (2011). *2010 NAEYC Standards for Initial & Advanced Early Childhood Professional Preparation Programs.* Retrieved from http://www.naeyc.org/ncate/files/ncate/file/faculty/Standards/NAEYC%20Initial%20and%20Advanced%20Standards%203_2012.pdf

National Down Syndrome Society (NDSS). (2018). About Down syndrome. Retrieved from https://www.ndss.org/about-down-syndrome/down-syndrome/

National Partnership for Women & Families. (2018). *Voters' views on paid family + medical leave: Findings from a national survey.* Washington, DC: Author. Retrieved from http://www.nationalpartnership.org/our-work/resources/workplace/paid-leave/voters-views-on-paid-family-medical-leave-survey-findings-august-2018.pdf

National Research Council. (2010). *Student mobility: Exploring the impact of frequent moves on achievement.* Washington, DC: National Academies Press.

National Science Foundation. (2017). Women, minorities, and persons with disabilities in science and engineering. Washington, DC: Author. Retrieved from www.nsf.gov/statistics/wmpd/

NCD Risk Factor Collaboration. (2017). Body-mass index: Evolution of BMI over time. Retrieved from http://www.ncdrisc.org/overweight-population-stacked-ado.html

Neblett, E. W., Rivas-Drake, D., & Umaña-Taylor, A. J. (2012). The promise of racial and ethnic protective factors in promoting ethnic minority youth development. *Child Development Perspectives, 6,* 295–303. doi:10.1111/j.1750-8606.2012.00239.x

Neblett, E. W., White, R. L., Ford, K. R., Philip, C. L., Nguyên, H. X., & Sellers, R. M. (2008). Patterns of racial socialization and psychological adjustment: Can parental communications about race reduce the impact of racial discrimination? *Journal of Research on Adolescence, 18,* 477–515. doi:10.1111/j.1532-7795.2008.00568.x

Nederhof, E., Belsky, J., Ormel, J., & Oldehinkel, A. J. (2012). Effects of divorce on Dutch boys' and girls' externalizing behavior in Gene × Environment perspective: Diathesis stress or differential susceptibility in the Dutch Tracking Adolescents' Individual Lives Survey study? *Development and Psychopathology, 24,* 929–939. doi:10.1017/S0954579412000454

Needham, A. (1997). Factors affecting infants' use of featural information in object segregation. *Current Directions in Psychological Science, 6,* 26–33. doi:10.2307/20182439

Needham, A., & Baillargeon, R. (1993). Intuitions about support in 4.5-month-old infants. *Cognition, 47,* 121–148. doi:10.1016/0010-0277(93)90002-D

Needham, A., & Baillargeon, R. (1997). Object segregation in 8-month-old infants. *Cognition, 62,* 121–149. doi:10.1016/S0010-0277(96)00727-5

Needham, A., & Baillargeon, R. (1998). Effects of prior experience on 4.5-month old infants' object segregation. *Infant Behavior and Development, 21,* 1–24. doi:10.1016/S0163-6383(98)90052-2

Needham, A., Barrett, T., & Peterman, K. (2002). A pick-me-up for infants' exploratory skills: Early simulated experiences reaching for objects using 'sticky mittens' enhances young infants' object exploration skills. *Infant Behavior and Development, 25,* 279–295. doi:10.1016/S0163-6383(02)00097-8

Needham, A. W. (2016). *Learning about objects in infancy* (1st ed.). New York: Routledge.

Nehring, I., Kostka, T., von Kries, R., & Rehfuess, E. A. (2015). Impacts of in utero and early infant taste experiences on later taste acceptance: A systematic review. *The Journal of Nutrition, 145*(6), 1271–1279.

Nelson, C. A., III, Bos, K., Gunnar, M. R., & Sonuga-Barke, E. J. S. (2011). The neurobiological toll of early human deprivation. *Monographs of the Society for Research in Child Development, 76*(4, Serial No. 301), 127–146. doi:10.1111/j.1540-5834.2011.00630.x

Nelson, C. A., III, Thomas, K. M., & de Haan, M. (2006). Neural bases of cognitive development. In W. Damon & R. M. Lerner (Series Eds.) & D. Kuhn & R. S. Siegler (Vol. Eds.), *Handbook of child psychology: Vol. 2. Cognition, perception, and language* (6th ed., pp. 3–57). Hoboken, NJ: Wiley.

Nelson, C. A., III, Zeanah, C. H., Fox, N. A., Marshall, P. J., Smyke, A. T., & Guthrie, D. (2007, December 21). Cognitive recovery in socially deprived young children: The Bucharest Early Intervention Project. *Science, 318,* 1937–1940.

Nelson, D. A., Mitchell, C., & Yang, C. (2008). Intent attributions and aggression: A study of children and their parents. *Journal of Abnormal Child Psychology, 36,* 793–806. doi:10.1007/s10802-007-9211-7

Nelson, D. A., Robinson, C. C., Hart, C. H., Albano, A. D., & Marshall, S. J. (2010). Italian preschoolers' peer-status linkages with sociability and subtypes of aggression and victimization. *Social Development, 19,* 698–720. doi:10.1111/j.1467-9507.2009.00551.x

Nelson, E. A., Schiefenhoevel, W., & Haimerl, F. (2000). Child care practices in nonindustrialized societies. *Pediatrics, 105,* e75. doi:10.1542/peds.105.6.e75

Nelson, J. K. (2005). Interference resolution in the left inferior frontal gyrus. *Dissertation Abstracts International: Section B: The Sciences and Engineering, 66*(10), 5703.

Nelson, K. (1973). Structure and strategy in learning to talk. *Monographs of the Society for Research in Child Development, 38*(1–2, Serial No. 149).

Neniskyte, U., & Gross, C. T. (2017). Errant gardeners: Glial-cell-dependent synaptic pruning and neurodevelopmental disorders. *Nature Reviews Neuroscience, 18*(11), 658.

Nesdale, D. (2007). Children's perceptions of social groups. In J. A. Zebrowski (Ed.), *New research on social perception* (pp. 1–45). Hauppauge, NY: Nova Science.

Newcomb, A. F., & Bukowski, W. M. (1984). A longitudinal study of the utility of social preference and social impact sociometric classification schemes. *Child Development, 55,* 1434–1447. doi:10.2307/1130013

Newcombe, N., Huttenlocher, J., Drummey, A. B., & Wiley, J. G. (1998). The development of spatial location coding: Place learning and dead reckoning in the second and third years. *Cognitive Development, 13,* 185–200. doi:10.1016/S0885-2014(98)90038-7

Newcombe, N. S. (2019). Navigation and the developing brain. *Journal of Experimental Biology, 222.* doi:10.1242/jeb.186460

Newcombe, N. S., Levine, S. C., & Mix, K. (2015). Thinking about quantity: The intertwined development of spatial and numerical cognition. *Wiley Interdisciplinary Reviews: Cognitive Science, 6,* 491–505. doi:10.1002/wcs.1369

Newcombe, N. S., Uttal, D. H. & Sauter, M. (2013). Spatial development. In P. Zelazo (Ed.), *Oxford handbook of developmental psychology, Vol. 1: Body and mind* (pp. 564–590). New York: Oxford University Press.

Newman, A. J., Supalla, T., Fernandez, N., Newport, E. L., & Bavelier, D. (2015). Neural systems supporting linguistic structure, linguistic experience, and symbolic communication in sign language and gesture. *Proceedings of the National Academy of Sciences, 112*(37), 11684–11689.

Newman, R. S. (2005). The cocktail party effect in infants revisited: Listening to one's name in noise. *Developmental Psychology, 41,* 352–362.

Newport, E. L. (1990). Maturational constraints on language learning. *Cognitive Science, 14,* 11–28.

Newport, E. L., & Meier, R. P. (1985). The acquisition of American Sign Language. In D. I. Slobin (Ed.), *The crosslinguistic study of language acquisition, Vol. 1. The data; Vol. 2. Theoretical issues* (pp. 881–938). Hillsdale, NJ: Erlbaum.

Newton, E. K., Laible, D., Carlo, G., Steele, J. S., & McGinley, M. (2014). Do sensitive parents foster kind children, or vice versa? Bidirectional influences between children's prosocial behavior and parental sensitivity. *Developmental Psychology, 50,* 1808–1816. doi:10.1037/a0036495

Ng-Knight, T., Shelton, K. H., Riglin, L., Frederickson, N., McManus, I. C., & Rice, F. (2018). "Best friends forever"? Friendship stability across school transition and associations with mental health and educational attainment. *British Journal of Educational Psychology.* doi:10.1111/bjep.12246

Ngun, T. C., & Vilain, E. (2014). The biological basis of human sexual orientation: Is there a role for epigenetics? *Advances in Genetics, 86,* 167–184. doi:10.1016/B978-0-12-800222-3.00008-5

Nguyen, M. (2011). Closing the education gap: A case for Aboriginal early childhood education in Canada, a look at the Aboriginal Head Start Program. *Canadian Journal of Education, 34*(3).

Nguyen, S. P., & Gelman, S. A. (2002). Four and 6-year olds' biological concept of death: The case of plants. *British Journal of Developmental Psychology, 20,* 495–513. doi:10.1348/026151002760390918

NICHD Early Child Care Research Network. (1997). Familial factors associated with the characteristics of nonmaternal care for infants. *Journal of Marriage and the Family, 59,* 389–408.

NICHD Early Child Care Research Network. (1998a). Early child care and self-control, compliance, and problem behavior at twenty-four and thirty-six months. *Child Development, 69,* 1145–1170.

NICHD Early Child Care Research Network. (1998b, April–May). *When child care classrooms meet recommended guidelines for quality.* Paper presented at the meeting, "Child Care in the New Policy Context," U.S. Department of Health and Human Services, Bethesda, MD.

NICHD Early Child Care Research Network. (2000a). Factors associated with fathers' caregiving activities and sensitivity with young children. *Journal of Family Psychology 14,* 200–219.

NICHD Early Child Care Research Network. (2000b). The relation of child care to cognitive and language development. *Child Development, 71,* 960–980.

NICHD Early Child Care Research Network. (2001). Child-care and family predictors of preschool attachment and stability from infancy. *Developmental Psychology, 37,* 847–862. doi:10.1037//0012-1649.37.6.847

NICHD Early Child Care Research Network. (2002). Early child care and children's development prior to school entry: Results from the NICHD Study of Early Child Care. *American Educational Research Journal, 39,* 133–164.

NICHD Early Child Care Research Network. (2003). Social functioning in first grade: Associations with earlier home and child care predictors and with current classroom experiences. *Child Development, 74,* 1639–1662.

NICHD Early Child Care Research Network. (2004). Trajectories of physical aggression from toddlerhood to middle childhood: Predictors, correlates, and outcomes. *Monographs of the Society for Research in Child Development, 69*(4, Serial No. 278), i–143. doi:10.2307/3701390

NICHD Early Child Care Research Network. (2006). Child-care effect sizes for the NICHD Study of Early Child Care and Youth Development. *American Psychologist, 61,* 99–116. doi:10.1037/0003-066X.61.2.99

NICHD Early Child Care Research Network, & Duncan, G. J. (2003). Modeling the impacts of child care quality on children's preschool cognitive development. *Child Development, 74,* 1454–1475. doi:10.1111/1467-8624.00617

Nicholson, T. (1999). Reading comprehension processes. In G. B. Thompson & T. Nicholson (Eds.), *Learning to read: Beyond phonics and whole language* (pp. 127–149). Newark, DE: International Reading Association.

Nicoladis, E., & Genesee, F. (1996). A longitudinal study of pragmatic differentiation in young bilingual children. *Language learning, 46*(3), 439–464.

Nicolopoulou, A. (2007). The interplay of play and narrative in children's development: Theoretical reflections and concrete examples. In A. Göncü & S. Gaskins (Eds.), *Play and development: Evolutionary, sociocultural, and functional perspectives* (pp. 247–273). New York: Erlbaum.

Nieder, A. (2012). Supramodal numerosity selectivity of neurons in primate prefrontal and posterior parietal cortices. *Proceedings of the National Academy of Sciences of the United States of America, 109,* 11860–11865. doi:10.1073/pnas.1204580109

Nieder, A., & Dehaene, S. (2009). Representation of number in the brain. *Annual Review of Neuroscience, 32,* 185–208. doi:10.1146/annurev.neuro.051508.135550

Nielsen, J. A., Zielinski, B. A., Ferguson, M. A., Lainhart, J. E., & Anderson, J. S. (2013). An evaluation of the left-brain vs. right-brain hypothesis with resting state functional connectivity magnetic resonance imaging. *PloS One, 8*(8), e71275.

Nielsen, M., Suddendorf, T., & Slaughter, V. (2006). Mirror self-recognition beyond the face. *Child Development, 77,* 176–185. doi:10.1111/j.1467-8624.2006.00863.x

Nigg, J. T., Lewis, K., Edinger, T., & Falk, M. (2012). Meta-analysis of attention-deficit/hyperactivity disorder or attention-deficit/hyperactivity disorder symptoms, restriction diet, and synthetic food color additives. *Journal of the American Academy of Child and Adolescent Psychiatry, 51,* 86–97, e88.

Nilsen, E. S., & Graham, S. A. (2009). The relations between children's communicative perspective-taking and executive functioning. *Cognitive Psychology, 58,* 220–249. doi:10.1016/j.cogpsych.2008.07.002

Nisan, M., & Kohlberg, L. (1982). Universality and variation in moral judgment: A longitudinal and cross-sectional study in Turkey. *Child Development, 53,* 865–876. doi:10.2307/1129123

Nisbett, R. E., Aronson, J., Blair, C., Dickens, W., Flynn, J., Halpern, D. F., & Turkheimer, E. (2012). Intelligence: New findings and theoretical developments. *American Psychologist, 67,* 130–159. doi:10.1037/a0026699

Nisbett, R. E., & Miyamoto, Y. (2005). The influence of culture: Holistic versus analytic perception. *Trends in Cognitive Sciences, 9*(10), 467–473.

Nishina, A., Bellmore, A., Witkow, M. R., & Nylund-Gibson, K. (2010). Longitudinal consistency of adolescent ethnic identification across varying school ethnic contexts. *Developmental Psychology, 46,* 1389–1401. doi:10.1037/a0020728

Nobes, G., Panagiotaki, G., & Jonsson, K. R. (2019). Child homicides by stepfathers: A replication and reassessment of the British evidence. *Journal of Experimental Psychology: General, 148*(6), 1091–1102.

Nobes, G., Panagiotaki, G., & Pawson, C. (2009). The influence of negligence, intention, and outcome on children's moral judgments. *Journal of Experimental Child Psychology, 104,* 382–397. doi:10.1016/j.jecp.2009.08.001

Noble, K. G., Houston, S. M., Brito, N. H., Bartsch, H., Kan, E., Kuperman, J. M., . . . Sowell, E. R. (2015). Family income, parental education and brain structure in children and adolescents. *Nature Neuroscience, 18*(5), 773–778. doi:10.1038/nn.3983

Nóblega, M., Bárrig-Jo, P., Gonzalez, L., Fourment, K., Salinas-Quiroz, F., Vizuet, A., & Posada, G. (2019). Secure base scripted knowledge and preschoolers' social competence in samples from Mexico and Peru. *Attachment & Human Development, 21,* 253–264. doi:10.1080/14616734.2019.1575548

Nolen-Hoeksema, S. (2012). Emotion regulation and psychopathology: The role of gender. *Annual Review of Clinical Psychology, 8,* 161–187. doi:10.1146/annurev-clinpsy-032511-143109

Nordenström, A., Servin, A., Bohlin, G., Larsson, A., & Wedell, A. (2002). Sex-typed toy play behavior correlates with the degree of prenatal androgen exposure assessed by CYP21 genotype in girls with congenital adrenal hyperplasia. *Journal of Clinical Endocrinology and Metabolism, 87,* 5119–5124. doi:10.1210/jc.2001-011531

Nordhov, S. M., Rønning, J. A., Ulvund, S. E., Dahl, L. B., & Kaaresen, P. I. (2012). Early intervention improves behavioral outcomes for preterm infants: Randomized controlled trial. *Pediatrics, 129*(1). doi:10.1542/peds.2011-0248

Novin, S., Banerjee, R., Dadkhah, A., & Rieffe, C. (2009). Self-reported use of emotional display rules in the Netherlands and Iran: Evidence for sociocultural influence. *Social Development, 18,* 397–411. doi:10.1111/j.1467-9507.2008.00485.x

Nowell, A., & Hedges, L. V. (1998). Trends in gender differences in academic achievement from 1960 to 1994: An analysis of differences in mean, variance, and extreme scores. *Sex Roles, 39,* 21–43. doi:10.1023/A:1018873615316

Nucci, L. (1997). Culture, universals, and the personal. In H. D. Saltzstein (Ed.), *New Directions for Child and Adolescent Development: No. 76. Culture as a context for moral development: New perspectives on the particular and the universal* (Vol. 1997, pp. 5–22). San Francisco: Jossey-Bass.

Nucci, L. P. (2001). *Education in the moral domain.* New York: Cambridge University Press.

Nucci, L. P., & Gingo, M. (2011). The development of moral reasoning. In U. Goswami (Ed.), *The Wiley-Blackwell handbook of childhood cognitive development* (2nd ed., pp. 420–445). Oxford: Wiley-Blackwell.

O'Connor, A., & Boag, S. (2010). Do stepparents experience more parental antagonism than biological parents? A test of evolutionary and socialization perspectives. *Journal of Divorce and Remarriage, 51,* 508–525. doi:10.1080/10502556.2010.504101

O'Leary, K. D., Slep, A. M. S., Avery-Leaf, S., & Cascardi, M. (2008). Gender differences in dating aggression among multiethnic high school students. *Journal of Adolescent Health, 42,* 473–479. doi:10.1016/j.jadohealth.2007.09.012

O'Neal, E. E., Jiang, Y., Franzen, L. J., Rahimian, P., Yon, J. P., Kearney, J. K., & Plumert, J. M. (2018). Changes in perception–action tuning over long time scales: How children and adults perceive and act on dynamic affordances when crossing roads. *Journal of Experimental Psychology: Human Perception and Performance, 44,* 18–26. doi:10.1037/xhp0000378

Oakes, L. M., & Cohen, L. B. (1995). Infant causal perception. In L. P. Lipsitt & C. K. Rovee-Collier (Eds.), *Advances in infancy research* (Vol. 9, pp. 1–54). Norwood, NJ: Ablex.

Oakes, L. M., Hurley, K. B., Ross-Sheehy, S., & Luck, S. J. (2011). Developmental changes in infants' visual short-term memory for location. *Cognition, 118*(3), 293–305.

Oberlander, T. F., Weinberg, J., Papsdorf, M., Grunau, R., Misri, S., & Devlin, A. M. (2008). Prenatal exposure to maternal depression, neonatal methylation of human glucocorticoid receptor gene (NR3C1) and infant cortisol stress responses. *Epigenetics, 3,* 97–106.

Obradović, J., & Hipwell, A. (2010). Psychopathology and social competence during the transition to adolescence: The role of family adversity and pubertal development. *Development and Psychopathology, 22,* 621–634. doi:10.1017/S0954579410000325

Obus, E. A., Brito, N. H., Sanlorenzo, L., Rea, C., Engelhardt, L., & Noble, K. G. (2017). Improving adherence to reach out and read: A bookmark intervention. *Journal of Pediatrics and Pediatric Medicine, 1,* 1–7.

Ocampo, K. A., Bernal, M. E., & Knight, G. P. (1993). Gender race and ethnicity: The sequencing of social constancies. In M. E. Bernal & G. P. Knight (Eds.), *Ethnic identity: Formation and transmission among Hispanics and other minorities* (pp. 11–30). Albany: State University of New York Press.

Odgers, C. L., Caspi, A., Russell, M. A., Sampson, R. J., Arseneault, L., & Moffitt, T. E. (2012). Supportive parenting mediates neighborhood socioeconomic disparities in children's antisocial behavior from ages 5 to 12. *Development and Psychopathology, 24,* 705–721. doi:10.1017/S0954579412000326

OECD. (2018, October). Policy brief on child well-being: Poor children in rich countries: Why we need policy action.

OECD Family Database. (2019). PF2.1. Parental leave systems. Retrieved from http://www.oecd.org/els/soc/PF2_1_Parental_leave_systems.pdf

Ofner, M., Coles, A., Decou, M. L., Minh, T. D., Bienek, A., Snider, J., & Ugnat, A. (2018). Autism Spectrum Disorder among children and youth in Canada 2018. Public Health Agency of Canada. Retrieved from https://www.canada.ca/en/public-health/services/publications/diseases-conditions/autism-spectrum-disorder-children-youth-canada-2018.html

Ogbu, J. U. (1981). Origins of human competence: A cultural-ecological perspective. *Child Development, 52,* 413–429. doi:10.2307/1129158

Ogden, C. L., Carroll, M. D., Lawman, H. G., Fryar, C. D., Kruszon-Moran, D., Kit, B. K., & Flegal, K. M. (2016). Trends in obesity prevalence among children and adolescents in the United States, 1988–1994 through 2013–2014. *Journal of the American Medical Association, 315*(21), 2292–2299.

Ohayon, M. M., Carskadon, M. A., Guilleminault, C., & Vitiello, M. V. (2004). Meta-analysis of quantitative sleep parameters from childhood to old age in healthy individuals: Developing normative sleep values across the human lifespan. *Sleep, 27,* 1255–1274.

Oliner, S. P., & Oliner, P. M. (1988). *The altruistic personality: Rescuers of Jews in Nazi Europe.* New York: Free Press.

Oliver, B., Dale, P. S., & Plomin, R. (2004). Verbal and nonverbal predictors of early language problems: An analysis of twins in early childhood back to infancy. *Journal of Child Language, 31,* 609–631.

Oller, D. K., & Pearson, B. Z. (2002). Assessing the effects of bilingualism: A background. In D. K. Oller & R. E. Eilers (Eds.), *Language and literacy in bilingual children* (pp. 3–21). Clevedon, England: Multilingual Matters.

Olson, K. R., & Enright, E. A. (2018). Do transgender children (gender) stereotype less than their peers and siblings? *Developmental Science, 21*(4), e12606. https://doi.org/10.1111/desc.12606

Olson, K. R., Durwood, L., DeMeules, M., & McLaughlin, K. A. (2016). Mental health of transgender children who are supported in their identities. *Pediatrics, 137*(3), 1–8. http://dx.doi.org/10.1542/peds.2015-3223

Olson, K. R., & Gülgöz, S. (2018). Early findings from the transyouth project: Gender development in transgender children. *Child Development Perspectives, 12*(2), 93–97. http://dx.doi.org/10.1111/cdep.12268

Olson, R. K., Keenan, J. M., Byrne, B., & Samuelsson, S. (2014). Why do children differ in their development of reading and related skills? *Scientific Studies of Reading, 18*(1), 38–54. doi:10.1080/10888438.2013.800521

Olson, S. L., Bates, J. E., & Kaskie, B. (1992). Caregiver–infant interaction antecedents of children's school-age cognitive ability. *Merrill-Palmer Quarterly, 38,* 309–330.

Olson, S. L., Lopez-Duran, N., Lunkenheimer, E. S., Chang, H., & Sameroff, A. J. (2011). Individual differences in the development of early peer aggression: Integrating contributions of self-regulation, theory of mind, and parenting. *Development and Psychopathology, 23,* 253–266. doi:10.1017/S0954579410000775

Oostenbroek, J., Redshaw, J., Davis, J., Kennedy-Costantini, S., Nielsen, M., Slaughter, V., & Suddendorf, T. (2018). Re-evaluating the neonatal imitation hypothesis. *Developmental Science,* e12720.

Oostenbroek, J., Suddendorf, T., Nielsen, M., Redshaw, J., Kennedy-Costantini, S., Davis, J., . . . Slaughter, V. (2016). Comprehensive longitudinal study challenges the existence of neonatal imitation in humans. *Current Biology, 26*(10), 1334–1338.

Opendak, M., & Gould, E. (2015). Adult neurogenesis: A substrate for experience-dependent change. *Trends in Cognitive Sciences, 19*(3), 151–161.

Opfer, J. E., & Gelman, S. A. (2001). Children's and adults' models for predicting teleological action: The development of a biology-based model. *Child Development, 72,* 1367–1381.

Opfer, J. E., & Siegler, R. S. (2004). Revisiting preschoolers' *living things* concept: A microgenetic analysis of conceptual change in basic biology. *Cognitive Psychology, 49,* 301–332. doi:10.1016/j.cogpsych.2004.01.002

Oppliger, P. A. (2007). Effects of gender stereotyping on socialization. In R. W. Preiss, B. M. Gayle, N. Burrell, M. Allen, & J. Bryant (Eds.), *Mass media effects research: Advances through meta-analysis* (pp. 199–214). Mahwah, NJ: Erlbaum.

Opportunity for All. (2018). Opportunity for all—Canada's first poverty reduction strategy. Retrieved from https://www.canada.ca/en/employment-social-development/programs/poverty-reduction/reports/strategy.html

Orben, A., Dienlin, T., & Przybylski, A. K. (2019). Social media's enduring effect on adolescent life satisfaction. *Proceedings of the National Academy of Sciences, 116*(21), 10226–10228.

Orben, A., & Przybylski, A. K. (2019). Screens, teens and psychological well-being: Evidence from three time-use diary studies. *Psychological Science, 30*(5): 682–696.

Organisation for Economic Co-operation and Development (OECD). (2017). *Starting strong 2017: Key OECD indicators on early childhood education and care.* Paris, France: OECD Publishing. Retrieved from https://read.oecd-ilibrary.org/education/starting-strong-2017_9789264276116-en#page3

Organisation for Economic Co-operation and Development. (n.d.). Gender equality: Length of maternity leave, parental leave and paid father-specific leave. Retrieved from http://www.oecd.org/gender/data/length-of-maternity-leave-parental-leave-and-paid-father-specific-leave.htm#

Orr, S. K., Dachner, N., Frank, L., & Tarasuk, V. (2018). Relation between household food insecurity and breastfeeding in Canada. *Canadian Medical Association Journal, 190*(11), E312–E319.

Orth, U., & Robins, R. W. (2014). The development of self-esteem. *Current Directions in Psychological Science, 23,* 381–387. doi:10.1177/0963721414547414

Orzack, S. H., Stubblefield, J. W., Akmaev, V. R., Colls, P., Munné, S., Scholl, T., . . . Zuckerman, J. E. (2015). The human sex ratio from conception to birth. *Proceedings of the National Academy of Sciences, 112*(16), E2102–E2111.

Osborne, C., & McLanahan, S. (2007). Partnership instability and child well-being. *Journal of Marriage and Family, 69,* 1065–1083. doi:10.1111/j.1741-3737.2007.00431.x

Ostrov, J. M., Ries, E. E., Stauffacher, K., Godleski, S. A., & Mullins, A. D. (2008). Relational aggression, physical aggression and deception during early childhood: A multimethod, multi-informant short-term longitudinal study. *Journal of Clinical Child and Adolescent Psychology, 37,* 664–675. doi:10.1080/15374410802148137

Otgaar, H., Howe, M. L., Merckelbach, H., & Muris, P. (2018). Who is the better eyewitness? Sometimes adults but at other times children. *Current Directions in Psychological Science, 27*(5), 378–385. doi:10.1177/0963721418770998

Oyserman, D., Elmore, K., & Smith, G. (2012). Self, self-concept, and identity. In M. R. Leary & J. P. Tangney (Eds.), *Handbook of self and identity,* 2nd ed. (pp. 69–104). New York: Guilford.

Ozonoff, S., Cook, I., Coon, H., Dawson, G., Joseph, R. M., Klin, A., . . . Wrathall, D. (2004). Performance on Cambridge Neuropsychological Test Automated Battery subtests sensitive to frontal lobe function in people with autistic disorder: Evidence from the Collaborative Programs of Excellence in Autism Network. *Journal of Autism and Developmental Disorders, 34,* 139–150. doi:10.1023/B:JADD.0000022605.81989.cc

Padilla-Walker, L. M., Carlo, G., Christensen, K. J., & Yorgason, J. B. (2012). Bidirectional relations between authoritative parenting and adolescents' prosocial behaviors. *Journal of Research on Adolescence, 22,* 400–408. doi:10.1111/j.1532-7795.2012.00807.x

Padilla-Walker, L. M., & Christensen, K. J. (2011). Empathy and self-regulation as mediators between parenting and adolescents' prosocial behavior toward strangers, friends, and family. *Journal of Research on Adolescence, 21,* 545–551. doi:10.1111/j.1532-7795.2010.00695.x

Padilla-Walker, L. M., Harper, J. M., & Jensen, A. C. (2010). Self-regulation as a mediator between sibling relationship quality and early adolescents' positive and negative outcomes. *Journal of Family Psychology, 24,* 419–428. doi:10.1037/a0020387

Padilla-Walker, L. M., & Nelson, L. J. (2010). Parenting and adolescents' values and behaviour: The moderating role of temperament. *Journal of Moral Education, 39,* 491–509. doi:10.1080/03057240.2010.521385

Pakulak, E., & Neville, H. J. (2011). Maturational constraints on the recruitment of early processes for syntactic processing. *Journal of Cognitive Neuroscience, 23,* 2752–2765. doi:10.1162/jocn.2010.21586

Paley, V. G. (1981). *Wally's stories.* Cambridge, MA: Harvard University Press.

Palincsar, A. S., & Magnusson, S. J. (2001). The interplay of first-hand and second-hand investigations to model and support the development of scientific knowledge and reasoning. In S. M. Carver & D. Klahr (Eds.), *Cognition and instruction: Twenty-five years of progress* (pp. 151–187). Mahwah, NJ: Erlbaum.

Palladino, B. E., Nocentini, A., & Menesini, E. (2016). Evidence-based intervention against bullying and cyberbullying: Evaluation of the NoTrap! program in two independent trials. *Aggressive Behavior, 42,* 194–206. doi:10.1002/ab.21636

Pallini, S., Baiocco, R., Schneider, B. H., Madigan, S., & Atkinson, L. (2014). Early child–parent attachment and peer relations: A meta-analysis of recent research. *Journal of Family Psychology, 28,* 118–123. doi:10.1037/a0035736

Palmen, H., Vermande, M. M., Deković, M., & van Aken, M. A. G. (2011). Competence, problem behavior, and the effects of having no friends, aggressive friends, or nonaggressive friends: A four-year longitudinal study. *Merrill-Palmer Quarterly, 57,* 186–213.

Panfile, T. M., & Laible, D. J. (2012). Attachment security and child's empathy: The mediating role of emotion regulation. *Merrill-Palmer Quarterly, 58,* 1–21.

Papale, L. A., Seltzer, L. J., Madrid, A., Pollak, S. D., & Alisch, R. S. (2018). Differentially methylated genes in saliva are linked to childhood stress. *Scientific Reports, 8.*

Papastergiou, M. (2008). Are computer science and information technology still masculine fields? High school students' perceptions and career choices. *Computers & Education, 51,* 594–608.

Pardini, D. A., & Byrd, A. L. (2012). Perceptions of aggressive conflicts and others' distress in children with callous-unemotional traits: 'I'll show you who's boss, even if you suffer and I get in trouble.' *Journal of Child Psychology and Psychiatry, 53,* 283–291. doi:10.1111/j.1469-7610.2011.02487.x

Parga, J. J., Daland, R., Kesavan, K., Macey, P. M., Zeltzer, L., & Harper, R. M. (2018). A description of externally recorded womb sounds in human subjects during gestation. *PloS One, 13*(5), e0197045.

Parke, R. D., & Buriel, R. (1998). Socialization in the family: Ethnic and ecological perspectives. In W. Damon (Series Ed.) & N. Eisenberg (Vol. Ed.), *Handbook of child psychology: Vol. 3. Social, emotional, and personality development* (5th ed., pp. 463–552). New York: Wiley.

Parke, R. D., O'Neil, R., Spitzer, S., Isley, S., Welsh, M., Wang, S., . . . Cupp, R. (1997). A longitudinal assessment of sociometric stability and the behavioral correlates of children's social acceptance. *Merrill-Palmer Quarterly, 43,* 635–662. doi:10.2307/23093363

Parker, J. G., & Asher, S. R. (1993). Friendship and friendship quality in middle childhood: Links with peer group acceptance and feelings of loneliness and social dissatisfaction. *Developmental Psychology, 29,* 611–621.

Parker, K. J., & Maestripieri, D. (2011). Identifying key features of early stressful experiences that produce stress vulnerability and resilience in primates. *Neuroscience & Biobehavioral Reviews, 35*(7), 1466–1483.

Partanen, E., Kujala, T., Näätänen, R., Liitola, A., Sambeth, A., & Huotilainen, M. (2013). Learning-induced neural plasticity of speech processing before birth. *Proceedings of the National Academy of Sciences, 110*(37), 15145–15150.

Partanen, E., Kujala, T., Tervaniemi, M., & Huotilainen, M. (2013). Prenatal music exposure induces long-term neural effects. *PloS One, 8*(10), e78946.

Parten, M. (1932). Social participation among preschool children. *Journal of Abnormal and Social Psychology, 27,* 243–269. doi:10.1037/H0074524

Partners United in the Fight Against Poverty. (2015). Towards the end of child poverty. Joint statement issued by the Global Coalition Against Child Poverty and other partners. Retrieved from https://blogs.unicef.org/blog/a-joint-vision-to-end-child-poverty/

Pas, E. T., & Bradshaw, C. P. (2012). Examining the association between implementation and outcomes: State-wide scale-up of school-wide Positive Behavior Intervention and Supports. *Journal of Behavioral Health Services & Research, 39,* 417–433. doi:10.1007/s11414-012-9290-2

Pascalis, O., de Haan, M., & Nelson, C. A. (2002, May 17). Is face processing species-specific during the first year of life? *Science, 296,* 1321–1323.

Pastorelli, C., Lansford, J. E., Luengo Kanacri, B. P., Malone, P. S., Di Giunta, L., Bacchini, D., . . . Sorbring, E. (2016). Positive parenting and children's prosocial behavior in eight countries. *Journal of Child Psychology and Psychiatry, 57,* 824–834. doi:10.1111/jcpp.12477

Patterson, F., & Linden, E. (1981). *The education of Koko.* New York: Holt, Rinehart, and Winston.

Patterson, G. R. (1982). *Coercive family process.* Eugene, OR: Castalia.

Patterson, G. R. (1995). Coercion as a basis for early age of onset for arrest. In J. McCord (Ed.), *Coercion and punishment in long-term perspectives* (pp. 81–105). New York: Cambridge University Press.

Patterson, G. R., Capaldi, D., & Bank, L. (1991). An early starter model for predicting delinquency. In D. J. Pepler & K. H. Rubin (Eds.), *The development and treatment of childhood aggression* (pp. 139–168). Hillsdale, NJ: Erlbaum.

Patterson, G. R., Reid, J. B., & Dishion, T. J. (1992). *A social interactional approach: Vol. 4. Antisocial boys.* Eugene, OR: Castalia.

Paus, T. (2010). Growth of white matter in the adolescent brain: Myelin or axon? *Brain and Cognition, 72,* 26–35. doi:10.1016/j.bandc.2009.06.002

Peake, P. K., Hebl, M., & Mischel, W. (2002). Strategic attention deployment for delay of gratification in working and waiting situations. *Developmental Psychology, 38,* 313–326. doi:10.1037/0012-1649.38.2.313

Pearson, D., Rouse, H., Doswell, S., Ainsworth, C., Dawson, O., Simms, K., . . . Faulconbridge, J. (2001). Prevalence of imaginary companions in a normal child population. *Child: Care, Health and Development, 27*(1), 13–22. doi:10.1046/j.1365-2214.2001.00167.x

Pease, A. S., Fleming, P. J., Hauck, F. R., Moon, R. Y., Horne, R. S., L'Hoir, M. P., . . . Blair, P. S. (2016). Swaddling and the risk of sudden infant death syndrome: A meta-analysis. *Pediatrics, 137*(6), e20153275.

Pedersen, S., Vitaro, F., Barker, E. D., & Borge, A. I. H. (2007). The timing of middle-childhood peer rejection and friendship: Linking early behavior to early-adolescent adjustment. *Child Development, 78,* 1037–1051. doi:10.1111/j.1467-8624.2007.01051.x

Pederson, D. R., & Moran, G. (1996). Expressions of the attachment relationship outside of the Strange Situation. *Child Development, 67,* 915–927.

Peets, K., Pöyhönen, V., Junvonen, J., & Salmivalli, C. (2015). Classroom norms of bullying alter the degree to which children defend in response to their affective empathy and power. *Developmental Psychology, 51,* 913–920. doi:10.1037/a0039287

Pegg, J. E., Werker, J. F., & McLeod, P. J. (1992). Preference for infant-directed over adult-directed speech: Evidence from 7-week-old infants. *Infant Behavior and Development, 15,* 325–345. doi:10.1016/0163-6383(92)80003-D

Peisner-Feinberg, E. S., Burchinal, M. R., Clifford, R. M., Culkin, M. L., Howes, C., Kagan, S. L., & Yazejian, N. (2001). The relation of preschool child-care quality to children's cognitive and social developmental trajectories through second grade. *Child Development, 72,* 1534–1553. doi:10.1111/1467-8624.00364

Pellegrini, A. D. (2009). *The role of play in human development.* New York: Oxford University Press.

Pellegrini, A. D., Long, J. D., Roseth, C. J., Bohn, C. M., & Van Ryzin, M. (2007). A short-term longitudinal study of preschoolers' (homo sapiens) sex segregation: The role of physical activity, sex, and time. *Journal of Comparative Psychology, 121,* 282–289.

Pellizzoni, S., Siegal, M., & Surian, L. (2009). Foreknowledge, caring, and the side-effect effect in young children. *Developmental Psychology, 45,* 289–295. doi:10.1037/a0014165

Pelsser, L. M., Frankena, K., Toorman, J., & Pereira, R. R. (2017). Diet and ADHD, reviewing the evidence: A systematic review of meta-analyses of double-blind placebo-controlled trials evaluating the efficacy of diet interventions on the behavior of children with ADHD. *PloS One, 12*(1), e0169277.

Pena, M., Maki, A., Kovacic, D., Dehaene-Lambertz, G., Koizumi, H., Bouquet, F., & Mehler, J. (2003). Sounds and silence: An optical topography study of language recognition at birth. *Proceedings of the National Academy of Sciences of the United States of America, 100,* 11702–11705. doi:10.1073/pnas.1934290100

Penman-Aguilar, A., Carter, M., Snead, M. C., & Kourtis, A. P. (2013). Socioeconomic disadvantage as a social determinant of teen childbearing in the U.S. *Public Health Reports, 128,* 5–22. Retrieved from http://www.jstor.org/stable/23646793

Pennestri, M. H., Laganière, C., Bouvette-Turcot, A. A., Pokhvisneva, I., Steiner, M., Meaney, M. J., . . . Mavan Research Team. (2018). Uninterrupted infant sleep, development, and maternal mood. *Pediatrics, 142*(6), e20174330.

Pepperberg, I. M. (2009). *The Alex studies: Cognitive and communicative abilities of grey parrots.* Cambridge, MA: Harvard University Press.

Pereira, A. F., Smith, L. B., & Yu, C. (2014). A bottom-up view of toddler word learning. *Psychonomic Bulletin & Review, 21*(1), 178–185.

Perera, F. P. (2016). Multiple threats to child health from fossil fuel combustion: Impacts of air pollution and climate change. *Environmental Health Perspectives, 125*(2), 141–148.

Perfetti, C., & Stafura, J. (2014). Word knowledge in a theory of reading comprehension. *Scientific Studies of Reading, 18*(1), 22–37. doi:10.1080/10888438.2013.827687

Perlman, S. B., Kalish, C. W., & Pollak, S. D. (2008). The role of maltreatment experience in children's understanding of the antecedents of emotion. *Cognition and Emotion, 22,* 651–670. doi:10.1080/02699930701461154

Perou, R., Bitsko, R. H., Blumberg, S. J., Pastor, P., Ghandour, R. M., Gfroerer, J. C., . . . Huang, L. N. (2013, May 17). Mental health surveillance among children—United States, 2005–2011. *Morbidity and Mortality Weekly Report, 62*(02), 1–35. Retrieved from http://www.cdc.gov/mmwr/preview/mmwrhtml/su6202a1.htm?s_cid=su6202a1_w#Ta7

Perris, E. E., & Clifton, R. K. (1988). Reaching in the dark toward sound as a measure of auditory localization in infants. *Infant Behavior and Development, 11,* 473–491. doi:10.1016/0163-6383(88)90007-0

Perron, J. L., Lee, C. M., LaRoche, K. J., Ateah, C., Clément, M. È., & Chan, K. (2014). Child and parent characteristics associated with Canadian parents' reports of spanking. *Canadian Journal of Community Mental Health, 33*(2), 31–45.

Perry, C., Zorzi, M., & Ziegler, J. C. (2019). Understanding dyslexia through personalized large-scale computational models. *Psychological Science, 30*(3), 386–395. doi:10.1177/0956797618823540

Perry, D. G., Bussey, K., & Freiberg, K. (1981). Impact of adults' appeals for sharing on the development of altruistic dispositions in children. *Journal of Experimental Child Psychology, 32,* 127–138. doi:10.1016/0022-0965(81)90098-9

Perry, D. G., Perry, L. C., & Rasmussen, P. (1986). Cognitive social learning mediators of aggression. *Child Development, 57,* 700–711. doi:10.2307/1130347

Perry, D. G., Perry, L. C., & Weiss, R. J. (1989). Sex differences in the consequences that children anticipate for aggression. *Developmental Psychology, 25,* 312–319. doi:10.1037/0012-1649.25.2.312

Perry, L. K., & Saffran, J. R. (2017). Is a pink cow still a cow? Individual differences in toddlers' vocabulary knowledge and lexical representations. *Cognitive science, 41*(4), 1090–1105.

Perry, L. K., Samuelson, L. K., & Burdinie, J. B. (2014). High-chair philosophers: The impact of seating context-dependent exploration on children's naming biases. *Developmental Science, 17*(5), 757–765.

Pester, D., Lenz, A. S., & Dell'Aquila, J. (2019). Meta-analysis of single-case evaluations of child-centered play therapy for treating mental health symptoms. *International Journal of Play Therapy.* https://doi-org.ezproxy.lib.utexas.edu/10.1037/pla0000098

Petanjek, Z., Judaš, M., Šimić, G., Rašin, M. R., Uylings, H. B., Rakic, P., & Kostović, I. (2011). Extraordinary neoteny of synaptic spines in the human prefrontal cortex. *Proceedings of the National Academy of Sciences, 108*(32), 13281–13286.

Peter, T., Edkins, T., Watson, R., Adjei, J., Homma, Y., & Saewyc, E. (2017). Trends in suicidality among sexual minority and heterosexual students in a Canadian population-based cohort study. *Psychology of Sexual Orientation and Gender Diversity, 4*(1), 115.

Peter, T., Taylor, C., & Chamberland, L. (2015). A queer day in Canada: Examining Canadian high school students' experiences with school-based homophobia in two large-scale studies. *Journal of Homosexuality, 62*(2), 186–206. doi:10.1080/00918369.2014.969057

Peters, R. D., Bradshaw, A. J., Petrunka, K., Nelson, G., Herry, Y., Craig, W., & Rossiter, M. (2010). The "Better Beginnings, Better Futures" ecological, community-based early childhood prevention project: Findings from grade 3 to grade 9. *Monographs of the Society for Research in Child Development, 75*(3), 1–176.

Peters, R. D., Petrunka, K., Khan, S., Howell-Moneta, A., Nelson, G., Pancer, S. M., & Loomis, C. (2016). Cost-savings analysis of the better beginnings, better futures community-based project for young children and their families: A 10-year follow-up. *Prevention Science, 17*(2), 237–247.

Peterson, C. C., Wellman, H. M., & Liu, D. (2005). Steps in theory-of-mind development for children with deafness or autism. *Child Development, 76,* 502–517. doi:10.1111/j.1467-8624.2005.00859.x

Peterson, R. L., Pennington, B. F., & Olson, R. K. (2013). Subtypes of developmental dyslexia: Testing the predictions of the dual-route and connectionist frameworks. *Cognition, 126*(1), 20–38. doi:10.1016/j.cognition.2012.08.007

Petitto, L. A., Holowka, S., Sergio, L. E., & Ostry, D. (2001, September 6). Language rhythms in baby hand movements. *Nature, 413,* 35–36. doi:10.1038/35092613

Petitto, L. A., & Marentette, P. F. (1991, March 22). Babbling in the manual mode: Evidence for the ontogeny of language. *Science, 251,* 1493–1496.

Petitto, L. A., Zatorre, R. J., Gauna, K., Nikelski, E. J., Dostie, D., & Evans, A. C. (2000). Speech-like cerebral activity in profoundly deaf people processing signed languages: Implications for the neural basis of human language. *Proceedings of the National Academy of Sciences, 97*(25), 13961–13966.

Petrides, K. V., Sangareau, Y., Furnham, A., & Frederickson, N. (2006). Trait emotional intelligence and children's peer relations at school. *Social Development, 15,* 537e547. doi:10.1111/j.1467-9507.2006.00355.x

Petrill, S. A., Deater-Deckard, K., Thompson, L. A., Schatschneider, C., Dethorne, L. S., & Vandenbergh, D. J. (2007). Longitudinal genetic analysis of early reading: The Western Reserve Reading Project. *Reading and Writing, 20,* 127–146. doi:10.1007/s11145-006-9021-2

Petrill, S. A., Lipton, P. A., Hewitt, J. K., Plomin, R., Cherny, S. S., Corley, R., & DeFries, J. C. (2004). Genetic and environmental contributions to general cognitive ability through the first 16 years of life. *Developmental Psychology, 40,* 805–812. doi:10.1037/0012-1649.40.5.805

Pettit, G. S., Brown, E. G., Mize, J., & Lindsey, E. (1998). Mothers' and fathers' socializing behaviors in three contexts: Links with children's peer competence. *Merrill-Palmer Quarterly, 44,* 173–193. doi:10.2307/23093665

Pettit, G. S., Lansford, J. E., Malone, P. S., Dodge, K. A., & Bates, J. E. (2010). Domain specificity in relationship history, social information processing, and violent behavior in early adulthood. *Journal of Personality and Social Psychology, 98*(2), 190–200.

Pew Research Center. (2015, December 17). Parenting in America: Outlook, worries, aspirations are strongly linked to financial situation. Retrieved from http://www.pewsocialtrends.org/files/2015/12/2015-12-17_parenting-in-america_FINAL.pdf

Pew Research Center. (2016, January 7). Parents, teens and digital monitoring. Retrieved from http://www.pewinternet.org/files/2016/01/PI_2016-01-07_Parents-Teens-Digital-Monitoring_FINAL.pdf

Phillips, A. T., Wellman, H. M., & Spelke, E. S. (2002). Infants' ability to connect gaze and emotional expression to intentional action. *Cognition, 85,* 53–78.

Phipps, M. G., Blume, J. D., & DeMonner, S. M. (2002). Young maternal age associated with increased risk of postneonatal death. *Obstetrics and Gynecology, 100,* 481–486.

Piaget, J. (1926). *The language and thought of the child* (M. Warden, Trans.). New York: Harcourt Brace & Company. (Original work published 1923)

Piaget, J. (1952a). *The child's concept of number* (C. Gattegno & F. M. Hodgson, Trans.). London: Routledge.

Piaget, J. (1952b). *The origins of intelligence in children* (M. Cook, Trans.). Oxford: International Universities Press.

Piaget, J. (1954). *The construction of reality in the child* (M. Cook, Trans.). New York: Basic Books.

Piaget, J. (1964). Development and learning. In R. E. Ripple & V. N. Rockcastle (Eds.), *Piaget rediscovered* (pp. 7–20). Ithaca, NY: Cornell University.

Piaget, J. (1965). *The moral judgment of the child* (M. Gabain, Trans.). New York: Free Press. (Original work published 1932)

Piaget, J. (1969). *The child's conception of time* (A. J. Pomerans, Trans.). London: Routledge & K. Paul.

Piaget, J. (1971). *The construction of reality in the child* (M. Cook, Trans.). New York: Ballantine. (Original work published 1954)

Piaget, J. (1972). *Psychology and epistemology: Towards a theory of knowledge* (P. A. Wells, Trans.). Harmondsworth, England: Penguin.

Piaget, J., & Inhelder, B. (1977). The child's conception of space. In H. E. Gruber & J. J. Vonèche (Eds.), *The essential Piaget* (pp. 576–642). New York: Basic Books. [Reprinted from *The child's conception of space* by Piaget, J., & Inhelder, B. (F. J. Langdon & J. L. Lunzer, Trans.), 1956, London: Routledge & K. Paul.]

Piasta, S. B., & Wagner, R. K. (2010). Developing early literacy skills: A meta-analysis of alphabet learning and instruction. *Reading Research Quarterly, 45,* 8–38. doi:10.1598/RRQ.45.1.2

Piazza, E. A., Hasenfratz, L., Hasson, U., & Lew-Williams, C. (2018). Infant and adult brains are coupled to the dynamics of natural communication. *bioRxiv,* 359810.

Piazza, E. A., Iordan, M. C., & Lew-Williams, C. (2017). Mothers consistently alter their unique vocal fingerprints when communicating with infants. *Current Biology, 27*(20), 3162–3167.

Piazza, M. (2011). Neurocognitive start-up tools for symbolic number representations. In S. Dehaene & E. Brannon (Eds.), *Space, time, and number in the brain: Searching for the foundations of mathematical thought* (pp. 267–285). London: Elsevier.

Pickron, C. B., Fava, E., & Scott, L. S. (2017). Follow my gaze: Face race and sex influence gaze-cued attention in infancy. *Infancy, 22*(5), 626–644.

Pierce, K., Marinero, S., Hazin, R., McKenna, B., Barnes, C. C., & Malige, A. (2016). Eye tracking reveals abnormal visual preference for geometric images as an early biomarker of an autism spectrum disorder subtype associated with increased symptom severity. *Biological Psychiatry, 79*(8), 657–666.

Pierce, T. (2009). Social anxiety and technology: Face-to-face communication versus technological communication among teens. *Computers in Human Behavior, 25,* 1367–1372. doi:10.1016/j.chb.2009.06.003

Pierroutsakos, S. L., & DeLoache, J. S. (2003). Infants' manual exploration of pictorial objects varying in realism. *Infancy, 4,* 141–156. doi:10.1207/S15327078IN0401_7

Pietschnig, J., & Voracek, M. (2015). One century of global IQ gains: A formal meta-analysis of the Flynn effect (1909–2013). *Perspectives on Psychological Science, 10*(3), 282–306. doi:10.1177/1745691615577701

Pike, A., & Oliver, B. R. (2017). Child behavior and sibling relationship quality: A cross-lagged analysis. *Journal of Family Psychology, 31,* 250–255. doi:10.1037/fam0000248

Pilgrim, C., Luo, Q., Urberg, K. A., & Fang, X. (1999). Influence of peers, parents, and individual characteristics on adolescent drug use in two cultures. *Merrill-Palmer Quarterly, 45,* 85–107. doi:10.2307/23093315

Pillow, B. H. (1988). The development of children's beliefs about the mental world. *Merrill-Palmer Quarterly, 34,* 1–32.

Pingault, J. B., Côté, S. M., Lacourse, E., Galéra, C., Vitaro, F., & Tremblay, R. E. (2013). Childhood hyperactivity, physical aggression and criminality: A 19-year prospective population-based study. *PloS One, 8*(5), e62594.

Pinker, S. (1994). *The language instinct: The new science of language and mind.* Harmondsworth, Middlesex, England: Allen Lane, Penguin Press.

Planalp, E. M., & Braungart-Rieker, J. M. (2015). Trajectories of regulatory behaviors in early infancy: Determinants of infant self-distraction and self-comforting. *Infancy, 20*(2), 129–159. doi:10.1111/infa.12068

Planalp, E. M., Van Hulle, C., Lemery-Chalfant, K., & Goldsmith, H. H. (2017). Genetic and environmental contributions to the development of positive affect in infancy. *Emotion, 17*(3), 412.

Plante, I., Théorêt, M., & Favreau, O. E. (2009). Student gender stereotypes: Contrasting the perceived maleness and femaleness of mathematics and language. *Educational Psychology, 29,* 385–405.

Plato. (1961). The laws. In E. Hamilton & H. Cairns (Eds.), *The collected dialogues of Plato.* Princeton, NJ: Princeton University Press.

Plomin, R. (2018). *Blueprint: How DNA makes us who we are.* Cambridge, MA: MIT Press.

Plomin, R., & Daniels, D. (2011). Why are children in the same family so different from one another? *International Journal of Epidemiology, 40*(3), 563–582. doi:10.1093/ije/dyq148

Plomin, R., & Deary, I. J. (2015). Genetics and intelligence differences: Five special findings. *Molecular Psychiatry, 20*(1), 98–108.

Plomin, R., DeFries, J. C., & McClearn, G. E. (2008). *Behavioral genetics.* New York: Macmillan.

Plomin, R., DeFries, J. C., Knopik, V. S., & Neiderhiser, J. M. (2012). *Behavioral genetics: A primer* (6th ed.). New York: Worth.

Plomin, R., DeFries, J. C., Knopik, V. S., & Neiderhiser, J. M. (2016). Top 10 replicated findings from behavioral genetics. *Perspectives on Psychological Science, 11*(1), 3–23.

Plomin, R., Fulker, D. W., Corley, R., & DeFries, J. C. (1997). Nature, nurture, and cognitive development from 1 to 16 years: A parent-offspring adoption study. *Psychological Science, 8,* 442–447.

Pluess, M., & Belsky, J. (2010). Differential susceptibility to parenting and quality child care. *Developmental Psychology, 46,* 379–390. doi:10.1037/a0015203

Plumert, J. M., & Kearney, J. K. (2018). Timing is almost everything: How children perceive and act on dynamic affordances. *Advances in Child Development and Behavior, 55,* 173–204. doi:10.1016/bs.acdb.2018.05.002

Polanczyk, G. V., Salum, G. A., Sugaya, L. S., Caye, A., & Rohde, L. A. (2015). Annual research review:

A meta-analysis of the worldwide prevalence of mental disorders in children and adolescents. *Journal of Child Psychology and Psychiatry, 56,* 345–365. doi:10.1111/jcpp.12381

Polderman, T. J., Benyamin, B., De Leeuw, C. A., Sullivan, P. F., Van Bochoven, A., Visscher, P. M., & Posthuma, D. (2015). Meta-analysis of the heritability of human traits based on fifty years of twin studies. *Nature Genetics, 47,* 702–709.

Polka, L., & Sundara, M. (2012). Word segmentation in monolingual infants acquiring Canadian English and Canadian French: Native language, cross dialect, and cross language comparisons. *Infancy, 17*(2), 198–232.

Polka, L., & Werker, J. F. (1994). Developmental changes in perception of nonnative vowel contrasts. *Journal of Experimental Psychology: Human Perception and Performance, 20,* 421–435.

Pollak, S. D., Cicchetti, D., Hornung, K., & Reed, A. (2000). Recognizing emotion in faces: Developmental effects of child abuse and neglect. *Developmental Psychology, 36,* 679–688.

Pollak, S. D., Messner, M., Kistler, D. J., & Cohn, J. F. (2009). Development of perceptual expertise in emotion recognition. *Cognition, 110,* 242–247. doi:10.1016/j.cognition.2008.10.010

Pons, F., Bosch, L., & Lewkowicz, D. J. (2015). Bilingualism modulates infants' selective attention to the mouth of a talking face. *Psychological Science, 26*(4), 490–498.

Pons, F., Lewkowicz, D. J., Soto-Faraco, S., & Sebastián-Gallés, N. (2009). Narrowing of intersensory speech perception in infancy. *Proceedings of the National Academy of Sciences of the United States of America, 106,* 10598–10602. doi:10.1073/pnas.0904134106

Poole, D. A., Bruck, M., & Pipe, M. E. (2011). Forensic interviewing aids: Do props help children answer questions about touching? *Current Directions in Psychological Science, 20,* 11–15. doi:10.1177/0963721410388804

Poon, C., Saewyc, E., & Chen, W. (2012). Enacted stigma, problem substance use, and protective factors among Asian sexual minority youth in British Columbia. *Canadian Journal of Community Mental Health, 30*(2), 47–64.

Popova, S., Lange, S., Chudley, A. E., Reynolds, J. N., & Rehm, J. (2018, April). World Health Organization International Study on the Prevalence of Fetal Alcohol Spectrum Disorder (FASD) Canadian Component. A report prepared by the Institute for Mental Health Policy Research, Centre for Addiction and Mental Health. Retrieved from https://canfasd.ca/wp-content/uploads/sites/35/2018/05/2018-Popova-WHO-FASD-Prevalance-Report.pdf

Popova, S., Lange, S., Probst, C., Gmel, G., & Rehm, J. (2017a). Estimation of national, regional, and global prevalence of alcohol use during pregnancy and fetal alcohol syndrome: A systematic review and meta-analysis. *Lancet Global Health, 5*(3), e290–e299.

Popova, S., Lange, S., Probst, C., Parunashvili, N., & Rehm, J. (2017b). Prevalence of alcohol consumption during pregnancy and fetal alcohol spectrum disorders among the general and Aboriginal populations in Canada and the United States. *European Journal of Medical Genetics, 60*(1), 32–48.

Popp, D., Laursen, B., Kerr, M., Stattin, H., & Burk, W. K. (2008). Modeling homophily over time with an actor-partner interdependence model. *Developmental Psychology, 44,* 1028–1039. doi:10.1037/0012-1649.44.4.1028

Porges, S. W. (2007). The polyvagal perspective. *Biological Psychology, 74,* 116–143. doi:10.1016/j.biopsycho.2006.06.009

Posada, G., Lu, T., Trumbell, J., Trudel, M., Plata, S. J., Peña, P. P., . . . Lay, K. (2013). Is the secure base phenomenon evident here, there, and anywhere? A cross-cultural study of child behavior and experts' definitions. *Child Development, 84,* 1896–1905. doi:10.111/cdev.12084

Posada, G., Trumbell, J., Noblega, M., Plata, S., Peña, P., Carbonell, O. A., & Lu, T. (2016). Maternal sensitivity and child secure base use in early childhood: Studies in different cultural contexts. *Child Development, 87,* 297–311. doi:10.111/cdev.12454

Posada, G., Vaughn, B. E., Veríssimo, M., Lu, T., Nichols, O. I., El-Sheikh, M., . . . Kaloustian, G. (2019). Preschoolers' secure base script representations predict teachers' ratings of social competence in two independent samples. *Attachment & Human Development, 21,* 238–252. doi:10.1080/14616734.2019.1575547

Posner, M. I., Rothbart, M. K., & Sheese, B. E. (2007). Attention genes. *Developmental Science, 10,* 24–29.

Potter, D. (2010). Psychosocial well-being and the relationship between divorce and children's academic achievement. *Journal of Marriage and Family, 72,* 933–946. doi:10.1111/j.1741-3737.2010.00740.x

Potter, D. (2012). Same-sex parent families and children's academic achievement. *Journal of Marriage & Family, 74,* 556–571. doi:10.1111/j.1741-3737.2012.00966.x

Poulin, F., & Pedersen, S. (2007). Developmental changes in gender composition of friendship networks in adolescent girls and boys. *Developmental Psychology, 43,* 1484–1496. doi:10.1037/0012-1649.43.6.1484

Poulin, F., Kiesner, J., Pedersen, S., & Dishion, T. J. (2011). A short-term longitudinal analysis of friendship selection on early adolescent substance use. *Journal of Adolescence, 34,* 249–256. doi:10.1016/j.adolescence.2010.05.006

Poulin-Dubois, D. (1999). Infants' distinction between animate and inanimate objects: The origins of naive psychology. In P. Rochat (Ed.), *Early social cognition: Understanding others in the first months of life* (pp. 257–280). Mahwah, NJ: Erlbaum.

Poulin-Dubois, D., Blaye, A., Coutya, J., & Bialystok, E. (2011). The effects of bilingualism on toddlers' executive functioning. *Journal of Experimental Child Psychology, 108,* 567–579. doi:10.1016/j.jecp.2010.10.009

Poulin-Dubois, D., Brooker, I., & Polonia, A. (2011). Infants prefer to imitate a reliable person. *Infant Behavior and Development, 34*(2), 303–309.

Poulin-Dubois, D., & Brosseau-Liard, P. (2016). The developmental origins of selective social learning. *Current Directions in Psychological Science, 25*(1), 60–64. doi:10.1177/0963721415613962

Poulin-Dubois, D., Serbin, L. A., Eichstedt, J. A., Sen, M. G., & Beissel, C. F. (2002). Men don't put on make-up: Toddlers' knowledge of the gender stereotyping of household activities. *Social Development, 11,* 166–181. doi:10.1111/1467-9507.00193

Powell, B., Cooper, G., Hoffman, K., & Marvin, B. (2014). *The Circle of Security Intervention: Enhancing attachment in early parent–child relationships.* New York: Guilford Press.

Power, T. G. (2004). Stress and coping in childhood: The parents' role. *Parenting: Science and Practice, 4,* 271–317.

Powers, K. L., Brooks, P. J., Aldrich, N. J., Palladino, M. A., & Alfieri, L. (2013). Effects of video-game play on information processing: A meta-analytic investigation. *Psychonomic Bulletin & Review, 20,* 1055–1079. doi:10.3758/s13423-013-0418-z

Powlishta, K. K. (1995). Intergroup processes in childhood: Social categorization and sex role development. *Developmental Psychology, 31,* 781–788. doi:10.1037/0012-1649.31.5.781

Pratt, M. W., Hunsberger, B., Pancer, S. M., & Alisat, S. (2003). A longitudinal analysis of personal values socialization: Correlates of a moral self-ideal in late adolescence. *Social Development, 12,* 563–585. doi:10.1111/1467-9507.00249

Pressley, M., & Hilden, K. (2006). Cognitive strategies: Production deficiencies and successful strategy instruction everywhere. In W. Damon & R. M. Lerner (Series Eds.) & D. Kuhn & R. S. Siegler (Vol. Eds.), *Handbook of child psychology: Vol. 2. Cognition, perception, and language* (6th ed., pp. 511–556). Hoboken, NJ: Wiley.

Preves, S. E. (2003). *Intersex and identity: The contested self.* New Brunswick, NJ: Rutgers University Press.

Price, C. S., Thompson, W. W., Goodson, B., Weintraub, E. S., Croen, L. A., Hinrichsen, V. L., . . . DeStefano, F. (2010). Prenatal and infant exposure to thimerosal from vaccines and immunoglobulins and risk of autism. *Pediatrics, 126,* 656–664. doi:10.1542/peds.2010-0309

Price, H. L., & Roberts, K. P. (2011). The effects of an intensive training and feedback program on police and social workers' investigative interviews of children. *Canadian Journal of Behavioural Science, 43,* 235–244.

Prinstein, M. J., & Cillessen, A. H. N. (2003). Forms and functions of adolescent peer aggression associated with high levels of peer status. *Merrill-Palmer Quarterly, 49,* 310–342. doi:10.2307/23096058

Prinstein, M. J., Rancourt, D., Adelman, C. B., Ahlich, E., Smith, J., & Guerry, J. D. (2018). Peer status and psychopathology. In W. M. Bukowski, B. Laursen, & K. H. Rubin (Eds.), *Handbook of peer interactions, relationships, and groups* (2nd ed., pp. 322–346). New York: Guilford.

Prinz, R. J., Sanders, M. R., Shapiro, C. J., Whitaker, D. J., & Lutzker, J. R. (2009). Population-based prevention of child maltreatment: The US Triple P System population trial. *Prevention Science, 10,* 1–12. doi:10.1007/s11121-009-0123-3

Provencher, C., Milan, A., Hallman, S., & D'Aoust, C. (2018). Fertility: Overview, 2012 to 2016. *Statistics Canada Catalogue, 91-209-X.* Retrieved from https://www150.statcan.gc.ca/n1/en/pub/91-209-x/2018001/article/54956-eng.pdf?st=4QXlSxwx

Provenzi, L., Giorda, R., Beri, S., & Montirosso, R. (2016). SLC6A4 methylation as an epigenetic marker of life adversity exposures in humans: A systematic review of literature. *Neuroscience & Biobehavioral Reviews, 71,* 7–20.

Przybylski, A. K., & Weinstein, N. (2017). A large-scale test of the Goldilocks Hypothesis: Quantifying the relations between digital-screen use and the mental well-being of adolescents. *Psychological Science, 28*(2), 204–215.

Public Health Agency of Canada. (2009). What mothers say: The Canadian maternity experiences survey. Retrieved from http://www.publichealth.gc.ca/ths-ssg-survey-eng.php

Public Health Agency of Canada. (2012a). Child maltreatment in Canada. Retrieved from https://www.canada.ca/en/public-health/services/health-promotion/stop-family-violence/prevention-resource-centre/children/child-maltreatment-canada.html#Chi

Public Health Agency of Canada. (2012b). The impact of the Aboriginal Head Start in Urban and Northern Communities (AHSUNC) program on school readiness skills. Retrieved from https://www.canada.ca/en/indigenous-services-canada/services/first-nations-inuit-health/family-health/healthy-child-development/aboriginal-head-start-reserve-first-nations-inuit-health-canada/school-readiness.html

Public Health Agency of Canada. (2013). Perinatal health indicators for Canada 2013: A report of the Canadian perinatal surveillance system. Ottawa, 2013.

Public Health Agency of Canada. (2017a). Evaluation of the Aboriginal Head Start in Urban and Northern Communities Program 2011–2012 to 2015–2016. Retrieved from https://www.canada.ca/en/public-health/corporate/transparency/corporate-management-reporting/evaluation/2011-2012-2015-2016-aboriginal-head-start-urban-and-northern-communities-program.html

Public Health Agency of Canada. (2017b). Perinatal health indicators for Canada 2017: A report from the Canadian perinatal surveillance system. Cat.: HP7-1E-PDF ISBN: 2371-9036 Pub.: 160323

Public Health England. (2018). Official statistics: Breastfeeding prevalence at 6–8 weeks after birth (experimental statistics): 2017/18 statistical commentary (October 2018 release). London: Crown. Retrieved from https://assets.publishing.service.gov.uk/government/uploads/system/uploads/attachment_data/file/750442/2017_2018_Annual_Breastfeeding_Statistical_Commentary.pdf

Puig, J., Englund, M. M., Simpson, J. A., & Collins, W. A. (2013). Predicting adult physical illness from infant attachment: A prospective longitudinal study. *Health Psychology, 32*(4), 409–417. doi:10.1037/a0028889

Puma, M., Bell, S., Cook, R., Heid, C., Broene, P., Jenkins, F., . . . Downer, J. T. (2012). *Third grade follow-up to the Head Start impact study: Final report* [Executive summary] (OPRE Report 2012-45b). Washington, DC: U.S. Administration for Children and Families, Office of Planning, Research and Evaluation. Retrieved from http://eric.ed.gov/?id=ED539264

Punamäki, R.-L., Wallenius, M., Hölttö, H., Nygård, C.-H., & Rimpelä, A. (2009). The associations between information and communication technology (ICT) and peer and parent relations in early adolescence. *International Journal of Behavioral Development, 33,* 556–564. doi:10.1177/0165025409343828

Qiu, A., Mori, S., & Miller, M. I. (2015). Diffusion tensor imaging for understanding brain development in early life. *Annual Review of Psychology, 66,* 853–876.

Quine, W. V. O. (1960). *Word and object.* Cambridge, MA: Technology Press of the Massachusetts Institute of Technology.

Quinn, G. E., Shin, C. H., Maguire, M. G., & Stone, R. A. (1999, May 1). Myopia and ambient lighting at night. *Nature, 399,* 113–114.

Quinn, J. M., Wagner, R. K., Petscher, Y., & Lopez, D. (2015). Developmental relations between vocabulary knowledge and reading comprehension: A latent change score modeling study. *Child Development, 86*(1), 159–175. doi:10.1111/cdev.12292

Quinn, M., & Hennessy, E. (2010). Peer relationships across the preschool to school transition. *Early Education and Development, 21,* 825–842. doi:10.1080/10409280903329013

Quinn, P. C. (2005). Developmental constraints on the representation of spatial relation information: Evidence from preverbal infants. In L. Carlson & E. van der Zee (Eds.), *Functional features in language and space: Insights from perception, categorization, and development* (pp. 293–309). New York: Oxford University Press.

Quinn, P. C., & Eimas, P. D. (1996). Perceptual organization and categorization in young infants. In C. Rovee-Collier & L. P. Lipsitt (Eds.), *Advances in infancy research* (Vol. 10, pp. 1–36). Westport, CT: Ablex.

Quinn, P. C., Lee, K., & Pascalis, O. (2019). Face processing in infancy and beyond: The case of social categories. *Annual Review of Psychology, 70,* 165–189.

Quinn, P. C., Yahr, J., Kuhn, A., Slater, A. M., & Pascalis, O. (2002). Representation of the gender of human faces by infants: A preference for female. *Perception, 31,* 1109–1121.

Raby, K. L., Cicchetti, D., Carlson, E. A., Egeland, B., & Collins, W. A. (2013). Genetic contributions to continuity and change in attachment security: A prospective, longitudinal investigation from infancy to young adulthood. *Journal of Child Psychology and Psychiatry, 54,* 1223–1230. doi:10.111/jcpp.12093

Radke-Yarrow, M., & Zahn-Waxler, C. (1984). Roots, motives, and patterns in children's prosocial behavior. In E. Staub, D. Bar-Tal, J. Karylowski, & J. Reykowski (Eds.), *Development and maintenance of prosocial behavior: International perspectives on positive behavior* (pp. 81–99). New York: Plenum Press.

Raffan, E., Dennis, R. J., O'Donovan, C. J., Becker, J. M., Scott, R. A., Smith, S. P., . . . Summers, K. M. (2016). A deletion in the canine POMC gene is associated with weight and appetite in obesity-prone Labrador retriever dogs. *Cell Metabolism, 23*(5), 893–900.

Rafferty, Y., & Shinn, M. (1991). The impact of homelessness on children. *American Psychologist, 46,* 1170–1179. doi:10.1037/0003-066X.46.11.1170

Raghavan, R., Camarata, S., White, K., Barbaresi, W., Parish, S., & Krahn, G. (2018). Population health in pediatric speech and language disorders: Available data sources and a research agenda for the field. *Journal of Speech, Language, and Hearing Research, 61*(5), 1279–1291.

Rai, R., & Regan, L. (2006, August 12). Recurrent miscarriage. *Lancet, 368,* 601–611. doi:10.1016/S0140-6736(06)69204-0

Raikes, H. A., & Thompson, R. A. (2008). Attachment security and parenting quality predict children's problem-solving, attributions, and loneliness with peers. *Attachment and Human Development, 10,* 319–344. doi:10.1080/14616730802113620

Rakison, D. H., & Krogh, L. (2012). Does causal action facilitate causal perception in infants younger than 6 months of age? *Developmental Science, 15*(1), 43–54. doi:10.1111/j.1467-7687.2011.01096.x

Rakison, D. H., & Lupyan, G. (2008). Developing object concepts in infancy: An associative learning perspective. *Monographs of the Society for Research in Child Development, 73*(1). doi:10.1111/j.1540-5834.2008.00454.x

Rakoczy, H., Behne, T., Clüver, A., Dallmann, S., Weidner, S., & Waldmann, M. R. (2015). The side-effect effect in children is robust and not specific to the moral status of action effects. *PloS ONE, 10*(7), e0132933. doi:10.1371/journal.pone.0132933

Ramani, G. B., & Siegler, R. S. (2008). Promoting broad and stable improvements in low-income children's numerical knowledge through playing number board games. *Child Development, 79,* 375–394. doi:10.1111/j.1467-8624.2007.01131.x

Ramenzoni, V. C., & Liszkowski, U. (2016). The social reach: 8-month-olds reach for unobtainable objects in the presence of another person. *Psychological Science, 27*(9), 1278–1285. doi:10.1177/0956797616659938

Ramey, C. T., Campbell, F. A., Burchinal, M., Skinner, M. L., Gardner, D. M., & Ramey, S. L. (2000). Persistent effects of early childhood education on high-risk children and their mothers. *Applied Developmental Science, 4,* 2–14.

Ramey, C. T., & Ramey, S. L. (2004). Early learning and school readiness: Can early intervention make a difference? *Merrill-Palmer Quarterly, 50,* 471–491.

Ramirez, G., & Beilock, S. L. (2011, January 14). Writing about testing worries boosts exam performance in the classroom. *Science, 331,* 211–213.

Ramirez, G., Gunderson, E. A., Levine, S. C., & Beilock, S. L. (2012). Spatial anxiety relates to spatial abilities as a function of working memory in children. *Quarterly Journal of Experimental Psychology, 65,* 474–487. doi:10.1080/17470218.2011.616214

Rao, N., & Stewart, S. M. (1999). Cultural influences on sharer and recipient behavior: Sharing in Chinese and Indian preschool children. *Journal of Cross-Cultural Psychology, 30,* 219–241. doi:10.1177/0022022199030002005

Rasbash, J., Jenkins, J., O'Connor, T. G., Tackett, J., & Reiss, D. (2011). A social relations model of observed family negativity and positivity using a genetically informative sample. *Journal of Personality and Social Psychology, 100,* 474–491. doi:10.1037/a0020931

Rasmi, S., Chuang, S. S., & Hennig, K. (2015). The acculturation gap-distress model: Extensions and application to Arab Canadian families. *Cultural Diversity and Ethnic Minority Psychology, 21*(4), 630–642. doi:10.1037/cdp0000014

Rasmussen, S. (2011). 31% believe in ghosts. *Rasmussen Reports.* Retrieved from http://www.rasmussenreports.com/public_content/-lifestyle/-holidays/october_2011/31_believe_in_ghosts

Ratner, N., & Bruner, J. (1978). Games, social exchange and the acquisition of language. *Journal of Child Language, 5,* 391–401.

Rattan, A., Good, C., & Dweck, C. S. (2012). "It's ok—Not everyone can be good at math": Instructors with an entity theory comfort (and demotivate) students. *Journal of Experimental Social Psychology, 48,* 731–737. doi:10.1016/j.jesp.2011.12.012

Raub, A., Nandi, A., Earle, A., Chorny, N. D. G., Wong, E., Chung, P., . . . Heyman, J. (2018). *Paid parental leave: A detailed look at approaches across OECD countries.* Los Angeles: WORLD Policy Analysis Center. Retrieved from https://www.worldpolicycenter.org/sites/default/files/WORLD%20Report%20-%20

Parental%20Leave%20OECD%20Country%20 Approaches_0.pdf

Raval, V. V., & Martini, T. S. (2009). Maternal socialization of children's anger, sadness, and physical pain in two communities in Gujarat, India. *International Journal of Behavioral Development, 33,* 215–229.

Raval, V. V., & Martini, T. S. (2011). "Making the child understand": Socialization of emotion in urban India. *Journal of Family Psychology, 25,* 847–856. doi:10.1037/a0025240

Ray, D. C. (2011). *Advanced play therapy: Essential conditions, knowledge, and skills for child practice.* New York: Routledge. doi:10.4324/9780203837269

Recchia, H. E. & Howe, N. (2009). Associations between social understanding, sibling relationship quality, and siblings' conflict strategies and outcomes. *Child Development, 80*(5), 1564–1578.

Recchia, H. E., Wainryb, C., Bourne, S., & Pasupathi, M. (2015), Children's and adolescents' accounts of helping and hurting others: Lessons about the development of moral agency. *Child Development, 86,* 864–876. doi:10.1111/cdev.12349

Reed, J., Hirsh-Pasek, K., & Golinkoff, R. M. (2017). Learning on hold: Cell phones sidetrack parent–child interactions. *Developmental psychology, 53*(8), 1428.

Reich, S. M., Subrahmanyam, K., & Espinoza, G. (2012). Friending, IMing, and hanging out face-to-face: Overlap in adolescents' online and offline social networks. *Developmental Psychology, 48,* 356–368. doi:10.1037/a0026980

Reid, V. M., Dunn, K., Young, R. J., Amu, J., Donovan, T., & Reissland, N. (2017). The human fetus preferentially engages with face-like visual stimuli. *Current Biology, 27*(12), 1825–1828.

Reijntjes, A., Thomaes, S., Kamphuis, J. H., Bushman, B. J., de Castro, B. O., & Telch, M. J. (2011). Explaining the paradoxical rejection-aggression link: The mediating effects of hostile intent attributions, anger, and decreases in state self-esteem on peer rejection-induced aggression in youth. *Personality and Social Psychology Bulletin, 37,* 955–963. doi:10.1177/0146167211410247

Reilly, D. (2012). Gender, culture, and sex-typed cognitive abilities. *PLoS ONE, 7*(7).

Reilly, D., Neumann, D. L., & Andrews, G. (2015). Sex differences in mathematics and science achievement: A meta-analysis of national assessment of educational progress assessments. *Journal of Educational Psychology, 107*(3), 645–662. http://dx.doi.org/10.1037/edu0000012

Reiser, B., & Faraggi, D. (1999). Confidence intervals for the overlapping coefficient: the normal equal variance case. *Journal of the Royal Statistical Society, 48*(3), 413–418.

Reissland, N., & Shepherd, J. (2006). The effect of maternal depressed mood on infant emotional reaction in a surprise-eliciting situation. *Infant Mental Health Journal, 27,* 173–187. doi:10.1002/imhj.20087

Ren, A., Qiu, X., Jin, L., Ma, J., Li, Z., Zhang, L., . . . Zhu, T. (2011). Association of selected persistent organic pollutants in the placenta with the risk of neural tube defects. *Proceedings of the National Academy of Sciences of the United States of America, 108,* 12770–12775. doi:10.1073/pnas.1105209108

Ren, H., Zhou, Z., Liu, W., Wang, X., & Yin, Z. (2017). Excessive homework, inadequate sleep, physical inactivity and screen viewing time are major contributors to high paediatric obesity. *Acta Paediatrica, 106*(1), 120–127.

Renken, B., Egeland, B., Marvinney, D., Mangelsdorf, S., & Sroufe, L. A. (1989). Early childhood antecedents of aggression and passive-withdrawal in early elementary school. *Journal of Personality, 57,* 257–281. doi:10.1111/j.1467-6494.1989.tb00483.x

Renouf, A., Brendgen, M., Séguin, J. R., Vitaro, F., Boivin, M., Dionne, G., . . . Pérusse, D. (2010). Interactive links between theory of mind, peer victimization, and reactive and proactive aggression. *Journal of Abnormal Child Psychology, 38,* 1109–1123. doi:10.1007/s10802-010-9432-z

Research America. (2018, June 18). *Americans view child abuse and neglect as a serious public health problem.* Retrieved from https://www.researchamerica.org/news-events/news/americans-view-child-abuse-and-neglect-serious-public-health-problem

Rest, J. (1983). Morality. In P. H. Mussen (Series Ed.) & J. Flavell & E. Markman (Vol. Eds.), *Handbook of child psychology: Vol. 3. Cognitive development* (4th ed., pp. 556–629). New York: Wiley.

Rest, J. R. (1979). *Development in judging moral issues.* Minneapolis: University of Minnesota Press.

Resurrección, D., Salguero, J., & Ruiz-Aranda, D. (2014). Emotional intelligence and psychological maladjustment in adolescence: A systematic review. *Journal of Adolescence, 37,* 461–472. doi:10.1016/j.adolescence.2014.03.012

Reynolds, A. J., Temple, J. A., & Ou, S. R. (2010). Preschool education, educational attainment, and crime prevention: Contributions of cognitive and non-cognitive skills. *Children and Youth Services Review, 32*(8), 1054–1063. doi:10.1016/j.childyouth.2009.10.019

Rhoades, K. A., Leve, L. D., Harold, G. T., Neiderhiser, J. M., Shaw, D. S., & Reiss, D. (2011). Longitudinal pathways from marital hostility to child anger during toddlerhood: Genetic susceptibility and indirect effects via harsh parenting. *Journal of Family Psychology, 25,* 282–291. doi:10.1037/a0022886

Rhodes, M., & Wellman, H. (2013). Constructing a new theory from old ideas and new evidence. *Cognitive Science, 37*(3), 592–604. doi:10.1111/cogs.12031

Ricard, M., & Allard, L. (1993). The reaction of 9- to 10-month-old infants to an unfamiliar animal. *Journal of Genetic Psychology, 154,* 5–16. doi:10.1080/00221325.1993.9914716

Rice, F., Harold, G. T., Boivin, J., Van den Bree, M., Hay, D. F., & Thapar, A. (2010). The links between prenatal stress and offspring development and psychopathology: Disentangling environmental and inherited influences. *Psychological Medicine, 40*(02), 335–345.

Richardson, K., & Norgate, S. (2005). The equal environments assumption of classical twin studies may not hold. *British Journal of Educational Psychology, 75*(3), 339–350.

Richman, C. L., Berry, C., Bittle, M., & Himan, M. (1988). Factors related to helping behavior in preschool-age children. *Journal of Applied Developmental Psychology, 9,* 151–165.

Rideout, V. (2012). *Social media, social life: How teens view their digital lives.* Retrieved from Common Sense Media website: https://www.commonsensemedia.org/research/social-media-social-life-how-teens-view-their-digital-lives

Rideout, V. (2014). *Learning at home: Families' educational media use in America.* New York: Joan Ganz Cooney Center.

Rideout, V. (2015). *The Common Sense census: Media use by tweens and teens.* Retrieved from Common Sense Media website: https://www.commonsensemedia.org/research/the-common-sense-census-media-use-by-tweens-and-teens

Rideout, V. J., Foehr, U. G., Roberts, D. F. (2010). Generation M^2: Media in the lives of 8 to 18 year-olds. Menlo Park, CA: Kaiser Family Foundation. Retrieved from http://www.kff.org/entmedia/upload/8010.pdf.

Ridge, K. E., Weisberg, D. S., Ilgaz, H., Hirsh-Pasek, K. A., & Golinkoff, R. M. (2015). Supermarket speak: Increasing talk among low-socioeconomic status families. *Mind, Brain, and Education, 9*(3), 127–135.

Rieger, S., Göllner, R., Trautwein, U., & Roberts, B. W. (2016). Low self-esteem prospectively predicts depression in the transition to young adulthood: A replication of Orth, Robins, and Roberts (2008). *Journal of Personality and Social Psychology, 110*(1), e16–e22. doi:10.1037/pspp0000037

Riegle-Crumb, C., & Humphries, M. (2012). Exploring bias in math teachers' perceptions of students' ability by gender and race/ethnicity. *Gender & Society, 26,* 290–322.

Riegle-Crumb, C., & Moore, C. (2014). The gender gap in high school physics: Considering the local communities. *Social Science Quarterly, 95,* 253–268.

Rieser, J. J., Garing, A. E., & Young, M. F. (1994). Imagery, action, and young children's spatial orientation: It's not being there that counts, it's what one has in mind. *Child Development, 65,* 1262–1278.

Riggs, N. R., Greenberg, M. T., Kusché, C. A., & Pentz, M. A. (2006). The mediational role of neurocognition in the behavioral outcomes of a social-emotional prevention program in elementary school students: Effects of the PATHS curriculum. *Prevention Science, 7,* 91–102. doi:10.1007/s11121-005-0022-1

Rinaldi, C. M., & Howe, N. (2012). Mothers' and fathers' parenting styles and associations with toddlers' externalizing, internalizing, and adaptive behaviors. *Early Childhood Research Quarterly, 27,* 266–273. doi:10.1016/j.ecresq.2011.08.001

Rioux, C., Castellanos-Ryan, N., Parent, S., & Séguin, J. R. (2016a). The interaction between temperament and the family environment in adolescent substance use and externalizing behaviors: Support for diathesis-stress or differential susceptibility? *Developmental Review.* Advance online publication. doi:10.1016/j.dr.2016.03.003.0273-2297

Rioux, C., Castellanos-Ryan, N., Parent, S., Vitaro, F., Tremblay, R. E., & Séguin, J. R. (2016b). Differential susceptibility to environmental influences: Interaction between child temperament and parenting in adolescent alcohol use. *Development and Psychopathology, 28,* 265–275. doi:10.1017/S0954579415000437.

Ritchie, S. J. (2016). *Intelligence: All that matters.* London: Hodder & Stoughton.

Ritchie, S. J., & Tucker-Drob, E. M. (2018). How much does education improve intelligence? A meta-analysis. *Psychological Science, 29*(8), 1358–1369. doi:10.1177/0956797618774253

Riva Crugnola, C., Tambelli, R., Spinelli, M., Gazzotti, S., Caprin, C., & Albizzati, A. (2011). Attachment patterns and emotion regulation strategies in the second year. *Infant Behavior and Development, 34,* 136–151. doi:10.1016/j.infbeh.2010.11.002

Rivas-Drake, D., Seaton, E. K., Markstrom, C., Quintana, S., Syed, M., Lee, R. M., . . . the Ethnic and Racial Identity in the 21st Century Study Group. (2014). Ethnic and racial identity in adolescence: Implications for psychosocial, academic, and health outcomes. *Child Development, 85,* 40–57. doi:10.1111/cdev.12200

Roberts, A. L., Gladish, N., Gatev, E., Jones, M. J., Chen, Y., MacIsaac, J. L., . . . Baccarelli, A. A. (2018). Exposure to childhood abuse is associated with human sperm DNA methylation. *Translational Psychiatry, 8*(1), 194.

Roberts, B. W., & DelVecchio, W. F. (2000). The rank-order consistency of personality traits from childhood to old age: A quantitative review of longitudinal studies. *Psychological Bulletin, 126,* 3–25. doi:10.1037/0033-2909.126.1.3

Robertson, D. L., Farmer, T. W., Fraser, M. W., Day, S. H., Duncan, T., Crowther, A., & Dadisman, K. A. (2010). Interpersonal competence configurations and peer relations in early elementary classrooms: Perceived popular and unpopular aggressive subtypes. *International Journal of Behavioral Development, 34,* 73–87. doi:10.1177/0165025409345074

Robertson, L. A., McAnally, H. M., & Hancox, R. J. (2013). Childhood and adolescent television viewing and antisocial behavior in early adulthood. *Pediatrics, 131*(3), 439–446.

Robnett, R. D., & Leaper, C. (2013). "Girls don't propose! Ew": A mixed-methods examination of marriage tradition preferences and benevolent sexism in emerging adults. *Journal of Adolescent Research, 28*(1), 96–121. http://dx.doi.org/10.1177/0743558412447871

Rochat, P. (2009). *Others in mind: Social origins of self-consciousness.* New York: Cambridge University Press.

Rochat, P. (2011). What is it like to be a newborn? In S. Gallagher (Ed.), *Oxford handbook of the self* (pp. 57–79). Oxford/NewYork: Oxford University Press. doi:10.1093/oxfordhb/9780199548019.003.0003

Rochat, P. (2018). The ontogeny of human self-consciousness. *Current Directions in Psychological Sciences, 27*(5), 345–350. doi:10.1177/0963721418760236

Roche, J., Petrunka, K., & Peters, R. D. (2008). *Investing in Our Future: Highlights of Better Beginnings, Better Futures Research Findings at Grade 9.* Kingston, ON: Better Beginnings, Better Futures Research Coordination Unit. Retrieved from http://bbbf.ca/Portals/15/pdfs/BB%20Report%20O31.pdf

Roche, K. M., Ghazarian, S. R., Little, T. D., & Leventhal, T. (2011). Understanding links between punitive parenting and adolescent adjustment: The relevance of context and reciprocal associations. *Journal of Research on Adolescence, 21,* 448–460. doi:10.1111/j.1532-7795.2010.00681.x

Rochman, D. (2011, December 12). Incredibly, world's tiniest preterm babies are doing just fine. *Time.* Retrieved from http://healthland.time.com/2011/12/12/worlds-tiniest-preterm-babies-are-doing-just-fine

Rodkin, P. C., Espelage, D. L., & Hanish, L. D. (2015). A relational framework for understanding bullying: Developmental antecedents and outcomes. *American Psychologist, 70,* 311–321. doi:10.1037/a0038658

Rodkin, P. C., Farmer, T. W., Pearl, R., & Van Acker, R. (2000). Heterogeneity of popular boys: Antisocial and prosocial configurations. *Developmental Psychology, 36,* 14–24. doi:10.1037/0012-1649.36.1.14

Rodkin, P. C., Farmer, T. W., Pearl, R., & Van Acker, R. (2006). They're cool: Social status and peer group supports for aggressive boys and girls. *Social Development, 15,* 175–204. doi:10.1046/j.1467-9507.2006.00336.x

Rogers, F. (1996). *Dear Mister Rogers: Does it ever rain in your neighborhood? Letters to Mister Rogers.* New York: Penguin Books.

Rogers, L. O., & Meltzoff, A. N. (2017). Is gender more important and meaningful than race? An analysis of racial and gender identity among Black, White, and Mixed-race children. *Cultural Diversity and Ethnic Minority Psychology, 23,* 323–334. doi:10.1037%2Fcdp0000125

Rogers, S. J., Vismara, L., Wagner, A. L., McCormick, C., Young, G., & Ozonoff, S. (2014). Autism treatment in the first year of life: A pilot study of infant start, a parent-implemented intervention for symptomatic infants. *Journal of Autism and Developmental Disorders, 44*(12), 2981–2995. doi:10.1007/s10803-014-2202-y

Rogers, T. T., & McClelland, J. L. (2004). *Semantic cognition: A parallel distributed processing approach.* Cambridge, MA: MIT Press.

Rogoff, B. (2003). *The cultural nature of human development.* Oxford: Oxford University Press.

Roisman, G. I., & Fraley, R. C. (2006). The limits of genetic influence: A behavior-genetic analysis of infant–caregiver relationship quality and temperament. *Child Development, 77,* 1656–1667. doi:10.1111/j.1467-8624.2006.00965.x

Romens, S. E., McDonald, J., Svaren, J., & Pollak, S. D. (2015). Associations between early life stress and gene methylation in children. *Child Development,* 86(1), 303–309.

Romeo, R. R., Leonard, J. A., Robinson, S. T., West, M. R., Mackey, A. P., Rowe, M. L., & Gabrieli, J. D. (2018). Beyond the 30-million-word gap: Children's conversational exposure is associated with language-related brain function. *Psychological Science, 29*(5), 700–710.

Ronald, A., & Hoekstra, R. A. (2011). Autism spectrum disorders and autistic traits: A decade of new twin studies. *American Journal of Medical Genetics Part B: Neuropsychiatric Genetics, 156,* 255–274. doi:10.1002/ajmg.b.31159

Roopnarine, J. L., & Davidson, K. L. (2015). Parent–child play across cultures: Advancing play research. *American Journal of Play, 7,* 228–252.

Rosander, K. (2007). Visual tracking and its relationship to cortical development. *Progress in Brain Research, 164,* 105–122.

Rosch, E., Mervis, C. B., Gray, W. D., Johnson, D. M., & Boyes-Braem, P. (1976). Basic objects in natural categories. *Cognitive Psychology, 8,* 382–439. doi:10.1016/0010-0285(76)90013-X

Rose, A. J. (2002). Co-rumination in the friendships of girls and boys. *Child Development, 73,* 1830–1843.

Rose, A. J., & Rudolph, K. D. (2006). A review of sex differences in peer relationship processes: Potential trade-offs for the emotional and behavioral development of girls and boys. *Psychological Bulletin, 132,* 98–131. doi:10.1037/0033-2909.132.1.98

Rose, A. J., Carlson, W., & Waller, E. M. (2007). Prospective associations of co-rumination with friendship and emotional adjustment: Considering the socioemotional trade-offs of co-rumination. *Developmental Psychology, 43,* 1019–1031. doi:10.1037/0012-1649.43.4.1019

Rose, A. J., Swenson, L. P., & Carlson, W. (2004). Friendships of aggressive youth: Considering the influences of being disliked and of being perceived as popular. *Journal of Experimental Child Psychology, 88,* 25–45. doi:10.1016/j.jecp.2004.02.005

Rose, A. J., Swenson, L. P., & Waller, E. M. (2004). Overt and relational aggression and perceived popularity: Developmental differences in concurrent and prospective relations. *Developmental Psychology, 40,* 378–387. doi:10.1037/0012-1649.40.3.378

Rose, S. A., & Feldman, J. F. (1997). Memory and speed: Their role in the relation of infant information processing to later IQ. *Child Development, 68,* 630–641. doi:10.2307/1132115

Roseberry, S., Hirsh-Pasek, K., & Golinkoff, R. M. (2014). Skype me! Socially contingent interactions help toddlers learn language. *Child Development, 85*(3), 956–970.

Rosen, L. H., Underwood, M. K., & Beron, K. J. (2011). Peer victimization as a mediator of the relation between facial attractiveness and internalizing problems. *Merrill-Palmer Quarterly, 57,* 319–347.

Rosenberg-Lee, M., Barth, M., & Menon, V. (2011). What difference does a year of schooling make? Maturation of brain response and connectivity between 2nd and 3rd grades during arithmetic problem. *NeuroImage, 57*(3), 796–808.

Rosengren, K. S., & Hickling, A. K. (2000). Metamorphosis and magic: The development of children's thinking about possible events and plausible mechanisms. In K. S. Rosengren, C. N. Johnson, & P. L. Harris (Eds.), *Imagining the impossible: Magical, scientific, and religious thinking in children* (pp. 75–98). Cambridge: Cambridge University Press.

Rosengren, K. S., Gelman, S. A., Kalish, C. W., & McCormick, M. (1991). As time goes by: Children's early understanding of growth in animals. *Child Development, 62,* 1302–1320. doi:10.1111/j.1467-8624.1991.tb01607.x

Rosenthal, J. A. (1996) Qualitative descriptors of strength of association and effect size. *Journal of Social Service Research, 21*(4), 37–59. doi:10.1300/J079v21n04_02

Ross, H. S., & Lazinski, M. J. (2014). Parent mediation empowers sibling conflict resolution. *Early Education and Development, 25*(2), 259–275. doi:10.1080/10409289.2013.788425

Ross, H. S., & Lollis, S. P. (1989). A social relations analysis of toddler peer relationships. *Child Development,* 1082–1091.

Ross, J., Yilmaz, M., Dale, R., Cassidy, R., Yildirim, I., & Zeedyk, M. S. (2016). Cultural differences in self-recognition: The early development of autonomous and related selves? *Developmental Science.* Advance online publication. doi:10.1111/desc.12387

Ross, N., Medin, D., Coley, J. D., & Atran, S. (2003). Cultural and experiential differences in the development of folk biological induction. *Cognitive Development, 18,* 25–47. doi:10.1016/S0885-2014(02)00142-9

Ross-Sheehy, S., Oakes, L. M., & Luck, S. J. (2003). The development of visual short-term memory capacity in infants. *Child Development, 74*(6), 1807–1822.

Rothbart, M. K. (2011). *Becoming who we are: Temperament and personality in development.* New York: Guilford Press.

Rothbart, M. K. (2012). Advances in temperament: History, concepts, and measures. In M. Zentner & R. L. Shiner (Eds.), *Handbook of temperament* (pp. 3–20). New York: Guilford.

Rothbart, M. K., Ahadi, S. A., Hershey, K. L., & Fisher, P. (2001). Investigations of temperament at three to seven years: The Children's Behavior Questionnaire. *Child Development, 72,* 1394–1408. doi:10.1111/1467-8624.00355

Rothbart, M. K., & Bates, J. E. (2006). Temperament. In W. Damon, R. M. Lerner, & N. Eisenberg (Eds.), *Handbook of child psychology: Vol. 3. Social, emotional, and personality development* (6th ed., pp. 99–166). Hoboken, NJ: Wiley.

Rothbart, M. K., Derryberry, D., & Hershey, K. (2000). Stability of temperament in childhood: Laboratory infant assessment to parent report at seven years. In V. J. Molfese & D. L. Molfese (Eds.), *Temperament and personality development across the life span* (pp. 85–119). Mahwah, NJ: Erlbaum.

Rothbart, M. K., Sheese, B. E., & Posner, M. I. (2007). Executive attention and effortful control: Linking temperament, brain networks, and genes. *Child Development Perspectives, 1,* 2–7. doi:10.1111/j.1750-8606.2007.00002.x

Roth-Hanania, R., Davidov, M., & Zahn-Waxler, C. (2011). Empathy development from 8 to 16 months: Early signs of concern for others. *Infant Behavior and Development, 34,* 447–458. doi:10.1016/j.infbeh.2011.04.007

Rothstein, H. R., & Bushman, B. J. (2015). Methodological and reporting errors in meta-analytic reviews make other meta-analysts angry: A commentary on Ferguson (2015). *Perspectives on Psychological Science, 10*(5), 677–679.

Rovee-Collier, C. (1997). Dissociations in infant memory: Rethinking the development of implicit and explicit memory. *Psychological Review, 104,* 467–498. doi:10.1037/0033-295X.104.3.467

Rovee-Collier, C. (1999). The development of infant memory. *Current Directions in Psychological Science, 8,* 80–85. doi:10.1111/1467-8721.00019

Rowe, D. W. (2008). Social contracts for writing: Negotiating shared understandings about text in the preschool years. *Reading Research Quarterly, 43,* 66–95.

Rowe, M. L. (2008). Child-directed speech: Relation to socioeconomic status, knowledge of child development and child vocabulary skill. *Journal of Child Language, 35*(01), 185–205.

Rowe, M. L. (2018). Understanding socioeconomic differences in parents' speech to children. *Child Development Perspectives, 12*(2), 122–127.

Rowe, M. L., & Goldin-Meadow, S. (2009, February 13). Differences in early gesture explain SES disparities in child vocabulary size at school entry. *Science, 323,* 951–953.

Rowe, M. L., Ozcaliskan, S., & Goldin-Meadow, S. (2008). Learning words by hand: Gesture's role in predicting vocabulary development. *First Language, 28,* 182–199. doi:10.1177/0142723707088310

Rowe, R., Costello, E. J., Angold, A., Copeland, W. E., & Maughan, B. (2010). Developmental pathways in oppositional defiant disorder and conduct disorder. *Journal of Abnormal Psychology, 119,* 726–738. doi:10.1037/a0020798

Rowley, S. J., Kurtz-Costes, B., Mistry, R., & Feagans, L. (2007). Social status as a predictor of race and gender stereotypes in late childhood and early adolescence. *Social Development, 16,* 150–168. doi:10.1111/j.1467-9507.2007.00376.x

Roy, B. C., Frank, M. C., DeCamp, P., Miller, M., & Roy, D. (2015). Predicting the birth of a spoken word. *Proceedings of the National Academy of Sciences, 112*(41), 12663–12668.

Rozin, P., Haidt, J., & McCauley, C. (2016). Disgust. In L. F. Barrett, M. Lewis, & J. M. Haviland-Jones (Eds.), *Handbook of emotions* (4th ed., pp. 815–834). New York: Guilford.

Rubenstein, A. J., Kalakanis, L., & Langlois, J. H. (1999). Infant preferences for attractive faces: A cognitive explanation. *Developmental Psychology, 35,* 848–855. doi:10.1037/0012-1649.35.3.848

Rubin, K. H., Bowker, J. C., Barstead, M. G., & Coplan, R. J. (2018). Avoiding and withdrawing from the peer group. In W. M. Bukowski, B. Laursen, & K. H. Rubin (Eds.), *Handbook of peer interactions, relationships, and groups* (2nd ed., pp. 617–636). New York: Guilford.

Rubin, K. H., Bukowski, W. M., & Bowker, J. C. (2015). Children in peer groups. In M. H. Bornstein & T. Leventhal (Vol. Eds.) & R. M. Lerner (Ed. in Chief), *Handbook of child psychology and developmental science* (7th ed., pp. 175–222). Hoboken, NJ: Wiley.

Rubin, K. H., Bukowski, W. M., & Parker, J. G. (2006). Peer interactions, relationships, and groups. In W. Damon & R. M. Lerner (Series Eds.) & N. Eisenberg (Vol. Ed.), *Handbook of child psychology: Vol. 3. Social, emotional, and personality development* (6th ed., pp. 571–645). Hoboken, NJ: Wiley.

Rubin, K. H., Bukowski, W., & Parker, J. G. (1998). Peer interactions, relationships, and groups. In W. Damon (Series Ed.) & N. Eisenberg (Vol. Ed.), *Handbook of child psychology: Vol. 3. Social, emotional, and personality development* (5th ed., pp. 619–700). Hoboken, NJ: Wiley.

Rubin, K. H., Fein, G. G., & Vandenberg, B. (1983). Play. In P. H. Mussen (Series Ed.) & E. M. Hetherington (Vol. Ed.), *Handbook of child psychology: Vol. 4. Socialization, personality, and social development* (4th ed., pp. 693–774). New York: Wiley.

Rubin, K. H., Lynch, D., Coplan, R., Rose-Krasnor, L., & Booth, C. L. (1994). "Birds of a feather . . .": Behavioral concordances and preferential personal attraction in children. *Child Development, 65,* 1778–1785. doi:10.1111/j.1467-8624.1994.tb00848.x

Ruble, D. N., Martin, C. L., & Berenbaum, S. A. (2006). Gender development. In W. Damon & R. M. Lerner (Series Eds.) & N. Eisenberg (Vol. Ed.), *Handbook of child psychology: Vol. 3. Social, emotional, and personality development* (6th ed., pp. 858–932). Hoboken, NJ: Wiley.

Rueda, M. R., Posner, M. I., & Rothbart, M. K. (2011). Attentional control and self-regulation. In K. D. Vohs & R. F. Baumeister (Eds.), *Handbook of self-regulation: Research, theory, and applications* (2nd ed., pp. 284–299). New York: Guilford Press.

Rueda, M. R., Rothbart, M. K., McCandliss, B. D., Saccomanno, L., & Posner, M. I. (2005). Training, maturation, and genetic influences on the development of executive attention. *Proceedings of the National Academy of Sciences of the United States of America, 102,* 14931–14936. doi:10.1073/pnas.0506897102

Ruffman, T., Slade, L., & Crowe, E. (2002). The relation between children's and mothers' mental state language and theory-of-mind understanding. *Child Development, 73,* 734–751. doi:10.1111/1467-8624.00435

Rumelhart, D. E., & McClelland, J. L. (1986). On learning the past tense of English verbs. In J. L. McClelland, D. E. Rumelhart, & PDP Research Group (Eds.), *Parallel distributed processing: Explorations in the microstructure of cognition: Vol. 2. Psychological and biological models* (pp. 170–215). Cambridge, MA: MIT Press.

Russell, A., & Finnie, V. (1990). Preschool children's social status and maternal instructions to assist group entry. *Developmental Psychology, 26,* 603–611. doi:10.1037/0012-1649.26.4.603

Rutgers, S. G., & Meyers, S. (2015). Skin-to-skin contact. *Journal of Alternative Medicine Research, 7*(3), 185.

Rutten, B. P., & Mill, J. (2009). Epigenetic mediation of environmental influences in major psychotic disorders. *Schizophrenia Bulletin, 35,* 1045–1056. doi:10.1093/schbul/sbp104

Rutter, M. (1979). Protective factors in children's responses to stress and disadvantage. In M. W. Kent & J. E. Rolf (Eds.), *Primary Prevention of Psychopathology: Vol. 3. Social Competence in Children* (pp. 49–74). Hanover, NH: University Press of New England.

Rutter, M., Beckett, C., Castle, J., Kreppner, J., Stevens, S., & Sonuga-Barke, E. (2009). *Policy and practice implications from the English and Romanian adoptees (ERA) study: Forty-five key questions.* London: British Association for Adoption & Fostering.

Rutter, M., O'Connor, T. G., & the English and Romanian Adoptees (ERA) Study Team. (2004). Are there biological programming effects for psychological development? Findings from a study of Romanian adoptees. *Developmental Psychology, 40,* 81–94.

Rutter, M., Sonuga-Barke, E. J., Beckett, C., Castle, J., Kreppner, J., Kumsta, R., . . . Gunnar, M. R. (2010). Deprivation-specific psychological patterns: Effects of institutional deprivation. *Monographs of the Society for Research in Child Development, 75*(1, Serial No. 295), 1–252.

Ruvolo, P., Messinger, D., & Movellan, J. (2015). Infants time their smiles to make their moms smile. *PLoS ONE 10*(9), e0136492. doi:10.1371/journal.pone.0136492

Ryan, S. A., Ammerman, S. D., & O'Connor, M. E. (2018). Marijuana use during pregnancy and breastfeeding: Implications for neonatal and childhood outcomes. *Pediatrics, 142*(3), e20181889.

Rymer, R. (1993). *Genie: An abused child's flight from silence.* New York: HarperCollins.

Rytioja, M., Lappalainen, K., & Savolainen, H. (2019). Behavioural and emotional strengths of sociometrically popular, rejected, controversial, neglected, and average children. *European Journal of Special Needs Education.* Advance online publication. doi:10.1080/08856257.2018.1560607

Saarni, C. (1979). Children's understanding of display rules for expressive behavior. *Developmental Psychology, 15,* 424–429.

Saarni, C., Campos, J. J., Camras, L. A., & Witherington, D. (2006). Emotional development: Action, communication, and understanding. In W. Damon & R. L. Lerner (Series Eds.) & N. Eisenberg (Vol. Ed.), *Handbook of child psychology: Vol. 3. Social, emotional, and personality development* (6th ed., pp. 226–299). Hoboken, NJ: Wiley.

Sabbagh, M. A., Xu, F., Carlson, S. M., Moses, L. J., & Lee, K. (2006). The development of executive functioning and theory of mind: A comparison of Chinese and U.S. preschoolers. *Psychological Science, 17,* 74–81. doi:10.1111/j.1467-9280.2005.01667.x

Sabongui, A. G., Bukowski, W. M., & Newcomb, A. F. (1998). The peer ecology of popularity: The network embeddedness of a child's friend predicts the child's subsequent popularity. In W. M. Bukowski & A. H. Cillessen (Eds.), *New directions for child and adolescent development: No. 80. Sociometry then and now: Building on 6 decades of measuring children's experiences with the peer group* (pp. 83–91). San Francisco: Jossey-Bass.

Sackett, P. R., Borneman, M. J., & Connelly, B. S. (2008). High stakes testing in higher education and employment: Appraising the evidence for validity and fairness. *American Psychologist, 63,* 215–227. doi:10.1037/0003-066X.63.4.215

Sadeh, A., Hen-Gal, S., & Tikotzky, L. (2008). Young children's reactions to war-related stress: A survey and assessment of an innovative intervention. *Pediatrics, 121*(1), 46–53. doi:10.1542/peds.2007-1348

Saewyc, E. M. (2011). Research on adolescent sexual orientation: Development, health disparities, stigma, and resilience. *Journal of Research on Adolescence, 21,* 256–272. doi:10.1111/j.1532-7795.2010.00727.x

Saewyc, E. M., Wu, A., Marshall, S., Li, G., Watson, R. J., & Adjei, J. K. (2019). Long-term effects of gay straight alliances on perceived school safety among LGB youth in western Canada: Using a novel analytical method to enhance causal inference for population health interventions. *Journal of Adolescent Health, 64*(2), S4–S5.

Saffran, J., Hauser, M., Seibel, R., Kapfhamer, J., Tsao, F., & Cushman, F. (2008). Grammatical pattern learning by human infants and cotton-top tamarin monkeys. *Cognition, 107,* 479–500. doi:10.1016/j.cognition.2007.10.010

Saffran, J. R., & Kirkham, N. Z. (2018). Infant statistical learning. *Annual Review of Psychology, 69,* 181–203.

Saffran, J. R., Aslin, R. N., & Newport, E. L. (1996, December 13). Statistical learning by 8-month-old infants. *Science, 274,* 1926–1928.

Sagi, A., Koren-Karie, N., Gini, M., Ziv, Y., & Joels, T. (2002). Shedding further light on the effects of various types and quality of early child care on infant–mother attachment relationship: The Haifa Study of Early Child Care. *Child Development, 73,* 1166–1186. doi:10.1111/1467-8624.00465

Sainio, M., Veenstra, R., Huitsing, G., & Salmivalli, C. (2011). Victims and their defenders: A dyadic approach. *International Journal of Behavioral Development, 35,* 144–151. doi:10.1177/0165025410378068

Saint Augustine. (2002). The confessions of Saint Augustine. Translator: E. B. Pusey (Edward Bouverie). Retrieved from Project Gutenberg website: http://www.gutenberg.org/files/3296/3296-h/3296-h.htm

Sale, A., Berardi, N., & Maffei, L. (2009). Enrich the environment to empower the brain. *Trends in Neurosciences, 32,* 233–239. doi:10.1016/j.tins.2008.12.004

Salguero, J. M., Palomera, R., & Fernández-Berrocal, P. (2012). Perceived emotional intelligence as predictor of psychological adjustment in adolescents: A 1-year prospective study. *European Journal of Psychology of Education, 27,* 21e34. doi:10.1007/s10212-011-0063-8

Salihovic, S., Kerr, M., Özdemir, M., & Pakalniskiene, V. (2012). Directions of effects between adolescent psychopathic traits and parental behavior. *Journal of Abnormal Child Psychology, 40,* 957–969. doi:10.1007/s10802-012-9623-x

Sallquist, J. V., Eisenberg, N., Spinrad, T. L., Reiser, M., Hofer, C., Zhou, Q., . . . Eggum, N. (2009). Positive and negative emotionality: Trajectories across six years and relations with social competence. *Emotion, 9,* 15–28. doi:10.1037/a0013970

Salmivalli, C., Kärnä, A., & Poskiparta, E. (2011). Counteracting bullying in Finland: The KiVa program and its effects on different forms of being bullied. *International Journal of Behavioral Development, 35,* 405–411. doi:10.1177/0165025411407457

Salo, V. C., Rowe, M. L., & Reeb-Sutherland, B. C. (2018). Exploring infant gesture and joint attention as related constructs and as predictors of later language. *Infancy, 23*(3), 432–452.

Salthouse, T. A. (2009). Decomposing age correlations on neuropsychological and cognitive variables. *Journal of the International Neuropsychological Society, 15,* 650–661. doi:10.1017/S1355617709990385

Salvadori, E., Blazsekova, T., Volein, A., Karap, Z., Tatone, D., Mascaro, O., & Csibra, G. (2015). Probing the strength of infants' preference for Helpers over Hinderers: Two replication attempts of Hamlin and Wynn (2011). *PloS One, 10*(11), e0140570.

Sameroff, A. J. (1998). Environmental risk factors in infancy. In J. G. Warhol (Ed.), *New perspectives in early emotional development* (pp. 159–171). Calverton, NY: Johnson & Johnson Pediatric Institute.

Sameroff, A. J., Seifer, R., Baldwin, A., & Baldwin, C. (1993). Stability of intelligence from preschool to adolescence: The influence of social and family risk factors. *Child Development, 64,* 80–97.

Samuelson, L. K. (2002). Statistical regularities in vocabulary guide language acquisition in connectionist models and 15–20-month-olds. *Developmental Psychology, 38,* 1016–1037.

Samuelson, L. K., & Horst, J. S. (2008). Confronting complexity: Insights from the details of behavior over multiple timescales. *Developmental Science, 11,* 209–215. doi:10.1111/j.1467-7687.2007.00667.x

Samuelson, L. K., Smith, L. B., Perry, L. K., & Spencer, J. P. (2011). Grounding word learning in space. *PLoS ONE, 6*(12), e28095. doi:10.1371/journal.pone.0028095

Sanders, J., & Munford, R. (2014). Youth-centered practice: Positive youth development practices and pathways to better outcomes for vulnerable youth. *Children and Youth Services Review, 46,* 160–167. doi:10.1016/j.childyouth.2014.08.020

Sandin, S., Schendel, D., Magnusson, P., Hultman, C., Surén, P., Susser, E., . . . Henning, M. (2016). Autism risk associated with parental age and with increasing difference in age between the parents. *Molecular Psychiatry, 21*(5), 693.

Sandler, I. N., Wheeler, L. A., & Braver, S. L. (2013). Relations of parenting quality, interparental conflict, and overnights with mental health problems of children in divorcing families with high legal conflict. *Journal of Family Psychology, 27,* 915–924. doi:10.1037/a0034449

Sandler, W., Meir, I., Padden, C., & Aronoff, M. (2005). The emergence of grammar: Systematic structure in a new language. *Proceedings of the National Academy of Sciences of the United States of America, 102,* 2661–2665. doi:10.1073/pnas.0405448102

Sanlorenzo, L. A., Stark, A. R., & Patrick, S. W. (2018). Neonatal abstinence syndrome: An update. *Current Opinion in Pediatrics, 30*(2), 182.

Santos, C. E., Galligan, K., Pahlke, E., & Fabes, R. A. (2013). Gender-typed behaviors, achievement, and adjustment among racially and ethnically diverse boys during early adolescence. *American Journal of Orthopsychiatry, 83*(2–3), 252–264. http://dx.doi.org/10.1111/ajop.12036

Saudino, K. J., & Wang, M. (2012). Quantitative and molecular genetic studies of temperament. In M. R. Zentner & R. L. Shiner (Eds.), *Handbook of temperament* (pp. 315–346). New York: Guilford Press.

Saunders, B. E., Berliner, L., & Hanson, R. F. (2004). *Child physical and sexual abuse: Guidelines for treatment* (revised report: April 26, 2004). Charleston, SC: National Crime Victims Research and Treatment Center.

Sauter, D. A., Eisner F., Ekman P., & Scott S. K. (2010). Cross-cultural recognition of basic emotions through nonverbal emotional vocalizations. *Proceedings of the National Academy of Sciences, USA, 107,* 2408–2412. doi:10.1073/pnas.0908239106

Savage-Rumbaugh, E. S., Murphy, J., Sevcik, R. A., Brakke, K. E., Williams, S. L., & Rumbaugh, D. M. (1993). Language comprehension in ape and child. *Monographs of the Society for Research in Child Development, 58*(3–4, Serial No. 233).

Savin-Williams, R. C. (1998b). The disclosure to families of same-sex attractions by lesbian, gay, and bisexual youths. *Journal of Research on Adolescence, 8,* 49–68. doi:10.1207/s15327795jra0801_3

Savin-Williams, R. C., & Cohen, K. M. (2007). Development of same-sex attracted youth. In I. H. Meyer & M. E. Northridge (Eds.), *The health of sexual minorities: Public health perspectives on lesbian, gay, bisexual and transgender populations* (pp. 27–47). New York: Springer.

Savin-Williams, R. C., & Ream, G. L. (2003). Sex variations in the disclosure to parents of same-sex attractions. *Journal of Family Psychology, 17,* 429–438. doi:10.1037/0893-3200.17.3.429

Savin-Williams, R. C., & Ream, G. L. (2007). Prevalence and stability of sexual orientation components during adolescence and young adulthood. *Archives of Sexual Behavior, 36,* 385–394. doi:10.1007/s10508-006-9088-5

Saxe, R., & Powell, L. J. (2006). It's the thought that counts: Specific brain regions for one component of theory of mind. *Psychological Science, 17,* 692–699. doi:10.1111/j.1467-9280.2006.01768.x

Scaramella, L. V., Conger, R. D., Spoth, R., & Simons, R. L. (2002). Evaluation of a social contextual model of delinquency: A cross-study replication. *Child Development, 73,* 175–195. doi:10.1111/1467-8624.00399

Scaramella, L. V., Neppl, T. K., Ontai, L. L., & Conger, R. D. (2008). Consequences of socioeconomic disadvantage across three generations: Parenting behavior and child externalizing problems. *Journal of Family Psychology, 22,* 725–733. doi:10.1037/a0013190

Scarf, D., Imuta, K., Colombo, M., & Hayne, H. (2012). Social evaluation or simple association? Simple associations may explain moral reasoning in infants. *PloS One, 7*(8), e42698. doi:10.1371/journal.pone.0042698

Scarr, S. (1992). Developmental theories for the 1990s: Development and individual differences. *Child Development, 63,* 1–19.

Schaefer, D. R., Simpkins, S. D., Vest, A. E., & Price, C. D. (2011). The contribution of extracurricular activities to adolescent friendships: New insights through social network analysis. *Developmental Psychology, 47,* 1141–1152. doi:10.1037/a0024091

Scharrer, E. L. (2013). Representations of gender in the media. *The Oxford handbook of media psychology* (pp. 267–284). New York: Oxford University Press.

Scheel, A. M., Ritchie, S. J., Brown, N. J., & Jacques, S. L. (2018). Methodological problems in a study of fetal visual perception. *Current Biology, 28*(10), R594–R596.

Schieffelin, B. B., & Ochs, E. (Eds.). (1987). *Studies in the social and cultural foundations of language: No. 3. Language socialization across cultures.* New York: Cambridge University Press.

Schlaggar, B. L., & Church, J. A. (2009). Functional neuroimaging insights into the development of skilled reading. *Current Directions in Psychological Science, 18,* 21–26.

Schmidt, F. L., & Hunter, J. (2004). General mental ability in the world of work: Occupational attainment and job performance. *Journal of Personality and Social Psychology, 86,* 162–173. doi:10.1037/0022-3514.86.1.162

Schmidt, J. A., Shumow, L., & Kackar, H. (2007). Adolescents' participation in service activities and its impact on academic, behavioral, and civic outcomes. *Journal of Youth and Adolescence, 36,* 127–140. doi:10.1007/s10964-006-9119-5

Schmidt, M. E., Pempek, T. A., Kirkorian, H. L., Lund, A. F., & Anderson, D. R. (2008). The effects of background television on the toy play behavior of very young children. *Child Development, 79,* 1137–1151.

Schneider, B. H. (2016). *Childhood friendships and peer relations: Friends and enemies* (2nd ed.). New York: Routledge.

Schneider, B. H., Atkinson, L., & Tardif, C. (2001). Child–parent attachment and children's peer relations: A quantitative review. *Developmental Psychology, 37,* 86–100. doi:10.1037/0012-1649.37.1.86

Schneider, B. H., Dixon, K., & Udvari, S. (2007). Closeness and competition in the inter-ethnic and co-ethnic friendships of early adolescents in Toronto and Montreal. *Journal of Early Adolescence, 27*(1), 115–138.

Schneider, M., Merz, S., Stricker, J., De Smedt, B., Torbeyns, J., Verschaffel, L., & Luwel, K. (2018). Associations of number line estimation with mathematical competence: A meta-analysis. *Child Development, 89*(5): 1467–1484. doi:10.1111/cdev.13068

Schneider, W., Körkel, J., & Weinert, F. E. (1989). Domain-specific knowledge and memory performance: A comparison of high- and low-aptitude children. *Journal of Educational Psychology, 81,* 306–312.

Schneider, W., & Ornstein, P. A. (2015). The development of children's memory. *Child Development Perspectives, 9*(3): 190–195. doi:10.1111/cdep.12129

Schnoll, J. S., Connolly, J., Josephson, W. J., Pepler, D., & Simkins-Strong, E. (2015). Same- and cross-gender sexual harassment victimization in middle school: A developmental-contextual perspective. *Journal of School Violence, 14*(2), 196–216.

Scholl, B. J., & Leslie, A. M. (2001). Minds, modules, and meta-analysis. *Child Development, 72,* 696–701. doi:10.1111/1467-8624.00308

Schonert-Reichl, K. A., Smith, V., Zaidman-Zait, A., & Hertzman, C. (2012). Promoting children's prosocial behaviors in school: Impact of the "Roots of Empathy" program on the social and emotional competence of school-aged children. *School Mental Health, 4*(1), 1–21.

Schult, C. A., & Wellman, H. M. (1997). Explaining human movements and actions: Children's understanding of the limits of psychological explanation. *Cognition, 62,* 291–324.

Schultze-Krumbholz, A., Schultze, M., Zagorscak, P., Wölfer, R., & Scheithauer, H. (2016). Feeling cybervictims' pain—The effect of empathy training on cyberbullying. *Aggressive Behavior, 42,* 147–156. doi:10.1002/ab.21613

Schulz, L. (2012). The origins of inquiry: Inductive inference and exploration in early childhood. *Trends in Cognitive Sciences, 16,* 382–389.

Schulz, L. C. (2010). The Dutch Hunger Winter and the developmental origins of health and disease. *Proceedings of the National Academy of Sciences, 107*(39), 16757–16758.

Schulz, L. E., & Sommerville, J. (2006). God does not play dice: Causal determinism and preschoolers' causal inferences. *Child Development, 77,* 427–442. doi:10.1111/j.1467-8624. 2006.00880.x

Schutte, A. R., Spencer, J. P., & Schöner, G. (2003). Testing the dynamic field theory: Working memory for locations becomes more spatially precise over development. *Child Development, 74,* 1393–1417.

Schwartz, D., Kelly, B. M., & Duong, M. T. (2013). Do academically-engaged adolescents experience social sanctions from the peer group? *Journal of Youth and Adolescence, 42*(9), 1319–1330. http://dx.doi.org/10.1007/s10964-012-9882-4

Schwartz, D., Tom, S. R., Chang, L., Xu, Y., Duong, M. T., & Kelly, B. M. (2010). Popularity and acceptance as distinct dimensions of social standing for Chinese children in Hong Kong. *Social Development, 19,* 681–697. doi:10.1111/j.1467-9507.2009.00558.x

Schwartz, O. S., Dudgeon, P., Sheeber, L. B., Yap, M. B., Simmons, J. G., & Allen, N. B. (2012). Parental behaviors during family interactions predict changes in depression and anxiety symptoms during adolescence. *Journal of Abnormal Child Psychology, 40,* 59–71. doi:10.1007/s10802-011-9542-2

Schwartz, P. D., Maynard, A. M., & Uzelac, S. M. (2008). Adolescent egocentrism: A contemporary view. *Adolescence, 43,* 441–448.

Schwartz, S., & Johnson, J. H. (1985). *Psychopathology of childhood: A clinical-experimental approach* (2nd ed.). New York: Pergamon Press.

Schwartz-Mette, R. A., & Rose, A. J. (2012). Co-rumination mediates contagion of internalizing symptoms within youths' friendships. *Developmental Psychology, 48,* 1355–1365. doi:10.1037/a0027484

Schwarz, B., Mayer, B., Trommsdorff, G., Ben-Arieh, A., Friedlmeier, M., Lubiewska, K., . . . Peltzer, K. (2012). Does the importance of parent and peer relationships for adolescents' life satisfaction vary across cultures? *Journal of Early Adolescence, 32,* 55–80. doi:10.1177/0272431611419508

Scott, K. M., Smith, D. R., & Ellis, P. M. (2010). Prospectively ascertained child maltreatment and its association with DSM-IV mental disorders in young adults. *Archives of General Psychiatry, 67,* 712–719. doi:10.1001/archgenpsychiatry.2010.71

Sears, M. S., Repetti, R. L., Reynolds, B. M., & Sperling, J. B. (2014). A naturalistic observational study of children's expressions of anger in the family context. *Emotion, 14*(2), 272–283. doi:10.1037/a0034753

Seaton, E. K., Yip, T., & Sellers, R. M. (2009). A longitudinal examination of racial identity and racial discrimination among African American adolescents. *Child Development, 80,* 406–417. doi:10.1111/j.1467-8624.2009.01268.x

Sebanc, A. M., Kearns, K. T., Hernandez, M. D., & Galvin, K. B. (2007). Predicting having a best friend in young children: Individual characteristics and friendship features. *Journal of Genetic Psychology, 168,* 81–96. doi:10.3200/GNTP.168.1.81-96

Sebastián-Gallés, N., Albareda-Castellot, B., Weikum, W. M., & Werker, J. F. (2012). A bilingual advantage in visual language discrimination in infancy. *Psychological Science, 23,* 994–999. doi:10.1177/0956797612436817

Seehagen, S., & Herbert, J. S. (2011). Infant imitation from televised peer and adult models. *Infancy, 16,* 113–136. doi:10.1111/j.1532-7078.2010.00045.x

Segaert, A. (2012). *The National Shelter Study: Emergency Shelter Use in Canada 2005–2009.* Ottawa: Homelessness Partnering Secretariat, Human Resources and Skills Development Canada.

Segal, N. L., McGuire, S. A., Havlena, J., Gill, P., & Hershberger, S. L. (2007). Intellectual similarity of virtual twin pairs: Developmental trends. *Personality and Individual Differences, 42,* 1209–1219. doi:10.1016/j.paid.2006.09.028

Seidenberg, M. S. (2005). Connectionist models of word reading. *Current Directions in Psychological Science, 14*(5), 238–242. doi:10.1111/j.0963-7214.2005.00372.x

Seidenberg, M. S., & Zevin, J. D. (2006). Connectionist models in developmental cognitive neuroscience: Critical periods and the paradox of success. In Y. Munakata & M. Johnson (Eds.), *Attention & Performance XXI: Processes of Change in Brain and Cognitive Development* (pp. 585–612). Oxford, UK: Oxford University Press.

Sekar, A., Bialas, A. R., de Rivera, H., Davis, A., Hammond, T. R., Kamitaki, N., . . . Genovese, G. (2016). Schizophrenia risk from complex variation of complement component 4. *Nature, 530*(7589), 177–183.

Selfhout, M. H. W., Branje, S. J. T., Delsing, M., ter Bogt, T. F. M., & Meeus, W. H. J. (2009). Different types of Internet use, depression, and social anxiety: The role of perceived friendship quality. *Journal of Adolescence, 32,* 819–833. doi:10.1016/j.adolescence.2008.10.011

Selman, R. L. (1980). *The growth of interpersonal understanding: Developmental and clinical analyses.* New York: Academic Press.

Sénéchal, M. (2016). Testing a nested skills model of the relations among invented spelling, accurate spelling, and word reading, from kindergarten to grade 1. *Early Child Development and Care,* 1–13.

Sénéchal, M., & LeFevre, J. (2002). Parental involvement in the development of children's reading skill: A 5-year longitudinal study. *Child Development, 73,* 445–460.

Sénéchal, M., Ouellette, G., Pagan, S., & Lever, R. (2012). The role of invented spelling on learning to read in low-phoneme awareness kindergartners: A randomized-control-trial study. *Reading and Writing, 25*(4), 917–934.

Senghas, A., & Coppola, M. (2001). Children creating language: How Nicaraguan sign language acquired a spatial grammar. *Psychological Science, 12,* 323–328.

Senghas, A., Kita, S., & Özyürek, A. (2004). Children creating core properties of language: Evidence from an emerging sign language in Nicaragua. *Science, 305*(5691), 1779–1782.

Sentse, M., Kretschmer, T., & Salmivalli, C. (2015). The longitudinal interplay between bullying, victimization, and social status: Age-related and gender differences. *Social Development, 24,* 659–677. doi:10.1111/sode.12115

Serbin, L. A., Poulin-Dubois, D., Colburne, K. A., Sen, M. G., & Eichstedt, J. A. (2001). Gender stereotyping in infancy: Visual preferences for and knowledge of gender-stereotyped toys in the second year. *International Journal of Behavioral Development, 25,* 7–15. doi:10.1080/01650250042000078

Serbin, L. A., Powlishta, K. K., & Gulko, J. (1993). The development of sex typing in middle childhood. *Monographs of the Society for Research in Child Development, 58*(2, Serial No. 232), i–95. doi:10.2307/1166118

Seyfarth, R. M., & Cheney, D. L. (1993). Meaning, reference, and intentionality in the natural vocalizations of monkeys. In H. L. Roitblat, L. M. Herman, & P. E. Nachtigall (Eds.), *Language and communication: Comparative perspectives* (pp. 195–220). Hillsdale, NJ: Erlbaum.

Shackman, J. E., & Pollak, S. D. (2014). Impact of physical maltreatment on the regulation of negative affect and aggression. *Development and Psychopathology, 26,* 1021–1033.

Shaffer, C. S., Adjei, J., Viljoen, J. L., Douglas, K. S., & Saewyc, E. M. (2018). Ten-year trends in physical dating violence victimization among adolescent boys and girls in British Columbia, Canada. *Journal of Interpersonal Violence.* Advance Online Publication. http://doi.org/10.1177/0886260518788367

Shalev, R. S. (2007). Prevalence of developmental dyscalculia. In D. B. Berch & M. M. M. Mazzocco (Eds.), *Why is math so hard for some children? The nature and origins of mathematical learning difficulties and disabilities* (pp. 49–60). Baltimore, MD: Paul H. Brookes.

Shanahan, L., McHale, S. M., Crouter, A. C., & Osgood, D. W. (2008). Linkages between parents' differential treatment, youth depressive symptoms, and sibling relationships. *Journal of Marriage and Family, 70,* 480–494. doi:10.1111/j.1741-3737.2008.00495.x

Shantz, C. U. (1987). Conflicts between children. *Child Development, 58,* 283–305. doi:10.2307/1130507

Share, D. L. (2004). Knowing letter names and learning letter sounds: A causal connection. *Journal of Experimental Child Psychology, 88,* 213–233. doi:10.1016/j.jecp.2004.03.005

Shaw, D. S., Gilliom, M., Ingoldsby, E. M., & Nagin, D. S. (2003). Trajectories leading to school-age conduct problems. *Developmental Psychology, 39,* 189–200. doi:10.1037/0012-1649.39.2.189

Shaywitz, S. E., Mody, M., & Shaywitz, B. A. (2006). Neural mechanisms in dyslexia. *Current Directions in Psychological Science, 15,* 278–281.

Sheehan, M. J., & Watson, M. W. (2008). Reciprocal influences between maternal discipline techniques and aggression in children and adolescents. *Aggressive Behavior, 34,* 245–255. doi:10.1002/ab.20241

Sheese, B. E., Voelker, P. M., Rothbart, M. K., & Posner, M. I. (2007). Parenting quality interacts with genetic variation in dopamine receptor D4 to influence temperament in early childhood. *Development and Psychopathology, 19,* 1039–1046. doi:10.1017/S0954579407000521

Shell, R., & Eisenberg, N. (1990). The role of peers' gender in children's naturally occurring interest in toys. *International Journal of Behavioral Development, 13,* 373–388. doi:10.1177/016502549001300309

Sheridan, M. A., Fox, N. A., Zeanah, C. H., McLaughlin, K. A., & Nelson, C. A. (2012). Variation in neural development as a result of exposure to institutionalization early in childhood. *Proceedings of the National Academy of Sciences, 109*(32), 12927–12932.

Shiell, M. M., Champoux, F., & Zatorre, R. J. (2016). The right hemisphere planum temporale supports enhanced visual motion detection ability in deaf people: Evidence from cortical thickness. *Neural Plasticity.* doi:10.1155/2016/7217630

Shiell, M. M., & Zatorre, R. J. (2016). White matter structure in the right planum temporale region correlates with visual motion detection thresholds in deaf people. *Hearing Research.* doi:10.1016/j.heares.2016.06.011

Shiner, R. L., Buss, K. A., McClowry, S. G., Putnam, S. P., Saudino, K. J., & Zentner, M. (2012). What is temperament now? Assessing progress in temperament research on the twenty-fifth anniversary of Goldsmith et al. *Child Development Perspectives, 6,* 436–444.

Shirtcliff, E. A., Coe, C. L., & Pollak, S. D. (2009). Early childhood stress is associated with elevated antibody levels to Herpes Simplex Virus Type 1. *Proceedings of the National Academy of Sciences, 106,* 2963–2967.

Shomaker, L. B., & Furman, W. (2009). Parent—adolescent relationship qualities, internal working models, and attachment styles as predictors of adolescents' interactions with friends. *Journal of Social and Personal Relationships, 26,* 579–603. doi:10.1177/0265407509354441

Shonkoff, J. P., Boyce, W. T., & McEwen, B. S. (2009). Neuroscience, molecular biology, and the childhood roots of health disparities: Building a new framework for health promotion and disease prevention. *JAMA, 301*(21), 2252–2259. doi:10.1001/jama.2009.754

Shonkoff, J. P., Garner, A. S., & the Committee on Psychosocial Aspects of Child and Family Health, Committee on Early Childhood, Adoption, and Dependent Care, and Section on Developmental and Behavioral Pediatrics. (2012). The lifelong effects of early childhood adversity and toxic stress. *Pediatrics, 129,* e232–e246. doi:10.1542/peds.2011-2663

Shutts, K., Kinzler, K. D., & DeJesus, J. M. (2013). Understanding infants' and children's social learning about foods: Previous research and new prospects. *Developmental Psychology, 49*(3), 419.

Shutts, K., Kinzler, K. D., McKee, C. B., & Spelke, E. S. (2009). Social information guides infants' selection of foods. *Journal of Cognition and Development, 10,* 1–17.

Shweder, R. A., Mahapatra, M., & Miller, J. G. (1987). Culture and moral development. In J. Kagan & S. Lamb (Eds.), *The emergence of morality in young children* (pp. 1–83). Chicago: University of Chicago Press.

Sibinga, E. M., Webb, L., Ghazarian, S. R., & Ellen, J. M. (2016). School-based mindfulness instruction: An RCT. *Pediatrics, 137*(1), e20152532.

Sickmund, M., & Puzzanchera, C. (Eds.). (2014). *Juvenile Offenders and Victims: 2014 National Report.* Pittsburgh, PA: National Center for Juvenile Justice. Retrieved from http://www.ncjj.org/nr2014/downloads/NR2014.pdf

Siegel, L. S. (1993). The cognitive basis of dyslexia. In M. L. Howe & R. Pasnak (Eds.), *Emerging themes in cognitive development: Vol. 2. Competencies* (pp. 33–52). New York: Springer-Verlag.

Siegler, R. S. (1976). The effects of simple necessity and sufficiency relationships on children's causal inferences. *Child Development, 47,* 1058–1063.

Siegler, R. S. (1986). Unities in strategy choices across domains. In M. Perlmutter (Ed.), *Minnesota Symposia on Child Psychology: Vol. 19. Perspectives on intellectual development* (pp. 1–48). Hillsdale, NJ: Erlbaum.

Siegler, R. S. (1987). The perils of averaging data over strategies: An example from children's addition. *Journal of Experimental Psychology: General, 116,* 250–264.

Siegler, R. S. (1995). How does change occur: A microgenetic study of number conservation. *Cognitive Psychology, 28,* 225–273. doi:10.1006/cogp.1995.1006

Siegler, R. S. (1996). *Emerging minds: The process of change in children's thinking.* New York: Oxford University Press.

Siegler, R. S. (2006). Microgenetic analyses of learning. In W. Damon & R. M. Lerner (Series Eds.) & D. Kuhn & R. S. Siegler (Vol. Eds.), *Handbook of child psychology: Vol. 2. Cognition, perception, and language* (6th ed., pp. 464–510). Hoboken, NJ: Wiley.

Siegler, R. S. (2016). Magnitude knowledge: The common core of numerical development. *Developmental Science, 19,* 341–361. doi:10.1111/desc.12395

Siegler, R. S., & Araya, R. (2005). A computational model of conscious and unconscious strategy discovery. In R. V. Kail (Ed.), *Advances in child development and behavior* (Vol. 33, pp. 1–42). Oxford: Elsevier.

Siegler, R. S., & Booth, J. L. (2004). Development of numerical estimation in young children. *Child Development, 75,* 428–444. doi:10.1111/j.1467-8624.2004.00684.x

Siegler, R. S., & Jenkins, E. (1989). *How children discover new strategies.* Hillsdale, NJ: Erlbaum.

Siegler, R. S., & Mu, Y. (2008). Chinese children excel on novel mathematics problems even before elementary school. *Psychological Science, 19,* 759–763. doi:10.1111/j.1467-9280.2008.02153.x

Siegler, R. S., & Ramani, G. B. (2009). Playing linear number board games—but not circular ones—improves low-income preschoolers' numerical understanding. *Journal of Educational Psychology, 101,* 545–560. doi:10.1037/a0014239

Sigman, M., & Ruskin, E. (1999). Continuity and change in the social competence of children with autism, Down syndrome, and developmental delays. *Monographs of the Society for Research in Child Development, 64*(1, Serial No. 256).

Signorella, M. L., Bigler, R. S., & Liben, L. S. (1997). A meta-analysis of children's memories for own-sex and other-sex information. *Journal of Applied Developmental Psychology, 18,* 429–445. doi:10.1016/S0193-3973(97)80009-3

Signorielli, N. (2012). Television's gender-role images and contribution to stereotyping: Past, present, future. *Handbook of children and the media* (2nd ed., pp. 321–339). Thousand Oaks, CA: Sage.

Sijtsema, J. J., Veenstra, R., Lindenberg, S., & Salmivalli, C. (2009). Empirical test of bullies' status goals: Assessing direct goals, aggression, and prestige. *Aggressive Behavior, 35,* 57–67. doi:10.1002/ab.20282

Sikora, J., & Pokropek, A. (2012). Gender segregation of adolescent science career plans in 50 countries. *Science Education, 96*(2), 234–264. http://dx.doi.org/10.1002/sce.20479

Silk, J. S., Tan, P. Z., Ladouceur, C. D., Meller, S., Siegle, G. J., McMakin, D. L., . . . Ryan, N. D. (2016). A randomized clinical trial comparing individual cognitive behavioral therapy and child-centered therapy for child anxiety disorders. *Journal of Clinical Child & Adolescent Psychology.* Advance online publication. doi:10.1080/15374416.2016.1138408

Simion, F., Valenza, E., Macchi Cassia, V., Turati, C., & Umiltà, C. (2002). Newborns' preference for up–down asymmetrical configurations. *Developmental Science, 5,* 427–434. doi:10.1111/1467-7687.00237

Simon, T. J., & Klahr, D. (1995). A computational theory of children's learning about number conservation. In T. J. Simon & G. S. Halford (Eds.), *Developing cognitive competence: New approaches to process modeling* (pp. 315–353). Hillsdale, NJ: Erlbaum.

Simon, T. J., & Rivera, S. M. (2007). Neuroanatomical approaches to the study of mathematical ability and disability. In D. B. Berch & M. M. M. Mazzocco (Eds.), *Why is math so hard for some children? The nature and origins of mathematical learning difficulties and disabilities* (pp. 283–305). Baltimore, MD: Paul H. Brookes.

Simons, K. D., & Klein, J. D. (2007). The impact of scaffolding and student achievement levels in a problem-based learning environment. *Instructional Science, 35*(1), 41–72. doi:10.1007/s11251-006-9002-5

Simons, R. L., Lei, M. K., Beach, S. R., Brody, G. H., Philibert, R. A., & Gibbons, F. X. (2011). Social environmental variation, plasticity genes, and aggression: Evidence for the differential susceptibility hypothesis. *American Sociological Review, 76,* 833–912. doi:10.1177/0003122411427580

Simons, R. L., Lei, M. K., Stewart, E. A., Brody, G. H., Beach, S. R., Philibert, R. A., & Gibbons, F. X. (2012). Social adversity, genetic variation, street code, and aggression: A genetically informed model of violent behavior. *Youth Violence and Juvenile Justice, 10,* 3–24. doi:10.1177/1541204011422087

Simpkins, S. D., Eccles, J. S., & Becnel, J. N. (2008). The mediational role of adolescents' friends in relations between activity breadth and adjustment. *Developmental Psychology, 44,* 1081–1094.

Simpkins, S. D., Fredricks, J. A., & Eccles, J. S. (2015). The role of parents in the ontogeny of achievement-related motivation and behavioral choices. *Monographs of the Society for Research in Child Development, 80*(2), 1–151.

Simpson, E. A., Murray, L., Paukner, A., & Ferrari, P. F. (2014). The mirror neuron system as revealed through neonatal imitation: Presence from birth, predictive power and evidence of plasticity. *Philosophical Transactions of the Royal Society B: Biological Sciences, 369*(1644). doi:10.1098/rstb.2013.0289

Simpson, J. A., Collins, W. A., Tran, S., & Haydon, K. C. (2007). Attachment and the experience and expression of emotions in romantic relationships: A developmental perspective. *Journal of Personality and Social Psychology, 92,* 355–367. doi:10.1037/0022-3514.92.2.355

Sims, M., Hutchins, T., & Taylor, M. (1998). Gender segregation in young children's conflict behavior in child care settings. *Child Study Journal, 28,* 1–16.

Singh, L. (2018). Bilingual infants demonstrate advantages in learning words in a third language. *Child Development, 89*(4), e397–e413.

Singh, L., Morgan, J. L., & Best, C. T. (2002). Infants' listening preferences: Baby talk or happy talk? *Infancy, 3,* 365–394. doi:10.1207/S15327078IN0303_5

Singh, L., Nestor, S., Parikh, C., & Yull, A. (2009). Influences of infant-directed speech on early word recognition. *Infancy, 14,* 654–666. doi:10.1080/15250000903263973

Sirois, S., & Jackson, I. R. (2012). Pupil dilation and object permanence in infants. *Infancy, 17*(1), 61–78.

Sisk, V. F., Burgoyne, A. P., Sun, J., Butler, J. L., & Macnamara, B. N. (2018). To what extent and under which circumstances are growth mind-sets important to academic achievement? Two meta-analyses. *Psychological Science, 29*(4), 549–571. doi:10.1177/0956797617739704

Skinner, B. F. (1953). *Science and human behavior.* New York: Macmillan.

Skinner, B. F. (1957). *Verbal behavior.* New York: Appleton-Century-Crofts.

Skinner, B. F. (1971). *Beyond freedom and dignity.* New York: Knopf.

Slaby, R. G., & Frey, K. S. (1975). Development of gender constancy and selective attention to same-sex models. *Child Development, 46,* 849–856. doi:10.2307/1128389

Slaby, R. G., & Guerra, N. G. (1988). Cognitive mediators of aggression in adolescent offenders: I. Assessment. *Developmental Psychology, 24,* 580–588. doi:10.1037/0012-1649.24.4.580

Slater, A., Bremner, G., Johnson, S. P., Sherwood, P., Hayes, R., & Brown, E. (2000). Newborn infants' preference for attractive faces: The role of internal and external facial features. *Infancy, 1,* 265–274. doi:10.1207/S15327078IN0102_8

Slater, A., Johnson, S. P., Brown, E., & Badenoch, M. (1996). Newborn infant's perception of partly occluded objects. *Infant Behavior and Development, 19,* 145–148. doi:10.1016/S0163-6383(96)90052-1

Slater, A., Mattock, A., & Brown, E. (1990). Size constancy at birth: Newborn infants' responses to retinal and real size. *Journal of Experimental Child Psychology, 49,* 314–322. doi:10.1016/0022-0965(90)90061-C

Slater, A., Morison, V., & Rose, D. (1984). Newborn infants' perception of similarities and differences between two- and three-dimensional stimuli. *British Journal of Developmental Psychology, 2,* 287–294. doi:10.1111/j.2044-835X.1984.tb00936.x

Slater, A., Von der Schulenburg, C., Brown, E., Badenoch, M., Butterworth, G., Parsons, S., & Samuels, C. (1998). Newborn infants prefer attractive faces. *Infant Behavior and Development, 21,* 345–354. doi:10.1016/S0163-6383(98)90011-X

Slaughter, V., Jaakkola, R., & Carey, S. (1999). Constructing a coherent theory: Children's biological understanding of life and death. In M. Siegal & C. C. Peterson (Eds.), *Children's understanding of biology and health* (pp. 71–96). Cambridge: Cambridge University Press.

Slavich, G. M., & Cole, S. W. (2013). The emerging field of human social genomics. *Clinical Psychological Science, 1*(3), 331–348. doi:10.1177/2167702613478594

Slone, L. K., Smith, L. B., & Yu, C. (2019). Self-generated variability in object images predicts vocabulary growth. *Developmental Science,* e12816. https://doi.org/10.1111/desc.12816

Sloutsky, V. M. (2010). From perceptual categories to concepts: What develops? *Cognitive Science, 34,* 1244–1286. doi:10.1111/j.1551-6709.2010.01129.x

Smahel, D., & Wright, M. F. (Eds.). (2014). *The meaning of online problematic situations for children: Results of qualitative cross-cultural investigation in nine European countries.* London: EU Kids Online, London School of Economics and Political Science.

Smetana, J. G. (1988). Adolescents' and parents' conceptions of parental authority. *Child Development, 59,* 321–335. doi:10.2307/1130313

Smetana, J. G., & Asquith, P. (1994). Adolescents' and parents' conceptions of parental authority and personal autonomy. *Child Development, 65,* 1147–1162. doi:10.2307/1131311

Smetana, J. G., & Ball, C. L. (2019). Heterogeneity in children's developing moral judgments about different types of harm. *Developmental Psychology, 55,* 1150–1163. doi:10.1037/dev0000718

Smetana, J. G., & Braeges, J. L. (1990). The development of toddlers' moral and conventional judgments. *Merrill-Palmer Quarterly, 36,* 329–346. doi:10.2307/23087284

Smetana, J. G., & Jambon, M. (2018). Parenting, morality and social development: New views on old questions. In C. C. Helwig (Ed.), *New perspectives on moral development* (pp. 121–140). New York: Routledge.

Smetana, J. G., Jambon, M., & Ball, C. (2014). The social domain approach to children's moral and social judgments. In M. Killen & J. G. Smetana (Eds.), *Handbook of moral development* (pp. 23–45). New York: Psychology Press.

Smiler, A. P., Frankel, L. B. W., & Savin-Williams, R. C. (2011). From kissing to coitus? Sex-of partner differences in the sexual milestone achievement of young men. *Journal of Adolescence, 34,* 727–735. doi:10.1016/j.adolescence.2010.08.009

Smiley, P. A., & Dweck, C. S. (1994). Individual differences in achievement goals among young children. *Child Development, 65,* 1723–1743. doi:10.1111/j.1467-8624.1994.tb00845.x

Smith, A., & Schneider, B. H. (2000). The inter-ethnic friendships of adolescent students: A Canadian study. *International Journal of Intercultural Relations, 24*(2), 247–258.

Smith, C. (2018). Family, academic, and peer group predictors of adolescent pregnancy expectations and young adult childbearing. *Journal of Family Issues, 39,* 1008–1029. doi:10.1177/0192513X16684894

Smith, C. L., Diaz, A., Day, K. L., & Bell, M. A. (2016). Infant frontal electroencephalogram asymmetry and negative emotional reactivity as predictors of toddlerhood effortful control. *Journal of Experimental Child Psychology, 142,* 262–273. doi:10.1016/j.jecp.2015.09.031

Smith, E. D., & Lillard, A. S. (2012). Play on: Retrospective reports of the persistence of pretend play into middle childhood. *Journal of Cognition and Development, 13,* 524–549. doi:10.1080/15248372.2011.608199

Smith, J. S. (1992). Women in charge: Politeness and directives in the speech of Japanese women. *Language in Society, 21,* 59–82.

Smith, L., & Yu, C. (2008). Infants rapidly learn word-referent mappings via cross-situational statistics. *Cognition, 106,* 1558–1568. doi:10.1016/j.cognition.2007.06.010

Smith, L. B. (2005). Action alters shape categories. *Cognitive Science, 29,* 665–679. doi:10.1207/s15516709cog0000_13

Smith, L. B., Thelen, E., Titzer, R., & McLin, D. (1999). Knowing in the context of acting: The task dynamics of the A-not-B error. *Psychological Review, 106,* 235–260.

Smith, R. L., & Rose, A. J. (2011). The "cost of caring" in youths' friendships: Considering associations among social perspective taking, co-rumination, and empathetic distress. *Developmental Psychology, 47,* 1792–1803. doi:10.1037/a0025309

Smith, S. A., & Murphy, V. A. (2015). Measuring productive elements of multi-word phrase vocabulary knowledge among children with English as an additional or only language. *Reading and Writing, 28*(3), 347–369. doi:10.1007/s11145-014-9527-y

Smith, S. L., Choueiti, M., Prescott, A., & Pieper, K. (2013a). *Gender roles and occupations: A look at character attributes and job-related aspirations in film and television.* Executive Report, Geena Davis Institute on Gender in Media. Retrieved from http://seejane.org/wp-content/uploads/full-study-gender-roles-and-occupations-v2.pdf

Smithson, L., Paradis, J., & Nicoladis, E. (2014). Bilingualism and receptive vocabulary achievement: Could sociocultural context make a difference? *Bilingualism: Language and Cognition, 17*(04), 810–821.

Smolina, K., Hanley, G. E., Mintzes, B., Oberlander, T. F., & Morgan, S. (2015). Trends and determinants of prescription drug use during pregnancy and postpartum in British Columbia, 2002–2011: A population-based cohort study. *PloS One, 10*(5), e0128312.

Snarey, J. R. (1985). Cross-cultural universality of social-moral development: A critical review of Kohlbergian research. *Psychological Bulletin, 97,* 202–232. doi:10.1037/0033-2909.97.2.202

Sniekers, S., Stringer, S., Watanabe, K., Jansen, P. R., Coleman, J. R., Krapohl, E., . . . Amin, N. (2017). Genome-wide association meta-analysis of 78,308 individuals identifies new loci and genes influencing human intelligence. *Nature Genetics, 49*(7), 1107.

Snow, C. (1972). Mothers' speech to children learning language. *Child Development, 43*(2), 549–565.

Snowling, M. J., & Melby-Lervåg, M. (2016). Oral language deficits in familial dyslexia: A meta-analysis and review. *Psychological Bulletin, 142*(5), 498.

Snyder, J., Cramer, A., Afrank, J., & Patterson, G. R. (2005). The contributions of ineffective discipline and parental hostile attributions of child misbehavior to the development of conduct problems at home and school. *Developmental Psychology, 41,* 30–41. doi:10.1037/0012-1649.41.1.30

Snyder, J., Reid, J., & Patterson, G. (2003). A social learning model of child and adolescent antisocial behavior. In B. B. Lahey, T. E. Moffitt, & A. Caspi (Eds.), *Causes of conduct disorder and juvenile delinquency* (pp. 27–48). New York: Guilford Press.

Snyder, J., Schrepferman, L., McEachern, A., Barner, S., Johnson, K., & Provines, J. (2008). Peer deviancy training and peer coercion: Dual processes associated with early-onset conduct problems. *Child Development, 79,* 252–268. doi:10.1111/j.1467-8624.2007.01124.x

Snyder, J. J., Schrepferman, L. P., Bullard, L., McEachern, A. D., & Patterson, G. R. (2012). Covert antisocial behavior, peer deviancy training, parenting processes, and sex differences in the development of antisocial behavior during childhood. *Development and Psychopathology, 24,* 1117–1138. doi:10.1017/S0954579412000570

Snyder, T. D., & Dillow, S. A. (2010). *Digest of education statistics, 2009* (NCES 2010–013). Washington, DC: National Center for Education Statistics.

Sobel, D. M., & Kirkham, N. Z. (2006). Blickets and babies: The development of causal reasoning in toddlers and infants. *Developmental Psychology, 42,* 1103–1115. doi:10.1037/0012-1649.42.6.1103

Society for Research in Child Development. (2019). Understanding and addressing the effect of digital games on cognitive development in middle childhood. *Social Policy Report Brief, 32*(1). Retrieved from https://www.srcd.org/sites/default/files/spr_brief_32-1_final.pdf

Soderstrom, M., Blossom, M., Foygel, R., & Morgan, J. L. (2008). Acoustical cues and grammatical units in speech to two preverbal infants. *Journal of Child Language, 35*(4), 869–902.

Solheim, E., Wichstrøm, L., Belsky, J., & Berg-Nielsen, T. S. (2013). Do time in child care and peer group exposure predict poor socioemotional adjustment in Norway? *Child Development, 84,* 1701–1715. doi:10.1111/cdev.12071

Solis, M., Ciullo, S., Vaughn, S., Pyle, N., Hassaram, B., & Leroux, A. (2012). Reading comprehension interventions for middle school students with learning disabilities: A synthesis of 30 years of research. *Journal of Learning Disabilities, 45*(4), 327–340. doi:10.1177/0022219411402691

Solmeyer, A. R., Killoren, S. E., McHale, S. M., & Updegraff, K. A. (2011). Coparenting around siblings' differential treatment in Mexican-origin families. *Journal of Family Psychology, 25,* 251–260. doi:10.1037/a0023201

Solomon, G. E., Johnson, S. C., Zaitchik, D., & Carey, S. (1996). Like father, like son: Young children's understanding of how and why offspring resemble their parents. *Child Development, 67,* 151–171.

Solomon, J., & George, C. (1999). The measurement of attachment security in infancy and childhood. In J. Cassidy & P. R. Shaver (Eds.), *Handbook of attachment: Theory, research, and clinical applications* (pp. 287–316). New York: Guilford Press.

Sommerville, J. A., & Crane, C. C. (2009). Ten-month-old infants use prior information to identify an actor's goal. *Developmental Science, 12,* 314–325. doi:10.1111/j.1467-7687.2008.00787.x

Song, C., Benin, M., & Glick, J. (2012). Dropping out of high school: The effects of family structure and family transitions. *Journal of Divorce and Remarriage, 53,* 18–33. doi:10.1080/10502556.2012.635964

Sonuga-Barke, E. J. S., Kennedy M., Kumsta, R., Knights, N., Golm, D., Rutler, M., . . . Kreppner, J. (2017). Child-to-adult neurodevelopmental and mental health trajectories after early life deprivation: The young adult follow-up of the longitudinal English and Romanian Adoptees study. *Lancet, 389*(10078), 1539–1548. doi:10.1016/S0140-6736(17)30045-4

Sorensen, L. C., Dodge, K. A., & Conduct Problems Prevention Research Group. (2016). How does the fast track intervention prevent adverse outcomes in young adulthood? *Child Development, 87*(2), 429–445.

Soska, K. C., Adolph, K. E., & Johnson, S. P. (2010). Systems in development: Motor skill acquisition facilitates three-dimensional object completion. *Developmental Psychology, 46,* 129–138. doi:10.1037/a0014618

Sowislo, J. F., & Orth, U. (2013). Does low self-esteem predict depression and anxiety? A meta-analysis of longitudinal studies. *Psychological Bulletin, 139,* 213–240. doi:10.1037/a0028931

Spearman, C. E. (1927). *The abilities of man, their nature and measurement.* New York: Macmillan.

Spelke, E., Lee, S. A., & Izard, V. (2010). Beyond core knowledge: Natural geometry. *Cognitive Science, 34*(5), 863–884. doi:10.1111/j.1551-6709.2010.01110.x

Spelke, E. S. (1976). Infants' intermodal perception of events. *Cognitive Psychology, 8,* 553–560.

Spelke, E. S. (1979). Perceiving bimodally specified events in infancy. *Developmental Psychology, 15,* 626–636. doi:10.1037/0012-1649.15.6.626

Spelke, E. S. (2003). What makes us smart? Core knowledge and natural language. In D. Gentner & S. Goldin-Meadow (Eds.), *Language in mind: Advances in the study of language and thought* (pp. 277–311). Cambridge, MA: MIT Press.

Spelke, E. S. (2004). Core knowledge. In N. Kanwisher & J. Duncan (Eds.), *Attention and performance: Functional neuroimaging of visual cognition* (Vol. 20, pp. 29–56). Oxford: Oxford University Press.

Spelke, E. S. (2011). Core systems and the growth of human knowledge: Natural geometry. In A. M. Battro, S. Dehaene, & W. J. Singer (Eds.), *The proceedings of the Working Group on Human Neuroplasticity and Education: Vol. 117. Human neuroplasticity and education* (pp. 73–99). Vatican City: Pontifical Academy of Sciences.

Spelke, E. S., & Kinzler, K. D. (2007). Core knowledge. *Developmental Science, 10,* 89–96. doi:10.1111/j.1467-7687.2007.00569.x

Spence, I., & Feng, J. (2010). Video games and spatial cognition. *Review of General Psychology, 14,* 92–104. doi:10.1037/a0019491

Spence, M. J., & Freeman, M. S. (1996). Newborn infants prefer the maternal low-pass filtered voice, but not the maternal whispered voice. *Infant Behavior and Development, 19,* 199–212. doi:10.1016/S0163-6383(96)90019-3

Spencer, J. P., Clearfield, M., Corbetta, D., Ulrich, B., Buchanan, P., & Schöner, G. (2006). Moving toward a grand theory of development: In memory of Esther Thelen. *Child Development, 77,* 1521–1538. doi:10.1111/j.1467-8624.2006.00955.x

Spencer, M. B., & Markstrom-Adams, C. (1990). Identity processes among racial and ethnic minority children in America. *Child Development, 61,* 290–310.

Spencer-Rodgers, J., Peng, K., Wang, L., & Hou, Y. (2004). Dialectical self-esteem and East-West differences in psychological well-being. *Personality and Social Psychology Bulletin, 30,* 1416–1432. doi:10.1177/0146167204264243

Sperry, D. E., Sperry, L. L., & Miller, P. J. (2018). Reexamining the verbal environments of children from different socioeconomic backgrounds. *Child Development.* https://doi.org/10.1111/cdev.13072

Springer, K., & Keil, F. C. (1991). Early differentiation of causal mechanisms appropriate to biological and nonbiological kinds. *Child Development, 62,* 767–781. doi:10.1111/j.1467-8624.1991.tb01568.x

Springer, K., Nguyen, T., & Samaniego, R. (1996). Early understanding of age- and environment-related noxiousness in biological kinds: Evidence for a naive theory. *Cognitive Development, 11,* 65–82. doi:10.1016/S0885-2014(96)90028-3

Srinivasan, M., & Carey, S. (2010). The long and the short of it: On the nature and origin of functional overlap between representations of space and time. *Cognition, 116,* 217–241. doi:10.1016/j.cognition.2010.05.005

Sroufe, L. A., Bennett, C., Englund, M., Urban, J., & Shulman, S. (1993). The significance of gender boundaries in preadolescence: Contemporary correlates and antecedents of boundary violation and maintenance. *Child Development, 64,* 455–466. doi:10.2307/1131262

Stack, D. M., Muir, D. W., Sherriff, F., & Roman, J. (1989). Development of infant reaching in the dark to luminous objects and 'invisible sounds.' *Perception, 18,* 69–82.

Stahl, A. E., & Feigenson, L. (2015). Observing the unexpected enhances infants' learning and exploration. *Science, 348*(6230), 91–94.

Stahl, A. E., & Feigenson, L. (2018). Violations of core knowledge shape early learning. *Topics in Cognitive Science.* https://doi.org/10.1111/tops.12389

Stake, J. E., & Mares, K. R. (2005). Evaluating the impact of science-enrichment programs on adolescents' science motivation and confidence: The splashdown effect. *Journal of Research in Science Teaching, 42,* 359–375.

Stanley, L. (2019). Is the preschool PATHS curriculum effective? A review. *Journal of Evidence-Based Social Work, 16,* 130–143. doi:10.1080/23761407.2018.1558141

Stapel, J. C., van Wijk, I., Bekkering, H., & Hunnius, S. (2017). Eighteen-month-old infants show distinct electrophysiological responses to their own faces. *Developmental Science, 20,* e12437. doi:10.1111/desc.12437

Statistics Canada. (2011). Family violence in Canada: A statistical profile. Retrieved from http://www.statcan.gc.ca/pub/85-224-x/85-224-x2010000-eng.pdf

Statistics Canada. (2014). Police-reported sexual offences against children and youth in Canada, 2012. Retrieved from http://www.statcan.gc.ca/daily-quotidien/140528/dq140528a-eng.htm

Statistics Canada. (2015a). Census family. Retrieved from http://www23.statcan.gc.ca/imdb/p3Var.pl?Function=Unit&Id=32746

Statistics Canada. (2015b). Table 13-10-0799-01: Children's screen time, 2 hours per day or less, by sex, household population aged 6 to 17, 2015. Canadian Community Health Survey: Nutrition, Canada and Provinces.

Statistics Canada. (2017a). Census in brief: English–French bilingualism reaches new heights. Ministry of the Industry. Retrieved from https://www12.statcan.gc.ca/census-recensement/2016/as-sa/98-200-x/2016009/98-200-x2016009-eng.cfm

Statistics Canada. (2017b). Portrait of children's family life in Canada in 2016. Retrieved from https://www12.statcan.gc.ca/census-recensement/2016/as-sa/98-200-x/2016006/98-200-x2016006-eng.cfm

Statistics Canada. (2017c). Postsecondary qualification holders aged 25 years and over by highest certificate, diploma or degree, major field of study, sex and other demographic characteristics. Retrieved from https://www150.statcan.gc.ca/t1/tbl1/en/cv.action?pid=3710014801

Statistics Canada. (2017d). Same-sex couples in Canada in 2016. *Statistics Canada Catalogue, 98-200-X2016007.*

Statistics Canada. (2018a). A portrait of Canadian youth. Catalogue no. 11-631-X ISBN 978-0-660-24687-1. Retrieved from https://www150.statcan.gc.ca/n1/pub/11-631-x/11-631-x2018001-eng.htm

Statistics Canada. (2018b). Canadian postsecondary enrolments and graduates, 2016/2017. Retrieved from https://www150.statcan.gc.ca/n1/daily-quotidien/181128/dq181128c-eng.htm

Statistics Canada. (2018c). Police-reported hate crime, 2017. Retrieved from https://www150.statcan.gc.ca/n1/en/daily-quotidien/181129/dq181129a-eng.pdf?st=xlM3n0Np

Statistics Canada. (2019a). Early learning and child care arrangements for children aged 0 to 5 years. Retrieved from https://www150.statcan.gc.ca/n1/pub/11-627-m/11-627-m2019026-eng.htm

Statistics Canada. (2019b). Family characteristics of children aged 0 to 14 including presence of grandparents in private households for the population by age group 0 to 14, % distribution 2016, Canada, provinces and territories, 2016 Census: 100% Data. Retrieved from https://www12.statcan.gc.ca/census-recensement/2016/dp-pd/hlt-fst/fam/Table.cfm?Lang=E&T=41&Geo=00&SP=1&view=5&age=1

Statistics Canada. (2019c). Persons living below Canada's official poverty line (market basket measure), 2013 to 2017. Retrieved from www150.statcan.gc.ca/n1/daily-quotidien/190226/t002b-eng.htm

Statistics Canada. (2019d). Table 13-10-0745-01: Birth-related indicators (low and high birth weight, small and large for gestational age, pre-term births), by sex, three-year period, health regions and peer groups. Retrieved from https://www150.statcan.gc.ca/t1/tbl1/en/tv.action?pid=1310074501

Statistics Canada. (2019e). Table 13-10-0096-01: Health characteristics, annual estimates. Retrieved from https://www150.statcan.gc.ca/t1/tbl1/en/tv.action?pid=1310009601

Statistics Canada. (2019f). Table 13-10-0424-01: Live births, birth weight indicators, by characteristics of the mother and child. Retrieved from https://www150.statcan.gc.ca/t1/tbl1/en/tv.action?pid=1310042401

Statistics Canada. (2019g). Table 13-10-0428-01: Live births and fetal deaths (stillbirths), by type of birth (single or multiple). Retrieved from https://www150.statcan.gc.ca/t1/tbl1/en/tv.action?pid=1310042801

Statistics Canada. (2019h). The Canadian Income Survey, 2017.

Statistics Canada. (2019i). The Daily: Canadian Income Survey, 2017. Released February 26, 2019. Retrieved from https://www150.statcan.gc.ca/n1/daily-quotidien/190226/dq190226b-eng.htm

Statistics Canada. (2019j). Table 42-10-0005-01: Type of child care arrangement, household population aged 0 to 5 years. Retrieved from https://www150.statcan.gc.ca/t1/tbl1/en/tv.action?pid=4210000501

Statistics Canada. (n.d.a). Table 13-10-0096-01: Health characteristics, annual estimates. Retrieved from https://www150.statcan.gc.ca/t1/tbl1/en/tv.action?pid=1310009601

Statistics Canada. (n.d.b). Table 13-10-0797-01: Measured children and youth body mass index (BMI) (Cole classification), by age group and sex, Canada and provinces, Canadian Community Health Survey—Nutrition. Retrieved from https://www150.statcan.gc.ca/t1/tbl1/en/tv.action?pid=1310079701.

Stecher, B. M., McCaffrey, D. F., & Bugliari, D. (2003, November 10). The relationship between exposure to class size reduction and student achievement in California. *Education Policy Analysis Archives, 11*(40). Retrieved from http://epaa.asu.edu/epaa/v11n40/

Steele, H., Steele, M., & Croft, C. (2008). Early attachment predicts emotion recognition at 6 and 11 years old. *Attachment and Human Development, 10,* 379–393. doi:10.1080/14616730802461409

Steenbeek, H., & van Geert, P. (2008). An empirical validation of a dynamic systems model of interaction: Do children of different sociometric statuses differ in their dyadic play? *Developmental Science, 11,* 253–281. doi:10.1111/j.1467-7687.2007.00655.x

Steinberg, L. (2010). A dual systems model of adolescent risk-taking. *Developmental Psychobiology, 52,* 216–224. doi:10.1002/dev.20445

Steinberg, L., Lamborn, S. D., Darling, N., Mounts, N. S., & Dornbusch, S. M. (1994). Over-time changes in adjustment and competence among adolescents from authoritative, authoritarian, indulgent, and neglectful families. *Child Development, 65,* 754–770. doi:10.1111/j.1467-8624.1994.tb00781.x

Steinberg, L., & Silverberg, S. B. (1986). The vicissitudes of autonomy in early adolescence. *Child Development, 57,* 841–851. doi:10.2307/1130361

Steinmayr, R., & Spinath, B. (2009). What explains boys' stronger confidence in their intelligence? *Sex Roles, 61,* 736–749. doi:10.1007/s11199-009-9675-8

Stenberg, G. (2013). Do 12-month-old infants trust a competent adult? *Infancy, 18,* 873–904. doi:10.1111/infa.12011

Stern, D. N. (1985). *The interpersonal world of the infant: A view from psychoanalysis and developmental psychology.* New York: Basic Books.

Sternberg, R. J. (1999). The theory of successful intelligence. *Review of General Psychology, 3,* 292–316. doi:10.1037/1089-2680.3.4.292

Sternberg, R. J. (2003). A broad view of intelligence: The theory of successful intelligence. *Consulting Psychology Journal: Practice and Research, 55,* 139–154. doi:10.1037/1061-4087.55.3.139

Sternberg, R. J. (2007). *Wisdom, intelligence, and creativity synthesized.* New York: Cambridge University Press.

Sternberg, R. J. (2008). *g*, g's, or Jeez: Which is the best model for developing abilities, competencies, and expertise? In P. C. Kyllonen, R. D. Roberts, & L. Stankov (Eds.), *Extending intelligence: Enhancement and new constructs* (pp. 225–266). New York: Erlbaum.

Sterrett, E. M., Jones, D. J., McKee, L. G., & Kincaid, C. (2011). Supportive non-parental adults and adolescent psychosocial functioning: Using social support as a theoretical framework. *American Journal of Community Psychology, 48,* 284–295. doi:10.1007/s10464-011-9429-y

Stevens, T., Wang, K., Olivárez, A., Jr., & Hamman, D. (2007). Use of self-perspectives and their sources to predict the mathematics enrollment intentions of girls and boys. *Sex Roles, 56,* 351–363. doi:10.1007/s11199-006-9180-2

Stevenson, H. W. (1991). The development of prosocial behavior in large-scale collective societies: China and Japan. In R. A. Hinde & J. Groebel (Eds.), *Cooperation and prosocial behaviour* (pp. 89–105). Cambridge: Cambridge University Press.

Stiles, J., & Jernigan, T. L. (2010). The basics of brain development. *Neuropsychology Review, 20*(4), 327–348.

Stocker, C. M., Richmond, M. K., Rhoades, G. K., & Kiang, L. (2007). Family emotional processes and adolescents' adjustment. *Social Development, 16,* 310–325.

Stoddart, T., & Turiel, E. (1985). Children's concepts of cross-gender activities. *Child Development, 56,* 1241–1252. doi:10.2307/1130239

Stoet, G., & Geary, D. C. (2018). The gender-equality paradox in science, technology, engineering, and mathematics education. *Psychological Science, 29*(4), 581–593. http://dx.doi.org/10.1177/0956797617741719

Stone, L. B., Hankin, B. L., Gibb, B. E., & Abela, J. R. Z. (2011). Co-rumination predicts the onset of depressive disorders during adolescence. *Journal of Abnormal Psychology, 120,* 752–757. doi:10.1037/a0023384

Stone, L. J., & Church, J. (1957). *Childhood and adolescence: A psychology of the growing person.* New York: Random House.

Stouthamer-Loeber, M., Loeber, R., Wei, E., Farrington, D. P., & Wikström, P.-O. H. (2002). Risk and promotive effects in the explanation of persistent serious delinquency in boys. *Journal of Consulting and Clinical Psychology, 70,* 111–123. doi:10.1037/0022-006X.70.1.111

Stover, C. S., Connell, C. M., Leve, L. D., Neiderhiser, J. M., Shaw, D. S., Scaramella, L. V., . . . Reiss, D. (2012). Fathering and mothering in the family system: Linking marital hostility and aggression in adopted toddlers. *Journal of Child Psychology and Psychiatry, 53,* 401–409. doi:10.1111/j.1469-7610.2011.02510.x

Strand-Brodd, K., Ewald, U., Grönqvist, H., Holmström, G., Strömberg, B., Grönqvist, E., . . . Rosander, K. (2011). Development of smooth pursuit eye movements in very preterm infants: 1. General aspects. *Acta Paediatrica, 100,* 983–991. doi:10.1111/j.1651-2227.2011.02218.x

Strazdins, L., O'Brien, L., Lucas, N., & Rodgers, B. (2013). Combining work and family: Rewards or risks for children's mental health? *Social Science and Medicine, 87,* 99–107. doi:10.1016/j.socscimed.2013.03.030

Striepens, N., Kendrick, K. M., Maier, W., & Hurlemann, R. (2011). Prosocial effects of oxytocin and clinical evidence for its therapeutic potential. *Frontiers in Neuroendocrinology, 32,* 426–450. doi:10.1016/j.yfrne.2011.07.001

Stronach, E. P., Toth, S. L., Rogosch, F., Oshri, A., Manly, J. T., & Cicchetti, D. (2011). Child maltreatment, attachment security, and internal representations of mother and mother–child relationships. *Child Maltreatment, 16,* 137–145. doi:10.1177/1077559511398294

Strong, D. D., Bean, R. A., & Feinauer, L. L. (2010). Trauma, attachment, and family therapy with grandfamilies: A model for treatment. *Children and Youth Services Review, 32*(1), 44–50. doi:10.1016/j.childyouth.2009.06.015

Strough, J., & Berg, C. A. (2000). Goals as a mediator of gender differences in high-affiliation dyadic conversations. *Developmental Psychology, 36,* 117–125. doi:10.1037/0012-1649.36.1.117

Strough, J., & Covatto, A. M. (2002). Context and age differences in same- and other-gender peer preferences. *Social Development, 11,* 346–361. doi:10.1111/1467-9507.00204

Stuewig, J., Tangney, J. P., Kendall, S., Folk, J. B., Meyer, C. R., & Dearing, R. L. (2015). Children's proneness to shame and guilt predict risk and illegal behaviors in young adulthood. *Child Psychiatry & Human Development, 46,* 217–227. doi:10.1007/s10578-014-0467-1

Stukas, A. A., Snyder, M., & Clary, E. G. (1999). The effects of "mandatory volunteerism" on intentions to volunteer. *Psychological Science, 10,* 59–64. doi:10.2307/40063378

Stukas, A. A., Switzer, G. E., Dew, M. A., Goycoolea, J. M., & Simmons, R. G. (1999). Parental helping models, gender, and service-learning. *Journal of Prevention and Intervention in the Community, 18,* 5–18. doi:10.1300/j005v18n01_02

Sturaro, C., van Lier, P. A. C., Cuijpers, P., & Koot, H. M. (2011). The role of peer relationships in the development of early school-age externalizing problems. *Child Development, 82,* 758–765. doi:10.1111/j.1467-8624.2010.01532.x

Subbotsky, E. (1994). Early rationality and magical thinking in preschoolers: Space and time. *British Journal of Developmental Psychology, 12,* 97–108. doi:10.1111/j.2044-835X.1994.tb00621.x

Subbotsky, E. (2005). The permanence of mental objects: Testing magical thinking on perceived and imaginary realities. *Developmental Psychology, 41,* 301–318. doi:10.1037/0012-1649.41.2.301

Subbotsky, E. V. (1993). *Foundations of the mind: Children's understanding of reality.* Cambridge, MA: Harvard University Press.

Substance Abuse and Mental Health Services Administration. (2018). *Helping children and youth who have traumatic experiences.* Retrieved from https://www.samhsa.gov/sites/default/files/brief_report_natl_childrens_mh_awareness_day.pdf

Sugai, G., & Horner, R. R. (2006). A promising approach for expanding and sustaining school-wide positive behavior support. *School Psychology Review, 35,* 245–259.

Sugden, N. A., Mohamed-Ali, M. I., & Moulson, M. C. (2014). I spy with my little eye: Typical, daily exposure to faces documented from a first-person infant perspective. *Developmental Psychobiology, 56*(2), 249–261.

Sukhodolsky, D. G., Smith, S. D., McCauley, S. A., Ibrahim, K., & Piasecka, J. B. (2016). Behavioral interventions for anger, irritability, and aggression in children and adolescents. *Journal of Child and Adolescent Psychopharmacology, 26,* 58–64. doi:10.1089/cap.2015.0120

Sullivan, K., & Winner, E. (1993). Three-year-olds' understanding of mental states: The influence of trickery. *Journal of Experimental Child Psychology, 56,* 135–148. doi:10.1006/jecp.1993.1029

Sullivan, M. W., & Lewis, M. (2003). Contextual determinants of anger and other negative expressions in young infants. *Developmental Psychology, 39,* 693–705.

Sun, Y., & Li, Y. (2011). Effects of family structure type and stability on children's academic performance trajectories. *Journal of Marriage and Family, 73,* 541–556. doi:10.1111/j.1741-3737.2011.00825.x

Sundara, M., Polka, L., & Molnar, M. (2008). Development of coronal stop perception: Bilingual infants keep pace with their monolingual peers. *Cognition, 108,* 232–242. doi:10.1016/j.cognition.2007.12.013

Super, C. M., & Harkness, S. (1986). The developmental niche: A conceptualization at the interface of child and culture. *International Journal of Behavioral Development, 9,* 545–569. doi:10.1177/016502548600900409

Suskind, D. L., Leffel, K. R., Graf, E., Hernandez, M. W., Gunderson, E. A., Sapolich, S. G., . . . Levine, S. C. (2015). A parent-directed language intervention for children of low socioeconomic status: A randomized controlled pilot study. *Journal of Child Language, 43*(02), 366–406.

Sutherland, K. E., Altenhofen, S., & Biringen, Z. (2012). Emotional availability during mother–child interactions in divorcing and intact married families. *Journal of Divorce and Remarriage, 53,* 126–141. doi:10.1080/10502556.2011.651974

Sutherland, S. L., & Friedman, O. (2012). Preschoolers acquire general knowledge by sharing in pretense. *Child Development, 83,* 1064–1071. doi:10.1111/j.1467-8624.2012.01748.x

Sutton, J. E., Joanisse, M. F., & Newcombe, N. S. (2010). Spinning in the scanner: Neural correlates of virtual reorientation. *Journal of Experimental Psychology: Learning, Memory, and Cognition, 36,* 1097–1107. doi:10.1037/a0019938

Suzuki, L. K., Davis, H. M., & Greenfield, P. M. (2008). Self-enhancement and self-effacement in reaction to praise and criticism: The case of multiethnic youth. *Ethos, 36,* 78–97. doi:10.1111/j.1548-1352.2008.00005.x

Swahn, M. H., Simon, T. R., Arias, I., & Bossarte, R. M. (2008). Measuring sex differences in violence victimization and perpetration within date and same-sex peer relationships. *Journal of Interpersonal Violence, 23,* 1120–1138. doi:10.1177/0886260508314086

Swearer, S. M., & Hymel, S. (2015). Understanding the psychology of bullying: Moving toward a social-ecological diathesis-stress model. *American Psychologist, 70,* 344–353. doi:10.1037/a0038929

Tager-Flusberg, H. (2007). Evaluating the theory-of-mind hypothesis of autism. *Current Directions in Psychological Science, 16,* 311–315. doi:10.1111/j.1467-8721.2007.00527.x

Tager-Flusberg, H., & Joseph, R. M. (2005). How language facilitates the acquisition of false-belief understanding in children with autism. In J. W. Astington & J. A. Baird (Eds.), *Why language matters for theory of mind* (pp. 298–318). New York: Oxford University Press.

Tajfel, H., & Turner, J. C. (1979). An integrative theory of intergroup conflict. In W. G. Austin & S. Worchel (Eds.), *The social psychology of intergroup relations* (pp. 33–47). Monterey, CA: Brooks/Cole.

Takaoka, S., Fujino, T., Hotta, N., Ueda, K., Hanada, M., Tajiri, M., & Inoue, Y. (2014). Signs and symptoms of methylmercury contamination in a First Nations community in Northwestern Ontario, Canada. *Science of the Total Environment, 468,* 950–957.

Tanaka, H., Black, J. M., Hulme, C., Stanley, L. M., Kesler, S. R., Whitfield-Gabrieli, S., . . .

Hoeft, F. (2011). The brain basis of the phonological deficit in dyslexia is independent of IQ. *Psychological Science, 22,* 1442–1451.

Taneja, V., Sriram., S., Beri, R., Sreenivas, V., Aggarwal, R., & Kaur, R. (2002). 'Not by bread alone': Impact of a structured 90-minute play session on development of children in an orphanage. *Child Care Health and Development, 28,* 95–100. doi:10.1046/j.1365-2214.2002.00246.x

Tang, H., Hammack, C., Ogden, S. C., Wen, Z., Qian, X., Li, Y., . . . Christian, K. M. (2016). Zika virus infects human cortical neural progenitors and attenuates their growth. *Cell Stem Cell, 18*(5), 587–590.

Tangney, J. P., & Dearing, R. L. (2002). *Shame and guilt.* New York: Guilford Press.

Tangney, J. P., Stuewig, J., & Mashek, D. J. (2007). Moral emotions and moral behavior. *Annual Review of Psychology, 58,* 345–372. doi:10.1146/annurev.psych.56.091103.070145

Tanner, J. M. (1961). *Education and physical growth: Implications of the study of children's growth for educational theory and practice.* London: University of London Press.

Tardif, T., Fletcher, P., Liang, W., Zhang, Z., Kaciroti, N., & Marchman, V. A. (2008). Baby's first 10 words. *Developmental Psychology, 44,* 929–938. doi:10.1037/0012-1649.44.4.929

Tasimi, A., & Wynn, K. (2016). Costly rejection of wrongdoers by infants and children. *Cognition, 151,* 76–79. doi:10.1016/j.cognition.2016.03.004

Taumoepeau, M., & Ruffman, T. (2006). Mother and infant talk about mental states relates to desire language and emotion understanding. *Child Development, 77,* 465–481.

Taumoepeau, M., & Ruffman, T. (2008). Stepping stones to others' minds: Maternal talk relates to child mental state language and emotion understanding at 15, 24, and 33 months. *Child Development, 79,* 284–302.

Taylor, J., Iacono, W. G., & McGue, M. (2000). Evidence for a genetic etiology of early-onset delinquency. *Journal of Abnormal Psychology, 109,* 634–643. doi:10.1037/0021-843X.109.4.634

Taylor, M. (1999). *Imaginary companions and the children who create them.* New York: Oxford University Press.

Taylor, M., & Mannering, A. M. (2007). Of Hobbes and Harvey: The imaginary companions created by children and adults. In A. Göncü & S. Gaskins (Eds.), *Play and development: Evolutionary, sociocultural, and functional perspectives* (pp. 227–246). New York: Erlbaum.

Taylor, M., Carlson, S. M., Maring, B. L., Gerow, L., & Charley, C. M. (2004). The characteristics and correlates of fantasy in school-age children: Imaginary companions, impersonation, and social understanding. *Developmental Psychology, 40,* 1173–1187. doi:10.1037/0012-1649.40.6.1173

Taylor, M., Hulette, A. C., & Dishion, T. J. (2010). Longitudinal outcomes of young high-risk adolescents with imaginary companions. *Developmental Psychology, 46*(6), 1632–1636. doi:10.1037/a0019815

Taylor, M. G. (1993). *Children's beliefs about the biological and social origins of gender differences* (Unpublished doctoral dissertation). University of Michigan, Ann Arbor.

Teglas, E., Girotto, V., Gonzalez, M., & Bonatti, L. L. (2007). Intuitions of probabilities shape expectations about the future at 12 months and beyond. *Proceedings of the National Academy of Sciences of the United States of America, 104,* 19156–19159. doi:10.1073/pnas.0700271104

Teglas, E., Vul, E., Girotto, V., Gonzalez, M., Tenenbaum, J. B., & Bonatti, L. L. (2011, May 27). Pure reasoning in 12-month-old infants as probabilistic inference. *Science, 332,* 1054–1059.

Teicher, M. H., & Blass, E. M. (1977). First suckling response of the newborn albino rat: The roles of olfaction and amniotic fluid. *Science, 198*(4317), 635–636.

Teicher, M. H., Samson, J. A., & Anderson, C. M., & Ohashi, K. (2016). The effects of childhood maltreatment on brain structure, function, and connectivity. *Nature Reviews: Neuroscience, 17,* 652–666.

Teinonen, T., Fellman, V., Näätänen, R., Alku, P., & Huotilainen, M. (2009). Statistical language learning in neonates revealed by event-related brain potentials. *BMC Neuroscience, 10,* 1–8. doi:10.1186/1471-2202-10-21

Tempelmann, S., Kaminski, J., & Tomasello, M. (2014). Do domestic dogs learn words based on humans' referential behaviour? *PloS One, 9*(3), e91014. doi:10.1371/journal.pone.0091014

Tenenbaum, H. R., & Leaper, C. (2003). Parent–child conversations about science: The socialization of gender inequities? *Developmental Psychology, 39,* 34–47. doi:10.1037/0012-1649.39.1.34

Teoh, S., Chin, L., Menon, V., Ng, M., Peat, N., Raper, M., . . . Savage, J. (2006). World records in obstetrics and gynaecology. *Journal of Obstetrics and Gynaecology, 26*(7), 607–611.

Terrace, H. S., Petitto, L.-A., Sanders, R. J., & Bever, T. G. (1979, November 23). Can an ape create a sentence? *Science, 206,* 891–902.

Terrett, G., White, R., & Spreckley, M. (2012). A preliminary evaluation of the Parent–Child Mother Goose Program in relation to children's language and parenting stress. *Journal of Early Childhood Research, 11,* 16–26.

Thamotharan, S., Lange, K., Zale, E. L., Huffhines, L., & Fields, S. (2013). The role of impulsivity in pediatric obesity and weight status. A meta-analytic review. *Clinical Psychology Review, 33*(2), 253–262.

Thapar, A., Cooper, M., Eyre, O., & Langley, K. (2013). Practitioner review: What have we learnt about the causes of ADHD? *Journal of Child Psychology and Psychiatry, 54*(1), 3–16.

The Annenberg Public Policy Center. (2017). Gun violence in PG-13 movies continues to climb past R-rated films. *The Annenberg Public Policy Center of the University of Pennsylvania.* Released January 11, 2017.

The ManyBabies Consortium. (2019). Quantifying sources of variability in infancy research using the infant-directed speech preference. *Advances in Methods and Practices in Psychological Science.* (Accepted pending data collection.)

Thelen, E. (1986). Treadmill-elicited stepping in seven-month-old infants. *Child Development, 57,* 1498–1506. doi:10.2307/1130427

Thelen, E. (1995). Motor development: A new synthesis. *American Psychologist, 50,* 79–95. doi:10.1037/0003-066X.50.2.79

Thelen, E. (2001). Dynamic mechanisms of change in early perceptual-motor development. In J. L. McClelland & R. Siegler (Eds.), *Mechanisms of cognitive development: Behavioral and neural perspectives* (pp. 161–184). Mahwah, NJ: Erlbaum.

Thelen, E., & Corbetta, D. (1994). Exploration and selection in the early acquisition of skill. *International Review of Neurobiology, 37,* 75–102.

Thelen, E., Corbetta, D., Kamm, K., Spencer, J. P., Schneider, K., & Zernicke, R. F. (1993). The transition to reaching: Mapping intention and intrinsic dynamics. *Child Development, 64*(4), 1058–1098.

Thelen, E., & Smith, L. B. (1998). Dynamic systems theories. In W. Damon (Series Ed.) & R. M. Lerner (Vol. Ed.), *Handbook of child psychology: Vol. 1. Theoretical models of human development* (5th ed., pp. 563–634). Hoboken, NJ: Wiley.

Thelen, E., & Smith, L. B. (2006). Dynamic systems theories. In W. Damon & R. M. Lerner (Series Eds.) & R. M. Lerner (Vol. Ed.), *Handbook of child psychology: Vol. 1. Theoretical models of human development* (6th ed., pp. 258–312). Hoboken, NJ: Wiley.

Therrell, B. L., Padilla, C. D., Loeber, J. G., Kneisser, I., Saadallah, A., Borrajo, G. J., & Adams, J. (2015, April). Current status of newborn screening worldwide: 2015. In *Seminars in perinatology* (Vol. 39, No. 3, pp. 171–187). WB Saunders.

Thiessen, E. D., Hill, E. A., & Saffran, J. R. (2005). Infant-directed speech facilitates word segmentation. *Infancy, 7,* 53–71. doi:10.1207/s15327078in0701_5

Thiessen, E. D., & Saffran, J. R. (2003). When cues collide: Statistical and stress cues in infant word segmentation. *Developmental Psychology, 39,* 706–716.

Thinus-Blanc, C., & Gaunet, F. (1997). Representation of space in blind persons: Vision as a spatial sense? *Psychological Bulletin, 121,* 20–42.

Thomaes, S., Bushman, B. J., Stegge, H., & Olthof, T. (2008). Trumping shame by blasts of noise: Narcissism, self-esteem, shame, and aggression in young adolescents. *Child Development, 79,* 1792–1801. doi:10.1111/j.1467-8624.2008.01226.x

Thomas, A., & Chess, S. (1977). *Temperament and development.* New York: Brunner/Mazel.

Thomas, A., Chess, S., & Birch, H. G. (1968). *Temperament and behavior disorders in children.* New York: New York University Press.

Thomas, J. R., & French, K. E. (1985). Gender differences across age in motor performance: A meta-analysis. *Psychological Bulletin, 98,* 260–282. doi:10.1037/0033-2909.98.2.260

Thompson, C. A., & Opfer, J. E. (2010). How 15 hundred is like 15 cherries: Effect of progressive alignment on representational changes in numerical cognition. *Child Development, 81,* 1768–1786. doi:10.1111/j.1467-8624.2010.01509.x

Thompson, R. A. (1998). Early sociopersonality development. In W. Damon (Series Ed.) & N. Eisenberg (Vol. Ed.), *Handbook of child psychology: Vol. 3. Social, emotional, and personality development* (5th ed., pp. 25–104). Hoboken, NJ: Wiley.

Thompson, R. A. (2006). The development of the person: Social understanding, relationships, conscience, self. In W. Damon & R. M. Lerner (Series Eds.) & N. Eisenberg (Vol. Ed.), *Handbook of child psychology: Vol. 3. Social, emotional, and personality development* (6th ed., pp. 24–98). Hoboken, NJ: Wiley.

Thompson, R. A. (2008). Early attachment and later development: Familiar questions, new answers. In J. Cassidy & P. R. Shaver (Eds.), *Handbook of attachment:*

Theory, research, and clinical applications (2nd ed., pp. 348–365). New York: Guilford Press.

Thompson, R. A. (2012). Whither the preconventional child? Toward a life-span moral development theory. *Child Development Perspectives, 6,* 423–429. doi:10.1111/j.1750-8606.2012.00245.x

Thompson, R. A. (2015). Relationships, regulation, and early development. In. M. E. Lamb & R. M. Lerner (Eds.), *Handbook of child psychology and developmental science* (7th ed., pp. 201–246). Hoboken, NJ: Wiley.

Thompson, R. A. (2016). Early attachment and later development: Reframing the questions. In J. Cassidy & P. R. Shaver (Eds.), *Handbook of attachment: Theory, research, and clinical applications, 3rd ed.* (pp. 333–348). New York: Guilford.

Thompson, R. A., & Newton, E. K. (2010). Emotion in early conscience. In W. F. Arsenio & E. A. Lemerise (Eds.), *Emotions, aggression, and morality in children: Bridging development and psychopathology* (pp. 13–31). Washington, DC: American Psychological Association.

Thornberry, T. P., Freeman-Gallant, A., Lizotte, A. J., Krohn, M. D., & Smith, C. A. (2003). Linked lives: The intergenerational transmission of antisocial behavior. *Journal of Abnormal Child Psychology, 31,* 171–184. doi:10.1023/A: 1022574208366

Thorne, B. (1993). *Gender play: Girls and boys in school.* New Brunswick, NJ: Rutgers University Press.

Thorne, B., & Luria, Z. (1986). Sexuality and gender in children's daily worlds. *Social Problems, 33,* 176–190. doi:10.2307/800703

Thurstone, L. L. (1938). *Primary mental abilities.* Chicago: The University of Chicago Press.

Tiedemann, J. (2000). Parents' gender stereotypes and teachers' beliefs as predictors of children's concept of their mathematical ability in elementary school. *Journal of Educational Psychology, 92,* 144–151. doi:10.1037/0022-0663.92.1.144

Tienari, P., Wahlberg, K.-E., & Wynne, L. C. (2006). Finnish adoption study of schizophrenia: Implications for family interventions. *Families, Systems, and Health, 24,* 442–451. doi:10.1037/1091-7527.24.4.442

Tincoff, R., & Jusczyk, P. W. (1999). Some beginnings of word comprehension in 6-month-olds. *Psychological Science, 10,* 172–175. doi:10.1111/1467-9280.00127

Tobin, D. D., Menon, M., Menon, M., Spatta, B. C., Hodges, E. V. E., & Perry, D. G. (2010). The intrapsychics of gender: A model of self-socialization. *Psychological Review, 117*(2), 601–622. http://dx.doi.org/10.1037/a0018936

Tobin, K., & Murphy, J. (2013). Addressing the challenges of child and family homelessness. *Journal of Applied Research on Children: Informing Policy for Children at Risk, 4*(1), Article 9. Retrieved from http://digitalcommons.library.tmc.edu/childrenatrisk/vol4/iss1/9

Todd, B. K., Fischer, R. A., Di Costa, S., Roestorf, A., Harbour, K., Hardiman, P., & Barry, J. A. (2017). Sex differences in children's toy preferences: A systematic review, meta-regression, and meta-analysis. *Infant and Child Development, 27:* e2064. http://dx.doi.org/10.1002/icd.2064

Tolan, P. H., Gorman-Smith, D., & Henry, D. B. (2003). The developmental ecology of urban males' youth violence. *Developmental Psychology, 39,* 274–291. doi:10.1037/0012-1649.39.2.274

Tolchinsky, L. (2003). *The cradle of culture and what children know about writing and numbers before being taught.* Mahwah, NJ: Erlbaum.

Tom, S. R., Schwartz, D., Chang, L., Farver, J. A. M., & Xu, Y. (2010). Correlates of victimization in Hong Kong children's peer groups. *Journal of Applied Developmental Psychology, 31,* 27–37. doi:10.1016/j.appdev.2009.06.002

Tomada, G., & Schneider, B. H. (1997). Relational aggression, gender, and peer acceptance: Invariance across culture, stability over time, and concordance among informants. *Developmental Psychology, 33,* 601–609. doi:10.1037/0012-1649.33.4.601

Tomasello, M. (1994). Can an ape understand a sentence? [Review of the monograph *Language comprehension in ape and child,* by E. S. Savage-Rumbaugh et al.]. *Language and Communication, 14,* 377–390.

Tomasello, M. (2008). *Origins of human communication.* Cambridge, MA: MIT Press.

Tomasello, M. (2014). *A natural history of human thinking.* Cambridge, MA: Harvard University Press.

Tomasello, M., Strosberg, R., & Akhtar, N. (1996). Eighteen-month-old children learn words in non-ostensive contexts. *Journal of Child Language, 23,* 157–176. doi:10.1017/S0305000900010138

Tomasello, M., & Vaish, A. (2013). Origins of human cooperation and morality. *Annual Review of Psychology, 64,* 231–255. doi:10.1146/annurev-psych-113011-143812

Tomblin, J. B., Records, N. L., Buckwalter, P., Zhang, X., Smith, E., & O'Brien, M. (1997, December). Prevalence of specific language impairment in kindergarten children. *Journal of Speech, Language, and Hearing Research, 40*(6), 1245–1260.

Tomlinson, H. B. (2009). Developmentally appropriate practice in the kindergarten year—Ages 5–6: An overview. In C. Copple & S. Bredekamp (Eds.), *Developmentally appropriate practice in early childhood programs serving children from birth through age 8* (3rd ed., pp. 187–216). Washington, DC: National Association for the Education of Young Children.

Tooby, J., & Cosmides, L. (2005). Conceptual foundations of evolutionary psychology. In D. M. Buss (Ed.), *The handbook of evolutionary psychology* (pp. 5–67). Hoboken, NJ: Wiley.

Tooley, G. A., Karakis, M., Stokes, M., & Ozanne-Smith, J. (2006). Generalising the Cinderella Effect to unintentional childhood fatalities. *Evolution and Human Behavior, 27,* 224–230.

Toomey, R. B., Ryan, C., Diaz, R. M., Card, N. A., & Russell, S. T. (2010). Gender-nonconforming lesbian, gay, bisexual, and transgender youth: School victimization and young adult psychosocial adjustment. *Developmental Psychology, 46*(6), 1580–1589. https://doi.org/10.1037/a0020705

Torassa, U. (2000, March 8). Leave it on: Study says night lighting won't harm children's eyesight. Retrieved from http://edition.cnn.com/2000/HEALTH/children/03/08/light.myopia.wmd/index.html

Totsika, V., & Sylva, K. (2004). The home observation for measurement of the environment revisited. *Child and Adolescent Mental Health, 9*(1), 25–35. doi:10.1046/j.1475-357X.2003.00073.x

Tottenham, N., Hare, T. A., Quinn, B. T., McCarry, T. W., Nurse, M., Gilhooly, T., . . . Casey, B. J. (2010). Prolonged institutional rearing is associated with atypically large amygdala volume and difficulties in emotion regulation. *Developmental Science, 13,* 46–61. doi:10.1111/j.1467-7687.2009.00852.x

Trainor, L. J. (1996). Infant preferences for infant-directed versus noninfant-directed playsongs and lullabies. *Infant Behavior and Development, 19,* 83–92. doi:10.1016/S0163-6383(96)90046-6

Trainor, L. J., & Desjardins, R. N. (2002). Pitch characteristics of infant-directed speech affect infants' ability to discriminate vowels. *Psychonomic Bulletin & Review, 9*(2), 335–340.

Trainor, L. J., & Heinmiller, B. M. (1998). The development of evaluative responses to music: Infants prefer to listen to consonance over dissonance. *Infant Behavior and Development, 21,* 77–88. doi:10.1016/S0163-6383(98)90055-8

Trainor, L. J., & Trehub, S. E. (1992). A comparison of infants' and adults' sensitivity to Western musical structure. *Journal of Experimental Psychology: Human Perception and Performance, 18,* 394–402. doi:10.1037/0096-1523.18.2.394

Tran, C. V., Cole, D. A., & Weiss, B. (2012). Testing reciprocal longitudinal relations between peer victimization and depressive symptoms in young adolescents. *Journal of Clinical Child & Adolescent Psychology, 41,* 353–360. doi:10.1080/15374416.2012.662674

Trehub, S. E., Plantinga, J., & Russo, F. A. (2015). Maternal vocal interactions with infants: Reciprocal visual influences. *Social Development, 25,* 665–683. doi:10.1111/sode.12164

Trehub, S. E., Unyk, A. M., Kamenetsky, S. B., Hill, D. S., Trainor, L. J., Henderson, J. L., & Saraza, M. (1997). Mothers' and fathers' singing to infants. *Developmental Psychology, 33*(3), 500–507.

Treiman, R., Hompluem, L., Gordon, J., Decker, K., & Markson, L. (2016). Young children's knowledge of the symbolic nature of writing. *Child Development, 87*(2), 583–592.

Treiman, R., & Yin, L. (2011). Early differentiation between drawing and writing in Chinese children. *Journal of Experimental Child Psychology, 108*(4), 786–801.

Tremblay, R. E., Pihl, R. O., Vitaro, F., & Dobkin, P. L. (1994). Predicting early onset of male antisocial behavior from preschool behavior. *Archives of General Psychiatry, 51,* 732–739. doi:10.1001/archpsyc.1994.03950090064009

Trentacosta, C. J., Hyde, L. W., Shaw, D. S., Dishion, T. J., Gardner, F., & Wilson, M. (2008). The relations among cumulative risk, parenting, and behavior problems during early childhood. *Journal of Child Psychology and Psychiatry, 49,* 1211–1219. doi:10.1111/j.1469-7610.2008.01941.x

Trivers, R. L. (1972). Parental investment and sexual selection, 1871–1971. In B. Campbell (Ed.), *Sexual selection and the descent of man* (pp. 136–179). Chicago: Aldine.

Trivers, R. L. (1983). The evolution of cooperation. In D. Bridgeman (Ed.), *The nature of prosocial development* (pp. 95–112). New York: Academic Press.

Trommsdorff, G., Friedlmeier, W., & Mayer, B. (2007). Sympathy, distress, and prosocial behavior of preschool children in four cultures. *International Journal of Behavioral Development, 31,* 284–293. doi:10.1177/0165025407076441

Tronick, E. Z., Als, H., Adamson, L., Wise, S., & Brazelton, T. B. (1978). The infant's response to entrapment between contradictory messages in face-to-face interaction. *Journal of American Academy of Child Psychiatry, 17,* 1–13. doi:10.1016/s0002-7138(09)62273-1

Tronick, E. Z., Thomas, R. B., & Daltabuit, M. (1994). The Quechua manta pouch: A caretaking practice for buffering the Peruvian infant against the multiple stressors of high altitude. *Child Development, 65,* 1005–1013.

Tryphonopoulos, P. D., Letourneau, N., & Ditommaso, E. (2014). Attachment and caregiver–infant interaction: A review of observational-assessment tools. *Infant Mental Health Journal, 35,* 642–656. doi:10.1002/imhj.21461

Trzaskowski, M., Yang, J., Visscher, P. M., & Plomin, R. (2014). DNA evidence for strong genetic stability and increasing heritability of intelligence from age 7 to 12. *Molecular Psychiatry, 19*(3), 380–384.

Trzesniewski, K. H., Kinal, M. P.-A., & Donnellan, M. B. (2010). Self-enhancement and self-protection in a developmental context. In M. D. Alicke & C. Sedikides (Eds.), *The handbook of self-enhancement and self-protection* (pp. 341–357). New York: Guilford Press.

Ttofi, M. M., & Farrington, D. P. (2011). Effectiveness of school-based programs to reduce bullying: A systematic and meta-analytic review. *Journal of Experimental Criminology, 7,* 27–56. doi:10.1007/s11292-010-9109-1

Tucker-Drob, E. M., & Bates, T. C. (2016). Large cross-national differences in gene × socioeconomic status interaction on intelligence. *Psychological Science, 27*(2), 138–149. doi:10.1177/0956797615612727

Tucker-Drob, E. M., Rhemtulla, M., Harden, K. P., Turkheimer, E., & Fask, D. (2011). Emergence of a gene × socioeconomic status interaction on infant mental ability between 10 months and 2 years. *Psychological Science, 22,* 125–133. doi:10.1177/0956797610392926

Tummeltshammer, K. S., Wu, R., Sobel, D. M., & Kirkham, N. Z. (2014). Infants track the reliability of potential informants. *Psychological Science, 25*(9), 1730–1738. doi:10.1177/0956797614540178

Tung, Y. L., Yeo, G. S., O'Rahilly, S., & Coll, A. P. (2014). Obesity and FTO: Changing focus at a complex locus. *Cell Metabolism, 20*(5), 710–718.

Turiel, E. (1987). Potential relations between the development of social reasoning and childhood aggression. In D. H. Crowell, I. M. Evans, & C. R. O'Donnell (Eds.), *Childhood aggression and violence: Sources of influence, prevention, and control* (pp. 95–114). New York: Plenum Press.

Turiel, E. (1998). Moral development. In W. Damon (Series Ed.) & R. M. Lerner & N. Eisenberg (Vol. Eds.), *Handbook of child psychology: Vol. 3. Social, emotional, and personality development* (pp. 863–932). New York: Wiley.

Turiel, E. (2006). The development of morality. In W. Damon & R. M. Lerner (Series Eds.) & N. Eisenberg (Vol. Ed.), *Handbook of child psychology: Vol. 3. Social, emotional, and personality development* (6th ed., pp. 789–857). Hoboken, NJ: Wiley.

Turiel, E. (2008). Thought about actions in social domains: Morality, social conventions, and social interactions. *Cognitive Development, 23,* 136–154. doi:10.1016/j.cogdev.2007.04.001

Turiel, E. (2014). Morality: Epistemology, development, and social opposition. In M. Killen & J. G. Smetana (Eds.), *Handbook of moral development* (2nd ed., pp. 3–22). New York: Psychology Press.

Turkheimer, E., Haley, A., Waldron, M., D'Onofrio, B., & Gottesman, I. I. (2003). Socioeconomic status modifies heritability of IQ in young children. *Psychological Science, 14,* 623–628.

Turner, S. D., Gomes, T., Camacho, X., Yao, Z., Guttmann, A., Mamdani, M. M., . . . Dhalla, I. A. (2015). Neonatal opioid withdrawal and antenatal opioid prescribing. *CMAJ Open, 3*(1), E55.

Turpel-Lafond, M. (2013, April). Still waiting. First-hand experiences with youth mental health services in B.C. Representative for Children and Youth report submitted to Legislative Assembly of British Columbia.

Tuvblad, C., Raine, A., Zheng, M., & Baker, L. A. (2009). Genetic and environmental stability differs in reactive and proactive aggression. *Aggressive Behavior, 35,* 437–452. doi:10.1002/ab.20319

Twenge, J. M., Joiner, T. E., Rogers, M. L., & Martin, G. N. (2018). Increases in depressive symptoms, suicide-related outcomes, and suicide rates among U.S. adolescents after 2010 and links to increased new media screen time. *Clinical Psychological Science, 6*(1), 3–17.

Twenge, J. M., & Nolen-Hoeksema, S. (2002). Age, gender, race, socioeconomic status, and birth cohort differences on the children's depression inventory: A meta-analysis. *Journal of Abnormal Psychology, 111,* 578–588.

Tyrka, A. R., Graber, J. A., & Brooks-Gunn, J. (2000). The development of disordered eating. In A. J. Sameroff, M. Lewis, & S. M. Miller (Eds.), *Handbook of developmental psychopathology* (pp. 607–624). New York: Springer.

U.S. Department of Health & Human Resources. (2019, April 24). Head Start program facts: Fiscal year 2018. Retrieved from https://eclkc.ohs.acf.hhs.gov/sites/default/files/pdf/no-search/hs-program-fact-sheet-2018.pdf.

U.S. Department of Health and Human Services, Administration for Children and Families. (2010). Head Start impact study: Final report, executive summary. Retrieved from http://www.acf.hhs.gov/sites/default/files/opre/executive_summary_final.pdf

U.S. Department of Health and Human Services Children's Bureau. (2019). Child maltreatment 2017. Retrieved from https://www.acf.hhs.gov/sites/default/files/cb/cm2017.pdf

U.S. Department of Health and Human Services, Health Resources and Services Administration, Maternal and Child Health Bureau. (2006). Child health USA 2006: Population characteristics: Working mothers and child care. Retrieved from http://www.mchb.hrsa.gov/chusa_06/popchar/0206wmcc.htm

Uhlhaas, P. J., Roux, F., Rodriguez, E., Rotarska-Jagiela, A., & Singer, W. (2010). Neural synchrony and the development of cortical networks. *Trends in Cognitive Sciences, 14*(2), 72–80. doi:10.1016/j.tics.2009.12.002

Ulusar, U., Sanhal, C. Y., & Mendilcioglu, I. (2017). OC18. 04: Ultrasound-based computer-aided tracking technique of fetal breathing movement analysis for intrauterine growth restriction. *Ultrasound in Obstetrics & Gynecology, 50,* 38.

Umaña-Taylor, A. J., & Guimond, A. B. (2010). A longitudinal examination of parenting behaviors and perceived discrimination predicting Latino adolescents' ethnic identity. *Developmental Psychology, 46,* 636–650. doi:10.1037/a0019376

Umaña-Taylor, A. J., Quintana, S. M., Lee, R. M., Cross, W. E., Rivas-Drake, D., Schwartz, S. J., . . . Seaton, E. (2014). Ethnic and racial identity during adolescence and into young adulthood: An integrated conceptualization. *Child Development, 85*(1), 21–39. doi:10.1111/cdev.12196

Underwood, B., & Moore, B. (1982). Perspective-taking and altruism. *Psychological Bulletin, 91,* 143–173. doi:10.1037/0033-2909.91.1.143

Underwood, M. K. (2003). *Social aggression among girls.* New York: Guilford Press.

UNICEF. (2013). *Improving child nutrition: The achievable imperative for global progress.* New York: United Nations Children's Fund. Retrieved from http://data.unicef.org/corecode/uploads/document6/uploaded_pdfs/corecode/NutritionReport_April2013_Final_29.pdf

UNICEF Innocenti Research Centre. (2012). *Measuring child poverty: New league tables of child poverty in the world's richest countries* (Innocenti Report Card 10). Florence, Italy: Author. Retrieved from https://www.unicef-irc.org/-publications/pdf/rc10_eng.pdf

United Nations Committee on the Rights of the Child. (2006). *General Comment No. 8 (2006): The right of the child to protection from corporal punishment and or cruel or degrading forms of punishment* (articles 1, 28(2), and 37, inter alia) (CRC/C/GC/8). Geneva, Switzerland: United Nations.

United Nations Convention on the Rights of the Child, G. A. Res. 44/25, U. N. GAOR, 44th Sess., at 3, U. N. Doc. A/RES/44/25 (1989, Nov. 20). Retrieved from http://www.unicef.org/crc/

Unsworth, N., Redick, T. S., McMillan, B. D., Hambrick, D. Z., Kane, M. J., & Engle, R. W. (2015). Is playing video games related to cognitive abilities? *Psychological Science, 26*(6), 759–774. doi:10.1177/0956797615570367

Updegraff, K. A., Kim, J.-Y., Killoren, S. E., & Thayer, S. M. (2010). Mexican American parents' involvement in adolescents' peer relationships: Exploring the role of culture and adolescents' peer experiences. *Journal of Research on Adolescence, 20,* 65–87. doi:10.1111/j.1532-7795.2009.00625.x

Updegraff, K. A., McHale, S. M., & Crouter, A. C. (1996). Gender roles in marriage: What do they mean for girls' and boys' school achievement? *Journal of Youth and Adolescence, 25,* 73–88. doi:10.1007/BF01537381

Uppal, S. (2017). Young men and women without a high school diploma. Retrieved from https://www150.statcan.gc.ca/n1/en/pub/75-006-x/2017001/article/14824-eng.pdf?st=_oVjjwKO

Uttal, D. H., Meadow, N. G., Tipton, E., Hand, L. L., Alden, A. R., Warren, C., & Newcombe, N. S. (2013). The malleability of spatial skills: A meta-analysis of training studies. *Psychological Bulletin, 139,* 352–402.

Uttal, D. H., & Yuan, L. (2014). Using symbols: Developmental perspectives. *Wiley Interdisciplinary Reviews: Cognitive Science, 5*(3), 295–304.

Vaillancourt, T., Brendgen, M., Boivin, M., & Tremblay, R. E. (2003). A longitudinal confirmatory factor analysis of indirect and physical aggression: Evidence of two factors over time? *Child Development, 74,* 1628–1638. doi:10.1046/j.1467-8624.2003.00628.x

Vaillant-Molina, M., & Bahrick, L. E. (2012). The role of intersensory redundancy in the emergence of social referencing in 5½-month-old infants. *Developmental Psychology, 48,* 1–9.

Vainio, A. (2011). Religious conviction, morality and social convention among Finnish adolescents. *Journal of Moral Education, 40,* 73–87. doi:10.1080/03057240.2010.521390

Vaish, A., Carpenter, M., & Tomasello, M. (2009). Sympathy through affective perspective taking and its relation to prosocial behavior in toddlers. *Developmental Psychology, 45,* 534–543. doi:10.1037/a0014322

Vaish, A., Carpenter, M., & Tomasello, M. (2010). Young children selectively avoid helping people with harmful intentions. *Child Development, 81,* 1661–1669. doi:10.1111/j.1467-8624.2010.01500.x

Vaish, A., & Striano, T. (2004). Is visual reference necessary? Contributions of facial versus vocal cues in 12-month-olds' social referencing behavior. *Developmental Science, 7,* 261–269.

Valkenburg, P. M. (2015). The limited informativeness of meta-analyses of media effects. *Perspectives on Psychological Science, 10*(5), 680–682.

Valkenburg, P. M., & Peter, J. (2009). The effects of instant messaging on the quality of adolescents' existing friendships: A longitudinal study. *Journal of Communication, 59,* 79–97. doi:10.1111/j.1460-2466.2008.01405.x

Valkenburg, P. M., & Peter, J. (2011). Online communication among adolescents: An integrated model of its attraction, opportunities, and risks. *Journal of Adolescent Health, 48,* 121–127. doi:10.1016/j.jadohealth.2010.08.020

Van Beek, Y., Van Dolderen, M. S. M., & Demon Dubas, J. J. S. (2006). Gender-specific development of nonverbal behaviours and mild depression in adolescence. *Journal of Child Psychology and Psychiatry, 47,* 1272–1283. doi:10.1111/j.1469-7610.2006.01663.x

Van Beijsterveldt, C. E. M., Overbeek, L. I. H., Rozendaal, L., McMaster, M. T. B., Glasner, T. J., Bartels, M., . . . Boomsma, D. I. (2016). Chorionicity and heritability estimates from twin studies: The prenatal environment of twins and their resemblance across a large number of traits. *Behavior Genetics, 46*(3), 304–314.

Van de Gaer, E., Pustjens, H., Van Damme, J., & De Munter, A. (2006). Tracking and the effects of school-related attitudes on the language achievement of boys and girls. *British Journal of Sociology of Education, 27,* 293–309. doi:10.1080/01425690600750478

Van den Bergh, B. R., Dahnke, R., & Mennes, M. (2018). Prenatal stress and the developing brain: Risks for neurodevelopmental disorders. *Development and Psychopathology, 30*(3), 743–762.

Van den Bergh, B. R., van den Heuvel, M. I., Lahti, M., Braeken, M., de Rooij, S. R., Entringer, S., . . . Schwab, M. (2017). Prenatal developmental origins of behavior and mental health: The influence of maternal stress in pregnancy. *Neuroscience & Biobehavioral Reviews, 2017.* doi:10.1016/j.neubiorev.2017.07.003

van den Boom, D. C., & Hoeksma, J. B. (1994). The effect of infant irritability on mother–infant interaction: A growth-curve analysis. *Developmental Psychology, 30,* 581–590.

Vandell, D. L., Belsky, J., Burchinal, M., Steinberg, L., Vandergrift, N., & NICHD Early Child Care Research Network. (2010). Do effects of early child care extend to age 15 years? Results from the NICHD Study of Early Child Care and Youth Development. *Child Development, 81,* 737–756. doi:10.1111/j.1467-8624.2010.01431.x

VanderLaan, D. P., Postema, L., Wood, H., Singh, D., Fantus, S., Hyun, J., Leef, J., Bradley, S. J., & Zucker, K. J. (2015). Do children with gender dysphoria have intense/obsessional interests? *Journal of Sex Research, 52*(2), 213–219. http://dx.doi.org/10.1080/00224499.2013.860073

Van der Ven, S. H., Boom, J., Kroesbergen, E. H., & Leseman, P. P. (2012). Microgenetic patterns of children's multiplication learning: Confirming the overlapping waves model by latent growth modeling. *Journal of Experimental Child Psychology, 113*(1), 1–19. doi:10.1016/j.jecp.2012.02.001

van der Zee, E., Zulch, H., & Mills, D. (2012). Word generalization by a dog (Canis familiaris): Is shape important? *PloS One, 7*(11), e49382. doi:10.1371/journal.pone.0049382

Vanfossen, B., Brown, C. H., Kellam, S., Sokoloff, N., & Doering, S. (2010). Neighborhood context and the development of aggression in boys and girls. *Journal of Community Psychology, 38,* 329–349. doi:10.1002/jcop.20367

Van Heugten, M., & Shi, R. (2009). French-learning toddlers use gender information on determiners during word recognition. *Developmental Science, 12,* 419–425. doi:10.1111/j.1467-7687.2008.00788.x

Van Houtte, M. (2004). Why boys achieve less at school than girls: The difference between boys' and girls' academic culture. *Educational Studies, 30,* 159–173. doi:10.1080/0305569032000159804

van IJzendoorn, M. H., Juffer, F., & Duyvesteyn, M. G. C. (1995). Breaking the intergenerational cycle of insecure attachment: A review of the effects of attachment-based interventions on maternal sensitivity and infant security. *Journal of Child Psychology and Psychiatry, 36,* 225–248. doi:10.1111/j.1469-7610.1995.tb01822.x

van IJzendoorn, M. H., & Sagi, A. (1999). Cross-cultural patterns of attachment: Universal and contextual dimensions. In J. Cassidy & P. R. Shaver (Eds.), *Handbook of attachment: Theory, research, and clinical applications* (pp. 713–734). New York: Guilford Press.

van IJzendoorn, M. H., Schuengel, C., & Bakermans-Kranenburg, M. J. (1999). Disorganized attachment in early childhood: Meta-analysis of precursors, concomitants, and sequelae. *Development and Psychopathology, 11,* 225–249.

van IJzendoorn, M. H., Vereijken, C. M., Bakermans-Kranenburg, M. J., & Riksen-Walraven, J. M. (2004). Assessing attachment security with the Attachment Q Sort: Meta-analytic evidence for the validity of the observer AQS. *Child Development, 75,* 1188–1213. doi:10.1111/j.1467-8624.2004.00733.x

van Lier, P. A. C., Vitaro, F., Barker, E. D., Brendgen, M., Tremblay, R. E., & Boivin, M. (2012). Peer victimization, poor academic achievement, and the link between childhood externalizing and internalizing problems. *Child Development, 83,* 1775–1788. doi:10.1111/j.1467-8624.2012.01802.x

Vannatta, K., Gartstein, M. A., Zeller, M., & Noll, R. B. (2009). Peer acceptance and social behavior during childhood and adolescence: How important are appearance, athleticism, and academic competence? *International Journal of Behavioral Development, 33,* 303–311. doi:10.1177/0165025408101275

Van Ryzin, M. J., & Dishion, T. J. (2012). The impact of a family-centered intervention on the ecology of adolescent antisocial behavior: Modeling developmental sequelae and trajectories during adolescence. *Development and Psychopathology, 24,* 1139–1155. doi:10.1017/S0954579412000582

van Wermeskerken, M., van der Kamp, J., Savelsbergh, G. J., & von Hofsten, C. (2013). Getting the closer object? An information-based dissociation between vision for perception and vision for movement in early infancy. *Developmental Science, 16,* 91–100. doi:10.1111/desc.12006

Van Zalk, M. H., Kerr, M., Branje, S. J., Stattin, H., & Meeus, W. H. (2010). It takes three: Selection, influence, and de-selection processes of depression in adolescent friendship networks. *Developmental Psychology, 46,* 927–938.

Van Zalk, N., Van Zalk, M., Kerr, M., & Stattin, H. (2011). Social anxiety as a basis for friendship selection and socialization in adolescents' social networks. *Journal of Personality, 79,* 499–525. doi:10.1111/j.1467-6494.2011.00682.x

Vaquera, E., & Kao, G. (2008). Do you like me as much as I like you? Friendship reciprocity and its effects on school outcomes among adolescents. *Social Science Research, 37,* 55–72. doi:10.1016/j.ssresearch.2006.11.002

Vasek, M. E. (1986). Lying as a skill: The development of deception in children. In R. W. Mitchell & N. S. Thompson (Eds.), *Deception: Perspectives on human and non-human deceit* (pp. 271–292). New York: SUNY Press.

Vasiliadis, H. M., Diallo, F. B., Rochette, L., Smith, M., Langille, D., Lin, E., . . . Lesage, A. (2017). Temporal trends in the prevalence and incidence of diagnosed ADHD in children and young adults between 1999 and 2012 in Canada: A data linkage study. *Canadian Journal of Psychiatry, 62*(12), 818–826.

Vaughn, B. E., Vollenweider, M., Bost, K. K., Azria-Evans, M. R., & Snider, J. B. (2003). Negative interactions and social competence for preschool children in two samples: Reconsidering the interpretation of aggressive behavior for young children. *Merrill-Palmer Quarterly, 49,* 245–278.

Vellutino, F. R., & Scanlon, D. M. (1987). Phonological coding, phonological awareness, and reading ability: Evidence from a longitudinal and experimental study. *Merrill-Palmer Quarterly, 33,* 321–363.

Venker, C. E., Haebig, E., Edwards, J., Saffran, J. R., & Weismer, S. E. (2016). Brief report: Early lexical comprehension in young children with ASD: Comparing eye-gaze methodology and parent report. *Journal of Autism and Developmental Disorders, 46*(6), 2260–2266.

Ventura, A. K., & Worobey, J. (2013). Early influences on the development of food preferences. *Current Biology, 23*(9), R401–R408.

Veríssimo, M., Santos, A. J., Vaughn, B. E., Torres, N., Monteiro, L., & Santos, O. (2011). Quality of attachment to father and mother and number of reciprocal friends. *Early Child Development and Care, 181,* 27–38. doi:10.1080/03004430903211208

Vernon, P. A., Wickett, J. C., Bazana, P. G., & Stelmack, R. M. (2000). The neuropsychology and psychophysiology of human intelligence. In R. J. Sternberg (Ed.), *Handbook of intelligence* (pp. 245–266). Cambridge: Cambridge University Press.

Véronneau, M.-H., Vitaro, F., Brendgen, M., Dishion, T. J., & Tremblay, R. E. (2010). Transactional analysis of the reciprocal links between peer experiences and academic achievement from middle childhood to early adolescence. *Developmental Psychology, 46,* 773–790. doi:10.1037/a0019816

Via, M. (2012). The malnutrition of obesity: Micronutrient deficiencies that promote diabetes. *ISRN (International Scholarly Research Network) Endocrinology, 2012,* Article ID 103472. doi:10.5402/2012/103472

Vicente, S., Veríssimo, M., & Diniz, E. (2017). Infant massage improves attitudes toward childbearing, maternal satisfaction and pleasure in parenting. *Infant Behavior and Development, 49,* 114–119.

Victora, C. G., Bahl, R., Barros, A. J., França, G. V., Horton, S., Krasevec, J., . . . Lancet Breastfeeding Series Group. (2016). Breastfeeding in the 21st century: Epidemiology, mechanisms, and lifelong effect. *Lancet, 387*(10017), 475–490.

Vikan, A., & Clausen, S. E. (1993). Freud, Piaget, or neither? Beliefs in controlling others by wishful thinking and magical behavior in young children. *Journal of Genetic Psychology, 154,* 297–314. doi:10.1080/00221325.1993.10532183

Vitaro, F., Barker, E. D., Boivin, M., Brendgen, M., & Tremblay, R. E. (2006). Do early difficult temperament and harsh parenting differentially predict reactive and proactive aggression? *Journal of Abnormal Child Psychology, 34,* 681–691. doi:10.1007/s10802-006-9055-6

Vitaro, F., Pedersen, S., & Brendgen, M. (2007). Children's disruptiveness, peer rejection, friends' deviancy, and delinquent behaviors: A process-oriented approach. *Development and Psychopathology, 19,* 433–453. doi:10.1017/S0954579407070216

Voegtline, K. M., Costigan, K. A., Pater, H. A., & DiPietro, J. A. (2013). Near-term fetal response to maternal spoken voice. *Infant Behavior and Development, 36*(4), 526–533.

Volbrecht, M. M., Lemery-Chalfant, K., Aksan, N., Zahn-Waxler, C., & Goldsmith, H. H. (2007). Examining the familial link between positive affect and empathy development in the second year. *Journal of Genetic Psychology, 168,* 105–130. doi:10.3200/GNTP.168.2.105-130

Volling, B. L., Mahoney, A., & Rauer, A. J. (2009). Sanctification of parenting, moral socialization, and young children's conscience development. *Psychology of Religion and Spirituality, 1,* 53–68. doi:10.1037/a0014958

von Bartheld, C. S., Bahney, J., & Herculano-Houzel, S. (2016). The search for true numbers of neurons and glial cells in the human brain: A review of 150 years of cell counting. *Journal of Comparative Neurology, 524*(18), 3865–3895. doi:10.1002/cne.24040

von Hofsten, C. (2007). Action in development. *Developmental Science, 10,* 54–60. doi:10.1111/j.1467-7687.2007.00564.x

Voos, A. C., Pelphrey, K. A., Tirrell, J., Bolling, D. Z., Vander Wyk, B., Kaiser, M. D., . . . Ventola, P. (2013). Neural mechanisms of improvements in social motivation after pivotal response treatment: Two case studies. *Journal of Autism and Developmental Disorders, 43,* 1–10. doi:10.1007/s10803-012-1683-9

Voss, W., Jungmann, T., Wachtendorf, M., & Neubauer, A. P. (2012). Long-term cognitive outcomes of extremely low-birth-weight infants: The influence of the maternal educational background. *Acta Paediatrica, 101*(6), 569–573.

Votruba-Drzal, E., Coley, R. L., & Chase-Lansdale, P. L. (2004). Child care and low-income children's development: Direct and moderated effects. *Child Development, 75,* 296–312. doi:10.1111/j.1467-8624.2004.00670.x

Vouloumanos, A., & Werker, J. F. (2009). Infants' learning of novel words in a stochastic environment. *Developmental Psychology, 45,* 1611–1617.

Vouloumanos, A., Hauser, M. D., Werker, J. F., & Martin, A. (2010). The tuning of human neonates' preference for speech. *Child Development, 81,* 517–527. doi:10.1111/j.1467-8624.2009.01412.x

Voyer, D., Voyer, S., & Bryden, M. P. (1995). Magnitude of sex differences in spatial abilities: A meta-analysis and consideration of critical variables. *Psychological Bulletin, 117,* 250–270.

Voyer, D., & Voyer, S. D. (2014). Gender differences in scholastic achievement: A meta-analysis. *Psychological Bulletin, 140,* 1174–1204.

Vukasović, T., & Bratko, D. (2015). Heritability of personality: A meta-analysis of behavior genetic studies. *Psychological Bulletin, 141*(4), 769.

Vygotsky, L. S. (1962). *Thought and language* (E. Hanfmann & G. Vakar, Trans.). Cambridge, MA: MIT Press. (Original work published 1934)

Vygotsky, L. S. (1978). *Mind in society: The development of higher psychological processes* (M. Cole, V. John-Steiner, S. Scribner, & E. Souberman, Eds.). Cambridge, MA: Harvard University Press.

Wade, M., Fox, N. A., Zeanah, C. H., & Nelson, C. A. (2019). Long-term effects of institutional rearing, foster care, and brain activity on memory and executive functioning. *Proceedings of the National Academy of Sciences, 116*(5), 1808–1813.

Wade, T. J., Cairney, J., & Pevalin, D. (2002). Emergence of gender differences in depression during adolescence: National panel results from three countries. *Journal of the American Academy of Child and Adolescent Psychiatry, 41,* 190–198. doi:10.1097/00004583-200202000-00013

Wagner, N. J., Camerota, M., & Propper, C. (2017). Prevalence and perceptions of electronic cigarette use during pregnancy. *Maternal and Child Health Journal, 21*(8), 1655–1661.

Wainright, J. L., & Patterson, C. J. (2008). Peer relations among adolescents with female same-sex parents. *Developmental Psychology, 44,* 117–126. doi:10.1037/0012-1649.44.1.117

Wainright, J. L., Russell, S. T., & Patterson, C. J. (2004). Psychosocial adjustment, school outcomes, and romantic relationships of adolescents with same-sex parents. *Child Development, 75,* 1886–1898. doi:10.1111/j.1467-8624.2004.00823.x

Wainryb, C., & Recchia, H. (2014). Moral lives across cultures: Heterogeneity and conflict. In M. Killen & J. G. Smetana (Eds.), *Handbook of moral development* (2nd ed., pp. 259–278). New York: Psychology Press.

Wainryb, C., & Turiel, E. (1995). Diversity in social development: Between or within cultures? In M. Killen & D. Hart (Eds.), *Morality in everyday life: Developmental perspectives* (pp. 283–313). New York: Cambridge University Press.

Wakefield, A. J., Murch, S. H., Anthony, A., Linnell, J., Casson, D. M., Malik, M., . . . Walker-Smith, J. A. (1998, February 28). Ileal-lymphoid-nodular hyperplasia, non-specific colitis, and pervasive developmental disorder in children. *The Lancet, 351,* 637–641. doi:10.1016/S0140-6736(97)11096-0 (Retraction published February 6, 2010, *Lancet, 375,* p. 445)

Waldman, I. D., Tackett, J. L., Van Hulle, C. A., Applegate, B., Pardini, D., Frick, P. J., & Lahey, B. B. (2011). Child and adolescent conduct disorder substantially shares genetic influences with three socioemotional dispositions. *Journal of Abnormal Psychology, 120,* 57–70. doi:10.1037/a0021351

Waldrip, A. M., Malcolm, K. T., & Jensen-Campbell, L. A. (2008). With a little help from your friends: The importance of high-quality friendships on early adolescent adjustment. *Social Development, 17,* 832–852. doi:10.1111/j.1467-9507.2008.00476.x

Walker, C. H. (1987). Relative importance of domain knowledge and overall aptitude on acquisition of domain-related information. *Cognition and Instruction, 4*(1), 25–42. doi:10.1207/s1532690xci0401_2

Walker, C. M., Walker, L. B., & Ganea, P. A. (2013). The role of symbol-based experience in early learning and transfer from pictures: Evidence from Tanzania. *Developmental Psychology, 49,* 1315–1324. doi:10.1037/a0029483

Walker, P., Bremner, J. G., Mason, U., Spring, J., Mattock, K., Slater, A., & Johnson, S. P. (2010). Preverbal infants' sensitivity to synaesthetic cross-modality correspondences. *Psychological Science, 21,* 21–25.

Walker, S. (2009). Sociometric stability and the behavioral correlates of peer acceptance in early childhood. *Journal of Genetic Psychology, 170,* 339–358. doi:10.1080/00221320903218364

Wall, J. A., Power, T. G., & Arbona, C. (1993). Susceptibility to antisocial peer pressure and its relation to acculturation in Mexican–American adolescents. *Journal of Adolescent Research, 8,* 403–418. doi:10.1177/074355489384004

Walle, E. A., & Campos, J. J. (2014). The development of infant detection of inauthentic emotion. *Emotion, 14,* 488–503. doi:10.1037/a0035305

Waller, R., Hyde, L. W., Klump, K. L., Burt, S. A. (2018). Parenting is an environmental predictor of callous-unemotional traits and aggression: A monozygotic twin differences study. *Journal of the American Academy of Child & Adolescent Psychiatry, 57,* 955–963. doi:10.1016/j.jaac.2018.07.882

Wallerstein, J., & Lewis, J. M. (2007). Sibling outcomes and disparate parenting and stepparenting after divorce: Report from a 10-year longitudinal study. *Psychoanalytic Psychology, 24,* 445–458. doi:10.1037/0736-9735.24.3.445

Wallman, J. (1992). *Aping language.* Cambridge: Cambridge University Press.

Walsh, A., & Leaper, C. (2017, April). *A content analysis of gender representations in preschool television.* Presentation at the Biennial Meeting of the Society for Research in Child Development, Austin.

Walsh, A., & Leaper, C. (in press). A content analysis of gender representations in preschool children's television. *Mass Communication & Society.* doi:10.1080/15205436.2019.1664593

Wang, M.-T., & Huguley, J. P. (2012). Parental racial socialization as a moderator of the effects of racial discrimination on educational success among African American adolescents. *Child Development, 83,* 1716–1731. doi:10.1111/j.1467-8624.2012.01808.x

Wang, Q., & Fivush, R. (2005). Mother–child conversations of emotionally salient events: Exploring the functions of emotional reminiscing in European-American and Chinese families. *Social Development, 14,* 473–495.

Wang, Z., Sabatini, J., O'Reilly, T., & Weeks, J. (2019). Decoding and reading comprehension: A test of the decoding threshold hypothesis. *Journal of Educational Psychology, 111*(3): 387-401. doi:10.1037/edu0000302

Ware, E. A., Uttal, D. H., Wetter, E. K., & DeLoache, J. S. (2006). Young children make scale errors when playing with dolls. *Developmental Science, 9,* 40–45. doi:10.1111/j.1467-7687.2005.00461.x

Warneken, F., & Tomasello, M. (2007). Helping and cooperation at 14 months of age. *Infancy, 11,* 271–294. doi:10.1111/j.1532-7078.2007.tb00227.x

Warneken, F., & Tomasello, M. (2008). Extrinsic rewards undermine altruistic tendencies in 20-month-olds. *Developmental Psychology, 44,* 1785–1788. doi:10.1037/a0013860

Wassenaer-Leemhuis, A. G., Jeukens-Visser, M., Hus, J. W., Meijssen, D., Wolf, M. J., Kok, J. H., . . . Koldewijn, K. (2016). Rethinking preventive post-discharge intervention programmes for very preterm infants and their parents. *Developmental Medicine & Child Neurology, 58*(S4), 67–73.

Waters, H. S. (1980). "Class news": A single-subject longitudinal study of prose production and schema formation during childhood. *Journal of Verbal Learning and Verbal Behavior, 19,* 152–167.

Waters, H. S. (1989, April). *Problem-solving at two: A year-long naturalistic study of two children.* Paper presented at the biennial meeting of the Society for Research in Child Development, Kansas City, MO.

Watson, J. B. (1924). *Behaviorism.* New York: Norton.

Watson, J. B. (1928). *Psychological care of infant and child.* New York: Norton.

Watson, J. B., & Rayner, R. (1920). Conditioned emotional reactions. *Journal of Experimental Psychology, 3,* 1–14. doi:10.1037/h0069608

Watson, R. J., Peter, T., McKay, T., Edkins, T., & Saewyc, E. (2018). Evidence of changing patterns in mental health and depressive symptoms for sexual minority adolescents. *Journal of Gay & Lesbian Mental Health, 22*(2), 120–138.

Watson-Gegeo, K. A., & Gegeo, D. W. (1986). Calling-out and repeating routines in Kwara'ae children's language socialization. In B. B. Schieffelin & E. Ochs (Eds.), *Studies in the social and cultural foundations of language: No. 3. Language socialization across cultures* (pp. 17–50). New York: Cambridge University Press.

Watt, H. M. G. (2010). Gender and occupational choice. In J. C. Chrisler & D. R. McCreary (Eds.), *Handbook of gender research in psychology, Vol. 2: Gender research in social and applied psychology* (pp. 379–400). New York: Springer Science+Business Media. doi:10.1007/978-1-4419-1467-5_16

Watts, T. W., Duncan, G. J., Chen, M., Claessens, A., Davis-Kean, P. E., Duckworth, P., . . . Susperreguy, M. I. (2015). The role of mediators in the development of longitudinal mathematics achievement associations. *Child Development, 86*(6), 1892–1907, doi:10.1111/cdev.12416

Watts, T. W., Duncan, G. J., Siegler, R. S., & Davis-Kean, P. E. (2014). What's past is prologue: Relations between early mathematics knowledge and high school achievement. *Educational Researcher, 43*(7), 352–360. doi:10.3102/0013189X14553660

Waxman, S. R., Fu, X., Ferguson, B., Geraghty, K., Leddon, E., Liang, J., & Zhao, M. F. (2016). How early is infants' attention to objects and actions shaped by culture? New evidence from 24-month-olds raised in the U.S. and China. *Frontiers in Psychology, 7,* 97. doi:10.3389/fpsyg.2016.00097

Waxman, S. R., & Senghas, A. (1992). Relations among word meanings in early lexical development. *Developmental Psychology, 28,* 862–873.

Way, N., & Greene, M. L. (2006). Trajectories of perceived friendship quality during adolescence: The patterns and contextual predictors. *Journal of Research on Adolescence, 16,* 293–320. doi:10.1111/j.1532-7795.2006.00133.x

Wazana, A., Moss, E., Jolicoeur-Martineau, A., Graffi, J., Tsabari, G., Lecompte, V., . . . Meaney, M. (2015). The interplay of birth weight, dopamine receptor D4 gene (DRD4), and early maternal care in the prediction of disorganized attachment at 36 months of age. *Development and Psychopathology, 27*(4pt1), 1145–1161. doi:10.1017/S0954579415000735

Weaver, I. C., Cervoni, N., Champagne, F. A., D'Alessio, A. C., Sharma, S., Seckl, J. R., . . . Meaney, M. J. (2004). Epigenetic programming by maternal behavior. *Nature Neuroscience, 7*(8), 847.

Webb, A. R., Heller, H. T., Benson, C. B., & Lahav, A. (2015). Mother's voice and heartbeat sounds elicit auditory plasticity in the human brain before full gestation. *Proceedings of the National Academy of Sciences of the United States of America, 112*(10), 3152–3157. https://doi.org/10.1073/pnas.1414924112.

Webster-Stratton, C. (1998). Preventing conduct problems in Head Start children: Strengthening parenting competencies. *Journal of Consulting and Clinical Psychology, 66,* 715–730. doi:10.1037/0022-006X.66.5.715

Weems, C. F., & Silverman, W. K. (2013). Anxiety disorders. In T. P. Beauchaine & S. P. Hinshaw (Eds.). *Child and adolescent psychopathology* (2nd ed., pp. 513–541). Hoboken, NJ: Wiley.

Weems, C. F., Taylor, L. K., Cannon, M. F., Marino, R. C., Romano, D. M., Scott, B. G., . . . Triplett, V. (2010). Post traumatic stress, context, and the lingering effects of the Hurricane Katrina disaster among ethnic minority youth. *Journal of Abnormal Child Psychology, 38,* 49–56. doi:10.1007/s10802-009-9352-y

Wei, X. & Nielsen, R. (2019). CCR5-[delta]32 is deleterious to the homozygous state in humans. *Nature Medicine, 25,* 909–910.

Weinburgh, M. (1995). Gender differences in student attitudes toward science: A meta-analysis of the literature from 1970 to 1991. *Journal of Research in Science Teaching, 32,* 387–398.

Weinraub, M., Bender, R. H., Friedman, S. L., Susman, E. J., Knoke, B., Bradley, R., . . . Williams, J. (2012). Patterns of developmental change in infants' nighttime sleep awakenings from 6 through 36 months of age. *Developmental Psychology, 48*(6), 1511–1528.

Weis, R., & Cerankosky, B. C. (2010). Effects of video-game ownership on young boys' academic and behavioral functioning: A randomized, controlled study. *Psychological Science, 21,* 463–470. doi:10.1177/0956797610362670

Weisgram, E. S., & Dinella, L. M. (Eds.) (2018). *Gender typing of children's toys: How early play experiences impact development.* Washington, DC: American Psychological Association. http://dx.doi.org/10.1037/0000077-000

Weisleder, A., & Fernald, A. (2013). Talking to children matters: Early language experience strengthens processing and builds vocabulary. *Psychological Science, 24*(11), 2143–2152.

Weiss, B., Dodge, K. A., Bates, J. E., & Pettit, G. S. (1992). Some consequences of early harsh discipline: Child aggression and a maladaptive social information processing style. *Child Development, 63,* 1321–1335. doi:10.2307/1131558

Weissman, M. D., & Kalish, C. W. (1999). The inheritance of desired characteristics: Children's view of the role of intention in parent–offspring resemblance. *Journal of Experimental Child Psychology, 73,* 245–265. doi:10.1006/jecp.1999.2505

Wellman, H. M., & Gelman, S. A. (1998). Knowledge acquisition in foundational domains. In W. Damon (Series Ed.) & D. Kuhn & R. S. Siegler (Vol. Eds.), *Handbook of child psychology: Vol. 2. Cognition, perception, and language* (5th ed., pp. 523–573). Hoboken, NJ: Wiley.

Wellman, H. M., Cross, D., & Watson, J. (2001). Meta-analysis of theory-of-mind development: The truth about false belief. *Child Development, 72,* 655–684. doi:10.1111/1467-8624.00304

Wentzel, K. R. (2009). Peers and academic functioning at school. In K. H. Rubin, W. M. Bukowski, & B. Laursen (Eds.), *Handbook of peer interactions, relationships, and groups* (pp. 531–547). New York: Guilford Press.

Wentzel, K. R., & Asher, S. R. (1995). The academic lives of neglected, rejected, popular, and controversial children. *Child Development, 66,* 754–763. doi:10.2307/1131948

Wentzel, K. R., & Caldwell, K. (1997). Friendships, peer acceptance, and group membership: Relations to academic achievement in middle school. *Child Development, 68,* 1198–1209. doi:10.1111/j.1467-8624.1997.tb01994.x

Werchan, D. M., & Gómez, R. L. (2014). Wakefulness (not sleep) promotes generalization of word learning in 2.5-year-old children. *Child Development, 85*(2), 429–436. doi:10.1111/cdev.12149

Werker, J. F. (1989, January–February). Becoming a native listener. *American Scientist, 77,* 54–59.

Werker, J. F., & Lalonde, C. E. (1988). Cross-language speech perception: Initial capabilities and developmental change. *Developmental Psychology, 24,* 672–683.

Werker, J. F., & Tees, R. C. (1984). Cross-language speech perception: Evidence for perceptual reorganization during the first year of life. *Infant Behavior and Development, 7,* 49–63. doi:10.1016/S0163-6383(84)80022-3

Werner, E. (2005). Resilience and recovery: Findings from the Kauai longitudinal study. *Focal Point: Research, Policy, and Practice in Children's Mental Health: Resilience and Recovery, 19*(1), 11–14. Retrieved from http://www.pathwaysrtc.pdx.edu/publications?terms=Werner%2C+Resilience+and+recovery&transition=on&author=&year1=&year2=&pubtype=&hide=hide

Werner, E. E. (1989, April). Children of the Garden Island. *Scientific American, 260*(4), 106–108, 108D, 110–111.

Werner, N. E., & Crick, N. R. (2004). Maladaptive peer relationships and the development of relational and physical aggression during middle childhood. *Social Development, 13,* 495–514. doi:10.1111/j.1467-9507.2004.00280.x

Werner, N. E., & Hill, L. G. (2010). Individual and peer group normative beliefs about relational aggression. *Child Development, 81,* 826–836. doi:10.1111/j.1467-8624.2010.01436.x

West, M. J., & Rheingold, H. L. (1978). Infant stimulation of maternal instruction. *Infant Behavior and Development, 1,* 205–215. doi:10.1016/S0163-6383(78)80031-9

Westinghouse Learning Corporation. (1969). *The impact of Head Start: An evaluation of the effects of Head Start on children's cognitive and affective development.* Springfield, VA: Clearinghouse for Federal Scientific & Technical Information.

Wethington, H., Pan, L., & Sherry, B. (2013). The association of screen time, television in the bedroom, and obesity among school-aged youth: 2007 National Survey of Children's Health. *Journal of School Health, 83*(8), 573–581.

Whitaker, K. J., Vértes, P. E., Romero-Garcia, R., Váša, F., Moutoussis, M., Prabhu, G., . . . Tait, R. (2016). Adolescence is associated with genomically patterned consolidation of the hubs of the human brain connectome. *Proceedings of the National Academy of Sciences, 113*(32), 9105–9110.

White, L. K., Lamm, C., Helfinstein, S. M., & Fox, N. A. (2012). Neurobiology and neurochemistry of temperament in children. In M. R. Zentner & R. L. Shiner (Eds.), *Handbook of temperament* (pp. 347–367). New York: Guilford Press.

Whitehurst, G. J., Zevenbergen, A. A., Crone, D. A., Schultz, M. D., Velting, O. N., & Fischel, J. E. (1999). Outcomes of an emergent literacy intervention from Head Start through second grade. *Journal of Educational Psychology, 91,* 261–272.

Whiting, B. B., & Edwards, C. P. (1988). *Children of different worlds: The formation of social behavior.* Cambridge, MA: Harvard University Press.

Whiting, B. B., & Whiting, J. W. (1975). *Children of six cultures: A psycho-cultural analysis.* Cambridge, MA: Harvard University Press.

Whitley, B. E. (1997). Gender differences in computer-related attitudes and behavior: A meta-analysis. *Computers in Human Behavior, 13,* 1–22. doi:10.1016/S0747-5632(96)00026-X

Wichstrom, L. (1999). The emergence of gender difference in depressed mood during adolescence: The role of intensified gender socialization. *Developmental Psychology, 35,* 232–245.

Widen, S. C., & Russell, J. A. (2003). A closer look at preschoolers' freely produced labels for facial expressions. *Developmental Psychology, 39,* 114–127.

Widen, S. C., & Russell, J. A. (2010). Children's scripts for social emotions: Causes and consequences are more central than are facial expressions. *British Journal of Developmental Psychology, 28,* 565–581.

Widen, S. C., & Russell, J. A. (2013). Children's recognition of disgust in others. *Psychological Bulletin, 139,* 271–299. doi:10.1037/a0031640

Widom, C. S., Czaja, S. J., & DuMont, K. A. (2015). Intergenerational transmission of child abuse and neglect: Real or detection bias? *Science, 347,* 1480–1485. doi:10.1126/science.1259917

Wiesel, T. N., & Hubel, D. H. (1963). Single-cell responses in striate cortex of kittens deprived of vision in one eye. *Journal of Neurophysiology, 26*(6), 1003–1017.

Wiesen, S. E., Watkins, R. M., & Needham, A. W. (2016). Active motor training has long-term effects on infants' object exploration. *Frontiers in Psychology, 7,* 599. doi:10.3389/fpsyg.2016.00599

Wigfield, A., Cambria, J., & Eccles, J. S. (2012). Motivation in education. In R. M. Ryan (Ed.), *The Oxford handbook of human motivation* (pp. 463–478). New York: Oxford University Press.

Wigfield, A., Eccles, J. S., Schiefele, U., Rosser, R. W., & Davis-Kean, P. (2006). Development of achievement motivation. In W. Damon & R. M. Lerner (Series Eds.) & N. Eisenberg (Vol. Ed.), *Handbook of child psychology: Vol. 3. Social, emotional, and personality development* (6th ed., pp. 933–1002). Hoboken, NJ: Wiley.

Wigger, J. B. (2018). Invisible friends across four countries: Kenya, Malawi, Nepal and the Dominican Republic. *International Journal of Psychology, 53,* 46–52.

Wilgenbusch, T., & Merrell, K. W. (1999). Gender differences in self-concept among children and adolescents: A meta-analysis of multidimensional studies. *School Psychology Quarterly, 14,* 101–120. doi:10.1037/h0089000

Williams, J. F., Smith, V. C., & Committee on Substance Abuse. (2015). Fetal alcohol spectrum disorders. *Pediatrics, 136,* e1395–e1406.

Williams, T., Connolly, J., Pepler, D., & Craig, W. (2005). Peer victimization, social support, and psychosocial adjustment of sexual minority adolescents. *Journal of Youth and Adolescence, 34,* 471–482. doi:10.1007/s10964-005-7264-x

Willingham, D. T. (2017). *The reading mind: A cognitive approach to understanding how the mind reads.* San Francisco, CA: Josey-Bass/Wiley.

Willis, C. (2009). *Teaching infants, toddlers, and twos with special needs.* Beltsville, MD: Gryphon House.

Willyard, C. (2018). New human gene tally ignites debate. *Nature, 558,* 354–355.

Wilson, B. J. (2008). Media violence and aggression in youth. In S. Calvert & B. Wilson (Eds.), *The handbook of children, media, and development* (pp. 237–267). West Sussex, England: Blackwell.

Wilson, B. J., Kunkel, D., Linz, D., Potter, J., Donnerstein, E., Smith, S., . . . Gray, T. (1997). Television violence and its context: University of California, Santa Barbara study. In J. Federman (Ed.), *National television violence study* (Vol. 1, pp. 3–268). Thousand Oaks, CA: Sage.

Wilson, E. O. (1975). *Sociobiology: The new synthesis.* Cambridge, MA: Belknap Press of Harvard University Press.

Wilson, T. D., & Dunn, E. W. (2004). Self-knowledge: Its limits, value, and potential for improvement. *Annual Review of Psychology, 55,* 493–518. doi:10.1146/annurev.psych.55.090902.141954

Winsler, A., De Leon, J. R., Wallace, B. A., Carlton, M. P., & Willson-Quayle, A. (2003). Private speech in preschool children: Developmental stability and change, across-task consistency, and relations with classroom behaviour. *Journal of Child Language, 30,* 583–608.

Wismer Fries, A. B., Shirtcliff, E. A., & Pollak, S. D. (2008). Neuroendocrine dysregulation following early social deprivation in children. *Developmental Psychobiology, 50,* 588–599.

Wismer Fries, A. B., Ziegler, T. E., Kurian, J. R., Jacoris, S., & Pollak, S. D. (2005). Early experience in humans is associated with changes in neuropeptides critical for regulating social behavior. *Proceedings of the National Academy of Sciences, 102*(47), 17237–17240.

Witherington, D. C., Campos, J. J., Harriger, J. A., Bryan, C., & Margett, T. E. (2010). Emotion and its development in infancy. In J. G. Bremner & T. D. Wachs (Eds.), *The Wiley-Blackwell handbook of infant development* (2nd ed., Vol. 1, pp. 569–591). Malden, MA: Blackwell.

Witt, S. D. (2000). The influence of peers on children's socialization to gender roles. *Early Child Development & Care, 162,* 1–7.

Witt, W. P., Wisk, L. E., Cheng, E. R., Mandell, K., Chatterjee, D., Wakeel, F., . . . Zarak, D. (2015). Determinants of cesarean delivery in the U.S.: A lifecourse approach. *Maternal and Child Health Journal, 19*(1), 84–93.

Wittmann, B. C., Daw, N. D., Seymour, B., & Dolan, R. J. (2008). Striatal activity underlies novelty-based choice in humans. *Neuron, 58,* 967–973. doi:10.1016/j.neuron.2008.04.027

Witvliet, M., Olthof, T., Hoeksma, J. B., Goossens, F. A., Smits, M. S. I., & Koot, H. M. (2010). Peer group affiliation of children: The role of perceived popularity, likeability, and behavioral similarity in bullying. *Social Development, 19,* 285–303. doi:10.1111/j.1467-9507.2009.00544.x

Wolitzky-Taylor, K. B., Ruggiero, K. J., Danielson, C. K., Resnick, H. S., Hanson, R. F., Smith, D. W., . . . Kilpatrick, D. G. (2008). Prevalence and correlates of dating violence in a national sample of adolescents. *Journal of the American Academy of Child and Adolescent Psychiatry, 47,* 755–762. doi:10.1097/CHI.0b013e318172ef5f

Wolke, D., Bilgin, A., & Samara, M. (2017). Systematic review and meta-analysis: Fussing and crying durations and prevalence of colic in infants. *Journal of Pediatrics, 185,* 55–61.

Wong, C. F., Clark, L. F., & Marlotte, L. (2016). The impact of specific and complex trauma on the mental health of homeless youth. *Journal of Interpersonal Violence, 31,* 831–854. doi:10.1177/0886260514556770

Wong, P. C., Skoe, E., Russo, N. M., Dees, T., & Kraus, N. (2007). Musical experience shapes human brainstem encoding of linguistic pitch patterns. *Nature Neuroscience, 10*(4), 420–422.

Wood, D., Bruner, J. S., & Ross, G. (1976). The role of tutoring in problem solving. *Journal of Child Psychology and Psychiatry, and Allied Disciplines, 17,* 89–100.

Wood, W., & Eagly, A. H. (2002). A cross-cultural analysis of the behavior of women and men: Implications for the origins of sex differences. *Psychological Bulletin, 128,* 699–727. doi:10.1037/0033-2909.128.5.699

Wood, W., & Eagly, A. H. (2012). Biosocial constructions of sex differences and similarities in behavior. In J. M. Olson & M. P. Zanna (Eds.), *Advances in experimental social psychology* (Vol. 46, pp. 55–123). San Diego, CA: Academic Press.

Woodhouse, S. S., Dykas, M. J., & Cassidy, J. (2012). Loneliness and peer relations in adolescence. *Social Development, 21,* 273–293. doi:10.1111/j.1467-9507.2011.00611.x

Woodward, A. L. (1998). Infants selectively encode the goal object of an actor's reach. *Cognition, 69,* 1–34. doi:10.1016/S0010-0277(98)00058-4

Woodward, A. L. (2005). Infants' understanding of the actions involved in joint attention. In N. Eilan, C. Hoerl, T. McCormack, & J. Roessler (Eds.), *Joint attention: Communication and other minds: Issues in philosophy and psychology* (pp. 110–128). Oxford: Oxford University Press.

Woodward, L. J., & Fergusson, D. M. (1999). Childhood peer relationship problems and psychosocial adjustment in late adolescence. *Journal of Abnormal Child Psychology, 27,* 87–104. doi:10.1023/A:1022618608802

Woolley, J. D. (1997). Thinking about fantasy: Are children fundamentally different thinkers and believers from adults? *Child Development, 68,* 991–1011. doi:10.1111/j.1467-8624.1997.tb01975.x

Woolley, J. D., Cornelius, C. A., & Lacy, W. (2011). Developmental changes in the use of supernatural explanations for unusual events. *Journal of Cognition and Culture, 11*(3–4), 311–337. doi:10.1163/156853711X591279

Woolley, J. D., & Phelps, K. E. (1994). Young children's practical reasoning about imagination. *British Journal of Developmental Psychology, 12,* 53–67. doi:10.1111/j.2044-835X.1994.tb00618.x

World Health Organization. (2017a). 1 in 10 infants worldwide did not receive any vaccinations in 2016. Retrieved from https://www.who.int/news-room/detail/17-07-2017-1-in-10-infants-worldwide-did-not-receive-any-vaccinations-in-2016

World Health Organization. (2017b). Commission on ending childhood obesity: Facts and figures on childhood obesity. Retrieved from https://www.who.int/end-childhood-obesity/facts/en/

World Health Organization. (2018a). Fact sheets: Malnutrition. Retrieved from https://www.who.int/news-room/fact-sheets/detail/malnutrition

World Health Organization. (2018b). Fact sheets: Obesity and overweight. Retrieved from https://www.who.int/en/news-room/fact-sheets/detail/obesity-and-overweight

World Health Organization. (2019). Guidelines on physical activity, sedentary behaviour and sleep for children under 5 years of age. Retrieved from https://apps.who.int/iris/handle/10665/311664

Wörmann, V., Holodynski, M., Kärtner, J., & Keller, H. (2012). A cross-cultural comparison of the development of the social smile: A longitudinal study of maternal and infant imitation in 6- and 12-week-old infants. *Infant Behavior & Development, 35,* 335–347. https://doi.org/10.1016/j.infeh.2012.03.002

Worobey, J., & Worobey, H. S. (2014). Body-size stigmatization by preschool girls: In a doll's world, it is good to be "Barbie." *Body Image, 11*(2), 171–174.

Wu, X., Wang, Y., & Liu, A. (2017). Maternal emotional expressiveness affects preschool children's development of knowledge of display rules. *Social Behavior and Personality: An International Journal, 45*(1), 93–104. https://doi.org/10.2224/sbp.5783

Wynn, K. (1992, August 27). Addition and subtraction by human infants. *Nature, 358,* 749–750. doi:10.1038/358749a0

Wynn, K. (2008). Some innate foundations of social and moral cognition. In P. Carruthers, S. Laurence, & S. Stich (Eds.), *The innate mind: Foundations and the future* (pp. 330–347). Oxford: Oxford University Press.

Xiao, N. G., Quinn, P. C., Liu, S., Ge, L., Pascalis, O., & Lee, K. (2018). Older but not younger infants associate own-race faces with happy music and other-race faces with sad music. *Developmental Science, 21*(2), e12537.

Xiao, N. G., Wu, R., Quinn, P. C., Liu, S., Tummeltshammer, K. S., Kirkham, N. Z., . . . Lee, K. (2018). Infants rely more on gaze cues from own-race than other-race adults for learning under uncertainty. *Child Development, 89*(3), e229–e244.

Xie, H., Drabick, D. A. G., & Chen, D. (2011). Developmental trajectories of aggression from late childhood through adolescence: Similarities and differences across gender. *Aggressive Behavior, 37,* 387–404. doi:10.1002/ab.20404

Xu, F., & Arriaga, R. I. (2007). Number discrimination in 10-month-old infants. *British Journal of Developmental Psychology, 25,* 103–108.

Xu, F., & Denison, S. (2009). Statistical inference and sensitivity to sampling in 11-month-old infants. *Cognition, 112,* 97–104. doi:10.1016/j.cognition.2009.04.006

Xu, F., & Garcia, V. (2008). Intuitive statistics by 8-month-old infants. *Proceedings of the National Academy of Sciences of the United States of America, 105,* 5012–5015. doi:10.1073/pnas.0704450105

Xu, F., & Kushnir, T. (2013). Infants are rational constructivist learners. *Current Directions in Psychological Science, 22,* 28–32. doi:10.1177/0963721412469396

Xu, F., & Spelke, E. S. (2000). Large number discrimination in 6-month-old infants. *Cognition, 74,* B1–B11.

Xu, Y. (2010). Children's social play sequence: Parten's classic theory revisited. *Early Child Development and Care, 180,* 489–498. doi:10.1080/03004430802090430

Xu, Y., Farver, J. A. M., Schwartz, D., & Chang, L. (2004). Social networks and aggressive behaviour in Chinese children. *International Journal of Behavioral Development, 28,* 401–410. doi:10.1080/01650250444000090

Xu, Y., Farver, J. A. M., & Zhang, Z. (2009). Temperament, harsh and indulgent parenting, and Chinese children's proactive and reactive aggression. *Child Development, 80,* 244–258. doi:10.1111/j.1467-8624.2008.01257.x

Xue, Y., & Meisels, S. J. (2004). Early literacy instruction and learning in kindergarten: Evidence from the Early Childhood Longitudinal Study—Kindergarten Class of 1998–1999. *American Educational Research Journal, 41,* 191–229.

Yamada, H. (2009). Japanese children's reasoning about conflicts with parents. *Social Development, 18,* 962–977. doi:10.1111/j.1467-9507.2008.00492.x

Yaman, A., Mesman, J., van IJzendoorn, M. H., & Bakermans–Kranenburg, M. J. (2010). Parenting and toddler aggression in second-generation immigrant families: The moderating role of child temperament. *Journal of Family Psychology, 24,* 208–211. doi:10.1037/a0019100

Yang, J., Kanazawa, S., Yamaguchi, M. K., & Kuriki, I. (2016). Cortical response to categorical color perception in infants investigated by near-infrared spectroscopy. *Proceedings of the National Academy of Sciences, 113*(9), 2370–2375.

Yang, Y. T., Mello, M. M., Subramanian, S. V., & Studdert, D. M. (2009). Relationship between malpractice litigation pressure and rates of cesarean section and vaginal birth after cesarean section. *Medical Care, 47,* 234–242. doi:10.1097/MLR.0b013e31818475de

Yarrow, M. R., Scott, P. M., & Zahn-Waxler, C. Z. (1973). Learning concern for others. *Developmental Psychology, 8,* 240–260. doi:10.1037/h0034159

Yau, J., Smetana, J. G., & Metzger, A. (2009). Young Chinese children's authority concepts. *Social Development, 18,* 210–229. doi:10.1111/j.1467-9507.2008.00463.x

Yavorsky, J. E., Kamp Dush, C. M., & Schoppe-Sullivan, S. J. (2015). The production of inequality: The gender division of labor across the transition to parenthood. *Journal of Marriage and Family, 77*(3), 662–679. doi:10.1111/jomf.12189

Ybarra, M. L., & Mitchell, K. J. (2007). Prevalence and frequency of internet harassment instigation: Implications for adolescent health. *Journal of Adolescent Health, 41,* 189–195. doi:10.1016/j.jadohealth.2007.03.005

Yeager, D. S., & Dweck, C. S. (2012). Mindsets that promote resilience: When students believe that personal characteristics can be developed. *Educational Psychologist, 47*(4), 302–314. doi:10.1080/00461520.2012.722805

Yeager, D. S., Miu, A. S., Powers, J., & Dweck, C. S. (2013). Implicit theories of personality and attributions of hostile intent: A meta-analysis, an experiment, and a longitudinal intervention. *Child Development, 84,* 1651–1667. doi:10.1111/cdev.12062

Yeates, K. O., & Selman, R. L. (1989). Social competence in the schools: Toward an integrative developmental model for intervention. *Developmental Review, 9,* 64–100. doi:10.1016/0273-2297(89)90024-5

Yip, T., Wang, Y., Mootoo, C., & Mirpuri, S. (2019, March 25). Moderating the association between discrimination and adjustment: A meta-analysis of ethnic/racial identity. *Developmental Psychology.* Advance online publication. http://dx.doi.org/10.1037/dev0000708

Yodanis, C. L. (2004). Gender inequality, violence against women, and fear: A cross-national test of the feminist theory of violence against women. *Journal of Interpersonal Violence, 19*(6), 655–675. https://doi.org/10.1177/0886260504263868

Yonas, A., Cleaves, W. T., & Pettersen, L. (1978). Development of sensitivity to pictorial depth. *Science, 200,* 77–79.

Yonas, A., Elieff, C. A., & Arterberry, M. E. (2002). Emergence of sensitivity to pictorial depth cues: Charting development in individual infants. *Infant Behavior and Development, 25,* 495–514. doi:10.1016/S0163-6383(02)00147-9

Yoon, Y., Cederbaum, J. A., Mennen, F. E., Traube, D. E., Chou, C., & Lee, J. O. (2019). Linkage between teen mothers' childhood adversity and externalizing behaviors in their children at age 11: Three aspects of parenting. *Child Abuse & Neglect, 88,* 326–336. doi:10.1016/j.chiabu.2018.12.005

Yoshikawa, H., Aber, J. L., & Beardslee, W. R. (2012). The effects of poverty on the mental, emotional, and behavioral health of children and youth: Implications for prevention. *American Psychologist, 67*(4), 272–284. doi:10.1037/a0028015

Young, C. B., Wu, S. S., & Menon, V. (2012). The neurodevelopmental basis of math anxiety. *Psychological Science, 23,* 492–501. doi:10.1177/0956797611429134

Youngblade, L. M., & Belsky, J. (1992). Parent-child antecedents of 5-year-olds' close friendships: A longitudinal analysis. *Developmental Psychology, 28,* 700–713. doi:10.1037/0012-1649.28.4.700

Youniss, J., & Smollar, J. (1985). *Adolescent relations with mothers, fathers, and friends.* Chicago: University of Chicago Press.

Yuan, S., & Fisher, C. (2009). "Really? She blicked the baby?": Two-year-olds learn combinatorial facts about verbs by listening. *Psychological Science, 20,* 619–626. doi:10.1111/j.1467-9280.2009.02341.x

Yuen, R. K., Merico, D., Bookman, M., Howe, J. L., Thiruvahindrapuram, B., Patel, R. V., . . . Pellecchia, G. (2017). Whole genome sequencing resource identifies 18 new candidate genes for autism spectrum disorder. *Nature Neuroscience, 20*(4), 602–611.

Yuill, N., & Perner, J. (1988). Intentionality and knowledge in children's judgments of actor's responsibility and recipient's emotional reaction. *Developmental Psychology, 24,* 358–365. doi:10.1037/0012-1649.24.3.358

Zachrisson, H. D., Dearing, E., Lekhal, R., & Toppelberg, C. O. (2013). Little evidence that time in child care causes externalizing problems during early childhood in Norway. *Child Development, 84,* 1152–1170. doi:10.1111/cdev.12040

Zadnik, K., Jones, L. A., Irvin, B. C., Kleinstein, R. N., Manny, R. E., Shin, J. A., & Mutti, D. O. (2000, March 9). Myopia and ambient night-time lighting. *Nature, 404,* 143–144. doi:10.1038/35004661

Zahn-Waxler, C., Friedman, R. J., Cole, P. M., Mizuta, I., & Hiruma, N. (1996). Japanese and United States preschool children's responses to conflict and distress. *Child Development, 67,* 2462–2477.

Zahn-Waxler, C., Radke-Yarrow, M., & King, R. A. (1979). Child rearing and children's prosocial initiations toward victims of distress. *Child Development, 50,* 319–330. doi:10.2307/1129406

Zakay, D. (1992). The role of attention in children's time perception. *Journal of Experimental Child Psychology, 54,* 355–371.

Zakay, D. (1993). The roles of non-temporal information processing load and temporal expectations in children's prospective time estimation. *Acta Psychologica, 84,* 271–280.

Zarbatany, L., McDougall, P., & Hymel, S. (2000). Gender-differentiated experience in the peer culture: Links to intimacy in preadolescence. *Social Development, 9,* 62–79. doi:10.1111/1467-9507.00111

Zelazo, P. D., & Carlson, S. M. (2012). Hot and cool executive function in childhood and adolescence: Development and plasticity. *Child Development Perspectives, 6*(4), 354–360. doi:10.1111/j.1750-8606.2012.00246.x

Zelazo, P. R., Zelazo, N. A., & Kolb, S. (1972, April 21). "Walking" in the newborn. *Science, 176,* 314–315.

Zeman, J., & Garber, J. (1996). Display rules for anger, sadness, and pain: It depends on who is watching. *Child Development, 67,* 957–973.

Zentner, M. R., & Kagan, J. (1996, September 5). Perception of music by infants [Letter to the editor]. *Nature, 383,* 29. doi:10.1038/383029a0

Zentner, M. R., & Kagan, J. (1998). Infants' perception of consonance and dissonance in music. *Infant Behavior and Development, 21,* 483–492. doi:10.1016/S0163-6383(98)90021-2

Zevenbergen, A. A., & Whitehurst, G. J. (2003). Dialogic reading: A shared picture book reading intervention for preschoolers. In A. van Kleeck, S. A. Stahl, & E. B. Bauer (Eds.), *On reading books to children: Parents and teachers* (pp. 177–200). Mahwah, NJ: Erlbaum.

Zhai, F., Brooks-Gunn, J., & Waldfogel, J. (2011). Head Start and urban children's school readiness: A birth cohort study in 18 cities. *Developmental Psychology, 47,* 134–152. doi:10.1037/a0020784

Zhao, T. C., & Kuhl, P. K. (2016). Musical intervention enhances infants' neural processing of temporal structure in music and speech. *Proceedings of the National Academy of Sciences, 113*(19), 5212–5217.

Zhou, Q., Eisenberg, N., Wang, Y., & Reiser, M. (2004). Chinese children's effortful control and dispositional anger/frustration: Relations to parenting styles and children's social functioning. *Developmental Psychology, 40,* 352–366. doi:10.1037/0012-1649.40.3.352

Zhou, Q., Wang, Y., Deng, X., Eisenberg, N., Wolchik, S. A., & Tein, J.-Y. (2008). Relations of parenting and temperament to Chinese children's experience of negative life events, coping efficacy, and externalizing problems. *Child Development, 79,* 493–513. doi:10.1111/j.1467-8624.2008.01139.x

Zhu, J. L., Olsen, J., Liew, Z., Li, J., Niclasen, J., & Obel, C. (2014). Parental smoking during pregnancy and ADHD in children: The Danish national birth cohort. *Pediatrics, 134*(2), e382–e388.

Ziemer, C. J., Plumert, J. M., & Pick, A. D. (2012). To grasp or not to grasp: Infants' actions toward objects and pictures. *Infancy, 17*(5), 479–497.

Zigler, E., & Styfco, S. J. (2004). The wisdom of a federal effort on behalf of impoverished children and their families. In E. Zigler & S. J. Styfco (Eds.), *The Head Start debates* (pp. 221–249). Baltimore, MD: Paul H. Brookes.

Zimmer-Gembeck, M. J., & Skinner, E. A. (2011). Review: The development of coping across childhood and adolescence: An integrative review and critique of research. *International Journal of Behavioral Development, 35,* 1–17. doi:10.1177/0165025410384923

Zisenwine, T., Kaplan, M., Kushnir, J., & Sadeh, A. (2013). Nighttime fears and fantasy-reality differentiation in preschool children. *Child Psychiatry and Human Development, 44,* 186–199. doi:10.1007/s10578-012-0318-x

Zolotor, A. J., Robinson, T. W., Runyan, D. K., Barr, R. G., & Murphy, R. A. (2011). The emergence of spanking among a representative sample of children under 2 years of age in North Carolina. *Frontiers in Psychiatry, 2,* 1–8. doi:10.2289/fpsyt.2011.00036

Name Index

Subject Index

Page numbers in **bold** indicate definitions.